Republic Grade School, built in 1893.
Photo circa 1920-21.

Republic High School, built in 1920.
Photo circa 1920-21.

**Turner**
Publishing Company

*Nashville, Tennessee • Paducah, Kentucky*

TURNER PUBLISHING COMPANY
200 4th Avenue North • Suite 950
Nashville, Tennessee 37219
(615) 255-2665

412 Broadway • P.O. Box 3101
Paducah, Kentucky 42002-3101
(270) 443-0121
www.turnerpublishing.com

Copyright 2007: Republic Historical Society
Publishing Rights: Turner Publishing Company
All rights reserved.

This book or any part there of may not be
reproduced or transmitted in any form or by
any means, electronic or mechanical, including
photocopying, recording, or by any information
storage and retrieval system, without permission
in writing from the authors and the publisher.

ISBN 978-1-63026-946-3
Library of Congress Control Number:
2006935515

0 9 8 7 6 5 4 3 2 1

# Table of Contents

Preface ............................................................................. 4
Tribute to the Armed Forces ............................................. 5
Early Native Americans & Early Settlers ........................... 6
Civil War & Rural Life Around Republic ........................ 17
Republic ......................................................................... 26
Area Schools .................................................................. 64
Republic Schools ............................................................ 73
Area Churches and Cemeteries ...................................... 89
Sponsors ........................................................................ 92
    Businesses ................................................................ 92
    Organizations ......................................................... 116
    Tributes .................................................................. 120
    Churches and Cemeteries ...................................... 129
Family Histories ........................................................... 147
Index ............................................................................ 272

*The R.C. Stone Milling Company, circa late 1800s. Featured in the buggy at right are Jack McPhayden and E.L. McDonald (light hat). Courtesy of Edna Mae Brashers' family.*

# Preface

The members of the Historical Society wish to say a special thanks to Bunny Sawyer Jones of Bolivar for convincing the society to try to produce an update to the 1971 Centennial Book, and to the community for helping to make this book an actuality. Thanks goes to those present and former Republic residents who contributed their biographies, to the wonderful sponsors, and all those who had enough faith in the undertaking to purchase books in advance.

There is also deep gratitude to all the individuals who gave hours and hours of their time in so many different ways. This was a huge undertaking for the small group of historical society members who gave their all to the project: Carolyn Meadors, Bill and Mary Sue Robertson, Helen Blades, Bill and Carolyn O'Neal, Mae Belle Fuhr, Jack and Patsy Trogdon, Buell and Betty Mason, and Alan and Rosemary Comisky. As the book was nearing completion the group was joined by Mary Strickrodt, Betty North, Anna Webb, Wilena Farwell and Harriet Cummins who spent time proofing and helping to organize the history section of the book.

As with any project there are always so many unnamed persons whose hard work is much appreciated, and without their help this project could not have become a reality.

With great anticipation, it is hoped many memories will be enjoyed and history remembered in the reading of this book.

Bill O'Neal
Historical Society President

Rosemary Comisky
Book Chairman

*The Republic Historical Society History Book Committee. Standing from left: Rosemary Comisky, Buell and Betty Mason, Mary Sue Robertson, Mary Strickrodt, Jack Trogdon, Carolyn Meadors, Betty North, Alan Comisky, Anna Webb, Patsy Trogdon, Wilena Farwell, and Bill Robertson. Sitting: Helen Blades, Mae Belle Fuhr, and Carolyn and Bill O'Neal.*

# A Tribute
# In Honor of Those Who Served Our Country

### Eleanor Roosevelt's Wartime Prayer

Dear Lord,
Lest I continue
My complacent way,
Help me to remember that somewhere,
Somehow out there
A man died for me today.
As long as there be war,
I then must
Ask and answer
Am I worth dying for?

*Poem Eleanor Roosevelt carried in her wallet during World War II*

# Early Native Americans and Early Settlers

*Private arrowhead collection of Bryan McElhaney*

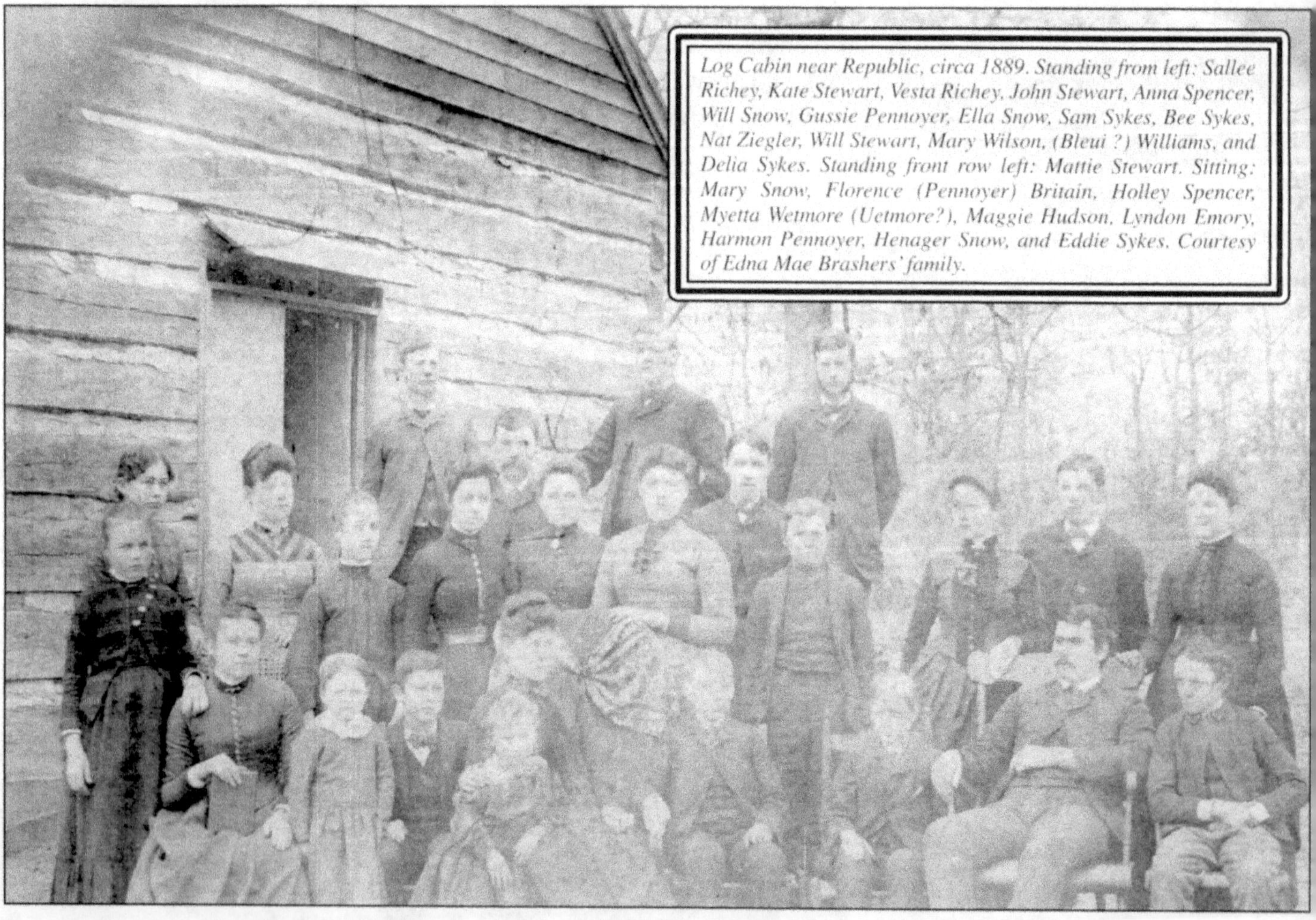

Log Cabin near Republic, circa 1889. Standing from left: Sallee Richey, Kate Stewart, Vesta Richey, John Stewart, Anna Spencer, Will Snow, Gussie Pennoyer, Ella Snow, Sam Sykes, Bee Sykes, Nat Ziegler, Will Stewart, Mary Wilson, (Bleui?) Williams, and Delia Sykes. Standing front row left: Mattie Stewart. Sitting: Mary Snow, Florence (Pennoyer) Britain, Holley Spencer, Myetta Wetmore (Uetmore?), Maggie Hudson, Lyndon Emory, Harmon Pennoyer, Henager Snow, and Eddie Sykes. Courtesy of Edna Mae Brashers' family.

# Early Native Americans

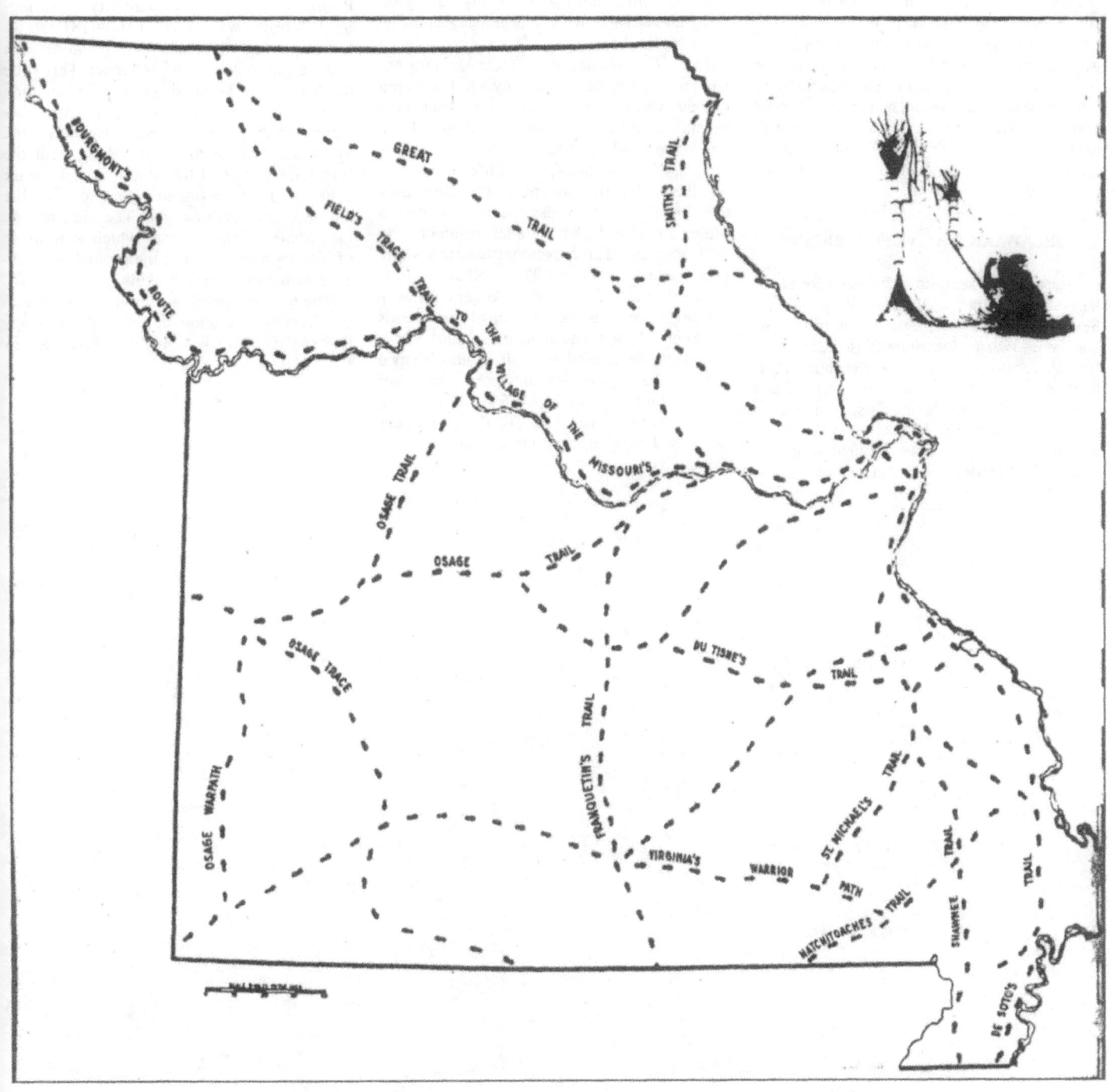

*Portions of the Osage Trail. Courtesy of Missouri Magazine.*

## OSAGE NATIVE AMERICANS

A report by the U.S. Department of the Interior showed that the Osage Indians were already living south of the Missouri River as early as 1500 A.D. This area of the rich Ozark prairie was known as Osage Country and served as a hunting and fishing ground for the Osage, Delaware and Kickapoo Indians. The abundance of game, water and a variety of grasses combined with moderate winters made this an ideal area.

The Osage men were known to be tall. Many were six to seven feet in height. They were very quick and graceful. They rejected civilized customs, especially whiskey. While living in Missouri, they dressed in skins, shaved their heads, and painted their bodies. They talked very little. They were peaceful, and seldom showed hostility towards whites. However, they could become very hostile if their hunting lands were invaded.

The Indian children were under the supervision of the mothers. Girls were taught to gather food and water, care for skins, make clothing, and set up the lodges on hunting trips.

Life was a well planned cycle. In April, they planted corn, beans and pumpkins by using a crude hoe. In May, the whole tribe left this region for their summer hunt, leaving their crops unattended. In August, they returned to harvest the crops and to store some of it in rock caches for later use. Then the tribe left for a fall hunt, which lasted the rest of the year. During the first months of the year, they hunted for bear and beaver until planting time again.

They left this region because of the treaties made with the white man. Each treaty drove them farther westward. The first to leave was

Big Track, who took half of the Big Osage Tribe and settled northeast Oklahoma on the Verdigris River. On October 10, 1808, the combined Big and Little Osage Tribes signed a treaty. The government paid the Big Osage tribe $800 in cash and $1,000 in merchandise for the land. The Little Osage got half that amount. By 1825, the government had taken 15.3 million acres and the Indians were crowded into a small area 50 by 30 miles in southeast Kansas. In 1867, the United State Senate ratified the treaty which brought all the Osage tribes together in the Indian Territory on a desolate area known as Osage Country. *Submitted by Betty Mason.*

## Delaware Native Americans

A large Delaware tribe of 500 had several villages along the James River and Wilson Creek. Several white men came with this tribe. One was James Wilson, for whom Wilson Creek was named, located southeast of Republic. Their hunting and fishing ground included a large part of the Republic area. James Wilson was known as the white man who had many squaw wives, but one at a time. When he got tired of one, he would take her back and get another one.

The homes of the Delaware were durable structures of logs with two or three rooms, good clapboard roofs, and puncheon floors.

By 1829, it was time, according to the white man, for them to move on. The treaty was signed at Delaware Town with George Washon as the Indian agent.

In 1830, about ten years after Missouri entered the Union, there were only a few scattered Indians who remained in this area. Their trails became the white man's roads and then beds for the railroads. Many of their skills were incorporated in the newcomers' way of life.

When the early farmers plowed their land, they found rock. They also found and collected Indian arrowheads that were left behind by the different tribes. This proves they used this whole area as a hunting ground. The small arrowheads were for smaller game and the larger ones were for larger game. Some very small arrowheads were curved and found along the streams. These may have been used for fish. Round shaped stones were used for grinding corn. The larger stones with an area at the top for a stick to fit in were used for tomahawks. The flat flint stones were used as scrapers to tan the hides or skin the animals.

## Kickapoo Native Americans

Around 1812, a band of Kickapoo Indians built a town on what is now called Kickapoo Prairie, located in the present city of Springfield. A treaty was signed in July 1819 in St. Louis, giving the Kickapoo Indian tribe a reservation in southwest Missouri. This tribe of four or five hundred was here when John Campbell came to this area. This town became a trading post between the Indians and the white man of the East. Along with the furs came stories of the beautiful, rich Ozark country. This tribe signed a treaty on October 24, 1832 and left this area. They left behind the remains of their houses which were made of hickory poles stuck in the ground and covered with bark, grass, or skins.

The Kickapoo Trail was used by the Federal Government as a guide for building a telegraph line and the "Old Wire Road." *Submitted by Betty Mason.*

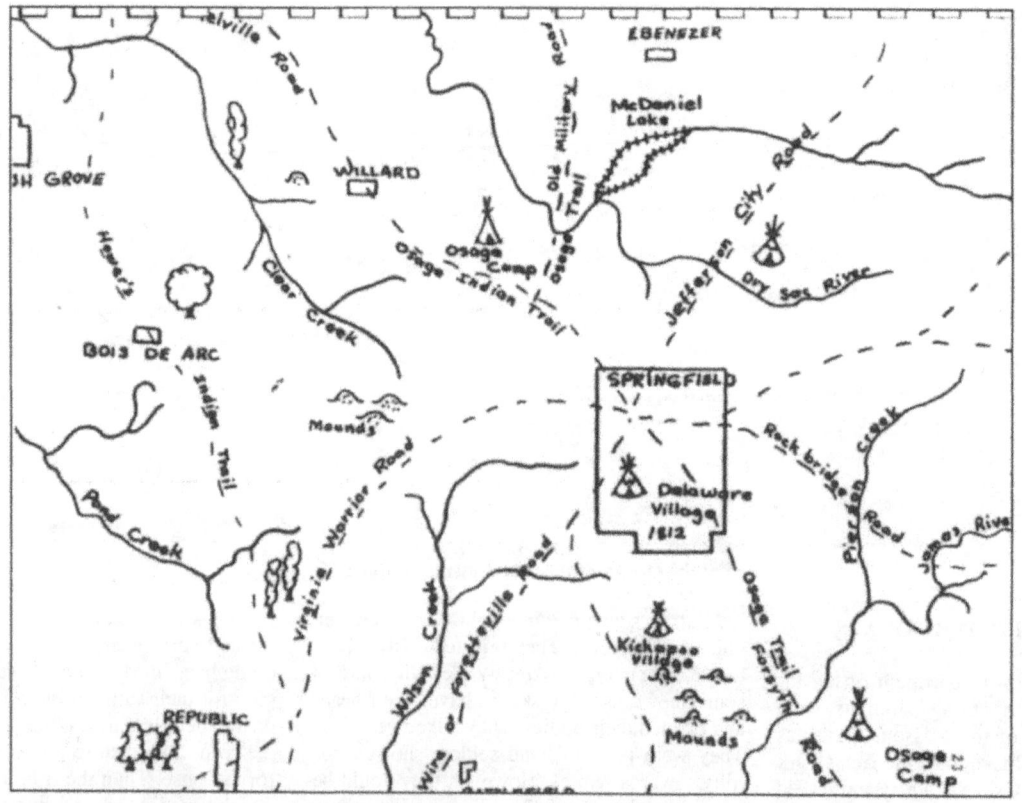

*Location of Delaware Village, 1812. Courtesy of Missouri Magazine.*

# Early Settlers

## First Settlers

When the Indians left the region, news spread rapidly that land was open for settlers. Word had come from the early explorers and fur traders about the rich, fertile land of the Ozark prairie. In the early 1830s, many families had already found their way to this area. Many came from Tennessee and Kentucky to settle along the spring fed streams on the grand prairie west of Springfield. The forest regions were full of deer, elk, bear, wild turkey and other game. Buffalo were occasionally seen. The soil along the rivers was rich but full of rocks. The trees had grown to an immense height, denoting strength of soil, adaptable to corn, wheat, oats and potatoes. Mining resources were found good for lead, zinc and some coal. The streams abounded with life. This became a challenge to the hardy explorers and home for the early settlers.

The first settlers to the Republic area were Thomas Haseltine and David Reynolds. Both families came in 1834 from Tennessee. Many others soon followed! The names of Ritter, Noe, White, Blades, Mooneyham, Garoutte, Cliborne, Hayes, O'Neal, Britain, Robertson, Anderson, McElhaney, Laney, Beal, Hagewood, Brooks, Criswell, Davis, House, Howard, Howell, Land, Lonon, McDaniel, Owen, O'Bryant, Pickering, Rainey, Richardson, Short, Sparkman, Thurman, Williams and Youngblood were some of the early arrivals. Many of our citizens can trace their family history from at least one of these families. These were farmers looking for rich farm land and a pleasant place to raise their families. Republic was located in the center of a rich prairie. The land had to be cleared and plowed. The bull tongue plow was what the settlers most commonly used. It had one sharply pointed and slightly curved blade of steel mounted on a plow stock and drawn by oxen. Corn was planted by marking off the rows at right angles across the field and dropping two or three kernels of corn in each cross. Small grain was sown by broadcasting by hand over the plowed field.

Most farmers had a fruit orchard, vegetable garden and strawberry patch. They owned various farm animals, such as horses, oxen, cows, hogs, sheep, chickens and geese and a faithful dog to help provide the needs of the family. They also relied on wild game and fish. Meal was made by pounding the corn in a stump mortar.

The first dwellings were made of logs. Floors were made of hard packed dirt or puncheon, (split logs.) Bedsteads were fastened to the walls in the corners of the house and had only one leg. Honey was used for sweetening and also as grease for the wagon wheels.

Churches and schools were established with great distances between them. Schools were sometimes held in homes, barns and churches. The early teachers received $1 a month per student. The teacher often stayed with a family of one of the students.

Hardships were a part of the pioneer life. In 1856 there was a crop failure. The weather that spring was wet, but a drought killed the crops in the fall. By 1857, there was a seed shortage. Seed sweet potatoes brought $7 a bushel; Irish potatoes, $2; and seed corn, $1.50. Many farmers could not buy corn and hay. Cattle died. In the first weeks of May and August, there was no flour for sale in the county. Corn meal was $1.50 a bushel. In those days, neighbors were few and far between, but everyone was friendly and willing to divide the last mouthful.

Thread and yarn were made by spinning wheel, then woven on great four posted looms. The looms were made of axe-hewn wood and pinned together with mortises and wooden pegs. Cotton was often combined with wool and the material was called "jeans." Weaving was an endless task for the women. The material was dyed with natural products of the woods such as walnut. If a linen dress was needed, the flax seed had to be planted, harvested, soaked for two weeks, dried for two weeks, beaten to release the fibers, combed and spun into linen thread. For everyday wear, men wore brown jeans called butternut, but the Sunday suit was indigo blue.

There were few doctors in the early days.

*Princess Finger Pattern quilt made by Lydia (Harshbarger) Foust in 1883.*

Home remedies were passed from generation to generation. For example, a toothache was thought to be cured by placing gunpowder in the cavity. Mixtures of different materials were cures from hangnails to lung congestion. Skunk or goose grease was rubbed on chests for deep colds. Asafetida in a bag was worn around the neck to prevent all types of diseases.

Spinach was believed to have a desired effect on kidney complaints. Asparagus was eaten to purify blood while celery was a cure for rheumatism and neuralgia. Lettuce and cucumbers cooled the body, and onions brought peaceful sleep.

There were "words of wisdom" heeded by the early settlers. No job was started on Friday that could not be completed that day. A broom was not to be moved from house to house lest it bring bad luck. A rabbit's foot brought good luck if carried on the body. Three chestnuts kept in the pocket stopped the pain of backaches. Water was located below the surface by the use of a willow branch.

These early settlers came and carved out a civilization. They asked only for an independent way of life and opportunity to provide for their family. They made many decisions by which we abide today. *Submitted by Betty Mason.*

## LITTLE YORK

In the year of 1835 John McCall, a veteran settler of Greene County, entered a tract of government land located about two miles west of the present town of Brookline. He sold this land to Chesley O. Rainey who came to Greene County in 1854 or 1855. Rainey secured the services of James H. Goodin, a surveyor from Cass Township. The two platted the town of Little York on Rainey land and became the second town platted in Greene County, recorded November 19, 1858. There were 20 lots in the town and within a very short time were taken by early settlers.

According to the 1860 and 1870 census of Greene County, some of the early residents were: John Potter and Stephen Phelps as merchants and Isaac King and Jesse Miller as blacksmiths. The three doctors were Dr. Theodore Youngblood, Dr. Phillips and Dr. Still. Little York was the post office for all of Pond Creek Township in 1860. The Baptist Church was organized in 1862, but later moved to Brookline. The "Blind Tigers" saloon was a gathering place for miles around.

During the Civil War, Little York was a thriving community. It was mentioned several times in a book <u>The Battle of Wilson's Creek</u> by Edwin C. Bears. General Lyon entered Greene County from the west and camped near Little York in Pond Creek Township. Some of the hungry soldiers plundered the neighborhoods. General Lyon followed the Little York Road into and out of Springfield just before the battle at Wilson Creek.

When the Frisco Railroad missed Little York by about two miles, the town of Little York came to an end. Most of the residents packed up their belongings and moved to the railroad town of Brookline.

George Rainey, son of C.O. Rainey, purchased many of the lots as the owners moved out. Corn was planted in the main street and Little York became a prosperous farm.

Brookline was laid out by the railroad upon the completion of the railroad to that point in the fall of 1871. *Submitted by Betty Mason.*

## BROOKLINE

The first settlers arrived in 1834 to this area. Some of the early settlers were: Haseltine, Youngblood, Potter, Phillips, Conley, Morris, Abernathy and Spellman. When settled, the village of Brookline was located halfway between Republic and Springfield. It was laid out by the railroad when the rails were completed to this point in the fall of 1871. Lots were sold for $1.25 each. The first building was built by T.M. Mills in October of that year. It was a store and dwelling combined. John Potter also built a store and dwelling. Some other houses and churches followed. January 23, 1873 the town itself came into being. It was named by a railroad worker from Brooklyn, NY, but because of the Ozark twang it became known as Brookline Station.

In 1875 there were zinc and lead mines nearby. The shipments from this station that year were: 74 car loads of zinc, 242,441 pounds of lead, 150 car loads of wheat plus other produce.

In 1883 there were two general stores, a drug store, a grain elevator and a schoolhouse east of town. There were three churches: Presbyterian, Congregational and Baptist, that had moved from Little York. A passenger train stopped twice a day.

The depression of the 1930s brought economic decline to the entire region. The bank closed and businesses dried up. Tragedy began when Harry Young killed the Republic Marshal. Circumstances led to the home of the Youngs. County law enforcement officers converged at the Brookline home where the "Young Brothers Massacre" occured.

Brookline survived the depression but by 1983 the population had declined from nearly 2000 to 390.

For generations there was general farming, cattle and dairy operations. The residents voluntarily worked to repair roads and keep the town alive. Today the town has grown to include a tractor distributor, bridge company, propane distributor, excavating company, variety store, small general store, Magellan Pipeline, a fire station and Carnahan Fencing Company. Brookline

*Brookline Post Office*

*Store at Brookline that has stood for generations.*

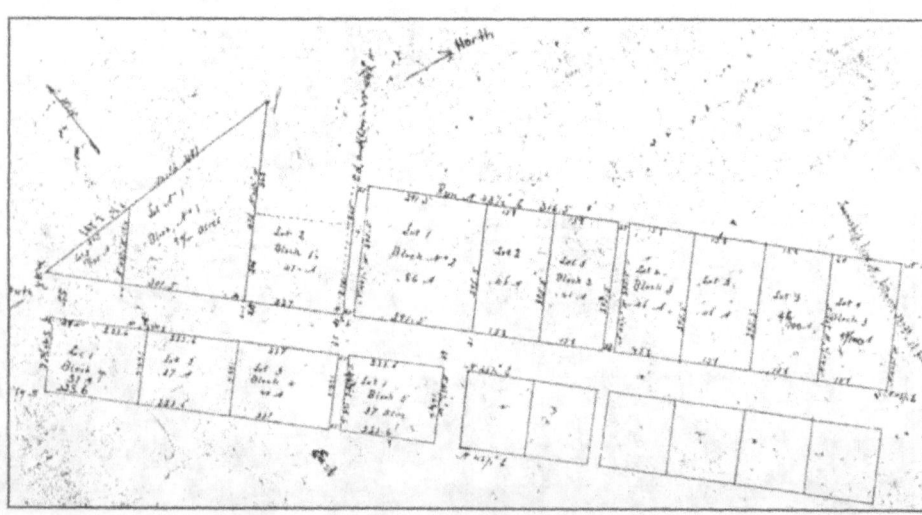
*Little York*

*This group picture was taken at the home of Jesse J. Kellough and Leah A. Kellough. Back row from left: unknown, ---- Byfield, C.C. (Allen) Neill, Etta Neill, Frank McElhaney, and Kate Phillips. Front row: Ethel Shelton, unknown, Jessie Bartley, ---- Byfield, Mary Shelton, and unknown. All of these young people lived near Brookline. Etta Neill, Allen Neill and Jessie Bartley were cousins. Allen married Kate Phillips and Etta married Ernest Hodge. Frank McElhaney married Florence Aven from Nixa. Picture made before 1907. Courtesy of Mary Neill.*

has remained a quiet little town that people here like to call home.

Brookline needed water and sewer service. They only had septic tanks and wells. Republic could provide that service. Republic and Brookline had a lot in common. They were in Republic School District. Brookline asked if the two cities could merge. The voters of both areas agreed and Republic and Brookline were consolidated on June 6, 2005. *Submitted by Betty Mason.*

## BATTLEFIELD

Battlefield features prominently in Greene County history as having the first settlement of people of European descent. In the spring and summer of 1822, just one year after statehood, John Pettijohn, traveling from Virginia and Ohio with family and Arkansas friends, settled near a spring on the north bank of James River in what would be Section 27 of Wilson Township (T 28, R 22), about two and one-half miles southeast of the future town of Battlefield. When a road finally crossed the James in that great bend in the river, it would be called Owens Ford.

Its historical link goes back even farther connecting to our country's fight for freedom.

One of the six Revolutionary War veterans settling in Greene County, Timothy Scruggs, died in the 1840s and is buried four miles south of Battlefield in the Griffin Cemetery.

In 1839 the St. Louis to Fayetteville road was established and passed about 1/2 mile north-west of the future town. After 1860 when the telegraph started southwest from Springfield, it would be called the Wire Road.

The 1904 atlas shows Wilson Township densely settled, mostly in ownership of 40 and 80 acre tracts with a few of 160 and 200. The largest land owner was Charles B. Owen, owning one piece of land totaling 983 acres on the bend of James River near the ford that would bear his name and near where Pettijohn settled.

In 1905 when the Missouri Pacific Railroad built a 35 mile branch from Crane in Stone County to Springfield, Ed Stewart donated land for a town. Finding out they couldn't name the town after him since it was already taken in Missouri, it was named Battlefield in honor of the Battle of Wilson's Creek fought August 10, 1861. A descendent of the Civil War "Ray House" owner and daughter of the man who donated land for the town, Verna Stewart McDaniel, age 10 when the railroad was built, remembered as a girl in her teens, getting on the train at Battlefield to go to Springfield and purchase sewing goods.

An unforeseen consequence of the town's name was people wanting to view the actual site of the Battle of Wilson's Creek and getting off the train thinking they had arrived there. This mistake gave the livery stable a good business providing transportation for the four mile trip.

On August 26, 1907 the Bank of Battlefield was organized with a capital stock of $10,000 and deposits of $35,000. Out of 11 banks in Greene County's small towns, only three had a larger capital stock. The bank directors were L.E. McCroskey, A.M. Howard, J.A. Walker, W.A. Fry and Will McElhaney.

The canning factory, which was near the tracks, may have been owned by the same people who had one almost one mile south that shows on the 1904 plat map.

Population by 1910 was 28 people. A map from 1920 shows Joe Sooter's blacksmith shop, Harve Garoutte's barber shop, C.T. Perkins' store, Walter McCroskey's pool hall, R.H. Jones' dry goods store, Bank of Battlefield, Red Barn livery stable, post office, canning factory and depot.

The town had the Methodist Episcopal Church with the Baptists meeting there also in the beginning.

Green Ridge School, one-half mile south of Battlefield, predated the town. Until its doors were closed in 1954 from consolidation, the school provided entertainment with pie and chili suppers and family nights for the entire community. Those wishing to attend high school went to

*The Battlefield Depot. Courtesy of Dixie Keltner.*

*Battlefield Methodist Church Gathering, 1951. Front row 1) Larry Vaughn, 2) ? Owen, 3), 4) ?, 5) Barbara Steele, 6) Marilyn Perkins, 7) Carolyn Zulauf, 8) Maurice Freeman, 9) Marian Zulauf, 10) Linda Green, 11) ?, 12) Shirley Inman, 13) Rocky Burmingham. Second and third rows (mostly ladies) 14, Sally Patterson, 15) June Vaughn, 16) Mary Jo Patton, 17) Evelyn Perkins, 18) Dora Stewart, 19) Alta Demonbrum, 20) Louise Demonbrum, 21) Ger ?, 22) Inez Owen, 23-25) ?, 26) Leona Noe, 27) ?, 28) Jessie Crabb, 29) Chris Steele, in black hat, 30) ?, 31) Grace Shelton, 32) Laura Herndon, 33, Beulah Patton, 34) ?, 35) Verna McDaniel, 36) Nettie Lou Crabb, 37-39) ?, 40) J.W. Steele, 41) Dixie Keltner, 42) Eugene Inman, 43) Charlene Stewart Back row: 44) ? Burmingham, 45) Holman Herndon, 46) Ray Crabb, 47) Charles Freeman, 48) Hershel Perkins, 49) ? Owen, 50) Clarence Howard, 51) Arve Shelton, 52) Pat Patterson, 53) Ralph Stewart, 54) Jerry Vaughn, 55) Lawrence Vaughn, 56) ?, 57) Bert Haslett, 58) Junior Perkins, 59) Verna Lee McDaniel, 60) Roy McDaniel, 61) Dorothy Burmingham, minister, 62) ? Demonbrum, guest minister. Courtesy of Dixie Keltner.*

Republic or Springfield. Merle Howard Zulauf boarded the train in Battlefield at the beginning of the week, attended high school in Springfield while staying with her aunt, and rode the train home on Friday night.

In the 1920s and 30s the businesses were: T. (Theodore) Young's store, Harve Garoutte's store/barbershop, Bank of Battlefield, tomato canning factory, Enoch Mooneyham's blacksmith shop, a bowling alley, post office and depot. The canning factory paid between 10 and 25 cents an hour in 1939. A haircut was 25 cents at Harve Garoutte's barbershop and gas was 10 cents a gallon. Both stores had glass topped gas pumps. There was a handle on the side that was pulled back and forth which pumped gas into the glass top. The nozzle was then put in the gas tank and gas gravity fed, emptying the glass top.

The mail was thrown from the moving train and picked up by Jessie Garoutte who carried it to the post office, at T. Young's store, for delivery. The last mail carrier for Battlefield, was Sam Hock. He was transferred to Republic when the Battlefield post office was closed in the early 30s. Just south across the tracks from the depot was the ball field where the Battlefield Indians played and slightly to the east was the stockyard.

Other than general farming, there were a great many tomatoes grown locally which were sold to the Battlefield canning factory. There were no doctors in Battlefield but Dr. Wasson from Nixa, Dr. French from Republic, Dr. LeCompte from Brookline and Dr. John Wood Williams from Springfield came when needed. In the 20s they were still traveling by horse and buggy.

Among the few automobile owners were Billy Sanders and T. Young who was driven by his wife, Mollie.

Jack Glidewell remembers he and some other boys getting a ride to Springfield on the milk truck. When it came time to go home, they pooled their money for one of them to buy a ticket at 25 cents. The train stopped for the one passenger, then before it had picked up speed, the rest of them jumped on to ride home.

The switchboard for the local phone service was in Nixa with William Glidewell's home having the ring of two longs and one short.

Roads were taken care of within the township by a poll tax. Each household was required to donate a certain amount of time toward road care with less time required if they also donated use of horses or equipment.

The first radio was purchased in the mid-20s by Rassie Patton. It had headphones and was battery powered.

The 1940s brought both electricity and war. Ozark Electric Co-op records indicate lines were laid in Battlefield in 1944. Mary Jo Patton remembers that they had bought a washing machine before the electricity was turned on and when it was, they washed everything in the house.

Lewis Davis was one of Battlefield's young men who went to World War II but didn't come back. He was killed in New Guinea by a Japanese machine gun while scouting enemy position.

A main difference coming in the late 40s and early 50s was people driving to Springfield to work. As America's industry mobilized to a peacetime economy, there was often more money to be made working in factories than in farming. This truth became more evident in those years with the droughts and high temperatures reaching a record 113 on July 14, 1954.

There were a few other noticeable changes. Trains quit stopping at Battlefield and the depot was removed. In 1952 there were only three businesses left in town: Harve Garoutte's store/barbershop, Leon and Irene Johnson's grocery store and Finis Robertson's automotive shop. Mail delivery was out of Brookline and the

*1906 sale bill offering lots for sale in Battlefield. Courtesy of Ralph McDaniel.*

phone system a Springfield exchange. All water still came from private wells and outhouses outnumbered indoor plumbing.

In 2006 Battlefield has grown to a population of about 4,500 with a four lane highway leading into it from James River Freeway. Incorporated as a 4th class city, the sewer system installed in 1993 caused the growth spurt from about 500 houses to 1,820 in 2006.

The city is governed by a mayor and six aldermen. Electricity is provided by either Springfield City Utilities or Ozark Electric Co-op with water from Greene County Water District #1

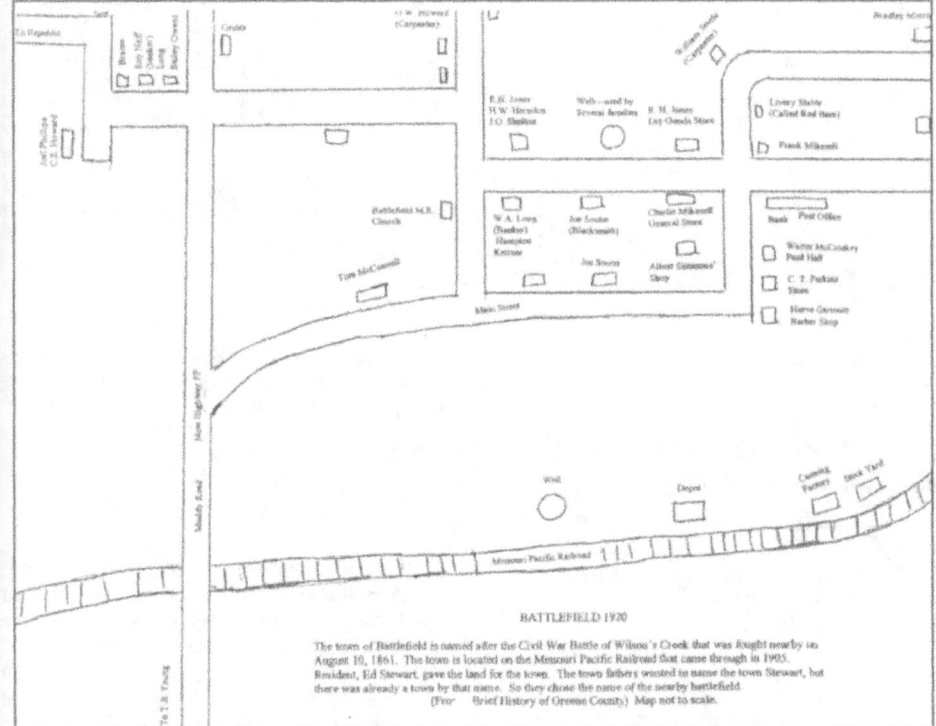

*Map of Battlefield in 1920. Courtesy of Merle Zulauf.*

The town's police department, with five officers, is in the City Hall which is located at the city's park. Battlefield residents have 911, coordinated by Greene County.

Fire protection is provided by the Battlefield Fire Department District, not under the governance of the city, which has 13 full-time firemen and 10 volunteers operating with two engine/pumper trucks, one tanker and one rescue truck.

The city limits are Farm Road (FR) 190 (south), Republic Road and FF (north), FR 131 (east) and Elm Street and FR 115 (west). Due to prior agreement with Springfield, Battlefield's growth will be to the south and west with four subdivisions either currently being developed or proposed.

Changing from an almost completely agrarian economy 50 years ago, Battlefield now has about 30 businesses with most of its population providing workforce for Springfield although there are still some beef cattle farmers in the area.

The town proper has three churches: Methodist celebrating its 100th anniversary in 2006, Battlefield Baptist and Assembly of God, with a fourth, the Wilson Creek Baptist Church, about one mile west and one and one-half miles south.

Connections to the past in Battlefield are lessening. Mary Hock Neill remembers being told as a child in the 20s and 30s to not talk about the Civil War. The community had people who had fought on both sides and it was still a sensitive issue. There are few people left who knew Civil War veterans. Jack Glidewell remembers Tim Maples and Bent Keltner, both of whom fought in that war.

After the 2003 tornado demolished T. Young's old store building, the Methodist church is the only public building left from Battlefield's beginning. *Submitted by Mary Strickrodt.*

## BUTTERFIELD OVERLAND STAGE COMPANY

The John A. Ray house was built in 1852 on the St. Louis-Springfield-Fayetteville Road that was originally established in 1838-39 from Jefferson Barracks in St. Louis and known as the Military Road to move supplies and correspondence on to the garrison in Fort Smith, Arkansas. As a new road in 1838, it saw thousands of Cherokee Indians as they neared the end of their forced westward travel from their homes in Georgia and the Carolinas, adding the name "Trail of Tears" to the road's history.

John A. Ray was appointed the first postmaster of Wilson Creek Post Office, Greene County, Missouri in January 1866 with the post office in his home. The post office was discontinued November 2, 1868.

On September 15, 1857 John Butterfield, owner of the Butterfield Overland Stage Company, was awarded the contract for transporting the U.S. Mail, and was given one year to have everything in order to start. Over 800 men, 139 relay stations, 1800 head of stock, and 250 Concord Overland Stage Coaches were obtained to provide service from St. Louis, Missouri to San Francisco, California. Being a southerner, Postmaster General Aaron Brown made sure the line took the southern route through Fort Smith, Arkansas, taking no longer than 25 days to reach the West Coast. John Butterfield used existing roads from Tipton, Missouri to Fort Smith, Arkansas. On September 15, 1858 the Butterfield Overland Stage began rolling, one starting at Tipton, Missouri and the other starting from San Francisco, California. The Ray's home became a flag stop for the stage line as it passed in front of the house.

Due to the large debts that Butterfield owed Wells Fargo, John Butterfield was forced out in March of 1860 and the Butterfield Overland Stage Company was taken over by Wells Fargo. The last Overland mail trip was made on March 21, 1861.

The Missouri and Western Telegraph Company, with a $1,000,000 capital, was chartered by the state of Missouri in 1859 to build, buy and operate lines west of the Mississippi River.

These and other lines were later absorbed by the Western Union Telegraph Company. The new telegraph lines that arrived in St. Louis on December 22, 1847 would leave there following the road to Springfield in 1860 and to Fort Smith in 1862 causing it thereafter to be known as the Wire Road. Every few miles a sign was placed on one of the poles to indicate how far to the next town.

The road passing in front of the Ray House had been known as the Military Road, the Springfield-Fayetteville Road, the Trail of Tears and the Wire Road. After the house was built it saw the Butterfield Overland Stage running for two and half years, the hanging of telegraph wire, the bloodiest Civil War battle west of the Mississippi and over 100 years of farm

*Main Street in Battlefield. Courtesy of Bill O'Neal.*

13

*Contract for the Wilson Creek Post Office, a delivery station for the Butterfield Overland Stage Company.*

*The Walter Stewart home in Terrell Creek. This house is still standing. Walter and Hattie Stewart with children Tressie, Roy and Elsie. Courtsey of Wanda Lea Hazen.*

## The Town Of Wilson Creek

Brookline Township was organized in January 1873. It was in a portion of this township that the Battle of Wilson's Creek was fought, and the town of Wilson Creek was built in 1907.

Wilson Township was organized in 1859 upon the formation of Christian County, and was named for James Wilson. James Wilson was one of the early settlers who came to Greene County with the Delaware Indians and lived with a squaw of that tribe on the creek that bears his name.

The town of Wilson Creek was built in Brookline Township on the southeast section and portions on Wilson Township.

On Jan. 21, 1907 Clarence Howell purchased land from M.C. and Pricilla McCroskey for the sum of $5,400 and from J.B. and Lucy Stewart for the sum of $260 (book 253 p. 28). On August 23, 1907 Clarence Howell of Republic filed with the Greene County Recorder of Deeds the plat for a town to be called Wilson Creek. The plat showed the proposed streets, their names and the subdivided lots. Under the terms of the land purchase, Howell was to have free use of the water from a spring in a small section of land still to be retained by the Stewarts. The town would be situated on level terrain on the east side of Wilson Creek on a bluff overlooking the stream. Clarence envisioned two things when he purchased this land, a lime kiln to be set up in the north section next to the railroad spur and a town to occupy the south portion. On July 25, 1907 the Rogers White Lime Company of Rogers, Arkansas, purchased about 29 acres from Clarence Howell for the sum of $1,188.00 (book 248 p. 354). The lime kiln business was not new to Clarence as he had started other such businesses. As the lime kiln came into full operation, eight or nine houses were built near the kiln for the employees. They were two room buildings framed of 2x4's and referred to as 2x4 houses.

Clarence Howell became

life. With the road now closed, it watches over a peaceful valley in the Wilson's Creek Battlefield National Park. *Submitted by Bill Robertson.*

## Terrell Creek Station

Terrell Creek Station was located on the Walter Stewart farm about seven miles southeast of Republic on what is now ZZ Highway and Terrell Creek. It was a stage stop on the Old Wire Road which went from Springfield to Fayetteville, Arkansas. It had a store, post office and a grist mill with a small under-shot wheel which was turned by ripples in the water. There was also a country school called Sharon Hill. In 1905 when the Missouri Pacific Railroad was built from Springfield to Crane, a depot was built at Terrell Creek Station.

In 1912 there were 12 buildings on Walter Stewart's place. *Submitted by Bill O'Neal.*

*Tressie Stewart Davis, Hattie Perkins Stewart, Elsie Stewart O'Neal, Walter Stewart, and Roy Stewart on horse. Courtesy of Wanda Lea Hazen.*

*George and sister Clara Cox's store in Wilson Creek, 1910. Courtesy of Wayne Glenn.*

the manager of the lime kiln with Henry Mizell as foreman. Those working at the lime kiln according to Joe Glidewell, who worked there as a youth, were Ed Garrett, Lum Branson, Arie Rolson, Lige Sanders, Bob Horton, Joe Sanders, Emmett Robins, Kelly Short, Fred Shelton, Tom Glidewell, Arthur Newton, Charlie Horton and Lum Bowman.

Clarence Howell's family was the first to live in Wilson Creek Town occupying a small house by the kiln. Later he built a large nine room dwelling on the southwest edge of the town. After Clarence's wife Minnie died April 4, 1907, his family consisted of three boys: George, Lou and Orville, and two girls, Florence and Edith. Lou Howell never lived in Wilson Creek having left Republic before the family moved. Florence and Orville came to Wilson Creek with their father. Florence Howell married Emmit Short, Edith Howell married William O'Bryant, and Orville married Blanche Pierce.

On September 28, 1907, Christopher C. Branson purchased three lots in the new town. The Wilson Creek post office was established with Branson appointed its first postmaster on October 19, 1908.

George Howell and his wife moved to this town in 1910 and opened a general store, staying for about two years. The store was closed, George and his wife moved to Springfield.

Clarence Howell's brother-in-law A.J. Brooks purchased two lots for a building. Brooks was a proprietor of a general store in Republic but before he could build a store Larry Bert Robinson moved into town and opened a general store. Bert and his wife, Alpha, lived in the back of the store at first. A daughter Fern was born in 1911 soon after they arrived, and may have been the first child born in Wilson Creek. Bert and Alpha had three other children: Freda, Huel and Raymond Buell. Huel died in infancy. On December 18, 1914, the Robinsons purchased the property belonging to A.J. Brooks along with five other lots and built a new house just behind the store building. The post office was also relocated to the store, and people from the surrounding area came to get their mail and do their shopping. The Robinson's store was a true general store. It stocked a wide variety of merchandise: a cracker barrel, penny candy and peanut butter in bulk.

When George Howell's family moved out, the Charles Stamps family on November 4, 1912 bought the lot and eventually made their home in the old store building. The Stamps family included wife Lottie and children: Doskie, Jennings, Carrie, Richard, Herschell and Wesley. The family remained in the town throughout the existence.

About 1913 the lime kiln ceased its operations.

Wilson Creek was only a whistle or flag stop on the railroad. The depot was a two room building on the west side of the railroad tracks. Bert Robinson operated the station. This building burned and was replaced with a converted boxcar. At some time Doc Bloom came to Wilson Creek. He too operated a small general store, most likely in the building built by C.C. Branson. The Bransons had moved in 1911.

On December 30, 1915 Clarence Howell's son Orville purchased about 32 acres comprising the old lime kiln from the Marblehead Lime Company.

In 1917 Clarence Howell's son-in-law William O'Bryant, moved into Wilson Creek and brought a new industry to replace the lime kiln.

Will O'Bryant, also a Republic resident, came to manage a tomato canning factory. This cannery was one of three owned by a man named Bridwell. The O'Bryant family consisted of five children: Jack, Victor, Paul and Floyd. A daughter Opal had died some years earlier. Tomatoes were brought in from growers within a 10 mile radius. Most of the tomatoes canned were shipped out and used by the army during World War I. The cannery also did custom canning for local gardeners. It provided work for many of the men and women of the community and even the youngsters could pick up spending money.

Tom and Mary Lentz moved into a house where Doc Bloom had lived. This was across the road from were the cannery would be located. Tom was a violin maker.

On May 16, 1918 Orville Howell purchased the entire town that still remained under the ownership of Clarence. He moved into the house that Clarence Howell had lived in down by the kiln. Orville's family consisted of wife Blanche, who died while living in Wilson Creek, and children Paul and Curtis. Orville remarried and had a daughter Marcella.

The canning factory operated only about five years, closing in 1924, with Will O'Bryant moving back to Republic. The shutting down of the canning factory and the lack of other industry to take its place marked the beginning of the end for the town of Wilson Creek. Clarence Howell died May 11, 1923. Orville and his sons moved into Clarence's house and lived there a short time before moving to Springfield.

Bert Robinson began to increase his holdings by buying any land that came up for sale. By 1924 he owned practically all the south end of the town site and the hills across the railroad tracks.

On May 15, 1926, the Wilson Creek post office was discontinued. In the spring of 1927 the Robinson's store burned and they moved to the O'Bryant's house. They reopened a store in a small building behind the old store, and operated it for a short time.

Only a few families ever came to Wilson Creek to live. the total population at the maximum occupancy was never more than perhaps 35 to 50 people. Most of the subdivided lots were never sold separately and remained as large tracts which were cultivated.

O.E. "Orie" Hart owned the 97 acres of Bert Robinson, Lester Davis had the three lots that Tom and Mary Lentz owned and I.W. "Jack" Gardner owned 33.55 acres that had been Clarence Howell's place. In 1960 the state of Missouri began a program of land acquisition for the future Wilson's Creek National Battlefield. These families were the last to live in what was the town of Wilson Creek. The site of where Wilson Creek town was is now part of the Wilson's Creek National Battlefield, managed by the National Park Service. All of the homes, buildings and foundation were removed by the Park Service. Now even those who lived and were part of this community are unable to find where buildings were.

Florence (Howell) Short's grandchildren, Greg and Gary, live in Republic and along with their sisters, DyAnna (Short) Shaver and LuDena (Short) Hunt, still have the farm where

*The Wilson Creek boxcar depot.*

*William O'Bryant house in Wilson Creek. Courtesy of Springfield Magazine.*

Florence and Samuel Emmit "Hop" Short (married about 1917) farmed and raised their children: Ivan who died young; Helen (Short) Wilkins, and Gene. Helen lives in Springfield, Missouri. Gene bought the farm and lived there until his death in 2005. The farm is located about two miles from where the town of Wilson Creek was. *Material came from History of Greene County 1883, Springfield Magazine 1981, and people who lived and were a part of the town of Wilson Creek whose stories were passed down. Submitted by Bill Robertson.*

# Civil War and Rural Life Around Republic

*A Civil War "Union" reunion likely on May 30th in the mid-1890s at the home of veteran Thomas Hagewood, near Republic. By this time widower Mr. Hagewood had married Widow Sophia Berry Payne. She was born and raised at Hooten Town in Stone County on the James River. She first married James Payne, who had been raised on the James River near the current Payne Cemetery, just south of the Christian/Greene County line west off Highway 160, north of Nixa. In this photo, Mrs. Hagewood is the lady with covered head on the extreme right in the front row, while Mr. Hagewood is just to her right. The man to Mrs. Hagewood's immediate left is Timothy Maples of Delaware Town, south of Wilson Creek. Courtesy of Wayne Glenn.*

*Above: Log cabin built in 1839 by the Spencer Kerr family, now owned by the Newlins.*
*At right: Jeff and Sherry Newlin home in 2006.*

# Civil War

## The Ray House

John A. Ray, a native of Tennessee, migrated to Missouri in the late 1840s. A widower with one daughter, Frances Elizabeth, transported all his possessions in a wagon pulled by a team of oxen. He met Roxanna Steele who had three daughters by her previous marriage to William Steele. After a brief courtship, they married September 24, 1849. Five more children were born to the family.

*John and Roxanna Ray house about 1882, built in 1852. Photo courtesy of National Park Service, Wilson's Creek National Battlefield.*

On October 1, 1852 John began a new house for his family. It was a sturdy house built of timber hewed and hauled from Arkansas. The house was constructed on the Telegraph Road. In 1860 part of the house was used as a post office when John Ray was named postmaster.

One day in August 1861 John and his family watched as a column of soldiers led by General Lyon marched down the Telegraph Road. Although there is no documented evidence, soldiers undoubtedly secured water from the spring, foraged in Ray's cornfield, and raided the family vegetable garden.

Olivia, one of the daughters who was age 7 at the time, tells about going to "herd horses" in a pasture along Wilson Creek with her 10-year-old sister Livonia and her 9-year-old brother John Wesley. It was before sunrise on August 10, 1861. A stranger came galloping up shouting, "Get out of here, children! They'll be fighting any minute!" The children mounted the horses and raced home to give the alarm.

The family was greatly alarmed because they knew the Confederate troops were camped in the valley a short distance away. They all took refuge in the cellar under the house, except for John Ray, who watched the battle from his front porch. The chicken house was hit, but the home was missed. A yellow hospital flag was displayed by the Confederates at the Ray House, and firing was ceased in that direction. The house was used as a hospital when the wounded were brought there. The Ray family carried water and placed blankets or knapsacks under their heads and tried to make them as comfortable as possible.

General Lyon was killed, and his body was brought to the house and left there until a detail from Springfield was sent to transport the body back to Springfield. Frances Elizabeth ran to pile rocks on the spot where General Lyon died. A marker now marks the spot.

Most of the original material of the house itself is still there. Roxanna died March 26, 1871. John died in July 1875. Frances Elizabeth married Clayborn Stewart. A granddaughter, Dorothy Stewart McElhaney, lived in the house until the land was purchased by the Wilson's Creek National Battleground Park Service.

Rhoda Jones was born in Georgia. She was the personal slave of Roxanna Steele who married William F. Steele in 1837. Rhoda came to Missouri with the Steeles when they moved here in the 1840s and settled just north of the future Christian and Greene County line, in Greene County. Rhoda was the "Mammy" of William Steele (a son of William F. and Roxanna Steele) who was murdered 60 plus years later. Owned by Roxanna Steele, Rhoda stayed with her mistress when Steele died. When Roxanna Steele married John Ray in 1849, Rhoda stayed on. When the Battle of Wilson's Creek took place in 1861, Rhoda and her four slave children hid with part of the Ray family in the cellar of their homestead. Rhoda would have been in the Ray House when General Nathaniel Lyon was brought to the home. After the war Rhoda married John Jones and moved to Springfield where she remained until her passing in November 1897 of throat disease. She is buried at Hazelwood Cemetery. *Submitted by Betty Mason.*

*John Ray's spring. Courtesy of National Park Service, Wilson's Creek National Battlefield.*

*Rhoda Jones, slave of Roxanna Steele Ray, brought from Georgia. Courtesy of Wayne Glenn.*

## The Sharp House

The Sharp house was located on the Telegraph Road, across the creek, on a hill west of the Ray House, and just across the county line into Christian County. Mary Horton (Montgomery) Howard was living with her daughter's family, Mary Frances and Joseph Sharp, at the time of the battle. The story told is that she refused to take refuge in the cellar with the rest of the family. They were young and had their lives ahead of them, while she was old and near the end of her life. Besides, she didn't believe a Yankee bullet could kill her anyway. A cannon ball and several musket bullets hit the house, but she was uninjured.

On August 10, 1861, Colonel Sigel's Union troops advanced from the south entering Terrell Creek Valley which extended northward about 3/4 miles to the Sharp house. Here, they observed that a strong force of about 3,000 Rebel Cavalry had taken position in the valley. Pushing ahead, Sigel's men advanced to several hundred yards southwest of the Sharp house, and this became a commanding position for Sigel's artillery. Colonel Sigel's troops were positioned in the fields behind and around the Sharp house. At times, the house was in the direct line of fire. The house, barn and other out buildings were riddled with cannon shot.

Confusion broke out when Sigel's battery fired on the Confederates from behind. Sigel moved his position near the Sharp house. The Confederates waded up the stream and started up the slope leading to the Sharp house. Sigel's column divided, and one gun withdrew down the road and set up a road block.

After the battle the Union Army retreated to Springfield. Those who were left searched the neighborhood for any hiding enemy. The Sharp house and out buildings were searched. All the buildings were badly damaged. The Sharp family was found crouched in the cellar. The soldiers were confronted by an old woman with a fiery tongue wanting to know if the fuss was over yet. They were left unharmed and were told it was safe to come out. The sight they saw with all the dead men and horses was not a pleasant sight to see.

The Sharp house was burned the following year by Bushwhackers and the family moved from the area. *Submitted by Betty Mason.*

## Wilson's Creek National Battleground

The battle of Wilson's Creek was fought on August 10, 1861 and was over in six short hours. On December 24, 1861 just four months after the battle, Congress passed a joint resolution honoring Lyon and all who had fought at Wilson's Creek. This was one of only five such resolutions passed during the entire war. After the war's end, veterans began coming to the battlefield to honor their comrades. They began piling rocks on the spot where Union General Nathaniel Lyon was killed, and then in 1928 The University Club of Springfield erected the monument on Bloody Hill honoring General Lyon.

The battle to make Wilson's Creek part of the National Park Service took much longer. A local group of citizens formed in 1950 and called themselves the Wilson's Creek Foundation, Inc. They realized the importance of Wilson's Creek and wanted to make it a national park. After purchasing 37 acres on Bloody Hill in 1951, they then lobbied the state of Missouri to buy the rest of the battlefield which turned out to be around 1700 acres. With this accomplished they then lobbied the federal government for recognition and in 1960 President Eisenhower signed the bill that created Wilson's Creek National Battlefield.

Since that time many improvements have been made to Wilson's Creek National Battlefield. The Visitor Center was built in the early 1980s as well as putting in the five mile tour road. Also in the early 1980s the John Ray house was restored to its 1861 appearance. In 2003, construction was completed on an addition to the existing Visitor Center. The main part of the addition is the Civil War research library which houses the largest collection of Civil War books on the Trans-Mississippi Theater of the Civil War in the National Park Service. Then, in 2005, General Sweeney Museum of Civil War History was acquired. This collection of over 5,000 objects makes Wilson's Creek one of the premier museums in the Midwest.

Today Wilson's Creek National Battlefield is facing many developmental pressures. A new housing subdivision is going in to the south boundary, and the surrounding communities are growing by leaps and bounds. Wilson's Creek National Battlefield is a prime example of partnerships that are successful. Without the local citizens getting involved, the park would not be a part of the National Park Service today. *Submitted by Connie Langum.*

## BATTLE OF WILSON'S CREEK

Most Missourians favored neutrality when the Civil War started April 12, 1861, probably hoping to keep their head down and avoid the coming conflict.

Knowing of the Confederate's plan to at-

*Stones stacked where General Lyon fell. Photo circa August 1897. Courtesy of Dixie Keltner.*

tack his army of 5,400 men, General Nathaniel Lyon felt that, outnumbered over 2 to 1, his best chance was a surprise attack on General Ben McCulloch's army at dawn the morning of August 10, 1861. Splitting his forces, Lyon sent Colonel Franz Sigel's column to meet the enemy on their south while he engaged them from the north.

McCulloch, who had the combined command of his army, Major General Sterling Price's and N. Bart Pearce's, totaling 12,000 soldiers, camped by the Wire Road ford over Wilson Creek near ripening cornfields. Due to threat of rain, he decided to cancel the next day's attack on General Lyon's army camped at Springfield.

The Union forces gained the high ground first, later known as Bloody Hill, but advantage in the battle would shift. Among the many things that would cause problems for both sides: part of the Union soldiers wore gray which caused confusion; approximately 2,000 of the Confederate soldiers were unarmed; General Lyon was killed and all Regular Army officers above the rank of captain were either killed or wounded.

After six hours of battle, much of it close-quarter fighting, the Confederates withdrew at 11:30 a.m. after their third attack. Union Major Samuel Sturgis, realizing his men were exhausted and ammunition low, ordered a retreat to Springfield. Poorly equipped and disorganized, the Confederates didn't pursue.

It should probably be known as the Battle of Oak Hills since named that by the victorious Confederacy. Instead, due to the number of troops engaged, length of the battle and percentage of men killed and wounded, 535 dead and 2,000 wounded or missing, 12% of the Confederate forces and almost 25% of the Union's, it is remembered as the bloodiest battle of the Civil War west of the Mississippi. It has been written in history as the Battle of Wilson's Creek. *Submitted by Mary Strickrodt.*

*Visitor Center at Wilson's Creek National Battlefield.*

*Wilson's Creek National Battlefield. "Don't Yield An Inch," by Andy Thomas. A critical moment in the Battle of Wilson's Creek, August 10, 1861.*

# Rural Life Around Republic

## Pond Creek Township
## The First Two Generations

The first settler in what would be Pond Creek Township was David Reynolds, coming in 1834, 13 years after statehood. Reynolds and most who followed were from Tennessee. William McDaniel, N.B. Neil and Edward Blades all settled there in 1836, about the same time Pond Creek's first 14 x 15 schoolhouse was built. Over the next six years George Britain; ___ Conner; Samuel, Anthony, William and James Garoutte; Robert and Stephen Batson; John Loose; Magruder Tannehill and Robert Carr all came. John Laney, James Wade, Joel Skelton and James McCarty had arrived by 1861 and George Jackson, James Hood and John Wallace by 1880. They are but a few of those who came, some before the Civil War hoping to escape it, and some after seeking rich land on which to raise their families.

Pond Creek was formed in 1859. It was 25 square miles in the corner of Greene County bordered by Christian County (south), Lawrence County (west), Center Twp. (north) and Republic Twp. (east). Elections were ordered held at Wade Chapel. In 1860 the post office called Pond Creek, where all area mail arrived to be picked up by the recipient, was changed to Little York.

With Civil War battles at Wilson's Creek, Springfield, Dug Springs, Newtonia and Carthage and the border war just two counties away, Pond Creek was poorly situated to stay out of trouble. John Reynolds, son of Pond Creek's first settler, was one of ten men who voted for Abraham Lincoln in 1860 in Pond Creek Township where it was said that there were "no secession votes." John was killed on the night of November 22, 1861 while Confederates headquartered at Springfield. Joel Skelton, a Georgia native, was killed November 8, 1862 with Andrew Owen killed the same night. Others killed were John Gower, Lum Johns and James Everhart.

With much of the land a rolling prairie, farming had been the only industry in Pond Creek Township, but in the 1880s, a great part was still timbered. Deposits of lead were found along Pickerel Creek and in the township's southeast part, but little mining was done.

Clearing the land of timber with a cross cut saw, supplying logs for building and, after the stumps were removed, left it ready to plant.

If land was planted in corn after clearing, sassafras tended to sprout thick. Cutting sprouts out of a field was necessary, but an aggravation for the farm children who had to do it. However, according to one farmer's journal, once a field began to be farmed in wheat, the sassafras gave it up. The turning of the ground with a turning plow for wheat happened to be at just the time of year so that cutting them with a plow share killed the sprouts.

Albert Skelton, born 1874, wrote that he had seen some grain cradled (cut by hand) but not much. The dropper had arrived within his first memory. It was a machine similar to a two horse mower that cut and held the grain until the driver thought he had enough for a bundle and "tripped" it. This caused the bundle to fall to the ground after which men known as binders came along and bound them, using a small handful of the straw to tie the bundles.

Horse powered threshers were used until Jim Reynolds bought a Garr Scott steam thresher about 1880 and moved it from job to job by horse power.

Getting rid of the corn stalks in the field was a job assigned to teenage boys early in the morning of the severest part of winter when everything was frozen hard. A horse was hitched to two chains, 5 or 6 ft. long, which were attached to a six inch diameter pole long enough to cover six rows of corn stalks, then dragging the field, the stalks snapped off.

The major part of farm income came from the harvest of the land or animals raised and sold. Some farmers bought calves in the fall when they were cheaper to keep and fatten. Extra butter and eggs were sold by the woman of the house. First taken to the nearest store, but after buggies and spring wagons (hacks) became commonly available, they were taken weekly to Springfield to regular customers. The butter was wrapped in damp cloths and eggs packed in large buckets of bran.

A smokehouse was necessary with an average family of eight, butchering at least one beef, and seven or eight hogs for large quantities of sausage made into links or patties and layered in lard in stone jars. Every family had an apple and peach orchard and anytime a neighbor came in during the winter, a pan or bucket of apples was set out. Apples and peaches were preserved by drying. Home canning started around the 1880's in tin cans and glass jars sealed with wax. Strawberry patches began to appear around this time. Potatoes and apples were stored in the cellar, peas and beans were dried, peppers, onions and garlic were dried and hung, and turnips, parsnips, carrots and cabbage were stored in a straw lined pit in the ground.

Homes were usually built as money and need came together. George and Mollie Skelton married in 1873 and moved into a one-room home, later adding a kitchen and using a trundle bed for the children. In the 80s, he built two more rooms on and in the next decade, another two rooms above.

Entertainment ran from singing schools taught by Wes Wade, to school literaries, to picnics held at the Caleb Thurman sassafras grove, about 3/4 mile west of Republic on the north side of the road. There was a swimming hole on Pickerel Creek at Jim and Hattie Reynolds place that drew boys on hot Sunday afternoons. In the late summer and fall, boys in early teens spent Sunday afternoons fighting bumblebees after plowing up their nests in the after harvest wheat stubble. About 1890 a group went fishing at Johnson's Hole on the Sac River in the two mile stretch between Whinrey's and John's grist mills and seined 110 lbs. of fish. Henry Reynolds hand caught three trout that day which weighed 10 lbs.

A "Cob Web Party" for teenagers at the Britain home in about 1892 was later referred to as "the time of our lives." All the furniture in one room had been removed with two chairs placed near the room's center back to back about one and one-half feet apart. Two long strings were then tied to something on the outside of the room (door hinge or wall hook), then ran all over the room in every direction and height, finally ending up, one on the back of one chair and one on the other with a corn cob tied to the end of each string. There were as many pairs of strings as couples of boys and girls. Before being allowed in the room, they had to pair off. Let into the room, the boys took a cob from one chair and the girls from the other. They had to follow their string, winding it up, running every direction

*John and Ann Wallace.*
*Courtesy of Bill Robertson.*

*John and Ann Wallace home about 1880, later owned by Gertrude and Forest Wade. Courtesy of Bill Robertson.*

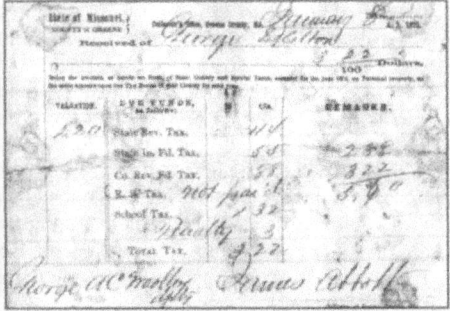

*Tax receipt of George Skelton.*

until they came to the end with no one ending up with who they started with. Fifty-five years later, Albert Skelton wrote, "I don't think I ever had so much fun in all my life, and everybody enjoyed themselves."

Peddlers walking the countryside and carrying their wares were a common sight in the decades after the Civil War. For 67 years after 1871, Republic's general store was the closest and it sold everything. The groceries it carried were sugar, salt, saleratus (baking soda) and a few other staple items.

Whinrey's and John's were the closest grist mills to Pond Creek Township. They were both located on the Sac River two to two and one-half miles apart and ground wheat into flour and corn into either meal for the table or chops for chicks.

Although during the Civil War, an old-timer said that prices were "all a fellow was a mind to ask!" Brown sugar is a good indicator of price changes due to circumstances. Just three years after the Civil War in 1868, it sold for 16-2/3 cents per lb. Six years later in 1874, four years after trains started running in Greene County, it was down to 12-1/2 cents per lb. By 1914, 40 years later when rail lines were moving produce across the entire United States, it had decreased to 4-1/2 cents per lb.

In 1876 the census (whites only, there were no blacks in Pond Creek) showed a ratio of people to horses (including mules) of about three to one, clearly a farming township. Of the 608 people, only 244 could read and write. There were 114 males under 21 and 197 over 21 with 127 females under 21 but only 80 over 21. This may attest to the number of women dying from childbirth. In 1880 the census was up to 1,009.

Attending church was always a part of life for the early settlers. The first sermon was preached by Methodist minister Rev. Thomas Ashley at the David Reynolds home in 1838.

Blades Chapel dates back to 1844 when the division took place in the Methodist Episcopal Church of the United States and they met at Old Bethel Church. The congregation broke up during the Civil War, then reorganized in 1867. When the church burned in May 1872, they met at the Grandview School. The building known as Blades Chapel was built in 1889.

Hopewell Baptist Church was organized on June 15, 1867 with their church building erected in 1873.

A Christian Church congregation was organized May 1, 1881, meeting at St. Elmo School. The annual camp meeting was held at Robertson's Springs about two miles southeast of Republic. There was also one held at Garoutte Spring, northwest of Blades Chapel Church.

Travel was first by foot, horseback or wagon. Except in the dry of summer when it was a deep bed of dust, the roads were always cut to pieces with ruts from the wagon's narrow tires. Roads in winter were either mud or ruts that fell in when they got deep or, in freezing weather, frozen ruts. There were no road graders at all until the late 1800s. Although the foundry whistle could often be heard in Pond Creek Township, a trip to Springfield in a wagon was a 3-3/4 hour trip starting at daybreak or before. A two-mile walk to Republic to attend church services, board the train or court a girl was considered nothing.

When the train came in 1871, it stopped in Republic between eight and nine in the morning and returned from Springfield about six in the evening. People could ride in to shop, go to the circus, fair or theatrical productions or they could take a trip somewhere. However, with so many train wrecks, they felt they were taking their lives in their hands to ride them.

After 1871, area mail would be picked up in Republic until 1903 when Mail Route No. 1 was established with Elmer Skelton the first carrier. Rural telephone service came about the same time with the switchboard in George Jackson's home.

Many of the later curable or treatable diseases and conditions still held horror for people of the late 1800s: typhoid, diphtheria, influenza and childbirth, besides the great number of farming accidents that occurred.

When people were sick, they "doctored" themselves and only sent for the doctor when it was serious, seldom ever going in to him. The doctors in Republic that were used were Dr. Bishop, Dr. White, Dr. Patterson, Dr. G.B. Dorrell and Dr. Beal. Three other doctors were occasionally called, Dr. Loudermilk of Bois D'Arc, Dr. Brown of Billings, Dr. Camp and a doctor from Brookline.

George Skelton bought the first spring wagon (hack) in the area about 1890. It had elliptical springs and removable seats, resembling a three seated buggy. Corpses were dressed at home and placed in coffins first made by William McDaniel and later by Wes Wade. Skelton's hack became the transportation for taking the deceased to the cemetery.

Except for the removal of timber, the land and weather have changed the least. The 21st century has no monopoly on extreme weather. In 1871 no rain fell in Greene County from August 1st to October 8th. In 1881 there was no rain from mid-July to September 10th, the stock being driven to Pickerel Creek which still had a hole of water in it. But in 1875, Springfield had an extraordinary rain storm and Wilson Creek, within the city, was 100 yards wide.

The greatest change in 2006 is the land usage. While there are still operating farms in Pond Creek Township, much of the ground is untilled and the trend is towards small acreages and large houses. *Submitted by Mary Strickrodt.*

## Nelson's Mill

This picture of Nelson's Mill which was taken in 1913 by Dick O'Conner was first built by Woodson Howard and a Mr. Ingram in 1840. It later burned in the 1920s. The mill

*Nelson's Mill, circa 1913. Courtesy of Bill O'Neal.*

site, which was located about five miles south of Battlefield, Missouri, and was first known as Howard and Ingram Mill, then Knowland, then Griffin, then Hawkins and last as Nelson's Mill. The dam was later converted into a low water crossing, and a bridge was built by Christian County. Nelson's Mill was on James River, east of Manley Cemetery. *Submitted by Bill O'Neal.*

## Schuyler Creek Salting Station

Farmers for miles around the Republic area planted acres of cucumbers to sell to Charley Cassy at the "pickle works" in the 1940s. The large wooden tanks were built on the Cassy farm on what is now Farm Rd. 101, east of Republic near Schuyler Creek. The cucumbers were placed in a brine in the tanks to begin the pickling process. They were then transferred to Springfield Pickle Works to finish the process.

*Schuyler Creek Salting Station, referred to as the Pickle Works, 1944. Courtesy of Margie (Cassy) Francis.*

## Early Farm Machinery

In the early years of farming when it came time to harvest grain, neighbors would work together, going from field to field cutting, bundling, shocking, then later coming back and threshing the wheat, oats, or barley. Shocks were eight to ten bundles set on end with the grain heads to the top and with bundles for a cap to shed the rain and weather. There were some farmers who chose not to shock the grain but instead would haul the bundles to a corner of a field and make a cone shaped stack. This would

*Steam engine tractor and threshing machine.*

open the field up so the threshing machine could be set up next to the stack. The women would work together preparing meals for the workers. The children old enough to work in the fields would do so and the younger ones would bring drinking water to the workers.

During the threshing season farmers would hire a threshing crew to come in and do their threshing. These crews would have their own people with them. Generally they had a cook shack, where meals would be prepared on site and a bunk shack, usually used by women. The men would sleep in the farmers' barns. As jobs were finished the crew would move from farm to farm. Pay for this service was a percentage of the harvest. As the years progressed and farm machinery improved, one farmer would purchase a binder, another a threshing machine, and share the work with all neighbors participating.

*Cook shack for threshing crew. Courtesy of Bill O'Neal.*

*Early tractor and combine. Courtesy of the Sparkman Family.*

The threshing machine separated the grain from the stem or straw of the wheat, oats, or barley. The kernels would go to a hopper where a sacker would sack the grain. The straw was blown through a tube to the ground, making a big straw stack. This straw could be used for bedding cattle, straw tics for family beds and many other uses. Some farmers would bale the straw, others would haul loose straw and stack it in a barn, and some left it in the fields. Some would haul the bundles of grain to a ditch that was prone to wash out, set the threshing machine up and blow the straw into this area; this would help prevent erosion. These straw stacks were fun to play on as a child, making tunnels, playing king on the mountain, jumping, falling, rolling and doing all kinds of things. It was quite a task to get to the top. The cattle would also use it to bed down around the base; the calves seemed to have fun playing around the straw stack too.

*Eight horse-drawn combine. Courtesy of the Sparkman Family.*

*Marion Gardner. Courtesy of Herbert Batson.*

*Threshing crew, 1913. Courtesy of Otto C. Fuhr Family.*

With the arrival of the combine, there was no longer the need for binding the grain, shocking the bundles, and then later threshing. This was now done by a horse or tractor drawn machine. The grain went into a hopper that would hold several bushels and could be dumped into a wagon and hauled to the barn. The straw was either scattered on the ground or windrowed up to be baled or picked up loose. With the progression of machinery, one farmer could do the work that previously took several people to perform. *Submitted by Bill Robertson.*

## SAWMILLS

Early settlers were able to use all of their land. The wooded area provided firewood, and wood for building homes, barns, outbuildings, and furniture. After the first settlers established the land, sawmills became an important part of building the community. A

*Local sawmill from the early 1900s. Courtesy of Otto C. Fuhr family.*

sawmill could be set up on a farm, and most every dimension of lumber could be cut out of a saw log.

The people who owned the sawmill would have their own crew; they would cut the trees and haul or drag them to the mill. There was a scale to show how many different pieces of lumber you could cut out of a log. This helped to fill what was needed to complete a home or barn. When the cut lumber was taken off the saw it was stacked in a manner so air could get between the layers to dry or cure.

It took several days to set up a sawmill. The owners of the sawmill would usually have an agreement with the landowner that other property owners could haul logs to be cut by the mill operators. Some sawmills would stay at one place for a year. The sawmill owners would work on shares, as they had a list of people needing to purchase lumber as well as selling ties to the railroad.

Some of the homes and businesses in Republic were built with this type of lumber. You can find lumber that was cut in the 1930s and 1940s stored in barns that can be planed and used today. Some of the hardest woods came from this area. This was another way early settlers survived by selling the lumber and wood from their land. Landowners are still harvesting trees from their land using new techniques.

The logs are hauled to a company that can saw and cure the lumber in days, where it once took months.

*Information obtained from those who had sawmills and people who had sawmills on their property, including Bill Misemer, John West and Charles Fuhr.*

## MAKING SORGHUM MOLASSES IN THE 1930s

Sorghum cane was grown as a food crop by several farmers around the Republic area. The leaves were stripped off the canes which were then cut and fed into the rollers where they were squeezed to extract the sap. The sap was channeled into a holding container, and then went by pipe to the evaporating pan where it was cooked down. The water was evaporated out of the sap leaving the sorghum molasses. It took about six gallons of sap to produce one gallon of sorghum molasses.

The pictures below show this process:

*1. The bare cane is fed into the sap extractor.*

2. *Piles of sorghum cane, after juice has been extracted.*

3. *The sap being cooked down by Bob Fuhr and Jim Selvey. Submitted by Mae Belle Fuhr.*

## DAIRIES

### COOPER DAIRY

Jim Cooper owned a small dairy just north of Republic in 1935. Today it would have been inside the city limits. Milk was bottled in quart bottles. After being bottled, the milk was placed in crates with dividers to prevent breakage, and loaded on the bed of the truck. Mr. Cooper owned a blue pickup truck with running boards and side handles for delivery boys to grasp while riding. Two of the delivery boys were Charles Wilhite and Kent DeWitt. Charles remembers the two of them riding on the running board, jumping off, running to the house, delivering milk, picking up the empty bottle, taking it back to the truck, placing the empty in the crate and grabbing a quart of milk ready for the next house. He and Kent could keep up with Mr. Cooper, who did not stop the truck for deliveries. Russell Payne was also employed to help with deliveries. *As remembered by Charles Wilhite.*

### MOONEYHAM DAIRY FARM

Ed and Maud Mooneyham owned and operated a dairy farm in the early 1900s, located west of Republic. They would bottle milk and sell it in Republic and the surrounding area to support their family of three sons. *As reported by Marilyn Mitchell.*

### PAUL MCCONNELL DAIRY FARM

The Paul McConnell family owned an 80 acre farm at the corner of Hines and Lynn Streets, going 1/4 mile east on Hines and 1/4 mile south on Lynn, with the exception of 10 acres of bottomland on Hines. Readying the land for farming, Paul David recalls picking up 120 wagon loads of rock on the 10 acres just north of the house. This section was then fertilized and sowed in alfalfa for an outstanding crop. Their dairy herd consisted of 28 head of cattle. Starting in 1958, the entire family; Paul, Juanita, Paul David and Richard, all worked together bottling one gallon jugs of whole milk, no pasteurization just whole milk, with lots of cream settling on the top of each jar. They filled around 40 to 50 gallons per day, placing each one in a chest type cooler for the public to serve themselves. You were asked to pay 50 cents for the milk, and pay a 50 cent deposit for the jug which was to be returned with each purchase, money was placed in a box completely on the honor system. They terminated this operation in 1963. At that time the price of milk had been increased to 75 cents per gallon. *As remembered by Paul David McConnell.*

### ALDEN MCCROSKEY DAIRY FARM

The Alden McCroskey Farm located on West Farm Road 170, east of Republic, had a dairy herd of 25 to 30 cows. They started the sale of whole milk later than the McConnells but used the honor system and self service also, ending their operation in the late 70s charging $1.00 per gallon at that time. *As remembered by Mrs. Alden McCroskey.*

### DAIRY PRODUCTS HOME DELIVERY

In the late 1940s or early 1950s Lloyd Garoutte operated the Daricraft Home Delivery which was a division of the Daricraft Creamery located in Monett, Missouri. A dairy truck would deliver your order to your home each week. This division of Daricraft ended in approximately 1955.

At a later date Hiland, Cloverleaf and Foremost Dairies offered home delivery service in the city of Republic. These dairies were located in Springfield. *As remembered by Mary Sue Robertson.*

### MAPLE GROVE PARK

At the turn of the century Maple Grove Park was located about two miles northeast of Republic on the main gravel road going toward Springfield. Maple Grove Park was on a tract of land with a large spring-fed lake surrounded by several cabins for changing one's clothes and selling food and drinks to the many youth and adults who came to enjoy swimming. Advertising pictures of the time showed large crowds of folk gathering by the cabins and under the shade of large maple trees all around the pool. The swimming pool had a homemade diving board and other attractions.

There was a large pavilion with covered porch which provided a dance floor. Many people came to enjoy an evening of music and dancing. It continued to be a social gathering place until liquor became a problem and a stabbing took place. The area was closed to visitors in the late 1920s, and a fire destroyed the last remaining building. Today the area is privately owned, and a smaller spring-fed lake remains at the location on the corner of what is now South Farm Road 93 and West Farm Road 168. *Submitted by Mae Belle Fuhr.*

*Scenes from Maple Grove Park. Courtesy of the Sparkman Family.*

23

## Traveling On Old Highway 60

In the late 1930s and early 1940s, the only paved road to Springfield was old Highway 60. Folks living in Aurora, Marionville and Billings all traveled through Republic. Republic's north city limit was at the rock home of Joe and Dolly Harris about one block north of now Hwy 174.

Driving north out of town, (now N Hwy) the Jim Dillon home and across from it, the Ronald Brashears family lived on one of Dr. E.L. Beal's fruit orchard farms. Many farms along this route had orchards and sold fruit to travelers.

The next farm on the left was John Coggin's on the west side of Hwy 60. It had the beacon light that led planes into Springfield airport, then on east Division. On the right was Harry Britain family home and then the Queen family before coming to "Buddy's Corner" (called two-mile corner). There one could fill up with gasoline at their pumps and buy food and other items.

Turning east, now Farm Road 168 the George Clarkson home was on the left. Also on the left was the one-room school, Mt. Etna, where Mr. E.B. Ferguson taught for many years while living on his farm a few miles east. Across the busy highway was the Ed McTaggart home among huge pine trees where he had a roadside stand, selling, in season, his apples, grapes and other produce.

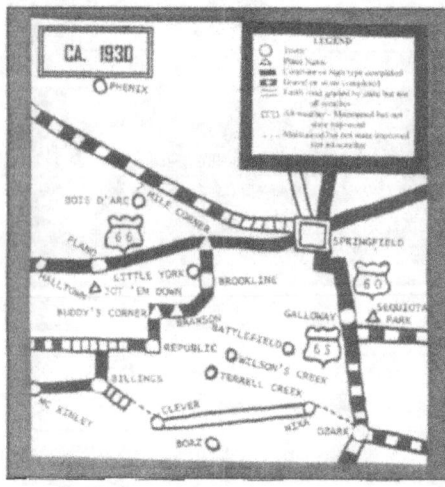

*Traveling on Old Hwy. 60, circa 1930.*

Next on the left was the old Wallace place and up a lane on the right was the Mastin home. Dan and Mary Hartman lived in the next home on the left. In the valley was the Linzee Wells farm where they processed their own turkeys for sale in the fall and shipped many each year across the country. His wife Daphne taught music at Republic for many years. On east the next hilltop was the Ragsdale home and across the highway was the Roy and Minnie Branson Store where they had gas pumps, a larger supply of groceries and kerosene for purchase. They also fixed flats, a convenience with the great number of flats in those days of inflated tires with tubes.

Nearby was the Harris place and on to where the highway turned almost directly left (north, now MM) and ran parallel with the old Frisco railroad tracks. Just a ways up the road and across the tracks on the right was the Glen Hendricks brick home. Continuing north the home on the left belonged to the Potters.

On up the road almost a mile was the town of Brookline, established in 1872 after the railroad came through. On the left in Brookline was the Kellogg's home and nearby were the homes of the Raper and Kennedy families.

At the crossroads past Brookline was the Tom Hendrick's home. Into a valley and up a small hill, each side of the road was lined with rows of mature walnut trees that had been planted. The Parish family lived on the west side at the top of the hill in a two story house. Across the highway was their two story barn. As one traveled through here, the children (and maybe the adults) played a "car game." One was supposed to make a wish and if you could hold your breath through the grove of walnut trees, your wish would come true. However, in the fall, when walnuts lay on the highway, the cars slowed so one would have to take a deeper breath of air or lose one's wish.

Past that, the one room Brick School was on the right and then the Trogdon farm on the left. Next was Conn's Corner where there were again gas pumps and also Mary's Beauty Shop. The Rainwater's home was on the left, next was the "Seven Mile Corner" where Hwy 60 met Route 66 and was said to be seven miles west of the Springfield square on that highway of song and story that went to the West Coast.

Farmers made the trip to Springfield about once a week to either sell or exchange their extra eggs, cream and poultry or to purchase their needed supplies of flour, sugar, corn meal, feed and clothing.

If there were farm chores at home to do, children didn't always get to make the trip "to town." However, when they were lucky and did get to go, they always went to the square to the 5 and 10 cent stores because the saved coins by now were "burning a hole in their pockets." *Submitted by Mae Belle Fuhr.*

## Route 66/Plano

Route 66 was "the" national highway when it was commissioned November 11, 1926, and was assigned its number by the federal government.

Historic Route 66 was recently commissioned by the state on May 5, 2006, as a Scenic Byway and is now presently shown on the maps as Highway 266. This road is along the northern boundary of the Republic School District.

Beginning at the corner of MM heading west, one can find the remains of Moore's Sinclair/Texaco filling station. It has been idle since the early 1970s.

Continuing west one mile on the right is Rainey's Garage. It has been in business since 1946. Further west 1.5 miles, Barnes General Store is on the left. John Barnes built the original two story, 34 by 36 foot store in 1934. He sold groceries and such. The building also had an attached residence below and behind. The business expanded to provide Sinclair gas, garage services, a barbershop, feed store, mill, slaughterhouse and locker, furniture and appliances. The station and hardware moved across the highway in the 1960s.

The rock buildings on the right (8673 MO 266) were part of Parkaway Camp and O'Dell Gas Station.

At 9323 MO 266 was once Graystone Heights built of native stone by Ben Brewer in 1935. There were six cabins with hot and cold running water, private toilets and showers, priced at $1.25- $1.75 a night. By 1939 it had grown to eight air cooled cabins and cafe with a Conoco Service. Prices were raised to $1.50-$3.00. It remained in business until I-44 bypassed old 66 in the mid-1960s. It is now used by R&S Floral.

At the junction of Farm Road 65 on the left is the 1887 Yeakley Chapel and Cemetery.

On the right, at the junction of Farm Road 59 is the site of the old Rose Hill Cafe and Station. Allan Rose built this cafe and Standard gas station in 1927. It sat above Pickerel Creek and in sight of his Camp Rose Auto Court. There were four tourist cabins, later turned into housing. Sam Holman bought the camp in the early 1960s and turned it into a Dude Ranch. The remains of the notorious roadhouse, Hillbilly Heaven, are down by the creek. The cafe was razed in the late 1960s for road construction. The court is now a private residence 11294 MO 266 S. Outer Road.

Old 66 veered left to descend Rose Hill and curved to cross the "Ol' Bloody" bridge over Pickerel Creek, then rejoined present 266 to cross the 1932 M.E. Gillioz Bridge over Pickerel Branch. Many accidents occurred in this area.

The town of Plano was located at the junction of Farm Road 45 and Route 66. It probably was named for Plano, Texas. The rock residence on the left was formerly Ray Hilton's grocery store and a Tydol gas station. On the right is the two story remains of what was once a thriving trading post operated by Alf Jackson and included a casket factory and mortuary and post office. The building was constructed from hand-cut blue limestone hauled from two miles away. The walls were two and a half feet thick. Neighbors joined together to complete the building in about three months. Later there was a saloon and a dance hall on the upper floor. The post office existed from 1895-1903.

At what is now 14257 MO 266 was the former location of Dutch's Tavern and Station. Alfred (Dutch) and his wife Mildred Hogenmiller converted their home into a tavern/station in the late 1920s. Originally it had Standard Oil hand pumps and later they used Mobil Oil electric pumps.

Most of the information for this article was obtained with permission from the book, <u>Birthplace of Route 66 Springfield, Mo</u>, by C.H. Skip Curtis, and a *News Leader* article dated July 23, 1972. *Submitted by Alan Comisky.*

## Jot 'Em Down Store

The country store named Jot 'Em Down was located on the northeast corner of PP and TT Highways, northwest of Republic. Jot 'Em Down was given its name from the "Lum 'N Abner" program which aired on the radio from April 1931 to 1955. This full-service store was built in 1938 by the new owners Vernie and Clara (Viles) Giles and Hollis Viles with the first day of business in November of that year. The community near St. Elmo School was excited about a grocery store opening in their neighborhood, as the closest stores were Plano, Halltown or Republic. Vernie and Clara made their home in the back of the store which was two rooms. Later Vernie and Clara paid Hollis for his share of the partnership and became full owners.

*From left: Norene Viles, Orten Pyeatt, Matty and Hollis Viles, Cleo and Leo Batson, and Bob Pyeatt (child), in front of the Jot 'Em Down store. Courtesy of Joan Viles.*

*Dorothy (Blades) Swinney (left) and Cleo (Blades) Batson at the Jot 'Em Down store, 1944. Courtesy of Cleo Batson.*

As told by Joan Viles, a sister-in-law, they had a great business. They would buy chickens and eggs from local farmers. Vernie had a pickup truck with racks and would take poultry or whatever he had purchased to town to sell; and at that time he purchased supplies for their store. There were two gas pumps used starting in 1920. The taller one in the picture is a Wayne Model 615, a 1920 model. This was a gravity or sometimes known as a visible pump, as one could see the gas as it was pumped. The second one in the picture, which was much shorter, was an electric Bowser Model 575 which was made from 1941 through 1948.

Leo and Cleo (Blades) Batson were the next couple to operate Jot 'Em Down beginning in the early 1940s. The store continued to thrive and was supported by neighbors as before. Farmers could purchase chicken and cow feed, all farm supplies, a full line of groceries as well as most household products. A kerosene refrigerator was used for their items that needed to be kept cold. The neighbors of the community developed a closer relationship because of this store.

In 1946 Gladys and Charlie Booth along with their children: Max, Ron and Sue, became the new proprietors of Jot 'Em Down and lived in a small house in the woods just east of the store. Since there was no heat in the house during the winter months, they moved into the back of the store which was only one room at

*Charley and Gladys Booth*

*Oren and Joan Viles in front of Jot 'Em Down, May 1939. Courtesy of Joan Viles.*

that time. The business was very good. They continued to buy eggs from the farmers which they took to town and sold. They also carried a full supply of farmer needs including feed for all farm animals and various supplies for the farm. A full grocery supply, home supplies and of course soda and candies were in stock.

Saturday evenings most everyone from the local community came to Jot 'Em Down to visit. Ralph and Merle Mooneyham and children: Dorothy, Carl, Ruby, Reva and Kay; Clyde and Bonnie Wade and children: Juanita, Rosie and Patsy; Orville and Lavonne Batson and boys: Sonny, Donnie and Ray; Clarence and Jewell Booth and daughters: Judy and Jane; True and Opal Sifferman, and their granddaughter Kay Miller when visiting; Burl and Edna Blades and children: Shirley and Gary. This is only to mention a few. All of the kids would play outside and the parents would sit inside talking about the weekly events in their lives. Everyone always looked forward to spending Saturday evening at Jot 'Em Down. The Booth children remember Glen Lee Norman coming into the store, buying a coke and drinking it with one swallow, then he would buy another coke and take his time drinking it. Another memory was John Jackson who lived east of the store. He made his home with his farm animals sharing the entire house with them. John always traveled on his BF Avery Tractor and when he would leave the store, the Booth children would jump on the back of the tractor and hang on, hitching a ride to their house just down the road.

The Avery Tractor Company discontinued business in the early 1950s being purchased by Minneapolis Moline.

During the time the Booths operated the store, on routine shopping trips to Springfield Grocery, Charlie would pick up commodities for the St. Elmo School hot lunch program. He was instrumental in starting the hot lunch program by volunteering this service.

May 18, 1950 the Booths left the store turning it over to Bill and Nettie Whittaker along with their sons, Bruce and Elmer, and daughter Linda.

They lived in the house south on PP where Elmer and Irene Sifferman last lived.

It is not known how long the Whittakers had the store but possibly only two or three years before it was rented by another couple. One memory from the store with the last proprietors was a cat clock hanging in the back of the store and with each tick of the clock, the cat's tail would move from side to side. Shortly after this the store was closed for the very last time. Many good memories belong to the Jot 'Em Down store. A place where neighbors took care of each other, laughed together, and cried together. The kids shared good times playing together and it all happened within a four-mile radius of their homes. *As shared by Joan Viles, Regina (Sifferman) Maness, Cleo (Blades) Batson, and Sue (Booth) Jackson.*

## Iron Ore Mine

Several years before 1957, William Craig, a hard rock miner with over 50 years of experience, became interested in the mineral deposits near Republic. After prospecting this section, and finding rich iron ore deposits extending from Bois D'Arc to Brown Springs, William obtained leases and title to much of this ore bearing land.

Two factors had changed the mining in Missouri, the exhausted mines in the Great Lakes and Canada, and modern, heavy mining machinery made pit mining a better paying proposition. These events made it possible to reactivate some of the old abandoned mines. The ore at the Republic mine was higher quality than that of other places in the state.

The mill was erected for approximately $150,000 and had a daily capacity of 300 ton. The ore was taken out by the open pit method, using power shovels to remove and a dragline to convey it to the mill. Here the ore bearing rocks and dirt were broken up, washed and cleaned until only the desired ore remained in nuggets from one inch in diameter to the size of a grain of corn. The mill and mine employed about 15 men.

*Iron Ore Mining. Courtesy of The Republic Monitor.*

In December 1957 the first car load of high-grade iron ore was shipped from the Craig-Siegrist Mining Co., located two and a half miles northwest of Republic. It was consigned to the smelters at Granite City, IL. It was hoped that the mining would continue for several years. Many years ago, iron was laboriously mined northwest of Republic, but due to the great effort required in mining, the expense of getting the ore to the smelters and the low price for the product, the mine was abandoned.

Information from *The Republic Monitor*, and those who remembered the mine. *Submitted by Bill Robertson.*

# Republic

*Different views of the Republic Depot.*

# Republic

## RAILROAD

The South Pacific Railroad came through Republic in 1870 and in October deeded the railroad to the Atlantic and Pacific Railroad Company. There was no town at that time and very few houses, and to make matters worse the railroad company refused to build a switch or a depot. Such men as Josiah F. Brooks, W.H. Noe, H.A. Noe, H.A. White, E.T. Anderson and perhaps others, raised one thousand dollars, to build and grade the ground for a switch. From these men's efforts the town of Republic grew and the railroad became very important. The depot shipped fresh fruit, canned goods from the canneries, cattle from the stockyard, flour from the mill, and mail from the US Post Office. Supplies were brought in by the railroad as well.

In November of 1876 the Atlantic and Pacific Railroad sold to the St. Louis San Francisco Railroad Company (Frisco).

The Frisco Railroad made it possible for area residents to attend the 1904 World's Fair in St. Louis, Missouri, and opened up the area for nation-wide travel.

There was a stockyard south of the railroad. Farmers would drive their cattle to the yard to be shipped out by rail. Carolyn O'Neal remembers the cattle drives coming by her house east of town in the 1930s.

The early refrigerated cars had bunkers on

*Train going through Republic, passenger train on side track. Courtesy of Tim Kubat.*

*Believed to be Guy Sparkman in front of Frisco Shops in Springfield. Courtesy of Mae Belle Fuhr.*

*Train coming through Republic. Courtesy of Springfield-Greene County Library and Louis Griesmer.*

*Engine 1510 built by Baldwin in 1923 for St. Louis-San Francisco Railroad. Courtesy of Springfield-Greene County Library and Louis Griesmer.*

each end with hatches at the top which opened up so that 500 pound blocks of ice could be lowered into these bunkers and salt would be added to the ice to keep the fruit fresh until it reached its destination. The walls of the cars were insulated with cork and horsehair, and at different stops on the route more ice could be added depending on the temperature. Many boxcar loads of apples, strawberries, peaches and produce were shipped to New Orleans and other areas.

There were local trains going to Springfield, also going west into Oklahoma. One could take the train to Springfield, get on an express train and go to just about any place in the United States. Most would ride to Springfield stopping at Brookline, Hazeltine Station, Nichols Junction and on to the depot in Springfield. One could shop and return on the afternoon local train. Beryl Batson remembers she and her girl friends taking the train to Springfield in the morning, shopping and returning on the afternoon train. Carolyn O'Neal and friends took the train to Springfield to see movies at the Gillioz Theater. On Friday evenings Bill O'Neal boarded the train in Springfield and came to Republic to spend the weekend with his grandparents.

During WWII many trains came through Republic, transporting troops, military equipment, and supplies for the war. It seemed there was a train every 17 minutes. People could tell where the heavy fighting was, in Europe or Japan, by which direction the trains were going with the supplies. After the war, service men and women returned home on the trains. Even in the 1960s the US government used the railroads to transport troops to and from bases.

In the 1940s all the area rural schools joined together and boarded a train in Springfield, on a trip to the St. Louis Zoo and Shaw's Garden. They boarded the train in the early morning and returned in the late evening. Several buses were waiting at the depot in St. Louis to transport everyone to the zoo. For children who had never been on a train or a MKO bus, this was quite an experience.

The Frisco Railroad was responsible for the beginning and prospering of the city of Republic.

## REPUBLIC

In 1830 almost all of the southern part of Missouri was known as Wayne County. As immigration flowed rapidly from Tennessee, Virginia and Kentucky, and some from other states to the southwestern part of Missouri, legislation was needed to readjust the counties of Missouri. On January 2, 1833, "Greene County" came into existence. It was named for Nathaniel Greene of Revolutionary times. This area was huge and covered what now constitutes McDonald, Newton, Jasper, Barton, Dade, Lawrence, Barry, Stone, Christian, Greene and Webster. It also included parts of Taney, Dallas, Polk, Cedar, Vernon, Laclede, Wright and Douglas.

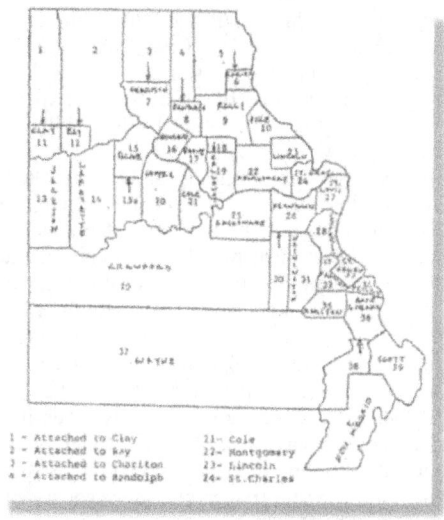

Legislation continued to readjust boundaries until 1857, and the above list of counties constitutes the counties as they appear on the maps of today.

The town of Republic is located in the southwest part of present Greene County and began its existence as a typical crossroads station dur-

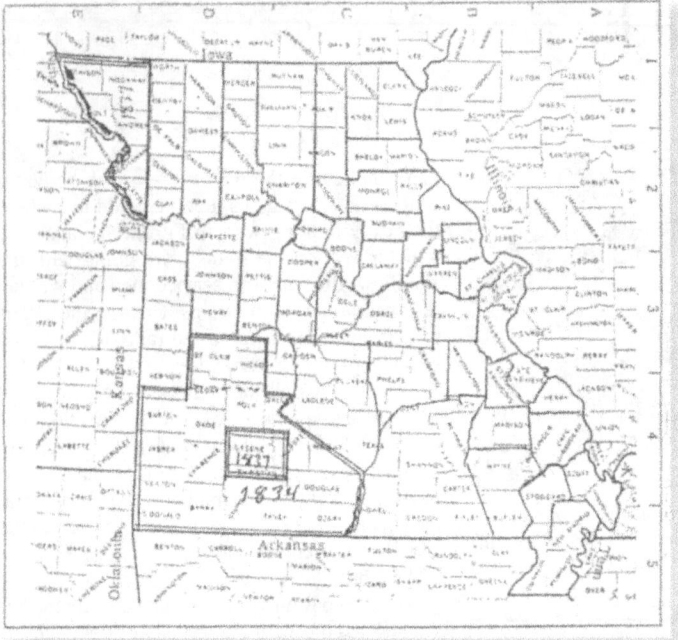
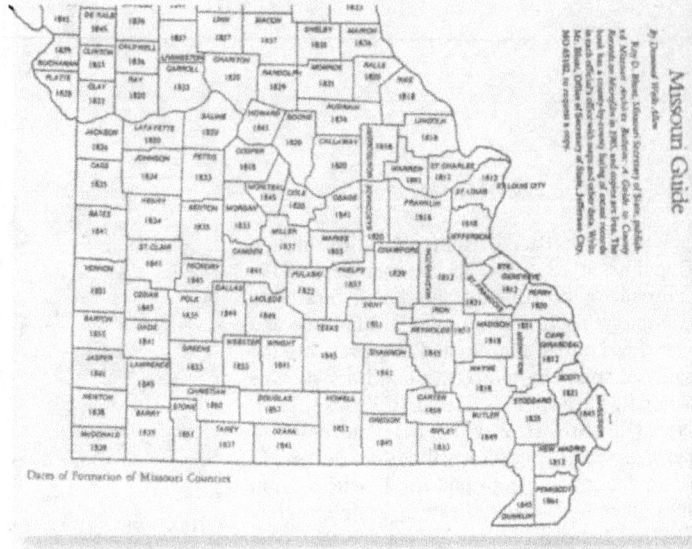

*County Map for the State of Missouri 1834*
Greene County, Missouri, established in 1833 from western parts of Crawford and Wayne counties. Note that the northern border of Greene was somewhat vague—part of the Cedar, St. Clair, Hickory and Benton areas were assigned for administration. (Note, also, that the extreme northwest part of Missouri—Platte, Buchanan, Andrews, Holt, Atchison, Nodaway, did not belong to Missouri until 1837.) By 1837, Greene County had been reduced to its present limits, plus parts of present Christian and Webster counties. Christian (1859), Webster (1856) were relatively new counties, and did not exist when our 1850 date line began.

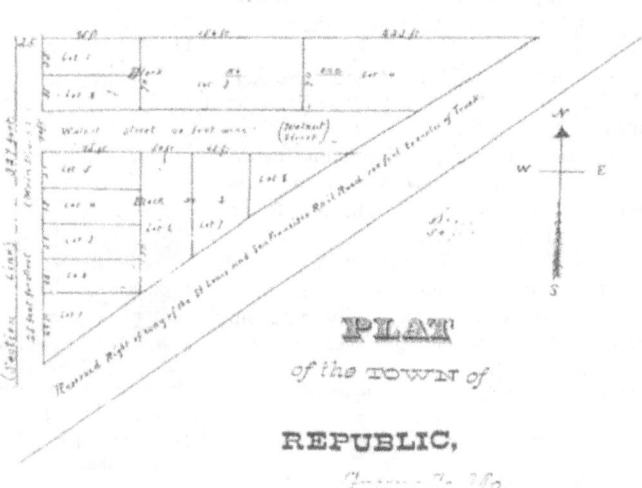

*First store building in Republic. Courtesy Republic Historical Society.*

ing the period of 1850-1860. The first plat of what is now Republic was filed on January 8, 1879, by William B. O'Neal.

Mr. O'Neal was a son of Jesse and Annie (Brown) O'Neal, and was born March 30, 1841, in Carroll County, Arkansas. In 1861 he enlisted in the 24th Missouri Volunteers and remained in the service three years and four months.

He was at the battles of Pea Ridge, Fredericktown and many other skirmishes, as well as various engagements of the Red River Expedition. His regiment was at the battle of Wilson's Creek, but was not called into action. He was mustered out at St. Louis in October 1864. At the close of the war he settled in Greene County to become the founder of the town by making the original plat. Besides farming and being a large property holder, he also engaged in the general merchandise business. In 1883 Mr. O'Neal had filled the office of constable of the township for 10 years, and had received the Greenback nomination for sheriff in 1878. On August 5, 1865 he married Miss Sophrina, daughter of John Luce, of Greene County. She died August 16, 1881, and Mr. O'Neal then married Elizabeth Hainer, also of the county, on January 30, 1882.

*The History of Greene County, Missouri 1883* states that the village of Republic was situated at about the center of the eastern line of section 19 (28-23). It was located in the midst of a rich, thickly-populated, and well-settled prairie, and had an excellent local trade.

W.H. Noe built the first store. This was followed by H.A. White who built a store and hall. The first dwelling house was erected by John Summer and Rev. Loping. The second dwelling was built by Dr. Barlett.

The First Baptist Church was organized June 11, 1874, by Elder J.M. Lappin. The original members were W.B. Searcy, W.H. Harrison, J.P. Youngblood, A.E. Searcy, T.J. Harrison, P.A. Youngblood, Anna Newberry, Cilia Stumps and Ella Decker. The church was a frame building, built at a cost of $1,200. It was beautifully located and out of debt. The pastors who had served the church by 1883 were Elders J.M. Lappin, J.W. Burgess, A.T. Eaton, George W. Black and D.T. Balcom. They had a membership of 36.

The Congregational Church was organized in September 1876. The original members were P.L. Anderson and wife, Edward Howell, Phoebe Tibbetts, W.S. McCleary and wife, Arminta Criswell, Mary Hackett, Mrs. J.F. Brooks, Minnie Smith and Hattie Brooks. The church building was completed in September 1880 at the cost of $2,000 and dedicated the same month by Rev. Robert West who was president of the Home Missionary Society. Pastors serving the church were Rev. S.G. Elliott and in 1883 Rev. N.M. Wheat.

In 1883, Republic contained two general merchandise stores, two drug stores, one hardware and agricultural implement house, one shoe shop, three blacksmith shops, a livery stable, two grain houses, a good grist mill with three runs of burrs and the two above mentioned churches. The population was 150.

At the October term of court in 1888, a new township was created under the name of Republic. It took parts of Pond Creek, Center and Brookline townships and covered the following described territory: "Republic—The west half of township 28, range 23; also section 28, 29, 30, 31, 32 and 33 of township 29, range 23; also sections 6, 7, 18, 19 and 30 of township 28, range 24."

Some dissatisfaction arose over those boundaries and at the July term in 1889, the first order was rescinded and the following order was made setting the boundaries of Republic township: "The west half of township 28, range 23; and sections 28, 29, 30, 31, 32 and 33 of township 29, range 23; also sections 25 and 36 of township 29, range 24 and sections 1, 12, 13, 24 and 25 of township 28, range 24." The town of Republic was designated as the voting place of Republic Township.

The small community grew rapidly after a request by the citizens of Republic to the Frisco railroad company to build a depot or a switch station at this site. The company refused. But a few hustling citizens secured $1,000 in subscriptions to obtain the switch.

Walter Coon, in an article written in 1915, credited Josiah F. Brooks as being the "Father of Republic." Mr. Coon felt that Josiah Brooks, born in New York state, was a century ahead of the times. Not only did he help lead the fight for the switch, he planted the shade trees on Elm Street, and along with W.H. Noe, and J.E. Decker founded and fostered the beautiful Evergreen Cemetery where the bodies of Mr. Brooks and his wife now rest.

Another very important influence in getting the railway subscriptions raised was William H. Noe. Mr. Noe was the son of L.F. and Catherine M. (Holmes) Noe, and was born in Monmouth County, New Jersey. He was educated in the public schools of Livingston County, New York, and followed farming until his 18th year, when he dealt in horses for some time. He then engaged in railroad building, taking charge of the horses used in the transportation of track and building material. After this he became a contractor and builder of railroads in Connecticut. He laid the foundation for the Rockland Print Works, taking a contract to remove seven thousand yards of "hard pan" in 30 days. He finished the work in just 20 days. He then came west, taking contracts and handling stock on the way to Missouri. He bought land in Greene County, and in 1833 had one of the best improved farms in the section, stocked with the finest breeds of horses, cattle, and hogs. He built the first building, a storehouse, located on the west side of Main Street where East Elm connects to Main Street. This building was often referred to as the "little red building."

He operated a general store stocked with such useful necessities as feed, flour, soap, harness, thread, kerosene, or almost anything needed in those days. It was the longest standing building of the original structures in Republic. After his first store he soon built a second store and a hall.

The only information found for another named dedicated worker in obtaining the tracks was that he was a tinsmith named H.A. Noe. Homer A. Noe also served as a postmaster from 1872-1874.

Another leader was Harvey A. White, who was born November 27, 1838 in the township of Westminster, Canada. His parents moved to Illinois in 1839 and settled in McHenry County, where his father was engaged in milling and merchandising. Harvey farmed until he was 21 years old and then enlisted in the army, joining at the first call for troops, and served until discharged because of disability. He then went to Chicago, where he engaged in carpentry for about four years. He moved to Missouri in the fall of 1866, stopping in Greene County for a short time, then going to the counties of Christian and Taney, building the Cedar Valley Mills located in Taney County, where he was employed in milling and the practice of his profession for about eight years. He then moved to Republic and took an active part in the building of the town, and was one of the first trustees. He is credited for building the second store and a hall. Mr. White received his medical education in the Eclectic Medical Institute of Cincinnati. The doctor was engaged in the mercantile business in Republic for seven years, but closed out in December 1880, and resumed his profession. He was married in February 1867 in Greene County to Miss Jane, daughter of P.L. Anderson. Their union was blessed with three children, two sons, and a daughter.

Peter L. Anderson was the son of James and Hetty (Looney) Anderson, and was born July 28, 1820 in Marion County, Tennessee. He grew to manhood in his native county, where he received his education. In 1850 he moved to Missouri and reached Greene County the 6th of December.

He rented land on which he raised six crops and then in 1856 he purchased his farm from a Mr. Rose and continued to live there and made improvements. He married in Marion County, Tennessee, in 1837 to Miss Martha Hollaway. They had five children: Hetty, William H., John, Joney and Elijah. Their son William H. was a member of the Kelson's Cavalry Company. He was taken prisoner in Newton County by some men disguised as Federal soldiers, and was never heard of again. Peter Andersen's first wife died in January 1853 and in December 1865 he married Mrs. Sarah Luce of Greene County. They had four children: Alexander, Henry, George and Martha Jane. He was a member of the Congregational Church.

Elijah Teague Anderson was also named as one of the influential citizens who worked to get the $1,000 subscription needed to bring the railroad to town. He married Melissa Jane Garoutte and was in the mercantile business in the 1880s. E.T. and Melissa had sons William Peter (Shorty), Charles and Teague; their daughters were Myrtle who married Will Brashear, Minnie who married Elmer Roop, and Zana who married Powell Lonon. E.T. and his sons built the Anderson house on Pine Street where it remains today still in the Anderson family. It is listed on the National Historical Register. He deeded to the city the land for Pine, Hines, Hampton, and Anderson Streets. He was instrumental in starting the first high school. He also helped with the purchase of land, plotting, and fencing Evergreen Cemetery.

By 1915 Dr. William P. Patterson was a well known physician and surgeon in the county and had practiced his profession for 28 years. He was born at Sale Creek, Hamilton County, Tennessee, on October 19, 1861. He was a son of J.A.N. and Elizabeth S. (Coulter) Patterson. Dr. Patterson attended the public schools, and the Sale Creek Academy. He entered the State University at Knoxville, then graduated from the medical department of Vanderbilt University in Nashville. He then did post-graduate work in the New York Polyclinic. He came to Greene County, Missouri in 1886 and built up an excellent practice. In 1891 Dr. Patterson married May Blackman, daughter of Wallace W. Blackman. In January 1897, when seeking a wider field for his talents, he moved his office to Springfield. The Pattersons had three daughters: Aldine, May and Elizabeth.

Walter A. Coon was another prominent early resident of Republic. Mr. Coon was born January 18, 1872 near Urbana in Dallas County, Missouri. His parents were William Benton and Harriet V. (Andrew) Coon. Mr. Coon began a teaching career at the age of 18. He felt pride in the fact that he taught three years at one place, two at another, and completed 13 months of public school in less than one school year by teaching at three different schools in three different counties while boarding at the same place during the whole year.

Mr. Coon was married November 27, 1895, to Mira A. Crudginton, the eldest daughter of T.B. Crudginton. They had two daughters and one son: Merle, born December 2, 1896; Faye, born January 5, 1899 and Teddy Benton, born February 12, 1903.

Mr. Coon learned the mercantile business under the care of "Uncle" Steve Burris, the "Merchant King" of Dallas County. After a thorough training in the mercantile and business world, he engaged in the newspaper business for two years before deciding to embark in the mercantile business and chose Republic as a desirable place to open a business. He located in Republic in the summer of 1899. He continued in the business until December of 1911 when the store was sold and William Delarue became the manager.

He then accepted the presidency of the Bank of Republic, which became the fourth oldest bank in Greene County.

He was appointed postmaster, but resigned after one year because of health.

He attended the Christian Church, and it was largely through his efforts that a Masonic Lodge was organized in Republic. He was very active in this group as well as the Shrine, Scottish Rite, Eastern Star, Woodmen of the World, Knights of the Maccabees, and Independent Order of Odd Fellows. He also served as president of the Republic School Board starting in 1903. He saw the school grow from a six months to a nine months term, from a two year course to a four year high school course, and from an unclassified school to a school of the first class.

Mr. William W. Coover was listed in the 1879-1880 *Gazeteer*, and a biography was found in the *Greene County History 1883*. William was the son of S.H. and Catherine (Wilhelm) Coover, and was born September 16, 1850 at Vandalia, Montgomery County, Ohio. His parents moved to Iowa and lived there about nine years, then came to Greene County, Missouri where his father was a contractor and builder for some time. He was educated in the common schools of the county. His first mercantile employment was with Sheppard and Co. in Springfield. After being in their employment for three years, they put him in charge of a stock of goods at Brookline, and he received one third of the profits. In 1878 Mr. Coover moved to Republic, and opened the same line of goods in partnership with M.P. Johnson, who was a commercial traveler and continued to travel. Mr. Coover managed the business. At the end of three years that partnership was dissolved and Mr. Coover took ownership of the business. Besides his merchandizing, Mr. Coover dealt largely in grain shipping and in one year shipped about 100,000 bushels of wheat. Mr. Coover was married December 27, 1876, to Miss Mary E., daughter of S.F. Gibson of Brookline. They had one child, Samuel Clyde.

James Wilson Bishop was also listed in the 1879-1880 *Gazetteer. The Greene County History of 1883* said he was the fourth son of David F. and Eunice (Wilson) Bishop, and was born May 27, 1828 in Derby Centre, Orleans County, Vermont. He leaned toward the medical profession when quite a young child and became interested in the study of anatomy of all animals killed on the farm. He received his education at Oberlin, Ohio and began the study of medicine under Dr. Baxter, where he took one course of lectures. He practiced one year, then entered Ann Arbor Medical School, graduating in the class of 1854. He resumed practice at Tower Hill in Shelby County, Illinois, where he lived six years, then moved to Story County, Iowa. He remained there in active practice for 13 years. He then took two courses of lectures at the Keokuk Medical College, where he graduated in medicine, surgery, and therapeutics. He returned to Story County, Iowa, and resumed practice, but at the end of eight months he came to Greene County, Missouri, and located his practice in Republic, specializing in obstetrics and diseases of women. He married February 22, 1850 in Williams County, Ohio, to Miss Mary Meade. They had two boys and one girl.

In the 1883 *Gazatteer* William McCleary was listed. *The Greene County History of 1883* tells that Mr. McCleary was the son of Joseph C. and Margaret (Smith) McCleary, and was born March 31, 1840 in Jefferson County, Ohio. He was educated at Liberty Academy, Virginia. He emigrated to Iowa, where he remained for four years, then came to Greene County, Missouri, where he engaged in farming, making a specialty of wheat farming. His health became impaired and he moved to Republic, engaging in the hardware and agricultural implement business. There was no station on the road where Republic now stands when Mr. McCleary first came, not even a switch. He was largely instrumental in building up the town and had a highway established to Springfield.

He was married the first time in Morgan County, Ohio, to Miss Annie, daughter of Robert Gray. They had three girls. He married the second time to Eliza K., daughter of David Smith, of Belmont County, Ohio. They had one boy and two girls.

In those same editions William Cliborne was listed. He was the son of Jubal and Charlotte (Willis) Cliborne. He was born January 30, 1820 in Knox County, Tennessee. He was reared on a farm in Tennessee and in 1851 emigrated to Missouri, settling in Greene County. When he arrived, there was abundant game so there was always plenty of fresh meat. When the war of the rebellion came he was elected second lieutenant of Captain V. Abernathy's company of Home Guards. After the Battle of Wilson's Creek, a party of rebels went to Mr. Cliborne's home and put a rope around his neck and threatened to hang him because they said he had signed a petition for the Dutch soldiers to come to the county. They released him upon the condition of his leaving the country. He went to Rolla, but returned with the army. He suffered at the hands of both armies who "pressed" his stock and feed. Mr. Cliborne was elected justice of the peace in 1860, and served until 1876. He was a soldier of the Black Hawk War. He was married the first time in Monroe County, Tennessee, to Miss Drucilla Ann Gilbreth. That union was blessed with four children. He married the second time in March 1885 to Mary Logan. They had two boys and a girl. He gave the first ground for the town site of Republic.

Another gentleman appearing in the 1883 biographies was Theodore F. Criswell. He was the third son of Gregory and Sarah (Baar) Criswell who had 10 children. He was born November 30, 1844 in Stark County, Ohio. He was educated in his native county, and enlisted in Company B, 115 Ohio Volunteer Infantry, in the Army of the Cumberland, under General "Pap" Thomas. He was mustered out July 6, 1866, at Cleveland, Ohio. In April 1867 he and his brother H.G. Criswell came to Greene County, Missouri, and bought the Sharp farm which was on the Wilson's Creek Battleground.

Previous to engaging here in farming, he taught school in Lawrence and Christian counties in Missouri. In March 1874, they sold the farm and moved two miles north of Republic, on the Mt. Vernon and Springfield road. It was a splendid farm containing 187 acres. Mr. Criswell was married February 4, 1869, to Miss Arrimba, daughter of Thomas Greene, one of the old settlers of Greene County. They had two sons and two daughters. They were members of the Congregational Church at Republic.

John Wesley Britain and Lucy A. Cox Britain lived on a farm northwest of Republic given to John by his father George. Mr. Britain decided to go into the mercantile business. About 1900 Mr. Britain sold the store to Mr. Godwin and daughter Anna and Bob Thurman who was working in the store and took over the undertaking business. In 1902 John Wesley was elected Representative to the Missouri Legislature. He had served as Justice of the Peace in Pond Creek Township while living on his farm.

Eli H. and Elizabeth Britain lived on the farm his father George W. gave them which was located just past the intersection of West Elm and Highway 174. The home was on the north side of what is now Highway 174 and the brick yard business was to the south side. This brick yard made the bricks for the Hood United Methodist Church and many of the brick buildings on Main Street. Eli and Elizabeth had four children. Besides farming and the brick business, he later built a grocery store where the Farmers Exchange was located and a number of years later a mercantile where the Masonic Lodge is today. Eli and his oldest sons ran the stores. He later decided to go into a fruit growing business. Eli died in 1920 and Elizabeth in 1930. *Compiled by Rosemary Comisky.*

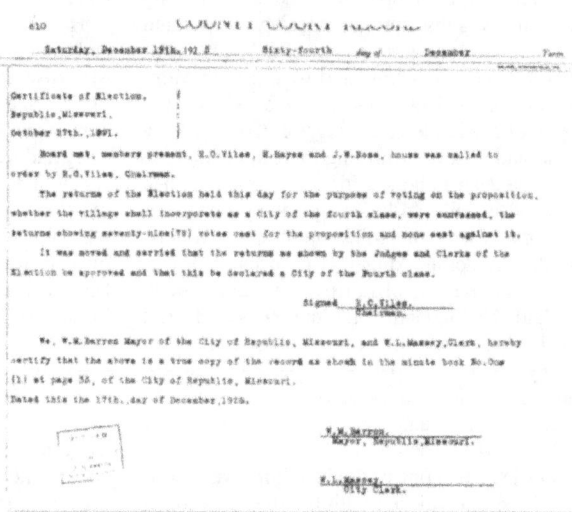

## Mayor's Comments For Historical Book

Since I became mayor in 2004, our overriding goal has been to create an autonomous community. We want Republic to be such a self-contained city that its residents can live, work, sleep, worship, play, and eat in Republic if they choose to do so. The other decisions and accomplishments have been done under this umbrella. The consolidation with Brookline, for example, provided Republic with commercial land that could be developed into a business park. The result is that hundreds of jobs are being created as the Brookline area develops. New restaurants are coming to town because we now have jobs in town so restaurants will have a guaranteed lunch crowd.

Other goals that can be realized because of this overriding goal are:

1) With citizens spending their money in Republic, the resulting tax money is used for our infrastructure improvements.

2) We are at the point that we can go to regional storm water run-off rather than the small detention ponds that attract mosquitoes.

3) We are at the point of re-vitalizing downtown, especially along Main Street.

4) The business structures provide a bigger tax structure for our schools.

5) We have a deepening and refreshing sense of community.

6) We are now moving to a Home Rule Charter form of government that brings the government closer to the people with less state interference.

Citizen government is at its best in Republic. It is a privilege and blessing to serve these years on the board and as mayor. *Submitted by Jim Collins.*

*Mayor Jim Collins*

## Mayors Of Republic, Missouri

The following list of mayors was complied from city council minutes and *The Republic Monitor.*

|  |  |
|---|---|
| Peter Chaffin | June 4, 1896-March 1898 |
| M.L. Howard | April 12, 1898-December 5, 1898 |
| D.R. O'Neal | December 12, 1898-April 5, 1899 |
| Henry Hayes | April 5, 1899-March 4, 1901 |
| James Watson | April 3, 1901-April 11, 1904 |
| Henry Hayes | May 2, 1904-April 3, 1905 |
| D.R. O'Neal | April 10, 1905-April 5, 1906 |
| Henry Hayes | April 5, 1906- |
| Adams | June 6, 1907 |
| Record book missing | |
| W.P. Anderson | April 1, 1909-April 8, 1912 |
| Sherman Robertson | April 8, 1912-April 13, 1914 |
| Fred R. Short | April 13, 1914-April 4, 1917 |
| W.A. Beal | April 4, 1917-April 8, 1918 |
| W.S. Phelps | April 8, 1918-April 12, 1920 |
| E.M. Winter | April 12, 1920-April 14, 1921 |
| W.A. Beal | April 14, 1921-April 10, 1922 |
| W.M. Barren | April 10, 1922-April 10, 1928 |
| W.A. Beal | April 10, 1928-April 13, 1936 |
| V.W. Stover | April 13, 1936-April 12, 1937 |
| B.W. Davis | April 12, 1937-April 11, 1938 |
| W. Harold Owen | April 11, 1938-April 9, 1945 |
| Russell J. Lynch | April 9, 1945-April 12, 1948 |
| W. Harold Owen | April 12, 1948-April 14, 1952 |
| Lavega Claiborn | April 14, 1952-July 1954 |
| L. Fred Jackson | July 1954-April 3, 1956 |
| Robert Bell | April 3, 1956-August 12, 1957 |
| Sheral Garoutte | August 12, 1957-April 3, 1964 |
| Carl Plummer | April 3, 1962-April 8, 1964 |
| Frank J. Comisky | April 13, 1964-April 10, 1967 |
| Gene McConnell | April 10, 1967-April 3, 1968 |
| Lester T. Sweckard | April 8, 1968-April 7, 1970 |
| Claudius Cope | April 2, 1974-May 28, 1974 |
| Larry Cox | appointed May 28, 1974-elected to July 19, 1979 Mayor Protem until |
| Kenneth Green | September 5, 1979-January 14, 1980 Mayor Protem until |
| Harold Thompson | April 1, 1980-June 22, 1982 |
| Charles W. Tennison | appointed June 28, 1982-1984 |
| Janet Thompson | 1984-1986 |
| Lester Sweckard | 1986-1988 |
| John Yocum | 1988-1990 |
| Gerry Pool | 1990-1992 |
| Harold Tindell | 1992-1996 |
| Doug Boatright | 1996-2000 |
| Keith Miller | 2000-2004 |
| Jim Collins | 2004-present |

## Republic's First Businesses

Copies of *The Missouri Gazetteer* and *Business Directory* published by R.M. Polk and Company of St. Louis can be viewed at the Missouri History Society Library in Columbia. The following excerpts are from those volumes on the history of Republic.

In 1876-1877 Republic was a station on the Atlantic and Pacific Railroad in Greene County, 15 miles southwest of Springfield, population 75, daily mail, John W. Johnson-postmaster.

Businesses listed were J. Castoe and Son, blacksmiths; B. Damerel, carpenter; Decker and Johnson, general store; Rev. C. Lappin; Rev. W.B. Searcy; John Sumner, carpenter; and H.A. White, general store.

The 1879-1880 volume states Republic was located on the highest point of this area of the Ozark mountains and was a village with a population of 100 in Brookline Township, southwestern part of Greene County. That volume also states Republic was a station of the St. Louis and San Francisco Railroad, 15 miles southwest of Springfield, the county seat, and was 254 miles from St. Louis. The railway company had erected a commodious depot; and during 1878 seven dwelling houses and three good store buildings were built; a new side track on the railroad was laid; and the shipments for the last 12 months were 200 cars of bulk wheat, 10 carloads of livestock, besides butter, eggs, and country produce. Wheat was the principal product of this region yielding 20-30 bushels per acre. The county was equally divided between timber and prairie, and was becoming settled by a good class of farmers. Also listed were Congregational and Baptist churches, Adams Express, daily mail, with John W. Johnson, postmaster.

*The Business Directory* listed William Arnold, blacksmith; J.W. Bishop, druggist and physician; G.W. Brim, blacksmith; B.C. Burgess, carpenter; F.W. Burgess, plasterer; Coover and Johnson, general store, grain and livestock; N.D. Davis, carpenter; Rev. S.G. Eliott, Congregational Church; M.F. Harrison, constable; Frederick King, lawyer; Samuel J. Logan, boot and shoe maker; William Rodecker, blacksmith; W.B. Searcy, Justice; John Sumner, carpenter; J.L. Sumner, butcher; White, Anderson, and

## Marshals And Police Chiefs

This list of marshals was taken from information gained in the minutes from the Republic City record books.

| | Marshal |
|---|---|
| John F. Cliborne | July 17, 1897 |
| Henry Hayes | September 9, 1897 |
| Bill Collison | April 12, 1898 |
| J.O. Kerr | April 5, 1899 |
| W.J. O'Neal | April 17, 1899 |
| John F.G. Claiborne | July 17, 1899 |
| William Collison | October 23, 1899 |
| Joseph Pearce | April 4, 1900 |
| J.M. Hill | December 22, 1900 |
| P.M. Young | April 7, 1902 |
| James G. Blades | April 11, 1904 |
| E.F. Collison | November 23, 1904 |
| Special Police | |
| J.A. Britain | August 7, 1905 |
| Marshal | |
| E.F. Collison | June 5, 1906-1910 |
| Records missing until | |
| Sam Williams | April 8, 1912 |
| Mose Jones | April 14, 1913 |
| J.T. Carr | appointed to Saturday and Sunday nights and other nights as needed. |
| W.H. Davis | July 14, 1913 |
| T.F. Plumlee | April 10, 1916 |
| Lou Carskaden | April 14, 1921 |
| Samual T. Harrison | April 14, 1924 |
| M.S. Noe | April 9, 1928 |
| E.A. Thurman | June 10, 1929 appointed to take M.S. Noe's place. Also council voted to place a grave marker to be inscribed "Killed in Service" |
| F.E. Royston | April 14, 1930 |
| Mose Jones | April 11, 1932 |
| G.W. Thurman | April 10, 1933 |
| Jim Perkins | April 13, 1936 |
| Frank Bridges | April 10, 1939 |
| Jim Perkins | April 13, 1942 |
| Joe Gaddy | April 4, 1946 won election but would not accept. Jim Perkins appointed |
| Jim Perkins | April 8, 1946 |
| Charlie Jones | April 14, 1947 |
| A.J. Hughes | April 14, 1952 |
| Joe Gaddy | April 3, 1955 |
| Leo Owen | April 14, 1958 |
| Police Chief | |
| Ray Mathews | April 11, 1966 |
| Bob Duvall | August 1, 1973 |
| Eugene Blades | August to November 1979 acting police chief |
| Sam Hartsell | December 1, 1979 |
| Roy Graves | April 1985 |
| Sam Hartsell | May 1986 |
| Darrell Crick | November 2001 Interim Police Chief |
| Mark Lowe | March 2002 to present |

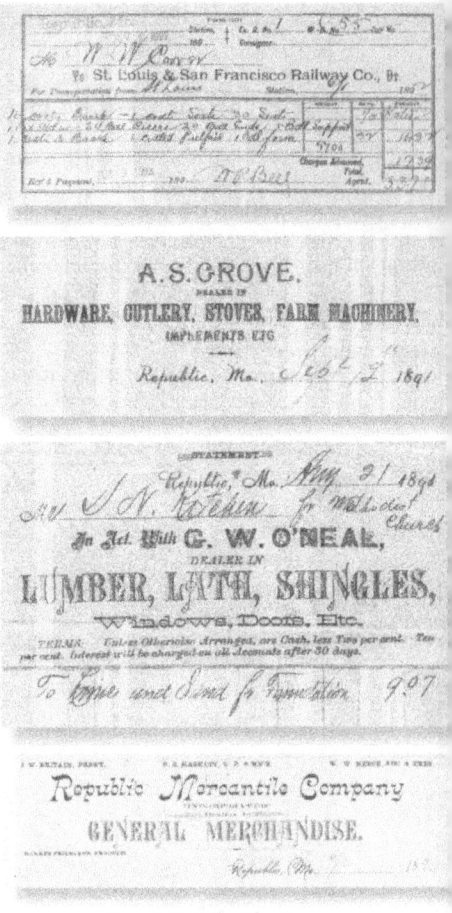

*Republic's first businesses*

Robertson, flour mill; H.A. White, express and station agent; H.A. White, general store and grain.

A copy of the 1881 *Gazetteer* found in the Springfield Library Center has the following account: "In 1873 in the county of Greene and upon the main line of the St. Louis and San Francisco railway, the town of Republic was first started. Its present population is about 150. Because of its situation and the fertility of the surrounding country its shipments to the St. Louis market are considerable, being distant from that city 254 miles. It contains a post office, two churches, school, two grain elevators, a flouring mill, and one hotel. The mercantile and minor industries are also well represented, and its people feel great encouragement for its future prosperity." Listed businesses included J.W. Bishop, physician and druggist; Bishop & Smith, wagon, yard and farming implements; J.W. Bishop, hotel and livery stable; Rev. G.W. Block, Baptist Church; Coover and Johnson, grain elevator; W.W. Coover, general merchandise; J.S. Colemen & Sons, general merchants; F. King, lawyer and postmaster; M.A. Mills, farm machinery; Mrs. C.E. Nichols, millinery; G.W. Patterson, physician; John Sallee, blacksmith; Rev. E.T. West, Congregational Church; A. Yoachum, grain elevator and flouring mill, and C.H. Young, druggist.

In the Columbia, MO, library, the *1883-1884 Missouri Gazetteer* and *Business Directory* stated Republic's population was 150. There was Western Union telegraph, daily mail and Adams Express. Lewis D. Brooks was postmaster.

The *Business Directory* listed J.W. Bishop, druggist; D. Lewis, general store; J.I. Coleman and Sons, general store; William W. Coover, general store and grain; J.M. Cotter, druggist; Berry Damene, carpenter; N.C. Davis, carpenter; A.S. Grove, farm implements; John House and Henry Hayes, blacksmiths; Frederick King, flour mill operator and lawyer; William S. McCleasy, hardware and farm implements; T.N Merrell, shoemaker; A.W. Montague, railroad and express agent; G.W. Patterson, physician; Rev. N.M. Wheat, Congregational Church; and William Wilkinson, wagonmaker.

The 1885-1886 volume has Republic station on the Center Division St. Louis and San Francisco Railroad with two churches, a school, a steam flouring mill, telegraph, Western Union, and Adams Express, population 200, daily mail. William W. Coover, postmaster.

The *Business Directory* listed Austin and Company, flour mill; Dr. J.W. Bishop, druggist and hotel; Rev. A. Burns, Methodist Church; William W. Coover, general store, stock and grain; W.S. Crayne, wagonmaker; A.S. Grove, farm implements; John House, blacksmith; J.W. Johnson, saloon; Frederick King, lawyer; W. McCleary, poulterer; T.N. Merrell, shoemaker; Park, King and Company, livestock and grain; G.W. Patterson, physician; Rev. S. Richards, Congregational Church; J.W. Rose, express, railroad and telegraph agent; William Wilkinson, wagonmaker.

The Columbia, Missouri, books in 1889-1890 list four churches, a school, canning works, a planing mill, a weekly newspaper *The Republic*, telegraph, Western Union, Adams Express, population 500; John W. Rose-postmaster.

The *Business Directory* lists H. Banister, photographer; M. Billings, barber; R.K. Bradfield, editor and publisher, *The Republic*; Brooks Brothers, general store; Rev. A. Burns, Methodist Church; J.T. Butlin, blacksmith; Rev. J.M. Cheeseman, Congregational Church; Cliborne Brothers, livery; William W. Coover, general store and grain; A.S. Grove, farm implements; Henry House, grocer; John House, blacksmith; J.W. Lebaw, hotel; Thomas Logan, harness; J.W. McNeil, tinner; T.N. Merrell, shoemaker; Mooneyham & Youngblood, lawyers; A.J. Oliver, druggist; G.W. O'Neal, lumber and planing mill; G.W. Patterson, physician; F.B. Pierce, railroad, express and telegraph agent; John Rayl, meats; Republic Canning Company, canned goods; Rose & Thurman, general store; William M. Ryder, poultry; W.B. Searcy, meats; Sparkman and Noe, hardware; Isaac Teague, drugs and hotel; Mrs. W.T. Weiss, milliner; J.W. Whitehurst, general store; William Wilkinson, wagonmaker; W.G. Williams, boarding house; Youngblood Grocer Company, groceries.

In 1891-1892 Republic had four churches, school, canning works, flour mill, bank and a weekly newspaper *The Republic*, telegraph, Western Union, Adams Express, population 500, C.R. Pickering, postmaster.

Listed businesses were Bank of Republic, W.W. Coover, proprietor; J.R. Bell, railroad, express and telegraph agent; Brooks Brothers, general store; J.T. Butlin, blacksmith; Rev. C. Combs, Congregational Church; W.W. Coover, banker and druggist; A.S. Grove, farm implements; Henry House, grocer; John House, blacksmith; C.A. Howell, wagonmaker; J.W. Leban, hotel; Thomas Logan, harness and shoemaker; Rev. C.A. Mitchell, Methodist Church; Mooneyham & Youngblood, lawyers; H.A. Noe, tinsmith; G.W. O'Neal, lumber and planing mill; G.W. Patterson, physician; Porter & Brooks, poultry and game; John Rayl, meat market; R.C. Viles, editor and publisher, *The Republic*; Republic Canning Company, canned goods; Rose & Thurman, general store; William Ryder, poultry; W.B. Searcy, meat market; Sparkman and Noe, hardware; Will Spencer, barber; Isaac Teague, drugs and hotel; Mrs. W.T. Weiss, milliner; J.W. Whitehurst, general store; William Wilkinson, wagonmaker; W.G. Williams, boarding house; Williams Brothers, livery stable; Youngblood Grocer Company.

In 1893-1894, Republic was listed as a fourth-class city with a population of 1,000. Republic had four churches, school, canning works, cheese factory, flour and planing mills, one bank and two weekly newspapers, *Greene County Republican* and *Imperialist*; lead and zinc ores were found two miles east of the city; telegraph, Western Union; express, W.F. & Company; Richard A. Gamble, postmaster.

The *Directory* lists W.P. Andrews, foundry; Bank of Republic (capital, $15,000), G.W. Britain-president, Paul Von Lossow-cashier; Edward D. Beal, physician; William R. Bell, railroad and express agent; J.T. Britain, blacksmith; James F. Brooks, general store; John Brownell, carpenter; William C. Chastain, general store; John Claiborne, Federal District Marshal; W.W. Coover, banker and druggist; William Creighton, cheese factory; Dr. Green B. Dorrell, druggist; William R. Gamble, grocer; Gardner, hotel; *Greene County Republic*, Robert C. Viles, proprietor; Abraham S. Grove, mayor and dealer in hardware and farm implements and agent for Milwaukee Binders, Springfield Wagon Company, Improved Indiana Grain Drills, South Bend Plows, John Dodd's Hay Rakes, US Corn Planters, Champion Mowers, Huber Threshing Machines, Reeves Straw Stacker, IXL Wind Mills, Superior Pumps, Heckel's Pioneer Steel Goods, Etc.; John Hay, hotel and meat market; Rev. W.S. Hills, Congregational Church; John House, blacksmith; John W. Houtz, justice; C.A. Howell, wagonmaker; Edward E. Hussey, carpenter; *Imperialist*, S.P. Smith, editor and publisher; Sherman Jones, grocer; Robert P. London, machinist; O.D. Lutz & C.A. Howell, grocers; G.A. Marsh, jeweler; Warren M. Mooneyham, justice; William Mooneyham, lawyer; Rev. Edward Moore, Christian Church; James M. Nelson & S.A. Williams, livery; H.A. Noe, tinsmith; Mrs. Olden hotel; George W. O'Neal, general lumber dealer and planing mill, dressed flooring, siding, ceiling, finishing lumber, joists, timber, shingles, lath, sash, doors, blinds, windows, molding, building paper, sewer pipe, glass, cement lime, hair, paints, oils, etc; Joseph O'Neal, shoemaker; George W. Patterson, physician; John Rayl, meat market; Republic Canning Company, G.W. O'Neal-president, John A. Youngblood-secretary; Republic Mercantile Company, J.W. Britain-president, E.E. Haskett-vice president, W.W. Neece-secretary and treasurer, dealers in staple and fancy groceries, dry goods, clothing, boots and shoes, hats and caps, furniture, undertakers' supplies, and millinery goods; Republic Roller Mills, R.C. Stone-proprietor; William Reynolds, blacksmith; W.R. Rose and J.D. Chapman, blacksmiths; Robert A. Sayers, physician; R.A. Sayers, mining company, Dr. G.B. Dorrell-president and W.R. Bell-secretary; W.J. Shadden, druggist; Rev. H. Smith, Methodist Church; Samuel P. Smith, editor and publisher of *Imperialist*; Sparkman & Noe (T.J. and John Sparkman and H.A. Noe) hardware; Eberlee Spyres, physician; William B. Stapp, horse dealer; G.A. Tinsour, barber; R.C. Viles, editor of *Greene County Republic*; Thomas J. Young, restaurant; George G. Youngblood, painter; John A. Youngblood, lawyer; J.M. Youngblood, general store; Youngblood and Norman, lumber.

In 1898-1899, Republic's population was 1,300. E.M. Hays was postmaster. Lead and zinc ores were found two miles east of the city.

The *Directory* lists B.B. Adams, baker; W.P. Andrews, founder, Bank of Republic, T.F. Creswell, president; C. Barber, produce; Edward D. Beal, physician; William R. Bell, railroad & express agent; J.T. Britain, blacksmith; James F. Brooks, general store; John Brownell, carpenter; Peter Chaffin, mayor; William C. Chastain, general store; W.W. Coleman, harness; J.C. Collison, shoemaker; Mrs. W.R. Davis, notions; Dribble and Rainey, livery; Dr. Green B. Dorrell, drugs; E.C. Duckman, drugs; Mrs. A.C. Farley, milliner; Goodwin H. Followill, general store; Abraham S. Grove, hardware; E.E. Hasket, druggist; Henry Hayes, marshal; Hayes House; R. Hayes, barber; John H. House, blacksmith; M.V. Ingram, meats; Jones Brothers, publisher of *The Monitor*; Jacob Krykendall, baker; Fred H. Lowing-cashier, Bank of Republic; O.D. Lutz, grocer; G.A. Marsh, jeweler; Noe Hardware Company; George W. O'Neal, lumber; George W. Patterson, physician; Republic Canning Company; Republic Cheese Company; Republic News Agency; Republic Roller Mills, R.C. Stone, proprietor; Thomas Robertson, livestock; Sparkman & Son, general store; Wilkinson Hotel; George G. Youngblood, painter; John A. Youngblood, lawyer; J.M. Youngblood, general store.

*This information was compiled by Harold Lloyd for The Republic Monitor in 1971.*

## Dr. Edward Beal

Dr. Edward L. Beal was born January 16, 1864, in what later became the town of Battlefield, Missouri. For a quarter of a century, the name of Dr. Beal was a household word in and around the Republic area where he was engaged in the general practice of medicine. He maintained his home in Republic. Doctor Beal grew up as the oldest child on the family homestead, enduring hard work as a boy. He received his education in public schools near Campbell Township, in Ozark College at Greenfield, and Morrisville College in Polk County. Dr. Beal began a teaching career at Roundtree School but later gave it up to study medicine. He received his medical education in the Missouri Medical College at St. Louis and in the Jefferson Medical College of Philadelphia, Pennsylvania. Dr. Beal received the highest honors of his class of 188 graduates, graduating April 8, 1888. He began his medical practice in Republic, Missouri, on March 16, 1889. Dr. Beal was ranked among the leading medical men of the county. He was an associate of Dr. J.E. Tefft, an eminent Springfield surgeon, for about five years.

On March 30, 1889, Dr. Beal was united in marriage to Mary E. Landers, born July 24, 1867, in Dade County, MO. She was the daughter of John N. and Ellen J. (Wilson) Landers.

They adopted a son, Luther Beal, who was born on January 30, 1894.

During this time he became interested in horticulture, and his advancement in that field attracted attention of horticulturists at the University of Missouri and throughout other sections of the state.

He was an outstanding orchardist and helped organize the Ozark Fruit Growers Association of which he was president for 30 years. After a careful study of different locations, from Re-

*Middle top: Dr. E.L. Beal. Top, second man from left: Fred Short. Courtesy of The Republic Monitor.*

*Dr. Beal's strawberry crop. Courtesy of the Historical Society.*

*East of Republic, McElhaney strawberry crop around 1900. Standing from left: Charley Lloyd, Bill Robertson, Lou McElhaney, George L. McElhaney. Seated: Maggie McElhaney (married John Ward), Dewey McElhaney, Bess McElhaney (married John Kimmons) and Bryan McElhaney. Courtesy of Betty Mason.*

public to the Pacific coast, Dr. Beal became convinced that Republic was ideal for apple growing and set out three large orchards of his own, one of which he retained until his death. These orchards became widely known for their beauty and fine quality of fruit. At one time he was the owner of an 82-acre apple orchard. He owned 30 acres of strawberries and was instrumental in advancing strawberry and grape production in this area.

Dr. Beal probably gave more time and energy toward the welfare and upbuilding of the town and its communities than any other citizen. Among the many civic and industrial enterprises which he helped to promote was the garment factory which had a very valuable payroll. Dr. Beal and Sherman Robertson were agents for Studebaker cars in Republic.

On January 16, 1946, a "Dr. Beal Day" was observed in the high school auditorium in honor of his 82nd birthday. He gave up his medical practice in 1944, but patients continued to call on him for advice and treatment almost until the time of his death. By the time he quit counting, Dr. Beal had delivered 2,500 babies.

*History of Greene County, Missouri*
*The Republic Monitor, March 30, 1950, edition*

## REPUBLIC – THE TWENTIES

Republic at the half century mark was a bustling little town. It had 800 people and sold just about everything those people would need to live.

There were stores that sold lumber to build a house, furniture to put in it, groceries, general merchandise, poultry, hardware and harness and a drug store with a band room in back. The town boasted two banks, a printing company, two butchers, a bakery, barber, cobbler, feed store, bottling works, restaurant, plumber, tin shop, hotel and place to purchase coal. Some of the business names have become obsolete. Cobblers are gone and shoe repair shops are hard to find.

Because the country's transportation was in transition from horse to a gasoline powered vehicle rated by horsepower, there was both a blacksmith shop, on the east side almost to Olive Street and a garage attached to it that apparently sold cars. It had a capacity for 30 cars with a repair shop in back. There were hitching sheds behind the stores on the west side of Main Street just north of the railroad tracks and a veterinary stable next to the car repair shop.

Besides all the personnel needed to work in the above stores, there were two flour mills that employed many and of course, the school which is usually one of the town's largest employers.

Most of the travel through Republic in 1920 was still by rail. The roads, unpaved and unreliable, also made the train the preferred mode of travel for salesmen. There were two hotels shown on the 1920 Sanborn map; one, on the west side of Walnut less than one-half block from the depot, the second on the third block north on Main on the east side, which hoped to catch the newer automobile traffic. There were three restaurants to serve the travelers and business people working in town. They would have also provided a

*Stickney's Store, later Plummer's Store. Courtesy of Zetta May Stickney Combs.*

*Stickney's Store, May 8, 1925. Courtesy of Zetta May Stickney Combs.*

treat for the farmers coming to town on Saturdays to sell their produce and buy their supplies.

There's not much evidence of second floor businesses, but those along the west side of Main Street had the most. A tin shop was in the first building south of Grant Street with the Masonic Hall beside it. The Teague Opera House came next, occupying the third and fourth buildings. The Republic Bank was next door to that but probably didn't want anything over it. Next south was Bob Thurman's Merchandise with his undertaking business over that.

But a good memory is as good as a map. In 1971, Otis Branson put his memories about Republic in the 1920s on paper. Courtesy of *The Republic Monitor* - he wrote:

"I was born on a farm four miles northeast of Republic, November 25, 1907 and made my home here until 1925. I was the youngest son of "Uncle Jeff" Branson, brother to "Clown," "Fiddler Jess," Tom, Homer and a half brother to Joe Branson who had a store and filling station on the old road to Brookline.

Starting at the railroad going north on the west side of Main, there was the Bill Russell grocery. He had a son Johnnie and a daughter, Wilma, who married Harold Owen, Glenn Owen's son. Next was Bob Thurman's furniture store. Bob was the undertaker for years and had a son Ellis and a daughter Daphne, who married the ex-postmaster, Linzee Wells, and bought the old Manford Bell place just over the hill west of Joe Branson's grocery and station. There was also the bank and the old Delarue clothing store, Harry and "Dutch" Chaffin's Cafe, Owen and Short Hardware. Across the street to the north was a vacant lot and Popcorn Pete Worthington had a stand there and sold popcorn and other goodies. He had a son, Little Joe, who moved to Pomona and worked at the Pomona Tile Company until he retired. There was also a daughter of Popcorn Pete who later married Grover Wells, who was the adopted son of the Normans near Brookline. Hub Norman was his brother. North of Popcorn Pete's was Grubaugh Hardware Company and there was also the Republic Theater owned and operated by Lawrence Coggin for years. For a few years on that side of the street there was the old Jim Howell's little grocery store. I believe Jim Blades had a little office in there some place; he was a well-known veterinarian. Dr. Beal's office was in that area. He was the father of Luther Beal; they had acres of apple orchards mostly west of Republic. Later Small Eagan and wife started a good size grocery in or near by the Grubaugh Hardware. Small's brother was Eddy and their father was Spike Eagan, railroad section foreman for a few years at Republic. The last business on that side was the Ford Garage owned by Sherm Robertson. His main salesman was Hot Shot Gaylor. He would trade for almost anything in the line of livestock. He had a farm west of Republic and took the stock there until he could sell them.

Across Main Street and little to the north was the old two-story frame hotel owned by Buck Hoffman, who had a son Little Buck. Then there was the Chevrolet Garage going back south on the east side of the street. There was a blacksmith shop next door south. My brother Lawrence "Clown" Branson owned an ice house and transfer there. He was married to Lillian DeVoge and had one son Oliver. Jack Carr and my other brother Homer worked for Clown and Homer sawed stove wood all over Republic and for the farmers all around. There were other businesses between there and the old Doc O'Dell drug store. Doc owned and operated that store for years. This was where we bought our school books and supplies and he was also a pharmacist. Across the street south was another bank. "L" Heying ran a grocery south of the bank. He had a son Clarence Heying who married Geneva Watson. Also in that area was the J.B. Stickney shoe shop. Burl and Bill Adams had a barber shop in there to the south; they also had some boys, Red and Pinky. The O'Neal Lumber Co. was there across the tracks before I was born in 1907. South of it across the street was the big mill where flour and bulk cream of wheat was manufactured. My brother-in-law, Laurel Hart, was engineer there for a long time and my brother Tom fired the boiler for him. After many years the mill shut down and all the machinery was shipped to Coffeyville, KS and the mill became a cold storage and storage. I can remember the little red building across the street west of O'Neal's Lumber that was at one time a saloon. Before it was torn down someone brought eggs and poultry there and Clown Branson trucked them to Springfield. Clown and Roll Ottendorf became partners after a number of years.

Laurel Hart married my sister Hannah and they had two sons and one daughter. Their daughter, now in Republic, is Mrs. Irieta Merrill. Their sons were Byron "Tuffy" Hart and Earl Hart. Laurel worked for the city of Republic and was superintendent of the waterworks for a few years. I suppose you have heard of Martha Youngblood who had three daughters: Grace, Cleo and Leota. They were all school teachers. And let's not forget Shrimp Bennett, who ran a barber shop for years there with his brother. I used to work for "Jug" Harve Snyder and Goldie when they had a farm northwest of Republic just west of Ralph DeBorde's and am well acquainted with Jug's sister Ruth. I was there in the way some of the time watching Harry Chaffin's brown bungalow being built that is now owned by "Sac" Swinney, During this period the old sheds for people to tie their horses were located north of this home. The wagons and buggies were out in the weather, but the horses were under roof with feed box and hay stalls for each horse. There were two double rows of them. The old cement jail was also here. Later these were torn away and a big feed and seed store was built there. Behind Owen and Short was the old "Mose" Jones blacksmith shop. Later it moved across the street north where the MFA now is or at least it used to be there.

I knew the Noe brothers: Mark, Frank and Clyde. Clyde had a red headed son, Paul, I went to grade school at Brookline with Harry Young who killed Mark Noe and later he and his brother murdered all of those officers, including Marcel Hendrix out at his mother's farm home. I also went to school with many at Beulah, Mt. Atena (Etna) and Republic High. The road coming west from the cemetery was a dead end at North Main and on the northwest corner was an old two-story brick house. East of that was the old Decker place, just west of the cemetery. They were in the "chips" and had a chauffeur, maids and electric car. They seemed to keep to themselves pretty much.

Duncan Brackens was mail carrier for years on rural route two. He had a son Glen who was one swell boy. There was Alvin Coggin who was known by many as "Lantern Jaw." He sold his place to Lonnie Green. He had several children who went to Republic High School. I'm sure "Kid" Garton owns that place now.

There was Jenks Harris who had a big family. His son, "Bus" Harris worked for the state highway department for years. He had sons Joe Harris, "Bulger" Harris, Bill Harris and Gladys, Maggie and Eula were the girls. There was also my cousin "Cracklin" Loge Branson. The Paul Goodwin place was the original "Bud" Chambers place.

My cousin Fyan "Poggy" Lloyd bought the old Roush place and raised a family there. I think his widow still lives there.

There was the old Bridwell Canning Factory that was just south of Republic. There were two Charley Jones: "Big" Charley and "Little" Charley, "Big" Charley was Mose Jones' brother and "Little" Charley was Mose's son and a brother to Johnnie Jones. Tommy Wallace was a well-known person around Republic. He had a big grape vineyard just west of the old Mt. Aetna (Etna) School. He was the one that bought the old Frank Youngblood place and started the big swimming pool (Maple Grove Park). They had an open air dance hall there and had a ball on the weekend. "Tuffy" Hart was the main attraction there as a rule. He would climb to the top of a 40 foot telephone pole and dive off into eight feet of water. This pool was fed by springs and was really cool and refreshing. Tommy had a daughter Lucille.

Cal Baxter and Monroe Mooneyham did all the threshing there for miles around. We can't forget Marvin Smith and his son Buster Smith who lived out south of Republic and was a good automobile mechanic. At one time good old Republic had one of the toughest baseball teams around. Offhand I can remember three or four: "Little" Charley Jones, Johnnie Jones, Walter Gaylor and Leonard Fugitt.

There was also Milt Paulsell who married Roxie DeBorde. They ran a canning factory out on his farm and he had a big dairy also. There were the Keatts brothers, Tom and Charley, and the Rainey brothers, Harold and Roscoe.

This is between 1907 and 1925 when I left for Indiana. I came to California in 1942."

## MILLS

The first small mill in Republic was built in 1890 by R.C. Stone and L.E. Prickett. After this

*R.C. Stone Milling Company*

*Becker and Langenberg Mills, October 25, 1915.*

mill burned in 1894 a large brick mill was built by R.C. Stone Milling Company at the southeast corner of Main and E. Elm Streets and was in full operation in 1902.

Most all "old-timers" think of the big mill as being the life stream of Republic because it was the main source of employment. In 1902 the mill capacity increased to 1,500 barrels and several hundred feet of warehouses with several large elevators, making this at one time the largest exclusive soft wheat mill in the United States. At its peak it had a running capacity of 2,000 barrels every 24 hours. During the years between 1900 and 1907, the mill operated night and day. It carried the slogan "The World Is Our Field."

Around 1913 it changed hands and was called the Langenberg Milling Company. In 1917 it was known as the Republic Flour Mills.

Then in about 1920 it sold to Rea-Patterson Milling Company with J.K. Woodfill as manager and Mrs. Florence Britain as office clerk. From about 1920 to 1925 this firm shipped flour all over the United States.

During this time, it was known as Missouri Flour Mills Company with a capacity of 800 barrels. The elevator on the northeast corner had a capacity of 30,000 bushels. Just to the west of it was a building divided into six "rooms" with the flour mill on the north end and the boiler room next to it. The next four rooms, going south, were Warehouses 1, 2, 3 and 4. A spur came off the railroad and ran south between O'Neal Lumber and Coal and the flour mill office, serving both businesses.

William Barron and Sons had a cooperage business for making barrels to ship the flour. This building was east of the big mill, next to the mill pond, with an overhead runway for rolling the barrels directly to the mill and to the floor where the packers were. This was also where empty barrels could be loaded into boxcars on the railroad for shipping. The same switch was used to load the barrels of flour. When R.C. Stone closed the mill, the machinery was moved to Kansas.

In 1925 the Producers Ice and Mfg. Co. bought the big mill building and made it into a cold storage. There was a need for this type of operation because of the many apple orchards, grape vineyards and strawberry patches in the area.

The Republic Fruit Growers Association was formed with Dr. E.L. Beal as president. Apple graders and juice pressers were bought and the mill storerooms became a very busy place during the fruit season. But 10 years later the market for apples and grapes got so low that they went out of business.

*Rea-Patterson Milling Company*

The building was sold to Schafffitzel who rented it to a blending products company which operated it for a few years. Then it was used for government storage.

*The back of Rea-Patterson Milling*

*Mill workers. Back row standing from left Night Watchman, Charles Anderson, next three unknown, Guy Davis, Nick Britain. Middle row W.P. Anderson, Ed Gill, unknown, Ollie Thurman, Warren Hunt, Lawson, and unknown Front row: Clay Coker, next two unknown, Elmer Ruckman, unknown, H.L. Pennoyer, and Walter Anderson. Picture taken in 1902.*

*McCleary House, lived in by mill managers.*

During the depression in the 1930s, cattle were selling for eight to ten dollars a head and hogs were two to three cents a pound. To help the farmers, the federal government bought the livestock. They were shipped to Republic stockyards located west of the depot, on the corner of North Main and West Elm Streets and then taken to the slaughterhouse on the south edge of town. After the animals were slaughtered and dressed, they were taken to the cold storage processing room. People who didn't have jobs were hired to strip the meat off the bones. From there the meat was taken to the canning factory located southwest of the depot. It was then shipped all over the United States.

After Mr. Schaffitzel's death, the building sold at auction and was purchased by Lester E. Cox, who had a sentimental feeling toward the old mill where he had worked as a young man.

The last occupant of the building was Solid State Circuits. After they went out of business, the building was destroyed by fire.

The citizens of Republic were always very grateful to R.C. Stone for building the mill and furnishing employment. *Submitted by Bill O'Neal.*

## The Little Mill

Always known as the "Little Mill," the Republic Custom Mill was located at the northeast corner of Walnut and Olive. Generally through the efforts of G.W. Thurman and P.A. Chaffin, it was organized in 1904 with a capital stock of $12,000.

By 1906, the mill was making White Lily

*Little Mill. Courtesy of Republic Centennial Book.*

*Wade Tomato Cannery, west of Hopewell Baptist Church.*

*Republic MFA, 1968. Courtesy of Vernon Sanders.*

Flour and graham flour, shipping its products throughout southern Missouri in addition to a large custom business.

After purchasing the relatively new electric lighting plant in 1911, the mill owners ran it in connection with the mill with G.W. Thurman as the manager. This plant furnished the electricity for the city.

Used in later years by MFA, the last grain holding bin survived the large brick structure but was razed in June 2006.

## Tomato Canneries

Beginning with the early 1900s and continuing through the 1930s, there has been no single industry having such a widespread impact on the lives of its citizens as the tomato cannery, other than perhaps farming and dairying. There were several in the area. Wades operated one west of Republic near Hopewell Church.

O'Bryants operated one owned by a man named Bridwell at Wilson Creek; there were two in Battlefield, one on the Greene, Christian County Line and three in Republic, including the Ed Fuhr Cannery. The Fuhr Cannery was located in the northwest part of Republic, north on a lane from West Hines Street. This cannery operated in the 1920s and into the mid-1930s.

The canneries had to locate by a spring or creek so water could be pumped or hauled in by wagon. O'Bryant used a two-cylinder steam engine fueled by cordwood to pump the water from a spring. Most of the canneries were constructed in a similar manner with open sides. The interior consisted of large scalding and cooking vats, usually one long section divided into four compartments: one for scalding, two for cooking, and one for other uses. It set atop a rock furnace large enough to accommodate four-foot logs. There were wooden peeling troughs which held the peelings, one at work level with a slide attached to a lower trough. There was a crimper, wire baskets and crates for scalding and cooking, wooden crates and buckets, peeling knives, cans and other supplies. In early spring, seeds were broadcast onto burnt seedbeds in preparation for transplanting in early June. During the winter months the land was cleared, usually from two to six acres, as it was believed the crop did better planted in new ground. The fields were prepared in a criss-cross fashion; one person dropped the plant in the cross and another came along with a spud and spudded it into the ground; then another followed with water.

In August, when the crops were ready to harvest, nearly everyone in the community worked. Tomatoes were picked, placed in wooden crates and carried by wagons to the factories. The tomatoes were unloaded and dumped into a wire cage and lowered into the scalding vat. This was done to loosen the skin on the tomatoes. From the scalding vat, they were placed on a table where women peelers peeled tomatoes and put them in buckets. The peelings were pushed into a trough to be deposed of. From the buckets they were poured out on another table where they were graded. The next step was packing them in Number 3 size cans (which held about a quart). After the cans were packed, they were moved to the crimping machine where a metal lid was put on and the contents sealed. Being highly acidic, it was not necessary that the tomatoes be cooked a long time. For short cooking, a retort was available that provided for cooking under pressure. There were other cookers for regular cooking. Labeling could be postponed until after the growing season.

Although most of the canned tomatoes at Wilson Creek were shipped out and used by the army in World War I, some did make it to local stores. These canneries also did custom canning for the communities. Some canned peaches, apples, green beans, corn, blackberries, pumpkins, etc.

The railroads played an important part in the canning industry, the Frisco Railroad in Republic, and the Springfield Southern Railroad (later to become Missouri Pacific Railroad) in Wilson Creek and Battlefield. These lines made it possible to ship almost anywhere.

Wages were low by today's standards. Peelers were paid 5 to 10 cents a bucket, and other workers earned 50 to 75 cents a day. Workers were given tokens which were redeemed for cash at the end of the season. One of the tokens from the Ed Fuhr Cannery is on display at the Republic Historical Museum. There were no child labor laws, so the entire family could work at the factories. The young children could earn spending money and help with the expense of getting ready for school; most considered themselves fortunate to have the work.

This industry dipped in the 30s because of the damaging droughts and blight. As the nation prepared for World War II in the 1940s, laborers began leaving the fields for better paying jobs in defense plants. The local industry finally lost out to growers in New Jersey, California, and southern states who could produce bigger and better crops more cheaply.

The industry had served the county well, providing jobs when there were no other jobs, and people were desperate for employment. The years have no doubt faded thoughts of the hardships that were endured, and perhaps only pleasant memories remain.

*Bill Robertson compiled material from Greene County Archives, Webster County Historical Soc. Journals, 1981 Springfield Magazine, and Mae Belle and Charles Fuhr.*

## Factories Of Republic

The factory building that was located in the 300 block of West Elm served Republic in a variety of capacities. It began as a shoe factory in the 1920s. There was a period of time the building remained vacant. During this time it was used for various community functions such as rehearsals of the Republic Community Band and was available for area church revivals. Then negotiations between the trustees of the building, which was still known as The Shoe Factory, and the Sovereign Tailors Company were finally concluded.

According to an article in the local newspaper (date unknown), these negotiations took over a year. The contract bound the company to expend not less than $50,000 a year for a period of 10 years for wages; and the rental, taxes, and upkeep of the property would "be properly taken care of." These guarantees were the best news Republic had received in a long time.

The Sovereign Tailors Co. was a manufacturer and distributor of men's clothing. They specialized in made-to-measure clothing and uniforms for employees of railroads, streetcar men, police and other uniformed employees.

The next company to occupy this building was Rubensteins. Rubenstein operated it as a men's cap factory. This change took place in the late 1930s. The wages paid were 25 cents an hour.

*Republic Factory in 1942. Courtesy of Helen Blades.*

*These women are making men's pants for the Army at the Wood Garment Factory, 1942. Courtesy of Helen Blades.*

By the early 1940s, the factory had changed owners again. The Wood Garment Factory, owned by C. Virgil Wood. Later the Nick Abramson and Tommy Weinsaft families took over. They made men's pants. The wage earned by its employees was 40 cents an hour. During World War II, they were making men's pants for the soldiers.

Although still owned by Abramson/Weinsaft, the factory's name changed to Crane Manufacturing for the production side of the factory, and Republic Garment for the sales and shipping side of the factory. The crane name does not refer to the city of Crane, but to their logo of the crane bird. In 1966 or 67 there were complications with silent investors and the family purchased the south end of the old cold storage building located on Main Street just south of the tracks becoming private owners. This was soon remodeled to house the Crane Manufacturing/Republic Garment's new location.

At this time the factory building on West Elm was sold to Anthony and John Hagale who started operations for the second garment factory in Republic, known as Hagale Industries. The building, once known as The Shoe Factory, remained an important part of Republic's economic growth until it was completely destroyed in 1971 by the most damaging tornado the city of Republic has seen to date. The Hagales purchased land on Highway 174 West and built a new building to house the Hagale Factory which continued in operation until around the year 2000.

Crane Manufacturing/Republic Garment eventually closed and moved all of their production to Crane, Missouri. *Submitted by Helen Blades.*

## THE TELEPHONE SWITCHBOARD

Anna Mae (Dennis) Bennett worked for the Southwestern Bell Telephone Company for 35 years and six months. She began working for the company on September 1, 1942 in the building on Main Street which later was acquired by the Plummer Store. At that time Miss Iva Haynie was chief operator. Other operators were Pauline Cason, Florabelle Wallace, Bernadine Marsh and Peggy Kirby. There was only one switchboard in the office. The telephone was of the "crank type" and the caller had to ring for the operator. There were only about 200 phones in the exchange.

The office grew with the community and in 1946 a second switchboard was added and Mrs. Callie Tourville and Mrs. Thelma Fraka were employed. Anna Mae acquired the nickname of "Myrt" from some of her patrons, probably copied from the old radio program of "Fibber McGee and Molly," whose telephone operator went by that name. In 1958 the dial system was installed and Anna Mae went to Springfield to work as an operator and also did other work as office and payroll clerk and ticket investigator, a job she held for 10 years.

At the same time as the Southwestern Bell Switchboard was in place there was a Gooseberry Line Switchboard located upstairs in the 200 block of North Main Street. It is thought that the Gooseberry Line was for the rural area.

## HOWARD'S FLOWER GARDEN

Anna (O'Neal) Howard was born June 6, 1870 in Republic. She met Martin Howard when he took his first job after schooling at a mercantile store in Republic. They married and were the parents of two sons, Arthur and Paul.

Martin served as postmaster and one term as mayor. He owned the Buick Agency in Republic. After being elected to public office in 1924 in Springfield, he continued to work there and was working at an abstract office when he died in 1934.

Anna was busy with their two sons but began planting and developing about three acres of beautiful flowers. She soon had a thriving floral business, selling her cut flowers, bulbs and plantings to her many customers, from her home and summer house located on the corner of Hampton and Harrison Streets. In 1947 she was still arranging and selling her flowers. She made beautiful baskets for services at the Christian Church on North Main Street.

Anna passed away April 22, 1953 at the age of 82.

Today, some of her plantings still bloom on lots where homes were built and her beautiful flowers were planted. The Martin Howard's home (now owned by others) and summer house bring back lovely memories of those who enjoyed Anna's labor of love for flowers. *Submitted by Mae Belle (Sparkman) Fuhr.*

## WPA

In May 1935 the federal government created the WPA (Works Progress Administration) by order of President Roosevelt. This program targeted recipients who were heads of households on relief, 15% of whom were women. Ninety percent of the workers for WPA were unemployed.

There were several projects around Republic. One was the building of the gymnasium for the high school. Other projects were digging sewer lines to serve major areas of the city and improving farm roads out of the city such as Highways M and P.

About the same time there was a government project to supply material for mattresses and quilts for the families that applied for them. Materials were shipped by Frisco Railroad to the Republic Depot and unloaded on a large platform close to the depot. It had a roof over it but the sides were open.

Families had to make their own mattress and took the quilt tops home to make. Each family received mattresses and quilts according to the size of the family. Four mattresses could be made in a day. Two tables were on the platform. They were marked with the size of the mattress to be made. Cotton came in large bales. Each family had someone that had already made one to teach them how. The cotton from the bale had to be torn apart in small pieces and placed on the marked table. The mattress cover came already made and was ready to slip and work the cotton into. Large needles were supplied to tack the mattress. Many local families took advantage of the program. *Submitted by Helen Blades.*

## LAUNDROMATS

The first known laundromat in Republic was owned by the Riddles on Olive Street. Charlie operated this from the late 1930s to the 1960s. The machines were the wringer types with separate rinsing tubs beside the washers. The washing machines were set up with two rinse tubs, both with clean water, one for the first rinse and the second where bluing could be added for that extra clean look, no fabric softener at that time. The wringer could be swiveled in a position over each rinse tub as well as the washing machine.

One tub of wash water was used for the entire wash. The white clothes were washed and rinsed first, next were colored clothes, then came the towels, the overalls and jeans came last. The wet clothes were placed in baskets, taken home, and hung on clotheslines to dry. Rain was the only factor to deter hanging them outside. Temperatures could be 0 to 100, clothes would freeze dry or dry very quickly.

One bit of information from the late 1800s; if clothes were dingy or had turned yellow, they were to be hung on the clothesline when the peach trees were blooming to whiten the fabric.

Charlie would drain, clean the tubs and washing machines for the next customer waiting for a machine. This was much faster than using the wash board at home.

Charlie also worked on radios and small appliances. The highway patrol brought their short wave radios to Charlie's shop for repairs. He had one of the first crystal radio sets in the area.

In the 1950s Ray Johnson built a similar laundromat on the south end of Republic by his feed mill. It was operated in the same manner as the Riddle's. These wringer washing machine laundries lost out to the new much faster laundromat started in the mid-1950s by Howard Davis on North Main Street using automatic washers and dryers.

## ENTERTAINMENT

A location for most kinds of entertainment was provided by a school or church. Sometimes a Chautautqua was scheduled to visit a town and provided plays, circus acts and concerts for several days.

The fees were often guaranteed by the merchants or paid by a local individual. The troupe came to town on the train with all equipment necessary to set up a show, including a large tent. In Republic it was sometimes set up in the spacious lot behind the school on West Elm Street. Other times, it was located in the pasture across from the mill on South Main Street.

Another setting for plays, and later, for "silent" movies, was the opera house. It was on the west side of Main Street, over what was then Chaffin's Cafe, extending over part of the Owen and Short Hardware, now known as Country Sunshine, In 1907, the ever-popular play, "In Old Missouri With the Younger Brothers," was scheduled and advertised as "coming directly from the Baldwin Theatre in Springfield." It was seldom seen in small towns. Another show advertised by the Davis Opera House was "The Spinsters Convention" on Friday night, March 3, 1916. This was to be given under the auspices of the Ladies Aid of the M.E. Church. A note added "If you want a good laugh, don't fail to see the old maids. Tickets on sale at the usual place."

Teague Anderson built an outdoor theatre in Anderson Park which was on North Main Street. Anderson Street was on the south edge and Pine Street was on the east. A baseball field was included in the area. Fourth of July celebrations were often held at the park. Recently, framed glass advertising panels, which were said to have been used at the outdoor theatre, were shared by the owner. Some were hand printed with names of coming attractions and some were typewritten. One was commercially prepared in New York City by the Excelsior Illustrating Company. It announced the Paramount Picture Company's coming attraction, "Chickens," featuring Douglas MacLean. This movie was made in 1921. By 1929, "Talkies" or movies with sound, were being made. Douglas MacLean made only one before retiring from acting.

*Glass advertising slide. Courtesy of Tim Kubat.*

In the fall of 1919, a new theatre was opened by H.B. Ingler believed to be on the west side of Main Street.

Apparently, this was after "movies" were popular, as *The Republic Monitor* states, "Mr. Ingler has been giving us good programs twice each week and plans to continue this for the movie lovers of the vicinity.

During the era of the silent movies, music was provided by the management. In Republic,

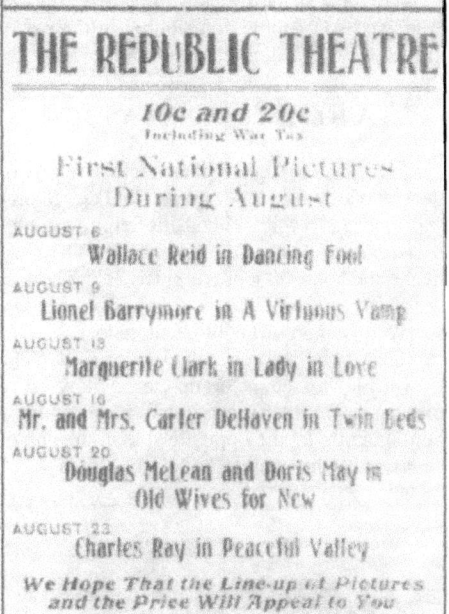

*Courtesy of The Republic Monitor.*

Wilma (Russell) Owen and Daphne (Thurman) Wells, piano players, and Buddy's Whizbangers provided that extra touch to the mood and story on the screen. In 1927, Chaffin and Thurman, next owners of the Republic Theatre, advertised a news reel and also the music of Buddy's Whizbangers. They provided a free Saturday matinee, courtesy of the town merchants. Later the theatre was owned by Lawrence and Lola Coggin, and finally, by the Cason family.

Lynn Martin started The Republic Theatre, in 1938. It was just north of the corner of Main and Grant Streets. By the time this theatre closed, easy access to Springfield theatres, television, and Drive Ins had changed the habits of the movie going public forever. *Submitted by Patsy Trogdon.*

*Irene Martin, assisted with the theatre.*

*The Republic Theatre on left.*

*Lynn Martin in front of theatre.*

## MOONEYHAM JUNCTION BARN

The Mooneyham Junction Barn just west of Republic was the place to go for good country music. The Barn, a large Quonset hut, was established in 1962 by farm owners Mr. and Mrs. Burel Mooneyham. It was a place for neighbors to go and enjoy their favorite gospel bluegrass or country music. Admission was free, but donations were accepted to cover the cost of lights and heat.

*Mr. and Mrs. Burel Mooneyham. Courtesy of The Republic Monitor.*

The first musicians to play at the Barn were Bill Slentz and Ernie Jackson. A local band, "The Country Generation," consisted of Republic residents Greg Moore, Roger Eitel, Buck Eaves and Rogersville resident, Roger Werle.

## SATURDAYS

Saturday was a busy day in Republic when farmers brought their produce to town to sell and buy their supplies for the coming week. There were stores to supply all their needs from bakery to grocery stores, dry goods, clothing, hardware, barber shops, feed stores and produce places which bought products such as chicken, eggs, cream and rabbits from the farmers.

There were theaters for entertainment and restaurants for eating out. On Saturday nights big crowds came to the band concerts. At one time the band played on a stand in the middle of the street at Main and Grant. It was a social gathering where friends met. Neighbors visited with friends and listened to the band. The youth strolled up and down the street visiting with friends and having a good time, dropping into the cafe for something to eat and buying five cent ice cream cones.

Later the bandstand was moved farther west to the corner of Grant and Walnut, east of the Hood United Methodist Church. This lot was owned by the Republic Masonic Lodge who leased it to the city for $1.00 per year. A bandstand was constructed and the crowd could sit, listen and visit. The rows of open back benches were made from tree limbs driven into the ground and topped with a slab of lumber.

On Saturday afternoon the merchants held a drawing. The first prize was $5.00 and several $1.00 prizes were given to lucky winners. If the name drawn was not present, the amount to be given away at the drawing would be higher the next week.

The crowd returned to hear the band play in the evening. It was an enjoyable day! *Submitted by Helen Blades.*

## POPCORN PETE

Pete Worthington, "Popcorn Pete" sold popcorn out of a popcorn machine in the late 20s and early 30s which was on a vendor cart. He pushed his cart to the center of downtown Republic every Saturday evening from his home located on Phelps and Summit Streets in northwest Republic. He would set his cart up on the northwest corner of Main and Grant Streets. There was a gazebo located there, and the first band concerts were played from this area. The popcorn was sold by the bag. After the band concert, "Popcorn Pete" would push his cart back to his house ready to return the next Saturday.

An interesting note regarding Pete: It is said that he put a zinc plate in one shoe and a piece of copper in the other shoe and always wore a short sleeve shirt with no coat. He stated that the power of the zinc and copper combined to always keep him warm.

Pete's son Archie Worthington worked for the U.S. Post Office. His responsibility was to hang the mail bag on the mail crane by the railroad track, located on the northeast side of the Main Street railroad crossing. The train had a mail car with a Railroad Post Office Clerk on board who would retrieve the mail as the train passed through town without stopping. If he should miss the bag no mail would go out for the day. Another responsibility of the RPO clerk would be to deliver the mail by throwing out a bag of mail for the community as the train passed through town. Archie always pushed a two-wheel cart carrying the mail to and from the tracks.

As diverse as their jobs were, both "Popcorn Pete" and son Archie contributed in their own unique way with their carts.

## A REPUBLIC CHARACTER

One of the most colorful characters of Republic was Vardeman R. "Shorty" Walker. Shorty was married to Mary Elizabeth Selph who preceded him in death, December 1948. They had made their home in Republic since 1923. Shorty's death was in April 1960, having one brother as a survivor, Delbert of Pueblo, Colorado.

Shorty was known by everyone as "The Cowboy," dressed in complete cowboy attire topping it off with his cap gun in a holster and a hunting knife on the opposite side of the gun or occasionally he would dress as an Indian.

*Shorty Walker, drawn by Greg Adamson of Springfield New-Leader.*

He loved to stop on the busiest street corners or the main highways and dance a jig for anyone who would watch, or catch a bus to Springfield and walk around the square. He was known to take his cap gun from his holster, point it to his head, pull the trigger and drop to the ground. In fact he pretended to shoot himself one day and someone called an ambulance to report a suicide. When the ambulance arrived they found Shorty having a good time. He always played a harmonica. One day Don Sneed, who was the manager of the Farmers Exchange, asked to show him the correct way to play the harmonica. After that he never would play for Don again. Alan Comisky remembers Shorty always smoking Red Dot cigars, with the paper ring still attached.

When Mrs. Walker passed away, he carried the mattress from her bed outside, took all of

*Shorty Walker with Barber Frank Babcock and Mike Kubat in the chair. Courtesy of John Parker.*

her possessions, placed them on top of the mattress and set fire to them. He thought this was what the Indians would have done.

Shorty never caused trouble, everyone loved to watch him with all his antics. A very colorful character of the past was laid to rest alongside his wife in Evergreen Cemetery.

## REPUBLIC BOTTLING WORKS

This Republic Bottling Works picture was taken about 1917 or 18. Ralph Landon is standing behind the truck, Orville Thurman is seated and Albert Rose is holding the ice chunk. The three men delivered ice from a Model T to Republic residents. Soda pop was made and bottled by the company. One of their bottles is on display at the Republic Historical Society Museum.

*Republic Bottling Works*

## SHERIFF MARK NOE

June 2, 1929 was not unlike many other late spring evenings Mark Noe had seen during his life in Republic. It was a warm Saturday night and the town was still bustling with activity at 10:00 p.m. Although he owned a local hardware store, he was also the town marshal. His job primarily was that of a night watchman but it also included taking care of any ruffians or local youths that got out of control. That evening he and several other citizens watched a grey, 1929 Ford coupe drive erratically up and down Main Street several times. Concerned they might be drunk, Noe decided to check them out before they hurt someone. Crossing over the street to the east side, he confronted one of the youths, Oval Lafollette and took a gun from him. He then ordered Lafollette to get back into the car and he slid in alongside of him.

The driver, a local Brookline tough by the name of Harry Young, was driving. Harry and his brothers had all served sentences in the Missouri state penitentiary and were well known to Noe. According to later testimony, Noe tried to disarm Young and a fight ensued. A shot rang out and the car took off north on Main Street until it reached Dr. Beal's house. Here it stopped and another shot rang out before Lafollette jumped clear and scampered off into the shadows of the night. The car then took off again and headed north out of town. Several bystanders became concerned and called first Judge Kerr to see if Noe had arrived at his house but he had not. They then called Sheriff Marcel Hendrix, who arrived later that evening to search for Noe. Lafollette was found at his brother-in-law's house, taken into custody and questioned. It was then authorities were told that Noe and Young had gotten into an altercation inside the car and that Young had shot the marshal.

The next morning Noe's lifeless body was found alongside the road south of Brookline with two bullet wounds—one to the head and one to the chest. Harry Young now became the focus of an area manhunt by law officers. However, he escaped to Houston, Texas where he and his two brothers, Jennings and Paul, started a huge auto theft ring for the next two years. Harry Young, understandably, stayed away from the Republic area for the next two years, knowing he would be arrested for murder if he was caught.

However, over Christmas of 1931, Harry, Jennings, their sister Lorena, and her husband, secretly spent two weeks at the family farm in Brookline, visiting with their mother and little sister Vinita. They remained undetected until Lorena and Vinita tried to sell a stolen car in Springfield on January 2, 1932. After questioning, they admitted that Harry and Jennings were at the farm. Sheriff Hendrix and 10 other men quickly headed to the farmhouse, arriving about 4:00 that afternoon. As the posse tried to break into the house, a gunfight erupted and within a few minutes, Hendrix, Ollie Crosswhite, Wiley Mashburn, Tony Oliver, Sid Meadows and Charley Houser all lay dead—the victims of the most prolific killing of police officers in American history.

Once again, Harry and Jennings escaped to Houston, only to be cornered in a rooming house three days later. Here, according to official reports, they committed a double suicide rather than be taken alive by the police. Some weeks later their bodies were buried in unmarked graves in Joplin. *Submitted by Tony Stephenson.*

## CORONER'S INQUEST
*Taken Before*
*Dr. Murray C. Stone*
*To inquire into the death of Mark S. Noe*
*Taken by Minnie M. Hanson*
*Republic, Missouri*

AT AN INQUEST: Taken before Dr. Murray C. Stone, Coroner of Greene County, on the 3rd day of June 1929, at the office of The Boy Scouts Room, in the city of Republic, Missouri, to inquire into the death of Mark S. Noe, the following proceedings were had:

APPEARANCES:
Dr. Murray C. Stone, Coroner, Greene County.
Mr. George Skidmore, Prosecuting Attorney.

D.E. MCNABB, being duly sworn, testified as follows:
DIRECT EXAMINATION BY DR. STONE:
There isn't much to tell. I was walking up the street, Mark was in Owen and Short's hardware store. He asked me to come in and have a friendly chat with him.
Q. What time was that?
A. Somewhere around ten o'clock. We saw a car parked in front of Ryan's cafe and Mark said he believed it was a stolen car.
Q. Did you see who got out of the car?
A. Yes.
Q. Did you know who they were?
A. I wasn't quite sure.
Q. What did Mark do?
A. We went in the back room of the hardware store and Mark checked the license number of the car. When we came back from the room, the car was gone. They drove up and down the street six or eight times. They first stopped at the cafe on the east side of the street, then they drove north, came back and stopped in the center of the street. One of the two got out of the car, spoke to some boys who were standing there, and went inside the restaurant. As he got out of the car, Mark said, "I believe that he has a bottle of whiskey in his shirt. I believe I'll just go out and get that gentleman." When he went out to the car he talked to the fellow driving. The fellow who got out of the car came out and went up the street about 50 yards, crossed the street and started back. Mark hollered to him and told him to come over there. Mark went inside his shirt and pulled out something. Either a gun or a bottle. I couldn't tell.
Q. How close was he to the car?
A. The fellow was out of the car, Mark got what he had, put the fellow in the car and got in with him.
Q. Mark got something that this fellow had and put it in his pocket?
A. Yes.
Q. Where was he sitting when he got in the car?
A. He was in the middle, Mark was on the right hand side.
Q. All three were in the same car?
A. Yes. It was a one seated car. Ford Coupe.
Q. Where did they go?
A. Went on north.
Q. About what time was this?
A. About eleven o'clock.
Q. Anybody following the car?
A. No.
Q. Was two shots all you heard?
A. That was all. I went to the Minute Cafe and asked where I could find Mark.
Q. Did you know that this was Mark in the car?
A. Yes. I then went to the Ford Garage and tried to get in connection with his office.
Q. Are you sure those were shots and not back fire?

A. Yes. Two shots and not back fire.
Q. During all this time there were three men in the car?
A. Yes, all three.
Q. When both shots were fired, all three were in the car?
A. Yes, I presume.
Q. How close were you when the first one was fired?
A. About 30 or 50 yards.
Q. When the second one was fired?
A. About one and a half blocks.
Q. You couldn't tell who fired the shots?
A. No sir.
Q. Did it sound like the same gun?
A. Same gun.
Q. When you went to use the phone did you notify someone?
A. Yes, Judge Kerr. I asked him if Mark had showed up and he said he never did.
Q. Did you see both men?
A. Yes.
Q. How were the men dressed?
A. One had on a light shirt, cap, light pants and soft collar.
Q. About the other one?
A. Light shirt and cap.
Q. Was he a small fellow?
A. Rather slim. Weighed about one hundred fifty pounds.
Q. Think that one could have had on overalls?
A. He could have had on waist overalls.
Q. Which one was driving?
A. The big fellow.
Q. Did you stay around the restaurant or go home?
A. I went to the Ford Garage and had the night man phone for me.
Q. Who did you call?
A. Judge Kerr.
Q. What did you do then?
A. Called Elvie Thurman.

BY THE JURY: What did you do after that?
A. Stayed at the garage all night with Elvie. In the morning I went home and ate breakfast.

BY MR. SKIDMORE: Were you with Mark when he was talking to these fellows?
A. I was standing near the curb about 15 feet.
Q. Did they appear to be drunk?
A. Neither one staggered when they got out of the car.

H.G. SNYDER, being duly sworn, testified as follows:
Q. Where do you live Mr. Snyder?
A. Here in Republic.
Q. Tell the jury what you can?
A. All that I know is what LaFollette told me after I arrested him.
Q. What is your commission?
A. Deputy Sheriff.
Q. Who called you?
A. Elvie Thurman.
Q. What time?
A. Eleven or twelve o'clock.
Q. You arrested LaFollette about what time?
A. About four or four-thirty.
Q. Where was he?
A. At his brother-in-law's six or seven miles from here. Brother-in-law's name is Kates.

41

Q. Was LaFollette in bed asleep?
A. Yes.
Q. What did LaFollette do?
A. The first thing I did when I went in and awoke him I asked him what he did. He said nothing. I told him that we had been sent after him and asked him if he didn't run off from the marshall last night.

He said, "Yes." We told him that he would have to go with us and that we would have to take him to town as we figured Young had bumped Mark off. He said that he didn't kill him when he was around. He said that Young and Noe were scuffling over a gun. He said that Young got his gun out of the car pocket. When they got down by Dr. Beal's they were still scuffling. Young was driving, LaFollette was in the middle and Noe was sitting on the right hand side. Mark was beating Young over the head with gun and was getting the best of Young. Two shots were fired and he slipped from under Mark and left the car.

Q. Was car going all this time?
A. Car was standing at the time the shot took place.
Q. Did you know LaFollette?
A. Yes.
Q. Did you know Harry Young?
A. Yes.
Q. Did he say Harry Young was in the car?
A. Yes.
Q. Did LaFollette explain how he got out of the car?
A. Yes, Harry Young was driving, Mark was leaning over him and they were fighting over gun, and he slipped out from under Mark and got out of the car.
Q. Do you know whether or not any gun had been found?
A. No, sir.
Q. Do you know what kind of a gun Mark had?
A. Mark had two or three guns. I don't know which one he had.
Q. Do you know if Young had been in the pen two or three years ago for filling station robbery?
A. Frisco searched his home and found Frisco property.
Q. Did you think that LaFollette was telling the truth?
A. I don't know.
Q. Do you know his reputation?
A. Don't know so much about it. He has been in the pen once, I don't think that he was a very mean boy.
Q. Were you around when Noe's body was found?
A. No. When I got there, there were a couple of men there.
Q. Who were the men?
A. I don't know there names. One lived on Marcel Hendricks place. One was a Boyd. I don't know his first name.
Q. What shape was the body in?
A. Looked like it had been thrown out of the car while car was going south. Head was lying north.
Q. Was there anything with the body?
A. Lap robe, papers, cushion, hat and a glass jar. The jar had something in it.
Q. Did you know that the boys had been around town?

A. Don't know. I went to Billings to the ball game.

LILLARD HENDRIX, being duly sworn, testified as follows.
DIRECT EXAMINATION BY DR. STONE:
Q. Where do you live Mr. Hendrix?
A. Brookline.
Q. Tell the jury what you know about this case?
A. This morning about six or fifteen after six I was standing outside and two men came up the road going north and stopped and hollered to come there right quick. They said a man was lying dead at the corner. So I got in the car and went to Brookline and called the Sheriff's office as I didn't know the Coroner's number and they told me that there had been a disturbance at Republic and the City Marshall was missing, so Elmer Boyd, Hugh Morton, Al Sagar followed in car. We drove down there. I was in the front car. As quick as I looked at the man I knew it was Mark Noe. That's all I know about it, so I started to leave but Hugh Morton went to Brookline and phoned down to Republic before I got there.
Q. Had it been raining?
A. It looked like it had. I don't know as I went to bed at ten thirty.
Q. Could you make out any tracks in the road?
A. None except the ones that these two men made that notified me.

BY THE JURY: Who were these two men?
A. I don't know. They were driving a Ford Truck. They had five or six Jersey veal calves in it. They said to phone somebody real quick, so I jumped in the car.

BERNICE ADAMS, being duly sworn, testified as follows:
DIRECT EXAMINATION BY DR. STONE:
Q. What's your name?
A. Bernice Adams.
Q. Where do you live?
A, Here.
Q. Tell what you know?
A. About eleven o'clock last night I was out in front at the gas tank and I heard what sounded like a pistol shot up the street. I looked up and I saw a Gray Ford Coupe coming down the street in low and passed by. I could see someone fighting in the car. They drove down by Fikes' and stopped and as soon as the car stopped one fellow jumped out and ran, came back up the street and turned the corner at the Baptist Church and went down the alley. About the time he got to the corner another shot was fired in the car.
Q. Was the car standing still?
A. Yes, and I heard someone call for help and then the car started again. The car was on the left hand side of the road, then crossed to the right hand and when they got over there they shot again. They then went right out of town.
Q. How many shots did you hear?
A. Three.
Q. One while car was moving?
A. Yes.
Q. One while car was standing?
A. Yes.
Q. Another one after it had started up?

A. Yes.
Q. All sounded like the same gun?
A. Same gun.
Q. Did you know this LaFollette?
A. I had seen him a few times but I didn't know him personally.
Q. Did you know any of the people in the car?
A. I saw LaFollette when they went down the street. I never saw anyone in the car. This car was down at the garage and LaFollette was in the car.
Q. Was Young in the car?
A. I don't know Young.
Q. What were the men at the garage for?
A. They stopped and called two boys out.
Q. Did they buy any gas?
A. No.
Q. Did you see Mark talk to them?
A. No.
Q. The first time you saw the car were the three together?
A. I don't know.
Q. You didn't pay any attention to the car until you heard the first shot?
A. I didn't pay any attention until I heard the first shot.

J.S. EVANS, being duly sworn, testified as follows:
DIRECT EXAMINATION BY DR. STONE:
About all I know is that it was about eleven o'clock last night as I was coming home from Springfield show and as I got down by Harve Snyder's and Fikes' and on the right hand side of the road there was a Ford Coupe parked. The right hand door of the coupe was opened and someone was scuffling, I heard a shot so I made the remark that we had better go up and get Mark Noe and as we drove up the street to the city garage. McNabb and the night man was sitting just inside the door. We drove on up and stopped at the Minute Cafe to see if I could see Mark. When I didn't see him I drove on up to Ryan's Cafe, went on up the street and turned around at the corner and drove down by and the car was gone.
Q. Only heard one shot?
A. One shot.
Q. How close were you to the car?
A. About fifteen or twenty feet.
Q. How many were in the car?
A. Two.
Q. Was door on the right hand side opened?
A. Yes.
Q. How far was this out of town?
A. Next block.
Q. Did you recognize anyone in the car?
A. No.
Q. Did you know Harry Young?
A. No.
Q. Are you quite positive that there wasn't three in the car?
A. Couldn't swear that there were three in the car.
Q. Do you live here in town?
A. Yes.
Q. What's your business?
A. Barber.

A.H. SAGAR, being duly sworn, testified as follows:

DIRECT EXAMINATION BY DR. STONE:
Q. Where do you live?
A. Brookline.
Q. Tell the jury what you know about this?
A. I don't know much. I got there about the time Hendrix did.
Q. Did you hear Hendrix testimony?
A. Yes.
Q. Can you add anything to it?
A. Nothing much. Only when I got there about five cars came.
Q. Anyone disturb the body?
A. No, sir.
Q. Were papers scattered around?
A. There seemed to be. Side curtains which I particularly noticed, a blanket, either a horse or army blanket, I couldn't tell, a hat which was lying two and a half feet from his head, a quart jar. The jar had something in it. Dr. Beal picked that up and a paper sack. This was about two and a half feet from his head.
Q. Was this car curtain or blanket bloody?
A. I couldn't say as they were all rolled up. Didn't pay much attention as I had to get back for other business.
Q. Did anyone touch the body?
A. No one except Dr. Beal and Harve G. Snyder.
Q. Were there any bruises on the face.
A. I didn't notice any. That's all I know.

OVAL LAFOLLETTE, being duly sworn, testified as follows:
DIRECT EXAMINATION BY DR, STONE:
Q. Where do you live?
A. About five miles NW from here. We were driving down the street a time or two.
Q. Who was with you?
A. Harry Young.
Q. About what time?
A. About eleven o'clock.
Q. Whose car?
A. Young's car.
Q. Did you ride around a while?
A. Yes. We saw some boys go into the cafe. We stopped car in the middle of the street.
Q. Which cafe?
A. Ryan's cafe. I went in the cafe, came out and started to get in the car and Mark Noe said to me, "Get in." I did.
Q. Did you see Mark before that?
A. No, sir.
Q. Did both you and he get in the car with Harry Young?
A. Yes. They started fighting, Harry Young and Mark, over Young's gun.
Q. Was that the first gun you saw in the mix up?
A. Yes.
Q. Did Mark have a gun out when he told you to get in the car?
A. Yes.
Q. Whose gun were they fighting over?
A. Couldn't swear.
Q. Tell about it?
A. I was in the middle, Mark was on the right hand side and Harry Young was driving. They were still fighting over gun. Mark reached over me trying to get Harry's gun. I then got out of the car and ran.
Q. Where did you run to and was car going when you got out?
A. I ran to my brother-in-law's west of town.
Q. How many shots did you hear fired?
A. One or two fired as I got out of town.
Q. Two and maybe three?
A. Yes.
Q. Where was the car when the first shot was fired?
A. By the Drug store.
Q. Was the car moving?
A. Yes.
Q. Where was car when you got out?
A. Below Sherman Robertson's Garage.
Q. Had the car stopped on its way down?
A. No.
Q. Was Harry scuffling and driving at the same time?
A. Yes.
Q. Was car wobbling?
A. Quite a bit.

BY MR. SKIDMORE: Repeat the talk between Harry and Mark?
A. Never had said a word.
Q. Did Mark say anything as he got in the car?
A. He said something to Harry. I didn't understand what he said.
Q. Did he say anything about you boys being under arrest?
A. Never said a word.
Q. What kind of a gun did Harry have?
A. 32-20 and 25 automatic.
Q. Did he have both of them with him last night?
A. Yes
Q. Was 32-20 lead bullet?
A. I don't know.
Q. What kind of a gun was fired?
A. I don't have any idea.
Q. What kind of a gun did you have?
A. Harry's automatic.
Q. Was it the one that the Marshal took away from you?
A. Yes.
Q. Did you meet Harry here?
A. Yes, about six o'clock.
Q. Where had you been from six till eleven?
A. Billings, Clever and then here.
Q. Driving around?
A. Yes
Q. Have anything in mind whatsoever?
A. No.
Q. Have any liquor?
A. No.
Q. Both sober.
A. Yes, so far as I know.
Q. Do you know if Harry was drinking?
A. If so, I didn't know it.
Q. Did Harry have two guns?
A. Yes
Q. Where did he have them?
A. In back on top of seat of Ford coupe.
Q. Both?
A. Yes.
Q. Where does Harry live?
A. Somewhere in Springfield?
Q. Did you see him often?
A. First time in over a year.
Q. Would you state for sure whether or not Noe had been wounded at the time you left the car?
A. I don't know. One shot was fired when I was in the car. Harry and Mark were scuffling over a gun.
Q. Did Mark have a gun in his hand when behind you?
A. Yes sir.
Q. What did he say to you?
A. He said, "Get in."
Q. He got a gun out of your shirt?
A. Yes sir,
Q. Did he search you?
A. Yes sir, that's what he did.
Q. Just where did you have the gun?
A. Sticking under my belt.
Q. You tell me, Oval, were there much scuffling and blows struck?
A. A few.
Q. Before the shooting?
A. A little ways.
Q. Was that one shot close to you?
A. Yes.
Q. Did you have a light in the car?
A. Dash light. I don't know whether it was lit or not.

BY MR. SKIDMORE: Tell again how you got out of the car?
A. Scooted from under Noe.
Q. Did you open the door or was it opened?
A. Yes, I opened the door.
Q. You stepped from running board and ran?
A. Yes.
Q. Did you tell anyone what happened?
A. I told my brother-in-law when I got home.
Q. Think of anything else you ought to tell.
A. That's all I know.

BY JURY: How many shots were fired when you were in the car.
A. One.
Q. Don't know who shot it?
A. No sir.

BOYD FUGITT, being duly sworn, testified as follows;
DIRECT EXAMINATION BY DR. STONE:
Q. Where do you live?
A. About three miles south of here. All I know is that I saw LaFollette as I was leaving. I was going to Billings to the ball game and as I turned the corner at Owen and Short's hardware, LaFollette and someone else was standing in the middle of the street between Owen and Short's and the Band Stand and LaFollette hollered at me and as I looked out of the side of the car as I was making the turn, I saw LaFollette and someone else standing by him, but I don't know who the fellow was, but I knew it to be LaFollette. I was going to Billings to the ball game.
Q. Did you know Harry Young?
A. No.

ALONZA BLADES, being duly sworn, testified as follows:
DIRECT EXAMINATION BY DR. STONE:
Q. Where do you live?
A. About four miles north from here. I can't add very much except what Snyder said as he and I were together in my car.
Q. You heard his testimony?
A. Yes, I stayed with this boy at his home (Snyder's) half an hour alone and he told me Mark was beating Young over the head with a

gun and he was getting the best of him. That's when he slipped from under Mark and in his opinion as he slipped he tore them apart. When Mark was shot, he did it then.

Q. When grappled together is that when he got out of car?

A. Yes. Said that Young got gun out of the pocket of the car and Mark was trying to get it. Also said that cartridges in the gun he had, had steel jacket with lead nose.

Q. Did he say anything about the other gun?

A. Told you what he told me.

Q. LaFollette gave Noe his gun and Noe kept it?

A. Yes.

Q. He said if he got shot it must have been when he was getting out of car?

A. Yes.

Q. Somebody found clothes. Were you along?

A. Fred Short and S.V. Eagan found the clothes. I tried to feed LaFollette his breakfast but he couldn't eat.

FRED SHORT, being duly sworn, testified as follows:
DIRECT EXAMINATION BY DR. STONE:

Q. Mr. Short, we have here some clothing and tools. You found these this morning?

A. Yes.

Q. Where?

A. On Hwy #66 about nine miles from here. Close to Plano the clothes were lying in the ditch and the tools before you went in the ditch.

Q. Did you find these going west?

A. Yes.

Q. About what time?

A. About eight thirty a.m.

Q. Did you look around and could you tell if car had stopped?

A. Couldn't tell if car had stopped. If it had it stopped on the concrete. The clothes were all bundled up. The cap was on the far side of the ditch, the tools inside next to the road and the clothes were in the ditch.

Q. Did it look like they were thrown out of the car?

A. Couldn't tell.

Q. Couldn't tell if car had stopped to make repairs?

A. No.

Q. Was there any gasoline in that jar?

A. Yes, jar smelled like gas.

Q. Was there any gasoline on the clothes?

A. Yes.

Q. Who was with you?

A. S.V. Eagan. We were west of junction of 66 and road north of the Republic road. Where the road intersects.

Q. See any evidence to burn clothes outside of the gasoline?

A. No, but there were some papers under the clothing?

Q. Did you bring the papers in?

A. Yes, I brought them to the store but I don't know where they are now.

JOHN SHIPLEY, being duly sworn, testified as follows:
DIRECT EXAMINATION BY DR. STONE:

Q. You know Oval LaFollette?

A. Yes.

Q. You know Harry Young?

A. Yes.

Q. When did you see Young last?

A. Last night about fifteen till ten. They were at the garage and Adams started out for me to look for a ride home. He said there were some boys in there and if they were going north the boys would like to ride out with them and he came back and said come on out, so I went and got in the car and the other boy got on it. He lives about three blocks from here. He got out at home and they drove me on home. We said a word or two, I bid them goodnight and went on in the house.

Q. What kind of clothes were worn by Young?

A. Cream colored shirt, light cap, dark pants. I didn't pay much attention.

Q. Did he have on overalls or jumper?

A. Not at the time I saw him.

Q. Could those pants, cap and shirt look like the ones he wore?

A. Could have. I didn't pay any particular attention.

Q. Had the boys been drinking?

A. Couldn't say. Weren't drunk when I met them.

BY MR. SKIDMORE: Did they have any liquor?

A. Never saw any. If they had they never produced any.

Q. What time did you get home?

A. About ten o'clock.

Q. Did you talk to them?

A. Only while they were turning around.

Q. You sat in the car?

A. No. Only while riding out.

Q. Did you see any gun?

A. No.

Q. How long have you known Young?

A. Not so very long. He said I should have known him but I remember him.

Q. Did he wear dark pants, light cap and cream colored shirt?

A. Best I can remember. It was dark and I didn't pay much attention.

OVAL LAFOLLETTE (called to stand again) being duly sworn, testified as follows:
DIRECT EXAMINATION BY MR. SKIDMORE:

Q. Do you remember the motor of the car going dead and someone getting out and cranking it?

A. No, sir.

Q. Do you remember saying to the officer as you got out of the car, if Mark got shot it was while you were getting out of the car?

A. Yes.

Q. You don't know what happened after?

A. No sir.

Q. Tell the jury that you didn't take any part in the fight?

A. No, sir. I did not take any part at all.

Q. You stated a while ago that you were not drinking?

A. Yes, sir.

Q. Had Harry Young ever gotten into any trouble?

A. Don't know if he did. Couldn't say cause I don't know.

Q. Were you any particular friend of his?

A. Never did run around with him much.

Q. Ever lived in the same neighborhood with him?

A. No sir.

Q. Are these the clothes Harry had on?

A. Resemble them I would say. Had on light cap, dark pants, cream colored shirt, but no overalls and jumper.

Q. Ever see these before? (screw driver and pliers).

A. Never before.

STATEMENT BY THE CORONER:

Let the records show that the fatal wound of the body of Mark S. Noe was a bullet wound of the head which entered on the left side three inches behind the left ear. The bullet went upward, through the brain and was found beneath the skull near top of the head on right side. There was also a wound half an inch behind the angle of jaw on the left side. This wound extended upward between the bones of the face and the base of the skull. No bullet was recovered from the wound. There was also a bullet wound through the right arm at the elbow. The cause of death was a bullet wound of the brain. There was found on the body, thirty cents in change, papers, pencil, badge, nothing else of special value.

I have examined this inquest and find it to be correct.

*Murray C. Stone*

## Downtown Republic In The 1950s
*See map on page 45*

1. John Arrington's Home
2. John Arrington's Garage
3. Hanson's Home
4. Funeral Home
5. Apartment Home
6. Armour and Fred McCullah's Ice House
7. Armour and Fred McCullah's Streetcars (used for storage)
8. Armour and Fred McCullah's DX Station
9. Sinclair Station (owned by Lloyd Sublett and Marvin Conroy)
10. Ford Garage (Paul Williams-Don Pollard-Floyd Harris)
11. Blacksmith Shop (Bob Fuhr)
12. City Service Garage (Almas Thompson)
13. *The Republic Monitor* (Mr. and Mrs. Dave Russell)
14a. Bennett Dry Goods
14b. Biglieni Plumbing and Hardware
15. Jewelry Store
16. O'Dell Drug Store (Doc and Ralph)
17. Bruce DeWitt's Attorney Office
18. Dr. R.C. Mitchell's first office later became a cafe, Republic Cleaners, and then remodeled and became Miller's Insurance Agency. Next door was a Ceramic Shop, Oil Painting Shop, Gift Shop, and at present a Chiropractor Clinic.
18.5 Dr. R.C. Mitchell's new office (later Dr. James Smith and Dr. Jon Clark)
19. MFA. Remember the back entrance to MFA where the feed, chickens, eggs etc. were all taken care of. No one has lived unless you chose the feed sack your parents purchased, as it would soon become the material for your new dress or shirt and if you were lucky you might get a new pair of underpants to match.

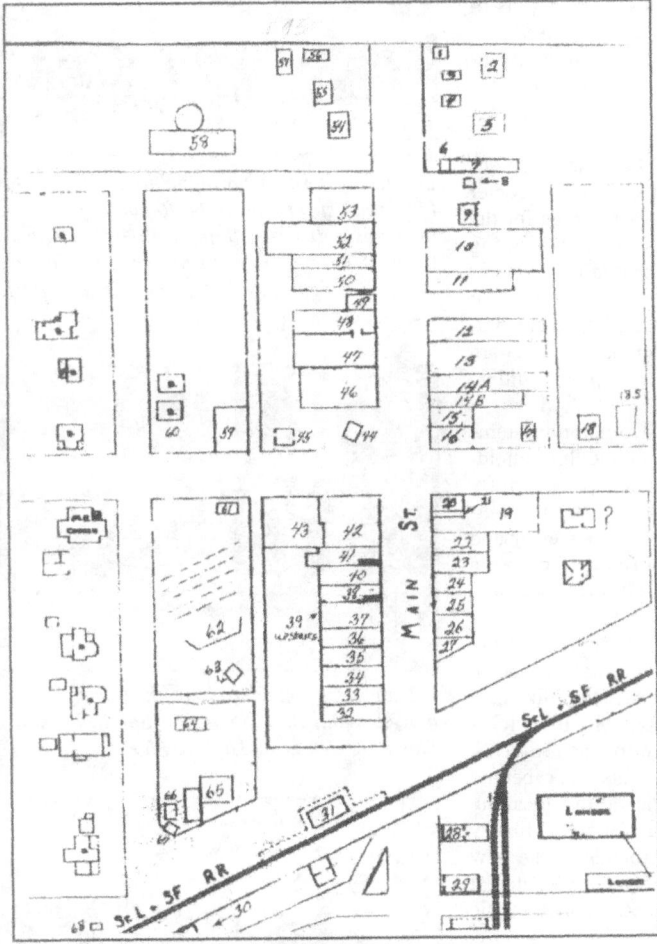

*Downtown Republic in the 1950s.*

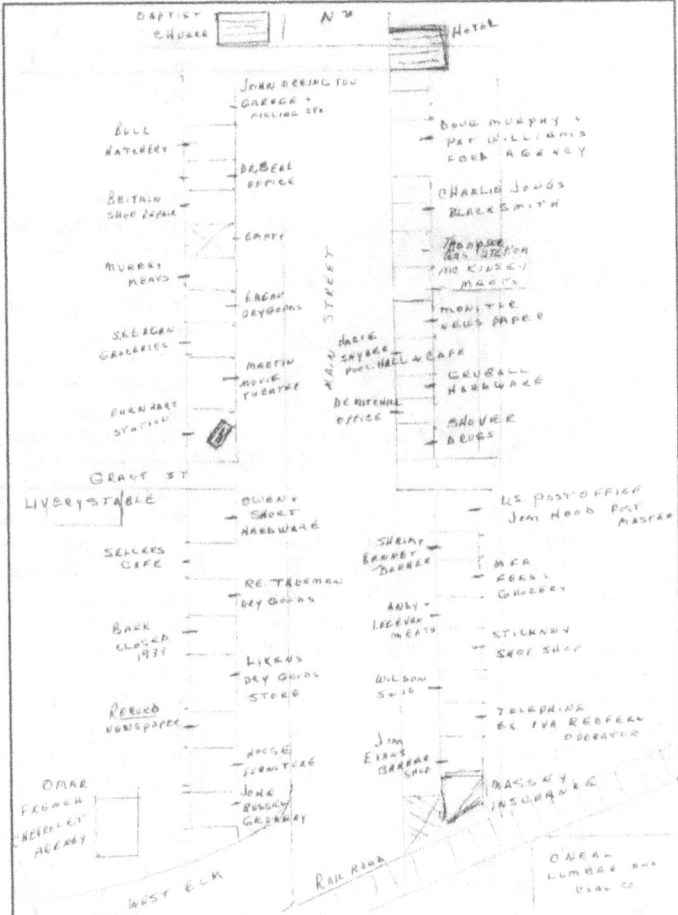

*Downtown Republic in the 1930s – As remembered by Howard (Wormey) and Jo Ann Eagan.*

20. U.S. Post Office (Linzee Wells was postmaster)
21. Curtis Packard Attorney Office
22. Evan's Market (Lee and Carl Evans. MFA purchased the Evans Market and expanded their building in the late 1950s or early 1960s)
23. Plummer's Dry Goods (Carl and Thelma Plummer, with living quarters in the back and upstairs)
24. Telephone Office with our own switchboard operators. This building later became Massey's Real Estate Office (Mr. Les Massey)
25. Beauty Shop (Eileen McCroskey)
26. Barber Shop (Frank Babcock)
27. Beauty Shop (Tonett Dial and Irene Sifferman were operators in 1958)
28. O'Neal Lumber Yard
29. Republic Bank or Farmers State Bank
30. Ramsey Feed Mill
31. Frisco Depot
32. Bacon Tire
33. Roy's Pool Hall
34. Liquor Store
35. *The Record* (owned by the Davis Family)
36. Barber Shop (owned and operated by Frank and Claude Bennett)
37. Logan's Market
38. Republic Locker Plant
39. Dr. Robert Brim (located upstairs)
40. Beauty Shop
41. Trailway's Cafe and Trailway Bus Stop (Owners: Chaffin Family, Lloyd and Hildred Garoutte, Harley and Lil Sublet, and finally the Pendergrass Family. The Western Auto was in this same building operated by Mr. and Mrs. Leonard Sims who lived upstairs.
42. Owen and Short Hardware (owners Glenn Owen and Fred Short and later purchased by Russell and Randall Sobotka). Above the hardware was the Woodsman of the World
43. Walden Insulation Company
44. Clyde Earnhart Standard Station
45. Clyde Earnhart Home
46. Republic Theater (owners Lynn and Irene Martin)
47. Eagan's Market (owner Edna Eagan later owned by Ray Mathews)
48. Eagan's Dime Store
49. Republic Sundries (owner Ruth Snyder). This was also the MKO Bus Stop. Mr. Lavega Claiborn operated a pharmacy in the back.
50. Beauty Shop later became Republic Automatic Laundry. Upstairs above the Beauty Shop was an apartment house.
51. Dr. Carl Leidenger's Office
52. Davis Hatchery (owner Howard Davis)
53. Jess Duvall's Garage (Jess owned several of the busses for the Republic School District)
54. First Baptist Church
55. Apartment House
56. John Manning Home
57. Manning Plumbing and Well Drilling
58. MFA Mill (MFA delivery truck garage)
59. Webb Hughes Second Hand Shop
60. Charley Jones Home
61. Breakbill TV Repair
62. Bandstand
63. Republic Jail
64. Rock Garage
65. Doc French Chevrolet Dealership and Garage
66. Leo Owen's Home (Republic marshal)
67. Service Station with gas pumps in front of Owen Home.
68. Shorty Walker Home (Dancing Cowboy)

## JUNE BUG DAY

E.A. "Pop" Witmer was a local Spanish American War veteran and editor of *The Ozark Hills and Hollers Magazine*, which was published locally, *The Ozark Hills and Hollers* was a magazine peculiar to the democratic way of life. It was started by Ed Witmer for the purpose of encouraging new poets, writers, and journalists; of introducing to others some of the ways and customs of the Ozarks and its people; and most of all to stress the importance of all people, both rich and poor, young and old, that go into the making of this great world.

He believed our religions, our government, and our very lives depended upon everyone, not just a chosen few. He believed the city was the local people.

It was for this reason that he asked for everyone's poems, essays, stories and criticisms. He wanted his magazine to express the people. Mr. Witmer believed that by providing a place for people who wanted to voice their opinions on

the problems of life, he would be furthering a better understanding which would lead to a life of peace and harmony for everyone.

Pop, after watching Junebugs busily zooming around, wondered why couldn't all Junebugs, including those people born in the month of June, get together and celebrate their special day. Since there is a day set aside for groundhogs and every dog has his day, why shouldn't there be a Junebug Day. So a plan was made to set a date, invite some real "buggy folk" from the region, writers, musicians, whistlers, poets, singers, fine speakers and plenty of folklore to help celebrate the day in a great way. The first celebration was held in June 1932.

From the first few dozen celebrations the crowds grew steadily, with a mix of local talent and out of town performers. It was an all day event with a carry in meal.

Junebug Day held June 8, 1958 was held in the high school gym. Entertainment was provided by Old Time Fiddlers, a famous banjo player from the Bluegrass Region, glee clubs, the Republic Accordin' Band, the Payne Wash Tub Band, an Arkansas String Band, the Tea Kettle Paraders, the Ozark Tomato Queen, Dell Doak with her Recording Machine; a play "Axin Her Father," and a ventriloquist. This was just the beginning of the program as printed by "Pop."

December 31, 1960 Mr. and Mrs. Witmer relocated to Springfield after living in Republic over 25 years. Junebug celebrations continued each year at the O'Reilly Gym on the corner of Glenstone and Division.

## HISTORY OF THE REPUBLIC BRANCH LIBRARY

The inhabitants of Republic, Missouri had no public library service until the Greene County Library, which was established in 1947, began bookmobile service to the bedroom community in 1955. After making its regular stop just off of Main Street, bookmobile driver Glen Norman would drop off large stacks of books at the home of the Wade sisters, who operated an informal library and would allow children and adults to check out the materials.

During the late 1950s discussions began over a possible merger of the Springfield and Greene County Public Libraries. A contractual agreement was reached in late 1960 allowing the two entities to share materials. The citizens of Republic were devoted users of the bookmobile and had expressed interest in having a city library. These ideas prompted the Greene County Library to establish a permanent facility in Republic.

The barn of the Lester E. Cox farm was donated to the city for use as a community center with a portion of the first floor reserved for the library. Remodeling work began in the spring of 1961 and was completed that fall. The board of trustees appointed Ethel Ely as librarian for the Republic Branch. An open house celebration was held on Tuesday, October 10. The barn sits at 410 S. Hampton next to Republic Middle School.

The consolidation of the two library systems did not occur until 1971, when the Springfield-Greene County Library District was formed. By that time the Republic Branch Library had outgrown its space in the Community Center and the decision was made to move the library to a building at 219 W. Highway 60 owned by Noel and Bonnie Quessenberry.

Continued growth prompted another move in 1985 to a storefront at 221 W. Highway 60 in the Southwest Plaza Shopping Center. Six years later, on June 17, 2001, the Republic Branch Library opened in another storefront at 1264 U.S. Highway 60 East in Merchants Park behind Ziggie's Cafe. After four years at this location, plans are currently under way for a new library facility to be built on the grounds of the new Republic High School, which will be located at the intersection of Highway ZZ and Republic Road.

*Photos courtesy of Springfield-Greene County Library.*

*The newly formed Springfield-Greene County Library District moved the Republic facility to the Quessenberry Building at 219 W. Highway 60 in 1974. Photo by Betty Miller for Springfield Magazine, February 1983, "From Carnegie To Kickapoo Prairie".*

*Due to space considerations, the library branch moved again in 1985 to the Southwest Plaza Shopping Center on Highway 60.*

*Having outgrown yet another facility, in 2001 the Republic Branch Library moved to its current home at 1264 U.S. Highway 60 East.*

*In 1961, the Greene County Library established this facility in the barn of Lester E. Cox at 410 S. Hampton. Photo from "Welcome To Republic: The Friendly Progressive City" pamphlet, published by the city in June 1964.*

# REPUBLIC COMMUNITY BAND

The Republic Community Band started in the 1930s when community members joined the high school band, under the direction of "Bud" Thurman, for weekly rehearsals and Saturday night concerts on the bandstand at the corner of Walnut and Grant Streets in Republic. The band was reorganized in the early 1980s when local and regional musicians sought a way to continue playing their instruments and occasionally performing in a musical ensemble. Ernie Pratt, former Republic High School music director was recruited to lead the group, and the membership quickly grew to over 60 persons.

*Bonnie Quessenberry and Herb Coggin in "Last Chance Saloon," during Centennial 1971.*

*Bandstand at Walnut and Grant, 1953.*

Through the years, this all-volunteer organization has drawn members not only from Republic but from Springfield, Bolivar, Cassville, Shell Knob, Monett, Verona, Clever, Nixa, Seymour, Diamond, Galena, Billings, and Ozark. Directors who followed Mr. Pratt include John Eubanks, Leon Bradley, Dan Updegrave, and current director, Dee Brake.

The band presents three regular indoor concerts each year - fall, holiday and spring. Outdoor performances during the summer include Artsfest and Cider Days on Walnut Street in Springfield, the annual Freistatt community picnic, Have-A-Blast and the Kiwanis Fall Festival in Republic. The band is supported by sponsor contributions and occasional donations for performances. They rehearse on Thursday nights at the Republic Middle School, and all musicians are welcome to join the group. *Submitted by Linda Leonard.*

# CENTENNIAL 1971

In February of 1971 a group of Republic Citizens began preparing for the August 27, 28, 29, 1971 Centennial Celebration for the city. Much time, effort, and care went into the planning for the event.

Centennial dresses for women and girls, Belle buttons, parasols, hoops, and petticoats were available at the Centennial Headquarters at 223 N. Main. Men could purchase hats, vests, ties, arm garters, the essential beard buttons, and shaving buttons. There were cups, plates, bumper stickers, and cookbooks for sale. Tickets for the Centennial ball, teen ball, and square dance could also be purchased. La Verne Boyer was in charge of the headquarters. Her volunteer assistants were Lorene Boyer, Kathy Lawrence, Patty Greene, Kathy Goodwin, Becky Ruckman, Cindy and Kerri Quessenberry, Lisa and Sally Engle, Helen Kubat, Becky Fault, Pat Stokes, Nancy Flanigan, and Valetta Kipper.

Formal swearing in ceremonies for the Centennial sheriff, judge, and a number of sheriff deputies were at the Republic City Hall. Judge of the Centennial was W.A. (Pete) Peterson. Orville Batson became official sheriff of the festivities with Gene Boatright, Joe White, John Day, Harley Hemphill, Tommy Thompson, Harold Blades, Dean Thomas, Charley Stokes and Don Batson sworn in as his deputies. Others were

*Ken Walker and Charley Schatz*

added after the main swearing date.

The Kangaroo Court was set up at the corner of Pine and Grant Street on a vacant corner lot behind the then Farmers Exchange. A water-filled cattle tank and a stockade were prepared for those brought before the judge. The dunking booth seemed appropriate to bring justice to those found in violation both of founded and unfounded offenses by the role playing centennial court. *The Monitor* owner Jim Smith was the public defender and Gary King was the prosecutor.

A beauty pageant was held at the Republic High School gym on June 22 to select a Queen for the Centennial. The honor went to Carol Carlson, daughter of John and Edith Carlson, a 20-year-old Southwest Missouri State sophomore. The three finalists were Debbie Hollis 3rd runner up, Lynn Bennett served as 2nd runner up and Debbie Cooper 1st runner up.

In the "Little Miss" Centennial Karen Elaine Sutherland, daughter of Mr. and Mrs. William Sutherland of Republic was selected from 30 contestants. Karen's attendants were Laurie Chilton, first runner up, and Gena Kay Espy, 2nd runner up.

The official crowning of Carol Carlson took place at the 8th annual Kiwanis Club sponsored Horse Show. She was crowned by Marcia Mossbarger, Miss Missouri of 1979.

The celebration officially got under way at 10 a.m. on Friday the 27th when the city's guest of honor, State Supreme Court Commissioner Alden Stockard, was presented the key to the city by Republic's Mayor Les Sweckard. This ceremony was conducted from the platform of a railroad caboose which was on a siding track at the O'Neal Lumber Company yard. The mayor was assisted in the welcome and presentation honors by Carol Carlson, Miss Centennial; Karen Sutherland, Little Miss Centennial; Ken Walker and Charles Schatz, Centennial Co-chairmen; Postmaster Herbert Coggin; and Representative Wayne Groner.

In Commissioner Stockard's remarks, he commented that he was born in Republic in a house at the corner of Grant and West. His father was the postmaster from 1900-1907. Commissioner Stockard resided in Jefferson City and had held his position as commissioner for 17 years. After the key presentation, activities went

*Candidates for the Centennial Queen, 1971. Back row from left: Cindy Evans, Brenda Biglieni, Sue Biglieni, Teresa Bridges, Judy Butler, Terri Courtney, Lynn Bennett, Carol Carlson, Debbie Cooper, Debbie Hollis, Patty Kinsey, Brenda Hemphill, Judy Latshaw, Patsy Ramsey, Beverly Rolufs, Terry Trogdon, and Kris Wood. Front row: Debbie Day, Jeanie Davis, Sally Engle, Debbie Hagler, Janie Lewis, Annis Maples, Mary Ann O'Neal, and Kerri Quessenberry.*

into full swing with displays and entertainment designed to provide almost constant attractions for all age groups.

Some of the contests and the winners names were:

Egg Contest: Obie Short, first place and Kent Cook, second place.

Sack Race: Steve Batson, first place and Billy Mooneyham, second place.

Tire Race: Beverly White, first place and Jeff Bruton, second place.

In the baby contest Shane Mooneyham, son of Mr. and Mrs. Terry Mooneyham, first place; Diane Denny, daughter of Mr. and Mrs. David Denny, second place; and Drenda Day, daughter of Mr. and Mrs. Kenneth Day, third place.

In the old-fashion dress contest, Elaine Kenny took first place; Carol Bennett, second place; and Vera Pollard, third place.

In authentic old-fashion dress first place went to Edith Carlson; Maro Hessee, second place; and Sharon Humphrey, third. Mrs. Humphrey's dress was authenticated to be 150 years old.

General dress winners were Sherry Thomas, first place; Opal Biglieni, second place; and Connie Carter, third place.

Children dress winners five years and under: first place, Melinda Arnold; second place, Kayla Garton; and third place, Drenda Day.

In ages 6 to 12 winners were: Gay Mooneyham, first place; Elizabeth Brownstone, second place, and Lisa Rowan, third place.

Ages 12 to 18 were Teresa Bridges, first place; Marti Coggin, second place; and Cheryl Jones, third place.

Prizes in the best costumed family were Bud Mooneyham family, first place; Richard Geren family, second place; and Ronnie Bennett family, third place.

The children's pet contest had a total of 38 entries with pets being judged in four categories:

Largest pet category, Scott Caldwell.

Smallest pet had joint winners, Lesley Pyeatt and Jeannie La Fon. They entered a pair of white mice fitted with tiny ribbon collars and tiny silver leashes.

Best trimmed and groomed pet winner was Traci Riggin.

Most unusual pet winner was Mark Hemphill with a pet opossum.

The longest beard contest was won by Terry Fugitt, first; Gene Boatright, second; and Gene Fair, third,

In the most unusual beard category first place went to Orville Batson; second to Lester Ray; and third to Bud Mooneyham.

In the best trimmed and groomed beard Herb Coggin took first, Hal Williams, second; and John Arnold, third.

Winners of the greased pole contest were Chris Waterman and Joe Schumerth.

There was only one barber shop quartet composed of Charley Schatz, Noel Quessenberry, Jim Smith and Gary King.

Grand champion of the pie eating contest was Dickie Hailey, with Alan Rader and Mr. Tanner runners-up.

Old fiddlers contest was won by Don Wright.

Window display: Plummer's Dry Goods, first place; second place to the 49's Extension Club display in Ken's TV window; and third place to Floyd Britain for his barbed wire displayed in the window of Republic Auto Supply.

An estimated crowd of at least six thousand watched the two mile long parade on Saturday afternoon at 2 p.m. The parade featured a number of steam engines and long lines of antique automobiles in addition to a number of floats and special interest entries. Float winners were Evangelical Methodist Church, first place; Jot 'Em Down 4-H, second place; American Home Club, third place; Billings Bluebirds, fourth place. Several saddle clubs participated, and there were a number of individual horse-drawn entries.

The Abou Ben Adhem Shrine group presented a large number of units with entries in band, motorcycles, small cars and auto cavalcade divisions.

A group of Centennial officials rode in a jeep-driven tram donated for the occasion by the Shepherd of the Hills Farm at Branson, and the tram was used to provide free rides around Republic for the children.

The awards ceremony for the oldest Republic citizens was won by Dr. Burd O'Dell at the age of 93. Horace Bell, age 95, arrived after the award and was given an additional trophy. Other recognition went to John Arnold, 92; Bertha Nance, 91; John Hicks, 91; Frank Scandrett, 87; David "Solly" Frazier, 91; Jessie Frazier, 87; and Ida Boothe, 88.

Those unable to attend the ceremony, but also receiving mention were Iri Jackson, 95; T.A. Sifferman, 94; Emmer Blades, 92; Minnie Squibb, 91; Ava Garoutte, 89; Cordie Thurman, 89; A.L. Swinney, 89; Hattie Brashers, 88; Mrs. Ira Wade, 88; Nancy Williams, 87; Claude Looney, 86; and Tura Coggin, 85.

Entertainment on virtually an hourly basis was provided by a number of bands, groups, and individuals throughout the celebration. Among those entertaining the crowds were the Greene County Ramblers, Foggy River Boys, the Forest Wasson band, the Marvin Cardwell band, the Aurora Rinky Dinks, Marilyn Killar, Evert Simmons, 135th Army Band, Wolf Creek, and other assorted acts.

A number of food and game stands were available, and several demonstrations of antique steam-driven farming equipment were given.

Gunfights between the "good guys" and the "bad guys" were staged several times daily with the participants firing blank ammunition and costumed for the occasion.

The grand finale of the centennial celebration was a community-wide church service for all denominations held Sunday morning in Republic City Park. About 600 attended the service and heard the principal address given by Dr. William Everheart, president of Drury College.

A large number of people remained at the park for an old-fashioned basket lunch shared on the grounds.

All the hard work proved to be a huge success. A Centennial book was published at this time with biographies and town history. *Submitted by Rosemary Comisky.*

## THE TORNADO OF 1971

It was a calm night on December 14, 1971 around 11:30 p.m. Some residents had already

*Scenes from the 1971 tornado: Northeast corner of Main and Hwy 174, church building southwest of city, destroyed businesses, the Frank Barnhart and Ralph Smart homes.*

retired for the night while others were working. All were soon to find out what it was like to be in the middle of a tornado. Homes were destroyed, businesses completely gone, churches leveled, and trees that had lined Main Street and Elm Street were no longer there. What seemed to go on forever was over in seconds, with destruction over most of the town.

The Assembly of God Church on West Street and Hwy 60 was leveled. Hagale Garment Mfg. Co. was destroyed, leaving 150 employees out of work. Charlie Riddle was working on the second floor when the tornado hit, he called Mr. Hagale as soon as possible, telling him, he better come down because the roof was gone and there was nothing he could do. The next morning the Republic citizens could see what damages had come to their town and homes. Neighbors who had not spoken to each other in years came together to take care of putting their homes and town back in order.

Ralph Smart's family was home alone on West Elm Street as he worked the night shift at Springday Corp. Helen Smart and their two boys were found after their home was completely destroyed. The boys were across the street knocking on Johnny Garton's door unharmed. Helen had started to get the boys when she saw a flash of light and screamed for help. She must have blacked out because the next she knew she was waking up in a neighbor's home. Helen was taken to St. John's Hospital with bruises but no broken bones. Police officers, Oren Sisco and Frank Hooten, were dispatched to Hwy 266 to watch for developing weather conditions. Ivoe Rogers, of Route 4, Republic, contacted police to inform them a tornado had touched down and several mobile homes were overturned. The officers found Mary Rucker standing beside her home. She told them her husband John was trapped between the roof and the bathroom wall. It took several officers to free John. He was unconscious and was taken to Cox Medical Center, where he was pronounced dead on arrival.

There had been storms and tornadoes before the 1971 tornado. This one served as a wake up call of the necessity to have early warning systems for Republic and Greene County. People who were not fearful of these types of storms before 1971, are now going to safe places at the first warnings.

Due to the curiosity seekers, deputies had to block off the streets coming into the city of Republic so cleanup and repairs could be done. The city opened the landfill for the clean up, but going through the roadblocks and with so many sightseers made getting to the landfill a challenge. Through the help of many people, the homes and town were put back in order. The loss of the big trees that lined each side of Main and East Elm Streets changed the looks of the city for a lifetime.

## PLANE CRASH FEBRUARY 22, 1973

Dollie Foust had just sat down at her kitchen table about 4:10 p.m. Thursday February 22, 1973 getting ready to eat, when she heard a noise that sounded like a shotgun blast.

Within seconds the smoke poured through her home at 545 North Main, Republic, Mis-

*Scenes from the plane crash. Courtesy of Springfield-News Leader.*

souri. A twin engine Beechcraft airplane had crashed into her garage, destroying the garage and setting her home on fire.

According to witnesses, the plane passed over Republic about 4 p.m. February 22. It circled the school twice according to Deputy Ray Mathews, and then it flew north, turned around and headed back south.

Eyewitnesses near the site indicated that the plane appeared to have attempted to land in an open field, but pulled up, passed over Highway 174 at tree-top altitude, suddenly banked left, and veered into the ground.

Jim Blades of Republic was driving a school bus toward the school when he observed the plane flying very low, apparently under full power. It looked like it was flying straight south following a street, when one wing dipped, and it crashed. One wing hit an old stump, which had been left from the tornado in December 1971; this kept the plane from crashing into the center of Mrs. Foust's home. One piece of a propeller landed atop the roof. One engine was on the north side of the stump, the other on the south side. The force of the impact instantly took the lives of both the pilot and the one passenger according to Deputy Mathews.

What caused the plane to crash is unclear. Randall Sobotka heard the aircraft and went outside to see what was going on. Mr. Sobotka was in the U.S. Air Force in WWII and still retained an active interest in flying. He observed that the plane was flying lower than normal, but nothing that would indicate the plane was having any trouble. Randall watched it heading south and then in a few moments, watched it come back in a northerly direction. Tom Short was probably the closest one to the scene to have observed what took place.

Tom was at Jack Wheeler's service station on Highway 174, when he observed the plane coming from the northwest heading in a southeasterly direction. He noted that the airplane just cleared the treetops and power lines near Ethel's Cafe and the nose of the plane dipped down as it banked to the left. The plane was flying very low, maybe 40 to 50 feet off the ground. Tom lost sight of the plane behind a couple of houses; when it came back in his sight, the wing that was down hit a small shed to the rear of a house and started to roll or cartwheel. As it rolled it blew up and a ball of fire went better than 100 feet into the air.

No explanation was given as to why the plane was off course. The plane had departed from East Kansas City, Missouri with an intended destination of Point Lookout Airport, Hollister. Losing their lives were Noel Wilber Atkinson, the pilot, and Harry T. Cooper, the passenger.

The Aviation Toxicology Laboratory stated there was a high blood alcohol content in both bodies. *Submitted by Bill Robertson.*

## REPUBLIC PUMPKIN DAZE
## A HISTORY IN THE GROWING

In 1992, a small group of Republic, Missouri citizens formed a committee to organize a harvest festival. They wanted something unique to draw interest and attendance from the far reaches of the region. The result of their brainstorming and hard work is now known worldwide as Republic Pumpkin Daze. Those men and women became the founding fathers and mothers of a growing festival that has captured the attention of giant pumpkin growers and curious onlookers.

The fascination with giant pumpkins first gained international attention at the turn of the 20th century when William Warnock of Goderich, Ontario, Canada, sent a 400 pound specimen to the Paris World's Fair of 1900. Warnock was awarded a special Bronze Medal and diploma from the French government. To further establish his place in the annals of world records, Warnock exhibited a 403-pound pumpkin at the St. Louis World's Fair of 1904. His record stood until 1976.

With a Missouri connection to giant pumpkin history and the overwhelming enthusiasm of the

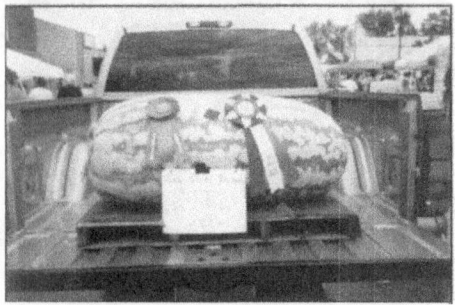

*State records were set during Pumpkin Daze, with this 838.5 lb. pumpkin and 249 lb. watermelon. Courtesy of James Taylor.*

committee, the Kiwanis Club of Republic sponsored the World Pumpkin Confederation Weigh-Off held in Republic on October 3, 1992.

From the beginning, the need for organization was recognized and the Giant Harvest Association, Inc. was created. This non-profit organization coordinated the World Pumpkin Confederation Weigh-Off and Pumpkin Daze Harvest Festival in 1993 and 1994. Then in 1995, the organizers of Pumpkin Daze switched to the Great Pumpkin Commonwealth as their official weigh-in sanctioning agency. At that time the coordinating non-profit organization became Republic Pumpkin Daze, Inc.

In 1992, money prizes were awarded for first through fifth place for pumpkins and watermelons, with ribbons for sixth through tenth places. Ribbons were also awarded for longest gourd, sunflower and bean, heaviest cabbage, muskmelon, onion, apple and radish. In 2005, money prizes were awarded for pumpkin, watermelon, squash, cantaloupe, tomato, long gourd and heaviest gourd, with both adult and youth (12 and under) divisions. Ribbons were awarded for the top five in each of the following categories: tallest sunflower, longest ear of corn, largest sunflower head, heaviest cabbage, heaviest turnip, tallest cornstalk and heaviest radish.

Some of the past weigh-off results for Republic Pumpkin Daze are as follows:

1992 World Pumpkin Confederation (first weigh-off held in Republic)
Pumpkin - Joe Kelley at 462.5 pounds
Watermelon - Waddell Estep at 179 pounds (ranking 2nd in national competition)
1995 Great Pumpkin Commonwealth (first year with GPC as national affiliation)
Pumpkin - Audie Starkey at 522.8 pounds
Watermelon - Eldon Pitcher at 148.8 pounds
2005 Great Pumpkin Commonwealth (latest results)
Pumpkin - Richard Bottorf at 838.5 pounds
Watermelon - David Miller at 249 pounds

As an officially sanctioned weigh-off site for the Great Pumpkin Commonwealth, Republic Pumpkin Daze entries are eligible for national prizes. Over the years several entries have received national ranking.

The festival continues to grow in reputation, participation and attendance. More growers are competing; more retail, game and activity; concessions and informational booths are lining up and down Main Avenue; and more people of all ages from near and far are flocking to the best place to be each year on the first Saturday in October.

With Pumpkin Daze being held on Main Avenue in downtown Republic, the cooperation of city officials has been crucial to the location as two blocks of State Highway N are cordoned off for the event.

Since 1993, one of the most anticipated publications for area residents and growers is the official Republic Pumpkin Daze booklet. The booklet contains information on the national and local prize schedules, also listing past winners of the weigh-in as well as the past years' winners of various other contests and pageants held during the festival, with a schedule of events for the current year, and acknowledgements of sponsors and contributors.

It is claimed that at the St. Louis World's Fair of 1904, several foods were invented, including the hamburger, the hot dog, the ice cream cone and cotton candy. Whether these claims are true or not is greatly debated, however, William Warnock and his world champion 403-pound pumpkin was real and a legacy thrives in Republic, Missouri.

On the first Saturday in October everyone is welcome to view the giant fruits and vegetables, meet the growers, shop the booths and munch on the now traditional hamburgers, hot dogs, ice cream cones and cotton candy.

Republic Pumpkin Daze 2006 Committee: Jane Boatright, Andrew Brown, Cindy Burks, Amy Cameron, Duane Compton, Vickie Hayward, Dana and Rita Hodges, Carl Huffman, Peggy King, Peggy Kubicek, Kathy Long, Ron Mark, Mark Mauss, Leon Medlin, Jack Muench, Cyndy Muench, Christine Parks, Mike Schumaker, David Stevens, Judy Towe, Sue Walter, Debbie Watson, Dan Westfall, Greg White, Chris Wilbers and Linda Womack. *Submitted by Leon Medlin and Peggy King.*

## People Helping People

In October 1987, Marcella Garner saw a need in Republic, Missouri. Through the Ladies Auxiliary of the local VFW she started the organization People Helping People. She believed no child should be hungry or without shoes or a coat. Marcella would see a family who appeared to be in need, she would then set up an interview with them to see what their wants, needs and wishes were. After the initial interview, she would ask for volunteers to adopt a child for Christmas. Those who gave their time to make it a success were churches, individuals, school organizations, youth programs, Boy Scouts, Girl Scouts, 4-H club members, to mention only a few.

They first met in a small office building on

*Marcie Garner's family. Charlie Garner, son; Penny Horn, daughter; Chuck Garner, husband; and Nancy Spencer, daughter.*

Main Street, which was donated by a secret Santa, asking to remain anonymous. That first year, they provided food baskets to 30 families at Christmas time. Next they used the Republic Housing Authority Building located on Olive Street. Later Marcella convinced the city of Republic to allow them to use the downstairs of the Cox Barn, located on Hampton Street for their housing, rent-free.

Marcella Garner devoted her time and her love to the needs of those less fortunate. She was the recipient of the Jefferson Award in recognition of outstanding public service, the National Daily Points of Light Award from President George Bush, a letter of recognition from President Bill Clinton, the Republic Woman of the Decade and the award Outstanding Citizen of Republic, presented by the Mayor and Board of Aldermen, to name only a few.

People Helping People was formally incorporated as its own entity in 1997 and received its 501(c)3, not for profit status, in 2000. It is overseen by a board of directors and operated through a host of volunteers and funded through the generosity of the Republic community. There is no paid staff; all work is entirely volunteered. The organization's mission is to provide under-privileged children and families with food, clothing, household items, medical care, seasonal gifts, etc.

Food baskets are available all year upon request. The building location is open weekly to the public to pick up food, clothing, household items and other basic necessities. Thanksgiving and Christmas baskets that include food, toiletries, hygiene items and toys for the children are prepared for the holiday season. During the 2005 holiday season alone, 94 families encompassing 217 children received gifts and food from the organization. School supplies for deserving children are available at all times. School nurses call PHP when they have children that need shoes, clothing, eyeglasses, and dental or medical needs. These items are provided without question or discrimination and at no cost.

After more than three years of planning, fundraising and construction, People Helping People of Republic, Missouri, Inc. became a homeowner. In May 2006 it moved into a new permanent home, "Marcie's Place" at 210 N. Pine, one block east of the four way stop on

*Ribbon cutting for People Helping People.*

*Marcie Garner at Cox Barn.*

Main and Grant Streets in downtown Republic.

The 1,800 square foot facility includes a food pantry, sorting and receiving area, space for used clothing and household items as well as enough land for future expansion. The new facility may well be unique to the area in that it is owned by a local community based not-for-profit organization and was funded entirely by the generosity of the community who gave of their money, time and services to make the dream of this building a reality. It truly "took a village" to raise the building. It was named after the organization's founder, Marcella Garner, who still inspires those she left behind.

People Helping People of Republic, Missouri, Inc. is unique to Republic in that it is the only organization within the city to provide this type relief to the general public's deserving families. Without this organization there are children of Republic who would not have food, clothing, school supplies or other basic necessities. Together a community can make a difference in a child's life. *Information provided by Elizabeth Horn, daughter of Marcella Garner and Lindy Maus, President, People Helping People Board of Directors.*

## Relay For Life

In May 1985 Dr. Gordy Klatt wanted to enhance the income of his local American Cancer Society office. He decided to personally raise money for the fight by doing something he enjoyed—running marathons. Dr. Klatt spent a grueling 24 hours circling the track at Baker Stadium for more than 83 miles. Throughout the night, friends paid $25 to run or walk 30 minutes with him. He raised $27,000 to fight cancer. That first year, nearly 300 of Dr. Klatt's friends, family, and patients watched as he ran and walked the course.

While he circled the track those 24 hours, he thought about how others could take part. He envisioned a 24-hour team relay event that could raise more money to fight cancer. Months later he pulled together a small committee to plan the first team relay event known as the City of Destiny Classic 24-Hour Run Against Cancer.

In 1986, 19 teams took part in the first team relay event on the track at the colorful, historical Stadium Bowl and raised $33,000. This is how the first Relay For Life began.

Relay For Life began in Republic in 1999. It was started by Kellie Jeffries along with Stacy Shultz an American Cancer Society Staff partner. The first Relay made $14,717 with only 11 teams participating. It has always been held at the Middle School football stadium and has continued to grow over the years. In 2006 the Relay earned over $115,000 with only 39 teams. This was a significant increase over the $104,000 raised in 2005. The 2005 Relay was considered a big success after it topped the 2004 Relay which raised $87,000. Each year it has continued to grow in numbers and dollars. The Relay truly represents the spirit and kindness of the people of Republic.

Relay For Life has continued to grow nationwide with over 4,500 held in the United States in 2006. Relay has also become an international program with several countries participating. The first Relay in Iraq was held in 2006. *Information provided by Vickie Hayward.*

## Miss Missouri

In 1993 Republic was proud that its own Shelly Kay Lehman was crowned Miss Missouri USA. Shelly, daughter of Rex and Judy Lehman, grew up in Republic and graduated from Republic in 1986. In 1991 she graduated

*Miss Missouri 1994, Shelly Lehman (Holt).*

from SMSU (now MSU) with a bachelor of science degree, and obtained her master's degree in education in 1996.

During her reign as Miss Missouri USA, Shelly divided her time between being a third grade teacher and the official duties of the title. As a first-year teacher her students were a big part of her life, but she also traveled all over Missouri talking to children about the importance of staying in school.

The highlight of her reigning year was the opportunity to participate in the nationally televised Miss USA Pageant held in 1994 in South Padre Island, Texas with her family and friends there supporting her. After making it to the top 12, Shelly finished seventh overall.

Shelly currently teaches in the Republic school system and is still involved in pageants and modeling. She and her husband, Jake Holt, live in Republic and have two beautiful daughters, Kamrynn and Kyra, who attend Republic schools.

## Town Teams

Down through the years baseball and softball have been a favorite recreation and pastime for summer activities. Hundreds of teams have spent their summers enjoying the sport with friends and family as fans. Baseball fields were often vacant lots or farmers fields and through continued use of running the bases, a path was soon created and the appearance of the desired field evolved. Often the school fields were used. As a result town teams were popular.

As more families began to own cars and community activities expanded, the sport and enthusiasm of the fans continued. The teams began playing in leagues in Springfield and surrounding area.

In February of 1975, Herbert Coggin (president of the American Legion Baseball Booster Club) and Neil Pittman (High School and American Legion baseball coach) appeared before Mayor Larry Cox and the City Council to ask permission to build a baseball field on property located on Miller Road. After several meetings, Coggin and Pittman convinced the Council that using the land for the youth was more important than selling it to developers as had been previously considered. The council agreed to the request.

Many volunteers from the Booster Club worked hard on the project and a field was built including backstops, fencing, and dugouts. Some bleachers from the old football field were donated by the school.

At the time it was hoped that this could be the beginning of a fine sports complex as indicated in a letter to the City Council by Coggin. However, it was never imagined that the Bervin White Memorial Complex along with the Saddle Club Arena, would develop into such a modern complex on Miller Road from such a meager start.

*Republic Independents, 1914.*

*From left: George Thurman, Manager; Aubyn French; Leonard Fugitt; Jim Hood; Ernest Ferguson; Bill Hood; Elmer Howell; H. Squibb; Ross Hood; Percy Delarue; Harve Snyder; and Claude Bennett. Donated by Ruth Snyder.*

*O'Neal Lumber, composed primarily of Republic products, came through in a dark horse role to gain third place in the district softball tournament in Springfield to attend the state tournament in St. Joseph, Missouri in 1961. Team members include, left to right, front row: Manager Joe Blades, Ken Blades, Ed Davis, Gary Johnson, Jim Blades, and bat boy Billy Todd. Standing: Alan Comisky, Howard Thurman, Jack Trogdon, Jack Fraka, Bob Duvall and sponsor Elton Todd. Courtesy of News and Leader staff photos.*

*Rowan Electric Softball Team, 1972. Back row from left: Bervin White, Bob Duvall, Mike Gammel, Larry Carter, Neil Pittman, and Bill Schatz. Middle row: Jim Duvall, Max Brown, Larry White, Jerry Daren, and Terry Noland. Bottom row: Tommy Owen, Mike Schatz, Mickey Owen, and Mark Brown. Not present, Alan Comisky.*

*Town team, 1948-49. Front row: David Comisky, Richard Randles, Alan Comisky (bat boy), and Fuzzy Jorden. Middle row: Jerry Randles, Max Booth, Tom Shook, Jerry Owen, and Wayne Sanders. Back row: Gordon Stewart, Bill Raper, Charles Comisky, Edward Davis, and Gary Baumberger.*

*American Legion Post 139. Front row: Head Coach Jerry Owen, Doug Ramsey, Mickey Owen, Allen Brown, Lon Bennett, Doug Davis. Back row: Gary Hill, Bill Gilbert, Jim Gray, John Stockstill, Jeff Burton, Harris Randles, Asst. Coach Robert Mahan.*

## AMERICAN LEGION BASEBALL

In 1978 Republic was fortunate to have an American Legion Baseball team participate in Central Plains Regional Tournament in Rapid City, South Dakota. They were given this privilege by winning the state title at Meador Park in Springfield.

*American Legion Booster Club President Herb Coggin. Courtesy of The Republic Monitor.*

## TRI-WAY COUNTRY CLUB

The first meeting of citizens from the area interested in building a golf course met May 31, 1967 with Mr. Joe Adams of the Farmers Home Administration. Mr. Adams explained how such a project might be financed with a rural recreational loan from the FHA.

After further meetings, a steering committee was chosen to follow up on the possible project. Those on the steering committee included Bill Cantrell and Arlie Little of Clever, and Herbert Coggin of Republic.

On May 6, 1968 an organization known as TRI-WAY Country Club, Inc. was formed and the members of the board of directors were elected. They were Joe Nelson, Rolland Andrews, Leroy Wood, Karl Leidinger, Arlie Little and Herbert Coggin. A charter was received and Herbert Coggin was elected president.

*Anderson, Brown, Koston & Deeds Post 139, 1978. First row, bat girls: Cathy Hancock and Toby Feltus. Second row: Doug Davis, Wesley Towe, Greg McCord, Jeff Burton, Mickey Owen, Bruce Bennett, Coach Ray Mahan. Third row: Manager Bill Schatz, Allen Brown, Kent Russell, Jim Winn, Tom Trogdon, Harris Randles, Steve Kirkwood, Lon Bennett, Coach Jerry Owen.*

*Courtesy of The Republic Monitor.*

The board received an option for 100 acres of land located two miles south of Republic on Highway P belonging to Boyd Fugitt as the site for the golf course.

An application was made to the FHA for a loan of two hundred thousand dollars for the project. After many months of delays the loan was secured.

Hood-Rich Architects and Consulting Engineers were hired to prepare plans for the facilities (club house, swimming pool, tennis courts, etc). J. Pres Maxwell of Morrison, Colorado was hired to design and build a nine hole golf course.

On April 16, 1971 a final inspection and approval of the project was made, and what begin as a dream some four years before became a reality for some two hundred families.

The country club later was expanded to 18 holes, and the corporation sold the course to Dale Boatright. It was renamed Island Green and now operates as a private club.

## REPUBLIC AREA CHAMBER OF COMMERCE

The Republic Area Chamber of Commerce (RACC) began in 1979. The following businessmen: Lyle Bebee, Don Dodson, Mac McKay, Ron Mark, Pete Peterson, Dale Meadors and Eual Moore held their first meeting at what is now the H&R Block building on Highway 60. They elected Lyle Bebee to be their first president. The second president, Dale Meadors, held the title of president for 15 years. He was followed by James Kelly.

RACC promotes and encourages new business and industrial development for the city. They meet monthly and have tax deductible annual dues to help finance their accomplishments. They have a "Welcome to Republic" program, sponsor an annual Business Expo, and a golf tournament.

The group is proud that the city of Republic's population continues to grow rapidly.

1960 - 1,519
1970 - 2,411
1980 - 4,485
1990 - 6,292
2000 - 8,438

## MAIL DELIVERY TO THIS AREA

Mail was delivered by the Butterfield Overland stage line in the early days of 1858. In September 1958 to commemorate the centennial run, the local post office received several pieces of mail for cancellation and to be placed on the special coach; postmaster Linzee Wells felt there would be a large amount of mail accumulated.

Much of this mail was sent in by stamp collectors who wanted the cancellation of the historical mail run for their files.

Mayor Shearl Garoutte arranged for the coach to pass by the Republic High School where the high school band would escort it on to the post office, and a waiting crowd of people. There are those today who as school children remember the stage coach stopping at the school.

*Mail carrier Duncan Bracken with "Jeff" the horse, May 4, 1911. When this picture was taken, "Jeff" had been on the job five years and four months, with 38,000 miles covered. Courtesy of Republic Historical Society.*

The stage lines lost their mail runs to a much faster rail service.

The railway started delivering mail in 1832, and continued to grow until the Civil War.

In 1862 railroads had Working Railway Post Office cars, that would kick out and pickup mail bags at each depot, with a crew sorting mail as the train traveled from town to town. In 1965 the railroad lost the mail contract due to the decline in passenger traffic.

To fill this void the United States Postal Service employed highway post offices (HPO) using large buses with a working crew on board.

The crew would sort the mail while traveling and have it ready for the next town. The first HPO run was from Washington, DC to Harrisburg, Virginia on February 10, 1941; the last was made on June 30, 1974.

Now the mail is all sorted at each post office and delivered by trucks with owners bidding for the routes from post office to post office.

*Information from the National Museum, websites and from people who saw this in operation.*

## REPUBLIC POST OFFICE

On October 10, 1871, the Republic fourth class post office was established.

The first post office building was located one half mile south of the Frisco Depot. In the early 1900s the office was moved to the east side of Main Street, in the center portion of what is now Main Street Antiques. In November 1919 the office was again moved, and this time it was located on the west side of North Main Street in the Dr. E.L. Beal building. It remained there until July 1931, when it was moved to the ground floor of the Masonic Lodge building on the corner of Main and Grant Streets. It remained at

*Butterfield Overland Stage anniversary run, 1958.*

*Railroad Post Office car.*

*Mail crane picking up mail bag. Courtesy of National Archives.*

that location 31 years. The Post Office moved to a newly constructed building at 116 W. Grant on August 1, 1962. The present location is at the corner of Highway 160 and Harrison. The move to this larger newly built location was made in July 1992.

The post office advanced to third class on

*Railroad Post Office postal employees sorting mail. Courtesy of National Archives.*

*Highway Post Office bus. Courtesy of National Archives.*

*Clerks working aboard the 1941 White Highway Post Office bus. Courtesy of National Archives.*

January 1, 1907, and to second class on July 1, 1951. City delivery was established in 1969. The post office in 2006 has 24 employees.

Postmasters who have served Republic and commissioned dates are:

|  |  |
|---|---|
| Marcus D. Ritter | October 10, 1871 |
| Homer A. Noe | June 10, 1872 |
| William H. Smith | November 24, 1874 |
| John W. Johnson | January 13, 1876 |
| Frederick King | January 2, 1880 |
| Lewis D. Brooks | January 11, 1882 |
| William W. Coover | January 16, 1883 |
| John W. Rose | May 25, 1885 |
| Claton R. Pickering | June 18, 1889 |
| Richard A. Gamble | May 1, 1893 |
| James T. Meek | September 6, 1895 |
| Enoch M. Hays | July 7, 1897 |
| Fenton T. Stockard | June 8, 1900 |
| Walter A. Coon | March 2, 1907 |
| Martin L. Howard | March 20, 1908 |
| Hugh B. Ingler | May 6, 1913 |
| James D.A. Hood, Jr. | February 17, 1922 |
| Herbert Linzee Wells | February 8, 1935 |
| Beth Cox | November 1, 1960 |
| Herbert L. Coggin | May 13, 1961 |
| Norma Cox | December 1, 1990 |
| Donna Rippee | February 3, 1993 |

## REPUBLIC FIRE DEPARTMENT

The 1922 Model T Fire Truck, often referred to as "Old Billy," was replaced with a 1947 Chevrolet fire truck that had a 500 gallons per minute pump.

In 1963 the 1947 model was replaced with a 1963 American La France with 750 gallons per minute pump.

In 1978 a new truck was purchased from Pierce Fire Company in Appleton, Wisconsin. This 1978 truck had a 1,000 gallons per minute pump loaded with hoses, ladders, and numerous pieces of fire equipment needed at the time.

In 1979 Pete Hansen was appointed fire chief, Lloyd Sublett was the 1st full-time paid fire chief for the city of Republic. Don Murray was hired as fire chief from September 1986 until 2004. In 2006 the department is headed by Duane Compton.

In 1995 a '95 Freightliner was purchased from Fire Master in Springfield, Missouri. It pumped 1,500 gallons per minute. Cox Health System donated a rescue truck and it was in service until 2005.

Beginning in the mid-1970s the fire department had fund raisers, such as chili suppers and the cook shack at the Fall Festival when it was held on Main Street. The money made at these events was used to purchase additional equipment for the trucks. The volunteer firemen spent many hours building and painting a truck donated by Melvin Reed 266 Auto Auction. The rescue truck was then in service equipped with Republic's first Jaws of Life and additional rescue equipment.

The fire trucks were housed in the round house that was once used as an old water storage tank next to Empire Electric on S. Main Street. A siren atop the water tower was used as the noon whistle for the workers to stop for lunch, and also used to alert the firemen of a fire. Later it was used as a storm siren to alert the citizens of approaching storms and severe weather. In 2006 the city is equipped with nine storm sirens.

Today the fire station is located at 701 Highway 60 East in a new modern facility.

Past Fire Chiefs not mentioned above were Carl Eubanks, Joe White, Richard Brewer who was assistant to Chief Dennis Morgan, and Bill Farr. *Submitted by Duane Compton.*

## WEST REPUBLIC FIRE DEPARTMENT

The West Republic Fire Department was organized in 1966 on Jackson Road, now Farm

*"Old Billy"*

*First and last purchased fire trucks for Republic.*

*Republic Fire Department, 1969. Standing from left: Bob Duvall, Chief; Charlie Schatz; Harley Hemphill; Joe White; John McNabb; Jerry Kelley; Bervin White; Carl Eubanks; and Bill Squirrel.*

*The West Republic Fire Department.*

Road 168. The following year on July 12, 1967, it was officially chartered by the state of Missouri as Greene County Fire Control Unit No. 16. The fire fighting equipment was housed in a small two bay garage just east of what is now the intersection of Farm Road 168 and Farm Road 59. In March 25, 1985 a one-acre tract of land at the corner of Farm Road 168 and Farm Road 59, was purchased from J. Leslie Hartz and his wife for a sum of $2,000.

The names of the original board members appearing on the state corporate charter were Billy J. Schmidt, Gordon S. Carter, and Sheral Denny.

A four bay partially in-ground fire station was built on this one acre tract of land to house the districts growing inventory of fire apparatus.

In 1989 the district fire crews responded to 27 emergencies for the entire year. The department had in its inventory five trucks with a total water capacity of 5,300 gallons.

As the West Republic Fire Department moved into the 21st century, the requests for assistance far exceeded what they had been in the past. The year 2003 saw the addition of three more bays added on to the existing four bay stations, the addition of a L8000 Ford engine with a 1,250 gallon per minute pump and a 1,000 gallon on board water supply tank came in November 2004.

The district's apparatus inventory now stands at seven trucks, one medium rescue, two engine units, and three tanker units with a total water capacity for the three units of approximately 7,500 gallons. And one four wheel drive brush unit for off the road wild land fire fighting.

The approximately 35 square miles of area served by the West Republic Fire Department has seven miles of interstate highway crossings. The sixteen volunteer members of the department answered over 175 calls for various types of assistance in the year 2005. These calls range from structure fires, wild land fires, motor vehicle accidents, medical assists and search and rescues.

As the number of calls increase so does the need for more volunteers, equipment, and resources in a growing community.

## BROOKLINE FIRE DEPARTMENT

The Brookline Fire Department was formed in 1963 with the help of then Sheriff Mickey Owens. Sheriff Owens helped start several of the county fire departments. Several local residents were involved with getting the department up and running. The first fire chief was Vinnie Simone while the first secretary-treasurer was Roland Baumberger. Some of the other founding firemen were Gene Gibson, Don Jackson, Charles Hutchinson, and Hank Datema. The first building was constructed in Brookline and would house two trucks. The first trucks were old Missouri Department of Conservation trucks. This was the start of the Brookline Fire Department (BFD). The department started with paid memberships and fund raisers to keep the department going. All the while the department was trying to add more equipment and training for the volunteers. BFD started the first arson unit in the county in April 1980 using a 1965 Dodge van that was a former Air Force ambulance. Two fireman were trained to do this duty.

In 1980 the department had eight volunteers to respond to calls in the area. This number has steadily grown over the years with more people becoming involved and the department constantly growing with the help of the community.

In 1988 the Brookline Fire Protection District was formed to serve the same area as the Brookline Fire Department. This has allowed the district to grow from a department with eight volunteers to a district with 35 volunteers. The training program has been stepped up so now there are over 30 state certified firefighters and 14 licensed EMTs.

In 1988 the Brookline Fire Protection District purchased the 2nd set of Jaws of Life in Greene County. These Jaws of Life were frequently requested to be used over a good portion of western Greene County.

In 1989 Station 2 was added on Hines Street in Rankin Acres to give better protection for residents in the south part of the district.

*Fire Chief Bill Farr, J.D. Shoemaker, Don Groves, Jim Shoemaker, Charles Shoemaker, Bob Trogdon, Rick Green, Gary Henry, Gary Shoemaker, John Rainey, Larry McConnell, and Doug Tutor.*

*Equipment of the Brookline Fire Department around 1975, including: Yellow 1952 Reo, the largest tanker in Greene County at that time. The red light on the Reo was from an airplane wing. Also shown is a white 1949 Dodge.*

*The current fire apparatus of BFD.*

*Old Station One, the first fire station in the district.*

*The Battlefield Fire Training Center.*

The Brookline Fire Protection District has grown from four trucks to the current fleet of 10 trucks. *Information provided by Larry McConnell.*

## BATTLEFIELD FIRE PROTECTION DISTRICT

The following information lists by years the highlights of the Battlefield Fire Department. In the late 1950s it became a volunteer fire department located in Battlefield but the area covered from Farm Road 115 on the west side, to old highway 65 on the east, and Springfield city limits to the county line both north and south. The department was supported by ham and bean suppers yearly.

1964: The first fire station was built. It was located in Battlefield near the railroad tracks at the southeast side of town.

1976: Volunteers started walking door-to-door collecting dues for fire department operations.

1982: A new Station One was built with four bays to house trucks next to the first station.

1985: It was voted to have a Fire Protection District governed by three elected board members.

1986: A new station was built on Evans Road near Springfield Lake, known as Station Two. In late 1986, Station One was added onto to provide a training room and offices. They allowed the Missouri Division of Fire Safety to use an office.

1991: They built a third station at Western and Farm Road 156, known as Station Three, continuing the use of volunteer staffing.

1998: They built the Administration and Training Center in Battlefield. This would house the administration personnel and be the training center for the district. The Division of Fire Safety also was allowed an office in this new building.

2002: They built Station Four on Plainview Road and staffed it with their first full-time personnel working 24 hours a day seven days a week. In May 2002, after the tornado destroyed the original fire station one, both old and new, they built what is now Station One located to the east of the two old stations destroyed.

January 2005: The new station became their second station staffed with firefighters working 24/7.

2006: Three battalion chiefs were hired to manage both stations, one per shift. At this time, the Battlefield Fire District has 15 full-time firefighters, three battalion chiefs, a deputy chief and a chief. They have one full-time mechanic, one full-time maintenance person, one part-time light-duty maintenance person and a full-time secretary. The District is governed by a staff of three elected board members, and meet on the second Tuesday of each month at 7 p.m.

## THE CITY LOGO

In 1989 the city of Republic held a contest to design a logo for the town. The winning entry, submitted by Marilyn Shexsnayder, consisted of an oval divided into four quadrants. Three of the sections represented values of the community: an outstretched hand, representing friendliness and the willingness to help a neighbor; a family in silhouette, symbolizing family values; and to portray the centrality and value of religion, an ichthus, the symbol of faith. The fourth section depicted the state of Missouri with a star representing Republic's location within the state. The city readily adopted this logo placing it on stationery, business cards, street signs, city vehicles and the city flag.

In February 1998, the city received a letter from the ACLU threatening a lawsuit if the ichthus was not removed from all city property. With support from a citizens committee, the Board of Aldermen voted not to change the logo. A legal battle ensued, drawing attention from national news media reaching throughout the United States and overseas. The "Support Republic" committee raised funds to cover expenses of the year-long legal battle but in July 1999, fearing exorbitant expenses to the city, the Board of Aldermen voted not to continue with the lawsuit.

The space where the ichthus was remains blank. Then Mayor, Doug Boatright said that's not a bad thing. "It's the opportunity to tell a story. This is what used to be here, and this is why it's not now. I think that will say a lot." *Submitted by Paula Howell.*

## REPUBLIC CITY PARKS AND PROGRAMS

Miller Park at 711 East Miller Road has 58 acres that has become the recreation hub of the city. The park is the home of Republic Community Center, Activities Building, and Aquatic Center. Miller Park also features the Bervin White Memorial baseball/softball complex, new playground equipment, and a 3/4 mile glasphalt walking trail.

Republic is very proud of its new Aquatic Center. It is a state of the art facility and opened on May 28, 2005. The Aquatic Center features, zero depth entry, splash/spray features and play structure, kids play area, water basketball, therapy area, floatable walkway, speed waterslide and corkscrew, lap lanes, designated "red" area for private parties, diving boards (1 meter and 3 meter), "The Huna" surfing simulator, shade structures, pool house with concessions and locker rooms, and over 100 "cruise style" lawn chairs.

Swimming and Huna lessons are offered for different ages and there are also water exercise classes. A Junior Lifeguard program is available.

The Community Center Building houses the Parks and Recreation Administrative Offices and Community Rooms, They have community rooms available to rent for meetings and parties; two wooden floor gymnasiums; indoor walking/running track (12-13 laps/mile), locker/chang-

*Original city logo.*

*Present city logo.*

ing rooms with showers; and a Cox Hospital sponsored Fitness Center.

The Activities Building also on Miller Road has community rooms, and one wooden floor gymnasium.

Leagues are offered both in the fall and winter for girls and boys basketball (Kindergarten-6th grade), spring junior high/high school basketball for 7th-12th grade. There is a winter Pee-Wee non-competitive league to work on basketball fundamentals and scrimmages for 4 and 5 year olds to learn the skills of the game. Men's fall and winter leagues are available also.

There are winter volleyball leagues for girls 3rd-8th grade. Fall and winter leagues are available for adult co-ed players ages 18 and over.

Baseball and softball are played at the Bervin White Memorial Complex. Boys baseball and girls softball leagues for ages 3-14 are available during the summer. Adult Men and co-ed softball leagues play during summer and fall evenings.

Flag football is played on the fields for 1st-2nd graders during the fall.

Garoutte Field at 210 East Hines has 10 acres that is home to all league play for the Republic Parks and Recreation Department's youth soccer program. A large soccer field and a smaller field are located on the property. Co-ed Youth soccer leagues are offered both spring and fall for ages 4-14. The field is also used for Republic's annual Fall Festival which is sponsored by the Kiwanis. The Kiwanis also has a pavilion that can be used for activities.

J.R. Martin Park is a 24 acre park located in the heart of the city. The park features several play structures, four tennis courts, two pavilions, rest room facilities, seven horseshoe pits, and a paved 10 foot wide walking trail which has a length of 9/10 of a mile along the perimeter. The park is host to the annual Easter Egg Hunt in the spring, and the Have a Blast 4th of July celebration.

McKee Park at 674 West O'Neal Road is a two acre park located on the west side of Republic within Countryside Terrace subdivision. The park features picnic tables and a play structure.

Shuyler Creek Trail is a 10 foot wide trail approximately 3/4 mile long and runs from the Wal-Mart Supercenter to a picnic resting area along Lee Street. It is ideal for walking and running.

The parks program also offers a House of Horror at 300 E. Hines at the old pool house at Halloween. City merchants provide after hour treats from their business locations to the small ghosts and goblins that come to celebrate the evening.

A Summer Recreation Day Camp provides a program designed for youth ages 6-11. There is also a School's Out Day program for the same age group. For the senior citizens, four trips a year are planned to various programs and events. An incentive walking program is encouraged for all ages. *Submitted by Rosemary Comisky.*

## REPUBLIC'S GROWTH

The original plat of Republic from 1871 appears to be one city block, irregularly shaped because its existence came about when the railroad came through at a northeast to southwest angle.

Growth was gradual, serving the farming community around it principally in three ways: providing supplies from fabric to food staples to farming needs, a high school for the surrounding one-room school districts and transportation to Springfield and the rest of the world.

Annexations, including the original plat before 1940, totaled about 378 acres, little more than one-half mile by one mile if laid out square. With over half of the next decade taken up with World War II, Republic's area only increased about one-third of its original size.

The next 10 years of 1950-59, the post-war decade that scrambled to find housing for soldiers coming home, showed the greatest growth Republic had seen (until 2005) when 923 acres were added. This growth was from a large piece on the north and east with three smaller on the south and west. Although the land for "Wormeyville," more properly known as Eagan-Buxton Addn. (orig.) and four subsequent additions, were annexed in the 1940s, it was in the mid-1950s that those very nice modern ranch style houses were built.

Growth in the 1960s was comparatively small with 318 acres added, three narrow bands on the north, south and west. The 1970s added 912 acres, almost all of it to the east and south and increasing its size by over a third.

Building and annexation slowed down in the 1980s with only 264 acres acquired, one piece on the east and a smaller one on the south. The 1990s added 649 acres which, except for land along the Hwy 60 corridor to and including a large parcel northeast of the city, is as scattered as chocolate chips on a cookie.

Annexations from 2000 to 2004 were again small and spread out but totaled almost 780 acres. At this point, the city occupied almost 6.8 square miles.

The June 6, 2005 consolidation of Brookline into Republic added 2,927.09 acres, bringing the city to a total area of a little over 11-1/3 square miles and an estimated population of 11,500. Long in contemplation and negotiation, the deal has benefited both. The value added with the additional residential tax base and new industries now moving in, far surpasses the initial outlay to provide services.

In 135 years Republic has gone from a support of the surrounding farming community, to a workforce provider to Springfield from the 1970s to 2006, to a new city with an rapidly increasing industrial tax base. Go-o-o Republic! *Submitted by Mary Strickrodt.*

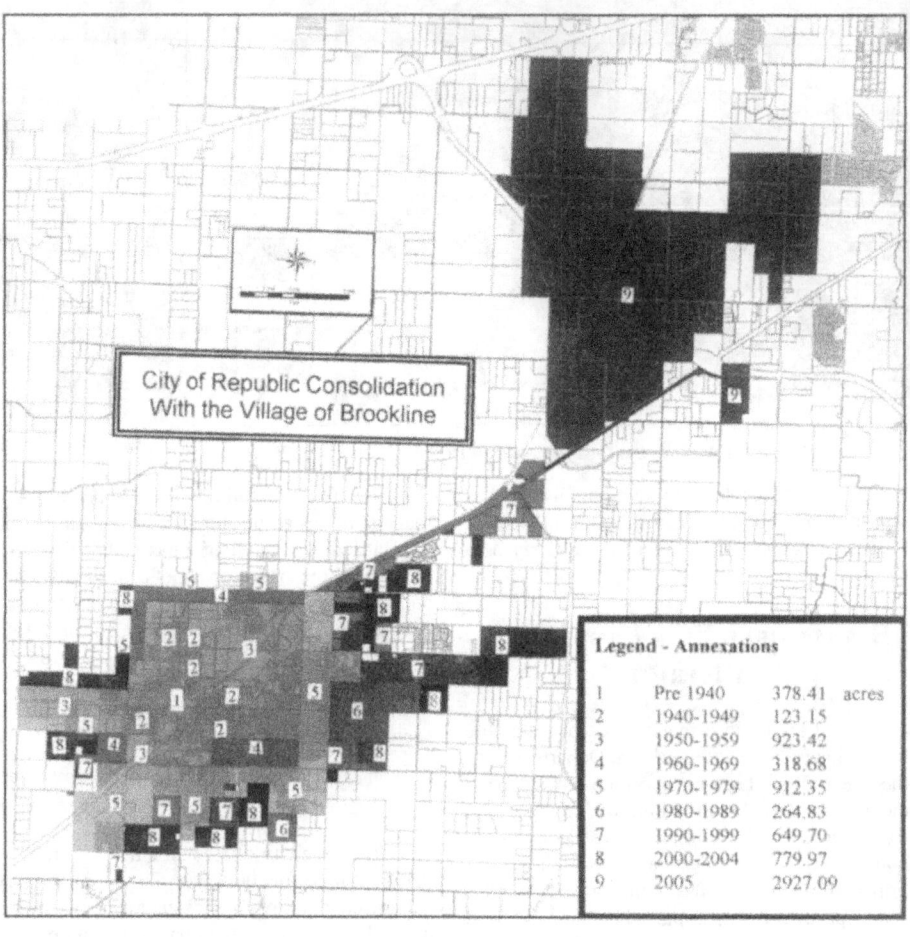

*Map of Republic*

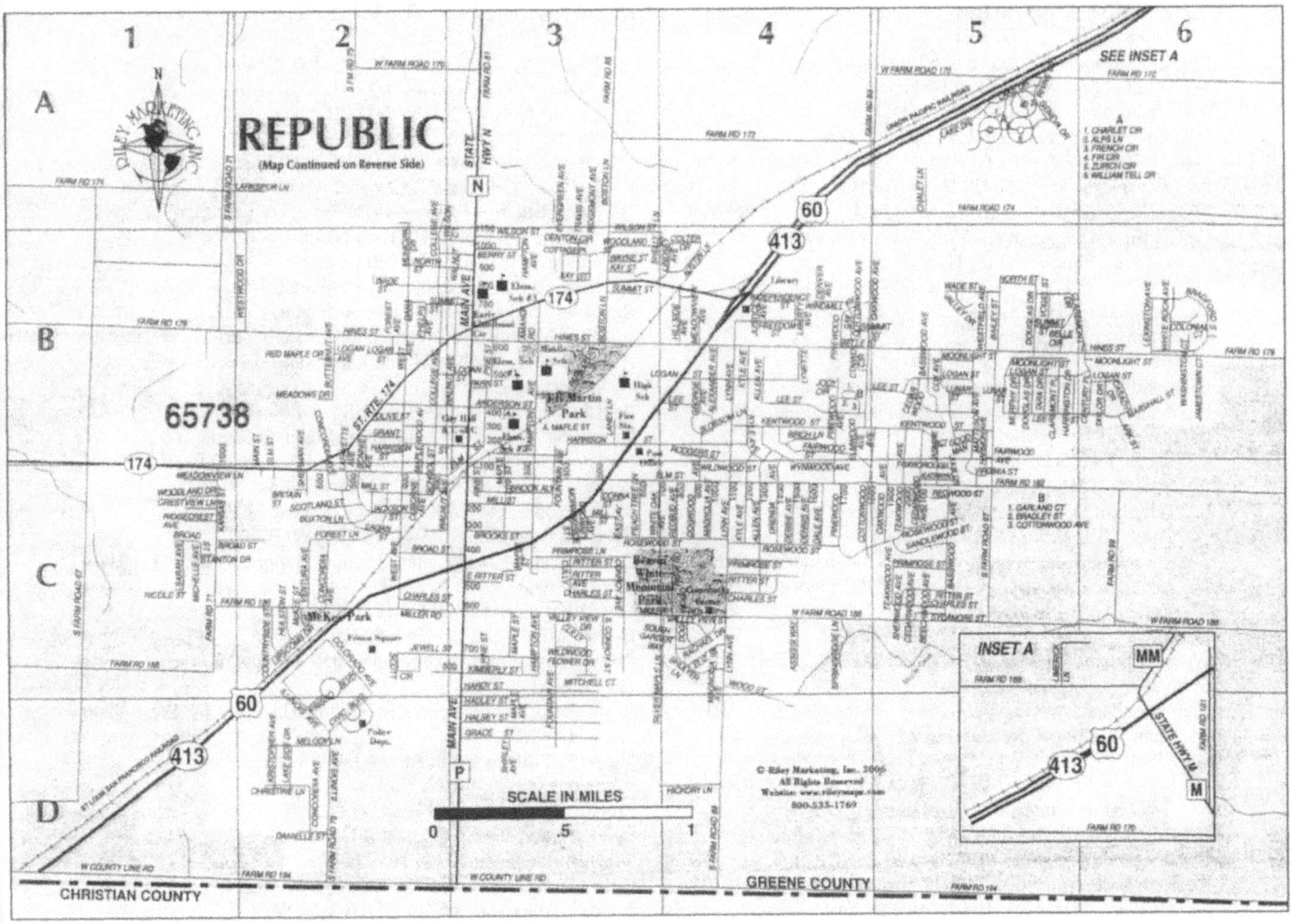

*Current map of Republic*

## BUSINESSES BEGINNING AT WEST CITY LIMITS OF HIGHWAY 60 SOUTH SIDE OF HIGHWAY

MFA Town & Country • 860 US Hwy 60 West
Frisco Square
    Republic Police Station • 540 Civic Blvd.
    Burger King • 808 S. Illinois
    Republic Family Health Care • 820 S. Illinois
    Cox Heath Physical Therapy • 830 S. Illinois
    Republic Dental Care • 834 S. Illinois
    Cox Ambulance Service • 838 S. Illinois
    Vance Chiropractic Clinic • 851 S. Colorado Ave.
Simmons Engineering • 458 US Hwy 60 West
Treasures Old and New • 418 US Hwy 60 West
Stocker Insurance • 314 US Hwy 60 West
Sharon Lakey Real Estate • 288 US Hwy 60 West
James Kelley Law Office • 316 US Hwy 60 West
Advance Tire and Wheel • 122 US Hwy 60 West
Main Street Intersection
Kwik 'N EZ Service • 168 US Hwy 60 East
Family Flowers & Greenhouse • 210 US Hwy 60 East
Cardin's Carpet & Closeouts • 210 US Hwy 60 East
Vacant
Stephen Maus DDS • 258 US Hwy 60 East
Supercars • 280 US Hwy 60 East
Chastain Construction • 480 US Hwy 60 East
Jerry's Cash Advance • 482 US Hwy 60 East
Studio 484 Hair Design • 484 US Hwy 60 East
Lindy Maus CPA • 496 US Hwy 60 East
Advance Motors, Inc. • 526 US Hwy 60 East
The Cottage House • 550 US Hwy 60 East

Animal House Veterinary Clinic • 564 US Hwy 60 East
Domino's Pizza • 586 US Hwy 60 East
Movie Gallery • 590 US Hwy 60 East
Elm Street Intersection (Right)
Lincoln-Evans Land Title • 600 E. Elm
Preston Family Dental • 604 E. Elm
Price Kellar & Shannon Bryant Attys. • 608 E. Elm
Vision Health Eye Center • 612 E. Elm
Sonshine Manor • 300 S. Cottonwood Ave.
Taco Bell • 610 US Hwy 60 East
Kum and Go • 638 US Hwy 60 East
Harrison Street Intersection
Republic US Post Office • 660 E. Harrison
Western Printing Company • 665 E. Harrison
Judy's Day Care • 720 US Hwy 60 East
Republic Dental Lab • 732 US Hwy 60 East
Republic Glass • 744 US Hwy 60 East
Pinegar Program Car Center • 766 US Hwy 60 East
Sonic Drive Inn • 790 US Hwy 60 East
Changsha Oriental Restaurant • 716 E. Lee
Pizza Hut • 806 US Hwy 60 East
E-Z Pawn • 814 US Hwy 60 East
Fred's Discount Store • 832 US Hwy 60 East
Kidco • 840 US Hwy 60 East
Family Dry Cleaners • 846 US Hwy 60 East
Wash House Laundromat • 852 US Hwy 60 East
Dollar General • 858 US Hwy 60 East
Vacant • 864 US Hwy 60 East

Vacant • 870 US Hwy 60 East
Vacant • 876 US Hwy 60 East
Empire Finance • 882 US Hwy 60 East
All About Hair • 892 US Hwy 60 East
Yocum Automotive • 906 US Hwy 60 East
O'Reilly Automotive • 920 US Hwy 60 East
Ken's TV • 932 US Hwy 60 East
Southwest Realtors • 938 US Hwy 60 East
Foreman Auctions • 938 US Hwy 60 East
Ornsby Insurance Agency • 938 US Hwy 60 East
Tiara Beauty Shop • 950 US Hwy 60 East
Fast Cash • 956 US Hwy 60 East
Vacant • 980 US Hwy 60 East
Hines Street Intersection
Walgreens • 1050 US Hwy 60 East
Diamond Head Restaurant • 1225 E. Hines
Hurricane Bay Car Wash • 1220 E. Freedom Street
Independence Strip Mall
    Vacant • 1212 E. Independence Street
    Vacant • 1216 E. Independence Street
    Tele Rent • 1220 E. Independence Street
    Cato • 1302 E. Independence Street
    Russell Cellular & Satellite • 1306 Independence Street
    Advance America Cash Select • 1310 Independence Street
    Vacant • 1314 Independence Street
Murphy's Gas Station • 1140 US Hwy 60 East
Walmart Super Center #1009 • 1050 US Hwy 60 East
Subway • 1150 US Hwy 60 East
Merchant Park
    Loan Machine • 1206 US Hwy 60 East
    Ziggie's Cafe • 1230 US Hwy 60 East
    Republic Printing • 1236 US Hwy 60 East
    Great American Title • 1244 US Hwy 60 East
    Republic Branch Library • 1264 US Hwy 60 East
Choice Auto Sales • 1234 US Hwy 60 East
Rapid Roberts Conoco • 1278 US Hwy 60 East
Austin Transmission • 1510 US Hwy 60 East
Republic Ornamental Concrete • 1530 US Hwy 60 East
Downtown Motors • 1560 US Hwy 60 East
Town East Shopping Center
    Riley's Sports Cafe • 1644 US Hwy 60 East
    Vacant • 1648 US Hwy 60 East
    Vacant • 1652 US Hwy 60 East
    Vacant • 1656 US Hwy 60 East
    Obert's Furniture • 1664 US Hwy 60 East
    El Charro Mexican Restaurant • 1668 US Hwy 60 East
    Worn But Not Forgotten • 1676 US Hwy 60 East
    Golden Tan • 1680 US Hwy 60 East
    Curves • 1684 US Hwy 60 East
    Mama Jo's Bakery & Cafe • 1688 US Hwy 60 East
Republic Ford • 1740 US Hwy 60 East
Just One More Brew & Cue Saloon • 7530 US Hwy 60 East
Alpine Village Mobile Home Park, Sales & Rental • 7534 US Hwy 60 East
Paul Jones Excavation • 2450 US Hwy 60 East
Ozarks Steam Engine Association Steam O Rama
Christopher's Import Service • 2910 US Hwy 60 East
Performance Cycle • 2926 US Hwy 60 East
MGM Properties • 2940 US Hwy 60 East
H&H Woodworking • 2944 US Hwy 60 East
Cunningham & Associates Building Supplies • 2958 US Hwy 60 East
Sew What Shop • 3020 US Hwy 60 East
B-Health-E • 3020 US Hwy 60 East
Rudy's Discount Smoke Shop • 3050 US Hwy 60 East
Highway M
Auto Performance Specialist • 6840 US Hwy 60 West State Hwy M
Victor L. Phillips Company • 6330 US Hwy West
Vermeer • 6260 US Hwy 60 West
Tractor Barn • 6154 US Hwy 60 West
DeVille Steel • 3325 S. Farm Rd. 107
B&B Builders • 5850 US Hwy 60 West
Dealer Auto Auction • 5750 US Hwy 60 West
Buddy's Auto Mall • 5740 US Hwy 60 West

## City Limits Beginning James River Freeway Along North Side of US Hwy 60

Ozark Structures • 5731 W US Hwy 60
Blades Classic Cars • 5759 W US Hwy 60
417 Motors • 5759 US Hwy West
M Square Construction Co • 5905 W US Hwy 60
Burk Bridge Company • 6021 US Hwy 60 West
All About Nature LLC • 6143 W US Hwy 60
Quality Outdoor Products, Inc. • 6229 US Hwy 60 West
MFA Propane
Anthony's Security Storage • 6625 W US Hwy 60
Ashcraft & Associates • 6657 W US Hwy 60
Conco • 6725 US Hwy 60 West
Springfield Aggregate Supply • 6725 US Hwy 60 West
Magellan Midstream Partners LP Pipeline Terminal • 3132 S State Hwy MM
Carnahan White, Inc. • 1845 S. State Hwy MM
Murphy Tractor & Equipment Company • 1401 S. State Hwy MM
Express Lane #7 • 6935 W US Hwy 60
Commercial Plastics Co. Signs • 7475 W US Hwy 60
Stringer Animal Clinic • 7523 W Farm Rd 170
Hales • US Hwy 60 East
Cars Across America • 1579 US Hwy 60 East
Ulrich Marine Center • 1455 US Hwy 60 East
Meek's Building Center • 1355 US Hwy 60 East
US Bank • 1261 US Hwy 60 East
Lowe's of Republic #2314 • 1225 US Hwy 60 East
Highway 174
Dogwood Center
Missouri Home Lenders • 1097 US Hwy 60 East
Dentist David K Budd DDS • 1093 US Hwy 60 East
Unique Nails • 1089 US Hwy 60 East
Subway • 1150 & 1085 US Hwy 60 East
Cingular Wireless • 1081 US Hwy 60 East
Pizza Inn • 1077 US Hwy 60 East
American Family Insurance • 1073 US Hwy 60
Orschen Farm & Home • 1055 US Hwy 60 East
Price Cutter #17 • 1013 US Hwy 60 East
Medicine Shoppe Pharmacy • 1013 US Hwy 60 East
Hines Intersection
Grace Place Hair Salon • 689 E. Hines
A Place to Store • 689B E. Hines
Sunny Bunz and Tanning Salon • 738 E. Hines
Hair Repair • 754 E. Hines
Mid-Missouri Bank • Corner of Hines & Hwy 60 East
Real Estate Pro's • 941 US Hwy 60 East
Farmers Insurance Group • 935 US Hwy 60 East
McDonald's Office • 929A US Hwy 60 East
Ozarks Cash Advance & Payday Loans • 929 US Hwy 60 East
Heaven's Scent • 923 US Hwy 60 East
Bailey Quarries, Inc. • 911 US Hwy 60 East
State Farm Insurance • 877 US Hwy 60 East
Security Finance • 871 US Hwy 60 East
KFC & Long John Silver's • 843 US Hwy 60 East
Regions Bank • 811 US Hwy 60 East
Pinegar Chevrolet • 769 US Hwy 60 East
Windfalls Restaurant • 747 US Hwy 60 East

Poorman's Appliance Center • 737 US Hwy 60 East
Republic Fire Department • 701 US Hwy 60 Esat
Great Southern Bank • Harrison & Hwy 60 East
5 Star Land and Title • 627 E. Harrison
Tips and Toes • 629 E. Harrison
Bee's Self Storage • 631 E. Harrison
Gibb's Upholstery • 615 E. Harrison
A+ Imports • 212 N. Laney Road
King Automotive Equipment • 216 N. Laney Road
Corner Construction • N. Laney Road
Ruckman Heating & Cooling • 215 N. Laney Road
Aaron's Fireplace • 611 E. Harrison
All About Storage • 505 E. Harrison
J & L Building & Development • 505 E. Harrison
J & R Construction & Siding • 505C E. Harrison
Martian Amusement • 505 E. Harrison
Layne Morgan Warehouse • 500 E. Harrison
Total Imaging Solutions • 514 E. Harrison
Radius Com Corporation • 520 E. Harrison
Ace-Hi Refrigeration, Inc. • 534 E. Harrison
Commerce Bank • 605 US Hwy 60 East
Elm Street Intersection
Town Center
    Scramblers • 533 E. Elm
    Life Mortgage Services • 545 E. Elm
    Vacant • 549, 553
    China King • 557 E. Elm
    Vacant • 561, 565, 569
    Guaranty Title Company of Southwest MO • 573 E. Elm
    Vacant • 577, 581, 585, 589, 591
Fidelity Title Agency • 509 E. Elm
Countryside Bank • Corner of Elm and US Hwy 60 East
H & R Block • 513 US Hwy 60 East
Romark Industries • 515 US Hwy 60 East
Sunlight Reflection • 517 US Hwy 60 East
Turbo Clean Car Wash • US Hwy 60 East
Hedrick Equipment Rent • 411 US Hwy 60 East
A1 Custom Muffler • 401 US Hwy 60 East

Garden Cafe • 389 US Hwy 60 East
Norris Flooring • 315 US Hwy 60 East
Spotless Car Wash • 210 S. Hampton
E's Inn • 253 US Hwy 60 East
Dairy Queen • 147 US Hwy 60 East
Main Street Intersection
B & S Heating and Cooling • 121 US Hwy 60 West
Vacant • 161 US Hwy 60 West
Plaza Shopping Center
    Bollinger Heating and Cooling • 201 US Hwy 60 West
    Video Playhouse • 205 US Hwy 60 West
    Bids and Boxes / Ebay Sales • 207 US Hwy 60 West
    Wollard Allstate Agency • 215 US Hwy 60 West
    Michelin Research • 217 US Hwy 60 West
    USDA AMS Poultry Program • 223 US Hwy 60 West
    Republic Chamber of Commerce • 225 US Hwy 60 West
    Ray Lower & Associates • 229 US Hwy 60 West
    Farm Bureau Insurance • 231 US Hwy 60 West
    O.K. Barber Shop • 235 US Hwy 60 West
    Republic License Office • 243 US Hwy 60 West
    Taylor Insurance Agency • 245 US Hwy 60 West
    Bos Insurance • 245 US Hwy 60 West
    The Republic Monitor • 249 US Hwy 60 West
    Edward Jones Investments • 253 US Hwy 60 West
    Dr. L.F. Pratt Optometrist • 255 US Hwy 60 West
    Hair Illusions • 259 US Hwy 60 West
    Relax & Renew Massage Therapy • 263 US Hwy 60 West
    Peggy King Advertising • 267 US Hwy 60 West
    King of Kash Signature Loans • 271 US Hwy 60 West
    Eagle Business Forms, Inc. • 275 US Hwy 60 West
    Family Medical Walk-In Clinic • 281 US Hwy 60 West
    Southwest MO Resource Conservation & Development • 283 US Hwy 60 West
    Family Pharmacy • 285 US Hwy 60 West
    Karl's Tuxedos & Bridal • 289 US Hwy 60 West
    Linda's Flowers • 291 US Hwy 60 West
Growing Kids Childcare • 341 US Hwy 60 West

## FROM US HWY 60 SOUTH EAST SIDE OF MAIN

St. John's Medical Clinic • 332 S. Main
Empire Electric District
Kidzone Child Care • 106 N. Main
Main Street/Railroad Tracks
Main Street Hair Salon • 128 N. Main
John's Barber Shop • 130 N. Main
Asher Framing Gallery • 132 N. Main
Main Street Furniture/Antiques • 136 N. Main
Masonic Lodge • 146 N. Main (upstairs)
Republic Historical Museum • 146 N. Main
Grant Street
Diversified Metalworks • 106 E. Grant

Shelter Insurance • 115 E. Grant
ABC Family Chiropractor • 113 E. Grant
Shapes Fitness for Women • 200 N. Main
Linda's Corner • 202 N. Main
City of Republic Planning and Development • 204 N. Main
Main Street Learning • 216 N. Main
EC Floor Covering • 224 N. Main
Custom Garage Door Company • 226 N. Main
Meadors Funeral Home • 314 N. Main
Casey's • 604 N. Main
Republic School Maintenance Building • 634 N. Main

## City Limits West Side of Main

Missouri Gas Energy Equipment • 901 N. Walnut
Bancsource • 931 N. Walnut
Boatright Trucking, Inc. • 221 W. North Street
Republic Security Storage • 118 W. North Street
Republic City Public Works Department • 225 N. Main Street
Republic City Hall • 213 N. Main
Office of the Mayor • 209 N. Main
Refrigeration Associates • 207 N. Main
NeNe's Beach Bunnies Tanning Salon • 203 N. Main
Grant Street
Link Construction Electric & Plumbing • 115 W. Grant
White Land Surveying LLC • 114 W. Grant
Springfield Stage & Gift Shop • 143 N. Main
DWO Destiny • 141 N. Main
Republic Locker Plant • 133 N. Main
VFW Post #44593 • 129 N. Main
Page Machine Company • 127 N. Main
Air Power of Missouri • 123 N. Main
West Elm
Dan's Welding Service • 115 West Elm
Tiffany's Performing Art Studio • 126 N. Walnut
ABC's & 123's • 139 N. Walnut
Creative Hair Design • 210 N. Walnut
Villars Automotive & Towing • 613 N. Walnut
Crossing Main Street Tracks
Commercial Warehouse Storage • 117 Main
Southwest Antiques • 127 N. Walnut
Diversified Metalworking • 155 S. Walnut
Fiber Management LLC • 225 S. Walnut
Downtown Mini Storage • 208 S. Walnut
Photos by Leah • 129 S. Main

## Highway 174 North Side

Christian Health Care • 901 E. Hwy 174
Highland Park Town Center
    AmericInn Lodge & Suites • 950 N. Austin Lane
    Uncle Fudd's Fun Park • 830 E. Colter
Bristol Manor Residential Care Center • 635 E. Hwy 174
Main Street
Village Green Square
    Rodgers Company Realty • 107 W. Hwy 174
    Beginning in Thyme • 113 W. Hwy 174
    A New You Salon • 121 W. Hwy 174
    Ikard and Brown Law Offices • 125 W. Hwy 174
    Williams Home Builders LLC • 145 W. Hwy 174
    Sherry & Rita's Hair Salon • 137 W. Hwy 174
Cole's Machine Quilting & Supplies • 291 W. Hwy 174
Gold Medal Gymnastics • 509 W. Hwy 174
Tots Spot • 220 N. Cedar
Oacac Head Start • 228 N. Cedar
Sys Self Storage • N. Cedar
Irwin Printing • 555 W. Hwy 174

## Highway 174 South Side

Gary's Sales, Inc. • 548 W. Hwy 174
Sweeper Shop • 324 W. Hwy 174
Painter's Corner • 108 W. Hwy 174
Main Street
Hope Day Care & Pre School • 218 E. Hwy 174
174 Complex
    Critters Taxidermy • 800 E. Hwy 174
    Daktronic Sales & Service • 812 E. Hwy 174
    Midwest Tae Kwon Do Association • 824 E. Hwy 174
    Control System Service Assembly Shop • 806 E. Hwy 174
    Cable America • 655 N. Hillside
    Control System Service Office • 720 N. Hillside
    PHD Painting, Inc. • 724 N. Hillside

# Scenes of Downtown Republic

*R.C. Stone Milling Company, Oct. 29, 1902.*

*Main Street, Republic.*

*Looking north from the top of the mill in Republic, Main Street, early 1920s. Courtesy of Woodfill family.*

*Main Street looking south, early 1920s. Courtesy of Woodfill family.*

*Automobile Day at Republic.*

*Main Street, west side near railroad tracks.*

*West side of Main Street, Republic.*

# Area Rural Schools

*Grandview School, circa 1895.*  *Courtesy of Helen Gammon.*

*Front row from left: Ada Wade, Oscar Wade, I.D. "Bud" Brown, Cleve Wade, Newt Porter, and Marcellus Hazelton. Second row: Elbert Wade, Edward Brittain, Ernest Hart, Lycurgus "Curgey" Guyette, Zoa Hart (Mrs. Brick Wade), Grace Wado (Mrs. Frank McCullah), Minnie (McDaniel) Blades, Etter Hart, Effie Swain, Ethel Miller (Mrs. John Reynolds), Bertha Miller, Laura Skelton (Mrs. Jim Walker), Lemie Hazelton. Third row: Brick Wade, Fred McDaniel, Pete Hays, Forrest Wade, Sally Termin, Otis Hazelton, Net Julian, Fred Tinsley, Cora (Hart) Adams, Will Hart, Emmer Ferguson (Mrs. Havey Britain and Mrs. Joe Blades), John Hart, Mabel McDaniel (Mrs. Don Collier), Henry Brittain, Pearl Skelton, Iri Guyette (Mrs. Marshall Jackson), Maggie McDaniel (Mrs. Elbert Denny), and Rilla Wade. Top row: Ernest Winter, John McDaniel, Gertrude Wallace (Mrs. Forrest Wade), Richard Sharp, Minnie Jackson (Mrs. Ben Squibb), Robert ???, Nora Skelton (Mrs. Aaron Carter), Amos Ferguson, May Winter (Mrs. Alva Reynolds), Simon Ferguson, Nellie Jackson (Mrs. Lawrence Coggin), Lafe Winter, Stella Porter, Frank Hayes, Maggie McDaniel (Mrs. John Hagewood), Frank Winter, Ava McDaniel (Mrs. Charles Garoutte), Bert Hazelton, Lucy Hazelton, Bias Batson, Gertie Winter (Mrs. Frank Carter), Verne Skelton, Iva Wade (Mrs. Joe Phillips) and Jim Batson.*

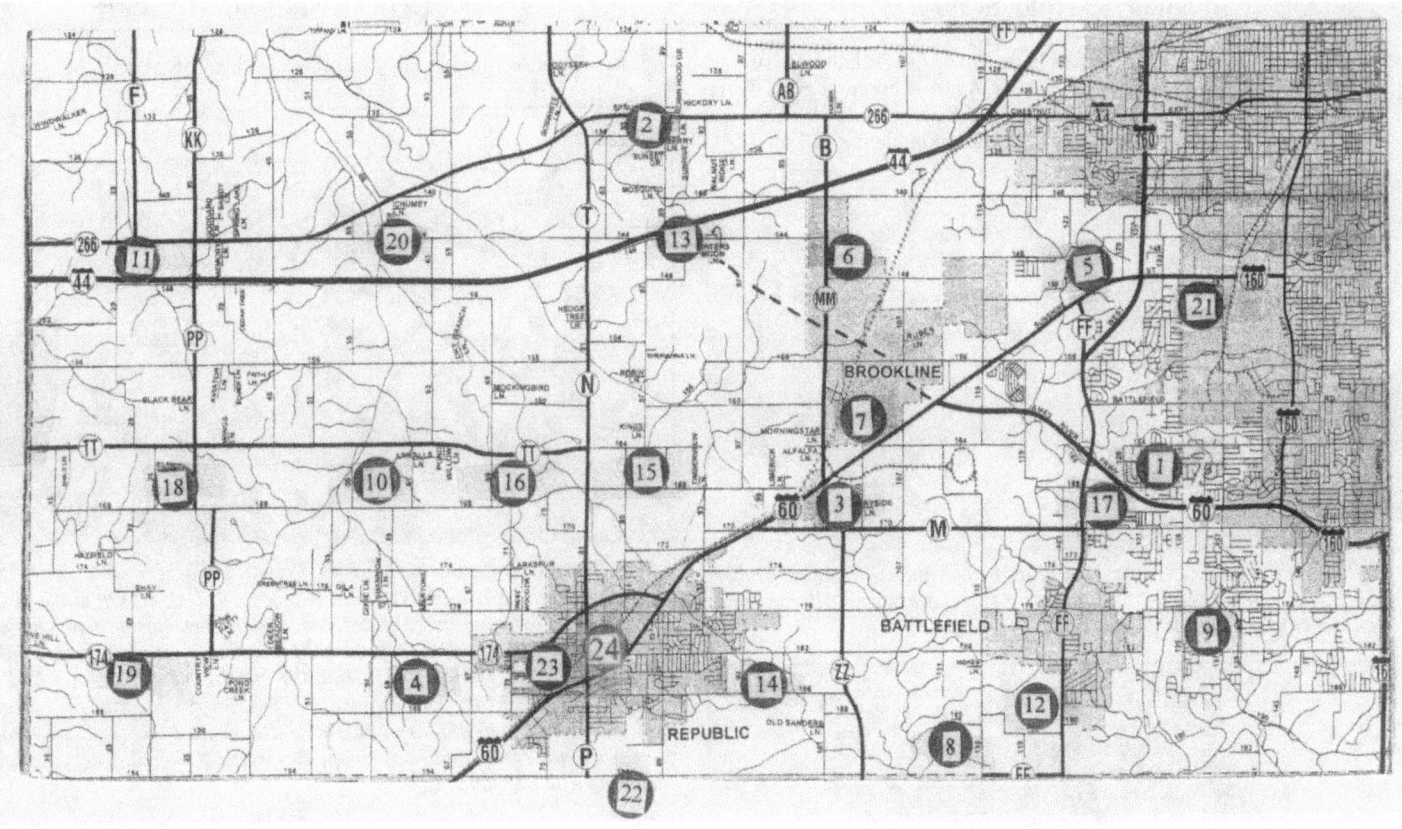

### Area Schools

Locations for the rural schools which surrounded Republic prior to the late 1940s and early 1950s are indicated on the map by a number which corresponds to the alphabetized list below. Some were consolidated with Republic R-3 district and others with nearby towns.

1. Bell Victory
2. Bennett
3. Beulah
4. Blades
5. Bluff
6. Brick
7. Brookline
8. Capernium
9. Central Point
10. Grandview
11. Gray
12. Green Ridge
13. Jones
14. Lindsey
15. Mt. Aetna (Mt. Etna)
16. Prairie View
17. Rountree
18. St. Elmo
19. St. Joe
20. Salem
21. Sherwood
22. Wise Hill
23. Republic Early Days
24. Republic Current

Thanks to David Burton. We relied greatly on the information in his book *Rural Schools of Greene County, MO*.

*This chapter courtesy of Patsy Trogdon, Compiler.*

## BELL VICTORY SCHOOL

Bell Victory was located south of Farm Road 164 (Walnut Lawn), west of FR 135 (Golden), at the corner of Doris. A new school was built by the WPA in 1930. High school students attended Republic until 1951. It was then reorganized into Kickapoo and later into Springfield R-XII in 1954.

*Bell Victory School, 1918 or 1920. Front row: Alma Kauffman, Hubert Johnson, one of the last two is Sherman Spencer. Back row: Gladys Johnson, Teacher–Judith McCorkle, and Loris Moore.*

*Bell Victory School, September 3, 1940. Front row: ??? Graves, Delphia Jean Short, Louise Burleson, Betty Burleson, Nancy Perkins, Norma Lee Sammons, Reba Kauffman, and Bobby Hyde. Middle row: ??? Henderson, Pat Casey, Richard Hyde, George Burleson, Edwin Lindsey, and Mrs. Pauline Musgrave–Teacher. Back row: Norman Kirby Kauffman, Miles Mustain, Aubrey Conrad, Edgar Graves, Warren Hoffman, and Gordon Langston.*

## BENNETT SCHOOL

The Bennett School was located on the southeast corner of Farm Road 85 and Hwy 266. A barn has been built over the original building and is on property owned by Gammon and Gammon Cattle Company. Reorganized as a part of Bois D'Arc in 1947 and then into Ash Grove R-IV in 1958.

*Bennett School, 1937-38. Front row: John Williams, Ed Wilson, Tom Strong, next 2 unknown, and Gene Bennett. Middle row: unknown, W.D. Pipkin, Jack Strong, Ernie Bennett, and Bill Kuhn. Back row: First 3 unknown, Mrs. Strong, Betty Kuhn, and Henrietta Kuhn.*

## BEULAH SCHOOL

Located north corner of Hwy M on west side of FR 103.

*Beulah School, 1940. Back row: Mrs. Reba Baumberger–Teacher, Betty Jean McElhaney, Wayne Davis, Burl McConnell, Delbert Orcutt, Jimmy Merritt, William Raper, and Eldon Salkil. Middle row: Norma Jean Green, Fred Harvill, Henry Salkil, Margaret Mae Jackson, Mary Lee Howard, Vanda Mae Bates, Wanda Rose Britain, Katie Jane Norman, and Audie Leonard Harvill. Front row: Rosena Green, Marilyn Merritt, Max Norman, Doris McConnell, Mary Lou Davis, Raymond Jackson, Lester Davis, Charlene Orcutt, Eugene Inman, Deloris McConnell, Leroy Raper, and Mary Lou McConnell.*

## BLADES SCHOOL

Located south of Hwy 174 on east side of FR 59. The first of three schools near this location was built in 1847 and the last one in 1899. The first was a log structure and was 14x15 feet in size.

## NOTES FOR BLADES SCHOOL:

Taken from ledger on file at Republic Historical Museum.
A Special School Meeting: April 17, 1871.
School House not named specifically, but described as Sub-District No. 4, Township No. 16, Range No, 24, County of Greene. William Scott, James A. Hays and James M. Logan were elected by those attending to be the School Directors.

On April 13, 1872, at the same described location, Jas. A. Hays, John Laney and I.T. Blades were elected to the board. Eight persons voted against the tax and one voted for the tax. The amount and purpose were not noted, Mitchell Eddy was chairman and S.F. Laney was secretary of the meeting.

A list of taxpayers in District 4, Township 16 and Range 24, on the 19th of April 1872.

| | |
|---|---|
| I.T. Blades | W.R. Logan |
| E.R. Blades | John Laney |
| George W. Browning | Samiel F. Laney |
| James A. Hays | Fredrick King |
| Joseph Hays | Thomas King |
| J.C. Hagwood | Jane King |
| Alpheus Hazelton | William T. Scott |
| Tarlton Logan | C.M. Rutherford |
| James M. Logan | George Anderson |
| Samiel Logan | Mitchell Morgan |

A contract dated 23rd day of July, 1872 and signed by James A. Hays and I.T. Blades stated that Robert Hathaway would be hired to teach for the term of four months for the sum of thirty-six dollars, per month, commencing on the 29th day of July, 1872. Mr. Hathaway was from Springfield.

In later reports of the same time period, it was noted that there was one primary school in the Sub-District and it was made of logs. The teacher was a male who was paid $40.00 per month for the four month term. There were

23 male and 21 female students, the value of the school house was estimated to be $199.00, the value of apparatus, including maps, globes, charts, etc, was $10.00.

*Blades School, 1927. Front row: Doris Ottendorf, Loren Ottendorf, Lee Blades, Max O'Neal, Louie Jr. Ottendorf, Ray Blades, Dee Blades, Jr., Florence Mae McElroy, and Betty Blades. Second row: Margie (Britain) Carson, Donna (Britain) Ruyle, Mildred (Britain) Bass, Helen Blades, Vernell (Wade) Cox, Maxine (Ottendorf) Wade, Frances (Wade) Thompson, Olive (Hacking) Blades, and Opal (Blades) Brashers. Third row: Carlos Garoutte, Lester Blades, Berl Hagewood, Carlos Hagewood, Eldon Norman–Teacher, Norwood O'Neal, Alice Hacking, Naomi (O'Neal) Berry, Opal McElroy, and Ina (Wade) Mooneyham*

## BLUFF SCHOOL

Located west of FR 129 on FR 148, just east of Wilson Creek. The building burned in 1970; however, the unique rock fence built around the school still exists.

*Bluff School, 1947-48. Back row from left: Marilyn Sterling, Nora Belle Prine, Edith Sterling, Norma Garrison, Margie Sterling, Mary Jean Meyers, Barbara Henson, Joy McGee, Geraldine Henson, next 2 unknown, and Edith True–Teacher. Middle row: Carline Sterling, Peggy Mooneyham, Nancy Garrison, Claudine Prine, unknown, Josephine Garrison, Marie Carter, Betty Garrison, Betty Carter, Linda McGee, and Barbara Garrison. Front row: unknown, Terry Henson, Herman Carter, Luther Deckard, Ray Prine, Robert Garrison, unknown, Jerry Garrison, Carol Garrison, Frank Sterling, and unknown.*

*Bluff School*

## BRICK SCHOOL

Located on the northeast corner of FR 148 and MM in the north part of Brookline. Reorganized as part of Republic in 1954.

*Brick School. Back row: #1-Ted Rumsey, #3-___McCroskey, #4-Sherman Rumsey. Front row: #3-Hubert Rumsey. (This was a Banner Year for Brick.)*

*Brick School*

## BROOKLINE SCHOOL

Location: From MM Hwy, turn east on Washington Street and continue across RR tracks to FR 103. The stone house, which is the second school to be built here, is on the southwest corner. The first was closed in the 1930s.

*Brookline School. Top row: Miss Crighton, Teacher, LeRoy Raper, Ann Kellough, Shirley Pittman, Donald Joe Sumner, Ferd Clouse, Jimmie Chastain, Paul Stewart, Donald Lee Chilcutt. 3rd row: Norma Pittman, Elnora Phillips, Glen Hardison, Sue Tyler, Jean Standlee, Ronald Richter. 2nd row: Gary Phillips, JoAnn Standlee, Kay Kellough, Butch Freeman, Rocky Kellough, J.W. Chilcutt. Bottom row: Loyd Chilcutt, Floyd Chilcutt, Karen Johnson, Howard Clouse, Nancy Sumner, Jackie Matherly.*

*Brookline School*

## CAPERNIUM SCHOOL

The school was first located on land belonging to W.B. Robertson on what is now FR 186 (Miller Road) and ZZ Hwy. According to a 1904 plat map, this is Section 23, and is now part of Wilson's Creek National Battleground. It is said to have been moved two more times, the last was east of FR 111 and one mile south of FR 182 (east of the park). FR 111 is closed at the 1/2 mile point.

*Capernium School, September 6, 1939. First row: Leo Gardner, Harold Dale LaFollett, Marcella Keltner, Marcella Davis, Wilma Lee Chastain, Vaunda Long, Eugene Edwards, and Wayne Sanders. Second row: Mamie Jo Salkil, David Noakes, Ruth Norman–Teacher, Howard Salkil, Mildred Parker, Ira Milford Clifton, and John A. Noakes. Back row: Jim Stewart, George Robert Good, and Keet Stewart.*

*Capernium School*

## CENTRAL POINT SCHOOL

The school was located on FR 178 (Weaver Road), west of FR 137 (Scenic) in the southwest part of Springfield. The school was reorganized as part of Kickapoo in 1951 and Springfield in 1954. The original school was east of Scenic before it burned in the early 40s.

*Central Point School, 1947-48. Front row: John Carpenter, Ted Schmidt, Francis Price, Glen Owen, Joe Russell, Jerry Pierce, next 2 unknown, and Joe Carpenter. Middle row: Norene Schmidt, Shirley Sanders, Kathryn Whitely, and Mary Price. Back row: Wanda Payne, Louise Payne, Marilyn Carpenter, Yvonne Schmidt, Zelma Russell, Janelle Boyts, Wanda Lewallen, Barbara Whitely, Carol Owen, and Dixie Keltner. Teacher–Mrs. Elenore Bareford.*

## GRANDVIEW SCHOOL

The most recent location of Grandview School was 1/4 mile south of Hwy TT on the east side of FR 55. It has been said that it was once located further east on or near the old Henry Rubison place. This area was called the Julian School District, where the West Republic Fire Department is now located. A new school was built, but within a month, it was destroyed in a suspicious fire. In 1894 or 1895, Grandview School was rebuilt on FR 55, and after 1951 was moved a short distance north and is used as a barn.

The old school bell, which was located in the bell tower of the building, has been donated to the Republic Historical Museum by Norval and JoAnn (Foust) Brown.

*Grandview School, 1947-48. Front row: Shirley Dean Patton, Kenny Blades, David Blades, Bud Williams, Carl Mooneyham, Danny Paul Blades, and unknown. Middle row: Kay Mooneyham, Mary Margaret Yount, Wanda O'Neal, Wilma O'Neal, JoAnn Foust, Mary Sue Foust, Kay Carter, and Vivian O'Neal. Back row: Colleen Williams, Rosie Wade, Virginia O'Neal, Anna Marie Blades, Juanita Wade, Roberta Williams, LaDane Patton, Margaret Wade, Ruby Mooneyham, Reva Mooneyham, and Eleanor Emhoff–Teacher.*

## Gray School

Located south of Hwy 266 and east of FR 29, Gray School was named for James Karr Gray, who owned land where the school was built. The building is now a home located 1/2 mile south of I-44, on the east side of Hwy PP.

## Jones School

Located east of Hwy N, north of Republic, between I-44 and FR 91, Reorganized as part of Republic in 1951. It was being used as a barn when it was destroyed in a fire.

*Gray School, 1939. Back row: Mamie Watson–Teacher, Charles Ryan, Wallace Biellier, Hester Grimmett, Drucilla Gray, ??? Mallicoat, and Wallace Elliott. Middle row: Don Carter, Ron Carter, ??? Mallicoat, Willie Elliott, Van Gray, James Gray, and Dale Gray. Front row: Rowena Biellier, Velma Gray, unknown, Vester Gray, unknown, and ??? Grimmett.*

*Jones School, early 1930s. Front row: Sonny Boatright, Louis Mills, Maxine Merritt, Douglas Anderson, Elene McConnell, Jimmie Biglieni, and Carol Biglieni. Middle row: Earnest Floyd, Joe Jones, Herbert Coggin, Benton Day, Beth Snyder, Huba Boatright, Jackie Anderson, and Shelia Boatright. Back row: Joe Swinney, Cletis Floyd, Elma Floyd, Fern Pendergrass, Imogene Day, Austin Boatright, and Raymond Sifferman–Teacher.*

## Green Ridge School

The building was originally located east of FF and FR 190. It was purchased in the 1950s and moved to present location .3 miles west of Hwy FF on the north side of FR 190. It is being used as a barn.

*Green Ridge School.*

*Green Ridge School, Grades 1-8, 1952-53. Top row: Sally Patterson–Teacher, LeRoy Patton, unknown, Carl Yocum, Carolyn Keltner, Joe Freeman, Jessie Jo Adams, and Stanley Yocum. Second row from top: Lawrence (Larry) Vaughn, Donna Johnson, Jerry Lee Keltner, Barbara Steele, Alfred Batson, and Mary Skelton. Third row from top: Marilyn Perkins, Lawrence Batson, Susan Skelton, Jerry Sparkman, Linda Kay Phillips, Larry Noe, Marian Zulauf, and Eugene Batson. Bottom row: Anna May Chastain, Dottie Powell, Susan Garrison, Gary Patton, Deana Yocum, and Carolyn Zulauf.*

## Lindsey School

The original school met in Lindsey Chapel located across the road from Lindsey Cemetery, on Lynn Steet on land owned by T.L. Robertson. Later in 1908 land was purchased and the school was located 1/4 mile east of FR 97 on the north side of FR 186 (Miller Road).

*Lindsey School, 1929. Lindsey parents and students along with guests, Capernium parents and students, attending a School Fair at Lindsey.*

*Lindsey School in 1922. Back row: Eva (McClure) Hayes, Elsie (Maness) Oliver, unknown, Sybil (Short) Hosey, Iona (Short) Wilson, Joy (Land) Hagewood, Deloris (Robertson) Sanders, Perl Glidewell–Teacher. Middle row: Luther Land, Bertha (DeWett) Gibson, Homer Boyd, unknown, Wilford Land, unknown, Finis Robertson, Lucille Boyd, and Ed DeWett. Front row: unknown, Alvin Sanders, next 2 unknown, Donald Maness, Kate McClure, unknown, Guy McElhaney, unknown.*

## Mt. Aetna School

Mt. Aetna School was located on the northeast corner of FR 168 and FR 85 and was later known as Mt. Etna.

*Mt. Aetna School, 1941. Back row: Junior Ross Sparkman, Leon Boatright, Henry Salkill, Rockford Owen, Denzil Keith, Leroy Bolton, and Orlis Keith. Middle row: Dorothy Rainey, Ola Mae Merritt, Inez Stephenson, Lawrence Bolton, Mrs. Mildred Howard–Teacher, Donald Elkins, Ross Boatright, Joan Duvall, Mrs. Grace Sumner–school cook, and Evelyn Elkins. Front row: Eldon Salkill, Billy Duvall, Donald Humphrey, Mary Sparkman, Peggy Duvall, Marjorie Hanson, Mae Belle Sparkman, Stella Rainey, Rita Belle Owen, Betty Rainey, Marjorie Sparkman, and Leroy Elkins.*

## Prairie View School

It was located south of FR TT on the east side of FR 69. A new home was built on the original site. The school building was sold, made into a home, but later destroyed by a fire.

*Prairie View School, 1938-39. Front row: Jewell Butler, Jean Danhauer, Cecil Robertson, Arbeleta Cook, Ray Butler, Ellis Mooneyham, and Earl Devries. Back row: Jack Cook, Donald Robertson, Charles Duff, Oma Jean Cook, Wayne Butler, Margaret Duff, Ruby Batson, and Valentine Kastendieck–Teacher.*

*Prairie View School, 1917.*

## Rountree School

Rountree School was located on the southeast corner of Hwy FF and FR 168. The building is still in use as a center for Indian culture. It is said that it was originally a Lodge Hall with two floors, the first being used for the school.

*Rountree School, 1905.*

## St. Elmo School

St. Elmo School was located 1/4 mile north of FR 168 on the east side of FR 31. The school is said to be over 120 years old. The first building was made of logs. A partition was added to the present school during the 1930s, which made two classrooms. A kitchen area was added in the 40s. After consolidation with Republic in 1951, the building was purchased by the area Women's Progressive Farming Association, and then sold to the Jot 'Em Down 4-H Club for a meeting place. It is also used as a community center and voting place.

St. Elmo School, 1931-32. Both classes of the two-room school are in this picture. Front row: Geneva Brown, Harold Breakbill, Dan Trogdon, James Clayton, unknown, ??? Page, Helen Pyeatt, and Wanda Gilliland. Second row: Jack Clayton, Lester Patton, Vester Patton, Earl Batson, Bryce Hendricks, Paul Souder, next 2 unknown, Dicky Brown, Glen Perkins, and Richard Carr. Third row: ??? Tabor, Pauline Batson, Ruby Brown, Norine Viles, Evelyn Gilliland, Virginia Trogdon, Rose Helen Brown, ??? Patton, Omel Brown, ??? Tabor, Marie Neil, Dorothy Blades, Anna May Page, Norma Gilliland, and Deloris Brown. Fourth row: John Hagerty–Teacher, Elnora Gilliland, Opaline Neil, Beatrice Viles, Garland Brown, Carl Batson, Jessie Souder, Virgil Batson, Tom Brown, Wayne Blades, Eugene Hendricks, Lorene Patton, Myrtle Evelyn LaFollett, Lucille Sifferman, and Chloe Blades–Teacher.

St. Elmo School, 1947-48. Back row: Mae (Howard) Brown–Teacher, Billy Mack Reed, Edna Lee Breakbill, Barbara Rubison, Donna Sue Sifferman, and Donna Cunningham. Middle row (starting in middle of picture): Gary Blades, Dale Blevins, Jerry McGeehee, Doris Reed, Becky Viles, Karen Sifferman, and Sue Booth. Front row: LeRoy Breakbill, Ronnie Booth, Donnie Batson, Dale Looney, Charlie Looney, Max Brown, Junior Breakbill, Ray Batson, and Don Brown.

## St. Joe School

Located 1/2 mile south of Hwy 174 on FR 31.

St. Joe School, 1937-38. Front row from left: Harold Keatts, Lola Fern Jewell, Fred Harvill, Harold Dale Kerr, Bonnie Jewell, Audie Harvill, Bill Fuhr (in back), Lucille Keatts, Mary Lou Hendricks, Louise Batson, and Glen Thayer. Second row: Leo Tiede, Don Batson, Richard Tiede, Charles Fuhr, James Thayer, Wayne Batson, Vivian Frazier, Ernestine Tiede, and Edith Jewell. Third row: Charles Lovett, Charley Laney, Ruth Harvill, Lena Mae Harvill, and Opal Kelly. Back row: Joe Fuhr, Maxine Kerr, Mary Lovett, and Jane Staley–Teacher.

## Salem

South of Hwy 266 and Yeakley Chapel at the T of FR 59 and FR 144, Salem School was built prior to 1890s. It was reorganized with Republic in 1951 and used as a community center and voting site in the 1970s.

Salem School, 1947-48. Front row from left: Cecil Sweeney, Jerry Randles, John Floyd, Richard Randles, Pete Lee, and Jerry McCarty. Middle row: Virginia McCarty, Beverly Holt, Doris Ricketts, Mary Ann Nelson, Orilla Viles, Morean Lee and unknown. Back row: Bonnie ???, Jewell Floyd, Wanda Nelson, Barbara Holt, Wilma Nelson, Effie Floyd, Helen Floyd, and Mrs. Maxey–teacher.

Salem School.

*Salem School, circa 1890-1900. Students unknown.*

## SHERWOOD SCHOOL

Located on the southwest corner of Scenic (FR 137) and West Sunshine Street in Springfield. The school was annexed into Springfield in 1952. Prior to that date, high school students attended Republic High School.

*Sherwood School, 1941-42. Front row: ??? Rowsey, John Tom Crighton, Gary Gunderson, James Looney, Richard Rowsey, Kay Brown, Lavelle Buckley, Dorothy Grisham, ??? Rowsey, unknown, Kathryn Dodson, Delores Davis, next 2 unknown. and Wilma Lisenby. Middle row; Grace Marie Kreider, Clara Crighton–Teacher, Kathryn Eppard, Esther ???, Naomi Lisenby, Betty Tennis, Junior Eppard, Kent Gunderson, Hobert McCroskey, James Buckley, Edwin Looney, Bill Cloud, Bob Cloud, and Bill Dodson. Back row: Bonnie Gault, Wilamenia Crighton, Rose Marie Brown, JoAnna Lisenby, Glenda Owen, Helen Davis, Patsy Wallis, Walter Clark, Richard Looney, James David Kreider, Louis Buckley, Billy Eppard, last 2 unknown.*

*Sherwood Orchestra, 1942. Front row: Walter Clark, Bob Cloud, Esther ???, Grace Marie Kreider, Patsy Wallis, Glenda Owen, and Wilhemina Crighton (at piano). Middle row: JoAnna Lisenby, Naomi Lisenby, Rose Marie Brown, unknown, Bill Cloud, Louis Buckley, Edwin Looney, and Kent Gunderson. Back row: Bill Dodson, Junior Eppard, James Buckley, Hobert McCroskey, and A.L. Lillard–Director.*

## WISE HILL SCHOOL

Located 2.2 miles south of Republic city limits on P Highway. Turn left at the top of Terrell Hill on Honeysuckle. The building was .2 miles north in the wooded area. Originally, the road was located north of the present bridge and curved back and forth up the hill. The school faced south. After consolidation, those students living on the north side of Terrell attended Republic schools while those on the south went to Clever.

*Wise Hill School, 1938-39. Front row: unknown, Billy Gilmore, Gene McConnell, Reva Sims, Burl Davis, Geneva Little, Margie Sims, Burton Gene Salchow, Herbert Sims, Inas McConnell, and Frankie Pierce. Middle row: Hershal Salchow, Charles Biglieni, Virgil Sims, J.B. Gray, Raymond Salchow, Harold Mooneyham, Gene Gilmore, Henrietta Davis, and Charles Little. Back row: unknown, Merlin Ottendorf, Lucille Salchow, Lenore Davis, Annabelle Gray, Ruth Nelson, Thelma Haworth, Verdalea Davis, Virgie Mae McConnell, and Mildred Ladd–Teacher.*

# Republic Schools ...

Excellence in Education

## List of Republic School Superintendents

| | |
|---|---|
| 1893 W.S. Moore | 1920-1922 J.F. Montague |
| 1894 George H. Redfearn | 1923 Pruitt Rogers |
| 1895-1896 C.A. Mitchell | 1924-1926 Rex Clarke |
| 1897-1898 A.C. Farley | 1927-1929 E.M. Edmondson |
| 1899 D.R. O'Neal | 1930-1934 M.S. Collings |
| 1900-1901 C.L.M. Stinnett | 1935-1937 Harry J. Siceluff |
| 1902 J.A. Galbraith | 1938 Dewey Hickman |
| 1903-1904 W.F. Aven | 1939-1956 C.K. Leonard |
| 1905-1907 F.R. Rice | 1957-1965 Amos McMurtrey |
| 1908-1910 F.J. Burney | 1966-1984 William (Bill) Schatz |
| 1911-1914 C.W. McCroskey | 1985-1996 Allan B. Crader |
| 1915-1917 W.R. Rice | 1997-2002 Howard Neeley |
| 1918-1919 L.M. Speaker | 2003- Pam Hedgpeth |

## Grade School Notes

Recently while re-hanging some pictures at the grade school, Mrs. Roop discovered on the back of a picture of Longfellow, the following names with the accompanying inscription: "Presented by the Fifth Reader Class in 1894. Elmer Ruckman, Finley Houtz, Ollie Gregory, Rilla Britain, Frank Noe, Hallie Searcy, Herrick Hathaway, George Buck, Floyd Mosley, Artie Moore, Ethel Sampson, Lula Watson, Cora Vance, Allie Robertson, Mila Batson, Ida Robertson, Cora Rayl, Anna Youngblood, Adie Ingler, Emma Sallee, Clara Britain, Alvin Crum, Deffa Batson, Myrtle O'Neal, Will Arehart, Grace Brimhall, Maude Gentry and Pearl White."

The third grade is progressing nicely with the books they are binding. Students entering school this week were Harold Livingston, second grade, and Frances Bottorff, first grade. Students leaving were James House, fourth grade, and Carroll Beal, sixth grade.

*Roberta Anderson and Margaret Best, Reporters (newspaper was dated prior to 1929).*

## 1893 Republic School

The year of 1893 marked a new era in the educational history of Republic, when, in keeping with the progressive age, her citizens decided to erect a $5,000 school building which stood a gem in architecture and the pride of every citizen of Republic. The site of this beautiful structure was a most desirable one. The ground contained two acres, which afforded ample room for the pupils to enjoy.

The building was a two-story 56 x 70 feet with a basement of seven feet and contained five large rooms conveniently arranged, and a spacious assembly room in which to hold chapel. In the belfry was a nice room used for the purpose of holding teacher's meetings. The library room was a cozy apartment 12 x 22 feet, neatly carpeted with a nice reading table covered with standard magazines and the best periodicals of the day. A book case 14 feet high contained about 400 volumes of inestimable value to every energetic student. Also a large map of Missouri adorned the wall, besides a number of beautiful pictures.

The entire building was heated with two large furnaces of the latest models. The assembly room was well seated and conveniently arranged. The walls were decorated with pictures of all kinds and maps, and a Webster International Dictionary on the table where all the students could have access. The cost of the premises, building, and fixtures aggregated to about $6,500.

Republic High School Class of 1903 Graduation held at Teague Opera House
Front Row: Flora Barron, Mina Davis, Cora Roop
Back Row Standing: George Edgar, Emma Wilkerson, Supt. W. F. Aven, Luella Anderson, Gail Houtz

Republic School Third and Fourth Grades, 1941. Top row: Barbara Leonard, Peggy Manners, Bobby Amsler, Wayne Hughes, Ned West, Becky Matt, and Helen Pope. Second row: Anne Hood, Norma Jean White, Gloria Fuhr, Greta Jean Maples, Everett Davis, Ada Marie Shields, Betty Lou James, and Jackie Bridges. Third row: Joanne Tiede, Nadine Payne, Clara Tiede, Patsy Woodfill, Juanita McSpadden, Virginia Looney, Leslie Berridge, Howard Luna, and Eddie Sims. Fourth row: Buddy Hays, Eugene Keith, Jerry McSpadden, Pat Brown, Robert Armstrong, and James Glidewell. Mary Spellman–Teacher.

Republic School Grades 2 and 3, 1947-48. Top row: Teacher–Bonnie Hadlock, Donald Hodge, Joyce Gaddy, Larry Brashers, Rosemary McMurtrey, and Bobby Burleson. Second row: Bob Brashears, unknown, John Brim, and Lorene Blades. Third row: Norma Gaddy, Johnny Hollyfield, Darlene Garoutte, DeWett, Janet Britain, unknown. Fourth row: Joe Boatright, DaMarous DeWett, Ted White, Jimmie Ann Hayes, Gary Hayes, and unknown. Fifth row: James Coker, Fred West, Connie Garbee, unknown, Robert Thurman, and Gary O'Bryant. Sixth row: Danny Danielson, Charlie Luna, David Warford, Timmy Tourville, unknown.

Republic School Second Grade Class, 1941. Back row: Jill Head, Bob Alderman, Nancy Lawrence, Edward Davis, Leland Brown, Charles Comisky, Marjorie Amsler, and unknown. Front row: Joann Hays, Frances Hughes, Patsy Logan, Jack Head, Jerry Herring, Don Alderman, ??? Glidewell, Dorothy Bull, Jessie ???, Frankie Armstrong, and Billy Luna. Rosa May Hadlock–Teacher.

At left: Republic School Grades 4 and 5, 1947-48. Top row: Mildred Howard–Teacher, Porter DeWitt (5), Barbara Fullerton (5), David Logan (5), Rosemary Maness (4), Jimmy Luna (5), Gladys Blades (5), Grandvall Ward (4), Helen Bertoldi (4), and Don Markel (4). Second row: Edward Piland (4), Anne Land (5), Dale Boatright (5), Donna Woodfill (5), Johnny Garton (4), Pearl Dial (5), Donald Rogers (4), and Dorothy Hagewood (4). Third row: Lucille Bertoldi (5), Bill Lawrence (5), Glenda Smith (4), David Merritt (5), Jackie Wiles (5), Gordon Wilson (5), Sue Powers (4), J.W. Biglieni (5), Shilah Adams (5), and Alan Comisky (4). Fourth row: Morris Combs (4), Shirlene Garoutte (4), Jerry Mason (4), Dee Cason (5), Leroy Garoutte (4), Edna Sneed (5), Eddie Hill (5), Patsy Hill (5), Jimmy Bell (5), and Norma Jean Walker (5). Bottom row: Joe Cole (5), Finis Salkill (4), Terry Dodson (4), Walter Larson (4), Bill Lynch (4), and Delano White (5).

## School Notes 1952
## The Republic Record Newspaper

High School News: The senior class went to Springfield to have individual pictures taken on Tuesday of this week. They were accompanied by Mr. McMurtrey who drove a bus.

Monday afternoon the regular monthly Chapel Service was conducted by the Ministerial Alliance in the High School Auditorium. The following ministers presented a very interesting and worthwhile service: Rev. Young, Rev. Coyle, Rev. Batson and Rev. Mahaney.

Friday night, Coach Mac is taking this year's edition of the Tigers for the initial outing at Ozark. The squad, starting with seniors, Robert Williams, Max Brown, Gary Baumberger, Jerry Fugitt, Dean Bruton, Roger Jordon, Charles Harper, J.W. Biglieni, Ronnie Parton, James Weatherwax, Porter DeWitt, David Logan, Donald Rogers, Alan Comisky, Jerry Mason, Ray Batson, Johnnie Garton, Ben Raper, and Keith Looney.

The newly formed Pep Squad, with their sponsor, Mrs. Garbee, will make the trip to encourage the Tigers to a victorious start.

Grade One: These children had perfect attendance records for the first quarter: Patrick Arnold, Bruce Brashers, John Cahill, Donna Sue Hagewood, Susan Jordon, Betty Land, Terry Mooneyham, and Kenny Wieland. We enjoyed our Halloween party Friday afternoon. Prizes were won by Janice O'Neal for the best costume, Carolyn Mason for being best disguised, and Susan Jordon for pinning the tail on the cat. We are grateful to the mothers who served orange pop and cookies. A new boy, Bobby Harter, enrolled Monday.

Grade Two: Friday we had a Halloween party. Many spooks visited our room. Tony Logan and Phyllis Cox won the prize for the best costumes, and Marilyn Maness won a prize for being the hardest to guess. We want to thank those who served us refreshments. Mothers present were Mrs. Chester Vaughn, Mrs. Bernard Davis, Mrs. Jojohn Gott, Mrs. June Kerr, Mrs. Dwight Blades, and Mrs. Adrian Cox. Sammy Orr moved to Kansas City last week. We are practicing songs to sing at the Request Program Friday night.

Grade Five: We all had a good time at our Halloween party. Terry Fugitt and Carol Ann O'Neal won the costume prizes in our room. We played games after we had removed our masks. Our room mothers served refreshments to us at the close of the party. We were glad to have Karen Gordon and Bobby Davis visit us for the party. Other visitors were the room mothers: Mrs. Howard Davis, Mrs. Sheral Garoutte, Mrs. Guy Sparkman, Mrs. Elden Hood, Mrs. Norwood O'Neal and Mrs. Frank Bennett.

We were sorry to lose Karen Gordon from our room last week. She now goes to Sunshine School in Springfield. Dorothy Mae Worthington started to our school last week. She comes from the Marionville School. We are working hard learning to divide by two numbers. Most of us are having good lessons in arithmetic. In history and reading, we are studying about the pioneers who first settled the Middle West. All of us enjoy learning about the first people who settled here.

## Republic High School
## 1920 – 1962

By 1920, Republic was offering four years of high school. Following the prevailing style, a two-story symmetrical brick structure was built with central outside steps to the first floor.

The new high school building saw its first students two years after World War I ended. It lasted through the Depression, World War II and the first of the Baby Boomers, moving those born in 1945 and 46 to graduate in the "new" high school. They were sometimes the grandchildren of the 1920 graduates. Girls, who five years before had dresses to their ankles, in 1920 were wearing them mid-calf and by 1925, up to their knee. Lucille Norman Pittman, 100, and Chloe Blades Neil, 102, are the oldest known living graduates of Republic High School remember those times having graduated in 1924 and 1926, respectively.

Much of the clothing, boys and girls alike was homemade, some from feed sacks. Boys wore both knee and long pants when the school opened and then later, overalls. As the Depression wore on and wore people down, clothing then became handed down, often mended and scarce for many.

Wristwatches had come about with WWI and few students had one. Roberta Anderson didn't have one until her first job after graduating from State Teachers College in 1937. By the time the school closed in 1962, many girls would have been given one for 8th grade graduation.

In 1920, few families owned a car. Anderson remembers in the 20s, a farm boy rented a spot in their barn on Pine at Anderson St. to keep his horse and buggy while he was in high school. By 1962, about 1/4 of the senior boys drove cars to school.

*Disclaimer: The information contained herein is based solely on the memories of students who attended that school between 40 and 70+ years ago, and is "hopefully" correct.*

The 1920 Republic High School was entered by climbing 6 to 8 concrete steps. Entrance through the front doors was on the main floor and about 16 feet beyond were wide stairs going down to another hall on the ground level. On that main floor, facing south, the home ec room was on the east side and typing on the west. Later the room on the right was changed to the office. By 1962 Mrs. Floried Mount had stately and efficiently presided there for more years than some who are retired can remember. She had her finger on the pulse of the entire school and knew where everyone was, teacher and student alike, and what they were doing. If you asked to use her phone (one of two in the school), you'd better have a good reason and be able to document it.

*Republic High School 1928.*

The room on the left (east) was then changed to the science and biology room and starting in the 50s, it was the typing, shorthand and bookkeeping room, taught by Miss Claudia Crumrine since at least 1939. With hair forever styled for the 1940s, she was neatly dressed, clear in her direction, kind in her teaching and intolerant of nonsense. Years of RHS graduates owe their typing skills on the computer to her. She also taught physical education for awhile.

Stairs to the top floor split around the central staircase going up to a landing. Ascending the right set of stairs, at the landing students turned left and went up the cen-

*Chloe Blades Neil*   *Lucille Norman Pittman*

*Republic High School Class of 1933. Front row from left: Reba Marsh, Mary Elizabeth O'Bryant, Edwina Jackson, Edna Mae Crume, Agnes Dennis, Bonnie Sharr, and Dennie Garoutte. Second row: Helen Ward, Beryl Payne, Mary O'Dell, Maxine Swinney, Margaret Best, Roberta Anderson, Martha Tuter, and Doris Hubbard. Back row: Roy Skelton, Earl Ray, Edna Moore, Luther Land, Margaret Criswell, Ural Richardson, and Guy McElhaney.*

tral staircase to the second floor. Turning around facing south again, on the right was the English room.

In the early 30s, English, Latin and choir were taught by Harry Siceluff (later Dr. Siceluff) fresh from college and always wearing a coat, tie and starched white shirt. He taught Shakespeare and Dickens and in 1933, directed the seniors in the play "Love A La Carte" on the small stage in the west end of the gym (home ec room after 1937.) The 1932 play had been "Love Pirates of Hawaii."

Other than English, Latin and choir, classes taken by Roberta Anderson Arnold from 1929-33 were World History, Citizenship, Algebra I and II, Geometry, American History, Home Ec (Clothing and Food taught by Mrs. Jimmie Evans), Typing, Bookkeeping and American Problems, an excellent choice for the world that was coming.

There were no school buses until sometime in the 30s and school was from 9 to 4 with an hour for lunch. The league for basketball included, Ash Grove, Bois D'Arc, Fair Grove, Strafford, Walnut Grove, and Willard. They also played Billings, Clever and Marionville.

Cheerleaders in 1938 were Jo Ann Stewart Fugitt, Maxine Riley Ferguson and Jo Ann Sellers Eagan.

*Margaret Best in her graduation dress, 1933.*

A summer job then usually meant working for your parents. Roberta Anderson Arnold's father, cashier at the Bank of Republic until Roosevelt closed the banks, let her help at the bank a couple of times but without pay. Mainly he wanted her to listen to the broadcast of the St. Louis Cardinals' baseball games and do a box score for him to read when he came home. In the late 30s Jo Ann Sellers Eagan and her sister Betty worked for their parents in the Sellers Cafe, just south of Owen and Short. Their mother bought their material at Likens Dry Goods, Betty designed the dresses and both girls sewed their school clothing throughout the summer. Summer fun included swimming in James River or Terrell Creek.

In the 40s and 50s, English was taught by Mildred Heagerty. Her students say she was a good teacher whose dresses were "the last word in New York fashion" and so classic in design they could be worn in 2007. She was followed in the 60s by Lucille Napper from whom countless students learned proper grammar. With life in the Ozarks influencing their speaking, Mrs. Napper realized the students could learn but she couldn't make them use it.

Still on the top floor, directly east across the staircase at the front of the building was originally the math room but changed to history and social studies room, in the 50s. The study hall and library (sparse in the beginning) ran across the south side of the second floor, watched over by whatever teacher didn't have a class. During WWII, the students leaned out the study hall windows and watched the troop trains and depending on which way they were headed, speculated on where the next big push in the war would be. It was also in the 40s that the new Highway 60 was being built through Republic and Bill O'Neal remembers the students being let out one day to watch.

At the bottom of the stairs coming down from the main floor and across a wide hall on the south side of the building was the original gymnasium with a door on its south side going outside.

Just east of that, was the room originally used for typing.

Mary Luttrell Woodfill, told her daughter Patsy Trogdon of playing basketball there in the late 20s and that the fans had to stand on

*Roberta Anderson, 1932-33, in her pink organdy dress with blue ribbon sash. She made this dress at school and wore it to the Jr.-Sr. Banquet.*

*Class of 1938, top row from left to right: Bryce Hendricks, Mae Kathryn Ghan, Willis Mae Norman, Marie Anderson, Marie Neil, Leon McElhany. Second row: Tom Brown, Lois Tuter, Myrtle LaFollette, Carl Garton, Mildred Medlin, Ellis Raney. Third row: James Harris, D.C. Hickman, Superintendent, Anna Mae Beal, Maxie James O'Neal. Fourth row: Everett E. Rubison, Lucille Sifferman, Wilbert Reynolds, Maxine Boatwright, Dick Hessee, Kathryn Chumbley. Fifth row: Mildred Britain, Irene Berry, Virginia Trogdon, Maxine Riley, Helen Short, Angie Merle McCroskey. Sixth row: Jo Ann Sellers, Wilma Byfield, LeVera Turpin, George Lay, Zalma Pauline Pearce, and Jo Ann Stewart.*

the sidelines since there were so few bleachers, all on the south side. Beryl Payne Batson, a 1933 grad, also remembers playing basketball there. The Junior-Senior Banquet for the 1933 graduating class was held on the second floor of the O'Neal Lumber Company with graduation at the Baptist Church. The lumber company's second floor apparently served several functions for Carolyn O'Bryant O'Neal remembers taking tap dancing lessons there.

In 1937-38, the WPA built a rock gymnasium on the west end of the high school, accessed north down the wide hall. Other than the place to congregate before school, it was where most students who brought their lunch sat to eat until the mid-50s when the new junior high was added on with its basement cafeteria. Some would also go downtown to O'Dell's Drug Store or Seller's Cafe while most of the town kids went home for lunch.

Jo Ann Sellers Eagan was in the first class to have a yearbook, called the Black and Gold, and graduate from the new gym in 1938. She was in band, chorus, a girls' quartet and performed solo. Drama was a popular class, taught by Virginia Patton who also taught Latin and Eng-

*Book from the 1933 Jr.–Sr. Banquet.*

77

lish. There were tournaments in which not only members of the newly formed debate club could compete but also entries in declamation, poetry and other speech events.

The Agriculture and Industrial Arts building was located east of the school and built of rock, believed to have been constructed by the WPA also.

Pearl Harbor was bombed Sunday, December 7, 1941, and the next day the Republic School Board met and decided that starting the following day, Tuesday, the students would attend a six day school week. Because of the need for produce generated by the war and its drain on manpower, they wanted the farm children out of school early to help put in the crops. The 1942 class graduated April 16.

Graduating in 1946, Mae Belle Sparkman Fuhr's entire high school experience was colored by WWII. Boys she attended school with, dropped out in order to enlist or did so after graduating. War rationing affected every part of their lives. Tires, gasoline, clothing and food (especially sugar) all had to be purchased with ration coupons. Away ballgames were only attended by people who could get a ride with someone who had gas to get there and field trips were restricted. Flat tires and repair kits were a way of life. Clothes were worn until grown out of, then handed down. Patterns were sold showing how to take garments apart and make them into other or smaller clothes. Coats were usually worn "for the duration." One benefit of the war was a home nursing course taught by a registered nurse. Mrs. Stewart and Cowan taught home ec with treadle sewing machines that were still there in 1958 with the addition of only one electric. The home ec room was also used during basketball games when the FHA girls sold pies and coffee. The junior class had the concession at the southeast corner of the gym.

Trying to make a list of where everything was at this late date will, more than anything, show that as enrollment increased, especially in the fall of 1959 when the baby boomers entered high school, the school scrambled to find places to hold classes. Ex: There was a basement room with pipes exposed in the low ceiling under the office where classes were held at different times for speech, journalism, health and psychology. Another unlikely classroom was the small room east off the stage originally intended for stage preparations. In the early 50s, it held a piano and instruments for band practice held on the stage. Later, it stored band uniforms and held the driver's education class.

Ellis "Bud" Thurman was the music teacher from 1936-37 into the 50s and a favorite from all accounts, apparently as much from personality as the high performance results achieved by his students. In 1936, when there wasn't a music department, he approached the school board and asked for one. When they said they had no money for it, he volunteered to serve for free. Leonard Fugitt, Harold Owen, Dr. R.C. Mitchell and Dr. Robert Brim donated the money for his salary with other people donating money for other needed musical equipment. Bud Thurman is still cited in the 21st century as a byword for excellence in teachers.

The room on the west side of the stage held music equipment but later became the coaches' office. Locker rooms, bathrooms and showers were tucked under the bleachers.

Wooden barracks from O'Reilly Army Hospital in Springfield were moved in behind the high school with classes starting in 1951. Seventh and eighth grades were held there until the addition was built, then music was held in the west end and science in the east.

Consolidation of the rural grade schools had started about 1950. The last of the rural schools voting to enter Republic's district came at the same time as construction bond issue approval near Christmas of 1952 on the fifth vote. Their students entered the brand new elementary school in the fall of 1954, just across the street from the high school.

The junior high was built on the east end of the high school close to the same time. It contained classrooms for English, Social Studies and Science and took the high school classroom east of the home ec room to be used for math. It also had a cafeteria underneath in which hot dogs and hamburgers were served to both the junior and senior high students. The pop machine was near the southeast outside doors to the gym. Some still went downtown to O'Dell's and Ruth's Sundries. After the new grade school was built across the street, hot lunches were available to all the school's students.

The 1950s and 60s math room in the southeast corner of the top floor was memorable because the students longed for a fire drill so they could climb out the window and walk out on the roof of the attached junior high building. How they would have gotten down from there is lost to

*Republic High School and gym, circa 1940.*

memory. That wish was seldom if ever realized and plans for a fire drill were interesting.

By the 60s, there were 40+ years of oil soaked wood floors and old schools were beginning to be warned about this extreme fire hazard. When they burned, they burned fast and this and overcrowding were two of the arguments used for a new school. In review, fire drill plans seem more an exercise in hope than implementation. Because stairways often served as chimneys when the old schools burned, the students in the top floor English room were told that a fire ladder truck would come to get them out. That sounded like fun, too. But...a ladder truck from where?

In the "new" gym where there were three sets of wooden bleachers, of the two on the east side, separated by the hall going down to the home economics room, Republic's students always sat on the ones to the south of the hallway. Behind the students, Bill Warford and Richard Blanche painted the Republic Tiger on the wall in the 50s. The bleachers on the north side, west of the gym's front door is where the "away" team's students sat. Over the hall doorway that separated the two east side bleachers was the time clock and the lucky people who got to run the scoreboard. The other set of bleachers on the east side held Republic's parents.

The outside of the gym was also used, unofficially. Boys, with slicked back hair and rolled up shirt sleeves, leaned against the west gym wall to smoke. Amazingly, the only thing they got in trouble for, occasionally, was not for smoking but doing it on school grounds.

The majority of the high school students in the 1950s and 60s were the last who attended one-room schools and whose mothers didn't work outside the home. They were also the first to benefit from the booming post war economy of having television, air conditioning and two cars in the family.

Girls wore pony tails and began to tease hair, they wore gathered skirts, cinch belts and variations of the same saddle oxfords worn in the 40s. Boys evolved from duck tails (frowned on by parents) to crew cuts, wore Levi's and highly polished Bostonians with heel taps. If a girl was going steady, she wore his letter jacket and senior ring, either on a chain or with enough adhesive tape or yarn around it to fit on her finger.

The Class of 1962 was the last to graduate from the old high school on Anderson Street. The Vietnam War started that year but no one knew its significance.

The new surroundings may have heightened awareness but the move seemed the turning of a corner. The popular song "There's A New World Coming" turned out to be true. By the end of the first year in the new school, Rachel Carson's *Silent Spring* was published, the first commercial satellite was launched, Marilyn Monroe died, the Cuban Missile Crisis scared us out of our wits, "personal computer" was first mentioned by the media, the UN condemned South Africa's apartheid, the first disco opened, the Alabama governor openly supported segregation, almost 20,000 people died in Peru, Bali and Yugoslavia in natural disasters, the CIA domestic operations was created, the Supreme Court ruled that the poor must have lawyers, the Birmingham riots shocked us, Alcatraz closed, zip codes were created, the first black person graduated from the University of Mississippi, the Beatles emerged and skirts rose above the knee.

It's probably just an illusion but the further in time we get from that old high school, the better it looks. *Submitted by Mary Skelton Strickrodt.*

*Courtesy of The Republic Monitor.*

*Courtesy of The Republic Monitor.*

## TIME CAPSULE

The kindergartners of Republic, in 1988 filled a time capsule to be opened in the year 2000 when they would be graduating, Allan Crader, superintendent of Republic Schools, and Pam Hedgpeth, principle of Republic Elementary I, buried the time capsule in the front of Elementary I building. During the ceremony students participated in a balloon release.

The year 2000, a new century and a step into a new millennium seemed to be worlds away. But 2000 came and those little kindergartners were making plans for college, and Pam Hedgpeth became Republic's assistant superintendent. Before they donned their cap and gown, seniors took a look back to the beginning of their school careers when they opened the 13-year-old time capsule.

The contents of the capsule were shared with parents and the public. The capsule was filled with a school T-shirt, artwork, newspaper clippings and videotape of the children singing. Some of the teachers had children put on their drawings what they wanted to be when they grew up. After asking some if they were still planning on the career they had put down, the answer was no. Most of the seniors had plenty of memories of kindergarten - one remembered having cookies and milk everyday, one putting on a play. The students even remembered a little mischief they got into with their foam nap mats when the teacher would walk out of the room, they would then use the mats as forts.

## ELEMENTARY I BUILDING

*235 E. Anderson. Elementary I is celebrating its 50th birthday. It was built in 1954 and remodeled in 2004-05. New classrooms added to the building include the media center, computer lab, music and art rooms. Currently there are 41 certified staff members, 613 first and second grade students housed in 25 sections. In addition, there are AmeriCorp and support staff so that Elementary I has 59 full-time staff to serve the needs of students.*

## ELEMENTARY II BUILDING

*234 E. Anderson. In April 2000, voters approved a bond issue to renovate Elementary II. The front of the existing building was imploded and replaced with a two-story structure that included the following new areas: media center, gymnasium, art room, music room, new offices, and several new classrooms (five regular classrooms and eight smaller-size classrooms for the downstairs area). The upstairs consists of seven additional classrooms. The two north wings and cafeteria were renovated with new cabinetry and tile. The building renovations were completed in 2002. Elementary II is home to a total of 634 third and fourth grade students and 55 Greene County Special Education Coopertives. This Elementary II building is located on the site of the 1920 High School.*

*720 N. Main. The Early Childhood Center was designed to meet the unique needs of children in preschool and kindergarten. Construction of E.C. was started in the spring of 1998 and opened for students on January 2, 2000. A new addition was built during the summer of 2005, so that the building now has a total of 25 classrooms.*

## ELEMENTARY III BUILDING

*The current attendance center for the fifth and sixth grade students of Republic is located at 201 E. Highway 174. The building was dedicated on February 7, 1993, although the district's fourth and fifth graders had occupied the building in December of 1992. There have been two additions to the building over the years; the first, adding two classrooms and a bandroom, and the most recent was the addition of two full-sized classrooms and one special education classroom, occupied in December of 2004. Mr. Steve Murdaugh was the first principal of the building, Mr. Jim Dykens served as principal for six years, and Mrs. Cynthia Crabtree has served as the building principal since 2002. Although the grade levels and the principals in the building have changed over the years, one constant has been the secretary. Libby West moved into the new building in 1992 and has been there since. Currently there are 22 classes in Elementary II, staffed by 40 teachers (including specialty teachers, the teachers of gifted, and special education teachers) and 15 other staff members.*

## MIDDLE SCHOOL BUILDING

*518 N. Hampton. When opened in 1962, the current building was the cadillac of high schools in the area. The gym was a show place, the vocational areas in the back were an instant hit and the spacious rooms and halls were filled with proud students and staff. Through the years the building had additions made and several renovations. As the district continued to grow, it became a middle school for 5th through 8th grade, then housed 6th through 8th, and now is again at the no vacancy point with only 7th and 8th grades inside its walls. It is a structure which holds warm memories and years of tradition for the community of Republic.*

## HIGH SCHOOL CAMPUS

*An aerial view of Republic High School, 1976.*

This building was first occupied in 1962 and the former High School, built in 1920, was restructured for the Junior High students.

North of Highway 174, at the top of the photo, is the location for the future Elementary Three, or ElII. The Kiwanis tennis courts are visible near the upper left corner where the Senior Center is now located. *Photo courtesy of Bill Schatz.*

## HIGH SCHOOL

*688 E. Hines. The school was built in 1980. The south wing was added in 1989 and included the fine arts, industrial arts, and the girl's gym. The cafeteria was added in 1997. The two-story north wing was added in 2001. There are 72 classrooms and 112 teachers and staff members. The alternative school is downtown at 216 N. Main Street.*

## NEW HIGH SCHOOL LOCATION

*Site of the proposed location for a new Republic High School.*

In September 2004, Republic schools purchased 148 acres at the southeast corner of M and ZZ Highways for a total of 1.5 million dollars.

Originally planning for construction to begin in 2010, school officials now anticipate an earlier date with their master plan committee currently at work on plans for the campus. Future expansion possibilities allow for the building of an elementary school there also,

The school anticipates keeping the existing farm buildings in order to have a school based farm for the students to have hands-on experience. They're also looking forward to the opportunity of offering increased technical classes and believe soccer will be one of the additional programs this expansion will allow.

The additional acreage also allows the school the option of selling parcels of land for development to help fund construction.

## REPUBLIC HIGH SCHOOL STUDENT BODY

The Republic High School student body gathered in response to news of the release of American hostages who had been taken prisoner in 1979. The Islamic militants, led by Ayatollah Khomeini, had deposed the government led by the Shah of Iran, who was a friend of the United

*Republic High School student body, 1980-81. This photo was made to celebrate the news of the U.S.A. hostages being released.*

States. Efforts by President Carter to get them released, including an aborted rescue attempt, had failed, as they refused to negotiate with him. The release came on the very day Ronald Reagan was inaugurated to the office of President, January 20, 1981. Tony Orlando's song "Tie A Yellow Ribbon Round The Old Oak Tree" became a tribute to the hostages and started a tradition using yellow ribbons as a symbol for honoring hostages. *Submitted by Tony Stephenson.*

## REPUBLIC HIGH SCHOOL
## TEAMS WITH STATE RECORDS

**Boys Basketball**
1948 Reached State Quarter Finals (there was only one division state wide)
1949 Qualified for state tournament. This was the final year for only one division state wide.
1963 Class M State Champions
1980 Class 3A State Runner-up

**Girls Basketball**
1993 Class 3A Runner-up
1994 Class 3A State Champions
2004 Class 4 State Champions

**Football**
1982 State Semi-finalists
1985 State Semi-finalists
1986 State Semi-finalists

**Girls Softball**
2005 State Quarter Finals

**Volleyball**
2005 Class 3 State Third Place

**Boys Golf**
2001 Class 3 State Third Place

## 1941-42 REPUBLIC HIGH SCHOOL GREENE COUNTY LEAGUE CHAMPIONS

*Greene County League Basketball Champs, 1941-42. Back row: Coach Chester Elmore, Carl Evans, George McNabb, E.L. Britain, Keith DeWitt, and Bob McNabb. Bottom row: Max Raper, Wuan "Turk" Green, Bill O'Neal, Harold "Unk" Bennett, and Wayne Manning.*

## 1948 REPUBLIC HIGH SCHOOL 1948 BOYS BASKETBALL FIRST TEAM FOR STATE TOURNEY PLAY

*1948 Basketball Team. With a record of 28 wins and 8 losses, this was the first time in history that Republic High School was represented in the State Tournament. Back row: Coach Amos McMurtrey, Jimmie Blades, Ray McNabb, Roy Wade, Hobart Stewart, and Joe O'Neal. Front row: Jack Fraka, Bob Manning, Jack Trogdon, Billy Williams, and Ray Butler.*

## 1954-55 Republic High School Boys Basketball

*1954-55 Basketball Tigers with a record of 24/8. Front row from left: Coach Amos McMurtrey, David Logan, Shearl Cook, Johnny Garton, J.W. Biglieni, and Porter DeWitt. Back row: Kenny Blades, Alan Comisky, Ray Batson, Ben Raper, Donald Rogers, James Bruton, and Eugene Harp.*

## 1961-62 Republic High School Boys Basketball

*1961-62 Basketball Team with a record of 30/2. From left: Terry Mooneyham, Jim Ferguson, Charles Cook, James Alford, Don Carlson, Tony Logan, Harold Harris, Butch Blades, and Darrel Mooneyham. Leland Brown–Coach.*

*Part of the "Cavalcade" parade as Class M State Champions, 1963.*

## 1963 Republic High School Class M State Champions

The 1962-63 *Springfield News and Leader* newspapers headline read "Republic Appears Sure To Challenge For State Title." The Tigers returning lettermen were seniors Tony Logan 6'1", Don Carlson 6'6-1/2", Butch Blades 5'10", Harold Harris 5'10", Charles Cook 6'2", junior Terry Mooneyham 5'10" and sophomore Howard Arndt 6'7" and a most important part of the team, manager John Thurman. They moved into a new high school building to start the year and a new gym in December.

The Tigers had 34 wins and 1 loss. The 75-73 loss was to Springfield Central High School in the finals of the Marshfield Tournament. The teams played again, one week later at Central's gym "The Pit." Republic won 79-53. In those days, Central didn't lose in "The Pit."

The team won the Blue-Gold Tournament and beat Ozark four times (Ozark's only losses for the year) two times in league play, the finals of the Greene County League Tournament and the finals of the Class "M" Regional Tournament by a score of 57-33.

In the Class "M" games at S.M.S. (state tournament first round) Republic beat Granby 94-58. Republic defeated Bolivar 61-38 in the state tournament quarter final. Republic advanced to the "Final Four" at the University of Missouri's Brewer Field House with the semi-final score of Republic 73 and Clopton 42. Republic Tigers played the Bernie Mules for the State Championship.

*Class M State Champions, 1963. Top row: Coach Leland Brown, John Thurman–Manager, Randy Coggin, Kenny Blades, John Wagner, Richard Brewer, Dan Chilton–Manager, and Clarke Brown–ball boy. Bottom row: Harold Harris, Tony Logan, Gary Johnson, Howard Arndt, Don Carlson, Charles Cook, Butch Blades, and Terry Mooneyham.*

Marty Eddlemon, *News and Leader* sports writer wrote "They just about burned up the baskets before a record crowd of an estimated 4,000 persons in the first half before the Republic Tigers took control to brush past Bernie 78-63 for the State Class "M" High School Basketball Championship."

"Bernie's race-horse boys with the deceiving nickname of Mules poured through four jumpers in the first 78 seconds of action." Coach Brown called a timeout. Years later, Howard Arndt remembers what he said, "We've got to let these guys settle down." Eddlemon continued "but after Howard Arndt's tip-in broke the ice with 6:18 left in the first quarter, Republic joined in the fun."

Republic behind 22-20 after the first quarter, ahead 40-36 at the half, ahead 60-47 after the third quarter and final score ahead 78-63.

*The Kansas City Star* headline "Bernie Loses Run-Gun Classic."

Fritz Kreisler, *Star's* sports staff "Republic answered fire with fire in a fabulous shooting match to defeat Bernie 78-63..."

"A roaring, standing-room only crowd of about 5,000 persons..."

"Big Don Carlson and unheralded Butch Blades led Republic in what has to rank with the finest finals in state history." *Submitted by Leland Brown.*

## 1979-80 REPUBLIC HIGH SCHOOL BOYS STATE CLASS AAA RUNNER UP

*Class AAA State Runner-up, 1979-80. Back row: Asst. Coach Leo Clanton, Steve Hargis–Manager, Steve Wagner, Kevin Long, Kevin Sanders, Greg Garton, Danny Johnson, and Coach Jerry Buescher. Middle row: Ryan Stewart, Jeff Sutton, Keith Blanche, Jeff Viebrock, Terry Swearengin, and Kevin Holmes. Front row: James Wagner–Manager, and Dan Shilling–Manager.*

## 1922 REPUBLIC HIGH SCHOOL GIRLS BASKETBALL TEAM

*Girl's Basketball Team, 1922.*

## 1993 REPUBLIC HIGH SCHOOL GIRLS STATE BASKETBALL RUNNER-UP

*1993 State Runner-up, Girl's Basketball, Class 3-A with a record of 25-6. Front row: Brandy Dipper, Kerry Ellis, and Cindy Wise. Middle row: Krista Dake, Glenna Mooneyham, Cindy Irvine, and Tori Mooneyham. Top row: Coach Dave McQuerter, Amber Kile, Amber Isminger, Ashley Fry, Vicky Smith, Melissa McGill, and Asst. Coach Greg Whittington.*

## 1994 REPUBLIC HIGH SCHOOL GIRLS STATE BASKETBALL CHAMPIONSHIP

*1994 State Basketball Champs, Class 3-A, with a record of 31-1. Front row: Cindy Wise and Brady Dipper. Middle row: Melissa McGill, Glenna Mooneyham, Julie Sanders and Tori Mooneyham. Top row: Asst. Coach Mike Thorne, Nikki Harrington, Vicky Smith, Ashley Fry, Stacy Evans, Amber Kile, and Coach Dave McQuerter.*

## 2004 REPUBLIC HIGH SCHOOL GIRLS STATE BASKETBALL CHAMPIONSHIP

*2004 State Basketball Champs, Class 4, with a record of 24-7. Front row: Krystal Glessner, Kelsey Lock, Holly Davidson, Stacy Edwards, and Jennifer Nichols. Middle row: Jocelyn Butler, Josie Sparkman, Alena Keller, Alaina Sparkman, Amanda Gimlin, Amanda Gardner, and Katherine Springston. Top row: Coach Kris Flood, Asst. Coach Tori Mooneyham, Asst. Coach Kayla England, and Trainer Kevin King.*

## 1923 REPUBLIC HIGH SCHOOL FOOTBALL SQUAD

*Republic High School Football Squad, September 12, 1923.*

## 1982-83 REPUBLIC HIGH SCHOOL FOOTBALL TEAM

The Republic High School Football Team of 1982-83 never lost a regular (COC) season game from their 7th grade year to the 12th grade year. They won every COC Title during this time. Front row: Rodney Yocum, Jeff Nimmo, Steve Rader, Kent Taylor, John Rote, Johnny Smith, and David Duvall. Second row: Mike Wojciechowski, Mike Lohkamp, Randy Williams, Scott Huff, Darin Cantrell, Aaron Hamilton, Cavin Cowan, Dale Murphy, and Asst. Coach Dan Penner. Third row: Asst. Coach Eddie Miller, Jamie Jenkins, Layne Cardner, Terry Doyle, Brad Garton, Dan Stocker, Lenny Housley, Tim Bender, Gary Fees, and Head Coach Jim Chambers. Top row: Earl Dutton, Roger Cowan, Keith Sutton, Jeff Hargrove, Greg Hargis, John Adcock, Scott Crockett, Pat Gallagher, and Bob Yunger.

## 2001 GOLF STATE TOURNAMENT 3RD PLACE

Boys Class 3-A, 3rd Place State Golf Tournament, Rivercut Golf Course in Springfield, May 15, 2001. From left: Coach Jim Newcomer, Ryan Blumenstock, Chad Letterman, Chris Stocker, Trent Ramsey, and Colter LaRue.

## CROSS COUNTRY TRACK AND KENNETH BOWLING

Kenneth Bowling, Cross Country and Track Champion. Cross Country, Class A: All State, 1999, 2000 and 2001; State Champion, 2002. 1600 Meters, Track, Class A: All State, 2001, State Champion, 2002 and 2003; 32 meters, Track, Class A: All State, 2000 and 2001; State Champion, 2002 and 2003.

## 1981-82 TRACK STATE CHAMPIONSHIPS

Cross Country State Champions, 1981-82. From left: David McNabb, William "Bill" Schatz, and Sherri Dunn.

## VOLLEYBALL 1948

1948 Volleyball Team. This team won first place in the three tournaments entered with a record of 12-0: Bois D'Arc Invitational, Greene County League, and Reeds Spring. Front row: Earline Alms, Bonita Blades, Mary Lou Hendricks, and Erma Batson. Middle row: Inas McConnell, Rose Marian Yount, Anne Hood, Rosalene Blades, Beth King, and Jewell Butler. Top row: Claudia Crumrine–Coach, Lou Dean Snowden, Imogene True, Barbara Leonard, Dixie Garton, and Lora Lee Foust.

## VOLLEYBALL 1961-62 GREENE COUNTY LEAGUE CHAMPIONSHIP

*Greene County League Volleyball Champs, 1961-62. Bottom row: Barbara Rice, Sharon Hagewood, Trudy Tolliver, and Jane McMurtrey. Middle row: Judy Sawyer, Charlotte Mooneyham, Frances Butcher, Linda Robertson, and Marilyn Maness. Top row: Jean Schaumann, Carol Hargrove, Cheryl Harris, Barbara Vaughn, Vernell Maness, and Linda Lewis. Bill Schatz–Coach.*

## 2005 VOLLEYBALL 3RD PLACE STATE

*2005 Class 3 State Volleyball, Third Place. Back row: Jennifer Nichols, Holly Davidson, Coach Richardon, Krystal Glessner, and Chelsea Brashers. Middle row: Emily Strusz, Danielle Holland, Coach Uzzell, Coach Miller, Kayna Daniel, and Brittney Day. Front row: Jackie Hungerford, Daryl Knetzer, Chelsea Mooneyham, Hannah Cummins, and Taylor Faulkner.*

## REPUBLIC HIGH SCHOOL MUSIC

In March of 1958 the R-III music department under the direction of Dan Palen, accompanied by Mrs. Daphne Wells, elementary music director, entered a sub-district music contest at Willard, Missouri. Republic participated in 44 events, winning 28 one ratings and 16 twos. The final results of the meet gave Republic musicians a higher standing on a percentage basis than the host Willard High School.

The following are the students who received one ratings in solo entries: Linda Wells, piano; Linda Rader, piano; Mary Ann Wells, flute and vocal; Mary Sue Dixon, flute; Charlotte Bennett, clarinet; LaDonna Schol-

*Jo Ann Gipson, La Donna Scholler, Anne Thurman, Sue Howard, Karen Kubert, Linda Wells, and Mary Anne Wells. Courtesy of Republic High School.*

*Donna Wilson, Kay Harrington, Larry Peterson, Lawrence Moore, Kelly Haile, and Beverly Bolin.*

ler, clarinet; Ann Thurman, oboe; Karen DeWitt, bassoon; Donna Wilson, cornet; John Thurman, cornet; and Kelly Haile, trombone. The group ensembles, the band, and girls quartet received honors as well.

Winners with one ratings were eligible to take part in the district meet held at SMS in Springfield. Those receiving one ratings at this meet advanced to the state contest held in Columbia.

## REPUBLIC HIGH SCHOOL CHOIR 1979-2006

When the current high school was opened in 1979, the music department changed from having one teacher to teach band and choir in junior high and one teacher to teach band and choir in high school to the teacher who taught vocal music taught choir in both junior and senior high. From 2001 through the present time, there has been a teacher for band and choir in each building.

In 1996, the choir was invited to New York by Mid-America Productions to participate in a concert at Carnegie Hall. Thirteen people from Republic sang at the Carnegie Concert. In 1998, an invitation from Field Studies was received to sing at Carnegie Hall. There were 35 people who went from Republic that time. Then in 2000, they went again with Field Studies to New York. That time 70 people participated in the Carnegie Concert.

Since 1979, Republic has been represented at State Music Contest by the Mixed Choir, Chamber Choir, Men's Choir and Women's Choir. Most years students have received "I" or superior ratings. Through the years there have been many good soloists and ensembles who have received "I" ratings.

Through the years a large number of students have auditioned for and made District and FFA Choirs. Hanging across the hall from the high school music room, are the pictures of Republic singers who have made All-State Choir. In order to try out, a person must be a junior or senior. Those who made the choir include Susan Riddle, Randy Tennison, Tom Bough, Dan Lohkamp, Ann Payton, Mike Van Wyk (2), Chris Ballard (2), Christy Payton (2), Nick Phillips, Devon Foster, Eric Messenger, Kristen Collins, Josh Thompson, Erin Anders, and Toni Hensley (alternate). *Submitted by Kathy Phillips.*

## 1959-60 Republic High School Marching Band

## McDonald's All-American High School Band

As a senior trombone player in the Republic High School Band in 1985, Greg Farwell was one of 104 young people in the country selected from a field of 5,000 nominees for the McDonald's All-American High School Band. The All-American Band was created in 1967 to recognize achievements of outstanding young musicians and consisted of two students from each state and the District of Columbia plus one member each from the Virgin Islands and Puerto Rico. The Band performed in the nationally televised Macy's Thanksgiving Day Parade in New York City, in the Chicago Christmas Parade, in the Fiesta Bowl Parade in Phoenix, and in the Tournament of Roses Parade on New Year's Day in Pasadena, California. All of the trip expenses were paid by McDonald's Corporation. *Submitted by Wilena Farwell.*

*Republic Marching Band, 1959-60. Courtesy of Sheral Kay Steere.*

*Greg Farwell, member of McDonald's All-American Marching Band.*

## 1938-39 Republic High School Band

*Republic High School Band, 1938-39. Front row: "Turk" Green, Harold Bennett, Bob Moore, Howard "Wormey" Eagan, Carolyn O'Bryant, Juanita Cantrell, Violet Hays, Phyllis Alderman, Bob Skelton, Ralph Poe, Don Winters, Mary Ruth Bassore, Earlene Barber, Loleta Eagan, and Evelyn Bull. Middle row: Ellis "Bud" Thurman–Director, Carol Elizabeth DeWitt, Mary Margaret Hill, Judy Robertson, Helen Brown, Ralph McDaniel, Peggy Sellers, Irving Damitz, Billy Miller, E.L. Britain, Edsel Day, Bobby Brim, Don Davis, Dorothy Massey, George McNabb, and David Russell. Top row: Keith DeWitt, Bill O'Neal, C.W. Wilhite, Wyville Miller, Bill Cantrell, Marvin Conroy, Maxine Bull, Ralph O'Dell, Margie Bennett, unknown, Glenda Hillhouse, Jean Bennett, Russell Payne, Mary Ellen Hock, and Jarvis O'Neal.*

## 1946-47 Republic High School Band

Republic High School Band, 1946-47. Back row: James Johnston, George Johnston, Loretta Rogers, Anne Hood, Betty Campbell, Ceytru Bentley, Hobert Stewart, Gene Bennett, Norma Lee Sammons, Gene McConnell, Eula Helton, Dorothea Clutter, Norma Brown, Vetha Etheridge, and Erlene Alms. Third row: Norma Jean Riley, Burnadine Marsh, Clara Tiede, Ruth Larson, Roy Wolfinbarger, Junior Carter, Sue Carpenter, JoAnn Tiede, Ruby Sanders, Dorothy Clark, Gordon Langston, Madge McDaniel, Jack Trogdon, Joe O'Neal, Vester Gray, Betty McElhaney, Dorothy Mooneyham, Jimmie Blades, Velma Gray, Rex Bennett, Wanda Phillips, Patsy Keltner, Charles Biglieni, Frankie Pierce, Eddie Wilson, Tom Shook, and Bud Thurman–Director. Second row: Patsy Woodfill, Beth King, Jackie Bridges, Peggy Manners, Betty Sue Walker, Bobby Amsler, Vonda Long, Peggy Kirby, Dorothy Larson, Wayne Sanders, Imogene True, Patty Harper, Jack Fraka, and Nell McDaniel. Front row: Jackie Woodfill, Nancy Green, Katy Norman, Rita Belle Owen, Reba Kauffman, and Barbara Leonard.

## 1953 Republic High School Concert Band

Republic High School Concert Band, 1953. Conductor—Robert Clarke. Pictured from left, Row 1: Donna Woodfill, J.W. Biglieni, Shilah Adams, Sue Tyler, Donna Sue Sifferman, Linda Wells, Mary Anne Wells, and Anne Land. Row 2: Charlotte O'Neal, Barbara Brashers, Phyllis Bashaw, Johnny Hollyfield, J.C. Carlson, Jimmy Bell, Joe Bentley, Myron Jenson, Rosie Wade, Charles Harper, Karen Sifferman, Dawna Evans, Margaret Wade, Reva Mooneyham, and Doris Reed. Row 3: Janet Britain, Rosemary McMurtrey, Anna May Raper, DaMarous DeWett, Margaret Howard, Larry Hopper, Donna Walker, Danny Danielson, Loyd Fishburn, Paul David McConnell, Kenny Blades, Donald Hodge, Donna Wilson, Ruby Mooneyham, Janet Harrington, Don Markel, Richard Blanche, Jerry Robertson, James Weatherwax, Lenard Sanders, Gordon Wilson, Porter DeWitt, Rex Hodge, Marshall Bryant, Bill Lynch, and Ed Howard. Row 4: Jimmie Mason, Robert Thurman, "Fuzzy" Jordon, Gary Baumberger, Edward Piland, Robert Blanche, David Logan, June McKeel, Sally Davis, Jimmy Mooneyham, and Rosemary Maness.

# 1990-91 Republic High School Marching Band

*Pictured from left, Row 1: Robin Bareis, Carrie Earnheart, Eric Johnson, Josh Wright, Caleb Rust, Chad Lugar, Scott Girth, Cindy Euler, Anthony Martin, Janet Davis, Becky Stark, Eric Latimer, John Harlan, Shane Gold, and Joel Trogdon. Row 2: Valerie Beldon, Alanna Comisky, Laura Iseminger, Amy Eubanks, Michelle King, Carrie Cox, Amber Iseminger, Kelly Jorgenson, Stephanie Sewell, Mark Buechler, Jonathan Hailey, Renee Batson, Stephanie Applequist, Jenna Croston, Jennifer Voules, Ryan Goheen, Lori Severson, Christie ----, Wendy Spoon, Genisse Dalla Rosa, Gina Cireco, Terri Campbell, and Michelle Hines. Row 3: Julie Harlan, Justin Knauer, ----, Stacy Smith, Brian Thrasher, Ryan Sample, Colby Tanner, Scott Duncan, Travis Little, Brian Rohlman, Krista Dickens, Greg Rowan, Kara O'Bryant, Nicole Berkner, Kelly Horton, Sherri Spillers, Jenny MacDonald, Chris Santhuff, Mike Van Wyk, Brad Worthy, Michaelea Tourville, Jayne Rogers, and Johnny Pippin. Row 4: ----, Adam Hindman, Vanessa Ferrell, Heather Workman, Angela Staires, Jenny Adams, Vickie Schatz, Julie Avery, Jamie Fanning, Mark Jorgenson, Jon Yordon, Don Goddard, Brandon Barnhart, David Bell, Courtney Cooper, Debbie Schatz, Christie Rabe, Jason Hastings, and Malanie Miller. Row 5: Brad Coker, Stacye Lisenby, Gail Appelquist, Vesta Sheridan, Lynn Hughes, Shelley Shackleford, Tara LaSalle, Danavee Kimmons, Malisa Sorrell, Krista Taylor, Brandy Rote, Gina Girth, Heather Chevalier, Angie Haddock, Ruthie Gloyd, Tricia Hawkins, Heather Fillback, Corleng Little, Renae Martin, ----, and Chris Updike.*

## Republic Future Farmers Of America

In April of 1958 six members of the Republic Future Farmers of America and their local advisor, Vencil Mount were in Columbia for the 30th annual state FFA convention and contest.

The local chapter placed fifth in the district contest held in Springfield, with 56 schools participating. Four members of the local FFA chapter were selected to represent the district in the state contest as judges of dairy products. They were Lawrence Moore, Clifford Ricketts, Jerry McCarty and Sammy McCroskey. There were about 1,500 FFA members from area schools.

The delegates from the local chapter were Terry Keltner and Joe Carpenter. Terry was also a member of the state FFA activity program committee. The four Republic FFA members participating in the contest won first at the dairy products judging and the right to compete and represent Missouri in the national contest. Individual top ratings for the dairy products judging team went to Lawrence Moore, Clifford Ricketts, and Jerry McCarty, with Sammy McCroskey serving as an alternate. Defeating five teams from the Kirksville district, five teams from the Warrensburg district, six teams from the Maryville district, twelve teams from the Springfield district, six teams from the Cape Girardeau district and five teams from the Rolla district. Winning gave them the right to represent Missouri in the National FFA dairy products judging contest in Waterloo, Iowa.

# Area Churches and Cemeteries

*Methodist Episcopal Church, Walnut and Grant, taken about 1908.*

*Hood Methodist Church, Built 1891
On National Historic Register
In 1908 was Methodist Episcopal Church*

*Old Congregational Church, North Main, no longer standing.*

## Area Churches

Anchor Baptist
206 N. Main
Pastor: Jim Collins
Founded June 1996

Battlefield Assembly of God
5145 FF Highway
Pastor: Richard Orrell
Founded 1978

Battlefield First Baptist
5010 South FF Highway
Pastor: Ray Smith
Founded 1970

Battlefield United Methodist
FF Highway and Third Street
Pastor: Fredrick Zahn
Congregation formed in late 1800s

Bible Baptist
227 E. Brooks
Pastor: Billy Pool
Organized October 18, 1955

Blades Chapel
Farm Road 51 off Hwy 174
Pastor: Terry Cunningham
Dates back to 1844

Brookline 1st Baptist
2044 State Highway MM
Pastor: Mitchell Wright
Organized 1882

Brookline Church of Christ
2630 S. Highway MM
Preacher: Tony Gentry
Began June 4, 2006

Calvary Baptist
804 W. U.S. 60
Pastor: Mike Green
Organized October 28, 1966

Calvary Chapel
711 E Miller Road
Pastor: Antonio Rivas
Established 1997

Calvary Christian Assembly of God
9048 W State Highway 266
Pastor: Gerald D. Horne
Organized 1976

Church of Christ
323 E Harrison
Pastor: David Maravilla
Established 1934

Church of the Nazarene
1003 E. Harrison
Reverend: Tommy Loving
Organized 1973

Church on the Rock
200 E Hwy 174
Pastor: Duane Goforth
Founded September 1995

First Baptist - Republic
305 N. Main
Pastor: Steve Ward
Organized June 11, 1874

First Christian Disciples of Christ
443 N. Main
Minister: Dr. Thomas Minton
Organized 1872

Free Will Baptist
437 N. Walnut
Reverend Donald Anderson
Church built 1948

Harvest Church
1404 E. Hines Street
Pastor: Mick Smith
Established 1987

Hood United Methodist
139 N. Walnut
Pastor: Steve Burbee
Organized 1881

Hope Lutheran
218 E. Hwy 174
Pastor: Brian Whittle
Organized 1983

Hopewell Baptist
Hwy 174 West to Farm Road 53 North
Pastor: Archie Conn
Organized June 1867

Liberty Gospel
Hwy 60 - Next to Brookline Auto Sales
Pastor: Dee Stogner

Meadowview Baptist
1100 Highway 174
Pastor: Josh Mathews
Organized 1982

Pleasant View Fundamental Baptist
13345 W. State Highway TT
Pastor: George Pettey
Established 1945

Republic Congregation of Jehovah's Witnesses
4421 S. Farm Rd. 85
Presiding Overseer: Dennis Geren
Organized 1925

Republic Assembly of God
341 W. Highway 60
Pastor: Rick Cockrell
Organized 1932

United Pentecostal
303 W. Highway 174
Pastor: Mark D. Morris
Established 1988

West Republic Baptist
W. Hwy 60
Pastor: Dr. Christopher Beck
Established March 12, 1974

Westside Christian
537 W. Elm
Minister: James Haenig
Organized 1967

Wilson Creek Baptist
6411 S. Farm Road 115
Pastor: Randall Moody
Founded May 1928

Yeakley Chapel
266 and Farm Road 65
Pastor: Millard Altis
Organized 1865

## Cemeteries

The early pioneer days were difficult. When a loved one died, they were buried in a pleasant spot on their farm or near a church. Often, the graves were only marked with a large rock. There are many such graveyards and cemeteries on private property in the Republic area.

It was not until the late 1800s that land was deeded for the purpose of establishing a cemetery.

1. Batson Family Cemetery is located northwest of Republic on private property once owned by Robert Batson in 1845.

2. Batson Memorial Cemetery is located west of Republic on Highway 266, near the Greene County line. The cemetery is located on the south side of the road, There is a chain link fence across the front with short columns at each side of the gate. The first burial was in 1877.

3. Blades Chapel Cemetery is located off Farm Road 51, southeast of Blades Chapel Church. The church was built in 1889.

4. Brookline Cemetery is located north of Brookline on Farm Road 156. Cumberland Union, a religious and educational incorporation, deeded the land to the Brookline Association to be used for a cemetery.

5. Edgar Cemetery is located on Farm Road 182. The land once was owned by John F. Edgar. The land is now owned by the Wilson's Creek Battleground.

6. Evergreen Cemetery is located on Hines Street in Republic. The land was deeded in August of 1892 by J.F. Brooks, W.H. Noe and J.E. Decker to Evergreen Cemetery.

7. Garoutte Cemetery is located on State Road TT, next to Pleasant View Fundamental Baptist Church. On November 7, 1889, the land was deeded by Mark and Allie Garoutte for a cemetery.

8. Glidewell Cemetery is located on Old Mill Road, south of Battlefield, in Christian County. It is on Boling family land. The Boling family are the caretakers of the cemetery.

9. Harrington Cemetery is located on Farm Road 178, east of Republic. In 1876, the land was owned by W.D. Sparkman and was formerly called Sparkman Cemetery. The land once belonged to Alfred and Ellen Harrington and is currently named Harrington Cemetery.

10. Kerr Springs Cemetery is located in the extreme southwest corner of Greene County and is surrounded by woods. One and a half acres was deeded on May 2, 1887 by R.C. and Elizabeth Kerr for public graves. The Kerr Springs Association was formed January 21, 1893. More land was donated by Spencer G. Kerr.

11. Laney Cemetery is located on private property on Farm Road 31 where the road comes to a "T." There is a lane on the left that leads to the cemetery.

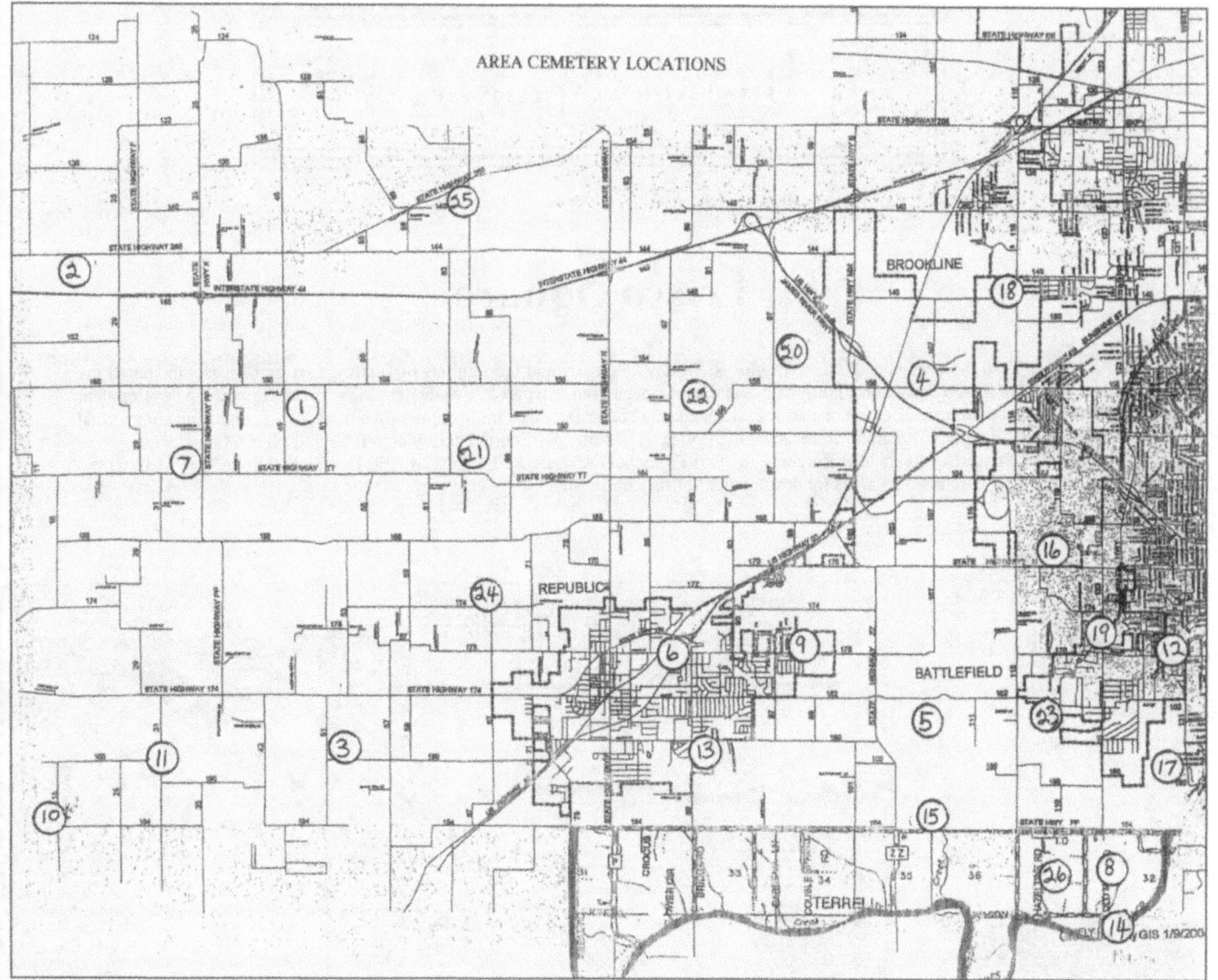

AREA CEMETERY LOCATIONS

12. Larkin-Payne Cemetery is located northeast of Battlefield on private property on Farm Road 178. The land was deeded in 1872 for a family burying ground.

13. Lindsey Cemetery is located on Lynn Street on the south side of Republic. It was formerly called Robertson graveyard and is the oldest burying ground near Republic. Lindsey Robertson owned the land and was pastor of Lindsey Chapel which was located across the road.

14. Manley Cemetery in Christian County is located on west Old Limey Road, near the Greene County line. Burials began in the 1860s on land donated by T.B. and Sarah J. Manley and the cemetery was officially established in 1901. The gazebo that sits in the cemetery was recently modernized and dedicated to the Rogers family. The cemetery has expanded to three acres through a donation of land by Lucille Baxter and is enclosed by a chain link fence.

15. Manley Cemetery in Greene County is located on the southern part of the Wilson's Creek Battleground. C.B. Manley once owned the land. Caleb Manley deeded the land on November 6, 1872 for a cemetery.

16. McElhaney Cemetery is located near Farm Road 168 on the Greene County Power Plant property on the east side along a walking path. The land was once owned by E.L McElhaney and was deeded in 1889. The first burial was William Jackson in 1874. He was the father-in-law of E.L.

17. Owen Cemetery is located in east Battlefield on Farm Road 131, about 100 yards behind a private residence and cannot be seen from the road.

18. Perkins Cemetery is located northeast of Brookline on Farm Road 148 near Farm Road 115 on private property near old cedar trees, The property was once owned by W.G. Perkins. There are no markers left. The gravestones found in 1960 were moved to the Brookline Cemetery.

19. Phillips Cemetery is located on Highway FF, in north Battlefield. The land was once owned by Joel and Lucy Phillips. Lucy was buried there on July 4, 1865. Their son, Columbus Phillips, deeded the land in 1889.

20. Ragsdale Cemetery is located northwest of Brookline on land once owned by Richard J. Ragsdale. The cemetery is located off Farm Road 157 in the middle of the pasture on private property.

21. Reynolds Cemetery is located on TT Highway on private property. There is a sign over the gate that says 1844. David Reynolds was the first settler in Pond Creek Township.

22. Small-DeBoard Family Cemetery is located northwest of Brookline on private property. There are only three gravestones.

23. An unnamed graveyard is located west of Battlefield on Farm Road 182 behind a barn in the corner of a field on private property. There are only three or four broken stone markers. The property was once owned by Sarah Perkins in 1876. The oldest grave is that of John B. Perkins, age one year in 1872. He was the grandson of Sarah Perkins.

24. Wade Chapel Cemetery is located northwest of Republic on Farm Road 174. The first buried was Nancy Hearn Wade on June 14, 1854. She was the wife of James Wade, a Methodist circuit rider (preacher). This cemetery was formerly known as Britain Graveyard.

25. Yeakley Chapel Cemetery is located on 266 Highway and Farm Road 65. Yeakley Chapel Methodist Church was established in 1865 by John Yeakley. The cemetery is located behind the church.

26. Yocum private cemetery is located on Stanley Yocum's property. The last person buried there was Baker Yocum in 1937 or 38. *Submitted by Betty Mason.*

# Business Sponsors

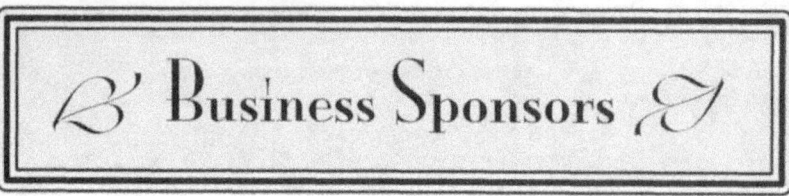

## Frisco Square

October 1996 the developer Modern Tractor & Supply Company and the families of Bussey, Cox and Lipscomb started the development of Frisco Square on a portion of land that had been used as a part of Cox-Davis Dairy. Frisco Square is a development with open and common area, common parking, sidewalks and other facilities, multi-family dwellings, office, retail and commercial sites for sale. The city of Republic constructed the Police and Municipal Courts Facility at 540 Civic Drive. Others locating their businesses at Frisco Square include Burger King, Cox Clinic and Ambulance Facility, Medlin Dental, and Lone Tree LLC. Crawford-Mace, LLC purchased 36 acres for development of residential sites.

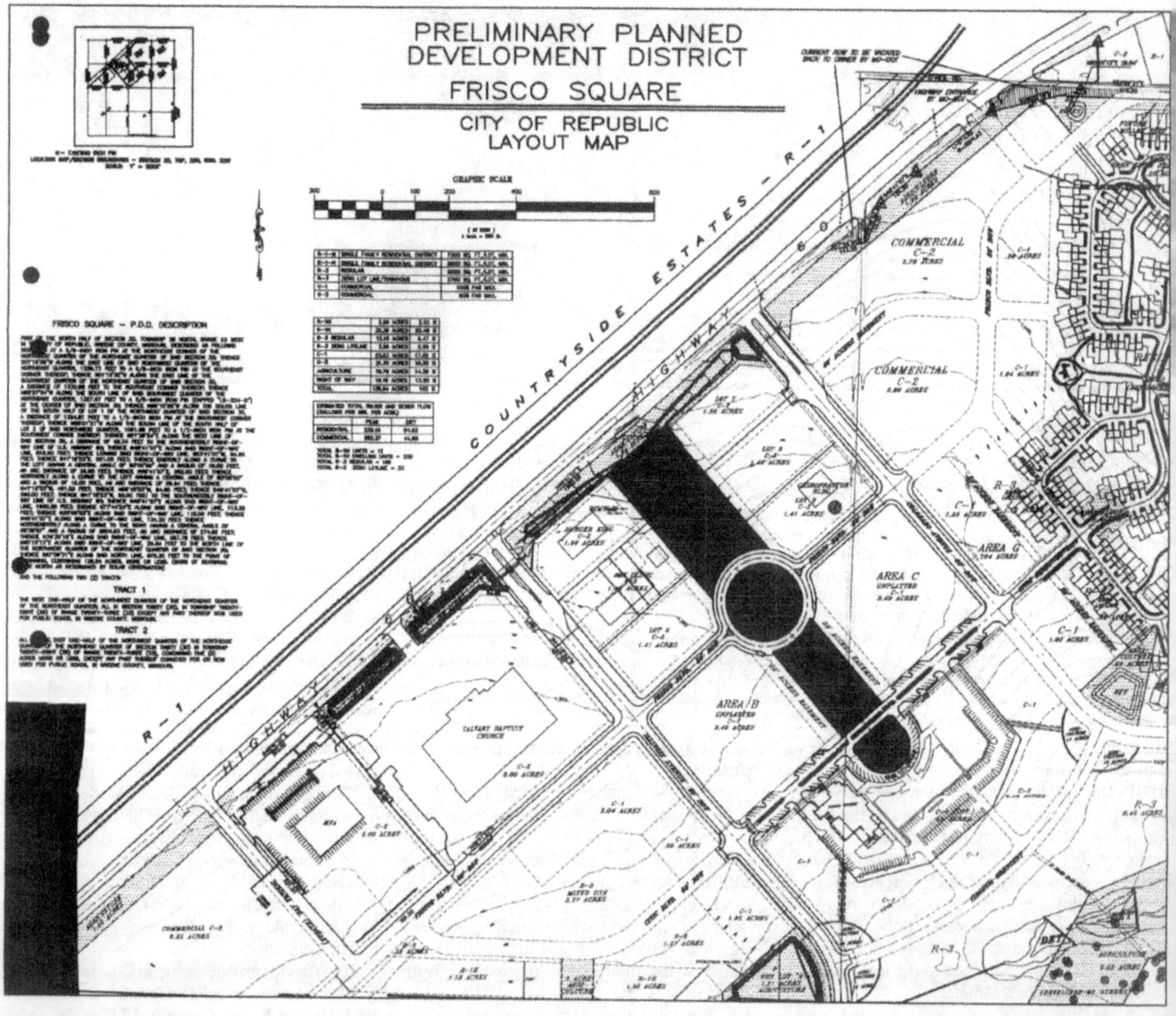

# Advance Tire and Wheel, Inc.

Advance Tire opened its doors on April 1, 1991. The original building was built in approximately 1976 by a local businessman named Norman Davis who operated a motorcycle shop at the location until sometime around 1981. At that time, Tom Bruton opened Bruton Tire Company. Bruton Tire stayed at this location until late 1990.

In early 1991 Calvin Sowder, Rodney Morgan and Randy Morgan opened its doors for the first time to Advance Tire and Wheel, Inc.

As time went by Calvin was bought out in 1992 and a year later Rod Morgan was bought out. That left Randy Morgan on his own by late 1993.

This resulted in Randy hiring his dad, Stan Morgan, in 1993 to run the store. Stan ran the store for 10 years before retiring in 2003. At that time Jerry Tindle Jr. was hired and quickly promoted to store manager in 2003. Jerry remains the store manager to this day.

Advance Tire specializes in new and used tire sales, custom wheels, brakes, shocks, state inspections, wheel alignments, and front-end work.

Advance Tire and Wheel, Inc. wishes everyone good luck and best wishes in the future, with many, many thanks to all their customers over the years.

*Advance Tire and Wheel, Inc. in 2006.*

*Jerry Tindle, Jr.*

*Randy Morgan*

*Looking back west from the old house.*

*The old house on Main Street.*

# Pinegar Chevrolet
## Growing with the Community

Pinegar Chevrolet has been Republic's family owned and operated Chevrolet dealer for 27 years. Ed Pinegar, president, opened the doors to Pinegar Chevrolet in September 1979 and was committed to satisfying the needs of all new and pre-owned vehicle buyers.

"Back then, there was no James River Expressway; the only way to get out here was to come down M Highway to Highway 60, and you might meet one to three cars," said Pinegar, "There was no Wal-Mart, no McDonald's; Ramey's had a small store and that was it. It's incredible to see how Republic and Springfield have grown."

Now, with an expanded staff, including Gary Fletcher as general manager, and Tad Pinegar, new sales manager, Pinegar Chevrolet has sales of over 2,500 annually. Pinegar still believes in handling every customer with both respect and dedication.

Republic has continued to grow through the years and Pinegar Chevrolet keeps up with the growth by not only expanding and updating their facilities, their inventory has also increased. Pinegar Chevrolet is dedicated to always satisfying the needs of this growing community and the surrounding areas. The most recent expansion is Pinegar's Pre-Owned Super Center directly across the street. With the various growing communities comes growing needs, the Super Center lot has not only quality GM products, but also a wide selection of import and other domestic models.

All of Pinegar Chevrolet's new cars and trucks guarantee GM quality. Pinegar Chevrolet offers competitive pricing and you will always find value for your money. Secondary financing is also offered in order to enable customers with impaired credit to get back on track.

"We like that when a customer purchases a vehicle, they will see familiar faces when they return for oil changes or when it is time to purchase again," says General Manager Gary Fletcher. Pinegar Chevrolet continues to be a winner of the GM Mark of Excellence in both sales and service. This is just another example of how the employees treat customers not only during the purchase of a vehicle, but also after with the full Service Center, Parts Department and Body Shop that offers free estimates.

Growing with the time also means moving forward with technology. This is why Pinegar Chevrolet now has the entire new and pre-owned inventory online at www.pinegarchevrolet.com.

Like Republic, the dealership will continue to grow and Pinegar Chevrolet will live up to the standard Ed set in 1979 when he created his trademark slogan: "Big Enough to Serve, Small Enough to Care."

# Ulrich Marine

Ulrich Marine is celebrating its 27th year in business, having started in Republic. In 1979 Fred Ulrich rented a service station on a three acre site and began repairing Mercury motors as well as doing car engine repairs. He earned a Mercury service contract and by 1983 had grown so big that he needed to expand to the five acres adjacent to the station. A 6,000 square foot facility and two large dry storage buildings were added. This past year Fred expanded to Ozark, opening Ulrich Marine Ozark.

Ulrich Marine, owned by Fred Ulrich, is a full sales and service marine center, offering fiberglass repair, boat and RV storage, a full line parts department, an award winning service department with premier dealer status, tournament support with a state-of-the-art mobile service van, state-of-the-art live release pontoon, and factory-trained service technicians.

The Marine Center also has propellers and offers propeller repairs; year-round boat storage; trolling motors and batteries; and outboard motors. Ulrich Marine features Champion bass boats, BassCat boats, Pro Craft boats, Tahoe Fish & Ski boats, Voyager pontoon boats, Fisher boats (both Mod V, Deep V hull and jon), and Princecraft deckboats and fishing boats. There is also a wide assortment of used Champion, Ranger and BassCat boats, and many more.

Those wanting to try out a boat before buying it can do so in the three acre test lake located behind the facility at Highway 60 East in Republic,

Ulrich has boats, motors and accessories for those serious about fishing or just getting away from it all. They also can take care of any storage needs that are wanted.

Ulrich Marine has built a nationwide reputation of excellence in service and repair as well as customer satisfaction. They are also involved in the community and host an annual Kid's Fishing Fair on the first Saturday in June from 10:00 a.m. to 2:00 p.m.

*This small service station was the original building where Ulrich Marine began doing boat and motor repair.*

*Photo from 1979 of Dennis, Al and Fred Ulrich.*

# Tractor Barn

The property now known as the Tractor Barn on West 60 Highway (or 413) was originally farm land with a large white farm house and a large barn owned by the Howards.

The highway was built in 1942, and the Howard farm was split, leaving a portion on the south side and a small portion on the north side of the highway. At a later date, thought to be 1954, the highway was widened to four lanes.

In 1976 Jim and Norma Champieux purchased the property for the purpose of beginning a business which was Southwest Tractor and Parts, Inc. on Highway 60 and Farm Road 107. Their daughter Terri, had just graduated from Republic High School and started working in the business on a temporary arrangement.

At the time Southwest Tractor was established, the customers were primarily farmers, who planted crops and cut and put up hay, including the introduction of round balers and centipede rakes, etc. In 1986, Southwest Tractor was sold and this property is now occupied by Vermeer.

At the time the Champieux' sold Southwest Tractor & Parts, they moved to the east and began a tractor salvage business called the Tractor Barn. Terri was still working in the business and she and her husband Mark Day took over the sole operation of the business. On Labor Day weekend in 1999, the old barn burned, with extensive loss, but Terri decided to rebuild and continue the operation of the business and has remained in the business for 30 years.

It is quite interesting to look back to 1976 when Southwest Tractor was started, and the farming industry as it was at that time, and then to look at 2007 as it exists today, the customers being primarily "hobby" farmers.

Tractors have a new meaning for most of the customers today, being used to mow or smaller jobs.

Farm land and farmers are becoming a memory and the land is rapidly being consumed by housing and commercial businesses. Progress? Yes, maybe! Very much so!

It is a blessing that our parents and grandparents aren't around to see the "progress."

*The old white farm house and barn where Tractor Barn is now located.*

# Republic License Office

In the late 1980s Marilyn Huffman was appointed contract agent for the Republic License Bureau. Republic was the second office in Greene County. The first office was in Springfield. It was run as a state office with state employees.

The Republic office assisted clients in getting their drivers license, titles and transfers of titles for motor vehicles, trailers, ATVs and trucks. The office also assisted in getting driving records and acted as a mediator between the Department of Revenue and the public offering solutions to title and plating problems. Marilyn as a Contract Fee Agent had a reputation of providing gracious service to clients.

In 1992 a change in state government administration came with the election of Governor Carnahan. Mr. Ray Bennett was appointed the Contract Fee Agent. He continued offering a friendly service to the Republic and Greene County area. The Republic office had a reputation for friendly service, where people could sit down and be waited upon with a smile. Many individuals drove from Springfield to Republic because of the atmosphere of the office. Republic became one of the largest contract offices of the state of Missouri. In the spring of 2005 a new governor, Matt Blunt, appointed Ronald Mark as the Contract Fee Agent. The Republic office has upgraded all the equipment and put in new desks to make it more efficient and a more pleasant place to work.

Governor Matt Blunt felt that contract agents could provide a more efficient service than the state run offices. He appointed three other officers as contract agents in Greene County.

Ron Mark, with Manager Alicia Tyler and Assistant Manager Jeremy Jett, try to provide the public with a friendly knowledgeable service to the public and a good image as they represent the state of Missouri in Republic.

*Ribbon Cutting for the Republic License Office*

# Edward Jones

Edward Jones got its start in 1922 when Edward D. Jones Sr. founded the firm that bears his name.

Until the 1950s, Edward Jones was typical of most New York Stock Exchange firms. In the '40s and '50s, the representatives from Edward Jones were called "TNT brokers" because they traveled the countryside surrounding the company's office in St. Louis from Tuesday until Thursday, serving their clients.

In 1948, Edward D. "Ted" Jones Jr., son of the founder, returned to the family business after studying agriculture at the University of Missouri and working on Wall Street. While working his territory in rural Missouri and Illinois, he began experimenting with the concept of locating offices in communities outside St. Louis.

In 1955, he hired a representative for Mexico, Missouri, and with the opening of this first branch office, a new era began.

By 1980, the branch-office network had grown to 304 offices. It was then that Ted Jones handed the reins of the firm over to John Bachmann, who served as managing partner until December 2003. John began his Edward Jones career in 1959 as a college intern, literally sweeping out the basement of the firm's headquarters. He was a successful investment representative in the 1960s before returning to the home office, where he gained experience in a number of areas before being named managing partner in 1980.

Under Bachmann's leadership, the firm built upon its philosophy of serving the needs of serious, long-term individual investors from one-investment-representative offices, and moved to the forefront of the industry in terms of technology and training. Those closest to Bachmann throughout his career credit his vision, strategic focus, leadership and commitment to Edward Jones' culture for making the firm one of the best places to work in America. Bachmann continues his contributions to the firm, the industry and the community in his role as senior partner.

For the past 50 years, Edward Jones has brought Wall Street to Main Street in communities across the country. Edward Jones' one-broker office strategy runs counter to that of virtually every other major securities firm in the United States and has helped fuel remarkable growth for the company. Revenue has grown from $16 million in 1977 to more than $2 billion annually. With more than 9,200 branch offices in all 50 states and through affiliates in Canada and the United Kingdom, Edward Jones' growth has been extraordinary.

Douglas E. Hill, chief operating officer from 1998 through 2003 and managing partner in 2004 and 2005, continued the firm's tradition of bringing personal investment services to an ever-increasing number of individual investors in suburban and rural communities across the country. With the firm's nationally recognized training program, which Hill helped develop after having been a successful investment representative, Edward Jones is adding about 200 new investment representatives each month. This growth would assure that the firm has the opportunity to continue offering investments tailored to the needs of individual investors in the communities in which they live and work.

In 2006, James D. Weddle became only the fifth managing partner in the firm's history. Weddle has spent his entire career at Edward Jones, beginning as an intern in 1976. As a successful investment representative, Weddle later assumed responsibility for the firm's growth on the East Coast. He then assumed responsibility for managing the firm's branch offices in late 1997. His responsibilities included not only the facilities themselves, but also investment representatives' compensation, recognition and leadership development.

Edward Jones continues to be distinguished by its unique brand. The firm remains focused on serving the serious, long-term individual investor. Its investment philosophy still emphasizes quality and diversification. Today, of course, TNT brokers no longer travel the countryside. Instead, Edward Jones locates its offices in communities so investment representatives can develop face-to-face, personal relationships with clients.

The Republic office of Edward Jones opened in 1993. Jasen Fronabarger is the investment representative assisted by senior branch office administrator, Sue Walter.

*Sue Walter and Jasen Fronabarger*

# Commerce Bank
## Celebrates a successful past and looks forward to an even brighter future in Republic

Commerce Bank's roots run deep in Republic and trace back more than half a century. While banking has changed dramatically over the past 50 years, some things remain the same including Commerce Bank's commitment to its customers and the communities they serve. From Farmers State Bank, to Security State Bank, to Commerce - they take pride in their growth and progress and that of their customers, and the community. For generations, they've served as a leading support team to families, individuals, farmers and businesses and continue to break new ground every day.

The officers, board members and staff of Commerce Bank, are proud to be a part of Republic and part of the partnership for prosperity that benefits all.

**A Brief History:**

1950 - Farmers State Bank received its charter and opened for business in April at the corner of Elm & Main Street.

1955 - New bank building built on Main Street.

1966 - Name was changed to Security State Bank.

1977 - New branch bank built on Highway 60.

1984 - Security State Bank expanded into Springfield with the M Highway/Republic Road branch.

1987 - New Year's Eve fire gutted Main Bank downtown. A temporary trailer (mobile office) was used to serve customers until the bank completed its restoration and re-opened of the facility.

1991 - Main Bank moved from downtown to Highway 60, after significant expansion of the facility.

1992 - Security State Bank merged with Commerce Bank, offering more convenience and more products solutions to growing customer needs and preferences in Republic, Southwest Missouri and beyond.

1998 - Steve Lohkamp rejoined Commerce Bank to serve as community president and continues to serve in 2007.

2000-2007 - Commerce Bank continues to expand its products and convenience. The bank moved its ATM from the back of the bank to the corner of the parking lot on Highway 60. Through commercebank.com, customers enjoy on-line banking and bill pay. Debit cards became popular for customers and widely accepted by merchants. Commerce established leadership position in student banking with information for students and parents at commercebank.com/learn. Commerce serves customers with a variety of financial needs from business and personal banking, to mortgage lending, brokerage, investment management, trust and more.

Commerce Bank takes pride in serving a vibrant and growing Republic community. The bank actively supports numerous initiatives to ensure a brighter future for Republic including support for education and the public school system, the chamber, local and regional economic development and more.

Community President, Steve Lohkamp, sums it up, "While so many things have changed at the bank and in our community, one thing that has never changed is the importance of taking care of our customers. I think our founders would be pleased with our mission statement: Be Accessible. Offer Solutions. Build Relationships. And, our customer promise, simply stated: Ask Listen Solve. These words guide how we do business every day. And, no matter how many locations or products we may have, it's how we serve - you - our individual customer that really counts."

*605 US Hwy. 60 East*

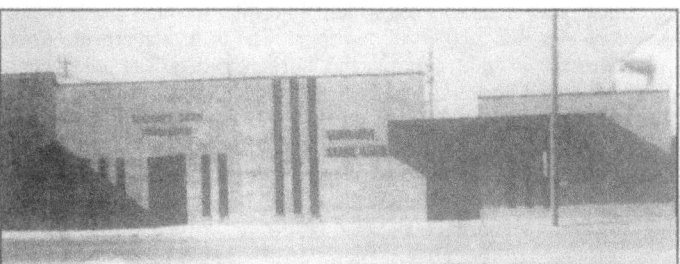
*Former Main Street location.*

*From left: Sandi Wilson, Teller Supervisor; Nita Martin, Financial Services Rep.; Steve Lohkamp, Community President; Suzy Gordon, Financial Services Rep.; Joyce Robbins, Financial Services Manager; and Dorothy Dale, Financial Services Assistant.*

# Countryside Bank

*Front row from left: Susi Boatright, Kathy Long, Cecelia Wilson, Oneida Smith, Darlene Dunning, Shelley Santhuff, Janice Burgess, Ranae Buxton, Lisa Crawford, and Maureen Waldron. Back row: Jerrod Gray, Ken Fitzpatrick, Dustin Royster, Joan Caldwell, Deborah Thompson, Ilene Glenn, Trish Ghan, Rita Ratliff, Rosy Wagner, Cliff Ricketts, Mark Kelley, Marcalene Befielb, Jack Muench–President, and Ben Spickard.*

Countryside Bank opened in Republic, MO on June 15, 1998 with six employees and $3,000,000 in capital. The bank was organized with a six member board of directors and 24 shareholders. The organizers of the bank were Charles L. Spangler, Jack R. Muench, L. Max Porter, W. Ronald Gammon, Jerry R. Carter and Curtis L. Plotner, who also served as the original board of directors. The officers were Jack Muench, President; Ilene Glenn, Vice President; and Shari Crews, Cashier. Rita Ratliff served as the first new accounts representative, Rosy Wagner was loan assistant and Rachel Smythe was teller.

The bank opened in a single-wide modular banking facility on the bank property at 520 E. Elm, at the corner of Elm Street and Highway 60, and after opening, immediately started construction of the permanent bank building. The bank moved into its permanent location the following March. Countryside Bank was the only independent bank in Republic when it opened in 1998, and is the only bank with its home office in Republic in 2007. It has grown from $3,000,000 in assets in 1998 to over $90,000,000 as of March 31, 2006.

# Great Southern

Great Southern has a long history of serving personal and business customers with their banking, investment, insurance and travel needs. Like the great town of Republic, Great Southern is proud of its heritage and deep roots in the Ozarks.

In the 1920s, Republic was a town of just over 1,500 people. Automobiles were beginning to make their debut and folks were keeping up with "The Married Life of Helen and Warren" in the local papers. In nearby Springfield, a business opened its doors for the first time in 1923 - Great Southern.

Great Southern Savings and Loan Association began with a $5,000 investment, four employees and 936 members. Today, Great Southern has grown to more than $2 billion in assets, 700 associates and nearly 150,000 customers. The company grew from one office in downtown Springfield to now operating 35 banking centers in 14 counties in southwest and central Missouri and four loan production offices in St. Louis, Kansas City and Columbia in Missouri and Rogers, Arkansas.

Back in the early days, Great Southern's founders had a simple charge: to foster thrift and homeownership by attracting savings deposits and investing those funds in local real estate loans. The founders also established enduring values and a proud philosophy of doing business that the company still holds dear. The basic principles of integrity, prudence, reliability and loyalty to customers helped Great Southern weather economic storms pre-dating even the Great Depression of 1929, and underscore a heritage of strength and reliability that continues to distinguish the company today.

Great Southern experienced steady growth during the subsequent decades with its focus on homeownership and savings, but as 70s decade came along, big changes began to take place at the company.

Like Republic, Great Southern began to flourish in the 70s. In 1974, the company's fifth president, William V. Turner, joined the association and ushered in a new operating philosophy. Under Mr. Turner's leadership, it instituted an aggressive service expansion program. In the late '70s and into the '80s, the association took advantage of its savings and loan charter to branch into complementary areas not allowed to commercial banks. During Mr. Turner's first five years, 14 new offices were added in eight Ozarks communities.

During this time, Great Southern also took advantage of further deregulation in the industry and began offering checking accounts, consumer and commercial loans. It also built a firm foundation for the future in offering customers "more for your money." The company was among the first in the area to introduce such novel industry milestones as late night and weekend banking hours, adjustable rate mortgages, and alternative investment products. In yet another progressive innovation and years ahead of its time, Great Southern introduced the "Cash Management Account," which was the forerunner to money market checking in the Ozarks.

Great Southern also differentiated itself by opening a full-service travel agency and investment division and by expanding its insurance agency. In fact, Great Southern was the first financial institution in southwest Missouri to offer investment products and services to retail customers.

The late '80s and '90s brought more change, and more opportunity. During this period, conversion to a bank charter allowed the bank to serve customers with an even broader range of products and services. For Great Southern to continue to grow, it needed a strong capital base. In 1989, history was made as it became a publicly held company listed on NASDAQ. In response to changing consumer demands, the company invested heavily into ATMs, telephone banking and online banking providing 24-hour access for customers throughout the Ozarks.

When bank consolidation that was occurring throughout the U.S. reached the Ozarks in the late '90s, Great Southern experienced dramatic growth. Great Southern had greatly strengthened its convenience and value proposition for customers and it was poised to take advantage of the changes occurring in the marketplace. In 1996, Great Southern held roughly six percent of the local deposit share according to FDIC figures. Today, that deposit share has grown to 21.10 percent.

In 2005, Great Southern made history again by building a new banking center in Republic on Harrison Street. The company had the privilege of serving many customers from Republic for years and the new banking center solidified these relationships and opened up new opportunities to attract new customers.

Graciously, the community of Republic welcomed Great Southern and its team of associates with open arms resulting in one of the company's most successful banking center openings ever.

Moving ahead, under the leadership of Joseph W. Turner, Great Southern will operate under the same philosophy that has guided it for decades: building winning relationships with its customers, associates, shareholders and communities. On any given day, the company and its associates will be hard at work helping young families realize the dream of homeownership, helping a business owner expand his or her business, or providing the right product or service to help an individual save for a future goal. It will also partner with the community to make it a better place to live for its citizens. It will make every effort for the Great Southern sun to be a familiar and welcome sight in Republic and throughout the Ozarks.

*Ribbon cutting for the new banking center in 2005.*

# Mid-Missouri Bank

*Mid-Missouri Bank in 2003 and its new home in 2006.*

Mid-Missouri Bank has only a recent history in Republic. Chartered in June 1998 as Town and Country Bank of the Ozarks, business was originally conducted in a temporary structure in the 200 block of West Broad Street. Seventy-one days after construction started on the permanent banking house it was completed and operations began at 161 US Highway 60 West. The bank was organized by Dale Meadors and capitalized by 96 members of the local and surrounding communities. Town and Country Bank of the Ozarks grew quickly reaching an asset size of nearly $55 million. In December 2003 Mid-Missouri Bancshares purchased Town and Country Bank of the Ozarks operating the bank as a wholly owned subsidiary until December 17, 2005 when the bank was fully merged into Mid-Missouri Bank and the name was changed to Mid-Missouri Bank, Republic. In the fall of 2006 the main banking house again moved into brand new and larger quarters at the corner of Hines and US 60 in the middle of Republic.

*Dale Meadors in front of Town and Country Bank of the Ozarks, 1988.*

# Regions Bank
## A Look Back at Regions Bank in Republic, MO

Looking at the financial industry you will see many banks have a complex and rich history mostly due to the trend of financial companies merging and consolidating. Regions Bank in Republic, MO, has deep roots dating back to 1888 when it was formed as the Mount Vernon Building and Loan Association. Over the years as it has transitioned through names, one underlying principle has remained constant, taking care of the customers.

The following is a look back at how Regions Bank has evolved over the years - along with the financial industry.

### First Savings Bank

First Savings Bank was started by several local businessmen, who saw the need for a Savings and Loan. They raised the necessary capital and opened the Mount Vernon Building and Loan Association in Mt. Vernon, MO, in 1888. To become a member of the association, one purchased stock and paid for it in monthly installments of $1 per share. According to newspaper reports, stockholders could own up to 10 shares and could borrow no more than $2000. At the time of incorporation, 400 shares were subscribed. Therefore, the first recorded assets amounted to one month's dues collected, or $400.

In 1947, the board of directors adopted a new set of bylaws that did away with the stock system of raising capital. All outstanding stock was converted to either an investment account on which dividends were paid in cash or a savings account on which dividends were credited. Also, the association moved to another building on the west side of the square where it remained until 1964. However, it was in 1962, the association changed its name to First Savings and Loan Association of Mt. Vernon.

Time marched on and the 1970s marked a period of growth and expansion for the association in southwest Missouri. Branches were opened in Aurora, Bolivar, Republic, El Dorado Springs, and Springfield. By the early 80s, the association underwent another name change to First Savings Bank but it maintained its state savings and loan charter.

### Union Planters Bank - Tennessee's Oldest Bank

In 1998 Union Planters Bank, a $15-billion holding company based in Memphis, TN, bought First Savings Bank for an estimated $59 million. The merged company had an asset base in southwest Missouri of $489 million with 18 bank locations.

### Regions Bank Enters the Picture

In January 2004 Regions Financial Corp. and Union Planters announced they had signed a definitive merger agreement, creating the 15th largest bank holding company in the nation. The merger was completed in 2005 creating a banking network with more than 1,300 locations and 1,400 ATMs across its now 16-state footprint.

*Regions Bank in Republic, 2007.*

### How Did Regions Start?

Regions' history is one that is founded on a community focus. In 1970, a small group of Alabama bankers and businessmen got together and proposed a daring plan - the formation of the first multi-banking holding company in Alabama. Their proposal was grounded in one simple idea - that sound banking principles and new growth opportunities could be combined to create a stronger financial institution for the state.

Regions became the state of Alabama's first multi-bank holding company when the First National Bank of Huntsville, First National Bank of Montgomery and Birmingham's Exchange Security Bank joined together. The company began operations with a total of $543 million in assets and 40 banking locations, and, in 1994, was renamed Regions Financial Corp. to reflect its growing presence throughout the South.

### What Regions is Today

Today, Regions provides everyday confidence to some five million customers throughout a 16-state footprint in the South, Midwest and Texas. Regions had $84.6 billion in assets as of September 30, 2005 making it one of the nation's Top 15 banks. But, with all of the change in names and evolution in banking there is one thing that hasn't changed, the focus on their customers. Regions works to help customers and communities realize their dreams by anticipating, understanding and meeting financial needs through effective solutions.

*Exchange Security Bank in Birmingham, Alabama.*

*First Savings and Loan in Republic.*

# H&R Block

In January 1955 the Internal Revenue Service made the decision to quit offering free tax preparation service. Two brothers, Henry and Richard Bloch, were in the accounting business, doing tax preparation free for their clients. A client who was a sales person for the *Kansas City Star* suggested that Henry and Richard run an ad for $7.50 advertising a tax service. The "Bloch" brothers were very busy after running the ad.

They named their new business H&R Block. They expanded the following year with a franchise to New York City. In 1965 when Ron Mark started preparing taxes for them, H&R Block had 600 offices in the United States. They now have over 9,000 offices throughout the world.

In 1966 Ron Mark left the post office and became a franchise director for H&R Block in Springfield, Missouri. In 1974 Ron established the Republic office as headquarters for southern Missouri and north Arkansas. Ron also participated in the training of many other directors of franchises. He assisted the manager of the Seoul, Korea branch making several trips to Korea to visit that office.

H&R Block has gone through many changes in its years of business. H&R Block continues to provide a needed service to the public and has become a world-wide company. It has expanded into many areas; electronic filing, instant loans on refunds and mortgage and financial services to become financial partners for their clients. The local H&R Block became part of the Springfield complex in 1999 when Ron Mark retired from the company.

# The Republic Monitor

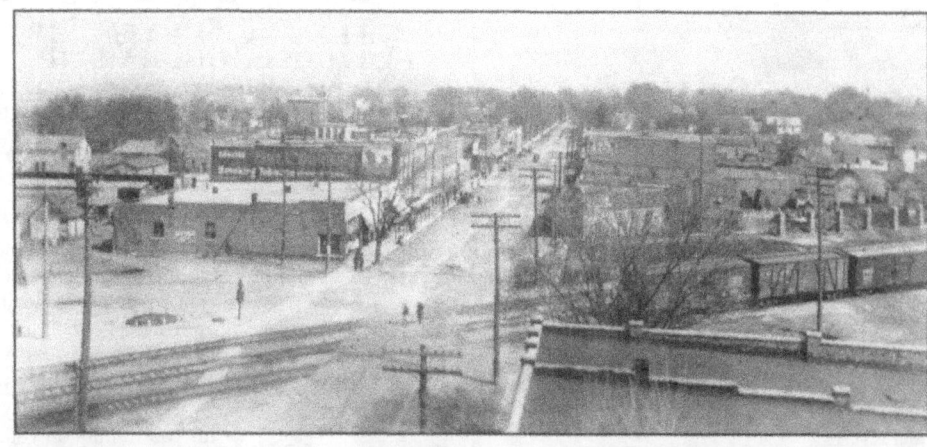

From its start on a Washington Hand Press in 1894 to today's computers and modern day printing procedures, *The Republic Monitor* has seen a lot of changes throughout its 112-year history in Republic.

Even through a long list of ownership, *The Monitor* has continued to bring the residents of Republic top-quality news coverage of the events and people of the town. The first copy of *The Monitor* was issued by J.J. and I.S. Jones on April 7, 1894. That first copy was printed on the Washington Hand Press, located in a small frame building on the east side of Main Street, which was known as "Smoky Row."

Charles E. Gentry was the first, and only, "paid up" subscriber. However, it wasn't long before the *Greene County Republic*, a paper published by R.C. Viles, was bought and added to *The Monitor.* With this purchase, the Jones' brothers used a part of the material to add to their office, while the balance was sent to Exeter, Missouri, where "Ike" Jones established the *Kodac*.

With *The Monitor's* subscription list continuing to grow, a country Campbell press and a gasoline engine were installed to keep up with it.

Then, after 10 years of strenuous work, the Jones' brothers sold the plant to F.E. Anderson. Anderson then sold it to Elder W.B. Cochran. The paper continued to change hands from R.C. Stone and others before falling into the hands of J.R. Derry in 1915. Since the early 1900's, *The Monitor* has gone through even more changes in ownership. Dave and Ethel Russell owned the paper from 1931 to 1967. Darrell Sumner of the Sumner Media Group, Inc., purchased it in 1996 from Jim Smith, who had owned and operated the paper for 26 years. Sumner moved the paper from its 102-year-old location downtown to 417 U.S. Highway 60 E. Then in December of 2003, Community Publishers Inc. (CPI) purchased the paper from Sumner and moved it to its current location at 249 U.S. Highway 60 W. in the Southwest Plaza.

CPI is an independent, privately held corporation owning a combination of 29 daily, twice-weekly, weekly, and niche publication in southwest Missouri, north central Arkansas, and in and around Tulsa, Oklahoma. CPI was founded in 1982, and does its commercial printing and all printing of *The Republic Monitor* at Missouri Color Web Printers, its commercial printing facility in Springfield.

*The Republic Monitor* is proud of its rich tradition as Republic's oldest continuing business.

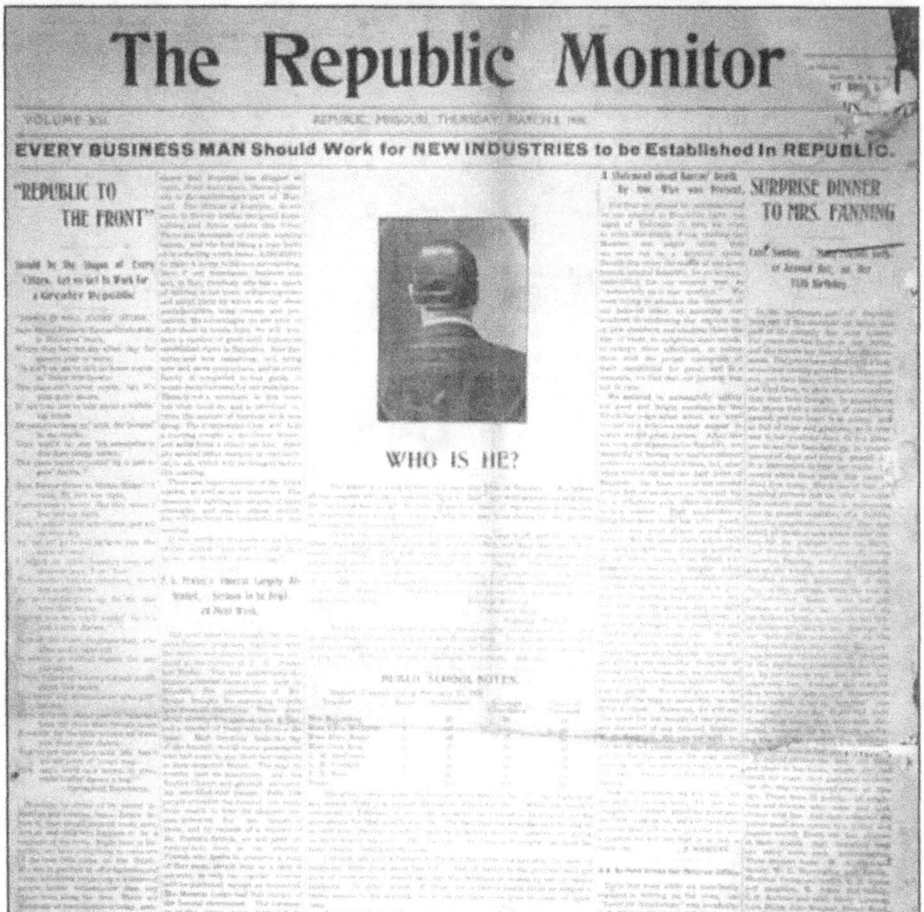

The Republic Monitor

EVERY BUSINESS MAN Should Work for NEW INDUSTRIES to be Established in REPUBLIC.

"REPUBLIC TO THE FRONT"

SURPRISE DINNER TO MRS. FANNING

WHO IS HE?

PUBLIC SCHOOL NOTES.

The Churches.

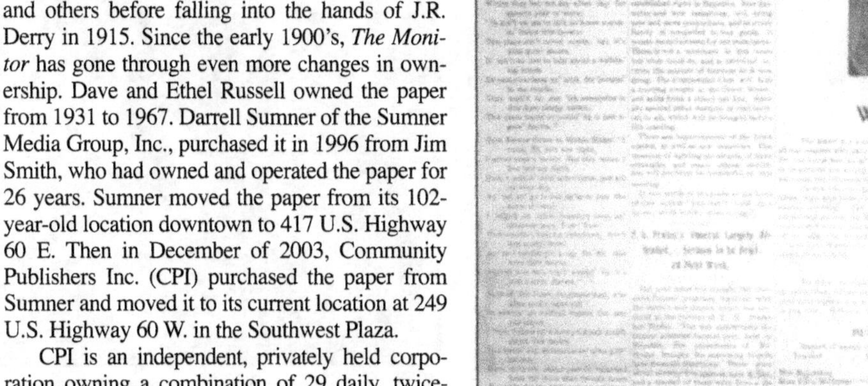

REPUBLIC, MO., 189

M

SUBSCRIPTION
$1.00 PER YEAR.
The best advertising medium in Greene County.

Bills payable monthly

IN ACCOUNT WITH

THE MONITOR.

JOB OFFICE IN CONNECTION
All Job Work Must be Paid for When Delivered

# Rodgers Co. Realty
## "A HouseSold Word"

Rodgers Co. Realty is the oldest continuous real estate company in Republic. Rodgers Co. Realty was founded in 1970 by Rex Rodgers. He was active in building homes and real estate sales until 1985. Rex and his wife Rosemary decided to retire and become snowbirds.

In the summer of 1986, Rex came out of retirement to help Elbert "Mac" McKay and his wife Reeda reopen and own Rodgers Co. Realty. It was located on the corner of Highway 60 and Elm Street (the building is now Domino's Pizza).

Mac and Reeda have been an awesome selling team in the Republic area. Mac started doing appraisals along with being the broker of the office. Reeda has always put her clients needs ahead of her own. She is now working on the second generation of buyers and sellers in the market!

Mac and Reeda's daughter Torre created the tag line "The HouseSold Word" for the company that is still used today.

In 1995, they were joined by Madge Blades who has lived and worked in the Republic area most of her life, raised a family, sold many houses to many people and can make about any Real Estate deal work. She has been listing and selling homes for area people since 1983.

In 1996, Torre (McKay) Conklin started working along side her parents as a full time Realtor. She works hard for her customers which shows up in her sales and listings performances.

Rodgers Co. Realty moved to its current location at 107 W. State Hwy 174, the corner of Hwy 174 and Main Street in January 1997.

Rodgers Co. Realty has prided itself on honesty, integrity and working for your family on your schedule.

*Madge Blades, Mac McKay, Reeda McKay, and Torre Conklin*

*Rex and Rosemary Rodgers*

*Rodgers Co. Realty, "The HouseSold Word"*

# Shelter Insurance Agency

In 1946, Billy Miller started the MFA Insurance Agency in Republic. The business was originally located on Main Street, next door to O'Dells Drug Store. Years later Billy bought a lot from Dr. R.C. Mitchell and built the current structure at 115 E. Grant. Mr. Miller wrote insurance for a large majority of the Republic community and also the adjoining farm area.

Lucille Miller, in the 1960s, started a ceramic's shop in the same building and taught classes to the public. The ceramic pieces were poured there and fired after the students had done all the finishing work. The business flourished for several years and in the mid-70s, Lucille decided to convert the business to a gift shop, thus All Seasons Gift Shop came onto the scene. Lucille and Billy traveled to various markets across the United States and brought gift and decorating items back to Republic. The shop offered a wide variety of merchandise and shoppers came from the surrounding area. The shop was one of the first of its kind in the city.

Joining the family business in 1976, daughter Kay Miller, worked in the insurance agency and gift shop until Billy's retirement in 1989 at which time Kay became the agent of record. The gift shop was soon closed due to the Miller's retirement.

This family run business has been proudly providing service to the community for the past 60 years and continues today.

# Heaven's Scent Flowers and Gifts

Heaven's Scent Flowers and Gifts opened in Republic 19 years ago on August 3, 1987 when owners Marlene Klepees and her mother Elsa Dirks decided to go into the floral design business. The mother-daughter combo did not purchase an existing floral company, but instead built their business from the ground up by selling one bouquet at a time. In the early, fledgling stages the staff consisted of only Marlene and Elsa. Since that time, however Heaven's Scent has steadily grown and flourished, increasing the number of both patrons and personnel. Currently they have seven staff members.

Heaven's Scent Flowers and Gifts has been in its current location at 923 US Highway 60 East for the last seven years and is a full-service florist shop. It specializes in cut flower bouquets, funeral and wedding arrangements, and seasonal bouquets as well as specialty bouquets, live plants, pre-designed silk arrangements, and non-floral gift items such as stuffed animals, candles, balloons and cards. Although Heaven's Scent is also associated with both FTD and Teleflora wire services, the largest percentage of business is generated from phone orders and walk-in purchases.

Heaven's Scent is open from 8:00 a.m. until 6:00 p.m. Mondays through Fridays and from 8:00 a.m. until 4:00 p.m. on Saturdays. Funeral deliveries are made seven days a week.

Both Marlene and Elsa have made Republic their home town and have formed close, personal bonds with many of their customers whom they now consider friends.

# Ken's TV
## (Owned by David Denny since 1989)

Ken's TV opened for business in August 1964 by Ken Walker. Ken's TV offered television and radio repair and new Zenith TV sales and service. Ken's TV was located at Grant Street next to the former Republic Post Office. Then moved to 200 N. Main (which originally was Doc O'Dell's Drug Store). In 1973 Ken built and moved into a commercial building on 450 West Highway 60 and that building is still owned by Ken today. In 1985 satellite dish sales and installation were added to the business.

David Denny graduated from Republic High School in 1967. David started working for Ken in the fall of 1968. At that time Ken was David's father-in-law. David attended Springfield College of Technology and received a diploma for completing the radio and tv repair electronics course. He would go to school during the mornings and worked for Ken in the afternoon. In about 1989 Ken decided to retire and transferred the business to David.

In 1990 David moved the business to its present location 932 U.S. Hwy. 60 East (next door to O'Reilly Automotive). David has seen many changes in the television repair and satellite business. The industry has changed from tube-type TVs to digital flat panel and digital LCDs; from small 27" up to 65" big screens. Large satellite dishes have been replaced by the small satellite dishes. VCRs have been replaced by DVD players. The electronics repair business is constantly changing. Ken's TV still repairs televisions and VCRs.

In 1996 Ken's TV became a Dish network retailer. David's wife Linda Denny was added to the business to help with sales and manage the store while David is out installing the Dish network systems. This is why you see the red truck around town that says, "My Man Does Dishes!"

*David Denny and Ken Walker*

*Ken's TV on May 12, 1967*

# Family Pharmacy
## Continues To Grow Starting Year 30

Family Pharmacy in Republic opened a week prior to September 11, which all Americans will always remember. From that beginning in Republic, the pharmacy has continued to grow and expand services. Lynn and Janet Morris, who own Family Pharmacy, Inc., own two nursing home pharmacies serving over 100 healthcare facilities, a complete home medical supply, a bargain outlet, a frozen custard and coffee shop, a photo shop, and manage a hospital pharmacy.

The independent chain's headquarters are in Ozark. They operate the original retail pharmacy in Ozark that started in 1977. The warehouse serving the chain is in Nixa.

Family Pharmacy is recognized as a Top 100 Chain Store in the United States, ranking 66 in 2005 for total sales. "The pharmacy in Joplin, Missouri, opens a completely new territory for us," states Morris. "We are excited for the opportunities as we operate a drive thru retail pharmacy, a nursing home pharmacy, and a one hour photo center in the same building," concludes Morris.

The newest pharmacy opened late 2005 in Marshfield and the newest Family Pharmacy will open in Bolivar in June 2006. Other new projects in 2006 include pharmacies in Theodosia and other selected areas as well as buying an existing pharmacy. They are looking at other sites as well, including Springfield. The chain already operates one pharmacy in Springfield in the Summer Fresh Market on Plainview Road.

The pharmacist manager for the Republic store is Emily Donnelson. The assistant store manager is Mary Doerr and the front-end manager is Pam Poe. Other employees include Rachel Kelsey, Bonnie Stroesenreuther, Natalie Short and Vickie Lang.

"The employees that we have are a major reason why Family Pharmacy is growing so fast in the Republic area," stated Morris. "We believe in giving great customer service, knowing you by name and doing special things for our customers," reports Morris.

Family Pharmacy in Republic features park-at-the-door convenience, free coffee, ice-cold water and a nice waiting area. Family Pharmacy rents and sells medical and hospital equipment and has a private counseling area. Flu shots and several disease state management programs are available. Family Pharmacy also provides screenings for osteoporosis, blood pressure and free hearing screenings.

Family Pharmacy's prescription department is a state-of-the-art system that monitors for drug interactions.

This is one of the few Family Pharmacy stores that doesn't have a drive thru, but the employees actually provide curbside service. "I feel like our pharmacists really care about their patients and are the best," said Morris.

Family Pharmacy features a TrueCare cash discount card program that saves people money. It is a free card that gives discounts on all prescriptions as well as private label items, sale items, photo finishing and much more. The TrueCare cash discount card is now being used by thousands of customers in their network of pharmacies.

Family Pharmacy has expanded their gift line. They now feature candles and more gifts in the $20-and-under range.

"Whether you need a birthday, wedding, anniversary, graduation, hospital or get-well gift, we will be able to serve you," said Morris. Family Pharmacy also features a $1 section, files Medicare for diabetic supplies and accepts all third-party insurance cards and Missouri Medicaid.

"We invite everyone to come and experience the Family Pharmacy difference," states Morris. "You can trade at bigger stores, but you can't call their owner at home or office like you can when you deal with us. The buck stops with me and I will always make time to listen and help everyone who calls and needs me or one of my management team members."

"We are extremely proud of our growth and success in Republic. We will always try to live up to 'Best Service and Low Prices,'" ended Morris.

*From left: Vickie Lang, West Reg. Manager; Mary Doerr, Asst. Manager; Dr. Tera Sanders, Pharmacist; Bonnie Stroesenreuther, Front End Manager; Pam Poe; and Rachel Kelsey. Additional staff: Emily Donnelson, Pharmacist and Holly Pressman, Technician.*

*Back row from left: BJ Jones, Mandy Jones, Tera Sanders, and Justin Sanders with Dylan Sanders. Middle row: Lynn Morris, Taylor Sanders, and Janet Morris. In front: Melissa Sanders with Olivia Sanders.*

# Christian Health Care

From growing a garden to raising rabbits, residents at Christian Health Care in Republic are made to feel like they are at home, according to Administrator Ray Thompson. They are also very active, going on outings within the community to places such as the Republic Senior Friendship Center.

Thompson said he started the animal therapy and gardening for the residents to be able to feel like they are a part of the facility, yet in a familiar atmosphere. The residents and their families provide for the care of the animals, which now include rabbits and will soon include a Banty rooster and hen.

But the involvement in the community doesn't end there. Christian Health Care takes cookies to all the banks and doctors offices in Republic, Billings and Clever; conducts blood pressure screenings at the Senior Center; takes food to the Ronald McDonald House on the second Wednesday of the month; and is active in the Republic events, such as the Christmas parade, Business Expo and Pumpkin Daze. Thompson, who has been administrator for almost a year, is also a member of the Kiwanis Club. Christian Health Care, located at 901 E. Highway 174, employs an average of 95 workers, and has a census of between 95 and 100 residents. Thompson said the census has been up since he's been administrator. The facility is state certified to accommodate 127 residents, including five private rooms. It offers skilled nursing services, palliative care, an Alzheimer's special care unit, and rehabilitation services. Thompson said under the palliative care unit, Christian Health Care provides a comprehensive program of pain management, comfort measures, support therapy and ongoing patient and family education and counseling for individuals diagnosed with a terminal illness. "Treating the person rather than the illness is our goal by supporting the patient and family through the final phase of illness," said Thompson. There is also bereavement counseling available.

Under the rehab unit, most residents return home after a while. Christian Health Care does a home evaluation before the person returns home and recommends whether he/she should go home or not. Christian Health Care has 11 other homes in southwest Missouri. The Republic one was built in 1989. Over the past year, new carpeting was placed in the community room, and some landscaping was added, along with maintenance and upkeep when residents move out. Thompson said one of the future goals is to make some renovations to the building and add more landscaping. Another one of his goals is to get the census a little higher, and have even more involvement in the community.

Thompson said it has been good to be able to come home and run his hometown location. He said he has a really good rapport with the residents, and feels that comes from his growing up in farming and his being in the Navy. He also plans to eventually teach a fly-tying class to the residents. "I like being out in the population with the residents and getting to know them," said Thompson, who also goes on some outings with them. "I like being involved in the whole facility." Christian Health Care not only takes care of its residents, but there are also special things for the employees as well. Thompson said on dietary day, the department heads cook the meal, and let the employees of the department off for the day with pay.

Thompson said he feels the facility gives the best care it can to the residents, and this is done through generating happy employees and having a clean facility.

Christian Health Care also honors its veterans on Veteran's Day. Thompson said this past Veteran's Day, each one was presented with a medal, and State Representative Jim Viebrock from the 134th District and Republic Mayor Jim Collins were present to visit with the veterans.

# Sonshine Manor

Sonshine Manor is nestled in the beautiful country setting of Republic, Missouri close to metropolitan Springfield, and an hour from Branson. Built in 1991 by Dr. Francis Maple, Sonshine is currently operated by the Eden Heritage Foundation, a nationally recognized not-for-profit corporation. Sonshine is a family-oriented facility with professional staff who provide the highest level of residential and skilled care in a home-like atmosphere. The beautiful community areas at the manor include—a spacious dining room, a living room with a fireplace, large windows, and a piano; an arts and crafts room; a TV room; and a beauty salon. At Sonshine Manor, safe and professional care is always provided in an intimate and personal setting.

### Medical Services

Sonshine Manor provides the full spectrum of medical care, from management of medications and personal services in residential care, to assistance with meals, personal care and medical intervention for residents in skilled nursing care. A licensed nurse is on duty 24 hours a day for both skilled and residential care. The medical director is available to serve as the resident's personal physician and to provide consultation to outside physicians who are unable to visit their patient at Sonshine Manor. The medical director makes weekly visits to the facility and maintains daily contact with the nursing staff.

*A friendly encouraging staff of professionals providing safe and dignified care to the elderly. From left: Gladys Crowe; Activity Director, Tomi Benedict; and Account Manager, Judy Thomas.*

### Professional Services

Dental care, podiatry, vision care, lab and X-ray services are all available at Sonshine Manor. Physical therapy, as well as occupational and speech therapies, are arranged with a physician's order. Progress made in therapy is maintained by their restorative therapy program.

### Other Services

Delicious and nutritious, home-cooked meals are a daily ritual. Special diets are accommodated, while a variety of snacks are provided between meals and each evening. The professional housekeeping staff keeps the manor squeaky clean. Laundry services are provided for the resident's personal laundry at no extra charge. A variety of beauty salon services are provided three days per week at reasonable rates. Community areas can be reserved for special occasions, holidays, and parties.

### Resident Rooms

The semi-private and private bedrooms are spacious with large closets, private bathrooms, and locked cabinets for privacy. Each room is equipped with an individual heating and cooling unit, as well as a ceiling fan for personal comfort. The screened windows allow residents to enjoy the country-fresh air. Cable TV and low-cost private phones are also available.

### Spiritual Growth and Care

Bible studies, church services, special music and pastoral visits are an on-going part of life at Sonshine. Volunteers from several denominations make weekly visits to the manor. Sonshine participates in the Ombudsman Program sponsored by the Council of Churches which provides a trained volunteer to listen to resident concerns and to serve as a liaison when requested.

### Sonshine Manor is Always Full of Life and Activity

Activities: A variety of activities are scheduled daily for Sonshine residents to meet social, intellectual, spiritual, and recreational needs—pet therapy, crafts, bingo, trivia, music and the bell choir are just a few. A monthly birthday party is provided by local ladies who bring delicious home-baked cakes for residents celebrating a birthday that month to enjoy with other residents. Sonshine is involved in the Y.E.S. (Youth Exchange with Seniors) Program. Students from Republic High School make weekly visits to the manor and develop special friendships with Sonshine residents. Outings are planned with input from the residents regarding their interests, whether it be a trip to a local orchard, library or community event.

A recent addition to the services provided at Sonshine Manor are the independent living duplexes called Sonshine Gardens. The one and two bedroom units provide a modern worry free home for each of its tenants. The tenants may choose to have meal service from Sonshine Manor at a nominal charge, and all maintenance, lawn care, housekeeping, available nursing support and utilities are provided in the basic monthly rent. Sonshine Gardens are spacious and very comfortable with a full garage and patio, fully equipped kitchens and are completely handicapped accessible.

Sonshine Manor and Sonshine Gardens are reflections of the mission of Eden Heritage Foundation which includes sensitivity to the physical, emotional, social and spiritual needs of those they serve and those they employ. We are proud to serve the Republic community with a vital service for our elderly.

*300 South Cottonwood Republic, MO*

# Meadors Funeral Home

There have been five different owners of the funeral home in Republic, MO from 1908 thru 1999. The current owner of Meadors Funeral Home, 314 N. Main is John McCulloch. Listed below are the past and current owners of the funeral home.

R.E. Thurman Funeral Home 1908-1950: R.E. (Bob) Thurman and wife, Anna, were the first owners of the funeral home. They purchased the general mercantile store on Main Street, one block north of the railroad tracks in 1900/01. He sold funeral supplies upstairs over the general store for several years, before he moved to the 200 block of East Elm.

Fossett Funeral Home 1950-1955: Max L. Fossett and wife Lelia were the second owners. He moved the funeral home back to Main Street.

Cantrell Funeral Home 1955-1974: Bill and Jean Cantrell were the third owners.

Meadors Funeral Home 1974-1999: Dale and Carolyn Meadors were the fourth owners. In 1978 the Meadors made major renovations to the facility and were also owners of the Clever and Billings Chapel. They started an ambulance service in Republic in 1974.

Meadors Funeral Home 1999-to present: In October 1999 Dale and Carolyn sold the business to John McCulloch because of health concerns. The name remains Meadors Funeral Home, serving the Republic, Billings, and Clever communities and surrounding area, with funeral chapels in those cities. The current Republic funeral home facility on Main Street is built around the house where Max Fossett operated the funeral home. A picture of the house is on display at the funeral home. Judy Ankrom, Russ Allen, Rick Lindsey, and Christina Sanders make up the full time staff with part-time assistants, Eva Burk, Barbara Kuhn and Ron Melton.

According to the Centennial publication in 1971, J.W. Britain was the first undertaker in Republic. His undertaker parlor was upstairs over his mercantile business. Bob Thurman worked in the store and learned the business from him and later purchased the undertaking business.

*Meadors Funeral Home, top to bottom: Clever (1994), Republic, and Billings (built in 1977 and remodeled in 2004).*

*J.W. Britain, Undertaker, covering a casket above his mercantile store.*

# Wal-Mart

On July 2, 1962, brothers Sam M. and James L. Walton opened the first Wal-Mart Store in Rogers, AR. The store made sales of $975,000 its first year.

By 1969, Wal-Mart had 32 stores and $10.8 million in sales. In October 1969 Wal-Mart became incorporated.

In 1976, sales reported $678.4 million for 195 stores. There were now 10,000 associates employed and stock split for a second time resulting in shares trading at $23 each on the New York Stock Exchange.

Wal-Mart opened its first store in Republic in 1987. Over the next 24 years in the year 2000, Wal-Mart had continued to grow stronger. Even with the loss of Sam Walton in April 1992 and Bud Walton in March 1995 Wal-Mart would close out the century with more than 4,100 stores worldwide including 1,079 internationally. At that time over 1.2 million associates were working worldwide.

In 2002, Wal-Mart opened a brand new supercenter in Republic, MO. The store employs 200+ associates now in 2007 and has enjoyed continued growth in customer base and in sales. They have very strong ties to the community and give away thousands in grant money each year to various organization. They are also corporate sponsors of Children's Miracle Network and are involved in projects around the community. They appreciate the community for allowing them to grow and prosper.

*The Wal-Mart Pledge*

*Wal-Mart in 1987*

*Wal-Mart in 2007*

# Peggy King

Peggy King has very diverse business interests. In 1984 she opened Peggy King Advertising at 267 US Highway 60 West in a new shopping center located in the southwest part of the city. Her slogan has become "We can put your logo on just about anything."

She does both embroidered and screen printed products such as caps, pens, calendars, T-shirts, and many more featured items in her business. The showroom is filled with products to promote business, school, church, or organizations. She can also design promotional business items for giveaways. Peggy does her very best to find just the right item for you. If it isn't available in her shop she will work to locate the item for you.

In 1992 she chose an old rock building close to Main Street at 127 South Walnut to open her Southwest Antiques business. This building in earlier times previously housed the Johnson's Feed Mill, and Johnson's New and Used Furniture.

Since 1984 Peggy is proud to have been a member of the Republic Chamber of Commerce, and is actively involved in community activities.

In 2005 she was honored by receiving the Chamber's Business of the Year Award.

# Organizations

## Order of the Eastern Star

Republic Chapter #370 Order of the Eastern Star was constituted in October 1914. It became a part of the largest fraternal organization in the world to which men and women may belong. Presently the order has membership throughout the USA, Canada, and 18 other countries. It is a social, charitable and fraternal organization. At this time Missouri has over 30,000 members and is divided into 50 regional districts. Membership in OES is open to women 18 years of age and older with specific Masonic relationships as well as Master Masons in good standing in their lodges. The organization is based on the lives of five biblical women: Adah, Ruth, Esther, Martha and Electa, whose lives reflected fidelity, loyalty, faith, constancy and love. The order is not a religion, even though it is religious in character. The members come from all religious denominations.

The local chapter is involved each year with the special community activities of Kiwanis Fall Festival, Pumpkin Daze, and Relay for Life. They also sponsor the Rainbow Assembly for Girls #84.

Those ladies serving the highest office of Worthy Matron from the time of its founding until present are:

| | | |
|---|---|---|
| 1914 Sadie Prater | 1945 Eula Arrington | 1976 Kay Inmon |
| 1915 Annie Howard | 1946 Grace Land | 1977 Carole Wiechert |
| 1916 Gail Pennoyer/Lydia Owen | 1947 Mattie Hock | 1978 Lou Compton |
| 1917 Martha Youngblood | 1948 Lucille Garbee | 1979 Mary Chambers |
| 1918 Grace Cantrell | 1949 Helen Jones | 1980 Sandy Maness |
| 1919 Ethel Cox O'Bryant | 1950 Helen Jackson | 1981 Nell Green |
| 1920 Georgia Woodfill | 1951 Hazel Dillon | 1982 Virginia Fanning |
| 1921 Amanda Britain Cox | 1952 Regina Maness | 1983 Penny Lake |
| 1922 Lola Brown | 1953 Carolyn O'Neal | 1984 Paula Howell |
| 1923 Alice Barron | 1954 Katherine Garoutte | 1985 Janet Thompson |
| 1924 Mary Beal | 1955 Irene Manning | 1986 Cindy Shipley |
| 1925 Frances O'Bryant | 1956 Ethel Bennett | 1987 Gladys McHatton |
| 1926 Tresa O'Dell | 1957 Carol Coggin | 1988 Lois Whitworth |
| 1927 Sallie French | 1958 Edith Breshears | 1989 Geraldine Foster |
| 1928 Ethel Blades | 1959 Dorothy J. Clark | 1990 Paula Farr |
| 1929 Carrie O'Bryant | 1960 Angie Sanders | 1991 Beverly Zieres |
| 1930 Minnie O'Neal | 1961 Virgie Logan | 1992 Lee Kromas |
| 1931 Lazeta Randolph | 1962 Tressye Buxton | 1993 Joy Smith |
| 1932 Pearl Bain | 1963 Irene Biglieni | 1994 Paula Howell |
| 1933 Ada Peebles | 1964 Juanita McConnell | 1995 Jennell Fredrick |
| 1934 Maxine Bain | 1965 Dorothy Owen | 1996 Rosemary Comisky |
| 1935 Muriel Ottendorf | 1966 Sue Duvall | 1997 Linda Humes |
| 1936 Ruth Brim | 1967 Marilyn Sanders | 1998 Sheral Kay Steere |
| 1937 Helen Britain | 1968 Sheral Kay Steere | 1999 Sheral Kay Steere |
| 1938 Celia Ann Williams | 1969 Genevieve McNabb | 2000 Shelley Wears |
| 1939 Amy Trautwein | 1970 Rose Krause | 2001 Ellen Shook |
| 1940 Jennie Pierce | 1971 Vanlora Boston | 2002 Ellen Shook |
| 1941 Grace Land | 1972 Evelyn Perkins | 2003 Paula Howell |
| 1942 Nettie Huckins | 1973 Donna Freeman | 2004 Amy Phillips |
| 1943 Velma Howard | 1974 Florence Armstrong | 2005 Sheral Kay Steere |
| 1944 Margaret Winter | 1975 Paula Harris | 2006 Tammy Weston |

# The Kiwanis Club

The Kiwanis Club of Republic was founded June 25, 1959, and held their Charter Night Dinner on August 6, 1959 at Dent's Dinner House located just west of Springfield on Hwy. 60. The initial Kiwanis Club of Republic, Missouri consisted of these 35 original members:

| Name | Occupation At The Time |
|---|---|
| Fay Bacon Jr. | Tire Service |
| V.W. Baldwin | Retail Venetian Blinds |
| Max Brashers | Refrigeration Service |
| Ralph Beaver | Automobile Sales Manager |
| Joe Blades | Dairy Farmer |
| Harold Breakbill | Radio and T.V. Sales |
| William Cantrell | Funeral Director |
| Frank Claiborne | Pastor of First Baptist Church |
| William Cundiff | Pastor of Hood Methodist Church |
| Vernon M. Davis | Real Estate Sales |
| Don Dodson | Assembly of God Print Shop |
| Paul Epps | Automobile Sales |
| Ray A. Francis | Lumber Company Book keeper |
| Jack French | Automobile Sales |
| Leonard Fugitt | Livestock Dealer |
| Sheral Garoutte | Locker Plant |
| Floyd Harris | Automobile Sales Manager |
| Perry Jones | Accountant |
| Stanley Land | Pastor of Christian Church |
| Lynn Martin | Insurance Agent |
| Ray Mathews | Grocery Store |
| George McCroskey | Furniture Sales |
| Amos McMurtrey | Republic Public Schools |
| Ross R. McPhail | Veterinarian |
| John Nelson | Service Manager |
| Leo Owen | City Marshal |
| Oral R. Owens | Book Binding |
| Carl Plummer | Dry Goods Store |
| Arthur Rolufs | Frisco Railway |
| Donald L. Scholler | Public Utilities Manager |
| Henry Sifferman | Oil and Gas Sales |
| Elton Ray Todd | Lumber Company Manager |
| Jack Trogdon | Department Store Credit Manager |
| John L. Wagner | Communications Manager for Southwestern Bell |
| Warren D. Wilson | Corrections Officer |

Kiwanis International is a world-wide service organization, dedicated to community service with an emphasis on youth.

The Kiwanis Club sponsors many projects in the community, probably best known for the Fall Festival which was started in 1960 and is still held annually. The Fall Festival is the Kiwanis Club's biggest project and also provides a venue for other local organizations to raise money for their projects with game and food booths. The Festival consists of three nights, Thursday through Saturday, spotlighting local talent and entertainment, family oriented games including bingo, and carnival rides for all ages. The festivities conclude with the crowning of the Fall Festival Queen.

In 1960 Kiwanis built the baseball field on what is now Garoutte Park. The next year they added lights as one of their projects. They also started the Republic Horse Show in 1963 which was successful for several years.

The Kiwanis Little League Baseball program was started in 1967 with 17 teams and 221 boys participating. It is interesting to note that the start-up initial cost for balls, bats and T-shirts was a whopping $325.85. Many boys growing up in Republic, Billings, Clever and Galena participated in this program and have many fond memories of "Kiwanis Baseball." The program outgrew the Kiwanis Club and was eventually turned over to the Republic Park Board.

The Kiwanis Club also publishes the Republic Area Telephone Directory which includes Republic, Billings, and Clever and is available to all residents. The Republic Car Show is the most recent project co-sponsored with the Republic Downtown Merchants Association and proves to be a success with over 100 current and vintage automobiles on display.

Throughout the years the Kiwanis Club of Republic has sponsored many chili suppers, pancake days, and other various events with the same goal in mind, to give back to their community. The Don Dodson Memorial Scholarship is awarded to a college-bound Republic High School senior, in the amount of $500, and is based on community service as well as academic grades. It is also matched by a Federal Grant. Additional donations are made to the Children's Miracle Network and Kiwanis International, but the majority of contributions are donated to local organizations to benefit the Republic area.

*Original Officers and Directors at the Kiwanis Club of Republic*
Taken at "Charter Night" held August 6, 1959 at Dent's Dinner House. Front, l-r: Joe Blades (director), Frank Claiborne (president), Oral Owens (secretary), Amos McMurtrey (treasurer), Elton Ray Todd (director) and Ross McPhail (director). Second Row l-r: John Wagner (director), Don Scholler (director), Bill Cantrell (director), Jack French (director) and Jack Trogdon (vice president).

*Current members of the Kiwanis Club*
Front Row l-r: George Minier, Tom Cobb (Lt. Gov. Division 13), Robert Nelson (secretary-treasurer), Rex Pittman (vice president), Jim Burks (president), Ron Melton (president-elect), Edward Walters and Gary Griffin; 2nd row, l-r: Kevin Ledford, Richard Williams, Ivan Stewart, Dale Meadors, Peggy King, Jim Collins, Eual Moore, Jim Osburn, Jeff Goodnight, and Hal Williams. Members not present include Tom Castor, Al Cummins, Tim Hamilton, Malcolm Oliver, Chad Pinson, George Reass and Ray Thompson.

# Republic Historical Society

A group of interested citizens met at the Republic City Hall and later at the conference room of the Republic Branch Library in January of 1997 to form a Republic Historical Society. These meetings were led by temporary chairman, Mark McConnell. This group met several times to write a charter and bylaws to be submitted at the first organizational meeting.

At the February 18, 1997 organizational meeting held at the Republic High School the following officers were elected. President Darrell Barr, 1st Vice President Kathy Kelly, 2nd Vice President Tony Stephenson, Recording Secretary Betty Mason, Corresponding Secretary Mark McConnell, Treasurer Paula Howell, Director (3 year term) Bill O'Neal, Director (2 year term) Alice McGilvery, and Director (1 year term) Herb Coggin. Standing committees chairmen were also appointed. Historian Patsy Trogdon, Librarian Mark Anderson, Membership Jane Boatright, Community Picnic Dana Cain, Program Tony Stephenson, Audio Video Taping Paula Howell, and Logo Design Mark Anderson. The group voted to meet the first Tuesday of each month at 6:30 in the evening. Dues were set at $10 per year.

Members have tried various means of fund raising for the group to remain in existence. For several years they did large chicken barbecues cooked by Bill O'Neal and his crew. The first year it was held in conjunction with the Founder's Day Celebration on Saturday July 26, 1997. Dana Cain secured the Senior Center Building on Hines Street where exhibits were both inside the building and on the outside grounds of the Kiwanis Park.

Now the group sponsors two money making events, the Spring Garden Tour and the Christmas House Tour.

The group continued to meet at the high school until December 1997 when the Masonic Lodge allowed the use of the downstairs of their building at Main and Grant. Once in that location, items were collected from the community, both donated and on loan to form a museum in connection with the society. The museum is open on Saturdays, or by request from the public. This is made possible by the generous donation of time from the membership.

One project the group enjoyed doing was the display in the Frisco Building during the Ozark Empire Fair in Springfield. This was done until the building was destroyed by an explosion.

When the group first started participating in the Kiwanis Fall Festival there were games and raffle tickets available. Now the booth is set up to be more informational.

The museum acts as host to the growers who come to the area to show off their pumpkins during Pumpkin Daze. The growers come with the hope of getting their name in *The Guinness Book of World Records* by having the largest pumpkin ever grown.

Clarice Lawrence and Mary Sue Robertson have been very good about writing articles for *The Republic Monitor* to keep the community aware of what the society has been doing and to share stories, memories, and events of the past.

The latest service project is the writing of this book. It is the desire of the society membership to try to record some of the history for future generation. It is hoped with the help that has come from the community that this book accomplishes that goal.

*Standing from left: Marty and Dean Bruton, Rosemary Comisky, Buell Mason, Mary Sue and Bill Robertson, Jack Trogdon, Carolyn Meadors, Alan Comisky, Patsy Trogdon, Tom Davidson, Lorene Davidson, and Betty Mason. Sitting: Helen Blades, Mae Belle Fuhr, and Carolyn and Bill O'Neal.*

*Republic Historical Society Garden Tour*

*Display at the Frisco Building during the Ozark Empire Fair.*

*Christmas Home Tour*

# Republic Masonic Lodge

Masons (also known as Freemasons) are the oldest and largest fraternal organization in the world. Today there are more than two million Freemasons in North America.

The actual origins of Freemasonry have been lost in time. Most scholars believe Masonry arose from the guilds of stonemasons who built majestic cathedrals in the Middle Ages.

Beyond its focus on individual development and growth to become better citizens, Masonry is deeply involved in helping people. Presently, two major state projects are the Foundation for Prevention of Substance Abuse, and three Scholarship Funds: the Ruth Lutes Backmann for nurses or schoolteachers, Merit Scholarship for any student at an accredited school, and one for Masonic youth members at an accredited school.

A man of 18 years or older may join the Masonic order if he expresses a desire to join. He may fill out a petition and present it to the lodge he wishes to join along with the fee for joining. He will be investigated by members of the lodge for approval. After he completes the three degrees, he may then join other Masonic organizations, if he so desires. Among them are the York Rite, Scottish Rite, and Nobles of the Mystic Shrine (Shriners). These organizations all have a special charity they support to aid the community in which they reside. Having a local working Masonic Lodge benefits all.

"Lodge" is where a group of Masons meet together, as well as the room or building in which they meet. In the lodge room, Masons share a variety of programs and here the bonds of friendship and fellowship are formed and strengthened.

The first Masonic Lodge was established in the US on November 14, 1807 in Pennsylvania. Missouri's Grand Lodge was established on April 21, 1821.

Republic Masonic Lodge #570 Ancient, Free, and Accepted Masons was chartered September 28, 1905. F.G. Prater was the first Worshipful Master. Their meeting place was above what is now known as the Owen and Short Hardware, until the present location at the southeast corner of Grant and Main was purchased. John House owned the lot in 1882 after buying it from John Sallee for $150. John House used the location for a blacksmith shop. Eli Britain purchased the land in 1905 and built the present building. He and his son operated a general store in the building until 1911 when it was sold to Republic State Bank. The bank remodeled the building, moving the stairway to the east and installed a vault. Members of the Masonic Lodge #570 AM & FM bought the building from the bank in 1930. The US Post Office moved into the ground floor on the north side and occupied the space for 31 years. After the post office vacated, a dairy supply store was located there. City Hall occupied the space beginning 1963 to 1979. The ground floor on the south side housed the Frank "Tooter" Young Barber Shop in 1930, later to become Frank Bennett's Barber Shop. Then Roy Wilson, Curtis Packard, Lynn Martin and Ben Mooneyham had insurance offices there. Stocker Propane occupied the space in 1971.

Before the Masons took over the second floor in 1930, it had been a cigar factory operated by brothers, Bent and Vern "Jocko" Britain. Bob Best had also operated a skating rink there. The Masons, Eastern Star, and Rainbow Girls continue to meet on the second floor. The Knights of Pythins are also using the meeting room. Because of the Mason's generosity and commitment to the community, the Republic Historical Society has a museum on the ground floor at the present time.

Before the 100th anniversary was celebrated in 2005, the outside of the building was refurbished. One of the special features celebrating the 100-year event was a postal cancellation in honor and recognition of the event. Sandy Maness designed the stamp and gained permission for the cancellation. There were also special Fenton Glass Masonic items for sale. Many members of the Grand Lodge and local members were present for a program and refreshments.

*1905 Building*

*#570 Ancient, Free, and Accepted Masons-2007*

# Tributes

## Dale Boatright

When Dale Boatright was very young he learned that you should always pay cash for your toys and borrow for your business. It did not take him long to realize that his father was a very wise man in the things he taught him. No matter what kind of work that was being done he was told to do the best he could and then do a little more. Dale's first real job was driving a team of horses from the hayfield when he was only seven; no job was too big. In 1954 and 1955 he drove a dump truck for Bridges and Company on the weekends while still in high school. After graduating from high school in 1955 he tried working at McCleary's in Chicago, IL and Caterpillar in Peoria, IL, but knew right away that this kind of work was not for him. When he returned home in 1957, he returned to work at Bridges and Company. He married Jane Carolyn (Owen) in 1958. A big year was 1959 as their first son Douglas Jay was born, and they purchased Boatright's Truck Stop located at Main and Hwy. 174. The truckstop was alright but not something he wanted to make his life's work. Dale's older brother Gene drove an 18-wheeler leased to Frozen Food Express out of Dallas, TX. After listening to his stories about all the places he had been and the different things he had seen, Dale thought maybe this could be a new adventure on the open road. He packed his clothes in two brown paper bags and a cardboard box, and headed out in his old Dodge pickup truck, which had big holes in the floor, and drove to Texas. The plan was to only drive until Doug started school. Then their second son, Aaron Todd, was born in 1967, and their daughter Beverly in 1970. He kept telling himself next year he would stop driving, next year, next year. This lasted until Doug graduated from college. He regrets that he missed a lot of his family events in those 20 years of driving. In 1982 he built Boatright Trucking and Repair Shop. He still had seven trucks leased to Frozen Food Express in Texas, six to Stoops Express in Indiana, and six to Consolidated Freight Inc. in Joplin, MO. In 1985 federal deregulation came into play. Dale thought this was the time to pull out of Stoops and CFI and get his own authority with permits for 48 states including Canada. Boatright Trucking then grew to 59 trucks on the road. It did not take long to realize that more trucks were needed so he started the owner-operator program. This worked well so the next step was to offer a lease-purchase program. These programs are still a part of the operation. Occasionally he takes to the road just to keep the feeling, the way the American cowboy must have felt many years ago. In 1991 Queen City Air Freight was started in Springfield. Dale likes new challenges and feels when opportunity comes along he wants to take the leap. The air freight took off so well in 1998 that he found it necessary to build the first freight terminal in Joplin. He was so glad he had two sons that could run each terminal. Next "9-11" had to be faced and remained a big shock for a year or so. Time changes and so do opportunities. Dale tried real estate and built his first subdivision in 1998. The year of 1998 held many great things, not only a new Joplin terminal but a new office for Boatright Trucking Inc. and a second subdivision. Then along came a once in a lifetime dream of playing golf on his own golf course. It was too good to be true. Island Green Golf Club and a subdivision south of Republic, on P Hwy opened in 2000. A reality that good hard work his dad taught him is the greatest feeling of accomplishment one can have. Island Green has hosted the Missouri State Boys and Girls Golf Championships and has seen many good golfers use the course. That gives him great pleasure to see so many have picked up the game. He learned you can tell a lot about a person while playing a round of golf with them.

He enjoys all the times he rides motorcycles with his sons and friends. He rides horses with his two brothers and friends and camps in the mountains. At one time he owned an airplane, but that is altogether a different story. Dale thinks you should live everyday as full as you can but remember to always put family first and never forget your livelihood. He never thought he was too good to load and unload his own truck, wash out the trailer or change tires; these things are money in the bank. He tries to live by the rule never to ask someone to do something that he would not do himself.

*Dale on his horse in the mountains of Mexico.*

*Aerial view of the Island Green Golf Course.*

*Island Green Golf Course club house across the lake.*

# Lester E. Cox

Lester Edmund Cox, the only son of Amanda Belle Britain Cox and James Mitchell Cox, was born in Republic, Missouri, August 22, 1896. His older sister, Ethel Mae Cox, married Clarence O'Bryant and lived in Republic with their two children. Later she married Charles Ghan. The Britain family had migrated to Republic, as did many other settlers prior to 1840, from McMinn County, Tennessee. A description of the Britain family can be found in an earlier edition of a Republic History. John Britain, great-grandfather of Lester, and his wife died leaving five young boys in Greene County. They became wards of the court, "Bond Boys," and were apprentices until age 21. Legal papers for these boys are found in the Greene County Courthouse. George Washington Britain, grandfather of Lester E. Cox, was named for the American hero. He had 1,400 acres in Pond Creek Township, and left much of it to his children. It was said he heard the battle of Wilson's Creek from his farm home. James M. Cox, of a farm family from Kentucky settled in Turon, Kansas, and later in Missouri. The home where Lester was born remains today on Main Street in Republic.

By the age of 12, Lester was working and buying his own clothes. One of the variety of jobs he held included school janitor. He played cornet in the Republic band instilling in him a love of music. He played first base on the Republic ball team. He earned the money for his tuition to Drury College and left Drury to work for the Langenberg Mill in Republic. As an enlistee in World War I, he became a pilot and lieutenant in the first Army Air Corps. An earlier chance meeting with Mildred Belle Lee, daughter of Springfield's former mayor, Robert E. Lee, led to their marriage on August 9, 1918. After returning to Springfield, the couple had three children: Virginia Belle married Lynn Bussey, Lester Lee married Claudine Barrett, and Cathryn Lee married Jack E. Lipscomb. A printed biography of Lester E. Cox is available at the Springfield Greene County Library. The author John K. Hulston, historian and family friend, compiled the book based on the many facets of Cox's life. A motto of Lester E. Cox was "find a need and fill it." For the ensuing years, until his death in 1968, at the age of 73, his life was filled with civic endeavors, business ventures, and a sincere desire to give others an opportunity. Of significance in the life of Lester E. Cox is the fact that at one time he ran 23 businesses. Some of these included Ozark Motor and Supply Company, Modern Tractor and Supply Company in Springfield, Cox-Davis Dairy Farm in Republic, a controlling interest in radio station KWTO, interest in stations KCMO, KOAM, and other directorships including Frisco Railway, Ozark Air Lines and Union National Bank. He was active in the Boy Scouts of America. He organized and became manager of the famed Boy Scout Band. He was a childhood member of Hood Methodist Church in Republic and later in life the St. Paul Methodist Church in Springfield. He was a guiding force for the Springfield Chamber of Commerce working toward the development of the airport and fair board, as well as spearheading Missouri's development potential. His interest in Wilson's Creek National Battlefield led him to secure state funds for the advancement of the park. His most notable legacy lives on by having the Lester E. Cox Medical Center, known now as Cox Medical Centers, reflecting his genuine interest in the health of the region.

The grandchildren include: Lester B. Cox. Linda (Bussey) Willard, Lewis E. Bussey, Cynthia (Lipscomb) Bayer, Lawrence "Larry" W. Lipscomb. His nine great-grandchildren are Amanda B. Cox, Lester E. Cox, Cathryn Lynn Willard, Colin Macway Bussey, Lauren Daniel Tew, Lanna Daniel Britt, Stephanie Amanda Lipscomb, Stuart Lipscomb and Andrew Lipscomb. The family of Lester E. Cox continues to perpetuate the many opportunities opened up by the extraordinary life of Lester E. Cox, including Chesterfield Village in Springfield, and Frisco Square in Republic.

*Lester E. Cox*

*James Mitchell Cox home. Pictured are: James Mitchell, Amanda, Ethel, unknown, Lester E., and unknown.*

*The home of James Mitchell Cox on Main Street. Pictured from left: Lester E., Ethel, James Mitchell, and Amanda Belle.*

# Howard Lee Eagan

Few men have had more involvement in Republic's history than Howard Lee "Wormey" Eagan. He had a financial interest in four businesses on Main Street before 1972. He developed Republic's first major housing subdivision in the mid-50s, which was quickly nicknamed "Wormeyville." Howard has also been active in local church activities as well as city and school politics.

His business career started shortly after graduating from Republic High School in 1939. He and his mother, the late Edna "Fanny" Eagan, owned Eagan's Market, which was one of five grocery stores on Main Street when the population of Republic was less than one thousand people. Wormey was attending Teacher's College, now Missouri State University, when their store manager died. He quit college to help manage the store. This was interrupted in 1944 when he left to serve his country in World War II. He left his wife of three years, the former Jo Ann Sellers, and their one-year-old son Gary to spend two years in Germany in the Combat Engineer Corps.

Sheral "Gose" Garoutte was hired to help Fannie operate the store. After his return from the war, Wormey and his mother opened a Ben Franklin store next door in 1948. Both businesses were sold by 1957.

In 1955 Howard Lee sensed that Republic was about to start growing and that new houses would be in demand so he began buying available land to develop. The original subdivision, which has been expanded several times, was a 28-acre orchard covered with dead apple trees. During the time of developing "Wormeyville," Howard also built several residential and commercial buildings outside the subdivision.

With partners Floyd Harris and Jack Trogdon, Wormey used his collateral to purchase the Ford franchise from Don Pollard in 1959. The dealership was moved across the street where Eagan Construction Company built a new showroom. The new business was named Harris Ford Sales as Floyd was the managing partner. Jack left the business after a short time. The dealership was sold to Dwight Legan in 1971.

Howard Lee's last connection to Republic business was the old Farmer's State Bank, which is now Commerce Bank. This was the first bank established in Republic since its two banks failed in the early 30s, opening in 1950. Wormey accumulated enough stock in the bank to become a member of the board of directors in the early 60s which led to a keen interest in the banking business,

An opportunity arose in 1966 whereby Wormey purchased controlling interest in the Pleasant Hope Bank at Pleasant Hope, MO. He hired M.A. Buxton, who had been cashier of Farmer's State Bank since its beginning to help him manage his new business. "Buck," as everyone called M.A., and his wife Tressye moved to Pleasant Hope to work in Wormey's bank. Buck retired in 1971 as executive vice president. Howard sold the bank in 1985 and retired.

He and Jo Ann built a new home shortly afterward in Wormeyville, located about 150 yards from the house they had lived in for 32 years. They are currently living there.

Wormey and Jo Ann have both been active members of the First Christian Church on Main Street since before they were married. How-

*Howard Lee "Wormey" Eagan*

ard Lee Eagan was on the church board when the current sanctuary was constructed in the late 40s. He is the only surviving member of the board when the cornerstone was laid in 1950. He now serves as board member, elder and trustee.

Wormey served two terms on the Republic City Council and one term on the school board when he was in the construction business.

Probably the most amazing thing about Howard Eagan has been his balanced lifestyle. He has always taken time for church, family, friends and recreation. Until recently he was an ardent fisherman. For many years Wormey, with his brother-in-law, the late J.W. Fugitt, would quail hunt every day except Sunday during quail season.

Nowadays you'll find him on the golf course with his buddies who have named their group what else but "The Wormey Tour." *Submitted by Terry Fugitt.*

*Wormey shown with Republic Mayor Frank Comisky at a ribbon cutting of the new Empire District Electric building on South Main Street, April 17, 1964. Eagan Construction built several commercial and residential buildings.*

*Wormey is the only surviving member of the First Christian Church board from this photo taken at the dedication of the new sanctuary in 1950. Note the wet mortar around the cornerstone, which had just been set. Pictured on the left side, standing from left: Howard Wakeman, J.W. Fugitt, Howard "Wormey" Eagan, Ellis "Bud" Thurman –Choir Director, Edgar Green, Troy Bedell, C.K. Leonard–Republic School Superintendent, and Boyd Fugitt. Sitting from left: E.D. McTaggert, Russell Lynch, Leonard Fugitt–Chairman of the Board and Chairman of the Building Committee, and Linzee Wells–Church Treasurer. Right side standing from left: Pastor A.T. Mahaney, J.E. King, unknown, Rev. George Myers, Clyde Davis, Wallace Ferguson, E.B. Ferguson, and Rev. Paul Downs–Immediate Past Minister. Seated is Arthur Larson.*

# History of Fugitt Farms

This is a history of 2,700 acres of land lying south and east of Republic from 1938 to the present. The tract stretches from Miller Road south 2.75 miles. From its western boundary along Terrell Creek it runs 3.75 miles east to Wilson Creek. All 2,700 acres were used for agricultural purposes by the Fugitt family until Terry Fugitt completely liquidated the business in 1990 for health reasons. The land acquisitions began in 1938 because J.W. Fugitt, Leonard's son, was planning to get married and as Leonard would say, "Son needed a place to get started."

Three generations of Fugitts were involved in the purchases of land and management of the farming and livestock operation. Leonard Fugitt, 1895-1967, negotiated every land deal and most of the livestock deals until his death. He owned Robertson Livestock Commission Co. at Union Stockyards in Springfield for 30 years before selling out in 1958. For several years before leaving, he led the six commission firms at the yards in cattle receipts. Leonard had a passion for buying run down farms and "cleaning them up." J.W. Fugitt, 1916-1983 was an excellent manager. He ran the farms in a sensible way, always trying to pay for them before his dad would buy another one. For instance, if a house wasn't needed on a purchased farm, they would quickly sell it off with a few acres to cheapen down the price of the land. Terry Fugitt, son of J.W., 1942-present, assumed the roll of his father in 1964 after graduating from college, of paying for the remaining farms his grandfather bought. After Leonard's death, J.W. indicated to Terry he was "burned out" and would like to sell out. In 1971 Terry made a deal with his father whereby he bought all his personal property, over half his land and assumed complete control of the business. J.W. retired and died 12 years later.

For the first 20 years the farm was primarily a dairy operation. Five full time employees lived on the farm. In 1958 the dairy operation was closed out and the farm was used for beef cattle. Steer backgrounding; buying a thin 500 pound steer, keeping it a year and moving it to a feed lot for finishing, was their preferred cattle enterprise. Because of his superior marketing ability, Leonard always felt it was more profitable than a cow-calf operation. After the dairy operation was dropped, their full time labor force was reduced to two.

*Terry, J.W. and Leonard Fugitt, Easter Sunday, 1964.*

Before the severe drought of the early 50s, which lasted three to four years, there was very little Fescue growing on the hillsides around Republic. Orchard Grass was the favorite forage but the drought killed it all. J.W. Fugitt harvested many acres of Orchard Grass seed. After the drought, about 1955, Fescue was introduced because dry weather wouldn't kill it. Several million pounds of Orchard Grass and Fescue seed have been harvested and sold from these 2,700 acres since 1938.

During the early 60s a situation arose which upset Leonard Fugitt considerably. The state of Missouri decided it wanted to buy what Leonard considered was the best 300-acre tract he had ever bought for a national park. Leonard and J.W. fought it as hard as they could but the state finally used eminent domain and condemned the Wilson Creek bottom farm for purchase. Leonard became very depressed and died the year before the state took it by court action. The state of Missouri donated the land to the U.S. government and it is now the southwest corner of Wilson's Creek National Battlefield. J.W. and Terry made a deal with the U.S. Department of Interior to rent the farm for a small fee and therefore had the use of it until Terry sold out in 1990.

In February 1990 Terry Fugitt sold 100 acres to John Sherron, an investor who sold it to the Henry family in 1996. That tract is now Valley Park Estates in Republic. Later in June 1990 Terry sold the remaining 2300 acres, of which 770 acres were owned by his mother Bette, to Charles Blount. Mr. Blount used it in much the same manner as the Fugitts. Missouri Partners Inc. purchased the property from Blount in 2005 and it has been referred to in the media as "The Terrell Creek Development." Cowherd Construction purchased 205 acres from MPI in 2005 that is now The Lakes of Shuyler Ridge subdivision which contains three lakes and 517 lots.

*Five loads of cattle loaded and ready to leave the farm headed for a feed lot. Approximately 280 head, mid-1970s.*

*Terry Fugitt, at right in light pants and dark jacket, explains his pasture management practices to a crowd of cattle producers at one of the many "field days" he hosted. Livestock and agronomy specialists of the Missouri Extension Service liked to use the Fugitt Farm as a model operation, early in the 1980s.*

*Drilling in red clover seed on a burned-off Fescue pasture in 1980.*

# Fugitt Farms
## 1938 • 1990

Leonard Fugitt 1895 - 1967
J.W. Fugitt 1916 - 1983
Terry Fugitt 1942 - Present
John Fugitt 1977 - Present

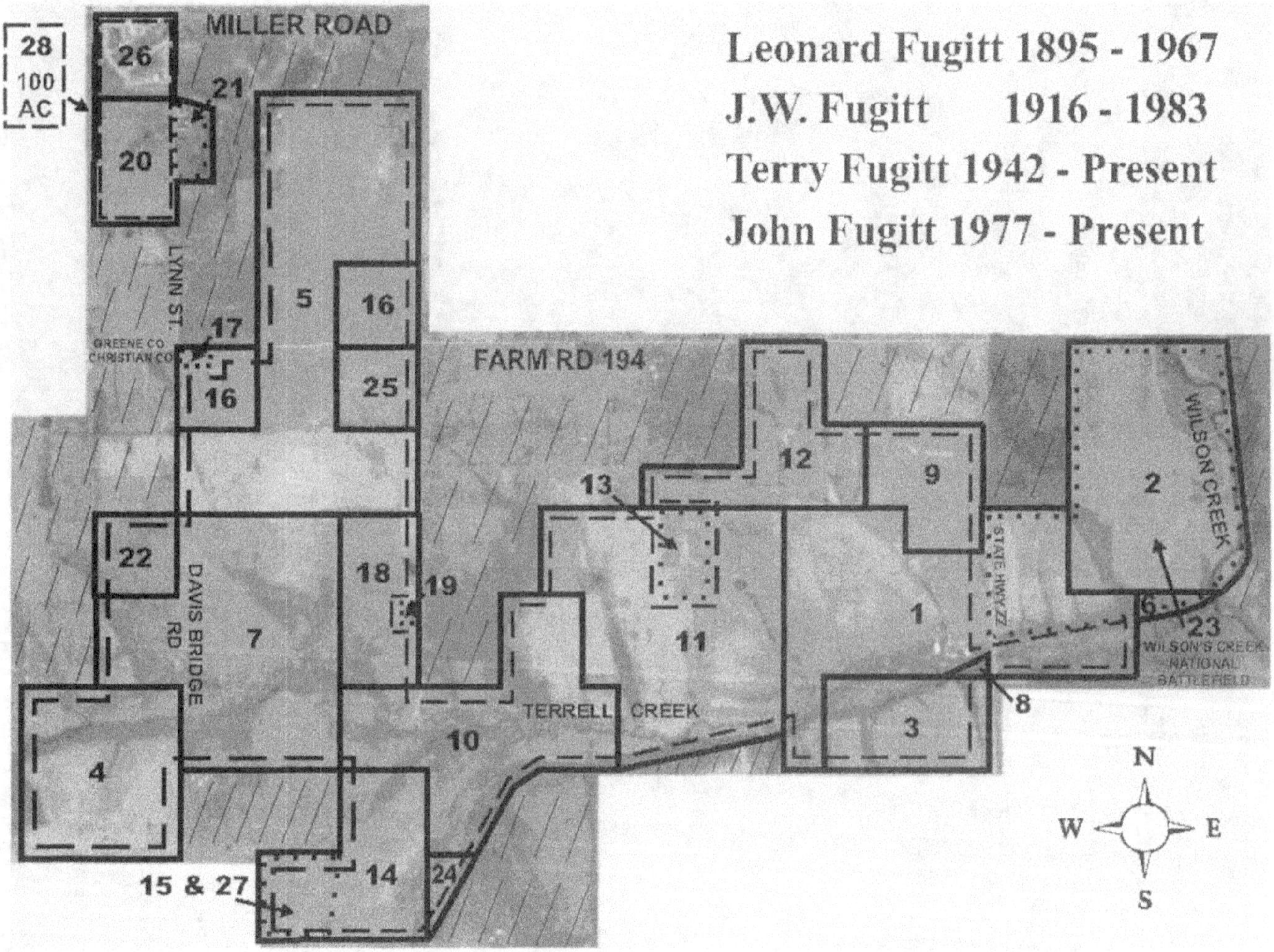

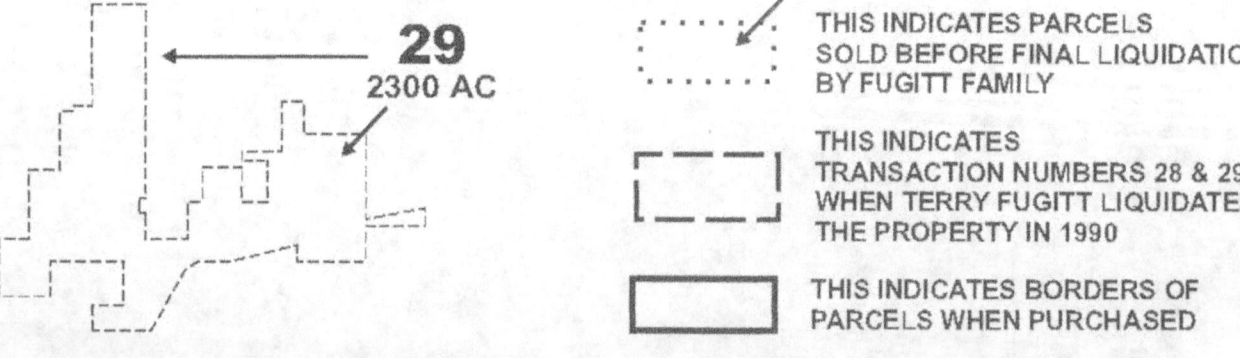

**MAP LEGEND:**

- ·······→ THIS INDICATES PARCELS SOLD BEFORE FINAL LIQUIDATION BY FUGITT FAMILY
- - - - - THIS INDICATES TRANSACTION NUMBERS 28 & 29 WHEN TERRY FUGITT LIQUIDATED THE PROPERTY IN 1990
- ─── THIS INDICATES BORDERS OF PARCELS WHEN PURCHASED

Below is a chronology of the year and size of each transaction involved. Twenty-one different landowners sold land to members of the Fugitt family from 1938 to 1979.
All transactions negotiated by Leonard Fugitt until his death in 1967.

| Map # | Seller | Buyer | Acres Bought | Acres Sold | Year |
|---|---|---|---|---|---|
| 1 | Joe Shipman* | | 320 | | 1938 |
| 2 | Blond Ward | | 240 | | 1942 |
| 3 | Jesse Forbis | | 80 | | 1943 |
| 4 | Andrew Pearce | | 161 | | 1943 |
| 5 | Chester Arthur | | 360 | | 1944 |
| 6 | Gene Hancock | | 20 | | 1946 |
| 7 | Harold Davis | | 280 | | 1946 |
| 8 | Clever School District | | 5 | | 1949 |
| 9 | Almus Thompson | | 80 | | 1953 |
| 10 | Barney Davis | | 225 | | 1956 |
| 11 | Clyde Davis | | 296 | | 1957 |
| 12 | Short Family | | 122 | | 1957 |
| 13 | | Gene McConnell (from 11) | | 20 | 1958 |
| 14 | Hobert Estes | | 120 | | 1961 |
| 15 | | J.D. Fitzpatrick (from 14) | | 33 | 1961 |
| 16 | Charles E. Riley | | 80 | | 1963 |
| 17 | | Everett Davis (from 16) | | 2.5 | 1963 |
| 18 | Calvin Blades | | 80 | | 1964 |
| 19 | | Alvie Bennett (from 18) | | 2 | 1965 |
| 20 | Frank Porter | | 77.5 | | 1966 |
| 21 | | Leroy Wood (from 20) | | 17.5 | 1967 |

*J.W. Fugitt made these deals.*

| Map # | Seller | Buyer | Acres Bought | Acres Sold | Year |
|---|---|---|---|---|---|
| 22 | Charles Talent | | 40 | | 1967 |
| 23 | | State of Missouri (from #1&2) sold under protest | | 320 | 1968 |
| 24 | Joe Nelson | | 10 | | 1969 |

*Terry Fugitt made three purchases and two sales.*

| Map # | Seller | Buyer | Acres Bought | Acres Sold | Year |
|---|---|---|---|---|---|
| 25 | Hazel Maxwell | | 40 | | 1977 |
| 26 | Diana "Corky" McGuire Knupp | | 40 | | 1978 |
| 27 | J.B. Gray (bought back #15) | | 33 | | 1979 |
| 28 | | John Sherron | | 100 | 1990 |
| 29 | | Charles Blount | | 2300 | 1990 |

*End of transactions made by the Fugitt family.*

*This 320 acre farm was owned by Walter Stewart for many years and was always rerferred to by the Fugitts as the "Stewart Place." Joe Shipman was a land speculator who owned the land briefly.

| | | |
|---|---|---|
| John Sherron sold #28 to the Henry family | 100 | 1996 |
| Charles Blount sold #29 to Missouri Partners Inc. | 2300 | 2005 |
| Missouri Partners Inc. sold part of #5 and #16 to Cowherd Construction Co. all in Greene County | 205 | 2005 |

# Gene and Jean (Gregg) Short

The Short family farm originated many years ago when William Franklin Short (July 15, 1851-August 27, 1924) from Tennessee and Nancy Thomas (Perkins) (December 23, 1850-April 15, 1936) from Kentucky, were united in marriage on September 22, 1882, relocating to Republic.

The two of them farmed setting up a wonderful home for generations to come. From this union came seven children: Idelar, Lutishe, Mary Frances, Martha Jane, Nancy Consadie, Alice and Samuel Emmit, who was born February 27, 1898. Samuel met Florence Lucille Howell, daughter of Clarence August and Minnie Annabell Howell from Michigan, Minnie dying in April 1907. On August 23, 1907, Clarence filed with the recorder of deeds the plat of a town to be called Wilson Creek. Clarence and three of his five children were the first family to call Wilson Creek home.

Samuel and Florence were married November 22, 1916, and began their life together on Samuel's home place, where they had three children: Ivan (July 18, 1918-August 15, 1920), Helen (February 10, 1920) and Gene (December 6, 1927-February 1, 2005). Helen and Gene graduated from Republic schools with Helen graduating in 1939, marrying Robert "Bob" Henry Wilkins of Clever in 1941. Bob died in March of 1997. Helen continues to live in their Springfield home.

Gene graduated in 1945, but after his father's sudden death on October 30, 1946, at age 18 he took over the farm. Gene met Betty Jean Gregg, daughter of George Wallace and Floy Gregg of Charity, Missouri, and the two were married in 1950. Gene and Jean always worked outside the home and farm. When Gene's mother Florence moved to Springfield, they purchased the farm, and continued the tradition of farming. They had four children: Greg (born 1953), DyAnna (born 1954), LuDena (born 1957) and Gary (born 1959). This generation raised, milked and showed Registered Holsteins as well as harvesting their own crops and hay. In earlier days such animals as hogs, sheep, chickens, ducks, geese and the loyal border collie were found watching over the farm and family. A joyous and important part of the farm was the garden Gene and Jean grew and harvested with the kids help, and Jean canning the majority of their winter food.

The family farm has seen several aesthetic changes over the years. The home has been enlarged, with a portion of the original homestead remaining. A new garage, hay barn and large pond were added to preserve and enhance the overall beauty of the Short Farm. Gene and Jean instilled the importance of hard work, education and religious roots within their four children. The family and descendents to come, were and are, members of the Republic First Christian Church.

Growing up Greg, DyAnna, LuDena and Gary were involved in such activities as 4-H, FFA, playing sports and showing their award winning Holsteins during the summer. Each of the children graduated from Republic: 1971 (Greg), 1972 (DyAnna), 1975 (LuDena) and 1977 (Gary). Once the children were married, they continued to raise cattle and help with farm operations. The farm received the Century Farm award in 1995. On May 21, 1996, Betty Jean suddenly passed away. Within the year the cows were sold. After that Gene, Greg and Gary started a beef cow and calf operation which continues today.

Gene died on February 1, 2005 following 77 years in a community he loved, leaving the farm on which he was born, raised and operated, raised his children and took great pride in everyday of his life. During his time in Republic he worked at Mid-Am Dairy for 40 years, and later Meadors Funeral Home. Gene also was involved in preserving Republic's history and was an active member of the community, being involved with the first rural fire department in Republic, Republic Kiwanis, First Christian Church, and Lindsey Cemetery where the family plot is located.

The Short lineage continues through the following families:

Greg and wife, Julianne, call Republic home with two daughters, Natalie and Megan. DyAnna and husband Ronald Shaver own a farm in Norwood, MO with their son Sheldon. LuDena and husband Mark Hunt live in Springfield with daughter Ashley. Gary owns the farm next door to the family farm with son, Eric.

Gene and Jean's grandchildren: Natalie graduated from Republic in 2003, Eric in 2004, and Megan in 2005; Ashley graduated from Kickapoo in 2003 and Sheldon in 2007 from Norwood. Eric and Megan are attending Missouri State University; Natalie graduated from MSU in December 2006 and Ashley in May 2007. Natalie will wed Nolan Sunderman from Republic on May 25, 2007. Ashley will wed Joel Gaisford from Ozark on July 7, 2007.

The children and their families continue the family tradition of farming by raising and running the beef cow and calf operation on the Short Farm.

*Jean and Gene Short*

*The Short home.*

*From left: Gene Short, Florence Howell Short, Samuel "Hop" Short, and Helen Short Wilkins.*

*From left: Greg Short, LuDena Short Hunt, Gene Short, DyAnna Short Shaver, and Gary Short.*

*Jean and Gene Short*

*From left: Natalie Short, Megan Short, Gene Short, Eric Short, Sheldon Shaver, and Ashley Hunt.*

# Churches and Cemeteries

## Republic Assembly of God

Republic Assembly's first service was held in an old brick building on Main St. which belonged to Sam Hughes. The first pastor was Seltha Bray of Marionville. She held a four week revival in which 75-100 attended nightly and over 25 were saved. In the early years, Republic Assembly held services in various buildings throughout Republic such as the old Ford Garage, the Carl Plummer building, the Biglieni building, and the rock building across from Hood Methodist. Then on May 3, 1940, the church dedicated its first church home on Pine St. under the leadership of Rev. Kalas. The church continued to see growth and in 1951 it added on a Sunday school annex. In January of 1960, the church decided to buy the property on the corner of Hwy. 60 and West Avenue. The land was purchased from Virgil Baldwin. Fourteen months later a new church would be dedicated to the Lord on March 5, 1961.

During the next 10 years the church continued to see growth in every area. Then on December 14, 1971 tragedy hit the church. The current pastor, Rev. Popejoy, had mentioned the problem of building capacity and how the church needed to "knock out one of the walls." Little did he or the church know on that December day a tornado would rip through Republic and destroy everything. The church found itself with a real problem because it was not covered by insurance. However, the people rallied together and found alternative ways to meet. They held services in the local high school on Sundays and a local Baptist church during the week. The church members would work hard and long to reconstruct a new building. In the midst of these difficult times the church experienced a marvelous spirit of unity and the church continued to grow. On November 5, 1972 the present building was dedicated to the Lord. In 1992 the church built a Family Life Center beside its current facility to house offices, classrooms, a kitchen and a banquet setting. Then in September of 2002 Growing Kids Child Care began operating out of the Family Life Center.

In 2002 the church felt the need to expand their facility once again. Under the leadership of Rev. Rick Cockrell, the church built an addition to the front of the current building which connected the church and the Family Life Center. The new addition is a two-story facility providing additional space for classrooms, offices, and larger foyer. It was dedicated to the Lord on Easter Sunday, 2003.

Republic Assembly now stands as a landmark in the community. They are thankful to all the pastors and members who have sacrificed through the years. They continue to follow their mission today, which is "Helping people connect with God, with their community, and with one another."

*First building on Pine Street and the present location.*

# First Christian Church
## (Disciples of Christ)

Around 1872, the Reverend John Lee organized the First Christian Church of Republic at the home of Clark Smith, two miles northeast of town. Worship continued in the Mount Etna vicinity until 1885, when a frame house of worship was built at the present location at the corner of North Main and Logan Streets in Republic.

In 1936, during the Depression, Clark McNeil was the pastor. A Love Offering was started because many of the church members were farmers and didn't know how much money they would have for their church offering. They now have only a few farmers, but this special offering remains a tradition on the 2nd Sunday of December.

Worship services were held in the building until March 5, 1950, when the corner stone was laid for the present structure. Rev. A.T. Mahanay was pastor at the time. The frame building was moved to the back of the lot for use during the construction of the new sanctuary. Mrs. Tura Coggin later purchased the old structure and moved it to the corner of Walnut and Anderson Streets. It was converted into apartments and remains so today.

A multi-purpose building was dedicated July 12, 1992. This addition also provided handicap accessible restrooms and an enclosed ramp to the sanctuary. This building will seat 150 at tables and chairs. Many fellowship festivities have been enjoyed with this addition. "Parson Bill" Harper was interim minister during the planning and construction of this building.

In the year 2000 at the 50th anniversary of the construction of the stone sanctuary, the corner stone was opened and the contents examined. It contained numerous artifacts, which brought back fond memories of earlier days such as a New Testament, the membership roll, Republic newspapers, a dedication program of the "Little White Church" from 1887, coins from 1950, and other memorabilia. When the time capsule was reset, the original contents and additional items from the year 2000 A.D. were placed back in the cornerstone and will not be opened again for another 50 years. The stone was reset where it remains to this day.

The Christian Women's Fellowship has provided a great variety of service for Christ and to the church family. In the past 25 years they have come to be recognized for their "ready to bake" apple pies. This started as a fund-raiser for outreach projects, the C.W.F. first made 25 pies. In 1998, with the help of many volunteers, 1,500 pies were made. Monies from the pies are used for outreach and church projects.

The Christian Church (Disciples of Christ) of Republic has been served by over 40 ministers including numerous evangelists and revivalists. Today the church is known as "a loving church growing in the heart of Republic."

Rev. Dr. Thomas D. Minton currently serves the church as pastor.

*Condensed from church records and previous histories on file in the church office.

*First Christian Church (Disciples Of Christ) Republic, Missouri*

*First Christian Church after 1992 addition.*

*First Christian Church prior to the multi-purpose addition.*

# Westside Christian Church

Independent New Testament Churches recognize the fellowship of other congregations throughout the world with a large membership represented who are known as Christian Churches.

They are independent of all ecclesiastical control from any organization, whether local, state or national.

They are under the rule of Christ and totally dependent on Him. They simply want to be Christians, offering the unity of all believers in Christ.

It is their desire to follow the Bible in all matters of faith, worship and practice. They believe in the Divine inspiration of the Scriptures, and therefore accept as true the Virgin Birth of Christ, His miracles, the resurrection, the second coming, etc. Christ's prayer was that all be one according to the Word: God's purpose for the church is to be united through the Word; their message is to offer this plan for Christian Unity.

Westside Christian Church started with a group of people meeting in the home of Fred Vander in April of 1967 to form a new church. Minister Don Gee, from Parkview Christian Church in Springfield, Bill Vernon from Kingsway Christian Church in Mount Vernon along with elders and deacons from these two churches served as advisors. This first worship service was held on Tuesday night with Don Gee conducting the service. After the service the group chose the name of Calvary Christian Church as a tentative name, and the first publicly announced service was scheduled for April 30, 1967 to be held at the Republic Community Center with Don Gee bringing the message. At the close of this service a unanimous vote was made to call Dr. M.E. Frank as their minister.

Parkview Christian Church was used for the first baptisms.

Property located at 537 West Elm was purchased on May 28, 1967 and at this time the name was changed to Westside Christian Church. Ground breaking ceremony was held on Nov. 18, 1967, and the first service was held at this location on September 8, 1968.

**Ministers who have served:**
Dr. M.E. Frank
Dwayne Witt
Stanley White
Mike Helms
John Raymond
John Oliver
Bill Raymond
Tim Carr
Carey Davidson
Jim Haenig

**Our Aim:**
No Book – But the Bible
No Creed – But Christ
No Plea – But the Gospel
In Matters of Faith – Unity
In Opinions – Liberty
In All Things – Love

**Charter members:**
Mrs. Karen Adams, Mr. and Mrs. Jerry Aton, Miss Phyllis Blanchard, Mr. and Mrs. Alvin Brown, Mr. and Mrs. Jim Boston, Mr. and Mrs. Russell Campbell, Linda, and Mike, Mrs. Karen Denny, Dr. and Mrs. M.E. Frank, Richard Alan Garton, Mr. and Mrs. Jerry Graves, Mrs. Mary Jane Hartman, Mr. and Mrs. Waldon Hoffman, Donna Faye Johnston, Mr. and Mrs. David Logan, Mr. and Mrs. Ira Latshaw, Mr. and Mrs. Harry Lee McConnell, Darrell, and Larry, Mr. and Mrs. Gary McConnell, Mr. and Mrs. Lester Pranger and Norene, Mr. and Mrs. Carl Plummer, Mrs. Patsy Ann Pyeatt, Marla and Jill, Mrs. Vera Robertson, Mr. and Mrs. Donnie Rodgers, Mr. and Mrs. David Russell, Robert Skelton and Mollie, Mrs. Mayme Stewart, Mrs. Dixie Stewart and Charles, Mr. and Mrs. Gene Shrum, Mrs. Bessie Swinney, Deann Thomas, Mr. and Mrs. Fred Vander, Terry and Freddie.

"A Growing Church for a Growing Community."

# Hope Lutheran Church

In 1983, a small group of Lutherans gathered for the first time around God's Word and Sacraments in a small house on Highway 60. Pastor Marvin Lilie presided over the service for the small congregation, whose members adopted the name "Hope Lutheran Church." The church soon outgrew its small meeting place, and the congregation arranged for a pre-fabricated building to be moved to a new site, on the south side of Highway 174. About 110 members belonged to Hope Lutheran when it held its first service in the new building on October 7, 1984.

In 1985, the congregation called Pastor Dale Bond, as God blessed the church with yet another phase of expansion. In January 1992, Hope moved into its current 200-seat sanctuary on an adjacent piece of land along Highway 174. At this time more than 200 baptized members belonged to the church.

A year later, members completed work on a basement kitchen and classroom area, which would eventually become home to the Hope Lutheran Child Care Center. The center continues to offer Christian care and education to children in pre-school and after-school programs. The facility is also serving the community as an emergency storm shelter.

During its history, Hope has been served by five resident pastors: Rev. Marvin Lilie, Rev. Dale Bond, Rev. Andrew Etzler, Rev. Dirk Reek, and Rev. Brian Whittle.

*Hope Lutheran Church, first, second and modern meeting places.*

# Battlefield United Methodist Church

Battlefield United Methodist Church is older than the town with which the church shares its name. The congregation was formed in the late 1800s during the days when preachers rode circuits through the countryside stopping to conduct services at local churches. The congregation was later named for the nearby Civil War site, Wilson's Creek Battlefield.

The plain, white-framed building was constructed on an acre of land which was donated to the church by J.T. Phillips in 1905. The lot was deeded to the church trustees, William Sheldon, T.B. Keltner, and C.T. Perkins, for as long as the property was used for church purposes.

The actual building of the Battlefield Methodist Episcopal Church began on November 1, 1905. Accounts kept during that period listed a load of lumber, a load of bricks, and a load of sand for $1.25 each. On June 17, 1906 a "rig" was hired to bring Dr. J.W. Stewart to the church for dedication services and a church dinner. Prior to this time pastor J.F. King and 66 members held services at the Green Ridge Schoolhouse.

A few years after the church building opened it was relocated to land provided by L. Stewart near present-day FF Highway and Third Street. The church remains on this land today.

For more than a decade the church sheltered an active congregation; however, in the 1920s the young people began to move away from the village of Battlefield, and the Great Depression of the 1930s took its toll on the congregation's membership as people continued to move away from the area.

By 1943 the situation for the church seemed to be improving, and Pastor Frank R. Nelson noted that interest in Battlefield Methodist Episcopal Church seemed to be increasing. By 1947 there were 32 active members. Later the church purchased and installed a stove for the church so that activities could continue at the church during the winter.

In 1951 there was a "church homecoming." Sixty-five people attended the event along with Pastor Dorothy Burmingham. By the late 1950s and the early 1960s attendance was so small that the congregation was put in the Republic, MO charge.

In July 1970 a committee of members remaining at the church voted to send its remaining membership to Hood United Methodist Church. The doors of Battlefield UMC were closed. During this time the church building was leased to the First Baptist Church of Battlefield while that congregation built its own church.

On June 1, 1975 a small, dedicated group of people including Faye Spindler, Alan Schmidt, Mike Clawson, Art Evans and Dale Snider formed what is now known as Battlefield United Methodist Church. Student Pastor Alan Schmidt was the first pastor of the newly reformed church.

The first Sunday for the new congregation was cold, rainy and finally it snowed. Undaunted, the groups huddled by the stove in the one-room building. The room was dull and drab, a musty odor filled the air, but the small group didn't mind; they were there to praise the Lord!

The congregation soon needed more room. The Sunday School grew and was using the City Hall next door. By September 1975, the church had grown so much that the members decided to build an addition. The church raised and borrowed $30,000, and the extension was added. Everyone in the church worked. Everything was carried by hand and laid in place. The addition was completed in 1976.

Alan Schmidt left the church in 1977. He was followed by Rod Kelley in 1978, Dustin Cooper in 1980 and Dr. Ray Drake in 1982. David Sears, Steve Counts, Kirby Holbrook, Jim Bryant, Mary Ann Ray, Treva Hall and Josh Langiller-Hoppe have followed.

In 1979 women's group known as FOCUS - Fellowship of Christians United in Service - formed. This group has been instrumental in raising funds for church improvements such as purchasing a new piano and hosting an annual chili supper.

As Battlefield United Methodist Church marks the 100th anniversary of its opening, its members continue to faithfully serve the Battlefield community.

# Hood United Methodist Church

The history of Hood United Methodist Church began some years prior to 1891 when the present building was erected. The first church was organized by Uncle Lindsey Robertson who was its pastor until his death. There was no one to pastor the church after his death, but a camp meeting was held each year at Robertson Springs to hold the group together.

In 1881 a six week revival was held at the Baptist Church by the Rev. Mr. Darby and Uncle Alex Lawson, during which time more than 100 persons professed the Christian faith. At the close of the revival those who wished to affiliate with the Baptist Church lined up on one side of the room and those who wished to form the Methodist group on the other side. Mary Kitchen was the first to step out for the Methodist side and the Methodist Episcopal group was formed. Rev. Darby served as pastor. Services were first held in the Baptist Church built in 1886 and later in the Congregational Church built in 1880.

When it was proposed that the group build a church, they decided to name it after the largest contributor and that honor fell to W.E. Hood. Others who helped with the building included D.N. Kitchen, E.H. Britain, George Britain and Richard Gamble. D.N. Kitchen and Sons laid the foundation. Bricks for the building were furnished at cost by the Britain brick yard. E.E. Hussey was hired as contractor and B.J. Price was the architect. R.L. Hasket did the brick work and Dr. E.L. Beal laid the cornerstone. The board of trustees included W.W. Lawson, E.H. Britain, Will Coover, Anthony Robertson and W.E. Hood.

The church and the first parsonage were completed in 1892 at a net cost, including lots, of $3,730. Improvements in 1906 brought the value of the property up to $4,000. $1800 was borrowed and another $600 when the building was completed. In November 1897 a debt of $1,450 was paid off amid much rejoicing and the mortgage was burned. In 1986, through the dedicated effort of Ruth Hodge, the Greene County Historical Society declared Hood United Methodist Church as a historic site, being the oldest original church building in Republic still in use. The church is also listed by the United Methodist Church as a historic site.

The first Sunday School was organized by Rev. Hervey Smith in 1882 with a membership of 100. A large pulpit Bible was presented to the church on July 3, 1892 by Mr. H.G. Criswell as a thank you "to the good old Mothers of the M.E. Church." It is now being restored. The Bible now in use was given in memory of Wilford and Grace Land by their daughter Anne E. Johnson.

Some items taken from the girlhood diary of Clara (Britain) Short reveal the place revivals played in the church in the early years. Sunday, January 19, 1896 "I went to Sunday School and heard Joe Jones preach. He is going to stay all week and preach." January 26, 1896 "I went to Sunday school and heard Joe Jones preach. The church was full and running over. We've had company at our house all week for meals—people from all over the country came in for morning service and stayed until evening service." February 1, 1896 "Mr. Jones preached his last sermon this evening to a packed house. There were 23 who joined the Methodist Church this morning".

In 1913 a terrific hail storm struck Republic doing much damage to homes and other buildings. It was at this time that the original belfry was damaged and the steeple torn down.

By August 1952 the dream of an education building was becoming a reality and Church School Superintendent, Paul Wilson, expressed the hope that plans and cost estimates might be presented to the next meeting of the Official Board. On April 3, 1953, ground was broken for the new facility under the direction of Rev. B.E. Dillon. Much of the labor was contributed by volunteers. This is the present Asbury Hall.

On February 16, 1964 the congregation decided to build a new parsonage on a lot donated by Mr. Jim Hood. Jack Hood was the architect and Jack Bridges was chairman of the building committee. The new parsonage was consecrated by Bishop Eugene M. Frank on January 3, 1965.

Late in 1968 a meeting of the board of trustees was called to inspect the church facilities to determine needed repairs and improvements. The Church Conference voted unanimously to accept the proposal presented by Mr. Art Evans and the pastor, Rev. Jim Ireland. The work included cleaning the bricks, tucking and pointing the bricks, repairing and repainting of exterior wood trim, installation of a new wood shingle roof, new windows, repair and repainting interior walls, new carpeting and new pews.

Much more space was needed in 1985 when plans were made to build a new educational and fellowship building to house Sunday School rooms, a new kitchen and large all purpose room.

William Cantrell was chairman of the building committee. Other members were Naoma Williams, Dorothy Owen, Jack and Valle Montgomery, Lloyd and Wanda Meacheam, Clifford Kubat, Larry and Linda Jones, Gailya Dow, Dorothy Decker, Stan Coggin and Jack and Juanita Bridges. The building was consecrated on March 2, 1986. In 1987 it was named in memory of Otho and Fay Bridges.

Planning for the Christian Life Center was started in 1995. David Budd and Sue Groves were co-chair of the building committee. The project was approved by the Church Conference in 1999. Joplin Construction and Design Management designed and built the building. The Consecration Service was held in October 2000 with Bishop Ann Scherer presiding.

The history of the church has been rich. Countless stories have been left untold. Countless sacrifices have gone untold. And by the grace of God many stories of love, service and sacrifice are yet to be acted out by those who follow in the footsteps of the many who have gone before us.

# Anchor Baptist Church

Anchor Baptist Church was founded the second Sunday in June 1996 in the home of Pastor Jim and Linda Collins. Four families started the church and met in the Collins' home, the Senior Friendship Center, a rented building on Main Street and even the Kiwanis pavilion before purchasing the 206 N. Main building from Sumner Media.

The building on N. Main was *The Republic Monitor* building for many years and had an apartment in the back. The church completely renovated the building creating the current facility which contains a 70 seat auditorium, four class rooms, a sound room/office, and a fellowship hall. The church had to redo the walls, floor, ceiling, and put on a new roof. The members did the work and had wonderful times of fellowship while doing it.

The church ministers to the community, has had many people accept Jesus as Savior, and holds in depth Bible studies. Jim Collins is still the senior pastor. Roy Ulrich is the church's deacon and treasurer. Tom Collins is the music director and Sunday school superintendent, Leon Hagewood is the trustee chairman, and his wife Susie is the clerk. The church meets for Sunday school at 9:30 and Sunday morning worship at 10:30. The church also has a Wednesday evening Prayer Meeting and Bible Study at 7:00 p.m. In the near future, they believe God will lead them to a larger facility or perhaps to build one. For now, they enjoy the blessings of God in a wonderful community.

*206 N. Main Republic, MO*

# Bible Baptist Church

Bible Baptist Church was organized October 18, 1955 with thirteen charter members. Rev. Chester Dunn was the first pastor.

The church began in a small house on Main and Elm Streets. The congregation grew and they purchased the present property on the corner of Brooks and Hampton Streets and built a small wood structure that housed the congregation until the need for more space pressed them to build a larger auditorium. Later the two buildings were connected with an all purpose type building used for Sunday school class rooms and a youth department. After this space was added the first building was turned into a kitchen and fellowship hall.

On August 30, 1986 all of the above structures were arsoned and burned. For the next two years the congregation met in the old Andrews Pharmacy building downtown across from the city hall while the present facility was constructed.

The new building was dedicated in 1988. The church celebrated its 50th anniversary September 18, 2005. Rev. Billy J. Pool has been pastor for the past 25 years.

Pastors preceding Rev. Pool were Chester Dunn, Samuel Freeman, Alton Chiles, Elmer Miller, Dr. John Ross, James Maggard, Oran Cobb and Loye Stone.

The population of Republic was 965 people when the first buildings were built and the last census, which was in the year 2000, the population had grown to 8,438.

In a growing city they are still known as, "The Church That Cares For Your Soul."

*227 E. Brooks St.
Republic, MO*

# First Baptist Church of Battlefield

In February 1970, a group of visionary Christians met in the heart of Battlefield with one purpose in mind, the birthing of a Baptist Church. Macedonia Baptist Church served as sponsor for the group which became known as the Battlefield Baptist Mission. By the summer of 1970, the congregation received permission to meet in the nearby, but vacant, Methodist Church building. On November 1, 1970, the constituting service was held for the First Baptist Church of Battlefield with 136 Charter Members on the roll. The Pastor was Rev. Jim Schudy with Scott Killingsworth as music director.

Groundbreaking was held March 14, 1971, on the first unit (Building A) on the corner of FF Highway and Weaver Road. Completion and occupation of this structure came on July 25, 1971. Quickly the need for more land and buildings became obvious. The Otis & Grace Keyes family were approached twice more about purchasing property until the present total of nearly 20 acres was secured. The second unit (Building B) was dedicated on March 23, 1975 and the third (Building C) on September 4, 1977. A ball field, children's playground equipment, paved parking lots, and basketball goals were added to provide a recreational area for the Church and Community. The sanctuary and fellowship hall were totally renovated in the late 1990s.

Our current ministerial staff is: Pastor - Ray Smith, Minister of Youth - Aaron Kruse, and Minister of Music - Marty Saner.

Proud of the past and excited about the future. First Baptist Church of Battlefield is presenting Christ in clear, contemporary ways and meeting the spiritual needs of the growing Battlefield and Republic communities. First Baptist of Battlefield is building, bonding, and bringing lives to God.

*Pointing people in the right direction.*

# Republic Free Will Baptist Church

The church building was erected in 1948 by a group of Fundamental Methodist led by Rev. Fred Cunningham. Some of the family names were Blades, Miller, Etheridge, Wade, Batson and Swinney. In 1968 they joined the Evangelical Methodist Church. In 1976 they became an independent Methodist church and was named Evangelical Community Church. In 1992 the Missouri State Mission Board of Free Will Baptist opened the church as a Free Will Baptist mission with Rev. Tony Butcher as pastor. It was called Republic Free Will Baptist Church. In 1995 Rev. Butcher left and Rev. Clarence Burton was interim pastor. In August 1995 Rev. Don Anderson came as pastor. Later in that year the church became an autonomous Free Will Baptist Church and remains such until this day. The church is doing well and contemplating a new sanctuary and fellowship hall. Thanks to all those (too numerous to mention) who over the years have been faithful to the Lord to provide a place of worship in Republic. Over the past 58 years 24 different pastors have ministered at this location. Only the Lord knows the number of souls that have come to know Christ as Savior while attending this House of Worship.

*437 North Walnut in Republic.*

# Brookline First Baptist Church

In 1862 the Union Baptist Church was organized in Little York, two miles southwest of the present village of Brookline. The community is rural, 12 miles west of Springfield. The little village of Brookline is one mile south of the present church. A frame house of worship, erected in 1872, was sold for debt to the carpenters, but was purchased and restored back to the church by Charles McClure.

The present church was organized in 1882 on ground donated by the St. Louis-San Francisco Railroad. The church had a reported membership of 35. The church and property was valued at $850.00. In 1948 the Baptist Training Union was organized and in 1963 the Brotherhood was organized under the leadership of Rev. Lynn Swadley. This same year, the property north of the church, including seven lots, a house, and a well was purchased with plans to build. In 1965, under the leadership of Rev. Bert Miller, a new parsonage was built. February 1, 1971 Rev. Bradley Allison was called as pastor. Rev. and Mrs. Allison owned their home in Springfield so the parsonage became rental property until the church voted to sell it and apply the money to building a new church. The new church was built on two acres of ground donated by the Wayne Trogdon family. It is now located one mile north of the village of Brookline on MM Highway.

The ground-breaking ceremony was held on Sunday, September 25, 1973, and the first service was held in the new building on March 3, 1974 with a week-long revival.

Rev. and Mrs. Allison were a blessing to the church in many ways. Besides leading the building of the new church, they led in becoming a mission-minded church in giving to home missions, state missions and foreign missions. A church library was dedicated in September. Bro. Allison retired in 1981 and Rev. Fred Lynn was called as pastor. In 1983 the church voted to build an addition consisting of six classrooms, a pastor's study, kitchen and fellowship hall. The church continued to grow and on December 20, 1991 the church purchased two more acres of land east of the present building. The new educational wing consists of four classrooms, choir room, restrooms, and four offices. The church was still debt free. A few years later more room was needed so on Aug. 1, 2000 an additional eight acres, on the north side of the church, was purchased from the Otha Hendrix Estate. A new Family Life Center was built, consisting of a large gym, an exercise room, a beautiful new kitchen, new offices, restrooms and showers, and several classrooms. Dedication and ribbon cutting ceremonies were held on August 31, 2003.

*Brookline Baptist Church — 124 years of history, 1882-2006.*

*Mabel Trogdon and her baptistry painting.*

# Calvary Baptist Church

On October 28, 1966, a group of 18 adults met in the home of Mr. and Mrs. Jim Girth to organize a church. The new Calvary Baptist Church first met on November 6, 1966, at the Lindsey Schoolhouse. There were 67 charter members, who recall meeting in a drafty building with a potbellied stove. The church was accepted into the Greene County Baptist Association in September 1967.

Property at the corner of Hines and Highway 60 was purchased in June 1967, and construction began on a new church building. The first services were conducted there on December 17, 1967. Several additions and renovations were made through the years, beginning with construction of a new sanctuary, dedicated in May 1972. Renovations completed in 1982 provided additional educational space, as well as space for a Day Care Ministry that was opened under the leadership of Shirley Day in 1982 and continued for 17 years. The dedication and laying of the cornerstone for a new two story educational wing were held at the 20th anniversary celebration on August 16-17, 1986. A note burning service on July 2, 2000, celebrated retiring the debt on the building at Hines and Highway 60. This was held in the sanctuary - fortunately, nothing else burned!

*Lindsey School, Farm Rd. 186*

Property consisting of 24 acres had been acquired on Hines Street in 1996, with the goal of building a new church building there, but God had other plans. A vacated grocery store on west Highway 60 was purchased in July 2003, and subsequently the other properties were sold. This building was renovated into a beautiful new worship center, educational facility, gymnasium, fellowship hall, youth and children's area, and was opened on March 6, 2005 with approximately 1,000 in attendance.

The church has had only four pastors: Rev. Floyd Creason (November 1966 to July 1970), Rev. Max Stark (August 1970 to April 1973) and Rev. Gene McBride (October 1973 to January 1982). Rev. Mike Green, current pastor, has served longer than any other, beginning his ministry in April of 1982.

*1967-2005
Corner of Hines and U.S. Highway 60 West.*

Since 1985, many teams of youth and adults have participated in numerous mission trips to various areas of the country. An annual missions conference has been held in recent years to raise awareness for missions.

A number of ministries to the community have become traditions. They include the Easter pageant and Christmas musicals, VBS, 4th of July celebrations, Fall Harvest Carnival, Cup of Cold Water at the Republic Fall Festival, the Clothes Closet, the Benevolence Ministry, the Grand Oak Food Drive, Operation Christmas Child, Pregnancy Care Center, Nursing Home Ministry, Car Care Clinic, and the Awana children's ministry. The church building has been used as a polling place since 1987, and for blood drives by the Community Blood Center of the Ozarks.

The average Sunday school attendance in 1967 was 60, and in 2005 has grown to 470. Current membership is 1,357.

After nearly 40 years, the church looks forward to continue serving God by "Touching Hearts; Changing Lives."

*Present location of Calvary Baptist Church
804 U.S. Highway 60 West.*

# First Baptist Church

First Baptist Church's commitment to helping people, offering hope and leading people to maturity in Christ has been evident throughout the church's long history in this community. On Sunday, June 11, 1874 seven individuals first came together to follow God's will, and held the church's first service. Mrs. Ella Decker, Mr. and Mrs. J.P. Youngblood, Mr. and Mrs. W.H. Harrison and Mr. and Mrs. W.B. Searcy first gathered in the Opera House on Main Street to worship God, fellowship and encourage one another. God designed something special for this group of believers and future generations.

These believers and others continued to gather in the Opera House during the early years in their history, eventually expanding to a railroad passenger car for Sunday school and Bible studies. Consistent efforts to reach out to the community along with a desire to follow God yielded growth in spirit and in number. In 1903 the church grew to a point that a new facility was needed. The church moved out of the railroad car and Opera House and into their new building, just north of downtown on the current property. God continued His blessing during the early 20th century as the church expanded ministries to include Women's Missionary Union (WMU), the Brotherhood ministry for men and the area's first Junior Union, a ministry for children.

As the church moved into the 1920s God allowed the church the opportunity to reap positive growth as they reached new heights. Adversity and challenges have also been a part of their past. These challenges include a fire that damaged the building, transition with pastors, and adjusting to changes within the community and nation. Little did they know they were being prepared to minister in a time of great need. By the end of this decade the nation was in the throws of the Great Depression and they, along with the community, struggled during this time. Despite these challenges, the church maintained a focus of helping people, offering hope and leading people to maturity in Christ.

They continued to grow in the 1930s and 1940s expanding their facilities and using new technology. They excavated a basement, built on educational space, and built a baptistry in the auditorium. There was no indoor plumbing at the time so the baptistry was filled with buckets of water and a hose connected to a hydrant outside. Trying to expand their outreach and impact they started broadcasting the Sunday services over the radio.

Three of their members caught a vision for what God was about to do in the community as they boldly put $300 into a building fund in 1954. By 1959 those $300 grew into an expansive educational space, a modern nursery, a fellowship hall and kitchen facilities. These events spurred further growth and on May 10, 1964 they broke ground for a new sanctuary, finally moving into the sanctuary in 1965. The old building was torn down after 62 years of service, leaving the structure they have today. When you obey God and follow His will it is amazing to see how big His blessings can be.

The 1970s, 1980s and 1990s brought many more opportunities to serve and to follow God. Forging ahead they reached out by utilizing new technologies and old fashion methods.

They began a tape ministry by recording the services to audio cassette tapes, making copies and distributing the copies to those who could not attend services. This ministry continues today with plans to broaden to CDs and internet broadcasts. With all of the technology in the world nothing can replace a friend inviting a friend to church. Focusing their attention on neighbors, friends and family they strive to impact Republic in a positive way through community involvement and outreach.

They are investing in the future with renewed attention on ministries for everyone. They look forward to expanded facilities, services and programs allowing them to commit all the more to helping people, offering hope and leading people to maturity in Christ.

*Members of First Baptist Church at a baptism ceremony at Decker Pond.*

*First Baptist Church in 2006*

*First Baptist Church in 1903*

# Meadowview Baptist Church

Throughout time, many significant changes and events began with just a few people joining together for a common cause. So it was with the Meadowview Baptist Church, where results show that many lives have been touched and changed, despite the church's humble beginnings and brief history.

In 1982 local people were meeting to worship in a storefront on Highway 60 and at the Wade Cemetery Chapel; they had dreams of building a church.

Members soon purchased 10 acres along State Highway 174, just west of town, and plans to build their first building got underway. Brother John Purselley was the pastor and encouraged members to change the church name to Meadowview Baptist Church, to reflect the surrounding area and its welcoming atmosphere. Meadowview built the current building debt-free, and in two phases, with worshippers meeting in the lower level of the building until the upstairs was finished in 1993. Today, Sunday School and worship are held in the auditorium, while the lower level is utilized for children's church, many fellowship activities, and serves as a tornado shelter for the community during inclement weather.

Brother Purselley led the church until 1993, when at 65, he retired and moved to become a missionary in England. Two other pastors followed Brother Purselley - Bill Sizemore and Bill Wiemer.

In 1997, Brother Jeff Copes from United Baptist Church in Springfield, and a professor at Baptist Bible College, came to Meadowview to pastor. Greg Mitchell was brought in as associate pastor and music director, and students from Baptist Bible College in Springfield began attending. Brother Mitchell and his wife, Jennifer, have been with the church since 1997, providing the stability and reliability subsequent pastors grew to count on.

Under Pastor Copes' leadership, people began to notice the activity at Meadowview and the church began to flourish. However, after a few years, another change was on the horizon. That change was good for both Brother Copes and Jason Gaddis, a student at BBC who had served his internship at Meadowview. In October 2000, Brother Copes moved to Oklahoma City, OK, to a ministry at Heartland Baptist Bible College. Brother Gaddis was then voted in as pastor and led Meadowview for three years. When he took a position at Southwest Baptist Church in Oklahoma City in 2003, Brother Joshua Mathews, Meadowview's youth pastor at the time, was voted in as pastor.

Under his guidance Meadowview remains a sound Bible preaching church, committed to proclaiming the gospel, making disciples of Christ, and equipping them to become spiritually mature, according to the church mission statement.

Meadowview Baptist Church strongly supports and encourages interest in foreign missions through the association with the Baptist Bible Fellowship International, but its major focus is to spread the gospel in the community. Members are encouraged to take part in activities at the church, but also to participate in community events such as Republic's Pumpkin Daze. The church offers many programs and activities for children, youth and adults. Biblical counseling for individuals and families is among Meadowview's beneficial outreach programs.

# Hopewell Baptist Church

Hopewell Baptist Church is located approximately three miles west of Republic on Farm Road 176.

On the Saturday before the third Sunday in June 1867, Elder E. Clark and George Long met with a body of Christians near the headwaters of Pickerel Creek and organized a church. The name Hopewell was suggested by John H. Jackson and accepted by the church.

The members proceeded to elect a minister. The first pastor was George Long, the first clerk was Robert P. Dillinger, and the first church caretaker was Elder E. Clark. All were elected for one year.

Part of the lumber for the church was hauled by wagon from Van Winkle's Mill in Arkansas by John Jackson and other members. The first benches were made of heavy timber with no backs. Many families came to church in wagons, using chairs for seats, and these chairs were often carried into the building and used instead of the benches.

The church had a dirt floor, and straw was placed in a corner for sleeping children. A large box stove with a drum was placed near the center of the room for heat.

The church records indicate the first soul saved after the church was organized was Triphany Blades. Eleven members were received in the next two years. These were Sarah H. Hood, Sarah McDaniel, Margaret Laney, Ellen Rickman, James E. Garoutte, Rose Rickman, Edward Blades, Martha H. Ray, Patience Blades, Mary L. Blades, and Elizabeth Howard.

Some of the early pastors were George Long, D.T. Baucom, Isaac Stanley, I.D. Lamb, Robert Long, E.T. Stone, J.W. Wallace, Thomas Baucom, Johnathan Stogdale, Thomas Milton, J.T. Holbert, William McPherson, H. Webster, J.J. Brashears, J.W. Smith, B.T. Melton and Henry I. Britain.

The first funeral at Hopewell Baptist Church was for John H. Jackson in June 1873. At the same time a funeral was held for him in Knox County, Tennessee, his former home.

A Sabbath school was organized in 1889, and Sunday school was organized March 26, 1905.

The church records mention that an organ was purchased in 1904.

Communion and foot washing were practiced in the afternoon service on Homecoming Day during the early years of the church. After a few years the church voted to discontinue the practice of foot washing. In recent years the Lord's Supper has been observed on the Sunday preceding Easter.

Through the years Hopewell has helped support missionaries in many foreign countries, including China, Pakistan, Mexico, France, Africa, Israel, Brazil, Iran, Ethiopia, England, New Guinea and the Philippines, as well as an Indian reservation in New Mexico.

# Blades Chapel Church

The church is located four and one-half miles west of Republic, MO on Highway 174 then one mile south on Farm Road 51.

The history of this church dates back to 1844 when the division took place in the Methodist Episcopal Church, but it cannot be definitely stated whether it was organized at that time, or at a later period as a Methodist Protestant Church. Among the early members occur the names Garoutte, Laney and Blades. After worshiping for a time in the home of Anthony Garoutte they erected a house of worship known as Old Bethel Church. During the Civil War the congregation was broken up, but was reorganized in 1867 with the names Brittain and McDaniel also appearing in the membership. In May 1872, the house of worship was destroyed by fire and worship was held for some years in the Grandview School House in Pond Creek Township. A recent statement dates the organization of this church in 1889, by Rev. James Turentine, in which year a frame house of worship was erected, valued at $2,000. Dudley Blades donated $400 to the building of the church. A new addition in 2006 is being added. There have been many pastors of the church; more recent is Rev. Roy Wade who served for several years, and at present Rev. Terry Cunningham. The 1885 cemetery predates the church, and is located southeast of the present building.

# Yeakley Chapel

Yeakley Chapel (now United Methodist) Church is the beneficiary of three notable and significant traditions. It is a part of the rich history of American Methodism, celebrating 200 years of ministry in the United States. It can proudly take its place in the history of the early development of religion in Greene County, and it is a living memorial to the dedication of far-sightedness of its pioneer founders.

In the *Past and Present of Greene County, Missouri*, published in 1915, Jonathan Fairbanks and Clyde Edwin Tuck make the following observation: "As is often the case in the newer portions of our country, the history of churches in Greene County…begins with the travels and activities of the man on horseback. A truly militant character he, carrying on in the name of his exalted master an aggressive warfare on the hosts of sin and Satan…All honor to the humble, faithful soldier of the cross, pioneer knight errant of salvation, armed with Bible and hymn book, the Methodist itinerant!" The beginning of ecclesiastical history in Greene County belongs to that of the Southern Methodist Church. A small congregation was formed at Ebenezer, north of Springfield in 1831, and there is evidence that the first sermon preached in Greene County was delivered prior to that date by Rev. James H. Slavens, himself an elder in the Methodist Church.

The history of Yeakley Chapel can be traced back to November 15, 1809. It was on that date that Henry and Susanna Yeakley celebrated the birth of a son, John, one of 13 children born to this early pioneer couple. For the first 30 years of his life, John grew up on the old homestead in Tennessee. When a young man he learned the blacksmith trade which he followed as his main vocation throughout the subsequent years of his active life. In 1829, John married Matilda Grills and 10 years later this young couple followed the westward migration of the nation, leaving their native Greene County, Tennessee, for a home in the wild and sparsely settled country of southwest Missouri. Traveling in a small, two-horse wagon, the Yeakleys spent their first Missouri winter in Polk County. In the spring of 1840, they moved south and settled on 80 acres in West Center Township of Greene County, Missouri.

Although his mother was a Quaker and his father a devout Lutheran, John Yeakley's religious beliefs always seemed to be Methodist. He was a tolerant man, and his study of the holy word and his dedication to the church were guiding forces in this life, and the lives of his family and friends. It was his strong belief in the Almighty, coupled with his pioneering spirit that inspired Yeakley to join with five other families in establishing the first Methodist Church in West Center Township. Also included in the first register of Yeakley members were J.N. and Martha Jones, Mr. and Mrs. B. Johnson and J.C. Richardson.

On January 29, 1883, the original church building was destroyed by fire, the victim of a stray spark from an old wood stove. Feeling a deep sense of personal loss, John Yeakley gave the land for a new church and assisted in the construction of a new building, built in 1887 west of the original location, in connection with a small local cemetery. Except for being turned to face the north, the addition of a basement and periodic maintenance, this building still serves the congregation today, and the grave of John Yeakley is located in the cemetery nearby.

The oldest existing records of the church are in an old register, dated 1890-93. The first entry is the minutes of The First Quarterly Conference for the year 1890-1891, conducted at Pearce Chapel on December 6, 1890. At the time; Yeakley Chapel was part of the Bois D'Arc circuit that also included the Bois D'Arc Church, Pearce Chapel and the church at a small settlement known as Wyandott. The preacher in charge of this early meeting was Jacob Shook, a name that has meant a great deal to the Yeakley congregation for many years.

While over the years Yeakley Chapel has experienced many changes, both in leadership and membership, it has always stood firm in its dedication to proclaiming the Gospel and ministering to the needs of its people. No one knows what John Yeakley envisioned the church that bears his name might become. However, one cannot help but suspect that he deeply believed in the words of Jesus when he quoted from Matthew 16:18 "…I will build my church and the powers of death shall not prevail against it."

*Virginia McCarty Norman, Donna Walker Wilson and Doris Ricketts Sell (front), September 1954.*

*Sunrise service at Yeakley Chapel, 1994.*

*Yeakley Chapel on April 2, 2006.*

# Brookline Cemetery Association

The citizens of the town of Brookline and adjacent county of the county of Greene and state of Missouri met at the Congregational Church house in Brookline, MO on May 6, 1883 at 1:00 p.m. to organize in convention by election Rev. W.H. Hicks, chairman and Judge T.N. Hosey, secretary. The object of the meeting was to take into consideration a proposition to transform the "Cumberland Union" religious and educational grounds to that of a public cemetery and that the land lying between said grounds and the Township line south, owned by Mr. David Anderson, be purchased and made an addition to the aforesaid ground for cemetery purposes, and that there be a Cemetery Society organized at the town of Brookline, Greene County, Missouri. The following resolution, offered by Rev. Mr. T.B. Fly, was read and adopted:

Resolved that there be a commission appointed composed of seven men, and they are hereby empowered to draft Articles of Association, and to incorporate under the laws of the state of Missouri, and that said corporate body shall be known and styled, Brookline Cemetery Association of Brookline Township of the County of Greene, State of Missouri.

The convention appointed Rev. Mr. A.A. Lawson, S.F. Gibson, T.C. McCall, David Anderson, T.A. McConnell, M.L. McClure and John Potter. This commission was instructed to investigate titles, terms of sale of land, obtain good and sufficient deeds, and when incorporated and the transfers of titles to lands are made, to call the people together again to hear this report.

S.F. Gibson, Secretary
W.H. Hicks, Chairman

The Brookline Cemetery Association met on Saturday the 7th day of July 1883 at the Cumberland Presbyterian Church House in Brookline, MO. Pursuant to the call of the Board of Trustees, the Rev. Mr. S. Forrester was chosen chairman of the meeting. The minutes of the conventional meeting and the minutes of the meetings of the commission were read and approved.

The commission appointed by the people in convention assembled on the 6th day of May 1883; having now become a Board of Trustees of Commission Society by incorporation, reported a charter from the Secretary of the State of Missouri authorizing and empowering an organization of the aforesaid and purposed Cemetery Society under the laws of the State aforesaid, and to be known by the name of and styled "Brookline Cemetery Association" of Brookline Township, Greene County, Missouri, also articles of association and bylaws for the regulation and government of said organization, all of which was received and approved and adopted.

As provided for in the above bylaws there were two more trustees elected making nine members of the board instead of seven as first appointed. Charles McClure and T.M. Sanford were chosen said trustees to serve as provided for in the bylaws of the association.

S.F. Gibson, Secretary
S. Forrester, Chairman

The Brookline Cemetery Association met at the C.P. Church House at 3:00 p.m., April 1885.

W.G. Perkins was employed to canvas the people for the purpose of raising money to pay the expenses of the Brookline Cemetery in the purchase of additions to and fencing the grounds and putting the cemetery in order. It was agreed to have a meeting of the people at large on the cemetery grounds on the third Saturday 16 of May 1885 for the purpose of consideration and expression of opinion of the best interests of the people in Brookline Cemetery, the selection adjusting and sale of lots, enlarging the numbers of the Society thereby providing for a more permanent establishment of the Brookline Cemetery Association.

The Brookline Cemetery Association met on May 16, 1885. The secretary ordered to invite David Anderson to have deed ready and be present at the meeting on May 23, and to have the indebtedness made to present at that time.

T.A. McConnell was instructed to have a quit-claim deed made by the "Cumberland Union" corporate board to the Brookline Cemetery Association," by May 16, 1885. This deed was recorded May 18, 1885, Book 65 page 610.

On motion, S.F. Gibson was ordered to have charge of the Brookline Cemetery and to sell lots and make certificates of purchase to parties buying them, giving price and descriptions of the lots purchased.

It was agreed that there be a called meeting of the Board of Trustees with the finance and deed parties to adjust indebtedness, titles and pay for the additions to cemetery grounds purchaser of Mr. David Anderson, on May 23, 1885. This deed was recorded in book 66 page 367 on May 23, 1885 for a tract of land containing 3 and 35/100 acres more or less.

On May 2, 1911 the committee, consisting of J.E. Wilson, Jeff Pierce and J.N. Hosey, appointed for the purpose of examining the records, books, accounts and other things of the Brookline Cemetery Association gave the following report: We find no Warranty Deeds to the ground, but find a quit-claim deed from Alfred P. Harwood and wife Margaret for five acres more or less of land the same being recorded September 24, 1887, Book 73, page 374, Greene County, Missouri. An examination of the books found them to be in good shape and properly kept. During this meeting it was decided to mow the cemetery twice a year instead of once.

In 1965 the bylaws were changed to have an annual meeting on the first Saturday of May each year. The Board of Trustees consists of seven members. The Board of Trustees has a secretary and treasurer to keep proper records. The treasurer is bound by a surety bond. The records are audited annually.

On May 2, 1992 the Board of Trustees added bylaws requiring a permanent marker on a concrete base to be placed on any grave within two years of burial. They also require a vault or concrete box for each burial.

The cemetery is non-endowed and operates on donations.

*The entrance to Brookline Cemetery.*

*Boy Scouts conducting Flag Raising Ceremony on Memorial Day.*

# Evergreen Cemetery

The Evergreen Cemetery was established in 1892 by Josiah F. Brooks, Allen Owen, W.H. Noe, and J.E. Decker on property in northeast Republic, MO. E.T. and W.P. Anderson are also credited for helping purchase land, plot and fence the cemetery. The block fence is across the front and west side of the cemetery.

The cemetery is governed by a 12 member board.

The beautiful maple trees make it a beauty spot in Republic. In the early years of the cemetery people would walk there on a Sunday afternoon. It was a nice, cool, and shady walk in a beautifully kept cemetery.

In 1965 Lester Cox donated the remaining land between the cemetery and Hampton Street so that the cemetery could be enlarged.

In 1993 the VFW Post #4593 erected three flag poles and a raised podium with the inscription: "This memorial is dedicated to the men and women who served in the Armed Forces of America." Because of damage a new stone was erected in 1997.

# Lindsey Chapel Cemetery

Lindsey Chapel Cemetery started with the burial of Mary C. Robertson, granddaughter of Lindsey and Delilah Robertson on a hill located on their farm on April 26, 1846, the grave could be seen from their home. It was known as the Robertson Graveyard.

At the death of Lindsey Robertson, his son Anthony M. Robertson was heir to this part of the farm. It remained the Robertson Graveyard until Anthony M. and his wife Hettie E. (Anderson) Robertson deeded this acreage to the trustees of Lindsey Chapel Cemetery on March 28, 1882, for the sum of $1.00 to be used as a public burying ground. The trustees R.L. Robertson, W.L. Gamble, R.A. Gamble, John E. Baxter, E.W. Keltner, E.B. Short, S.W. Riley, J.M. Payne, W.C. Short, E.J. Bryant, J.T. O'Bryant, James Short, Sam Short, A.J. O'Bryant, and William Hagewood, agreed to keep in good repair by fencing and maintaining and cleaning off said ground in a good husbandly manner. A second deed dated April 29, 1887 by A.M. and H.E. Robertson to the trustees, for $1.00 more land was added. A third deed dated March 19, 1900, by A.M. and H.E. Robertson, for the sum of $9.00; this deed is to correct a former deed to the above named cemetery so as to revise in former deed two acres in the cemetery. The cemetery had a chapel across the road, which would line up with the middle of the cemetery, This building was known as Lindsey School as well as a chapel for church and funeral services.

There have been several different trustees, directors, and caretakers through the years. Luther Land and his wife Josephine were in charge from the 1960s to the 2000s; much was accomplished during this time. A perpetual care account was instituted; a descendant of Lindsey Robertson donated funds to purchase two acres and install a chain link fence in February 2001. The watchful eyes of Luther kept the cemetery in good repair. There are now over 570 graves at Lindsey Chapel Cemetery.

# Wade Chapel Cemetery

Wade Chapel Cemetery is located northwest of Republic, MO. The cemetery had its beginning in 1854 when Nancy (Herren) Wade, who was born in 1805, was buried in the churchyard of Wade Chapel, a Methodist church located in the northeast part of what is now the cemetery. She was the wife of James (Jimmie) Wade, Methodist circuit rider, who held services at the church. It is not known when the church was built, but it was destroyed by fire at an unknown date. The second grave in the churchyard was that of Allen Newton Bailey, who was born in 1830. "A travelers' baby" was the next burial to take place in 1854. The travelers went on their way after the child was laid to rest, and though the name has apparently been lost, the cemetery association has recently placed a marker at the grave. Since that time on, the cemetery has been an establishment in the community where many families' loved ones have been laid to rest.

Several of the early graves in the burial ground have covers built over them for protection, since there was no stock law at the time. These coverings were made of flat sandstone and seven of them are still in place.

The Wade Chapel churchyard contained approximately one acre of land. There is no record as to the year that the plot was obtained from the landowner or why that the site was chosen for the church. Records do show that the 40-acre tract, of which the churchyard was a part, was owned by C.F. Dryden in 1839. Mr. Dryden had purchased the land for the sum of $1.25 per acre. It is also recorded that he sold the land to D.W. Burford in 1857. Before the plot was sold, the C.F. Dryden gave or sold the land for the churchyard on October 8, 1885, and the community held their first meeting in regards to the cemetery. The purpose was to establish guidelines and organize the care of the cemetery. Minutes of this meeting were found in an old daybook that belonged to George W. Jackson. The minutes were copied into a ledger used for cemetery records. Records show that additional land was purchased in 1888 and 1946.

Improvements have been made over the years. In the early 1900s, pine trees were either donated or purchased and planted throughout the cemetery. The chapel was erected in 1907. This was made possible by cash donations and donated labor from interested parties. The chapel has been used for funerals, programs on Decoration Day and business meetings pertaining to the cemetery. The first funeral service held in the chapel was in March 1909. About the first of the century, one Sunday in May was designated as an annual Decoration Day. This practice continues today. In the early days, many families who visited the cemetery on that day took a basket dinner. A barrel of water was hauled to the yard and placed in a shady spot, provided drinking water for the crowd. A memorial sermon by a visiting minister and a program of songs and recitations by children and adults were well attended. Decoration Day in 1909 was of special interest to those who planned and worked to make the chapel a reality, since the building was dedicated on that day.

The cemetery is the final resting place of many of our veterans who died in service to our country. Some of these veterans date back to the Civil War. Confederate and Union Army veterans alike are buried here. Today, the operation and care of the cemetery is still a function of the community. A board of directors is chosen yearly at the annual meeting. Along with the patrons of the community, they oversee the care and up keep of the cemetery.

*Wade Chapel in 1968*

*Entrance to Wade Chapel Cemetery*

# Family Histories

1920's Short Gathering. The house stood on the southeast corner of where Farm Road 101 T's with the Greene-Christian County Line Road now Farm Road 194.

**ALDERMAN** - Until the mid-1950s, the St. Louis-San Francisco Railway Company depot near Main Street was a familiar sight to residents of Republic. The old gray-painted building had occupied that location for more than half a century, and in 1933 it acquired a new depot agent when J.W. Alderman moved his family to Republic.

*Frisco Depot 1954, Republic, MO.*

The Aldermans had previously lived in Ozark, MO, where Mr. Alderman had served as the Frisco agent there for 15 years. When they arrived in Republic, the Aldermans had three daughters: Jean, 16; Phyllis, 10; and Patricia, 6. During the first month of 1934, Mrs. Alderman gave birth to twin sons, Bob and Don.

In 1956, after 23 years as Republic's depot agent, Mr. Alderman retired, ending a nearly 50-year career with Frisco. During his years in Republic, he was active in community affairs and had served on the city council, the local board of education and the board of Hood Methodist Church. Mr. Alderman served terms as president of both the board of education and the church board. He passed away in 1957.

Mrs. Alderman also was active in the local community as a member of the Eastern Star, the Arts and Crafts Guild and other women's organizations. During her years in Ozark, and later in Republic, she gained regional recognition as a poet, and one of her poems was selected for an anthology of American poetry at the 1939 World's Fair in New York. Mrs. Alderman died in 1986.

All of the Alderman children graduated from Republic High School. During World War II, Jean married Malcolm Alloway, now deceased, and they had two daughters, Ann Stingle of Fairfax, VA and Jane Flinn of Friendswood, TX. Jean lives in Houston, TX and has four grandchildren and two great-grandchildren.

Phyllis married George Droke, also during World War II, and they had three children: Thomas, of Fort Worth, TX; Linda Cafiero of Colorado Springs, CO; and Margaret Mitchell of Seattle, WA. Phyllis and George live in Austin, TX, and have seven grandchildren and one great-grandchild.

Patricia married Wayne Chronister of Springfield, both are now deceased. They had four children: Gary, Judy Matteson, now deceased, and Mark, of Springfield, and Cindy Eckley of Ozark. There are five grandchildren and one great-grandchild.

Bob lives with his wife Linda in Leavenworth, KS. Children include Curt, of Frisco, TX; Janice Garner, of Lebanon; Cathy Griesel of Winona, MN; and Keith, of Laguna San Miguel, CA. There are four grandchildren.

Don and his wife Colleen live in Houston, TX. Children include Bruce, of Concord, CA; Laurie Myhill, of Fayetteville, NY; Amy, of Sedona, AZ; and Carrie Dalton, of Fort Worth, TX. The Aldermans have four grandchildren. *Submitted by Don Alderman.*

**ALLEY** - Jess and Opal Alley moved to Republic in 1941. Jess lived in Oklahoma, Arkansas and Missouri. Opal is from Berryville, AR. They had three sons and two daughters. The children attended school in Republic.

Troy Paul was in the Navy and Army; he is buried in the National Cemetery, Springfield, MO. Philip is a disabled veteran living in Monett and will also be buried in the National Cemetery. Virgil Silas lives in Aurora, MO. Veta lives in Chesapeake, MO. Mary lives in Kentucky.

Jess died in 1980 and Opal lives in Republic. Jess and Opal have eight grandchildren and several great-great-grandchildren. *Submitted by Opal Alley.*

**ALLMAN** - Norma Blevins, at the age of 10 years, moved to Republic with her father and mother. Norma lived on West Elm Street in the second house on the left from Main Street, near the old elementary school for about two years, before moving, to her grandparents', Jimmie and Susie Hilton's farm in Crane, MO. She lived there until marrying. When her youngest child was a baby, they returned to Republic on the old park spot purchasing a new home.

While living in Kansas City, Bob would stop by the park to let his children play after visiting his parents in Aurora, MO and never thought he would someday be living there. The Allmans have lived at this location for approximately 30 years and have been very happy with Republic seeing many changes. Their children attended Republic schools the entire time.

Bob and Norma have 13 children between them, referred to as his and mine. Norma's all live close around with one in Athens, TX. Bob's are all out of state. Bob was Navy and Army, and grew up in Aurora, MO. Norma has been a housewife, graduating from Crane High School.

They are members of the Republic Free Will Baptist Church which they love, enjoying many happy times with wonderful people. Their children and family love Republic and intend to stay in this area. *Submitted by Norma and Bob Allman.*

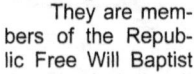

*Bob and Norma Allman – 1981.*

**AMBS/MADEN** - In May of 1955 the Ambs family, which consisted of Michael P., his wife Dicie L. (Maden) and daughters Martha Jane, Susan and Mary Elizabeth, moved from Springfield to Republic. They purchased the Annie Howard place from Doc and Mrs. French.

The French family had purchased the place a few years earlier and had done considerable repair to the house which was built about 1890 by a person in the lumber business in Republic.

Over the next six years the Ambs did a lot of remodeling until they moved to O'Fallon, MO in 1961. They enjoyed their stay in Republic and made many friends while in the city. *Submitted by Michael Ambs.*

**ANDERSON** - William Peter Anderson was born in 1871, the year Republic became a town. W.P., who would spend most of his life known as "Shorty", was a well-built 5'7". He was the grandson of Peter L. Anderson, who owned a farm north of Republic, and the eldest son of Elijah Teague Anderson and Melissa Garoutte. The Andersons came to Greene County from

*Anderson Family, l-r: E.T. Anderson, Peter L. Anderson, W.P. Anderson, baby Glen Anderson.*

Tennessee in 1855. Melissa was the daughter of William Babington Garoutte. Her grandfather, James Smith Garoutte, came to Greene County in 1837, the 7th son of Michael Garoutte who came from Marseilles, France in 1775 to aid the colonists in the Revolution.

E.T. Anderson and Melissa had three sons and four daughters. Della was stillborn and two sons, W.P. and Charles, were Missourians all their lives. Teague lived and died in Oklahoma. The daughters followed their husbands: Myrtle moved with Will Brashear to Moline, IL; Minnie and Charles Roop settled in Webster Groves, where she made a career as a Red Cross executive; and Zana "Coosie" and Powell Lonon lived in Santa Ana, CA where her parents retired. Minnie and Myrtle each had two daughters and "Coosie" had one.

In January 1899, W.P. married Theresa Houtz. Their son Glen was born in 1900. Sadly, Theresa died before Glen was two, and the Andersons and Houtz families cared for Glen until W.P. married Emma Nance who died in 1908. In 1915 Ella Nance and W.P. were married on St. Patrick's Day and celebrated 39 anniversaries until his death in December 1954. They were parents of two daughters, Roberta and Joan, who graduated from Republic High School, as did Glen. Charles married Kate Costello and they adopted a son, James. Teague married Jenn Rawlings and they had sons, Jack and Eugene, and a daughter, Rebecca.

E.T. and W.P. Anderson were involved in the growth and welfare of Republic during their lifetimes. E.T. helped secure the Frisco Depot and a train stop, which helped Republic become an incorporated town. E.T. and his son helped start the Bank of Republic in 1899, and "Shorty" later became cashier for 35 years, until the bank was closed during the Depression of the 1930s. He also served variously as mayor, councilman and school board member.

At one time Anderson land reached from Main Street east to the railroad and north to Hines. Land then south of Anderson Avenue was donated for the high school which the Andersons helped start. "Coosie" was the first Anderson graduate in the class of 1904. The Andersons were also instrumental in the development of Evergreen Cemetery, where on two Anderson lots E.T. and Melissa, W.P. and his wives and daughter, Teague, his son and family members representing five generations are buried.

The E.T. Anderson house at 406 North Pine was built in the late 1880s. It was the home of W.P. and Ella as long as they lived. In 1979 after Ella's death, Joan Anderson and her husband Ransom Ellis Jr. restored the house and it was accepted into the National Register of Historic Places. It is now the home of Ransom Ellis III, their son, and his family. Members of the Anderson family have now lived there for almost 120 years. *Submitted by Roberta Anderson Arnold.*

**ANDERSON/HINSHAW -** George Edward "Ed" Anderson was born Oct. 9, 1877 in Greene County, MO and died Sept. 23, 1962. He was the son of Henry Small Anderson and Jessie Mary "Wiley" Anderson. On March 27, 1912 in Greene County, MO, Ed married Elsie Lee Hinshaw, born June 19, 1890 and died Nov. 22, 1974. Elsie was the daughter of Jackson Ramsey Hinshaw and Mary A. (Mills) Hinshaw. They spent their married life on a farm north of Republic, Greene County, MO. They had two daughters: Mary Lorilla, born Feb. 7, 1913, and Stella M., born and died Aug. 13, 1923. Ed and Elsie Anderson and their daughter Stella are buried at Yeakley Chapel Cemetery near Halltown, MO next to Elsie's parents, Jackson Ramsey and Mary A. (Mills) Hinshaw. Henry Anderson is buried at Brookline Cemetery near his second wife, Mary C. (Robertson) Anderson, and a son, Lynn Anderson.

*Elsie Lee (Hinshaw) and George Anderson.*

George Edward Anderson was the grandson of Peter Looney Anderson who came to the Republic area in 1850 and remained in the area until his death on June 9, 1903. Peter was first married to Martha Holloway, who died about 1853. His second wife was Sarah (Hazelton) Luce, who died April 7, 1884. Peter was married a third time to Nannie Payne.

George Edward and Elsie Anderson's daughter Mary grew up and attended Jones School north of Republic. She was married to Noel Eugene Bolin on July 8, 1939 at Mary's parents' home north of Republic. Noel was born Oct. 5, 1919 and died Feb. 22, 1982. Noel was living with his family on land adjacent to the Anderson farm when they met. When Noel and his brothers were working in the fields Mary would take water to them. Noel and Mary raised two daughters, Beverly Ann and Beatrice Louise.

Noel served his country during World War II and came back to the farm north of Republic, MO. Noel farmed and worked as a salesman for Fuller Brush. He later sold tractors for Engle Tractor for a time and then spent many years selling new and used cars. For many years he owned and operated his own used car lot in Springfield, MO. Mary devoted her life to taking care of the family and the farm. She kept busy with milking cows, gardening, cooking, cleaning, sewing and caring for the girls. Their daughters grew up on the farm and attended school at Republic. *Submitted by Beatrice L. Addison.*

**ANDERSON/STEPHENSON** – Douglas Anderson's family came from Marion County, TN before the Civil War. The first ancestor was Peter Looney Anderson, born July 28, 1820 to James and Hetty (Looney) Anderson. According to family oral history James and Hetty died on the way here and are buried in the Pea Ridge, AR area. Peter served in the 74th Regiment, Company A, Missouri Militia from 1862-63. He homesteaded land on Pond Creek. Peter was married several times. Doug's line starts from Peter's marriage to Sara Hazelton Luce in 1855. They had four children, including Doug's grandfather, Henry Small Anderson. Henry married Clemmie McCullah Robertson on Oct. 28, 1894. To this union came three children, the oldest was Doug's father, Earl Roscoe.

*Henry Small Anderson and Mary Clementine (McCullah) Robertson. This is their wedding picture, Oct. 28, 1894.*

*Doug and Mary Jo Anderson on their wedding day in October 1952.*

Earl married Floss Isabelle Chumbley on Nov. 20, 1920. They had three children: Jacquelyn Lou, Pascal Douglas and Breta Jane.

Pascal Douglas "Doug" Anderson married Mary Jo Stephenson, daughter of Joe and Jane Stephenson. She was born on March 22, 1934, the last of seven children and the only one birthed by a doctor! She said it took almost a year to pay her off. The Stephenson family were of Scotch-Irish and Native American blood, having come up the Trail of Tears.

Douglas met Mary Jo while she was still in high school at Republic. She worked as a waitress at the Trailways Cafe on the north side of town. After returning from the Army in World War II, Doug became a truck driver and his favorite stop-over was the Trailways to see a very dark-haired young lady.

They married October 18, 1952. Doug continued to drive long hauls for awhile. However, a few years later he purchased a can milk route from Ab Norman. Doug and Mary Jo lived just off south Main Street in Republic. They purchased several Jersey heifers. In the summer of 1959, their son Mark was announced. Doug decided he had to have a home and farm for his new kid. They purchased the old Clarence and Hettie Ghan place in October 1959. Their herd of cows trailed behind a pickup truck out P Highway with Mary Jo sitting on the tailgate, holding a tree limb covered with leaves. They lived there the rest of their lives.

Mary Jo was some lady, out-spoken, loving, fair, and a prolific writer. But most of the time she enjoyed making people wonder what was going on. Many, to this day, remember her Christmas tree in the front window, lighted in July. She left this world in January 1994.

Doug was a very strong man who farmed most of his life while working first at Dayco in Springfield, and in later years as a greeter at

*Doug Anderson at his farm south of Republic – Fall 2002.*

Wal-Mart in Republic. He was known for his knowledge of cattle and horses, but mostly for his mules, Miss Kitty and Rufus. He left us in March 2004.

Many people remember the Andersons because of the big outdoor cookouts and bluegrass music. Many people came to their place unknown and left as friends. Now Mark never knows if he's feeding 20 or 100, but hopes to keep up the tradition of the "Mule Man" and "Murt." *Submitted by Mark Anderson.*

**ANDRUS -** Earl "Chick" George Andrus was born in Hurley, MO to George Edward and Sarah Arminta (Jones) Andrus on Feb. 26, 1912. He was the fifth born of eight children. George Andrus' ancestors had moved from northern Indiana to Stone County, MO in the 1860s.

Mary Louise Conrad was born in Hurley, MO, to Samuel Labrenth "Brent" and Mary Elizabeth (Simpkins) Conrad on Dec. 13, 1915. She was the ninth of 11 children. Brent's parents had moved from northern Indiana to a farm one mile north of Billings in 1877. They later donated a part of their land to become Rose Hill Cemetery. Many of the Conrad family are buried there.

The couple married Oct. 19, 1933. They farmed around Hurley and Ash Grove until moving to Billings in 1949.

The Andrus family: Earl, Louise, son Ralph, and daughter Erlene, moved from Billings to the second home completed in the Eagan-Buxton addition on the west side of Republic in the fall of 1955. Their older son, Raymond, had finished his barber apprenticeship, part of it in a shop on Main Street in Republic owned by Frank Babcock, and had opened his own shop in Billings. Ralph opened a new Phillips 66 service station on Highway 174 in Republic and later worked for Hoffman-Taff. Erlene was a freshman at Republic High School and graduated in 1959.

*Earl and Louise Andrus and children: Raymond, Ralph and Erlene in 1942.*

Earl sold farm equipment for Sears, and Louise worked at the local garment factory. Earl served on the Republic City Council for a time before Republic started its tremendous growth of the past several years. Louise retired from the garment factory, and they started raising dogs and tropical fish. They opened Earl's Pet Shop where they sold tropical fish and pet supplies for several years. After living on West Street for 15 years, they moved to a new home on East Rosewood where they lived until their deaths, Earl in 1980 and Louise in 2002.

The three children all live in the Billings area where they raised their families. Raymond retired after being a barber in Billings for 50 years. Ralph is semi-retired and in the construction business. Erlene is retired after being a secretary with the public school system for 25 years. *Submitted by Erlene Nelson.*

**ARMSTRONG -** Orland Kay Armstrong, who was usually called "O.K." was a prominent Ozarkier who was born in Willow Springs, MO in 1893 and passed from the scene at the age of 93 in his home near Republic. He was widely known as a patriot, educator, journalist, politician, speech writer, orator, peace activist, historian, world traveler, pornography fighter, family man and Baptist Sunday school teacher.

"OK" was the third of nine children born to Rev. William Calvin Armstrong and Agnes (Brockhaus) Armstrong. He was gifted with high energy and leadership from his youth. He received Summa Cum Laude honors from Drury College. Later, he earned a law degree from Cumberland University and a master's degree at the University of Missouri School of Journalism, under the famous Dean Walter Williams. OK then went to the University of Florida in Gainesville as the founder of their School of Journalism, now one of the largest and most respected in the nation. After about four years there, he returned to Springfield and began writing and teaching at Drury College.

O.K. Armstrong.

During World War I, OK enlisted in the United States Army Signal Corps, Aviation Section, predecessor to the Air Force. Following the armistice, he joined the American Red Cross and served in France working with Russian prisoners of war.

Upon returning, he met the love of his life, Louise McCool, daughter of Rev. A.M. McCool. Louise and OK married, and together they had four sons and one daughter. She was beautiful and gracious, but cancer took her away in 1947, while she was still young.

OK interviewed about 1,200 surviving former slaves in the 1920s, and wrote a book entitled *"Ole Massa's People."* His journalism career produced many articles in national magazines, and his national audience blossomed through his association with the *Reader's Digest*. For 35 years he traveled the world, producing "articles of lasting interest" *(Reader's Digest* theme). He wrote about world leaders, wartime generals, political situations and the series on the American Revolution. He produced more articles for *Reader's Digest* than any other writer of his time.

OK went to Washington, D.C. in 1927 to witness the triumphant return of Charles Lindbergh after his famous solo flight from New York to Paris. He got into the McLean House, where Lindbergh was the guest of President Calvin Coolidge; OK got the only interview during Lindbergh's Washington visit, published in newspapers throughout the nation. Thus began a lifelong friendship with Charles Lindbergh.

From age 14, OK taught Sunday school classes, here in Springfield and in Washington, D.C. During 1938, OK worked undercover for Missouri's Governor Stark, investigating the Pendergast political machine in Kansas City.

Armstrong was always a champion for decency and equal rights. He wrote articles about equal rights for women, for African Americans, for American Indians, and for Japanese Americans interned during World War II. He co-authored *Baptists In America* with his second wife Marjorie Moore Armstrong, a book about prominent Baptists' influence in the founding of America. He also authored *Fifteen Decisive Battles of the United States,* tracing the history of victories from Gen. Oglethorpe (1742) in Georgia, to the air power victory over Germany (1945).

As an orator, Armstrong was outstanding. Usually, OK would start by telling a funny story about himself, getting the audience to warm up to him. Using only skeletal outlines, he never read a speech, but with a crescendo of voice inflection, gestures, and pace, he would thunder his point home to rousing applause. He ran for the State Legislature and was elected three times. During his terms in office, he investigated the Missouri State Penitentiary, exposing the abuses there. He organized trips to the State Capitol in Jefferson City on school busses for all the grade school kids of his district, with a stop at Bagnel Dam along the way. This was a great treat during the 1930s Depression, remembered fondly by many who went on the trips. He wrote speeches for President Eisenhower and produced dozens of "speech of the week" for Republican Congressional candidates.

OK was elected to the U.S. House of Representatives in 1951. His victory was attributed to a debate with the incumbent. Congressman Armstrong was selected the "Outstanding Freshman" in Congress by Congressional Quarterly. His term in Congress happened during the Korean War. OK flew to Japan, had a two-hour interview with Gen. Douglas MacArthur, then went over to Korea. He was given a tour of the front lines by Gen. Matthew Ridgeway, and their Jeep got too close to combat and had its windshield blown out.

In 1951, during his term in Congress, OK flew to San Francisco to attend the Peace Conference to formally end the war with Japan. OK took a map of Russia which showed the locations of dozens of slave labor camps, compiled by the CIO-AFL labor union, and presented it to Soviet Ambassador Andre Gromyko. This embarrassed Gromyko, and the event was published all over the world. OK believed "holding up the truth to their lies" would have gone far toward winning the cold war sooner. Leadership was an integral part of OK's makeup. Like the Old Testament prophets, OK did not wait for a trend to develop, but boldly held forth the truth and led the way.

Most of his adult life was lived in Springfield at Benton and Lynn, in a house built in 1873. In 1963, OK dismantled the house and moved its elegant materials just north of Wilson's Creek National Battlefield, where he designed and built a house modeled after Mt. Vernon (Washington's home). He lovingly called it "The Highlands," in reference to his Scottish heritage.

O.K. Armstrong was born before the invention of the automobile, radio, television, airplanes, computers, or many other things which have transformed our world. The fastest travel was by train. He grew up to utilize jet planes to travel the world, and he witnessed Neil Armstrong land on the moon. He visited every country in Central America, and spoke before all their legislative bodies; he also visited most every country in South America, Europe, the Balkins and most African nations. He visited most Asian nations; writing and speaking. He was once asked where he had not yet been; he responded, "Well, I missed Lithuania."

Most of all, OK was a patriot who loved America and championed freedom, democracy, decency, honesty and hard work. Most of his peers are gone now, and most of those who knew him personally miss him and the influence he had for good causes. *Submitted by OK Armstrong's son.*

**ARNDT** – Wilford Arndt was the youngest of eight children born to Robert F. and Hulda E. (Bengsch) Arndt, born in Clever, MO on March 1, 1921 and died Feb. 16, 2005. Wilford married Maxine (Bull), the oldest of five children born to Olan and Clora (Hargas) Bull in 1940, and had three children: James O., Robert O. and Paula K. Arndt, all born in Republic. Wilford and Maxine purchased a farm on what was then Route 2, Republic, MO, now known as FR 178 in 1944. Wilford worked for his father-in-law, Olan Bull, who had a chicken hatchery on Main St. in Republic while milking cows and growing crops on his farm. Maxine went to work in 1948 for the garment factory in Republic and helped on the farm. Wilford entered the U.S. Army during World War II and served his country in Europe returning with a Purple Heart after being wounded.

Wilford Arndt.

Wilford then went to work for the state of Missouri testing livestock, retiring after many years to farm full time. Wilford and his oldest son Jim purchased the farm of Olan Bull in 1966 to raise beef cattle, selling full sides of beef to many Republic residents for years. Most of the farm was sold in 2003 after being annexed into the city of Republic and now is a housing development. The original farm house and barn are on the remaining property still owned by Jim. Olan Bull purchased that farm in 1928 when Maxine was 5 years old.

Wilford served the community helping the local VFW Post become an active part of Main St. in Republic and serving many veterans in need of help and supporting Christmas programs in Fort Leonard Wood, MO. Wilford purchased one of the first bricks used on the Main Street sidewalk restoration.

During the 1940, 50, 60, 70, 80 and 90 decades Wilford was always helping local farmers when hay needed to be hauled, or any other request made of him as a neighbor and friend. Wilford and Jim both lived on the farm helping each other eke out a living until Wilford's death in 2005.

All of Wilford and Maxine's children reside in Republic and continue to honor his memory helping support the VFW and keeping his spirit alive. *Submitted by Frances Arndt.*

**ARNDT/GEBHARDS -** Lloyd George and Edna Grace Arndt moved to Republic from Springfield, MO in early 1953, locating at 423 North Main Street. Lloyd was born in 1918 to Robert Frederick and Hulda Elizabeth (Bengsch) Arndt, in Clever, MO. The family included brothers: Ernest, Clarence, Albert, Howard, Otis, Earl and Wilford and sister Sylvia.

Lloyd and Edna Arndt.   Howard and Amber Arndt.

Edna was born in 1923 to Bernhard Frederick and Anna Carolina (Rother) Gebhards of Langdon, MO. The family included brothers: Edwin, Frederick and Harry, and sisters: Tina, Etta and Wilma. During WWII Lloyd served from 1942-45 in the U.S. Army's 2nd Armored Division, "Hell on Wheels," participating in campaigns in North Africa, Italy, Normandy, Belgium and Germany. The couple met through Edwin Gebhards, who was Lloyd's service buddy and Edna's brother, and they were married Jan. 5, 1946.

Lloyd worked at the U.S. Federal Medical Center in Springfield, where he served as a corrections officer for over 24 years. He was a member of the American Legion and the Veterans of Foreign Wars. Edna was a homemaker and a cook at three of the Republic schools. She was a member of the Hood Methodist Church, and was noted for her handcrafted quilts. Lloyd passed away in 1982 followed by Edna in 1986. Both are buried in Smart Cemetery, Clever, MO.

The couple was blessed with two children, Howard David in 1947 and Amber Anne in 1951. Both attended Republic schools for 12 years. Howard was a starter on Republic's 1963 State Championship basketball team. He graduated in 1965 as salutatorian of this class and earned All-State Basketball Honors in 1964 and 1965. The 6'8" Arndt was also named to *Parade Magazine's* 1965 High School All-America Basketball Squad. He attended the University of Kansas on a basketball scholarship and played four years for the Jayhawks. He earned a bachelor and a master of science in electrical engineering in 1970 and 1971. He also earned a master of business administration from Syracuse University in 1977. Howard served in the U.S. Army Reserves for six years.

Amber graduated from high school in 1969 and attended the University of Missouri earning a bachelor of science in merchandising in 1973. Subsequently, she earned a master of science in accounting from Southern New Hampshire University in 1989. *Submitted by Howard and Amber Arndt.*

**ATON -** John Aton was born Oct. 7, 1834 to John and Margaret Heaton Aton in Union County, KY. When John was a young boy, the family moved to Belleville, IL. There he was a shop foreman for the Ohio and Mississippi Railroad. It was also where he met and married his wife, Frances Wyles, on April 24, 1855. Two sons, Benjamin Franklin, born Aug. 30, 1859, and John Jr., born Oct. 18, 1862, were born before the family moved to Greene County, MO in 1862. John had purchased property located south of Springfield, west of Campbell Street Road, between Weaver and Plainview Roads, in 1851 for $1.25 per acre.

*Thomas Nelson Aton Family in 1910, l-r: Ira, Clara, Ruth, Sidney, Lois, Billy, Rosa and Tom. Taken at the farm on Plainview Road, Springfield, MO.*

It was at this location that John set up a blacksmith's shop and began farming. It was his blacksmith's shop that both the Confederate and Union Armies used on their journeys from Springfield to Wilson's Creek during the Civil War. He also raised, stood and sold jacks. Mares were brought in from as far away as Lockwood and Golden City to be serviced.

After settling in Greene County, four more children were born to John and Margaret: Mary E. (Feb. 17, 1865), Walter W. (May 3, 1872), Thomas Nelson (Feb. 18, 1875) and George (Feb. 17, 1878).

At the time of his death the daily news stated, "John Aton, one of the old settlers of Greene County, is critically ill at his home. He was stricken with paralysis on Saturday and has not uttered a word since that time." His death occurred a short time later. Thomas "Tom" Nelson Aton, from birth to death, lived on the property that had been established as the family farm. He too farmed and did blacksmith work. In the 1900s, Tom was a foreman for the county road construction department. He supervised the initial construction of Scenic and major revisions and improvements of Campbell, Weaver and Plainview Roads as well. This was accomplished with horses, mules, and manpower. In the late teens he took over the 320-acre George McDaniel farm which was located east and west of Campbell and north of M Highway.

Tom married Rosa Belle Munhollon Feb. 23, 1898. Four children were born to this union: Ira Ervin (April 7, 1899), Tina Lois (Jan. 18, 1902), Sidney Millard (March 25, 1904) and Ruth Irene (Dec. 16, 1906). Ira and Sid worked with their father in the farming operation starting at a young age. Ira was employed by Standard Oil as a young adult. He was killed in an auto accident at the age of 32.

Sid married Georgia Utley on Sept. 7, 1927. Sid and Georgia became the parents of three sons: Joe Bob (March 23, 1929), Jerry Max (Jan. 27, 1933) and John Perry (Nov. 14, 1934). Sid, with the assistance of his sons, continued to farm as well as doing carpentry work. Georgia was an elementary teacher for the Springfield public school system. They lived at the farm until each passed away, Georgia in 1984 and Sid in 1985.

Bob, Jerry and John each married, had children and have remained in Greene County. To this day, Bobby Aton, son of John, continues to live on property that was originally purchased five generations ago in 1851. *Submitted by Jerry Aton.*

**BATSON/BLADES -** Leo Arthur Batson was born April 12, 1912, to Lawrence Batson and Bertha (Blades) Batson. Leo was the first-born son with a younger brother, Orville Batson. On April 13, 1935, Leo married Cleo Lavaughn Blades (born April 17, 1915), daughter of John Leroy "Roy" Blades and Malissa "Lissa" Jane (Mooneyham) Blades. Leo and Cleo were married in Monett, MO by Pastor Alvin Erickson. Cleo was one of six children: Clara (Blades) Parker, Wayne Blades, Dorothy (Blades) Swinney, Thelma (Blades) Dorrell and Jimmie Blades.

Leo and Cleo initially lived in a house on the Blades family farm and later in a home near Plano. Leo took over the milk route of his brother-in-law, Wayne Blades, when Wayne went into the military during WWII. Cleo worked for Cline and Mary Clark at their grocery store in Halltown. It was there that she developed the "itch" to have her own store. She got that opportunity when she and Leo purchased the Jot 'Em Down store from Clara and Vernie Giles.

The Jot 'Em Down store, named after a popular radio show at the time, was located at the intersection of PP and TT Highways northwest of Republic. The store had a filling station, and inventory included groceries and livestock feed. On Saturday evenings farmers would pick up groceries and feed and congregate there to visit with neighbors. Leo and Cleo lived

*Cleo's Women's Apparel Store, Main Street, Republic, MO.*

just down the road from the store and milked a number of cattle in addition to running the store and milk route. In the 1950s they sold the store to Charlie and Gladys Booth. Leo went to work for Tony Thornton hauling cattle to the sale barn in Springfield and Cleo worked in Thornton's Cafe at the sale barn.

In 1959 they built a home on Hines Street in Republic. They also leased the former movie theater on Main Street in Republic from Lynn Martin. The theater had evolved into a dime store, and they purchased its inventory from the current owner, Edna Eagan. Over the years, the inventory transitioned to ladies' clothing from markets in Kansas City and Dallas, and the store's name was changed to Cleo's Women's Apparel. Leo and Cleo worked together in the store for three decades before retiring in 1988.

Leo and Cleo had 14 nieces and nephews whom they claimed as "their own." Likewise the nieces and nephews thought of their aunt and uncle as "second parents." Leo and Cleo enjoyed retirement years and celebrated 59 years of marriage prior to Leo's death on Nov. 13, 1994, at age 82. Cleo continues to reside in their Hines Street home and is passionate about her family and her faith. Her hobbies have resulted in many family heirlooms such as crocheted doilies and afghans and handmade quilts. *Submitted by Lynette Chastain.*

**BATSON/GARDNER -** Thomas Blackstone Blades (1857-1950), son of Ransom Dudley Blades was married to Eliza (1863-1941). Their children were Albert, Efton, Earl, Floyd, Bertha, Eva, Lilly and Ethel.

Bertha (1889-1972) married Lawrence Batson (1889-1915). They had two sons, Leo and Orville Lesley. Lawrence died after being operated on for appendicitis at his father's home on the kitchen table. Orville was eight months old at the time. After Lawrence's death Bertha made her home with her parents.

Leo married Cleo Blades. Orville married G. Lavon Gardner in 1917. Orville and Lavon had four sons: Herbert "Sonny" Lawrence in 1934, Donald Eugene in 1936, Ray Leon in 1937 and Willis Lesley in 1938. After Orville and Lavon were married they relocated to California.

Sonny was born in Pomono and Donnie, Ray and Willis in Ontario. The family returned to Missouri to live on part of the Blades homestead. Sonny attended St. Joe School until he was spanked by the teacher. When he refused to go back his parents sent him to Billings to finish the year.

The follow-

*Marion and Rosa Gardner with children: Hershal, Otto, Noel, Ola and Ailene ca. 1909.*

ing summer the Batson family along with the teacher and her husband, Tom Brown, returned to California. There were eight passengers in a five passenger coupe. The back of the rear seat had been removed so some could ride in the trunk.

In 1945 they once again returned to Missouri, locating in Greenfield. While in California the kids were used to hearing air raid warnings. While living in Greenfield sirens were heard. The family rushed into town fearing it would be bombed. When they arrived they saw a big bonfire on the square of Greenfield and found out the war was over.

In 1946 their fourth son Lesley was killed getting off the school bus. He was seven years old at the time.

In 1947 the family rented part of the Blades homestead from their uncle, Earl Blades, on Pickerel Creek in Greene County. Another uncle, Floyd Blades, continued to live on Thomas' farm building a pipeline milk barn, probably one of the first in Greene County. Moving there, Orville, Lavon and the boys operated the farm with Floyd from 1948 to 1954. Sonny remembers working for Monroe Mooneyham thrashing grain. Monroe always wore a bow tie when working in the field; this was a holdover from the 1860s.

Lavon worked in the garment industry for Republic Garment and Hagle Manufacturing. Orville worked for Greene County Road and Bridge, Owen and Short Hardware and for the city of Republic in charge of the streets, sewer, parks, and water. Orville died in 1995 and is buried at Wade Chapel Cemetery. Lavon continues to live in Republic.

Lavon's father was Marion Gardner (1874-1947). He was the son of George Gardner. Marion was a Methodist preacher. His first wife, Lettie Batson, bore two children, Otto and Hershel, before she died. He then married Rosa Etheridge (1877-1962). Their children were Noel, Herbert, Ola, Ailene, Bonnie, Alma, Lavon, Gladys, Ferrell and Evilana (Evalee). They lived on the county line road, south of Republic. When Marion went to town by wagon, Rosa could hear him singing as he left town and knew to start supper.

Sonny married Violet Ray Smith, born in 1956. They have three children: Lawrence Wade, Joy Lee and Daniel Paul. *Submitted by Herbert "Sonny" Batson.*

**BEARD/DOUGHERTY** – Tony Herbert Beard, son of James and Clara Hambelton Beard, and Alma Alice Dougherty, daughter of John and Dora Harris Dougherty, were married in Gainesville, MO in 1941. After his time in the Army, serving in World War II, Tony and Alma settled in Gainesville, MO, where Tony helped to build Bull Shoals Dam. The couple had three children: Gerald Roger and Rita Carol were born in Gainesville and Cathie Sue was born in Mountain Home, AR.

Tony began driving a truck for Mountain Truckline out of Mountain Home, AR. In 1956, Mountain Truckline sold to Voss and the Beards relocated to Springfield, and thus brought the Beard family to Republic. The family first lived on College Street and one year later moved to 206 East Elm where they resided until 1964.

During these years, Gerald graduated from Republic High School, worked at Fred McCullah's Service Station and later was a butcher at "Gose" Garoutte's Locker Plant on Main Street. In 1963 Gerald married Nancy Evans and had one daughter, Melanie, now married to Casey Yunger. Later Gerald married Christina Fugitt and had two daughters: Lisa, now married to Allen Shevey, and Lori, now married to Billy Viles. In 1964, Voss Truckline sold out to Western Gillette, and the Beards moved to Miami, OK where Rita and Cathie graduated high school. Both girls graduated from Miami's NEO A&M College, and then Rita graduated from Tahlequah.

Rita married and had three boys: Jason, Brent and Matthew Billows. In 1973, Western Gillette sold out to Roadway and brought Tony and Alma back to Springfield where they once again made their home in Republic. Cathie married Stan Coggin and they have one son, Zachary, and a daughter, Beth, now married to Jacob Nelson. Zachary has one son, Brady.

After retiring from Roadway at 62, Tony then began driving a Republic school bus. When he retired from that job, he began mowing the school yards. In December 2000, at the age of 80, Tony passed away. Alma, his wife of almost 60 years, still resides in Republic. Gerald resides in Florida. Rita and her son Matt make their home in Republic where Rita is a Title I reading aide in the Elementary III building. Cathie and her husband Stan still reside on the Coggin family's century farm just north of Republic. Cathie is in her fourteenth year of teaching second grade at Republic's Elementary I, and Stan works as a controller for Friend Tire Co. in Monett, MO. Stan is currently serving his 19th year on Republic's School Board.

Tony and Alma's family has grown to include eight grandchildren and seven great-grandchildren to this date. *Submitted by Cathie Beard Coggin.*

**BECK** – "One of the most exciting experiences I have had was attending a White House briefing with President Reagan in the East Room," says Republic resident Dr. Christopher Beck. Dr. Beck moved to Republic from Springfield, MO with his parents, Raymond and Anita, in 1976. He graduated from Republic High School in 1980 and attended Baptist Bible College (BBC) in Springfield, earning a bachelor's degree in 1984.

*Dr. Christopher and Dana Beck with Lincoln Christopher Ray.*

After graduation Beck became executive director, then state chairman of the Missouri's Moral Majority. In that capacity, Beck had a number of exciting experiences including the White House briefing, hosting a syndicated radio broadcast and hosting meetings with nationally known personalities.

Later, Beck was hired as an on-air personality at KWFC radio. Eventually, he became full-time news reporter. His experiences in this post were exciting and varied. Beck was the only broadcast journalist from southwest Missouri to be allowed into the Supreme Court to hear oral arguments in the historic Webster versus Reproductive Health Services case in l989. Beck reported on this case for KWFC, but also for the USA Radio Network, and Focus on the Family's "Family News In Focus."

While at KWFC, Beck met Dana Burrell. She hailed from Marshfield and graduated from Southwest Baptist University with bachelor's degrees in both elementary education and home economics. Upon graduation, she was hired as a kindergarten teacher in Niangua. Christopher and Dana were married in 1992 and initially moved to Springfield.

Christopher pursued graduate work, graduating in 1992 with a master's degree in communication. Christopher became a professor at Baptist Bible College (BBC) where he eventually would be named chair of the Communication Department.

Dana continued teaching, moving to Marshfield Schools. She also pursued a graduate degree, obtaining her master's degree in early childhood education. Once Dana's graduate work was completed, Christopher began to pursue his doctorate at Regent University in Virginia, earning a Ph.D. in communication with an emphasis in political communication. Dana obtained a kindergarten teaching position in the Willard school system where she continues to teach.

Christopher and Dana began attending West Republic Baptist Church (WRBC), located on West Highway 60 (one mile west of Republic's Burger King). After years of ministering in the adult class, Beck was called by a unanimous vote to serve as pastor. He also continued his work at Baptist Bible College.

"As pastor of WRBC." Christopher says, "I felt that my wife Dana and I should live in the community in which I was called to share the gospel of Christ—the good news that one can find forgiveness and salvation by placing one's faith in Jesus and what He did on the cross. So, soon I had 'come back home' to Republic."

On Nov. 24, 2004, Dr. and Mrs. Christopher Beck were blessed with the addition of a son, Lincoln Christopher Ray Beck. Though he has health issues that are an ongoing concern, Lincoln is a blessing to the family and to all who have come to know him and his story. *Submitted by Christopher Beck.*

**BECK/GRIFFITH** - Raymond and Anita Beck were married in 1959 and moved to Missouri from northwest Arkansas at that time. Raymond had been born in Indiana, but the family moved to Mountain Home, AR when he was in elementary school. Anita (Griffith) Beck was born in Cotter, AR, and grew up in that small, close-knit community.

*Raymond and Anita Beck and sons, Christopher and Clayton.*

Raymond graduated from Mountain Home High School in 1958 and moved to Missouri immediately. He and Anita were engaged at the time, and immediately after her graduation from Cotter High School in Cotter, AR, they were married on June 13, 1959. They initially lived and worked in St. Joseph, MO, but soon found their way to southwest Missouri settling in Springfield.

While living in Springfield, the Beck's two

sons, Christopher and Clayton, were born. As the boys grew older, Raymond and Anita desired to move outside of Springfield in a more rural setting with a good school system. After looking at many homes in many different surrounding communities, the Becks found "the perfect home" in Republic, MO. They made the move to Republic in 1976. Their sons attended Republic Middle School and Republic High. Christopher graduated in 1980 and Clayton in 1985.

Raymond continued working in Springfield at the Paul Mueller Company from where he eventually retired in 2005. Anita was employed with Springfield Public Schools and Republic Schools. She also ran for the state legislature in 1992. Currently, she holds a real estate and brokers license.

Clayton's career eventually took him to places such as St. Louis, Racine, WI, and Las Vegas. Clayton became a missionary to Belize for a brief while, before moving to Michigan with his wife, Rebekah. Clayton has six children: Jessica, Lauren, Isaac, Anna, Jericho and Bethany.

Christopher resides in Republic with his wife Dana and their son Lincoln. Christopher received his bachelor's degree from Baptist Bible College, his master's degree from Missouri State University, and a Ph.D. from Regent University in Virginia. Christopher is chair of the Communication Department of Baptist Bible College and also serves as pastor of West Republic Baptist Church (WRBC), located between Republic and Billings on West Highway 60.

Serving the Lord in church is a priority in the Beck's household. Raymond and Anita are both active members of WRBC. *Submitted by Raymond and Anita Beck.*

**BELL/KING** – In the late 1800s, Benjamon H. Bell and Minty J. (King) Bell came cross country in a covered wagon on the wagon train from North Carolina to Republic, MO with their children: Nora, Horace, George, John, Sarah, Mary, Abbie and Joseph. William, Elsie and Lawton were born in Republic.

*Picture taken at the foot of the pump house on Terrell Creek that supplied water for Frisco RR. From l-r: Myrtle Paaree, Sarah Schmidt, Will Schmidt, George Schmidt, Culetta Schmidt McGehee.*

Horace stayed in Republic and raised his children there. Sarah married William Schmidt and she moved to Billings, where he ran the pump house at Terrell Creek for the Frisco RR. It pumped water to Billings (town) to run the steam train that came through Republic and Billings. He retired from Frisco in the middle of 1940. *Submitted by Betty Hale.*

**BENNETT** - With an occasional jog for short acres, the County Line Road stretches east-west some six miles ever mindful of her purpose as a boundary between Greene and Christian counties since their separation in 1859. A continuous flow of energy, this venerable old road

*James and Susan Bennett and family at home in Christian County circa 1907.*

*James and Susan Bennett at home in Greene County circa 1925.*

*The Bennett home 2002.*

south of Republic has been home to the Bennett family for approximately 120 years. Today, a sixth generation of descendants from John and Sarah Bennett still calls the road home.

John Wesley Bennett, a native of Tennessee, and Sarah Elizabeth Moore, his bride in 1854, resided first along the banks of the James River at Delaware Town. Having four children at that location from 1856-62 and another after the Civil War in 1869, the Bennett parents did not move from Delaware Town to the county line until the 1890s. Youngest son James Martin and wife Susan (Hays) Bennett purchased their own land in Christian County in 1907. Perched on opposing hilltops and a mile apart, each small Bennett farm could be viewed from the other, an aspect of the range of observation the County Line Road offers.

After the purchase of their farm, James and Susan Bennett became increasingly aware of the Republic reorganized school system but the county line served as a boundary for the new district. Thus, their four children: Claude, Carl, Edith and Frank, were unable to attend. With the purchase of 10 acres in 1912 on the north side of the road, Mr. Bennett promptly lifted his house from its foundation, positioned it on logs, and rolled it creaking and groaning across the road into Greene county! The children no longer attended a one-room school miles away. With a new address the house also received two new rooms and a wide rounded front porch with columns. This house came to be known as the Bennett place even though the original home of parents John and Sarah lay a hilltop to the east.

Through the 1930s strawberry fields abounded on much of the Bennett land with produce being shipped by rail from Republic. The home played host to many Saturday night card parties with neighbors. Music was also a form of entertainment among the Bennetts as sons, Frank and Claude, played in local bands.

Fulfilling his childhood dream Harold (Unk) Bennett, great-grandson of John and Sarah, purchased the home in 1973. He and his wife Ila completely remodeled the old house. At this writing the old home yet stands, the road still jogs, and Bennetts still call the County Line Road home. *Submitted by Kay Bennett.*

**BENNETT/CLICK** - George Franklin "Shrimp" Bennett was born on July 25, 1905, to James Martin and Susan Adaline Bennett at the farmhouse located south and west of Republic, MO, on the northwest corner of County Line Road and Beal Road. Frank liked to play tricks on his mother and once climbed into a tree to toss a dead snake around her shoulder when she was walking to the barn. During the winter of 1911 or 1912, he became very sick with diphtheria and almost died. He missed two years of school at that time but went ahead to graduate from Republic High School in 1925.

*1925 Class Photo.*

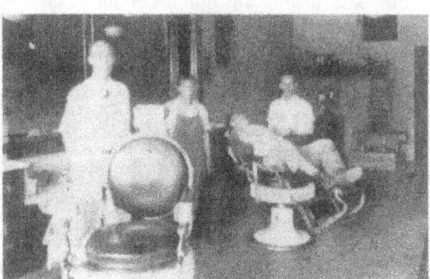

*Late 1920s or early 30s, Frank is standing behind second chair in old barbershop, SE corner of Main and Grant*

A year after high school graduation, Frank worked as a shoeshine boy in the local barbershop. The owner asked Frank if he would like to shave necks and before long Frank was also cutting hair and shaving faces. That was the beginning of 46 years in the barber business. The first shop where Frank worked was located on the southeast corner of Main and Grant Street. Frank was also quite a musician and enjoyed playing tenor banjo and drums in several local orchestras.

*Ethel, Frank, and Charlotte at old house on South Main in Spring 1946.*

In 1936 a young woman, Ethel Click, came from Oklahoma to Republic to visit friends. She was introduced to Frank and in February of 1937 they were married. Frank and Ethel lived in an apartment next to the old water tower on South Main for several years but soon bought a home north of the tower on the opposite side of the street. The Republic Milling Company, sometimes called the Cold Storage Building, was across the street from that house. Frank and Ethel became the proud parents of a baby girl, Charlotte Jean, in December of '42.

Soon after Charlotte's birth Frank was drafted into the Army and served in the South Pacific for over a year during WWII. When Frank returned home he bought his own shop, located next to the locker plant on the west side of Main south of Grant. He and his brother, Claude, barbered there for many years. He cut hair morning, noon and night when a haircut and shave cost 30 cents. One of the added attractions at Bennett's Barber Shop was the shower in the back. The farmers would come to town for supplies then get a haircut and shave, take a shower and be ready for Saturday night activities. In the mid-50s, Frank and his family moved to 425 N. Main where he lived until 1996. He remembered that across the street from that North Main location had been the Anderson Park where Fourth of July and Labor Day picnics were held.

Frank never owned a car until the late 40s. Even after owning a car, he walked to work every day. Because of his small stature, he got the nickname "Shrimp." He used to joke about his height by saying that he was 6 feet tall at one time but he had walked around the barber chair so much that he wore his legs down.

Frank was a 50-year member of the Republic Masonic Lodge #570 and Ethel was an active member of the Republic Eastern Star. Both were members of First Baptist Church. Frank once served as the choir director of the church and Ethel taught Sunday school for many years. Ethel was also a 4th grade school teacher at Republic for more than 20 years. Ethel died in August of 1986. In August of 1996 Frank moved to Broken Arrow, OK, to be near his daughter and family. He died August 2, 1998, seven days after his 93rd birthday. He and Ethel are buried in Evergreen Cemetery in Republic.

One of Frank's favorite sayings was "If you get there first, you make a mark. If I get there first, I'll rub it out." He lived in Republic all his life and was very knowledgeable concerning its history and its people. He remembered many events and had great stories to tell. He definitely "made the mark." *Submitted by Charlotte (Bennett) Parker.*

**BENNETT/HOOD** - William E. "Gene" Bennett was born March 15, 1932, son of David S. and Ilene C. (White) Bennett, and grandson of W.P. and Martha (Mooney) Bennett and Ed and Beulah (Carter) White. Gene married Anne T. (Hood) Bennett on Oct. 4, 1953. Anne was born Jan. 18, 1932 and passed away on Oct. 16, 2001. She was the daughter of Roscoe and Lucille (Turner) Hood and granddaughter of Wm. E. and Grace T. (Cheatham) Hood.

Gene graduated from Republic High School in 1949, continuing his education at the Missouri School of Mines in Rolla, MO, graduating with a BS in mechanical engineering. After working two years in Indiana they returned to Republic in 1960 purchasing their home at 408 E. Elm. Anne graduated from Republic High School in 1950, continuing her education at St. John's School of Nursing, graduating in May 1953 as a registered nurse. She had a lifetime love for antiques shown by her collection. She operated two antique stores, one in downtown Republic and one on Hwy. 60 West.

Gene and Anne had three beautiful daughters: Lynette "Lyn," born in December 1955, graduated from Republic, attended Tulsa University and graduated with a BS and a RN, degree. "Lyn" married Robert J. Carter, and they have a daughter Allison, who graduated from Glendale High School, continued to Trinity College and received a BS degree in philosophy. Allison married Erick Twist, and they have one son Carter. "Lyn" and Robert's daughter Jessica graduated from Glendale High School also, attended Kansas State University receiving a BS degree in architecture. She is living in Austin, TX and is practicing architecture.

Louann was born in February 1958 and married Ernie Giddens in 1977. They have a daughter, Rhiannon, who graduated from Baker University with a BS degree in business in 2005 and will be living in Republic. Their son Ben is attending Southern Illinois University located in Carbondale, IL and is studying for a BS degree in aeronautical management. Ernie and Louann own Redneck Trailer Supply, located in Springfield, MO. They started this business in 1979 and continue the operation today. Ernie and Louann live on their farm northwest of Republic.

Leah was born in January 1960 and passed in February 1998. Leah graduated from Republic High School, attended SMSU after graduation, and married Tommy Butler. They had one daughter Danielle Anne, born May 1993. Danielle is attending RMS and is in the 7th grade. She and her father continue to live in Republic.

Gene and Anne moved their family to a home on East Elm Street in 1966. Four years after Anne's death, Gene moved to a home on Farm Road 45, continuing to live in the Republic area. Anne is buried at Evergreen Cemetery. *Submitted by Gene Bennett. Editor's note: Gene passed away Oct. 20, 2006.*

**BENNETT/WADE** - Max was born Aug. 22, 1934 at Pleasant Hope, MO. He was the son of David Samuel and Ilene White Bennett who moved to Republic in 1947 from a farm north of Republic. They purchased an interest in the Owen and Short Hardware store and were an active part of this business until his death. David had diphtheria as a child and suffered from the effects of this illness most of his life. David was born July 4, 1905 to William P. and Francis Alice (Mooney) Bennett and died on April 16, 1949. He had six siblings: John, Floyd, Bert, Hershel, Gola and Leila.

Ilene was born Oct. 22, 1908 to Ernest D. and Beulah Carter White and died June 5, 1990. She had five siblings: Vernon, Harold, Thelma, Betty and Barbara. Ilene operated a dry goods store on Main Street in Republic for several years after the death of her husband. It was a favorite hangout for many of the high school girls. Max had two siblings: Ernie, born April 12, 1928 and Gene, born March 15, 1932. Max was diagnosed with a brain tumor in June 2002 and died on Aug. 9, 2003 at the age of 68.

*Rosie and Max Bennett, Christmas 1996.*

Max attended Bennett Grade School and Republic High School where he graduated in 1951. He went to work for Caterpillar Tractor Co. in Joliet, IL in 1952. Max spent four years in a work/study tool and die apprenticeship. He was the first to graduate from this school at the Joliet facility. He worked as a tool designer and supervisor in the shop at Caterpillar. Later in his career he served on the Board of Equipment Manufacturer Institute, chaired by the president of Caterpillar.

In 1966 the adventures continued for the Bennett family with a move to Kansas. Through his hard work and ingenuity his expertise took them to many places around the country, Wilmington, IL; Lewis, KS; Hesston, KS; Logan, UT; Oregon, IL; Newton, KS; Great Bend, KS; and Wichita, KS. In 1977 Max attended a special 13-week management school at the Harvard Business School with 160 business men from around the world. It was a great experience and opportunity for life long friendships. However, they were no more important to Max than keeping in touch with his friends at home. He loved coming back for his high school reunion and was often the MC for the event.

He married Rosalene (Rosie) Wade on Sept. 5, 1954. Rosie was born in Ontario, CA, Jan. 2, 1937. She was the daughter of Clyde D. and Bonnie Gardner Wade and the sister of Juanita Bridges and Patricia Altman. She attended Grandview Grade School and graduated from Republic High School in 1954. They had four children: twins, David E. and Neisha L. (1956); Daniel M. (1957); and Tracy B. (1960). David married Karen Schickram Duggan. Karen has two daughters, Kelly and Alyssa Duggan. Neisha married Hugo Dahlstrom and they have four children: Chris, Tara, Kelly and Britt. Daniel married Jennifer Jameson Dyer. Jennifer has one daughter Jamen Dyer, and Daniel and Jennifer have two sons, Max and John. Tracy married Edmund Berry IV and they have two children, Yana and Dimitry. Ed has two children, Kimberly and Edmund V.

Max and Rosie were always on the go, they traveled many miles to visit friends, play a round of golf, and enjoy their family. It was never too far to travel, be it Mexico, China, Scotland, England, France, Italy, Belgium, Jamaica or a town just down the road. *Submitted by Rosie Bennett.*

**BEST/TYLER** - Edythe (Cutbirth) Tyler and Orvie O. Best were married on Feb. 2, 1985 in the home of her daughter Sue and son-in-law Leland Brown, here in Republic. Following a honeymoon trip to Hawaii, they have lived in Republic.

Edythe Cutbirth was born on Feb. 22, 1914 in Dit, MO

*Edythe and Orvie Best.*

*Back Row, l-r: Jessica Carter, Gene Bennett, Ernie Giddens; 2nd row: Allison Carter Twist, Lyn Carter, Anne Bennett, Rhiannon Giddens, LouAnn Giddens, Ben Giddens; front is Dani Butler.*

to Andrew Jackson Cutbirth and Myrtle (Ryles) Cutbirth. She had two sisters and one brother: Edrie McGinnis, Gladys Brumley and Herbert Cutbirth. Edythe's mother died of tuberculosis when Edythe was 2 years old. Her father never remarried.

Edythe graduated from Rogersville High School in 1932. Edythe married Harwood H. Tyler on Oct. 10, 1936. Harwood was born Jan. 11, 1916 in Pocahontas, AR to George Tyler and Leona (Staton) Tyler. Edythe and Harwood had one child, Evelyn Sue, born Aug. 17, 1937. They were living in Springfield, MO at that time. Harwood worked for Lipscomb Feed and Mill Co. driving a delivery truck. He was killed in a car-truck accident on July 16, 1940, at Valley Water Mill Road in Springfield as he returned from delivering feed to Buffalo, MO. He was 24 years old.

Edythe and Sue moved to Brookline, MO to live near her sister Edrie and her husband, May McGinnis who owned and operated one of two grocery and feed stores in Brookline. Edythe began working in garment factories in Springfield and Edrie and May took care of Sue. In the early 1950s she began working at the Woods Garment Factory in Republic and worked there for several years.

Edythe's father, Andrew Jackson Cutbirth, moved to Brookline to live with Edythe and Sue. He died of a stroke in 1951 at the age of 67. Sue attended grades one through eight at Brookline School, which was a one-room school. Following eighth grade she attended high school at Republic and graduated in 1955. In 1956 she married Leland Brown, a 1952 Republic graduate who had attended all 12 years in the Republic school system.

During the 1960s Edythe moved into the home of her sister Edrie and May to assist in the care of Edrie. Edrie died Sept. 2, 1970. Following this time Edythe moved to Republic, renting an apartment from Earl and Ruby Brown, parents of her son-in-law Leland. When her brother Herbert became ill, he purchased the lot next door to Earl and Ruby and Leland built a house for them to share. Edythe took care of Herbert until his death in 1981 at the age of 72. Edythe continues to live in the same house. Her sister Gladys passed away in Oct. 28, 1997.

Orvie Best was born Oct. 12, 1910 in Willard, MO. His parents were Leroy J. and Mary B. Best. His brothers were Tony, Leroy, James and Troy. His sisters were Eva and Bertha. Orvie's father was gatekeeper and guard for Doling Park in Springfield. Orvie worked for Ajax Pipeline Co. He worked for 12 years laying gas line from Oklahoma to Illinois. He felt God calling him to be a pastor and entered the ministry in 1935. For a time he combined his work with Ajax Pipeline and being a pastor.

Orvie was married to Mildred White in 1928. They had four daughters, all of whom are now living in Springfield. Mary and Sam Headlee, Bonnie and Jack Fuzzell, Betty Letterman and Ab (deceased) and Dot Vestal and Gene (deceased). Orvie pastored in the area and held many revivals. He became the pastor of Broadway Bible Church, Springfield, MO in 1956 and served them for 21 years, retiring in 1977. Mildred passed away on Dec. 25, 1982.

Edythe and Orvie have continued to have a ministry of encouragement to many area pastors and missionaries as well as friends and family. They attend Calvary Baptist Church in Republic. *Submitted by Edythe and Orvie Best. Editor's note: Orvie Best died 2006.*

**BIGLIENI/MCGUIRE** - Charles Anthony Biglieni, a native of Italy, was born Dec. 19, 1852 to Joseph Biglieni and Angie Compfortie Biglieni in Lake Como, Italy. He emigrated to this country in 1881 with his cousin Frank Duroni who settled in Marionville, MO. Three years later his younger brother Joseph joined him here. Joseph was born Jan. 16, 1864 and died Oct. 27, 1922 when a team of horses ran away with him while sowing grain. He settled on land three miles east of Republic. They all became naturalized citizens.

*Charles Biglieni Family. Iva being held by Charles, Florella, Laura holding Wesley; standing: Josie, Carl, Ethel, Clint and Eunice. (William was born after this picture.)*

Charles settled on land two miles east of Republic, MO. Wal-Mart is built on a parcel of the land today. He married Laura McGuire of Cave Springs, MO May 22, 1888. She was born March 17, 1864 to John W. McGuire and Catharine McGuire in Seymour, IN. They farmed as long as health permitted and remained on the same farm until their death, she on Aug. 7, 1930 and he Sept. 24, 1932. They had nine children: Ethel, Josephine, Clinton, Carl, Eunice, Florella, Iva, Wesley, and William.

Ethel was born in 1889 and died in 1953. She married in 1905 to Edd Ruhl who was born in 1879 and died in 1961. They had three children: Paul, Marie and Clyde.

Josephine, born in 1890, died in 1975, never married. She was the housekeeper for the Lester E. Cox family for over 30 years.

Clinton, born 1892, died 1925 when killed by a bull. He married in 1916 to Mae Phillips, no children.

Carl, born 1893, died 1961, married in 1911 to Eva Hunt, born 1894, died 1976. They had six children: Oblene, Maxine, Madine, Carol, Geralee and C.A. "Bud."

Eunice, born 1895, died 1966, married in 1917 to John Chilcutt, born 1889, died 1982. They had a son Dale.

Florella, born 1898, died 1982, married in 1918 to Ralph Blades, born 1899, died 1987. They had a daughter Helen.

Iva, born 1899, died 1967, married in 1921 to Hobart Bean, born 1897, died 1961. They had a daughter Marjorie Lee.

Wesley, born 1901, died 1987, married Opal McCroskey, born 1902, died 1992. They had a son Joseph Wesley known as J.W. He was killed in a car accident in 1957 in Houston, TX.

William, born 1904, died 1971, married 1928 to Irene Squibb, born 1909, died 1994. They had a son Charles. William owned W.R. Biglieni and Son Hardware from 1946 until 1961. It was located at 204 N. Main Street.

All the families followed farming for an occupation. *Submitted by Sue Morris.*

**BIGLIENI/MOSIER** - Charles William Biglieni was born in 1929. He was the only son of W.R. (Bill) and Irene Biglieni. Charles was raised south of Republic and graduated from Republic High School. In 1948 he married Norma Jean Mosier. They continued to live on the homeplace and Charles did plumbing and electrical work out of Republic Hardware that was owned by his father and mother until 1961. Then Charles started maintenance work for Reyco Industries. In 1972 Charles had an accident with the hay baler. He was in the hospital all summer. Because his hands and arms did not work well after that, he retired from Reyco and started full time farming. Charles and Norma had seven children.

1) Charles Robert, the oldest, married Karen Robertson. Robert was a sergeant and medic in the army. He was killed in battle in March 1971. His name can be found on the Vietnam Wall Memorial.

2) Danny Gene, the second son, married Becky Salchow. They had three children: Suzanne, Lindy and Joshua. Danny was employed with Security State and Commerce Bank for 29 years. Danny and Becky now run a cattle operation west of Republic, storage unit and hair salon.

*Back LR-Robert, Charles, Billy, Danny. Front: Norma, Sue, Brenda and Tommy.*

3) William Lee, third son, after finishing high school, attended University of Missouri for one year. After that he went to Nebraska to work on a cattle ranch. There he had an accident where he had his leg caught in a power take off and had to return to Missouri for surgery. After recovery, he joined a cattle fitting service where he worked 26 states and Canada, where he met his wife Nancy Triggs. They have made their home in Canada where they have raised two boys, Travis and Anthony. They now own their own cattle ranch.

4-5) Linda and Brenda, twins. Linda, the oldest, decided to go back to heaven five days after being sent here. Until just recently Brenda has lived in southwest Missouri all her life, where her four children also grew up. Michelle, the oldest, is now in Chillicothe, MO with her husband Shawn Sewell and their children, Tristen and Colten. Abi is the second child, but eight years younger, and is finishing college this year at Missouri Southern University in Joplin, MO. Cody, the only son, is a junior in high school, and Elizabeth, better known as Lizzie to her friends, is the youngest and a sophomore in high school. Cody and Lizzie reside in Newton, KS with their mom and her husband, David Milller, who is also a native of Republic.

6) Margaret Sue, after graduating from high school, married Dennis Morris from Ash Grove, MO. They own and operate Morris Brothers Embroidery Business and a cattle farm. They have two sons, Chad and Dusty, and their only grandchild, Ryleigh Rae.

7) Tommy is the fourth son in the Charles Biglieni family. After graduating high school, he made his occupation showing and judging cattle. He has two daughters, Brooke and Belle. Tom has spent most of his life in this area. He operates a cattle farm and is a field man for Joplin Regional Stockyards.

Charles and his family have received numerous awards related to farming. He was SW MO Seedstock producer of 1982. Governor John Ashcroft visited Charles and Norma's farm in 1985. In 1986 the family was chosen as farm family of the year by Springfield Chamber of Commerce. Charles was inducted in the Missouri Polled Hereford Hall of Fame in 1998. *Submitted by Charles and Norma Biglieni.*

**BLACKWELL/TROGDON** - The Charles R. Blackwell family has lived in Republic and the surrounding areas all of their lives. Charlie Russell Blackwell and Dois Louise (Trogdon) Blackwell were married on Nov. 26, 1949 in Willard, MO. Charlie was born and raised in Willard, MO on Oct. 30, 1928 to Joe Oliver Blackwell, born Jan. 17, 1909, died Dec. 30, 1971, and Clara Virginia (Russell) Blackwell, born Dec. 29, 1910, died July 26, 1997.

Louise (Trogdon) Blackwell was born and raised in Bois D'Arc, MO on June 25, 1934 to Orville Trogdon (Aug. 23, 1899-Oct. 21, 1951) and Myrtle (Hendricks) Trogdon (Feb. 10, 1915-Dec. 22, 1992). Charlie and Louise raised two sons in Republic, Steven Lynn (July 29, 1952) and Charles David (April 20, 1955), both of whom graduated from Republic High School - Steve in 1970 and David in 1973.

*Louise and Charlie with sons David and Steve Blackwell – 1977.*

Charlie and his brother Jim, born July 31, 1930, died June 22, 1995, were carpenters in Republic for over 45 years. Before retiring, Charlie drove a school bus and worked in the maintenance department for the Republic school system. Louise was a homemaker and also became a school bus driver. She currently works as a cook at Republic Elementary II.

Steve Blackwell married Linda Conn, born May 7, 1953, of Nixa, on Sept. 25, 1970. Linda is the daughter of Robert and Aileen Conn. Steve has been employed by Kraft Foods in Springfield, MO for over 35 years. Linda is employed as a housekeeper. Steve and Linda raised two children in Republic, Lori Lynn, born Dec. 14, 1971, and Charles Robert, born Jan. 10, 1976, both of whom graduated from Republic High School - Lori in 1990 and Robby in 1994. Lori Blackwell married Shannon Utchman, of Fordland, MO, on Nov. 2, 2002. Shannon was born Sept. 20, 1971, the son of Jim and Janice Utchman. Shannon and Lori currently reside in Fordland, MO, and are both employed by Kraft Foods in Springfield. The couple has one son, Riley Dean, born Sept. 1, 2004. Robby Blackwell is engaged to be married to Chance Taylor of Billings, MO. Robby currently resides in Battlefield, MO, and is employed by Life Mortgage in Springfield.

David Blackwell married Sherry (Borovicka), born Feb. 11, 1956, of Republic, on April 24, 1976. Sherry is the daughter of I.E. "Ben" and Reba (Hild) Borovicka. David has been employed at BNSF Railway as a conductor for over 32 years. Sherry has owned and operated a beauty salon in their home for over 24 years. David and Sherry raised one daughter in Republic, Tasha Ann, born Aug. 20, 1981, who graduated from Republic High School in 1999, from Southwest Missouri State with a BS in Marketing in 2003 and received her MBA in marketing from SMS in 2004. Tasha currently resides in Springfield, MO, and is employed at *417 Magazine* in Springfield.

Sadly, Charlie passed away on Oct. 28, 1990. The Blackwell family continues to live in and around Republic, carrying on his name with great pride for all his accomplishments and the family he created in his 62 years as a Republic resident. *Submitted by Steve Blackwell.*

**BLADES** - Burl L. and Myrtle M. Blades met in 1956 and soon became friends. They both had previous marriages, so were blessed to start their lives with five great children-- Burl having two, Shirley B. Hammons and Gary Blades, and Myrtle having Margarette, Ora Mae and Gail. They all became friends.

After 46 years of marriage Burl passed away very suddenly Oct. 5, 2003 at the age of 92 years, 8 months and 4 days. He was a farmer and truck hauler working with Springfield Stockyards close to 40 years. Burl is buried in Wade Chapel Cemetery by his loving parents, Ira and Annie Blades, and a grandson Baby Hammonds. Burl had four grandchildren, four great grandchildren and two great-great-grandchildren. His sister Chole (Blades) Neil was 100 years old in 2005; living near Republic, walking, visiting, eating well and feeling great.

*This picture of Burl and Myrtle was taken at Senior Center Feb. 1, 2001 for Burl's 90th birthday.*

Burl and Myrtle's home was located at 818 Rosewood Street in Republic; their yard showed both their love for flowers and Burl's ground keeping expertise. Both attended Blades Chapel Church while living in Republic. After Burl's death Myrtle returned to Carthage, MO, which was her birthplace. Myrtle was a 1935 Carthage High School graduate. *Submitted by Myrtle M. Blades.*

**BLADES/DAVIS** - John Henry Blades was born in 1876 in Greene County, MO. He was the son of James Reynolds Blades and Louisa Faye (Rickman) Blades. John married Nellie May Davis in 1911. She was the daughter of Henry Clay Davis and Lizzie Alice (Clark) Davis. They owned and operated a farm west of Republic, MO. John was one of 10 children. He and Nellie had four children.

Their first two children were boys who died at birth.

Reathel Wanda was born in 1918 and married Willard Leon Mooneyham in 1937. He was the son of Edward Leon Mooneyham and Maud (Butler) Mooneyham. Together they had eight children: 1) Velma Faye, born in 1938, never married and had no children. 2) Wilda Louise, born in 1939, married Clinton Maggard and has four children: Doris Jean, Marietta, Patricia (died at birth) and Timmy. Wilda has eight grandchildren. 3) Jerry Leon, born in 1940, married Sue Wade and has two children, Lisa and Christina. Jerry has five grandchildren. 4) Marilyn Ilene, born in 1942, married Eugene Mitchell and has two children, Rhonda and Ronald. Marilyn has one grandchild. 5) John Edward, born in 1944, married Jean Studebaker and has one stepson, Don, and two step-grandchildren. 6) Charlotte Elaine, born in 1945, married Gary Rippee and has three children: Sandra, Cathy and Jeffrey. Charlotte has four grandchildren. 7) Ray Dean, born in 1950, married Janet Herndon. Together they have three children: Aaron, Melinda and Casey. Ray Dean has a son, Marty, by a previous marriage. Ray Dean has five grandchildren. 8) Donald Lee, born in 1951, married Linda Bussard and they have one son, Curtis, and four grandchildren.

*Nellie and John Blades and children, Reathel and Faye Blades.*

Willard and Reathel owned and operated a farm west of Republic where they raised their eight children. Willard is deceased and Reathel now resides in Billings, MO.

Louisa Faye was born in 1920 and married Clyde Leroy Mooneyham in 1941. He was the son of Edward Leon Mooneyham and Maud (Butler) Mooneyham. Together they have four children. 1) Darrell Lee, born in 1944, married Judy Baum. They have four children. Ty, Kassie, Ashley and Dustin. They have five grandchildren. 2) Terry Lynn, born in 1946, married Norma McCord. They have three children: Shane, Ryan and Chad. They have five grandchildren and one step-grandchild. 3) Glen Ray born in 1949, married Lynn Landers and they have five children: Melissa, Glenna, Tracey, Brett and Chelsea. They have seven grandchildren. 4) Max Randall, born in 1951, married Linda Childress. Together they have five children: Nicole, Carrie. Tori, Lindsey and Lake. They have six grandchildren.

Clyde and Faye own and operated a dairy farm west of Republic where they raised their four children. Clyde is now a resident of Mercy Villa Nursing Home in Springfield, MO. Faye still resides on the farm. Five generations have been raised on this farm.

Both Reathel and Faye attended grade school at St Joe, a little country school near where they lived, and graduated from Billings High School. Their children all graduated from Republic High School. The ancestors of this family originated from England. *Submitted by Reathel (Blades) Mooneyham. Editor's note: Clyde passed away in 2006 and Faye in 2007.*

**BLADES/HOWARD** - The Blades, Howard, Denny and Rubison families settled in the Republic and Brookline area several generations ago.

*Front Row: Madison Schon (4), Dorothy Blades, Kelsey Blades (6-1/2), Nathan Blades (9-1/2); back row: Paul Schon, Margaret Blades, Ken Blades, Cynthia Schon, Maria Blades, Jeff Blades - Thanksgiving 2004.*

Kenneth Dale Blades, born Sept. 29, 1938, and Margaret Alice Howard, born Sept. 15, 1940, were married Sept. 26, 1958. Their children are Jeffrey Wayne Blades, born Jan. 26, 1961, and Cynthia Lee Blades, born April 17, 1964. Jeffrey and Ann Maria Lieser, born Feb. 20, 1962, were married July 23, 1988. Cynthia and Paul Otto Schon, born March 28, 1962, were married Nov. 16, 1985. Jeffrey and Maria's son and daughter are Nathan Alexander Blades, born July 2, 1995, and Kelsey Elizabeth Blades, born April 5, 1998. Cynthia and Paul's daughter is Madison Dale Schon, born Sept. 8, 2000.

Ken was born to JW Wayne Blades, Sept. 29, 1918, and Dorothy Vernell (Rubison)

Blades, Jan. 24, 1922, who were married Sept. 28, 1936. Their first child, Rex Wayne, was born July 8, 1937 but died as an infant Jan. 9, 1938. Wayne died Feb. 5, 1979.

Margaret was born to Lee Howard, born Sept. 13, 1897, and Velma Irene (Denny) Howard, born Sept. 18, 1902, who were married Dec. 24, 1923. Also born to Lee and Velma were twins, Thelma Faye Howard and Velma Mae Howard, born Dec. 5, 1926, and Mary Lee Howard, born Nov. 28, 1928. Thelma Faye died within a few days of birth. Lee died Nov. 5, 1984 and Velma died Oct. 22, 1978.

Ken (1956) and Margaret (1957) are graduates of Republic High School. *Submitted by Ken and Margaret.*

**BLADES/LOVETT -** Earl Blades was the son of Thomas Blades, grandson of Ransom Dudley Blades, and great-grandson of Edward A. and Penelope Blades. Earl was born Oct. 6, 1897. He was the fifth child of Thomas and Louisa (Gibson) Blades. His older siblings were Alfred, Bertha, Lillie and William (Efton). Younger siblings were Eva, Ethel and Floyd.

As a young adult, Earl married Myrtle Angus. The marriage didn't last long, but produced a son, Lawrence Blades. He was raised by his mother and still resides in Memphis, TN. Earl then married Tressie Lovett on Feb. 1, 1920. Tressie and Earl began their family in a house that sat on two acres (probably a gift from Thomas Blades) at the edge of the family farm. Their first child, Lorene, was born Aug. 8, 1921, two months premature. She was so small she could be held in one hand, and they said a teacup would fit on her head. When the doctor arrived he said that she probably would not make it through the night. He left without filling out a birth certificate. Her grandmother stayed up all night with her, blowing into her face to make her take a breath and keep her lungs going. Lorene's sister Bonnie was born June 17, 1925, and her brother Donald was born Aug. 9, 1928.

*Tressie and Earl Blades in 1930 with children: Lorene, Bonnie and Donald. They left for Lamar, CO soon after this picture was taken.*

On Christmas Eve, 1929, the house burned to the ground. The family lived in the smoke house until October 1930, at which time they moved to Lamar, CO, where Earl continued farming. Their final child, Pauline, was born May 30, 1933. Earl, Tressie, Donald and Pauline returned to Missouri in 1946. Soon they were living back on the two acres in the house that replaced the one that had burned.

Lorene married James Davidson and has four sons: Jerrold, Allan, Steven and Thomas. She has spent her life as a nurse, homemaker and care provider for her siblings and parents. Lorene Blades Davidson lives in the little stone house on Farm Road 43, one mile south of Highway 174, that sits at the same location where Earl and Tressie began. From the back yard you can see where Earl was born, where Thomas Blackstone lived and was probably born, and where Ransom Dudley Blades lived. Surrounding the stone house are the huge shade trees planted by Earl in the early 1900s.

Bonnie married Robert Garrett and had five children: Robert Jr., Donna, Robin, Richard and Ronald. They lived primarily in California where she was a homemaker and nurse.

Donald served in the Army during the Korean War. He returned and farmed with his father.

Pauline graduated from Republic High School at 16 and SMS at 20. She was an English teacher for almost 30 years.

Earl lived to be 93 and Tressie lived to be 97. Being a member of the Blades family has been a source of countless stories. There is great pride in being part of one of the first families of this region. *Submitted by Tom Davidson.*

**BLADES/MAYNARD -** Edward A. Blades and his wife Ellen Penelope Maynard with their family came to Greene County, MO in 1836 taking about two months by ox team from McMinn or Monroe County, TN. They settled on Section 10, Township 28, Range 24, near a spring on Pickeral Creek, west of Republic, MO on land granted by the government. Later he purchased an additional 480 acres ranging in price from 50 cents to $2.50 an acre. The southwest part of the county was at that time almost without inhabitants. At that time there were only six families in Pond Creek Township: Reynolds, Blades, Garoutte, Batson, McDaniel and Skelton.

*Edward A., George W., Ransom D., Isaac T., James R. and William W. Blades.*

Mr. Blades built a rude log cabin, put a small quantity of land under cultivation and it was amid but few of the conveniences of modern civilizations. A considerable part of the grinding of their corn for bread was done with the old fashioned pestle, and when they did go to mill it was a distance of from eight to 40 miles from home. Such facts are in strange contrast to the conveniences and comforts of the present day. No one except those who experienced them can realize the trouble and inconveniences to which the earliest settlers were subjected.

Edward A. was born in 1780 and died in 1844. Ellen was born in 1801 and died in 1856. Their children were Sarah McDaniel, Ransom Dudley, Nancy Hood, Isaac, Cynthia Hood, Edward Jr., William Willis, Elizabeth Blades, Rebecca Batson, James R.. Frances Lile and George Washington.

The first school was in a private house built by Ransom Dudley Blades on his father's land. Later Blades School was built on Isaac Blades' land near Blades Chapel Cemetery. Ransom Dudley gave $400 to build Blades Chapel Church in 1889, which continues to have services today. These were well attended by the Blades families since it was primarily populated by these families, many of whom lived back to back within a four mile radius of the school and church.

Ransom Dudley, son of Edward and Ellen, was born in 1821 and died in 1902. He came to Missouri with his parents when he was 15 years old. Farming was his principal occupation. In 1841 he married Frances Garoutte. She was born in 1824 and died in 1863. Their children were Samuel, Nancy Lafollette, John M., Isaac T., Sarah Brashears, Patience Gardner, Mary Rickman, William, Thomas Blackstone, Elizabeth Coker and James.

During the Civil War. Mr. Blades was an outspoken Union man. He voted for Lincoln in 1864. John M., son of Ransom, was born in 1844 and died in 1941. In 1866 he married Polly French who was born in 1844 and died in 1916. Their children were Arena Foster, James M., Sarah O'Neal, Joseph, Monroe, Rosetta Lovett, Mary Garoutte and William.

Monroe, son of John M. was born in 1876 and died in 1950. In 1898 he married Emma Browning, born 1877, died 1960. Their children were Ralph and Velma. Ralph was born in 1899 and died in 1987. In 1918 he married Florella Biglieni who was born in 1898 and died in 1982. Their only child Helen, born in 1921, never married.

*Ralph, Helen and Florella Blades.*

Velma was born in 1902 and died in 1997. In 1918 she married Royal Britain, born 1898 and died in 1987. They had eight children. *Submitted by Helen Blades.*

**BLADES/MCDANIEL -** Jimmie Blades and Madge McDaniel, high school sweethearts, were married on Oct. 7, 1950 at the Fundamental Methodist Church in Republic, MO. That was the beginning of this family history. Jimmie was the sixth child of Roy and Malissa Blades of the Republic area and Madge was the sixth child of Roy and Verna McDaniel who resided near Battlefield, MO.

*l-r: Jana Kendrick, Stan Blades, Jimmie Blades, Madge Blades, Julie Randles, Susan Blades.*

Both attended one-room schools for grades one through eight. After they graduated from Republic High School in 1949, Jimmie was employed by Producers Creamery and Madge attended Draughon Business College, then worked at an insurance agency and a food brokerage, all in Springfield, MO.

In 1951, during the Korean War, Jimmie joined the Navy. After completing boot camp at the Great Lakes Naval Training Center in Illinois, he was stationed at the U.S. Naval Operating Base in Bermuda. Madge joined him there and worked on the base in the Naval Administrative Offices. Their first child, Stan, was born on this tropical island in 1954. After his tour in Bermuda, Jimmie was sent to San Juan, Puerto Rico and then to Chincoteague, VA, where he was discharged in August of 1955.

The family returned home to Republic, MO and they were blessed with three more children: Jana, Julie and Susan. After a few years they moved to the farm where Jimmie grew up and, shortly after, purchased it from his father. Jimmie raised cattle and ran a bulldozing business for several years. Among the many excavating jobs he did in the area was the Garoutte Field in Republic. He then worked out of the Operating Engineers Union from which he retired in 1986. During this time Madge was busy raising the children and doing the many chores involved in farm life. She also operated a kindergarten in the church basement for several years and later worked as a secretary for the Republic Middle School.

In 1983 they built a Grade A dairy barn. Family and other employees operated the dairy from that time until the present, and it is now operated by their son-in-law, Mike Kendrick and grandson, Kolby. Jimmie retired from dairying two years ago but still enjoys helping in the field at harvest time.

Stan has also made his living on this family farm for several years. He operates a crankshaft grinding business and has customers in many states around the country.

Madge started selling real estate 22 years ago and is still working fulltime.

Jimmie was a member of the Republic Kiwanis Club in its early years, serving one term as president, and was also a charter member of the Greene County Planning and Zoning Board. He is an avid sportsman and participated in basketball and fast-pitch softball for many years.

Jimmie and Madge are very proud of their family. Stan married Deborah Finn and they had two children, Ranson and Micah. He is presently married to Florence (Erickson) and has two stepchildren, Matt and Erica. Jana, a housewife, married Michael Kendrick and they have three children: Kurt, Kolby, Amy and one beloved foster son, Kolt. Julie, a teacher, is married to Harris Randles and their children are Jason, Adam and Tara. Susan, a computer specialist, married Robert Gardner Jr. and they have two sons, Eric and Alex. She then married Raymond Maynard and they had a son, Phillip, and a daughter, Melissa.

Jimmie and Madge still attend the church where they were married, now the Republic Free Will Baptist Church. The family has always been active in their church and also in school activities, both for their children and now for the grandchildren. They love life and hope to be around for a long while to come. *Submitted by the Blades family.*

**BLADES/MOONEYHAM** - John Leroy "Roy" Blades was born in 1892, the first child of James Melton Blades and Columbia Ann Browning Blades, at their farm home southwest of Republic. His siblings were Alma (Miller), Ona (Potts), Elene (McCroskey), Everett and Harold. On May 22, 1912, he married Malissa "Lissa" Jane Mooneyham, born 1893, daughter of William J. Mooneyham and Elizabeth Jane Logan Mooneyham. Her siblings were Monroe, William, Charley, John, Ada (Miller), Ed, Pearl (Miller), Clara, George, and half-sister Delia.

Roy met Lissa at a revival at the First Baptist Church in Republic. After a brief courtship, Roy proposed and 16 months later they were married. They lived with Roy's parents for a month until renting their first home. That sum-

*Front, l-r: Cleo Batson, Roy Blades, Lissa Blades, Dorothy Swinney; back: Thelma Dorrell, Wayne Blades, Clara Parker and Jimmie Blades.*

mer and fall they were hired as part of George Batson's threshing crew - Roy and his wagon and team of horses to haul water for the steam engine and Lissa to help cook for the crew. They slept on pallets on the ground beneath a tent. While not the typical life of newlyweds, they recalled this season with fond memories.

Roy and Lissa had seven children: Clara (Parker), Cleo (Batson), Wayne, Drextle, Dorothy (Swinney), Thelma (Dorrell) and Jimmie. They were blessed with 14 grandchildren, 29 great-grandchildren, and 23 great-great-grandchildren. While raising their family, they moved 12 times in and around the Republic area. Upon retirement, their final move was from their 120-acre farm, where their son Jimmie now lives, to their home at Logan and Walnut in Republic. They resided there until Roy's death in 1984 at age 92, and Lissa's death in 1989 at age 95.

They made a living from many different sources: farming, cutting and selling firewood, bailing hay, stud fees from breeding their stallion, selling eggs, milk, honey, and garden produce, raising and selling rabbits, and making and selling quilts. Over the years they owned and operated a grocery store, a tire shop and filling station and a feed mill. Roy was employed by the railroad and the Greene County Road and Bridge Department.

The family butchered their own beef and pork and Lissa canned fruits and vegetables. She also made many of the family's clothes from feed sacks. Beds consisted of straw ticks filled with fresh straw. Geese were plucked for making feather pillows. Laundry was done once a week in a black iron kettle and on the washboard. Baths in the old washtub were weekly starting with the youngest, changing the scarce water periodically. The ice man came in the summer along with the Raleigh and Watkins men who peddled their wares: flavorings, spices, toiletries, liniment, salve, etc.

Signs of changing times were evidenced when the entire countryside ran outdoors to see the first airplane fly over. Likewise everyone rushed to see Dr. Beal's car drive by.

Roy and Lissa saw many dramatic changes in the world during their 90-year lifetimes and felt they'd lived good, long lives. Their final resting place is Wade Chapel Cemetery where they are buried alongside their son, Drextle, who died at birth. Their immediate and extended family cherish the legacy they left behind. *Submitted by Thelma Dorrell.*

**BLADES/ROLUFS** - Larry Michael Blades and Patricia Anne Rolufs were married on Dec. 30, 1965. They have two daughters: Teresa Ann, born April 8, 1969, and Lucinda Sue, born Feb. 21, 1970. Teresa married Jeffrey Strickland on Dec. 28, 1990. They now have two children, Amanda Lynn, born Nov. 14, 1992, and Christopher Lee, born Jan. 23, 1995. They live in Stella, MO. Lucinda "Cindy" is unmarried at this time and lives in Republic.

Larry is the eldest of three children born to Claude "Sonny" Blades, born Aug. 29, 1925, expired Feb. 28, 1990, and June Farmer Blades, born Feb. 28, 1929. Claude "Sonny" and Margaret June were married on Aug. 18, 1945. Their children are Larry Michael, born Oct. 12, 1946; Terry Wayne, born Aug. 7, 1952; and Claudia Sue "Suzy," born May 21, 1957.

Claude "Sonny" was the youngest son of Jess Blades, born Sept. 20, 1885, died Dec. 20, 1960, and Nora Hayes Blades, born May 30, 1887, died July 16, 1957.

Jess Blades was the son of Gid Blades and Rachael Ray Blades. They married Jan. 23, 1872.

Gid Blades was the son of Isaac Tillman Blades who died in 1896 and Nancy Ann Hood Blades who passed away in 1894.

Nora Hayes Blades was the daughter of Melissa Britain Hayes and George Hayes. All lived in the Republic area.

June Farmer Blades is the only child of Carl Celo Farmer born May 18, 1907, died Jan. 30, 1987 and Pauline Nicholson Farmer, born Sept. 20, 1908, died Jan. 22, 1987. They were married on Feb. 25, 1928.

Carl Celo Farmer was the son of James A. Farmer, born in 1852 and Olive Ann Porter Farmer, born in 1864, and married on Feb. 21, 1852.

James A. Farmer was the son of Christopher Farmer and Mary Elizabeth Willmington, who married on April 15, 1825.

Olive Ann Farmer was the daughter of Presley Porter and Zeilda Morning Bently Porter.

Pauline Nicholson Farmer was the daughter of Walter David Nicholson, born Feb. 27, 1880 and died on March 25, 1963, and Jessie Irene Frame Nicholson, born Oct. 30, 1880 and died on July 26, 1969. They married Feb. 5, 1902.

Walter David Nicholson was the son of Johnathon Jefferson Nicholson, born Dec. 13, 1839 and died March 17, 1912, and Mary Elizabeth Johns Nicholson, born June 6, 1843, died Jan. 16, 1926. They were married in 1860.

Jessie Irene Frame Nicholson was the daughter of John Parker Frame, born Feb. 17, 1853, died Nov. 18, 1942, and Venelia O. Elson, born May 12, 1847 and died July 19, 1925. They were married on Jan. 27, 1876. All lived in the Ash Grove and Bois D'Arc, MO area.

Patricia is the eldest of three daughters born to Arthur Lloyd Rolufs, born Sept. 6, 1919 and expired Sept. 22, 1986, and Delighta Bell Vanderpool Rolufs, born July 19, 1927 and died Nov. 27, 2001. Arthur and Delighta "Dee" were married on Dec. 8, 1943. They moved to Republic from Springfield in October 1957. Their children are Patricia Anne, born Oct. 9, 1944; Sandra Sue, born Nov. 28, 1948; and Beverly Jean, born July 22, 1955.

Arthur L. Rolufs was the youngest son of Henry Rolufs and Phina Lang Rolufs of the Rolla, MO area.

Delighta "Dee" was the daughter of Ed E. Vanderpool and Irene Bishop Vanderpool of the Highlandville, MO area. *Submitted by Larry Blades.*

**BLANTON/ANDERSON** - Frank Blanton was born in 1884 to John Blanton and Elizabeth McAmis. In 1908 he married Maude Anderson, who was born in 1885. Her parents were Henry Anderson and Jessie (Wiley) Anderson. When Frank and Maude were married they had seven children: Joe Rubison, Bert Blanton, Jessie Batson, Frank Jr. Blanton, Dorothy Gandy,

Thelma Maude Etheridge and Lester Blanton. All of the children attended Brick School and a few attended Republic High School.

Frank Blanton was a farmer and cattleman, Maude was a homemaker. They owned 380 acres north of Republic, MO. Maude died in October 1959 and Frank died in February 1965.

Joe Hazel married Homer Rubison; their children are Wilma Roberts, Sharon Eaves and Barbara Rubison.

Bert married Janie Wolfe; their children were Glen Blanton and Betty Crocker(both deceased).

Jessie Elizabeth married Earl Batson; their children are Cora Lee Allred and Jimmy Batson (deceased).

Frank Jr. married Louella Gale; their children are Jeannie and Patrick and they all lived in the state of Washington.

Dorothy Mae married Raymond Gandy; they had one son, Sidney who lives in the State of Maryland.

Thelma married Harold Etheridge; their children are Gary Etheridge and Sandy Deragowski.

Lester married Virginia Dameron; their son is Bob Blanton. *Submitted by Gary Etheridge.*

**BLOOD/SIPLINGER** - The third time was a charm for Terry (Blood) Griffin. Terry lived in Republic from 1961 until moving to Springfield in 1964. She attended church and youth activities in Republic during her teen-age years and returned there to live once again in 1994.

Terry first moved to Republic when she was in the second grade and lived in a new section of town coined Wormeyville. The developer's nickname was Wormey and the name for the new sub-division stuck. Terry's parents are Keith and Alma "Johnnie" (Siplinger) Blood. Keith worked as a construction worker and is now retired and lives in Springfield. Johnnie was a homemaker. She joined her parents in heaven in 1998.

*Blood Family, back l-r: Johnnie, Jane; front: Terry, Keith and Penny.*

Terry's older sister, Jane (Blood) Tuck, married Larry Tuck. He is a Republic graduate. Larry is retired from the Army and now works with computers. Jane is a nurse with St. John's.

Terry's younger sister Penny (Blood) Goodwin married Ed Goodwin. Ed is a Republic police reserve officer and also security officer for the Springfield school system. Penny works as a nurse with the same school system. All three attended school in Republic for three years.

Terry remembers her elementary classes in what is now E-I, being divided into A, B and C students based on their achievement in school. Her first two years, Terry and her sister walked to school. Her third year, the school decided that anyone who lived one mile or more away from school could ride the bus. Terry lived exactly one mile and was then able to ride the bus to school. Terry and her family attended the Fall Festival each year which was then held on Main Street. She also remembers when a neighbor's burning trash blew into their back yard starting a grass fire. Fortunately, the fire chief lived next door and put out the fire long before the fire truck arrived.

Terry's second experience in Republic occurred in the early 70s when she began to attend the Hood United Methodist Church and teach an elementary Sunday school class. This rekindled many friendships, and Terry made numerous new friends. Soon she was attending overnight lock-ins and spiritual weekends with her new friends. It was during this time that she met and later married Gary Griffin. During this time in her life Terry's faith in God grew tremendously.

In 1994, Terry returned to Republic to live. Her husband had been appointed to pastor the Hood United Methodist Church. Once again, Terry renewed friendships and made many new friends as she became involved in the church, community, and school activities. Terry had already made one connection with Republic prior to moving. She has been a member of the Republic Community Band for 18 years.

In 1998, Terry began teaching kindergarten and later first grade at Billings. The third time has been a charm for Terry as she has watched her daughter, Amy, graduate with distinction from Republic and attend Missouri State on an academic scholarship. Amy is following in her mother's footsteps in preparing to be an elementary school teacher. *Submitted by Terry Griffin.*

**BOATRIGHT/OWEN** - The Owen family and the Boatright family in 1958 were joined by the marriage of Jane Carolyn Owen to Oscar Dale Boatright, both graduates of Republic High School. Their marriage was blessed with three children: Douglas Jay, Aaron Todd and Beverly Ann, all three graduated from Republic High School.

Douglas went on to graduate from SMSU in Springfield. Douglas married Deborah Michele Evans in 1982; they have three children: Ashley Michele, Stefanie Marie and Evan Owen. Ashley and Stefanie are both graduates of Republic High School and Evan is currently enrolled at Republic Middle School. Doug was appointed to Republic City Council in 1990 and served three terms. He was elected mayor of the city of Republic in 1996 and served two terms in that capacity.

In 1990 Todd married Lorie Lynn Moreland, also a graduate of Republic High School. They have two children, Derek Todd and Alexa Lynn, and presently live in Carl Junction, MO. Doug and Todd now operate Queen City Air Freight with two locations in Springfield and Joplin. The Springfield location originated in 1990 with Doug and Todd both operating the company; Todd began the Joplin branch in 1997, and built a warehouse facility at the Joplin Regional Airport in 2000.

Beverly married Douglas Conner in 1995; they currently live in Stuart, FL with their two children, Elijah Vess and Isabella Blue. Douglas operates his own construction business, and Beverly is a flight attendant with American Air Lines.

After years of service to Frozen Food Express, Dale built his own trucking company in 1982, operating as Boatright Trucking Co. Inc. In 2000, Dale and Jane built Island Green Golf Club, an 18-hole premiere course and subdivision just south of Republic. Dale and Jane still live in the Republic area where both are active members of the community. Jane is a charter life member of the Republic Historical Society. *Submitted by Jane Boatright.*

**BOATRIGHT/SHORT** - Gene Boatright was the first son of Roscoe and Eathel (Gaddy) Boatright born March 1, 1931, in the Gainesville, MO area. Gene was married on May 26, 1949 to Lorene Short, the sixth child of Clell and Ollie Elizabeth (Pope) Short. She was born May 10, 1930, in southern Christian County. Gene and Lorene lived in the Republic area most of their married life. Gene worked at various jobs, owning his own dump truck, hauling coal and hay during the drought years of 1952-53, construction work including ground work on Parkview High School and Lake Springfield, and doing finish work on I-44 in Joplin, MO.

*Lorene and Gene Boatright.*

In 1956 he started work for Frozen Food Express in Dallas, TX as an over-the-road truck driver, until his death April 3, 1974. He had the "gift of gab" making friends all over the country. He was awarded a safe driving pin for each year, and a gold watch at 25 years. He loved telling jokes and playing jokes on his fellow truck drivers. Gene was an honest and decent person who helped many with money, machinery, vehicles, and just a good conversation. He loved camping and cooking ham on outings at the lake. He loved to ride horses and to play dominos with friends from Texas and neighbors, Randall and Annabelle Gleghorn, from across the street. Some of these sessions lasted from 6 p.m. until 2 or 3:00 a.m. in the morning. He liked the local police - he affectionately referred to them as "Fuzz." If there was pie or cake, he would call and say, "Fuzz, come on down for coffee and dessert." Gene and Lorene had many friends they visited in Dallas and loved having them return the visit to Republic.

He and Lorene purchased a travel trailer to travel when he retired, but due to his unexpected death they were unable to fulfill that dream. Gene and Lorene had six children: Vicky Girth, Michael Gene, Nancy Cunningham and Kayla Philpott. Two infants preceded Gene in death.

Lorene was always a stay-at-home Mom taking care of the home and their children. This was Gene's wish. She planted a garden, canned and froze vegetables and fruits, raised chickens and calves, milked the cow and was always available to make home-made ice cream. She took the children to the drive-in movies, to the swimming pool, and just driving around the countryside. All four of the children helped with the chores. This was a very good time in their lives.

Gene's love of trucking was passed down to Michael, until his untimely death in October 1979. The love for truck driving continues to his grandson, Scott Girth, who now owns Legacy, Inc.

After Gene's death, Lorene kept the family home on North Main until 1986; she now lives on South Main. They have 10 grandchildren and nine great-grandchildren. Seven of the nine grandchildren live in the surrounding area. Gene, Michael and the two infant children are buried at Wade Chapel Cemetery. *Submitted by Lorene Boatright.*

**BOCK/CARLSON** - Carol Carlson was born June 15, 1951 in Springfield with Dr. Mitchell as the attending physician. She was the last child and only daughter of John and Edith Carlson. Carol attended Republic Schools where she enjoyed speech club, cheerleading and volleyball. After graduating from Republic she continued her education at Southwest Missouri State and graduated with an education degree. Upon graduation she moved to Dallas, TX and taught in the Dallas school system for several years.

In 1977, she met Kurt Bock, an Air Force pilot who was an instructor pilot training in San Antonio. Kurt was a graduate of the class of 1975 of the Air Force Academy and a native of central Illinois. Carol and Kurt were married on Sept. 2, 1977, the same September 2nd date chosen by her mother Edith, her grandmother Tressie and her great-grandmother Ellen. She was the fourth generation married on that date.

Jonathan, Carol, Kurt and Rebecca Bock.

After their wedding in the Republic Christian Church, Carol and Kurt began a 28-year-military career that took them to Mississippi, Illinois, Alabama (twice), Washington, DC (twice), Germany, Georgia and Belgium. Kurt retired as a colonel in 2003 and the family moved to Bloomington, IL where Kurt is the vice president of finance and treasurer of the Illinois Farm Bureau and Country Insurance. Carol and Kurt have two children, Jonathan and Rebecca.

Jonathan was born on Jan. 1, 1982 at Scott AFB, IL. During his family's travels, Jon attended five different elementary schools, went to a Christmas party at Vice President Qualyes' home, learned to ski in the Alps, played football and wrestled for Brussels American School in Belgium. After graduation from the University of Illinois, Jon became an equity analyst for Main Street Trust Bank in Champaign, IL. He was recently married to Jennifer Ardeu of Arad, Romania.

Rebecca was born on June 17, 1991 in Florsheim, Germany and is the proud holder of a German birth certificate. During Carol and Kurt's travels, Rebecca learned to ski in the Alps, traveled in France and England, and learned how to shop in European markets and order dinner in five different languages. She is now attending Normal, IL public schools and playing piano and flute. *Submitted by Jonathan Bock.*

**BOOTH/CHERRY -** Charles Noel Boothe was born in Kentucky the 5th child of Spencer and Ida Boothe. The family moved to this area in the early 1900s and Charley attended school at St. Elmo and Halltown. In 1931 he married Gladys Fay Cherry of Greensburg, KS. Shortly after their marriage they moved to Spencer, MO. Charley had an automotive garage. He dropped the E from his name.

In 1936 during the Great Depression they went to California and were there for about three years. Gladys' dad, Clem Cherry, went for a visit and told them it was time to come home. They moved back to this area and stayed on the farm for a while.

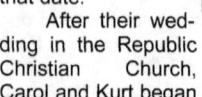
Charley and Gladys (Cherry) Booth.

During the war Charley worked at Boeing Aircraft in Wichita, KS. In 1946 Charley and Gladys became the proprietors of Jot 'Em Down store (this was the name of the store in the popular radio show *Lum and Abner*). They were there for about 10 years. It was a community gathering place and a lot of fond memories are from that time period in their lives. They moved to a dairy farm and lived there until Charley and Gladys started working in Springfield and moved to Republic.

In 1975 they purchased the house on Harrison Street from Spence and Ida's estate. Charley and Gladys celebrated 50 years of marriage in 1981 with lots of friends and relatives attending. In their later years they did a lot of fishing. They enjoyed going to the lakes with friends and relatives. Charley's lifetime hobby was hunting and fishing. Gladys loved to cook and care for her family. They represent one of the oldest pioneer families. Through their many moves and their love for people they gathered many friends.

Charley lived until 1983 and Gladys continued to live on Harrison Street until 2000 when she moved to Prescott, KS to be near her daughter. She lived until 2002. They raised four children: Max, Ron, Sue and Steve. Max lived until 1999 and his wife Mary lived until 2003. Ron lives with his wife Irma in Columbia, South Carolina. Sue lives with her husband George Jackson in Prescott, KS. Steve lives with his wife Nancy in Virginia Beach, VA. *Submitted by Sue Jackson.*

**BOOTHE/KELTNER -** Spencer and Ida Boothe spent their childhood in Kentucky. As a young man he was part of the Oklahoma Land Rush. He acquired some land and the rest of the family decided to follow. When they reached Oklahoma the land was gone so they returned home leaving Spence. A fellow came along and offered him two mules for the land, and he was on his way home.

Front: Spence and Ida; back: Charley, Loyd, Bessie, Clarence, Winnie and Oral Boothe.

He married Ida Keltner in 1898. They moved to the Greene County area in the early 1900s. They purchased 40 acres of land in Greene County, Section 7, Township 28, north of Range 24. They added to that land another 60 acres and were able to care for their family with this land. They also had the only gas station between Springfield and Joplin on Route 66 at Halltown, MO. They raised six children: Bessie, Oral, Charles, Loyd, Winnie and Clarence.

The children attended St. Elmo and Halltown Schools. Bessie, Oral and Loyd, moved to California. Winnie moved to the Steelville, MO area. Only Charley and Clarence remained in this area. Spence and Ida lived on the farm until 1946. They purchased a house in Republic from Harold and Thelma Mooneyham, Lot #10 in the W.B. Scarcys addition 151 Harrison Street. They lived the rest of their lives at that address.

Spence lived until 1951 and Ida lived until 1974. They were hard working honest people and loved by many, especially their family. You could always expect a good meal and a tune on a fiddle with your visit. No person ever left Ida's house hungry. She even fed the railroad hoboes. *Submitted by Ron Booth.*

**BOROVICKA -** The I.E. "Ben" Borovicka family moved to Republic in the summer of 1973. Ben was transferred to Republic with Western Gillette Trucking. Ben Borovicka and Reba Maxine (Hild) were married on Dec. 10, 1954 in Coffeyville, KS. Ben was born in Parker, KS on Dec. 26, 1927 to Charley (March 26, 1899 to Nov. 17, 1988) and Maggie (Caylor) Borovicka (May 22, 1903 to March 7, 1998).

Ben and Reba (Hild) Borovicka and children: Bruce, Sherry and Brian in 1965.

Reba (Hild) Borovicka was born in Cherryville, KS on Oct. 12, 1934 to Kenneth Edgar Hild (Feb. 10, 1909 to Feb. 22, 1970) and Joanne Maxine (Testerman) Hild (Feb. 4, 1914 to Nov. 13, 1973). Ben and Reba raised three children: Sherry Ann (born Feb. 11, 1956), Bruce Edward (born March 13, 1957) and Brian Lee (born July 17, 1960), all of whom graduated from Republic High School: Sherry in 1974, Bruce in 1975 and Brian in 1978. Ben was an over-the-road trucker for over 40 years, doing everything from driving a cattle truck in his early years to retiring from Roadway Express in 1989. Reba is a homemaker who has raised both children and grandchildren and has had a hand in her great-grandchildren's lives as well.

Sherry Borovicka married David Blackwell (born April 20, 1955) of Republic, on April 24, 1976. David is the son of Charlie (Oct. 30, 1928 to Oct. 28, 1990) and Louise (Trogdon) Blackwell (born June 25, 1934). David graduated in 1973 from Republic High School. David has been employed at BNSF Railway as a conductor for over 32 years and Sherry has owned and operated a beauty salon in their home for over 24 years. David and Sherry have one daughter, Tasha Ann (born Aug. 20, 1981), who graduated from Republic High School in 1999, from Southwest Missouri State in 2003 with a BS in marketing and received her MBA in marketing from SMS in 2004. She currently resides in Springfield, MO and is employed at *417 Magazine*.

Bruce Borovicka married Karen (Hopkins) (born Aug. 2, 1960) of Springfield, MO on Nov. 24, 1984. The couple currently resides in Howe, TX after being transferred with Yellow Transportation, where Bruce has been employed for over 20 years. Karen is currently employed by the Howe school system. Bruce and Karen have one son, Bruce Edward Jr. (born June 18, 1985), who graduated from Howe High School in 2003 and is currently a sophomore at Collin County College in Texas. Bruce has a daughter from a previous marriage, Shannon Lynn (born Oct. 9, 1978), who currently resides in Springfield, MO, and is employed at Grand Crown Leisure Travel. Shannon has two children, Rhianna Narelle (born Feb. 19, 2000) and Keegan Ander (born Aug. 1, 2001).

Brian Borovicka married Brenda (McKinney) (born Dec. 17, 1953) on June 23, 1986. The couple resides in Springfield, MO, and are both currently employed at Bass Pro Shops. Brian has a son from a previous marriage, Joseph Lee (born June 9, 1980), who graduated from Republic High School in 1998 and from Southwest Missouri State with a bachelor of fine arts. Joe is currently employed at the Greene County Library Center and plans to move to Chicago in the fall of 2006 to pursue his master of fine arts degree and to one day teach his skill to others.

Sadly, Ben passed away on June 30, 2004, following a courageous short battle with cancer. Ben's family continues to live in and around Republic, carrying with them the pride of the fulfilling life he lived and began for them in this small town. *Submitted by David Blackwell.*

**BOYD/LAND** - Margaret Anna Boyd, nee Land, as a young girl came with her family from Tennessee in the late 1800s in a covered wagon pulled by a team of oxen. She brought from Tennessee seeds which she planted in Lindsey Cemetery, and are now the big pine trees that sound so mournful when the wind blows through them. She later met and married John Boyd and they raised a family of two girls, Grace and Lucille, and three boys: Homer, John R. and James.

In later years after her husband died, she inherited a 20-acre farm about one mile east of Republic in the Lindsey School District, It had a large two-story house on it, which stood on a

*Lindsey School. Front l-r: James Sparkman, Neal Boyd, Burl McConnell, Vera Lea Mooneyham, Kay Maxwell, Betty Pitchford, Norma Lee Sparkman, Calvin Turpin; 2nd row: Lois Wallace, Virginia Lloyd, Billy Magers, Betty Maxwell, G.W. Turpin, _, _,; 3rd row: Carol Joe Loyd, Harry Lee McConnell, Leo Sparkman, Geraldine Sparkman, Bob Pitchford, Esther Mae Headley and Irene Turpin. Teacher-Crystal McCorkle.*

rock foundation, it had no electricity and kerosene lamps were used at night for light, commonly known as coal oil lamps. Sometimes at night when the wind would blow hard, it would slosh the oil in upstairs lamps. Homer and James were both drafted in the Army in WWII, Homer serving in the European Theater in North Africa and France, and James in the Pacific. John R. was married with a family and was not drafted.

*Margaret Boyd.*

Homer married Martha Blades after the war and they had four children: David, Steve, Mike and Nancy. James married Betty Cassy after the war and they had three children: Larry, Darrel and Julie. John R. was married to Iva Mae Spurgeon and they had five children: Barbara, Freddie, Johnnie, and twins, Gary and Terry. Lucille was married to Jesse Teague and had three daughters: Evelyn, Catherine and Gladys, and two sons, Robert and Earl. Earl died in childhood. Grace was married to Ellis Hilton and had three children: Carl, Pauline and Joseph. She died in childbirth when Joseph was born. He was taken to live with his grandmother in Republic. His mother had wanted to name him Neal, so he became Neal Boyd and carried this name until he enlisted in the Army in 1949 and has been Joseph Hilton since.

Homer and James had a cane mill before the war which consisted of two large meshing cylinders that had a long pole attached to one of them and was hitched to a horse that walked round and round turning the cylinders, squeezing out the cane juice, which was then put into a large pan and boiled down to make molasses. People came from all around with wagon loads of cane. The cane mill was sold for scrap during the war.

Lucille's husband died in 1944 and she moved with her children to the old homeplace in Republic, eventually inheriting it when Grandma Boyd died in 1955. She is buried in Lindsey Cemetery with son John R. and daughter Lucille. *Submitted by Joe Hilton.*

**BOYD/ZUMWALT** - David Boyd and his wife Catherine obtained a Spanish land grant in what is now Lincoln County, MO in 1799. Catherine was a sister to the Zumwalt brothers for whom Fort Zumwalt in St. Charles County is named. Their oldest son John (born 1792 in Kentucky) married 19-year-old Margaret Harryman in 1814. Earlier, Margaret and two other girls had been kidnapped by Indians and held for several months before being ransomed.

John served in a Missouri Militia company commanded by Daniel Morgan Boone during the War of 1812. Later, John was able to claim 160 acres of public land in what is now Republic as a reward for his service. His land ran for a mile north from the intersection of Hines Street and Lynn Avenue and for a quarter mile to the west. John and his family moved here no later than 1849. John lived until 1868 and Margaret lived until 1885 when she died at age 90. They are buried in Lindsey Cemetery.

John's son David taught the first school in the Republic area. It met in the barn of a Mr. Haseltine. David received $1.00 a month per student.

John's son Hugh served in the Missouri Home Guards during the Battle of Wilson's Creek in August 1861. General Lyon did not trust the loyalty of the Home Guards, and left them in Springfield while his outnumbered Union troops attacked the Confederate forces. After Lyon's defeat the Home Guard covered the Union retreat. Hugh served the remainder of the war as a lieutenant in Co. G of the 8th Regiment of the Missouri Calvary.

The Civil War was a terrible time for all the people living in the area including John and Margaret who had their house burned by Confederate raiders. Hugh's sister Eleanor wrote him a letter that expressed the thoughts of many families:

"We trust in the higher powers that you may never receive any bodily injury from the evil traitors and that you may be blessed with health and strength, that you may be able to overcome all the hardships of a poor weary soldier's life. We all sigh deeply for your welfare and safety and often implore the mercy of God in your behalf. I hope we will all out live our troubles and hardships that this wicked rebellion has brought on us all. You must write every opportunity for we are always uneasy about you. We all join in fervent prayer for your safety and in true love to you may kind heaven bless and protect you in all your distress and lonesome hours. So farewell dear brother for this time."

After the war, Hugh was involved in politics as a Radical Republican. He was appointed by the governor to supervise registration of voters in Center Township and as a cattle inspector. In 1870 he was a delegate to the state Republican convention. Families related to the Boyds by marriage include Land, Logan and Teague. *Submitted by Larry Land.*

**BRASHERS/BLADES** - James Basham Brashers fought in the Civil War in the Union Army. Although the records show him to have been inducted at the age of 18, he was actually inducted on his 16th birthday, Aug. 20, 1862. The story was told that he had been a drummer boy at the age of 13. While James was serving in the Army, his father, Walter Brashers, was killed by bushwhackers in May 1863. This act prompted his two other sons, Jessie Rankin and William Walter, to obtain leave from the Army so they could track down their father's killer. Their mother Elizabeth (Basham) had died in February 1863.

*Front: James and Sarah Blades Brashers; 2nd row: Ella Brashers Logan, Della Brashers Cash, Bettie Brashers Rose and Bill Brashers, children of James and Sarah.*

After the war James married 15-year-old Sarah Jane Blades, daughter of Ranson Dudley and Frances (Garoutte) Blades. Because of his having contracted rheumatism from sleeping on the cold wet ground while in the service, James was never able to do extensive farming. Therefore, he applied for and received a pension in the year 1879. He and Sarah had four children: Ella Brashers Logan, Della Brashers Cash, Bettie Brashers Rose and Bill Brashers.

Sarah Jane was remembered as being a spunky woman, even at the age of 80. One story passed down by family members was that she had wanted to go into town for the Saturday night concert and Mr. Brashers had declined the invitation to accompany her because of his rheumatism. Mrs. Brashers, however, tossing her head, said, "Well I'm going! I may be old someday and can't go." She is also remembered as being a petite woman, friendly and proud of her clothes and pretty shoes. On the other hand, Mr. Brashers was rather reticent and used a cane in getting around.

At the weekly band concerts a truck with removable sides was parked at the curb. The band members seated on its bed would play all evening as the people crowded the sidewalks. visiting with one another, and wandering in and out of the stores.

Republic at this time was a small country town without street lights, paved streets, and having wooden sidewalks. Saturday night was the busiest day of the week, when all the farmers brought in their produce and there were more horses, buggies and wagons than cars. These were the days of the Chautauqua Societies and the traveling tent shows. Republic had one movie house that had a big audience although the pictures were old.

When Mr. and Mrs. Brashers felt they could no longer live alone, they moved to Wichita, KS to live with their daughter Ella until his death in 1935. Mrs. Brashers then lived with the son in Hurley until her death in 1940 at the age of 91. *Submitted by Ada Copeland.*

**BRIDGES -** The Marvin Bridges family has lived in the eastern area of Republic School District since building a home near Battlefield in 1971. Superintendent Amos McMurtrey hired Marvin in 1962 as Republic's first industrial arts teacher in the new high school building (now the middle school). Marvin taught there until 1967. After serving a three-year stint in Springfield Public Schools, he was re-hired by Superintendent Bill Schatz as the assistant principal and coordinator of federal programs where he worked with Principal Don Farwell, Counselor Jim Klingebiel and other excellent staff. He held that position until 1975. He thoroughly enjoyed his 10-year contact with the Republic teachers, administrators, staff, students and parents. He enjoyed supervising the high school lunch line, supervising at football and basketball games and listening to the reasons why students were tardy to school when he filled out tardy slips. He completed his teaching career in Springfield Public Schools, mostly at Kickapoo High School.

Marvin's son Mike attended four years at Republic High School, graduating in 1975. He participated in football, dramatics, as well as other activities and organizations. He was student body president his senior year. Mike graduated from SMSU and MU Law School and is now a partner at Blackwell Sanders Peper Martin law firm in Springfield. He and his wife Kelly live in Springfield with their daughter Emilie. Their blended family has five children: Amos and Phillip Bridges, Kay Gates and her husband Rick, Sarah Vance, and Emilie Bridges. They have two lively grandchildren, Madeline and Benjamin Gates. They are active in Christ Episcopal Church and Mike serves on the Springfield Art Museum and Little Theatre boards.

Marvin's wife, Audrey, entered SMSU in 1962 and spent 30 years as a business teacher in Springfield. They are members of the Republic Retired School Personnel Association and the Missouri Retired Teachers Association. They continue to live in the same home where they do cattle farming and take care of rental property. *Submitted by Audrey Bridges.*

**BRIDGES/LAWSON -** Otho and Fay Bridges and their son Jack moved to rural Republic in 1934 when they lost their home in Springfield due to the Depression. They rented the Adams place south of town. They next lived on the Shelton place and then the Porter place. In 1940 they bought the Duncan Bracken place, then another 80 acres in 1943 which was part of the Pearce property. The 160-acre farm, located at the corner of P Highway and Farm Road 194, has been in the family since then and is called Rolling Acres.

Otho Bridges was born Sept. 11, 1903 in Walnut Grove, MO to Fide and Clementine Bridges and died March 24, 1987. He had seven siblings: Gene, Frank, Dixie, Ruby, Golden, Fanny, and Johnny. He drove teams of horses and operated a steam shovel, and was a charter member of the Operating Engineers Union in Springfield. Otho was known as "Humpy" from his early days in construction. A horse he worked was hump-backed and called "Humpy." The workers applied the name to Otho and it's the nickname he was known by the rest of his life. While working construction, he continued farming in Republic.

*Fay, Otho and Jack.*

Fay was born Aug. 4, 1905 in Bakersfield, MO to Lorenzo W. and Cora (Powers) Lawson and died Dec. 24, 1976. Her parents died in the 1918 flu epidemic. She lived with her only brother, Guy, later moving to Springfield where she worked as a hired girl in a large house on the northwest corner of St. Louis and Kimbrough. She met Otho at her uncle's house and they married in 1922.

Jack was born Feb. 22, 1932, and adopted by Otho and Fay through Springfield Children's Home. He died Aug. 20, 2002. He attended Republic Elementary and graduated from RHS in 1950. Jack attended Southwest Missouri State before joining the Army where he was stationed in Colorado and Alaska and attained the rank of sergeant. He returned to SMS on the GI Bill, graduating in 1958.

In 1952 Otho and Jack started Bridges and Company, Inc., a successful heavy-highway construction company. Jack served in numerous community and industry organizations, including president of the Missouri Associated General Contractors in 1977. The company worked on most roads leading to Springfield. Other projects included Lily-Tulip, Zenith, Springfield Airport and the Corps of Engineers.

Jack married Juanita Marie Wade June 10, 1951. Juanita is the daughter of Clyde D. and Bonnie Bell (Gardner) Wade of Republic. Juanita graduated from RHS in 1952. She has two sisters, Rosalene Wade Bennett and Patricia Sue Wade Altman. Jack and Nita raised three children: Teresa (born 1953), Jack Jr. (born 1956) and Greg (born l960). Teresa married Harold Poole and has two children, Natalie and Lucas. Jack married Mary Clegg and has one daughter, Margaret. Greg married Pam Wilcox and has two children, Amber and Bryant.

Otho and Fay loved horses and the three grandchildren spent their happy childhood years training and showing ponies at area horse shows. The boys often presented the American flag at shows riding their pony Billy with his fancy silver saddle. They showed in English, Western, and Roadster classes and won many blue ribbons throughout the years. The Bridges have been members of the Hood United Methodist Church since the 1930s. *Submitted by Teresa Poole.*

**BRITAIN/BAILEY -** George W. Britain and Betsy Ann Bailey were married in 1849 being among the early settlers in Pond Creek Township. When George was 9 years old his father John W. Britain brought his family from McMinn County, TN, to Greene County, MO. At age 12 George was orphaned and lived with Royal Haseltine near Brookline. He married Betsy, whose family lived near where the Wade Chapel Cemetery is now. They purchased 80 acres south of the cemetery, having a team of horses and a wagon to start with. They first lived in a small log house, later building a two story house, barn and granary.

George and Betsy reared nine children on this farm: Mark, John Wesley, Eli, Aleck, Melissa, Sarah, Amanda Belle, Abert and Mary Jane. They also raised two of his brother's children, John Thomas and Sarah Jane. Their children all married and settled in and around Republic.

George W. was one of the largest tax payers in Greene County owning 1,400 acres and giving his children more than 1,000 acres. Aunt Betsy was well known as a children's doctor. She would put the side-saddle on her gray mare and travel in any kind of weather day or night to treat a sick child with her home-made medicine. Mark F. Britain married Mary Jackson and they raised six children. All married and raised their families in or near Republic. Mark was sheriff of Pond Creek Township about 1883. Later they bought a small acreage and house on Elm Street where they lived until their deaths.

John Wesley and Lucy (Cox) Britain lived on a farm his father gave him. Mr. Britain went into the mercantile business. He built a 9-room house on North Main St. where their three children were born. He and his wife lived in this house until their deaths. About 1900 he sold his store to Mr. Godwin and Bob Thurman.

Eli and Elizabeth Britain lived on a farm his father gave him west of Republic where they raised four children. He owned and operated a brick yard on his farm making bricks for the Hood Methodist Church and many other buildings on Main Street. Later, he built a grocery store on Main St. where the Farmers Exchange was and at present Sherman Thompson operates Main Street Antiques and Furniture. Later he built the building where the Masonic Lodge and the Republic Historical Society are located and added a mercantile store. He and his son, Ira, also operated a large fruit farm. Aleck Britain married Diamma Sallee; they had five children. He and Levi Sallee bought a threshing machine along with a cook shack, doing custom threshing in Greene, Christian and Lawrence counties.

Malissa Britain married George Hayes and they lived on the farm her father gave her. They had four children.

Sarah Britain married a Gamble.

Amanda Britain married James Cox, and they had two children, Ethel M. and Lester E. They built a house on the east side of North Main Street.

Albert married Sarah Garrison and they lived south of his father. *Submitted by Jack Britain.*

**BROWN/BOWEN -** Earl Sylvester Brown was born in Richland, MO in 1901, the son of Jefferson Davis Brown and Clara Alice (Carter) Brown. In 1922, Earl married Ruby Margaret Bowen in Laclede County, MO. Ruby was born in Lynchburg, MO in 1900, the daughter of George Sylvester Bowen and Ida Augusta (Bradford) Bowen.

Earl and Ruby moved to Republic with their infant daughter, Ruby Mae, who was born in 1924. A son, Alvin Earl, was born in 1928 in a rented home on East Elm. In 1934, son Leland Davis was born in the same home—although the family had moved in-between. In 1937 the family purchased a home at the corner of Harrison and Hampton for the sum of $300 from Lester E. Cox and Ethel M. O'Bryant.

Earl worked in orchards, vineyards and on farms in the area. He was custodian at Republic High School in the early 40s. He owned and operated the MFA oil truck from the mid-40s to about 1960.

*Earl and Ruby Brown's 50th wedding anniversary with children: Alvin, Leland and Ruby Mae.*

All three children attended Republic schools. Ruby Mae graduated in 1942 and married classmate James Arnold. They had three children: Rolland, Max and Margaret Ann. Alvin graduated in 1946 and married classmate Angie Harris in 1949. They had three children: Clarke, Marilyn and Scott. Leland graduated in 1952 and married Sue Tyler, also a Republic graduate, in 1956. They have two sons, Stephen and Michael.

Earl Brown died in 1980. His daughter Ruby Mae died in January 1986, and his wife Ruby died in June 1986. Son-in-law James Arnold died in 1993 and grandson Rolland Arnold died in 1996. His son Alvin died in 1999 and Alvin's wife Angie died in 2003. His son Leland, and Leland's wife Sue, reside in Republic. *Submitted by Leland Brown.*

**BROWN/FOUST** - Lestle Victor Brown, born Jan. 17, 1906, son of Samuel "Buzz" and Elsie (Butler) Brown. Buzz had three sisters: Ola Woods, Pauline Woods, Dorothy Haden, and one brother Sheridan Brown. Lestle married Osha Jackson, daughter of Jason and Della (Batson) Jackson. Osha had two sisters, Ila Rubison, Golda Gilland, and one brother, Emmett Jackson.

Lestle and Osha had two children, Nova born Nov. l9, 1925 and Norval born Sept. 9, 1929. Norval attended Grandview School located in Pond Creek Township northwest of Republic, his mother and father also attended Grandview. At the age of 18 years Norval enlisted in the Army serving six years. Norval married Joyce Hayworth in 1951, they had a son Michael. Norval and Joyce divorced in 1955.

*Back: Norval, JoAnn and Mike; front: Susan, Bea and Ray.*

*Lestle and Osha (Jackson) Brown.*

He married JoAnn Foust in 1956. JoAnn was the daughter of Sam and Dollie (Garoutte) Foust. JoAnn had two sisters, Lora Lee (Day—Bacon) and Mary Sue (Robertson). JoAnn attended Grandview School, graduating from Republic High School in 1956. Norval and JoAnn had three children: Kenneth Ray, born Feb. 20, 1957; Beatrice Ann (Cox), born March 27, 1958; and Susan Marie (Jenkins-Rapp) born Nov. l2, 1959. They have nine grandchildren and 14 great-grandchildren. *Submitted by JoAnn Brown.*

**BROWN/HARRIS** - Alvin E. Brown was the son of Earl and Ruby Brown who lived in Republic since early in the 1900s. Angie L. (Harris) Brown was born and raised in the Battlefield area. Her parents, John W. Harris and Ora (Payne) Harris, lived and farmed in that area since the late 1800s or very early 1900s. Alvin and Angie attended the Republic schools from the first grade thru graduation from high school. They married in 1949 and had three children: Clarke, Marilyn and Scott.

*Angie and Alvin with their children: Clarke, Marilyn and Scott.*

Alvin worked at the Federal Medical Center in Springfield and eventually retired from the Bureau of Prisons while living in Atlanta, GA. He and Angie owned and operated a business on Main St. in Republic, Republic Decorator Supply. It was originally on the west side of the street by the theater and eventually moved to the other side next to the newspaper office. Alvin was instrumental in organizing the Republic Community Band and was master sergeant in the Missouri Army National Guard Band.

Angie worked at the Arrow Shirt Outlet store for many years and also was involved in the banking business in Springfield for quite a while. Their son Clarke lived in Republic, where he attended school from grades 1 thru 12. Their daughter Marilyn (Brown) Cotner moved to Springfield with the family in 1968 and graduated from Parkview H.S. Scott moved again with the family to Lompoc, CA and then to Atlanta, GA in 1973 where he finished high school and attended college.

Alvin and Angie have passed on - Alvin in 1999 and Angie in 2003. As of this writing Clarke lives in Springfield, Marilyn in rural Republic and Scott in Mableton, GA. *Submitted by Clarke Brown.*

**BROWN/NEWTON** - Smith Brown, born June 22, 1890 in Billings, MO, died in December 1944, was one of six children born to Thomas Toliver (May 20, 1856-Sept. 4, 1909) and Nancy Elizabeth Brown (May 5, 1858-Feb. 12, 1924), both are buried at the Garoutte Cemetery. They married Sept. 16, 1875.

Rose Belle Brown, one of six children born

*Back: Smithy, Don, Tom, Garland, Max; front: Nancy, Rose Helen, Lucille, Belle, Geneva, Ruby and Norma.*

to Bud Newton and Sarah Glowson Newton, was born Sept. 25, 1895 and died in December 1985 at the age of 90. As children, Smith "Sandy" and Belle lived in the same area north of Republic attending St. Elmo School. They were married in 1913 starting life together on the Brown

*Belle and Smith.*

family farm, purchased in 1879. The Brown farm received the Century Farm award years later. A team of horses and wagon served as Smith's transportation to and from work helping build Highway 66.

Upon Smith's death Dec. 18, 1944, Belle was left to raise their 11 children and three nieces and nephews by herself. There were 27 grandchildren, 11 living close by, having Sunday dinner at the Brown farm often. The grandchildren enjoyed eating watermelon, and arguing as to who was going to sit on the ice cream freezer while another turned the handle to freeze the ice cream. Paper sack box kites were a treasure to fly, being made at Belle's home. Every grandchild took a turn pushing the push mower, no motor on this one, to help Grandma cut her grass. Another delight was to snuggle in the featherbed during the cold winter months.

The farm house burned in 1963, a very sad day. Belle moved to Republic continuing to work at Wood Garment Factory where she was employed for over 30 years. Belle loved her family and was always ready to spend time with them. Her son Smithy took her to a St. Louis Cardinal baseball game in 1968 where she was chosen "Cardinal Mother of the Year," being honored with roses, gifts and special box seats.

Belle always drove a pickup. One time she ordered a new pickup and there was a $25 charge for a heater and $25 for a spare tire; she asked they be omitted. During cold weather she placed a lantern in the floorboard of the truck for heat.

Belle was always ready to sit with children or to care for elderly residents in and around the area during evening hours or on weekends, continuing to work days at the garment factory. When a family was in need Belle was the first to send a donation or take food. She was a very caring person. Many members of the community knew if they stopped by Belle's home there would be fried apple pies on the stove.

Smith and Belle's children: Lucille Brown Darling, Tom, Garland, twins - Rose Helen Brown Goff and Mildred (died at birth), Ruby Brown Moore, Wynona (died at age 7), Geneva Brown Fuhr, twins-Smithy and Nancy Brown Demanche, Norma Brown Gray, Max and Don. Belle Brown was a true mother, grandmother and friend to the entire Republic community. *Submitted by Smithy Brown.*

**BROWN/TYLER** - Leland Davis Brown was born in Republic, MO in 1934, the son of Earl Sylvester Brown and Ruby Margaret (Bowen) Brown. The youngest of three children, Leland graduated from Republic High School in 1952. He attended and played basketball for Southwest Missouri State College, Southwest Baptist College and Drury College. Leland graduated from Drury in 1958 and earned his master of education from University of Missouri in 1967.

*Leland and Sue Brown with sons Mike (left) and Steve (right).*

Evelyn Sue (Tyler) Brown was born in Springfield, MO in 1937, the daughter of Herman Harwood Tyler and Edythe Evelyna (Cutbirth) Tyler. Sue attended Brookline School and graduated from Republic High School in 1955. On May 25, 1956, Reverend Charles M. Fahl married Leland and Sue at First Christian Church in Republic. Their first son, Stephen Max Brown, was born March 12, 1957 and Michael Davis Brown was born April 11, 1959. Steve and Mike attended Republic Schools and graduated from Republic High School in 1975 and 1977 respectively.

Steve graduated from Southwest Missouri State University in 1980 with a bachelor of science in education. He student taught and student coached at Republic High School. He earned a master of science in guidance and counseling degree from SMSU and is currently a counselor at Republic. Steve married Cynthia Lynn Hough on June 4, 1983. They have three children: Andrew Tyler, Natalie Anne and Alexander Elliott.

Mike was employed by the Springfield Public Schools transportation department for several years and is now employed by City Utilities of Springfield. He married Margaret Porter on July 30, 2004 and has two step children and six step grandchildren.

Sue enjoyed staying at home with Steve and Mike in their early years. She cared for many children in her home. After Steve entered high school and Mike was in junior high, Sue became a secretary in the high school principal's office. She enjoyed this position for seven years before taking a position with City Utilities of Springfield in 1978. She continued to work for CU until retiring at the end of 2004.

Leland taught at Republic High School and coached junior high basketball, junior varsity basketball, and later served as the head basketball coach. The highlight of his career with Republic was in 1963 when he lead the varsity basketball team to the State Class M Championship. Leland retired from Springfield Public Schools in 1988. Following his retirement, Leland owned and operated Leland Brown Construction, building homes in and around Republic.

Leland and Sue actively serve in their church, Calvary Baptist. Leland was a member of the Relocation Committee, which coordinated the remodeling of the former Albertson's grocery store into their present church. Sue works in AWANA and the church library.

Leland and Sue enjoy Republic High School athletics and university basketball. They frequently travel with the Lady Bears. *Submitted by Steve Brown.*

**BRUTON/PECK** - The family of James C. Bruton came to the Republic area in 1947. The Brutons were some of the earliest settlers of Greene County having moved from northern Mississippi in 1841 to the area where Fordland and Rogersville later developed when the railroad came through the county. Webster County was later divided from Greene County, which at the time covered a large part of southwest Missouri. Jim was born near Cody Junction in 1908.

James Bruton and Clara Jane Peck were married July 3, 1933. In the early years of their marriage they lived in the Rogersville community. By the time of World War II they lived in Galloway just south of Springfield. At age 44 and the father of four children, he was drafted into the military but a suspected health problem kept him home.

*James and Clara Bruton.*

James and Clara became the parents of four children. Willard Dean was born in Webster County north of Rogersville in July 1935. James Earl was born in 1938 and Effie Deloris in 1940 near the Palmento community in eastern Greene County. Thomas Delbert was born in Springfield in 1943.

In 1946 the family moved to the Wise Hill area just south of Republic. The children attended the one-room Wise Hill School until a problem closed the school and the children finished the year at Clever. In 1947 the family moved to the Brookline and Republic area. The children attended Beulah School where a long-time teacher E.B. Ferguson was school master.

Jim Bruton was employed for over 25 years as a Teamster for the John Drennon & Sons heavy hauling and crane work. He was retired from the company. Clara was a home maker and never worked away from the home.

All four of the children attended Republic High School. Dean was a freshman in 1950 and Tom was the last to graduate in 1961. All the boys were involved in sports and many other school activities. Softball and basketball were all the sports the school offered in those years.

With the exception of Deloris who married Joy Dallas Brigman and moved to southern California, the family of Jim and Clara Bruton stayed close to home. Dean joined the Marines in 1955 for three years and came back to Republic in 1959 after having married a Republic girl, Marthella Kline, in June 1958. Dean worked for Campbell 66 and lived in Rogersville area for several years before moving to Kansas City for seven years. In 1975 Dean & Marty moved back to the Brookline area with their three children: Jeff, Helen and Rachel. All three of their children graduated from Republic High School.

James Earl married Kay Ratcliff from Aurora, MO and moved his family to Springfield and worked many years for Coke and food brokers. Jim and Kay have two boys, Jim Jr. and Timothy. Jim and Kay moved to Republic a few years ago and are retired.

Tom married Judy Cox from Republic and has lived in the area where their four children all attended high school. Their children are Dana Machell, Paula Dawn, Mary Beth and Thomas Delbert Jr. For many years Tom operated a tire shop in Republic. He currently runs a lawn and maintenance service.

Deloris and Dallas Brigman became parents of five children: Joy Dallas Jr., Dale, Carrie, Angela and Davin. Dallas was raised in the Battlefield and Republic area and is retired from the automotive tire business in El Centre, CA.

Clara Jane Peck Bruton died at age 49 in 1967 and is buried at White Oak in Webster County near Rogersville. James Clyde Bruton died in 1978 at age 70 and is next to his wife at White Oak. *Submitted by Dean Bruton.*

**BRYAN/KEMPER** - The Bryans and the Kempers are believed to have traveled to Missouri together. Jefferson Scott Bryan was born Oct. 17, 1849 in Carroll County, MO.

Frances "Fanny" Kemper was born in 1853 and raised in Bates County at Pappenville, MO, the daughter of Jonathon and Rebecca Jane Sutor Kemper. Their home, during the Civil War, became part of the area covering Order No. 11 executed in August of 1863. The order required that all persons living in Jackson, Cass, Bates and part of Vernon counties, except those living within one mile of a Union outpost, had to leave within 15 days. Because of the extreme vandalism that then surged unchecked into this area, it became known as the Burnt District.

*Frances Ann (Kemper) Bryan and Jefferson Scott Bryan.*

The Kempers loaded everything they could carry onto an ox cart and headed northeast to the oldest daughter, Eliza Hornbuckle's house in adjoining Callaway County. Fanny was 10. They returned to a burned house and devastation.

Jefferson Scott Bryan and Frances Ann Kemper were married on Aug. 11, 1872 and soon after, he went to St. Louis to work on construction of the Eads Bridge.

After twin boys and another son dying, Florence was born in Nevada in 1876. Into her old age, she would laugh and tell the story of stopping her father's habit of swearing as a small child by having repeated one of his phrases.

By 1892, Jeff and Fanny had moved to Republic with their children: Florence, Alice, Lois, Miles, Nell, Edna and Ruth. While living in Republic on N. College St. (441 N. is current address but the old house was further back on the lot), Jeff, a master carpenter, constructed the interior cabinetry and woodwork on the drugstore, northeast corner of Main and Grant.

In late 1893 or early '94, Jeff had a severe chronic cough that was diagnosed as grippe. After an extended time, Dr. Beal concluded that he had tuberculosis and recommended he move west to a dry climate for a cure. He refused to leave his wife, pregnant with their 11th child, until the baby was born. The baby, named after his father, was born on July 8, 1894 and Jeff left for Arizona within 20 days but died three or four days after arriving. The headline in the *Phoenix Daily Herald* of July 28, 1894 read, *"Died Among Strangers."* The newspaper account stated that when he had traveled to near Mesa, Jeff had insisted on going to a hospital. They put him in a large wagon with hay covered by a mattress and started out at 10 o'clock at night. At about 5 o'clock in the morning "near the Five Corners (northwest of Phoenix) the sick man called on the drivers to stop and in a moment expired." He was buried in the Pioneer Cemetery in Phoenix next to the owner of the Lost Dutchman Mine.

Shortly after 1901, following her oldest daughter Florence and husband Albert Skelton, Fanny Bryan moved to Indian Territory in Oklahoma, bought 80 acres of land and, except for

Alice who had also married, finished raising her family. She died there in 1930. *Submitted by Mollie Skelton Smith.*

**BUELL** - Anthony "Tony" Brian Buell was born on May 20, 1977, to Jack Carroll and Connie (Thompson) Buell. A fast and early learner (he started learning to read when he was two), he showed an aptitude for technology, from programming VCRs/digital clocks, playing computer games, and later, programming on computers. He displayed this interest throughout his time at school - first at Hurley Elementary (his mother taught there), and later the Republic school system. He participated in activities/competitions for clubs/groups, such as FBLA, the Industrial Technology Club and the Spanish Club, in which he was involved in competitions on district and state levels. Later in high school he took an interest in sports by being an athletic supporter (no pun intended) by traveling to football away games as a member of the Pep Club. Tony graduated in 1995 from Republic High School as one of the top students in his class.

Upon graduation, he was awarded a full scholarship to Southwest Missouri State University (now Missouri State) where he ultimately pursued a degree in Computer Information Systems (CIS). While working toward this goal, he also participated in clubs/organizations such as Phi Beta Lambda, AITP (Association of Information Technology Professionals), and Beta Gamma Sigma (an Information Technology Honors Society), where he was involved in competitions on the state and national level. He also continued his support of student athletics, especially basketball, as part of the Bear Hair fan organization (even becoming the group's unofficial webmaster). Tony finally received his BS in CIS, graduating from SMS in May of 2000.

*Anthony "Tony" Brian Buell.*

While in college, Tony also had part-time employment working on small, temporary jobs in moving, manufacturing, publishing, and banking. For one year, he worked as a computer lab assistant at SMS, and then spent the year after that as an intern at American National Property and Casualty Company (ANPAC). Upon his graduation from SMS, Tony accepted a full-time position as a computer programmer/analyst, and has remained there since. In that time he's received INS, AIT and AIS certifications from the Insurance Institute of America (IIA).

Actually, Tony isn't the first member of the family to work in the insurance business. The Buell family has had its hands in the insurance industry for around a century, starting in 1908 with Tony's great-grandfather, Albert Dunlavy (1884-1966), who co-founded Farmers Mutual Insurance and NW Arkansas Farmers Mutual Tornado Insurance Company. He served as secretary-treasurer (1939-55) and was on the Board of Directors. Tony's grandfather, Jasper "Jap" Bledsoe (1909-98), also worked at Farmers Insurance, serving as the company's vice-president (1960-64) and president (1964-94).

Tony also has the support of his family, which consists of his parents, Jack and Connie Buell, his sister Teri, brother-in-law Michael C. Watts, and grandmother Winnie Thompson, who all reside in Republic. Also living in the Ozarks area are his paternal grandmother, Loine Duncan Buell, and aunt, Jill Jackson, who reside in Ozark, MO. *Submitted by Tony Buell.*

**BUELL/THOMPSON** - Jack Carroll Buell was born May 2, 1942, at Green Forest, AR, son of J.B. and Loine Duncan Buell. He attended a one-room school house at Brawley, AR. His mother was Jack and his sister's (Jill Jackson) first teacher. He graduated from Green Forest High School in 1959, attended Arkansas Tech University, served with U.S. Army in Germany 1963-65, and graduated from the Neosho Water and Wastewater Technical School in 1972.

*Jack and Connie (Thompson) Buell.*

In September 1972 he moved to Republic as Republic's Wastewater Superintendent, where he was employed for two and a half years.

On Dec. 1, 1973, Jack and Connie Thompson were married on Magnolia Street by Bro. Harry McCullough. The couple have lived in Republic all of their married life. Connie was born Dec. 23, 1946, at Alpena, AR, daughter of M. Dean and Winnie Disheroon Thompson. She graduated from Alpena High School in 1964, University of Arkansas in 1968 and Southwest Missouri State University in 1983.

Their first home was at 226 S. Maple, behind the Snow White Drive-In. In the 1970s orders were called out over a speaker and could be heard throughout the neighborhood until closing time. Jack and Connie always knew who was ordering, what and how much the bill was. Snow White Drive-in is now E's Inn. Connie and Jack moved to 420 Concordia in 1974 and to their present home near Island Green Country Club in 1986.

Jack worked for the Department of Natural Resources for 28-1/2 years as a Waste Water Treatment Specialist, and retired in 2003. Connie taught school at Hurley R-I District for 12 years as a librarian/business teacher, and nine years at Republic R-III as a librarian, and retired in 2005. Jack and Connie have served as officers and members in local, district, and state professional organizations during their working years. They are active members of the Wesley United Methodist Church in Springfield, MO.

Jack was raised on a farm north of Green Forest, AR on Yocum Creek, and Connie was raised on a dairy farm north of Alpena, AR on Long Creek. Their family roots are in Boone and Carroll County, AR.

They have two children, Anthony Brian "Tony," who is employed by American National Property and Casualty Insurance (ANPAC) in Springfield, and Teri Dawn (Mrs. Michael C. Watts), who is employed with Cox Health Systems in Springfield. Both children live in Republic. *Submitted by Connie Buell.*

**BULL** - Charles Olan Bull was born and raised with his two younger brothers near Humansville, MO where his father John Bull, a Civil War veteran, was the local blacksmith and also served as the local peace officer following the war. When John died in the early 1900s, the boys moved with their mother Nina to Springfield where Olan began working for the Frisco Railroad at age 17. While working for the railroad, Olan was involved in a serious roundhouse accident in 1921 that earned him a lengthy stay in the Frisco Hospital, which was affiliated with St. John's Hospital at the time. During his recovery in the hospital, he met a young nurse named Clora who would become his wife just one year later.

Clora Hargis was born in 1895 in Webster County, MO, one of eight children born to Rasberry and Laura Thompson Hargis. She attended the Silver Shade School in Marshfield, then moved to Springfield shortly after her mother's death. A short time later, with some help and encouragement from Judge Keets of Springfield, Clora began training as a nurse at St. John's Hospital. After her marriage to Olan in 1922, Clora became a homemaker and Olan continued with what would eventually be 48 years of service with Frisco.

*Clora Hargis, Olan Bull and his Model T in 1921.*

In 1928 Olan moved Clora and their three young children from their modest home in Springfield to a 60-acre farm three miles east of Republic on Hines Street. The farm, complete with a barn, chicken house, smokehouse, plenty of pasture land and orchards, had been known by locals for years as "The Hays Place" and was nestled between Troy Bedell's farm on the east and Lester Phillips' property on the west. At the time of the move, the children: Maxine, Evelyn and Charles (or Bud as he was known to everyone) were too young to help with many of the chores, but Olan and Clora somehow got the work done. The farm would be home to the Bull family for more than three decades and would be the birthplace of two more children, Betty and Dorothy.

It would seem that five children, a farm and a full-time job at the railroad would be enough to keep a person busy, but Olan's entrepreneurial spirit would lead him to other projects over the years such as raising pedigreed Barred Plymouth Rock chickens, raising Jersey cattle and developing crop improvement programs. Then, in the mid-30s, Olan bought and operated the poultry hatchery on Main Street in Republic. He bought eggs from local farmers by running a weekly "egg route," incubating and hatching the eggs, then selling the baby chicks three weeks later. The hatchery business was severely tested in the Depression years of the 1930s, but it survived and was eventually sold to Howard and Bernard Davis in the 1940s. After his retirement from the railroad in 1954, Olan continued to work on the farm where he raised Hereford cattle and worked in his machine shop until his death in 1961. Clora remained on the farm for a few years following Olan's death, then sold the farm in 1965. Clora continued to be active until her death in 1975.

Although some of the Bull siblings moved out of the area as adults, they all attended local schools, including Lindsey and Blades Schools. Many of them married local residents and have children and grandchildren still living in the Republic area. Maxine married Wilford Arndt. Their children are Jim, Robert and Paula (Sherman). Evelyn married Gene Ruckman of Billings and had six children: Kenneth, Patricia (Gott), Becky (Loonsfoot), Mark, Jeffrey and Dan. Bud, who died in 1992, married Jean Alpheri and had two children, Susie (McAnally) and Steve. Betty's marriage to Max Kirkes produced two sons, Russell and Bill. Betty died in 1960. Dorothy married Craig Smith in 1956 and lived most of her life in Los Angeles, CA until her death in 1997. *Submitted by Evelyn Ruckman.*

**BURKS/JOULE** - Robert "Bob" was raised in New Mexico and came to Missouri in 1945 after he was discharged from the Navy in WWII. His parents, Ethel (Slagle) and Sonnie Burks, were originally from the Bolivar, MO area and had retired to a farm on the southwestern edge of Springfield. The abstract for 80 acres of this area was filed by Radford Cannefax at the Recorder's Office of Greene County Dec. 4, 1838. East of the home is the old family Cannefax Cemetery. Slaves belonging to the family were also buried there. The first elected sheriff of Greene County was a Cannefax and is buried there.

*Barbara (Joule) Burks and Robert E. with sons (l-r): Thomas, James and Edward at Silver Dollar City in 1964.*

Barbara was a Missouri native and moved to Springfield with her parents, Ted and Aretha Joule, in 1947 when her father took a position as county agent for Greene County.

Bob and Barbara met through mutual friends and married in 1949. They have lived for the past 53 years on the southwestern edge of Springfield which is in the Republic school district. Their home is located on part of 160 acres Radford Cannefax purchased in 1846 for 25 cents an acre.

Their three sons: Edward "Ed," James "Jim" and Thomas "Tom," attended all their school years in the Republic schools through high school graduation. All three then went on to graduate at SMU in Springfield.

Currently Ed is living in Arlington, TX with wife, Patricia, and daughters, Andrea and Melinda. He is a retired US Naval Air Intelligence Captain and now is the Director of Manpower for the same.

Jim lives in the Republic area with wife Cindy and daughter, Katie. He is employed at the Southwest Treatment Plant as a chemist and supervisor of the lab there. Jim and Cindy are very active in Republic's community affairs.

Tom lives near Washington, D.C. at Haymarket, VA with wife, Kimberly. and children, Julia and Nathan. Tom is employed with the FBI.

Bob is retired from the Justice Department after being employed at the Federal Medical Center for prisoners in Springfield. He and Barbara, along with Jim's family, attend the First Christian Church in Republic. *Submitted by Barbara Burks.*

**BUTLER** - Nelson Garrett Butler was born on a farm near Ozark, MO Oct. 24, 1857. He was the youngest son of Benjamin and Emily (Moreland) Butler, both of whom came from Michigan to Christian County during the Civil War period. Benjamin joined the Union Army and fought in several battles. Due to illness, Benjamin returned home; shortly thereafter, he and his wife contracted smallpox and died - Nelson Butler was five-years old.

*Nelson and Martha Butler.*

Nelson was taken in by different families following the death of his parents. Nelson traveled to Texas with a childless couple and worked on their farm for six years. When a teenager, he returned to Missouri, crossing Indian Territory by himself. In his early 20s, Nelson and one of his brothers went to California. Nelson lived there four years, working on a farm, then returned to Missouri.

Nelson rented and operated Mr. G.W. O'Neal's farm near Republic after Mr. O'Neal moved to town to look after his lumberyard. Nelson purchased 80 acres of land in Section 13; Republic Township and built a home. He soon purchased more acreage. Nelson married Martha Jane Britain in September 1886. Martha was the daughter of James and Elizabeth (Wade) Britain. James was born in Greene County and Elizabeth was born in Georgia. Martha received her education in the common schools of Pond Creek Township where she grew to womanhood.

Nelson and Martha had four children: Elsie (married Sam Brown), Nadie (married George O'Neal), Maude (married Edward Mooneyham), and Frank (married Mirta Mooneyham). Frank attended Prairie View Elementary School and Lester E. Cox was his 8th grade teacher.

In 1922 Frank Butler married Mirta Mooneyham, daughter of Monroe and Martha Jane (Mynatt) Mooneyham. During her childhood, Mirta worked in her father's cook shack and picked strawberries for a neighbor. She worked in the canning factory in Republic before she and Frank were married. They lived in the home built by Nelson Butler (Nelson and Martha moved to Republic) and Frank continued to work the family farm, an occupation he loved. They milked cows, raised hogs, sheep, and chickens. They supplied eggs to local hatcheries, including Gamble's Hatchery in Springfield. In later years, Frank raised beef cattle and produced hay. Frank also owned property in Kansas, which he later sold. In the early years of their marriage, Frank and Mirta would travel to Kansas for the wheat harvest.

Frank and Mirta had four children: Wayne (married Joretta Bullard), Ray (married Ernestine Tiede), Jewell (married Robert L. Wimmer), and Maxine (married Kenneth McGruder). All four children attended Prairie View Elementary School and were graduates of Republic High School.

Nelson (1857-1941) and Martha (1865-1958) Butler were faithful members of Hopewell Baptist Church, located four miles west of Republic. Nelson served as deacon for several years. Frank (1900-1983) and Mirta (1902-1987) Butler also attended Hopewell. Frank was a deacon and taught the young adult Sunday school class for over 40 years. Seven generations of this family attended Hopewell and members of four generations still attend. *Submitted by Jewell Wimmer.*

**BUTLER/BULLARD** – E. Wayne Butler (1926-2003) and Joretta A. Bullard (1931-) were married on March 6, 1949 in her parent's home in Mt. Vernon, MO. They made their home on a 200-acre farm, northwest of Republic, which they bought from Charlie Garoutte. Two rooms of their house were the original building of a stagecoach line. Traces of the old road can still be found as it wandered through the farm. Years later they purchased Jim Wade's 60-acre farm which joined their property.

They started their farm life by growing corn and small grains and milking Holstein cows. Wayne also continued showing sheep for a couple of years after they married. Several years later when their children joined 4-H, they showed Registered Polled Herefords. In 1993, they stopped their dairy operation and started raising more beef cattle and producing more alfalfa hay to sell.

Growing up, Wayne always attended Hopewell Baptist Church with his parents, Frank and Mirta Butler, and grandparents, Nelson and Martha Butler. He was saved at an early age and became a member at Hopewell. Wayne served his church as a deacon and song leader from 1957-2003. Joretta joined Hopewell after they were married and has taught a Sunday school class for more than 40 years.

Over the years, they have served their community in a number of volunteer associations. Wayne was a school board member for 15 years and Joretta worked in PTA for 17 years in Republic and Greene County Council. They both were Farm Bureau members for many years, serving in several offices. Wayne served on the Greene County Republican Central Committee from 1963 until his death in 2003.

They have three children: Janet, born March 9, 1951, married Dale Sanders in 1973. Their children are Jeffrey and Julie. Jeffrey married Jamie Ball and has a son, Jacob Cole. Julie married Jeremy Thompson and they have a daughter, Jenna Layne.

Judy, born March 5, 1954, married Darrell McConnell in 1973. Their children are Jennifer, Jill and Jessica. Jennifer married Michael Bowers and has two sons, Jett Ellis and Jasper Hoyt. Jill married Jason Beltz.

Jimmie, born July 1, 1957, married Andrea Hendricks in 1981; their children are Jocelyn and Joel. Jimmie started farming with his father as he was growing up and continues to operate the family farm today. *Submitted by Joretta Butler. Editor's note: Janet passed away in 2007.*

**CANTRELL** - William "Raymond" Cantrell, originally from Bakersfield, MO and Etta Mae (Bodine) Cantrell, originally from Shelbyville, IL moved to Republic in 1924 from Clever, MO where Raymond managed the Republic MFA store. In 1934 Raymond opened the Cantrell Produce Store, which he ran for approximately 12 years. Etta's parents, Eli and Sarah (Gray) Bodine resided on a farm near Republic, where they moved to in 1923. Raymond and Etta had three children: Rayetta, Jaunita Lula and William Bodine.

*Parents, Raymond and Etta, Bill (on lap), Rayetta and Juanita Cantrell*

Rayetta married Fred Beyer and moved to Chicago Heights, IL where Fred pastored the United Church of Christ. Rayetta and Fred had two children, Judith Ann and John Raymond.

Jaunita married Bryce Hendricks and had

two children, Beverly Carman and Jay Lynn. Jaunita worked as a nurse at Burge Hospital, which is currently Cox Medical Centers in Springfield, MO. Jaunita died in 1981.

*Standing l-r: Thomas Darin, Nancy Buenta, Pamela Ann, James William, Gilda Sue and Edward Raymond; sitting, Shirley Jean and William Bodine Cantrell.*

William "Bill" Bodine was born at Republic in 1926. Bill attended for 12 years and graduated from Republic schools. In his boyhood Bill enjoyed bicycling (all over Republic); swimming in Terrell Creek with friends (even in wintertime) and Boy Scouts. Bill enlisted in the U.S. Navy in 1944 where he served his country in WWII. Bill returned in 1946 to attend Drury College prior to enrolling in Mortuary School in St. Louis, MO where he graduated in 1948. Bill married Shirley Jean Tooley of Mountain Grove, MO in 1947. Bill and Jean had six children: Gilda Sue, Pamela Ann, James William, Nancy Buenta, Edward Raymond and Thomas Darin.

Bill and Jean purchased Fossett Funeral Home, later to become Cantrell Funeral Home, in Republic in 1955. In 1962 they purchased funeral homes in Clever and Billings, MO. Bill, Jean and their family were members of the Republic Hood United Methodist Church. Bill was a member of the Masonic Lodge, was active with the Shriners, and Jean was a member of the Eastern Star organization. Bill and Jean retired from the funeral homes in 1974 and resided in Republic. After retirement, Bill drove a school bus for the Republic school system for many years. Bill and Jean were proud of their children and enjoyed following and supporting them in a variety of Republic school events. After 52 years of marriage, Bill lost Jean to cancer in 1999. Bill later married Jeannie Whittaker of Springfield, MO.

Bill and Jean's daughter, Gilda Sue, married Mike Frazier and had two children, Christopher Thomas, who graduated from Republic High School, and Lori Ann who attended Republic schools for most of her school years.

Daughter Pamela Ann married Otto Jones of Republic and had two children, Shannon and Shanni. Pam later married Carl Blades and had two more children, Becky and Carla.

Son Jim married Cindy Wilson and they had one son James Mathew, who is currently residing in Republic. Jim is now residing in Kansas City, MO with his wife Margie where he is a funeral director, following in his father's footsteps.

Daughter Nancy married David White of Republic and had one daughter Jennifer Jean, who graduated from Republic High School. David passed away in 1998. Nancy resides in Republic and has worked for the Republic school system as a lunchroom attendant for many years.

Son Edward "Ed" Raymond, a Republic graduate, married Michelle Gardner of Republic and had three sons: Brent Raymond, Bryce William and Blake Edward, who all three graduated from Republic High School. Ed resides in Republic with his wife Amanda and is a member of the Springfield Fire Department. Ed also builds homes in the Republic area with his father Bill, under Cantrell Homes.

Son, Thomas Darin "Darin" graduated from Republic High School where he played football for the Republic Tigers. Darin married Valerie Culley from Republic and had one daughter Brittnay. Later Darin married Patty (Crabb) and had two more daughters, Morgan and Addison. Morgan and Addison attend Republic schools. Darin is active in Republic sports activities with his daughters and is employed at Cox South.

Before Etta Mae Cantrell died in 1992 there were five generations of Cantrells living.

In 2006 there were still four generations of Cantrells residing in Republic. *Submitted by Gilda Martin.*

**CARLSON/COX -** Phyllis Cox, daughter of Beth "Puge" Snyder and Adrian "Heavy" Cox, was one of the many Republic babies delivered by Dr. R.C. Mitchell at the Springfield Osteopathic Hospital, located on Sunshine Street in Springfield, MO. Phyllis was born June 16, 1945.

Donald Carlson, son of John and Edith (Shelton) Carlson, was born April 17, 1945 in California although the family soon relocated to the Republic area,

Growing up in Republic, they attended 10-cent movies at the Republic Theater located at 207 North Main in Republic, which was owned and operated by Lynn and Irene Martin, and ate hot dog coneys and drank five-cent Pepsi at O'Dell Drug located on the northeast corner of Main and Grant Streets.

Phyllis cheered for Donald through elementary school as he played basketball for the R-3 Kittens at the Springfield Boys Club, Donald's mother, Edith, planned parties for the junior high kids in her basement with "spin-the-bottle," being the anticipated final game. Phyllis danced with a local youth square dance group, the Jig-A-Longs, having regular performances on the "Ozark Jubilee," broadcast from the Jewell Theater located on Jefferson Street in downtown Springfield, MO. While Donald worked summers hauling hay and mowing lawns, Phyllis worked as a waitress at her Aunt Ruth Snyder's shop, Republic Sundries. At this shop, her Aunt Ruth taught her how to cook and Phyllis learned to make 15 to 20 pie crusts at a time.

During their high school years, Phyllis cheered for Donald, who was 6'6" tall, and played on the Republic High School State Championship basketball team. After high school, Donald and Phyllis attended SMS where Donald continued his basketball career. After graduating from college, the two were married on her dad's birthday, Aug. 18, 1967.

Donald became a basketball coach, teaching in Joplin and Springfield at Hickory Hills, Kickapoo, Jarrett and Glendale. Phyllis taught English at Parkview High School and also served as chairperson of the English departments at Central and Kickapoo High Schools in Springfield.

Donald and Phyllis had two daughters, Natalie Beth, born Aug. 22, 1973 and Christine Caroline, born Sept. 17, 1975. The daughters loved to come to Republic to visit their Grandma "Puge" Cox and Grandma Edith Carlson. Both daughters now live in St. Louis where Natalie Carlson Allen is a dietician for Barnes Hospital and Christine Carlson Keller is an elementary teacher at Webster Groves.

Phyllis and Donald have grandchildren who also love to return to Republic to visit their Aunt Libby West. *Submitted by Barbie Luttrell.*

**CARLSON/SHELTON -** John Carlson was born Dec. 29, 1915 in Bock, MN. After high school graduation, he left for sunny California, leaving behind two feet of snow on the ground. John moved to California to apprentice in his Uncle Bolier's hardware store. During the same period, Edith Shelton traveled from Nixa, MO to Visalia, CA to continue her college education while living with her Aunt Ercell. During her college years, Edith was a member of the girls basketball team and to this day her love of the sport continues. John and Edith met in 1934 during a Youth Fellowship Meeting at the Presbyterian Church they attended in Visalia, CA.

*Front row: Don and J.C.; back: John, Carol and Edith Carlson.*

Upon their marriage in 1936, John and Edith decided to settle close to her parents and bought their first home on West Elm Street in Republic. In 1953, the family moved to 521 North Main. John was employed as a salesman for Biedermans Furniture in Springfield.

Their life in Republic included a local pinochle group which played cards monthly and included Bud and Virgie Logan, Cliff and Helen Kubat, Jim and Millie Houston, Jay and Mildred White and Bill and Jean Cantrell. John was also a member of the Masonic Lodge located on Main Street in Republic and became a Master Mason in 1953. In 1967, John was installed as Worshipful Master of Republic #570.

John and Edith had three children. John Carlson (JC) was born in August 1940, Donald Carlson in April 1945 and Carol Carlson in June 1951. Both JC and Donald excelled in sports, especially basketball. John and Edith were loyal fans and followed the Republic basketball team to watch their sons play. John was a very vocal supporter and would shout his support from the stands while Edith would nervously cover her eyes during a difficult game. Occasionally, she and her friend Virgie Logan would become so anxious during a basketball game they would vacate their seats to pace in the hallways.

John and Edith's oldest son, John Charles, was an active member of the Boy Scouts led by Dr. Brim. During John's 8th grade year, he and a friend, John Brim, attended the National Boy Scout Jamboree in Los Angeles, CA. These two friends rode the train by themselves to California where 50,000 Boy Scouts were gathered; this was the largest jamboree ever held to that date. John was a member of the U.S. Navy and a graduate of Drury College. John is married to Carol Van Gelder and they make their home in Springfield.

Donald Carlson was a member of the Republic 1963 basketball team which won the state championship. Donald continued to play sports during his college years at Southwest Missouri State, where he was voted into the SMS Hall of Fame. Donald married his high school sweetheart, Phyllis Cox, and they reside in Springfield.

Carol graduated from Republic High School in 1969 and graduated from Southwest Missouri State. She is married to Kurt Bock and they reside in Bloomington, IL. *Submitted by Carol Carlson Bock.*

**CARTER -** The first members of the Carter family to settle in the Republic area were Stephen Carter (1853-1927) and his wife Sarah (Richard) Carter who farmed and kept the store at Plano for many years. Mr. Carter was the son of Rolla and Elizabeth (Dorrell) Carter, who owned over 500 acres of land in Center Township near Bois D'Arc. His grandparents, Caleb and Nancy (Ferguson) Carter, operated a blacksmith shop from their farm and were among the area's first settlers, coming to Greene County from Monroe County, TN in 1838.

*Back Row l-r: William, Gerald, Gordon, Dwight; front: Wayne, Gertrude and Frank. Picture taken in 1953 at Gertrude and Frank Carter's 50th anniversary.*

Stephen and Sarah's son, Frank Carter (1880-1959), married Gertrude M. Winter (1885-1981) in Republic in 1903. Frank and Gertrude bought a farm near Republic where they raised five sons: William Rudolf "Pat" (1904-1999), Gerald Lafayette "Jerry" (1906-1990), Gordon Stephen "Peck" (1909-1996), Dwight Halbert "Dude" (1912-1995) and Ernest Wayne "Buck" (1915-1962).

The family's farm thrived for over 30 years and sold fruit to distributors in Springfield and Kansas City, but it failed in the Depression. Frank, Gertrude, and Ernest lived briefly in Clever, then moved to their son Gerald's farm on the James River near Nixa, where they lived for the rest of their lives. William "Pat" Carter married Delphia "Dell" Keltner in 1929 and the two farmed in Republic and later in Ash Grove. Dwight Carter married Cleo V. Kerr in 1934 and moved to Kansas City, where he founded a successful commercial refrigeration business.

Gordon Stephen Carter graduated from Republic High School in 1928. He worked on his family's farms in Republic and Nixa and later for the Civilian Conservation Corps. On March 18, 1939, he married Phyllis W. O'Kelley (1916-2004), daughter of Halltown farmers, Charles and Ada (Hollingsworth) O'Kelley. A 1935 graduate of Halltown High School, Miss O'Kelley had worked as a nanny in Springfield before her marriage. In 1944, Gordon and Phyllis returned to Republic, buying a 20-acre farm on West Farm Road 168.

Over the next 50 years, Gordon and Phyllis Carter operated their land; first as a dairy, also raising pigs, cows, chickens, an acre of tomatoes, four acres of cucumbers and a pear orchard, and later as a beef cattle farm. Gordon also worked as a carpenter, helping to build and repair many houses in Republic, and co-founded the West Republic Volunteer Fire Department, serving as its fire chief for over 20 years. For several years Phyllis served as secretary of The Happy Hens Extension Club and wrote the club's regular reports for *The Republic Monitor*.

The Carters had three daughters, all of whom graduated from Republic High School. Linda Kay "Kaye" (1941) married James Robbins (1942-2002) of Oklahoma City and settled in St. Louis, MO where they raised two daughters, Kelly Lynn (1965) of Bethesda, MD and Lori Ann (1968) of Evanston, IL.

Cheryl Sue "Sue" (1945) operated a gift shop in Republic in the early 1970s and later worked as a hairdresser in Springfield; she now lives in Springfield with her husband, James Clemenson. Her son, Kevin Carter (1971-1992) who attended Republic Elementary School, was caring for his great-uncle Gerald Carter's Nixa farm at the time of his death at age 20.

Steva Lynn (1950) worked for many years at the Republic and Springfield Public Libraries and now lives in Springfield. She raised two sons in Springfield: Courtney "Cory" Carter Smith (1978), who lives on the Republic farm that belonged to his grandparents, and Casey Carter Smith (1981), who lives in Republic.

Kelly, Lori, Kevin, Cory and Casey loved spending time at their grandparents' farm, helping their grandpa feed his cattle, eating their grandma's homemade ice cream and playing baseball with their cousins, uncles and aunts in the field east of the house. *Written by Lori Robbins.*

**CASSY –** Charley Cassy was born in Sedalia and his wife Roxie was born in Fort Scott, KS. They met while he was in the Navy and later married in Springfield in 1919. They lived in the Rogersville area several years where seven of their children were born. They moved to Republic in 1935/36 where their eighth child was born.

*Schuyler Creek Salting Station – 1944.*

Times were very hard back then to live and raise a family because of the Great Depression and the area of the big dust bowl. He bought a dump truck and worked for the WPA. Their children attended the Republic, Mt. Etna and Lindsey Grade Schools, also the Republic High later on. In 1938/39 he bought a 40-acre farm on Route 2 east of Republic. He later bought 40 more acres east of the original acreage, which is now part of the Wilson's Creek National Battlefield area.

In 1941 he began raising cucumbers on five acres of land (later 20 acres or more) and selling them to the Springfield Pickle Works. In 1943 he was contracted by the Springfield Pickle Works to have a salting station to be located on his farm. It was called the Schuyler Creek Salting Station. He ran and operated this business and also contracted other farmers in and around Republic and the surrounding communities, also down south in Arkansas, to grow cucumbers. He sold them the proper seed, etc.

Over the years he had 300-500 acres contracted out. The farmers made pretty good money doing this back then. The small cucumbers (gerkins) sold at $5.00 bushel, regular size $2.50 bushel, the larger ones (not yellow) 50 cents a bushel that were used to make relish. The cucumbers had to stay in the brine for three months before they were shipped by trucks to the Springfield Pickle Works to be processed further. They were sold under the brand name Mountain Treat. He had up to 53 huge tanks or vats that each held from 375-1,250 bushels. He operated this salting station for nine years.

In 1952 he moved his family and the station to Aurora to be more centrally located to his customers. In 1956 he retired from this operation. Later he sold real estate and did a lot of painting. Other times he enjoyed fishing and country music. They moved to Arkansas, Branson, Aurora and then back to Springfield, where Roxie, born in 1902, died in 1983 and Charley, born in 1899, died in 1986.

Their eight children: Herschel lives in Springfield, Bob died in 2001, Betty died in 1955, Billy died in 1945, Virginia died in 1970, Margie lives in Independence, MO, Wilma lives in Wynona, MN and Joann lives in Aurora. There are 21 grandchildren, 40 great-grandchildren and 27 great-great-grandchildren so far. The remaining families still call Republic home. *Submitted by Margie (Cassy) Francis.*

**CHASTAIN/JONES –** Dr. Pierre Chastain left England on the English ship *"Mary and Anne"* on April 19, 1700, arriving in America at the mouth of the James River in Virginia on July 23, 1700. From Pierre came the Chastain descendants who live in the Republic-Clever area.

James Thomas Chastain and Mary Jane Offuitt were united in marriage in 1888 in Calhoun, GA. They moved to Missouri settling near the Christian, Greene County line, southeast of Republic in 1892/93. The second of nine children born to this union was Joseph Robert Chastain, born December 1890, died November 1969 and buried at Brookline Cemetery.

*Joe Chastain with sons, l-r: Claude, Clyde and Clay.*

Joseph married Maude Mae Gildewell in 1910. Maude was born in May 1894 and died in December 1918. Joseph retired from the Frisco Railroad where he worked for many years. They had three sons born in Republic: Claude Oren Chastain, born in August 1911; Clyde Ray Chastain, born in November 1912; and Clay Thomas Chastain, born in June 1915.

Clyde married Reathel Maize Jones, daughter of Ralph Jones and Anna (Carsten) Jones in 1932. Reathel was born in Maize, KS, in

*Clyde and Reathel Chastain with daughters, Dorothy Jean (left) and Anna May (right).*

March 1912, being named after her birth city of Maize, KS. She was given a beautiful layette and baby buggy by the town. Clyde worked as a truck driver and Reathel a housewife in the early years of their marriage. They journeyed to California in the 1930s during the Depression, living in a tent, picking fruit and vegetables for a living, later returning to the Republic area.

Entertainment for Saturday night was always playing cards with neighbors and friends. Reathel later worked in garment factories in Republic and Springfield and at Lily Tulip Cup Factory in Springfield. They purchased a farm on what is now the Wilson's Creek Battlefield in the 1940s; this farm was located just south of Sweeney's Museum. While living there their home on the battlegrounds burned in the early 1950s. The family relocated to Battlefield.

Clyde and Reathel divorced in 1955, at which time Clyde moved to Springfield and Reathel and Anna May relocated to Republic. Born to Clyde and Reathel were three daughters; Dorothy Jean Boyd, Betty Lou (died as an infant) and Anna May Bishop.

Dorothy Jean attended Republic Schools grades 7-12. Anna May, their youngest daughter attended Capernium School, located northeast of the Ray House on the battlegrounds. After consolidation of the area schools, she attended Beulah School on M Highway. After their move to Battlefield, she attended Green Ridge School located south of Battlefield, later attending Republic Elementary and High School.

Clyde died in January l979. Clyde, his mother Maude and two brothers are buried at Manley Cemetery, south of Battlefield.

Reathel continues to live in Republic and will be 94 years young the first day of March 2006. Reathel was one of the founding members of the first Parent Teachers Association in Republic school system donating all of her free time to this organization. *Submitted by Anna May Bishop. Editor's note: Reathel died in 2006 just before her birthday.*

**CHUMBLEY/GOODMAN -** Samuel was born March 25, 1843 in Claiborne County, TN the son of John and Malinda (Sharp) Chumbley. Sam died March 8, 1928 in Pasadena, CA. He is buried in Evergreen Cemetery, Republic, MO. Mary Eliza Goodman was born April 12, 1844, the daughter of Sampson and Sarah (Lyngar) Goodman. She died Dec. l4, 1911 and is also buried in Evergreen Cemetery.

*The Chumbley Boys, top row l-r: Ben, Lon, Ernest, Victor; seated: Clinton, Albert, Grandpa Samuel and Ed.*

Samuel and Eliza were married Feb. 1, 1863 in Greene County, MO. They had seven sons: Ben, Lon, Ernest, Victor, Clinton, Albert and Ed. The Anderson family is descended from Benjamin Thomas Chumbley, born Jan. 7, 1875. He married Lucy Emily Wester, daughter of Henry Clay and Sarah Elizabeth (Ellis) Wester, on July 28, 1895 in Polk County, MO. Ben died and is buried in Mission Park, San Antonio, TX.

*l-r: Janie Wyn (child), Doug, Mary Jo Anderson, Charles Chumbley, Breta Jane, Floss, Earl Anderson and Lucy Chumbley.*

For a time, Ben ran a dairy farm somewhere in the Republic area, known as the Silver Leaf. He and Lucy had three children: Charles, Ward and Floss Isabelle. Charles married and had three children: Bonnie Jean, Gladys and Wayne. Ward died at a young age. Floss married Earl Roscoe Anderson. *Submitted by Breta Holmes.*

**CLARK/DEMANCHE -** Phyllis Ann Demanche, daughter of Nancy and "Dick" Demanche was born June 29, 1948. She attended all 12 years in the Republic R-III schools. At the age of 19 she met Roger William Clark from Verona, MO. Roger was born July 13, 1948. Roger and Phyllis were both employed at Marionville Shoe Factory. Three months after they met, they were married on Aug. 18, 1967. August 2006 will be 39 years of marriage.

*Roger and Phyllis (Demanche) Clark.*

They started their life together with two cars, both of them having a car, a lamp from S & H Green Stamps and a mixer received from having a Stanley Party. They had no place to live. Belle Brown, Phyllis' grandmother, was in California visiting her three older daughters and after a telephone conversation with Phyllis she let them stay in her house until she returned home. Quite some time after Belle returned home, she moved Phyllis and Roger into one of her rental houses on Olive Street. At their new home on Olive Street most every Saturday night was spent with the four-room house being packed full of friends and family playing country music.

In 1968 Roger started to work for Mid-America Dairy in Springfield. Their first child was born the very first day he started working there. William "Bill" Clark was born on Phyllis' birthday, June 29, 1968. Four years later their second child, Richard "Dick" Joseph Clark was born Sept. 7, 1972.

Roger and Phyllis purchased a house at 428 N. College. Roger started work for Harry Cooper Supply during the day and Roadway Express at night. Eventually he chose to work with Roadway alone and continues with them after 33 years of service. Phyllis worked at the Republic Garment Factory at different times. With Roger being raised on a farm, they rented property from Annie Skelton, which was across the street from their home on North College, where they raised cattle and chickens. Later they purchased the Skelton place and remodeled it and continue to live there. It will be a century home in 2008. Phyllis being a stay-at-home wife and mother did a great deal of the remodeling. She always raised a garden including strawberries.

Phyllis loved being at home with their two sons and enjoyed many other kids who came over daily. Today they are both married but continue to be very close. The family closeness generated from Dick and Nancy Demanche, who were Phyllis's mom and dad, has continued with this family. Phyllis and her brother Tom continue to have very close family ties.

Bill Clark married Natalie Maus on June 7, 1997. They have sons Cooper Douglas Clark, born August 6, 2002, and Collin Maus Clark, born June 9, 2006. They reside in Springfield. Dick Clark married Laura Albough on June 28, 1997. They have a daughter Mariah Sha'e Clark, born Dec. 30, 1994; a son Cole Joseph Clark, born Feb. 1, 1999, and a daughter, Madison Dawn Clark, born Dec. 6, 2001. They reside in Fair Grove. *Submitted by Roger and Phyllis Clark.*

**CLARK/GOODWIN -** Volney "Vollie" Clark (born 1891, died 1968), son of Volney and Serilda Clark of Taney County, and Martha (Goodwin) Clark (born 1895, died 1985), daughter of Marion and Louisa Goodwin, moved to Republic in 1931, with their children: Volney Jr., Joanna, Howard and Donald. They moved to help care for Martha's mother, after a fire destroyed their home in Taney County.

Martha had several relatives in the Republic area including her brother Laurel Hart and wife Hannah (Branson) Hart. Laurel was in charge of the water and streets in Republic. Other relatives included brother Paul Goodwin, sister Ida Cunningham, aunts Victoria and Theodosia Ragsdale, Martha Youngblood, Lura Lonon, Nora Tillou, Ella Watson, and uncles John and Jordan Ragsdale.

Vollie was the janitor for Republic schools for many years and Martha cared for many Republic children in her home.

Vollie Jr., born 1918, died 1983, worked in construction work for many years.

Joanna, born 1920, died 1990, married Loarn Ottendorf. She worked in the garment industry and Loarn was an area mechanic and retired from Lily Tulip. They farmed for several years. Joan had one son Jack Clark, who retired after a long career in the Air Force. Jack and wife Coral reside in Bakersfield, CA. Jack had four children. Loarn lives in Republic.

*The Clarks. Front l-r: Martha, Joanne, Vollie; back: Donald, Vollie Jr. and Howard.*

Howard, born 1923, died 2003, married Jeanette Merritt of Clever. He worked in the garment industry in Parsons, KS and Joplin, MO until retiring in 1985, and moved back to Republic. They had one son, Gary, who is the Golf Pro at Milburn Hills Country Club in Overland Park, KS. Gary, wife Diane and children, Jeffrey and Jennifer, reside in Kansas City, KS. Jeanette lives in Republic.

Donald, born 1929, died 1995, married Dixie Allhands of Marionville, MO. He worked in the garment industry, then worked many years in the nursery/landscape business until his health forced early retirement. He was a Boy Scout leader during Jim's scouting years. They had two children.

Jim, a 1971 Republic graduate, is a retired master sergeant after a career in the Air Force, and lives in Republic.

Rita, a 1980 Republic graduate, also graduated from Southeastern Academy in Kissimmee, FL in 1981. In 1982 she became a travel agent with AAA Travel in Springfield, MO where she is currently employed. She married Kenneth Roetto in 1991. They own Roetto Insurance Agency and live in Springfield. They have two adult children, Nathan and Amanda.

Donald was severely injured in a hunting accident in 1988. He spent the remaining years of his life in the Missouri Veteran's Home in Mt. Vernon, MO. Donald was a Korean War Army veteran.

Dixie worked for years in offices of Wood Garment and Crane Mfg. Companies. She was secretary for Dr. Samuel Wittmer until his retirement, then was an accounting clerk for Springfield public schools until her health forced early retirement. She lives in Republic and is a charter member of Calvary Baptist Church and is active in the American Home Club. *Submitted by Dixie L. Clark.*

**CLUTTER/HAUN** - Lewis Clutter was born Jan. 26, 1889 and died Oct. 5, 1951. He married Laura Haun, who was born July 22, 1893 and died Nov. 8, 1974. Lewis and Laura Clutter moved from the Willard, MO area to Rt. 7. Springfield, MO in August 1943 to what was known as the Young Farm. The farm was located east of Brick School, north of Brookline, MO. They purchased the farm from a family named Moore who had purchased it from the Young family.

The house was a two-story house which still showed the gun shot holes in the front and back of house as a result of the gun battle and death of local city and Greene County law officers in the infamous shoot out between the officers and the Young boys in January 1932. The red barn was unique as there was a driveway leading from the ground up into the loft. Their grandchildren still remember riding their trikes down the steep incline. There was a large pond which was said to be the hiding place for the Young boys' stolen articles. Nothing was ever found to prove this correct.

They moved there with their two daughters. 1) Gladys (born June 3, 1927) graduated from Republic High School in 1945 as valedictorian of the class. She married Carson O'Dell in 1951 and presently lives in the Fair Grove, MO area. 2) Dorothea Jean (born Oct. 22, 1930, died Aug. 29, 2001) graduated from Republic High School in 1948. She married Harold Barker in 1949 and lived in the Dallas, TX area until returning to Springfield, MO in 1993. Their other daughter Marjorie (born Oct. 19, 1918, died Nov. 5, 1994) was married to Carl Wallis and lived in the Willard, MO area.

Lewis was a farmer who took great pride in keeping his place neat. He was known for the pretty alfalfa fields on the farm. At the time they moved to this farm there was no electricity. In 1944 he took on the job of getting REA to extend electricity to all the farms and homes in the area.

They sold the farm in 1958 to a family named Miller and quit farming due to health reasons. They returned to the Willard, MO area on Highway 13 where they lived until Lewis' death in 1961. Laura then moved to Springfield, MO where she lived until her death in 1974, *Submitted by Gladys O'Dell.*

**COCHRAN** - Floyd and Edna Cochran came to Republic in the early 1940s, buying the C.H. and Sarilda Boehm acreage. Prior to coming to Republic they lived in Springfield and a short time in Nixa. They had six children: Amber had a son and a daughter, Lucille had two daughters, Wanda had two sons and two daughters, Maurine had two sons, James had one son, and Richard had a son and a daughter.

Floyd was a retired streetcar conductor in Springfield. He had instruments from the Springfield weather bureau and phoned in the weather conditions in Republic every day. Edna was an active member of the Hood Methodist Church and was Republican Committeewoman from West Republic.

James was in the Merchant Marines. He and close friend, Billy Miller, accidentally met each other in the Philippines during WWII.

After the war he owned an air conditioning business in Kansas City. He and his wife Evelyn were active in the Gideons Bible Society, a group which places Bibles in all hotel rooms. James also helped with the Ozark Empire Fair in the Agriculture Department. *Submitted by Evelyn Cochran.*

**COCHRAN/GRAY** - Terry L. Cochran and Debra J. Gray were married Aug. 28, 1987 by Jimmie E. Cochran, Republic, MO. Debra had two sons by a previous marriage to Dale Wilson: Douglas (born Sept. 24, 1974) and Dustin Anthony (born June 14, 1978). They resided in Republic and had a lake home at Stockton for several years. Terry was born July 1, 1948 in El Dorado Springs, MO to Jimmie and Nathalee Cochran. Debra was born Nov. 3, 1952 to Henry and Norma Gray in Springfield, MO. Terry served in Vietnam for 14 months beginning June 1966.

*Terry and Debra (Gray) Cochran.*

Terry and Deb met when Deb worked with Terry's mother in a garment factory in the summers, but went separate ways until 1987 when Terry's mother discovered they lived a few houses apart. Terry and Debbie were both single. They started dating and were soon married. The boys welcomed Terry with open arms and respected him very much.

*l-r: Jimmie E. Cochran, Doug Wilson, Stacie Wilson, Makenna Wilson, Wendy Allen Wilson, Dustin Wilson, Debra Cochran, Terry Cochran and Henry "Van" Gray.*

They went to Stockton Lake as much as possible on the weekends and for mini vacations, always fishing and riding the Silver Bullet, later selling the residence. Terry and Deb wanted the boys to experience all of the surrounding fairs and events. This is one thing they enjoyed and wanted to say, they had been to each event at least once. They enjoyed many one day trips to St. Louis, Kansas City and many other places.

When each son went away to college, road trips were extended to Manhattan, KS (KSU) to see Doug and to St. Joseph, MO (Missouri Western) to see Dustin. Not only were these trips to see the boys, but to move them in and out of their college homes each spring and fall. Each trip was taking a different route than the last, just to make the trip more interesting. One trip to Kansas was to repair Doug's car when Garth Brooks was in town. They were able to fix Doug's car and see Garth in the same trip. Most trips included Grandpa and Grandma Gray.

Douglas married Stacie Wolden June 27, 1998, they have a daughter Makenna Lynn Wilson, born Oct. 4, 2004, and they reside in Kansas City, MO. Both are architects.

Dustin and Wendy Alien married on May 21, 2005. Dustin, an apprentice locksmith, and Wendy, who works with a Foreign Exchange Work Program, reside in Cape Girardeau, MO. Both boys met

*Makenna Wilson.*

their wives while at college. In 2003 Terry was laid off from work and later diagnosed with cancer in October 2003. This turned their lives upside down. The first of many surgeries began in St. Louis, MO with several return trips. Other surgeries followed in Springfield. Terry is currently surviving the many treatments of radiation and chemotherapy. Always with a positive attitude and determined to beat the cancer. You never see him without a smile. Terry's career was a machinist for several companies and Debra works with insurance at St. John's. Terry and Deb help care for each of their fathers as both mothers have passed away. Now they have Makenna to brighten up their life. What a bundle of joy! *Submitted by Debbie Gray Cochran. Editor's note: Terry passed away July 4, 2006 after a courageous battle with cancer. He is buried at Wade Chapel Cemetery.*

**COGGIN** - James A. Coggin (1832-1911) was born in Georgia, migrated with his family through Tennessee to Missouri. James and Mary Brown were the parents of three sons: George W., Martin L. and Levi. Mary Brown Coggin died before the family left Tennessee and James married Mary A. Shropshire. Two daughters, Melvina and Stella, were born to this union. In

*Front Row: Ora Coggin Jones, Myrtle Coggin Harralson, Clara Coggin Ivins, Frank Coggin, Laura Coggin O'Neal; back row: John Coggin, Gladys Coggin McCoy, Lawrence Coggin, Mrs. Alvin Coggin, Mada Maxine (baby) held by Alvin Coggin, Elizabeth Ellen Rose Coggin and George Washington Coggin. (Picture taken at their farm home.)*

the late 1880s, James A. and Mary moved to Greene County with their family. About 1900, James and Mary moved with sons, Martin and Levi and their wives, to Oklahoma. James died in 1911 and is buried in Harper County, OK.

George V. Coggin (1861-1922) and wife Elizabeth Ellen Rose (1862-1940), daughter of Richard Rose and Nancy Elizabeth Hosman, established their home north of Republic. George was known for his expertise in breeding and selling horses. Eleven children were born to this couple: Lafayette Alvin (1882-1961), Lawrence Hershel (1883-1974), Mattie B. (1884-1886), William E. (1886-1888), John Leon (1887-1957), Myrtle M. (1888-1982), Ora Ellen (1891-1985), Clara Elizabeth (1895-1964), Clarence B. (1896-1896), Laura Adrian (1898-1987) and Joseph Frank (1901-1981).

Four of the children: John, Lawrence, Ora (Jones) and Frank, remained in this area. Ora had two daughters, Ruth and Kathleen, and one son, Joe Donald. John had one daughter, Ina Mae. Lawrence had one daughter, Gladys.

Frank married Pauline Yeakley and they had a daughter, Helen Louise, who died on her 14th birthday in 1931 and a son, Herbert Lee. Herbert still lives in Republic having served as Postmaster for 30 years in Republic and Monett. He married Carol Elizabeth DeWitt, daughter of Attorney Bruce T. DeWitt and Thirza (Garbee) DeWitt, on Feb. 27, 1945. Carol is an accomplished pianist and piano teacher. Herbert and Carol have three sons: Randolph Joe, Stanley Kent and James Bradley, and one daughter, Martha Louise (Towe).

Front Row: Carol Elizabeth (DeWitt) Coggin, Herbert Lee Coggin; Back: Randolph Joe, Stanley Kent, Martha Louise (Towe), James Bradley.

Randy married Barbara Search of New Jersey. They have one son, Seth Alexander, one grandson, Garrett Alexander, and one granddaughter, Laura Elizabeth. Randy lives in Branson and Seth lives in Ozark.

Stan married Cathie Sue Beard of Republic and they have one son, Zachery Kent; one daughter, Beth Allison; and one grandson, Brady Kent. Stan lives on part of the family farm north of Republic. Zac lives in Republic.

Marti married Randy Lee Towe of Nixa. They have three sons: Trevor Paul, Blake Andrew and Caleb Michael. They live in Nixa.

Brad married Susan Diane Wimmer of Republic and they have twin sons, Daron Bradley and Quentin Nathaniel. They live in Republic. *Submitted by Herbert L. Coggin.*

**COKER/FUHR** - Holly Roberta (Fuhr) Coker was the second and youngest child of Roger Leo Fuhr (1947) and Nina Roberta (Warden) Fuhr (1947). Born on March 21, 1973 in Springfield, MO, her only sibling is Eric Roger Fuhr (1971).

Holly attended Marionville schools, graduating as salutatorian in 1991. She completed a bachelor of science in sociology at Missouri Southern State University graduating Magna Cum Laude in December 1994. She married Sterling Wade Coker in August 1993 in Springfield, MO.

Sterling is the eldest child of Robert Joseph Coker (1931-2006) and Virginia Irene (Vanderhoof) Coker (1949). Born in Springfield, MO on June 5, 1970, his only sibling is Jeremy Blaine Coker (1973). Sterling attended Marionville schools, graduating in 1988. In 2004 he completed a master's of business administration from Missouri State University.

*Holly, Sterling and Dalton Coker.*

Sterling and Holly moved from Springfield to Republic in October 2005. They have one son, Dalton Wade Coker, born June 7, 2000. They are active members of the Mt. Vernon Church of Christ where Sterling serves as the Deacon of Education and Holly teaches Sunday school.

Sterling is employed by St. John's Health Systems as the St. John's Clinic Business Office Director and Holly is employed by Tri-County Counseling, Mt. Vernon. *Submitted by Holly Coker.*

**COLE** – The Walter and Novella Cole family relocated to Republic in late August 1944. They moved from Lebanon, MO, and Mr. Cole found work at the garment factory. Mrs. Cole was a homemaker.

Mr. Cole was born in North Carolina and his family moved to Missouri in the spring of 1902. They settled on a farm near Eldridge, MO. Mrs. Cole was born and raised on a farm in the same area. They married in 1932 and raised four children: Margaret, Joe, Dan and Marilyn.

Mr. Cole died in 1953 and Mrs. Cole found employment with Dr. R.C. Brim, a local dentist. She remained in the family home on Brooks Street. She retired when ill health forced Dr. Brim to close his office (which he had moved to Springfield). She stayed in her home until her passing in 2004.

Margaret and Dan have spent their adult years in Southern California, and both had careers in the banking industry. Joe lives in Brookline and he and his wife, Anna Raper Cole, owned and operated the Family Cleaners in Republic until retirement in 2003. Marilyn is a homemaker and resides in Seymour, MO. *Submitted by Anna and Joe Cole.*

**COLLINS/HARALSON** - Jim and Linda Collins were married at the Calvary Baptist Church in Republic when it was located at the corner of Hines and Hwy. 60 on Oct. 27, 1990. This was the 2nd marriage for both of them. Linda has lived in Republic since 1978 while Jim moved here in 1990. Jim is originally from Walnut Grove and Linda from Bolivar. Linda has three children who graduated from Republic High School. Shannon Haralson in 1985, Darren Haralson in 1987 and Tricia Sifferman in 1991. Shannon lives in Ozark, Darren still lives in Republic, and Tricia lives in Springfield. Jim has two children. Daniel lives in Joplin and Lisa lives in Springfield.

*Jim and Linda Collins.*

Jim and Linda worked for many years as realtors in the Republic area. In addition, Jim was the associate pastor at Calvary Baptist Church from 1993-95 and at Bible Baptist church, 1995-96. They started the Anchor Baptist Church in Republic in 1996 and are still there at this writing. They bought a home on N. Kyle 12 years ago and still reside there. Their home has become the gathering place for family and friends.

In 2001, Jim got involved in local government and ran for Ward I Alderman. He won that race and served in that position for three years until he ran successfully for the position of mayor in 2004. He still serves at that post. His priorities include the opening of government to the citizens, establishing ad-hoc committees in areas such as business, communication, city/county relationships, community values, and downtown revitalization. This approach has created a positive direction for the city and involved hundreds of volunteers.

Linda went to work for St. John's Health Care in November 2002 and works in Patient Access. Her primary reason for taking the job was the necessity of having health benefits. Jim used those a lot. He had some strokes and in September 2003 had open heart surgery. Linda still works there.

Jim and Linda have nine grandchildren. All but one are boys. Five of the grandchildren are residents of Republic. The others aren't far away. The farthest away is in Joplin, so Jim and Linda get to see their grandchildren regularly. That is great with Linda who creates all sorts of special days and occasions to spend with the grandchildren - some individually and some as a group. The only requirement Grandpa has with the boys is that they learn to play at least a little golf so they can play with him occasionally. Grandma's house is a favorite with the kids for many reasons, not the least of which is her abilities as a cook.

Jim and Linda also like to travel. They have been on some great trips together and anticipate more in coming years. It is, however, always great to come back home to Republic. Most of their friends are in Republic and they have forged many lasting relationships. *Submitted by Jim Collins.*

**COMISKY/GILLHAM** - Charles Edward Comisky was the first child born to Frank Joseph and Irene Myrtle Comisky in November 1934. He grew up in Republic, MO and graduated from Republic schools. Charles, his siblings, and friends played games that children in a small mid-western town post WWII era played. They rode their bicycles and often hitched rides to Terrell Creek to camp and swim at the "Old Blue Hole."

After graduating from high school, Charles enrolled at Southwest Missouri State where he played basketball for the Bears. After his second year at SMS he enlisted in the U.S. Navy.

His tour of duty was with the Commander of the 7th Fleet and the Taiwan Defense Command in the Western Pacific. Ports of call included Japan, Hong Kong, Wake Island, the Philippines, Midway and Guam. He participated in the Tachin Island Evacuation in 1955. Charles played for the 7th Fleet basketball team which won the Far East basketball title. Ships he served on included USS *Helena*, *St. Paul*, *Bremerton*, *Rochester*, and *Eldorado*. After discharge he was employed by the Western Electric Co. installing telephone equipment for Bell Telephone. He worked for one year before returning to SMS where he received his degree in accounting and marketing in 1960. Charles was again employed by Western Electric at the Kansas City Works, located in Lee's Summit, MO. He held numerous supervisory and management positions associated with the manufacture of equipment used by the Bell Telephone System. He retired in 1989 after 30 years of service.

Since retirement, he has served as a volunteer at the Longview Golf Course and plays golf three or four times a week with friends who also volunteer their services to the Jackson County Parks and Recreation Department. Charles' hobbies have included canoeing and kayaking many rivers in Missouri and Arkansas. He also has rafted rivers in Colorado and has restored several classic autos. Charles coached basketball, baseball, and softball for many years in Lee's Summit Little League programs. He served several years as Director of the South Suburban Baseball Association.

In 1958 Charles married Jeannette Elizabeth Gillham from Fair Grove, MO. She was employed by Southwestern Bell when they met. She later worked for Royal McBee while Charles finished school. They have two children.

Michael Aaron born in 1964 is a graduate of Missouri and Arkansas Universities. In his last year of law school, his Marine Corps Reserve Unit was activated and he was sent to the Gulf War. Mike's unit was in the first Marine unit to cross the "Berms" into Kuwait. All of his unit returned home safely. He received his law degree in 1992. He is licensed to practice in Missouri, Kansas and Arkansas. Mike married Charlotte Freeman from Fort Smith, AR. She is a graduate of Arkansas University and is a Marine Corps Lieutenant Colonel stationed at 29 Palms, CA. She is planning to retire in early 2007. They make their home north of Smithville, MO.

Anne Elizabeth was born in 1968. She and her brother are graduates of the Lee's Summit school system. Anne graduated from Missouri and Kansas Universities with BS, BA and MS degrees in civil engineering. She is a licensed professional engineer. She worked for Bishop Engineering, and the past 11 years for Burns and McDonald in Kansas City. Anne is married to Michael Brincks from Carrol, IA. He is a graduate of Iowa University School of Law. He is currently a Director for the Government Services Administration in Kansas City. They have two children: Caroline Elizabeth, born February 2004, and Benjamin Wyatt, born January 2006. *Submitted by Charles Comisky.*

**COMISKY/MANESS** - Alan, son of Frank J. and Irene Comisky, grew up in Republic. He began his first grade school year in the two-story Republic school building on West Elm Street. During his 8th grade year the rural one-room schools consolidated. As a result the 8th graders were moved to old WWII Army barracks which were moved to the high school campus from the former O'Reilly General Hospital in Springfield. The barracks had become part of the Evangel College campus and they sold them to Republic. He graduated from the high school building that was torn down to become the E-2 building on Anderson Street.

*Front l-r: Alan and Rosemary Comisky, Alyssa Strader; standing in back is Steve and Alanna Strader.*

Alan married Rosemary Maness, daughter of Homer and and Lois Pope Maness, on July 23, 1960. Rosemary attended first grade in Richmond, CA while her dad worked in the shipyards during WWII, then attended second and third grade at Lindsey. Her parents paid tuition for her to attend Republic beginning her fourth grade year. After graduation from Republic High the same year as Alan, she attended SMS, now Missouri State University, and received her BS in education.

Rosemary began her teaching career in Republic and Alan worked for Bacon Tire. When he was drafted in the Army and sent to Germany, she resigned and joined him. They lived in Germany for 18 months. While in Germany she taught GIs studying for their GED.

Alan was with Headquarters Company 12th Engineers Battalion and worked in the water purification unit. They traveled extensively throughout Europe visiting cities in France, Italy, Belgium, Luxembourg, Austria, Monaco, Switzerland, England, Holland and Denmark.

When they returned to the States Alan began working for Don Brown's Glass Company, later for PPG, and retired from Builder's Glass. Rosemary began substituting in Republic and Springfield. Springfield put her on as a full-time sub at Hickory Hills. She began work on her master's degree completing it from Drury in 1969. During her 36 years with the Springfield Schools, she taught at Holland, Sequiota, and retired from Watkins. After retirement she taught for Grace Classical Academy.

Alan and Rosemary regularly attend Hood United Methodist Church. They are active in three car clubs. They own a Model T and two Model A's. Alan kept the 1959 Ford station wagon his dad used when be was working construction jobs. They enjoy working with the Republic Historical Society.

In addition to those activities, Rosemary is active in Alpha Delta Kappa, an honorary teacher sorority, retired teacher groups, Republic Community Band, and Republic Eastern Star #370.

They have one daughter Alanna Rose born May 4, 1974. She also graduated from Republic High. Travel was an important part of Alanna's growing up. Vacations were a must and she has traveled to most of the continental states as well as Alaska and Hawaii. On a trip to Europe she saw the house her parents lived in while in Ulversheim, Germany and the Army base in Dexheim, Germany. In HS Alanna enjoyed playing flute with the band, French Club, and journalism classes.

While attending Drury she continued to play in the band and joined Kappa Delta Sorority. She met her husband, Steven James Strader, a Willard High graduate, while they attended Drury together. His fraternity was Kappa Alpha. Alanna received a BA in business administration from Drury. She and Steve were married March 20, 1999. They have a daughter Alyssa Rose, born Feb. 19, 2003, and a son James Alan, born Jan. 12, 2006. Alanna works for O'Reilly Automotive in the corporate offices and Steve is employed by Builders Glass as a glazier. *Submitted by Alanna Strader.*

**COMISKY/WADE** - Frank Joseph Comisky (1908-2000) was born in St. Louis, MO. His parents were Francis and Barbara (Malecek) Komrska. Frank had a sister Mildred Barbara (1906-1961) who married Edward John Muir in 1934. Mildred and Ed are buried in Saints Peter and Paul Cemetery in St. Louis. Mildred and Frank's parents died young. Barbara died in December 1909 and Francis passed in June 1914. They are buried in Saints Peter and Paul Cemetery. Frank lived both in an orphanage and with his grandfather Wencelaus. Wencelaus was born in Volyne, Republic of Czechoslovakia and came to America in 1881.

*Irene and Frank Comisky.*

As a youth Frank decided to come to southwest Missouri. When he arrived in this area Komrska was not easily pronounced so he decided to legally change the spelling of his name to Comisky. He worked on the farm of Mr. and Mrs. Charlie Miller. He married Irene Myrtle Wade (1908-1999) daughter of George Calvin and Rosie Alice (Laney) Wade on Nov. 21, 1933. The Wades were pioneer families of this area. Her brothers and sisters were (twins) Clara Ennis (Hendrix) and Clarence Emmet, Ruby Susan, James Ralph, Clyde Dee, Ina Gladys (Mooneyham) and Dorothy Vernell (Cox).

Irene enjoyed gardening, canning, quilting and homemaking.

Frank worked various jobs after farming with the Millers. He drove a milk truck route for Daricraft and a school bus for Republic, but made carpentry his chosen occupation. He also enjoyed community service. He served for many years on the city council and as mayor from 1962-64. After serving as Worshipful Master of Republic Lodge #570 he served 25 years as secretary.

Frank and Irene had four children: Charles Edward, James David, Frank Alan and Lynda Sue.

Their son Charles married Jeannette Elizabeth Gillham June 21, 1958. Charles graduated from SMS, served in the US Navy, and worked for Western Electric until his retirement. Jan also attended SMS but chose to be a stay at home mom for their two children, Michael Aaron and Anne Elizabeth. Mike is an attorney and married Charlotte Freeman. Anne is a professional engineer. She married Michael Brincks. They have a daughter Caroline Elizabeth and a son Benjamin Wyatt.

David served in the U.S. Army in Germany and married Evelyn "Kitty" (Allen) Koch April 7, 1969. Before retirement she enjoyed working as a beautician. She has a son from a previous marriage named Larry Koch. At the time of David's death, June 12, 2001, he drove a gasoline tanker truck for Texas Trans Eastern in Houston, Texas. He is buried in Texas in the Houston National Cemetery.

Alan married Rosemary Maness July 23, 1960. He graduated from Republic High School. After serving in the US Army he became a glazier and retired from Builders Glass. Rosemary graduated from RHS, SMS and Drury and taught in Republic and Springfield. They have one daughter Alanna Rose and she graduated from Republic and Drury. She works in the corporate offices of O'Reilly Automotive, Inc. She married Steven James Strader March 20, 1999. They have a daughter Alyssa Rose and a son James Alan.

Lynda graduated from Republic High School. She married Charles Richard "Dick" Davis April 7, 1966. Dick graduated Republic High School and retired from Sweetheart Cup. They have two children, Jayme Beth and Jared Blane. Jayme graduated from Republic High

School and works for the Dept. of Energy. She was married to Patrick Hayes for 14 years, and they have three children: Connor Patrick, Emily Nichole and Lauren Elizabeth. Jayme is now married to Sheldon McNeil. Dick and Lynda's son Jared graduated from SMSU and works for Data Tronics in Fort Smith, AR. He married Penney Wilson July 16, 2005. *Submitted by Alan and Rosemary Comisky.*

**COOK/SIFFERMAN** – Daisy Sifferman, born in 1902, was the eldest of eight children born to Alex and Birdie (Smith) Sifferman. She was born in the large two-story home at the corner of PP and TT in Greene County. Her brothers and sisters were Minnie, Henry, Ray, Grace, Ruth and Ruby (twins), and Alice. Daisy spent most of her life in southwest Missouri attending Springfield Teacher's College and teaching in rural schools in Greene County.

*Daisy Sifferman Cook.*

During her marriage to Robert Warren Cook, she taught mathematics at the high school level off and on between obligations of raising five children. She taught at Branson, Hollister, Marionville and Stella. During their retirement years, Warren and Daisy returned to live in Republic in the Sifferman addition in a home built by her brother Ray.

Daisy, a self-taught painter, began her hobby at the age of 61 after her youngest daughter gave her some leftover oils from her last college class. She painted for 13 of the last 15 years of her life. She worked with compulsion to document those forces that held society together at the turn of the century: faith, hope, love and concern, family, home, church and community; farming activities at the time when hand tools were beginning to be replaced by power machinery; the growing, gathering and preparation of food; making clothing at home; raising crops and animals for use and for sale; social events; the use of schools for church meetings before churches were built – all these were subjects Daisy included among nearly 300 paintings she completed. Many of Daisy's paintings are displayed at Crowder College near Neosho, MO.

After Warren's retirement he found pleasure working on a farm near Chesapeake and developing it into a walnut plantation. He became a member of the Walnut Council of Missouri #87. Daisy passed away in 1977 and Warren in 1984. They are buried at White Chapel Cemetery. *Submitted by Kevin Medlin.*

**COX/DAVIS** - The Cox-Davis Dairy was a part of the Republic business community from 1954 to 1988. Lester E. Cox, one of the partners, had served as a school boy janitor in Republic's grade school which was adjacent to the Frisco Railroad. Mr. Cox owned land in Republic and farm land on the southwest edge of Republic. He first had a partnership with the Carl Schad family. Later, he deeded some of the land to the school district on which to build a school. Still later he deeded more land to the Evergreen Cemetery Association. Though living in Springfield he still maintained a partnership in the Cox-Schad dairy operation and an orchard in Republic.

The second partner, Warren Davis, a son-in-law of the Schads, used his GI Bill to obtain training for operating a dairy. He attended the Springfield Senior High School's institutional on-farm vocational training course. He finished this training in August 1954.

*Warren Davis' herd of Holsteins.*   *Warren milking cows.*

He and Mabel Schad married in 1950. The couple moved to the Ford Tractor farm on Cox Road in Springfield. In 1952 they bought an interest in the Cox-Schad Dairy. In 1954 they purchased the rest of the Schad interest and the partnership became the Cox-Davis Dairy. At that time the dairy was located on Hampton Street in the city.

Land north of Hines Street from Main to Boston Lane and across Highway 174 was pasture land and most days the cattle were driven down Hampton Street then a dirt road and across Hines Street, under Highway 174 from the milk barn to their pasture.

*Cox-Davis Dairy Holsteins crossing Hines Street at Hampton in 1954.*

The dairy had two identical barns - one was used for the dairy operation and for storage and processing the fruit from the adjacent orchard. The barn had 16 stall stanchions, which was quite a large operation for that day and time. It was further renovated into an elevated milk parlor with a bulk tank.

The other barn was used to store hay, as a loafing shed for the cows, and a machine shed. The second barn was damaged by a tornado in 1971 and later torn down. The milk barn is still standing and has since been used as a community center, library and most recently, as "People Helping People." Between Hampton Street and the railroad track, a grape vineyard and an apple orchard existed. These areas later became the Republic City Park and a swimming pool was built there in the early 1960s.

When the land was deeded over to the Republic school district and the city in 1960, the dairy operation was moved south of town.

This dairy operation involved the joint planning of Warren Davis, Lester E. Cox, and Lynn Bussey, a son-in-law of Mr. Cox, and an industrial engineer by profession. The dairy herd began with 60 head of cows, mostly Holsteins. Eventually with additions of registered Holsteins from Wisconsin, the Missouri University Experimental Farm at Mount Vernon, and other purchases, the herd reached a total of 310. The dairy was a member of the Dairy Herd Improvement Association from 1960-88 and Warren Davis served on the DHIA Federation Board for several years.

Because of the innovations and modernization facilities and techniques, the new dairy became widely known. Some of these innovations were pipeline milkers, mechanical feeders, and electric door openers. The *1963 World Book Yearbook* included a picture of Warren and Mabel Davis working in their modern dairy barn. *Hoard's Dairyman,* a national dairy farm magazine, pictured the farm on its cover in its May 10, 1966 edition. The February 1962 issue of *Farm Journal* magazine also featured an article with color pictures of the Davis couple working in their dairy operation.

Over the years the dairy employed many local young men, four regular employees at a time. Many of these were young high school boys wanting summer/weekend employment. During its years of operation many farmers, representatives of various dairy organizations and other interested persons came from many places for a tour of the "Cow Palace." This nickname was given to the dairy barn by the Davis children.

Though Lester E. Cox died in 1968, the dairy operation continued under the same name. The story is told that after his death his son Bud received a call asking if he would like to have the old grade school bell his dad had rung while working at the school. Bud, then asked Warren Davis to go pick up the bell. When he got there Bud got another call telling him there was a guy about to steal his bell. The caller continued, "Says his name is Davis."

The dairy operation continued until 1988 when the milking herd and calves were sold, and the Davis family moved into a new home on South Main. *Submitted by Janie Kuehn.*

**COX/SNYDER** - Beth "Puge" Snyder and Adrian Ervin "Heavy" Cox were married on Christmas Eve 1940. Heavy grew up in Jamesville, MO with his four brothers: Charlie, Dick, Roy and Clifford. While serving in the U.S. Army, Heavy obtained a leave for Christmas Eve in order to marry Beth, daughter of Golda (Allen) and Harve Snyder. After completing his term in the Army, Heavy joined Puge at Nevada, MO where she was secretary to the executive director of the State Institution for the Mentally Handicapped. Upon the birth of their oldest daughter Phyllis in 1945, they returned to Republic to become merchants on Main Street. They assumed ownership of Juggy's Cigar and Tobacco. In addition to the sale of tobacco and beverages, the establishment was also the home for a watch repair service operated by Paul Lloyd and later Nick Consalvo. Edward Britain also maintained an insurance office in the establishment. At one time Heavy operated a service station on North Main Street, north of Highway 174.

*Paul Lloyd and A.E. "Heavy" Cox behind bar.*

After years of being merchants on Main Street, Heavy and Puge were grateful for the many friends they had come to know. Heavy, who suffered from severe rheumatoid arthritis, left the business to take up small amounts of farming on a place he had purchased at the northeast corner of town. The acreage is now considered to be in the central part of the city limits located at 613 East Hines. Puge worked as a financial manager at the Springfield Postal Facility, and later served a tenure as the Post Master for the Republic Post Office. She returned to work at the Springfield Post Office where she retired after 35 years of service.

Puge and Heavy were the parents of two daughters, Phyllis Cox Carlson, who married Donald Carlson and at present is living in Springfield, and Libby (Cox) West, who married Joe West and continues to live in Republic. Puge and Heavy were grandparents of six granddaughters.

Heavy died at the young age of 47 years and Puge died at age 69. Both were laid to rest in the Evergreen Cemetery in Republic. *Submitted by Mindy Kelley. Editor's note: Joe West died 2007.*

**CRAWFORD** - In 1929 Melvin and Angie Crawford moved their family two miles East of Brookline on old Brookline Road. This house is still resided in by a member of the family, Jim and Janet Shoemaker, daughter of Roland Crawford. Melvin was in the plastering business. In later years they owned a gas station, ceramic and pottery shop on Highway 60 just east of the intersection of what is now James River Freeway. Their shop is still there doing business as Pumpers Print Shop.

*Back l-r: Dorothy Crawford, Chester Crawford, Mike Crawford, Richard Viles; middle: Tina Viles, Susan Viles and Patty Crawford; front: Becky Viles and Kim Viles.*

They had four sons and one daughter: Melvin "Orville," Chester, Roland "Tuffy" and Robert (twins), and Viola Crawford Parkhurst.

Chester rode the first school bus to Republic High School. He married Dorothy Hubbard on April 19, 1947 and they moved into a basement house originally owned by Viola and Parky Parkhurst on a portion of the Crawford property. They resided in this house until they passed away. Chester was a pipefitter and Dorothy was a stay-at-home mom. As funds were available they improved the house. They had three children: Susan, Patty and Mike.

When Susan was ready to start school in 1954, Brookline had just consolidated with Republic, so she went to the school that was on W. Elm Street. During Christmas break the elementary school was moved to Anderson Street. In 1962 she was a freshman in the new high school on Hampton Street. She graduated in 1966. Patty graduated in 1967 and Mike graduated in 1971.

In 1967 Susan married Richard Viles who graduated in 1964. They have three daughters: Tina, Kim and Becky. They wanted their daughters to go to Republic since it was a small school; but that began to change by the time they were ready to go to school. They all graduated from Republic High School: Tina in 1987, Kim in 1990 and Becky in 1991.

Patty Crawford never married and resides in Branson where she has been for the past several years. She works for the Grand Palace and Remington Theaters as a bookkeeper.

Mike Crawford never married and currently resides in Springfield. He is a real estate appraiser.

Tina Viles is still in the Brookline/Republic area. She has two children: Shawn Viles (15) who is a freshman at Republic High School and Shania Ulmer (6) who is in first grade at Republic E-1.

Kim married Dale Shelton and resides in the southwest Springfield area. They have two children: Levi (9) and Abbie (7). They go to Jefferies Elementary.

Becky married Kevin Edmonds and resides in Branson. They have three daughters: Kala (12), Paige (11) and Loryn (8). They are all enrolled in Branson schools. *Submitted by Susan Viles.*

**CRESON** - Ralph Creson was born May 31, 1902 and was raised by his grandmother who was a full-blooded Cherokee. She was on the Trail of Tears when she got sick along the way and was left with a family who was willing to take care of her. The family who took care of her settled near what is now Strafford.

Ralph as a young man got a job at the broom factory in Springfield. He bought a farm just outside of Republic. He married Hazel Flood Jan. 3, 1975. Hazel was born and raised in Nixa. Ralph worked at Billings bowl factory. He loved his work and was good at it.

Hazel remembers Republic as a very small place (it has grown a lot since then). They used to walk everyplace they went and often stopped to visit with his mother who liked to sit on the front porch.

Ralph and Hazel vacationed in Europe, Switzerland, Italy, and London. Ralph did not care for the food and was anxious to get back home. He said he hadn't seen anything as good as Republic. They liked living in Republic because they were close to the stores and everything they needed. Ralph died Feb. 13, 1992.

Hazel enjoys her volunteer work at the Republic Senior Friendship Center, especially the crafts, and has made a lot of lasting friendships there. *Submitted by Hazel Creson.*

**CROW** - Bryant Crow moved to Greene County in 1833 from Williamson County, TN. In 1838, Bryant Crow bought 80 acres near Republic from the U.S. Government in Section 8, Township 28, Range 22, for $1.25 per acre. He married Isabinda Cannefax in 1852. Isabinda's Uncle Chesley Cannefax was the first sheriff of Greene County.

Bryant and Isabinda Crow had two chil-

*1927 – Children of Joseph Bryant and Laura Belle Crow. Front l-r: Jesse, Wilbert, Laura Belle, Geraldine and Clifton; back: Melissa, Georgia, Lester, Henry, Mary Aileen and Maggie.*

dren: Joseph Bryant Crow, born March 5, 1855 in Springfield, and Visa Jane Crow, born Sept. 8, 1858 in Wilson Township. The Crows lived in a log cabin on Wilson Creek. Bryant Crow was born in 1800 and died in March 1859 in a logging accident in Wilson Township. Although there is no marker, it is believed he is buried in the Cannefax family cemetery off West Sunshine, Springfield.

In 1869, Isabinda Crow married Jefferson Russell and moved to the Russell farm in Wilson Township with her son Joseph Bryant and daughter Visa Jane. About 1888, Isabinda became ill and her son Joseph Bryant Crow, needed someone to help care for her. He hired 17-year-old Laura Taylor who lived on a farm north of them.

Laura Taylor was the daughter of Andrew Jackson Taylor and Isabel Lewis.

Andrew Jackson Taylor was a Civil War veteran whose discharge papers are on file in the Wilson's Creek National Battlefield Museum. After his discharge from the Union Army in 1865, Andrew Jackson Taylor and wife Isabel moved to Greene County. They lived in a log house by a cave near present day FR 178, southwest of Harrington Cemetery near Republic. Their eight children were all born there.

During the time that Laura Taylor was caring for Isabinda Crow Russell, she and Joseph Bryant Crow fell in love and were married at his home east of Battlefield on Aug. 22, 1889. Isabinda Crow Russell died in 1890 and is buried in Brookline Cemetery.

Joseph Bryant and Laura Crow had 11 children: Georgia, Jessie, Monta, Mary, Lester, Maggie, Melissa, Clifton, Henry, Wilbur and Geraldine. Eight of their children were born on the Crow family farm in Greene County Section 23, Township 28, Range 23 on land that was purchased in 1965 by the U.S. Government to become part of the Wilson's Creek National Battlefield.

Following Joseph Crow's death in 1925, Laura Crow sold the farm to her son-in-law Melvin Garrison and moved to Zion, IL. Laura Crow returned to Greene County in 1947 and died in 1951 in Billings, MO. Joseph Bryant and Laura Belle Crow are buried in Brookline Cemetery.

Crow family descendants have lived continuously in the area. Joseph and Laura's children: Lester Crow, Maggie Crow Garrison, and Melissa Crow Shaw, settled in Clever, MO and raised several children. Grandchildren: Winson Crow, Donna Shaw Teague, Mary Garrison Arndt, Gilbert Garrison, Russell Shaw, and Bill Garrison still live either in Greene or Christian counties, as well as several great-grandchildren.

In all, Joseph and Laura Taylor Crow had 38 grandchildren who lived to adulthood and over 30 are still living across the United States. *Submitted by Bryant L. McNiece.*

**CUNNINGHAM/BURNS** – The William "Bill" Perry Cunningham family moved to Republic Aug. 1, 1975 after living one year in Springfield, MO. Before that the family, Bill and Nancy (Burns), Nelson Perry and Carol Ann, had lived in the Maryland suburbs of Washington, D.C. Bill was a cartographer at the U.S. Naval Oceongraphic Office, Suitland, MD, and Nancy was a cytologist at the Anne Arendel General Hospital, Annapolis, MD.

In Republic Bill was the cartographer at the Southwest MO Local Government Advisory Council, and Nancy was a teacher's aide at the Developmental Center of the Ozarks. Nelson was a junior and Carol was a freshman at Republic High.

After Bill retired, he managed the family's rental properties, refinished antiques and was a Red Cross disaster volunteer. He died Sept. 17, 1991 of a heart attack.

*The William Perry Cunningham family: Bill, Nancy, Carol, Lee, Jeanne and Nelson.*

Bill's father, Wilbur Perry Cunningham Jr., was born in Scammon, KS but grew up in Rogers, AR. As a young man he moved to Kansas City, MO where he met and married Bill's mother Genevieve Austin. Bill had one sister Peggy.

Nancy's parents, Calvin Ernest and Effie Sisk Burns, were farmers living all their married life on a farm near Milan, TN. She had three brothers: Ray Edwin, Bruce Warren and Carey Eugene.

Bill and Nancy's son, Nelson, is a graduate of Southwest Missouri State. He married Jeanne Lischer and they have three children: Katherine Rebecca, Elizabeth Perry and Robert William. He works for Union Pacific Railroad and lives in Omaha, NE.

Bill and Nancy's daughter, Carol, is a graduate of the University of Tulsa. She married Lee Randell Ward and they have two children, Max Perry and Austin Daniel. She has worked in the public relations field but is now a stay-at-home mom and lives in Houston, TX.

The family adjusted to living in a small town quickly but did wonder how long they would have to live in their house for it to be their house and not "the Glenn Owen house." When they painted the house gray after it had been white for 70 years they realized that old houses in Republic were special and the people wanted them to stay the way they remembered them when they were children. *Submitted by Nancy Cunningham.*

**DAVIS** - Warren Davis, a young farm boy from a large farm family who lived in the Niangua and Conway area of Missouri, was drafted into the Army in 1944. He served in combat on Luzon in the Philippines. Three weeks after the atomic bomb was dropped on Hiroshima, he was sent to Japan. He saw Hiroshima twice. He is a member of the American Legion and the VFW.

*Warren and Mabel Davis*

Honorably discharged in 1946, he returned home and for awhile operated the general store in Rader Town with his brother, Walter. His first date with a young farm girl, Mabel Schad, from the Purdy area, was at the Springfield Fair.

They were married in 1950 and they and their small daughter, Janie, moved to Republic in 1952. They bought the Schad interests her father and brother had in the Cox-Schad Dairy located on Hampton Street. In 1954 the dairy became known as the Cox-Davis Dairy. Warren entered into what became a very successful business partnership and personal relationship with Lester E. Cox. The Davis family operated the dairy and raised various crops on the acreage. They also tended a vineyard and an orchard located there.

*Barns at Cox-Davis Farm*

At that time Republic had a population of about one thousand. It had only a grade school and a high school. Within five years there was a need for a new school. In 1959 Mr. Cox purchased additional land south of town for the dairy and then deeded the land occupied by the dairy to the city of Republic for a new school and other facilities. The Davis family moved to the new location with their three children.

The couple worked hard and the dairy became known for its innovations and its herd of registered Holsteins. As Republic grew, so did the dairy — becoming nationally known as a showplace of efficiency in the dairy industry.

Featured in magazines like *The Farm Journal* and *Hoard's Dairyman,* and pictured in the 1963 *World Book Encyclopedia Yearbook,* it brought visitors from far and wide to Republic.

In 1967 the Davis family won a cow judging contest sponsored by the *Hoard's Dairyman* magazine. They took first place in the family division contest which had 105,682 entries. In 1972 the family was named "Farm Family of the Year" at the Missouri State Fair. The four Davis children were active in 4-H and participated in its cattle showing activities - showing registered Holsteins from the farm. In 1988 the dairy herd was sold and the Davis family moved to 634 S Main Ave.

The family was active in community activities. Warren served on both the board of directors of the Republic MFA and the Security State Bank. He was named an Honorary Member of the FFA. Mabel received special honor for her many years of volunteer work at the Cox Hospitals in Springfield. She was instrumental in initiating the Republic "People Helping People" organization and the "Relay for Life" cancer fundraising event.

The four Davis children: Janie, Julie, Carl and Chris, attended Republic schools and all graduated from Republic High School. Janie, the oldest, was active in drama activities starring in several plays at the high school. Both she and Julie loved sports events and were active in the Pep Club. Julie was class president of her freshman class. She excelled academically, making the Honor Roll. The two boys played in the high school band. Chris, the youngest, was also active in FFA - receiving the honor of being named a Star Chapter Farmer in that organization.

There are four Davis grandchildren: Michael Kuehn, Justin Trout, Dana Salkill and Candice Davis - three of whom also attended Republic schools. There are also two great-grandchildren, Addison Mabel Salkill and Zoie Salkill.

In 1984 Warren and Mabel were charter members in the founding of Hope Lutheran Church, located on Highway 174, and remained very active in all its activities. They celebrated their 50th anniversary on Oct. 10, 2000. Mabel passed away in April of 2001.

Warren, age 82, continues caring for the Cox property and oversees the production of hay from the farm. He married Virginia Marshall of Springfield in December 2002 and the couple make their home at 634 S Main. They are regular bowlers, occasional golfers and do some traveling. *Submitted by Warren Davis.*

**DAVIS/HARRINGTON** - Vernon Monroe Davis (1904-1989) son of Thomas David (1871-1951) and Mary Matilda Johnson Davis (1895-1926) came to this area from Ozark. He met his future wife while working in a strawberry patch. He married Eva Ann Harrington (1908-1979) May 3, 1925. Eva Ann was the daughter of William Sigel "Sig" and Martha Louella Link Harrington.

During their marriage they ran Brookline Grocery Store and Sublett's Truck Stop and Restaurant at the corner of Main and Hwy. 174. In 1947 Wilson Creek Baptist Church was ready to build a new church. Vernon purchased the old building and had it moved to the east corner of Hwy. 60 and FR 101. It was added on to and remodeled and became Little York Gas Station and Grocery. Vernon also worked for the Frisco Railroad and sold real estate. Eva spent her time managing the businesses and rearing their seven children.

Donald Lee (1926-1975) married Mary Lou Tipton (May 31, 1944), daughter of George and Blanche Tipton. Their children are Stephen Lee (1945) and Sherry Lynn (1948).

Harold Wayne (1928-1999) married Alma Lorene Jones, daughter of Willis and Artie Hicks Jones, on May 9, 1948. Their children are Sandra Jean (1949), Danny Wayne (1953-1972), Bruce Allen (1957) and Kimberly Ann (1962-1975).

*Seated: Vernon and Eva. Standing: Bob, Don, Maxine, Dick, Mary Lou, Wayne and Lester.*

Mary Louella (1932-1994) married Jack William Wood, son of Henry and Alma Wood, on Feb. 4, 1951. They had no children.

Vernon Lester (1934-1984) married Wilma Lee Chastain, daughter of Claude and Helen Parker Chastain, on Sept. 2, 1951. Their children are Jerry Leslie (1952) and Stanley Dale (1956).

Viola Maxine (1939) married Sheral Max Cook, son of Irvin and Icia Marie Cook, on May 3, 1956. Their children are Michael Kent (1959-1975), Kevin Brent (1962) and Darren Keith (1969). Maxine is presently married to Harold Ginn.

James Robert (1941) married Marti Jenan Worley on May 27, 1961. Bob and Marti had a daughter, Lisa Ann (1965). He married Betty

Jo Secrest (1936-1996), daughter of Louis Otto and Edna Lindsey Secrest, on Oct. 5, 1968. They had a son, Jeffrey Robert (1970). Betty had three children when they married: Kenny, Rick and Pam Weatherford.

Charles Richard "Dick" (1943) married Lynda Sue Comisky, daughter of Frank and Irene Wade Comisky, on April 7, 1966. Dick and Lynda have a daughter Jayme Beth (1968) and a son Jared Blane (1974). *Submitted by Dick Davis.*

**DAVIS/O'DELL** – Barney Wilson Davis (Aug. 21, 1867-May 30, 1956) married Harriet (Hawkins) O'Dell (July 20, 1872-Sept. 2, 1963) on June 7, 1891. Barney was the youngest child of Sarah "Sally" Elizabeth Hart (Sept. 1, 1823-July 2, 1918) and George Davis (Nov. 15, 1818-April 25, 1900) who were married on March 3, 1840. Sarah and George met at a dance in Bedford County, TN and moved to Greene County (now Christian County) by wagon train. Barney's parents' home was about two miles from the Battle of Wilson's Creek, and they heard the first shots as the war began. Many soldiers came to their home asking for or demanding food. One time Sarah served them large platters of ham and the hominy she made outside in a large kettle over an open fire. A soldier left his leather powder bag hanging on the loom. The bag stayed in the family for years and was eventually donated to the Wilson's Creek Battlefield by Barney.

*Barney Davis Family – 1907, l-r: Walter Davis, Vesta Davis Gray, Barney holding Tressie Davis, Betty Davis Newcomb, Harriett Davis holding Bernice Davis Bassore, Lydia Davis Edwards, Hollie Davis Gray and Grace Davis Adams.*

For many years Barney and Harriet lived near Terrell Creek south of the Greene/Christian County line where Gardenia Lane now ends. They farmed as their family increased to eight living children. In later years Barney and Harriet moved into Republic and lived on E Elm Street near Hwy. 60. The house was later remodeled and used as commercial property (The French Hen) after the death of their daughter, Tressie, who had continued to live in the house after the death of her parents.

Tressie was a teacher for many years both out of state and in local schools, including Republic and Billings, where she taught home economics and science until her retirement.

Barney and Harriet's children are as follows: Hollie Jane (March 18, 1893-Jan. 20, 1990) married Joe Emmett Gray (July 15, 1887-Jan. 11, 1971) on Nov. 26, 1913. They had one son, Dallas Barney, who married Elizabeth Grace Nelson, and one granddaughter Jane Ruth Gray Smith (see Gray/Davis).

Walter McKinley (Sept. 29, 1894-Sept. 2, 1968) married Louisa Little on Dec. 17, 1897. Their daughter, Helen (Feb. 16, 1920), married Arthur Tess who was born Dec. 14, 1915. Helen's children: Michael (Jan. 28, 1949) and Kathy (July 20, 1951).

Bettie Sarah (Dec. 6, 1895) married Victor A. Newcomb (July 2, 1896). They had one son, Carl Eugene (Dec. 12, 1920), who married Donna Tierholm (June 26, 1919). Carl's children: John Davis (Oct. 18, 1946), Katherine Ann (June 9, 1948), Scott Timothy (May 16, 1951), Carol Lynn (May 2, 1953).

Laura "Vesta" (Aug. 19, 1897-Nov. 27, 1954) married William Jefferson Gray (June 12, 1893) on Dec. 15, 1918. Vesta's children: Juanita Lucille Evatt, J.B. Gray, Annabelle Gleghorn. Grandchildren: Carolyn Jo Gray Heavin, DeWayne B. Gray, Terry Lynn Gleghorn Yake and Lisa Kay Gleghorn Clemons (see Gray/Russell).

Lydia (Feb. 22, 1899) married Hubert Edwards (Oct. 26, 1894-Dec. 13, 1958). They had one daughter, Elizabeth Jean (Oct. 16, 1921), who married George C. "Sam" Little (June 21, 1916).

Grace (Jan. 2, 1902) married Oran Adams (Oct. 26, 1897-Aug. 29, 1951). Grace's children: Joetta (Nov. 6, 1922) married first, John Paul Engler and second, Ray Phillip Dorrah; Sallie Lou (March 24, 1934) married Tom Davidson. Grandchildren: Joan Paula Engler, Phillip Ray Dorrah, James Alan Dorrah.

Tressie Alta (July 1, 1905-Dec. 21, 1998) was single.

Bernice (March 12, 1907) married Russell Bassore (March 6, 1905). Bernice's children and grandchildren:

Virginia Lee (Oct. 23, 1926) married Hal James Richardson; children: Cheryl Kay (July 22, 1947), Lee Ann (Nov. 26, 1954), Jeffry Davis (Jan. 14, 1959).

Mary Ruth (Nov. 21, 1927) married Donald Max Powell; daughter, Kathy Nell (May 5, 1959).

Bill Davis (June 5, 1930) married Kay Nations. Children: Brad Davis (Nov. 25, 1956), Brenda Kay (April 21, 1958), Kerry Grey (June 30, 1960).

Barbara Ellen (April 26, 1932) married Donald Mathias Pruente. Children: Jill Ann (June 19, 1956), Beth Catherine (Aug. 12, 1957), Jan Ellen (Nov. 23, 1958), Matt Donald (Oct. 27, 1959), Dona Maria (Nov. 14, 1960).

Patricia Joan (Dec. 2, 1933) married Richard Lee Neely. Children: Richard Brent (May 30, 1954), Bruce Keven (Oct. 27, 1957), Brian Scott (July 20, 1959) and Nancy.

Donald James (Aug. 18, 1935) married Bettie Rapp. Children: David Rapp (Dec. 29, 1954), Julie (Aug. 24, 1962), Christopher "Todd" (May 13, 1964).

Carolyn Sue (Feb. 21, 1937) married John Wesley Wise. Children: Kimberly Sue (Aug. 3, 1958) and Sally Ann (June 26, 1960).

Two of Bernice's grandchildren, Todd Bassore and Julie Bassore Heinzler, and their families reside in Republic. Some information from *The Lambert/Lambeth Family of North Carolina.* Submitted by Carolyn Heavin.

**DAVIS/O'NEAL** - Howard Leroy Davis was born Sept. 14, 1912 to William L. and Della Marie (Bentley) Davis in Manchester, IA. Howard had one brother, Bernard Davis. Their mother passed away unexpectedly with a heart attack after having pneumonia in 1932.

Howard, his father (who had remarried) and brother came to Republic in December 1943 to go into the hatchery business. The Republic Hatchery, building and business, located on North Main Street, was purchased from Mr. and Mrs. Olan Bull and became Davis Hatchery and Feed. Howard and his father had previous experience in a poultry plant in Iowa.

Howard attended the State University of Iowa and graduated with a BS degree in mechanical engineering June 1, 1936. He was employed at Remington Arms Co., Lake Ordinance Plant, in Independence, MO from 1941 to January 1, 1944. On Jan 28, 1944, he enlisted in the U.S. Navy as a commissioned officer, LT(JG). He served in the Asiatic-Pacific and was discharged to inactive duty under honorable conditions May 22, 1946 at which time he returned to the hatchery.

*Howard and Margaret Davis.*

The hatchery bought eggs from the farmers in the 40s. Hatchery employees worked closely with the farmers to ensure healthy flocks and enjoyed the friendly visits with the farmers. The Davis family bought and sold chickens to hatcheries in southwest Missouri and northwest Arkansas, having their own delivery trucks. Children with their parents enjoyed visiting the hatchery to see the baby chicks. Both Howard and his father "Bill" were nicknamed "Chick." Howard's brother was with the business a few years, then left for other employment.

*Howard, W.L. Davis (father) and Bernard Davis (brother) bought this building and hatchery business from Olan Bull – December 1943.*

During the years of WWII, chicken feed was shipped in 100 lb. cotton bags instead of the paper or burlap. These cotton bags were flowered print and plain white, and ladies made dresses and many household items out of the bags. At one time the hatchery had a fashion show for the ladies to model the feed sack dresses they had made.

In 1947 Howard married Margaret (Freeman) O'Neal, widow of Maxie J. O'Neal and mother of Carol Ann O'Neal Shatz. Maxie died Feb. 2, 1945 of wounds received in action in France during WWII. Maxie's body was returned in 1948 and buried at Wade Chapel Cemetery. Howard and Margaret lived west of Republic, having two children, Robert Leroy and Jean Elaine. Margaret was born in Billings, MO, graduating from school there.

After his dad passed away in May 1953, Howard continued the hatchery business. He built a broiler house on his farm to raise broilers. Later he raised hens for an egg supply for the hatchery and hatching turkeys for an out-of-town hatchery. After that he quit hatching eggs and sold feed, seeds etc. He opened a coin operated laundry a couple of doors from the hatchery. In 1974 Howard sold the buildings and retired after 31 years of business on Main Street.

Howard passed away in the Veterans Home, Mt Vernon, MO, in October 1997 and was buried at Wade Chapel Cemetery. Margaret continues to live on their home place. *Submitted by Margaret Davis.*

**DAY/BOHANNON** - December 8, 1960 was a cold rainy day, but the Day family considered it beautiful. They were moving to Republic, MO and would become homeowners. Their home was located on South Main, next to Bacon Tire Co. The family included John V. (Oct. 10, 1936), Shirley J. (Bohannon) (Sept. 6, 1935); Deborah Ann (May 13, 1954); John Michael (Dec. 4, 1955). A baby girl, Johnna Lynn, was added to their home on Oct. 5, 1961.

*Shirley (Bohannon) and John V. Day*

After moving, they discovered they had no mail delivery. The post office, now the Historical Museum, provided mailboxes. They also had a Logan's Market, which delivered groceries, an MFA, Locker Plant, Bennett Barber Shop and the 1st Baptist Church. Everyone was very friendly.

In August 1971, Republic celebrated their 100th anniversary with a centennial. A tornado hit Republic in December of the same year. Everyone helped each other through these times.

In 1972 Deborah graduated from Republic High School. She married Ronnie Melton in May 1973. They had one daughter, Tiffany Lynn, born Aug. 12, 1977. In 1983 they divorced and she married Donald Clutter later that year. Donald has two daughters, Paula (March 17, 1974) and Ramona (May 21, 1976). Ramona has one son, Seth Kozemezak, born Sept. 27, 1996. Tiffany married Jason Booth (March 4, 1975) on Jan. 18, 1997. They have two daughters, Madilynn Grace (Feb. 13, 2001) and Kensington Elizabeth (Jan. 31, 2006).

John Michael graduated in 1974 from Republic High School and married Mary Alice Brown (May 18, 1954) from Elk Creek, MO on Aug. 7, 1976. They have one son, John Ryan (Jan. 29, 1982) who married Jennifer Davidson (March 11, 1979) on June 5, 2004.

Johnna Lynn graduated from Republic in 1979. On Jan. 26, 1980 she married Darcy Murr. They had two sons, Jacob Christopher (Dec. 25, 1982) and Adam Scott (Dec. 1, 1986). They divorced in 2003 and she remarried on June 12, 2004 to Mitchell Couch. He has a son, James (Sept. 9, 1982) and a daughter, Stephanie (May 18, 1985).

John and Shirley (Bohannon) Day observed their 50th anniversary on Aug. 19, 2003. John retired from Roadway on Sept. 30, 2001, and Shirley retired June 30, 1998 from Calvary Baptist Church Early Education Program. It was located at the corner of Hines and Hwy. 60 but that property was bought by Mid-Missouri Bank after Calvary Baptist purchased and relocated to the old Albertson's building on West Highway 60.

They have seen a tremendous amount of growth and change and eagerly wait for more in the future. *Submitted by Shirley Day.*

**DAY/BROWN** - John Michael "Mike" Day (Dec. 4, 1955) moved with his parents, John V. and Shirley J. Day, to Republic in December 1960, along with his older sister, Deborah Ann. They lived in the first house south of Bacon Tire Co., which was later relocated to Broad Street. The family had already moved to a larger two-story house on Elm Street to accommodate the addition of a little sister Johnna Lynn in 1961, and eventually an in-home day-care. A later move to Buxton Lane in Wormeyville allowed for more children in the day-care and the creation of Shirley's Wee Folks.

As a youngster growing up, Mike remembers very few activities, except attending the movies in downtown with his sister and playing with the neighbor kids. Occasionally, he would listen to the "older men" tell stories at the back of the MFA. The Fall Festival on Main Street was always a highlight.

Working hard to earn money kept him busy mowing yards, which he started after 4th grade. He then hauled hay for the Grays and worked at Greene County Propane before following in the steps of his grandfather, uncles, and dad and started driving a truck in 1975 for Jim Girth at Standard Rendering Co. He still has the passion for driving and is now an independent owner/operator.

Graduating in 1974, he always liked country music and wore jeans and boots, which a lot of people made fun of, but it never bothered him because he was always just himself, being friends with everyone. He always had a fast car that he had to work on often because of some drag racing done out on Hwy. 174.

God has always been a focus of the family, and he is a charter member of Calvary Baptist Church, where he serves as deacon and attends regularly.

Mike married Mary Alice Brown (May 18, 1954) from Elk Creek, MO on Aug. 7, 1976. She worked for Lee Roberts Chevrolet for three years before he sold the dealership to Ed Pinegar in 1979. She has been the office manager of Pinegar Chevrolet, Inc. since that time. They have one son, John Ryan Day (Jan. 29, 1982) who married Jennifer C. Davidson (March 11, 1979) on June 5, 2004 and they reside in Springfield, MO.

The Day family has enjoyed watching the growth of Republic and are looking forward to the future here. *Submitted by Mary Day.*

**DAY/PARKER** - Kenneth Day, the youngest child of Marion and Maude Day, and Marie Parker, the third child of Henry Parker and Lolla Yingst, were married in 1953. They both attended Republic schools and were childhood sweethearts. They lived in Golden City and in Kansas City, but knew that city life was not where they wanted to raise their children. So in 1962 they moved back to Republic. Ken was the manager of Tapjac Home Center, which was the town's lumberyard for 27 years, and Marie worked as the interior decorator for the Home Center for 15 years. They had three daughters. The eldest daughter Debbie graduated from Republic schools and married Dennis Sanders also a Republic graduate in 1973. They had three children: Stephanie (Sanders) Bishop, Joshua Sanders and Lucas Sanders.

Their second daughter Dana, also a graduate of Republic, married Mark Hubbard, a 1982 Republic graduate. They have three children: Kendra (Hubbard) Anderson, Cody Hubbard, and Katelin Hubbard.

Their third daughter Drenda, a graduate of Republic, married Kevin Rusenstrom from Michigan in 1991. They have three children, all girls just like her parents had: Grace Rusenstrom, Rose Rusenstrom and Ireland Rusenstrom.

In 1991 Marie launched her T.V. talk show called *"Keeping in Touch."* She currently produces it with her son-in-law Kevin. The show's name was later changed to *"Keeping in Truth"* and is seen on local stations, cable, and on satellite in several other states.

Ken's dad, Marion Day, met and married Maude Looney in Gainesville, MO. They moved to Republic in 1928. They had five children: the oldest was Emogene, Benton (a son who died in childhood), Bearl, Leo and Kenneth. Marion worked as a custom farmer. This meant that he would farm out land for people. He would till the ground, plant the seed, tend it, come back and harvest whatever crop they had. He had all his own equipment. He had binders to cut grain, thrashers which took the grain from the straw and is similar to combines today, and other machinery as well. Maude was a housewife. Her grandmother was a full-blooded Cherokee Indian. All their children attended Republic schools.

Marie's parents, Henry Parker and Lolla Yingst, were married in Arkansas and moved to Springfield in 1941 and to Republic in 1950. Henry bought and sold cattle while Lolla milked cows and tended a garden that seemed to stretch on for miles. She would also can most of her vegetables and meats. She was a seamstress that would put store bought items to shame. Henry and Lolla had four daughters. The first daughter, Vera, married Max Schaefer in 1935 and had one daughter, Barbara. The second daughter, Berniece, married Frank Comstock and had a son, Kenny. They divorced and she married Chloe Pierce. They had a daughter Norma (Pierce) Chilcutt. Their third daughter, Marie, married Ken Day in 1953. They had three children: Debbie (Day) Sanders, Dana (Day) Hubbard and Drenda (Day) Rusenstrom. Their fourth daughter Henrietta married Harold Smith. They had two sons: Wayne Smith and Michael Smith. *Submitted by Drenda Rusenstrom.*

**DEAN** - Eli Pendleton Dean, son of Thomas Jr. and Mary (Patterson) Dean, along with his brother Hardy Dean, walked from Union County, GA to Greene County, MO to find new homes for their families in 1883.

Eli Dean had married Mary Catherine Hayes, daughter of Jeremiah and Nancy (Lowe) Hayes. Mary Catherine and the three children: Ted, Adeline and Lura, along with their possessions came by train from Georgia to join Eli in Missouri. Nine children were born after they made Missouri their home - Jess, Tom, Rufus, Elisha, Melton Ratio, Naomi, Maggie, Vanner and Mary Zephi.

*Eli Pendleton Dean and family.*

After reaching adulthood only five children stayed in Missouri: Adeline who married Marion Blades, Lura who married Gilbert Poe, Tom who married Delphia Carter, Naomi who married Earl Hagewood and Maggie who married Monroe Mooneyham.

Ted married Ella Lafollette and moved to Utah. Rufus married Mae Martin and moved to Nebraska. Jess married Nancy Tinsley and Elisha married Nerva Garoutte. They moved to Nebraska but later moved to Scott County, KS. Ratio married Pearly Garoutte and had already moved to Kansas. Mary Zephi married Gus Case and moved to Canada. Vanner married Walter Logan and moved to Kansas then on to Delta, CO.

After Mary Catherine's death in 1923. Eli P. Dean came to Scott County, KS and bought a farm in northeast Scott County. He built homes for Ratio and Elisha. He remained in Kansas until his death in March 1935. His body was returned to Missouri to be buried by his wife in Rose Hill Cemetery close to Billings, MO. *Submitted by Martha Berry.*

**DEBOARD/HARRALSON** - Elisha "Lish" DeBoard was born in Mt. Vernon, KY on Jan. 25, 1860 and died Oct. 16, 1934. He was born to Abner Copeland and Susan (Sewell) DeBoard. He was one of 12 children, having four brothers and seven sisters. Elisha left Kentucky when he was 21 years old coming to Greene County, MO to become a farmer. He purchased a farm of 320 acres northeast of Republic from Nancy Small, widow of Henry Small, on Sept. 3, 1896, at the age of 25. This land continues to be owned in the year 2006 by his descendants. Being one of the major stockholders of the Republic State Bank, he became the bank president in 1912. Elisha was well known for being one of the leading citizens of Republic.

He married Mary Elizabeth Harralson (Feb. 13, 1865-May 8, 1960) in July 1884. She was one of five children born to James Harralson who was one of the earliest pioneers of Greene County, MO, coming to this area in 1825. James was a well-known farmer and liked by all. James and his wife had three sons and two daughters.

*Home of Elisha DeBoard.*

Elisha and Mary had eight children: Ralph (Dec. 16, 1885-Dec. 9, 1967) farmed in Republic; Roxie (September 1887) married Milton Paulson, a farmer; Susie (Aug. 1, 1890-Jan. 9, 1986) married Arthur H. House; Ruby (April 1892) married Lawrence Ellis Britain (Nov. 2, 1891-July 26, 1941), also a farmer; daughter Glynn (October 1894) married a Robertson and moved to Aurora, working for the Shendon-Robinson Hardware; Lucy (November 1899) married an Esterling; William not married; and Fay married a Bell.

Politically Elisha was a Republican, but never sought to be a leader in public affairs. He and his family attended the Christian Church.

Lish and Mary celebrated their 50th wedding anniversary in June 1934 in order to have a double celebration with Mary's brother and wife, Sterling and Amanda Harralson from California. As reported they were the center of interest in the golden wedding celebration at the farm home four miles north of Republic. Valuable presents were received including sets of dishes, silverware, ear rings and gold iced teaspoons. Dinner was served on the shady lawn with an angel food wedding cake baked by Lea Baker of Bois D'Arc. Both brides were attired in white silk dresses and accessories to match.

Approximately three months later, Oct. 16, 1934, Elisha DeBoard made a trip to Republic on business. After visiting with Leonard Fugitt and H.G. Snyder, with the topic of conversation being hogs, he traveled south on Main Street and attempted to cross the railroad track following a truck. *The Springfield News* reported, he apparently became confused when he looked up and saw the approaching train and attempted to stop with the car stalling midway on the tracks, with impact following immediately. Dr. E.L. Beal and Dr. R.C. Mitchell were on the scene and stated he was killed instantly. *Submitted by Peggy Ann O'Neill.*

**DEMANCHE/BROWN** - Nancy Ann Brown, daughter of Smith and Belle Brown, was born with her twin brother Smithy on Nov. 20, 1928, at the Brown homeplace located on PP Highway West of Republic. Nancy and Smithy attended St. Elmo School and Republic High School.

*Dick Demanche and Nancy (Brown) Demanche.*

Nancy lived in a boarding house at 212 W. Elm and worked at the Trailways Restaurant and Bus Stop located on Main Street downtown Republic. There, she met Richard "Dick" Eugene Demanche, who was working construction on Hwy. 60. At that time Hwy. 60 was what is now called West Elm Street and continued east through town.

Dick was born in Billings on Aug. 11, 1921 but spent his youth in Marionville, MO. He served in WWII from 1942-45 as a technical sergeant in the 14th Emergency Rescue Boat Squadron. He was a rifle marksman. While serving in the Air Offensive, he was in Japan, China, Southern Philippines, Luzon, Western Pacific, Ryukyus and Borneo.

He received a Bronze Star, several ribbons of honor, along with many other commendations with badges and pins, and was also given the original flag that flew on his ship.

Nancy and Dick met at the Trailways Cafe and married on Sept. 9, 1947. They lived in the boarding house which accommodated seven families. There were only seven rooms and one bathroom. The boarding house at 212 W. Elm was open in 1896. They were blessed with two children, a daughter Phyllis Ann (Demanche) Clark born June 29, 1948 and a son Thomas Eugene Demanche, born Oct. 4, 1951. Moving to the northeast corner of South Main and Highway 60, where they raised chickens and cattle at this location.

Dick and Nancy always had a lot of company and many friends, everyone wanting to enjoy a taste of her cooking. Nancy having 10 brothers and sisters made family get-togethers a large gathering. Nancy gave birth to twin boys on July 11, 1957, they only lived one hour and were buried at the Garoutte Cemetery located on West TT Hwy. In the 1960s the boarding house was for sale. Nancy and Dick purchased it and made it a beautiful family home.

Nancy was well known for her pies, her hot bread and being a great seamstress. Dick was known for his humor. They both worked very hard for many years. Their three grandchildren were loved very much by both of them. A fourth grandchild was added after Nancy's death.

Nancy was employed at Dayco in Springfield at the time of her death on April 7, 1980. Richard worked as superintendent over Greene County Road and Bridge, retiring when Nancy became ill in 1979. Dick passed away April 8, 1994. Both are buried in Garoutte Cemetery.

The Demanche's were a very close family and always filled with love, they left behind a treasure of memories for their children and grandchildren. Their grandchildren in the area today are Bill Clark, Richard "Dick" Clark, Shane Gold and Richard S. Demanche. *Submitted by Bill and Dick Clark.*

**DEMANCHE/GOLD** - Thomas E. Demanche is the son of Richard E. Demanche and Nancy A. (Brown) Demanche of Republic, MO. He was born in Springfield, MO on Oct. 4, 1951 and raised in Republic, graduating from Republic High School in 1969.

*Thomas and Deborah Demanche.*

Thomas' life vocation has been a truck driver and he currently works for Yellow Transportation in Springfield, MO. He married Deborah L. (Nakano) Gold on Sept. 15, 1979. They have two sons, Shane E. Gold, born April 29, 1976, and Richard S. Demanche, born June 20, 1981.

Deborah was born in Springfield, MO Jan. 6, 1954 and is the daughter of Stanley S. Nakano and J. June (Gullett) Nakano. Deborah has worked in Springfield and Republic as a banker.

Their son Shane married Jacqueline D. Fletcher Aug. 13, 2005. Jacqueline is the daughter of Allen M. and Marcella C. Fletcher of Billings, MO. Shane and Jacqueline have two daughters, Sydni, born July 12, 1999, and Morgan, born Oct. 24, 2000. They live in Springfield, MO.

Their son Richard is single and lives in Republic, MO. *Submitted by Thomas and Deborah Demanche.*

**DENNIS/OWEN** - Judith Ann is the third child of Charles Oscar Owen and Martha Allene Stevenson. She graduated from Republic High School and was married to Jack Dennis of Springfield in 1962. Jack operated Dennis Oil Company the business his father Hugh Dennis founded in 1940. They had two children, Jeffery Mitchel and Robin Denise Dennis, both graduates from Willard High School and SMSU in Springfield, MO.

Robin married Dean Patrick Thompson in 1990, and they currently live in Republic where Dean holds the position of Republic's first city administrator. They have four children: Megan LeeAnn, Molly Ashton, Malise Carrie and Ryan Patrick. Megan and Molly currently attend Republic schools.

Jeff was married to Darla Suzanne Highfill in 1997, they have two daughters, Sidney Claire and Kaitlyn Suzanne, and currently live in Springfield.

After Jack's retirement Jeff took over operation of the family business. Judy and Jack now live north of Willard, MO. *Submitted by Judy Dennis.*

**DENNIS/SMITH** - George Dennis (born 1890, died 1973) and his wife Ollie Mae Smith (born 1892, died 1974) moved to Republic from Vanzant, MO in 1915 with a baby girl, Agnes (born 1915, died 1999). George was born in Trenton, MO to David and Anna. David was from Kentucky. They had six boys and six girls. George was the oldest boy (3rd child) and only got to go to the 4th grade, then had to help support the large family.

After moving to Republic, George worked

at the flour mill on S. Main between E. Elm and Mill Street. When it shut down the depression was bad. The family, which now consisted of two more girls, Anna Mae (born 1922, died 2005) and Gladys (born 1925), moved to California for almost two years, 1928-30. There George worked on the Horse Shoe Pier. Just a few years ago it was demolished. Then he worked on a dairy farm in Whittier.

After returning to Republic, WPA was started and he dug ditches by hand-shovel for the sewer line. Then he helped build the high school which was just recently torn down. Some say it took longer to tear down than it took to build it, as it was built so strong. When WPA was stopped he went to work for Glenn Owen in his strawberry patch, grape vineyard and apple orchard, pruning, spraying, picking and packing.

When Owen sold his fruit farm, WWII was going strong and George again went to California to work in the shipyards. The family stayed in Republic. Agnes married Alfred Criswell in 1937. Anna Mae married Claude Bennett in 1955 and Gladys married Robert Mooneyham in 1951.

The Mooneyhams had eight children. Dennis, Robert A., Bill, Tim, Donna Roberts, Peggy Hicks, Janice Brown and Susie Ladd. All but Donna and Susie live in Greene County. *Submitted by Robert Mooneyham.*

**DENNY** - The Dennys immigrated from Ireland in the middle 1700s. Clayborn Denny left the east and settled around Eureka Springs, AR. Clayborn and his wife Eva had 12 children. Three of these children came to Missouri in 1870 and settled in Pond Creek Township. They were Darthula, Elbert and Calvin Leroy.

Darthula married James Benson Wade in June 1871 and from this union came 14 children. None of whom stayed in the Republic area.

Elbert Denny married Maggie McDaniel and they had four daughters: Velma Howard, Ina Sifferman, Gladys Parnell and Eva (died in infancy) and one son Shearl. Elbert purchased George W. Britain's farm of approximately 180 acres, tore down the old house and in 1919 built the house that still stands on that property.

*Picture taken in 1911 in front of the Jesse McDaniel home, four miles northwest of Republic. Front row: Ransom T., Elizabeth, Jesse, Mary, Elizah A., Ellen (Blades) McDaniel, William, Mary Jane (Sis Burk), Jane McDaniel Burk, Jackson and Elmon Burk. 2nd Row: Minnie McDaniel Blades, Ava McDaniel Garoutte, Maggie McDaniel Hagewood, Emmett, Lester Miller, Billie Miller, Nancy Miller, Olive Blades McDaniel, Maggie McDaniel Denny, Elsie, Elbert Denny, Ruby and Ollie Burk. 3rd Row: Dollie Garoutte, Mae Hagewood, Ocie Hagewood, Shearl Denny, Ina Denny and Velma Denny*

Elbert's son, Shearl Denny, married Helen M. Britain on June 1, 1941; they lived there all their life and had one son, David. Shearl Denny taught school for 40 years and was a dairy farmer. An interesting fact is that Helen Britain was the great-granddaughter of George W. Britain. Hence Helen Britain Denny acquired her inheritance through marriage.

David Denny married Karen Walker and they had two daughters, Lisa and Diane. Lisa married Barry Fabro and had two sons, Ryan and Joshua; they live in Billings, MO. Diane married Wes Enyart and had a son Blake and daughter Aubrey. They live on 10 acres east of the Denny house, which was part of the Denny farm.

As of this date, David and his wife Linda have lived in the Denny house since 1997. They continue to update and preserve the Denny family farm.

Calvin Leroy Denny married Artie Hart and three children were born to them. They were Earl, Eula (Dorriss) and Leo. Leroy and Artie owned and operated the hotel that was once located where the Davis Laundry was. *Submitted by David Denny.*

**DEVORE/NELSON** - Edwina Ruth Nelson DeVore (Sept. 8, 1928-Dec. 19, 1975) was the third child of Edgar Elijah Nelson (June 30, 1900-Aug. 23, 1979) and Ethel Ruth Maples (March 4, 1898-Feb. 3, 1981). (See Nelson/Maples.) She married Walter Eugene DeVore (Sept. 3, 1927-June 13, 1989) and they published newspapers in several area towns. After publishing the newspaper in Marionville in the early 1950s, Ruth and her husband began publishing the *Republic Record* in the mid-1950s.

*The DeVore children in 1995. Karen Sue "Susie" Alexander, Walter Eugene "Sonny" DeVore Jr. and Nancy Craig.*

During the time they were publishing the newspaper in Republic, they bought a new home on Eagan Street in what at the time was the new Eagan subdivision. The DeVores then published the *Nixa Enterprise* and moved south of Republic on the southeast corner of Honeysuckle and Oleander Roads. Ruth finished her bachelor's degree at what was previously Southwest Missouri State College and entered the teaching profession. She was a teacher for many years in the Clever schools, where she taught first grade.

Ruth's children are Walter Eugene "Sonny" DeVore Jr. (Oct. 14, 1951), Karen Sue "Susie" (June 28, 1956) and Nancy Ruth (May 13, 1958). An infant daughter, Elizabeth Ann (September 1954), is deceased.

Sonny married Brenda Kay Vanderhoof (Oct. 10, 1954) on Aug. 28, 1971. Their children are Cherie Christine (April 24, 1972), Angela "Angie" Kay (Sept. 20, 1974) and Derek Michael (Feb. 19, 1990). Cherie married Patrick John Wankum. Their children are Zachary Allan (June 18, 1992), Christopher John (Feb. 9, 1996) and Allison Rose (July 7, 1998). Angie married Clinton "Rex" Campbell. Their son, Carson David, was born Sept. 24, 2003. Rex's children are Morgan Rose and Samuel. Sonny and his family reside in Jefferson City where he is self-employed as a service business owner.

Susie married Patrick Lorne Kemppainen (Sept. 17, 1950-November 1999) on Aug. 27, 1978. Their children are Carl Ryan (Dec. 21, 1984) and Lauren Nicole (Sept. 22, 1986). Susie married Willis "Gregory" Alexander (Sept. 29, 1951) on June 1, 2000. Susie lives in Reeds Spring where she is a middle school art teacher.

Nancy married Jeffrey Allen Craig (Oct. 15, 1958) on April 28, 2001. His son is Colton Hamlin Craig (March 4, 1989). Nancy has lived in Republic since 1979 and has been employed by Kraft nearly 30 years. *Submitted by Nancy Craig.*

**DEWITT** - Bruce Tinsley DeWitt came to Republic in 1926 from Billings, MO, where he served as cashier of the Bank of Billings. Bruce lived in Oklahoma where he married Nanny Kaye Eichenberger. They had three sons: Bruce Jr., William Drew and Edward Harper (died in infancy), and two daughters, Cecil Virginia (died at age 16) and Nanny Kaye. Kaye's mother died at the time Kaye was born.

Bruce Jr. had one son, Robert Allen, who was killed during World War II.

Drew had four daughters: Gwendolyn Ann, Barbara Jean, Linda Erlene and Virginia Sue, and one son William Drew Jr.

*Front Row: Don Porter. 2nd Row: Henry Kent, Carol Elizabeth (Coggin), Keith Garbee. Back Row: William Drew, Bruce Jr. and Bruce Sr. DeWitt.*

*Shown at his desk is Attorney Bruce T. DeWitt. He practiced law in Republic from 1925 until his death in 1965. He served as city attorney for 27 years.*

Nanny Kaye had one daughter, Trenna Kay.

Bruce married Thirza May Garbee in 1920. Their three sons (Kent, Keith and Porter) graduated from Republic High School and were outstanding athletes. Henry Kent (died in 1999) had no children. Keith Garbee has three daughters and three sons: Janet Sue, Patricia Lynn, Carol Elizabeth, Michael Leon, Steven Keith and Gary Bruce. He has 18 grandchildren and three great-grandchildren. Don Porter has two sons, Brian David and Robert Allen, one daughter Alecia Kay, two granddaughters and one grandson.

Daughter Carol Elizabeth married Herbert Lee Coggin and lives in Republic. They have three sons and one daughter: Randolph Joe, Stanley Kent, James Bradley and Martha Louise (Towe). Herbert and Carol have seven grandsons, one granddaughter, three great-grandsons and one great-granddaughter. *Submitted by Martha Louise Coggin Towe.*

**DORRELL/BLADES** - Charles Leon Dorrell was born Aug. 22, 1926 to Verbin Daniel Dorrell and Delta Edna Swinney-Dorrell in Halltown, MO. He attended grade school in Lawrenceburg and high school in nearby Ash Grove. Leon was the middle son with an older brother Verbin "Junior" and younger brother Kenneth. Leon was drafted into the U.S. Army, training in Texas and serving in Japan during WWII. After a three-year engagement he married Thelma Blades, daughter of Roy Blades and Lissa Mooneyham-Blades of Billings, MO. Their wed-

179

*Dorrell Family at Leon and Thelma's 50th wedding anniversary celebration (May 22, 1997). L-R: Lyndle Dorrell, Karen Dorrell, Leon Dorrell, Jeremy "J.J." Dorrell, Thelma Dorrell, Lynette Chastain and Vernon Chastain.*

ding on May 22, 1947 was on Thelma's parents' wedding anniversary.

Thelma, born Feb. 15, 1927, was one of six children: Clara (Blades) Parker, Cleo (Blades) Batson, Wayne Blades, Dorothy (Blades) Swinney and Jimmie Blades. They were raised on their farm six miles west of Republic. Thelma graduated from Republic High School in 1945, the first of her family to complete high school.

Leon was a manager at Milk Haulers' Service and 39 years later retired from the parent company, Mid-America Dairy, in 1988. Following graduation, Thelma worked at garment factories in Republic and Springfield. After the birth of her children, she became a full-time mother. When the children reached school-age, she returned to work and for 24 years was employed by the Republic school district where she retired as food service director in 1987. Leon and Thelma bought 80 acres joining the Blades family farm where they raised their two children: Charles Lyndle (born April 28, 1954) and Jane Lynette (born May 2, 1957). They both graduated from Republic High School.

Lyndle graduated from Burge School of Nursing with a registered nursing degree and completed his BS and master's degrees at Drury College. He was employed at Cox Health where he was a part of the nursing school faculty, nursing administration, and currently is administrative director, materials management. Lyndle married Karen Davis of Willard, MO on June 24, 1978. They have one son Jeremy James "J.J." Dorrell, born Sept. 14, 1993.

After 21 years employment with Wal-Mart, Karen retired as a regional manager. In addition to being a full-time mom, she volunteers in various community, church and school organizations, including serving as president of the Ozark PTA. Lyndle, Karen and J.J. reside in Ozark, MO, where Jeremy attends school and participates on the wrestling team, in the school orchestra, and is a leader in the Fellowship of Christian Athletes.

Lynette and Vernon Chastain were married Jan. 12, 1980, and reside in Republic. Lynette graduated Summa Cum Laude from Drury College and retired after 30 years with Bank of America where she was a senior vice president. Vernon attended Southwest Missouri State University and is a local builder/developer specializing in residential and commercial projects.

In 1995 Leon and Thelma sold their farm and moved into a new home in Republic built by their son-in-law, Vernon. They had been married 53 years when Leon was diagnosed with colon cancer and died one month later on Oct. 16, 2000. Thelma continues to reside in their home on South Parkhill Drive, a street she had the opportunity to name. *Submitted by Lyndle Dorrell.*

**DUNN/JONES** - Craig Elvin Dunn, the third child of Elvin W. Dunn and Sharon Gail (Utke) Dunn, was born in Springfield, MO, Feb. 11, 1971. Craig grew up on their farm two and a half miles north of Republic where the family raised both commercial beef cows and registered Simmental cattle. He showed Simmental cattle with his father and brother Kevin through the 80s and learned the value of hard work from their farm. As a young boy he was active in sports, and his father faithfully took him to Little League baseball and Boys Club basketball games year around while growing up.

Craig remembers as a child getting out of school and going to his mother's classroom in the old high school on Hampton Street in the late 70s where the high school boys, with their long hair and bell-bottom jeans, would play basketball with him in the hallways and classrooms. When Craig's mother moved to the new high school on Hines Street, Craig would run as fast as he could through the park and across the railroad tracks hoping to cool down in front of her box fan in her classroom for there was no air conditioning in the schools at that time. Craig also has fond memories of proudly watching his sister Sherri win multiple track meets including state meets. Craig hauled hay in the summer for area farmers for extra money. His high school business teacher was his mother, who also happened to be his favorite teacher, and he always enjoyed having his mother around him while growing up in the Republic school system.

*Craig and Tricia Dunn and sons, Connor and Caden.*

Upon graduating from high school in 1989, Craig enrolled at SMSU and graduated with honors in 1993 with a BS in agricultural economics. Immediately upon graduating he went to work for Farm Credit Services in Springfield and in 1996 he moved to Empire Bank. He received his master's of science degree in administration from SBU in 1999. In 2004 Craig accepted a position as senior vice president at Citizens National Bank in Springfield, and in 2006 received his graduate degree from the Graduate School of Banking. Craig also serves on the Ozark Empire Fair Board and the Wilson's Creek National Battlefield Foundation Board.

Tricia Jo Dunn is the third child of Willis Dean Jones and Joyce Marie (DeVasure) Jones, born in Springfield, MO, Dec. 8, 1970. Tricia spent her childhood in the small community of Lebanon, MO. She especially enjoyed the six years the family lived on a farm near Bennett Springs State Park where she had fun riding horses and motorcycles. She also has fond memories of Sunday dinners with her grandparents and other family at her mother's home place, a dairy farm in southeast Laclede County. She attended church at Tabernacle Baptist Church and also attended school there for seven years. During her school years Tricia was active in sports playing on the high school volleyball team and community softball leagues.

After graduating from the Lebanon High School in 1988, Tricia attended the University of Missouri one semester and then SMSU. Tricia lost her father Willis in 1991 after a long battle with cancer. She graduated from SMSU in 1994 with a BS in psychology and minors in biomedical sciences and healthcare management. After working in a children's home sponsored by Burrell Behavioral Center in Springfield, Tricia began her career in insurance working for Humana Health Plans, a health maintenance organization. In 1999 Tricia accepted a position with the Arthur J. Gallagher Co. in Springfield and is an employee benefit consultant.

Craig and Tricia met at SMSU in a chemistry class in 1991 and started dating in 1992. They were married March 8, 1998, and moved out to the family farm in Republic. Between the times they were engaged and married, they remodeled a home on the family farm that was built by Craig's great aunt and uncle, Thelma and Ray Mathews. On Feb. 25, 2002, they were blessed with the birth of their first son, Connor Craig Dunn. Two years later on March 4, 2004, they were blessed with their second son, Caden Craig Dunn.

Connor and Caden spend their days during the week with their Grandmother Sharon where she teaches them many things, including Spanish, and they help her in her "Nature Center" where they get to experience such things as flowers, butterflies and birds. At home they have a lot of fun riding 4-wheelers in the woods, playing ball, and playing with the many animals and pets that they have on the farm. One of their favorite events is to ride around with their Pa (Elvin) while he feeds and checks the cows. Connor and Caden also love it when their Grammy Jones from Lebanon comes for a visit, and it is a special treat for them if their cousin Shayna joins her. They are members of Seminole Baptist Temple, and Connor has no fear when it comes time to sing with the other kids in front of the whole church. In the summertime, Craig gets the boat out, and the family spends time at the lake, along with some other favorites of Connor and Caden, which include Silver Dollar City and White Water. *Submitted by Craig and Tricia Dunn.*

**DUNN/UTKE** – Elvin W. Dunn was the third child of William Lester Dunn and Norma Blanche (Hargis) Dunn, born in Rogersville, MO, July 9, 1935. Elvin grew up on a dairy farm and attended his first four years of school in the one-room country school of Mount Pleasant, then grades 5-12 in the Rogersville Schools. His senior year he was on four national FFA judging teams. Upon graduating from high school in 1953, Elvin farmed for three years before enrolling at SMS in 1956. He continued milking cows morning and night while driving to classes during the day. In 1957 he took time out from college for six months active duty in the Army with five and a half years of active reserve time. He graduated in 1960 with a BS in accounting, then took an accounting position with the Dayco Corporation.

*Front Row, l-r: Craig, Sharon and Elvin Dunn; back row, Kevin and Sherri Dunn.*

Sharon Gail Utke was the first child of Lloyd S. Utke and Winona Gail (Willis) Utke, born in Marionville, MO, Oct. 23, 1939. Sharon spent her childhood in the rural German community of Billings. Her first memories of Republic were when she would stay at the home of her grandparents, Charles Arthur and Gail (Mead) Willis, west of Republic when she was a little girl. Sharon attended SMS where she met Elvin her sophomore year. She graduated with BS in education in May 1961 and in the fall she started Spanish and English at Jarrett Jr. High.

Elvin and Sharon were married June 23, 1961 and lived in Springfield for the first two years of their marriage. In October 1962 they purchased 40 acres north of Republic where they have lived until now. In 1965 Elvin accepted an accounting position with Litton Industries. After having three children: Sherri, Kevin and Craig, Sharon taught business and later Spanish in the Republic Schools for many years. During that time she acquired her MS in business education.

After taking early retirement in 1991 from Litton, Elvin worked at the Republic License Bureau and is still doing accounting for various businesses. Over the years he increased his farming operation to 400 acres. In 2004 Elvin received the Greene County Grassland Farmer of the Year Award for his efforts in a rotational grazing system. He has worked with 4-H and is currently on the Greene County Foundation Board. He served in the 1980s on the Republic R-III School Board.

First Baptist Church of Republic has always played an important role in the lives of the Dunn family. Sharon taught 5th and 6th grades for many years and still works with preschool. She also now gets to take care of her two little grandsons, Connor and Caden, during the day at her home.

The Dunn family is appreciative of all of the family, friends, neighbors, classmates, teachers and students who have been a part of their lives and have helped give them so many happy memories. *Submitted by Elvin and Sharon Dunn.*

The following poem Sherri wrote expresses the fond memories Sharon has of hearing the trains both as a little girl and later while teaching at Republic High School, as well as Sherri's own sentiment for her hometown of Republic.

**The Passing Train**
*by Sherri (Dunn) Drain, March 2006*

Republic, Republic, my hometown
What I remember is the train's faithful sound.
Every day the train whistle blew
Perhaps at ten, or maybe two.
And at the railroad crossings you would
   have to wait
For the train to pass with all its freight.

As down the track the train cars flew
So as well the years did, too.
And as each train car would go by
Each year seemed to faster fly.
And many people you once would greet
Are no longer seen upon the street.

And other citizens of our town
Those whose voices the train would drown
Likewise are no longer found.
For the lifeblood of each busy day
Changes form along the way.
And while you'll always hear a baby's cry
While some are born, others die.
But they leave a memory along the way
Like the trains that passed each day.

**DUVALL/KELTNER -** Jessie Albert Duvall was born in Texas County in 1907. He moved to Republic at the age of 13. He married Ethel Keltner in April 1927. They had five children: daughters Lucille Gann, Jo Ann McConnell, and Peggy Hyde, and sons Bill, Bob and Jim Duvall. Ethel spent her time caring for the home and her family.

Jess invested a lot of hard work and time as a mechanic for Republic Motor Company where he also sold Model Ts. He also worked hard for Paul Williams Garage as a mechanic, and over time he managed the company and later bought it.

He purchased 20 acres of land east of town for only $700. There he built a home for his family.

He later worked for the Republic school system as a mechanic and was manager of the school bus barn until his retirement.

He began his love of bus driving at the age of 18. He drove one of the first school buses, which Jess referred to as a "cracker jack box" because the entire body of the bus was made out of wood. It had rows of single seats that ran down each side and down the middle ran double seats. The bus was about 18-19 feet long and belonged to the Williams Motor Company. This love of bus driving continued for over 40 years. Another job he had in the 1920s was delivering ice with a one horse wagon. People would post in the window a sign telling the block size of ice they wanted that day. He got a salary of $1.50 for the day, which was about the most a young man in the early 1920s could receive. He quit that job in 1929 because refrigeration came to town.

Jess was truly a "people person." He cared about everyone and would do anything to help someone. His bus students have fond memories of the friendship they developed over the years as they spent time riding the long bus route. Students enjoyed interviewing him for class assignments because he would always take the time to talk and share information. *Submitted by Bob Duvall.*

**EAGAN -** The Eagans came to America from County Tipparary, Ireland in the early 1800s where they were part of the McEagan clan. The Mc was dropped upon entering America.

They own a castle there that was built by later followers of William the Conqueror in 1210 to help control the Irish people. After the castle passed to the McEagan Clan it became a school for gifted young men where they were schooled in history and law. The clan chieftain lives in the castle part time today, and it is opened to the public for three months. Howard, Jo Ann, and Gary Eagan have all visited the castle.

*The Michael Eagan Family, Back l-r: Parolee, Mabel, Merle, Michael (father), Patrick, Small and Edgar; front: Loleta and Harold (half siblings).*

Many Eagan men helped to build the transcontinental railroad after coming to this country.

Michael Eagan's family settled in the Dixon, MO area in the mid-1800s. Michael married Launa Bacon and with their baby son, Patrick, came to live in Republic, MO in 1885 where he was section foreman for the Frisco Railroad for many years. They had six children, five of whom were born in Republic. They were Patrick, Small, Merle, Edgar (who became a prominent lawyer in Jefferson City), Mable and Parolee. All of them left Republic except Small who was a well-known grocer man. Launa died in 1918 during the Spanish flu epidemic which took the lives of over two million people. Michael then married Elsie Merritt in 1922. They had two children, Loleta and Harold.

Smallwood "Small" Van Buren Eagan married Edna Brown of Springfield, MO in 1920. They had one son, Howard Lee, nicknamed "Wormey" because he was so wiggly as a kid. Everyone called him Wormey, even the teachers. Small operated his grocery store in Republic until 1935 when he went to live in Texas.

After a year in college Wormey left school to manage his mother's grocery store. He married Jo Ann Sellers in 1941 and they had one son, Gary Lee in 1943. Wormey went to the army in 1944 where he served with the 1264th Combat Engineers in Europe. He returned from Germany in 1946 and seeing a need for new housing in Republic for returning GIs who wanted to start families, he bought the old Dr. Beal orchard southwest of town and began the building boom in Republic.

In 1966 he bought the Pleasant Hope Bank and was president and chairman of the board. He built a second bank in Fair Grove, MO in 1982, and in 1985 sold both banks and retired.

Howard and Jo Ann traveled extensively but never found a place they had rather live. Howard Lee Eagan was born in Republic Sept. 9, 1921 and has lived here all of his life. His son, Gary Lee, earned a master's degree in art at the University of Missouri. He now lives in Eureka Springs, AR, where he owns an art studio. *Submitted by Gary Eagan.*

**ELLIOTT –** Dr. Elliott and his wife Betty moved to Republic from St. Paul, MN in December 1977. Prior to their move to Republic, Dr. Elliott was employed by the University of Minnesota. When Dr Elliott accepted a position as Department Chairman for the Agriculture Department at Southwest Missouri State University (now Missouri State) he and his wife Betty were looking for a good environment to raise their two adopted daughters, Marilynn and Barbie. Anson and Betty were natives of Missouri; he from Houston, MO and Betty from Mexico, MO. Both had attended the University of Missouri where Anson received his Ph.D. After surveying many of the surrounding areas, they felt Republic offered the best advantages. They were impressed with the friendliness of the community, the schools and the close proximity to Springfield.

*Betty and Dr. W. Anson Elliott*

Dr. Elliott and his family soon became involved in the Republic community. Dr. Elliott was elected to the school board in 1984 and was re-elected for a second term in 1988. His foresight into the rapid growth Republic would soon experience, led him and other school board members to think beyond "pulling in extra trailers" to handle the rapid growth the schools would soon encounter.

The Elliott family was active in the Hood Methodist Church where Anson served as chairman of the pastor-parish relations committee and Betty taught Sunday school for many years. Betty also did substitute teaching and served a short term as the city clerk before accepting a position at Missouri State University as office manager for Women's Athletics.

Their daughter, Hollie, was born in 1985. In 1989 Betty purchased ABC's & 123's Preschool from Dr. Pam Hedgpeth. The preschool is housed in the Hood Methodist Church and Betty continues to serve as director and owner.

In 1989 the Elliott family moved to Springfield, MO, but have remained involved in the Republic community. Through their respective educational endeavors, they have touched the lives of hundreds of students from Republic. *Submitted by Betty Elliott.*

**ETHERIDGE/BLANTON** - Harold Etheridge was born Sept. 28, 1923 to Frank and Myrtle (Wade) Etheridge. Harold attended Blades School, first through eighth grades and graduated from Republic High School.

After graduation, he was employed by MFA in Republic until he joined the U.S. Navy in June 1944. He was a storekeeper on the USS *Bowie* (APA-137) until June 1946. He saw action on Okinawa and occupational duty in Japan. His ship was close by the battleship *Missouri* anchored in Tokyo Bay where the official surrender ceremonies took place Sept. 2, 1945.

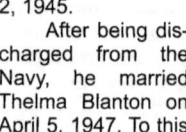

*Thelma and Harold L. Etheridge.*

After being discharged from the Navy, he married Thelma Blanton on April 5, 1947. To this union two children were born, Gary and Sandra "Sandy." Each summer they took a nice vacation and have been in every state except North Carolina and have also visited Mexico and Canada. Two of their favorite places to visit were the ocean in Florida and Washington D.C. because there is so much history there. Gary Etheridge married Debra Whittimore and they have two children, Sarah and Matthew. They live in the state of Minnesota. Sandy Etheridge married Davis Deragowski and they have two children, Lauryn and Lance. They live in Republic, MO.

Harold and Thelma, their children and two of their grandchildren all graduated from Republic High School. Harold worked for Reynolds Manufacturing Company and Paul Mueller Company as a supervisor, retiring in 1982. Thelma is a homemaker and the bookkeeper for the farm. They own 138 acres north of Republic where they raise cattle and hay. Harold continues his farming today even at the age of 82. *Submitted by Sandy Deragowski.*

**ETHERIDGE/LOGAN** - Caleb Etheridge married Milinda Logan and to this union seven children were born, four sons and three daughters: Lonnie, George, Frank, Lewis, Rosie, Mary and Sally.

Lonnie married Rilla Mayfield. They had two daughters, Hazel and Jewel. Hazel married John Yarberry and they had one son, Donnie Lee. They all lived east of Pleasant Hope, MO.

George married Ethel Brown and they had one daughter Gertrude. They lived at Chesapeake, MO.

*Back row, standing: Lonnie, Sally, Mary, Rose and George; seated: Frank, Caleb, Melinda and Lewis Etheridge.*

Frank married Myrtle Wade and they had four sons and four daughters: Everett, Ray, Ralph, Harold, Cleta, Dorothy, Eva and Vetha. Vetha married Leslie Faucett and they lived near Halfway, MO. Dorothy married Lester Martin and lives in Nixa. They had two boys, Jimmy and Danny, and two girls, Darlene and Milinda. Eva married Denzil Batson and they live in Republic, MO. They had one son, Dennie and one daughter, Connie. Vetha married Bob Colson and they live in Springfield, MO. They had one son Larry and one daughter Patty. Everett married Louise Easterday. They live in Springfield, MO. They had one son Joe and two daughters, Janet and Jill. Ray married Iona Maness and they live in Medicine Lodge, KS. They had two sons, Steven and Warren. Ralph married Betty Wells and they lived in Aurora. They had five daughters: Vonda, Alfreda, Linda, Brenda and Nina Kay. Harold married Thelma Blanton and they live in rural Springfield. They had one son Gary and a daughter Sandy.

Lewis married Jeerly Salee and they lived in Springfield. They had one daughter Jeerl Dean who married Earl Biggers and lived in Springfield, MO also. They had one daughter Gloria Ann.

Mary married Matt Garoutte and lived in Republic, MO. They had three sons: Sheral, Elve, Melvin, and one daughter Olive Jackson.

Sally married Bill Estes and lived in Oklahoma. They had one daughter Gracie who married Ray Durham. They had two daughters, Mary Sue and Lora Mae, and one son, Billie.

Rosie married Marion Gardner and had 12 children. *Submitted by Harold Etheridge.*

**ETHERIDGE/MANESS** – Ray, son of Frank Etheridge and Myrtle Wade, and Iona, daughter of Homer Maness and Lois Pope, grew up near Republic, attended the Republic schools, and graduated from Republic High School. Ray attended grade school at Blades Elementary and graduated from Republic High in 1938. Iona attended Lindsey Grade School and graduated

*Aaron Etheridge on Ray Etheridge's lap and Iona Etheridge; in back, l-r: Steve, Vanessa, Jacob, Erik, Jennie and Warren Etheridge.*

from Republic High in 1941. They were married Aug. 31, 1941.

Ray served in the Army during WWII. He was a member of Headquarters 8th Corps, and was in Europe from 1943-45, earning five Battle Stars and was decorated with a Bronze Star. During this time, Iona worked as secretary in the Kaiser Shipyards north of San Francisco, CA (Richmond).

After returning home, Ray enrolled at the University of Missouri where he graduated with a BS in agriculture in 1949. While in Columbia, Iona worked as secretary to the business manager of three hospitals.

After graduating from MU, they moved to Mansfield, MO in 1949 and resided there until 1955. Ray taught veterans agricultural skills through the Veterans Administration.

In 1949, they began raising a family when son Steve arrived and added a second son, Warren, in 1955. Iona became a stay-at-home mother while the boys were growing up.

Ray worked for the Kansas State Agricultural Extension Agency (branch of Kansas State University) beginning in 1955. From 1955-59, he was assistant county agent in Greenwood County, KS.

From 1959-86, Ray served as the Barber County Director of Extension and Extension Agricultural Agent in Medicine Lodge, KS. Involvement in 4-H flourished during this time with over 300 4-H members in the county.

Ray and Iona's activities and time were consumed by attending county fairs, National County Agent Association Conventions, and coaching numerous 4-H related judging teams. Ray coached national winning teams in National Pasture and Range judging contests twice (also winning the Adult Division once himself), as well as a national winning team in livestock judging. Ray was honored by his colleagues in 1970 when he received the Distinguished Service Award. Retirement plans were cut short by his death in 1988. Iona has continued to reside in Medicine Lodge.

Ray and Iona had five grandsons and a great-granddaughter. *Submitted by Warren Etheridge.*

**EUBANKS** - William Frederick Aderhold, born Jan. 4, 1825, his bride being Johanna Christina Helling. They immigrated to the United States from Prussia, Germany now Poland, landing in New York in 1845. They were on their honeymoon bringing along two of William's brothers. One stayed in the east, one went south, and William and Johanna settled in Alma, KS.

*Jeanie Eubanks and family – 2004.*

In the following years they owned many acres of farmland. William held the position of president with the First National Bank. They raised one daughter and three sons. Clarence William, born Nov. 4, 1868, was the youngest and christened in the German Lutheran Church. The family has his prayer book which was printed in 1890 in the High German language. He married Ellen Frances Richardson.

They owned several businesses, and he also worked as a station agent and telegrapher for the Missouri North Arkansas Railroad. He was initiated into the Grand Lodge in Searcy, AR, May 11, 1899 being a very active member. He organized several other lodges, including Modern Woodmen, Knights of Pythian, Woodmen of the World, and other Grand Lodges.

Carl Eubanks and Jeanie Bates were married June 1, 1959 moving to Republic. He worked as a calibrator for the Paul Mueller Co. in Springfield. The paternal great-grandparents of Jeanie (Bates) Eubanks came from Ireland to Sumner County, TN and then to southwest Missouri. Their surname was Bates. Most of her maternal and paternal ancestors owned businesses and several worked for the railroads. One was a postmaster and one helped to establish the first Methodist Church in northern Iowa.

Jeanie's first cousin Ronald Willard Aderhold married Laura Ann Courdin, whose ancestors were one of the eight original families from France and Italy coming to the United States for freedom of religion. They established the Waldension (Presbyterian) Church south of Monett, MO, and all are buried in the church cemetery.

Carl's ancestors immigrated through Canada to the United States from England. The name of Henry Eubanks appears among a list of 100 colonists transported to this country by Colonel William Clayborne Sept. 1, 1653. In return for his services, Clayborne was given 5000 acres of land in Virginia. The many descendants of this Eubanks family scattered to all parts of this country, with many settling in N W Arkansas and SW Missouri. Many fought in all of our wars.

When the Eubanks relocated to Republic some of their first neighbors were Warren and Kathy Wilson. Jeanie continues to live in the same neighborhood. Their two sons, Martie Lee and Tony Scott Eubanks, were born in Springfield hospitals and attended all of their school years in Republic.

After a divorce Carl remarried to Ramona Harris. Between the two they have 10 grandchildren. Carl was fire chief during the 1970s, being called to several emergencies during those years, including the tornado of December 1971 which destroyed a large portion of the city. It was declared a disaster area by Governor Warren E. Hearnes. Ninety percent of the damaged or destroyed houses belonged to homeowners. This storm also damaged Springfield Municipal Airport stopping its clock at 11:26 p.m.

Another publicized event happened Feb. 22, 1973 when a plane crashed into the home of Dollie Foust at 545 North Main, both men in the plane were killed.

The Security State Bank located on Main Street was damaged by fire Dec. 31, 1988, being rebuilt as soon as possible.

Republic has grown in all directions in the 47 years since the Eubanks came to Republic. They are very proud of the progress that Republic has made between 1871 and the present 2007. *Submitted by Jeanie Eubanks.*

**EVANS -** Lee Evans' grandfather Hart was born in 1843 into a very large family in Illinois. He was given away and brought to the Ozarks. After fighting for the Union in the Civil War, he married Martha Stephenson and settled on a farm south of Galena. He made a living by transporting goods from Springfield to sell to the hill folks. Hart's son Andy (1872) opened a grocery store in Hurley and fathered three children: Crystal, 1896; Lee, 1897; and Jimmy,

*Lee Evans with fox hounds; his dad Andy Evans, and the store delivery truck.*

1899. Lee married Fay Likens, the daughter of a Crane business family.

In 1924 Lee Evans and his father left Hurley to open a meat market/grocery store in Republic on the east side of Main Street. That same year; his brother Jimmy opened a barber shop two doors down, and Fay's family opened the Likens Family Dry Goods store across the street.

From its start the store did well, giving Lee and Fay the means to start a family and enjoy hunting and fishing. During the depression Lee implemented a customer credit system making loans to the locals. Poker and dice games helped ease the stress and attracted traveling salesmen and others. Lee financed the purchase of most of the land that is now the Terrell Creek project properties.

Lee's love of dogs is legendary. He always kept eight or ten fox hounds. Two thirds of his remaining pictures are of dogs! During the mid-30s, "Old Booze" spent his days at the store, delivering fresh meat home for supper and meeting the kids after school. Lee so loved hunting and fishing that a likely meal at the Evans' home would be fresh fish, quail or rabbit. Entertainment was a good card game, a day on the lake or a night listening to a crackling fire and the baying of dogs on a trail. Lee whittled trumpets from cow horns and used these to signal his dogs to return to camp. He could identify each of his dogs and tell how hot or cold the trail was by their distant sounds.

Gene (1919) and Carl (1926) helped at the store. In 1942 Lee helped Gene and wife Marjorie (Squibb) buy a small farm on the west side of Republic. Carl returned from the Navy in 1946 and continued working at the store until 1957. In 1965 Lee sold the store to the MFA and retired. He lost Fay in 1969 and passed away in December 1978. Carl retired from the Federal Medical Center and moved to Springfield with wife Donna. Gene died in 1990. Marjorie still lives on the original farm.

Carl and Donna's son Steve and wife Terry live in Springfield; daughter Cindy and husband Marty live in Houston, TX. Gene and Marjorie's son Jim and wife Terri live on the family farm. Daughter Nancy lives in Hermitage with her husband Terry Johnson. Nancy's daughter Melanie and husband Casey Yunger live in Kansas with their daughters, Carlie and Alison. *Submitted by Jim Evans.*

**FARWELL -** In the fall of 1966, Don Farwell with his wife Wilena and small son Jeff moved to Republic and filled the position of principal of Republic High School. Republic is close to Don's hometown of Cassville and Wilena's hometown of Anderson where both grew up on farms. They enjoyed the small town of Republic. During the summers Don sometimes worked hauling hay from the nearby fields that later became housing developments; during the fall he hunted quail in the surrounding areas. Farwells had ties to nearby Springfield for it was there at Southwest Missouri State University that Don and Wilena met. After both graduated from SMSU, they were married and moved to Killeen, TX, where Don was serving as an officer in the U.S. Army and Wilena began her teaching career. From there the couple moved to Weaubleau, MO, working in the schools of that area for two years before moving to Republic.

*The Don Farwell Family, l-r: Jeff, Wilena, Greg, Don, Derek and Wildon – abt. 1995.*

For the next 31 years, Don and Wilena enjoyed their association with the school. Every August Don eagerly anticipated the beginning of a new year enjoying interaction with students and faculty. Wilena joined the high school faculty in the vocational business department in 1979. She enjoyed interacting with the students and observing their successes in FBLA and beyond.

During Don's years as the high school principal, enrollment of the school more than doubled from around 300 to more than 600 students. Several additions were made to the high school building where he began as principal. In 1979 a new high school was built, and over the years more additions were necessary as the school continued to grow.

As the years passed, the family grew with the addition of three more sons: Greg, Derek and Wildon. All four sons completed all 13 years of their schooling in the Republic Schools. With four sons in the school and both parents working in the school, the family became very involved in the school and its activities at different levels. Both Don and Wilena were staunch supporters of the performing arts and academic and sports teams, sharing their joys of winning and suffering with them in their defeats. It was a special enjoyment for them to be able to support their sons in these activities at the same time.

Life away from the school included frequent family trips to Anderson and Cassville and the Roaring River area where Don and his boys enjoyed fishing. The family also enjoyed visiting and walking the trails of Wilson's Creek Battlefield Park and being involved in church activities. Republic has been a good hometown for the Farwells providing many good times and many kindnesses to the family in difficult times. After a courageous year-long battle with cancer, Don died in August 2004. The boys' careers sent Wildon to the east coast, Greg with his wife and daughters to the west coast, and left Jeff in Republic and Derek with his wife and two sons in Stockton, MO. *Submitted by Wilena Farwell.*

**FERGUSON -** Ernest Bly Ferguson, known to most in the Republic area as E.B., came to Republic from Barry County after marrying a native Republic girl, Edna Bessie Wallace in 1910. E.B. was born in Butterfield, MO (near Cassville) to Thomas and Azie (McNally) Ferguson in 1890. His mother died in 1902 when

E.B. was 12 years old. He attended elementary school at Butterfield, high school at Cassville and Monett, and college at State Teachers College, now Missouri State University.

Edna B. Wallace was born in 1892 to Thomas B. and Nancy J. (Wade) Wallace in Republic, MO. Edna's father, Thomas B. Wallace, died in 1900. Nancy (Wade) Wallace then married Thomas Ferguson in 1906 and relocated to Barry County. E.B. and Edna became acquainted when their parents married and they fell in love and were married in 1910.

After teaching school for a few years in Barry County, E.B. and Edna came to the Republic area and established a dairy farm northeast of town. Besides farming, E.B. had a long teaching career in Greene County. Countless hundreds of children enjoyed his rigorous and capable instruction until the end of the 1953-54 school year when schools were reorganized into the Republic school system. Some of the area schools in which he taught include Beulah, Blades, Grandview, Capernium, Mt. Aetna, and Brick. E.B. said, "In 40 years of teaching, I never had a child I couldn't teach to read." E.B. enjoyed organizing school children into competing teams of all kinds, from spelling bees to baseball teams. He was a left-handed pitcher in his own early school years and loved to participate as a player and as a coach during his teaching career. While at Mt. Aetna School, he coached a baseball team to win a tournament held at Springfield Teachers College. This is just one example of the many sports teams he led in participation and to victory.

E.B. and Edna Ferguson with their children, Thomas Wallace Ferguson and Mildred Ferguson – circa 1923.

While he was still teaching and farming, he became a State Farm Insurance agent and sold insurance in the area for many years. In 1954 he sold insurance full time, continuing to live on the farm for a few years. In the late 1950s he moved from his farm with Edna into the city of Republic.

He was a very active member of the First Christian Church in Republic, well known as a song leader and Sunday school superintendent.

E.B. and Edna had two children, Mildred, born in 1914, and Thomas Wallace Ferguson, born in 1918. Both graduated from Republic High School and the State Teachers College, now Missouri State University, in Springfield. Mildred moved away, began teaching, and married Woodson Fishback. They had two children, Wayne and Robert Fishback. T. Wallace, after serving in the U.S. Army Air Corps during WWII, settled in Republic with his wife, Maxine (Riley), who was the daughter of Republic area farmer C. Earnest "Earn" and Mary Iona "Onie" Riley. Wallace and Maxine Ferguson had two children, James "Jim" Wallace Ferguson and Jeanie Diane (Ferguson) Stark, who both graduated from Republic High School.

Jim married a Republic native, Marilyn (Maness), daughter of Donald S. and Regina (Sifferman) Maness. Jim and Marilyn had two children, David Wallace Ferguson and John Charles Ferguson. David married Julie Hedger of Marshall, MO, and in May 2005 had a daughter, Madison Nicole Ferguson, who at present is the youngest descendant of E.B. and Edna Ferguson. Jeanie married John E. Stark, who also is a Republic graduate.

Edna Ferguson died in January 1961 and E.B. passed away in November 1978. They are both buried in Wade Chapel Cemetery west of Republic. Submitted by Jim and Marilyn Ferguson.

**FISHER** - The marriage of Payton Townsend Fisher and Mary Ellen Adams produced five children: Joseph Franklin, Mertie, Nelson "Nelse," Ida and John Fisher.

On Oct 28, 1881 in Galloway Township, Christian County, MO, William Monroe Howard, born in January 1857 in Missouri and whose family came from Tennessee, married Rachel Luzzi Noe who was born Feb. 18, 1865 in Missouri and whose family came from Virginia and Arkansas. They had 13 children: Nerva born Oct. 16, 1882, John Ranson born August 1883, Alice born October 1885, Jasper born May 1888, David born March 1890, Lonnie born January 1892, Katie born March 1894, Oled born February 1896, Arch born February 1900 (from 1900 census), Ollie Delena born July 1902 and Mollie Mae born February 1906 (from family records.)

Rachel's parents were A.S., born 1836 in Virginia, and Margratt Noe, born 1838 in Illinois, and settled in Galloway Township in Christian County, MO. Rachel's siblings were John born 1860, Thomas born 1863, Violet born 1867, David born 1868, Lutecia born 1870, William born 1872 and Margaret born 1874. Christian County marriage record from 1859-76 states Archibald S. Noe married Martha Wade, a housewife from Tennessee, on Sept. 29, 1876.

L-R: Merle, Lena, Sherman, Lamen, Earmel, Velva; Minerva and Joe Fisher seated in front.

Joseph Franklin Fisher was born May 17, 1879 and Minerva Jane Howard, born Oct. 16, 1882, died April 1964, were married at her father's home on Oct. 28, 1900 in Bengal, MO. Their union produced 11 children: Payton Townsend born Dec. 6, 1901, died Jan. 29, 1921; Johnny Robert born Aug. 12, 1903, died Dec. 11, 1952; Lamen Leslie born June 27, 1905, died Nov. 3, 1979; Gladys Mae born Feb. 13, 1907, died Feb. 5, 2003; Malena born July 23, 1909, died May 28, 1969; Sherman Earl born May 10, 1911, died March 19, 1977; Lula Irene born March 1, 1913, died Sept. 25, 2005; William "Bill" Deulen born Oct. 22, 1916, died Aug. 20, 1997; Velva Lavanda born Sept. 15, 1918, died Oct. 13, 1972; Merle Evelyn born Nov. 10, 1920, died late 1990s; Earmel Ada Evelene born Oct. 1, 1922, died late 1990s (from family records).

The Fisher family lived around the Highlandville, MO area for several years. At age six in 1913, Gladys walked to Torey School with her brothers Pate, Johnny and Lamen. They moved to Stone County and the children continued their education at Craig Hollow. The parents' employment took them to a ranch in Ponce DeLeon. They walked to Jamesville School which had nine grades. This walk proved to be dangerous and Minerva Fisher developed her fear of water. They used a boat to cross James River. It was flooding one day and being unable to cross the river, the children waited several hours for their father to find them and take them home in a wagon. After two years of crossing the James River and a number of scary adventures, the family moved west of Republic.

Their new school was Blades which was approximately two and one half miles from their home. Gladys remembered the Fridays when they had spelling and arithmetic bees. They enjoyed the Christmas plays and games like Annie Over, Blackman and ball games. She also remembered the great food her mother prepared especially for breakfast and school lunches. Gladys graduated from the eighth grade at Blades School before moving into Republic with her family.

Gladys remembered when others were dying of smallpox, and her father inoculated his family with the cowpox infection. No one in her family contracted smallpox. Gladys had lots of great memories of her childhood. Being the eldest, she started cooking, baking and baby sitting at an early age. She continued these motherly duties with her family after she met and married Oca Hagewood. They celebrated 77 anniversaries together. Compiled from Family Records and submitted by Ermal L. Vernick, a daughter.

**FORTNER** - Sometime before 1860, several Fortner families moved from Greene County, TN to Lawrence and Greene County, MO. James Fortner (1818-1886) and his wife Lydia Cotter; his brothers, Pleasant Witt and Jacob Lee, all three brought their families with them. The 1850 Federal Census of Greene County, TN shows James 31, Lidia 31, Jacob 10, James 9, William 7, Elizabeth J. 5, Rebecca A. 2 and John 8 months. After moving to Missouri, James and Lydia's family continued to grow. Their children born in Missouri were Hannah 1857, Monroe 1859, Samuel 1861 and Mary 1863.

Bob and Doris (McConnell) Fortner.

James and Lydia's oldest son, Jacob, returned to Greene County, TN to marry Sarah Jane Haney/Haynie. They were married July 14, 1861. The other sons of James and Lydia and their marriages are as follows: James "Jim" to Mary Baty, William to Aganeth Eddington, John to Mary Susan Steeley, Monroe "Roe" to Rachel Fortner and Samuel "Sam" to Margaret Jones. Their daughter's marriages are as follows: Elizabeth married Thomas Marshall, Hannah married Wayland Ruark and Mary married Sterling Collins.

Jacob and Sarah raised a family of six children: Martha 1863-1923, Lewis 1869-1939, Elick "Ek" 1871-1953, Alva 1877-(?), Bert 1878-1963 and Robert "Bob" 1883-1973. Martha married Grant Ruark, Lewis married Eva ?, Ek married Lula Demore, Alva married Mattie Olinger, Bert married 1st, Bertha Marsh and 2nd, Effie Jones. Jacob and Sarah were living in Center Township, Greene County, MO in 1909 when their youngest son, Robert Lee Bob, 1883-1973, married Alta May (McSpadden) Fagg, 1888-1965. Alta's first husband, Cecil Fagg, had died following a farm accident.

Alta was the daughter of Thomas "Tom," 1859-1938, and Mary (Young) McSpadden, 1863-1949. Tom had homesteaded and built the family home at the corner of Highways N and 266 (Historic Route 66). The house still stands there today. Tom had a service station at that corner for many years, and that corner became known as "McSpadden Corner." Jacob and Sarah Fortner, and Tom and Mary McSpadden, all are buried at Yeakley Chapel Cemetery.

The Bob Fortner family and his father, Jacob, moved from Greene County to Dade County before 1919. Bob and Alta raised a family of seven children: Ramon, Alma, Eula, Thomas, Norma, JoAn and Robert "Bobby."

Their youngest, Bobby, attended King's Point School (a one-room school), near Lockwood, MO for his first two years. Then he completed his education at Lockwood High School. Following graduation he spent two years in the U.S. Army and later attended a vo-tech school and became an auto mechanic. Eventually he went into his own business. He was part owner and operator of North Side Automotive on West Kearney for several years. In 1963, Bobby married Doris McConnell of the Wilson's Creek Battlefield area east of Republic. Bobby and Doris moved to that area during the first years of their marriage. Their two daughters, Connie and Tammy, attended all 12 years at the Republic schools.

Connie married Jack Davis, and they have a service station at the west edge of Republic. Tammy lives in Republic and is an assistant manager for Wal-Mart. Connie and Jack are the parents of Bryan and Katy Davis. Bobby succumbed to cancer July 19, 2004 and was interred in Evergreen Cemetery in Republic. *Submitted by JoAn Clayton.*

**FOSTER** - In the summer of 1976, Robert Foster Sr. had the choice of moving his family to Halfway or Republic. Republic winning out, this native family from New Jersey packed their belongings from the short residence they had in Illinois, and settled in the little town of Republic. The culture shock was livid, but the family was determined to enjoy the little town's way of life.

Robert brought his second wife Karen, and a slew of kids to the Boston Lane residence, where he still resides, in retirement, from the auto body trade. Most of the family has moved away, but his sons Robert Jr. and Anthony still make the Republic area their home,

Robert Jr. married Karen Fuhr on Sept. 22, 1979 in Republic. They were blessed with three children: Jason born Sept. 3, 1980, Jennifer May 6, 1982, and Jessica Aug. 3, 1986. Jennifer married Michael Schulte, also a native of Republic, on June 17, 2004. At this writing, Jason currently is a high school teacher. Jennifer, Michael, and Jessica are currently obtaining their college degrees. Robert Jr. works for the *Springfield News-Leader*, Karen works for Missouri State University. Robert also is the building facilitator for the Sunset Church of Christ, where he and Karen are very active in the work there.

Anthony Foster married Sheila Ford on March l3, 1992. They have one child Samantha Foster born July 22, 1988. As of this writing, Anthony works for Kraft Foods. Sheila works for the Dairy Queen in Republic. Samantha is a junior at Republic High School. *Submitted by Karen Foster.*

**FOUST/GAROUTTE** - Sam Foust was the third child of Charles B. Foust and Ollie (Kimmons) Foust, born in Lawrenceburg, MO in February 1908 and died in May 1987. Sam married Dollie Garoutte, first child of Charlie and Ava (McDaniel) Garoutte in October 1930; she was born in October 1908 and died in April 1977.

*Dollie and Sam Foust.*

Sam and Dollie purchased the farm on which Dollie's great-grandfather William McDaniel had homesteaded, located about five miles northwest of Republic, in the 1940s. They were blessed with three daughters: Lora Lee (Day) Bacon, JoAnn Brown and Mary Sue Robertson. Sam and Dollie worked together along with their girls, starting a milk producing herd, building one of the first Grade A dairy barns in the area. This magnificent barn had a cement floor in the loft and could be driven into from ground level; the roof was covered with shank cedar shingles. Harry and Mary Misemer (Sam's sister) used their saw mill to cut the lumber for this barn from the wooded area on the north section of the Foust farm. The cattle entered on a cement floor for milking, accommodations for 16 at one time, milking approximately 60 head. The barn had a cedar lined tack room, one room for the team of horses, one room for a special horse, Mike, and one room for baby calves. There was a three grain bin drop from the loft to the milking area.

Sam and Dollie stabled horses for friends, building a track for everyone's pleasure to spend Saturday or Sunday afternoons riding their horses. Sam was an avid sportsman, loving to hunt, fish, training dogs and horses, his marksmanship was perfect. He also custom butchered for family and friends. Dollie was always working with the outside chores, raising chickens, tending the garden, canning and freezing produce, always ready to butcher a chicken for a wonderful meal at any time guests should arrive.

*Sam and Dollie Foust's barn.*

Sam was a devoted member of the Republic Masonic Lodge #570 becoming a Worshipful Master; Dollie was a member of the Republic Eastern Star #370.

In the mid-1940s Sam purchased two milk routes, employing one driver and driving one himself, picking up milk from area farmers and hauling it to MFA Creamery in Springfield. In the early 1950s Sam took a position with MFA/Producers Creamery/MidAmerican Dairy, now DFA Dairies in Springfield. At this time the milking herd was cut back and a Black Angus beef herd was started.

In 1956 Sam and Dollie agreed to a divorce, Sam relocating to Springfield marrying Donna Blankenship and Dollie along with her youngest daughter Mary Sue to Republic. Dollie worked at the local garment factory days and cooked in her brother's cafe in the evenings, Lloyd's Drive Inn, located on North Main/Hwy 174. Her cream pies were savored by many.

She was disabled with cancer in 1963 and spent the rest of her life loving her grandchildren and her family to the fullest.

In 1974 a twin engine Cessna plane crashed into her home on North Main Street, leaving her home a total ruin. The pilot and passenger were both killed, but Dollie escaped with only a terrific scare and lots of memories burned in flames. She was caring for her mother, Ava Garoutte, at the time of her death in 1977. Dollie is buried at Wade Chapel Cemetery.

Sam's death was in 1987, also being buried at Wade Chapel. *Submitted by Bill and Mary Sue Robertson.*

**FRANKS** - In 1942 Ivan and Alice Franks purchased 40 acres about one mile north of the Republic City Park on a dirt road, now Farm Road 85. Ivan and Alice owned a business in Springfield, Franks Electric Company, but Ivan had always had a love for horses and cattle and missed the country. He also wanted to contribute to the "war effort." Alice, who also grew up on a farm, was happier living in Springfield where there were more conveniences. However, Ivan did make some improvements before moving in. He had a well dug (before the house had only a cistern) and plumbed water to a pump at the back door. He also wired the house for electricity. However, Alice had to make do with no phone, no insulation, and no indoor plumbing.

*Ivan Franks in 1945 with one of his plow horses.*

Ivan and Alice moved to the farm with their daughter, Shirley, where they began farming with a good team of plow horses, since tractors were not available during WWII. Ivan still drove to Springfield daily to operate the electrical business.

Over time, the war ended, Ivan bought a new Oliver 60 tractor and established a herd of registered Jersey cattle. He also raised registered Landrace hogs and enjoyed his Missouri Fox Trotter horses. He purchased additional land adjacent to the original 40, built a larger barn, and helped pay for the road, now Farm Road 85, to be paved.

After living on the farm only about 18 months, the Franks moved back to Springfield and rented out the house on the farm. However, they kept farming and milking by driving to the farm twice daily until Ivan gave up milking in the early 1970s and concentrated on breeding miniature mules. The farm was Ivan's passion until his death in 1978.

After his death, Alice had a farm sale, keeping the Oliver 60 tractor and the hay baler, but selling all the livestock and other equipment. She continued to operate Franks Electric Company in Springfield until 1990. She died in 1992. Their farm is now owned by their youngest daughter Sondra Franks Hagerman and her husband Jerry Hagerman and the descendants of their oldest daughter, Shirley Franks Goforth. *Submitted by Sondra Hagerman.*

**FRENCH** - Dr. Ulysses "Gann" Simpson French and wife Sarah "Sallie" Alcinda (Turner) French, settled in Republic in the early 1900s, upon marrying in 1895. He began a medical practice around 1902, after graduating from Barnes Hospital in the 1900s (St. Louis, MO). He was one of the first doctors in Republic with wide practice as a physician and a surgeon. His dedication to his practice was shown when he saw patients up until the day before his death after being diagnosed with a critical condition. His office was located over the barber shop on Main Street next to Dr. Brim's Dentist Office. He was affiliated with Burge (Cox) Hospital, Springfield, MO. He was a founding charter member of the local Masonic Lodge and became both a Worshipful Master in 1908 and then a Past Master. Dr. French was very active in the community. Both were members of the Christian Church in Republic with their children.

Jack E. French.

Ulysses was born in Strafford, MO, 1869-1940, Republic. Sarah born in Smithfield, TX, 1874-1952, Republic. Their children were Opal 1897-1959, twins-Aubyn and Omar "Doc" 1899-1967. They were all born in Griffin, MO, and raised in Republic. Both Omar and Aubyn became Masons in 1921.

Back Row: Aubyn, Jack, Omar (Doc) French; front: Inez, Pauline, Sallie French.

Opal married Guy Homer Pickering and moved to Springfield, MO. They had one son, Jim Pickering, in 1931 who now resides in Springfield.

Aubyn married Clarissa Johnson and had two children, Inez 1925 and Richard Ulysses 1931.

Omar married Pauline Louise Greismer of Billings. Their children were Jack Eugene 1928-2005, Sallie Ann 1930, and Larry Omar 1933. All of Omar's children were delivered by their Grandfather Ulysses. Omar's second wife was named Freda O. Miller and they were married in 1954. They had no children. He owned land in the Republic area and the French Motor Company (Chevrolet Dealership) in Republic in the late 1930s. He sold the business to his son Jack in 1955 when he retired and Jack ran the business until selling it in 1963.

French Motor Co.

Jack married Betty Jean Conroy of Republic. Their children were Sandra Faye 1947, Steven Eugene 1950, Ronald Dean 1953-1972, Julia Ann 1955 and Diana Kay 1960. Betty now resides in her family's Republic homestead circa 1889. Betty is a descendent of the Goodin family of Republic.

Sandra had one daughter Shelly. Sandy lives in Republic with her husband Bob Williams.

Steven had two children, Brian and Deanna. Steve resides in Republic. Brian has one son Dakota. Deanna has three sons: Dustin, Derrick and Christopher.

Julia had two children, John "J.J." and Sabrina. Julia lives in Republic with her husband Robert West. John and his wife Beth Anne (McElwain) reside in Republic.

Diana Kay had twins Roni and Max with her husband Preston Norbury. His children from a previous marrage are Ivy and triplets Tyler, Curtis and Hayes (Hayes 1990-2003). They live in Springfield.

Jack had two other children from a second marriage to Sally Louise Johnson of Texas, Jennifer Louise and David Clifton, who both reside in Texas. *Submitted by Sandra, Steve, Julia, Diana, Jennifer and Cliff.*

**FUGITT** - It is believed the first Fugitt in America was a French Huguenot who settled in Maryland in the mid-1600s. The first American Fugitts owned land in Maryland and Virginia before moving to Tennessee and ultimately to Missouri.

Five generations after coming to America, Bedford Fugitt was the family's first ancestor to move to Missouri. He settled south of Clever near Stone County. He and the next three generations of Fugitts are buried in Wise Hill Cemetery north of Clever.

The first Fugitt to live in Republic was James William "Uncle Jimmy." He is shown here with his siblings, the first Fugitts born in Missouri and parents. Back, l-r: Frank, "Uncle Jimmy" and Wiley; Center: Parents, John H. and wife Mary; seated l-r: Mary Fugitt Wise, Della Fugitt Hodges and standing is Laura Fugitt Pearce. John H. was the son of Bedford who came to Missouri from Tennessee in the early 1800s. All pictured are buried in Wise Hill Cemetery, north of Clever.

Bedford's grandson, James William, "Uncle Jimmy" to his friends, was the first Fugitt to live in the Republic area having purchased a farm on Terrell Creek in the late 1800s. He married Martha Ella Davis and they raised two sons, Leonard and Boyd. After "Uncle Jimmy" died Boyd kept the farm and eventually sold 100 acres to the Tri-Way Country Club which is part of Island Green today. Boyd's son Jack lives on the farm today. He is the only Fugitt alive today who owns property with a Republic address. At one time there were four Fugitt households on East Elm Street.

Boyd Fugitt had another son Bill, who lived in the Republic area for several years before moving to Rogers, AR. Bill has a son Kim and two daughters, Kayla and Kathy. Boyd also had two daughters, Jo Ann Long, deceased, and Wanda Lee Durbin of Kansas City.

Leonard Fugitt owned Robertson Livestock Commission Co. at Union Stockyards for 30 years. He is pictured on the right. With him are his salesmen Francis "Speck" Jordan in center, and his nephew Bill Fugitt on left. This picture was taken in 1952 for the calendar Leonard had made to give to customers. Leonard sold the firm in 1958 to Speck Jordan. In 1974 Bill with his brother Jack, bought the commission company from Speck and changed the name to Fugitt Brothers Livestock Commission Co.

Leonard is best known as the one most responsible for assembling the large tract of land south of Republic, part of which became known as the 2200 acre "Terrell Creek Development." All land belonging to Leonard's family was sold in 1990.

Leonard had one son, J.W., who died in 1983. His widow, Bette Sellers Fugitt, now lives in Springfield. J.W. and Bette had one son Terry who with his dad spent most of his life involved in the farm Leonard bought. Terry and his children, Sarah Kizer, Mary Beth Stewart and John Fugitt live near Springfield, his other daughter, Kitty Flatt, lives east of Clever.

J.W. and Bette had one daughter Christina who raised two daughters, Lisa (Beard) Shevey now resides in Williamston, SC and Lori Beard Viles lives in Springfield. Christina also lives in Springfield after having lived and worked for eight years in Europe.

Who knows, maybe her facility to speak French is in her genes! In addition to her Fugitt ancestor, her paternal grandmother, Cecil Louise Garoutte, also gave her French ancestry. *Submitted by Christina Fugitt Griffiths.*

**FUHR** - Robert W. "Bob" Fuhr had a blacksmith shop in Republic, MO for over 20 years. He was of German descent, a hard working, industrious man. He married Ota Ermine Brashears when they were ages 20 and 17, respectively. They had 10 healthy children.

Bob Fuhr.

In those years it was a struggle to feed such a large family. Bob could do many things other than blacksmithing. He sheared sheep for the neighbors, sawed wood, threshed grain around the country side, made molasses in his mill, put up hay and farmed, raising most of the food supply for his family. His children also worked hard, helping with many chores. They grew strawberries and would pick them and ship them from the little town of Logan to other parts of the country.

When the draft was started for WWII, six of Bob and Ota's sons served and were in the service at the same time. They all six returned home safely with Boyd being the only one seriously wounded. At this time the Fuhr's lived northwest of Billings on a farm in the area known as Huckleberry Ridge. Bob had his blacksmith shop there, but since they were getting older and Ota's health was not the best and the family all gone from home, they decided to move into Republic. It was there that Bob opened his blacksmith shop on Main Street. He loved making and creating things. He made miniature, operable farm machinery such as wagons, balers, tractors, etc. They were quite authentic and were shown in some of the local fairs.

*Bob Fuhr Family. Bob, Ota, Vesta, Kyle, Ted, Boyd, Clara, Ray, Leo, Joe, Bill and Charles.*

All of the children grew up to be honest, hard working Christians, respecting their parents. Bob and Ota were a "God fearing couple," always in church, teaching Sunday school and enjoying life with their family. They had many grand and great-grandchildren who loved going to Grandma and Grandpa Fuhr's home. Six of their children are deceased now.

Bob was born March 19, 1891 and died Jan. 22, 1976. Ota was born April 16, 1894 and died Sept. 18, 1969. They are both buried in Kerr Cemetery. *Submitted by their oldest granddaughter, Leota Mae Ross Sawyer Recknor.*

**FUHR/BROWN** - Robert "Leo" Fuhr was born on Dec. 10, 1921 on a farm in northeast Lawrence County. He was the seventh child born to Robert William Fuhr (1895-1976) and Ota Ermine Fuhr (1899-1969). Leo's siblings were Vesta, Kyle, Boyd, Ted, Clara, Ray, Joe, Bill, Charlie.

*Geneva, Roger and Leo Fuhr.*

Geneva Mae Brown was born on July 2, 1926 on a farm in western Greene County near Republic. She was the eighth child born to Smith Brown (1890-1944) and Rose Belle Brown (1895-1985). Geneva's siblings were Lucille, Tom, Garland, Rose Helen, Mildred, Ruby, Wynonna, Smithy, Nancy, Norma, Max and Don.

Leo attended elementary school at Pleasant Valley School (Lawrence County) and high school at Republic. He graduated from Republic High School in 1938. Geneva attended elementary school at St. Elmo School (Greene County) and high school at Republic. She graduated from Republic High School in 1944. It was at Republic High School where they met. They were married in Columbus, KS in 1945.

For a period of time, Leo and Geneva lived and worked in California in the 1940s.

In 1947 their only child, Roger Leo, was born. From 1947 to 1969, Leo worked at various jobs, and Geneva worked at the garment factory. Roger attended Republic Schools and graduated from Republic High School in 1965.

The years of 1969-73 were memorable for Leo and Geneva. Roger graduated from Missouri State University in 1969. Roger married Nina Warden from Republic in 1969. Also, in 1969 Roger was drafted into the U.S. Army to serve in Vietnam. He served his country for two years and earned a Bronze Star. In January 1971 Leo and Geneva's first grandchild, Eric Roger was born. In December 1971, their home was damaged from a tornado and Geneva suffered minor injuries. In March 1973, their second and last grandchild, Holly Roberta, was born.

Throughout the 1970s and early 1980s, Leo worked at Great Western Meat Company in Republic and Geneva worked at Crane Manufacturing in Republic, then Marionville. For most of their lives, Leo and Geneva attended the Church of Christ in Republic. During much of this time, Leo taught adult Bible class. Geneva was active in women's bowling in Springfield and played in several leagues. Both Leo and Geneva enjoyed spending time with friends and family, especially their grandchildren.

In 1981, Geneva developed cancer and died a year later on Feb. 24, 1982. Leo retired from Great Western Meat Company in the mid-1980s. From that time on he spent much of his life with his family, tending to his son's farm in southeast Lawrence County, and in church. Leo moved to Marionville, MO in 1996. Leo died Nov. 8, 2003. Both Leo and Geneva are interred at Kerr Cemetery in southwest Greene County. *Submitted by Roger Fuhr.*

**FUHR/ENLOW** - Eric Roger Fuhr, born Jan. 5, 1971 at St. John's Hospital in Springfield, was the first child born to Roger Leo Fuhr (born 1947) and Nina Roberta (Warden) Fuhr (born 1947). His only sibling is Holly Roberta (Fuhr) Coker (born 1973).

Michelle Diane Enlow was the third child born to Manford Edward Enlow (born 1944) and Linda Grace (Hayley) Enlow (born 1947). Her siblings are Leslie Dale Enlow (born 1967) and Timothy Scott Enlow (born 1969).

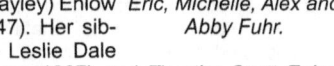
*Eric, Michelle, Alex and Abby Fuhr.*

Eric was raised on a farm in northeast Lawrence County, one mile south of Hwy. 174 on T Highway. He attended school at Marionville and graduated from Marionville High School in 1989.

Michelle was raised in Joplin. She attended West Central Elementary, North Junior High and Joplin High School. She graduated from Joplin High School in 1989.

Eric attended Missouri Southern State University from 1989-93 and graduated with a bachelor of science degree in secondary business education and obtained a Missouri State Teacher's License. In December 2004 he received his MBA from Missouri State University.

Eric and Michelle met through a mutual employer in Joplin in 1991. They were married in December 1993 in Galena, KS.

They moved to Republic from Springfield in 1995. They have two children, Abby Nicole Fuhr was born May 5, 2000 and Alex Leo Fuhr was born March 18, 2003. Eric and Michelle are members of Republic First Christian Church.

In 2006, Eric is employed as Director of Clinic Operations by St. John's Health System and Michelle is employed by Regions Bank. *Submitted by Eric and Michelle Fuhr.*

**FUHR/PHILLIPPI** - John Ernest Fuhr was born in Frankfurt, Germany near the Rhine River in the year 1825. He had three siblings - one brother and two sisters. Approximately in the year 1854, he emigrated from Germany by stowing away aboard a ship bound for the United States. Six days later, he became so hungry, he had to come out of hiding and was allowed to work his passage from Germany to the United States. He landed in Virginia.

*Fuhr Family - Front, l to r: Boyd, Vesta, Ota, Bob, Clara and Kyle. Back: Bill, Charlie, Joe, Leo, Ray and Ted.*

Four years later he met and married Louisa Phillippi on Feb. 13, 1858 in Bardstown, Cass County, IL. Louisa was born in 1836 to German parents. She had two brothers and one sister.

The "Fuhr" name first came to the southwest corner of Greene County with John and Louisa when they settled on a farm about seven miles southwest of Republic.

John and Louisa had six children: Edd, Otto, Clara, Caroline, Alice and Anna. John died in 1909 and Louisa died in 1916.

Otto C. Fuhr was born 1860 and was married to Margaret Jane Kerr (born 1856). Otto was a farmer, thrasher-man, sawmill operator and carpenter. Otto and his brother Edd worked together building houses, business buildings and barns in the Republic area. Edd ran a canning factory in Republic for several years.

Otto and Margaret Jane had seven children: Geruisha, Minnie, Robert William, Charles Thomas (Albert, Marcus and Mary all died young). Otto and Margaret Jane both died in 1936.

Robert or "Bob" Fuhr was born in 1891 and married Ota E. Brashears (born 1894) on Aug. 7, 1911. They had 10 children: Vesta, Kyle, Ted, Boyd, Clara, Ray, Leo, Joe, Bill and Charles.

Bob worked with his dad, Otto, in farming, thrashing and running a sawmill. Bob was a blacksmith by trade for many years. About 1944, he moved his shop from the farm on Huckleberry Ridge to the Main Street of Republic. Bob did many repair jobs for the farming community until 1974 when his health failed him. Bob and Ota saw six of their eight sons report for military duty during WWII. All six were in service at the same time. Ota died in 1969 and Bob died in 1976.

Charles E. Fuhr (born 1927) married Mae Belle Sparkman on Oct. 15, 1947. She was born in 1928 to Ross and Sallie Sparkman, who lived on a farm northeast of Republic. Charlie and Mae Belle had three children: twins-Judy and Jerry (born 1951) and another daughter Karen (born 1960).

There are eight grandchildren from this

family (four boys, four girls), one great-granddaughter and two great-grandsons. Most all have been or are currently being educated in the Republic school system.

John Ernest and Louisa, Otto and Margaret Jane, Robert and Ota Fuhr, along with their children and grandchildren lie at rest in the Kerr Cemetery in the southwest corner of Greene County, southwest of Republic, MO. *Submitted by Charles and Mae Belle Fuhr.*

### Wanting To Remember
*by Mae Belle Fuhr*

Wanting to remember them will preserve our priceless treasure.

Wanting to remember their fight for freedom from fear of seizure.

Wanting to remember their joys bring all of us much pleasure.

Wanting to remember their courage that we too be granted double measure.

**FUHR/SPARKMAN** - Charles Elbert Fuhr (Aug. 29, 1927) is the youngest child of Robert W. (1891-1976) and Ota (Brashears) Fuhr(1894-1969). The family home was at McKinley, MO, where his father had a blacksmith shop. Their children were Vesta, Kyle, Ted, Boyd, Clara, Ray, Leo, Joe, Bill and "Charlie". The family lived on different farms, then moved to live with Charlie's grandparents, Otto and Jane (Kerr) Fuhr, on Huckleberry Ridge in southwestern Greene County and NW of Billings. The younger children then attended St. Joe, a one-room country school.

Charlie's folks moved into Republic to a home on North Walnut in 1944. Robert "Bob" opened a blacksmith, welding, and repair business. The Republic Machine Works was on North Main. Bob had his shop there until 1974, when ill health forced his retirement. In 1975, his building and contents sold at public auction.

*Charles and Mae Belle Fuhr children, grandchildren and great-grandchildren – December 2005.*

Charlie at the age of 17, enlisted in the U.S. Navy in 1945. He already had five brothers serving in WWII - Kyle, Boyd and Ray were in the U.S. Army, and Joe and Bill in the U.S. Navy.

Mae Belle (Sparkman) Fuhr (born Sept. 29, 1928) was born in the family farm home, one and a half miles NE of Republic, that had belonged to her grandparents John A. and Minnie (Roush) Sparkman. Her parents were Ross (1900-1979) and Sallie (Owen) Sparkman (1902-1984). She is the oldest daughter of their five children: John A. (1925-2003), Mae Belle (1928), Junior Ross (1931-1990), Marjorie (1934) and Mary (1936). All attended Mt. Etna, a one-room school located two miles NE of Republic.

After Charlie returned from service in August 1946, he met Mae Belle, who had graduated in May from Republic High School. Charlie and Mae Belle were married Oct. 15, 1947 in Mt. Vernon. Charlie went to welding school under the GI Bill. He worked some in his father's shop and pumped gas at a local station at 16 cents a gallon. He was employed in businesses in Springfield for 45 years as a stainless steel fabricator and retired in 1992.

Mae Belle was a stay-at-home mom to their three children: twins-Judy Mae and Jerry Charles (born July 27, 1951) and another daughter, Karen Melinda (born Nov. 23, 1960). Their children attended Republic schools and graduated 1969 and 1979. Jerry enlisted in the Navy while a junior, and saw service in the Pacific and off the coast of Vietnam, returning in September 1971. He enrolled at SMSU and graduated four years later, working nights at Foremost Dairy. Judy received her degree later, going back after being the mother of three children: Cynthia (1973), Mark (1975) and Matthew (1977) Bruner.

The Fuhr's daughter Karen graduated in May and married in September 1979 to Robert Foster, a son of neighbors, who had moved to Missouri from New Jersey. Bobby had graduated two years earlier. They are the parents of three children: Jason (1980), Jennifer (1982) and Jessica (1986). Their home is on land Karen's great-grandparents owned at the turn of the 20th century on Sparkman Drive.

All their grandchildren attended Republic schools, and now two great-grandsons, Caleb (1993) and his brother Lucas (1999) are attending. One great-granddaughter Regan (1998) is in Rolla schools.

Charlie and Mae Belle equally love and appreciate their extended family: Jerry's wife Cheryl (Morin) and Judy's husband Paul Steward. Also their two granddaughters-in-law, Kara (Dade) and Angie (Hiller) Bruner; two grandsons-in-law, Michael Schulte and Greg Spaethe; and two step grandchildren, Ginger (mother of Regan) and her brother Jeremiah Steward.

The Fuhr family enjoyed planning many vacation trips across the country while the children were living at home. Their home has always been close to Mae Belle's birthplace. They have had the privilege of babysitting their grandchildren and great-grandchildren over the years, leaving them precious memories of fun times together! *Submitted by Jason Foster.*

**FUHR/WARDEN** - Roger Leo Fuhr was born on Jan. 10, 1947 in Springfield, MO. He was the only child born to Robert "Leo" Fuhr (1921-2003) and Geneva Mae Brown Fuhr (1926-1982). Roger attended Republic Schools and graduated in 1965. He attended Missouri State University and graduated in 1969 with a degree in business management. He married Nina Roberta Warden on June 6, 1969 in Springfield, MO.

*Fuhr Family. Front row, l to r: Alex and Abby Fuhr. Center row: Sterling Coker, Roger and Nina Fuhr and Eric Fuhr. Back row: Holly Coker, Dalton Coker and Michelle Fuhr.*

Nina Roberta Warden was born on June 2, 1947 in Elk City, OK. She was the first child of Albert "Reese" Warden (1923) and Roberta May Cruise (1924-1956). She spent her early years in Oklahoma and Texas. She moved to Marshfield, MO in 1960 and graduated from Marshfield High in 1965. Nina's siblings are Tim and Roger.

Shortly after Roger and Nina were married, Roger was drafted into the Army. Nina continued working for Southwestern Bell, where she had worked for five years. She then moved with Roger to Texas and California, where Roger was stationed while receiving training and working in Army hospitals. Nina returned home when Roger was sent to Vietnam.

Roger served as a senior combat medic with an infantry unit of the 101st Airborne Division near the DMZ between North and South Vietnam. For his service he was awarded the Bronze Star, Combat Medical Badge, Army Commendation Medal and numerous unit citations. While serving in Vietnam, their oldest child, Eric Roger Fuhr, was born on Jan. 5, 1971. On March 21, 1973 their second child, Holly Roberta, was born.

Roger and Nina have resided at the northeast Lawrence county farm they named Pleasant Valley Ranch since their marriage in 1969. The old Pleasant Valley Elementary School adjoins the farm. Roger's great-grandfather, Joe Brashears, previously owned this property. It had gotten out of the family for over 50 years until Roger's parents purchased it in 1968. Roger and Nina have since added two adjoining properties to it.

After returning from the Army, Roger was employed with Zenith Electronics in Springfield, MO for 20 years in various management positions. During that time, he made numerous trips to Chicago, IL as a member of a Corporate Task Force to the home office of Zenith Electronics and to the Texas-Mexican border where Zenith eventually relocated its manufacturing operations. Currently, Roger is an employee of American National Property and Casualty Insurance Company in Springfield, MO. He manages the mailing and warehousing operations.

Roger served six years on the Marionville, MO, R-9 School Board. He served two years as president and held other positions as well. He also served on the board for the Republic Farmer's Exchange (MFA), Lawrence County Cattleman's Association and the Kerr Springs Cemetery Board.

Nina was a stay-at-home mom and ran the farm operation while the children were young. In 1983, Nina went to work at the Missouri State Rehabilitation Center in Mt. Vernon, MO. She is now retired and enjoys spending her time with their three grandchildren. *Submitted by Roger Fuhr.*

**GADDY/NORMAN** - Ottie Bervin Gaddy came to Greene County from Ozark County when he was about 22 and met Miss Willas May Norman at a street fair in Republic. They were soon married and lived in Republic until 1959 when they moved to Springfield. Ottie Gaddy had a construction business for many years and was well known in the Republic area. He also worked for years in construction at Branson. He was born Jan. 15, 1915 in Ozark County and died May 19, 1993 at Springfield.

*Ottie Bervin Gaddy and Willas May (Norman) Gaddy.*

Willas May Norman, daughter of William

Willis Norman and Della Estella Lindsey, was born Jan. 25, 1919 in Brookline and died April 13, 2004 in Springfield. Children: Norma Hovey, Jerry Gaddy, Mary Cain, Sandra Calhoun and Paul Gaddy, were all born at Republic. The family always had a large garden, giving opportunity for the children to learn to work, a great blessing in later years. In later life, Mr. and Mrs. Gaddy bought a home in Ozark, then in Nixa where they lived the rest of their lives.

Ottie's parents, Bletcher Holden Gaddy, son of Elisha Holden Gaddy and Willie Marie Looney, was born Jan. 17, 1888 in Walnut Grove, Greene County and died May 25, 1961 at Republic, and Sarah Marvilla Luna, daughter of Jessie Richard Luna and Permelia Jane Beard of Ozark County, was born Dec. 28, 1895 and died Feb. 11, 1917, living all her life in Ozark County. Bletch and Marvilla were the parents of four children: Nola Careful Gaddy White, Eathel Agnes Gaddy Boatright, and Ottie Bervin Gaddy. The 4th child died as an infant along with their mother, Marvilla.

Bletcher married 2nd to Ida May Runion born Feb. 6, 1892 at Gainesville and died Jan. 2, 1968 at Republic. Ida was a good step-mother and grandmother to the children. They lived on a farm near a creek in the Gainesville area where they raised tobacco. It was a simpler life in a simpler time when work was hard but life was sweet. They drew water from a well, never had a refrigerator, kept meat in the smoke house, made soap in a large kettle over a fire in the yard, and had outdoor plumbing. But Ida always had time to take the grandchildren to the creek for a swim, wearing whatever clothes they had on at the time.

Bletcher drove a wagon and a team of horses to the store once a week for supplies up a rough mountain road. The trip took all day. They went to bed at sundown and arose at 4:00 a.m. to prepare for the day and milk the cows. Ida cooked on an old wood burning stove in the corner of the kitchen and her food was wonderful. Her grandchildren have many wonderful memories of her. Bletcher Holden Gaddy's parents moved from Walnut Grove to Ozark County in 1899. *Submitted by Norma Della Gaddy Hovey.*

**GARDNER** – William Marion Gardner was born in 1874 in Pond Creek Township northwest of Republic. His father was George Gardner, his mother Elizabeth Laney Gardner died when Marion was a year old. He was raised by his grandparents, George Marion Laney and Amy Bethia Garoutte Laney.

*Gardner Family, November 1955. Standing l-r: Gladys, Lavon, Alma, Bonnie, Herbert, Ailene, Ola, Noel; seated: Evalee, Rosa and Ferrell.*

Marion's first wife was Rutha Vileta Batson. Lettie died in 1902 leaving two sons, Herschel and Otto. March 13, 1904 Marion and Rosa Elmeda Etheridge were married. Rosa's parents were Caleb and Malinda Logan Etheridge. Their children were Noel Juanita 1905, Ola 1907, Ailene 1908, Herbert 1910, Bonnie Bell 1913, Alma 1915, Lavon 1917, Gladys 1919, Ferrell 1922, and Evalee 1924.

Noel and Jerry Wade's children were Helen and Roy; Ola and Howard Yount's children were Kenneth, Homer, Rose Marion and Mary Margaret; Ailene and Lloyd Shinn's children were Wanda, Vernon, Marcia and Charles; Herbert was married to Oda Fay Tinsley who died at an early age, they had no children; Bonnie and Clyde (Cotton) Wade's children were Juanita, Rosalene and Patricia; Alma and Frank Schmidt's children were Lee Roy and Jimmy; Lavon and Orville Batson's children were Herbert, Donnie, Ray and Leslie; Gladys and Earl Williams' children were Leon, Jim, Bill, Shirley, Johnny, Julia, Linda, Jack, Carl and Kathy; Ferrell and Ronald Williams' children were Debora, Bobby, Donnie, Fay, Wanda and Sharon; Evalee and Lyman Dempsey's son was Rodney.

William Marion Gardner was elected Constable of Pond Creek Township in 1898 with 82 votes. Reverend W.M. Gardner served until his death as a minister of the Methodist Protestant Church. While serving area churches, the family lived in Greene, Stone, Dade and Barry counties. Herbert lived with his parents and cared for them until Marion's death in 1947 and Rosa's death in 1962. Many members of this family are buried at Wade Cemetery.

After the death of Marion and Rosa their children celebrated their birthdays with a big potluck dinner for many years. About 80 members of this family gathered for a reunion June 25, 2005 at the J.R. Martin Park in Republic. Those from California, Oklahoma, Kansas and all points in Missouri enjoyed a great day. *Submitted by Juanita Bridges.*

**GARDNER/LONG** – Richard (Leo) Gardner was born March 19, 1933 at the home of his grandfather and step-grandmother, Marion Richard and Ollie Gardner. The farm was located at what is now the Christian-Greene County Line Road and Highway ZZ. Leo was the son of Ishmael William "Jack" and Lucille Annis (Glidewell) Gardner. Jack was born Sept. 9, 1911, the son of Marion and Alta Gertrude (Pope) Gardner. Gertie died in 1912 and Marion then married Ollie (Robertson) Phillips in 1913, moving to her farm where they lived until their deaths. Lucille was born Aug. 20, 1913, the daughter of William Davis and LaVada Emaline (Stiffler) Glidewell. Jack and Lucille were married Oct. 31, 1931 and in the late 1930s purchased a 40-acre farm from Cordelia Scroggs. After losing their first child, Marcella at birth, they raised their four sons: Leo, Lendsie, Archie and Jim there until the farm was purchased by the government to become a part of the Wilson's Creek Battleground.

*Bud Glidewell home circa 1910.*

Leo Gardner married Vaunda Noreene (Long) Gardner on May 6, 1955. Vaunda was born April 27, 1932 in Springfield, MO, the daughter of B.L. "Buck" and Laura Clarice (Franks) Long. Buck and Clarice also had one son, Lee Russell, who died shortly after birth. Buck was born June 11, 1912 in Springfield, MO, the son of Charles W. and Della (Riley) Long. Clarice was born March 9, 1912, the daughter of James Russell and Rosa (Ennis) Franks. Clarice was born in Arkansas and after being left an orphan at the age of nine, she moved to Springfield, MO where she was raised by an aunt and uncle.

In 1938 Buck and Clarice purchased an 80-acre farm from the William B. "Bud" Glidewell estate. Bud was the paternal grandfather of Lucille Annis (Glidewell) Gardner. Bud Glidewell's parents were Wilson Peter and Rebecca (Jennings) Glidewell. Wilson Peter's parents were Davis Peter and Ann Lavina (Perkins) Glidewell. Rebecca's parents were William and Ardelia Ann (Manley) Jennings. The Jennings and Manley families had owned the farm and surrounding land during the Civil War. Buck and Clarice Long lived on the battleground farm until 1950 when they sold the land to Dick O'Connor, who then opened a Civil War Museum on the property. The farm is now a part of the Wilson's Creek Battleground.

Leo and Vaunda grew up as neighbors attending Capernium School and later Republic High School together. As children, a favorite past time was collecting Civil War bullets and Minie balls that came to the surface in their yards and fields after heavy rains. One of the favorite get-togethers for the Gardners and Longs, along with the Ray Hampton family, was hamburgers and home-made ice cream. Buck had been a chef as a young man and no one could fry better hamburgers than he. Buck and Ray farmed together and raised cucumbers for the local pickle plant, at one time having about eight acres planted along Wilson Creek. The children from the three families picked cucumbers during the summer for their spending money.

Leo served his country in the Army during the Korean War, and a week after returning home from Korea, he and Vaunda were married. They raised their family in the Battlefield, MO area. Their children, Brenda Kay Gardner, Mark Allen Gardner and LaVada Ann (Gardner) Mooneyham Carnahan graduated from Republic High School. They have three grandchildren: Rance William Gardner, Zane Leroy Gardner, and Alysha Nikolet Mooneyham. *Submitted by Vaunda (Long) Gardner.*

**GAROUTTE** - Michael Garoutte came from France in 1775 in his own ship to help the 13 colonies in the Revolutionary War. William D. being his son, the father of Warren W. Garoutte came to Missouri in 1840. He had a large family.

*Back: Nerva, Harry, Anna, Warren, Pearly and John; front: Mark and Rosa Garoutte.*

Warren's son, Mark Garoutte, married Rosa Blades, daughter of Gideon and Rachel (Ray) Blades. They lived on the Christian and Greene County line where they raised their family. Warren wed Clejo Bray, Nerva wed Elisha Dean. Pearly wed Melton Ratio Dean. Melton and Elisha were brothers. Harry wed Leola Williams.

189

Leonard wed Pearl Watson. Cecil John wed Delores Wright. Anna wed Albert Wilson. One daughter died at birth. Mark Garoutte and his wife Rosa and the baby daughter are buried at Wade Chapel Cemetery near Republic, MO.

Warren, John and Anna are the only ones to stay in Missouri. Nerva, Pearly, Harry and Leonard all moved to Kansas. *Submitted by Sondra Berry.*

**GAROUTTE/BABINGTON** - In 1837, James Smith Garoutte moved his family to the Pond Creek Township in western Greene County six years after his wife Mary (Babington) Garoutte died. James donated land for the Garoutte Cemetery. Two of his 11 children, Nancy and William, remained in the area.

Nancy Caroline, the 5th child of James and Mary, married Richard Owens. They had 11 children. Among descendants staying in this area, Nancy Elizabeth married Thomas Tolivar Brown. From this lineage, numerous Browns and LaFollettes remain in the Republic area.

*Back Row, l-r: Ethel Sifferman and Homer Garoutte; front row: Louis Garoutte, Cecil Fugitt (J.W.'s mother), Hettie Ghan (Gimmie) and Hershel Garoutte.*

William Babington, the 4th child of James and Mary, married Amanda Hazleton in 1841 and by this union five children were born. After Amanda's death in 1857, he married Mehetable Tannahill and by this union nine children were born.

By the age of 21, William was a Justice of the Peace and was teaching school. In 1849, William and three brothers crossed the plains for the "Gold Rush." He returned in time for the Civil War, at which time he was offered and refused a brigadier general's commission. In 1862 he served with General Price, but returned to Greene County the same year to serve as Provost Marshall. He was taken prisoner and held captive for two years.

While in St. Louis in 1874, a hotel burned causing a large number of deaths. This led William to invent a fire escape. He sold the patent for $2,000. He also invented a corn planter ("Daddy" of the present-day corn planter) in a patent dated July 6, 1875 and a cotton seed planter in a patent dated Feb. 10, 1880. He also invented the grain binder "Knotter," but an employee in the machine shop where William was developing the prototype stole the idea. William spent his later years until his death in 1892 on the 560-acre Big Spring farm writing for the Journal of Agriculture.

William's 7th child, Thomas Waldo, moved his family from Stone County to the Big Spring farm after William's death.

Thomas had one of the larger milking operations in the area, largely because the spring allowed the milk to be cooled until it could be transported.

Thomas and his wife, Sallie Robertson had eight children: Homer, Ethel May, Herschel, Hettie, Lewis, Cecil and twins-Eric and Opal Jeanne.

Ethel married Roy Sifferman and they had two children, Don and Helen. They owned a farm near the Garoutte Cemetery.

Herschel married Mildred McCoy and they had one child, Mary Eloise. They lived near Halltown.

Hettie married Clarence Ghan and they had one child, Kathryn Mae. They owned a farm south of Republic at Lynn and County Line Road. Clarence and neighbor Carl Bennett built the rock barn which is still standing.

Lewis "Lou" married June Thigpein and they had four children: Jay D., Eric B. "E.B.," Francis and Glen.

Cecil married Leonard Fugitt and they had one son, James Waldo (JW or "Sheep").

Opal married Harold Swanson and they had one son, Harold Jr.

Eric married Marlynn Miller and they adopted Eric. B., Lou's son. *Submitted by Rusty Swift.*

**GAROUTTE/HICKS** - The Garoutte family has been in or around Republic for more than 100 years. Many may remember Sheral Joseph "Gose" Garoutte, who owned and operated the Locker Plant on Main Street from 1951 until his death in 1965. Gose Garoutte also served as a city council member and as mayor of Republic from 1957-62. He was very active in the community's Little League program. The ballpark at Hines St. and Hampton Ave. is named after Gose.

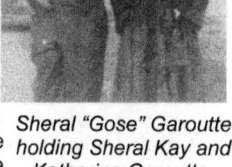

*Sheral "Gose" Garoutte holding Sheral Kay and Katherine Garoutte.*

Gose's father, Joseph Mathias "Matt" Garoutte, was raised on a farm on Farm Road 57, north of Billings. Matt married Mary Ellen Etheridge in 1904 and they had five children: Laurence, who died at a very young age; Elva Emery, who died in 1945; Gose who died in 1965; Melvin Anderson, who died in 1983; and Olive Louelia Jackson, who lives in the area. Melvin married Pauline Maness and had one son, Jimmy. Olive married Earl Jackson and had two children, Billy Joe and Betty Jane Tyndall.

*Todd Steere, James Steere, Sheral Kay Steere and Doug Steere, April 21, 1986, James and Sheral's 25th anniversary.*

Matt and Mary owned a large strawberry farm just west of Republic, where pickers came in wagons, camped, and picked berries. The farm was lost during the depression when many of the banks closed. The family moved to Republic. Later they bought a two-story home on Walnut and rented upstairs rooms to many of the young women who came to work at Woods Garment Factory. A major fire destroyed that home in 1945 and it was renovated.

In 1941, Gose married Katherine Hicks, of Springfield. Gose and Katherine operated the Locker Plant together, selling hamburger for 55 cents a pound, making their own sausage, rendering lard, and curing bacon and hams. Customers could also rent lockers, or refrigerated drawers, at the Locker Plant to store meats or frozen goods. A locker rented for $12-15 a year. The Locker Plant was next door to Logan's Market, operated by Lester Bud Logan, who was Gose's cousin. Katherine, who is now retired and resides in Republic, remembers the many calls that neighbors would place directly to the mayor's home. The population of the town at that time was small, around 1,000 people, but that was enough to keep the phone ringing. Katherine herself was later employed by the city from 1975-85, serving as the assistant city collector. She was also previously employed as a sales clerk in Springfield.

*Mary Ellen Etheridge Garoutte and Joseph Mathias "Matt: Garoutte at their home on Walnut St.*

Gose and Katherine had one child, Sheral Kay. Sheral Kay married James Steere in 1961 after their graduation from Republic High School. Sheral Kay is presently the city collector for Republic. James worked at the Locker Plant for a few years and also as a firefighter in Springfield. James later retired from Roadway, Inc. and presently works part-time for St. John's Regional Health Center. Sheral Kay and James had two children, Doug Steere and Todd Steere. Doug is an attorney with the United States Court of Appeals for the Federal Circuit in Washington, D.C. Todd has a master's degree in social work and is a social worker. *Submitted by Sheral Kay Steere.*

**GAROUTTE/MCDANIEL** - Samuel Garoutte was the ninth child of Michael Garoutte and Sophia Smith, born in New Jersey in 1796, married Jane Reynolds in 1822. They came to Missouri in 1837 being the first settler in the area, settling three miles north of Billings on the old Republic, Billings road, living nine months in an old Tennessee wagon bed set on two logs (according to Garoutte History, by Thiesen). They had 16 children, Michael their third child born in 1827, came with them at the age of 10 years.

*Charley Garoutte and Ava (McDaniel) Garoutte.*

Michael married Elizabeth Smith and farmed land next to his father. He served in the Civil War, Company B, Unit 15 Missouri Cavalry, with the Union, at the age of 37. They had six children, Columbus "Lum" Garoutte being their second child born in 1854, who married Sarah Cavener in 1880. They had seven children, Charles Elmer Garoutte being their first child, born in 1880. When Charles was four days old, a cyclone blew the house completely away, with Charlie being found in a feather bed in the middle of a field. Baby and mother were unharmed but Grandmother Cavener received a back injury and was a cripple for the rest of her life.

*Charley Garoutte.*

Charles married Ava McDaniel, daughter of Ransom T. and Eliza (Jameson) McDaniel in 1908. They had six children. Charles purchased and farmed land, which was the home place of Anthony Garoutte. The farm was located on the banks of Pickerel Creek northwest of Republic (currently owned by the Wayne Butler family). Children of Charles and Ava Garoutte were Dollie (Foust) born in 1908, Gladys (Grimmett) 1912, Lloyd 1914, Jim 1915 and two children died as infants. Charley and Ava worked together with their children and were very prosperous on this farm having purchased two area farms for a total of approximately 600 acres. Ava worked side by side with her husband raising large flocks of turkeys while on the farm. She was an avid homemaker and cook.

Upon leaving the farm in 1945 and selling most of his farm equipment and livestock, the auction was one of the largest the area had seen. He kept one cow and his Farmall (McCormick Derring) tractor and equipment to do custom work after relocating to the southwest corner of Harrison and Hampton Streets in Republic. Charley continued custom plowing and cultivating until his early 70s. He and Ava had one of the most beautiful and well kept gardens in the city, and a well kept barn lot, raising their own beef, chickens and produce.

Ava took care of all the produce from the garden, butchered chickens for freezing, and was a wonderful cook. She loved to sew on her treadle sewing machine, piecing quilts by hand, but crocheting was her most loved. Every item she crocheted was to perfection. She crocheted for several different individuals upon their request, especially Thelma Plummer with Plummers Dry Goods Store where she purchased all of her supplies. Charley and Ava were loved by family and friends. Everyone enjoyed watching their beautiful yard and flowers, especially one rose which covered the entire east side of their house. Charlie lived to the age of 85 years and Ava lived to be 96, both are buried in Wade Chapel Cemetery. *Submitted by Terry Bacon*

**GARTON/INMAN** – Ralph Sterling "Jake" Garton was born Sept. 3, 1908 in Springfield, MO. His father, Jacob Warren Garton Jr., was born Feb. 18, 1862 in Greene County, MO and died Jan. 7, 1933. His mother, Awilda Owen, was born May 6, 1872 and died March 20, 1942. His parents were married January 31, 1865. Awilda was the daughter of Charles Baker Owen and Nancy Caroline (McCroskey) Owen.

Jake attended the Crenshaw School in Springfield along with his younger sister Thelma. Aunt Thelma said Jake was held back from 2nd grade for fighting. The teacher tied a string from her apron to his overalls and told Jake if the string ever broke he would get in big trouble. Jake caught up and graduated the 8th grade with his classmates. As was the case with many large families in those days, they could only afford to send every other child to high school or college.

*Ralph Sterling Garton and Grace Pauline Garton.*

Jake grew up in a large 2-story farmhouse on South Kansas Avenue with five brothers and three sisters. He married Grace Pauline Inman on Oct. 29, 1927. She was born Feb. 3, 1910. Her father was John Henry Inman, son of John Watts Inman and Isabell Carrol. Her mother was Sophrena McCroskey, daughter of Matthew Carson McCroskey and Priscilla Jane Harris.

Five children were born to Grace and Jake: Roberta "Bobbie" married Dwight "Mac" McGuire. Bobbie's children are Cindy, Corki and Penny. Dixie Joan married Robert "Bob" Reynolds. Dixie's children are Paula, Chuck, Kenny and Pam. Sterling "Wayne" married Shirley Ann Walker. Wayne's children are Steve, Kathy, Laurie, Tim, Brad, Jamie and Stacy. John married Janice Earls. John's children are Angie, Greg and Kayla. Rick married Lura. Rick's children are Marty, Michelle, Mike and Melissa.

Jake and Grace moved to Republic, MO around 1945 and purchased a farm. Jake did custom hay work and raised cattle. He purchased real estate and built apartments, Grace worked at the Hagle Garment Factory even though she graduated from Draughon Business College with a teaching certificate. Jake ran for county commissioner at one time and carried the Democratic ticket but lost the election.

Jake's first cousin was Mickey Owen, former Greene County Sheriff and St. Louis Cardinal's catcher. Their grandfather was Charles Baker Owen, Civil War hero and fourth Greene County Sheriff. Jake's son Wayne remembers listening to the Cardinals on the radio and how exciting it was when Mickey would come and visit during the off season and sit by the wood stove visiting with Jake.

In later years Jake built a home on Maplewood Lane in Republic near Wayne and John's homes. The grandkids spent time helping out on the farm with Grandpa Jake. They sometimes got to drive the hay truck in the fields and play in the barn. Their moms would protest when Grandpa dropped them off and they had a little pinch of chew, but it was cool to spit! Grandma Grace always made great meals. They were wonderful grandparents. Jake drove a Republic school bus for many years and all the kids loved him.

Jake passed away June 9, 1977 and Grace passed away December 30, 1977. They will never be forgotten. *Submitted by Tim Garton.*

**GARTON/RAMBO** – Robert and Bertha Rambo were married in 1930. They lived with Bertha's dad for a short time, then moved to the area west of Brookline, MO, onto the Adams farm. They arranged with the Adams family to be caregivers to the elderly Mrs. Adams for use of the house and land. While living in this area, they became close friends with Buddy "J.B." and Elsie Garton, who were the parents of Glen Garton.

In 1936, a son Garry Rambo was born and in 1938, a daughter Donna was born. The Rambos moved their family to the farm on Farm Road 190, where Garry continues to live today. Garry and Donna started school at the country school named Green Ridge in 1944, and both graduated in 1952. By this time it had been decided by the Republic school district to consolidate the one-room schools. Thus, Robert Rambo bought the old schoolhouse and moved it across John Young's pasture to his farm, where it remains today. The one room appeared so small after the move compared to the large size it seemed when everyone attended the one-room school.

While Garry and Donna attended school at Green Ridge, they made a lot of friends in Battlefield. To name a few: Rosalind Kelly, Lynn and Richard White, Junior, Jimmie and George Earl Sparkman, Landon Adams and Harold Lee Morrow. The two of them walked to school together each day with Carolyn and Marion Zulauf, who lived just across the field. Donna's favorite teacher was Mrs. Sally Patterson.

In 1952 Garry and Donna started Republic High School, this was a big step for them. The next four years were very exciting for them. They created many good memories and established good friendships. After graduation, Donna and Glen Garton were married, moving to Kansas City. The two worked at the University of Kansas Medical Center until late summer 1959, when they returned to Springfield. Donna started working for Springfield City Utilities in the customer billing section. She continued employment with CU for 20 years leaving in 1983, becoming a housekeeper, which she continues part time.

In 1972, Glen and Donna's daughter Lorena was born. She married Paul R. Wood in 1996. They have one son Austin Paul who was born in 1999. They live in Rogers, AR. Glen and Donna spend as much time with their grandson as possible.

Glen retired in 1997 and Donna is semi-retired. They have lived on Dayton Street in Springfield for 41 years. Their parents, Robert and Bertha Rambo and Buddy and Elsie Garton, are all deceased. Robert died on May 3, 2004, and the tornado came through on May 4, 2004 destroying all of the timber, but leaving his farm buildings.

Glen and Donna enjoy their retirement, keeping busy with family plus sharing weekly in their congregation meetings at the Kingdom Hall and their door-to-door ministry, which they truly enjoy. They continue to ask, "Where have the last 50 years gone?" *Submitted by Donna (Rambo) Garton.*

**GEILERT** – Paul and Elsa Geilert and Elsa's Mother, Emilie Auguste (Fritsch) Guenther, immigrated from Greiz, Germany in 1913. They sailed aboard the SS *Lincoln,* arriving at Ellis Island, NY on Sept. 27, 1913.

They traveled to Dexter, MO, where Elsa's brother Edward and family were living. In 1915 they moved to Springfield, MO living on Elizabeth Street. Paul worked for the Frisco Railroad. In 1924 they decided to purchase a farm in Greene County. Their farm was located three miles northeast of Republic, MO. They farmed and lived the rest of their life there.

*Paul and Elsa Geilert.*

191

They had five children: Nellie Ackerman, born May 29, 1914, died March 6, 1985; Emil, born Aug. 4, 1916; Herbert, born Dec. 4, 1917, died March 5, 1996 and buried in Harrington Cemetery; Helen McGinnis, born July 23, 1925, died Aug. 2, 2003 and buried in Harrington Cemetery; Juanita Hamilton, born Jan. 13, 1928.

Paul was born May 6, 1888 in Doula, Germany and died June 19, 1978. Elsa was born July 9, 1890 in Irchwitz, Germany and died Oct. 26, 1984. They are buried in Harrington Cemetery. They became citizens of the United States of America on Dec. 9, 1919. They both are listed on the American Immigration Wall of Honor at Ellis Island, NY.

Elsa'a Mother returned to Greiz, Germany in the late 1920s. *Submitted by Juanita Hamilton.*

**GHAN** - Thomas Andrew and Jennie Guthrie Ghan moved from Christian County to a farm south of Republic at County Line Road and Lynn Street with children Charles Curtis, William Leslie, Clarence Talmadge and Edith. When Thomas' health deteriorated, he sold the farm to Clarence. Clarence married Republic native Hettie Garroutte and they had one daughter Kathryn Mae. The farm is noted these days by the old rock barn built by Clarence with the help of neighbor Carl Bennett near the site of the homestead log cabin. The rocks for the barn came off the fields - imagine finding rocks in an Ozark's field!

Besides milking cows, Hettie raised turkeys and dressed and sold them for Thanksgiving. They had a big garden with watermelon and strawberry patches. Clarence was in charge of the watermelons which he would trade to Mr. McDonald, owner of the Model grocery store in Springfield, for groceries.

Kathryn walked to school many days until bus service began in 1935. The school was a two-story brick building, built with bricks made from the brick factory in Republic. The same bricks were used to build the Hood Methodist Church.

Kathryn's grandson, Cory Swift, salvaged bricks from the sidewalk in front of the Hood Church to build a prayer garden for Cory's Eagle Scout project.

Kathryn met Bob Swift from Billings in 1937 and the two married in 1941. The following was written by Kathryn before their 50th wedding anniversary.

"In my day, eight grades were in one building. Mrs. Alice Roop was the principal. Some of my favorite teachers in grade school were Daphnie Thurman Wells and Edna Frame. We were assigned certain areas to play and had a dirt tennis court. None of us turned out to be a Chris Evert.

"I played clarinet in the community band directed by Bud Thurman. We had summer concerts at Republic every Saturday night and practice every Tuesday. When school started we only played for basketball games. Several people came from Billings to play in the band. That's where I met Bob. He didn't play in the band, but after practice we would always go to Sellers to dance to records. Since his dad owned the phone company in Billings, he would call me often. One day he called at school. The superintendent said, 'Ghan, it's your Billings boy friend.' I blushed a crimson red.

"My home economics teacher was my cousin Cletis Baker Lentz. We made uniforms for class. Sewing wasn't my favorite, but my mother sewed beautifully and made most of my clothes. I was in lots of plays and played Miss Tillie in our senior play, *"Miss Tillie Goes To Town."* Our practices were lots of fun. For graduation, the folks gave me a train trip to New York to the Worlds Fair in 1938.

"I went to Drury College for two years and it was nice, but I was in love with Bob and didn't put my heart in school." *Submitted by Larry Swift.*

**GLIDEWELL** – Wilson Peter Glidewell homesteaded a large plot of land from the government before the Civil War. He had come from Halifax, VA through Tennessee where he married a Cherokee Indian by the name of Sarah Perkins. He was a farmer. Their son Peter Wilson "Bud" Glidewell married Rebecca Jennings whose father was W.P. Jennings. Their son William David

*Jack Glidewell, born Oct. 8, 1917.*

"W.D." Glidewell first married Ida Pratt from the Elwood area and they had two sons, Wilson Peter and Charles Thomas. After she died, he married Lavada Stiffler from Nixa whose parents had built the first log cabin in Nixa. Lavada had lost her husband (John Johnson) and had one son, Gaylord Johnson. W.D. and Lavada had six more children: Eula, Lucille, Emma, Albert "Jack," Archie and Vernie "Jiggs," making nine children in all.

They lived during the depression. If they didn't raise it, they didn't have it. The boys caught rabbits and other small animals. They walked or rode a horse to Republic to sell animal furs for a dime apiece. Jack's first job was weighing tomatoes when the farmers brought them to the tomato canning factory located northeast of the train depot in Battlefield. All the Glidewell children went to Capernium School.

Jack was in the Army in WWII for four years and seven months. He served under Gen. MacArthur and spent 45 days in a fox hole in New Guinea with only one "D-Ration" a day. This ration was like a candy bar with all the vitamins they needed in it. Fifty years after the war, Jack was awarded the Congressional Medal of Honor and the flag flew over the U.S. Capitol in his honor on Nov. 17, 2005.

After the war, Jack came home and bought a farm which included battleground land known as "Bloody Hill," and built a Grade A milk barn. In 1952 he had to sell the farm to the state so the Wilson's Creek Battlefield could be established. He then moved to Battlefield, where he was a charter member of the First Baptist Church of Battlefield. The church started as a Mission in an old store building belonging to T. Young, an early settler of Greene County. Jack married Myrtle Trogdon.

Before retirement Jack had been a farmer, grocery man and worked for Springfield public schools in charge of maintenance of Kickapoo High School.

One of Jack's great-great-grandfathers was Caleb Manley. *Submitted by Albert "Jack" Glidewell.*

**GOLD** - Charles Gold was born in Crane, MO in 1937, son of Charley Efton and Sarah Gray Gold. He attended school in Crane then attended Draughon's Business College in Springfield, MO, and joined the Army in 1958. He met Nellie Heldstab (born 1940 in Tuscumbia, MO), the daughter of George Rayford and Anna Mabel Martin Heldstab, while she was attending Draughon's Business College in 1958.

After completing his service in the Army in 1962, where he received his computer programming skills, Charles returned to Springfield and began his 27 years of service as assistant manager, then manager of the computer department at Associated Wholesale Grocers in

*Front Row: Nellie and Charles Gold; back: Gregory and Cynthia "Cyndi" Gold – 1986.*

Springfield. He married Nellie in July 1962. The six years before his death in October 1995, he worked for Cuddy Farms.

Nellie attended school in Eldon, MO, before moving to Springfield. She worked as a medical secretary for Drs. Napper, Anthony & Sturdevant for seven years and then served as business office manager for Litton & Giddings Radiological Associates for 31 years. After retirement, she went back to work part-time as a secretary for St. John's Hospital.

In 1962 Charles and Nellie bought their first home in Republic on Eagan Avenue from Howard "Wormey" Eagan, and in 1967 had Wormey build their final home on Buxton Lane.

They had two children who attended the Republic school system from K through 12. Gregory Lee, born in 1967, graduated from Drury University in 1990 and married Kathryn Sitzes (from Farmington, MO) in 2002. Cynthia Marie, born in 1972, married Mark Giacin in 1995. They had a daughter, Madison Paige, born in 1996, and divorced in 2000. Cyndi graduated from Missouri State University in 2006.

Charles and Nellie loved the Republic community, their neighbors, the school system and their church home, Republic First Christian Church. Charles and Nellie both served as deacons in their church and were supportive parents of their childrens' scouting, band, music, poms, and dancing activities. Charles served as a Republic city councilman for several years. Nellie was active in the Springfield Chapter of the Medical Group Managers Association and the Missouri State, Midwest Regional and National Radiological Business Managers Association. Nellie is still living in the family home, is a member of the Republic Business and Community Women's group and enjoys being a grandmother.

Charles was a brother to Louise Harris (husband Floyd) who lived in the Republic community along with their children, Harold, Cheryl and Donnie. Louise and Floyd were a strong influence in Charles and Nellie's decision to make their home in the Republic community. *Submitted by Nellie Gold.*

**GRAY/BROWN** – Henry Van Gray (born Feb. 1, 1926) and Norma Francis Brown (born Nov. 28,1931, died July 8, 2003) were united in marriage on Jan. 12, 1949 in Eureka Springs, AR. Henry is the 4th child of Roy C. and Ava O. Skelton Gray of rural Halltown. Norma is the 11th child of Smith and Rose Belle Newton Brown. To this union two daughters were born, Vandeana June (born Dec. 7, 1949) and Debra Jean (born Nov. 3, 1952).

On Jan. 12, 1949, Norma rode the school bus to her brother's house, just down the road from home, and got off of the bus meeting Henry to elope. They drove to Arkansas in Ernie Gray's (Henry's brother) car. He was their witness too. They returned to Republic in time to go to the weekly Wednesday night wrestling matches at the Shrine Mosque. They began their life together living in Springfield on the family farm east of Halltown, and settling in Republic. Henry began working for Producers Creamery (now Dairy Farmers of America) in October 1949 and retired 39+ years later at age 62.

Norma (Brown) Gray and Henry "Van" Gray.

Norma worked for Brooks Potato Chips, Henningson Egg, Royal McBee, and several garment factories in Republic and Springfield, retiring at 65 after being diagnosed with cancer.

They always put out a big garden and prepared for the winter. Henry's most noted crop was the large strawberry patch he harvested each spring. Henry liked to garden and refinish furniture while Norma liked to crochet, knit and sew. Many were blessed to have a dishcloth or other item she made by hand. They always enjoyed the Fall Festival, as their home was open to everyone. They always had a pot of chili and a ham cooked for all to share. Grandchildren were of great joy to Henry and Norma. They were blessed with five grandchildren: Brandi Renee Core (born May 19, 1974, died May 22, 1974); Douglas Grant Wilson (born June 24, 1974); Amber Dawn Core (born Nov. 24, 1975); Dustin Anthony Wilson (born June 14, 1978) and Autumn Brooke Core (born June 22, 1984). Henry and Norma spent many miles and hours on the road to see the grandchildren in most events in which they participated.

Vandeana married Andy O. Core on Jan. 8, 1971 in Republic and Debra married Dale Wilson on July 17, 1971, divorcing in 1984. Debra later married Terry L. Cochran on Aug. 28, 1987. One day they found a note in their front door that read "Grandpa and Grandma, this is your starving college grandson. If it would not break you and put you in the poor house, I would like to have lunch with you. If it's ok, I'll be at Mom's house, if not, I'll just eat some bread and water. Love, Doug." Needless to say, Doug didn't have bread and water for lunch.

Many fun times were had pulling pranks and growing up in the Gray family, but you knew you were loved and had what was needed. Both grandparents were a big part of their lives as well as brothers and sisters and their families. Those were the more simple times in life that one reflects back on as the Good Ole Days. What great memories. *Submitted by Van Gray.*

**GRAY/DAVIS** - Joe Emmett Gray (born July 15, 1887, died Jan. 11, 1971) and his wife Hollie Jane Davis (born March 18, 1893, died Jan. 20, 1990) lived on a farm adjoining his parent's farm in the Wilson's Creek Battlefield area prior to purchasing a farm in Christian County east of the Wise Hill area on the road now named Honeysuckle in April 1917. They farmed and had dairy cattle before transitioning to beef cattle in later years. In the late 1960s Emmett and Hollie moved to Republic and lived on Brooks Street until their deaths. They had met at a last-day-of-school social at the old Sharon School, and their romance began the next night when Emmett came to Hollie's parents' home with a friend for a neighborhood music party. They were married on Nov. 26, 1913 while sitting in their buggy, and they enjoyed 57 years together.

*Emmett and Hollie at their 57th anniversary in 1970. Back: Dallas and Elizabeth Nelson Gray; front: Emmett Gray, Jane Gray Smith and Hollie Davis Gray.*

Emmett's parents were Josiah Jefferson Gray (born Jan. 16, 1851, died Dec. 23, 1922) and Arena Jane Russell (born Oct. 5, 1852, died Sept. 25, 1924). Josiah's parents were George Washington Gray and Sarah Jane Edgar. Arena was the daughter of J.N. Russell and Nancy Elizabeth Grimmer. Both families settled in Greene County after arriving from Tennessee (see Gray/Russell).

Hollie was the oldest daughter of Christian County natives Barney Wilson Davis (born Aug. 21, 1867, died May 30, 1956) and Harriet Hawkins O'Dell (born July 20, 1872, died Sept. 2, 1963) (see Davis/O'Dell).

The Grays had one son, Dallas Barney (born Dec. 20, 1914, died Nov. 4, 1992). Dallas married Elizabeth Grace Nelson (born Oct. 4, 1933, died Aug. 21, 1992 (see Nelson/Maples) who grew up on a neighboring farm, daughter of Edgar Elijah Nelson (born June 30, 1900, died Aug. 23, 1979) and Ethel Ruth Maples (born March 4, 1898, died Feb. 3, 1981) on Dec. 16, 1944. They were married in their automobile because Rev. Blades' child was ill, so they could not go into his house. They spent their 48 years together in a home built on the Gray farm on Honeysuckle Road.

As a young man Dallas worked at the Republic Farmers Exchange. Later, in addition to farming, Dallas worked at Producers Creamery/Mid-America Dairies until his retirement. He then enjoyed his hobby of gardening while he produced a large variety of fruits and vegetables for the family. He also enjoyed keeping hives of bees as had been passed down from his mother and grandfather, Barney Davis. Elizabeth taught briefly at Ozark and Marionville schools before spending over 30 years teaching in the Clever Schools, primarily in the fourth grade. Elizabeth was a wonderful seamstress and also enjoyed crocheting and quilting.

The Grays were devoted parents to their daughter, Jane Ruth Gray Smith (born Nov 22, 1948). Jane followed her mother into the field of education. She earned bachelor's, master's, and specialist's degrees from Southwest Missouri State University, and she spent her entire career as a teacher and elementary counselor in the Republic Schools. She retired in 1997 with 27 years of service and continued to work part time for the Republic Schools doing individual testing. Jane moved to Republic in 1979 and was a member of the founding board of the Republic Community Foundation. Jane married Walter Luther Smith (born Dec. 8, 1934, died Dec. 23, 1999) on June 10, 1983. His children are Douglas Allen (born Jan. 14, 1959); David Elliott (born April 30, 1961); and Diane Adele, (born Dec. 19, 1963). Diane married Brian Corbett Buckner (born Sept. 2, 1967) on Sept. 14, 1996. Her children are Nichole Gayle Bolin (born June 6, 1986) and Ian Bradley Buckner (born Nov. 3, 1997). (see Smith, Walter Luther). *Submitted by Jane Smith*

**GRAY/RUSSELL** – Josiah Jefferson Gray (born Jan. 16, 1851, died Dec. 23, 1922) was a second generation Greene County farmer who was born in the area that was to become Wilson's Creek National Battlefield in Greene County. His parents were George Washington Gray and Sarah Jane Edgar. His father was born in Tennessee and moved to Greene County in 1833. George settled in the area where he was among the first pioneers to clear the land and establish a farm. He died about 1906. Josiah's grandfather, Samuel Gray, was a native of Ireland, and he immigrated with his father to America soon after the Revolutionary War.

*Josiah Gray family in 1898. Back: Emmett, John, Ada, Emma; front: Josiah, Bill and Avena.*

Josiah was 10 years old at the time of the Battle of Wilson's Creek. Family stories indicated that he stood on General Lyon's horse where it lay at Bloody Hill. Josiah married Arena Jane Russell (born Oct. 5, 1852, died Sept. 25, 1924) on Aug. 22, 1878. Her parents, J.N. Russell and Nancy Elizabeth Grimmer, came to Greene County from Tennessee in the early 1840s. Josiah and Arena bought their own farm of 120 acres in 1882. It was a part of the Wilson's Creek Battlefield area southwest of what is now ZZ Highway and Farm Road 188. On "The Oak Hill Stock Farm" Josiah raised cattle and hogs. He also was involved in law enforcement as a constable in the Brookline Township.

*Gray grandsons, double cousins Dallas Gray and J.B. Gray – 1972.*

Josiah and Arena were the parents of five children who lived to be adults. Their oldest son, John T. (born in 1880) married Margaret L. McNabb in 1901. John farmed in Stone and Greene counties and served as a constable while they lived in Stone County. John applied his farming skills in orange groves after he moved with his family to California. He also worked with his sons in the heating and air conditioning business. John's sons were Earl V., Archie and Theodore.

Joe Emmett (born June 15, 1887, died Jan. 11, 1971) married Hollie Jane Davis (born March 18, 1893, died Jan. 20, 1990) on Nov. 24, 1913. Emmett's son, Dallas Barney (born Dec. 20, 1914, died Nov. 3, 1992) married Elizabeth Grace Nelson (born Oct. 4, 1922, died Aug. 23, 1992). Granddaughter, Jane Ruth Gray Smith (born Nov. 22, 1948) (see Gray/Davis and Davis/O'Dell).

William Jefferson (born June 12, 1893, died Feb. 1, 1964) married Laura "Vesta" Davis (born Aug. 19, 1897, died Nov. 27, 1954) on Dec. 15, 1918 (see Davis/O'Dell). Bill and Vesta lived for many years on the farm where Vesta was born that belonged to her parents, Barney and Harriett Davis. They later purchased their own farm on what is now Highway TT. Bill and Vesta then bought another farm and moved to Highway N just north of Republic where they farmed and managed an apple orchard. Bill and Vesta had three children: Juanita, J.B., and Annabelle. Juanita Lucille (born Dec. 20, 1923, died April 5, 2002) married Lloyd Thomas Evatt (born Jan. 23, 1922) on April 6, 1945. Juanita and Lloyd lived for many years on the northeast corner of Elm and Lynn Streets in Republic before moving to Springfield.

*Gray sons and spouses, l-r: Bill and Vesta Davis Gray, Emmett and Hollie Davis Gray, John and Maggie McNabb Gray.*

J.B. (born July 22, 1925, died July 10, 2002) married Lois June Swaney (born Nov. 11, 1928) on Aug. 27, 1947. J.B. and Lois had two children, Carolyn Jo and DeWayne B. Carolyn (born Feb. 25, 1950) married Donald Gene Heavin (born March 17, 1949) on Feb. 8, 1969. Carolyn's children: Kent Allen (born Sept. 23, 1969); Bradley J. (born June 22, 1972) and Geni Jo (born Nov. 19, 1977). Kent's son, Garrett Blayne was born Aug. 13, 1997. Brad married Janelle Renee Dickson (born March 3, 1973) on Dec. 6, 1997. Their daughter, Megan Erin was born Feb. 14, 2004. DeWayne's sons are Jason Bryan (born May 4, 1978) and Travis "Jared" (born April 17, 1979). Jason married Heather "Nichole" Hoskins (born July 16, 1978) on Oct. 26, 2002. Their son, Jake Bower, was born Sept. 13, 2005.

J.B. and Lois purchased their farm on Highway TT from Bill and Vesta in 1949. The Gray tradition of working in agriculture in Greene County continues as fifth generation DeWayne now owns and manages the Gray Farm. He is engaged in both cattle and crop production assisted by his nephews, Kent and Brad. Both Carolyn and DeWayne have a home on the family farm. The family has also been involved in managing delivery routes for the U.S. Post Office. DeWayne emphasizes that success on the farm is directly related to generations of neighboring families who have befriended and assisted one another through the years. Life in the Republic area has been enriched by continued friendships with these families.

Annabelle (born July 19, 1927) married Randall Wiley Gleghorn (born Nov. 17, 1928, died July 22, 1994) on Feb. 20, 1955. Annabelle's children: Terry Lynn (born July 29, 1959) married Mark Randall Yake (born Aug. 13, 1957) on Oct. 19, 1991; Lisa Kay (born July 24, 1963) married Donald Edward Clemons (born Feb. 7, 1955) on Dec. 28, 1990. Annabelle's grandchildren: Taylor Anne Yake (born March 4, 1993) and Shelby Lynn Yake (born May 21, 1996). Annabelle and Randall purchased Bill and Vesta's farm on Highway N. Annabelle moved into Republic, and Lisa lives on the farm.

Josiah and Arena also had two daughters: Sarah Ada (born Aug. 18, 1883, died 1957) married George Taylor (born 1885, died 1957) and lived on the Gray homestead until her death. Emma E. (born June 21, 1885, died Dec. 30, 1932) was single. Three additional children died at birth or in infancy. *Submitted by DeWayne Gray.*

**GREEN** - John Wesley Green, son of Elijah and Sarah "Dean" Green, born in Franklin County, AL on Sept, 12, 1845. He and his family moved to Cerro Gordo, TN in 1850. John ran away from home at the age of 14 and worked as a cabin boy on a steamboat. When the Civil War broke out, he enlisted in the Union Army on Jan. 20, 1864, serving in the Missouri State Militia Cavalry. He reenlisted in the Company E 13th Regiment Missouri Cavalry on Sept. 13, 1864. He was discharged on Sept. 16, 1865 and settled in Rolla, MO, where he met and married Elizabeth Mahulda Mitchell (born Oct. 22, 1850) on Jan. 16, 1866. According to the 1900 census, they were living in Greene County and listed his occupation as a farmer. The 1910 census showed them living in Republic Township. They had eight children: James Columbus, Martha Etta, Susan Adella, Alonzo, Alice Viola, Ernest, Lawrence Loren and Myrtle Eva. John and Elizabeth are both buried in Wade Chapel Cemetery.

*John Wesley Green and Elizabeth Mahulda (Mitchell) Green.*

Lawrence Loren (born Sept. 5, 1889, died Jan. 21, 1968) married Mary Eliza Garoutte (born May 18, 1888, died Nov. 28, 1973) on Dec. l2, 1907. They had 10 children: Ralph Arthur, Victor Wayne and a daughter, all died in infancy; Lawrence Edgar (born March 22, 1911, died April 26, 1990); Mary Elizabeth (Banham) (born June 19, 1913, died March 6, 1995); Dorothy Marie (Benson) (born Jan. 14, 1916, died Sept. 7, 2005); John Willard (born April 8, 1918, died Aug. 3, 2005); Harold Eugene (born April 30, 1921); Everett Wan (born April 30, 1925, died April 30, 1997) and Kenneth Lee (born June 18, 1929).

Lawrence Edgar was the only child who lived his entire life in the Republic area. He married Elma Jane Sparkman (born April 6, 1908) also a life-long resident of Republic, on June 2, 1930. After their marriage, they lived on a farm, located just east of Republic, that had been in Elma's family since before the Civil War. They had four children, all born on the home place: Norma Jean (born Feb. 22, 1933); Rosena Lou (born May 5, 1935) married Loy Hilton Dec. 19, 1978; Roberta Elma (born June 5, 1942) married Jimmie Lynn O'Neal April 8, 1961; and Wanda Sue (born Oct. 11, 1944, died Nov. 5, 1944). Roberta has also always lived in the Republic area.

Jim and Roberta had three children: Darrell Edward (born June 13, 1966) married first to Myra Haden on Jan. 27, 1986 and they had one son, Nickolas Alan (born Aug. 23, 1991). He then married Carrie Billings on Sept. 7, 1996, and they had two sons, Skylar Andrew (born Aug. 6, 1997) and Brayden Isaac (born Dec. 5, 2002).

Kathryn Sue (born Sept. 20, 1969) married Andrew Leitz on July 5, 1991. They had two sons, Kaleb Nathaniel (born July 23, 1993) and Kolby James (born July 18, 1998).

Dustin Ray (born Dec. 27, 1981) married Katie Dent on May 22, 2004. *Submitted by Roberta O'Neal.*

**GREEN/WOOD** — On Sept. 4, 1898, Alonzo "Loney" Green and Ida Alice Wood exchanged vows and began their married life in Republic, MO. Loney was a successful farmer in Greene County for a number of years. As the family began to grow he built a new home on one of the farms west of Republic. He cultivated most of his land without any of today's modern equipment. There was always a big garden and lots of canning to fill the cellar shelves for the "rainy days" ahead.

*Ida Alice and Alonzo Green Sr.*

As each child came along they were taught good work ethics and love of family and country. Loney and Ida were strong advocates for good schools and church attendance and found this in the Republic community.

Around 1920 the family moved to a small farm about a mile north of Republic where Loney grew and sold all kinds of fruits and vegetables. He was a good businessman. He owned a restaurant in Republic and was a partner with Jim Kitchen, operating the general/grocery store which was located directly behind the Green's house. The red brick house they called "home" is still located on the corner of Elm and Walnut Streets.

The Greens enjoyed visiting with many of their neighbors and friends: the Garoutte family, LaFollettes, Thurmans, Blades and many others. The band concerts on Saturday night were a "big thing" in those days and after the family moved from Republic they continued to come back for the concerts.

Their grandparents, John and Elizabeth Green, were also residents of Republic.

In 1924, the ninth and last child was born to Loney and Ida. Their children were Berry Wesley, Thomas Jefferson, Halland Ernest, Lucille Rivlet, Alonzo Jr., Edna Maxine, Mary Louise, Helen Mae and Willie Madine.

Berry married Jewel Blades. They had two daughters, Willa LaFon and Dora Lee. Their only living child, Dora Lee Thompson, still lives in Republic with her daughter Wilma.

Tom married Iris Thurman and had one daughter, Nancy. They lived in Republic almost all of their married life.

Halland married Helen Sager. They had one son, Billy Joe. They were divorced and he later married Agnes Jarmin. They had one daughter, Kay Ann, who lives in Springfield.

Lucille married Victor Mason. They were fortunate to adopt their only child, Gary, who now lives in the Springfield area. Lucille also lives in the Springfield area.

Alonzo Jr. married Imogene Whitehead. They had two sons, Marvin Lee and Max Douglas. Both sons now live in Bois D'Arc.

Edna married Leslie Brown and had one daughter Joyce and one son Jerald. Joyce lives in the Springfield area and Jerald lives in Bois D'Arc.

Louise married Vee Brower and had two daughters, Ramona Jean and Mary Joan. She still has a home in Republic.

Helen married Buck Waddle and had four children: Phillip, Idanna, Lonnie and Kit. Helen lives in Washington.

Willie Madine "Joni" married James Burton Collins. They had three children: Alexis Dianne, Kathryn Jean and Craig Steven. Joni lives in California.

One of the best stories remembered was when Loney would tell about the times he and Ida would go to the store before school started and buy 21 pairs of shoes (for seven children).

He would always say, "a pair for 'everyday,' a pair for 'church,' and galoshes for rainy and snowy days."

Loney and Ida are buried at Wade Chapel. There are sweet memories of "Memorial Day" Sundays at Wade Chapel with basket dinners shared by many and afternoon programs in the Chapel.

Republic holds many dear memories for the members of the Alonzo Green family. *Submitted by Louise (Green) Brower.*

**GRIFFIN** - In April 1994, the District Superintendent of the United Methodist Church called Gary Griffin to ask if he would consider moving to Republic to serve as pastor of the Hood United Methodist Church. In the Methodist system, the superintendent serves under the bishop. The bishop has the authority to appoint every pastor to any church in Missouri. At present, the superintendent consults with pastors concerning their appointment each year.

*Gary and Terry Griffin's family. L-R: Adam, Terry, Aaron, Gary, Amy and Eric.*

Gary had been serving at the Willard United Methodist Church for the past nine years. The church was having its best year of his ministry. The Griffin family had grown up in Willard. Gary's wife Terry had taught kindergarten for eight years. There were four children. Aaron was 17, Adam was 15, Eric was 13 and Amy was 11. However, there were signs that Gary had done all that he could do in leading the church. In fact, a few years prior to the superintendent's call, Terry had mentioned to the children about the possibility that the family might be moving sometime. Adam's remark was, "It is all right if we move as long as it is not to Republic." This was because of the fierce rivalry between the high schools.

Gary asked the superintendent if he could pray about the potential move. The superintendent responded that he needed an answer in one hour. Gary took Eric to the dentist that morning and prayed mightily as he drove. When he returned from the dentist, God had given Gary his answer that they should accept the appointment to serve in Republic.

With Two Men and a Truck, the Griffins moved to Republic in June 1994 despite Adam's misgivings. Republic brought back many memories for Gary. During his teen-age years, Gary would often attend weekend youth retreats with other youth from the Methodist and Christian Churches. Jim Ireland was the pastor and became a life-long friend. Gary had often thought that he would like to go to Republic.

During the first year of Gary's pastorate, the church averaged 150 people in attendance. Over the next few years, the attendance began to increase and there was a need for a larger worship area. In August 2000, the Christian Life Center was completed which doubled the physical size of the church. The slogan for the building campaign was, "It is not a building, but a ministry." The church took this slogan to heart. Within five years, the attendance at Hood Church had doubled with 300 people attending and there was an excitement about serving God.

Gary finished his twelfth year as pastor of the Hood Church in 2006. Terry taught first grade at Billings and will complete her requirements to be a principal. Aaron is a teacher and varsity basketball coach at Houston and married Bobbie in 2003. Adam is the Housing Director at Missouri Southern and married Sarah in 2005. Eric is an accountant at Reynolds, Inc. Amy is a junior at Missouri State and will be an elementary teacher. *Submitted by Aaron Griffin.*

**GROVES/HODGE** - Donald Louis and Sharon Sue (Hodge) Groves established their home north of Republic on part of the Jones-Hodge family land following their marriage in 1963 at Hood United Methodist Church. Don was born in Tuscumbia, MO to Louis G. (1914-1987) and Ruby K. (Klug) Groves (1922-1981). He recalls going fishing and trucking with his grandfather John Klug (1888-1954), an immigrant from Germany in the late l800s. His grandmother Eva McNeely Klug (1894-1978) was known for her coconut and chocolate cream pies and kind words. He remembers his grandfather Robert E. (l889-1971) and grandmother Nellie (Teaverbaugh) Groves (1891-1967) who lived near in Iberia, MO.

*Don and Sue Groves.*

Following his dad's discharge from Army service in WWII, the family moved to Greene County. After being the only child for nine years, Don had a little brother arrive that needed his attention. Roger Lee Groves was born in 1952. The Groves family moved to the north side of Interstate 44 between Highways N and MM after Don's marriage. Louis worked for *Springfield Newspapers* until his retirement. He was an avid gardener and horseman. Ruby worked at Lily Tulip, Federal Land Bank and as office manager for Graven Concrete. She enjoyed her sewing, painting and church. Ruby and Louis enjoyed traveling and camping.

Both of the Groves brothers graduated from Willard HS. Don attended SMS. Roger joined the Missouri National Guard and is currently serving in Iraq. Don worked at Springday, a Dayco Company, for 25 years. He was one of seven who made the first serpentine belts for which Ford bought the patent. After leaving Dayco, he began a career in over-the-road driving. He purchased his first truck from Dale Boatright. He went on to own several trucks and became a partner in G & S Trucking. He continues to drive.

Sharon Sue, daughter of William Orin and Ruth M. Jones Hodge and sister of Rex E. and Donald Ray, graduated from Republic HS. She attended Drury College receiving her AB degree and master's in education. Sue taught in Springfield public schools (SPS) for 30 years with 29 of those at Fremont Elementary. During that time she also taught at Drury College and SMS. She presented many workshops for Missouri Department of Elementary and Secondary Education across southwest Missouri and served as a Class 1 Missouri Assessment Program Senior Leader. After retirement she continues working part time for SPS Title 1 Program.

Don and Sue bred and showed cocker spaniels for 15 years, finishing several champions. Both are members of Ozarks Kennel Club where they work for the betterment of purebred dogs. They share interests in NASCAR, motorcycles, and Cardinal ballgames. Don's passion is trapshooting, taking part in local, state and national events. Don enjoys watching most sports. Sue is active in Delta Kappa Gamma, Springfield Area Retired Teachers Association and various church groups. She also is a member of Republic Order of Eastern Star. She enjoys sewing, crafts and anything to do with her lifelong love, horses. *Submitted by Sue Grove.*

**GUENTHER/WILSON** - Paul Arno Güenther, only son of Lina Becker Rost Günther and Otto Günther, was born in Jena, Germany Feb. 28, 1903 and died May 1, 1987. He had an older half-sister, Elsa. Paul came to the U.S. in January 1924 to assist in a new method of oil exploration for Gulf Oil Co., and soon met Edris Laura Wilson at a Valentine's party in Leedey, (NW) OK. He played the piano and she sang. They were married in December 1929.

*Arno Guenther, son of Paul and Edris, getting ready for hunting.*

Edris was born Sept. 12, 1907 near Leedey and died Sept. 3, 2000. Her mother, Laura Alice (Wrinkle) Wilson was born in Richland, MO Oct. 4, 1888 and died May 4, 1984. Laura's parents, Thomas E. and Nancy S. Wrinkle, older brother Alan, and two half-sisters, Virginia and Hattie, came from Knoxville, TN, descended from one of five Winkler brothers who fled Prussia as political dissidents during Napolean's reign, changing their name to Wrinkle. Edris' father, Kenneth Frank Wilson, born in Frankfurt, KS in 1883, was a young family participant at age 12, during the "Land Run" into Oklahoma to claim property. A great-great-grandson of James Wilson (PA) signer of the Declaration of Independence and the Constitution who emigrated from Scotland in 1765, was instrumental in getting the bridge built across the S. Canadian River on the Chisholm Trail, north of Leedey on SH34 in 1949. He was involved in oil and gas exploration and worked for the State Land Office in Oklahoma City. He was the first president of the Longhorn Chisholm Trail Assoc. and was commissioned an Honorary Colonel on the staff of Oklahoma Governor Johnston Murray in 1953 for his many years of service. He died in 1954.

Edris and Paul's son, Kenneth Arno Guen-

*Edris (Wilson) Guenther, Carole (Guenther) Wilmoth and Paul Arno Guenther in front of family home.*

195

ther, was born Oct. 26, 1930 and died Nov. 25, 1986. Carole Lina Guenther was born Oct. 25, 1934 in Pittsburgh, PA. The family moved to Enid, OK in 1936, Lubbock, TX in 1938, then Houston in 1940, where Paul eventually owned a machine tool shop. There he developed several patented inventions for the oil industry and worked for the government on the first radar developed during WWII. During the Korean conflict and a recession, he sold his home and business in Houston, and the family moved to a 365-acre farm on the James River off of FF Hwy., south of Battlefield, MO in August of 1955. The Manley Cemetery took the NE corner of the property. Each funeral included the curious Guenther cows lined up, respectfully observing across the fence line! Grandmother Wilson knew how to milk a cow, so everyone relied on her advice. Paul loved petting the cows and pigs (he named them all) and driving the little Ford tractor around the farm, but soon left the farming for others and took a job with Reynolds, the only manufacturing plant in Springfield in the 1950s.

After living in a big city, moving to a farm with so many animals, including white rabbits, was a dream for Carole and Arno, not to mention the beautiful chrysanthemums (used for RHS Homecoming floats), asters, bleeding hearts and lilacs. Even cleaning the barn was fun. There was always an afternoon swim in the very cold, clear James River with a "blue hole" nearby. The old house had burned down, so the first project was to build a new one. Living for two months in two "cabins" with the only plumbing a faucet outside, was an adventure. The memory of loons calling in the spring, and even a female mountain lion one moonlit night would stay with Carole forever.

Carole entered Republic High School in September 1950 as a 15-year-old junior and Arno attended Drury College in Springfield. Living outside the bus route, she rode with neighbor Loretta Rogers every morning at 7 a.m. to the school bus, driven by Frank Comisky. Loretta, at 19, taught in a one-room school nearby. The only drawback was not having a phone. They were just outside Greene County and across the river in Christian. Edris would not give up, and eventually got a phone from Greene County after five years.

Paul's niece, Helene, and her husband Kurt Heineman, walked to Switzerland from East Germany in 1951 before the Berlin Wall was built, bringing only what they could carry. Paul drove to NYC to pick them up and drove them back to the farm. They lived with the family for two years before moving to Houston. Carole was an accomplished pianist at 15, having studied since she was 4. Her favorite classes were choir under Bud Thurman and journalism with Mrs. Roberta Arnold. She studied piano at Drury from Robert Wharton and made a one rating at the state her senior year. She performed a piano solo with the RHS Band on tour, and did the processional for Baccalaureate during her class' graduation exercises in May 1952. As third in her class of 57, she received a scholarship to Southwest Missouri State College (now Missouri State U). She remembers tuition then was $27 a term (3 terms a year). She graduated in three years (1955) with a BS in Education (Music Ed. major and Diploma in Piano). Mr. Thurman and Mrs. Arnold attended her senior piano recital. Carole was selected as Musician of the Year by the SMS music faculty and performed at the graduation ceremony. Her brother, Arno, also graduated at the same time, having served two years in the Navy.

Arno and Loretta (Rogers) were married during that period, and Paul Lee Guenther was born Aug. 25, 1954 in Florida. They later had three more children, Diana (born Jan. 14, 1955, died April 27, 2005); Debbie (born Feb. 11, 1958) and Laura (born Feb. 11, 1961). Arno taught one year at a Springfield Jr. High then moved to Oxnard, CA, where he became a school principal and later superintendent. Loretta also taught school until her retirement. Arno had one more child, Eric K.A. Guenther (born Nov. 7, 1984) by his second wife, Marilyn, of Ojai, CA.

After graduation from SMS, Carole taught piano and band one year at Labette Co. Community H.S. in Altamont, KS. After a brief marriage in December 1955 to Roger Wayne Mitchell, an SMS music classmate from Thayer, MO, she received her master's in music degree, in piano performance from LSU in 1957. With great regret, Paul and Edris sold the farm that year and moved back to Houston with Carole, where Paul had a new job waiting. They later moved from Houston to Fort Worth where Paul worked for General Dynamics until his retirement in 1968 at age 65. They moved to Oxnard, CA, to be near Arno and grandchildren, and a new job for Paul at Point Mugu Naval Base in Port Hueneme, CA. They lived there the rest of their lives - their yard filled with fruit trees, berries and other beautiful plants.

Carole continued her studies in Houston with former teacher, Ruth Burr, who helped her begin her long teaching career in piano. She married an engineer (M.E.), L. Martin Everett Jr. in 1959. Martin had worked for Rocketdyne in Canoga Park, CA, a designer of the gearbox for the Saturn missile. They moved to Dallas where they both worked briefly at Texas Instruments, and their son, Mark Tobin Everett, was born Sept. 21, 1960. They moved to Sherman, TX, in 1963 where Martin worked for Johnson & Johnson. A second son, James Wilson Everett, was born Nov. 19, 1964 and lived to age 22 (June 21, 1987). They were married nine years.

In 1969 she married Allan G. Smith Jr., a writer *(The History of Grayson County)*, teacher of English at Grayson Co. College, and grandson of the first president of Austin College. He was also the Director of the Sherman Little Theater. They were married six years. Carole taught piano at home and part time at Grayson County College and Austin College. She was president of the local music club, the Sherman Musical Arts Women's Group, the Grayson Co. Music Teachers Assoc. and was musical director and pianist for over 12 productions at the Sherman Little Theater. She gave piano recitals for the music club and both colleges and accompanied many student and faculty recitals. She also was the pianist for, and played viola in the Sherman Symphony Orchestra for five years. Her civic interest extended to helping reorganize the Grayson County Humane Society 1976-79.

Carole moved to Richardson in 1979 and was married for 21 years to Stephen Reece Wilmoth, head of the Technical Dept. for Steinway-Hall Dallas. She continued to teach piano at home and often served as a judge for various piano festivals including National Guild Auditions. Carole was president of the Dallas Music Teachers Assoc. 1980-82, the DFW Metroplex President's Council of MTA's, and on the board of the Texas Music Teachers Assoc. She also had a deep love of nature, conservation, animals and especially birds. She attributed her interests to her early years on the farm in Missouri. She was president of the local Audubon Society in 1990 and later the Audubon Council of Texas. She was listed for many years in *"Who's Who in American Women."*

Mark Everett, Carole's son, received his M.E. degree in 1983 from the Rochester Institute of Technology in New York, and later his master's degree from Duke University. In 1988 he married Lynn Caryl Yanyo of Pittsburgh, PA, PhD in polymer science. They live in Cary, NC, with their two children, Colin, born Jan. 20, 1990, and Elise, born Sept. 15, 1993. Mark works for SAS, a computer software company, and Lynn with Lord Corp. in Research Triangle Park.

On Jan. 3, 2003, Carole married Dr. Harold "Hal" Eugene Freeland (born Feb. 9, 1930 in Hubbard, TX), a retired physician (GP) and moved to Keene, TX, a small town south of Fort Worth, to live an idyllic and quiet rural life with their six cats. They shared a love of music, gardening, birding, boating and motor home trips to scenic areas. *Submitted by Carole Guenther Wilmoth Freeland.*

**HAGERMAN -** In 1979 Sondra Franks Hagerman and Jerry Hagerman made the decision to return to the Republic area from Atlanta. Jerry and Sondra had both grown up and graduated from high school and college in Springfield, but had moved to Atlanta so that Jerry could earn two more college degrees in architecture from Georgia Tech.

*Jerry and Sondra Hagerman's house.*

When Ivan Franks, Sondra's father, suffered a heart attack, Sondra returned to assist her mother Alice with her multiple jobs of managing Franks Electric Company and keeping up with chores at the farm. It was while doing chores at the farm, stargazing and enjoying the quiet and absence of city noise that Sondra realized their children, Bo and Heather, would have a childhood richer in multiple activities and responsibilities living here than in Atlanta and they could be near family. Jerry agreed and the family moved to Republic in 1979 and began building their house in 1980 on land which was once part of her parent's dairy farm.

The Franks had lived in Springfield and driven daily to the farm to do chores for nearly 40 years. Now Sondra and Jerry lived on the same property but drove to Springfield to work, church and social commitments. They enjoyed the tranquility and freedom of living in the country. Bo and Heather grew up in an atmosphere of small town and suburban acreage life. They had as many pets as they wanted, bottle fed calves, camped out, helped sometimes with planting the vegetable and flower gardens, had fun on the ATV four wheeler, viewed stars through a telescope, caught minnows at the pond, stocked the cattle tank with goldfish, picked up pears for jelly (called pear honey) and picked up walnuts, all while staying right at home!

Bo and Heather graduated from Republic High School. Bo is now an architect in business with Jerry. Their company, Hagerman New-Urbanism, is in Springfield. Sondra is a realtor after retiring as an administrator from Springfield public schools, and Heather is an MD living in Nashville, TN.

The Republic area is changing. Sondra remembers not that long ago when she saw more cars than usual on her road at the same time, three! Now the road has been widened. The address has changed from a rural route number to S. Farm Road 85. The big barn burned in 2003. There are often more cars than three on the road at one time. Sondra and Jerry now share their acreage with many more deer and wild turkeys than cattle and horses, and the peace and tranquility which drew them back to the family farm are fading. The traffic noise from Highway 60 is constant now. And the stars? What happened to the stars? Yet the land still holds family memories dating back to 1942. *Submitted by Bo Hagerman.*

**HAGEWOOD/FISHER** – The Hagewood family has been in the Republic area for many years having come from Virginia and Tennessee. The Fisher family came from Tennessee, Virginia and Arkansas, also living in Highlandville, Stone County and California.

Oca Hagewood grew up on a farm west of Republic and married Gladys Mae Fisher on Oct. 30, 1925. Their family started on Jan. 6, 1927 when their first son Roy Lee was born. The early family was living in California when Johnie Joseph was born on Oct. 24, 1928.

*Standing l-r: Dorothy High, Faye Hagewood, June Hagewood, Ruby Hagewood, Gladys Hagewood; sitting: Ermal Hagewood, Glen High, Jimmy Hagewood, Johnie Hagewood, Roy Hagewood, Oca Hagewood, Sharon Hagewood; children: Ronnie Hagewood, Roy Allen Hagewood and Judy Hagewood.*

In 1933, another son was born on Aug. 20 who was named Jimmie Gene. Three daughters completed the family when Dorothy Mae was born on June 1, 1938, Ermal Lucille on June 24, 1941 and Sharon Kay on Nov. 6, 1945. Another daughter, Helen Irene was born on April 16, 1940 and expired with meningitis at age six weeks and was buried at Wade Chapel Cemetery.

Family members still attend Hopewell Baptist Church where the Hagewoods attended for years. The siblings attended Blades and Republic Schools for their education where the Hagewood girls were active in sports and music programs. They participated a few years in a 4-H organization and worked in two of the local businesses while in school.

After marrying, most of the children lived in the Republic area. On Aug. 22, 1946, Roy and Ruby Lee Batson of Republic married. Roy spent 16 months in the Army in 1946-1947 at Fort Dix, NJ. Two sons were born, Ronald Lee "Ron" on Sept. 16, 1954 and Roy on March 24, 1957.

On April 18, 1954 Johnie married Carolyn "June" Cave from Springfield. They had one daughter born on Feb. 2, 1955 whose name was Linda Kay. She loved to sing *"Tom Dooley"* when she was young.

The family continued when Jimmie married Juanita "Faye" Brashers of Republic on Aug. 27, 1954. They were blessed with Michael Gene born on Dec. 8, 1959 and Ann Michelle born on Dec. 27, 1965.

On Aug. 31, 1956 Dorothy married Glen Logan High of Republic. They reared their family in Republic and Marionville. The siblings included Margie Anne (born Dec. 12, 1958) and Kayla Sue (born Feb. 13, 1960) who was born on her grandmother's birthday and enjoyed many celebrations with her grandmother. Douglas Glen was welcomed on June 29, 1961, his brother Bradley was born on Oct. 28, 1962 and Robbie Don arrived on July 13, 1966. The family was complete when Brian "Dink" Oca (his grandfather's namesake) was born on May 9, 1968 and Leslie "Shawn" arrived July 10, 1972.

On Aug. 28, 1964 Ermal married Robert Luther Wheeler from Aurora, MO. Robert Kelly was born on Nov. 25, 1965. Living in Aurora and four other states, Ermal retired from the Naval Reserves after 20 years, serving in Desert Storm.

Sharon was married on June 16, 1964 to Garry Eugene Wilson of Republic. They had three children. Kathy Ann (born May 23, 1966) and Jason Ryan (born Nov. 28, 1974). Kathy drowned on Aug. 23, 1974 and Jason Ryan expired from a congenital heart defect Dec. 3, 1974. Both are buried at Wade Chapel Cemetery. Andrea Annette arrived on June 1, 1976 much to the delight of the Wilson family.

Wade Chapel Cemetery has become the resting place for the Hagewood family and other family members. The family continues today because of the Hagewoods and the Fishers. *Submitted by Robert Kelly Wheeler.*

**HAGEWOOD/ROBERTSON** - Benjamin Hagewood arrived from Tennessee to Brookline, MO in 1838. He was born June 2, 1791 in Virginia. On April 10, 1819 he married Mary Polly Robertson, who was born 1791 in Amherst County, VA. Ben had been married to Patsy Stephens in Tennessee who died in childbirth. Ben Jr. was born in 1817 or 1818.

*Maggie Hagewood and John T. Hagewood.*

Thomas Hagewood was born March 20, 1820 in Tennessee and married Nancy Jane Reynolds on Feb. 16, 1841 in Greene County. He died Dec. 3, 1904 and she died on Nov. 16, 1885, both are interred at Lindsey Cemetery. He served in the Civil War with Co. G. Missouri Home Guard. Their children: John C., Marion, Mary A., Sarah R., Nancy E., Matilda F., William M., James W. and Marvellus M.

John Calvin Hagewood was born in Missouri on July 25, 1842. He married Martha F. Cavener who was born on Feb. 19, 1848 in Lincoln County, TN. They were married Nov. 6, 1866 in Greene County. Martha Cavener arrived from Tennessee in 1852 on the Johnathan Gold Wagon Train. John C. served in the Civil War with the 46th Missouri Infantry. He served with Gen. Lyons at the Wilson's Creek Battle-field and helped to carry Gen. Lyons to the Ray house where the General expired. The Infantry marched to Pea Ridge, AR where John C. was injured. Four men who were from the Republic area carried him to Republic.

John C. and Martha deeded one acre of land to build the Blades Chapel in 1888. Also found, was a deed from John and Elizabeth Laney deeding one acre plus 70 rods for the Blades cemetery. A widow's claim on July 12, 1890 from Martha was for six children. She was to receive $8.00 a month plus $2.00 a month for each child until they reached the age of 16.

Their children: Gillian "Gillie," Marion L., Sarah L, John T., William, Lucy, Emma J., Emmett and Cordelia. Five of the children died from contaminated well water before they were 25 years of age.

Martha, who was a retired farmer, died at age 65 on Feb. 16, 1913 from tuberculosis. She and John C., who died on March 20, 1890, are both interred at Lindsey Cemetery.

John T. Hagewood was born Nov. 5, 1875 and married Maggie Ada McDaniel, born on June 15, 1882. They married March 17, 1902 in Springfield, MO. Children include Emmett Wesley, "Toad" died at age 32 from an auto accident. Oca "Monk," Delta May, Callie Marie, Raymond "Burl," Edith Merle, Margaret (died two days after birth), two male infants (stillborns), Anna Lucille and Hazel Pauline.

The couple lived and farmed most of their lives west of Republic on Hwy. 174. John T. died of tuberculosis on Jan. 9, 1939 and Maggie died Nov. 6, 1964. Both are interred at Lindsey Cemetery.

This information was compiled from the *History of Greene County,* Census, Marriage Records, Tax Records, Deed of Records, Sloan Robertson, Lucille Sifferman and family. *Submitted by Jo Ann Kackley.*

**HAILE/WADE** - James and Nancy (Hearn) Wade came to Missouri from Georgia in 1852. Nancy was one of the first people buried at Wade Chapel Cemetery in 1854. James died in Hindsville, AR in 1880 and his body was brought to Wade Cemetery and buried beside his wife Nancy in 1901. James and Nancy had 11 children: Joshua, John Fletcher, Sarah Ann, Mary Elizabeth, William P., James Benson, Martha, Wesley Osborne, Thomas Washington, Nancy and Samuel.

*Hazel and Bert Haile on 50th anniversary, Oct. 4, 1985.*

Wesley Osborne married Elizabeth Skelton. Their children were William L., Joel Bence, George Calvin, Ella, James and Ervey.

Joel Bence married Nellie B. Sims. They had four daughters: Ruth, Gussie, Hazel and Frances.

Meade Haile II came from Tennessee to Billings, MO about 1850 and is buried in Marionville, MO.

One of Meade's sons was Jackson Overstreet Haile. He ran the hotel in Billings, MO. One of Jackson's 12 children was Columbus Haile.

Columbus married Della Newton. They were the parents of Arthur Burton "Bert" Haile who was born in 1909.

The Wade/Haile families were joined when

Hazel and Bert were married Oct. 5, 1935. They had two sons, Kelly Wade Haile and Kirby Dale. Kirby died in 1948, seven months after birth from pneumonia.

Bert and Hazel farmed around the Republic and Billings area. Hazel was a school teacher in the rural one-room schools as well as Republic R-3. She retired in 1971 after 29 years of teaching.

Kelly graduated from Republic High in 1961. He married Juanita Simpson. She was born in the Neosho, MO area in 1943. They have two sons, Benson Columbus and Eric Kelly, born in 1976 and 1981 respectively.

Bert and Hazel, along with son Kelly and Juanita, operated the golf pro shop at Tri-Way Country Club from 1971 to 1975. It later became Island Green Country Club in Republic. The two families then operated Haile's General (Grocery) Store in the village of Brookline, MO from 1976 to 1995. Brookline has now merged into Republic. Kelly was the local village tax collector for 27 years, as well as notary public, accepted voter registration and did income tax preparation. He retired in 2005. *Submitted by Kelly Wade Haile.*

**HAMILTON/DALE -** The Dale family moved into Republic in 1981. Cheri entered fifth grade. The school seemed huge to her compared to the school she attended in Arkansas. There Cheri had one fourth grade class and practically knew everyone in the whole school, in Republic there were six fifth grade classes, so she felt quite lost. Cheri graduated from Republic High School in 1988. She had been active in band and flags while in school. Having lived her entire life on a farm she wanted some type of a degree in agriculture. She started at SMSU in the fall of 1988. During her freshman year, she decided to major in agronomy, which is the study of soil and crops. She graduated within four years from SMSU.

*C&N Plants. Standing, Cheri and Clayton. Under table, Kendall and Katie.*

During her last year in school she started to date another graduate of Republic, Tim Hamilton. He was attending school in Rolla, MO. Both of them were set to graduate in the spring of 1992, but in February Tim had asked Cheri to marry him. She enthusiastically said yes. They both agreed to move to wherever the first one got a job. This turned out to be Tim. He got a job in Jonesboro, AR, as an engineer for the GE Plant there. Cheri graduated on a Friday in May and on Saturday moved to Jonesboro and started work on Monday for Agri Pro, a company that did research on wheat. By August she had gotten a better job working for Anheuser Busch doing tissue culture and cross hybridization on rice.

During the 2-1/2 years that they lived in Jonesboro she got her master's in plant science. Then Tim got an opportunity to move jobs and come back to southwest Missouri which had always been their ultimate goal. They moved home. Cheri got a job at a local greenhouse and worked for a year and a half and then got pregnant with their first child, Clayton. Tim and Cheri discussed what they would do when the baby was born. For at least a year they had been contemplating opening their greenhouse. So once she found out she was pregnant it just seemed like the ideal time to go into business for herself. She had already grown two seasons of mums in the backyard and sold those wholesale.

So in 1996, at the age of 26 and being married for four years, she got a small business loan and the whole time she was pregnant worked at the startup process of opening a business. For the first seven years that she was in business, she was a wholesaler and supplied local greenhouses, some landscapers and grew baskets for Silver Dollar City. Wholesaling was the perfect job for her and her growing family, because within the five years following 1996 she had two more children, Katie and Kendall, giving them three total.

The kids have grown up in the greenhouse. They have gone to work with her everyday. They have learned how to count, because 12 four packs are in a flat of flowers. They have learned colors--orange marigolds to red geraniums. They have learned how important it is to be a part of the community where you live and to support that community. They know that the money they spend with small business owners support the community where they live. Cheri feels that small business won't die entirely because they offer personal service from someone who not only knows but cares about the customers and their families.

Cheri realizes that she could have a business in a large town, but would lose the small town atmosphere. She hopes the business that she started and the community in which she has loved being a part of, will be here for generations to come to deepen her family's history in the community. *Submitted by Cheri Hamilton*

**HARPER -** Nancy Wilson Harper (1822-1900) came to Greene County from Dayton, OH in 187? accompanied by son William Reilly Harper (1854-1935), his wife Minnie (1866-1900), daughters, Ella Mae (1863-1940), Mattie (1856-1909) and Emma (1852-_) and John Sims. William's father, James, died in 1870 at age 48. Nancy purchased land including 40 acres now intersected by Hwy. 60 and M Highway. William took this acreage for the care of his handicapped sister, Ella Mae.

William and Minnie bore Grace (Hodge) (l883-1967), Maude (Butler), Lula Harper (1888-1950) and Charles Earl Harper (1896-1968). They farmed and traded in small animal furs. He regularly competed in Brookline horseshoe games.

*L-R: Maude, Charles, Lulu, William R. and Grace Harper.*

Daughter Grace married William Orin Hodge. See "Hodge" family history.

Daughter Maude married Joshua Butler, a RR worker. They moved to Colorado with sons Clifford, Ted and Merton. Maude owned a boarding house following the death of her husband. Ted was a prospector who found uranium. The national news reported the ore value at $150/ton. He sold his claim and prospected until his death. Cliff managed resorts in Nevada and California. Merton worked through college driving ore trucks on the mountain mining roads. He owned businesses in Florence and Gunnison, CO, and loved trout fishing at his Gunnison River cabin.

Daughter Lula Harper became an RN and was a statuesque 6 feet tall. She became a private nurse to the mentally ill wife of a wealthy industrialist, living in Colorado Springs. She worked with the world's leading psychiatrists treating her employer's wife. Lula became mentally imbalanced following cranial surgery in 1939, requiring family care and institutional confinement. Her size, beautiful penmanship and psychiatric experience intimidated care providers, confounded diagnosis and frustrated state officials who received her letters, objecting to her confinement.

Son, Charles E. Harper and family moved to the acreage at 60 and M in 1946. Neighbors told extraordinary stories of his throwing arm and pranks which he would not confirm. Charles E. worked through aircraft mechanics school as a piano mover. He returned to Springfield and married his first wife Mary. He worked for Wheat's Electric Co. for over 40 years. Mary developed diabetes during her second pregnancy and died shortly after the birth of John, who died weeks later. Three-year-old daughter, Betty, died of cancer the following year. He married Annalee Franklin (1906-1967) and had Patty Jean (1932-) and Charles W. (1936-)

Patty married Jerold Scarlett, an architect, upon graduation from SMS. She teaches and plays oboe in ensembles and symphonies in Jefferson City. Daughter, Christy Kitrell teaches kindergarten and plays mandolin in a blue grass band. Dr. Todd Scarlet is a professor of earth sciences at University of South Carolina and loves self destructive sports, including mountain climbing and sea kayaking.

Charles W. married Patricia Nicholson, RN, and has three children and five grandchildren. He graduated from Rolla and Drury, following his service in the VII Army Band in Germany. He lives at Tablerock Lake following a career in research, engineering and manufacturing management. His children include a CPA, a managerial accountant, and an industrial software training supervisor.

William's children and many grandchildren attended Beulah, Brookline and Jones Grade Schools and Republic High School. *Submitted by Charles Harper.*

**HARPER/RIEHN -** Parson Bill and Frances Harper first came to Republic, MO in 1971 when Bill was called to be the pastor of First Christian Church in this community. William Charles was attending the University of Missouri at Columbia. Judith Ann had completed

*Harper family in 1971, l-r: Judy Harper, Parson Bill, Francis and Charlie.*

her college work and was living in St. Joseph, MO. She was the director of the RSVP program at Interfaith Community Services. It was there she met and married Kim Doverspike.

In November of 1971 at 567 Buxton Lane, a home was built for Bill and Frances that has been the home of three generations of this family. Charlie's oldest son Lyndal was born when his parents were living there. Judy and her husband Kim Doverspike are now living there with Frances. Judy is now the Executive Director of CASA in Springfield and Kim is on the staff of the Discovery Center.

*Harper family home at 567 Buxton Lane – Christmas 1998.*

In 1976 Bill and Frances moved to northeast Missouri where both of their mothers lived. Bill served a church and Frances taught in the area schools. She also taught at Crane, MO from 1971-76. After 10 years they returned to their home in Republic. Bill again had an interim pastorate at the Christian Church. The fellowship hall was added during this time.

*Frances and Bill, retired and tired.*   *Charlie Harper home to see mom and dad and cut wood for the fireplace.*

Bill and Frances Riehn met at Culver Stockton College in Canton, MO. They were married in 1947 by Dr. John B. Alexander a religion professor of the College. They left Missouri for Lexington Theological Seminary in Kentucky. Their daughter Judith Ann was born in Versailles, KY near Lexington. Bill's pastor at his home church at Mexico, MO and Dr. Daniel C. Troxel of the seminary ordained him as a minister of the Christian Church, Disciples of Christ in 1950. William Charles was born in Freeport, IL in 1952 near Mount Morris, IL where Bill was serving a Christian Church and the family lived in the parsonage.

There are many branches of the Harper

*Parson Bill at his favorite sport – fishing.*   *Will Harper, grandpa's fishing buddy.*

*Lyndal Harper, high school graduation.*   *Judy and Kim Doverspike home for Christmas in 1998.*

family. Charlie has the Harper family history. Five generations of this family share William as a part of their name. In almost every area of Missouri one could find Harpers living. In 1832 a James William Harper from Virginia came to Callaway County, MO. By 1888 his name appeared in print as living at Mexico, MO in Audrain County. His son was given the name William Jule. William Jule married Grace Knoebel. They were the parents of William Louis who married Frances Riehn. Their son was named William Charles after the two grandfathers. As of this writing, Charlie is living in Oklahoma. His son Lyndal Vernell calls Oklahoma City home and William Anthony's home is the campus of OSU at Stillwater. Frances Harper has one brother, Eugene Vernell Riehn. Lyndal was given a part of his name.

William L. Harper (Parson Bill) died in 1999 and is buried at Evergreen Cemetery in Republic. *Submitted by Frances Harper.*

**HARRIS/GOLD** – Floyd L. Harris arrived in Republic in early 1955 in search of a job. His first stop was at Don Pollard Ford Motors and he was hired. His employment in Republic required a one-hour drive of 55 miles from where the family lived in Cassville, MO. They owned a home there and Anna Louise (Gold) Harris worked for a feed company in Purdy.

In January 1956 they moved the family consisting of children: Harold, Cheryl and Donald, to Republic. They lived the next three years on North Main Street. In 1959 they moved to a house in the new subdivision known as "Wormeyville."

Floyd's employment changed when Don Pollard decided to sell the Ford dealership. Floyd wanted to keep his roots in Republic, so he and good friends, Howard Lee Eagan and Jack Trogdon formed a partnership to purchase the dealership. The name of the dealership would become Harris Ford Sales. The new dealership location was established on North Main across the street from the original Pollard Motor Sales. Harris Ford Sales would remain in existence until September 1973.

Floyd and Louise were active in clubs and youth sport sponsorships and community involvement which included support for the new high school, city swimming pool, city parks and a new 9-hole golf course south of Republic. All of these were important for growth to Republic and its future.

After retirement, Floyd and Louise enjoyed their remaining years as Republic residents. Sons, Harold and Donald, both remain in Republic and daughter Cheryl lives in Kansas City. *Submitted by Harold Harris.*

**HAYES** - In 1978, Lois Hayes and her four children moved to Republic. They found a community that was welcoming and friendly, excellent schools that cared about children, where they could participate in activities they liked and a wonderful church family.

Pleasant memories of life in Republic included summers at the Garoutte and Miller fields for baseball and softball, basketball at the elementary, middle and high school gyms, Fall Festival, and Calvary Baptist's Fourth of July picnics and fireworks. Sending teenage drivers for milk resulted in a two-hour trip cruising Highway 60 to see if friends were around. There was the winter with 15 inches of snow and not able to get out of the driveway and, of course, the great ice storm of the late 1980s. Most people had no water or electricity, but they made it to SMS for the Blue and Gold Tournament!

*The Hayes family in 2003.*

Suzanne "Suzy" graduated from Republic High School in 1982, Patrick "Pat" in 1983, Kelly in 1986 and Thomas "Tom" in 1989. Suzy was editor of *Tiger Tracks,* Pat played baseball, Kelly was in journalism and Tom played basketball for the Tigers. All four had their first jobs in Republic: Suzy at Pat's Pizza, Pat at Sip-N-Flip, Kelly at Tastee Freeze and Tom was one of the first employees when Dairy Queen opened.

Suzy graduated from SMS and has been teaching English at Ozark High School for 19 years, is married and has two children, Brittany and Benjamin, and two stepchildren. Pat has a degree in finance from SMS, is with the finance division of BKD and has three children in the Republic school system: Connor, Emily and Lauren. Kelly is married to Greg Shoemaker, also a graduate in the class of 1989, and they have three children: Adam, Rachel and Olivia. They recently moved to Dallas, TX, where Greg is with Town North Bank and Kelly is a homemaker. Tom was youth director at Calvary Baptist Church for several years and graduated from Southwest Baptist University in Bolivar, where he met his wife, Katie. They continue in the ministry and recently moved to Dallas for Tom to attend Seminary.

Republic provided a foundation and an education that helped these children to become productive, caring and responsible adults. They all have long-lasting friendships with former schoolmates. Although all of them do not live in Republic now, it will always be home. *Submitted by Lois Hayes.*

**HAYS** - James Arthur Hays was born 1837 in Arkansas. The family moved to Lawrence County where he married Malinda Caroline Mooneyham in 1861. Malinda was the daughter of Thomas Jefferson Mooneyham and his first wife, a Cherokee Indian.

James and Malinda made their home on a farm near the settlement called Little York. Family legend has it that James was known to partake of the spirits and ride his horse down Main Street, Republic, shooting off doorknobs. He and Malinda were living near Little York during the Battle of Wilson's Creek. James enlisted in 1862 and served until 1865. Fact or fiction also has it that James befriended a man by the name of Bill Hickok while in the service as they both worked as scouts. Bill Hickok, as we all know, later became known as "Wild Bill Hickok."

After his discharge, James' family moved to a farm near Boaz. He and Malinda had nine children, three dying early.

James continued farming until his death, a "fishing accident" on the James River in 1882. The truth be told, he was killed while fishing with dynamite, apparently slipping on a muddy bank and unable to get away from the dynamite. He left Malinda with six sons to raise.

*Malinda (Mooneyham) Hays and her six sons: front row, Bert and John; middle row: Henry, Malinda Hays, Purd; back row, Enoch and Tillman.*

Malinda moved to 40 acres near the county line next to her half-brother, Jeff Mooneyham, and finished raising her sons. It has been said that she set high standards for her sons and was known to discipline them with a blacksnake whip. It had been James and Malinda's goal that their sons be educated.

Those sons were William Henry Hays (1864-1935) who married Bonnie Ziegler.

George Purdy Hays (1865-1952) attended Drury in Springfield. When Purd left to attend school, he owned one pair of shoes, so walked barefoot from Republic to Springfield to save them. He married Hulda Dee Keller. Purd was admitted to the bar about 1902 and practiced law in Ozark 50 years.

John Thomas Hays (1870-1937) received a degree from University of Michigan. He married Martha Paulsell. For a short time, John and brother, Tillman, had a farm on Terrell Creek. Then he moved to Ozark and served two terms as prosecuting attorney.

James Tillman Hays (1870-1944) was the only Hays brother who didn't marry. He taught school in Oklahoma in the winter and returned to his farm in Missouri in the summers.

Enoch Monroe Hays (1872-1835) married Lou Phelps, who died after the birth of their son. He then married Agnes McCord. He was school administrator in Stone County and in Oklahoma.

Rutherford Berchard "Bert" Hays (1879-1939) married Lillie King in 1907. (History of Lillie's family in a separate article.) Bert worked as a carpenter and a farmer. He and Lillie are buried in Evergreen Cemetery, Republic. All of Bert and Lillie's six children attended school in Republic, at least four of them graduating. Those children were: Rose (grad. 1927), Ed, R.B. Jr., Purd (grad. 1932), Ervin (grad. 1939) and Violet (grad. 1941). (More history of Bert's children to follow in a separate article.) Many of Bert's grandchildren, great-grandchildren, etc, still live in the Republic and Clever area. *Submitted by Susan Hays Compton, granddaughter of Bert and daughter of R.B. Jr.*

**HAYS/KING -** Lilly May King, daughter of Andrew David "Dave" King and Martha Elizabeth "Mattie" Lonon, married Rutherford Berchard "Bert" Hays, son of Malinda Caroline Mooneyham and James Arthur Hays, in December 1907 in Ozark, MO. Lilly was born in September 1886 in Mountain Home, AR and moved with her family to Republic in the late 1800s. Bert was born in May 1870 in Boaz, Christian County, MO, but had moved to a farm just south of the Greene County line when his father died.

Lilly and Bert spent most of their married life in Republic raising their six children. All of the children attended Republic schools. Bert always said he had a flower garden, including his wife Lilly and his daughters, Rose and Violet.

*Ervin, Violet, Ed, Lily, Berchard Jr., Rose and Purd Hays.*

Bert died in July 1939 and was buried in Evergreen Cemetery; Lilly died in Tulsa, OK in April 1968 and was buried beside Bert in Evergreen Cemetery.

Their children were Rose May (born October 1908) married Wesley Earl Spain in 1939. His work on the railroad took them to Tulsa where Rose lived the rest of her life. They raised two children Jean Alice and Tommy. Jean Alice died suddenly at the age of 16 in 1959. They are buried in Tulsa.

Edward Lester (born February 1910) was in the army during WWII and when he returned home he met and married Bessie Applegate. They lived in Tulsa for a while before returning to Republic. In their later years they moved south of Ozark to be near Bessie's daughter. When Edward died he was buried in the Old Boston Cemetery.

Rutherford Berchard "R.B." (born 1911) married Roxie Mae Pope. When WWII came along he already had two children, but nevertheless did his part by working at the army camp in Camp Crowder. It had been said about R.B. that he never met a stranger. He died in October 1979 in Springfield, MO and was buried in the Delaware Cemetery in Christian County.

James Purd (born August 1913 in Republic) was an ordained Southern Baptist minister. He also taught English in Lansing, KS. He moved to Texas to be near his daughter a year and a half before he died. He was buried in Lansing, KS.

Ervin David (born September 1919 in Republic) was a graduate of Republic High School. After serving in the military he made his home in Tulsa where he married Sue Fletcher in February 1940. He was retired from Oklahoma Natural Gas. Ervin died in September 1999 and was buried in Broken Arrow, OK. Their children were Rose May (born October 1908) married Wesley Earl Spain in 1939. His work on the railroad took them to Tulsa where they lived their lives. They raised two children Jean Alice and Tommy. Jean Alice died suddenly at the age of 16 in 1959. They are buried in Tulsa.

Violet Elizabeth (born March 1923 in Billings) grew up in Republic, graduating from Republic High School. She followed her sister Rose and brother Ervin to Tulsa where she became interested in photography and begin to reproduce old family photos. She also took some outstanding pictures of her own. She married Lawrence Morgan in August 1947. She and Larry now reside in Owasso, OK. *Submitted by Jane Stevens. Editor's note: Violet died Dec. 25, 2006.*

**HENDERSON/GRAINGE -** Jim Henderson was the first child of Donald R. and Fern Pendergrass Henderson, born in Bois D' Arc, MO in July 1939. Jim started first grade at Republic. During his first grade, Jim's dad, who worked for Frisco Railways, was transferred to Birmingham, AL. They transferred later to Springfield, MO with Frisco. Fern began working at Lily Tulip when it first opened. Don passed away in January 1983 and Fern passed in September 2002.

Jim and Carolyn met while attending Central High School and married in November 1959. They lived in Springfield 25 years. Carolyn is the daughter of Emil and Lois Wasson Grainge and was raised south of Nixa in the farm house built by her grandfather, Jim Wasson. The Grainge family later moved to Springfield and owned and operated the Heart of the Ozarks Motel. Emil passed away in December 1964. Lois passed in August 1991.

In 1967 Jim and Carolyn, along with Don and Fern, purchased a farm east of Republic. They raised cattle and harvested the hay while living in Springfield. In February 1984, Jim and Carolyn started building their dream home on the farm. They moved in, along with their two children, Richard and Cathy, in December of 1984 and became residents of Republic.

Fern Henderson was the daughter of David and Elsie Melton Pendergrass Hammons. After David's death, Elsie married Roy Hammons. Elsie lived on a farm northwest of Republic. She passed in December 1979.

Jim retired from Nabisco after 34 years of service in December of 2001. Carolyn taught school for Springfield public schools for 21 years, retiring in June of 2001. Since Carolyn's retirement, she has substituted in Republic.

Richard and his wife Annette live in Nixa with their two children, Kayla and Ryan. Richard is an engineer for Burlington-Northern. Annette is an Ultra-sound Technician.

Cathy and her husband, Brad Barrett, live east of Republic with their two children, Allyson and Shealyn. Cathy teaches at Gray Elementary in Springfield. Brad is a MRI Technician. Cathy graduated from Republic High School in 1987. *Submitted by Carolyn Henderson.*

**HENSON/JANES -** Lloyd Joseph "Jack" Henson was the second born child of Lee Henson and Josephine Medlin Henson born on Oct. 8, 1914. Jack married Laura Janes, youngest of six children (born March 28, 1916) of Charles Boyd Janes and Nancy Louraina Pendelton Janes on Oct. 19, 1935. Jack died March 29, 1986 and Laura died July 7, 1998. They are both buried at Marionville, MO. They were parents of two children, Charles Wayne Henson (born Oct. 18, 1938, died Feb. 13, 1997) and Sharon Sue Henson (born Sept. 21, 1940) who lives in Arkansas.

During those early years Jack did labor for WPA helping to build roads for wages less than one can imagine today and eventually carpenter work in the surrounding area. He built a four-room house for his family and later had it moved to the county line road, now known as FR 194 where it still stands on the 39 wooded acres he purchased from Earl Ray in the early 1950s. At that time he added on to the house a new kitchen, bathroom and one bedroom. The house sits on the north side of the road putting it in Greene County and Republic school district where his children attended school.

*Jack and Laura Henson.*

Jack and Laura were hard working country people who carved out a place in the woods on Huckleberry Ridge to spend their entire lives. They were people who could have had a new home but chose instead to be thankful for what they had and tended it as if it were the nicest farm around. They sacrificed many things to be able to save for the future. Remembering the hard times they had come through during the Depression they were never wasteful. They made a living from gardening, milking a few cows, selling to a creamery and by raising chickens, ducks and pigs. Laura cooked, canned and sewed as most country women did; however, at one point she did work a short time out of the home at the "Egg" factory in Marionville, MO. Jack later went to work for Carnation Milk Plant in the early 1950s.

Together they cultivated a huge garden sharing with family, friends and neighbors, all the bounty of their labors. Laura was known for her natural ability for flower gardening and Jack for his talent for budding and grafting. He developed his own apple orchard from small seedlings while still working nights as a "pan man" at Carnation Milk Plant. Jack retired from there after 20 years, and he and Laura maintained the orchard for several years selling to customers and sharing with many people. The day after his retirement Jack suffered his first heart attack. He survived it to live another 12 years although he had many other health problems and was hospitalized several times. During those 12 years Laura continued to fulfill his wishes as far as helping to keep the orchard running and various other tasks which he could no longer perform alone.

They were blessed with seven grandchildren. Charles and his wife Helen Tiede Henson had two boys, Kevin and Brandon. Sharon and her husband Dwayne Hook had four daughters and one son: Kim, Karla, Kelly, Dwayne II and Cindy. Pa Pa Jack built a huge wooden patio table to be able to seat all of them plus their parents, and his main highlight of the summer was to feed them watermelons from his garden.

Jack was a member of Billings Masonic Lodge #328. They were both members of Curtis Chapel Baptist Church where Laura (Me Maw) spent much time seeing to it that her grandchildren were able to visit the little country church and attend Vacation Bible School there.

The old "home place" still stands. It is the only house Jack and Laura ever had. By family members it is known as "The House that Jack Built." The property was sold, and the house was re-sided after their deaths. The flowers still bloom in the gardens, and the apple blossoms burst forth each spring. The birds still sing while the wind whispers through the oak trees, and the memories are alive and well. *Submitted by Sharon Henson Hook Corbett.*

**HILL/PATTERSON** - Albion B. and Margret Hanna (Patterson) Hill were married in 1900. He was 44 and she was 19. They lived in a house built by them on North Main Street next door to Mrs. Eliza J. Patterson, Margret's mother. Six children were born to them between 1903 and 1922: Lorine, Maurice, Douglas, George (died at 8 years), Bryce (died at 8 months) and Mary

*Margret and A.B.*

Margret who was delivered in the Hill house on North Main by the legendary Doctor Beal.

A.B. died in 1932 in San Francisco and Margret reared the children with help from her mother next door. Mrs. Patterson had a bathtub, and she did some hard scrubbing on all of Margret's children. Margret became a hair stylist during the Depression and had a shop on North Main in town.

Lorine was selected "Miss San Francisco" while she was living with Inez, Margret's sister. She later married and lived in Australia. She performed as an "interpretive dancer". She came back to California and married Walter Schoenfeldon and lived in Arroyo Grande, CA where she died.

Maurice lost his right arm well above the elbow trying to outguess a through train. He was running home from his girlfriend Daphne Thurman's house. Emotionally drained, he left Republic for California, finishing his schooling there without any other help. He later married Betty

*Maurice Hill.*

and two girls were born to them, Jennifer and Shellie. He was a salesman like his father and his real estate office was one of the top in an extensive area in northern California. He was also a very good tennis player. Maurice Hill is buried in the Evergreen Cemetery in Republic.

*Hill residence. Kent DeWitt and pony and Mary on bike.*

Douglas Hill volunteered for the Army Air Corps and served as a captain in WWII. He married Erma from Washington and three sons were born to them: Rodney, Scott and Douglas.

Douglas was also a salesman like his father and brother Maurice, and had a very successful real estate business in Palo Alto, CA, their home. Douglas is buried in Palo Alto, CA where he had lived his adult life.

*Douglas and Mary Margret*

Mary Margret (Hill) Cox was born in Republic and completed all early schooling there, graduating from high school in 1940. She received a scholarship and attended St. Louis University. When WWII started she volunteered for service in the

*Carol DeWitt, Mary Hill on bike, Alice Whitram, Norma Lee Payne and Martha Whitram.*

U.S. Navy, serving from 1943 to 1945 and when discharged, attended the University of California at Los Angeles. Upon graduation in 1949, she went back into the navy and served 37 years in both regular and reserve, retiring as a lieutenant commander in 1982. She lives in Temecula, CA.

Margret (Patterson) Hill was hit by an automobile in 1959 and is buried in the Hill plot in Evergreen Cemetery. *Submitted by Mary M. Cox, only survivor of William D. Patterson, grandson of Robert Patterson.*

**HOCK/DAVIS** - Sam Hock, son of William Francis Hock and Catherine (Reeves) Hock, had three brothers: Jess, Will and Edward Joe and three sisters: Pearl, Myrtle and Lida. Sam's father was a Civil War veteran serving with Company G, 150th Regiment, 2nd Indiana Volunteers. Sam married Mattie Davis in September 1921. She was the daughter of Ira and Sarah (Glenn) Davis,

*Sam Hock.*

She had three brothers: Charles, Edward and Henry and one sister, Leona. Mattie's father also served in the Civil War with the Wisconsin Infantry Company I, 3rd Regular Volunteers.

Sam carried mail in Douglas, AZ. Part of his route was across the Mexican border in the town of Aguafrieta. This was a foot route, as all city routes were at that time. He learned a few Spanish words to be able to talk to the patrons on the route. When the Battlefield, MO position opened in 1928 he was glad to return to Missouri because he and Mattie had grown up in St. Clair, MO. Sam was the only mail carrier out of the Battlefield Post Office. When it closed he was transferred to Republic where he was the carrier on Route 2 which was the east side of Republic.

They moved to Republic in 1933. He retired in April 1953 and moved to Texas for a few years, but returned in the early 1960s where they remained the rest of their lives.

Sam and Mattie were active in the Methodist Church in Battlefield when they lived there and then in Republic. He was also active in the Masonic Lodge. Sam passed away on July 4, 1966 and Mattie on Jan. 30, 1981. They are buried in the Evergreen Cemetery in Republic.

Sam and Mattie had one daughter, Mary Ellen, who attended all 12 years at Republic graduating in 1944. She married classmate Tommy Neill on May 27, 1945 while he was in the service. After he returned from Army Air Force duty they lived in Republic for a few years with their children: Karen (born 1947), Jim (born 1949) and Barbara (born 1950).

They moved to near Springfield where

Tommy was employed at the Buick Agency in Springfield and had two more children, Joe (born 1957) and Jerry (born 1960).

Tommy died in December 1995 and Joe died in April 1999. Both are buried in the Brookline Cemetery. *Submitted by Mary Ellen Hock Neill.*

**HODGE** - George Franklin Hodge (June 11, 1848-June 18, 1918), son of William Stewart Hodge and Harriett Taylor, migrated from Golconda, IL to the Kansas Territory where he met and married Mary Elizabeth Harrison, daughter of John and Sarah Chaney Harrison (Aug. 10, 1857-Jan. 7, 1934) on Dec. 17, 1874. Five children were born to this family: Chester Aaron Stewart (1876-1888), John Aubrey (1878-??), Jesse Ethel (1880-1881), Reason Ernest (1882-1933) and William Orin (1884-1946).

*William Orin Sr. and Grace Harper Hodge – 1907.*

George Franklin Hodge spent many years as superintendent of schools in Decatur County, KS before moving his family to the Brookline area of Greene County in the late 1890s. Sons, Reason Ernest and William Orin, remained in the Brookline area and engaged in farming. Ernest served as a deputy in the Greene County sheriff's department under Sheriff Marcell Hendrix. William Orin attended veterinary school and served for many years as a veterinarian in the Greene and Lawrence County area.

*William Orin Sr. and Grace Harper Hodge – ca. 1942.*

Reason Ernest Hodge (1882-1933) was born in Decatur County, KS, moving to Missouri with his parents in late 1890s. He married Mary Etta Elizabeth Neill (1884-1985) on Nov. 25, 1907 in Greene County, MO. They had one son, Wilbur. Following the death of Sheriff Hendrix in the "Young Massacre," Ernest served as chief deputy. Following Ernest's sudden death, Mary Etta continued living in Brookline until her death.

William Orin Hodge (June 14, 1884-July 13, 1946) born in Decatur County, KS, moved to the Brookline area with his parents in the late 1890s. On July 4, 1907, he married Grace Elena Harper (Nov. 18, 1883-Jan. 8, 1967), daughter of William Riley Harper and Minnie Erskin. William Orin and Grace Elena were the parents of four children: Mary Elizabeth (1908), Jesse Ethel (1910-1988), William Orin Junior (1912-1981) and George Franklin (1919-1984).

William Orin Hodge Jr. (Dec. 10, 1912-May 16, 1981) born in Brookline, MO, graduated from Republic High School. On Dec. 25,

*Ruth Jones and Orin Hodge Family ca. 1950, seated l-r: Sharon Sue, Orin, Ruth, Rex Eugene; standing is Donald Ray.*

1934, he and Ruth Mildred Jones, daughter of Bert Isaac and Ora Ellen Coggin Jones, were married in Willard, MO. They established their home in the Jones School community, north of Republic, and engaged in farming. For many years they raised turkeys, laying hens, and maintained a dairy herd.

Ruth completed the 8th grade and always yearned for her high school diploma. Once her children completed their college degrees and were working on advanced degrees, she returned to the classroom and completed the long desired certificate of completion of high school studies. For a few years, Ruth was employed as a cook with Republic Schools before working for the Springfield R-12 Schools. Orin was known for his friendliness and willingness to help his neighbors. He was able to remedy many problems with his mechanical skill. He always joked that almost everything could be repaired with bubblegum and bailing wire.

Ruth and Orin were members of Hood United Methodist Church in Republic. Three children were born to this family: Rex Eugene, Donald Ray and Sharon Sue. A foster son, Charlie Brandenburg, joined the family in the early 1940s and stayed with them until he enlisted in the Navy following graduation from high school. *Submitted by Rex Hodge.*

**HODGE/SEVERN** - Rex Eugene Hodge, son of William Orin and Ruth Mildred Jones Hodge, attended the one-room Jones School (established on his great-great-grandfather's land in the late 1800s for his first three years of school. He continued his education in Republic when Jones and Republic Schools consolidated, graduating in the class of 1954.

*Rex Hodge family (1999), l-r standing: Rachel Hodge, Robert and Susan (Holster) Hodge. Seated: Rex and Mary (Severn) Hodge.*

Rex dreamed of establishing a registered milking Shorthorn herd and showing cattle. During his high school years, he began building a herd in conjunction with his parents. The direction of his future changed in 1953 when he felt the call to the ministry in the Methodist Church. Rex received his A.B. degree from Drury College and attended St. Paul School of Theology in Kansas City.

He was admitted as a full member of the Southwest Missouri Conference of the Methodist Church and was ordained an Elder in the church in 1963. His student appointments included Pearl, Mt. Olive, Hurley, Ebenezer and Conway churches in the Springfield District. While at seminary, he served Faubion Chapel. Following that appointment he and his family returned to southwest Missouri, where he served Conway-Warden Chapel, Fairview, Stella, and Muncie Chapel congregations. In 1970, he was appointed to Mt. Carmel, Springfield and served that congregation until 1982 when he was granted disability leave.

While attending school in Kansas City, Rex met Mary Elizabeth Severn, daughter of Edwin and Elizabeth Boggs Severn, a native of Maryland. They were married July 3, 1959, in Arbutus, MD. Mary received her A.B. degree from National College, Kansas City, MO and her master's in education from Drury in Springfield. Following 34 years as an elementary teacher, she retired in 1999, 29 years were spent with the Springfield R-12 system.

In 1976, this family began building their home on a portion of the family farm north of Republic; it became their permanent residence in 1982. Rex and Mary have two children, Robert Eugene and Rachel Emilee.

Robert graduated from Parkview High School, attended Drury College and the University of Southern California, Washington D.C. campus. A life-long love of sailing led him to tall sail ships and motorized yachts. Currently he is captain of a private yacht on the Atlantic coast.

Robert and Susan Holster Hodge were married in Springfield, Jan. 7, 1996. Susan, a registered dietician, completed her college work in dietetics, served an internship with the National Institute of Health, Bethesda, MD, and is an excellent chef, receiving awards for her culinary presentations. Robert and Susan maintain their permanent residence in the Brookline area.

Rachel graduated from Parkview High School, Burge School of Nursing and Drury College. She received her masters of science degree in nursing from the University of Oklahoma. Following 10 years of critical care nursing at Cox Health System, she accepted a position on the faculty of the school of nursing. Her current position is associate professor with Cox College of Nursing and Health Sciences. Rachel's home is in the Brookline area.

Donald Ray Hodge, son of W.O. and Ruth Jones Hodge, graduated from Republic High School, Drury College and received his doctors degree from the University of Wisconsin. He and his wife Ann Brown Hodge, parents of daughters, Kristin Marie and Carrie Lynn, make their home in Florida. *Submitted by Robert Hodge.*

**HOOD/BLADES** - Duncan spent his boyhood in McMinn, TN before coming to Missouri. He married Nancy Ellen Blades, daughter of Edward A. and Ellen L. (Maynard) Blades, Feb. 21, 1841. Four children were born to this mar-

*Hood family. Standing l-r: Margaret, Clyde, Knox, Mary Hicklin. Seated is Mary E. and James Duncan.*

riage: Ellen E., Sarah A., William E. and James Duncan. Duncan settled on a farm in Greene County, where he spent the rest of his life, dying at the age of 31 in 1849, when James Duncan was an infant.

James Duncan Hood was born Dec. 31, 1848 in Little York, Greene County, MO. He grew to manhood on the farm in his native community and worked hard helping support the family. His education was limited to the rural schools, which he attended a few months each winter. Throughout his life, he followed general farming and stock raising pursuits. At the age of 29, he purchased his first farm in Pond Creek Township. He bought, occupied and sold a number of farms before becoming owner of a valuable and well-improved place consisting of 359 acres, known as "The Sunrise Stock Farm," where he carried on general farming and stock raising on a large scale, which was ranked with the best farmers in every respect. He kept an excellent grade of livestock, had a very pleasant home with numerous outbuildings for housing his stock, various grains, grasses and farm machinery.

James Duncan married Mary E. Clack, Oct. 24, 1872. Mary had received a common school education. She was a daughter of Robert Clack, a carpenter and builder, who, when the Civil War began, enlisted in the Confederate Army and fought in the Battle of Wilson's Creek. Robert married Racheal Bonham on Sept. 10; 1835, both from Blount County, TN. To this union two daughters were born, Mary E. and Tennessee, who died as a young woman.

Eight children were born to Mr. and Mrs. Hood: Margaret "Maggie" (born July 31, 1873) married Henry O'Bryant, who was in the U.S. Postal Service; Micagah E.A. (born May 29, 1875, died Feb. 27, 1877); Edward (born May 29, 1876, died February 1878); Eva M. (born March 25, 1878, died Sept. 15, 1888); Clyde Henderson (born March 16, 1882, died Nov. 16, 1944); Nora E. (born Sept. 26, 1884, died Oct. 10, 1884); and Knox H. (born Sept. 15, 1888, died Sept. 17, 1918). Knox traveled for the International Harvester Company selling farm equipment. Mr. and Mrs. Hood also reared Mary Elizabeth Hicklin, daughter of William and Mary (Stogsdill) Hicklin. Mary Elizabeth was born in Lawrence County on May 7, 1882. After losing her mother at age 7 and her father at age 12, Mary was taken in by Mr. and Mrs. Hood who were friends of the Hicklin family.

Mr. Hood was a member of the Ancient Free and Accepted Masons, and he attended the Methodist Episcopal Church. *Submitted by Jim Hood.*

**HOOD/GADDY** - Howard Wayne, eldest son of Elden and Fern (Tuter) Hood was born on Dec. 7, 1938, in Brookline, MO. Howard received his education in the Republic school system while living on his parent's farm northwest of Republic. The rural lifestyle provided the necessary values and a lifetime of memories as he helped his father and mother with the farming and livestock operations.

*Howard Hood.*

Before graduating high school, at age 17, Howard joined the Navy, along with his best buddy, Edward "Pete" Lee. They were soon on their way to Chicago, IL, where they would receive their basic boot camp training. Howard soon found himself headed for a Navy base in San Diego, CA. Shortly after arrival, he shipped out to another base on the Philippine Islands.

After returning from serving two years of active duty in the Philippine Islands, Howard returned to Missouri and soon married Norma Gaddy in December 1960. To this union four children were born: Christina, Howard Jr., Jimmy and Brandee.

The 1966 Sailor of the Year at Olathe, Kansas Naval Air Station was Howard W. Hood, Yeoman 1st class, son of Mrs. Fern Hood and the late Elden Hood. He was chosen on the basis of leadership, appearance and attitude by Capt. W.F. Culley, commanding officer of the air station. Howard reported to ONAS June 6, 1965, when he was assigned to the administration department while living in Spring Hill, KS, with his wife and three children.

His Navy career would take him to many Naval stations around the country including, California, Texas, Missouri, Kansas, Washington and the Philippine Islands.

Being an avid hunter and outdoorsman during his younger years, living in many different locations throughout the country gave him an opportunity to enjoy hunting and fishing when and wherever time permitted. Not only did he have a passion for big game hunting such as deer, elk and antelope, but he also enjoyed wing shooting. Among other hobbies, Howard was interested and very knowledgeable in history and the American Indian culture.

After his retirement from the Navy in 1980, Howard moved his family to Omaha, NE where he joined his brother in the newly established Specialty Manufacturing Company, Inc. where he worked as a machinist. However, this corporate lifestyle did not provide the fulfillment he was looking for. Feeling the need for freedom, and wanting to see what this great country of ours had to offer, he decided to join the transportation industry. After driving the big trucks for several different companies, he took a leap of faith and purchased an 18-wheeler which he proudly named "Faith."

In June 1991, life took another turn for Howard when he married his second wife, Sharon Sargent. Together, they continued in the transportation industry until trading the "big rig" for a one-ton van and began transporting express packages around the country.

Howard passed away May 31, 2002 at his home in La Vista, NE and is buried beside his father at Evergreen Cemetery in Republic. He was the proud father of four children and grandfather of 17. *Submitted by Julie Dan Clark.*

**HOOD/HUGHES** - Clyde Henderson Hood was born March 16, 1882 in Billings, Christian County, MO, son of James Duncan and Mary E. Hood. He married Mae Lenora Hughes April 6, 1905 in Republic, MO. Mae was born June 23, 1882 in Bois D'Arc, MO, daughter of Samuel Meridieth and Lucy (Hendrix) Hughes. Their children were Hildred Hadely "Ted" (born Jan. 28, 1908, died March 11, 1960); Wanda Mae (born Jan. 21, 1914, died March 30, 1974); Victor (born Nov. 22, 1915, died Aug. 4, 1964). They lived in Springfield for a while, before moving to a farm just south of their parent's farm northwest of Republic.

In the early 1900s, Clyde was involved in the construction of the Greene County Courthouse located on Boonville Street in Springfield, which was completed in 1912. With his team and stone wagon, Clyde hauled Phenix stone columns for the basement of the courthouse which were all quarried and cut in Greene County.

Clyde and Mae spent most of their lives in Greene County, except for a few years when they homesteaded a ranch at Two Buttes, CO. From a sod house on the prairie, they ran their ranching operations until the drought and dust storms in the 1930s made it impossible to make a go of ranching. Clyde also owned and operated a freighting business out of Lamar, CO, hauling supplies to local communities and other ranchers. Afterward, they returned to Missouri where they inherited a portion of a 100-acre farm from James and Mary Duncan. Later he purchased the balance of the farm from his sister Maggie O'Bryant. This land was located to the north, just across what is now TT Highway, 4-1/2 miles northwest of Republic, which is still inhabited by their descendents.

*Clyde Hood and his team.*

Clyde and Mae managed to make a living and raise a family of five from the normal farming operations, which included raising small grain crops, selling milk from their dairy cows, and eggs from Mae's prized flock of chickens. They had a large barn that was built in 1915 that housed hay and grains to feed the cattle and provide shelter for Clyde's work and saddle horses.

*L-R: Elden, Wanda, Clyde, Mae and Ted Hood.*

Clyde, Mae, Maggie and her husband Henry, Knox, Ted and Elden, as well as J.D. and Mary, are all buried in the Evergreen Cemetery in Republic.

Mr. Hood was a member of the Ancient Free and Accepted Masons. *Submitted by John and Beverly Hood.*

**HOOD/MINK** - Jimmy Elden, son of Elden and Fern (Tuter) Hood, was born on Aug. 17, 1941 in Springfield, MO. Shortly after Jimmy's birth, Elden was involved in carpenter work in the construction of military bases around the country. They were soon located near Leadville, CO and later near Salt Lake, UT. The family returned to Missouri in 1943 when Jimmy was about 1-1/2 years old, buying a farm located 4-1/2 miles northwest of Republic between Clyde and James Duncan's farms.

Jimmy and his older brother Howard attended grade school at Prairie View School District, about 1/4 mile from home, until the school districts were consolidated. He finished his schooling in Republic High School, Reorganized District No. 3.

After graduation in 1960, Jimmy worked at the normal odd jobs before embarking in the professional world. In the fall of 1960, he took a job with an international food processing company, Henningsen Foods, Inc., headquartered in White Plains, NY. Working in food research and research engineering gave him a broad background for building his future.

Jami, Jim's mom (Fern), John, Jennifer, Julie and Jim Hood.

In September 1961, he was married to Judith Mink and ready to start the family life. He continued working in Springfield until 1963 when he was transferred to south central Nebraska. Upon his father's death in August 1964, Jimmy returned to Republic to assist his mother with the family farming operations. While living on his original home place, their first two children arrived, Julie Robin (born May 16, 1965) and Johnny Elden (born June 14, 1966).

After trying his hand in beef production for a few years, he decided to continue his professional career with Henningsen Foods. He was transferred to the company's district office in Omaha, NE in 1968 where a new division had opened. While living in Omaha, their younger two children were born, Jami Dawn (born Dec. 20, 1971 and Jennifer Rebecca (born Jan. 29, 1974). During this period, Jimmy was promoted to International Customer Service Manager for Henningsen Systems, Inc. This position required both domestic and international travel throughout the United States, Canada and several countries overseas. After 18 years of service, he left Henningsen's to establish his own companies, Specialty Manufacturing Company, Inc. and later J.H. Enterprises, Inc., both in Omaha, NE. Both companies were involved in stainless steel fabrication, building and marketing food processing equipment and spray drying systems for their customers throughout the United States and abroad. Upon retirement in 1995, he moved back to Missouri and is living on the old homestead of his grandparents.

Among his many hobbies, Jimmy enjoyed serving as chapter director in the Gold Wing Touring Association both in Nebraska and Missouri. He also served as state director in Missouri and enjoyed over 100,000 miles touring all 48 states and most of Canada. After retiring his Honda Gold Wing, he is now enjoying his Ezgo golf cart and hitting the links when and wherever possible.

Jimmy is the proud father of four children and grandfather of 10, all living in Nebraska and Iowa. *Submitted by Jennifer and Keith Harvey.*

**HOOD/TUTER** – Elden Hood married Fern Tuter, daughter of Solomon and Edna Earl (Boyd) Tuter, Dec. 23, 1937, at Mt. Vernon, MO. To this union two sons were born, Howard Wayne (born Dec. 7, 1938) and Jimmy Elden (born Aug. 17, 1941).

After working as a carpenter at Camp Crowder, Camp Carson, near Leadville, CO, and on into Utah near Salt Lake, they returned to Springfield, MO.

They soon found a 100-acre farm for sale south of Clyde and Mae Hood's farm. It was also bordered by the farm owned by James Duncan and Mary Hood. On Feb. 15, 1943 they bought it and settled down to make it home. They began working on the house, yard, fences, and stocking it with livestock. The three "Hood" houses were about 1/4 mile apart.

Fern (Tuter) and Elden Hood.

Fern canned everything from their garden and soon the cellar was full and ready for winter. They butchered their own meat, sold honey, milk and eggs to supplement their farming income. Elden owned a portable feed mill and did custom grinding and hay baling around the area. He worked nights for Holsum Bakery and Producer's Creamery in Springfield. He also owned a milk route, hauled cattle, and later drove a truck for Lily Tulip Corp. At 48 years old, Elden lost his life in an accident on Aug. 6, 1964 while helping build Highway 65, between Springfield and Branson, in Taney County.

While attending high school Howard joined the Naval Reserves and soon after graduation he found himself in the Philippine Islands serving his active duty tour. Returning home two years later, he married and became the proud parent of four children: Christina, Howard Jr., Jimmy and Brandee. Howard continued serving his country until his retirement.

After graduating high school, Jimmy was employed by Henningsen Foods, Inc. In 1996 he moved back to Missouri and is living on the old homestead of his grandparents. He is also the father of four children: Julie, Johnny, Jami and Jennifer.

After 26 years of marriage and Elden's death, Fern completed the house they were building on Clyde and Mae's farm which they had purchased. Their original "hill farm" was sold a few years later and Fern purchased the parsonage house in Brookline. Later purchasing the old Brookline Baptist Church building and converted it into a 20 room home. Both her grandfathers, George Boyd and Ballard Tuter, served as deacons in 1905, and where she had accepted the Lord as her personal Savior at the age of 12 and was baptized in Pond Creek by Rev. Stovall at the age of 17. In 1989 she moved back to the farm and sold the church home.

At the age of 65, she bought a cabin on 10 wooded acres at Mack's Creek, MO and enjoyed summer visits there for a few years. She now lives in Republic and often reflects on her life that began in her log cabin birthplace near Bolivar, which is now part of the museum in Bolivar, MO. *Submitted by Fern Hood.*

**HOPPER** - Wally and Roberta Hopper moved to Republic in July 1966. Wally had accepted a position with Security State Bank, which was the only bank in town at that time. He was employed there for 15 years as vice president. They have three children: Brian, Julie and Kelly. They bought a home on Scotland Street in the Wormeyville area and it was the last house that Howard "Wormey" Eagan built during his many years of construction. Their children all completed their education in the Republic Schools.

Wally belonged to many organizations and was president of Kiwanis from 1969-1970. Wally and Roberta were active in community affairs and attended Calvary Baptist Church. Their children have all married and have children of their own. Brian married Janet Hilton and they have a daughter Brandie and twins, Jake and Rachel. Julie married Larry White and they have a daughter Lacy, who has twin sons. They were divorced and Julie is now married to Ernie Dake. Kelly is a cosmetologist in Springfield and has a son Lake and a daughter Soncie. Roberta died in 1979 of cancer.

Donna and Wally Hopper.

After that, Wally married Donna Lacey. They moved from Republic in 1980 to pursue other banking opportunities in Houston and Lebanon. Upon retiring from United Savings and Loan in Lebanon in 1990, they returned to Republic. Wally went back to banking at Town and Country Bank and retired again in 2005. Donna retired from Famous Barr in 2001, after working there for 12 years. They still live in Republic and have a combined family of six children, 14 grandchildren and eight great-grandchildren. All family members live in and around the Republic area. This is their home and has been a great place to raise family and make friends. *Submitted by Wally and Donna Hopper.*

**HOWARD/CLARK -** Louis Howard and Mildred Clark drove to the courthouse in Buffalo, MO on Dec. 10, 1932. It was very cold and lots of snow on the ground. But, when you are in love, the weather is a "never-mind" in your heart. Louis and Mildred were married that day by the Buffalo County Judge and became Mr. and Mrs. Louis E. Howard. However, Louis and Mildred's friends knew them as "Curly" and "Bird." Many years ago a newspaper comic strip character was named "Bird" and as a result, this was the name Louis gave Mildred. Since Louis had been bald for most of his adult life, it didn't take much guessing to figure out "Curly."

Mildred (Clark) and Louis Howard.

Louis and Mildred started a home in rural Greene County, south of Brookline. Louis was a well respected farmer and Mildred a well-known public school teacher in rural Greene County.

Louis was always a farmer at heart. He loved the outdoors, the soil and what he could grow in it. He was noted for having a neat yard to grow many kinds of flowers, especially hybrid roses. He always had a beautiful garden in the summer with more vegetables than he and his family could use. He never sold anything from his garden but gave it to his neighbors and friends.

Louis and Mildred were good and faithful supporters of the Democrat Party. They received a plaque of Recognition from the Greene County Democratic Party for "Excellence and Dedication to Public Service from 1970-88."

Louis and Mildred became faithful members of Republic First Christian Church in 1950. Louis actively participated as a Deacon. He never wanted to be seen, but wanted his church to always be ready for whatever the occasion presented, such as: maintenance of the baptistery which meant filling it several days in advance of its use. He was always willing to take new ministers under his wing and go with them to visit shut-ins and other members of the church. He always laughed about how fast the ministers drove over the country roads and would he get home safely. Mildred's faithful endeavors brought about many children's programs. She was an active participant in the CWF, which was local as well as state. She played the organ or piano, whichever was needed. Mildred taught a Sunday school class for many years. She usually roasted a turkey for the annual Thanksgiving dinners and baked many pies for pie suppers.

Mildred taught public school in southwest Missouri for 40 years. Part of it in one-room school houses in rural Greene County. The rest was in Mt. Vernon, Republic, and Springfield. In her later years of teaching, she had the honor of being selected by the State Department of Elementary and Secondary Education to be a member of the committee that re-wrote guide lines for the special education curriculum. She always had an interest in her past students and their families and kept abreast of their achievements in the Republic community. Had she lived, she would be proud to know that her family has a part in the education of students in the Republic school system. And last but not least, that her great-grandchildren are and will be educated in the Republic school system.

*Ed and Mary Howard acknowledge Louis and Mildred were the best parents and in-laws a son and daughter-in-law could ever have.*

**HUGHES/ROSS** – Webster "Web" Wayne Hughes was born July 16, 1893 at Bois D'Arc, MO. He was the only son born to Samuel and Lucy Hughes. He had three sisters: Mae, Ethel and Rayben. Their grandparents were Sarah and N.J. Hendrix. A few years later the Hughes family moved to Republic, MO where they lived out their lives. Web was a veteran of WWI, serving his country well.

Discharged Jan. 28, 1919, he returned home to Republic. One evening he decided to attend a pie supper in Brookline, MO meeting the pretty red-headed Irish school teacher named Elta Virginia Ross, from Morrisville, MO. She was a descendant of Betsy Ross, the lady who designed and sewed the first American flag. Web bought Elta's cherry pie, and the rest is history.

They were married Feb. 13, 1923 in Greene County, MO. To this union, two boys and two girls were born in Republic. Blanche Eulalia (born Nov. 30, 1926), Frances Zana (born Nov. 30, 1934). Although there were eight years difference in their ages, Web always considered he had twin girls. Their sons were Wayne Woodard (born May 12, 1929) and Chester Monroe, who died in infancy.

For many years Web owned and operated a produce company, located on Grant Street across from the old band stand. He bought eggs, cream, chickens, rabbits, varmint hides in season, and livestock hides. All the kids from miles around knew Web, for he bought their rabbits and hides. Once he told his wife he thought one of the Jones (fictitious name) boys was selling him the same rabbits over and over again. The kid would enter the front door, sell his rabbits to Web, then as he left through the back door, he would grab his rabbits, come back the next day, or maybe a few hours later and resell them.

Web knew his rabbits, one that was clean shot brought five cents and others that were shot and mangled two cents. Web was more amused than angry, for he said "that kid will make a good business man someday."

Elta was a good wife and mother. She was kind, gentle and generous, until you made her angry. She believed; "spare the rod, and spoil the child." She was a hard worker, helped her husband, made sure her children attended Sunday school and church, did their chores and home work after school.

Elta belonged to Hood Methodist Church and Web belonged to First Baptist Church. Elta was a Democrat and Web a Republican. There were plenty of hot arguments around the Hughes house, but there was also plenty of love.

Web and Lester E. Cox (founder of Cox Medical Center) were school chums in Bois D'Arc and remained friends throughout their lives. On Dec. 3, 1971 Web was admitted to Cox Medical Center North following a stroke, and requested to see Lester before going to his room. His daughters, Blanche and Frances, wheeled him into Mr. Cox's office. Mr. Cox stood up, shook Web's hand, reached for the telephone, spoke with his chief of staff saying, "Mr. Web Hughes will be a patient here; please see that he receives the best of care." Web remained at Cox until his death on Jan. 18, 1972.

His wife Elta died July 19, 1983, at age 83, while living with daughter Frances in Dallas, TX. Distraught, Frances called Bill Cantrell of Cantrell Funeral Home in Republic. Mr. Cantrell said, "not to worry, he would come get Elta." Late that night, he drove his hearse to Dallas and brought Elta home. Good humanitarians like this make up the Republic area.

Web, Elta, Wayne Hughes Jr. and Wayne Hughes III are buried in Evergreen Cemetery, Republic. Baby Chester is buried along side his grandparents, Samual and Lucy Hughes. Blanche Hughes Havener is buried at Greenlawn Cemetery, Springfield. Frances Hughes Stinger no longer lives in Republic but remembers friends and classmates. She cherishes the memories of growing up and becoming a citizen of the great city of Republic, in her words, "God Bless Republic." *Submitted by Frances Stinger.*

**HUNTSINGER** - James C. "Jim" Huntsinger was born in Council Grove, KS on Dec. 8, 1932. His parents were both teachers in the local school system. They moved to St. Louis, MO in 1938. When World War II started, both of his parents worked in a small arms plant. They moved back to Kansas in 1944 where his parents were distributors for the *Kansas City Star* in Ottawa, KS.

At 14 Jim joined the Navy reserve, lasting only four days until his mother came and got him. He thinks he knew even then that he wanted to serve in the military. He again lied about his age and this time didn't tell anyone and at just under 16 years of age found himself in the Army.

He went to Radio Repair School in Georgia. He served in Vietnam, Africa, Newfoundland and Germany during his 27 years. He retired as Chief Warrant 4. He and his wife Doris were married in 1955; she was in the Navy and they were both stationed in Seattle, WA. They raised three boys, one of whom retired from the Army after 20 years and now works for the Defense Intelligence Agency in Hawaii. The other two have held various jobs to support their wives.

*James C. Huntsinger.*

After Jim's retirement, they settled in El Paso, TX. He worked for an office supply firm and then purchased a garage. His health deteriorated and they sold the garage and bought an Airstream trailer and started to see the United States. It was not to be, however, as his mother broke her hip and needed their help so they moved back to Kansas. Shortly after that, Jim developed heart problems. His wife was afraid that he would need long term care so they sold the trailer and bought a house that had a small house on the back of their property to care for his mother. When she died in 1989 they decided to move to Missouri closer to the fishing.

They purchased a house on Table Rock Lake and Jim loved being able to put his boat in the water and fish to his heart's content. When he again started having heart problems, they looked for someplace closer to the hospital. After looking over the area around Springfield, they settled in Republic. They have never been sorry; Republic is a great place to live. Jim ran for alderman and won, served two years and then lost when he ran again. He ran for mayor, lost that race too but bitten by the desire to serve "his city," he ran for alderman again and is serving on the council and as Mayor Pro Tem until 2006. He ran again and continues to serve the citizens of Republic in 2007. *Submitted by Jim Huntsinger.*

**INMON** - Raymond L. Inmon was born to Charles H. and Beula M. (Payne) Inmon on June 21, 1920 in Battlefield, MO. He married Loretta Faye Hilton on Dec. 21, 1939 in Springfield, MO. Charles Richard Inmon arrived to the newlyweds on Aug. 7, 1940, followed by Peggy Ann Inmon on Nov. 29, 1943. Raymond joined the Navy in 1944 where he served until 1946. Their third child, Ray Lee Inmon, was born

*Raymond and Faye Inmon.*

on March 17, 1947. Shortly after that Raymond served in the Army for the next year.

After his military service Raymond worked as a short order cook, a car salesman and a

*Webster Hughes, WWI, Jan. 28, 1919.*

*Elta Virginia Ross and Webster Wayne Hughes on their wedding day, Feb. 13, 1923.*

few other occupations. John Michael Inmon was born Nov. 7, 1955. In 1958 Raymond began his career at the Federal Medical Center as a correctional officer and his eldest son Charles joined the Army and served for eight years. A short time later the family moved to Republic where Peggy and Ray Lee graduated from high school. Peggy married and moved away from Republic. After his graduation Ray Lee served his country in the Army as a heavy equipment operator in Vietnam.

During the following years in Republic Raymond served as Little League coach and assisted with the local Cub and Boy Scout programs. Faye served as a Den Mother and was heavily involved in the First Christian Church in Republic. Just before John graduated from high school at Republic the family moved to the Brookline area where they lived in 1974 when John graduated from Republic High School and started attending Southwest Missouri State College. In 1976 John joined the Marine Corps as an air traffic controller where he served for 17-1/2 years until receiving a medical discharge.

In 1978 Raymond retired from the Medical Center and opened a Swap Shop in the Brookline area. In 1979 Raymond and Faye moved to Billings where they lived until his death in July 1999. Faye continues to reside in Billings. *Submitted by John Inmon.*

**JACKSON -** In the 18th century in Cantabary, Germany, Charles and Peter Cantabary decided to go to America. They boarded a ship and when they arrived in the U.S. were sold as indentured workers. The two brothers were separated and were never able to make contact. Peter Cantabary worked at various places and finally went to Knottsville, KY. He married a girl from Ireland and they had five children. One of their daughters, Christine Cantabary married John (Harry) Jackson and one of their sons was named John Samuel Corum Jackson who later became known as JSC Jackson.

*Grandpa Jackson's home built in 1885. Aunt Mollie, Aunt Hattie, Grandma Nancy, Grandpa John S.C., Elmer O'Banion, Uncle Bill Jackson, Uncle Carlos Jackson, unknown.*

JSC Jackson drove an ammunition wagon during the Civil War. When the war ended he and two brothers were brakemen on the train. They decided to join a wagon going west. While waiting for the wagon they decided to visit relatives near Republic where they heard about right-of-way land for sale near Republic. They purchased several hundred acres where they settled with their parents. JSC helped establish the Wade Chapel Cemetery and the Hopewell Church.

Early in the 18th century the O'Banion family migrated from Marrowbone, KY and while going through Missouri enroute to Kansas, they discovered a spring and spent the winter near the spring. After the winter, they purchased land near the spring and later the Grandview School house was built near the spring.

Before leaving Kentucky Alfred O'Banion had married the sister of Nancy Liles. Nancy's sister died leaving Alfred and several boys. Nancy Liles' husband had died before their daughter Nancy Jane was born. In time Nancy Liles and Alfred O'Banion were married and their total family came to Missouri.

Nancy Jane Liles and JSC Jackson were married in 1871. They settled on the land JSC Jackson had purchased and raised their large family, five boys and four girls, as well as two local orphans and two grandchildren.

The Jackson family, many of their grand, great-grand, and great-great-great-grandchildren still live in the Republic and Springfield areas. *Submitted by Joan O'Neal Varland.*

**JACKSON -** At least two Jackson lines came to the Republic area from Barry County, MO in the 1850s. This narrative covers only the one Jackson line of the great-great-grandfather, Andrew J. Jackson, born 1830 in Tennessee. His parents were also born in Tennessee, their names are yet unproven.

Andrew was first recognized in Barry County when he married Emaline Williams July 16, 1856. Their first four children were born there, including the great-grandfather, John M. Jackson Sr. in 1857. They moved on to Wilson Township, Greene County, MO by 1870 where they spent the remainder of their lives.

*circa 1935, Riley Jackson with wife Nellie, daughter Jean and sons: Leroy, Don and Bob.*

Their children (in addition to John M.) were Levina Elizabeth "Betty" (1859-1932) married Henry Cooper; William Andrew Jackson (1864-1931) married Carrie Gardner; Ida Belle (1870-1955) married John Rose; Minnie (1871-1893) married Timotheus T. Basnett; Lula (1872-1931) married Luther Byram; Anna (1876-1932) married Hugh Thurston; and Edward R. (1879-1922) wife's name uncertain.

The 12 children of John M. Jackson (1857-1937) and Nettie Idella Newell (1865-1922) included the grandfather, Riley Deputy Jackson (1897-1955) who married Nellie Looney Dec. 24, 1923. Grandaddy Riley lost a leg when a young boy, but excelled at handling horses. When fairs were held at Republic, Riley was the fastest to harness a horse. His siblings were Hattie Mae (1882-1946), Clarence Newton (1885-1955), Bessie (1886-1910), Ethel (1888-1970), Walter Andrew (1891-abt. 1956), Nellie (1893-1925), Laura Edith "Lilie" (1895-1919), John Marion Jr. (1899-1979), Glenn Edward (1902-1903), Hazel (1903-1904), and Mildred (1906-1992).

The family were mainly farmers in the Brookline area. Many of the family are at rest in the Brookline Cemetery, including the first two children of Riley and Nellie, Edith Idella (1925-1925) and Leroy (1927-1936). The three surviving siblings from that marriage are Jean (Kirby), Bob (the writer's father and Past Master of the Republic Masonic Lodge) and Don. *Submitted by Karen Jackson Meads and Deborah Jackson.*

**JACKSON -** George W. Jackson and his brothers: John, Joseph and Edward, were among the earliest settlers in the Republic area, arriving soon after the Civil War by horseback from Tennessee. They settled on land northwest of Republic on what is now Farm Road 168. Their names and acreages, located in Section 12, Township 28, Range 24, appear in the official lists of residents and maps of voting townships in the book *Statistics of the Population of Greene County by Civil Townships* from *the Census of 1870 and 1875.* George W. Jackson served as official census-taker for Pond Creek Township and used this book to carry out his duties for the county.

John and Christiana Castleberry Jackson, the parents of George W. and his brothers, with their two daughters, soon followed their sons to Missouri and settled nearby. Later the family's extended holdings made it so that "you could walk from Halltown to Republic and never be off Jackson land," recalls one descendant. Christiana brought with her the thick manual of herbal medicine, *The Botanic Physician Manual or Family Medical Advisor* (1835), from which she ministered to the ills and infirmities of her family and neighbors back in Tennessee. This well-worn manual was found in an old shed on the original homeplace.

*Luther Wade, Mertie Wade (child), Mattie Jackson Wade (holding baby Jerry), Nellie Jackson (on stepladder), Minnie Jackson, George W. Jackson, wife Charlotte O'Neal Jackson, Jason Jackson, Ila and Golda Jackson (on stepladder), Della Batson Jackson.*

George W. Jackson married Charlotte O'Neal, whose father and brother established and operated the O'Neal Lumber Yard in Republic for many years. To George W. and Charlotte four children were born: Mattie, Jason, Minnie, and Nellie. George W. was a prominent individual in the community. In addition to being the census-taker and justice of the peace for his township, he and his father John were instrumental in establishing the Hopewell Baptist Church in 1867. He also served many years as secretary for nearby Wade Chapel Cemetery.

George W. demonstrated a keen interest in developing his fine orchard and experimenting with grafting and other innovative procedures. His vegetable and flower gardens were outstanding. He had his own sassafras grove and hives of bees therein, also growing a wide variety of herbs and plants necessary for carrying on the practice of herbal medicine begun by his mother.

The original two-story home of George W. and Charlotte Jackson (shown in photograph) was built by George W. in 1899 for $1,000. It still stands on the land they occupied in the 1800s. They, along with George W.'s parents and many other family members, are buried in nearby Wade Chapel Cemetery. Their four children and immediate descendants are:

1) Mattie Jackson Wade (husband Luther; children: Mertie, Jerry, Marvin).

2) Jason Jackson (wife Della, children: Ila, Golda, Osha, Emmett).

3) Minnie Jackson Squibb (husband Benjamin, children: George, Johnnie Lucille, Chester, Burchie, Dorothy, June, Ruel and Marjorie).

4) Nellie Jackson Coggins (husband Laurence) died very shortly after the birth of daughter Gladys. *Submitted by Marjorie Evans.*

**JAMES/LUNA -** In 1902 Frank Luther James was born into the family of Freeman and Augusta (White) James. He was the second of 10 children. Frank married Opal Luna in 1931. They had three daughters: Betty, Mary Ann and Judy James. Frank and Opal lived near Gainsville, MO, on a farm for many years. Frank's father passed away in 1937, and Augusta and her son, Charlie James, moved to Republic. In later years, Augusta married Horrace Bell in Republic.

Frank and Opal moved to Republic in 1966. He was a hard worker, and he loved to work in the orchards picking grapes and apples. He also worked on farms around Republic. Opal also worked right beside him, and they were always together. They both loved to sing and play music.

Betty married Bron Morrison in 1949, and they had two children. Their son, Elwyn, was killed in 1969 at the age of 16 in a car wreck. Diana, their daughter, was 9 years old when Elwyn died. She is married to Michael Hunt, and they have two daughters.

Mary Ann is married to Delbert Strong, and they have two sons, Edward and Jack Strong. They live in Baldwin City, KS, where they have lived since 1960. Delbert and Mary Ann have four living grandsons. They lost one grandson, Judson, in a car accident. Mary Ann is a cosmetologist, and Delbert is retired.

Judy is married to Clifton Jewell, and they live in Springfield, MO. They lived in Republic some years ago. They have two children. Their daughter Kandi is married, and their son Jerry died as a teenager. Judy and Clifton have five grandchildren.

Frank passed away in 1970. He was a kind person who loved the church he and Opal attended, the Church of Christ in Republic.

Opal married Wayne Eaglin, and they lived in Republic until they departed this life. Opal passed away in 1994. *Submitted by Betty Morrison.*

**THE JIG-A-LONGS -** A lucky group of Republic youths danced their way through adolescence. Proud parents arranged for dance lessons, and a once in a lifetime opportunity to canvas the Midwest and Southern United States from the 1950s through 1960s. Mothers designed and made custom costumes for the dancers. Their parents packed and drove cars from state to state to meet all the scheduled bookings.

*Front l-r: Pat and Mike Arnold, Bob Arndt, Terry Gott, Jim Ferguson, Tony Logan; back: Libby Cox, Carla Massey, Linda Stewert, Sandy French, Phyllis Cox, Paula Arndt.*

Many summers were spent dancing and traveling. Year-round Saturdays ushered in all day rehearsals in order to dance on *The Ozark Jubilee,* which was a nationally televised country western show with many of the best-known stars of that day.

This article is a tribute to these families that invested so much in the youth of Republic. Parents of the Jig-A-Longs included the

*Tony Logan, Sandy French, Rex Burdett, Jackie Payne, Carla Massey, Phyllis Cox, Jimmy Ferguson, Terry Gott, Linda Stewart, Libby Cox.*

following: Jim and Roberta Arnold, Wilford and Maxine Arndt, Jojohn and Geri Gott, Wallace and Maxine Ferguson, Lester "Bud" and Virgie Logan, A.E. "Heavy" and Beth "Puge" Cox, Carl and Bonnie Massey, Jo Stewart, Jack and Betty French.

Other later members from Springfield included the following: Cordelia Colbertson, Ona Edwards, Rex Burdett and Jackie Payne. *Submitted by Sandy Williams.*

**JOHNSON/SPARKMAN -** Lawrence Norva Johnson was born near Clear Creek, MO in 1911, but moved to the Republic area at a young age. He often spoke of hunting and trapping as some of his main childhood activities. Lawrence's mother Hallie ran a chuck wagon when he was a child. He helped prepare the meals for the farm hands. Lawrence's wife, Stella, was always considered an excellent cook by everyone who enjoyed one of her meals. Before they were married, however, she didn't know how to cook, so he taught her and he barely touched a pan after she learned.

During Lawrence's early adulthood, he made a living doing contract farm labor. Later in life his labors were directed toward building his own farm. Over the years he established a sizable dairy herd, and later switched to raising beef cattle. Before the Rural Electric Associations were established in the late 1930s, few rural areas had access to electricity. Lawrence foresaw the advantages that electricity could bring to the farm and became involved with getting farmers to sign up with the REA. As electricity was brought in, he helped wire many of the farms in the Republic area.

During the Depression, he and other area farmers worked at a local lead mine located just to the southwest of the farm. His job at the mine was to push a wheelbarrow up a tall ramp and dump the ore into a separator. Other farmers worked both in and above the shaft. While the mine was a bust and only produced a very small amount of ore, it was like a gold mine for the local farmers. Mining provided them with a way to keep their farms at a time when many were struggling here and across the country.

*Stella, Lawrence, Jimmy and Kenneth Johnson at their farm near Republic in the early 1940s.*

Lawrence had a strong religious conviction and was a deacon at the Wilson Creek Baptist Church where he was a member for all his adult life. Lawrence lived to the age of 79 and is buried in the Evergreen Cemetery in Republic.

Stella Mae Johnson was born in 1911 to John and Minnie Sparkman, and spent her entire life in and around Republic. She was considered a hard-working woman, and one would rarely find her idle. Much of her day would consist of performing the chores of a typical farmer's wife: cooking, cleaning, canning and gardening; but Stella also had an artistic side. She enjoyed drawing, and later in her life, painting. She also enjoyed collecting and adorning dolls. Stella lived to the age of 89 and is buried next to Lawrence in the Evergreen Cemetery.

Lawrence and Stella had four children: Jimmy, Kenneth, Joyce and Don. Joyce died as an infant, but the rest have married and their families reside in the Republic, Springfield and Tulsa, OK areas. *Submitted by Don Johnson.*

**JONES -** Isaac Newton Jones, youngest son of the Rev. Joshua and Edna Bingham Jones, was born near Sweetwater, Monroe County, TN, April 20, 1825 and died in Greene County, MO June 17, 1882. He is buried in the Brookline Cemetery. On Sept. 11, 1851 he married Martha McClure (Oct. 25, 1834 TN), daughter of Charles and Keturah Moon McClure. Eleven children were born to this union: Sarah E. (1853-1886), Edna J. (1856), James Luther (1858-1940), Henry Bascomb (1860-1950), Charles W. (1861), Effie Keturah (1864-1890), Martha (1867), Alice (1868), Katherine (1869), Joshua Lyman (1872-1845) and Benjamin G.W. (1875-1969).

*H.B. Jones Family – 1930. 1st row l-r: Joe Donald, Henry Bascomb, Jack, Hannah Florence, Harold, Florence Kathleen; 2nd row: Ruth Mildred, Ora Ellen Coggin, Bert Isaac Jones, Fred Samuel and Mabel Keith.*

Isaac and his older brother Benjamin George Whitfield Jones sold the family farm in Tennessee following the death of their mother in 1849. They secured positions as representatives of the Seth Thomas Clock Co. and set out with a wagon train for Missouri. Their destination was the Webster County home of their brother who had migrated to Missouri with his family in the 1840s. The Jones brothers originally purchased land in the Ash Grove area of Greene County. Prior to 1851, Isaac sold his interest in the Ash Grove property to his brother Ben and began to purchase land in the Pond Creek area north of Republic eventually owning a large acreage for farming. Pension records indicate Isaac Newton served with Co. A Phelps Regiment from 1861-62. A history of Yeakley Chapel United Methodist Church lists Isaac N. and Martha among the founding members of that congregation. A small home, still in use, south of the junction of Highway N and Interstate 44 was the center of activity for this family and their agricultural endeavors.

Henry Bascomb Jones was born March 21, 1860 in Greene County, MO and died Sept. 27, 1950. He married Hannah Florence Pickering, born Jan. 20, 1863, died Aug. 7, 1937, daughter of Samuel Benton Pickering and Margaretta Gray. They had two sons: Fred Samuel (1886-) and Bert Isaac (1888-1971). Henry and Florence built a large home and barn just east of the original family home in Pond Creek Township and continued farming the land his father had secured. The home still stands on one of the highest spots in Greene County. Henry Bascomb, known as "Hank" to many and as "little grandpa" to his great-grandchildren, was a Bible student who frequently read and told stories to his great-grandchildren. Fred and his wife, Mabel Keith, made their home and reared their family in California. Bert married Ora Ellen Coggin, daughter of George W. and Elizabeth Ellen Rose Coggin and continued operating the family farm.

Bert Isaac Jones (Nov. 18, 1888-April 19, 1971) and Ora Ellen Coggin (Sept. 3, 1891-Nov. 14, 1985) were married April 18, 1911. They made their home on the Jones family farm north of Republic. Children Ruth Mildred (1912-1999), Florence Kathleen (1916) and Joe Donald (1923- 2000) were born to this couple. When health problems made living on the farm and working the land difficult, the farm was sold and Bert and Ora purchased a duplex and moved to Republic. Ora's sister, Laura, and husband, Oran O'Neal, also made their home in the duplex. *Submitted by Rachel Hodge.*

**JONES/WALLACE -** Raymond R. Jones was born Jan. 13, 1928 at Washington (Franklin County) MO, the son of Franklin R. Jones and Gertrude Sarah (Hollis) Jones. Eula Faye (Wallace) and twin brother, Ray, were born to George Washington (G.W.) Wallace and Edna Mae (Boston) Wallace April 22, 1929 at Roubidoux, Texas County, MO.

*Faye and Raymond Jones.*

Faye attended a one-room elementary school, three years at Plato High School, graduating from Houston High, Houston, MO. Faye enrolled at Missouri State University, earning a BS in elementary education. She began teaching, attending summer school to earn a minimum of 10 college hours and by passing a Missouri State written test, being a standard procedure for certification.

Raymond attended a one-room elementary school (Lambeth) in Maries County, MO, and graduated from Vienna High School, Vienna, MO. Raymond's parents did not enroll him in school until reaching his eighth birthday due to living three miles from school. He walked to school alone through a dense forest most of the way, with only a wagon trail as a road.

Upon graduation in 1948, a contract was signed to teach in a one-room school (Terry School District), Maries County, MO, for approximately $1,400 a term, providing 10 hours college credit was earned during the summer and a Missouri State test passed for a one-year certification. In 1950 he signed a contract to teach 6th grade at Dixon, MO.

In August of that summer he was enrolled at Missouri State University when notification came from the local draft board to report for military service, limiting teaching to seven school days. On Sept. 12, 1950 he began military service in the Korean Conflict, serving two years. He was assigned to Headquarters Company of the 3rd Inf. Div. in the area of Seoul. He earned the rank of sergeant as a personnel record specialist, and was awarded a Commendation Medal for meritorious service.

Faye and Raymond were married April 21, 1951 in Gainesville, GA at Camp Stewart, an army basic training center for soldiers.

In 1954, while Raymond was teaching school in Houston, MO, and Faye was teaching in a rural school (Texas County), their son Darrell was born. In 1956, daughter Lois was born and in 1958 the family moved to Republic, MO.

Raymond was employed as 6th grade teacher and school bus driver, then later as elementary principal (1958-68). He was employed as principal for seven years and superintendent of schools for 13 years in area public schools, including Spokane, Strafford and Everton. His total career in public education was 33 years.

Raymond attended Southwest Baptist College in Bolivar, Missouri, Missouri State University, graduating with a BS in education, a master's degree in education from Drury University, certified as elementary principal, course work beyond the master's degree to receive certification in public school administration as superintendent of schools.

Faye was not only homemaker, but was employed at Crane Public Schools for 24 years, during which time she taught 2nd, 3rd and 4th grades as well as special math and language arts. Her total career teaching was 32 years.

Faye is a member of Daughters of American Revolution (DAR) and Colonial Dames, qualified by being a certified descendant of John Hart, a signer of the Declaration of Independence.

Children: Darrell Raymond, Lois Faye, Sharon Elaine and LaRae Dawn. Darrell, Lois and LaRae are graduates of Missouri State University; Sharon a graduate of Evangel University.

Grandchildren: Whitney (Jones) Hoodenpyle is a teacher in the Republic R-3 School District; Sarah is a student in Bolivar schools; Jordan Kersee Jones is a student in Republic schools. *Submitted by Raymond Jones.*

**KELTNER/STEELE -** Victor and Mary Keltner both grew up around the Battlefield and Wilson's Creek area. Vick went to school at Capernium and Mary attended Green Ridge. Victor was the son of John Keltner and Ethyl Pierce. He had one brother Kenneth and two sisters, Flo and Dorothy. Victor's mother died in childbirth when he was about 2 years old.

*Dixie, Mary, Victor and Jo Ann Keltner of Battlefield.*

After Ethyl's death, John married again and once again became a widower. Next, he married Grace (Gillian) Norman. Grace was a widow with five children: Laura, Albert, Bertha, Alta and Clara. John and Grace also had Margie Lee and Marcella to add to the Keltner family.

Mary Steele was the daughter of John Almus Steele and Christie McConnell Steele. Her brothers were Glen, Harry and Clyde.

Victor and Mary Keltner lived in Battlefield when their daughter Dixie was born in 1938. That house still remains. Shortly after Dixie's birth, Mary and Vick bought a 40-acre farm east of Battlefield. They lived for nine years in a house made from boxcars. In 1947, they began building a new house while anticipating the birth of their second daughter Jo Ann. Victor and Mary lived on the family farm for over 56 years.

Dixie attended Central Point School eight years, then Republic High School. She went on to SMS and came back to Republic to teach five years before teaching in a Department of Defense school in Braccone, France. After teaching one year there, she returned home to teach 24 years in the Marshfield school system. Dixie retired from teaching in 1990 and now owns an antique shop in Springfield, MO.

Jo Ann went to school one year at Central Point before it was consolidated. For seven years she went to school at Kickapoo (now Walt Disney), then attended Republic High School. Jo Ann married Terry Wester and had four children: Sam, Terri, Krissi and Merle. *Submitted by Jo Ann Keltner.*

**KERR -** Robert Kerr Sr. was born in 1732 at Mecklenburg County, VA. His son Robert Kerr Jr. was born May 1758 in North Carolina. In King's Mountain papers (Missouri State Historical Society in Columbia) we see Robert Kerr Sr. and Robert Kerr Jr. fighting in the Revolutionary War with the Shelbies at the battle of King's Mountain in 1780.

Robert Kerr Jr. married Amy George in December 1786 in Greene County, TN. Amy (born November 1767 in Tennessee) was the gg-granddaughter of Samuel and Elizabeth (Verch Rees) Humphery. Samuel and Elizabeth were married February 1658 and had eight children. After Samuel's death in September 1677 in Bayn Tallwym, Wales, Elizabeth and her children came to Haverford, PA in 1683. Robert Kerr Jr. and Amy (George) Kerr had nine children: Martha, William, Robert III, Margaret, Rebecca, John George, Thomas Jefferson, Anderson and Amy.

William, Robert III and Thomas Jefferson came to Greene County, MO from Sevier County, TN in 1841. Robert Kerr III gave the land for Kerr Springs Cemetery.

William, Robert III and wife Elizabeth, Thomas Jefferson and wife Martha are buried at Kerr Springs Cemetery, west of Republic.

William Kerr (born March 1791, died March 1875 in Greene County, MO) married Nancy "Anne" Hubbert in January 1812 in Sevier County, TN. Nancy was born in August 1793 and died in September 1853 in Greene County, MO. William then married Mary Steele in September 1854. Mary was born in October 1811 and died in November 1895. William and Mary (Steele) Kerr had no children. William served in the War of 1812. His service pension request states he was drafted in Captain Williams company, Colonel Bunch regiment, Daugherty 5th Brigade, Jackson's Division January 1813 and honorably discharged in June 1813.

William and Nancy Anne (Hubbert) Kerr had five children all born in Tennessee.

1) Alexander Preston (born April 1813, died February 1855) is buried at Kerr Springs Cemetery. He married Margaret Hubbert in October 1835 in Talladega County, AL. Margaret (born January 1814, died in 1888) is buried at Short Cemetery, Hurley, MO. They had four sons and three daughters.

2) Amy (born July 1815, died February 1895) married Walter Cowden in February 1836 in Sevier County, TN. They had two sons and two daughters. After Walter's death in November 1843, Amy and her children came to Greene County, MO. She married John Steele in July 1845 and they had two sons and one daughter.

3) Robert (born March 1818, died December 1838 in Sevier County, TN).

4) James Jackson (born June 1820, died November 1838 in Bradley County, TN) married Liza Cowden. Their daughter Sarah R. Kerr married John Land in Tennessee. John and Sarah Land came to Republic in 1879 after the death of her grandfather, William Kerr. The 1904 Greene County Plat Book shows John and Sarah's family owning part of William Kerr's property.

5) Matthew H. (born March 1824, died February 1895) married Sarah Ann Ellis in January 1848 in Greene County, MO. Sarah was born June 1832 and died April 1900 in Christian County, MO. They had six sons and five daughters. Matthew and Sarah are buried in Kerr Cemetery on Kerr Road near Clever, MO.

William and his sons, Alexander and Matthew, owned property in the Republic area in Township 28, Range 23 and Section 21, 22, 24, 29 and 30. In 2005, 240 of the 320 acres William owned is covered with houses. This area is on the east side of Lynn and the north side of Elm Street to Bailey Road, which includes the Stoney Creek Estates.

In 2005 William and Nancy Kerr have descendents in Greene, Christian, Lawrence and Stone counties. Living in the Republic area are their gg-grandchildren, Luther Land and Opal McCroskey; their ggg-grandchildren; Anne (Land) Johnson, Betty (Truman) Silva, Lela (Lane) Laney, Lacey (Kerr) Flood, Allen McCroskey and Joe Lakins. *Submitted by Joe L. Lakins, ggg-grandson of William and Nancy Kerr.*

**KERR** – Amy, the daughter of William and Nancy (Hubbert) Kerr, was born July 1815 in Sevier County, TN and died in February 1895. In February 1836 Amy married Walter Cowden who was born in 1816 and died in November 1843. Amy and her four children came to the Republic area after the death of Walter. The Greene County Marriages Book A lists Amy Cowden married John Steele in July 1846 by Thomas Dodds JP recorded on page 143 certificate #611.

Amy's parents and brother Matthew came to Republic, MO in 1841. Her brother Alexander and family came to Republic from Alabama in 1843. In 1838 her brothers, Robert Clack Kerr and James Jackson Kerr, died in Tennessee.

Amy Kerr and Walter Cowden had four children all born in Tennessee.

John Albert Cowden (born April 1837, died June 1907) married Mary Frances Sullivan (born January 1841, died February 1915). John and Mary were married in October 1857 in Greene County. They had five children: Their first child died at birth in 1858; Amy Anne (born June 1860, died November 1930) married twice (1) Thomas Davis and (2) Isaac McCain; Matilda "Tillie" Frances (born September 1865, died June 1947); Rachel Katie (born June 1867, died in 1906) married James Jones in 1885; and Lena "Lennie" (born 1880, died January 1893).

William Cowden was born in June 1859.

Nancy Cowden (born June 1841, died November 1910) married James W. Sullivan in October 1856 in Christian County. James was born in November 1834 and died in February 1914. They had eight children: Their first child born in 1858 (name not known); John G. (born October 1860); Sarah A. (born December 1864) married Kinsey C. "Kims" Geren; George D. (born June 1866), Amy T. (born April 1868); Eliza E. (born April 1871); Samuel J. (born March 1874) and Lavina "Vina" J. (born November 1876).

Elizabeth "Lizzie" Cowden was born in August 1843.

Amy Kerr and John Steele had three children all born in Greene County, MO.

Robert Kerr Steele (born in 1847 in Greene County, MO, died in 1890) married Helen Cassett. Robert and Helen had four daughters: Grace married Fred Lehman, Avis married Harry Adams, Nelle married Leslie Naylor, and Belva married Nick Keatts. Grace and Fred Lehman had a daughter Dorothy that married Claude Thummel.

Samuel Ferguson Steele was born December 1848 in Greene County, MO. During the Civil War he went to Wisconsin with his family and in February 1865 he enlisted in Co. A, 153rd Illinois Voluntary Infantry under Captain Giles D. Walker. He was discharged at Memphis, TN in September 1865. He married Lavina McCann in 1873. Lavina died in 1880. In 1881 he married Sarah McDougal. Sarah and daughter May died in 1883. In 1885 he married Viola Pett Cave. Samuel and Viola had five children: Oscar Kenneth, Bessie, Emory Irl, Della Ione and Viva Dee. Viola died in July 1939 in Snohomish, WA. Samuel died in March 1940 at Buckley, WA. Both are buried at the GAR Cemetery in Snohomish, WA.

Ann Elizabeth Steele was born in 1850.

When Amy's father, William Kerr's, estate was settled, a lawyer, James W. Sullivan, represented John and Amy Steele. Amy's daughter, Nancy (Cowden), married a James W. Sullivan. This may have been the lawyer representing John and Amy. From letters written by John and Amy's son Samuel to the War Department concerning his Civil War pension, it appears they did not live in this area after 1865. *Submitted by Ellen Carr, ggg-niece of Amy (Kerr) (Cowden) Steele.*

**KERR/ELLIS** – Matthew, the son of William and Nancy (Hubbert) Kerr, was born March 1822 and died February 1895. He married Sarah Ann Elizabeth Ellis in January 1848 in Greene County, MO. Sarah was born June 1832 and died April 1900. Matthew and Sarah are buried at Kerr Cemetery on Kerr Road near Clever, MO. Matthew and his parents came to the Republic area from Sevier County, TN in 1841. His brother Alexander and family came to the Republic area in 1843. His sister Amy (Kerr) Cowden and her children came to the Republic area in 1844. Matthew and Sarah had 11 children:

1) Nancy Kerr, born April 1849.

2) James Wiley Kerr, born November 1850, died May 1924, married Agnes C. Howard in August 1874. She died September 1876. They had a son Jefferson Calvin who married Rosa Phillips. After Agnes death James married Mary Lavona O'Bryant. They had three sons: Clarence, Joseph and Clyde.

3) William T. Kerr, born March 1852, married Mary Jane Hodges in December 1872.

4) Sarah Frances Kerr, born July 1854, died July 1938, married Summerfield Jones in January 1879. They had two children: (1) Howard Lee Jones, born July 1890, died February 1946, married Rose Etta Rhodes August 1910. They had four children: Margaret married William Martien, Rosa married Kenneth Hines, Sarah married Thomas Williams, and William married Joan Mudd. (2) Forrest K. Jones, born February 1882, died August 1902.

5) Matthew Kerr, born September 1856.

6) Rebecca Kerr, born February 1858, died April 1858.

7) John T. Kerr, born April 1860, died 1941, married Mary Susan Pope in April 1885. They had three children: (1) Wesley Matthew "Matt" Kerr, born February 1885, married Lilly May Little. They had eight children: Orville born January 1904, David, Cecile born February 1909, Edna born May 1911, Stella Mae born January 1913, Earl born November 1914, Doyle John born September 1917, and Ruth born August 1921. (2) Sarah Lou "Stella" Kerr, born May 1888, died July 1952, married Johnnie Little. (3) John Ernest Kerr, born September 1889, died March 1911.

8) Andrew J. Kerr, born November 1862, died April 1875.

9) Mary E. Kerr, born March 1865.

10) Amy E. Kerr, born August 1867, died September 1922, married William Ellison Little.

11) Marion C. Kerr, born May 1870, died August 1915, married Lennie M. Nelson in November 1894. They had four children.

(1) Edward Matthew "Eddie" Kerr, born October 1897, died May 1972, married Nellie Jewel Washam, born June 1899, died January 1993. Children: (a) Marion Lee Kerr, born October 1932, married Jacqueline Jane "Jackie" Little in August 1952. Their children are Stacey Lee and Lacey Jane. (b) John Ed Kerr, born in 1936, married Zella June Hale, born in 1935. Their children are Johni Lynn, Kelli June (born December 1960, died December 1964) and Lisa Jo.

(2) Loyd M. Kerr, born March 1901, died October 1916.

(3) A child born August 1904 died at birth.

(4) Mary Lucille Kerr was born in May 1906.

Matthew and his brother Alexander owned property west of Lynn Street and on the south side of Miller Road. His father William owned property east of Lynn Street and on the north side of Elm Street.

In 2005 Matthew and Sarah had descendents in Greene and Christian counties. Their g-granddaughter, Opal McCroskey, and gg-grandchildren, Lacey (Kerr) Flood and Allen McCroskey and their families, live in the Republic area. *Submitted by Stacey Kerr.*

**KERR/HUBBERT** – Alexander, son of William and Nancy (Hubbert) Kerr, born April 1813, died February 1855 and is buried at Kerr Springs Cemetery. He married Margaret Hubbert October 1835 in Talladega County, AL. Margaret, daughter of Benjamin and Rebecca Calvert Hubbert, was born January 1814, died in 1888, and is buried at Short Cemetery, Hurley, MO. Alexander, his parents and brother Matthew, came to the Republic area in 1841. Alexander and Margaret came to Republic from Alabama in 1843. His sister Amy (Kerr) Cowden and children came to Republic after the death of her husband Walter in November 1843. Alexander and Margaret had seven children:

1) William H. Kerr, born November 1836, died in Republic December 5, 1855, and buried at Wade Cemetery.

2) Benjamin Anderson Kerr, born February 1838 in Alabama, died May 1909. He married Sarah Ann Reynolds, daughter of Henry and Sarah (Miller) Reynolds, born May 1836 in Missouri and died January 1892. Civil War record states he enlisted in March 1862 in Stone

209

County, MO, Co. F, 8th Regimental Cav. He was promoted to sergeant in April 1865 and mustered out July 1865. Benjamin and Sarah had five children: Sarah, William, Rachael, Amanda and Lutrecia. Benjamin and Sarah are buried at Short Cemetery, Hurley, MO.

3) Andrew Jackson Kerr was born May 1840 in Alabama. He served in the Civil War. Family legend says Andrew died in the war.

4) Matthew Thomas Kerr, born December 1843 in Republic, died in Ellis County, OK in December 1912 and buried at Arnett, OK. Matthew's Civil War file shows he enlisted March 1862 in Stone County, MO and was paid for furnishing his own horse with a valuation of $65.00. The record also shows he mustered out April 1865. In May 1864 Matthew married Mary Lacey, born August 1846, died May 1877 in Neosho, MO. They had three children: Britta Mart, Almeda and Marguerite Duerinda. After Mary's death he married Rosa Nina Laderach. Nina was born May 1853 in Cahors, NY and died February 1897 in Newton County, MO. They had five children: Edith May, Stella Martha, James Clifford, William Preston and Agnes Leota.

5) Nancy J. Kerr was born in May 1846 in Republic.

6) Martha Elizabeth Kerr, born April 1848 in Republic and died March 1876, is buried at Short Cemetery, Hurley, MO. She married James Madison Houser in March 1866 in Stone County, MO. James was born in 1847 and died in 1893. They had four children: John Sherman, Sarah, George Washington and Clara.

Rebecca Amanda Kerr, born June 1850 in Republic, died 1871 in Stone County, is buried at Short Cemetery, Hurley, MO.

Alexander and his brother Matthew owned property in Township 28, Range 23, Sections 29 and 30. This area is on the south side of Miller Road and west of Lynn Street

Alexander's father, William Kerr, owned property in Sections 21, 22 and 24. Section 24 property owners were William Kerr, William Steel and John A. Ray. After Alexander's death in February 1855, Margaret married Henry Reynolds in October 1857 and they moved to Stone County north of Hurley, MO before 1860. Henry and Margaret are listed in the 1860 Stone County census with seven of Henry's 10 children, ranging in age from 11 to 20 years and three of Margaret's seven children age 10, 12 and 17. Margaret and Henry had no children together. Margaret's son, Benjamin Anderson Kerr, married Henry's daughter, Sarah Ann Reynolds.

In 2005, Alexander and Margaret have descendents in Greene, Christian, Lawrence, Newton and Stone counties. Three of Benjamin and Sarah (Reynolds) Kerr's great-grandchildren and their families live in the Republic area: Betty (Truman) Silva, Lela (Lane) Laney and her husband Charley, and Joe Lakins and his wife, Bonnie. *Submitted by Linda Holt, ggg-granddaughter of Alexander Preston Kerr.*

**KERR-IRVIN,** James A. and Sarah J. (Irvin) Kerr with their seven children, settled in the neighborhood of Republic in late 1880. James and Sarah were both born and reared in Fountain County, IN. James was born 1842, died in 1903 and Sarah was born 1846, died in 1922. They were married Sept. 9, 1865 soon after James arrived home from the Civil War. He served in an Indiana regiment "of which he was an honorable member" of the Union Army.

On April 30, 1881, they purchased a 160 acre farm for $1,200 located midway between Republic and Brookline that partly bordered the South Pacific (Frisco) Railroad. This farm would become known and referred to locally as the Kerr family farm. Located in Brookline Township, Section 15, Township 28, Range 23, on the old Brookline-Galloway Road (now Farm Road 170), this farm would be the home of four generations of the Kerr family during the next 124 years. The Kerr farm was originally settled in 1863 by the William E. and Mary A. Thompson family of Wilson Creek who purchased it on Aug. 6, 1863 for $350. Among other outbuildings, they constructed a wood frame house (as shown in photo, burned in 1885) and a log barn that still remains.

*Sarah Kerr by original house on farm in mid-1880s.*

The children of James and Sarah Kerr were Elmer E. (born 1866, died 1894 on the Kerr family farm) never married; Mary E. (born 1868) married D.F. Leabo; James Owen (born 1870, died 1935) married Sarah J. Phelps; Emma V. (born 1872) married R.A. Bowland; Charles Walter (born 1874) married Frances Short of Republic; Olive M. (born 1877) married H.H. McElhaney of Brookline; and Edna A. (born 1880, died 1957 on the Kerr family farm) married Ira J. Treesh of Republic.

James Owen was the third of seven children and was 11 years old when his parents moved to the Kerr family farm. He married Sarah Jane Phelps of Republic on July 1, 1896. Sarah was born 1875 and died in 1957. James Owen was associated with the city of Republic for many years. He was appointed Justice of the Peace in 1911, elected Police Judge in 1926 and served a number of years as a member of the board of aldermen. They had six children: Elda Gertrude Cunningham (born 1900, died 1973) had no children. Bertha Frances Sharp (born 1908, died 1994) had one daughter, Sharron A. Johnson (born 1940). Sharron has one daughter, Sara Jo, who married Raymond Gilbert. Sara Jo has one daughter, Annie Jo Brown. Isabelle Jane Anderson (born 1922) married Reed Anderson. They have one son, James W. "Jim" (born 1949) who married Barbara Haladay. Their children are Carrie Jo, Marci Jane and Wesley Reed. Wesley died in 1997. Marci married Mark Creed, they have one child, Wesley James.

Elmer Irvin (born 1897, died 1965) married Julianne Terigan. They have one daughter, Sally Jane Taylor (born 1939). Wilber Herbert "Bill" (born 1913, died unknown) had no children. Junior Owen "June" (born 1917, died 2005) married LeVera Turpin. They had two children, Deanna K. (born 1941) married Bill Warford. They have one daughter, Julie K., who married Kirk Phillips. Julie has one child, Andrea K. Harris. Jim L. Kerr (born 1945) married Sandra L. Muench. They have one son, Kelly L. Kerr. *Submitted by Deanna K. Warford.*

**KING/GRIMES -** Breakfast at a Republic restaurant is a good way to start the day, that is, unless Peggy King is sitting at your table. In that case, you have a jumpstart on the day because with Peggy everyday is a celebration of life and she is happy to share her enthusiasm. Peggy was born in 1947 in Lebanon, MO to James and Merle Grimes. She has a younger brother Rickey. In 1952 the Grimes family moved to Crane, where they owned and operated Crane Shoe Store for 33 years. Those formative years spent in the company of her father and his customers helped to shape a community-minded businesswoman. Peggy attended school in Crane for 11 years, transferring her senior year to Galena High School where she graduated.

*Peggy King Family, l-r: James King, Peggy King holding Justine Scroggins, Josie Scroggins, Jeff Scroggins, Jayma King, Jenna Scroggins, Kim King and Joe King; front row: Will King, Chandler King, Jaycee King, Jayde King.*

In 1964 Peggy married Jerry King. To this union were born three children: James Lynn, Joe Lee and Josie Lea. Jerry died in 1983, making Peggy a widow at 36 years of age. In the fall of 1984, Peggy moved to Republic.

As a young bride she had traveled through Republic on the way to Springfield for doctor appointments and shopping. As a young widow, she made a new home in Republic for herself and her two youngest children. She enrolled Joe and Josie in the Republic school system. Her eldest son, James, was attending Labette Community College in Parsons, Kansas.

Peggy worked at the Southwest Regional Stockyards from 1979 to 2000. When she moved to Republic in 1984, she also started Peggy King Advertising, then in 2000 she opened a storefront in the Southwest Plaza Center.

In addition to her children, Peggy has the joy of her grandchildren: Jayma Lanae King, Jayde Lyndsay King, Jaycee Lynn King, Williams James King, Chandler Colt King, Jenna Layne Scroggins and Justine Logan (Buttercup) Scroggins.

In the spring of 1985, Peggy joined Calvary Baptist Church in Republic, thus having laid claim to her new community she got involved as a civic-minded citizen.

Highlights of her involvement include: Missouri High School Rodeo Association, secretary from 1985-90; co-chair of the National Knife Collectors Annual Show in Springfield for 12 years; publicity chair for the Republic Pumpkin Daze Committee; served by appointment of the mayor of Republic to the Communication Commission (The vote in 2005 for consolidation of the Village of Brookline with the city of Republic was the act of informed citizens; the Communication Commission was the vehicle for education on the issue.); member of the Kiwanis Club of Republic; 2005 recipient of the Republic Area Chamber of Commerce Business of the Year award.

For Peggy, Republic changed from a place to drive through to a place to call home. Even in 1984, it afforded the opportunity for a businesswoman and a mother to start a new career and continue raising her family. Today, Peggy is an enthusiastic supporter and promoter of what Republic has to offer and the tremendous future that lies ahead: business and population growth; continued excellence for the Republic R-III School District; the unceasing care and compassion of the spiritual community; and leadership that works for and with its citizens.

In Republic, community spirit is contagious and anyone can catch it, just sit at the breakfast table with Peggy King. *Submitted by Peggy King.*

**KING/LONON -** Andrew David "Dave" King was born in Murphy, NC in 1862, the same place and year as his future wife Martha Elizabeth "Mattie" Lonon. They were married in Maysville, Banks County, GA, then moved to Mountain Home, AR where most of their children were born. They moved to Republic in the late 1800s where two more children were born.

*Andrew David "Dave" King and Martha "Mattie" (Lonon) King.*

Dave and Mattie had a farm east of Republic on what is now Lynn Ave. He also did plasterwork.

Their children were: Lilly May, born Sept. 13, 1886 in Mountain Home, AR, died April 4, 1968 in Tulsa, OK and was buried in Evergreen Cemetery; Lula Jane, born Oct. 13, 1884-died 1885 in Mountain Home, AR; William H., born Nov. 9, 1888 in Mountain Home, AR-died 1890 in Republic, MO, buried in Evergreen Cemetery; Hattie Caroline, born April 15, 1890 in Missouri-died June 23, 1976 in California, buried in Evergreen Cemetery; Roy Edward, born May 30, 1892 in Republic, MO-died Feb. 5, 1964, married Velma Short; Jetta Irene, born July 13, 1894-died Oct. 29, 1982 in California and buried in California; Orville F., born June 3, 1897 in Republic, MO-died Oct. 19, 1918 of influenza-pneumonia while serving in the military in WWI at Camp McArthur, TX and buried at Evergreen Cemetery; Baby born and died on July 7, 1902 in Republic is buried in Evergreen Cemetery with his brother Willie.

Dave died in December 1940 and was buried in the Evergreen Cemetery next to Mattie who had died two years before on May 18, 1938. *Submitted by Jo Ann Hays Adams.*

**KIRBY -** Yolanda Moore (formerly known as Peggy Kirby) came to Republic, MO in 1944 to live with her newly wed father, Marion Kirby, and stepmother, Viola Cason. They bought a house on South Main Street across from the water tower and spent many years remodeling. Marion worked as a laborer out of the Springfield Union Hall and Viola worked in the garment factory. She later became a beautician and had a shop in her home for many years.

*Peggy and Paul Moore*

Peggy entered high school as a freshman, made friends quickly with her classmates and other towns folk. She joined the school band and participated in school activities. It wasn't long before Peggy got a job at Doc O'Dell's Drug Store working a few hours after school and some weekends, along with her life long friends, Burnadine Marsh and Jackie Woodfill. The three of them used to take summer evening bike rides and enjoyed many good times with band activities and slumber parties with other classmates. Senior year had many high lights for Peggy: she was chosen queen of her class, started a new relationship with a young man, Paul Moore, and also got a part-time job at the local telephone co. She continued working as an operator after graduation for about a year before leaving for Berkeley, CA, where she went to work for the Pacific Telephone Co.

Before leaving Republic, the Lions Club chose Peggy to compete in a national horse show queen contest in Springfield. She did not win, but was flattered and honored to be chosen to compete. Fond memories remain with Peggy even though she was a resident for only six years. Republic was good to her and she is grateful for all the experiences provided her.

In California Peggy found favor with the telephone company when she was one of 16 chosen to demonstrate their new Air Raid Warning System at the state fair in Sacramento. While still working for the telephone company, she completed a self-improvement course, and was hired for a variety of modeling jobs. Her husband returned from serving a year in Japan, and they started their family, and bought a home in Concord, CA, where they still live today. Paul retired from Pacific Telephone Co. and Peggy from Mt. Diablo Medical Center. They are both active with their church and serve in several areas. *Submitted by Yolanda Moore.*

**KITCHEN -** Daniel Newton Kitchen (born July 2, 1837, died Oct. 22, 1914) and Margaret Harriet (born July 11, 1836, died July 16, 1922) married Nov. 2, 1858. Sometime between 1859 and 1870, the Kitchen family immigrated to Greene County. They had eight children: Ruth B.C.S. Kitchen, William Lilburn D.D. Kitchen, Mary Eliza M.E. Kitchen, James Perry Daniel Lee Kitchen, Sarah Myra Amanda Jane Kitchen, John Chapman Samuel Wra Kitchen, Isaac Young David Houston Kitchen and Charles Ezekiel Burrow Fines Kitchen.

*Daniel Newton Kitchen*    *Margaret Harriet Kitchen*

James Perry Daniel Lee Kitchen married Nellie Anderson in October 1937. They owned and operated a grocery store in Republic, MO in the early 1900s. They had no children.

Sarah Myra Amanda Jane Kitchen married Rev. David Simmons from Marionville, MO. They had six children: Paul Wesley, Ruth Durham, Freddie, Robert, Esther Housley and James Leroy. Both David's father and grandfather were Methodist ministers. David also preached at times at the Hood Methodist Church. David and his sons helped lay the foundation for the Methodist Episcopal Church.

Mary Eliza M.E. Kitchen was married to Ben Bethel. They had no children.

John Chapman Samuel Wra Kitchen married Maude Erminie Adams in Marshfield, MO on Nov. 26, 1902. They had three children: Clara, Jessie and Bernice.

Charles Ezekiel Burrow Fines Kitchen married Mary Thieme. They had two children, Nellie Louise and Mable Irene.

Both John and Charles had farms just west of Springfield, MO and just east of what is now known as the Springfield-Branson Regional Airport.

Ruth B.C.S. Kitchen married Winfield Lawson in Greene County, MO on Aug. 17, 1878 and they had three children: Ernest Campbell, Walter and Willie.

Isaac Young David Houston Kitchen married Anna Caroline Lullau Sept. 28, 1904, and they had three children: William Earl, Mary Celeste and Margaret Irene.

William Lilburn D.D. Kitchen was born April 4, 1862 and died as an infant six months later on Oct. 10, 1862.

*Norman Cooper of Republic, MO, the grandson of John Chapman Samuel Wra Kitchen and great-grandson of Daniel Newton Kitchen, reported this history and pictures.*

**KUBAT -** Joseph Edward Kubat and Elsie Regina (Kasper) Kubat moved to Republic in the late 1950s. They grew up and married in Owatonna, MN. Both their great-grandparents came from Bohemia (now Czechoslovakia) and were early settlers and merchants in Owatonna. Edward and Elsie later moved to Chippewa Falls, WI, where Edward was a successful partner in St. Claire-Kubat Clothing Store. In 1913, Clifford Kubat was born and a few years later Rosemary was born. Edward's father retired in Cromwell, MN, and after his father passed away they moved to the family farm at Cromwell and ran the family store with his mother. Clifford and Rosemary graduated from Cromwell School and Clifford graduated Valedictorian of his class.

Rosemary married Erling Varnes, a WWII Merchant Marine Chief Engineer who survived several torpedo attacks. After Erling's demise, Rosemary moved to Republic in the 1970s.

Cliff Kubat married Helen Kubat in 1939. Helen's grandparents were from Sweden. Cliff had an American Standard service station and raised children, Karen and Mike, prior to being drafted into WWII. He fought in the Battle of the Bulge and went into Buchenwald Concentration Camp while the ovens were still warm and witnessed the Nazi atrocities. After the war he worked for International Paper in Cloquet, MN. Tim was born in 1948. In 1950 both Kubat families moved to a farm south of Harrison, AR. A few years later Cliff and his family moved to Republic, and Edward and Elsie moved near Mt. Vernon. Cliff milked cows for a few years, then went to work at the new Lily-Tulip plant. They were members of the Hood Methodist Church. In 1954 Cliff and Helen's family moved to 400 North Main in Republic. Cliff became plant and grounds foreman at Lily-Tulip, Helen was active in various clubs, an accomplished pianist and a self-taught organist at the church where she played for many years. After Cliff retired, he was active in the church, Meals on Wheels, City Council, Planning and Zoning Commission, Evergreen Cemetery Board, the City Park Board and was instrumental in developing J.R. Martin Park. Both Cliff and Helen are deceased.

Karen married Porter Dewitt and they had two boys, Bryan and Rob. She later re-married and moved to the Chicago area and had another son, Randy Freeman. Bryan is in the printing business and Rob has a produce business in the Tulsa area. All boys are married and have children. Randy is in the military service and Karen currently lives in Republic.

After high school Mike joined the Air Force and was stationed in Duluth, MN. He later married Suzanne and they have four children and two grandchildren. Mike is now retired and they currently live in Lincoln, IL.

Tim graduated from SMS with a BS in industrial technology. He married Marcia and they have two sons, Stan and Jason. Stan is an executive chef and Jason lives in Springfield. Tim and Marcia currently live in Republic. Tim works in industrial sales and Marcia is employed at a local hospital. *Submitted by Karen Freeman.*

**LACEY -** In June of 1970, the Fred and Donna Lacey family moved from Colorado Springs, CO to Republic, MO. There was a housing shortage that year and it was difficult to find rentals. After searching for several days, there was an ad in the paper for a rental in Republic. After driving through the town and looking at the house, they decided it might be a nice place for their three children to go to school. They liked the idea of a small town, and it was close enough to find work in Springfield. They have two sons and a daughter: Freddy was going to be a sophomore, Greg would be in the 8th grade and Kim would be in the 7th grade. The kids were amazed at how friendly the people were. "Everyone waved at us and didn't even know who we were!"

*Sitting l-r: Wally and Donna Hopper; standing in back: Julie Dake, Kelly Mann, Brian Hopper, Greg Lacey, Freddy Lacey and Kim Wolken.*

Fred went to work at Loveland's Transmission in Springfield and Donna went to work at Zenith. After about a year, Fred decided to open his own business and called it Fred's Auto Repair. It was located in an old Quonset hut behind Republic Auto Parts on Highway 60. He was in business there for several years. Donna went to work at General Electric when they moved to Springfield and worked there for 12 years. Their children completed their education in the Republic Schools and are now married and have children of their own.

Freddy married Susie Hicks and they have one daughter. They were divorced and he married Carolyn Propps. They have a son Adam, a daughter Amy and three grandchildren.

Greg married Diane Jackson and they have a son Jason, daughter Kerri and two granddaughters.

Kim married Danny Brown and they have two sons, Josh and Gabe, daughter Erin and one grandson. Kim and Danny were divorced and Kim is now married to Alan Wolken.

Fred and Donna were divorced in 1979. They all still live in the Republic area. Fred always had a great love for country music. He plays the guitar, sings, and formed his own band, which includes son Freddy. They still play at several Senior Center dances in the area.

They made the right decision. Republic was a nice place to raise their family and they are very fortunate to have them all still living here. *Submitted by Kim Wolken.*

**LAKINS/RUSSELL -** Joe and Bonnie (Russell) Lakins moved to Republic in 1960 and lived on Mill Street for two years. In 1962 they purchased a home in Republic on White Oak Street and lived there for 17 years; in 1977 they purchased 20 acres south of the West Republic Fire Station; and in 1979 they built a house and still reside there in 2006.

Joe and Bonnie have two children, Joe Dean and Douglas Wayne, who live in Clever.

Joe Dean married Mary Ann Logan, daughter of John and Joan (Andrus) Logan. They have a daughter Jennifer Ann. Jennifer married Darrell Watson and they have two children, Logan and Lane.

Douglas Wayne married Sandra Eitel and they have one son, Micheal Wayne. Douglas then married Pam Hoffman. Micheal first married Amy Brashers and they have two children, Ethan and Chandler. Micheal then married Christy Bilbo.

Joe and Bonnie were born in Stone County, MO. Joe's parents were Frank and Hulda (Lane) Lakins. His great-grandparents were Wiley and Lousia Lakins who came from Claiborne County, TN in 1851 to Phelps County (Rolla, MO). In 1899 his grandparents, Joseph Frank and Frusa Lakins, moved to Stone County, west of Hurley, MO. Joe's mother's parents were Lander and Rachel (Kerr) Lane. Rachel's grandfather Alexander and great-grandfather William Kerr were early settlers (1841) to the Republic area.

Joe's mother Hulda Ellen Lane first married William Deboard and they had three children: Mabel Irene, William Claude and a daughter who died at birth. After William Deboard's death, she married Frank Monroe Lakins and they had nine children: Robert, Norma, Carl, Juanita, Wilda, Joe, David and two sons who died at birth. Joe's brothers and sisters are deceased except Wilda Jean Holt who lives in the Hurley area.

Bonnie's parents were Paul William and Lena Elizabeth (Langley) (Camron) Russell. Paul's parents were James and Laura (Johnson) Russell. They lived in the Elsey, MO area where eight children were born. Lena's parents were Thomas and Ethel (Epps) Langley. They lived in the Hurley, MO area. Thomas, Ethel and two young sons traveled to Longmont, CO in a covered wagon where Thomas worked in the logging industry. While living there in the covered wagon Lena was born in 1910. The family returned to Hurley, MO in the covered wagon. Lena had three brothers and three sisters. Her youngest sister, Clarice (Langley) Lawrence, and husband Clifford have lived in Republic for the last 45 years.

Bonnie had two half brothers, Paul Densil Russell and Thomas Eugene Camron, both are deceased. She has a brother William Ruel Russell who lives at Clever, MO.

Joe and Bonnie have lived in the Republic area for 45 years and have seen many changes. When their sons started to school there were two buildings. The biggest change has been to Main Street business. They were customers of Bacon Tire, O'Neal Lumber, the barbershop, locker plant, Logan's Market and Farmers Exchange. They purchased the boys first bikes, Western Flyers, at the Western Auto Store, shopped at Batson's five and dime, Plummers Dry Goods store, did business at the bank and bought at least two cars from Harris Ford. Fred McCullah was always so cheerful when he pumped your gas and washed your windshield. That is all gone, but the good memories remain. *Submitted by Douglas Wayne Lakins.*

**LAND –** When William Kerr died in 1875, he left his farm to his granddaughter Sarah. The farm was 1.5 miles east of the center of Republic. In 1879 Sarah, her husband John Land, their children and extended family members left Monroe County, TN in covered wagons for Republic. It was a difficult journey with children dying along the way.

*John and Sarah Land and their family in 1910.*

John, who died in 1910 at age 76, was a well-respected Baptist deacon. Sarah, who died in 1927 at age 89, is remembered as a woman who loved hard candy. Upon their death, the farm was divided among their children. John's grandson Charles sold the last of the property in the early 1970s. Subdivisions now cover the farm.

Seven of their 10 children grew to adulthood and married. James married Manerva Couch, Ab married William Harrington, Charles married Edna Earl, Sarah married Lee Payton, Anna married John Boyd, Jesse married Sarah Robertson, and Will married Lilly Crum.

Jesse farmed and worked as a carpenter for the Frisco Railroad. He died in 1952 at age 76 after falling from the roof of a barn that he was building. Two of Jesse and Sarah Robertson's three children, Herbert and Ralph, lived to adulthood. Both lived most of their lives in California. After Sarah died in 1904, Jesse married Bessie Jackson. Both of their children died young. After Bessie died in 1910, Jesse married Sarah Boyd. Jesse and Sarah had three children: Wilfred, Luther and Edith. Sarah died in 1931 leaving three teenage children at home.

The countryside and a keen eye provided abundant quail, rabbit and squirrel for the table and for pocket money. The pocket money helped pay the tuition to attend the city high school.

Edith married James Marcy and lived most of her life in Kansas. She died in 1990 at age 73.

Wilfred married Grace Ottendorf. Wilfred was a Navy corpsman in WWII. He worked for the Federal Prison System, ending his career as associate warden of the Atlanta Federal Penitentiary. In 1962 he led a group of federal prison guards to Oxford, MS to assist deputy federal marshals in protecting James Meredith during the integration of the University of Mississippi. Wilfred died in 1999 at age 86. Grace, who also died in 1999, taught in the Republic school system for many years. They had one daughter, Anne Johnson, who lives in Republic.

Luther married Josephine House. He is 91 years old and has lived in Republic most of his life. During WWII Luther served in Patton's Third Army as a combat engineer. He took part in seven battles including the Battle of the Bulge. He was awarded a Purple Heart and a Bronze Star. Luther is a master carpenter and built numerous houses in Republic from the 1950s to the mid-1970s. Josephine was church pianist and a Sunday school teacher at First Baptist for many years.

Luther and Josephine have three children: Larry and Ron live in St. Louis and Betty Kinkel lives in Gardnerville, NV. *Submitted by Luther Land.*

**LAND/BOYD/TEAGUE/MITCHELL** - John and Sara Land came from Tennessee and settled on 40 acres three miles east of Republic. They are known to have had at least five children: Anna, Sarah, Abigail, Jess and Willie.

Anna married John Boyd and inherited the home place from her parents. Anna and John had five children: Grace, Lucile, Homer, John R. and James. Grace died early in life in childbirth. Homer and James both fought in WWII with both coming home and raising families. Lucile later told of the Young Brother's Massacre on Jan. 2, 1932 on the farm near Brookline.

*Evelyn Teague.*

Lucile, born March 16, 1907, married Jess Teague and had five children: Robert, Earl, Anna Evelyn (born May 8, 1937), Katherine and Gladys.

In 1944 while living in Sarcoxie, Jess Teague died of complications from having worked in the mines in Joplin. His and Lucile's 11-year-old son Earl Teague died one week later of complications from an ear infection. Lucile brought her three daughters back to the Republic area to live with her mother, Anna Boyd, on her farm. The girls attended Lindsey School with Evelyn the only 8th grader to graduate in 1950.

The winters were cold and snowy and the summers long and hot. They used coal oil lamps for light and used wood for both the heating and cook stoves. They went to town in a wagon with two horses, usually making the trip on Saturday when almost everyone else was there. At home for door stops, they used cannon balls from the Battle of Wilson's Creek that they found in a fence row near their house.

There were many happy memories made for this family during this time. Band concerts were held on Saturday night at the bandstand behind Owen and Short Hardware. Once Evelyn had a bad stomachache and Doc O'Dell gave her a purple colored mixture which stopped the pain immediately.

At Christmas they saw the high school band march in the parade, saw Santa (who was usually Hazel Maxwell) and received a wonderful sack of Christmas candy. A carnival, which was a lot of fun, came to town about every summer. Evelyn usually won two or three little celluloid dolls with colored feathers for their dress.

Anna Evelyn Teague married Edward Mitchell April 15, 1973, He worked at Kraft Food in Springfield. Evelyn worked at Zenith Mfg. in Springfield and at the Juvenile Shoe factory in Aurora. They had four children: Judy Essary who has two children, Vicky Gitson has two children, June Sharp has three children and Charles has one child. *Submitted by Anna Evelyn (Teague) Mitchell.*

**LAND/OTTENDORF** - J. Wilfred Land was born Aug. 11, 1912 on a farm east of Republic near the old Lindsey School, which he attended until high school age. Grace B. Ottendorf was born Nov. 16, 1913 in Republic and attended elementary and high school at the local school.

They were married June 1, 1936. Wilfred found work as he could locally, while Grace taught in several of the rural schools around Republic. Wilfred was called to serve his country as a Navy Medical Corpsman and was stationed his entire tour of duty in the United States. Grace joined him during the summertime and attended the college near where he was stationed each summer.

*Grace and J. Wilfred Land.*

Upon returning from the service, he found employment at the Federal Medical Center in Springfield and worked there as a correctional officer until his daughter, Anne, graduated from the local high school. Grace taught elementary school in the local school and attended what is now MSU each summer until she received her teaching degree. Both Grace and Wilfred loved high school sports and followed the teams closely. Wilfred was the time and scorekeeper for many years for the basketball teams.

After Anne graduated from high school Wilfred accepted a promotion and transfer with the Federal Prison System. They were sent to Leavenworth Penitentiary where he was assigned as lieutenant. He was training officer as well and trained many area local young men as they began their career in the correctional service.

Grace continued to teach school in Leavenworth, but unlike the local systems, she was not totally happy teaching and retired. She did, however, agree to substitute, and as it turned out, completed several sessions for teachers unable to continue their positions.

Wilfred was promoted once again to captain, and was sent to the Federal Training School for Juvenile offenders in Washington D.C. Grace was encouraged to accept a teaching position at the training school and taught there for a short period of time.

Wilfred was again promoted to a position with the Federal Bureau of Prisons. This called for a great deal of traveling, which neither of them liked very well. He accepted the position of associate warden at Atlanta, another maximum security prison. Grace did not teach in Atlanta. Wilfred was held hostage for 18 hours with several other personnel. Although it was a very dangerous situation, all were released safely.

When they retired from Atlanta, they returned to Republic to be near their daughter and her family. They remodeled the "old home place" of Grace's parents and lived there until the grounds and stairs became too much. Wilfred had a prize garden and he loved to compete with his brother, Luther. Grace enjoyed being a member of several social clubs and many bridge clubs.

They were very active in the Hood United Methodist Church until their health prevented their attending weekly services. Grace taught many Sunday school classes, and Wilfred did a great deal of conference work as lay speaker at various area churches. They each passed away in 1999 and were buried in Evergreen Cemetery. *Submitted by Gregg Johnson.*

**LANNING/HAMILTON** – Charles J. Lanning married Emma Hawkins on May 25, 1907 in Elwood, MO. They were the parents of eight children: Ralph "Doss" (born Aug. 22, 1916), Charles "Ted," Forrest, Jim, Dorothy (Lanning) Hammer, Edith (Lanning) (Martin) Johnson, Bertha (Lanning) Allen and Delores (Lanning) Peters.

Ralph "Doss" married Betty Burleson, and they had a son Charles (born in 1950) who now lives in Kansas City, and a step-daughter Carolotte Burleson. Ralph and Betty were divorced in the 1950s. Ralph has a daughter Williedean Poindexter who was born in 1964 and now lives in Billings.

Ralph's grandmother, Edith O'Neal, lived in Republic and owned and operated the boarding house located at 212 W. Elm Street, she made bread in her home for the local restaurants in Republic.

Ralph's mother Emma was raised in Republic working in the canning factory, peeling tomatoes. His dad, Charles, served in the Spanish American War, a veteran of the Philippine Uprising and San Juan Hill, serving in the Cavalry during WWI. Ralph also served his country in the military during WWII, taking part in D-Day, Battle of the Bulge, Omaha Beach and the Rhine.

Ralph's second marriage was to Gretchen Marcia Hamilton (born July 18, 1917) in December 1983. They have made their home on Hwy. 60 east of Republic since 1963; before this time they lived on Olive Street in Republic for 10 years. He worked in construction of bridges and dams until his retirement, working on Stockton Dam for three and one half years, and for a period of one year he worked for the civil service in Guam.

*Ralph and Gretchen Lanning.*

Gretchen spends her time crocheting and knitting, making beautiful crocheted dresses for children. She worked as a waitress for Bessie Swearengin at Bessie's Cafe on Hwy. 60 and at the Seven Gables Cafe on Hwy. 266.

Ralph started his art career at the age of 57. He decided to make things to decorate his yard, teaching himself the art of sculpturing. Ralph has been acknowledged and received awards from The Folk Art Society of America, giving him the Award of Distinction; ENVISION Folk Art of Missouri, giving him its first Award of Distinction; Missouri Folk Art Society's, giving him the outstanding achievement award, and he has had articles printed in various magazines all over the world. His most cherished rewards are the thank-you letters from school children who have visited the Lanning Gardens at his home. His work has been displayed at the Springfield Art Museum, the Intuit Center in Chicago, featured in the book *Rare Visions and Roadside Revelations* and was the subject of a PBS television show on folk art.

Ralph is among the top five folk art artists in Missouri and one of the few folk artists carving stone in the United States. *Submitted by Ralph Lanning.*

**LAWSON/TRUE** - Nelson Lawson was born Aug. 8, 1820, in Tennessee, probably Hawkins County, son of Isham Lawson and Mary Martin. Nelson married his first wife, Joanna Martin, 1846 in McMinn County, TN, and they had two children before she died in 1851. He then married his second wife, Lumitta Elmina Long, Sep. 14, 1854, in Bradley County, TN, and together they had 11 children. She was daughter of Tandy W. Long and Sarah Ellen Daniels.

Nelson enlisted in 1864 as a private with the Civil War Union forces from Bradley County in Company I, 10th Cavalry, Tennessee Volunteers, and was discharged as a first lieutenant in 1865. He and Lumitta left Bradley County about 1869, traveled to Rolla, MO, where they remained until the railroad was completed to Springfield. They and their children arrived in north Springfield on the first "iron horse" the morning of April 21, 1870. They settled in Center Township in the Yeakley Chapel vicinity. Later they lived briefly near Hutchinson, KS, then returned to Greene County. He died June 9, 1885 and was buried in Brookline Cemetery. Most of the children remained in Kansas. After Nelson's death, Lumitta returned to Kansas where she died Dec. 29, 1896 and was buried in Sego Cemetery near Hutchinson.

One brother and one sister of Nelson's moved to Greene County, MO, prior to his arrival. His brother was Alexander Ayers Lawson and wife, Catherine Dodd. His sister was Patience Ann Lawson and husband, William Lee Chilcutt.

Only three of Nelson Lawson's children lived in Greene County after they married. A son from his first marriage, James Harvey Lawson (1847-1889), is buried in Brookline Cemetery. A daughter from his second marriage, Arilla E. Lawson and husband David C. Waddle, lived in the Phenix community near Walnut Grove.

Their daughter, Martha Elizabeth Lawson, was born June 1, 1858 in Bradley County, TN, and married William Henry True in 1875 in the home of her father. The marriage was performed by her uncle, Rev. Alexander Ayers Lawson, a minister who served various Methodist churches in Greene County. William Henry True was born April 22, 1855, Johnson County, IN, son of James Nathan True and Rebecca Roberts.

William Henry died on the Greene County Courthouse steps in 1913 and Martha Elizabeth died in Republic in 1932, both are buried in Evergreen Cemetery, Republic. Their children were: Alice is buried Yeakley Cemetery. Emma May married Richard William Cunningham, who is buried in Clear Creek Cemetery. Katherine Rebecca married Bernard Owen Cunningham, buried in Clear Creek Cemetery. Maudie is buried in Yeakley Cemetery. Lula Leota married Ora Sanford Ratcliff and is buried Evergreen Cemetery. Ruth Lumitta had a meat market in Republic at one time and married Frank McKinstry. William Albert married Edith Clara Fry. Bertha Ethel is buried in Evergreen Cemetery. Jessie Pearl married Benjamin Harrison Robertson and is buried in Evergreen Cemetery. Ralph Almus married Lillie Pearl Williams and is buried Yeakley Cemetery. Hubert Paul married Gladys Marie Wright. Zachary Taylor married Irene Amelia Wright and is buried in Evergreen Cemetery. Sybil Justine married Thomas John Donnelly and is buried in Evergreen Cemetery. Mabel Madeline married W. Earl Carson.

Children of the following attended schools in Republic: Ruth, William and Jessie. *Submitted by Imogene (True) Bennett.*

**LEHMAN/BACON** – Joe Rex Lehman, son of Leo and Maxine Lehman of Clever, MO, was united in marriage to Judy Kay Bacon, daughter of Garley and Reathel Bacon of Billings, MO on Jan. 16, 1964. They established their residence in Republic, MO in January 1964 on West Street in the Wormeyville addition.

They have been residents of Republic, MO, all of their married life with the exception of Rex's military tour. Most of their residence was at 527 Scotland Street and 578 Ritter Street. They now reside at 193 Crocus Road in the Republic area.

Rex was a barber at Frank Bennett's (Shrimp's) Barber Shop and John's Barber Shop with John Harrington and John Parker from 1961-66. Rex then went to work at United Parcel Service Sept. 26, 1966 and retired Oct. 1, 2002. Rex also retired at the rank of first sergeant from the Missouri Army National Guard with 33 years of service.

Judy Lehman worked at Crank's Drug Store offices until she was pregnant with their first child, Shelly Kay Lehman, born April 6, 1968. She remained a housewife with the birth of their son, Stacy Kent Lehman Jan. 7, 1972. She remained a stay-at-home housewife until their son was in the 8th grade. Judy then went to work at Security Bank as a teller. Judy worked at Security State Bank until it was sold to Commerce Bank. She continued to work there for a while, then became a nail technician at Nita's Nail Shop, where she worked until she retired.

Their daughter, Shelly Kay Lehman, was a graduate of Republic High School and Southwest Missouri State University, with a master's degree in education. She is an elementary teacher in the Republic school system. She was crowned for the title of Miss Missouri USA 1994 in Columbia, MO. She competed in the Miss USA Pageant and was a top-10 finalist for the title which was held in South Padre Island, TX. Shelly Lehman was united in marriage to Rodney "Jake" Holt and to this marriage daughters, Kamrynn Riley and Kyra Paige were born.

Their son, Stacy Kent Lehman, was a graduate of Republic High School and Southwest Missouri State University with degrees in business and chemistry. He is now a medical representative for Zimmer Medical Co. Stacy Lehman was united in marriage to Alicia Fisher and to this marriage was born a son, Kolton Kent Fisher Lehman and a daughter, Kinley Kae Lehman. *Submitted by Judy Lehman.*

**LEIDINGER/LUCE** - Dr. Karl Josef Leidinger Jr. was born on Aug. 5, 1921 and grew up in Monticello, AR. After graduating from the University of Arkansas, he joined the Army Medical Corps where he served his internship. He opened his first office in Clever, MO in the late 40s. He moved to this area because there was not a doctor available. He practiced there for many years before moving his office to Billings and Republic, dividing his time between the two. After some time, he closed the office in Billings and kept the one in Republic. He married Lovetta Luce and they had three children.

Dr. Karl Leidinger Jr.

When he first arrived to the area, he drove a Karmann Ghia. No one had ever seen a car like that and most found it interesting. At that time, being the only doctor in the area, he did it all including delivering babies.

There was not a charge for the office call, only a charge for whatever was taken care of. A flu shot might cost you $2. If you were unable to pay, there was no charge. When the phone rang day or night, if someone needed him, he would go to them. Elizabeth remembers going with him, after he had worked at the office all day, to visit some of his patients that were home bound before he went home. He was very patriotic and had a small cannon that he enjoyed firing. It went with him sometimes when visiting friends. He would also fire it on holidays like the 4th of July or New Years. In the winter when there was a deep snow on the ground, he could be seen going to work on his tractor.

He passed away Jan. 21, 1985. He was a good friend, a humanitarian, and a loving father. *Submitted by his children: Elizabeth, Lee, and Alan.*

**LEWIS** - Leonard Max and Lena Lorie Lewis moved to Republic in 1953 with their four children: Larry, Linda (Sue), James and Karen (Faye). Three more children were born while residing in Republic: Mike, Paula and Ilonna. Max, as everyone knew him, worked for the Ford agency, first owned by Don Pollard and later by Floyd Harris.

Following a house fire and a divorce in 1963, Max started working out of the undamaged one car garage of the fire-damaged house. He began construction on a 28 by 40 garage behind the house and facing highway 174. With the help of many friends (and the slogan of "Built by drunks and material by thieves") he was able to complete and open the shop and ran it for several years until his death in 1980. He had a loyal following of car owners who wanted only Max to work on their cars.

Lorie (a gifted pianist) moved to Springfield after the divorce and lived there until her death in 2000. All the children attended and graduated from Republic Schools: Larry in 1965, Sue in 1966, James in 1967, Faye in 1969, Mike in 1971, Paula in 1973 and finally, Ilonna in 1974. All the children still live in Missouri, and most live near Republic. Several of Max and Lorie's grandchildren have attended and graduated from Republic. *Submitted by Michael Lewis.*

**LOGAN** - Tarlton Logan and his wife, Jane Campbell Logan, and their children along with extended family members, left Bedford County, TN in 1835 to resettle in the west.

The summer of 1836 brought them to Grand Prairie, a place in Greene County, MO, located just west of the present location of Republic, MO. Their 40-acre farm in Section 24, Township 28, Range 24, was located on what is now FR 67, between West State Hwy. 174 and FR 178. There they raised four girls and seven boys. Tarlton, age 74, and Jane, age 77, died within two weeks of each other in May 1877. They are buried on the Anderson Hampton place on Wilson Creek.

*Lester "Bud" Logan and Virginia "Virgie" Logan, June 22, 1983, their 50th wedding anniversary.*

Tarlton L. Logan (1803-1877) married Jane Campbell Logan (1800-1877). Their children were David Manuel, Mary, Nancy, Elizabeth, Benjamin, John, Agnes, James Monroe, Wesley Robert, William Hood and Samuel Jasper.

Benjamin joined the Union Army prior to his father's and brother's joining, but was discharged before the Battle of Wilson's Creek, Aug. 10, 1861, because he had a "wind" on the side of his neck and couldn't carry a knapsack. Tarlton and the other six boys enlisted at Rolla, MO Oct. 7, 1861 for six months. They all fought and survived the Battle of Pea Ridge, March 6-7, 1862. They were mustered out on April 17, 1862.

Benjamin Logan (1829-1900) was married to Ruth Boyd (1830-1918). They are buried in Evergreen Cemetery. They had 13 children: Alice, Jane, Malinda, James, Frank, Thomas, Fronia, Mary, Victoria, Martha, John, George and Hugh.

Thomas Logan-twin (1861-1924) married Sadie Meyer (1864-1941). They are buried in Republic, MO. They had three children: Lawrence, Hattie and Clarence.

Clarence "Bud" Logan (1895-1915) married Callie Hayes (1895-1971). Clarence and Callie had one child, Lester "Bud" Logan. Lester "Bud" was 18 months old when his father passed away and his Grandmother Hayes raised him. Callie later married Jim Tourville.

Lester "Bud" Logan (1914-1989) was married to Virginia "Virgie" Boatright (1914-1983). They are buried at Wade Chapel Cemetery. They were owners and operators of Logan's Market located on Main Street from 1952-1978. Their children are Patricia Ann "Patsy" Pyeatt Yount, David Roy and Anthony "Tony" Mac.

David Roy Logan (1937) is married to Donna Sue Sifferman (1938). They have two sons, Douglas "Doug" Mark (1959) and Don David (1964). David served four years in the Air Force. David and Donna returned to Republic where David worked with his parents at Logan's Market then at HandiRak Drug Co. Donna worked at Security State Bank in Republic for 23 years. They are retired and live on a farm west of Republic.

Douglas "Doug" Mark Logan (1959) is married to Kayla Pauline Word (1958). Doug works at Harry Cooper Supply Co. and Kayla is a dental hygienist. They have two sons, Daniel Lee (1987) and Benjamin "Ben" Levi (1990).

Don David Logan (1964) lives and farms west of Republic. *Submitted by Kayla Logan. Editor's note: David passed away June 4, 2006.*

**LOGAN/PASCHALL** - Clarence Lee Logan was born and reared near Hurley, MO. Lem and Liddie Logan reared him as his mother Viva Lee (Smart) Logan died in childbirth. Everette, son of Lem and Liddie, was Clarence Lee's dad. Clarence Lee attended Hurley Schools and took part in basketball, softball and track.

Emily May (Paschall) Logan was born near Peace Valley, MO and reared in Springfield. They met at Broadway Baptist Church, Springfield, MO. Clarence Lee came up from Hurley to hear one of his school teachers hold a spring revival. He saw a blond in the choir and kept coming back. Emily was 16 and Clarence was 22. Uncle Sam came calling and Clarence served two years. Emily gave him several names and addresses of girls to write to, but he chose Emily. They were later married at Broadway Baptist Church.

Hurley was too small for Emily, and Springfield was much too big for Clarence. He wanted

*Emily and Clarence – 1999.*

to be on a farm. So on September 1965 they chose Republic to be their adopted town when they moved to Route 2. They had four children: James, Sarah, Robert and Kathy, then eight years later were blessed with Judy.

*Clarence and Emily Logan's children. Front: Judy, Robert, Kathy; back is James and Sarah.*

*Clarence and Emily Logan's grandchildren. Back is David and Clarence; front: Janna, Monica and Desiree.*

James started 1st grade at Republic Elementary in the fall of 1965 and graduated May 1977 from Republic High School. Sarah graduated in 1979, Robert in 1980, Kathy in 1982 and Judy in 1990. Emily was pleased to hear Mr. Farwell, principal, say at Judy's graduation that he knew that her parents had been behind their children getting a good education and that they also backed the teachers. He said they should be proud of their children as they moved forth to achieve their goals. The children had been active in the Lindsey 4-H Club, dog training, sewing, cooking, outdoorsmanship, entomology and swimming at the Boy's Club in Springfield.

The boys built a tree house while they lived on the farm. Judy wanted to join them. When her mother looked out the window to check on the children she saw Judy suspended in mid-air with rope attached to arms, legs and waist. Her brothers and sisters had made a way for her to be in the tree house they thought—but it didn't happen. They were told to lower her back to the ground.

Each of the children picked walnuts and sold them to either start or increase their savings accounts.

Terrell Creek was nearby and provided many adventures, some more exciting than others.

Republic was there for them when their house burned in June 1976. Calvary Baptist Church, Happy Hens and individuals helped them in a lot of ways.

The summer sports programs, softball and swimming, encouraged their children to reach their goals; as did the public library with their summer reading program; pet shows etc. as well as the resources they offered year around.

Emily has been involved in the school system since the graduation of their children. She has volunteered to teach origami, be a reading coach, and help in other ways.

Clarence Lee's grandparents moved to Republic in 1959. They were active members at the Fundamental Methodist Church which was right next door to them. Their names are on a sidewalk brick on Main Street in their memory.

Clarence and Emily moved to town in September 1983. They are so glad they chose Republic as their adopted town in 1965. *Submitted by Emily Logan.*

**LOHKAMP/SAUNDERS** - Steve and Carol Lohkamp have been residents of Republic, MO since childhood. Steve lived at 1007 East Elm Street. His parents, Albert and Wanda Lohkamp, grew up near Monett and in Aurora. Carol's parents, R.V. and Gail Saunders, moved to Republic when Carol was five. Coming from Cassville and Crane, they purchased the house at 128 Kimberly from Bill and Wilma Wilkerson.

Steve Lohkamp and Carol Saunders started kindergarten in 1971, continued in Republic schools, and graduated in 1984. Two weeks later, Steve Lohkamp began working at Security State Bank. At its present location is Commerce Bank, where Steve serves as Community President. Carol Lohkamp is now the principal of the Republic R-III Early Childhood Center.

These two local kids grew into adulthood here and have continued by serving the public here. Steve Lohkamp is presently on the Republic School Board and is a member of the Chamber of Commerce. Carol Lohkamp is a former Republic city councilwoman and is currently on the mayor's Communication Commission.

Carol remembers that a trip downtown would always include buying a bottle of grape Nehi soda from the cooler at MFA. As an only child, she played with friends in her neighborhood and rode her bike daily. Steve and his brothers mowed lawns for people all over town, averaging 23 yards a week. Carol was in band and on the pom squad. Steve played three sports. They married and lived at 111 South Oakwood, then 504 East Ritter, and now at 1220 East Charles. They have a son, Austin, who graduated from Republic High School in 2004 and is now attending Missouri Southern State University in Joplin.

Steve and Carol Lohkamp still have that "Tiger Pride" in their school and community and continue to enjoy living in Republic. *Submitted by Steve and Carol Lohkamp.*

**LOONEY/EAVES** - Ben Looney was born Feb. 2, 1860 in Grasen County, TX and died Dec. 7, 1961 in Republic, MO. He and Etna Dallas Eaves were married Nov. 14, 1880 by Harrison M. Sewell, Magistrate. Witnesses were Marshall F. Sewell and Annie Sewell, a sister of Ben F. Looney. Etna, daughter of James Patrick Eaves and Violettie King Hamilton Eaves, was born Oct. 18, 1860 in Polk County, MO and died Jan. 17, 1947 in Republic, MO.

Uncle Ben, as he was affectionately known, was born in a "one-room shanty with a big fireplace" which furnished heat for all purposes. The family came to Missouri in 1866 and settled on the Sac River near Walnut Grove. He was one of a family of eight children. He started school in Texas when he was four years old.

At 20 years of age he married Etna and they started out life together near the Greene-Polk County line. He got his Cherokee Indian blood from his mother. His father was Irish. Ben's early church was the General Baptist. He farmed all of his life and never owned a car, but owned many horses.

The Ozark County Looney family moved from Greene County, MO to Ozark County, MO in the summer of 1900. The family consisted of Ben, Etna, and their seven children: Clyde, Claud, Glen, Dewey, Lelia, Merle and Maude. Ben was a seventh generation American, a descendant of Robert and Elizabeth Looney who arrived in America from the Isle of Mann in 1731. Descendants of at least two of the 14 sons of Robert Looney made their way to Ozark County, MO.

Ben farmed in the Sand Ridge and Lick Creek communities in Ozark County. He also freighted from Gainesville and West Plains. He served Gainesville as Justice of the Peace for many years.

All of Ben and Etna's children married Ozark County spouses.

Ben and Etna moved back to Greene County and Republic, MO in 1928, along with their daughter Maude and her husband, Marion Day, and her family. They lived with Maude for 42 years. On Nov. 30, 1929, Dewey and his wife Jessie, along with their three older children, moved to Republic. In the early 1940s, Claud, his wife Ruby, their four sons: Odin, Dolen, Lloyd, Newell and their families, moved to Republic.

Descendants of Ben and Etna Looney are still making themselves known in the Republic community. Some are business owners. Many have served the town and school in different capacities and some are just retired and living the "good life" in Republic.

In 1960 Ben was honored on his 100th birthday with a huge party at the MFA Hall in Republic. Over 200 relatives and friends from far and near crowded the hall and many remained outside.

Ben will always be remembered as a "cheery" fellow who had a wonderful memory. *Submitted by Gladene Looney White, great-granddaughter.*

**LOVETT/OWENS,** Michael G. Lovett was born April 21, 1827 in New Jersey. He moved to Missouri from Tennessee in 1858 and married Melissa Owens (b. Nov. 22, 1841) on Dec. 20, 1858. They had 10 children: AC or Commadore, Eliza, Diana, Sophia, Charles, Valentine, Loretta, Bethia, Mary and an unnamed baby. In 1865 he obtained 80 acres of land through a federal land grant. The land was located four miles west of Republic at the junction of Highway 174 and Farm Road 43. Michael died in 1878.

Eventually Charles became a landowner. He was the only child of Michael and Melissa to have children. Charles married Rosetta Blades the great-granddaughter of Edward A. Blades. They had five children: Tressie, Olen, Acie (Dutch), Floyd (Cap), and Stanford (Spide). Tressie married Earl Blades and they had four children: Lorene Davidson, Bonnie Garrett, Donald and Pauline. Lorene Blades Davidson lives on Farm Road 43 and owns the northern 40 acres of the original Lovett farm. Olen married Lela Sifferman and they had two children, Charles Lovett living in Salinas, CA and Mary Hannan living in Broken Arrow, OK. Acie married Lucy Farris and they had two children, Alberta Sparkman living in Marionville, MO and Jane Kokai living in Denver, CO. Floyd married Ruth Crum. Stanford never married.

*Tressie Lovett Blades, 18 years old in 1916, sitting in front of what is believed to be the original cabin of Michael and Melissa Lovett.*

Michael and Melissa were typical pioneers that overcame the hardships of the times to eke out a living while raising a family. Many stories have been passed down through the generations. The portion of the farm now owned by Lorene Davidson contains the cave that was an attraction for young local explorers in the late 1800s and early 1900s and still has the markings of some of its early adventures. One explorer got lost and after several hours of wandering emerged from a different entrance on the Trogdon farm. Pickerel Creek was the site of many church baptisms in the early 1900s, while people picnicked on its banks. Also at the farm is the farm house built by Michael's son Charles around 1915. Behind the farmhouse the foundation of the original family cabin can still be seen under the weeds. It would have been approximately a 10 by 10 one-room space. It was said that Melissa enjoyed her tobacco. She would first chew a little plug and then dry it out under the cushion of her rocking chair. Once dry, she would smoke it in her clay pipes. The pipes are the few treasures that survived the hard life.

One story passed from Michael to Charles to Tressie to Lorene, was that in the early years Indians would camp near the spring as they passed through the region. In 1946 Tressie and Earl Blades began farming the old farm. It was the first time a tractor had ever been used to break the soil. The new depth at which the ground was turned brought up hundreds of Indian artifacts. Even today, pieces of the past can be spotted while walking where Michael and Melissa once walked. *Submitted by Steve Davidson.*

**LUTTRELL/DUNCAN** - John J Luttrell and Nancy Duncan were married in Hawkeye, Pulaski County, MO in 1895. They were natives of the Brumley area in Miller County. Their first child, Alonzo, was born in 1896 and died in 1897. Burley was born in 1898 in Mountain View. Nancy's parents, George and Mary Ann (Shelton) Duncan, were living there, as well as her grandparents, Hayden and Sarah Duncan. They were back in Miller County when Dora was born in 1906 and Mary Ann in 1912.

*John J and Nancy (Duncan) Luttrell.*

The family lived for a time in Blackwell, OK, but moved home because of the terrible dust storms. They opened a grocery store in Brumley. Dora was in school when she became ill and died during the flu epidemic of 1918. She was buried beside her little brother in Mt. Union Cemetery.

It became a pattern for them to move away and start over. They went back to Oklahoma where they lived west of Miami. Mary Ann started school there, Burley became a mailman, and in 1920, married Josephine Holt. John and Nancy had another store.

In 1923, they came through Republic and learned the Eagans would sell their grocery business. They made the deal and later, they moved to North College Street in Republic. After a time, they moved to the home of Lindsey Robertson on South Main. In 1926, Burley and his wife had a daughter, Mary Jo. In March 1927, Nancy died after a lingering illness.

Mary Ann learned to cook and kept house for her dad. She attended high school, where she played basketball, studied agriculture and began dating Jack Woodfill. About that time, John married Faye Sharp and they talked about going to California. Jack decided if Mary was leaving, he would leave with her. They were married in 1929 and all left together. They got as far as Claremore, OK, found a new building which would soon be available, and made an agreement to put in a grocery. They settled into the new life and Jack learned the grocery business from the ground up. He and Mary started their family, a daughter, Jackie. All was well until the banks closed their doors. Times became so bad, Jack and Mary came back to Republic.

John and Burley went to Springfield. They opened another grocery at 1616 College Street. In 1933, just after Mary had the second daughter, Patsy, John suffered a stroke and died at his store. He was only 60 years old. Burley took over the location and Jack eventually went up and worked with him. Their third daughter, Donna, was their last. In 1946, Jack and Mary opened their own business. Burley moved over to Kearney Street for several years and when he became ill, it was agreed to have a partnership at Jack and Mary's location. It became the L and W Market, and continued the long history of the Luttrell family grocery business. *Submitted by Jerry Trogdon.*

**MANESS/JULIAN** - In 1883, a handsome young man of Scotch-Irish descent, arrived in the area of Bois D'Arc, MO. His name was John Baldwin Maness. A single man, he was the son of Arthur L. and Eliza Ann Berry Maness, being born Aug. 9, 1856 in Scott County, VA. He was a Presbyterian by faith, but served as a circuit rider to various churches.

In the same year as his arrival to the area, while at a camp meeting, he met Sylvania Jane Julian, whom he would marry on Dec. 31, 1883. In later years, John would tell about his meeting of Sylvania. She and another young lady were crossing the creek. Her long skirt had gotten wet and she was holding it up, just enough that her very white petticoat was showing. Seeing how white it was, he said he knew she must be a clean person.

*John B., Sylvania Jane and grandson, Donald Maness.*

Sylvania Jane was born March 27, 1858 in Indiana and came to Missouri in the 1860s with her parents, Benjamin Elliott and Mary Ann Diffie Julian. They lived in the Cave Springs area of Greene County. Sylvania had attended the Drury Academy in Springfield and was a school teacher before her marriage to John.

John and Sylvania had seven children, the first dying before he was two and the last dying at birth. The children were born in the Bois D'Arc and Elwood areas, except for Henry. The children were Glenarven Everett (born 1885, died 1887); Homer Elliott (born 1887, died 1981); Sterling Edward (born 1889, died 1975); Mary Cordelia McElhany (born 1891, died 1967); Eula Lorene Bertino (born 1894, died 1973); Laura Ellen Forbis (born 1897, died 1971); and Henry Billingly (born and died 1901).

Before 1900, the family moved to a farm a short distance east of Republic where they raised their family. As the children grew up and married, some left the area. Sterling and Mary were in Kansas and Oklahoma, and Eula went to California and remained there. Homer and Laura remained in the area for most of their lives. John died in 1922 and Sylvainia died in

1934. They are buried in Lindsey Cemetery in Republic, as are several of their descendents.

Laura married Jesse Greene Forbis in 1914 and had one child, Vernice Floyd Forbis, who married Alta Carolyn King, and after her death he married Wanda Ottendorf. Floyd had two sons, Ronnie and Glen.

Homer graduated from Republic High School in 1904 and married Etta May Short later that year. Her family lived near the Maness family. Homer and Etta May had three children: Raymond Everett (born 1905, died 1982); Henry Elliott (born 1906, died 1980); and Elsie Gwendola Oliver (born 1909, died 2006).

Henry married Velma Martin and lived in the McGirk, MO area. Their children were Etta Jane Wood who is deceased, Virginia Lee McGill, and Henry Elliott Jr.

Elsie married Donald Oliver and lived several places as Donald had a Naval career. They later settled in Charleston, SC. Their children were Donald Wesley Jr., Mary Deloris and Charlotte Mae Creech. Their children are all deceased.

Raymond married Flossie DeWett in 1925 and they had the following children: Mildred May Hilliard, Raymond Everett, Rayetta Elizabeth Brashers, Iris Edwina Jones Duke and Luther Edwin. Mildred, Rayetta and Luther live in the Billings area and Iris is in Republic. Raymond and Flossie lived in the Clever area.

After Etta May's death in 1915, Homer Maness married Lois Iona Pope in June 1916. Lois was from the Delaware community near Clever. Homer and Lois spent most of their married life on the same family farm near Republic. They had three children born there. They were Donald Sterling, Frances Iona Etheridge and Rosemary Comisky. They were long time members of the Hood United Methodist Church.

Homer and Lois were married almost 65 years when he passed away in 1981. Lois was born in February 1900 and lived to the age of 105, passing away in 2005.

Donald has spent most of his life on a farm east of Republic. He lives on the family farm, which has been a "Century Farm" for several years. Donald married Regina Vernell Sifferman in 1939 and they had three children: Harold Don Maness, Marilyn Kay Ferguson, and Iona Vernell Ward. Harold Don lives in Republic, Marilyn in Springfield, and Vernell in Oklahoma.

Iona married Ray Wade Etheridge of Republic, lived in Mansfield, MO for a time, then moved to Medicine Lodge, KS. Ray is deceased, but Iona has remained there for many years. They have two sons, Steve and Warren.

Rosemary married Alan Comisky. They spent time in Germany in their early married life, as Alan was in the service, but otherwise have lived in Republic. They have a daughter, Alanna Rose Strader, who lives near Springfield. *Submitted by Harold Don Maness.*

**MANESS/POPE -** Homer Elliott Maness, born 1887 in Elwood, Greene County, MO, was one of seven children born to John Baldwin and Sylvania Jane (Julian) Maness. His brothers and sisters included Glenarvan, Sterling, Mary, Eula, Laura and Henry.

Homer first married Etta Mae Short, daughter of James Monroe Short and Mary Alice Sparkman, on Aug. 18, 1904. Etta was born on May 4, 1886 in Republic, Greene County, MO. Homer and Etta had three children: Raymond Everett, Henry Elliott and Elsie Gwendola. Homer and Etta traveled to Oklahoma seeking a new life with their oldest son Raymond. Their middle child Henry was born near Meeker, OK. After discovering that Oklahoma was not the place for them, they returned to the Republic area where Elsie was born,

Unfortunately, Etta died March 16, 1915 before the children were grown. She is buried at Lindsey Chapel Cemetery.

Homer met his future bride in a strawberry patch where she had come to pick berries, and he was the foreman. This young girl was Lois Iona Pope. Lois was born Feb. 27, 1900 in Christian County, MO. She was one of 10 children. Her brothers and sisters were Myrtle Rebecca King, David Clarence, Alta Gertrude Gardner, Flossie Mary Gardner, Jesse Stephen, Lou Agnes Hunt, Eula Pearl Young, and Geneva Wilma "Bennie" Little.

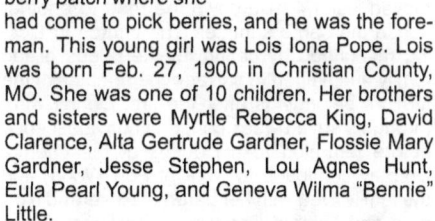
*Homer and Lois Maness – 50th anniversary, 1966.*

Homer and Lois were married June 24, 1916. Lois took on the responsibility of helping rear his three children, and they had three children: Donald Sterling, Frances Iona Etheridge, and Rosemary Comisky.

Homer built on to the small house where he brought his bride until they had a two story home overlooking Shuyler Creek in what is now on the corner of Farm Rd. 187 and 99. They attended Cumberland Presbyterian Church that sat on the corner of ZZ and Farm Rd. 99. When it closed they moved their membership to Hood United Methodist Church where they both taught Sunday school. Homer helped with the construction of Asbury Hall and then helped with the sanctuary renovation project in 1969. Homer served as Worshipful Master of the Republic Lodge #560. Homer and Lois were also members of Republic Eastern Star #370. From the early years of marriage their home was always an important place for friends and families to gather especially on Saturday evenings and after church on Sundays.

Their children grew up on the family farm where they grew grapes and strawberries that were shipped on the Frisco Railroad. They raised chickens and turkeys, operated a dairy farm, and finally, Angus cattle. They also grew cucumbers one year for the Cassy Pickle Works a few miles from their home. Homer began working construction jobs during the war working at Camp Crowder and Fort Leonard Wood, During this time of WWII, Lois and Iona kept the farm going.

They won the Skelly Award for outstanding work. After Lois fell and broke her arm, Donald returned from Wichita, KS to take over the farm responsibilities. Lois, Iona, and Rosemary took the train to Richmond, CA to join Homer near the shipyards. After the war, Lois and Rosemary joined Homer in Miamisburg, OH for another construction job.

Lois and Homer always returned to the farm where they celebrated life together with 64 years of marriage. Homer died March 30, 1981. Lois moved to Maranatha Village, Springfield, where she lived until she passed away July 9, 2005, at the age of 105. While she was at Maranatha, Lois began the hobby of making pillows that found their way around the world because of the missionary ties of Maranatha. She also enjoyed writing and memorizing poetry. Lois and Homer are buried at Lindsey Chapel Cemetery. *Submitted by Vernell Maness Ward.*

**MANESS/SIFFERMAN -** Donald S. Maness was born near Republic in 1917 and Regina V. (Sifferman) Maness was born in Greene County in 1922, They were married in June 1939 at Mount Vernon, MO shortly after Regina graduated from Republic High School. Donald had graduated from there a few years earlier.

Donald and Regina had three children: Harold Don, Marilyn Ferguson and Vernell Ward. They also attended and graduated from Republic High

*Donald and Regina Maness.*

School. They have five grandsons: Scott and Paul Maness, David and John Ferguson, and Jeremy Ward. They had one grandson, Keith Maness, who is deceased. They also have one great-granddaughter, Madison Ferguson.

Donald farmed and worked at Kraft, from which he retired. Regina retired from the MFA in Republic. They are long time members of Hood United Methodist Church and have been very active in many Masonic organizations.

Donald and Regina live on a "Century Farm" east of Republic. The farm belonged to his parents and grandparents before them.

Scott and Paul are happy that they lived close enough to see their Grandpa and Grandma often when they were growing up. *Submitted by Scott and Paul Maness.*

**MARK/PETERSON -** Ronald L. Mark was born Aug. 9, 1933 in Santa Ana, CA. He has a sister Marcellene, an older brother Gene and a younger brother Paul. Ron's father was a manager of an oil refinery in Huntington Beach, CA. Having been raised on a farm in Oklahoma he had always wanted to be a farmer. Ron's father W.B. Mark and Ron's mother Wyomia (Marriott) Mark spent their vacation time looking for a farm in Oklahoma, Arkansas and Missouri.

*Phyllis and Ron Mark.*

In 1936, Ron's father bought a farm near Montevallo, in Vernon County, MO. The Marks moved to the farm in 1938, where Ron started the first grade in a one-room school. Ron's father's health caused him to move back to California in the fall of 1939. It was later determined that his emphysema was caused by the asbestos used in filtering in the refineries. His father regretted selling the farm and was able to repurchase the same farm and moved back to Missouri in 1943.

Ron finished the 8th grade in a one-room school. He graduated from high school in El Dorado Springs. Ron started to school in Santa Ana, CA, and then moved to Ventura, CA, where he met Phyllis Peterson, a native of Nebraska.

Ron, working as a "roughneck" in the oil fields, was drafted by the army and went to Korea in 1953. Returning home from Korea, Ron purchased a herd of milk cows and started a dairy farm near Montevallo, MO. Ron had written to Phyllis all the time he was in the service. He and Phyllis were married Oct. 23, 1955 in Ventura, CA.

Ron applied for and was appointed post-

217

master in Montevallo, MO. In 1961, the farm that Ron was renting was placed in the soil bank and he sold his dairy herd. The postal department was downsizing smaller post offices, and the Montevallo Rural Carrier was transferred to El Dorado Springs. Ron received a transfer to the Springfield Post Office where he worked until 1965. Not being happy in the post office, Ron was looking for something that he would enjoy doing to make a living. Ron had assisted some of his postal patrons in Montevallo with the preparation of their income taxes. Ron took the H&R Block Tax School course and left the post office. He accepted the position as area director of franchises of southern Missouri, north east Arkansas and southern Kansas.

While working at the post office, Ron became acquainted with Ray Sifferman of Republic, a contract mail hauler. In 1974, H&R Block felt that having two managers in Springfield was not in the best interest of the company. It was suggested Ron relocate to Ozark, MO. Ron recommended moving his office to Republic, MO. Ron rented space from Ray Sifferman until 1985. Then he purchased the former Republic Library building and moved the office to its current location. Ron's wife, Phyllis, was also very active in the tax business; Ron retired in 1999 but continues doing income taxes for H&R Block. Phyllis, after having a stroke, was no longer involved with the business.

Ron Mark was not aware of his ties to Missouri, until an interest in family history caused him to find that his great-great-grandmother Douglass, was born in Jackson County, MO with some relatives in Polk County and that his great-grandmother, Rachel Hendricks, was born near Waldo, south of Lebanon, MO.

Ron's son Jeffrey Mark and his wife Imelda Joy have two children, Jacob and Emma. His daughter Anita has three children: Brittany, Garrett and Colleen.

Ron, a charter member of the Chamber of Commence, has been active in politics, Crime Stoppers, Pumpkin Daze and a promoter of the city of Republic.

Ron and Phyllis live north of Republic in the Elwood community. They attend Second Baptist Church in Springfield and have traveled in the United States and overseas on several mission trips. *Submitted by Ron Mark.*

**MARR -** Denny and Dorothy Marr moved to Republic in August 1995 with their children, Emily and Aaron. Another daughter Amy remained in Cape Girardeau to finish her education. The Marrs came in response to an offer to Denny to serve on staff at Calvary Baptist Church.

Denny and Dorothy met at First Baptist Church in St. Robert, MO, where he was serving as minister of music and youth, and she was serving as the church's pianist for worship. At that time he was a student commuting twice each week from Southwest Baptist University. Dorothy was at that time employed at Fort Leonard Wood with the U.S. Civil Service, Department of the Army. They were married at First Baptist, St. Robert on Oct. 26, 1979.

In January 1982, Denny accepted a call to First Baptist Church, Licking, MO. The Marrs moved there in the spring of that year with their daughters, Amy and Emily. While serving the church in Licking, the Lord blessed them with a son, Aaron. Dorothy continued with her job, commuting five days a week to Fort Leonard Wood. The family experienced both deep crisis and rich blessings in the community and church. In February 1984 Denny was diagnosed with an acoustic tumor on the left side of his brain. In addition to the call from the doctor, that same night the Marr's house was gutted by a fire. They lost most of their earthly belongings. Dorothy was eight month pregnant, and the baby did not move for several days after the fire.

Aaron was born quite healthy in May. Denny came through the surgery with a simple loss of hearing in the left ear, and the family moved just 1/4 mile down the road to another house the same summer. The church in Licking responded by caring for the needs of the family and helped to salvage the remains of the family's belongings after the fire. Denny went through a seven week period of convalescence before returning to his duties at the church. Dorothy continued to work at Fort Wood, and the family lived with her parents, Reverend Norman and Mildred Sanders at Buckhorn. Then the Marrs moved back to the country.

In August 1995, the family moved to Cape Girardeau, MO where Denny became minister of music and youth at Red Star Baptist Church. The family moved to the church's parsonage not far from the banks of the Mississippi River. The summer of 1993 was one of the most unique times of the family's lives. The Mississippi flooded the neighborhood up to 50 feet from the front porch of the parsonage. Denny did ministry that summer almost exclusively leading sand bagging crews out of the church parking lot in an attempt to save the neighbors' homes. Some were saved, some were lost. The neighborhood was decimated by the flood, and the Marrs had to live with friends for seven weeks until the river level subsided and the three feet of raw sewage in the parsonage basement was eliminated.

The church met for services some weeks across town at another unused church building and some weeks at the Baptist Student Center on the campus of Southeast Missouri State University. Although many homes in the neighborhood were destroyed by the flood, the church pulled together and attempted to minister to those who remained and to those who later moved in to begin a new life.

The process of moving out of the parsonage and back again repeated itself due to the flood of 1995. But this time the family was removed for four weeks and lived in the apartments above the Baptist Student Center on the University campus. Later that summer the move to Republic took place.

Currently Denny is still minister of education/administration at Calvary Baptist Church. Dorothy is secretary for the Sports Medicine Department at Missouri State University. Their daughters, Amy and Emily, are married, live in Republic, and have given them five grandchildren. Aaron is a painter in Springfield. *Submitted by Denny Marr.*

**MARTIN/CRAIG -** Charles Lyndell Martin and Irene Bonita Craig were married April 5, 1942 at the Boston Avenue Methodist Church in Tulsa, OK. They had been going together on and off since 1927. Lynn was born and raised in the Springfield area and Irene was born on a farm in Washington, IA. She later moved with her family to Springfield, MO. In 1929, the family moved to Tulsa, OK.

Lynn bought the Republic Theater and the adjoining building in 1938. An appliance store is now located in that space.

Irene moved to Republic at the time they were married. In 1943 they built what at that time was quite a show place home on the northwest corner of Harrison and Hampton Streets. It is still attractive, but quite different in appearance.

*Lynn and Irene (Craig) Martin home.*

The same year, Irene bought a home for her parents at what is now 414 East Elm Street. Her parents were Charles E. Craig Sr. and Lana (Lundt) Craig. Charles passed away in 1951 and Lana in 1953, leaving many friends and family to mourn their passing.

Lynn and Irene ran the theater for many years. Many a romance was started there on a Saturday night. Tickets started at 10 cents and popcorn was five cents. When they closed the theater, it was converted into a variety store. They started the Martin Insurance Agency in the building north of the theater and ran it until they retired.

They bought a 40 acre "farm" on the northeast corner of what is now Lynn and Miller. They raised Angus cattle for Lynn to play with and they all had names instead of numbers. It was very hard for Irene to send them to market. This area is now known as Martin Estates and is covered with new homes.

In 1961 they bought property on Table Rock Lake at Aunts Creek. They built a beautiful cabin there and dearly enjoyed it from 1962 until Lynn's death in 1992.

They both were active in Republic's betterment projects. They received an official proclamation from the conservation department naming a tree in their lawn as the State Champion Basswood, or Linden, tree. It measured 65 feet tall with a girth of 13 feet. They loved their home and their town. It was nearly impossible to get Lynn any further away from Republic than Aunts Creek.

*Mr. and Mrs. Lynn Martin – dwarfed by the huge tree.*

They were members and staunch supporters of the Hood Methodist Church. Lynn was an active member of the Masonic Lodge and the Shrine. He served in the Missouri National Guard. He was discharged due to tuberculosis and spent four years at Mt. Vernon Sanatorium before being cured. Irene was in the Eastern Star, Garden Club, ABC and every bridge group in town.

They had no children of their own, but loved everyone else's. This writer considered "Auntie" Irene, a mother and she treated him as her own son. *Submitted by Ronald Craig Brashear.*

*Marr Family.*

**MATHEWS/WILLIS** - Ray Mathews was born July 18, 1916 in Muldrow, OK and died April 21, 1977. He married Lillian (Willis) Mecker, daughter of Charles A. Willis and Gail (Mead) Willis from Glenns Ferry, ID, in 1939. They had two children, Leon, born May 3, 1941, in Boise, ID and Betty, born April 11, 1944, in San Bernardino, CA. Lillian died May 29, 1944. Ray's second marriage was to Thelma Meeker, from Champion, NE. She died Feb. 25, 1994.

The family moved from Redlands, CA to the Republic area in 1956 and was the owner/operator of Hi-way Motel located on Hwy. 60 east of Republic in Brookline. They relocated to Republic in 1958 and were the owner/operators of Mathews Market located on North Main Street next to the old theater building.

Ray Mathews served as chief of police for the city of Republic during the 1960s as well as being a Greene County Deputy Sheriff. He was in Civil Defense, Republic Kiwanis President and volunteered at the Republic Fire Department. His last working years were at Bacon Tire Service as inside service manager.

*Republic Fire Dept. volunteers. Bob Duvall, Don Brown, Harley Hemphill, Joe White, Jack Crawford, Charles Schatz, Bervin White, Ray Mathews and Billy Squirrel.*

Upon graduation from Republic High School in 1959, Leon relocated to Redlands, CA, to be near his grandmother Mathews. He married Sharri Sittler and had two children, Sean and Noel. Leon died Feb. 16, 1992. Upon graduation from Republic High School in 1962, Betty relocated to Palm Springs, CA, and married Ray Schnell on Nov. 2, 1962. They had two children, Kim and Kevin, and three grandchildren: Rebecca, Miranda and Kalina. Ray and Betty live in Upland, CA. *Submitted by Betty Schnell.*

**MCCONNELL** - The family of Henry Burl and Ida Mae (Inman) McConnell of Republic descends from the earliest settlers of Christian County. The McConnell line is traced to 1762 when Henry's great-great-great-grandparents, William and Jane McConnell, opened an inn at the main crossroads in Salisbury, the county seat for most of western North Carolina.

Grandson Walter (1784-1854), a War of 1812 veteran, and wife Polly Parker (1787-1860) lived in Maury and Giles Counties, TN, but moved their family northwest of Nixa in late 1845.

Their son John Walter (1829-1907) married Matilda Edwards (1838-1873), the daughter of Rev. James Wright Edwards (1807-1893), in 1853. Edwards, a Christian County official during the Civil War, owned much of northern modern Nixa and the Riverdale Mill.

Son William Alexander (1867-1952) was the first McConnell to live in the Republic area, moving by 1910 to a Wilson's Creek Battlefield farm. In 1886, he married Mary Bell Ray (1870-1927), the daughter of Christian County Assessor George M. Ray.

Youngest son Henry (1905-1955) married in 1925 to Mae Inman, whose family came to Missouri from Giles County. Mae's line of descents dates back to Lazarus Inman (1730-1781) of Virginia. Grandson Elkanah Inman (1814-1866) moved his family to a tobacco farm west of Nixa in late 1852.

Son John Wesley Inman (1842-1927), a Union soldier, married Nancy Lavanda Wilson (1846-1929) as the war was coming to an end in 1865. Their son, Finley Glover Inman (1869-1914), in 1896 married Mary Alice Dewitt (1881-1939) and had eight children, including Mae.

Henry, a county road worker, and Mae McConnell, in 1941, bought the family farm that straddles the Greene-Christian County line near the Wilson's Creek Battlefield. They had five children:

1) Harry Lee, a retired construction supervisor, married Jo Ann Duvall, daughter of Jesse and Ethel Keltner Duvall of Republic, and they settled on a farm east of Republic. They have three sons: Gary Lee (married Linda Schroeder); Larry Gene (married Fredona Tuter) and Darrell Dean (married Judy Butler).

2) Burl Russell married Barbara Jean Miller of Clearwater, NE, and they bought a farm near the battlefield although he worked for a Springfield dairy. They have three children: Randy Lee, Sharon Jean (married Don Murray) and Dennis Russell (married Carla Buoy).

3) Mary Lou married Leon McElhany (1920-1986), the son of Warry McElhany and Ralsie Inman. Mary Lou and Leon farmed extensively east of Republic while Leon worked at Springfield firms. They had four children: Danny Leon (married Janice Flood), Ronnie Lynn (married Tammy Nolte), Kathy (married Bill White) and Linna Mae.

4) Deloris Mae married Everett L. Davis, son of Lester Davis and Edith Johnson of the old village of Wilson Creek, and they bought a rural home south of Republic. They have three daughters: Linda Louise (married Bruce Scroggins), Teresa Fay and Melody Ann (married Larry Stevens).

5) Doris Fay married Robert D. Fortner (1936-2004), who owned an auto repair shop, and they bought a farm adjacent to her mother's home. They had two daughters: Connie Mae (married Jack Davis) and Tammy Fay. *Submitted by Burl McConnell.*

**MCCONNELL/BUTLER** - Darrell Dean McConnell and Judy Elaine Butler were united in marriage on Feb. 2, 1973 at Hopewell Baptist Church. Darrell is the son of Harry and Jo Ann McConnell of Republic. Judy is the daughter of Wayne and Joretta Butler, Republic. Darrell and Judy both graduated from Republic High School. After high school Darrell joined the National Guard, while Judy attended Missouri School of Cosmetology.

Darrell has worked as a diesel mechanic at Jenkins Diesel, Boatright Trucking and continues to run his own mechanic business from his home. Judy, a homemaker, has also worked part-time as a hair-stylist for Grace Place. Both Darrell and Judy own and manage an over-the-road trucking business, as well as overseeing their farm, which consists of Polled Hereford cattle.

Darrell and Judy built their home on approximately five acres of land west of Republic, joining the Butler farm owned by Judy's father, Wayne Butler. In 1992 they purchased the Brown farm and homestead, which included 50 acres and the 100 year-old-home in which Osha Brown was born. A portion of this property includes land traveled by many on the Trail of Tears.

Darrell and Judy have three girls: Jennifer Jo, Jill Renee and Jessica Lyn. Jennifer was born on Dec. 24, 1973. Jill was born four years later on Dec. 5, 1977. On Sept. 23, 1983, Jessica was born.

Jennifer graduated from Republic High School in 1992 and continued her education at Southwest Missouri State University, where she graduated in 1996 with a BS in elementary education. Jennifer was united in marriage to Michael James Bowers on June 15, 1996. Michael, from Thayer, MO, earned an agriculture business degree from SMSU in 1995. Jennifer, who also received a master's degree in guidance and counseling, has been teaching kindergarten in Republic since August of 1996.

Michael works at GrayBar Electric and maintains state certification as a soil scientist.

Michael and Jennifer have two sons, Jett Ellis Bowers, born April 8, 2001, and Jasper Hoyt, born Dec. 28, 2005. The Bowers family attends Hopewell Baptist Church, where Michael serves as a deacon.

Jill graduated from Republic High School in 1996 and continued her education at NEO in Miami, OK, before transferring to and graduating from Central Missouri State University. In 2001, Jill received her BS in agriculture business from CMSU. On June 8, 2002, Jill was united in marriage to Jason Wendell Beltz, from Mountain View, MO. Jason earned an animal science degree from MU. Jason and Jill now reside in Rising Fawn, GA, where Jason manages Colmore Farms and Jill works for Crystal Springs Print Works. Jason and Jill are active members of New Salem Baptist Church.

Jessica graduated from Republic High School in May 2002 and continued her education at OTC before transferring to Missouri State University, Springfield. She is actively pursuing an education degree. Jessica continues to work on the family farm and shows Polled Hereford cattle. Jessica is currently the editor for the *Missouri Hereford News* publication. She continues to attend Hopewell Baptist Church, where she is an active member. *Submitted by Darrell McConnell.*

**MCCONNELL/ROBERTS** - The first McConnells came to this country in 1757 and settled in Maryland. Over time some moved to Virginia, the Carolinas, and Tennessee. John Knox McConnell came to Greene County, MO along with his father, settling about two miles north of Brookline. John married and had several sons and daughters; one of the sons was C.H. McConnell, born in 1874. C.H. married Gertrude Roberts from Oldfield, MO. Farming was his occupation; they lived about four miles due north of Republic. C.H. and Gertrude had three children: Russell, Paul and Edith.

*Clarence McConnell, Gertrude McConnel, Edith, Paul and Russell.*

Russell married Altha Pearce, daughter of Ben and Mary Davis Pearce who lived near Terrell Creek. To this union Gene McConnell was born in 1930. Gene married Norma Sammons and to this union were born Mark, Randy, John and Mike.

Several of the McConnells that first came to this country served in the Revolutionary War, one receiving a pension from that war. During the Civil War some fought for the South and some for the North. Several were judges and some were lawyers, but for the most part they were farmers.

Gene's grandmother was Mary Davis Pearce. In the very early 1800s her grandfather came to this area and settled many acres along and on both sides of Terrell Creek from what is now called Davis Road almost to Wilson Creek. They were all farmers, and these farms passed from generation to generation down through the years. As they retired from farming, they sold their farms to different farmers. All of these farms will be taken in by the now planned Terrell Creek Sub-Division.

There are other McConnell families in the area around Republic, but no relation was ever claimed although the family feels most certain they are related through genealogy. Altha Pearce McConnell had a sister Nell who also married a McConnell who lived in Battlefield, MO. They were not related to Gene's dad Russell McConnell.

Gene McConnell graduated from Republic High School in 1948. He served four years in the Marines and fought in the Korean Conflict He later joined the National Guard to finish 20 years of service. Gene worked for the state of Missouri for 22 years, retiring from the National Guard and the state in March 1990. He and his wife Phyllis now reside near Billings, MO. *Submitted by Phyllis McConnell.*

**MCCROSKEY/DAVIS -** Eual L. (born 1925 in Springfield) and Mildred E. Davis McCroskey (b. 1926 in Christian County), both grew up on dairy farms. Eual attended Sherwood country school in the Springfield area, and Mildred attended a country school called Sharon Hill located in Christian County. Both later attended Republic High School. After graduation in 1945, Eual was employed by Edge Supply Company, Springfield, MO. This same year he purchased his first registered Jersey cow.

Eual and Mildred were married June 7, 1946. Eual left Edge Supply Co. for a better position as salesman with Peer Hardware, where he remained for five years. Living on a rented farm near Springfield, they now had raised five more head of Jersey cattle. At this time they had the opportunity to start full-time farming with Mildred's dad. Within six years their registered Jersey herd was large enough to start farming on their own.

*L-R: David , Bruce and Steven McCroskey.*

In 1956 they purchased 92 acres 2-1/2 miles southwest of Republic in Christian County. After milking full time for two years, Eual took a position with Rhodes Supply where he continued working for the next 20 years. He retired in 1977. During this time a Grade A dairy barn was built. Mildred stayed home to help with the dairy cattle and to take care of their three sons: Steven, Bruce and David.

Upon Eual's retirement the family was back to full time farming but on a smaller scale. They had milked registered Jerseys over a period of 52 years. They were long-time members of the Missouri Jersey Club. The club nominated Eual to receive the Hall of Honors Pioneer Dairy Award in 1999, giving the award to his family.

Their sons became interested in dairying as they grew up and son Steven started showing Jerseys in 1957. Bruce and David followed suit as they became old enough and showed their Jerseys for 25 years. They won many awards, showing their champions. As a high school student David took two animals to the All American Jersey Show in Ohio and placed very well. All of the boys belonged to Billings 4-H Club and the FFA. David, as an FFA member, won the State Farmers Degree. All three boys graduated from Billings High School.

Mildred was 4-H Community Leader for 15 years and also Christian County 4-H President for two years. She also worked several years in the Billings Fair and always liked to help her sons at the dairy shows.

Steven and Bruce now raise Jerseys on their own farms near Marionville, David, the youngest, completed college and is employed as a salesman for Nutrena. To honor his dad, Steven acquired a rotating Premier Breeder Award,which was established at the Ozark Empire Fair in all of the boys' names in 1999. Eual died as a result of heart trouble July 25, 1999. Mildred continues to live on the farm they purchased in 1956 southwest of Republic in Christian County. She has seven grandchildren and five great-grandchildren. *Submitted by Mildred McCroskey.*

**MCCULLAH/FEASTER -** Armor Bascombe Bates McCullah (born Nov. 7, 1885, died July 17, 1960) married Clemma Ethel Feaster (born July 7, 1885, died May 17, 1976) on Oct. 10, 1906. Clemma was born and raised near Crane, MO. Both graduated from Osa High School and were sweethearts during their senior year. Their children: Fred Leroy (born Nov. 11, 1916, died May 5, 1990) and Edith May (born March 26, 1919, died Sept. 4, 1991), graduated from Marionville High School.

Edith married Donald Brashears (born Feb. 23, 1916, died June 15, 1980) on May 28, 1938 and lived on a farm west of Republic near Turnback Creek. They had one child, Robert (born Sept. 28, 1940). Donald served in the Navy during World War II and they divorced before the end of the war. Edith married Cecil Henson (born May 11, 1911, died March 9, 2005) on Jan. 20, 1983. Edith, Donald and Cecil were childhood friends.

Armor and Fred worked in Marionville apple orchards until the late 1930s. They relocated to Republic to operate a service station owned by Clemma's maternal uncle, James Howell. That business was located one door north of Paul Williams's Ford Agency. In the early 1940s they purchased the adjoining lot north of that location and opened their own business: two gas pumps, a one-room store with a lean-to on the rear, two retired Springfield city buses for storage, and a small building insulated with sawdust for an icehouse. The ice was bought in Springfield from a plant near the MFA Creamery.

Fred was drafted into the Army Air Force and stationed in Victorville, CA. He married Zelda Elaine Carr (born June 5, 1923, died Oct. 7, 1975) on Sept. 5, 1942. They had one child, Gary Leroy (born Jan. 5, 1954). Armor continued to operate the station during Fred's absence. At the end of World War II, Fred returned to work with his father. Their station was open seven days a week. Tires were sold and flats fixed. Infinite gallons of gasoline were pumped into five-gallon cans in the trunks of farmers' wives' cars, often for less than 20 cents per gallon. Soda pop was a dollar for 24 returnable bottles or a six-pack for two-bits (25¢). Candy bars, chewing gum, and peanuts were a nickel. Cigarettes were $1.90 per carton. Ice was 13 cents for 12-1/2 pounds or a quarter for 25 pounds. Kerosene was pumped by hand in the lean-to for 15 cents per gallon. For several years Republic's school buses were fueled, serviced, and parked at the rear of the station. Charged purchases were recorded on a Big Chief tablet with a yellow #2 lead pencil bought at Eagan's Dime Store. Monthly statements were not mailed. Customers paid their bills when they got the money.

About 1950 the station was relocated to its original location, 226 North Main Street. Armor retired soon afterwards and Fred continued the family business until his death. Armor, Clemma, Fred, Zelda, Edith and Cecil are buried in Evergreen Cemetery. Donald is buried in Kerr Cemetery west of Republic. *Submitted by Bob Brashears.*

**MCDANIEL/BLADES -** Thomas McDaniel was a soldier in the War of 1812, where he fought with General Jackson at the Battle of New Orleans. He was married to Rebecca (Britian) McDaniel. To this marriage William McDaniel was born June 23, 1810 in Jefferson County, TN. In 1818, the McDaniel family moved to Roane County, TN, living there until 1821, moving to McMinn County, TN, living there and in Monroe County until 1836. The summer of 1836, the Blades and McDaniel families started their two month journey to Missouri.

William McDaniel and Sara Blades McDaniel married Aug. 28, 1836 during the trip to Missouri, William was 26 and Sara 17. Sara was the daughter of Edward and Penelope Blades, born on June 13, 1819. Penelope was a Cherokee Indian who spoke no English, using Indian sign language to talk to her family. The government opened up this land formerly inhabited by the Delaware, Kickapoo and Osage Indians to settlers in 1831.

When they arrived, there was only one family living in Pond Creek Township (a township being six square miles), David Reynolds along with his wife Polly Kelly Reynolds who had arrived in 1834. On Nov. 22, 1861 John Reynolds, son of David and Polly was murdered for voting for Abraham Lincoln by men who came to his home. William McDaniel experienced all the hardships and excitement of pioneer life. It took a great deal of time to accomplish anything in the wilderness because they were so far from civilization. In order for William to get his milling done, he had to take it 40 miles away, the trip took a week by ox team. Life proved to be very hard and tedious. He settled his farm of 240 acres in 1838, rearing a large family having eight boys and two girls. His first son, Jackson, was born Aug. 30, 1837; making him the first white child (non Indian) born in Pond Creek Township. The other children were John, James, Rebecca Eleanor "Ellen," Jesse, Ransom T., Elijah, William, Henderson and Sara Jane Missouri.

William was a member of the Methodist church for over 40 years, serving as class leader part of the time. Sara died in 1891 leaving behind her husband of 54 years.

William was a wealthy man leaving each of his children $360 and his grandchildren $160; with many heirs this totaled a tidy sum. He died in 1893 at the age of 83. He and Sara are buried in Wade Cemetery.

In 1870 there were 868 whites, 14 blacks, 251 horses and 50 mules in Pond Creek Township. William served as an election judge on Nov. 3, 1868 along with John Laney and Thomas J. Wallace. This election was held at George Britain's in Pond Creek Township, 89 people voted.

*House still stands on McDaniel homestead. Ransom and Liza (Jameson) McDaniel in photo.*

From the McDaniels, many local families are descendants: Rebecca McDaniel Miller's descendents are Miller, Potts and Manning families; Ransom McDaniel's descendents are Garoutte, Hagewood and Blades families; and William McDaniel's descendents are the Denny families. *Submitted by Charles McDaniel.*

**MCDANIEL/HAGEWOOD -** Benjamin Hagewood was one of the first settlers in Brookline between 1834 and 1849 from Tennessee. Thomas McDaniel was born in McMinn County, TN and moved to Greene County, MO in 1836. John C. and Martha C. Hagewood deeded an acre of land for the Blades Chapel Church on Dec. 3, 1888.

Ava Ann and her twin sister, Maggie Ada McDaniel, were born on June 15, 1882 near Republic. Maggie married John T. Hagewood on March 17, 1902 in Springfield, MO. His parents were John C. and Martha (Cavener) Hagewood. Her parents were Ransom McDaniel and Liza (Jameson) McDaniel. To this union the following children were born: Emmett Wesley "Toad," Oca "Monk," Delta May, Callie Marie, Raymond "Burl," Edith Merle, Margaret (died two days after birth), two male (stillborn) infants, Anna Lucille and Hazel Pauline.

The couple lived and farmed most of their lives west of Republic on Hwy 174. The family attended Hopewell Baptist and Blades Chapel for church services. They raised wheat and corn using a team of mules. They milked cows and cared for turkeys, chickens and hogs. They always had a large garden, which was canned to provide food during the year. They had a peach orchard and walked long distances to pick blackberries. It was always hot when picking berries and they usually got more chiggers than berries.

One time when Pauline and Anna went hunting for blackberries they found a plum tree that had delicious looking fruit. Being warm, thirsty and hungry they ate several plums and walked home. All got real sick and vomited after reaching the house. In the springtime they would search for sassafras roots to make tea. They had no electricity or water in the house and had to cut wood for cooking and heating.

The children attended Blades School and walked the approximate one and one-half mile to the school. Oca told the story about a verse he had to memorize for school. The poem, "Little fishes in a brook. Papa caught them with a hook, Mama fried them in a pan and I ate them like a little man." His memorization did well until he changed the ending to "And I ate them like a little hog," and he got a spanking. He was disciplined another time for putting a skunk in the schoolhouse, and the school had to be closed for a few days.

*L-R: Maggie (McDaniel) Hagewood, Marie (Hagewood) Wade, Anna (Hagewood) Lee, Gladys (Fisher) Hagewood, Pauline (Hagewood) Bowling and Mae (Hagewood) Tinsley.*

The children eventually all married and in 1942 Maggie moved to the Crane area. John T. expired Jan. 9, 1939 and was buried in Lindsey Cemetery. Maggie died Nov. 6, 1964 and was buried at Lindsey Cemetery. Anna Lucille Lee is the only sibling living at this time and resides with her family in Crane.

This information was collected from the *"History of Greene County,* Census, Marriage Records, Greene County Tax and Deed of Records" information, Sloan Robertson, Lucille Sifferman and family. *Submitted by Anna Lee.*

**MCELHANEY/HOWARD -** Birdie Pauline Howard was born May 7, 1898 in a farmhouse in Battlefield. She was the third child of Albert Marion and Sarah Permelia (Shelton) Howard. Birdie went to grade school at Green Ridge Elementary School. Green Ridge stood on Hwy. FF and was reorganized as part of Republic R-III in 1951.

*Birdie McElhaney*

In 1913, when Birdie was 15 years old, her family decided to visit the Shepherd of the Hills Country, now known as Branson, MO. The family had finished reading *Shepherd of the Hills* by Harold Bell Wright, and thought it would be a fun and educational trip. The family loaded up a covered wagon for the trip. The road was rough, and sometimes the children had to get out to help push the wagons up the steep hills. They camped near Marvel Cave. Albert found a guide to show the family the cave. Birdie remembers climbing down a 75-foot ladder into the cave. The family toured the cave with the guide using torches to light their way.

Around 1914, Birdie had the opportunity to go to the Fourth District Normal School, currently named Missouri State University, to a home economics class for high school girls. Birdie considered it a privilege to be able to attend the school.

Birdie married Bryan McElhaney Oct. 23, 1920. They lived in a house on the corner of Hwy. ZZ and Farm Road 178 that sat on 80 acres of farmland. Bryan farmed the land and built the little log chicken house. The home and the chicken house are still standing.

Birdie and Bryan had two children: Robert "Bob" was born Feb. 12, 1923. Betty Jean was born Dec. 23, 1931. In addition to being a farmer's wife and a mother, Birdie worked at the Shoe Factory in Republic, and later worked at the Garment Factory, which is now called Hagales.

Birdie and Bryan had three grandchildren. Bob married Mary Fadra Batson and had two children, Kay and Ginger. Robert and his family settled in Brookline. Betty Jean married Buell Mason and had one child, Rebecca "Becky." Betty and Buell settled in St. Louis County where they taught school for over 25 years.

One night in the early 1950s, Bryan and Birdie watched a meteor shower. They watched as one falling star hit the ground out in their field. Bryan dug it out of the small crater it made when it landed. The meteorite is currently in Becky's family.

Buell and Betty Mason moved back to Republic in 1982. Birdie sold the farm to her nephew, George McElhaney, and lived with Buell and Betty for the remainder of her life. Becky and her family moved to Republic in 1987. Birdie enjoyed helping to take care of the four great-grandchildren with Betty when Becky returned to work. Birdie passed away April 9, 1994. *Submitted by Rebecca Shaw*

**MCELHANEY/MCELHANY -** Warham "Warry" A. McElhany was one of five McElhany brothers who came to Greene County, MO from Grainger County, TN in 1837 with their mother and step father Joel Phillips and Lucy Pollard McElhany and their children. Warry was three years old when his father died in Tennessee and was 17 when he came to Missouri. They first settled near Battlefield. Joel and Lucy are buried in the Phillips Cemetery off FF Highway.

Warry was born in 1820 in Grainger County, TN. He married Stella Jane Robertson, daughter of Lindsey Robertson and Delilah Jones. They had three children: Delilah Lloyd, Mary Appline Rose and George L. McElhany. Warry was a farmer and the house he built is still standing on ZZ Highway. Warry and Stella are buried in the Lindsey Cemetery.

*George L. McElhany Family. Back Row: Lucy, Henry, Jane; middle: Warry, Myrtle, Maggie, Robert; front: Charley, Bryan, George L., Bess.*

George L. McElhany, son of Warry McElhany and Stella Robertson, was born in 1852. He first married Alice Garton, daughter of Jacob W. Garton and Penelope Elizabeth Rainey. They had 11 children: Henry, Myrtle Shelton, Jane Norman, Lucy Wiley, Charley, Maggie Ward, Warry J., Robert, Bessie Kimmons, Bryan and Alice, who died in infancy. Jane Norman, Warry and Bryan remained in the Republic area the rest of their lives.

Jane married George Norman and had five children: Eldon, Ethel Ely, Mary Dulin, Lucille Pittman and Ruth Roberts.

Warry married Rolsie Inmon and had three boys: Guy, Leon and George.

Alice died in 1901 leaving a house full of

children. She and baby Alice are buried in the Brookline Cemetery.

George married Emma Manley in 1907 and she helped raise the children. George and Emma are buried in the Republic Evergreen Cemetery.

William Bryan McElhaney was born in 1897, the 10th child of George and Alice. He married Birdie Howard, daughter of Albert Howard and Sarah Permelia Shelton. Bryan grew up in the house his grandfather built. He was a farmer all of his life, and lived on part of his father's farm, at the corner of ZZ and Farm Road 178.

Bryan and Birdie had two children, Bob and Betty Mason.

Bob married Mary Fadra Batson and has two girls, Kay Weaver and Ginger Davis.

Betty married Buell Mason and has one daughter Rebecca "Becky" Shaw.

Betty, daughter of Bryan McElhaney and Birdie Howard, attended Beulah, a one-room grade school, and graduated from Republic High School in 1949. She went on to SMSU and graduated in 1955. She taught school for 31 years. Three of those years were at Republic Elementary and the remainder was in St. Louis County.

Buell and Betty retired from teaching in 1982 and moved back to Republic. They are members of Calvary Baptist Church, where Buell is a deacon and Betty is the librarian. Betty helps with the quilting at the Republic Fellowship Center. They are members of the Republic Historical Society and are enjoying their retirement and grandchildren: Danny and Sarah Weaver, David and Jonathan Shaw. *Submitted by Betty Mason. Editor's note: Buell Mason died 2007.*

**MCMURTREY/GORDON -** Amos McMurtrey, born Oct 13, 1915 in Richville, MO, and Olivia (Gordon) McMurtrey, born Jan. 3, 1916 in Dora, MO were married July 15, 1938 while students at Southwest Missouri State Teachers College. They were graduates of Cabool HS and Ava HS, respectively. In 1947 they moved from Alton, MO to Republic, MO with their three daughters: Rosemary, Patsy and Jane. They were later joined by a brother Alan on Dec. 7, 1950.

*Amos and Olivia McMurtrey Family. Summer 1955, l-r: Olivia, Jane Carol, Rosemary, Patsy Ann, Amos Eugene; front: Alan Edward.*

Mr. "Mac," as he was commonly called, began the 1947-48 school year as a teacher, coach and bus driver. His first boys basketball team at Republic went 27-8 and went to the quarter final round in state tournament play, competing with all class schools at that time. In 1948-49 the team entered state tournament play at 27-3 losing in the first round play, again with all class schools competing. He remained as coach through 1955 when he took the position of principal of the Republic High School system with C.K. Leonard as superintendent. In 1956 he became superintendent of schools and in 1963 the new high school was built. This building now is occupied by the middle school.

In 1963 Republic became the Class M champions in basketball, coached by Leland Brown. Mr. McMurtrey loved all sports: track meets, basketball, softball, volleyball and he loved fishing. Story goes that if there is a fish in the lake "Mac" will catch it. During his last years at Republic, he helped start the football program and remained as superintendent until 1964-65.

Olivia and Amos McMurtrey became active members of the First Christian Church in 1953. Mrs. McMurtrey was a member of the Homemakers Club and taught Sunday school. "Mac" was active in Lions Club and Kiwanis Club. He actively worked with the members of the Kiwanis Club that led to the building of the first lighted baseball field in Republic.

The McMurtrey family while in Republic bought the two story brick house on N. Pine Street and years later would be known as the "old McMurtrey house." Alan McMurtrey and wife Debbie (Trogdon) and son Andy remain in the Republic area; Rosemary Otte, Patsy Patrick and Jane Green who graduated in 1958, 1961 and 1963 live in Overland Park, KS, Bolivar, MO and Springfield, MO, respectively.

Mr. McMurtrey died on Aug. 20, 1970 at age 54 after his retirement as superintendent of schools at Clever, MO. Olivia McMurtrey died in Republic on Aug. 16, 2002 at age 86 after having been able to enjoy her six grandchildren and two great-grandchildren. During Mr. "Mac's" short life, he touched so many young peoples lives, and there are many, many "Mr. Mac stories" told about how he helped people in their young formative years.

Amos and Olivia McMurtrey contributed a great deal to the Republic schools and community and won't soon be forgotten. *Submitted by Jane Green.*

**MCNABB -** Phyllis Jean McNabb was born on April 21, 1951 at Springfield Osteopathic Hospital to John Isaac and Genevieve McNabb. Phyllis is sister to Janet Thompson, John Allen McNabb and Linda Kay Pullen. Phyllis attended Republic Schools, graduating in 1969. From 1961 to 1966 she attended school in Tulsa, OK when her family moved there.

From her first marriage Phyllis had three children: Herbert Richard Bluebaum III, Jennifer Kay (Bluebaum) Elkins and Ashley Missy-Dawn Bluebaum. Phyllis divorced in 1989 and married Darrell Wayne Taylor from Willard, MO on Feb. 9, 2004 in Eureka Springs, AR. To this union Darrell's four children and numerous grandchildren and four great-grandchildren have made her family grow. Phyllis always wanted a large family and grandbabies and now has that. Currently they reside in Brighton, MO and also have a home in Viola, MO.

Herbie was born Sept. 22, 1978 at Cox Medical Center in Springfield, MO. He attended grade school in Billings and later moved to Republic with his mother and sisters and attended school there graduating in 1997. Herbie played baseball, football, was a Boy Scout and was active in church. He is a member of Republic First Christian Church. Herbie currently lives in Billings, MO, where he is involved with the Billings Volunteer Fire Department, helps on his dad's dairy farm and is currently working out of Fayetteville, AR.

Jennifer Kay was born Sept. 23, 1980 at Cox Medical Center in Springfield, MO. She attended grade school in Billings and later attended Republic schools where she graduated in 1999. Jennifer played softball, basketball and was active in church, Girl Scouts and is a Past Worthy Advisor of the Republic Rainbow Girls. She is a member of First Christian Church. On March 26, 2005 she married Russell "Rusty" Elkins in Eureka Springs, AR. Together they have three children: Kody Lane Keithley (born Aug. 31, 2001 at St. John's Hospital in Springfield, MO; Karlie Kay Elkins (born Nov. 25, 2004 at St. John's Hospital in Springfield, MO); and Stephen Berry Elkins (born Dec. 24, 1992). Together they live in Republic, MO.

Ashley Missy-Dawn Bluebaum was born Jan. 10, 1984 at Cox Medical Center in Springfield, MO. She attended kindergarten in Billings and later attended Republic Schools graduating in 2001. She was active in Girl Scouts and is a Past Worthy Advisor of the Republic Rainbow Girls. Ashley played softball, basketball and was active in church. She is a member of First Christian Church. She is currently residing in Billings, MO with her two children, Geoffrey Allen-Isaac Bluebaum (born Sept. 7, 2003 at St. John's Hospital in Springfield, MO) and Lily Jean Maggard (born Feb. 9, 2005 at St. John's Hospital in Springfield, MO). *Submitted by Jennifer Elkins.*

**MCNABB/ALLEN -** John Isaac McNabb was the oldest son born to Elsie Belle Edmonson McNabb and Virgil Lafayette McNabb on Jan. 29, 1923. His siblings were Evelyn, Bob and Keet. Raised in a single parent household, John quit high school to join the Army Air Corps during World War II. He returned to Republic and graduated from Republic High School. He attended Mortuary School in St. Louis. John was a funeral director at Max Fossett Funeral Home in Republic for many years. He changed professions, working for Paul Mueller Company as a calibrator, then going into management there in 1966. John had his pilot's license and flew small planes. He was an avid photographer and passed on his love of photography to his children.

*Genevieve Allen and John McNabb – 1941 Kentwood Arms Jr. & Sr. Prom.*

John served as municipal court judge, served on the Republic Rural Volunteer Fire Department, drove the ambulance and did many other jobs of community service, such as hanging Christmas lights on Main Street.

Genevieve Josephine Allen was also a graduate of Republic High School. She was the youngest child of Mabel Jenkins Allen and James Edward Allen. Her brothers were Glenn and Lawrence Allen. John married Genevieve in 1946, and they had four children: Janet Sue (1947), John Allen (1949), Phyllis Jean (1951), and Linda Kay, who was born on her dad's birthday in 1958. They were active members of the Republic First Christian Church, where John served as a deacon and elder. After moving to Tulsa, OK for six years, they returned to Republic in 1966 and became charter members of Westside Christian Church. After John's death, the family moved their membership back to the First Christian Church. John was a member of the Republic Masonic Lodge. He and Genny were active members of Republic Eastern Star where they served as Worthy Matron and Worthy Patron in 1969. Genny worked with John in the funeral home and then for Dr.

R.C. Mitchell as an assistant for several years. John died on March 13, 1969 and Genny died on Dec. 8, 1971.

Janet is married to Harold Lee Thompson, and they reside in Springfield. They have three children: Michelle Johnson, Michael Thompson and Gina Thompson, and nine grandchildren. Janet and Harold have both been active in Republic government. She is a retired office manager.

John Allen lives in Springfield and has two children, Andrea Lynn McNabb Batey and John Michael. John's wife, Lilly McMillan McNabb, died in 2001. He is a retired stockbroker.

Phyllis is married to Darrell Taylor and lives in Brighton. She works at Doctors Hospital. She has three children: Herbie Bluebaum III, Jennifer Elkins and Ashley Bluebaum, several stepchildren and several grandchildren.

Linda lives in Republic and has two children, Amanda and Heather Pullen, and three grandchildren. Her husband, Joe Allen Pullen, died in 1994. She has been an x-ray tech for over 27 years and is now in the MRI department at St. John's Surgery Center. *Submitted by John Allen McNabb.*

**MCPHAIL/MCKIMENS** - Ross K. McPhail, DVM was the first licensed veterinarian to practice in Republic. He was born in 1925, one of six boys and one girl born to Ross and Ethel McPhail. Dr. McPhail grew up in Strong City, KS. The older boys served in the Army during WWII and the younger ones in the Army and Navy during the Korean War. They all attended college on the GI Bill.

It was while attending K State that Dr. McPhail met and fell in love with Patrica Ann McKimens. They were married June 8, 1952 in Westmoreland, KS. The next day they moved to Springfield, MO, where Dr. McPhail went to work for Dr. C.C. Moore. Dr. Moore rented an office in Republic and hired Earline Neil as a secretary, and the McPhails moved to Republic. When Dr. Stam left Crane, MO. Dr. Moore bought his office equipment and opened an office there, and so Dr. McPhail's practice area included Republic, Billings, Crane, Hurley and Clever with occasional calls as far away as Blue Eye and Cape Fair.

*Ross McPhail.*

The area was much different in 1952. Missouri had no veterinary practice law at the time and lay practitioners had no training, so their diagnosis and treatments were quite crude and of little value. Most of the country roads were unpaved and when making calls down in the hills, Dr. McPhail would often have to stop and drive the goats, chickens and dogs out of the road before he could continue. Children would stop playing and run out to the road and wave as he drove by.

In 1955, Dr. McPhail bought the Republic practice from Dr. Moore and moved his office over to his home on Fountain Ave., where Mrs. McPhail managed the office and the home and reared three boys: Kevin, Kent and Kendall.

When other veterinarians moved into the area, Dr. McPhail closed the office at Crane and limited his practice to the Halltown, Republic, Billings,and Clever areas, treating mostly dairy cows and emphasizing herd health programs. Although on call 24/7, he made time to serve on the school board, the city council, was a charter member of the Kiwanis Club, and taught Sunday school for years.

He sold the practice in 1988 to Dr. Brown and retired. The next eight years he volunteered at the elementary school where he worked with children with learning problems. *Submitted by Ross McPhail.*

**MCSPADDEN** - James Walker McSpadden was born in Monroe County, TN. He was a teacher, married to Susan Caroline Bird. He served in the Mexican War and in the Civil War. James and family moved first to Lawrence County, MO, near Verona. Before 1856, they moved to Greene County where he purchased 80 acres from George Wiley.

Susan died about 1856 leaving children: Mary, Martha, Samuel, Sarah and Charlotte. James later married Nancy Bennett. James and Nancy had two sons, James Bennett and Thomas Matthew.

*Back: Howard McSpadden, Jack McSpadden, Leonard McSpadden, Tommy McSpadden; middle: Opha Helton, Hattie Voile, Jessie Potter, Margaret Cotter, Alta Fortner, Lillie Mills; front: Thomas Matthew and Mary Matilda McSpadden on their 50th anniversary, October 1929.*

James Walker served in the Civil War, including the Battle of Wilson's Creek. He was wounded at Corinth, MS and later died from his wounds.

Thomas Matthew was the youngest son of James Walker and Nancy McSpadden. He married Mary Matilda Young and they had 11 children who lived to adulthood. They were Lillie (Mills), Jack, Dee, Alta (Fortner), Opha (Helton), Tommy, Jessie (Potter), Hattie (Vaile), Leonard, Howard and Margaret (Cotter-Grant).

Jack, Howard, Lillie and Margaret spent most of their lives in Greene County. Dee, Alta, Opha and Leonard lived many years in Colorado; Tommy in Kansas; Jessie in Polk County; and Hattie near Miller, MO. The children attended Bennett School just east of their farm.

Howard Vinton was second from youngest of Tom and Mary McSpadden's children. Howard moved to Colorado when about 16 and, along with his brother Leonard, lived in brother Dee's home.

Howard married Leola Brown in August 1928 in Wiley, CO. They moved back to Missouri and lived with his parents on the family farm at McSpadden Corner which is 10 miles west of Springfield on Historic Route 66. Howard helped his dad operate a Shell Service Station which was one of the first in the area. Jerry Vinton, oldest son of

*Howard and Leola McSpadden – October 1929.*

Howard and Leola, was born at McSpadden Corner, making the third generation born there (including Thomas and Howard).

Howard and Leola moved to Republic prior to 1933 where daughter, Juanita, was born. Howard worked for Greene County operating a road grader. He always appreciated that job because during the Depression not many jobs were available. Howard was a great admirer of President Franklin Roosevelt. Later, Howard commuted to Fort Wood while the army base was being constructed.

In 1941 the family moved to a farm near Halltown, and later a farm south of Lockwood near sister, Alta Fortner and family. Youngest son, Rex, was born in 1944.

Howard and Leola returned to Republic following retirement in 1974, and lived there until Howard's death in 1982. Both Howard and Leola, along with many family members, are buried at Yeakley Cemetery west of McSpadden Corner. They spent many happy times at the Republic Senior Center and appreciated their many friends there.

Son Jerry and wife Doris live near Strafford. Rex and wife, Sharon, live in St. Louis. Juanita (McSpadden) Steinbaugh and husband, Arthur, live near Billings. *Some material was taken from McSpadden and Ullom by Dale McSpadden. Submitted by Juanita Steinbaugh.*

**MEADORS/ENGLEDOW** – Dale, Carolyn and Vicki Meadors moved from Bolivar, MO to Republic in April 1974, after purchasing the Funeral Homes in Republic, Billings and Clever. Dale was born at Sentinal, MO, Sept. 18, 1937, the youngest son of Elva Ray and Bessie (Brashers) Meadors.

Carolyn was born at Fillmore, CA Oct. 28, 1937, the oldest daughter of Clarence Eugene and Grace (Slagle) Engledow. They were

*Dale and Carolyn Meadors.*

united in marriage Nov. 19, 1955 at the home of Rev. W.M. Hines in Boliver. To this union were born two children a son Jackie Dale (died at birth) and a daughter Vicki Carol.

Vicki was in her junior year of high school during the move and she graduated from Republic High School. The family started getting acquainted with their new friends and neighbors in the community that they would serve. One of the first projects taken on was a much-needed ambulance service to serve the rural area and area cities. Vicki married Roger Lee in November 1975 and they made their home in the Republic area for a few years, then moved to Boliver were they still reside. They have two sons, Justin and Jared, both are students at MSU in Springfield.

Helping in community activities has been a big part of their lives. Dale is an active member in the Kiwanis Club, helping to organize the Republic Chamber of Commerce, Republic Senior Center and Pumpkin Daze. He also served on the Board of Directors of Southwest Bank, established Town and Country Bank of the Ozarks and served as chairman of board until the bank was purchased by Mid-Missouri Bank. Dale also served on the Board of Directors for Republic, and Billings Housing Authority, Evergreen Cemetery Assoc. and People Helping People.

Carolyn is a member of the American Home Club, Downtown Merchants Assoc. and the Republic Historical Society.

They are enjoying their retirement but are still active in helping out with community projects. *Submitted by Carolyn Meadors.*

**MEDLIN** - The Leon and Jane Medlin family consists of Leon, Jane, and their two sons, Kevin and Kent. Leon was employed by International Harvester Motor Truck division in Kansas City, MO when he was transferred to the Springfield, MO branch as parts-manager.

They were able to find a home in Republic June 1, 1970. Leon became involved in the community. He served on the Planning and Zoning Committee, and later on the city council for nine years.

The parts branch of IHC was sold in 1982 but Leon continued to be employed by the company until 1986 when he retired. Leon attended MU extension classes to become a master gardener in 1987. In 1990 he was placed on the membership honor roll. He did volunteer work until 1999 and received emeritus status.

*Front: Allie; 2nd row: Lacey, Ronda, Angie; 3rd row: Jane, Laura, Jarred; 4th row: Kent, Kevin, Leon Medlin.*

Jane was employed by M.F.A. Grocery Store on Main Street until it closed in 1981. In 1982 she became city collector and served in that position until retiring in 1996. Later she was employed at H&R Block in Republic until retiring from that position in 2005.

Kevin, their oldest son, graduated from Republic High School in 1978. He was a member of the National Honor Society. He attended SMSU (now MSU) and graduated in 1982. He graduated from University of Missouri Dental School in Kansas City in 1988. He enlisted in U.S. Air Force and was commissioned as a captain. He served at the Strategic Air Command at Omaha, NE. Later he served during the Gulf War at the base in Enid, OK until he was discharged. He opened a dental office in Crane, MO in 1991. Later he built an office in Republic where he is presently located. Kevin married Ronda Bray in 1981. She is also a graduate of MSU and is employed there as a teacher. They have a daughter, Laura, now a sophomore in Republic High School. She is active in school activities.

Kent their youngest son spent 12 years in the Republic R-III School System, graduating in 1982, He attended MSU and received his BS in education in 1987, master's in 1990, and specialist in 1992. He was employed by Springfield schools to teach chemistry at Hillcrest High School and later as assistant principal at Reed Jr. High School. He received his doctorate degree from the University of Arkansas in 1995. Later that year he received the position as high school principal at Lamar and served there for nine years. He applied for the position as high school principal in Willard and was appointed there in 2003. In 2004 he became the superintendent at Willard. Kent married Angela Jones in 1984. She graduated from nursing school as an LPN with honors at Nevada, MO, They have three children. Lacey, the oldest daughter, is a St. Jude cancer survivor. Their son Jarred is attending OTC in Springfield. The youngest daughter Allie is a 6th grader in Willard.

Jane and Leon attend Hood United Methodist Church. *Submitted by Leon Medlin.*

**MILLER/SIFFERMAN** – Billy Miller and Lucille Sifferman were married April 10, 1940. Both were descendants of pioneer families who settled in the Pond Creek area in the early 1800s.

The Sifferman clan traces back to Nichola Sifferman, born 1823, who immigrated to the United States from the Alsace-Lorraine region. During the crossing Nichola met his future wife, Louisa Meyer, a person of German descent. On arrival to the United States they started their trek to the Midwest and ended up settling in the Chesapeake area. He was hard-working and strong minded. A story is told that one Saturday he went to Lawrenceburg to spend the night with a friend. When he got up on Sunday morning, the friend was hoeing his potatoes. Nichola got on his horse and came home before they had their breakfast. He said, "Got in Hemil (God in Heaven) if he has to work on Sunday I'll never go back," and he didn't. A grandson, True Sifferman and wife, Opal Montgomery, were the parents of Lucille, born in 1921.

Hiram Montgomery, ancestor of Opal was born 1796 and settled in the Pierce City area. He was originally from North Carolina and had 12 children.

Ancestor, James Miller, was born in Tennessee. He remained in his native state until the Civil War when he moved to Greene County. He fought in the Confederate Army.

Billy's maternal side of the family was descended from the English family of Edward Blades, born 1780 in North Carolina. Edward married Ellen Maynor, who was either full bloodied Cherokee or half Cherokee and half French. In 1836 they moved to Missouri. The trip took two long months. They had to carry live embers with them since there were no matches to start fires. Edward and his family settled on Pickerel Creek. There were no other settlers to the south for 40 miles. Billy's father, Emmett Miller, was married to Alma Blades and Billy was born in 1921.

Three children were born to the Millers: Kay Miller (born 1941) before Billy left for a tour of duty in the Philippines; Janice Miller (born 1948) and David Miller (born 1953).

Lucille opened a gift shop called All Seasons Gifts in 1975 and it operated until 1990. Billy started an insurance agency in 1955 and his daughter, Kay, is still active in that agency, one of few 50-year-old family businesses still operating in Republic.

Kay has two children, daughter Kathy Jones resides in Joplin, MO and Kelley Jones in Phoenix, AZ. He has three boys: Cameron, Trevor and Dylan. Janice moved to Wichita, KS with husband, Jim Boone, after her graduation from Drury College. They currently own and operate Wichita Insulation. They have one son Jeffrey and his wife Shannon, daughter Alexandra, and son Tanner. David and wife Brenda reside in Newton, KS and own Midwest Electric. David's son, Daniel, just entered Emporia State College and children: Cody, Lizzie and Abby, are members of their household. *Submitted by Kay Miller.*

**MITCHELL/WILLIAMS** - Dr. Robert Clarence Mitchell was born March 11, 1907 in Oklahoma. He loved to joke with his son, John, that he grew up on an Indian reservation (because he was born before Oklahoma was a state). Dr. Mitchell's family then moved to Cherryville, KS, where his parents opened a bakery. Robert and his brother, Norris, worked in the bakery also. Additionally, Dr. Mitchell's father was a millwright and Robert developed his love of tinkering from watching his dad.

*Dr. R.C. Mitchell, Republic, MO, 1942.*

*School day at Republic Elementary in 1950s.*

Dr. Mitchell came to Republic in 1931, driving a Model A Ford Coupe. His first office was next door to O'Dell's Drug Store located at the corner of Grant and Main. His next office was across the street above the dry goods store. The dentist, Dr. R.C. Brim, was also in this building. His next move was to a small building on the north side of Grant Street where Miller's Insurance Agency is located. He then built an office next door on the corner of Grant and Pine Street around 1950, where he practiced until he retired. Dr. Mitchell had lots of patients and delivered many of the people now residing in the Republic area. He did not make appointments; you sat in a full waiting room for your turn. His son John remembers that every year he gave all of the school children their required vaccinations.

Dr. Mitchell's son John Norris also remembers his dad recollecting how in 1931, when he was just starting his practice, he was nervously carrying around all of his earnings in his pants pocket, ($400). He was worried that someone would steal his money, so he put all of it in the local bank in spite of the economy spiraling downward. The very next day the bank closed and he lost all of his money!

*Dr. R.C. Mitchell in early 60s back of Martin Insurance Building.*

Dr. Mitchell had many unusual hobbies, one of which was ham radio (his call number was W9WTG). When WWII started, his ham radio was physically taken away by the government after it was known that ham radio operators had heard about the bombing of Pearl Harbor before anyone else. He enjoyed racing speed boats on Lake Taneycomo, sail boating on Fellows Lake in Springfield, building a telescope in his backyard that was donated to the Republic High School Science Department after his death. He built a sailboat in the back of the building on the west side of Main Street where the Refrigeration Associates is now located. When finished, they had to tear out the back of the building to get the boat out. He played clarinet in the community band. He was an avid photographer and took many pictures which he developed and printed in his own dark room. He made gun barrels in his garage workshop where he lived at 500 E. Elm.

In the late 1930s, he married a local girl and school teacher, Lucille Williams, daughter of Ralph (Rass) and Nancy Williams. Their son, John Norris, was born on Feb. 19, 1944. John has two daughters, Nancy and Jennifer, and three grandchildren: Jennifer, Randall John and Forest John.

Dr. Mitchell passed away on June 5, 1978 and is buried in Evergreen Cemetery. *Respectfully submitted by Jennifer Hill Rogers, niece.*

**MONHOLLAND** - The Monholland family: Clue, Jean, Cathy and Bill, moved to Republic in the summer of 1961 for Clue's job with Peter Kiewit. Kiewit Construction helped build I-44. The family anticipated staying in Republic only while Kiewit was involved in this project.

On March 6, 1962, however, Clue was involved in a serious construction accident. This accident ensured the family's permanent relocation to Republic when Cathy was in the fifth grade and Billy was in the first. Jean worked in Springfield at the old Royal McBee typewriter factory and later at Zenith until it finally left Springfield. The Monhollands are originally from Tahlequah, OK. Since Republic is only 150 miles from that city, they remained close to family.

*L-R: Bill, Audrey, Lucas, Vicki, Cathy and Jean Monholland.*

Cathy and Bill both graduated from Republic High School in 1969 and 1973, respectively. Cathy received numerous University of Missouri scholarships and earned a bachelor's in English from Mizzou in Columbia in 1974; a master's from The University of Tulsa (English, 1979); a master's from Rice University (history, 1989); and she is currently completing her Ph.D. dissertation in English at The University of Tulsa. Cathy, a professional writer, editor, and college teacher, is also an avid hockey fan. She is well-known in national hockey circles for her hockey publications. Throughout the years, Cathy has remained friends with her RHS best friend, Glenda Carter Crews, and others. Cathy also stayed in touch with RHS's favorite English teacher, Lucille Napper, until Mrs. Napper's death in 2004. She saw Mrs. Napper two months before she died and showed Mrs. Napper her most recent academic publication in a French periodical. Cathy, who is divorced, has lived in Houston, TX for the last 24 years.

Bill attended SMS and married his RHS sweetheart, Vicki Metcalf Monholland. After living in Athens, TX for years, Bill and Vicki returned to Billings, MO several years ago and bought a house where they are raising their teenagers, Lucas and Audrey. Lucas and Audrey enjoy music, sports and school. Bill works at 3M in Springfield and is a master mechanic and also a prize-winning artist and sculptor known among family members for his fabulous metal sculptures, while Vicki works in the Billings area.

Clue recovered from his construction accident but never fully regained his good health. He died at the Missouri State Chest Hospital in Mt. Vernon in January 1982. Jean retired from Zenith and for the last 15 years has lived in Tahlequah, OK, where she works part-time in Northeastern State University's Placement Office. She is 78 years old and in excellent health.

Jean and Cathy love the years they spent in Republic and visit Bill and his family as often as possible. Both want to move back to Springfield, and Cathy hopes to retire in the Republic area. Jean, Cathy and Bill will always treasure their memories of the 35 years they lived in Republic and all the good friends they still have there. *Submitted by Cathy Monholland.*

**MOONEYHAM/BUTLER** - Edward Leon Mooneyham was born in Republic, MO in 1891. His parents were William J. Mooneyham and Elizabeth Jane (Logan) Mooneyham. Ed married Maud Butler, daughter of Nelson Butler and Martha Britain Butler in 1912. They owned and operated a dairy farm west of Republic, MO, where they would bottle milk and sell it in Republic and the surrounding area to support their family of three sons: Willard Leon (born 1917), Clyde Leroy (born 1920) and Edward Ellis (born 1929).

*Edward and Maud Mooneyham.*

Willard married Reathel Wanda Blades, daughter of John Henry Blades and Nellie Davis Blades, in 1937. Together they had eight children: 1) Velma Faye never married and has no children. 2) Wilda Louise married Clinton Maggard and has four children: Doris Jean, Marietta, Patricia (died at birth), Timmy, and eight grandchildren. 3) Jerry Leon married Sue Wade and has two children, Lisa and Christina, and five grandchildren. 4) Marilyn Ilene married Eugene Mitchell and has two children, Rhonda and Ronald, and one grandchild. 5) John Edward married Jean Studebaker and has one stepson, Don, and two step grandchildren. 6) Charlotte Elaine married Gary Rippee and has three children: Sandy, Cathy, Jeff, and four grandchildren. 7) Ray Dean married Janet Herndon. Together they have three children: Aaron, Mindy and Casey. Ray Dean has a son, Marty, by a previous marriage. Ray Dean has five grandchildren. 8) Donald Lee married Linda Bussard and they have one son, Curtis, and four grandchildren. Willard and Reathel owned and operated a dairy farm west of Republic where they raised their eight children. Willard is deceased and Reathel now resides in Billings, MO.

Clyde married Louisa Faye Blades, daughter of John Henry Blades and Nellie Davis Blades, in 1941. Together they have four children: 1) Darrell Lee married Judy Baum. They have four children: Ty, Kassie, Ashley, Dustin, and five grandchildren. 2) Terry Lynn married Norma McCord. They have three children: Shane, Ryan, Chad, five grandchildren and one step grandchild. 3) Glen Ray married Lynn Landers and they have five children: Melissa, Glenna, Tracey, Brett, Chelsea, and seven grandchildren. 4) Max Randall married Linda Childress. Together they have five children: Nicole, Carrie, Tori, Lyndsey, Lake, and six grandchildren.

Clyde and Faye own and operate a dairy farm west of Republic where they raised their four children. Clyde passed away July 6, 2006. Faye passed away March 30, 2007.

Ellis was married to Elizabeth Velma King, daughter of Roy King and Velma Short King, in 1950. Together they have two children: Roger Ellis never married and has no children. Alan Lee married Deidra Barnhart and has one child, Eric.

Ellis and Beth own and operate a dairy farm west of Republic. They raised their two children on this farm and the two of them still reside there.

Willard, Clyde and Ellis spent many long hours in the hot fields, custom filling silos and baling hay for many people. They have many friends. *Submitted by Marilyn Mitchell.*

**MOONEYHAM/MCCORD** - Terry Lynn Mooneyham was born Dec. 22, 1946, one of four sons born to Clyde and Faye (Blades) Mooneyham. His three brothers were Darrell, Glen and Randy. The family home was a farm six miles west of Republic where the boys learned farm work at a very young age.

*Terry Mooneyham (standing), Norma (McCord) Mooneyham (sitting).*

Terry graduated from Republic High School, where he played basketball and baseball. He married Norma McCord from Clever on June 30, 1967. They have three sons: Shane and his wife Barbie, who are residents of Ash Grove with their four sons: Cody, Taylor, Brock and Nick; Ryan resides in Springfield and has a son Christopher and a daughter Michaela; Chad also lives in Springfield and is not married.

Terry coached a variety of sports, coaching the youth division ages 1 to 13 in Republic from 1968-94. Norma coached girl's youth softball fast pitch during the 1970s.

Terry currently is employed by Paul Mueller Company as a journeyman machinist, where he has worked for 40 years. Norma has been a cosmetologist for 38 years. During this time she has owned and operated her own shop, located on Main Street in Republic and also owned a dress shop on Highway 60 in the 1970s. Norma is currently working for Christian Health Care as their beautician.

Terry and Norma spend a lot of their time traveling; spending time at their home in Shell Knob, MO; enjoying boating; and traveling to the Colorado Rocky Mountains where they ride their ATVs. *Submitted by Terry Mooneyham.*

**MOONEYHAM/VAUGHN** - The following information is adapted from an article in the 1971 Republic Centennial Book. The author is unknown to this writer who appreciates their work.

Thomas Jefferson Mooneyham, born 1818 in Tennessee, served in the Mexican War, discharged with rank of captain. Then served as sheriff of Marion and Franklin Counties and pursued a career as lawyer.

Thomas and his first wife, a Cherokee Indian, had two daughters, Malinda and Lucinda. His first wife is said to have left the family, returning to the reservation in Oklahoma. He then married Elander Vaughn in Illinois in 1846.

In 1861, Thomas enlisted in the Union Army and Elander and the children set out for

Missouri in a covered wagon as they felt she and the children would be safer there during the Civil War. The family now included his two daughters, their own seven children, and a nephew, Lewis Mooneyham. The ages of the children ranged from 3 to 15 years.

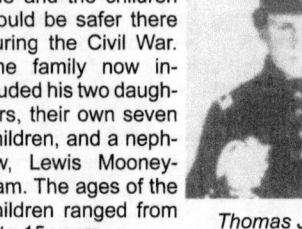

Thomas Jefferson Mooneyham, 1818-1861.

On the journey, Elander was sold molded feed near St. Louis, which killed one of the horses. However, she purchased another horse to make a team and they continued to land just west of Republic.

Elander reared the large family as Thomas Jefferson was killed in battle in October 1861. His sword was returned to the family. Elander, 1826-1894, is buried in Lindsey Cemetery, Republic. The children all married and continued to live in the Republic community. Thomas Jefferson Jr. married Elizabeth Gray. Daniel married Elizabeth Jane Dodd. Warren married Leila Harrington. William married Elizabeth Jane Logan. Dellie married John Arnie Campbell. Fannie married W.J. Skelton. Malinda married James Hays (more on Malinda and James in separate article). Lewis, the nephew, married Pernisa Reynolds. Lucinda and the youngest Mooneyham son died young.

William and Warren, attorneys, had an office on the west side of Main Street in 1895. Thomas "Jeff," Daniel, and Malinda had farms on the south side of Republic. *Submitted by Audrey Vaught, ggg-granddaughter of Thomas Jefferson Mooneyham and gg-granddaughter of Malinda Mooneyham Hays.*

**MOONEYHAM/WADE** - Paul was the fourth born of eight children to Charlie and Jean Neill Mooneyham. He was born in Missouri, moved to California in 1937 and then back to the farm on west County Line Road where he farmed and remained until his death in 2000.

Paul married Ina Wade in 1934. Ina was the seventh born of eight children to Calvin and Alice (Laney) Wade. To this union five children were born: Dale (married Joan Reinert); Kathy (married Ralph Andrus); Ray (married Deanna Toynton); Pauline (married Howard Shuler); and Judy (married Charles Padgett).

Mooneyham Family. Clockwise from left: Judy, Paul, Dale, Kathy, Ina, Pauline, Ray (in center).

Paul and Ina had 11 grandchildren and 23 great-grandchildren. Ina passed away in 1991 and Ray passed in 1997. *Submitted by Kathryn Andrus.*

**MORGAN/GUY** - Sidney Alfred Morgan was the second child of his family. He was born in West Plains, MO, in November 1946. Sidney married Sandy Guy in July 1967. He was drafted into the Army in 1969 spending basic training at Fort Leonard Wood, MO. From there he was assigned to Fort Eustis in Virginia. Sidney and Sandy were blessed with one son, Sidney Lynn born in January 1970 in West Plains, MO. While stationed at Hunter Army Airfield Base in Savannah, GA, Sandy and Lynn joined him so the family could be together.

The family left the military life in September 1971, relocating from Savannah to Republic. Purchasing a mobile home and setting it in a mobile home park located in the 300 block of West Elm. The tornado of December 1971, which caused tremendous damage to the city, took out one side of their home. Another mobile home was purchased and set in French's Trailer Court located on Hwy. 60, where the US Bank is currently located; at this time Sidney's employer, Greene County Propane, was located just across the highway.

In 1976 they purchased their first home in Republic on Magnolia Street where they currently live. Sidney continued to drive a propane delivery truck until retirement in 1996. During his employment he saw the company change ownership several times.

Sidney served with the Republic Fire Department for 24 years. He started with the department in 1973 when Carl Eubanks was fire chief, watching the department's growth from having two or three sets of gear to wear, to the fire department Republic has at this time. Sidney was there when the 1978 Pierce Fire Truck came in, and he and his brother Dennis were on the committee to hire the new fire chief when Bill Farr resigned to take another position.

Sandy worked at Zenith until the plant was moved to Mexico. She then started working for Kentucky Fried Chicken in Republic. She is presently employed with Luggage Works in Aurora, formerly Purdy Neat Things in Republic.

Their son Lynn graduated from Republic High School in 1988. He married a former classmate, Lori Womack, who moved with her parents to Republic in 1976. They were married in October 1997, making their home in Republic also. Lynn is currently a full time employee with the Republic Fire Department where he started in 1988 as a volunteer reserve. They have a son Tyler Allen and a daughter Hannah Kay. *Submitted by Lynn Morgan.*

**MOUNT/ESTES** - Amos Green Mount, son of Amos Mount and Charaletta (Woodsmall) Mount, was born May 17, 1841 in Oldham County, KY. He was educated in the rural school of his area, and in October 1861 enlisted in Company B, 6th Kentucky Regiment Infantry USA. After serving three years, he was discharged in October 1864. After returning to Kentucky he migrated to Scotland County, MO; then in 1867 to Greene County, MO, where he located on a farm north of the present town of Brookline, MO. While living in this area he became charter member and Tyler of the local Masonic Lodge. Dissatisfied in this location he moved to a 120 acre farm eight miles west of Springfield on West High Street Road and AB Road. In 1885 he and Mary Elizabeth Douglas were married. To this marriage three children were born: Rufus Walter, Kate and Moses Asberry "Berry."

Moses Asberry "Berry" Mount grew up attending Elwood country school. On Feb. 18, 1913 Berry and Letha Viola "Ola" Smith were united in marriage. To this union two sons were born, Vencil Geoffrey and Lloyd Russell. During the years of 1919 and 1920, Berry and Ola Mount with their two sons, Vencil and Lloyd,

Vencil Mount.     Floried Mount.

lived and farmed east of Republic, MO. In this location Vencil attended the first and second grade in the Beulah rural school with E.B. Ferguson as teacher. The next year Berry and Ola Mount with their two sons moved back to the home farm on AB and High Street Road. Both boys graduated from the Elwood rural school. Vencil attended the Bois D'Arc High School and Lloyd attended the Willard High School. During the years 1926-28 Vencil exhibited registered Jersey cattle at the Republic Street Fair.

Vencil Mount graduated from the Bois D'Arc High School in May 1932 when he started working on the farm with his father and attended SMS (Southwest Missouri State University) winter term (3 months). In the fall of 1935 he enrolled at the University of Missouri at Columbia. In 1938 Vencil graduated with a BS degree in agricultural education. He then accepted a job as vocational agriculture instructor in the high school at Clever, MO. The next year he became fascinated with a young local lady by the name of Floried Pearce Estes. The fascination ended in a mutual attraction and marriage on June 11, 1939 in the First Baptist Church at Clever, MO.

In 1946 they moved to Republic, MO, where he became the vocational agriculture instructor, remaining for a tenure of 34 years. He was a charter member of the local Kiwanis. He was a 50-year-member of the local Masonic Lodge No. 570 AF&AM and a 50-year-member of the Abou Ben Adhem Shrine. He retired June 30, 1980.

Shortly after their move, during a Saturday evening stroll around the public square in Springfield, MO, they met Mr. and Mrs. C.K. Leonard. Mr. Leonard was the superintendent of schools at Republic. After a short visit Mr. Leonard asked Mrs. Mount if she would be interested in a job as school secretary. After an interview she was told to report to his office the following Monday morning. She did and the job lasted 36 years. She retired in 1982. *Submitted by Vencil G. Mount. Editors Note: Vencil Mount passed away June 18, 2006, with interment in White Chapel Memorial Gardens.*

**MUENCH/OWSLEY** - Jack Muench and Cyndy Owsley were married on June 11, 1983 in North Kansas City, MO. Their first child, Bryan, was born on Feb. 10, 1985 in Springfield, MO; Robert was born Feb. 21, 1987; and Leslie on Sept. 27, 1990, also in Springfield.

Jack was born Dec. 6, 1953 in Aurora, MO. His father, Jackie Muench, was also born in Aurora and lived there until his death in 1965. His mother, Jeannie Burnett, was born and raised in Aurora as well. Both sets of grandparents were from Aurora, Ray and Effie Muench and Leon and Virginia Spangler. Jack attended high school in Aurora and graduated from the University of Missouri in Columbia with degrees in accounting and law.

Cyndy was born on Dec. 23, 1956 in North Kansas City, MO, to Charles and Maurine Owsley. She lived her childhood in North Kansas City and graduated from North Kansas City High School. She later graduated from the University of Missouri, Columbia, where she and Jack first met.

Her father, Charles, was born in North Kansas City and lived his entire life there until moving to Republic in 2003. He died in 2005. Her mother, Maurine Owsley was born in Mountain View, OK and grew up in Edmond, OK. Maurine attended Central State Lab School while her mother, Eula (Dean) Nix, attended Central State College. Mrs. Nix received her teaching certificate from Central State. Cyndy's mother also graduated from Central State with a degree in art education. Maurine moved to North Kansas City after graduation to teach high school where she met and married Charles.

Cyndy's maternal grandfather, John W. Spencer, died in 1930. Her maternal grandmother raised the three children and taught school in Oklahoma until retiring to north Kansas City. Her paternal grandparents, Charles Owsley and Carolyn Thompson lived in north Kansas City and were owners of the North Kansas City Electric Company. *Submitted by Jack and Cyndy Muench.*

**NANCE** - Sidney Johnson Nance, his wife Charlotte Parker and their five children, moved from Arkansas to Republic about 1885 and settled on a farm southwest of town. Two daughters and two sons were born in Republic, where five of the children and their mother spent their lives. Twenty members of the Nance family are buried in Evergreen and Wade Chapel cemeteries.

Clement Nance came from Wales about the time of the American Revolution. Sidney Nance's father, John Calvin, was Clement's grandson, born in 1824 in Lincoln County, NC where Sidney was also born in 1852. John Calvin, his wife Anne Jones, and their family moved to Nashville, TN at the time of the Civil War, and after to Arkansas.

Sidney was 10 at the time of the war and migrated with his parents to Arkansas. There on Christmas Eve, 1876, he and Charlotte Parker were married. The Nances farmed near Republic from the 1880s until the early 1900s when they homesteaded near Portales, NM. There, Sidney Nance died in 1909 and was buried. Charlotte returned to Republic and made her home with her daughter, Flora, and son, Cleve, until her death in November 1921.

The Nance children, who married and lived in Republic all their lives, included Lon (1879-1962), who married Lucinda Doty (1881-1913), mother of Grace and Roy, and later in life he married Bertha Britain (1879-1978); Lillie (1880-1952), wife of Ollie Thurman and mother of Raymond, Marie and Ewell; Emma (1882-1908), who was the second wife of W.P. Anderson; Cleve (1886-1973), who married Dora Johnson in 1930; and Ella (1888-1979), who married W.P. Anderson in 1915 and had two daughters, Roberta and Joan.

Edgar (1877-1966) and George (1893-1985), the oldest and youngest sons, both married in Republic, but Edgar, his wife Anna King, and daughters Helen, Josephine and Charlotte, moved to Ontario, CA in the 1920s. George and his wife Elizabeth Tilson, son Gerald and daughter Kathleen, lived most of their lives in Pueblo, CO. Pearl (1891-1982), the youngest daughter, married Day Brockerman, a railroad man, and with their daughter Margaret lived in various railroad towns, but finally in St. Louis. Flora "Flo" (1884-1956) married Robert Herbert, a retailer from Bad Axe, MI, and they also retired to St. Louis.

Nance descendents now living in Republic number three: Lillie's granddaughter and great-grand-daughter, Shirley Swinehart and Mary Jo Cruse. Shirley is the daughter of Raymond Thurman and Mary Elizabeth Dixon. The third Nance descendent still a resident is Ransom Ellis III, great-grandson of Sidney and Charlotte, whose grandmother was Ella Nance Anderson.

Other descendents of Sidney and Charlotte include grandchildren and great-grandchildren of Lillie, who live in Springfield, St. Louis, and near Monett; Marsha Phelps, granddaughter of George in Pueblo; and three of the third generation: Pearl's daughter Margaret Moody of Bridgeton, MO; Roberta Arnold of Tucson, AZ, daughter of Ella; and Charlotte Dickerson, Upland, CA, youngest daughter of Edgar. *Submitted by Mary Cruse.*

**NAPIER/FOSTER** - On Oct. 1, 2004. Clyde and Maxine Napier moved into their home at 812 E. Harrison in Republic. From that very first day, they have been very happy living here. Because their daughter lived in Springfield and medical facilities were close by, this community was chosen. They have found the people to be very friendly.

For 42 years they lived in McDonald County in southwest Missouri while Clyde was employed by USDA at the poultry plant in Noel from which he retired in 1989.

*Maxine and Clyde Napier.*

Clyde was born in Shannon County, MO to William Ashford and Grace Ernestine (Gulley) Napier. When he was 10 years of age he moved to Oregon County with his parents and attended school there. From 1951-53 he served in the Army during the Korean War. He graduated from Southwest Missouri State University, Springfield, MO in 1959.

Maxine was born in Fulton County, AR to Roy and Evelyn (Brown) Foster and attended school at West Plains, Missouri after her family moved there in 1941. She attended Draughon's Business College in Springfield before being employed at the ASC Office at West Plains, MO in 1951.

Clyde and Maxine were married Aug. 11, 1957 and have two children, Mark was born at West Plains, MO and Shelley Jean was born at Gravette, AR.

Mark and his wife, Marijo (Cheek) Napier have three children: Bryan Paul, Sara Michelle and Emily Grace Napier. Bryan and his wife, Amy Jo (Countryman) Napier, have a daughter Dacey Abagale, born on her great-great-grandfather Napier's birthday. Clyde and Maxine are members of First Baptist Church here in Republic. *Submitted by Clyde and Maxine Napier.*

**NEIL/BLADES** - Chloe Susan (Blades) Neil was born northwest of Republic on April 23, 1905 to Ira Harmon Blades and Annie Bethar Laney. She had one sibling, Burl Lester Blades, born Feb. 1, 1911 and died Oct. 5, 2003. Chloe married Earl David Neil April 2, 1932. The two of them farmed and taught in one-room rural schools for several years.

*Earl David Neil and Chloe Susan Blades, April 2, 1932.*

Earl and twin brother Mearl B. were born Dec. 3. 1902 to Lillie Mae (White), born 1865 and died 1955, and David Baldwin "Doc" Neil, born 1861 and died 1945. Doc was not a doctor or a veterinarian, so unsure as to why he was called Doc. Earl was a long time Democratic committee man and Chloe was a Republican committee woman. They either had to come to a mutual agreement or kill each others votes on election days.

Earl and Chloe took the assessments for Pond Creek area for many years and also the periodic census. They also volunteered at Republic Senior Center, and various local cemeteries, serving on the boards, as secretary, and in other positions.

Chloe was Sunday school teacher at Blades Chapel Church many years, where she is still attending at age 101+ (at the time of submitting article for this book). Earl and Chloe had one daughter, Earline Sue, born Oct. 26, 1937, who married Dale Eugene Brashers in 1955. They were married for 13 years.

Earline married Oliver "George" Minier Sept. 24, 1971. George was born Nov. 20, 1927 in Dushore (Sullivan County), PA to Jennie Cordelia (Vogel) and Daniel George "Dewey" Minier. Dewey and Jennie had 11 other children: Harry, Ellrey, Florence, Mary Ellen, Howard, Irene, Donna, Samuel, Ora Mae, Janet and Danny, who died at birth.

George had two daughters by a previous marriage, Tammi Lynn born Dec. 31, 1957 and Terri Sue born April 13, 1958. Both girls are currently living in Midland, TX.

George and Earline have a granddaughter Stephanie and grandsons, Casey and Cullen, plus several step-grand children. *Submitted by Earline Minier.*

**NELSON/MAPLES** - Edgar Elijah Nelson (June 30, 1900-Aug. 23, 1979) was a son of Elijah A. Nelson (Aug. 5, 1869-Sept. l9, 1903) and Minerva Elizabeth Pearce (June 25, 1870-Jan. 22, 1947). Nelson married Ethel Ruth Maples (March 4, 1898-Feb. 3, 198l), daughter of Elias L. Maples (Dec. 10, 1873-Sept. 6, 1955) and Gracie Paralee Tabor (Oct. 2, 1880-Jan. 14,1965), on July 2, 1921. Edgar, Ethel and their parents were born in Christian County and their families likely migrated from Tennessee and Kentucky.

The couple met in Clever and courted via horse and buggy. Ethel was a teacher and continued teaching a few years after their marriage before devoting all of her time with Edgar to their farm and family. They lived south of Republic in the old Wise Hill

*Nance Family, l-r: Emma, Lillie, Flora, Lon, Charlotte holding baby Pearl and Ella standing beside her; standing in rear: Cleve, Sidney and Edgar.*

*Nelson family 1974 – top l-r: Mary Nelson, Jack Nelson, Joe Nelson; middle: Jane Nelson, Edgar Nelson, Ethel Nelson, Dallas Gray; front: Elizabeth Gray, Ruth DeVore.*

area throughout their 58 years of marriage. They first lived south of the Greene-Christian County line on what is now Davis Bridge Road before moving south and east on the road now named Honeysuckle.

*Nelson grandchildren – 1977. Top, l-r: Kerry Nelson, Philip Nelson, David Nelson, Walter "Sonny" DeVore Jr., Karen "Susie" DeVore Alexander; bottom, l-r: Greg McCord, Kathleen McCord Williams, Nancy DeVore Craig, Jane Gray Smith, Kevin Nelson.*

Edgar and Ethel were proud parents of four children who lived nearby with their spouses and families. Their lives revolved around their farm, their family, and their church. They were long-time members of Clever First Baptist Church.

1) Elizabeth Grace Nelson Gray (Oct 4, 1922-Aug. 21, 1992), the Nelson's first child, married Dallas Barney Gray (Dec. 20, 1914-Nov. 4, 1992) on Dec. 16, 1944. They had one daughter, Jane Ruth Gray Smith, Nov. 22, 1948. (See Joe Emmett Gray.)

2) Edgar Jack Nelson was born Dec. 9, 1924. He was stationed in Germany while serving in the Army as a member of the Ozark Division of the 102nd Inf. Div. Jack married Mary Dawn Fleming (born Sept. 9, 1929) on June 9, 1949. They had two sons, Philip David (Oct. 30, 1950-Feb. 20, 2003) and Kevin Jack (Oct. 29, 1954-June 26, 1994).

*Nelson brothers and spouses – 2004. Mary Nelson, Jack Nelson, Joe Nelson, Ruth Ellen Nelson.*

Philip bought a neighboring farm and worked with his dad in beef and dairy farming. Philip was an entrepreneur, starting several businesses, including Holsteins Antiques in Billings and The Original Pop's Kettle Korn, which he was operating at the time of his death. Philip's daughter, Diane Kay, was born May 1, 1979.

Kevin remodeled a home on the Nelson farm where he resided when he returned to the area from Texas. He enjoyed antiques and traveled to purchase and sell unique items through his antique businesses. Jack and Mary continue to raise beef cattle on Davis Bridge Road south of Republic on the original Nelson homestead, where Edgar and Ethel lived when they married and where Jack was born. Mary worked a number of years at the Republic Farmers Exchange.

3) Edwina Ruth DeVore (Sept. 8, 1928-Dec. 19, 1975) was a teacher for many years in the Clever School where she taught first grade. Her children: Walter Eugene "Sonny" Jr. (Oct. 14, 1951); Karen Sue "Susie," (June, 28, 1956); and Nancy Ruth (May 13, 1958). (See DeVore, Edwina Ruth)

4) Joe Ward Nelson was born Dec. 26, 1934 and married his first wife, Martha Jane Hale (Feb. 16, 1934-Dec. 19, 1975) on Sept. 13, 1953. They had two sons, David Joe (Feb. 16, 1962) and Kerry Jon (April 8, 1964). An infant daughter, Frances Ann (Oct. 16, 1960), is deceased. David built a home on the Nelson farm with his wife Angela Lou Roy (May 1, 1964), who married on Aug. 6, 1982, and their sons, Andrew David (Oct. 22, 1985) and Matthew Elijah (March 1, 1988). David is a supervisor for Springfield City Utilities at Southwest Power Plant. Kerry married Leslie Edgar (Sept. 8, 1968) on June 13, 1992; and they live in Fremont Hills with their daughter Chloe Belle (Sept. 21, 2000). Kerry is the district administrator for the Missouri Board of Probation and Parole.

Tragedy struck the Nelsons when five family members were involved in an automobile accident on Dec. 19, 1975, on their way to Clever School for a PTA Christmas program. Their daughter Ruth and daughter-in-law Jane were killed, while Elizabeth, David, and Kerry were seriously injured.

Joe was married to Ruth Ellen Brown McCord, (Jan. 22, 1938), on Oct. 5, 1977. Ruth Ellen's son is Gregory Lane McCord (Oct. 13, 1959) who married Marlene Annette Crain (Oct. 15, 1963) on Oct. 12, 1991. Their children are Raymond Gene (May 16, 1983), Bryan Keith (March 26, 1985) and Meagan Lane (June 4, 1995). Ruth Ellen's daughter is Kathleen Ruth McCord (Jan. 7, 1961) who married Daniel Lowell Williams (March 20, 1958) on July 10, 1998. Their daughter is Sarah Catherine (Jan. 4, 1987).

Joe and his family spent many years in dairy farming, and he continues to live with his wife on the farm Edgar and Ethel purchased in 1942. Joe served as Christian County Presiding Commissioner and Western Commissioner for a number of years. He was a founding board member of TriWay Country Club, now Island Green Golf Club, south of Republic. *Submitted by Jack Nelson.*

**NELSON/MORENO** - John A. and Avelina (Moreno) Nelson and their three young sons: Jimmie, Lamont and Greg, moved to Republic, MO, in September 1954 from Joplin, MO. When they moved to Republic on Hampton Street, the population was just over 900, and their oldest son, Jimmie, was just beginning second grade. While looking for a home in the Springfield vicinity, they were told that Republic had good farm land nearby and, most importantly, a good school system for their children.

*L-R: John, Greg, Jimmie (standing behind), Lamont and Avelina Nelson – 1956.*

At the time of their move to Republic, John was employed at Terrill-Phelps Chevrolet as the service manager, where he remained employed for 14 years. In 1967, John left Terrill-Phelps and opened his own garage business, Nelson's Quality Auto Service, located on North National Avenue in Springfield, which became a successful business for John. His youngest son Greg later began working at the garage, and when John retired, he turned the business over to him. John enjoyed several years of retirement before passing away in November 2004.

Both John and Avelina were born and raised in the Webb City/Joplin area: John, the middle child of three, and Avelina, the fifth of ten children. Beginning in 1943, John joined the Army and served in WWII as a tank crewman in Europe. John and Avelina were married on Aug. 16, 1945, after he returned to the States when the war ended.

John served on the Republic School Board for several terms and also served as president of the school board. He was a charter member of the Republic Kiwanis and was involved in many of their initial projects. One of their projects, which required many hours of hard work, was the development of the Garoutte Ball Field at the corner of Hampton and Hines. Another of the organization's projects in which John was involved was the organizing of the first Republic Fall Festival, which has now become a yearly event in Republic.

In John's spare time, he built a cabin on Table Rock Lake for his children and grandchildren to enjoy. He also enjoyed raising cattle and horses on his farm north of Republic. Avelina was a full-time homemaker and was a home-room mother for all her sons. She continues to live in the same house she and John bought when they moved to Republic.

John and Avelina's three sons: Jimmie, Lamont and Greg, all graduated from Republic in the 1960s. Presently Jimmie lives in Springfield and runs his own business. Lamont is married to Virginia Tiede Nelson and has two sons, Todd and Jacob, both of whom also graduated from Republic. Lamont followed in his dad's footsteps by serving on the Republic School Board for two terms. In 2002, he retired from United Parcel Service after 33 years of service. Greg is married to Cindy Burke Nelson and has two sons, Rowdy and Kris, and two step-children, Myndi and Shawn. Greg and Cindy presently reside in the Willard community, and both of them stay busy working at their business in Springfield. *Submitted by Avelina Nelson.*

**NOE/ALLEN** - Mark Noe and Bernice Allen Noe lived on Mill Street in Republic. She loved making braided rugs and piecing quilts. Mark, after operating a hardware store, worked as a city marshall for the city of Republic. Sudden tragedy came to the Noe family when Mark was murdered on June 2, 1929. His body was found in a ditch along the highway one and half miles south of Brookline. The following story is an account from the local Republic newspaper:

"Late on a Sunday night Mark S. Noe noticed two men who had been drinking being disorderly, ordering one of the men to give up his gun, Noe got into the car with Oval LaFollette, 20 years old, and Harry Young, 25, ordering Young to drive to the home of Judge Kerr, who lived on Main Street. Before the car had gone as far as the Shover Drug Store, Young produced a gun from the door pocket of his Ford Coupe. He and Marshall Noe scuffled for the possession of the gun. As they drove north on Main Street, Young and Noe continued to scuffle. When the car reached the middle of the next block, in front of Dr. Beal's residence, LaFollette slid out of the car.

Mark Noe.

When residents heard gun shots and could not find Marshall Noe in town, they feared that he had met with foul play. Harve Snyder, deputy sheriff, was notified and a number of men searched for Marshall Noe the remainder of the night. Early Monday morning two men came upon a body on a side road running south from the Hendrix farm, and notifying L.V. Hendrix that a man lay dead in the ditch about one-half mile south of his house. As soon as he saw the body, he knew it was Marshall Noe and notified his brother Marcell Hendrix, Greene County Sheriff, and Republic officers. Marshall Noe had been shot three times.

LaFollette was taken into custody at the home of his brother-in-law about five miles west of Republic. A warrant was issued for the arrest of Young, and a search began. The death of Marshall Noe and the search for Harry Young led to the largest massacre in police history, that is now known as the "Young Brothers Massacre." Six officers from the Springfield Police Department and the Greene County Sheriffs Department were killed.

Harry and Jennings Young escaped to Houston, TX. A Texas man informed Texas officers that the brothers were in his home, identifying Harry Young from a newspaper picture. It was reported that when officers trapped the brothers in the house, they slew each other rather than surrender."

After the death of her husband, Bernice lived the remainder of her life on Mill Street in Republic. Her mother, Sally Allen, lived with her. They pieced and quilted many quilts and braided many rugs.

Bernice was a sister to Goldie Allen Snyder, aunt to "Puge" Snyder, and a great aunt to Phyllis Cox Carlson and Libby Cox West. *Submitted by Marti Clark.*

**O'BRYANT** - The O'Bryant family is one of the earlier settlers in this area, predating the founding of Republic. The O'Bryants were some of the "Scotch-Irish" immigrants that came to America at or before Revolutionary War times. Like many of these immigrants, they settled first on the east coast, moved west into Kentucky and Tennessee, and then moved further west.

Elias O'Bryant and Sarah Jones were married in Tennessee in 1813. There, they raised their children until around 1840 when, along with some of their children, they moved west and settled in Cedar County, MO. Elias died there (the family story is that he was killed by Indians) and around 1845 Sarah and four of her grown children moved here, homesteading an area along Terrell Creek southeast of Republic.

Modern day members of the O'Bryant family in Republic are descended through Elias and Sarah's youngest son, Elias Jackson O'Bryant, also known as E.J. who married Louisa Phillips. They had 12 children. Their two oldest were brothers, Andrew and Joel, who married two sisters from the Short family that settled around Hurley, MO, Nancy and Sarah Short. Joel and Sarah had seven children, among whom were Lydia and Fred.

O'Bryant family. Back: Fred and John; middle: Sarah (Short) mother, Lydia (Owen), Joel (father); Mae (Bledsoe) in front.

Lydia married Glenn Owen, who co-owned Owen and Short Hardware on Main Street for many years. Lydia and Glenn had two children, Harold and Wayne. Harold Owen served as Mayor of Republic in the 1940s. He married Wilma Russell, daughter of William Russell, who moved to Republic about 1891. William was a carpenter and businessman. Harold and Wilma had one daughter, Jane, who taught elementary school in Republic before retiring, and who lives in Republic. Jane has three daughters: Pam Day and Carrie and Sarah Cox.

Fred O'Bryant was a farmer, orchard grower and businessman in Republic during the first half of the 1900s. He at one time owned and operated the Republic Locker Plant, which is still in business on Main Street. Fred married Carrie Russell, another daughter of William Russell and sister to Wilma. Fred and Carrie had three children: Eleanor, Russell and Carolyn.

Eleanor taught first grade for many years in Republic before she and her husband, Bill Robertson, moved to Harrison, AR. Carolyn married Bill O'Neal, son of Clarence "Shorty" and Adith O'Neal, who were farmers in the Republic area. Bill was a rural mail carrier for many years for the Republic Post Office, and is now the President of the Republic Historical Society. Carolyn and Bill have four children: Joe Bob, Jim, Linda and Mary Ann. Mary Ann lives in Republic and is the nurse at the Republic E-1 School, and has one son, Michael Schmitt, a student at Republic High School.

Russell O'Bryant married Irene Medlin, daughter of Clyde and Emily Medlin of Billings. Russell operated the family farm and orchard in Republic until the drought years of the 1950s forced their closure. He later worked and retired from Hiland Dairy in Springfield.

Russell and Irene had three children: Gary, Sharon and Patrick. Patrick lives in the Republic area, having retired from City Utilities in Springfield and is a civil engineer. He married Carolyn Rainey of Brookline, and they have two children, Kelly, who presently lives in Nixa, and Kara. Kara lives in Republic, is in real estate, and has two children, Isaiah, who is in second grade in Republic, and pre-schooler Isabella Gillham. Going back to Sarah O'Bryant, Elias's widow, Isaiah and Isabella represent the eighth generation of their family to be in Republic! It is doubtful that very many other families can boast of eight generations living in the same town! *Submitted by Pat O'Bryant.*

**O'DELL** - Dr. Burd O'Dell was born March 11, 1878 in Carroll County, MO. He moved to Dade County in 1891, then to Billings, MO in 1903

L to R: Andy Marsh, Sherman Robertson, unknown (man with dog), Doc O'Dell.

where he was a dentist. Within a short time he moved his dental practice to Republic. In 1907 "Doc" married Tresa Anderson, a native of Republic. Burd and Tresa had two children: Ralph, born in 1922, and a daughter who is deceased.

He then went to Miller and owned a drug store for three years, returning to Billings where he was mayor for part of a year in 1922. Dr. Burd and Tresa O'Dell moved to Republic about 1924 where he bought and started the operation of O'Dell Drug Store on the northeast corner of Main Street at Grant.

Ralph O'Dell served in the Army. He met and married his wife Dette in 1945 and they had three children: Mike, Keith and Margie. They have two grandchildren. In 1951, Ralph purchased the drug store from his father, but Burd continued in the business until 1960. Ralph served as pharmacist until 1963.

At the 1971 centennial celebration, Dr. Burd O'Dell was the oldest living person in Republic at age 93. *Submitted by Ralph O'Dell.*

**O'DELL/BILLS** - Wilma O'Dell was born on a small farm about 40 miles outside of St. Louis on March 1, 1926. They were a family of seven. Her father, the town sheriff; mother, a dedicated housewife; herself; one older sister, Lillian; two older brothers, John and Ralph; a younger sister Loraine; and a younger brother Willard. She was a hard-working girl, who strived to assist with the family farm. After her mother passed away she moved out on her own. She lived off and on again between St. Louis and Chicago. She made up for what she lacked in childhood now. She danced, read, listened to music, etc. She listened to the radio every chance that she got and adored going to see old time movies and those are still her favorite kinds of movies. She finally settled down when she married in 1944 to a Charles Bills. With him she had two boys, Charles "Chuck" and Dennis. Charles was born in 1945 and Dennis in 1946.

She says that her kids made her life. Now she has four grandchildren and five great-grandchildren. She moved to Republic in 2004 and currently resides in Bristol Manor with her dog Bengi, whom she has had for 5 years. She says that her greatest accomplishment of life was surviving and that's all that anyone can hope for. Her advice to all people out there is to finish school and make something out of yourself. *Submitted by Sara Hodge, Kelsey Jones and Brenden Smith.*

**O'NEAL** - Moses O'Neal, born 1804 in Georgia, married Nancy Logan. They had 12 children after moving to Tennessee. Three of his sons came to Greene County, MO around 1860. Moses came to visit them and died while here. He is buried in Maple Park Cemetery in Springfield. One of his sons was William W. who married Martha Bristow. They homesteaded on land southwest of Republic. Their children were 1) Ellen, who married James M. Britain. Their children were Edward L. who married Marie Hedrick. Their son Edward L. Jr. married Kathleen Wilson and had sons, Edward L. III and Stephen. 2) William Curtis "Curt," who married Fronia Thurman and had the following seven children:

*Seated: Wm. W. and Martha (Bristow) O'Neal; standing: Frank, Curt, Ellen (Britain), Etta, George.*

1) Finis married Lettie Blades, their son John married Irene Rapp and had twin sons, Stan and Steve.

2) Ernest married Nora Stowe.

3) Clarence "Shorty" married Adith Sallee, their children: Robert married Elsia Edwards and has a daughter Peggy who married Joel Brown. Billy Gene married Carolyn O'Bryant and their children: Joe Bob married Betsy Townsend and has daughter Sylvia; Jim; Linda married Paul Lanning; Mary Ann married Rusty Swift and she has son Michael. Joe married Billie Saylers and has daughter Patty.

4) Fred married Vergie Robertson and they have daughters, Joan and Jeanette. Joan married Tom Varland and has son Tom. Jeanette married Charles Hartzog and has daughter Jennifer.

5) Lester married Alma Joplin.

6-7) Victor and Dorris.

Frank married Rilla Britain, his son Ellis married Elsie Stewart and their children were Charlotte, who married Bob Sifferman and their daughter Karen married Darrel Rand; Tony married first, Carolyn Carskaddon and had sons, Greg and Ron. Tony married second, Cheryl Kneal. Etta married Albert Hemphill. George married Nadie Butler and has children: Guy, Joy and Duane. *Submitted by Bill O'Neal.*

**O'NEAL** - Tony Ellis O'Neal was born on June 30, 1942 in Republic, MO to Ellis and Elsie O'Neal. He accepted Jesus Christ into his life at a young age and was baptized. He was a member of the Hood Methodist Church where he attended all his life.

He spent his entire life as a resident of rural Republic attending all 12 years at Republic public schools graduating in 1962. He farmed with his father Ellis; they had dairy, beef, hogs and crops. He received his American Farmer Degree in 1962. He was also honored and recognized as outstanding young farmer in the *Outstanding Young Men in America* publication in 1966. He served several years on the Greene County ASCS Farm Board. Tony continued to farm until health reasons forced him into retirement in 1998.

*Cheryl and Tony O'Neal.*

Tony married Carolyn Carskaddon in 1963 and two sons were born to this union, Gregory in 1964 and Ron in 1968. This marriage was dissolved in 1981. Tony married Cheryl Kneale of Jasper, MO in 1986. She was also a farmer and had two daughters from a previous marriage: Tauna (born 1964) and Misha (born 1968). They raised their four children and farmed together.

*First row: Nathan, Allison, Hunter, Brady O'Neal – Regan and Payton Smith – Justin and Jason Frieden; 2nd row: Lisa, Greg, Paula and Ron O'Neal – Misha and Stephen Smith – Tauna and Tom Frieden.*

Greg O'Neal married Lisa Hendrickson of Republic in 1984. They have two children together, Nathan and Allison O'Neal, of the home. They live near Republic on part of the Tony O'Neal Farm.

Ron O'Neal married Paula Albright of Bradleyville, MO in 1993. They have two sons, Hunter and Brady, of the home. They also live near Republic on part of the Tony O'Neal Farm.

Tauna Kneale married Tom Frieden of rural Lamar, MO in 1989. They have two sons, Jason and Justin, of the home near Lamar, MO.

Misha Kneale married Steven Smith of Jasper, MO in 1990. They have two children, a son and a daughter, Payton and Regan. They live on part of Misha's grandparents', Leonard and Wilma Kneale, farm.

Tony O'Neal passed away on May 8, 2005, leaving a much loved family and life he so enjoyed. Cheryl, his widow, moved back closer to her daughters and their families. *Submitted by Cheryl O'Neal.*

**O'NEAL/STEWART** - Frank O'Neal was born Oct. 4, 1875 and died June 2, 1947. He married Rilla Britain who was born April 9, 1879 and died Jan. 6, 1929. They are both buried in Wade Cemetery in Republic, MO. They had one son Ellis O'Neal, who was born Nov. 3, 1898 and died Jan. 3, 1978. He married Elsie Stewart, who was born June 1, 1899 and died June 22, 1989. They are also buried in Wade Cemetery. Elsie's parents were Walter Stewart (1874-1947) and Hattie Perkins (1877-1964). They are buried in Patterson Cemetery.

*Ellis and Elsie O'Neal.*

*Frank and Rilla O'Neal.*

Elsie had three children by a former marriage. Jo Ann Fugitt married Stanley Long. Jo passed away in 1997. She is buried in Greenlawn Cemetery in Springfield. Stanley is currently living in Tulsa, OK. Jo and Stanley had two daughters. Their first daughter Pat married John Kiefner and resided in Columbus, OH. They adopted two children, Andy and Beth Kiefner. Pat passed away in 2001. Bonnie, Jo and Stanley's second daughter, married Thomas Brienner and they now reside in Broken Arrow,

*Walter and Hattie Stewart.*

OK. Their son Tim resides in Chicago, IL with his wife Lori Glenn and three sons: Harris and twins, Grant and Henry. Their second son Bill married Kimberly Perkins and resides in Oklahoma City, OK with their two daughters, Jordan (adopted) and Jillian (biological).

Bill Fugitt married Barbara Lemons and they reside in Rogers, AR. They have two daughters, Kayla and Kathy. Kayla has two sons and a daughter: Matt, Mandy and Mitch. Kathy has two children, Alicia and Will. They all reside in Rogers, AR. Kim is Bill and Barbara's son. He married Connie Allred and has a daughter and two sons: Jessica and twins, Beau and Bill. They also live in Rogers, AR.

*Seated: Elsie O'Neal; standing: Wanda Hazen, Bill Fugitt, Charlotte O'Neal, JoAnn Long, Tony O'Neal.*

Wanda Fugitt married Bill Hazen. She has three daughters and two sons. Their first son William Hazen married Edith Payne and they reside in Kansas City. They had four children: Lori and Michael, who live in Blue Springs; Anna who lives in Kansas City and Matthew who resides in Rogersville. Bill Fugitt and Wanda Fugitt are twins.

*Front row: Ryan, Van Sifferman, Charlotte O'Neal, Karen Rand, Jayme Sifferman. Back row: Cayla Sifferman, Alyssa, Darrel, Deidra Rand.*

Elsie and Ellis were married and had two children, Charlotte and Tony O'Neal. Charlotte married and later divorced Robert Sifferman. During the marriage they had two children, Karen and Van Sifferman. Karen married Darrel Rand of Rogersville, MO and they have two children, Deidra and Alyssa Rand of Republic, MO. Van Sifferman has three children: Cayla, Jayme and Ryan Sifferman. Charlotte now resides on the homeplace where she was born and raised. She is retired from Dillard's. She also owns apartments in Republic.

Ellis, Elsie and Frank worked together with their family. They had a large fruit farm full of apples and peaches along with grape vines. All Ellis and Elsie's children helped pick, package and sell the fruit. In the late 1940s they sold the fruit farm. Ellis and Tony went into just dairy, beef and crops. Elsie also raised turkeys and chickens and sold eggs.

Ellis and Elsie enjoyed traveling in their later years and enjoyed the company of their family. *Submitted by Charlotte O'Neal.*

**OSWALT/SNEED** - Linda Sneed went to Republic schools all her life, and the old grade school where she attended through the 3rd grade was on West Elm near the garment factory. A new school was built on Anderson and the old school was torn down. Children from Brookline and Battlefield were consolidated into the new school. The senior class of 1962 was the last class in the old rock and brick high school before a new one was built.

In 1960 Linda met Ron Oswalt, who was serving in the U.S. Army at Fort Leonard Wood. They fell in love and were married in 1961 at Republic First Baptist on Main Street. She graduated in 1962 while Ron was gone to Germany during the Berlin Crisis. Their four daughters: Ronda, Sonya, Kristina and Leslie, all attended Republic schools.

During the 21 years Ron spent in the military, he served all over the world. The family, however, was only able to go with him stateside. They lived in Massachusetts, New York, Fort Leonard Wood and Maryland, before settling in Republic in 1977. They lived on the old Cockran farm for seven years before they bought a home on N. Allen. Very few houses were on their street at the time and even horses ran in a big field near their home.

After the military, Ron got on at the post office where he worked for over 21 years, and Linda continued working at Montgomery Wards. They still call Republic home and so do three of their four daughters. Six of the eight grandchildren go to Republic schools.

The area around the Oswalt home is surrounded by houses now. From 1984 to 2006, Republic has taken on many projects. Some good and some not so good. The downtown area has lost its glitter and everything has moved to the outer edges, which keeps growing. The citizens of Republic are fortunate to have good schools and decent management. People who live here care and we have "People Helping People" to show for their efforts. The Senior Citizen Center is one of the best and the Historical Society preserves the history. Hats off to the citizens of Republic and let's keep working for a strong future. *Submitted by Sonya Oswalt.*

**OTTENDORF/BLADES** – Lue Ottendorf (1892-1969) and Bessie Blades Ottendorf (1898-1955) were honest, hardworking people whose interests were friends, family, and helping their neighbors. Lue's father was Fred Ottendorf and Lue's mother was Elizabeth (Hines) Ottendorf. Lue came from a family of four boys and two girls. His mother died at a young age and he was the one who had to assume the responsibility of cooking for the younger children. The names of the children were Clyde, Anne, Stella, Roll, Elmer and, of course, Lue. Stella married Will Sims and lived on a farm near Clever. Clyde married Cloris Nelson and lived on a farm near Boaz. Roll married Mearl Hutchenson. Anne married a man named Robinson. Lue married Bessie Blades. They all stayed in Republic or on farms right outside of Republic

*Lue is on the front row and the first one on the left.*

Bessie came from a very large family which included 13 children. Two of the children died at a very young age and their names were not available. The remaining 11 included Rose Ann, Roe, Elyjah, Eliza Jane, Louise, Jessie, James "Jim," Oliver, Hershel, Bessie and Lena. Bessie's father was Gideon Blades and her mother was Rachel (Ray) Blades.

Lue and Bessie Blades were married Sept. 29, 1915 in Springfield, MO. Six children were born to their union. Doris, the first born, was killed when he was 18 years old while working in Idaho for the Conservation Corps under President Roosevelt's New Deal Plan. Don, Loarn and Louie were the remaining boys. Louise and Wanda were the girls. The three boys all served their country during the second World War. Loarn and Louie (Junior) were stationed in the European Theater of the war and Don was stationed in the Pacific for two and a half years. Don was awarded the Bronze Star medal for bravery under fire. Lue and Bessie were very relieved and happy when their sons returned at the end of the war.

Lue and Bessie lived in and around Republic except for a few years when they lived in Marionville. Around 1938, they bought a home on South Main Street. They continued to live there for the remainder of their lives.

During the early years of their marriage, Lue worked on the section crew of the railroad. He worked at farm jobs of many kinds and provided for his family. All of their children grew up to be honest and hardworking. Louise married Dale Little of Clever. Wanda married Floyd Forbis. Loarn married Joan Clark. Don married Ruby Cunningham and Louie married Juanita Baker of Billings. All three boys were farmers at some period in their lives.

Later in Lue's life, he fulfilled a needed service to the people of Republic. Most residents had gardens in their backyards. Lue had an old white horse named "Nelly." He hitched up his two-wheeled trailer and loaded his turning plow onto it and would go all over town plowing gardens.

The Ottendorf name is not found in the younger generation in the Republic area, but will always be remembered by those who knew and loved them. The Blades name is still well-known in Republic and very much respected. *Submitted by Ruby Kimmons.*

**OTTENDORF/HUTCHISON** - On Dec. 24, 1912, Rollie Eugene Ottendorf and Anna Muriel Hutchison were married and settled in Republic. Two daughters, Grace B. (Land) and Hazel L. (Cox) were born. Roll was a first generation American, born to Fredrick Ottendorf and Elizabeth Hines, a Republic girl. Muriel was from Bolivar.

Rollie and Anna Muriel managed the hotel that was located just south of the present Hood United Methodist Church. This is the reason the family became Methodist because the little girls could walk to Sunday school without crossing the street while Muriel baked 30 pies each weekend for the local cafe on Main Street.

Roll drove a drayage truck for local merchants hauling merchandise to Springfield daily. They saved enough to purchase a small home in the city, which he later traded for 10 acres east of the city near Stickney's grape vineyard.

During the Great Depression, times became very hard for the family and they lost the farm and were forced to move back into town to find work any place they could. The girls often spoke in later years of picking strawberries, grapes and apples. After things began to get better, they were able to purchase a small grocery store on the corner of Main and West Elm. They both worked in the store and made many friends.

They eventually purchased a home on the corner of West Mill and West Ave. This had nice lots for a large garden and a place for a cow, chickens and a horse. Roll would plow gardens for the locals, while Muriel would sell milk, butter and eggs. The garden produced lots of vegetables for their own use as well as products to sell.

The house was large enough that they almost always had renters either living in the basement or in boarding rooms. Many of the men working on the highway between Republic and Springfield boarded with the family, as well as workers at the garment factory.

Grace married J. Wilfred Land and Anne Elizabeth (Johnson) was born to the couple. Hazel married Dan Danielson and gave birth to a son, Danny. Grace attended college and became a school teacher, teaching many years in local area schools. Hazel attended Beauty College and was a local beautician, having a beauty shop in the same building Roll and Muriel had their grocery store.

The Ottendorfs were active in community affairs, especially Eastern Star and the Masons. Muriel was well known as a great instructor in Eastern Star and her home was often used to instruct new members. Roll belonged to the Scottish Rite. They were often Worthy Patron and Worthy Matron of the Star.

They each became employed by the Republic school system as janitors before they were forced to retire. They were en route home from a visit with Kansas relatives when they were involved in a terrible automobile accident which left them physically impaired for the rest of their lives. Muriel recovered better than Roll, whom the doctors said would never walk again. The German temper came out and he told them to just sit and watch. He did as he promised and did walk, but with quite a limp.

In their later years, Roll developed emphysema and Muriel suffered a paralyzing stroke making each of them homebound until death. Muriel passed away in 1969 and Roll passed away almost exactly one year later.

Grace and Wilfred raised Anne in Republic and in 1956 were transferred with Wilfred's employment with the Federal Prison System. They retired in Republic in 1971 and lived for many years in the "old home place" on West Mill. They were very active in Hood United Methodist Church, where a scholarship was established in their memory after their deaths in 1999. Anne resides in Republic. She has three children: Kathryn (Iman), Mark and Gregg Johnson.

Hazel raised Danny in Republic, never living too far from the city. They own a lake home near Cedar Creek where Hazel lived with

Danny for a period of time after her retirement as a long time employee with the city of Republic. Due to ill health, she now resides back in Republic. *Submitted by Anne E. Land Johnson, granddaughter of Roll and Muriel Ottendorf.*

**OWEN** – Charles Baker Owen was 9 years old when his family arrived in Greene County, MO in an oxen-pulled schooner in 1836. He was the fourth child of Solomon H. Owen (born Dec. 12, 1797, Sullivan County, TN, died May 9, 1874) and Mary Elizabeth Bushong (born Feb. 17, 1797, died March 31, 1876). His parents were married in 1821. Although his mother was born in America, she always spoke German, never English.

*Charles Baker Owen.    Nancy McCroskey.*

Charles (known as Baker) grew up on the family farm and was educated in the neighborhood schools. At 27 he was appointed deputy sheriff of Greene County under Sheriff Fulbright. In 1854 he went on a gold hunting expedition with 400 men, 800 oxen, and nearly 80 wagons. He later returned to Greene County and continued raising livestock. He went to Texas in 1856, traded for a herd of cattle and drove them to Kansas to sell.

Baker was married Sept. 18, 1856 to Sarah Yarborough and settled on a farm near Battlefield, MO. This farm grew to include approximately 2,000 acres spanning both sides of the James River. Rivercut Golf Course is now located on this site. Baker and Sarah had two sons, John Solomon (born Sept. 11, 1857, died Oct. 24, 1899) and Steven A. Douglas (born Jan. 6, 1861, died Jan. 28, 1915).

Life changed quickly in 1861. Baker was a Union man, but two of his brothers were southern supporters causing a family feud. General Lyon appointed Baker as the chief guide for Colonel Sigel and his German speaking troops. During the battle of Wilson's Creek, Colonel Sigel had to withdraw his men under heavy fire. Family historians claim that Baker picked up the flag and returned to Springfield. When asked how he escaped he said. "I had a damn fast horse."

After the battle he stopped by the Sanders' farm where his family was staying to tell them goodbye. This was the last time he would see his first wife. She passed away during the war on March 18, 1862. Baker joined the Union Army at Rolla, MO, enlisting in the Missouri 24th Volunteer Infantry. He was commissioned as 1st lieutenant by the Missouri governor and was later promoted to captain of Company D. His unit participated in many major campaigns. After serving three years he was mustered out at St. Louis, MO on Oct. 14, l864. He was once hit by a spent bullet but never wounded.

Baker returned to his farm and married Nancy McCroskey Jan. 31, 1865. Their eight children were Charles J., Rachel M., Margaret S., Alwilda M.J., George D., Francis W., William E. and Joseph L. Second wife Nancy passed away at home on Sept. 22, 1886.

Baker Owen bravely served as the fourth sheriff of Greene County during the turbulent years following the Civil War after being elected to the office in 1870 and re-elected in 1874. That was the beginning of a succession of Owen family sheriffs including son, John S. (1897-98), grandson Alfred (1925-28) and great-grandson Mickey (1965-81). Charles Baker Owen passed away March 15, 1907. First wife Sarah and second wife Nancy were buried at the Owen Family Cemetery in Battlefield, MO. *Submitted by Paula Howell.*

**OWEN** – The year 1957 saw a big change in the lives of Leo and Dorothy Owen. They decided to move their furniture store from Warsaw, MO to Republic, MO to be closer to family in Springfield, MO and Republic. This was a big gamble that fizzled. They then decided to get back into politics. Leo became city marshall of Republic and Greene County deputy sheriff for his cousin Mickey Owen, and Dorothy got the nod as city collector for Republic following Florence Britain, a sweet lady who was retiring and who helped Dorothy a lot to get settled in her job. This wasn't exactly a new experience for Dorothy. She had worked in the Greene County Assessor's office since she was 21 years of age, thanks to her Uncle E.J. Cogley who was Springfield's Revenue Collector.

*Leo and Dorothy Owen.*

One day in 1940, a nice man named P.W. Owen came into the office and told her he had a bachelor son, Leo, and wondered if she would be interested in meeting him. Not willing to let anyone get Dorothy's goat, she said sure, and a short time later they married. Dorothy had an 8-year-old daughter, JoAnn, and Leo and JoAnn became instant partners and members of their own admiration society.

After high school, JoAnn worked for the Red Cross for five years, then pursued her true calling and received a teaching degree from SMSU and a master's in education from University of Missouri, Columbia. JoAnn taught in Springfield for five years then moved to a two year college in Park Hills, MO, where she taught and coached athletics for 33 years. She has now retired from teaching and lives in Farmington, MO. JoAnn is an active member in the Methodist Church choir, Sunday school, UMW and teaches from one to three Bible study classes each year.

The Owen family found so many good friends in town and in the Hood Methodist Church, the Masons and the Eastern Star. They felt blessed to be in a community of caring, Christian people.

Leo Owen departed this life on Oct. 3, 1978 and Dorothy March 29, 1994, *Submitted by: JoAnn Owen.*

**OWEN/RUSSELL** - Allen M. and Mary Owen moved to Republic, MO in 1871 from Lake Geneva, WI. They came to Republic as young newlyweds looking for a new start, purchasing farms immediately north of Republic which are now remembered and known as the John Coggin and Randal Gleghorn farms. Allen and Mary as one of the early pioneer families were instrumental in the building of Republic. Allen helped to establish the present Evergreen Cemetery and also helped to build the first railroad spur for the Frisco Railroad in Republic.

Allen and Mary had four children: Forrest, Glenn, Margie and Lottie. Glenn remained in the Republic community his entire life. He later was partnered with his good friend, Fred Short. Glenn and Fred owned and operated Owen and Short Hardware Store for over 40 years located on Main Street in Republic. Glenn married Lydia O'Bryant around 1905. To this union two sons were born, Harold and Wayne.

*Harold Owen.*

Wayne lived his entire life in Seattle, WA. Harold chose to live his life in Republic where he was born. Harold Owen son of Glenn was born in Republic in 1906. He graduated from Republic High School, and attended Missouri University in Columbia, MO majoring in engineering and architecture earning his BFA degree. Upon graduation Harold was employed by Harry Cooper Supply Company in Springfield and remained employed as general manager for 40 years until his retirement.

Harold was best known as a community and civic leader in Republic and for his work in Masonic organizations, particularly with the Shriners Crippled Childrens Hospital. He served as mayor for the city of Republic from 1938-1945, a member of the Republic School Board for 15 years and a member of the Greene County School Board for six years which reorganized all of the school districts in Greene County from 1949-55. He was a Past Potentate of the Abou Ben Adhem Shrine, starting his career in Masonry as a high school sophomore, when he became a charter member of the first De-Molay Chapter in Republic, becoming a member of the Republic Masonic Lodge #570 in 1933. During the next 55 years Harold received many of Masonry's highest honors.

Harold married Wilma Russell, born 1906, daughter of William "Bill" and Laura (Palmer) Russell, locating in Republic from Tennessee. The Russell family operated a small grocery store located on Main Street in Republic for many years. Wilma was an accomplished pianist and well known for this outstanding talent. She played piano for the silent movies in the Republic Theater and at the Gillioz Theater located in Springfield, MO. She was a member of the very popular "Buddy's Whizbangers" Orchestra traveling all over the state of Missouri entertaining, and she eagerly gave of her talent throughout the community.

Wilma and Harold had one daughter, Jane Owen Cox. Jane has three daughters: Pam, Carrie and Sarah. Jane still resides in Republic. *Submitted by Jane Owen Cox.*

**OWEN/STEVENSON** - The Owen Family originated in Wales and migrated to America in the early 1700s. They moved to Greene County, MO in the early 1800s. Many served in public office, including four generations that served as sheriffs of Greene County. The most recent was Mickey Owen. Charles Baker Owen served as a captain in the Union Army and fought in the Battle of Wilson's Creek.

In October 1950, Charles Oscar and Martha Allene (Stevenson) Owen moved to Republic from Monett, MO. They had three children: Charles Sherman, Jane Carolyn and Judith Ann. The children attended a small country school named Mt. Etna, which was later consolidated into the Republic School District. Charles graduated from Republic High School in 1956 and graduated from SMSU in Springfield, MO. He was commissioned into the Army as an officer in 1962. He married Lynne Hopper while in college and later had two children, Charles Russell and Kathleen Marie. Russell is a graduate of Northwestern University and Kathleen is a graduate of SMSU. Russell is currently serving as a lieutenant colonel in the U.S. Air Force and is stationed in Tucson, AZ with his wife Elizabeth and their two children, Charles Thatcher and Olivia. Kathleen and her husband Steven Johnson currently live in Denver, CO with their new son Trevor. Charles retired from the US Army and is now a banker in Ft. Leavenworth, KS. His wife, Lynne, recently retired as the coordinator of the Parents As Teachers Program for the state of Kansas. *Submitted by Charles Owen.*

*Charles Sherman Owen, Martha Alene Owen, Charles Oscar Owen, Judith Ann (Owen) Dennis, Jane Carolyn (Owen) Boatright.*

**OWENS/GAROUTTE/WHITE/SCOTT** - Richard W. Owens (born Feb. 16, 1818) was the son of James Henry Owens and Catherine E. Moore. He married Nancy Garoutte (born April 9, 1822), the fifth child of James Smith Garoutte (born July 22, 1792) and Mary Babbington. James was the seventh child of Michael Antoine Garoutte and Sophia (Smith). Richard and Nancy (Garoutte) had 11 children. When the youngest, Jeremiah (born April 1, 1863), was 9-1/2 months old, his father was shot in the back by two Union soldiers near Fort Springfield on Jan. 16, 1864. Nancy was left with 11 children to raise by herself. Records show that she rose to the task.

*Jeremiah M. Owens, Lydia Ellen (Porter) Owens, Terry Owens, Nell Owens, Nancy Ellen (Owens) White.*

Jeremiah M. Owens married Lydia Ellen (Porter) born March 27, 1864. They had 11 children (eight grew to full adulthood), all lived around Halltown. Jerry, as he was called, was a main stay of the Halltown Christian Church. Their seventh child Nancy Ellen married Ora Lee White on Dec 24, 1924.

John Wesley White (born in North Carolina) married Mary Frances Jones (born in Kentucky) and lived in Greencastle, IN before coming to Greene County. John was asked by Union soldiers to go with them to give directions. He never returned. Their son Edwin D. was born May 28, 1846. Relocating to a farm northwest of Republic, he married Martha Hester Ann Skelton who was born April 26, 1856 in Republic and was buried at Wade Chapel Sept. 8, 1931. Her parents were Joel M. and Martha E.A. (Rucker) Skelton of Georgia. Ed and Martha's fifth child, Ora Lee (born Nov. 14, 1890) worked on the family farm and cared for his mother. He was introduced to his future wife Nancy Ellen (Owens) born June 26, 1898, by her cousin, Johnny Breakbill, a lifelong Republic area resident.

Ora and Nan were married Dec. 24, 1924, purchasing the John Sifferman farm 10 miles northwest of Republic in 1925. There they farmed and lived their 44 years of married life and raised their two sons: Stanley L. (born Aug. 16, 1928) and Jerry E. (born July 26, 1933). Ora died March 19, 1967 and Nan Nov. 20, 1978. They were placed in the Mausoleum at Rock Prairie Cemetery. They were members of the Halltown Christian Church.

Stanley attended grade school at Halltown, Roper and St. Elmo. He went two years to Republic High and graduated from Mt. Vernon in 1946. He attended SMS for 1-1/3 years, transferring to Ozark Bible College where he met Georgia Ellan Scott. He proposed to Georgia Ellan March 15, 1950 and they were married at Phillipsburg Christian Church by Roger Tribble on Aug. 30, 1950. Stanley graduated in 1951. Georgia was the daughter of J.E. Walter Scott and Ann Josephine (Ingersoll), of Lebanon, MO. They later moved to Springfield where Georgia's mother was a charter member of the Glendale Christian Church. Walter (born April 8, 1905, died June 14, 1979) and Josephine (born Nov. 17, 1905, died July 12, 2004) are buried at the Washington Cemetery, south of Lebanon. *Submitted by Stanley White.*

*Georgia and Stanley White.*

**PARKER** - John "J.C." Parker was born in Golden City, MO into a family of eight boys and three girls. They grew up in grain farming country and milked Jersey cows. Everybody had chores to do twice a day and knew they had to be done - or else! Farm kids had lots of fun also. The old farm pond was used a lot for fun - fishing, swimming and some fussing too.

*Joe Parker on left and John Parker on right in 2005.*

After high school, John worked construction for a year or so then decided to attend Moler Barber College in Kansas City, MO. He then barbered in Kansas City for about six years. While in Kansas City he met his wife Margie. Together they had two cute little girls. Lori was 4 years old and Kelly 2 years old when they made the move to Republic, MO in February 1965.

John and Margie purchased John's Barber Shop at 130 North Main Street from John Harrington. Five years later they purchased the building the barbershop was in from Roland Harrington. John soon became known to many as "John the Barber," John and Margie then added two little boys to their family, John Jr. and Joe. Republic was a growing town at that time and hasn't stopped growing to this day. Republic was, and continues to be, a very nice place to live and raise a family.

By working many hours (usually 12-hour days), the barber business was good enough that John and Margie were able to raise their four kids and build their first home on Summit Street in 1967. John also bought his red 1965 Chevrolet truck soon after moving into their new home. They continue to live in this same home today, and John is still driving his "old red pickup." Their home was a good one over the years with many happy memories. As the kids grew, married, and had kids of their own, John and Margie's home continued to be the "gathering place" for the entire family: Jeff and Lori Robinson and their kids Brooke, Jessica and Marcus; Jeff and Kelly Christian, Sean and Kristina, and grandson Parker; Johnny and Krisi Parker and boys Jake, Chad and Scott; Joe Parker and his girls: Laighton, Kayla, Valissa, and Katelyn.

The barbershop has been on Main Street Republic for years and years and has had many barbers working it. John knows as far back as 1934 when Jimmy Evans worked the shop. Other barbers who followed were Annette Wheelis, Claude Bennett, Frank Babcock, John Harrington, and Rex Lehman.

John watched first hand from his barber window on Main Street the many changes Republic experienced over the years. Even though time has changed much of Republic, many can still walk into John's Barber Shop and see the shop where they had their hair cut as kids. The walls are covered with items brought in by customers over the years, such as photos, cartoons, inventions, maps, calendars (as old as 1967), and other "items of interest". John was able to watch many kids grow up to have families of their own and then bring their own children, and sometimes grandchildren, back in for haircuts, suckers and Tootsie Rolls.

As of October 2005, after almost 41 years of cutting hair in John's Barber Shop, John now works the shop with his son Joe. The "old red pickup" parked on the corner still serves as a signal to many of his customers that "John is open." *Submitted by John C. Parker.*

**PATTERSON** - Robert Patterson was an American Revolutionary war soldier who at age 16 fought in the Battle of Kings Mountain located in Hamilton County, TN. He was the first white man in this Indian Territory. He was asked by the U.S. Government to build a mill for the Indians. He also helped with building schools and the Presbyterian Church for the people that followed. Robert Patterson was the ancestor

*Enoch Williams, Civil War Veteran (obituary dated May 3, 1939).*

*Jimmy Patterson, WWI, buried in France.*

that originated the families that came to the Republic area. His grandson William Douglas and Eliza Jane (Ingram) Patterson migrated to Republic from the Patterson Plantation in Tennessee in 1880. Robert should have a special mention in the history of Republic as he began a military family that served this country in the various wars participated in by the United States of America:

American Revolutionary War: Robert Patterson served in the U.S. Army.

Civil War: William Douglas Patterson, grandson of Robert, Confederate States of America, buried in Evergreen Cemetery at Republic, MO. Alexander Hill, father-in-law of Margret (Patterson) Hill, Confederate States of America, buried in Nevada, MO. Enoch Williams, father-in-law of Nannie (Patterson) Williams, Union soldier, buried in Evergreen Cemetery.

World War I: James Patterson, son of W.D. Patterson, U.S. Army, was killed and buried in France. John A. Patterson, son of W.D. Patterson, U.S. Navy, buried in Evergreen. Inez (Patterson) Corbin, U.S. Navy, buried in Arroyo Grande, CA.

World War II: Douglas Patterson Hill, son of Margret (Patterson) Hill, Army Air Corps, buried in Palo Alto, CA. Mary Margret (Hill) Cox, daughter of Margret (Patterson) Hill, U.S. Navy, born in Republic and graduated from Republic High in 1940. Mary volunteered for the U.S. Navy in 1942 and retired from the regular Navy and Reserves in 1982. She also served during the Korean and Vietnam Wars.

Mary M. Cox, LCDR, USN (Ret.)

Douglas (left), WWII Captain in USAAF and Maurice (right).

Vietnam: Rodney Douglas Hill, son of Douglas Patterson Hill, volunteered for U.S. Navy and mustered out for medical reasons. Scott Patterson Hill, son of Douglas Patterson Hill, U.S. Navy. Douglas Bohman Hill, son of Douglas Patterson Hill, volunteered for U.S. Navy, but at the time there was not a war time recruitment need. *Submitted by Mary M. Cox, LCDR, USN (Ret.), the only survivor of Missouri William D. Patterson, grandson of Robert Patterson.*

**PATTERSON/INGRAM** - In 1880 William Douglas "W.D." and Eliza Jane (Ingram) Patterson migrated to Republic, MO from Hamilton County, TN where they had been married in 1873. W.D. was 33 and Eliza 17. When they arrived in Missouri with two children, Alfred and Mary, Eliza was 24 and W.D. was 40.

W.D. was a native of Tennessee and Eliza was born in Frankfort, KY. While in Tennessee in 1861 at age 19, W.D. served in the Civil War as a Confederate States of America soldier. Six more children were born to them between 1880 and 1893: Margret, Nannie, Pearl, Jimmy, Inez and John.

In 1893 he purchased 80 acres of land and built their home on North Main. It is assumed he farmed the remainder of the land.

W.D. died from appendicitis at age 53. Eliza, who was 37 when he died, then reared the eight children, ages 1 through 17, by herself.

Her son Jimmy was killed in WWI in the Battle of Soisson, France and is buried there. Mrs. Patterson became a "Gold Star" mother and the Republic post of Veterans of Foreign Wars was named in Jimmy's honor as the Patterson-Sanders Post.

Margret and Nannie remained in Republic as the other children went to various states.

Eliza Jane, living most of her life in Republic, died in 1941 at age 85 of a fall in her home on North Main St. She was a really public spirited citizen and strong both mentally and physically. Originally a Presbyterian from Tennessee, she became a member of the old Congregational Church of Republic, then she became a lifelong member of Hood Methodist Church.

She was particularly remembered as an avid reader. Her grandchildren lived next door and could see her reading in bed into early morning hours.

William Douglas and Eliza Jane Patterson are interred in the Evergreen Cemetery in the Patterson plot. *Submitted by Scott Hill.*

**PENNOYER/BILBRUCK** - John B. Pennoyer was born in Sherbrook, Canada and migrated to Minnesota. He married Mary Frances Bilbruck, who was born in England, coming to America in 1857 at the age of 12 years. John and Mary came to Missouri in 1889 and settled south of Republic. They later moved to Republic in the 1890s, living in a house at 119 Mill Street where their five children were born: Harmon, Florence and Eugene. Two of their children died when they were small.

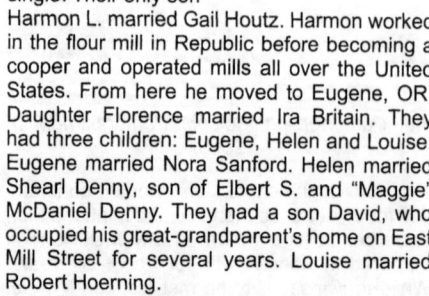
*John and Mary moved into this house in the 1890s. Harmon Pennoyer and an unidentified friend are on the front porch. The house is located at 119 Mill Street, Republic.*

Their daughter, Augusta, remained single. Their only son Harmon L. married Gail Houtz. Harmon worked in the flour mill in Republic before becoming a cooper and operated mills all over the United States. From here he moved to Eugene, OR. Daughter Florence married Ira Britain. They had three children: Eugene, Helen and Louise. Eugene married Nora Sanford. Helen married Shearl Denny, son of Elbert S. and "Maggie" McDaniel Denny. They had a son David, who occupied his great-grandparent's home on East Mill Street for several years. Louise married Robert Hoerning.

Florence Pennoyer Britain was employed by the city of Republic in the position of city collector, retiring in 1957. Ira traveled the United States as a U.S. fruit inspector. *Submitted by Terah Richardson.*

*Eliza Jane Patterson.*

*Wm. Douglas Patterson.*

**PHILLIPS** - Joseph Phillips was born March 3, 1806 in Granger County, TN. He married Lucy Pollard McElhaney of Virginia in 1828. They had five children: Nathan, Louisa, Thomas, Elizabeth and Columbus. They later moved to Greene County, MO. Joseph died Feb. 14, 1882 and Lucy died July 1, 1865. Both are buried in the Phillips Cemetery north of Battlefield, MO.

*Ross Phillips with children: Elnora, Gary and Janie Sue, ca. 1949.*

Columbus was born June 20, 1838. After the death of two wives, Columbus married Manilla McGinnis. They had six children: Emilla, Nancy, Joel, Mary, Katie and Zina. Columbus died Nov. 15, 1902 and Manilla died Aug. 15, 1938. Both are buried in the Phillips Cemetery.

Joel R. Phillips was born June 19, 1880 and married Iva Jane Bussard on Aug. 16, 1903. Iva was born July 25, 1886. To this union were born 11 children: Clellia Austin, Hershel Owen, Lee Thelmar, Thetta Cynthia Manilla, Loren Lester, Roscoe Emery, Odie Oren, Helen Pauline, Earnest Ray, Doris Isabell and Finis Eugene. All are deceased except Doris and Eugene. There were many happy family gatherings on the farm northeast of Clever. Joel died Oct. 11, 1949 and Iva died March 8, 1968. They are both buried at Patterson Cemetery.

Roscoe Emery Phillips was born Jan. 14, 1914. He married Doris Keltner, daughter of Fulton and Anna McCroskey Keltner, on Oct. 27, 1937. Doris was born Sept. 27, 1912. Ross and Doris attended Green Ridge School south of Battlefield. To this union were born Elnora Joyce (born Nov. 1, 1938), Gary Melvin (born June 29, 1941) and Janie Sue (born March 22, 1946). Ross started farming with a team of horses walking behind the plow. Ross also worked for Frisco Railroad from which he retired. They were members of the First Baptist Church of Republic. They were highly respected in the community. Elnora, Gary and Janie graduated from Republic High School. Ross died May 26, 1980 from cancer. Doris moved from the farm on East Hines to Republic in 1981. She lived on East Elm until her death July 23, 1988. They are buried at Patterson Cemetery.

Elnora Joyce Phillips was born Nov. 1, 1938 just about 100 yards south of where she has lived since 1959 which is just east of Brookline. She attended the rural schools of Mt. Etna, Rountree, Brookline and Beulah and graduated from Republic High School. Elnora married Hank C. Datema on April 18, 1959. Hank was born Sept. 24, 1933 in Baflo, Holland to Hommo and Alice Datema. Hommo and Alice immigrated to Springfield, MO Jan. 29, 1949 with their children: Sue, Peter, Hank, Alice, Cornelius and Ralph. Hank spent 16 months in Korea with the U.S. Army. Hank was a wonderful designer of homes and builder. Hank and Elnora owned and operated Datema Construction at the time of Hank's death. Hank was killed in a tragic construction accident March 10, 1995, and is buried in the Brookline Cemetery. Hank and Elnora had two children, Homer Richard (born Aug. 27, 1967) and Joyce Anne (born Sept. 25, 1969). They are graduates of Republic High School and SMSU.

Richard married Mia Rae Weirich of Gerald, MO on June 9, 1990. Their children are Michael Ross (born Aug. 28, 1992), Joshua Hank (born July 31, 1996), Mariah Elnora (born Dec. 27, 1999) and Emma Grace (born March 18, 2004).

Joyce Anne married Danny Burton of Crane, MO on Dec. 12, 1998. They have two sons, Clinton Earl (born Aug. 13, 2000) and Keith William (born Sept. 29, 2003). Danny has two other children, Coy (born May 9, 1989) and Eryn (born June 18, 1994). *Submitted by Elnora Phillips Datema.*

**PHILLIPS/GRANTHAM -** Raymond Phillips was born to Franklin and Reitha (Maine) Phillips in March of 1950 at Aurora, MO. There were 12 children in the family: Delmar, Sharon, Frankie, Janet, James, Teddy, Patsy, Raymond, Jerry Lee, Jimmy, Martha and Tony. They lived in Marionville and Aurora. Kathy Phillips was born to Joe and Katherine (Brewer) Grantham in July 1949 at Lubbock, TX. The family, which included two children, Kathy and Larry, moved to Aurora, MO in 1955.

*Chris, Nick, Kathy and Raymond Phillips.*

Raymond and Kathy both graduated from Aurora High School. Raymond attended one year of college at Okmulgee, OK. Kathy graduated from (then) Southwest Baptist College in 1971 and was hired by Republic R-III School District to teach band and choir in junior high and general music for fifth and sixth grade. She taught there for 10 years and when the new high school was built in 1979, she began teaching only vocal music in junior high and high school, which she continued to do until retirement in 2001. Raymond was hired by (then) SMS in 1977 and has continued to work there.

From 1971 until 1980, Kathy was the choir director for the Aurora United Methodist Church. In 1980, Raymond and Kathy joined Hood UMC when Kathy was hired as choir director. She served in that capacity until 2002.

In 1981 Nicholas Phillips was born and in 1985 Christopher was born. Both were born in Springfield, MO. Both graduated from Republic High School.

Raymond continues to work at Missouri State University and Kathy continues to teach vocal music part time at Republic High School. *Submitted by Raymond and Kathy Phillips.*

**PLUMMER-** In May 1946, Carl and Thelma Plummer were looking for a shoe repair shop when they came to Republic. They ate lunch at the Sublett Cafe on Main St. Thelma said "This is the best water I've ever tasted. Let's relocate here." They purchased the J.B. Stickney Shoe Store at 136 S. Main St. At the end of the Branson school year Carl and Thelma Plummer, daughters, Earline and Ernestine Alms, moved to Republic, living in the back of the store.

*Thelma and Carl Plummer.*

The store grew from only shoes and repair to including dry goods and notions. Key overalls ($1.99 a pair) and Levi jeans ($2.99 a pair) were soon added. In the 1950s they purchased the building just south from Maude Lamb when she closed her grocery store. Later, the building known as the Les Massey building was added. Lots of changes took place with each addition but not the friendly service. The slogan for the store became "WHERE FRIENDS MEET."

In the early years they opened about 6:30 a.m. and closed about 12 hours later. That accommodated the garment factory workers before work and farmers in the evenings. Saturday nights closing was after the band concerts and the movies let out. Parents shopped while kids went to the movies. Long hours with great memories.

Earline graduated from Republic and attended SMS. She married Phillip Sneed and they were both killed in a car accident just three weeks later. It was a shock to the whole community.

Ernestine moved to California to live with her father and family. She graduated from Woodrow Wilson High School in 1951. She returned to Republic and in 1954 married Donald L. Sifferman. Donald was in the Air Force. They spent 20 years as an Air Force family. After retirement they and their children: Carl, Ceann, Craig and Cathy, returned to Republic. Ernestine once again worked in Plummer's store.

All of Ernestine and Donald's children and five of their grandchildren graduated from Republic High School. Daughters, Ceann McGowan and Cathy Rausch, live here. Lots of changes have come about just on Main St. since 1946. Businesses on Main Street at that time were: two drug stores, MFA Grocery and Feeds, Bud Logan Grocery, Locker Plant, hardware, theater, barber shop, beauty shop, liquor store, car dealership, *Monitor* and *Republic Record* newspapers, two cafes, dime store and hatchery. The bank was south of the railroad tracks. The Post Office was on the corner of Main and Grant. There was a blacksmith shop and gas station.

Both Carl and Thelma were active in the city, community and church. Upon retirement they lived at 607 S. Main just a few blocks from the store. Both are deceased but still thought of with great respect. *Submitted by Ernestine Sifferman.*

**POOL -** In 1957 while attending Baptist Bible College, Billy Pool's family would drive through Republic going to visit their parents in Arkansas and Oklahoma. At that time Republic's population was about 965. They enjoyed stopping at Imperial Isle Shopping Center and eating when they could afford to stop and eat. Hamburgers were 15 cents, but at that price, many times they could not afford to stop and eat.

*Gerry and Billy Pool.*

Gasoline was 18 cents a gallon and his salary working for 7up Bottling Company was $27.50 per week plus a case of 7up as a bonus. Gerry worked for F.W. Woolworth on the square in Springfield.

While in college, Billy was pastor of Grace Baptist Church in Rogersville, MO. After College, they spent 10 years at Bible Baptist Church in Ottumwa, Iowa; seven and one half years at Grace Baptist Temple in Pinellas Park, FL; back to Ottumwa for four and one half years at Calvary Baptist Church; and from there they went to Childersburg, AL. In 1980 Bible Baptist Church here contacted him to see if he would consider coming to Republic. He preached his first message in November 1980, and that night was voted to become their pastor. He moved to Republic in January 1981 and has served this congregation for the past 25 years.

They were excited to move here since they would be closer to the college they attended in the 1950s and of course, closer to their roots.

They were welcomed by their church family and a very sweet neighbor Miss Iva Ray. She made sure that the Pools were well cared for. She even let them stay at her house during an ice and snow storm. She cooked and heated with gas and the Pool's house was electric. This was an ice storm they well remember, but the best memory was the good times they had at their neighbor's house.

The population of Republic was now 4,485. They were here four or five years when Gerry started attending city council meetings. She developed a keen interest in the affairs of the city and ran for Council Ward 3 in 1988 and won. She then was elected mayor and served from 1990 until 1992. She has served on numerous committees and maintained her interest in the welfare of the citizens here as well as her duties as a pastor's wife. In April 2005 she was elected to the board of Alderman Ward II.

Rev. Pool became involved in the city and its needs. He served on the board of Alderman for six years. They both believe in getting involved and make an effort to serve the community whether in the church or city. They love Republic and are looking forward to its future growth. *Submitted by Bill and Gerry Pool. Editor's note: Billy passed away unexpectedly Dec. 10, 2006.*

**PORTER/MATNEY -** Orris and Clara (Lorenze) Porter had one son Albert, born Jan. 4, 1922, whom they raised on a farm near the small town of Seymour, MO. Albert married Edith Matney on Sept. 28, 1940. Edith, born Oct. 16, 1924, was the daughter of Thomas and Latty (Becker) Matney and was also raised on a farm near Seymour, MO. On March 28, 1942, Albert and Edith had a wonderful daughter, Dorthy.

*Albert and Edith's 60th wedding anniversary in September 2000. Daughter Dorthy, standing.*

In 1943 the family packed their bags and moved to a farm in the Brookline area where the power plant is currently located. In 1946 they moved to a farm in the Billings area and then in 1951 bought a farm on the Greene and Christian County line south of Republic where they continue to reside.

In 1952 Albert went to work for Bridges Construction where he worked for 16 years. Edith started work at Woods Garment Factory but in 1959 changed jobs and went to work at Dayco Belt Manufacturing Company from which she retired.

Albert and Edith have two grandchildren, Ronda (Hawk) McLaughlin and William St. Clair.

Ronda married Keith McLaughlin and had twins, a boy, Jordan, and a girl, Jaclyn, born Jan. 1, 1986. Both graduated from Clever High

School in 2004. In 1999 Keith passed away due to cancer.

William married Angie (Green) St. Clair. They have three children: Justin (born Aug. 30, 1995), Brandon (born Sept. 22, 1997) and Nathan (born Jan. 11, 1999). William also has one stepson, Travis Cotter (born Aug. 10, 1992).

Albert and Edith enjoy the farm life very much and everything that comes with it even when times are hard. They worked very hard to keep their farm during the drought of the early 1950s. After all the years, Albert still enjoys cutting and bailing hay and Edith enjoys cooking, sewing, quilting, canning and gardening. *Submitted by Edith and Albert Porter.*

**PORTER/OWENS** - Simeon Hall Porter (born March 14, 1799 in Kentucky, died Jan. 30, 1887) married Nancy P. Richards (born Aug 23, 1831, Washington, IN). They had six children. One of them James Linden Porter (born Sept. 19, 1843, died Nov. 29, 1930) married Mary Emily Moore (born 1845), a full blooded Indian, in 1863. They had a daughter Lydia Ellen Porter (born March 27, 1864 in Xenia, IL). Mary Emily died during childbirth, so Lydia lived with her grandparents. They

*Jeremiah M. and Lydia Ellen (Porter) Owens.*

moved to Missouri when she was four, arriving there in a big snowstorm. They camped in Lawrence County near the Union Hall School northwest of Halltown. The snow was so deep you could walk right over the fences. They bought land about one mile north of Halltown, on what is called the Martin and Helton places.

A family by the name of Oldham came to Missouri with them. When Lydia Ellen was six her dad married one of the Oldham girls (Polly Ann) and he took Lydia home with him. The next day she said she had to go get a clean dress. When she got there she held on to her grandma and cried till her father let her stay. She never lived with her father after that. Both families moved to Greene County near St. Elmo School when Lydia was 11. She met Jeremiah M. Owens when she started to school that fall. He was 12 and he said the first time he met her that she was the girl for him. "I'll marry her some day," which he did on Oct 24, 1883.

They lived with her grandparents about seven years. Then they bought a place and moved. Her grandfather died, so her grandmother lived with them until her death in 1908. Jeremiah was born April 1, 1863. They were for a time in Oklahoma (territory) when a daughter, Nancy Ellen, was born on June 26, 1898. She was born in a dugout because she couldn't wait for her dad to get the house built. They came back to the Halltown area that winter. A dog kept Lydia's feet warm and she kept her baby warm.

Later they bought land 1-1/4 miles northwest of Halltown and stayed there the rest of their days and continued to raise their family. Jeremiah was a solid part of the beginning of the Halltown Christian Church around 1900. He died Jan. 17, 1949. Lydia had lost her love and she said she was going to die on his birthday, and she did on April 1, 1949. Both are buried in the Garoutte Cemetery.

They had 11 children, eight grew to full adulthood, seven married and lived around Halltown. Their last child was Ruth Owens (born Feb. 8, 1907, died July 24, 1989). She married Loyd Alonzo Richards Nov. 8, 1927. They had two children, Loyd Alonzo Richards Jr. (born April 18, 1935, died Dec 13, 2005) and Nell Elisabeth (Richards) Hughes (born May 1, 1941). *Submitted by Nell Elisabeth (Richards) Hughes*

**PULLEN/MCNABB** - Joe Allen Pullen was born in Clarinda, IA to Harl and Mary Pullen on Aug. 13, 1955. He is the grandson of Harold Murren and Lady Alice McKinley. He is a brother to Linda Rainey, Robin Lane, Michael Harl Pullen and Wren Elliott. Joe and his family moved to Springfield in 1964 and then to Republic in 1969. Joe left Republic High School to join the U.S. Navy and served for three years on the USS LaSalle. He traveled to Karachi, Pakistan, Bahrain and Saudi Arabia. He also crossed the equator.

*Front, l to r: Mandy Heather and Linda. Standing: Joe Pullen.*

Linda Kay McNabb was born on Jan. 29, 1958, at the Springfield Osteopathic Hospital. Linda is the daughter of John Isaac and Genevieve Josephine McNabb. She is the youngest sister to Janet Sue Thompson, John Allen McNabb, and Phyllis Jean Taylor. In 1961, her family moved to Tulsa, OK and then returned to Republic in 1966. John McNabb died in March of 1969 and Genevieve McNabb died in 1971.

Janet, her daughter Michelle Gwin, and Linda lived in their parents' house and went to school in Republic until the middle of her freshman year in 1973. Then she lived with her brother John McNabb and his wife Lilly in Springfield. She went to Central High School through her sophomore year. Linda's junior year (1974-75) was spent at Kickapoo High School. Linda moved back to Republic in 1975 and graduated in 1976, the first class to have their graduation outside. At each school she attended, she made many good friends and had the "best teachers."

Joe and Linda met in December 1975. He had just returned from the Navy and started work as a carman apprentice at Frisco Railroad. After a layoff, he worked for a while at Republic Vans, Advanced Plating, and then became a branch manager at Redneck Trailer Supplies. Joe loved to golf and play softball. After high school graduation, Linda started X-ray School at St John's School of Radiologic Technology and graduated in 1978. She and Joe were married on June 30,1978.

On May 1, 1980, Amanda Jo Pullen was born and on Sept. 28, 1981, Heather Nichole Pullen was born. The Pullen family lived in town for a while and then bought 20 acres south of Republic. They loved to entertain friends and family at their house especially on July 4th. Joe died of a brain aneurysm on May 13, 1994.

Mandy graduated from Republic High School in 1998 and Heather in 2000. Mandy has one daughter, McKayla Jo Pullen-Simpson and a son Breckin Allyn Hughes. Heather has one daughter, Taylor Paige Melton. Both Mandy and Heather work at Cox North. Linda started doing Magnetic Resonance Imaging (MRI) in 1987 and is still working for St. John's Health System. Linda enjoys photography and singing in the choir at First Christian Church. They all still reside in Republic. *Submitted by Linda Pullen.*

**RADER** - In 1940, Oscar and Julia Rader moved from Rader, MO with their family to a farm located on Highway M and ZZ. They set up a dairy operation and raised beef cattle. Bill also did custom threshing along Campbell Street which has become the Medical Mile.

*Oscar and Julia Rader family. Front: David, Linda, Sam, Don; back: Georgia, Oscar, Julia, Bill.*

All six children graduated from Republic High School. Part of the original farm has been selected as the site for the new high school.

Georgia Mae married Richard Heinemann and moved to the Chicago area where she worked as a medical transcriptionist.

Bill moved a mile west of the home place where he set up a dairy business and continued doing custom silo filling.

Don ran an egg operation.

Sam went into construction.

David, now deceased, ran a yard grading business.

Linda became a teacher and later a counselor.

Georgia, Bill, Sam and Linda live in or near Republic. Don lives in Vero Beach, FL. *Submitted by Judith Rader.*

**RAINEY** - The Greene County Raineys originally came from Scotland to North Carolina about 1735. Chesley Oren Rainey (born 1802 North Carolina) and Sarah Barbara (White) Rainey (born 1805) moved from Maury County, TN to Greene County, MO about 1854. Chesley Oren originated the town of Little York which was the 2nd largest town in Greene County at the time. Little York was located about two miles west of Brookline. Little York flourished until 1872 when the railroad came through and offered the residents of Little York incentive to relocate along the new railroad station of Brookline. The entire town was relocated leaving nothing much to indicate a town ever existed.

*Harold Rainey Family in 1959.*

Chesley Oren and Sarah had 13 children, all born in Tennessee. The oldest child was Jane Catherine (Rainey) Sparkman (born 1826), Minerva P. Rainey, Narcissus W. (Rainey) Mease, Jethro B. Rainey, Josephine A. (Rainey) Rose, Jefferson W. Rainey, James E.P. Rainey, Nancy C. (Rainey) Young, Sarah M. (Rainey) Thompson, Margaret (Rainey) Killingsworth, P.E. (Rainey) Garton, one girl who passed on at age

13, and the youngest child George Anderson Rainey (born 1847) who was 7 years old when the family moved to Missouri.

George married Mary Francis (Chestnut) in 1874. George and Mary had five children all born in the same house one mile west of Brookline. Their children's names were Rosa, Estella, Lawrence, Roscoe and Harold Ellis.

George and Mary's youngest son Harold Ellis married Edith Anne (Jeffery), from Billings area and all of their children were born and raised in the same Rainey house. Their children's names are Ellis Jeffery, Harold Ellis Jr., Dee Owen, Dorothy Edith, Stella Jean and twins, Mary Lou and Betty Sue.

In the proximity of Little York there are three children and several grandchildren of Harold and Edith still living on Rainey land including Betty Sue their youngest daughter who lives in the original Rainey farmhouse at this writing.

Patriarch of the Greene County Raineys, Chesley Oren and Sarah, and their youngest son, George Anderson and wife Mary Francis Rainey, as well as other Raineys are buried in the Harrington Cemetery near Republic. *Submitted by Betty Rainey.*

**RAPER** - Charles Arthur "Charlie" Raper is a 1964 graduate of Republic High School and his children, James Bradley and Angela Michelle "Missy," also attended Republic schools, as did Brad's wife, Stacy (Grubbs). Brad and Missy's mother, Beverly (Copeland) Cox, is a 1963 graduate of RHS. Charlie's wife, Susan (Albaugh), is a teacher in Ozark where their son, Charles Arthur Raper II, attends high school. Charlie lives and works in Springfield.

Charlie's sister, Donna Jean (Raper) Freeman is a 1962 graduate of RHS. In high school Donna was active in band, choir, student council, cheerleading, and the Rainbow Girls. Both Charlie and Donna attended Brookline and Republic Elementary Schools. Donna married Charles Jay "Butch" Freeman in 1963. Butch and Donna live in Springfield and have two daughters, Shelley Wears and Sarah Odom, one grandson Charles Jay Wears and one granddaughter Sophia Odom. Infant twin daughters died in 1968. Donna is retired from the Springfield Public Schools. Butch, Donna, and their daughters are members of Republic Eastern Star, Butch is a Past Master of Republic Lodge, and Butch and Donna serve on the board of the Republic Rainbow Assembly.

Charlie and Donna Raper were born on the Fugitt farm near Terrell Creek to James Arthur Raper Jr. and Vera Louise (Kennedy) Raper and later moved to Brookline. James is a 1941 graduate and Vera was a 1942 graduate of Republic High School, James was born in Springfield and currently resides there. Vera was born in Caplinger Mills and died in 2001 in Springfield.

Charlie's and Donna's paternal grandparents, James Arthur Raper Sr. and Bonnie (Cook) Raper, moved to the Yeakley community in 1933. The Raper family then lived on south Main Street in Republic from 1938 until 1943. During WWII, Bonnie Raper was appointed and served as supervisor over the weaving room in Republic—a government project to assist area families.

*James Arthur Raper Jr. and Vera Louise Kennedy – 1942.*

*Charles Arthur Raper, James Arthur Raper Jr. and Donna Raper Freeman - 2003.*

She also cooked at the grade school in one of the first hot lunch programs. Payment for a lunch ticket was a nickel or a sack of sugar due to the rationing of sugar during wartime. The four Raper children: James, Max, Roger and Maryan, attended Salem and Republic elementary schools. All three boys were good athletes, and James and Max were invited to try out for the Springfield Cardinals while students at RHS.

Granddad Raper's ancestors settled in Stone County, and the Raper lineage includes the names Rhodes, Odom, Ingram and McDaniel. Mam-ma Bonnie descended from pioneers of Christian, Greene and Stone counties--namely the Cook, Coffer, Estes, Lee, Payne, Berry and Gideon families.

Charlie's and Donna's maternal grandparents were Arthur and Mary (Flanagan) Kennedy. The Kennedy ancestors settled in Cedar County, and pioneer families of Grandma Mary include the Haineys, Redfearns and Flanagans of Greene County.

Ancestors number in the hundreds in Greene and surrounding counties, and the Republic area has been a significant component in the Raper family history and legacy. *Submitted by Donna (Raper) Freeman; Raper family information provided by Maryan (Raper) Smith. Editor's note: James Arthur Raper, Jr. died Dec. 29, 2006.*

**RAUCH** - In the late fall of 1880 four brothers by the name of Rauch relocated their families to the Billings community. Another brother would join them later. John, Nikolaus, Philipp, Peter and George Rauch were born in the German hamlet of Mittershausen in a region of west-central Germany known as the Odenwald. Three of the brothers initially settled in Piqua and Urbana, OH in the 1870s. When the last two emigrated from Germany in the summer of 1880, they and two of the other brothers decided to seek out inexpensive and relatively fertile farm land in southwest Missouri along the route of the newly completed Frisco Railway corridor.

*L-R: Peter, Nikolaus, John, Philipp, George Rauch and their families in October 1886.*

Four of the five brothers purchased land and established farm operations. The oldest brother, John, a bachelor who later returned to Germany shortly before his death, was a carpenter and woodworker by trade. Nikolaus was also a carpenter, as well as a farmer. Philipp farmed and for years maintained a threshing machine and crew, traveling the area and providing services to other area farmers. He also donated land on which the Billings Cooperative Creamery would be established in the 1890s. In addition to farming, George was one of the founding members of the Billings Mutual Insurance Company, the charter of which was written in the German language. Peter, who remained in Ohio with his tobacco shop after the other brothers relocated to Missouri, eventually settled on a farm east of Billings.

After their arrival in the Billings community all of the Rauch brothers and their families became involved in the then newly organized St. Peter's Evangelical Church. In early 1881, George, the youngest of the brothers, and his bride, Swiss immigrant Elisabeth Hutter, would be the first couple to be married in the church after its official organization.

Between the four Rauch brothers that married and their wives, they would raise 29 children, many of whom would live out their lives in the southwest Missouri region. All four of the brothers who remained in the United States, their wives and many of their children and their grandchildren are buried in St. Peter's Cemetery outside of Billings.

Descendents of these German speaking pioneers remain in the Billings community and other communities throughout the Ozarks, as well as quite literally throughout the United States and even beyond. Just as the original brothers and their children pursued varied careers and involved themselves in their communities, so it has been with the generations of descendents that have followed.

Over the years and today these descendents include award winning farmers and cattlemen, carpenters and tradesmen, engineers, doctors and dentists, lawyers, teachers, professors and other professionals, ministers and missionaries, professional musicians and entertainers; government employees and those who have served on local school boards and city councils as well as in other elected and appointive positions, both on the local and state level; business persons and entrepreneurs, as well as laborers and professional homemakers.

All of this followed after these five brothers sought new opportunities in the Missouri Ozarks. *Submitted by David Rauch.*

**RAYBOURN** – The first traceable Raybourn to immigrate to America was Joseph Raybourn, coming from Ireland or England and landing in Virginia in 1698. Migrating west through Tennessee and Kentucky, many of the later descendents settled in rural Bates County, MO, 90 miles south of Kansas City. Traditionally, the Raybourn family have agricultural backgrounds; most of them engaged in farming and cattle ranching. Much of the Raybourn land in Bates County has been in the family over a 100 years.

*Joy and John Raybourn.*

J.T. Raybourn left the area for a short period of time, about 1910, to cowboy in Wyoming and then homestead a place in Durant, NM, before returning to Bates County. He remained there the rest of his life, raising three children: Loreese, John T. and Eugene.

John R. Rayburn, son of John T. Raybourn, came to the Republic area in the mid-1970s as a trooper with the Missouri State Highway Patrol. He met an emergency department nurse, Joy Cope, and they were married in 1975. Joy grew up in Barry County and attended nursing school in Springfield, MO. J.R. and Joy built on a small acreage west of Republic on Farm Road 53. They had two daughters, Leslie (born Oct. 11, 1980) and Johnna (born July 17, 1983). They were killed Nov. 29, 1998 as they were stopped, waiting to make a left turn into a church parking lot west of Republic on U.S. 60.

Leslie was an honor student at RHS and would have been valedictorian of the Class of 1999. She was also an enthusiastic volunteer with the West Republic Fire Department and worked at Albertson's in Republic.

Johnna was a freshman at Park Avenue Christian School in Springfield. Both girls were Christians who loved the Lord and were involved in church activities throughout their lives. Leslie and Johnna were buried together in Wade Chapel Cemetery on Dec. 2, 1998.

J.R. and Joy still reside in the house they built 30 years ago. J.R. is now a commercial photographer and Joy continues to be employed in emergency trauma nursing. Since the death of her daughters, she had become involved in medical missions, and is currently furthering her education at Missouri State University.

J.R. and Joy continue their work here in Republic, secure in the hope that when its done, they will rejoin their daughters to spend an eternity with the Lord. *Submitted by John Rayburn.*

**REDFEARN** - George H. Redfearn and his wife Lora Belle Haynie Redfearn came to Republic probably in 1908 from the Bois D'Arc area. Both families had worked their way from Virginia and North Carolina and across Tennessee to settle in Greene County and Bois D'Arc. George was a schoolteacher and also dabbled in real estate. He became the first telephone operator for Southwestern Bell in Republic and had that position until 1918 when he was disabled by a severe stroke. He was an amateur musician, singing and playing the fiddle.

*George H. and Lora Belle Redfearn.*

Lora Belle was a hard-working housewife with the added care of her invalid husband. Both were dedicated to the importance of education for the children.

The family first lived on North Walnut in a small house, then they moved to a larger house next door. With George and Lora Belle were three daughters: Iva Haynie (Belle's daughter), Ruth and LaZeta. Iva was working in Oklahoma when George had his stroke, but she returned to Republic to run the telephone office until her retirement, Ruth married, lived in California and had no children. LaZeta first married Wm. Randolph and had a daughter Margaret. She later married Clark Cunningham and had a daughter Nancy.

The Redfearn house was occupied by a member of the family until 1974 when LaZeta moved to Aurora, MO. The house was sold to Hood Methodist Church and razed. Margaret Randolph Key lives in Golden, CO. Nancy Cunningham Seaton lives in Springfield, MO. *Submitted by Margaret Key.*

**REYNOLDS/BLADES** - The following information gathered by Darleen Nave and Marlene (Blades) Adams will show the direct lineage of Harold J. Blades and Vesta (Batson) Blades to the very first families (Reynolds/Blades) to settle in this area.

David D. and wife Polly Reynolds and family from East Tennessee were first to settle in Pond Creek Township in 1834. Theirs was Section 2 of Township 28, Range 24.

*Picture taken in 1983 at Reynolds Cemetery clean-up project. Harold J. Blades and daughter Marlene (Blades) Adams standing by Edward A. Blades tombstone.*

Edward A. Blades, wife Penelope, and their children were next to settle (1836) near Pickeral Creek close to Walter Blades' farm. The Blades emigrated here from McMinn County, east Tennessee, although Edward was a native of North Carolina. Edward's eldest son, Ranson Dudley Blades, was 15 years of age at that time.

Vesta (Batson) Blades' (1913-2005) parents were Benton W. Batson (1872) and Effie Jane (Reynolds) Batson (1879). Effie was the daughter of James H. Reynolds (born 1853) and Martha J. Mason (born 1856). James H. Reynolds' father was John S. Reynolds (1824 TN-1861 MO) and Hannah E. Likins (1830 TN-1913 MO) and John's parents were David D. Reynolds and Polly Reynolds who moved here from Tennessee.

Edward A. Blades (Jan. 6, 1779 NC) married Penelope Ellen Maynard about 1817 in Rowan County, NC. Penelope was said to have been full blood Cherokee. According to the 1840 census Greene County, MO, three in the household were engaged in farming, Edward and older sons, Ranson D. and Ike. Closest neighbors were the Garouttes, Wm. McDaniel, David Reynolds and the Laneys.

Harold J. Blades' (1910-2004) parents were James M. "Big Jim" Blades (1869) and Columbia A. Browning (1871). James' father was John M. Blades (1844). John M. Blades was one of the sons of Ranson D. Blades (1821) who came here with his parents, Edward A. Blades and Penelope E. Blades.

In 1836 when the Blades came to Greene County, the southwest part of the county was almost without inhabitants. At the same time with the Blades came William McDaniel. The Reynolds were also living in the township, and for nearly a year these three families were the only residents of what is known as Pond Creek Township.

The first school in this township was taught by Robert Batson in a private house built by Ranson D. Blades on his father's place. Stephen Batson also taught in the township as did William B. Garoutte. Stephen Batson came from Ohio in 1842 and lived on Pickeral near the south line of the county.

The Reynolds Cemetery is the final resting place of Edward A. Blades and some of his family members. There also lies David D. Reynolds with some of his family. This cemetery was established in 1844, the year of Edward's death.

According to the census 1870-1875 there were 868 whites, 14 blacks, 251 horses and 50 mules in Pond Creek Township. *Compiled by Marlene (Blades) Adams.*

**REYNOLDS/O'NEAL** - This story is about the descendants of David Reynolds who was the first settler in Pond Creek Township northwest of Republic, emigrating from Tennessee in 1834. David was the great-great-grandfather of Helen (Reynolds) O'Neal who was a life-long resident of Republic. The first sermon preached in the township was delivered in David's home by a Methodist minister in 1838. Continuing in the Methodist tradition, Helen (Reynolds) O'Neal had been a member of the Hood United Methodist Church in Republic since 1918, joining when she was 10 years old.

One of David and wife Polly's children, John S. Reynolds, was a respected Union man and one of 10 men in Pond Creek Township who voted for President Lincoln in 1860. He was the first victim of some of the fearful murders perpetrated in this township which grew out of the Civil War. On the night of Nov. 22, 1861, he was bushwhacked and killed, allegedly by Confederates, because he voted for President Abraham Lincoln. He was holding his cabin door shut against intruders when one of them broke through a window and shot him with a musket while his wife, Hannah, looked on. Hannah sprang from her bed and caught him as he tragically died in her arms. John and Hannah (1830-1913) had six children: W.F., James H., Sarah E., Susan J., and two other siblings (no information).

In 1877, John Reynolds' daughter, Sarah (1857-1881), married William Winter (1855-1942), who emigrated from Illinois at the age of 14. William and Sarah had two children: Frank A. and Lafayette. Sarah died at age 24 and in 1882 William married his second wife, Lizzie Gilliland. They had three children: Ernest M., Mary F. Gertrude and Jennie Willie Mae, who was called Mae. She always told people her full name was "Janie" Willie Mae. In those days a female mule was called a "Jennie" and she certainly didn't want to be named after a mule!

Sarah Reynolds, William's first wife, had a nephew by the name of David Alva Reynolds, son of James H. and grandson of John S. Reynolds (1876-1944) and Mae Winter (1886-1974) who he married in the early 1900s. Thus David's Uncle William became his father-in-law when he married Mae. Their children were Harold William (1906-1980) and Helen Lucille (1908-2006). Harold never married and worked the family farm until his death.

In 1941, Helen married Elwin "Norwood" O'Neal (1912-1975), descendent of another pioneer family (see Caleb and Mary Thurman history - Norwood's mother was Georgia Thurman, great-great-granddaughter of Caleb and Mary. The O'Neal children were Jimmie Lynn "Jim" (1942-) and Janice Lea "Jan" (1946-). Jim and wife Roberta (Green) and two of his children, Darrell, wife Carrie and children Nicholas, Skylar, and Brayden, and Kathy (O'Neal) Leitz, husband Andy and sons, Kaleb and Kolby, still live on part of the original Reynolds' homestead adjacent to the location of the 1861 bushwhacking. Jim's third child, Dustin R. "Dusty" and wife Anna Katherine "Katie" (Dent) live in Springfield, MO. Jan and husband John A. "Tony" Atkinson live in Springfield but retain ownership of part of the family homestead as well.

Researching the Reynolds' history has given the family a sense of how deep their

Greene County roots go. It is overwhelming to think about their great-great-grandfather being bushwhacked and killed in 1861; but the family is proud of his stand for President Lincoln and for his belief in freedom for all people. The expression "freedom is not free" was as true during the Civil War as it is true today. *Submitted by Jan Atkinson, daughter of Helen Reynolds O'Neal.*

**REYNOLDS/WILES** - Wilbert Levi Reynolds was born June 13, 1918 in Forsyth, MO to Bert and Laura Reynolds. He grew up partly in Ohio and mostly in Republic, MO. He graduated from high school in 1938. He was voted "Mr. Republic" by his senior class. He met Nellie Jo Wiles in 1940 and they were married in 1942. He was sent to England and was a corporal in the U.S. Air Force for two years. Their first daughter, Katy Ann, was born in 1943. Wilbert, "Webb" or "Jitter" as he was called by his Republic friends, returned from Europe in 1945. Rebecca was born in September 1946 and Patty Sue in 1948.

*Wilbert Levi Reynolds.*

When Webb returned from the service some of his close friends helped him get started in business. He had a cafe, bus route and milk route to make ends meet. He and Nell bought a home on Main St. next to the Christian Church. In 1954 he sold his home to the Carlson family and moved to Covina, CA. He put in a small cafe. He and his family never really thought of California as their home. Missouri was where they wanted to come back to. Five years after buying the cafe, he sold it and went into the Winchell's Donut Shop franchise. He kept it for 17 years, and retired back to Springfield.

His daughters followed with their husbands and children. Becky and husband Gary were partners with Webb and Nell in the Orange Julius in Springfield. Webb sold his half to Patty and husband Don. They kept it for 17 years.

Katy St. George has six children. Her husband George passed away in 1985. Katy has two donut shops and one bar-b-que café.

Becky Hartmayer and husband Gary have three children. Becky and Gary are both realtors with Re/Max.

Patty and husband Don Mummert have three children. Don works for Jackson Bros. and Patty is a marketing director with Capital Senior Living at The Waterford in Springfield.

After Webb retired, he took up a bus route again after 35 years. In July 2001 he found out he had lung cancer and died four weeks and two days later on Aug. 30, 2001. He was a wonderful man and worked hard all his life. He believed that hard work would always pay off as it did for him. Nell lives at The Waterford Independent Retirement Community in Springfield. She is 85 years old and still going strong. *Submitted by Patty Mummert.*

**RICHARDS/HUGHES** - Ike Richards was born in Germany about 1785. He had six sons probably born in Indiana. The sixth son, David, was born May 3, 1820 and died June 1914. He married Rebecca Groves about 1845 and they had seven children. The seventh child, Andrew Jackson Richards, was born Aug. 25, 1861 in Indiana and died May 13, 1942. He married Mayflower Melissa Williams in 1904. She was born Oct. 13, 1889 and died July 19, 1943. They had six children. The eldest, Loyd Alonzo Richards, was born Dec. 3, 1905 and died Jan. 13, 1979. He married Ruth Owens Nov. 8, 1927. She was born Feb. 8, 1907 and died July 26, 1989.

*Kristi, Danny, Nell, Don, Dawnnell, "Cody"; Michael, Zachary, Taylor Richards.*

Loyd and Ruth raised their family one-quarter mile west of Ruth's home place. They were faithful members of the Halltown Christian Church for over 50 years. Ruth was a direct descendent of the Henry Garoutte family of southern France, considered to be a royal family. This is the same family that produced Willard Benton Garoutte who married Mary Jane Richards on Jan. 15, 1871 and James E.D. Garoutte who married Charity Richards in 1871. These are two sisters of Andrew Jackson Richards.

Loyd and Ruth had a son Loyd Alonzo Richards Jr. (born April 18, 1935, died Dec. 13, 2005) who married Beverly Evans on May 29, 1955. She was born Nov. 3, 1938. Alonzo and Beverly had three children: Virginia Ruth (born Aug. 12, 1956), Andrew Alonzo (born Feb. 4, 1961) and Lisa Beth (born July 25, 1965).

Loyd and Ruth had a daughter Nell Elisabeth Richards (born May 1, 1941) who married Donald Ray Hughes on Sept. 8, 1963. He was born Oct. 19, 1938 in Springfield. He was in the last graduating class of Springfield High School in 1956, now Central High School. He worked for Western Electric. Nell will soon retire from J.C. Penney. They are members of College Heights Christian Church in Joplin. They have a son Danny Ray who was born April 18, 1965 and married Kristina Ann Smith on Aug. 1, 1986.

Danny graduated from Ozark Christian College in 1988 and has been in the ministry since. He is now minister of music at Northside Christian Church in Broken Arrow, OK. They have two sons, Zachary Loyd (born Aug. 5, 1994) and Michael Aaron (born Sept. 24, 1996) and a daughter Dawnnell Lea (born Aug. 14, 1972). She has a daughter Taylor Jo Hughes (born April 23, 1995). Dawnnell married Cliff (Cody) Holmes April 1, 2002. Dawnnell helps with Christmas musicals for children. Her family does quite a lot of playing and singing at church. She is a rancher's wife and home schools her daughter. *Submitted by Danny Ray Hughes.*

**RICKETTS** - Josephus and Eliza Ricketts arrived near the Plano General Store (located north of Republic on Highway 266) in the late winter of 1891, broke and homeless. They were traveling from Butler County, KY to California but ran out of money to continue their westward travel and settled on 40 acres near the Plano store. Traveling with them were their nine children: Jim, Jennie, Lydia, Asbury, Annie, Josie, Rebecca, Gilbert and Christopher Columbus "Lum."

*Photo of the children of Josephus and Eliza Ricketts believed to be taken around 1905.*

The Ricketts family had no relatives in the area and lived on Josephus' Civil War pension until they could find jobs and begin supporting themselves. A few of Josephus' daughters married men from other families in the area, including Jennie Ricketts who married Green Liles, Lydia Ricketts married Frank Batson, and Asbury Ricketts married Roe Blades. Josephus, his wife and all of his children (except Josie and Annie) are buried in Prospect Cemetery, north of Republic.

Josephus' oldest son Lum Ricketts married Florie Smith from near Hartville, MO, and Lum's brother Gilbert Ricketts married Florie's sister, Sara Bertha. Therefore, the children from these marriages were "double cousins." Lum and Florie Ricketts had three children: Herman, Eva and Artie Ricketts. In 1902, Lum and Florie settled on land 1.5 miles to the east of Plano General Store.

Josephus' middle son Gilbert had four children: Claude Vernon, Lawrence, Ralph and Raymond Ricketts. After living in Kansas for awhile, Gilbert and Sara settled on land near Fair Grove, MO in 1929. Gilbert's sons, Ralph and Raymond Ricketts, are still living. Ralph now lives near Centralia, MO and is 95 years old. Raymond lives on his farm near Fair Grove, MO and is 92 years old. Claude Vernon graduated from the U.S. Naval Academy and retired as a rear admiral from the Navy. Although now decommissioned, the Navy did have a warship named after Claude. The ship was named the USS *Claude V. Ricketts.*

Josephus' youngest son Jim Ricketts remained a bachelor all his life.

Through faith and trust in God, hard work, perseverance and a little luck, Lum Ricketts' family has flourished on the land where he originally settled. The property which Lum acquired in 1902 is still owned and occupied by his descendants today. Tragically, Lum died on May 24, 1915 from a blood infection at the age of 45. His wife and children moved to Colorado and homesteaded with relatives near Walsenburg, CO until the end of World War I, when Lum's oldest son Herman Ricketts returned from the war. Lum's widow, Florie, and her children that were still living with her, Eva and Artie, then moved back to the farm in Missouri about 1919.

Florie's oldest son Herman married Hattie Yeakley and her youngest son Artie married Bertha Merritt. Eva married Frank Brewer and moved with him to Colorado. Eva died shortly after delivering her only child, Franklin. Franklin was then raised by Herman and Hattie Ricketts. Herman and Hattie lived the remainder of their lives on property directly north of the property originally acquired by Lum Ricketts. One of Eva Ricketts' great-grandson's, Tim Lakey, still lives in the house that Herman and Hattie built on their property. Herman was a prominent farmer throughout the 1940s, 50s and 60s and at one time farmed over 1,500 acres which surrounded the original farm.

Artie and Bertha Ricketts had two children, Doris and Clifford. Doris married Ron Sell and lives in Springfield, MO. Ron and Doris have two children, Andrea O'Brien of Ozark, MO, and Kevin Sell of Rogers, AR. Clifford married Janice Gott. They have two children, Kristen Mason of Lee's Summit, MO and Ryan Ricketts of Bois D'Arc, MO.

In addition to farming, Artie Ricketts worked for contractors on jobs throughout Southwest Missouri during the road construction boom of the 1940s and 1950s. After being buried alive during a ditch collapse at a road construction site in the late 50s and suffering severe injuries to his hips, Artie began farming full time and continued to farm several hundred acres, until his death in 1994, which included and adjoined the original property acquired by Lum Ricketts in 1902. *Submitted by Ryan Ricketts.*

**RIPPEE** - The Rippee family have lived in Republic for 31 years, not long enough to be called a "native" but long enough to grow to love the community and its residents. Their history started with Bill and will end with Donna. Bill's first Republic claim to fame was selling cars at the "Little Cheaper Dealer." He worked with Dwight Legan at the local Ford Dealership until around 1984. Around that time Bill had a very serious heart attack. The family is very thankful to God for his recovery and being

*Bill and Donna Rippee.*

blessed with reasonably good health. He then began driving a bus for the Republic School District and has loved doing that for the past 20 or more years. At present he does grounds keeping work for the school district during the summer break.

Bill and Donna have been blessed with three lovely daughters: Gina, Amy and Billie. The girls each attended the Republic R-3 School System from K-12 grades, and made contributions to the community along the way. Donna has served the citizens of Republic as their postmaster. She has been with the United States Postal Service for 37 years, 14 of those years as Republic Postmaster.

Donna believes in the Republic community and strives to give back with service. She belongs to the Republic Area Chamber of Commerce, serving as president for four years; the Republic Business and Community Women; served on several committees with the Republic R-3 School District; and is a past member of the Republic Historical Society. Serving on the board of People Helping People, learning at the knee of Marcella Garner, she claims this to have been one of her favorite experiences.

Bill and Donna's daughters, Amy and Billie, and Billie's husband Mike Johnson, volunteer with People Helping People trying to give back to the community they love. Although their children have long since graduated, Bill and Donna continue to believe their obligation to education never ends. The Rippee family is very thankful for their church family at First Baptist Church in Brookline, which is now in the Republic city limits. God continues to be the center of their lives and they love living in the wonderful community of Republic.. They plan for another great 31 years for the Rippee family. *Submitted by Donna Rippee.*

**RITTER** - Michael Ritter was born July 8, 1807 in Montgomery County, OH, and died April 21, 1898 in Republic, MO, Greene County. He married Rachael Parsons Feb. 11, 1830, daughter of Benjamin Parson and Martha Garretson. She was born Jan. 27, 1811 in New Jersey and died Jan. 9, 1896 in Republic, MO, Greene County. He was the first postmaster in Republic, MO. He moved to Greene County, MO from St Joseph County, IN. Evergreen Cemetery in Republic, MO is where Michael, Rachael, Mary Ann and Marcus are buried. Michael and Rachael's children are John P., Adaline, Harriet, Marcus L. David, Phoebe Ann, Martha, Larrinda J., Lorinda A, Eliza, Ellen and Mary Ann.

*John Ritter and Barbara Garber, parents of Michael.*

Michael's parents are John Ritter (born April 3, 1777) and Barbara Garber (born Sept. 1, 1785) in Rockingham County, VA. Barbara's parents are John Garber and Barbara Zook. John and Barbara's children are Jacob, Michael, John Jr., Sarah, Benjamin Franklin, David, Susan, Samuel and Martin.

Michael's father, John Ritter, was born in North Carolina and grew to manhood. At a young age he learned the cooper's trade making this his main occupation. He resided near Nashville, TN for a short time then went to Kentucky. Since he was married in Montgomery, OH in 1805, he was probably a settler of that locality about the year 1803. He crossed the Ohio River at Cincinnati on his way to Ohio.

There was only a block house and a few cabins where that city now stands. The principal inhabitants at that point were soldiers. John was in the War of 1812 and served under General William Henry Harrison. About 1818 the Ritter family moved to Wayne County, IN and were pioneers of that county and owners of 160 acres of land. He then moved to St. Joseph County, IN where he lived until his death. Michael's mother, Barbara Garber Ritter, lived with her daughter in Floyd County, IA to the advanced age of 102 years, when she died.

Michael's son Marcus served in the Civil War and is buried in Evergreen Cemetery. Michael's family was German Baptist and his grandfather, John Garber, was one of the preachers who started churches in Rockingham County, VA known as "Dunkers" (German for immersion) referring to baptism. Michael has two nephews who lived in Springfield, MO, David and Aaron Ritter, who were founding fathers of Greene County. A nephew in Columbus, KS also was a founding father. John Newton Ritter was a lawyer, banker, state rep. and the first postmaster in that county. *Submitted by Teresa Barker.*

**ROBERTS** – Lee and Georgia Roberts moved to Republic, MO in the fall of 1967 after purchasing Engle Chev. He established Lee Roberts Chevrolet and was the Chevrolet dealer until September 1979.

Georgia, an RN and graduate of Springfield Baptist Hospital, worked for St. John's Hospital until her retirement in May 2002. The couple has four children: Margaret (Roberts) Brown, Fair Play, MO; Lee Melvin Roberts Jr., Takoma Park, MD; Alice (Roberts) Dickover, Flemington, MO; and Ellen (Roberts) Evans, San Antonio, TX.

*Lee and Georgia Roberts.*

Lee was active in the Republic Kiwanis Club and continues to play in the Republic Community Band. Both Lee and Georgia are active members of the Springfield Seventh-Day Adventist Church.

Contributions the Roberts have made to Republic have been: the first modern automotive dealership, and helping to secure First Savings and Loan, Kentucky Fried Chicken and McDonalds for the community. *Submitted by Lee Roberts.*

**ROBERTSON** - Lindsey and Delilah (Jones) Robertson and their family, moved from Monroe County, TN, to Greene County, MO, in 1837. They settled southwest of Springfield about one mile east of what would become Republic. Lindsey owned 660 acres in various parcels at the time of his death in 1861. The family home was southwest of the corner of Lynn Avenue and Miller Road. Water was obtained from a spring at the northeast corner of Lynn Avenue and Wood Street.

*Robertson tombstone.*

What would become the Lindsey Chapel Cemetery probably had its beginning with the earliest known grave and tombstone for Mary C. Robertson (born Dec. 5, 1845, died April 26, 1846), the daughter of Thomas Edward and Jane Caroline (Jarrett) Robertson, and a granddaughter of Lindsey and Delilah. She was probably the first death in the Robertson family after their move to Missouri. It was probably Lindsey who selected the high area across from the family home which is now just southeast of the corner of Lynn Avenue and Miller Road. Whether Lindsey and Delilah envisioned growth of their family burial site to a cemetery of over 570 graves will never be known.

The next burial was probably about two years later. William F. Steele (born May 8, 1809, died July 22, 1848) was apparently a family friend with no direct relationship to the Robertson family. His widow, Roxanna, later married John Andrew Ray. Both were buried at the cemetery in 1875 and 1876. William's daughter from his earlier marriage, Anna Elizabeth Steele, had been buried next to her father in 1862.

The third burial at the cemetery was probably Lindsey's sister, Lucy Robertson (born Feb. 14, 1799, died Dec. 1, 1849). Lucy was the wife of Alexander McCullah Jr. (born July 16, 1793, died April 18, 1856). They had arrived in Greene County about a month before her death. Alexander was buried beside her in 1856. The fourth burial was probably Lindsey's third son, Samuel H. Robertson (born Dec. 12, 1823, died Sept. 22, 1853). The fifth burial was probably an infant grandson of Lindsey (born June 6, 1855, died June 12, 1855). His parents were Warham A. and Stella Jane (Robertson) McElhany.

Burials in the next decade included Lindsey's sister, Mary "Polly" (Robertson) Hagewood (born 1791, died Feb. 24, 1861); Lindsey Robertson (born Oct. 13, 1792, died July 29, 1861); Lindsey's second son, Thomas Edward Robertson (born Dec. 17, 1821, died Feb. 2, 1863); and Sarah (Jones) O'Bryant (born July 29, 1797, died Jan. 12, 1867). Sarah, wife of Elias O'Bryant, was a sister to Delilah (Jones) Robertson. Another sister to Lindsey, Mickey (Robertson) Smith, died in the early 1850s. Her grave has not been located, but a burial in the family cemetery would have been likely.

These early burials at Lindsey Chapel Cemetery are identified by their tombstones. There may have been other early burials in unmarked graves, or their tombstones have been lost or are illegible. *Submitted by Sloan L. Robertson.*

**ROBERTSON/ALBRECHT -** Linda (Robertson) Albrecht was born Dec. 9, 1945, the fifth child of Gladys and William Finis Robertson. Linda lived in Republic her first three years, then again at age six. She started Republic Schools in second grade and continued to live in Republic until age 22. She attended Springfield Business School after high school then worked at the Frisco Railroad Office in Springfield, MO.

She met Gene Albrecht, a student engineer from University of Missouri at Rolla, while he was working summers at Frisco. They were married in August 1968. They lived in Maryland for one year while Gene was in the Army. Gene spent the next year in Korea with Linda living back in Missouri.

After the service commitment, Linda and Gene lived in Missouri, Illinois, Texas and back again to Illinois, all with Gene working with PPG Industries (glass plant). They have two children: daughter Jana (born Sept. 9, 1972 in Decatur, IL) and a son Ryan (born Dec. 29, 1974 in Wichita Falls, TX).

Linda and Gene currently reside in Mt. Zion, IL. Linda and family feel very connected to Republic and look forward to many more visits. *Submitted by Gene and Linda Albrecht.*

**ROBERTSON/FOUST –** William Finis "Bill" Robertson Jr., third child of Finis and Gladys (Wallace) Robertson, was born in November 1941 in Springfield, MO. The Robertson family moved to Republic in 1945. Bill attended two area one-room schools, Lindsey and Green Ridge and later attended the Republic Schools, graduating in 1959. He married Mary Sue Foust in August 1961. Mary Sue was the third child of Sam and Dollie (Garoutte) Foust, born March 1941. Dr. R.C. Mitchell delivered Mary Sue on his birthday in the house that her great-grandparents, Ransom and Liza Jane (Jameson) McDaniel, homesteaded northwest of Republic. She attended Grandview School until Republic Schools consolidated in the early 1950s, graduating from Republic High School in 1958 and from Draughons Business College in 1960.

Bill joined the U.S. Air Force in July 1960, serving a four year enlistment. The last 15 months were spent in Sault St. Marie, MI. At this location their first child was born, Debra Sue (Robertson) Cooney, in 1964. After leaving the Air Force, they returned to Republic. Bill was employed by United Parcel Service in 1966, retiring after 35-1/2 years of service in May 2002. During this time a son, William Foust Robertson, was born in May 1968. Mary Sue was employed by the Republic R-III School District in 1978, serving as high school principal's secretary for 13 years and secretary to the superintendent for 10 years, retiring in 2001.

*Bill and Mary Sue Robertson.*

Bill and Mary Sue served as youth directors: Bill as an elder and Mary Sue as church pianist for many years at Westside Christian Church. Bill was an active member with Teamsters Local #245, serving as trustee until his retirement in 2002.

During teen age years, Bill worked at various locations in Republic: at the age of 14, riding a Cushman Motor Scooter, he delivered the *Springfield News Leader* to all subscribers in the city of Republic; he worked as a Phillips 66 Service Station attendant for Don Brown, the station was located on West Hwy. 174 next door to the Westside Christian Church; and he was a station attendant for Dale Boatright's Truck Stop (formerly Lloyd's Drive Inn), located at the southeast corner of Main and Hwy. 174. Mary Sue was employed during her teen age years at Lloyd's Drive Inn, owned and operated by her Uncle Lloyd Garoutte; also working at Republic's first Tastee Freeze, owned by Jack Haptner, located at the northeast corner of Main and Hwy. 174 and the Republic Garment Factory, located on West Elm Street, operated by Tommy Weinsaft.

*L-R: Jeff, Alex, Debbie and Drew Cooney.*

Debra Sue (Robertson) Cooney, their first child, was born in April 1964, in Sault Ste. Marie, MI. Debbie graduated from Republic High School in 1982, attending Southwest Missouri State University and graduating from Missouri Southern State College in Joplin. She married Thomas Jeffery "Jeff" Cooney in 1986, relocating to Joplin, MO. They currently reside in Texas. Jeff is employed as director of safety for LoneStar Trucking and Debbie is a full-time teacher. They have two children, Alexandra Nicole (born June 1992) and Andrew Thomas (born March 1994).

William Foust "Bill" Robertson, their second child, was born in Springfield, MO, May 1968, and graduated from Southwest Missouri State University. He relocated to Las Vegas, NV in 1996, where he married Kerri Lee Ruth in June 1997. They currently reside in Dardenne Prairie, MO. Bill is employed as a senior professional specialty pharmaceutical sales representative with Johnson and Johnson. They have two children, Jack Samuel (born October 1999) and Abigail Ruth (born May 2002), in Las Vegas, NV. *Submitted by Bill and Kerri Robertson.*

*Back: Bill and Kerri; front: Jack and Abigail Robertson.*

**ROBERTSON/WALLACE -** William Finis Robertson was the second child of Marvin and Zade (Short) Robertson born May 1913 on the banks of Terrell Creek in Christian County. The family relocated to a 40-acre farm, on a portion of what is now the Wilson's Creek Battlefield Park, in 1915; this was purchased from William B. Robertson, father of Marvin. In 1927 Marvin died suddenly, leaving his wife Zade and two children, Delores (Robertson) Sanders and Finis, and one to be born six months later, Marvie Lee (Robertson) Napier. Finis gave up school at the age of 14 years to help his mother support the family.

Finis married Gladys Wallace (born January 1914), second child of Wm. Ernest and Myrtle (Land) Wallace, Cassville, MO, in November 1936. His mother was fighting a battle with cancer, with high medical expenses, which forced the farm to be sold and the family to relocate to Springfield. Finis took a position in Springfield to help support the family. His mother lost her battle with cancer in 1937. Delores married shortly thereafter, taking Marvie Lee to care for.

*Robertson family sitting Gladys (Wallace) Robertson; standing l-r: Mary (Robertson) West, Linda (Robertson) Albrecht, William F. "Bill" Robertson Jr., William Finis Robertson, Judy (Robertson) Walz.*

In 1941 Finis and his family, Gladys, Mary (Robertson) West (born in 1939) and Bill (born in 1941), moved to the west coast where Finis worked in the shipyards. Gladys did neighborhood laundry and cooked for fellow workers to help support the family. In 1945 they relocated to Republic, opening automotive garages in Republic and then in Battlefield. Finis and his family which now had Judy (Robertson) (Scott) Walz (born in 1944) and Linda (Robertson) Albrecht (born in 1945), returned to Republic from Battlefield, taking a position with Trailmobile in Springfield as a journeyman welder. After the plant closed, Finis and Gladys followed the company to Kansas City for several years but returned to Republic to take a position with Bacon Tire. While employed with Bacon Tire, Finis designed and built the first closed aluminum tire delivery truck in the area.

The family home was purchased in 1956

241

on West Elm Street in Republic, formerly Sam Robertson's property next to the old school. Gladys sewed for all of her children, teaching herself how to knit and crochet. Gladys and Finis spent 65 years of married life together, enjoying life to the fullest until poor health forced them to a nursing home. They were very active in the Westside Christian Church as long as their health permitted. Gladys died in 2002 and Finis in 2003; both are buried at Lindsey Chapel Cemetery, along with an infant daughter born in 1937.

Finis was an avid fisherman, having fished every stream in the area. He had fished in Wilson Creek as a child when it was a pure stream with large fish. He also went on numerous float trips on the James and White Rivers before they were dammed. Gladys and Finis spent every weekend at the lake in later years; this was truly the love of their life. The two of them were great gardeners, always having a very large garden. Gladys canned and froze all of their produce and Finis loved giving it away.

One of Finis' favorite childhood stories was seeing the first automobile. The noise scared him so badly he ran a mile to get back home. *Submitted by Debbie Cooney.*

**ROBERTSON/WALZ** – Judy (Robertson) Walz grew up in Republic. She was born Jan. 28, 1944 in Richmond, CA, returning with her family back to Republic, their original home, after Judy's birth.

The Robertson family lived at nearby Battlefield for awhile. Judy started elementary school at Green Ridge, a one-room country school in Battlefield. Judy, along with her two sisters, Mary, Linda and a brother Bill, walked to school together, along with other children who lived in Battlefield. Green Ridge was located about a mile and a half south of Battlefield. The children walked "uphill" in snow, rain or sunshine all the way.

*Pete and Judy (Robertson) Walz family photo – 1997. Back: Blake Walz, Tracey (Walz) Vandelicht, Ashley Myers, Shana Myers, Shelly (Walz) Adams, Brandon Adams; front: Reid Walz, Pete Walz, Kaycee Vandelicht, Judy (Robertson) Walz, Taylor Adams, Britney Cordone.*

Green Ridge School consolidated with Republic Schools in the early 1950s. At this time, the family relocated to Republic. Judy started 3rd grade in the old brick school located on West Elm Street next door to the family home at 321 West Elm Street. In 1954, Republic built a new elementary school located on Anderson Street. In 1962, Judy graduated from the Republic High School on Anderson Street. The class of 1962 was the last class to graduate from this building. The Republic R-3 School system had a great music program, and Judy thoroughly enjoyed being a part of the chorus, marching band and baton twirling.

In 1962, Judy married Donald Scott from Hurley, MO. They lived in Republic and their daughter Shelly was born in May 1966. Judy and Don agreed to a divorce, and in 1972, Judy and daughter Shelly relocated to Jefferson City, MO, where Judy received a transfer with the Division of Employment Security.

In December 1972, Judy married Franklin "Pete" Walz, a native of Jefferson City. Pete adopted Shelly, and Judy became stepmother to Pete's two children, Tracey and Blake. Judy has a very loving, blended family. God has always been a big part of their lives.

Judy worked for the Division of Employment Security (Department of Labor) for 25 years and retired from the state in 1999. Pete is retired from Von Hoffmann Press where he worked 40 years.

Judy and Pete have three children: (1) daughter, Shelly Adams and her husband Paul live in Lohman, MO with their son Brandon and daughter Taylor. (2) Daughter, Tracey Vandelicht is married to Mike and they live near Tebbets, MO. The Vandelichts three daughters are Shana, Ashley, and Kaycee. Shana has two daughters, Savannah and Sydney, and one son, Samuel. (3) Son, Blake Walz lives in Castaic Lake Area, CA with his son Reid. Pete and Judy vacation with them on trips to California.

Judy and Pete owned and operated a restaurant (Pedro's) in Jefferson City for a few years where they made homemade hot tamales and other specialty recipes handed down by Pete's father, Buck Walz, who was a great cook and well-known statesman. Although retired, Pete and Judy still make the hot tamales for their family and friends to enjoy. *Submitted by Shelly Adams.*

**ROSE -** William R. Rose came to Greene County about 1844 from Robertson County, TN with his wife Elizabeth Johns and seven children. He settled in what is now Pond Creek Township, Section 1. His father was Meredith Reddick Rose of Nash County, NC and Robertson County, TN. His mother was Nancy Manning of Nash County, NC and Robertson County, TN. Elizabeth Johns' father was Reese S. Johns and her mother was Milbury Redfearn.

*Townley Rose family. Back: Albert, Thaddeus, Edward, Walter; front: Leroy, Townley, Gay Otto, Eglantine, Arthur holding Flora Rose, Urith Goodin Rose and Lula.*

William R. and Elizabeth Rose's children were 1) Meredith Marion Rose, who married Margaret Ann Redfearn, daughter of Isaac Redfearn and Penelope Taylor. They had five children. 2) Nancy Sarah Rose married Isaac Anthony Redfearn, son of Isaac Redfearn and Penelope Taylor. They had 12 children. 3) Milbury Rose was married twice. Her first husband was Adophus Hugh Hazelton, son of Royal Hazelton and Mahetable Arms. They had at least six children. Her second husband was John Hines, son of William Hines. They had three children. 4) Richard Rose married Elizabeth Hosman, daughter of Alfred Hosman and Martha H. Cox. They had three children. 5) Temperance Rose married Thomas Forsythe, son of William Forsythe and Sarah McCray. They had five children. 6) Townley Rose's first wife was Josephine Ann Rainey, daughter of Chesley Oren Rainey and Sarah Barbara White. They had three children. His second marriage was to Eglantine Smith, daughter of William P. Smith and Sarah Julian. They had 10 children. 7) John William Rose married Sarah Elizabeth Laney, daughter of Jeremiah H. Laney and Sophia McAfee. They had two children.

Townley Rose was a charter member of the Republic Masonic Lodge. Townley and Josephine had three children, two died young, the third was Arabelle "Bell" who married John Tolliver Carter, son of John Carter and Rhoda Dorrell O'Banion. Josephine died in 1863. Townley married second, Eglantine Smith McClure, widow of Charles L. McClure. Charles and Eglantine McClure had one daughter, Sarah Alice. Alice married James Lafayette Britain, son of Marcellus L. Britain and Mary A. Paine. They lived in Republic and had four children: Charles (died young); Edward married Bettie Jones; Frank married three times: Delia Hagewood, Bessie, Elsa, respectively; and Cassius married Anna Johnson in Seattle, WA.

Townley and Eglantine Rose had 10 children: Arthur D., Franklin, Edward Y., Walter, unnamed son, Albert, Thaddeus, Leroy, Lula, and Gay Otto.

Albert Rose (born Jan. 1, 1878, died Oct. 14, 1958) married Bettie Brashers, daughter of James Basham Brashers and Sarah Jane Blades, daughter of Ranson Dudley Blades and Frances Garoutte. Albert and Bettie had four children: Eula Odessa Rose married William Earnest Riddle, son of James Edmond Riddle and Cora Elizabeth Bailey, who lived in Republic until 1929 when they moved to Calfornia; Burl Efton Rose married Theresa Dorothy Hadlin in California; Beulah Helen married Henry Lee Waddle; Mona Marie married first, Stanley William Cox and second, Orrin Smith Maybee.

Albert and Bettie Rose lived in and around Republic until 1923 when they moved to Springfield. Albert worked and retired from the Frisco Shops. Both are buried in Maple Park Cemetery in Springfield. Townley Rose is buried in Evergreen Cemetery in Republic. *Submitted by Mona Marie Rose Maybee.*

**ROSS/MANESS -** Ruby Eulalia Ross was the second child, first daughter, born to Thomas Francis and Eulalia Monroe (Woodard) Ross. Her father was the son of John Jacob and Susan Catherine (Cargile) Ross. Her mother was the daughter of Monroe and Martha Ann (Bland) Woodard, all Polk County, MO, natives.

Ruby was born Feb. 21, 1893 in Morrisville, Polk County, MO, the second of 10 children. She married George Robert Booher on Dec. 25, 1927. They had two daughters, Virginia June (born Dec. 11, 1929) and JoAnne (born April 23, 1931), both born in Morrisville, Polk County, MO.

Ruby was a school teacher for 31 years. In 1923 she was teaching school in Republic, Greene County, MO. at Lindsey School. Her class of 1923 was comprised of 43 students. Some of the students were of the following families: Salkil, Jones, Boatright, Williams, Land, McClure, Maness, Baldwin, Squibb, McElhany, Sanders, DeWett, Coward, Boyd, Robertson, Myers and Short. During this same time frame, there was a man named Homer E. Maness who was the District Clerk for the Lindsey School in Republic.

Homer was the son of John Baldwin and

Sylvania Jane (Julian) Maness. He was born Jan. 26, 1887 near Bois D'Arc, Greene County, MO. He married Etta Mae Short on Aug. 18, 1904. Etta was the daughter of James Monroe and Alice (Sparkman) Short. Etta was born May 24, 1886. Homer and Etta were the parents of Raymond Everett, Henry Elliott and Elsie Gwendola.

Ruby Ross had a brother, Marvin, who married Vesta Fuhr, daughter of Robert and Ota (Brashears) Fuhr, at that time from Lawrence County, MO, later living in Republic. Marvin and Vesta had four children, the first born being Leota Ross. Leota married Charles Sawyer, son of Charles Ervin and Mattie Ethel (Harris) Sawyer of Cedar County, MO. Leota and Guy had five children. The first born, Bunny, married Mike Jones, son of Orvil E. and Iris (Maness) Jones. Iris was the daughter of Raymond and Flossie (DeWett) Maness and granddaughter of John and Sylvania Jane (Julian) Maness.

One day while Bunny and Mike were in Greene County visiting cousin JoAnne Booher, they discovered among some paperwork that Bunny's great aunt Ruby had taught at Lindsey School and that Mike's great-grandfather, Homer Maness, was the person who signed Ruby's paychecks.

Who would have thought all those years ago, when Ruby and Homer were in the same vicinity, that nearly 50 years later, in 1972, Ruby's great-niece Bunny and Homer's great-grandson Mike would have ended up marrying each other! When Bunny and Mike married they lived briefly in Republic, not far from the Lindsey School where their ancestors had served the community. Bunny and Mike now live in Bolivar, Polk County, MO, where most of Bunny's forefathers on the Ross side were natives of Polk county. They raised their two children, Michael and Angela, on their farm where they have now lived for over 25 years. Bunny and Mike are active members of the Polk County Genealogical Society, Inc. and Bunny spent three years compiling the recently published family history book of Polk County, MO. It was the first of its kind in over 115 years. It holds over 700 family histories submitted by families with Polk County roots and many pages and pictures of actual county history. The county history section was graciously compiled by Linda Crawford of Tin Town, MO, a sister to Sandy Maness of Republic.

Bunny contributes her love of genealogy to her great aunt Ruby Ross Booher. She remembers as a young girl the letters her aunt Ruby wrote to her explaining the family tree and their family connections to such historical people as President Zachary Taylor, Henry Clay and Betsy Ross.

Most of Ruby's students mentioned earlier are in one way or another related to Bunny's husband Mike. It truly is a small world. Mike and Bunny Jones are glad that they can live close to all their relatives and that they have been blessed with large families to love. *Submitted by Bunny Sawyer Jones.*

**RUSSELL** - William Riley Russell was born in 1859 in Tennessee. He married Laura Jane Palmer in 1880. They had four daughters while living in Tennessee: Mary, Carrie, Mabel and Lillian. In 1894 they came by train to Republic, MO and two sons and a daughter were born here: Paul, John and Wilma.

William's brother John had already come to Republic and was a carpenter, helping to build some of the early buildings, including the first school house on West Elm Street and the Hood Methodist Church. William, or Bill as he was called, was also a carpenter and built houses - still standing are the ones at 430 East Elm and 132 South Hampton. During the First World War, Bill went into the grocery business on the west side of Main Street.

*Wilma Owen with sister Carrie O'Bryant, and great niece Sharon O'Bryant.*

Mary married Charlie Britain. Carrie married Fred O'Bryant (they are listed in the O'Bryants). Mabel married Albert Peterson and they had one son John Russell Peterson. Lillian married Harry Chaffin. They had Chaffin's Cafe on the west side of Main Street (later Sellar's Cafe). John married Mabel Barren and they had a son David Russell. John went into the grocery business with his father. Wilma married Harold Owen (they are listed in the Owens). Shortly after graduation Paul contracted tuberculosis and lived only a few months. He is buried in Evergreen Cemetery. *Submitted by Pamela Day.*

**SALLEE** - John Sallee was born in 1829 in Morgan County, IL. He married Permelia McClendon in 1847 and to this union nine children were born. He was a private in the Arkansas Cavalry during the Civil War. One of their children was Levi, born in 1854 in Carroll County, AR. After coming to Greene County, MO he married America McClendon in 1880. She was the daughter of Robert McClendon and was a teacher. She taught in a rural school northwest of Republic.

*Levi Sallee, wife America, and daughter, Adieth O'Neal.*

Levi and America had 10 children, some of whom married in Greene County. Mae married Jessie Young; Dollie married Wesley Roush; Jerlie married Lewis Etheridge (their daughter is Jeerl Dean); Berlie married Hazel Bell; Aideth married Clarence O'Neal (they are listed in the O'Neals).

Levi and America lived in Republic. He owned a steam engine, thrashing machine and a saw mill. In the summer he went from farm to farm and threshed their grain. In the winter he used the saw mill and made lumber. At one time he loaded the steam engine and saw mill on a railroad flat-car and went to Cuba, MO. There, he unloaded the steam engine and saw mill and drove them to Steelville.

At Christmas time, his wife America and daughter Aideth rode the train to Cuba to spend two weeks with him. *Submitted by James O'Neal.*

**SANDERS/BORUD** – Vernon A. Sanders was born Oct. 17, 1918, east of Republic, MO, to Samuel G. Sanders and Mae (Perkins) Sanders. His paternal grandparents were Franklin M. Sanders and Sarah A. (Wallace) Sanders. They farmed in the Nixa area. His maternal grandparents were Conce Perkins and Mary E. (Stewart) Perkins. They farmed in the Battlefield area. Vernon's great-grandpa, Clayborn Stewart, married Francis Elizabeth Ray in 1865, daughter of John Ray (John's house is the "Ray House" at Wilson's Creek National Battlefield).

*L-R: Vernon Sanders, Lester "Bud" Logan, Dallas Gray, Sam Sanders at Farmers Exchange about 1940/41.*

Vernon grew up on a 120-acre farm in the Lindsey School district where he attended school through the seventh grade. He then went to Republic in the eighth grade because the school bus came by their house. His eighth grade teacher was Alice Roop. He graduated from Republic High School in 1937. After graduation he worked for the Farmer's Exchange in Republic.

In 1942 Vernon was inducted into the U.S. Army at Jefferson Barracks in St. Louis. He was transferred to Seattle, WA, Port of Embarkation as company clerk. In 1943 Vernon was assigned to the Army Administration School at Hattiesburg, MS and later returned to Seattle as 1st sergeant. He transferred to Prince Rupert, British Columbia, and was discharged in February 1946 at Fort Lewis, WA.

Vernon returned to work at the Farmer's Exchange and in April he went to North Dakota to marry his Norwegian wife, Nora Angeline "Angie" Borud, whom he had met in Seattle. She had been working for Boeing. Angie was born July 28, 1921, in Park Rapids, MN. Her family moved to Fargo, ND when she was 5. Angie's dad and his parents came to America from Lillehammer, Norway.

*Angie and Vernon Sanders wedding picture April 17, 1946.*

In 1950 Vernon resigned as manager of Republic Farmer's Exchange and went to work in the office of M.F.A. Fertilizer Plant. In 1953 he went to work for Mr. Linzee Wells, at the Republic Post Office. Vernon worked as a rural mail carrier on Route 2 until his retirement in 1979.

Vernon joined the Hood Methodist Church in 1938 and for several years sang in the choir.

Angie joined the church after they were married and they have both been members of the Eastern Star for 50 years. Vernon has been a member in the Masonic Lodge for more than 50 years.

Vernon and Angie have three sons: (1) Dale (born Sept. 20, 1948) married Janet Butler in 1973. Their children are Jeffrey and Julie. (2) Dennis (born June 2, 1953) married Debbie Day in 1973. Their children are Stephanie, Joshua and Lucas. (3) Duane (born Sept. 4, 1957) married Melissa Miekley in 1982. Their daughter is Amanda.

Vernon and Angie also have seven great-grandchildren. *Submitted by Angie Sanders.*

**SANDERS/BUTLER** - V. Dale Sanders (born Sept. 20, 1948) and Janet M. Butler (born March 9, 1951) were married on Nov. 9, 1973 at Hopewell Baptist Church, west of Republic. They both graduated from Republic High School and had attended all 12 years at Republic.

Dale served in the Air Force as a crew chief on a C-130 airplane from 1968-1972. He was then employed by the Federal Medical Center in Springfield where he worked until retirement in December 1998. Janet worked for five years, until 1975, at Security State Bank on Main Street in Republic.

They live on a farm east of Republic that had belonged to his parents, Vernon and Angie Sanders. His parents bought the 112 acre farm in April 1949, from Mrs. John E. O'Bryant. Dale and Janet raise beef cattle and produce all the needed hay for their cow/calf operation.

*Back: Julie and Jeremy Thompson; front: Jeffrey, Janet, Dale, Jamie and Jacob Sanders.*

They have two children, Jeffrey Dale (born Feb. 8, 1975) and Julie Dawn (born Aug. 19, 1978). Both children attended school at Republic and graduated college from SMSU. Dale and Janet were active in their children's education and did volunteer work in PTA and the Booster Club. As a family, they attended Hopewell Baptist Church, where the children are the sixth generation, on their mother's side, to attend Hopewell. Janet has served as a Sunday school teacher and Dale is a deacon of the church.

Jeffrey married Jamie Ball in May 2001, and has a son, Jacob Cole. Jeffrey is a lawyer with the District Attorney's office in Tyler, TX and Jamie is a homemaker. Julie married Jeremy Thompson in June 2002 and is a kindergarten teacher at Republic. Jeremy teaches fifth and sixth grade math at Clever. They have one daughter, Jena Layne. *Submitted by Dale Sanders. Editor's note: Janet died 2007.*

**SANDERS/DAY** - In 1953 Dennis was born to Vernon and Angie Sanders of Republic, MO. Dennis lived on Elm Street by O'Neal Lumber Company, where as a kid, he used to go over and turn on the big saw. He thought this was fun and it was also fun to make the manager Ken Day mad! (Keep this name in mind for later on.)

Angie Sanders' family were large farmers in North Dakota and in the summers, Dennis would visit and help farm. He loved it! Growing up in Republic, Dennis's dad Vernon also farmed, (in addition to his day job) and Dennis enjoyed getting together with the neighbors and filling silos with corn. Back in those days, corn was put up right on Elm Street, where houses are on both sides of the road now.

Dennis loved fast cars and motorcycles in his teen years. He built a 1957, custom Chevy, which remained one of a kind. Pat Ray and Bob Lisenby helped and people ask about that car to this day!

Dennis went to work for Fred McCullah at McCullahs Service Station on North Main when he was 16 years old. He used to pump gas for Ken and Marie Day, and sometimes their daughter, Debbie. If you remember, Ken was the one to get onto Dennis for turning on his saw! Deb and Dennis married in 1973 and have three children: Stephanie, Joshua and Lucas. Dennis and Debbie are very proud of their children and their work ethics. Stephanie married Mike Bishop and they have three children: Sierra-7, Camille-3 and Savana-7 weeks old. Mike works for the railroad and Steph runs a commercial greenhouse. Josh works for the same company Dennis works for, CCX, except Josh works out of the Rolla terminal. While working for CCX, Josh met Marissa Tolliver, who worked at the Salem, IL terminal and they married. They have a son Jordan-5, and are expecting another child in June 2006. Luke worked at John's 4x4 And More for five years and is now working for Offroad Safari. Luke and Tessa have a daughter Ava, who is 4 months old. Dennis and Debbie feel they are very blessed with their children and grandchildren!

Debbie enjoyed growing up in Republic, where her dad Ken was manager of the lumber yard. Marie, Debbie's mom, also worked at the lumber yard, selling carpet and keeping the books. While Dennis attended Hood Methodist Church, Debbie's family attended the Assembly of God church where her mom played the piano and her dad was a deacon.

Debbie stayed with her grandmother, Lolla Parker, while her mom worked and Debbie developed a love of farm life from Mrs. Parker. Mrs. Parker sewed, gardened, made soap and had many varieties of farm animals

When newly married, Dennis and Debbie bought a 40 acre farm, north of town. In 1985 a mouse chewed some wires, the house caught fire and was a total loss. Dennis and Debbie have always been very thankful to the people of Republic for their generosity and support in this time of need. It was very humbling to be on the receiving end of so much kindness from the residents of Republic - but that's our town! *Submitted by Stehanie Bishop.*

**SANDERS/MIEKLEY** - Duane Alan Sanders was born Sept. 4, 1957 to Vernon and Angeline Sanders. Melissa Rene Miekley became his wife on July 16, 1982 at the home of her mother June Miekley in Clever, MO. Melissa was born Aug. 27, 1962.

Duane attended Republic School system and Melissa attended Clever School system. Duane worked for TapJac Lumber Yard for three years before buying his first semi-truck and trailer. He was an owner and operator for 20 years. He has worked for Estes Express Truck Lines for the last three years. Melissa

*Melissa, Amanda and Duane Sanders.*

was a Republic school bus driver for 12 years and currently is a nail technician at Hair Illusion in Republic.

Duane and Melissa live one block east of Main on Pine in Republic. This home is the first house that Vernon and Angie bought March 7, 1947. Vernon bought it from J.P. and Orpha Howell.

Duane and Melissa have one daughter Amanda Brooke, born Sept. 28, 1986. She is currently attending Ozarks Technical Community College as a freshman. *Submitted by Duane and Melissa Sanders.*

**SANDERS/ROBERTSON** - Alvin Lenard Sanders was born Aug. 1, 1914, the first son of Samuel Grant Sanders and Virgie Mae Perkins Sanders. He grew up on a farm east of Republic and attended school at Lindsey. Alvin worked a short time for Frisco Railroad before becoming a full time dairyman and farmer.

In 1937 Alvin married Mary Delores Robertson (born March 3, 1911), the daughter of Marvin Robertson and Nancy Conzadie (Short) Robertson. Delores grew up on a farm east of Republic that is now part of Wilson's Creek Park. Before she married she worked at Brown's Candy Factory in Springfield.

*Alvin and Delores Sanders with Lenard and Don – 1944.*

Alvin and Dolores's first home was just south of the Greene and Christian County line where their first son, Lenard Grant, was born on Sept. 17, 1938. Later they moved to the farm on what is now Farm Road 101 where they engaged in farming, raising beef cattle, and milking Holsteins. Their second son, Howard Don, was born there on May 3, 1942.

Starting in 1946 Alvin ran a can milk route to Producers Creamery in Springfield until they stopped receiving milk in cans. He then worked at Tap Jac Lumber Company until he retired in 1976.

Alvin and Delores enjoyed a few years of retirement before Delores passed away April 4, 1979 and Alvin Dec. 24, 1988. Both are buried at Lindsey Cemetery at Republic.

Lenard and Don attended school at Lindsey until it consolidated with Republic; Lenard graduated in 1956 and Don in 1959. After high school Lenard worked for a short time at Caterpillar in Illinois, then went to work at Producers Creamery in 1957.

Lenard married Marilyn Daniel (born Oct. 30, 1940) on April 24, 1959. They live in Republic. Lenard continued helping his parents on the farm as well as working at the creamery. Lenard and Marilyn had two children, Andrea (born May 23, 1962) and Brad (born Aug. 30, 1968). Lenard bought a farm southeast of Republic in 1964 where he raised hay and beef cattle. They built a house there in 1972.

Marilyn worked at the Farmers Exchange before the children were born then stayed home until both were in school. She then returned to work at the Farmer's Exchange until it closed. She then worked at Republic Floral until 2000.

Their daughter Andrea and her husband Jeff Allen have four children: Christopher and Heath Luttrull, Kylie and Daylie. They live in Marionville where she teaches 4th grade.

Brad is an officer in the U.S. Marine Corp and presently stationed in Florida with his wife Mary.

Lenard retired from Dairy Farmers of America in 1999 after 42 years of service. He continued farming his parents' farm as well as his own until 2004.

Don moved to Kansas City after graduation and married Joyce Hartline on June 11, 1961. She was born Nov. 1, 1941. They returned to Republic where they raised their children, Kevin (born Jan. 7, 1962) and Kim (born Oct. 17, 1965).

Kevin lives in Liberty, MO and is employed as vice president at Dairy Farmers of America. He and his wife Cheryl have two daughters, Abby and Holly.

Kim is a nurse at Nevada Regional Hospital at Nevada, MO; she has two children, Lindsay and Kody.

Don and Joyce moved to Harwood, MO in 1983 to help on her parents' farm. Joyce returned to school and became a registered nurse and retired from Nevada Regional Hospital in 2005 and Don continues to farm. *Submitted by Lenard G. Sanders.*

**SANDERS/SISSEL** – Shirley's history with Republic, as the daughter of Oran Robert Sanders and Opal Sissel Sanders, began as a child visiting her grandparents, Wilford Joel and Francis Ellen (Davis) Sissel, near Republic. Their farm was just west of Wilson's Creek Battleground and next door to the Cassy pickle factory. The Cassy family lived across the creek, up the hill, from her grandparents. What great fun for all the grandchildren to climb around the huge pickle barrels, however, they were only allowed to go there when the barrels were empty! It was also quite a treat while visiting, to make the trip to Republic.

After graduating from eighth grade at Central Point, east of Battlefield, MO, she entered Republic High School in 1952, riding the bus several miles each day with one of their favorite drivers, Jess Duvall. So many friendships were made in those four years that endure today. At that time Main Street was, indeed, the "main street" of Republic. O'Dell's Drug Store, Martin's Movie Theatre, Plummers Store, Trailway's Cafe, Bennett's Barber Shop and Dr. Brim's Dental Office were some of the businesses located on Main Street.

A classmate at RHS, Don Truman Brown, son of Smith and Belle Brown, would become her husband. They were married in 1957 by Rev. Al Smith at the Hood Methodist Church and became the parents of Suzanne Myree, Robert Allen, Mary Patricia "Tricia," Beth Elaine and William Michael. After living in Springfield, MO for a short time, they returned to Republic to raise their children, living first on West Elm Street and then on a farm just west of Republic. Their children attended and graduated from Republic.

Suzanne is a teacher in Seneca, MO, following her work with the state of Missouri as an advocate for MR/DD individuals. She has two children, Mischa Myree (Admire) Long and William Timothy Creel Admire. Mischa and her husband, Josey Long, have a daughter, Alyssa Myree.

Allen and his wife Marcia are currently stationed at Fort Wood, MO as they look forward to retirement following his career in the Army. He has one son, Gerald Allen; two step-children, Douglas and Jennifer, and two grandchildren, Cody and Breanna.

Tricia and her husband, Terry Don Phillips, live in Seneca, SC, where he is athletic director at Clemson University. After a career in marketing/public relations, Tricia is a full time mom with three teenagers: Meagan, Marshall and Madison Stone, and has two step-children, John Dennis and Sarah Jane.

Michael and his wife Lavinia live in Springfield, MO where he is with Howell Commercial Refrigeration and she is with Elfindale. He has one son, Blake Austin; two step-children, Jason and Alisha; and two grandchildren, Madison and Lily.

Beth lives in Springfield, MO in a MR/DD group home.

In the years the family has lived here, Republic has certainly changed as it continues to grow. One of the recent changes she's been privileged to be a part of, was the relocation of her church, Calvary Baptist, from its long time home on the corner of Hines and Hwy. 60 to West Hwy. 60 in the former Albertson's store after extensive renovation.

Republic was, and is, a great place to live and raise a family. After driving daily to Springfield for 25 years as manager of a pediatric clinic and as much as she loves to travel, it's always great for her to come home to Republic. *Submitted by Shirley Sanders Brown.*

**SCHATZ** - The William "Bill" Schatz family, natives of Billings, MO and Christian County, MO, moved across the county line in 1960 to Republic. The primary reason was that Bill was going to work for the Republic R-III Schools and he believed that he should be a resident of the district in which he worked.

*Bill Schatz.*

Bill, his sister Rosemary and his brother John, are children of William Louis Schatz, who died in 1988, and Lela Vival (Butler) Schatz, who died in 1978.

Bill spent a quarter of a century as the chief administrator of the Republic school system. During this time the school received a triple A rating, won state championship in basketball, and football was started. Also during this time, there was much new construction and many new programs became a reality.

His four children: Gail, Mike, Karen and Sarah, attended Republic K - 12 for their early education. All reside in this area with Gail and Sarah in Mt. Vernon and Mike and Karen in Republic. His seven grandchildren are Tara, Stuart, Clark, Eric, Kyle, Hope and Ryan.

After retirement from the school system. Bill spent time selling school supplies, working for a state senator and a funeral home, attending athletic events and doing volunteer work. *Submitted by Bill Schatz.*

**SELLERS** - The first Sellers came from England in the early 19th century. The name means "Maker of Saddles." They settled in the Piedmont area of Virginia where they raised saddle horses. During the Civil War Thomas E. Sellers joined the Confederate Army as a colonel under General Stone. They sold their gaited horses to the Confederate Army and were paid in Confederate Script. Their property was lost to them after the war, so they came west to settle in Springfield, MO.

Thomas E. Sellers' son, Robert M. Sellers, was the father of Melvin E. Sellers who came to Republic. Robert M. Sellers made the run in the Oklahoma Cherokee strip. He staked a plot, but later sold it.

*Maude and Melvin Sellers' wedding picture – June 16, 1917.*   *L-R: Jo Ann, Peggy and Bette Sellers dressed for Easter – 1934 behind the Baptist parsonage.*

Melvin E. Sellers married Maude Silvers in 1917. They lived in Springfield until 1933 when they came to Republic with their three daughters: Bette Jane, Jo Ann and Peggy Louise. They bought the Green Tree Cafe from Merlin Pearce and Bill Head. It was street fair time when they came, so Merlin and Bill stayed on to help them. They worked long, hard hours for a week, and Maude said she wondered what they had gotten themselves into. They rented the Baptist parsonage to live in as there was no pastor there.

After a few months they moved their business into the Chaffin building next to Owen and Short Hardware Store. That building had an old fashioned soda fountain with back bar and a counter with stools in the front part. The back section was a dining room with marble top tables and wire "ice cream" chairs. White hexagon tiles covered the floor throughout. There was also a juke box in the dining room, and it was the perfect place for the young people to learn to dance to the music of the "Big Bands."

The high school students would eat their lunches at school, run to Sellers Cafe, dance to the juke box, and run back to school when Maude stopped the music and shooed them out. They were not overweight in those days.

Most of the older high school boys worked at Sellers Cafe during the summer at one time or another. After the lunch hour, Maude would go home to rest to get ready for the dinner hour and to stay open until midnight. One summer afternoon Gene Evans was working when Maude left to rest. A man came about 3:00 p.m. and ordered a BLT. Gene didn't know what that was, so he slipped out the back door, ran the two blocks to his parents home, asked his mother how to make it, ran back, made and served the sandwich. It was a good thing he was the champion sprinter in school. Such was life, with few phones during the depression in a small town.

The Sellers sold the cafe in 1944 to the

Sublett family and went to live in Eldon, MO, for a few months, then both went to Hawaii as civilian employees in the armed service. Melvin was with the Army, and Maude was with the Navy. They really loved Hawaii, but returned to live in California at the war's end and lived there until they returned to Republic, MO to spend their retirement years.

Bette Jane Sellers married J.W. Fugitt, a Republic native in 1938. They lived on a farm by Terrell Creek as newlyweds where they had a large dairy herd. Gradually they bought small adjoining farms along the creek until they had 2,300 acres where they later raised beef cattle for several years. It is this property that is planned for a large development to be part of Republic at this time. They had two children, Terry and Christina, both of whom now reside in Springfield. Bette lives at One Parkway Place there, also.

Jo Ann married Howard Lee Eagan, also a native of Republic, in 1941. He managed his mother's grocery store until called to serve in the Army in 1944. They have one son, Gary Lee, who lives in Eureka Springs, AR. At the end of the war they found a need for housing in Republic and built over 100 homes and other buildings in Republic and Greene County. Later they bought the bank in Pleasant Hope, MO, but they have always lived in Republic.

Peggy Louise Sellers married Robert L. Harris in 1945. He served in the Air Force during the war. Upon earning an engineering degree at the University of Arkansas, he worked for the Public Health Service. He earned a doctorate and taught chemistry at the University of North Carolina. They have three children: Linda, Jim and Robert. They live in Raleigh, NC. *Submitted by Jo Ann Eagan.*

**SHORT** - Aaron Short was the great-great-great-great-grandfather to Iris Maness Jones Duke. His parents are unknown. He was born in 1750 in Kentucky. He married Ann Forbis and they settled in Tennessee. Their only known son was Willis Short. Both Aaron and Ann's fathers fought in the Revolutionary War. Their son Willis was born May 18, 1795 and died May 22, 1879 in Tennessee. He married Nancy Kendricks on Nov. 20, 1818 in Roane County, TN. Nancy was born May 25, 1800 and died July 6, 1853 in Kingston, Roane County, TN. She was the daughter of Samuel James and Margaret Fruby Kendricks. Their 14 children were Jasper Newton, Francis Smiley, Elias Bates, Mary Malcena, Samuel, John A., Larriett, Eldon, Julius, William, Jackson, Diana, Letha Margaret and Standifer Rice.

The Short family name has long been noted in Republic and throughout the Ozarks. The Greene County census of 1860 listed home owners and their families that lived near Wilson's Creek Battlefield. Elias Bates Short lived on what is today, the National Park Visitors Center. He was one of the first families to settle in the Wilson's Creek area, and brought his family here from Kentucky.

Elias was born Jan. 9, 1821 in Tennessee and died June 23, 1914 in Greene County, MO. He married Rebecca McCullah, the daughter of Alexander and Lucy Robertson. She was born July 18, 1822 in Roane County, TN and died June 27, 1888. Elias's military service was in Co. B, 72nd MO Militia. Both Elias and Rebecca are buried in Lindsey Chapel Cemetery east of Republic. Their nine children were a nameless babe, Francis Alexander, Sarah Elizabeth, Samantha Caroline, John Asbury, Willis Calvin, James Monroe, Wesley Bascombe and an infant son.

James Monroe Short, son of Elias and Rebecca (McCullah) Short, was born Sept. 19, 1855 and died Feb. 19, 1917. He married Mary Alice Sparkman on Feb. 22, 1882. She was born Dec. 21, 1864, the daughter of William David and Jane Catherine (Rainey) Sparkman. She died Feb. 29, 1904 in Republic, Greene County, MO. Both James and Mary are buried in the Lindsey Chapel Cemetery. Their four children were: Etta Mae, Glenn Alice, Raymond James and Willis Bascombe.

Etta Mae Short, the daughter of James Monroe and Mary Alice (Sparkman) Short, was born May 24, 1886 and died March 16, 1915 in Republic, MO.

*Etta Mae Short Maness with sons, Raymond and Henry. Photo by Ferrell in Republic, MO, abt. 1907.*

*Children of Homer and Etta Mae Short Maness. Elsie (6), Henry (9) and Raymond (10) dressed to go to their mother's funeral in March 1915.*

She married Homer Elliott Maness on Aug. 18, 1904 in Republic, Greene County, MO. Homer was the son of John Baldwin and Sylvania Jane (Julian) Maness. He was born Jan. 26, 1887 and died March 30, 1981. They are both buried in the Lindsey Chapel Cemetery. Their three children were Raymond Everett (born Oct. 9, 1905, died Oct. 28, 1982); Henry Elliott (born Dec. 4, 1906, died March 22, 1980) married Velma Irene Martin and settled in McGirk, MO near Jefferson City. Velma was the daughter of Thomas McNeese and Eliza Jane Martin. Their three children were Etta Jane, Virginia Lee and Henry Elliott Jr.

Elsie Gwendola was born July 18, 1909 and passed away Jan. 5, 2006. She lived in South Carolina and was a very sweet, thoughtful and caring lady. She married Donald Oliver and their three children were Donald Wesley Jr., Mary Deloris and Charlotte May. Raymond Everett married Flossie Ann DeWett. She was the daughter of George Lewis DeWett and Mildred Ruhamah (Harrington) DeWett. Their five children are Mildred Mae, Raymond Everett Jr., Rayetta Elizabeth, Iris Edwina and Luther Edwin.

Iris's family has deep roots in the Republic area, where both her parents grew up. Iris was the first baby born on New Years Day in Republic in 1934. The family moved to Stone County sometime after her birth. She married and raised her family in surrounding counties. She retired from a printing company where she had worked as an artist for 30 years. Iris once again came to live in Republic. This was a place she always felt at home, close to family that helped make Republic history. Some fond memories of her early years are of downtown Republic on Main Street. A drug store where her Grandfather DeWett took her for an ice cream cone, and of Saturday nights when her father brought the family to the movie theater on Main Street, and listened to the band play on the street. Sitting and watching the trains pass and counting the cars was exciting as they didn't see trains down on the farm where they lived. Later in her teen years her date took her to the same theater on Saturday nights. She later married him. He was Orvil Eugene Jones, son of Otis and Reathel Jones. Their four children are Michael, Rickie, Dwayne and Yvonne. Orvil passed away on April 18, 1979 and Iris married David L. Duke in 1983. For the past 22 years they have lived about six miles from the house where Iris was born. *Submitted by Iris Maness Jones Duke.*

**SHORT** - On Aug. 2, 1861 the north and south met for the first time in actual combat at The Battle of Dug Spring, in southwest Missouri, located on the outskirts of Clever in Christian County.

John Short, know as Gran "Pap" Short, was a guide for the Union troops; his home was located in Hurley, MO. When the troops camped for the night after the battle, Gran Pap asked to visit his family and the leave was granted. He reached home before dark, had supper with his folks and just as darkness settled over the valley, he sat down in the door to rest and visit for a while. Two men on horses rode up and shouted hello! When Gran Pap answered, they asked to be directed to the Union lines. Not suspecting any treachery, Gran Pap walked quickly to the fence and jumped over. As soon as his feet hit the ground, one of the men grabbed him. He reached for his pistol but as he did, the second man seized his wrist and tried to twist the pistol out of his hand. Gran Pap was on his knees, one man on his back trying to choke him and the other one attempting to get the pistol out of his hand. Suddenly the man on his back rolled off, the grip on the pistol loosened and the second man fled down the road. Gran Pap sprang to his feet to see what had happened. There on the ground, sprawled out on his face, lay the man who was trying to choke him, an axe sunk almost out of sight between his shoulders, leaning against the fence ready to faint was Lydia Elizabeth "Granny" Short. Their 8-year-old son George had grabbed an axe which she used on the bushwhacker. She insisted that Gran Pap go to the woods to spend the night for his safety. Then Granny, George, and perhaps other children, buried the man temporarily in a straw stack not far from the house.

Morning came and so did a gang of 24 or 25 men. The gang swarmed in asking questions and demanding to know where her husband was, pillaging through the bureau drawers and taking what they chose. Granny continued being her sassy self all the while. The leader took a shovel full of live coals from the fireplace, ripped open the straw tick and dumped the coals in the straw. Granny picked up the burning straw tick in her arms, carried it outside and dumped it over the fence into the road. Seeing the bravery, the leader advised his men to leave stating that no woman this brave deserves to have her house burned.

A permanent grave for the bushwhacker was dug by a sycamore tree in a little thicket under the hill, quite a distance from the house. No one returned to search for his body.

*Aaron, Linda and Paul Lanning.*

Lydia Elizabeth "Granny" Short was the great-grandmother of Carolyn O'Bryant O'Neal and great-great-grandmother of Linda O'Neal Lanning. *Submitted by Linda Lanning.*

**SHORT/COLEMAN -** John Short was the fifth child of Willis and Nancy Kendrick Short, born May 2, 1826. He married Lydia Coleman on Oct. 10, 1850. Lydia was born Sept. 13, 1832 to Elizabeth Shaw Coleman and was stepdaughter to Alexander McCullah. Elizabeth and Alexander both had previous marriages.

Soon after John and Lydia were married, they left (along with Lydia's mother) their home near Kingston, Roane County, TN for newer country and elbow room. The trio traveled down the Tennessee and Mississippi Rivers by flat bottom boat to New Orleans. From there they traveled by dug-out boat to Buffalo Shoals and to Searcy County, AR. John left his family in Arkansas and walked to Greene County, MO. He planted crops, and between tending them and making trips south to look for a homestead, the summer passed and he went back to Arkansas for his wife and mother-in-law.

With their worldly possessions in a two wheeled cart (included was a dye kettle brought from the old home), the three hardy pioneers came to the present site of Hurley. Here they settled down and reared a large family of 13 children. After Lydia's death in 1876, John married Isabelle Farmer, born Aug. 30, 1842. John, Lydia, Elizabeth Shaw Coleman and Isabelle are all buried side-by-side in the Short Cemetery on the John Short homestead. John died Jan. 2, 1906; Lydia died July 4, 1876; Elizabeth Shaw Coleman, born April 5, 1803, died March 30, 1873; and Isabelle died April 1, 1929.

Sarah Melcena Short, John and Lydia's fifth child, was born April 26, 1857 and died Aug. 23, 1933. She was interred at Lindsey Chapel Cemetery, Republic. She married Joel O'Bryant in February 1877, who was born Nov. 30, 1852 and died May 21, 1932. He was interred at Lindsey Chapel Cemetery, Republic.

Fred Washington O'Bryant, Sarah and Joel's fourth child, was born Jan. 1, 1884 and died Feb. 7, 1956. He was interred at Evergreen Cemetery, Republic. He married Carrie Maude Russell in March 1913, who was born Oct. 2, 1886 and died June 10, 1947. She was interred at Evergreen Cemetery, Republic.

*Betsy, Sylvia and Joe Bob O'Neal.*

Carolyn Jane O'Bryant, Fred and Carrie's third child, was born March 14, 1924 and married Billy Gene O'Neal on June 4, 1943. He was born May 2, 1924. Carolyn Jane and Bill's first child, Joe Bob O'Neal was born July 31, 1948. He married Anna Bess "Betsy" Townsend in October 1995. She was born June 29, 1951. Joe Bob is a great-great-grandson of John and Lydia Short. *Submitted by Joe Bob O'Neal.*

**SHRUM -** Eugene Thurman Shrum, from Schell City, MO married Elsie Ellen Freeman, from Roscoe, MO on Nov. 29, 1935. Before their marriage, Elsie taught in one-room rural schools near Roscoe and Taberville and Gene was a truck driver. One daughter, Dorothy Ellen Shrum, was born on April 13, 1938. Gene and Elsie first settled in Taberville, MO then later they rented a farm near Schell City, MO where Gene worked as a farmer and Elsie as a homemaker. In March 1942, they

*Elsie and Gene Shrum in April 1975.*

purchased a farm northwest of Metz, MO where they continued to farm and raise livestock. Later they had a dairy herd and sold milk as part of their income. While at Metz, Elsie taught school, including first and second, third and fourth, and seventh and eighth grades. She had earned her teaching certificate from Southwest Missouri Teachers College after graduating from Roscoe High School in 1929.

Dorothy married Charles C. Morris on June 28, 1955. After she graduated from high school, Dorothy joined her husband in Germany where he was stationed in the military. This meant that Gene and Elsie were "empty nesters." They operated the filling station in Metz, MO for a while, but decided they needed to make a move.

In 1962, Gene and Elsie moved from their farm near Metz, MO to Springfield, MO. Gene found employment with Chapman Construction and Elsie enrolled in Southwest Missouri State University to finish her degree. She graduated in May 1964 (at age 53) and was hired to teach first grade in the Republic school system.

They had purchased a home in Republic and moved there in April 1964. Gene stopped working in Springfield and became self-employed. He did carpentry work in Republic and the surrounding area, had a saw-sharpening business and a well-equipped workshop. He loved doing all kinds of woodwork, including Grandmother clocks, ceiling light fixtures, cedar chests, card tables, kitchen cabinets, end tables, sewing cabinets and a variety of other items.

They were charter members of Westside Christian Church and enjoyed being a part of that congregation. Gene was one of the carpenters who helped build that church, taking special care on the baptistery. They dearly loved that little church and all its faithful members.

Gene had a fatal heart attack May 12, 1975, and Elsie had to face the future without him. She retired from teaching in 1976 and continued to live in Republic until 1984. She realized that she needed to be closer to her family, so she sold her home and bought a home in Harrisonville, MO. She moved there in December 1984, where she immediately became active in the First Christian Church.

Her daughter Dorothy and son-in-law Chuck live in Peculiar, MO; grandson Gary, wife Dori and their daughter Skyler, live in Raymore, MO; granddaughter Tricia, husband Bill, children Michelle and John, live in Lenexa, KS; granddaughter Cindy and her daughter Jessica live in Belton, MO.

Elsie has many fond memories of all her little first grade students and their supportive parents from her teaching experience in Republic, MO. It was hard for her to leave Republic and all her friends, but she is real happy in her new home; Harrisonville is a nice place to live.

Thanks to the help of her wonderful family and an abundance of good friends and neighbors, she is still able to live in her own home. Every day she fills her time with projects to help her community - quilting group at church, sewing cancer turbans for cancer patients, walker caddies and lap robes for nursing homes. She is a very caring and giving individual. She celebrated her 95th birthday on Oct. 9, 2005. God has richly blessed her in so many ways. *Written by Dorothy (Shrum) Morris for Elsie E. Shrum. Editor's Note: Elsie Shrum passed away Oct. 24, 2005. Her interment was at Benton Green Cemetery at Roscoe, MO.*

**SHY -** Janet Shy and her three children came to Greene County in 1973 from Warrensburg in Johnson County, MO where Jan had attended Central Missouri State College. Their previous home had been in Lowry City, MO where the youngest of the children, Ann-Marie, was born in 1966. Douglas Roy was born in Kansas City, MO in 1962, and Tami Jeanette in Clinton, MO in 1964.

After living in Springfield for five years, the family moved to a new house on Dennis Street, Republic in May 1978, when across the street was still a meadow. The children enrolled in the Republic schools that fall and finished their schooling there over the next few years.

In 1983, Jan took photography courses at SMS, and in 1986 she enrolled at Drury College. After four years of night school, she graduated with a bachelor of science degree in 1990. Jan retired from Carlisle Power Transmission Products, Inc. (formerly Dayco) in the fall of 2003, after 27 years of service and enjoys dabbling in painting, writing and family history, (and gardening as required) interspersed with occasional days at "her old desk" when needed.

*Shy family gathering on March 28, 2005. On the couch: Doug's family: Brandi, Matthew, Doug, Cheryl and Beth Shy. In front is Ann-Marie Shy, Tami Neal, Jan Shy, Chris Neal.*

Douglas graduated from Republic High School in 1980 and joined the Missouri Army National Guard in 1981. He received basic training at Fort Gordon, GA, where he was designated high scorer in Basic Rifle Marksmanship of Company A, 1st Battalion, 1st Signal Training Brigade. Doug married Cheryl Ruth Miller in December 1985. Their children are Brandi Ruth (born 1986), Elizabeth Ann (born 1988) and Matthew Douglas (born 1994).

Brandi graduated from Republic High School in 2005 and works at Big Lots in Springfield. Elizabeth still attends RHS and works part time at the J.C. Penney Home Store in Springfield. Matthew is in the sixth grade at E-III in Republic and is currently patrol leader of the 676 troop of the Ozark Trails Council Boy Scouts.

Doug has worked for the Greene County Circuit Court since 1989; and Cheryl works at Paul Mueller Company. Doug served as Ward II Alderman 1997-2000. He graduated from OTC in 2002 with an associate degree.

In December 1982, Tami married Marty Neal and they had three children: Marty Robert II (born 1984), Zachary Allen (born 1986) and Christopher James (born 1990). Tami and Marty later divorced and Mr. Neal died in 2003. Tami attended OTC and was on the President's and Dean's List for the spring semester in 1994. Tami now resides and works in Branson.

Ann-Marie graduated from RHS in 1985. She participated in sports, was secretary of the National Honor Society, and received the Presidential Academic Fitness Award. Ann-Marie attended Drury College, graduating in 1989. After working four years in Kansas City, MO, and other employment in Springfield, she is now office manager for Lacey Bros. Construction, Inc. in Springfield. She joined the Navy Reserves in 2003 and attended Navy Reserve Accession Course (NRAC) at Recruit Training Command, Great Lakes, IL in 2003. *Submitted by Janet Shy.*

**SIFFERMAN** - John Sifferman and his wife Lundy were the first Siffermans to settle in the Republic area. Their farm was located on the Lawrence-Greene County Line near Halltown. They settled there after traveling from Iowa around the middle of the 1800s. They had six children.

*T.A. "Alex" and Birdie Sifferman.*

Thomas Alex Sifferman was born in 1877 and attended college in Marionville, MO. He married Birdie Smith of the Halltown area in 1901. They purchased a farm eight miles northwest of Republic. They had eight children: Daisy, Minnie, Henry, Ray, Grace, twins-Ruth and Ruby, and Alice. Three of the girls and both boys were schoolteachers. Grace taught in Republic several years, then continued teaching in Springfield until her retirement. Daisy was one of the area's sought after artists; those who have one of her paintings treasure her beautiful work. Henry taught in the area and owned and operated the International Harvester business on North Boonville in Springfield for many years. Ray operated a large dairy farm northwest of Republic. Thomas Alex had a total of 20 grandchildren.

Daisy Sifferman Cook remembered that she had to drive a horse and buggy to high school in Republic. One day she had tied the horse in a shed near an alley; after school she decided the alley was too rough, so she turned down Main Street. Immediately the horse took his head and ran the length of Main Street, with Daisy struggling to get control, but in vain. It was so embarrassing to her that thereafter she always used the alley as her main street to the school. Later her father bought her a car, which she drove to school. During this time she was sorry to report that three unfortunate dogs lost their lives.

Ray's son Robert and his son Van still farm the homestead. Grace's son Jack Taylor has a machine shop in Ozark, MO. Jack and his wife Kathy (Barton) have four children: son Jeremy, and a daughter Laura (Taylor) Korage. Kathy has two children from a previous marriage, a son Ryan Barton and a daughter Brook (Barton) Smith. Together Jack and Kathy have five grandchildren. *Submitted by Jack Taylor.*

**SIFFERMAN-BIELLIER** - Lewis Dale Sifferman and Nellie Frances Biellier were married in 1920 in Greene County, MO. Both were born in the year of 1899 - he at Brown Springs in Stone County and she at Bois D'Arc in Greene County. They would live their lives in the area, including Pond Creek, and the Halltown areas. Lew and Nellie would have six children: Hildred (Sifferman) Wayman Watson, Regina (Sifferman) Maness, Dale, Wayne, Norreva (Sifferman) Carter Simmons and Norris Sifferman. They would be married for more than 67 years when Lew passed away in 1988, and Nellie followed in 1996.

*Lewis and Nellie (Biellier) Sifferman – 50th wedding anniversary.*

*Children of Lewis and Nellie (Biellier) Sifferman in 2005: Hildred, Norris, Regina, Wayne, Norreva, Dale.*

Lew was the son of Elmer Nathaniel and Ella Mae (Carson) Sifferman. Elmer was born in Greene County in 1874 and died in Greene County in 1910. Ella Mae was born in Lawrence County in 1877 and died in Greene County in 1954. They would have six children: Myrtle S. (Sifferman) Crumpley, Lewis Dale, Lundy Ann (Sifferman) Lafollette, Lela (Sifferman) Lovett, Hazel (Sifferman) Wilson and Elmer Sifferman. Elmer and Ella Mae are buried at Rock Prairie Cemetery at Halltown, as are all their children and spouses. Many other Siffermans are also buried there.

Elmer Nathaniel Sifferman's parents were John Adams and Lunda Sophia (Kirk) Sifferman. John was born in Illinois but came with his family to Lawrence County, MO in the early 1860s. John Adams Sifferman and Lunda "Lundy" Sophia Kirk were married in 1870 at Fidelity, MO. They would have the following children: Lewis Lafayette, Elmer Nathaniel, Thomas Alexander, Daisy (Sifferman) White, John Alonzo, Lillie (Sifferman) and Stella (Sifferman) Drum Zimmerman.

Lundy was born in North Carolina. She came to the Newton and Jasper County area with her parents, Alexander and Emaline (Earnhardt) Kirk, before 1860. John Adams Sifferman's parents were Nicholas and Louisa (Meyer) Sifferman. Nicholas and Louisa came to the United States on the same ship and landed in New York in 1845. They were of German descendant. They were married in 1846 and their first child, John Adams, was born in Illinois. The remainder of their children were born in Iowa. They were Catherine (Sifferman) Ward, Rosina (Sifferman) Baker, Henry, George, Mary (Sifferman) Burney and Caroline (Sifferman) Ward. The family was in Lawrence County before 1870. Louisa died in 1869 and Nicholas married Elizabeth Brown. Nicholas died in 1894 in Lawrence County, MO. He is also buried in the Rock Prairie Cemetery at Halltown, MO.

Lewis Dale Sifferman's mother, Ella Mae Carson, was the child of George Enoch and Martha Ellen (Raynor) Carson. George Enoch was born in Missouri in 1849 and died in Greene County in 1928. Martha Ellen was born in Indiana in 1847 and died at Pierce City, MO in 1882. George and Martha were married in Harrison County, MO, but came to this area. They would have the following children: Lilly Olive (Carson) Lovejoy, William Raynor, Ella Mae (Carson) Sifferman and Drucilla Ann (Carson) Hartley. The oldest child was barely nine when Martha Ellen died. She is buried at Monett, and George is buried at Wade Chapel Cemetery. After Martha Ellen's death; George married Melvina Porter and they had a daughter Alta Beatrice (Carson) Carter.

George's parents were William Phillip and Theresa Ann (Evins) Carson. They were both born in Kentucky - he in 1812 and she in 1814. They were in this area by 1849. He died in Lawrence County in 1893 and she at Chesapeake in Lawrence County in 1892. Their children were Richard H., Nancy Jane (Carson) Bruise, Sarah E. (Carson), William Henry, Lucretia M. (Carson) Anderson, James A., George Enoch, John S., Elijah C. and Charles T. The last four being born in Lawrence County.

Nellie Frances (Biellier) Sifferman was the daughter of William Alexander Hamilton and Nancy Ellen (Lile) Biellier. Both parents were born in Greene County, MO. He was born in 1867 and she in 1869. They were married in Greene County in 1887. William died in 1959 in Lawrence County and Nancy died in Greene County in 1956. Their children were Ernest (born and died 1888), Gertrude Mae (Biellier) Carter, Christian Alvin, Elijah Dee, Ivy Marshall, Nellie Frances (Biellier) Sifferman, Anna(Biellier) born and died 1903, and Ralph Onas. All the children lived in Greene County. Dee lived in Republic but most of the children lived closer to the Ash Grove area.

Nancy Ellen Lile was the daughter of John Alvin and Frances Catherine (Blades) Lile. They were married in Greene County in 1864. John had been born in Kentucky. He served in the Civil War with the Missouri Volunteers. John and Frances had nine children: Margaret S.J. (Lile) Ruhl Dickinson, Allie Ann (Lile) Graves, Nancy Ellen (Lile) Biellier, John Alvin Jr., Thomas Tillman, James Green, William Elijah, Rosa A. (Lile) Shipley Reynolds Hunt and Lucy Victoria (Lile) Potts Cunningham. William Elijah and Rosa went to Kansas, but the rest remained in the area.

John Alvin Lile's father, Green Lile, had died in Kentucky, but his mother, Nancy Jane Collins, later married Alfred O'Banion, who was the widower of her sister Betsy. Nancy died near Republic in 1888.

Frances Catherine Blades was the daughter of Edward Alvin Franklin and Eleanor Penelope (Maynard) Blades. They were both born in North Carolina. She was born in the Cherokee Nation. Both died in Greene County. Edward had been married twice before he married Eleanor and had at least four daughters. Edward and Eleanor had at least 12 children: Sarah Ann

(Blades) McDaniel, Ransom Dudley, Nancy Emiline (Blades) Hood Batson Brown, Isaac Tillman, Cynthia Ann (Blades) Hood, Edward Alvin Franklin Jr., Rebecca L. (Blades) Batson, William Willis, Elizabeth Blades, James Reynolds, Frances Catherine (Blades) Lile and George Washington Blades. George Washington went to Stone County, MO and it was thought that Sarah went to Texas. The others all stayed in the area near Republic. This large family had many, many descendents and a large number of them are still in the Republic area. *Submitted by Regina V. Maness.*

**SIMMONS** - The Claude Simmons family moved to Republic, after having lived in Springfield five years. They came with one daughter and four sons. They chose Republic because of location, growth, a small town like Claude and Bea had lived in as children, and a fine school system that would give their children an education that would allow them knowledge for college entrance and completion, as well as many pleasant memories of activities and friendships. This was accomplished as Nancy went into nursing, Andy into engineering, Craig into geology, Chad into mortician/funeral director and business, and Blake into electronics.

Claude, a Kansas graduate in civil engineering, chose to start and own Simmons Engineering Company in Republic in 1960. He operated it to his retirement in 1986. He did engineering work for the city of Republic, both large and small projects in water, sewer, advising, etc. Andy and his wife Viva have owned the business since 1986, still in Republic.

When the Simmons moved to Republic in 1959 the population was 1,519; at present it is 11,000+. Main Street was the hub of the city, grocery stores, clothing stores, farmers exchange, barber and beauty shops, bank, insurance company, dime store, hardware, meat market, and more. Each fall the Fall Festival was held on Main Street. It was blocked off for a parade, food, cake walk, and queen candidates, and with a special feel about it with all businesses participating and all very joyful. The Fall Festival continues but is now held at the Kiwanis and Garoutte Field.

There were two fine doctors. Appointments were not made, instead one went to the office and waited his or her turn, unless there was an emergency which received immediate attention. If one needed further attention they had close ties to doctors in Springfield and would make arrangements. They also were available for night or off hours, as well as home calls when needed. This of course is not possible or practical now, but what a "blessing" then.

Andy recently recalled the preparation for the first baseball diamond. He remembered one Saturday morning many fathers and their sons met at the site to start work. The son's job was to pick up rocks. They said they had never seen so many! This Saturday work went on until the baseball field was finished. Later it became a practice field and is today known as Garoutte Field on which soccer games are played.

During many years it was a common practice if you were going to be gone a few days you would notify the police to watch your house. On one of these weekends, probably about 1978, one of the Simmons' son and wife came to spend a quiet weekend at the family home. The police noting a strange car and lights on, checked on this, and the son had to prove who he was and that permission had been granted for their stay. This was much appreciated by all.

The Simmons found it a pleasure to live and raise their family in Republic — a bit frustrating at times, but rewarding to those responsible for the growth both residentially and commercially, the churches, schools, utilities as needed, road system, police and fire departments, and more recently, sidewalks, and a very fine Republic Civic Center. *Submitted by Bea Simmons.*

**SKELTON/MASON** - George V. Skelton and Mary "Mollie" Lockridge Mason were married Nov. 16, 1873. George, born in 1850, was a seventh generation American and the son of Martha E.A. Rucker and Joel M. Skelton, who was killed by bushwhackers in his dooryard in 1863. Mollie, born in 1854, was the daughter of Sarah Erwin Benson and Jeptha Mason, who had come to Greene County by 1838. They started their family in Pond Creek Township in l874 with Albert and added six more children over the next 20 years: Elmer, Pearl, Vern, Nora, Laura and Ava.

*Skelton family. Standing: Ava, Pearl, Vern, Laura, Nora; sitting: Albert, George, Mollie Mason, Elmer Skelton.*

As their brothers, sisters, aunts and uncles had mostly stayed in the area, they were surrounded by relatives: Wades, Julians, Masons, Mooneyhams, Laneys, Wallaces, Roses, Browns, Gillilands, Whinreys, Greens, Moses, Jacksons, Reynolds, Ruckers and others.

Their first house was one room. After adding a kitchen and two more rooms over the next 15 years, the house eventually had two rooms upstairs and four rooms down.

Mollie made all her and the children's clothes and most of her husband's. She began her marriage preserving fruits by drying, but later canned in both tin cans and glass jars sealed with wax. Vegetables kept through the winter were only dried or root crops. They butchered seven to eight hogs and a yearling beef every fall. The wheat and corn for eating was taken to Whinrey's water mill for grinding. Water came from both a dug well and a cistern. Mollie sold butter and eggs locally at first, but later she sold to families who were weekly customers in Springfield. The eggs were transported in buckets of bran.

Albert started at age 5 at a subscription school in Hopewell Church with the teacher paid in food. He later attended other subscription schools and Grandview and Republic Schools and Marionville College. An ordinary teacher's salary was $40 per month.

The annual gatherings of 4th of July picnics were sometimes held at Caleb Thurman's sassafras grove about 3/4 mile west of Republic on the south side of the road and the camp meeting was usually at Robertson's Springs, about two miles southeast of Republic or Garoutte Spring near Blades Chapel Church. Entertainment for the boys was swimming in Pickerel Creek, hunting, fishing and a contraption called a Flying Jenny. It was made by cutting off a 6-inch diameter tree at waist level and sharpened to a point 1-1/2 inch thick. Cutting another 6-inch tree to a length of 14 feet, a hole was bored midways about halfway through, then set on the point of the upright tree. One boy got on one end and one on the other and they went around as fast as they could.

Local travel was limited to wagon, buggy, sleigh, horseback and walking. Albert considered himself a "great walker" and thought nothing of walking to Republic and back for Sunday evening services, and later to court Florence Bryan. Even though a wagon trip to Springfield took 3-3/4 hours necessitating starting at daybreak or before, the foundry whistle in Springfield could be heard at their home. The train to Springfield could be caught at 8:00 or 9:00 a.m., returning at about 6:00 p.m.

Mollie died in 1925 and George in 1937. Albert married Florence Bryan in 1896. In 1944 he wrote a short book of his life entitled *Seventy Years of Memories*. It is from that book that all information here was taken. *Submitted by Elizabeth Skelton Copley.*

**SKELTON/RUCKER** – Seven years before the Civil War, Joel M., born March 1, 1823 and Martha E.A. Rucker Skelton, born Jan. 11, 1828, could hear the beginning rumblings in Franklin County, GA and wanted to ensure their family was far away from the coming conflict. Joel, a sixth generation American, was the son of Noel (a soldier in the War of 1812) and Margy McGee Skelton and descended from Jeremiah, Robert, John Jr. and John Sr.

*Martha E.A. Rucker Skelton, widow of Joel Skelton.*

In 1854 they came to Missouri and settled on 80 acres in Pond Creek Township of Greene County, almost four miles northwest of present-day Republic. They traveled with her parents, Tavner and Elizabeth Wade Rucker, whose youngest children, Joshua and Frances, also came, following Elizabeth's people, the Wades.

Leaving the grave of their third child Sarah who had died as an infant, they brought their five remaining children with them: Mary-8, Sarepta Ellen-6, George-4, Annie-2 and William-a baby. The only part of the trip George would later remember was crossing the Mississippi River. Two children, Martha and James, were born two and five years after they arrived.

In addition to the border outlaws, there were battles all around in Springfield, Carthage and Dug Springs besides the larger ones at Wilson's Creek in August 1861 and Pea Ridge just over the line in Arkansas in March 1862.

Joel didn't fight in the war. He had come home on Nov. 7, 1862 from working in Springfield which was under control of the South at that time. Toward the end of the next day, an area group of bushwhackers with northern sympathies rode into Joel's dooryard and (in front of his children) according to a later account by Joel's grandson Albert, they "...compelled him at the point of a gun to submit to all sort of indignities. Grandmother (Martha) pleaded with them not to kill him and offered to go and get 'Uncle' Dave Reynolds, a Northern neighbor to vouch for the fact that he had taken no part in the war. They agreed but as she got to Mr. Reynold's house, she heard the shot that killed him. Pa told me that after she got home, the neighbors of both sides were afraid to help. But finally his sister, Aunt Ellen (14 at the time), dragged and worked one way and another and got the corpse inside the house. After they got it in the house, the neighbors helped them then." Leaving Georgia hadn't kept them safe.

At the time of their father's death the children ranged from ages 3 to 16 with the oldest boy, George, age 12 and the burden of farming fell on him. Martha finished raising her family by herself with most of them settling nearby. She died three days before her 60th birthday in 1888. *Submitted by Mary Skelton Strickrodt.*

**SMITH** - Gene and Anita Smith came to Republic in 1999 from Alton, MO. Anita got sick in 1998 and wanted to move closer to medical facilities. They had both retired from a garment factory in California. Anita's mother and sister still live in California. One sister lives in San Antonio, TX. She and Gene make frequent trips to visit them. Anita had done volunteer work in Thayer, MO in the nursing home and belonged to the Silver and Gold Extension Home Makers.

When they decided to move to this area they had already looked over several places. While driving around Republic, they found the Republic Senior Friendship Center and stopped to visit and to eat. While shopping with a friend at Hobby Lobby in Springfield, Anita saw a free Realtors Book of Homes. She took it home to show Gene and to look at it. They found a picture of a house in Republic they liked. They decided to come to Republic and check it out and bought it.

Gene and Anita have three daughters and two grandchildren, a boy and a girl.

Anita's first friend in Republic was Hazel Creson. They met at the Senior Friendship Center and have remained friends all these years. Anita enjoys doing crafts and sewing at the Center. *Submitted by Anita Smith.*

**SMITH** - The family of Henry and Martha Smith moved from Vanzant, MO to Republic in 1915. The Smith family consists of Emma, who later married Joe Chastain, Ollie Mae, who married George Dennis and Leona who married Leon Barber. The Barbers had three boys and moved to California in 1935 to make their home there. Opal married Friday Dean and also moved to California to make a home. A boy, Norman "Smokey", was a year old when they came to Republic. He later married Mildred Harvill.

Front row: Ollie Dennis, Opal Smith, Agnes Dennis, Earl Ray, Norman Smith, Alma Ray, Ethel Smith, Clarence Smith; 2nd row: Willie Ray, Leona Smith, Iva Ray, Martha Smith, Henry Smith, unknown; 3rd row: Charley Ray, unknown, George Dennis, Buddy Smith, Jimmy Smith, Ransom Smith, unknown. Taken Christmas Day 1922.

Also moving to Republic about this same time were three of Henry's brothers. Jimmy was a bachelor. Buddy was divorced with a daughter Ethel and a son Clarence. Ethel married Glen Logan. Their grandson, Mike Logan, is now living in Republic. Clarence moved to California as a young man.

Henry and Martha and the three brothers lived out their lives here.

Norman and a neighbor boy, Earl Hart, in their later teens or 20s worked for John Russell in his grocery store. They drove John's truck home for lunch. The first one who finished eating ran out and laid in the seat. The last one out had to stand on the running board to steer the truck while the one laying in the seat worked the gas peddle and brakes with hands. Once Earl went on vacation to California. He sent a postal card to Russell's store. At the end of the message he wrote "John Price quit reading this card!" John worked at the Post Office. *Submitted by Gladys Mooneyham.*

**SMITH** - Walter Luther Smith (Dec. 8, 1934-Dec. 23, 1999) was born and reared in Springfield, MO. He was the second son of Walter Sherman Smith (Nov. 21, 1908-April 1963), son of Dennis Smith and Hattie Lamb Smith, and Hazel Gladys Wilson (March 14, 1916), daughter of David William Wilson and Rosa Isabell Turner Wilson. Walter's siblings: Edward Myron (May 12, 1933-July 5, 1988) and Cheryl Rosa (July 2, 1946). After attending Central High School, Walter joined the Navy and served on the USS *Castor*. Following military service Walter returned to Springfield where he began employment with Springfield City Utilities as a bus driver. He later transferred to James River Power Plant and continued his service in power production at Southwest Power Plant when it was constructed near Republic. Walter had 33 years of service with City Utilities when he retired as a supervisor of Power Production in 1992. Walter was talented in woodworking and also enjoyed golf during his retirement.

Republic provided Walter a convenient location for commuting to work, but he was more concerned about a good environment for rearing his children when he moved his family to Republic in 1972. They lived in one of the first houses built on West Jewell Street.

Walter and his wife, Linda Rae Clayton, married June 7, 1958 and divorced March 15, 1979. They had three children: Douglas Allen (Jan. 14, 1959), David Elliott (April 30, 1961) and Diane Adele (Dec. 19, 1963). Diane married Brian Corbett Buckner (Sept. 2, 1967) on Sept. 14, 1996. Her children are Nichole Gayle Bolin (June 6, 1986) and Ian Bradley Buckner (Nov. 3, 1997).

Doug manages boat facilities and delivery and lives in Springfield. David lives in Republic and is a sergeant with the Springfield Police Department where he has been employed over 20 years. Diane has worked for various Springfield radio and television stations in the traffic department, and she lives in Republic with her family. Diane's husband, Brian, serves on the Republic City Council.

On June 10, 1983, Walter married Jane Ruth Gray (Nov. 22, 1948) (see Joe Emmett Gray). Walter and Jane met during a neighborhood float trip. They enjoyed travel in their fifth-wheel, especially trips to National Parks, and were able to visit forty-eight states before Walter's illness. Their family was a priority, and

*Smith grandchildren: Ian Buckner and Nicole Bolin - 2003.*

*Smith Family in 1996, back l-r: Brian Buckner, Doug Smith, Walter Smith, David Smith. Front: Diane Buckner, Nichole Bolin, Hazel Smith, Jane Smith.*

many special memories were made on a family cruise in 1997. Walter and Jane built a new home on Miller Road in 1994 when it was one of a few on the south side of Miller Road. *Submitted by Diane Buckner.*

**SNEED/TURNER** - Don Sneed moved to Republic in 1939 with his parents, Carl and Lillie Sneed, and nine brothers and sisters. He was still in high school and graduated from Republic. It was fair time and Don had his eyes on Helen Turner of Republic to take to the "Greene County Fair." Two months later, on Nov. 22, 1941, Don and Helen were married by Judge Denny Pickel at the Greene County Courthouse. It rained, snowed and sleeted that day, but these two didn't care. The first part of their marriage was spent on other people's farms doing whatever jobs needed to be done. Don finally landed a job as a seed cleaner at the Farmer's Exchange Grainery just off Main Street in Republic. In 1944, their first daughter, Linda, was born on the Bill Robertson place north of Republic. That same year Don was drafted into the Army.

Helen was fortunate enough to buy a small home on Olive Street adjoining Carl Sneed's land. She and Linda moved there on practically nothing as the Army paid very little. They ate lots of meals with the Sneed clan. A larger home on another side of Carl's land became available, so Helen bought it on West Street. It was a surprise to Don when he got home from the service in 1945. He went back to work for MFA and in 1947 their second daughter, Peggy, was born on West Street.

The home on West Street had three acres with good pasture. Don had a pet cow named "Guernsey" that gave tons of milk, which provided for his family and some of the neighbors. He and Helen also put out huge gardens and raised pigs for meat. This was all within three blocks from Main Street inside the city limits.

There were no indoor toilets at that time and you burned wood for heat or had fuel oil brought to your home. There was no air conditioning and in 1953 Republic experienced a torrid summer that still holds records. There was a bus line that connected to Springfield and a train station on West Elm.

On Saturday nights Republic had band concerts and the stores stayed open late for the farmers to shop. On Main Street was O'Dell's Drug Store, a movie house, two hardware stores, two gas stations, a post office, a bank, a doctor's and a dentist's office, churches, and even a chicken hatchery.

The MFA provided groceries, produce, meats, feed, live chickens, fertilizer and even gasoline.

At Christmas, bulk candy and fresh trees scented the whole store. In 1950, Don became store manager and retired in 1984. The Sneeds still live in Republic and have been married for

64 years. Linda married Ron Oswalt and they have four daughters and eight grandchildren. Peggy lives in Kansas City and has two sons and three granddaughters. *Submitted by Linda (Sneed) Oswalt.*

**SNEED/WHEATLEY -** This is the Republic history of the Carl Sneed family, which began here in 1939. Carl and Lillie (Wheatley) Sneed moved from Springfield to north of Republic near the beacon light. They had 10 children at that time. Their oldest son, Ted, had already died in 1935. Their children were Phillip, Don, Lloyd, Raymond, Evelyn, John, Barbara, Wanda, Bob and Edna.

Carl was a farmer for many years, and Lillie took care of the home and children. In 1945, the Sneeds moved into Republic on West Elm. Even though it was only three blocks from downtown (which consisted of East Elm, West Elm and Main Street), Carl had 11 acres on which he raised cattle, horses and chickens. He had a huge garden to help feed his family and later he also raised oats on part of his land. There was an old apple orchard that had knurled limbs that provided hours of fun for the children. A huge catalpa tree gave them catalpa worms for fishing and a mulberry tree had sweet berries which were a summer delight. A lot of delicious meals were provided in that home and a lot of Christmases were enjoyed over the years by the large family and their offspring.

*Carl and Lillie Sneed seated in back row, l-r: Johnny, Raymond, Bob, Don; front row: Edna, Evelyn, Barbara, Wanda – middle 1950s.*

Their son, Phillip and his wife were killed in a car wreck. He and his bride of only three weeks, Earlene (Alms), taught school and were missed by many people; Lloyd was killed in WW II by a sniper in Italy who did not know the war was over; Raymond lived in California for over 40 years and passed away Dec. 29, 2005 in California; Evelyn and her husband, Harold Wampler, have called Clever home all their married lives. They have two children, two grandchildren, and six great-grandchildren; John and his wife Sandy have five sons. John lives in Republic on old Sneed land and is retired from Kraft. They have five grandchildren and one great-grandchild; Barbara passed away in 1993 and Bob passed away in 2003, both had children and grandchildren; Edna and her husband Paul Dean live in Republic and have both retired. They have three children, seven grandchildren and one great-grandchild; Wanda lives in Mt. Vernon. She has eight children, 25 grandchildren and eight great-grandchildren; Don and wife Helen have two daughters, six grandchildren and 11 great-grandchildren.

Carl and Lillie Sneed both passed away in the 1970s, but their lives reflected the wholesome living that a hometown quality like Republic provides for its citizens. Today there are lots of banks, churches, restaurants, great schools, Wal-Mart, Lowes, etc., and Republic is still a great place to call home. *Submitted by Don Sneed.*

**SNYDER -** Ruth Marie Snyder was born Dec. 1, 1904. After growing up in Republic, Ruth relocated to California as a young adult becoming an automobile mechanic. She was part of the large service department of San Francisco's Hudson Motor dealer, Glen C. Stater. At this time, she was thought to be the only woman mechanic in California and possibly in the nation, serving in this position. Ruth, being an expert auto mechanic, developed the motor check up system that later became a standard procedure for dealers.

*Ruth Snyder*

After Ruth's success with Ford Motor Co., she returned to her hometown, Republic, to establish a very different business of her own. She opened Republic Sundries, a small drug store and eatery. She became well-known for her homemade pies, plate lunches and sandwiches, like her unique grilled pimento cheese. She became the cook for the local Kiwanis Club, preparing special meals for their regular meetings and enthusiastically supported their club activities. Despite a knee disability that had resulted from an injury received in a car accident during her youth, Ruth enthusiastically played in softball games to help the Kiwanis in fund raising for local parks.

Always loyal to her commitments, she was forever a very devoted Ford owner, family member, a very faithful Disciple of Christ Christian Church member, supporter of school sports and activities, and very proud to be a citizen of Republic.

Her sisters and brother, Keturah Snyder Coggin, Naomi Snyder Carter and Harve Snyder also lived most of their lives in the Republic area. Ruth Snyder died Feb. 17, 1990 and is buried in Evergreen Cemetery. *Submitted by Christy Keller.*

**SNYDER/ALLEN -** Golda (Allen) and Harve Snyder, also known as Goldie and Juggy, were life long residents of the Republic area. They owned and operated a pool hall and Juggy's Cigar and Tobacco Store on Main Street Republic. Golda was known for her hamburgers and chili, and Harve was known for his jolly, friendly spirit. After Harve's death, their daughter, Beth "Puge" and her husband, Adrian "Heavy" Cox, relocated to Republic to help with the businesses.

*Golda Allen Snyder.*   *Harve Snyder.*

Golda lived with Beth and "Heavy" caring for their young daughters, Libby and Phyllis. The granddaughters have fond memories of their grandmother, sewing identical dresses for them for every occasion. The girls were close in age, 12 months and four days difference in age, and Golda often dressed them like they were twins. She sewed dresses, play clothes and beautiful winter coats. Golda could crochet beautifully making gifts for others such as crocheted dish towels and pillowcases.

She enjoyed going to the home of her sister in Republic, Bernice Allen Noe, and her mother, Sally Allen; they would piece quilts and braid rugs. She also loved to visit her

*Phyllis Cox Carlson and Libby Cox West.*

sister, Audrey Allen Britian, in Mountain Grove, MO, taking the train from the Republic Depot to the Mountain Grove Depot. The granddaughters talk about their grandmother taking the "trip of her life" to visit the World's Fair, New York and Niagara Falls.

While living at home with their Grandma Goldie, Phyllis and Libby watched her "wring" the necks of chickens, pluck the feathers, and make golden fried chicken. In the summer when the family butchered a beef, Grandma Goldie would can the meat. In the winter, she would open a jar of the flavorful canned beef and make delicious hot stew or vegetable soup. She also made the famous "Grandma Goldie Cake," a rich, moist chocolate cake that she often frosted with caramel icing.

A special treat for the granddaughters was for Grandma Goldie to let them sleep with her and listen to her favorite radio program, *"Fibber McGee and Molly."* Grandma Goldie took great care of her granddaughters, Phyllis (Cox) Carlson and Libby (Cox) West, and taught them much that would prepare them for raising their own daughters: Natalie and Christine Carlson, and Jerri, Barbie, Mindy and Marti West. *Submitted by Natalie Allen.*

**SOBOTKA -** In August 1949, Russell B. Sobotka sold his hardware in Ridgeway, MO and moved with his wife Reva and their infant daughter Andrea to Republic, MO. He joined his twin brother, Randall J. Sobotka, in the ownership and operation of Owen and Short Hardware. Randall, a WWII hero, had completed his tour of duty and moved to Republic previously with his wife Bea and their young son Stephen Randall. Stephen was born in March 1945. Their daughter Susan Kay was born in July 1949.

*Russell Sobotka at Owen & Short Hardware, Republic, MO.*

The identical twin brothers were born March 27, 1916, in Cainsville, MO, on the family farm. Owen and Short, named for former owners, Glenn Owen and Fred Short, was located at the southwest corner of Main Street and Grant. Russell and Randall operated a plumbing and electrical contracting business in addition to hardware sales from that site. Their contract work included the construction of new schools for numerous area towns, including Republic. The hardware was one of the Republic businesses that remained open late on Saturday evenings. A line of old theater seats was provided inside the building for "loafing." Outside, in front of the store, benches were often filled with town residents, including the colorful Shorty Walker.

In December 1959, Russell moved across Main Street to the Post Office and became Republic's postal clerk under Postmaster Linzee Wells. He continued as an employee of the postal service, becoming assistant postmaster of Republic in 1970. In 1972 he was appointed postmaster for Billings, MO.

In the mid-1970s Reva and Russell Sobotka purchased a house on east Elm Street in Republic. Reva and a group of friends renovated the former Thurman Funeral Home with Russell's help and created "Elm House." Reva (Alexander), born in Cainsville, MO in September 1920, had been interested in hand crafts for many years. At Elm House amid other talented crafters, she taught needlework to many eager learners.

Russell retired in 1985 and the couple moved to Joplin, MO where Russell died in January 1992 and Reva in January 2005. After Russell moved to the Post Office, Randall continued at Owen and Short with the help of his wife Bea.

Bea (Ridley) Sobotka was born in July 1920, in the state of Georgia. She was an active member of the First Christian Church in Republic, where she served in many capacities and was a loyal choir member. Bea loved books and reading. She was a member of the Greene County Library Board.

In the early 1980s Randall sold Owen and Short, but remained in the contracting business. Later he worked part-time from his home in Republic, unable to retire due to the demand for his skill and expertise. Randall died in October 1986. *Submitted by Andrea Logan.*

**SPARKMAN/DICKERSON -** John was born Aug. 28, 1925 in Chillicothe, OH to William Ross and Sallie (Owen) Sparkman. He moved to Missouri at one year of age. He attended Mt. Etna School, later Republic High School, where he graduated in 1943. He served in the U.S. Army from 1944-47. He graduated from MU with a master in agriculture education and dairy science and graduated from Drury with a master in business. He was elected to the Dairy Hall of Honor at MU in 1968, served as president of Missouri and American Milking Shorthorn Society, and he was a charter member and president of the Missouri Dairy Fieldman and Sanitarians. He also served as 4-H leader for over 30 years while he coached many state and national dairy teams and judged state and international dairy shows. The children and John showed dairy cattle for years. The grandchildren also enjoyed showing cattle.

*Front: John and Dottie Sparkman, Sally; Back: John, Don and Glen.*

John joined Kraft field department in January 1955, serving until he retired in 1990 with 37 years of service. He received the Kraft Presidential Award of Excellence.

On Aug. 3, 1952 he married Dorothy Dickerson in Catlin, IL. They lived in Shoemaker, PA where their daughter Sally Jean was born Sept. 9, 1953. After John joined Kraft and was living in Springfield, John Allen was born March 16, 1955 and Don Lee was born Sept. 30, 1958. While living in Galena, William Glen was born Sept. 3, 1961.

In the mid-1960s John and Dorothy moved their family to the Sparkman family farm, northeast of Republic. There they raised their family and that is where Dorothy and two of her sons and their families still reside.

John served as livestock superintendent and was on the advisory board at the Ozark Empire Fair. He also was past president and legislative chairman on Greene County Farm Bureau Board of Directors. He also served on Roy Blunt's advisory board.

John's 12 grandchildren were his pride and joy: Sarah, Kerry, Ross, Susan, Li'l John, Michael, Josie, Shanna, Christian, Patricia, Alaina and Stephanie. John loved watching Alaina, Josie and Stephanie play sports; to him all the team's members were his grandchildren.

John passed away on March 13, 2003 in his home, burial was in the Sparkman family plot in Evergreen Cemetery. *Submitted by Dorothy Sparkman.*

**SPARKMAN/OWEN -** William Ross Sparkman (1900-1979) grew up one and half miles northeast of Republic, MO on the family farm of his parents, John Alexander (1861-1925) and Minnie Mae (Roush) Sparkman (1872-1951). Ross, the first born, had one brother Guy and four sisters: Leora, Elma, Stella and Lucy. All were born in the two-story home, and attended the one-room Mt. Etna School over a mile away. Ross married Sarah "Sallie" Edith (Owen) (1902-1984), then moved to Lynchburg, OH where his Roush grandparents lived. Their first son John Arthur (1925-2003) was born there. Ross's father died that same year. Returning to Republic, Ross and Sallie purchased most of the farm from his mother, and Minnie moved into Republic. Ross and Sallie's other children were: stillborn twin daughters in 1927, Mae Belle (1928), Junior Ross (1931-1990), Marjorie (1934), and Mary (1936). All were born at home, with the same family doctor, Dr. E.L. Beal, a longtime Republic physician.

*Front: Ross, Mary, Sallie. Back: Junior, Marjorie, Mae Belle, and John Sparkman.*

Sarah "Sallie" Sparkman, born northwest of Springfield, MO in the family home near the old zoo park. Her parents, Pleasant Wade (1866-1941) and Myrtle (Owen) (1874-1944) were cousins.

"P.W." was a cattleman, had a butcher shop on the east side of old Highway 13, north of the zoo. Myrtle was a homemaker. They had six children: Lela, Leo, Anna, Sallie, Harry and Irma. P.W., a campaigner, was well known around the courthouse and was committee man on Route #5. His grandchildren helped him pass out Roosevelt-Garner buttons. Many families survived because of WPA jobs building roads, buildings, and bridges during the lean hard times of the 1930s, and into the WWII years. His grandchildren remember his struggle to walk and climb the hill on their Sunday afternoon trips to the zoo. They remember nickels he had in his pocket for the Grapette pop and candy bar treat on the way home. He died in 1941 of a heart attack. They didn't get to say goodbye or get another hug. Sallie's great-grandfather, Solomon Owen was the first judge in Greene County. The Scotch-Irish Owen family came in 1836 from Sullivan County in southern Tennessee. Several other members of her family held public office as sheriffs, and her brother Leo Owen was the Republic Marshal from 1958 thru 1970.

Living through drought years of 1935 and 1936 was a daily struggle for both man and beast. Because of the crop losses, mortgage payments were hard to come by. The rains returned, the family had stacked their wheat and oats into huge stacks in the center of one field, waiting on the thrashing machine to come. Lightening struck the stacks, and all the grain crop for the year was lost! The farm was saved only because the bank delayed payment until the following year. One lesson learned, never stack all the crops in one place.

All five children attended the same one-room school at Mt. Etna, as did their father and his siblings. Because of farm chores and the bus schedule, many times they walked to Republic High until they could drive an old 1932 Chevrolet car. John graduated in 1943, Mae Belle in 1946, Junior in 1949, Marjorie and Mary in 1952. (Mary started school at age 5, skipping a grade and went thru with her sister Marjorie.) Junior purchased Mt. Etna School building in 1954 moving it to his acreage. He lowered the roof and it became a home for himself, his wife Burma Jean and their four children. They sold it to his brother John and it remains Dorothy's home today.

The Sparkman family had a narrow escape before 5:00 a.m. on April 27, 1946 when their home caught fire in an upstairs storeroom. Something fell, and the noise awoke the sleeping family. The homeplace was gone in minutes. Ross, Sallie, and their four children were not injured and very thankful to be alive. Their son John was away in the service for WWII.

*Sparkman-Owen family in front of Sparkman home 1945.*

Both John and Junior served their country. John in Europe and Junior in the Air Force during the Korean War. Junior met his future wife, Burma McMullan, while stationed in Albany, GA. John met his wife, Dorothy Dickerson from Illinois, while he was at MU and she was attending Stephen's College in Columbia, MO. Ross and Sallie's daughters found their mates in local families.

The Sparkmans rebuilt in 1947. The oak lumber came from timber on the farm. The exterior of native stone was hauled from Halltown. Ross and Sallie continued to live there until their passing. A tornado in 1971 downed cedar trees planted by John Alexander, in the early 1900s. These trees saved the home from damage, but the storm took the roof off the barn. Their grandson John Allen and wife

Cassie did major remodeling, but saved most of the exterior and live there today with their three children. Also living on the homeplace are: another grandson Glen and wife Jo and their two granddaughters; granddaughters, Diana (Davis) Perryman and her two sons; and Karen (Fuhr) and her husband Robert Foster and their three children. All are grateful that the Sparkmans were good stewards of their land on Sparkman Drive. Ross and Sallie enjoyed and spoiled 17 grandchildren: (John's four, Mae Belle's three, Junior's four, Marjorie's two and Mary's four).

Ross and Sallie Sparkman were buried in the Sparkman family plot at Evergreen Cemetery. Their son John Arthur was buried there and their twin infant daughters. Their son Junior Ross was buried in Moultrie, GA near his family there. *Submitted by Cynthia Spaethe.*

**SPARKMAN/RAINEY** - William David (1825-1910) married Jane C. (Rainey) Sparkman (1825-1908) in Maury County, TN. In 1856, they came by wagon train to Greene County with their children Allen (1848-1903), Oren "Iron" (1850), S. Elizabeth (1852-1863), Thomas Jefferson (1854-1919) and a baby daughter S. A. who died on the trip.

In 1857, the Sparkman home was built on their land two miles east of Republic, behind the Harrington Cemetery. Children born in Missouri were Minerva (1857-1924), James M. (1859-?), John A. (1861-1925) and Mary A. (1864-1904). They also cared for a foster daughter, Edna (Sturman) Land (1876-?), and an orphaned nephew, Johnny Meese.

Jane Sparkman, the oldest daughter of Chesley O. (1802-1866) and Sarah B. (White) Rainey (1805-1878), had come to Greene County in 1854, also from Maury County, TN. They purchased land from John McCall in 1855, two miles west of Brookline, and there James H. Goodwin, a surveyor, and Chesley O. Rainey plotted out the early settlement of Little York. Chesley and Jane had 13 children.

The Sparkmans came to America in 1636, landing in Virginia, and were Scottish. In 1728, John A. Sparkman filed a will in Raleigh, NC. After fighting in early American wars, some had land grants. The Sparkmans came by wagon to middle Tennessee in 1794. A maiden name was used in naming the county of Williamson. That Sparkman family was William III (1764-1832) and his wife Rosanna (Williams) Sparkman (1769-1861), who were parents of Williams Sparkman (1799-1847) and Elizabeth (Vestal) Sparkman (1800-1910). They married April 1820. They were parents of William David (the subject of this tracing). William David's father, Williams, died in 1847, and in December he married Jane C. Rainey. They lived in Maury County, until there was need of more land to provide for their family. In 1856 they came to Greene County. They left behind many family members, that they would never see again. W.D.'s mother, Elizabeth, lived on to be 110, when she died the same year as her son William David in Missouri (at age 85).

Most Sparkmans were farmers, having orchards and grain fields, in Tennessee and again, north and east of Republic. Many of this Tennessee Sparkman family are at rest in the beautiful sloping hillside Sparkman Cemetery in Boston, TN. Seth Sparkman (l797-1884), uncle to William David, was an early teacher and preacher in the church. In 1854, Seth and wife Rebecca (Latta) donated land to the town of Boston to have a meeting house and country school. Seth wrote in his papers this motto: "Live as if you expect to remain here, and be ready to go tomorrow!"

William David served in the Home Guard during the Civil War. Their home was only one and a half miles (as the crow flies) from the Battle of Wilson's Creek. Hearing cannon fire the morning of Aug. 10, 1861, the Sparkman family became very frightened. The noise was so loud, Jane in her excitement, raced outside to retrieve the featherbed she had airing on her clothesline. She ran back inside, tossing it on her bed, before she realized her baby was there! Baby John, only 3 weeks old, was quickly rescued! The family didn't learn until later, what a horrible battle had been fought, so close to their home and the terrible loss of life that day!

In 1863, the Sparkman family became very ill with the measles and their daughter Elizabeth (age 11) died and was buried nearby in the Harrington Cemetery. Her father W.D. went AWOL during this time to help care for his family.

William David and Jane had 60 years together and were laid to rest in the Harrington Cemetery as were her parents, Chesley and Sarah Rainey, and many other family members.

Elma (Sparkman) Green and husband Edgar and daughters Norma, Rosena and Roberta made their home on the homestead that her grandfather William David had built. Elma is 98, now living in Springfield, but the homeplace still provides shelter for others and is now 150 years old. *Submitted by Judy Steward.*

**SPARKMAN/ROUSH** - John Alexander Sparkman (1861-1925), the youngest son of William David (1825-1910) and Jane Catherine (Rainey) Sparkman (1825-1908), purchased a home about one and a half miles northeast of Republic, MO from John A. Youngblood, a surveyor, in the late 1800s. On April 6, 1899, John married Minnie Mae (Roush) Sparkman (1872-1951).

Minnie's parents were John Allen (1850-1927) and Mary "Mollie" (Troutwine) Roush (1850-1948) coming to Republic in 1894. John and Mollie were born in Russell, OH, but had lived in Halstead, KS for several years. They purchased a farm that joined John Sparkman's land; however, in 1919, the Roushs, because of ill health and age, returned to live near their birthplace, Lynchburg, OH. Some of their seven children were living there. John and Mollie were buried there in 1927 and 1948, respectively.

John and Minnie Sparkman had two sons and four daughters, all born at home. Their children were: Ross (1900-1979), Leora (1903-1990), Guy (1905-1998), Elma (1908), Stella (1911-1999) and Lucy (1913-1985). The family worked long hours caring for farm animals, orchards, and harvesting grain crops to supply the basic needs for food the year around. A large cellar was built to store the produce thru winter months. It also served as a storm shelter many times and is still being used by John and Minnie's great-grandson John Allen and Cassie Sparkman, and their three children, who make their home on the homeplace on Sparkman Drive.

John and Minnie were founding members of the early Christian Church in Republic. John's great uncle, Seth Sparkman (l797-1884) was an early circuit rider preacher in middle Tennessee. Before the Civil War in 1854, he donated land to construct a meeting place in Boston, TN and the family and others also helped.

There is an active group meeting in the original structure walls in Williamson County. Some Sparkman relatives still worship there. Boston was a thriving town until the mill shut down and the rail line moved. Only the meeting house and a small country store remain near the clear running stream. Among the peaceful valley, grain fields, on a sloping hillside, there is a beautifully kept Sparkman Cemetery.

After John's death in 1925, his widow Minnie, leased parts of farms to local men, testing her land for enough ore to be profitable to mine. This was fruitless, so when the leases ran out, she sold some and leased other farms to family members. Minnie and children moved into Republic, where the younger daughters finished school. The Sparkman children had attended Mt. Etna, a one-room country school.

*Minnie Sparkman and family, 1938/39.*

Minnie became active in several clubs and attended church services regularly. Her relatives have many quilts, woven rugs, and crocheted items, that she spent many hours of loving labor making. John and Minnie had 26 grandchildren. Minnie's last home was on West Avenue, that her son Guy built and where her grandson James and Kelly Sparkman, and their three children make their home today. Several grandchildren and great-grandchildren continue being good stewards of the Sparkman land on which they live.

John and Minnie Sparkman are at rest at Evergreen Cemetery, in Republic, as are his siblings, and three of their children and mates, including son, Ross and wife Sallie Sparkman, son Guy and wife Lorene (Mills) Sparkman, daughter Stella Johnson and husband Lawrence, son-in-law Edgar Green, and several grandchildren.

Their daughter Lucy Blades and husband Haven are buried at Wade Chapel, west of Republic. Their daughter Leora Ramsey and husband Hugh were laid to rest at Clear Creek Cemetery in northern Greene County. Their daughter-in-law Cletis (Ramsey) Sparkman was buried in the Ramsey Cemetery, near Rogersville. *Submitted by Jerry C. Fuhr.*

**STEELE** - The Steele family first came to America in 1801 from northern Ireland. Robert Steele met Nancy Dunshee on the *Strafford*. The ship strayed from its course before landing in Philadelphia. Robert fell ill to typhoid fever and was delirious for weeks. When he became aware of his surroundings he discovered his money had been stolen, so he had to work before he and Nancy could marry.

*Steele family about 1954. Back: Christie Steele, Glen Steele, Mary Keltner, Dixie Keltner, Harry Steele, Clyde Steele, John Steele; front: J.W. Steele with dog, Barbara Steele, Steve Steele, and Jo Ann Keltner.*

Robert and Nancy settled in the Catskills of New York where they had 12 children. Two of the Steele children, William and John, migrated in 1840 to Greene County, MO, by way of Georgia and settled in the Wilson's Creek area. William had married Roxanna Neal in Georgia. They brought with them two slaves, Rhoda and Wiley, who they had received as wedding gifts. William and Roxanna had four children: William Fletcher, Anne Elizabeth, Andrew McCord and Mary Cornelia.

William Fletcher was born Oct. 24, 1842. On Oct. 8, 1865 he married Mary Catherine Moore. Five children were born: William Jr., Savilla Belle Rose, Lena Leota Young, John Almus and Robbie.

Ann Elizabeth Steele was born March 29, 1842 and died in 1862.

Andrew McCord Steele was born May 9, 1846. He enlisted July 1, 1864 in the 16th Cavalry at Marionville, MO. He was mustered in Aug. 23, 1864 at Springfield, MO. Andrew was a bugler under Capt. W.F. McCullah's Company H. After being mustered out in Springfield on July 1, 1865, Andrew traveled a lot working on the telegraph lines. He married in Oil City, PA and had four children. At the time of his death in 1888, Andrew was nearly deaf, experiencing numerous headaches, probably as a result of the war.

Mary Cornelia Steele married Jerome Yarbrough, a Civil War veteran, July 22, 1866 and had 16 children.

Before the Civil War had begun, the elder William F. Steele died on July 22, 1848. Roxanna married John A. Ray, a widower with one daughter, Frances Elizabeth. Mr. and Mrs. Ray had seven more children: Appolina, Livonia, John Wesley, Olivia, Marshall, Marcellus and Charles Edward.

William Fletcher Steele's family remained in the Battlefield and Wilson's Creek area for many years.

William Fletcher Steele Jr.'s murder has become the oldest unsolved murder in Christian County. While eating supper May 2, 1913, someone shot him from behind.

The son of William and Mary Steele, John Almus, married Christie McConnell from Nixa. They had four children: Glen, who migrated to California in the 40s, Mary married Victor Keltner, Harry married Evelyn Torrence from Kansas when he was in WWII, and Clyde who also served in WWII and the Korean conflict

The children of Harry carry on the family name in this area. *Submitted by Dixie Keltner.*

**STEPHENSON** - John Stephenson, an Irish immigrant and veteran of the War of 1812, traveled in a wagon train to Greene County from Roane County, TN in 1843. John and his wife Sarah homesteaded land west of Nixa, at the northwest corner of present day Hwy. M and Hwy. 14, and began farming. One of his sons, Matthew, who was raised on the family farm, eventually saw two of his own sons fight for the Union during the Civil War. John was killed at the battle of Pleasant Hill, LA, and Jacob was seriously wounded at Franklin, TN.

When the war ended Jacob returned to Christian County, married Harriet Keltner and raised his own family, which included eight children. One of his sons, Joseph Lonzo, married Mary Jane Sanders and moved to a rock house overlooking the James River near his relatives, the Steinerts. Here, Joe and Jane raised their family of seven children, including Ruby, "Jack," Enid, Billy, Anna, "Dock" and Mary Jo. Eventually Joe and Jane moved to Republic along with Jack, Dock and Mary Jo.

Dock continued to live with his parents and cared for them until their death. Mary Jo graduated from RHS and married Doug Anderson. They eventually purchased a farm on the Greene-Christian County line where their son Mark still lives. Jack worked in the local orchards for several years until he enlisted in the Army during WWII. He was stationed for the duration of the war at Edwards AFB in Victorville, CA, along with several other Republic residents. While in the Army he met and married Rozella Freeman.

Upon returning to Republic after the war, he was employed as a meat-cutter and store clerk at Eagan's Market on Main Street for several years until he retired because of ill health. He and Rozella, raised two children, Jim Young, Rozella's son from a previous marriage, and "Tony" Stephenson, in their humble home on South Main Street. Jack passed away in 1973 and Rozella in 1996. Jim eventually moved to Fresno, CA and lived there for the rest of his life, passing away in 2002. Tony attended the College of the Ozarks and after receiving his degree, married Janet Van Da Griff of Verona, MO. They returned to Republic where Tony became a teacher and administrator at RHS and Janet had a long career in the health services area. They have one daughter, Kristen, who also became a teacher. She married Adam Owens, son of the late Bob and Roberta Owens, in 2000 and they now reside in St. Louis where Adam is a firefighter and Kristen is a homemaker. Tony and Janet currently reside in the Battlefield area and although both are retired, Tony still teaches history part-time at RHS.

Most of the Stephenson family is buried at Payne Cemetery on the banks of the James River and the family is related to several of the older area families in Greene and Christian counties, including the Anderson, Breazeale, Faught, Haguewood, Hicks, Keltner, Maynard, Slay, Steinert and Young families. *Submitted by Clifford Stephenson.*

**STEWART/GUYTON** - William Stewart born 1758 in Carlow, Ireland died in 1834. His wife Elizabeth Guyton was born in 1765 and died 1807 in Baltimore, MD. They had eight children.

John was born 1789 in Baltimore, MD and died 1873 in Greene County, MO. Wife Sarah Davis was born in 1792 and died 1880 in Greene County. They were married in 1811 in Bledsoe, TN. They had nine children.

Claiborne was born April 1840 in Bledsoe, TN, dying September 1908 in Ash Grove, MO. Claiborne married Frances Elizabeth Ray, born in 1844 in TN died in July 1895 in Patterson, Greene County, MO. They were married in 1865 in Springfield, MO and had 10 children.

Jonathan born 1859; Henryettea born 1866 in Patterson, Greene County, MO; Edwin J. born July 24, 1869 in Springfield, MO, mar-

*Back, l-r: Tommy, Elizabeth, Edwin, Walter; front: Jimmy, Grace, Claiborne, Frances Elizabeth, and Martha Stewart.*

ried Betty Young. They had two children, Verna married Roy McDaniel and Ralph marrying Dora Perkins. This family lived two miles south of the town of Battlefield. Edwin was a big stockman and horse trader. He platted the land for the city of Battlefield.

Edmond born 1870 in Springfield, MO; Walter was born June 1873 in Wilson Township, Greene County, MO, marrying Hattie Perkins. They had four children: Elsie M. married Ellis O'Neal; Tressie married Clyde Davis; Paul and Roy. Walter's family lived at Terrell Creek Station, which was a stop for the stage coach on the Old Wire Road. It had a grist mill, a store, post office, depot and a country school named Sharon Hill.

James, born December 1876 in Wilson Township, Greene County, MO, married Lisa. They had two children: Hubert who married Lucy Meese, and Dorothy who married Glen McElhaney. Jim was a good stockman and his place was next to the Wilson's Creek Battlegrounds.

Tommy married Josie, they had no children. Their home was on the hill by Wilson Creek Bridge on East Elm Street Road, daughter Martha was born in 1881, Grace was born in August 1882, and Elizabeth and Martha, no dates available. *Submitted by Nell Green.*

**STEWART/RAY** - Claiborne Jerome Stewart married Frances Elizabeth Ray Sept. 7, 1865 at the Ray House on the Wilson's Creek Battlefield. They had eight children, one of them was Walter Lafayette Stewart. Walter (June 14, 1873-Feb. 3, 1947) married Hattie Perkins (l877-Sept. 23, 1964) on Feb, 2, 1896. They had four children: Tressie R., Elsie, Roy and Paul. They had a large farm in Christian County with Terrell Creek running thru the farm. Walter was a farmer and a retail merchant, building a stockyard by the Missouri Pacific Railroad and calling it Terrell Station; farmers brought their animals there to ship them to the stockyards in Springfield. There was also a grocery store not far away.

George Henry Davis (Sept. 30, 1869-June 26, 1971) married Emily Cordelia Pearce (1866-Aug. 25, 1927) and they had three children: Clyde, Blanche and Harold. Henry and Emily were full time farmers and had a large farm on Terrell Creek in Christian County. George died at the age of 101 years, Emily was 61 at her death, both are buried at Wise Hill Cemetery, one mile north of Clever, MO in Christian County.

Tressie Stewart married Clyde V. Davis, son of George Henry Davis, Dec. 23, 1915. They had three children: Marcella, Don and Mildred. Clyde and

*Tressie and Clyde Davis.*

*Stephenson family photo taken in the late 1940s or early 50s at Brooks Street home of Joe and Jane Stephenson. Front, l-r: Dock, Jane, Joe, Ruby (Jernigan); back: Mary Joe (Anderson), Jack, Enid (Steinert).*

Tressie owned a farm with approximately 300 acres in Christian County with Terrell Creek running thru their land, and there was a large cave on the land. Clyde and Tressie farmed full time, having a milking herd, beef cattle, hogs and sheep. Retiring in 1956, they sold the farm to Leonard Fugitt of Republic. Tressie and Clyde moved to Republic after the sale. Clyde Davis (Aug. 23, 1895-Nov. 2, 1963) was 68 when he died and Tressie Stewart Davis (Nov. 4, 1896-May 17, 1980) was 83 when she died.

Mildred Davis, daughter of Clyde and Tressie Stewart Davis, granddaughter of Walter Layfette and Hattie Perkins Stewart, married Eual L. McCroskey on June 7, 1946.

James Madison McCroskey was one of three brothers settling in Christian and Greene County from Virginia and Tennessee. James Madison McCroskey and Rachel Gibson had 10 children. James and Rachel were the great-grandparents of Eual McCroskey. One of James' sons, Matthew Carson McCroskey and wife Priscilla Jane Harris, were well-known in Greene County. His occupation was farming and he and Priscilla owned 100 acres around Springfield, MO. Matthew and Priscilla had 12 children. Their son June (June 16, 1891-March 12, 1973) was married to Edna Thomas (April 25, 1890-Feb. 1, 1958) Nov 1, 1914 in Ozark, MO; they had six children, which at this time two are still living. June and Edna were Eual McCroskey's parents.

Edna was a nurse at the Springfield Baptist Hospital for several years. June's occupation was farming. He was a long time deacon in the Macedonia Baptist Church and served on the Greene County Sales Association Board. *Submitted by Bruce McCroskey.*

**STEWART/SHELTON** - Tommy Stewart and Josie Shelton met at the Nelson Mill in Christian County. During their courtship, Tommy would make frequent trips in his buggy to see Josie. He would wrap heated bricks in newspaper to keep Josie's feet warm during their buggy ride. After their marriage in 1906, they settled on a farm on East Elm Street across from the Wilson's Creek Battlefield in Republic. Tommy was a well dressed man who emphasized the importance of never going cheap on his cowboy hat and cowboy boots, so he was never without his Stetson hat. Tommy and Josie attended the Wilson Creek Church. When Tommy passed away, Josie's brother, William Shelton and his wife Tressie, bought the farm and cared for Josie. Josie and Tressie were both accomplished horsewomen who loved riding side saddle on their horses. William Shelton enjoyed gaited horses and felt that any good horse would roll on its back from side to side.

*Back, l-r: Katie Shelton, Wallace Shelton, Edith Shelton. Front: Tressie Shelton, John Charles Carlson "J.C.", and Will Shelton.*

William and Tressie Shelton entered a 'calling contest' which was held at the Shrine Mosque in Springfield. William took first place in the contest with his hog calling and won $5.00 while Tressie placed second in the husband calling contest and won $2.50.

William and Tressie were the proud parents of Wallace Shelton (born 1912), Edith Shelton (born 1916) and Katie Shelton (born 1918).

Tressie Shelton was very social and enjoyed visiting with her neighbor friends. Tressie and her neighbors, Blanche Hampton, Bessie McElhaney, Helen Chastain, Lucille Cook, Elsie Thomas and Dorothy Stewart McElhaney and others, would gather monthly for a quilting party. The women would work on their patch quilts and talk; then their husbands would join them for a big noon dinner. *Submitted by Edith Shelton Carlson.*

**STEWART/YOUNG** - Edwin Jasper "E.J." Stewart, as he was known by friends and family, married Betty Young, living two miles south of what is now known as the city of Battlefield. They had two children, Verna who married Roy McDaniel and Ralph Stewart who married Dora Perkins.

E.J. made trips out west to Texas, New Mexico, Colorado and Wyoming to buy cattle and horses. He would then ship them by rail to Battlefield. At that time there were stock pens next to the Missouri Pacific Depot in Battlefield. E.J. also ran a livery stable in Battlefield.

E.J. is responsible for platting the land and originating the city of Battlefield in 1906. The original plat was made naming the town "Stewart", but there was another town in Missouri named Stewartville so the name was changed to Battlefield. The residence lots were advertised for $15.00 to $35.00 and business lots for $35.00 to $50.00. These were for sale for 30 days only from Aug. 1 to Sept. 1, 1906. Terms were cash or easy terms on time payments. Battlefield was advertised as a station on the Missouri Pacific Railroad in sight of the famous Wilson's Creek Battleground, where the next Congress was to establish a National Park. It was also within two miles of the great Blue Springs fishing resort on James River, near Nelson's Water Mill.

The advertisement read "In the heart of one of the greatest farm, fruit, and stock growing localities in southwest Missouri. A healthy suburban resort, with the best public roads for business and retired persons, and the best of locations for small business enterprises. In the neighborhood of wealthy and enterprising farmers with no town east, south, or southwest within 10 miles of the city."

Ralph and Dora Stewart had no children. Verna and Roy McDaniel had six children: Doris, Leon, Ralph, Vernalee, Nell and Madge.

*Pam, Charles, Virginia and Ralph McDaniel.*

Ralph McDaniel was a 1941 graduate of RHS. He then joined the Air Force and was stationed in England. After the war he married Virginia Jordan. They had two children, Pam and Charles. Ralph worked at the Federal Medical Center until retirement. *Submitted by Ralph McDaniel, grandson of E.J. Stewart.*

**STICKNEY** - The Stickney Fruit Farm was on the east side of Highway 60 where the present Sonic and all the businesses north along the highway are located. The farm consisted of 12 acres of concord grapes, several acres of strawberries, and a small peach orchard. In the 1920s there were many acres of grapes in this area and at that time there was a Grape Growers Association.

*John B. Stickney in front of his store in Mtn. Grove. Picture taken before moving to Republic.*

The grapes were picked and packed in wooden baskets that held six pounds of grapes. These baskets were then placed in refrigerated Frisco cars and shipped to various parts of the United States. Several years later the grapes were picked and put in wooden beer lugs and trucked to Arkansas, maybe Tontitown, where grapes are now picked by machines. When Zetta May's father died in 1950, she and her mother, also named Zetta, were unable to continue with the farm.

John B. Stickney and family also had a general dry goods, shoe store, and shoe repair shop on the east side of Main Street in town. For several years the elder Zetta Stickney was city clerk and later worked for Curtis Packard Insurance Agency. They were faithful members of the Hood Methodist Church.

Zetta, the daughter, graduated from Republic High School in 1932. Later she attended State Teachers College in Springfield and Missouri University earning a degree in Vocational Home Economics. She taught three years at Republic High School and in 1941 moved to Lamar, MO where she taught at Lamar High School until retiring from teaching.

Zetta has many great memories of growing up in Republic, a town which at that time had a population of less than 1,000. *Submitted by Zetta May Combs.*

**STUFFLEBEAM** - Dr. Charles E. Stufflebeam was elected to the Republic Board of Education in 1979. He served five years as secretary of the board and one year as president; a new high school building was constructed and dedicated during his term as president.

*Charles Stufflebeam.*

Stufflebeam attended the University of Missouri's College of Agriculture where he obtained a BS degree in agriculture and MS and PhD degrees in animal breeding. He was employed as professor of animal science at Missouri State University's School of Agricultural Sciences.

Stufflebeam enjoyed his time of service with the Republic School Board particularly because of the involvement of his family. His wife Pat was an elementary teacher for 20 years. He also has three sons who graduated from Republic High School, Jim in 1971, Ken in 1975 and Mark in 1977. Each of them was involved in sports, particularly football and track. All three sons graduated from college and are now living in the Springfield/Republic area. Dr. and Mrs. Stufflebeam are especially proud of their three daughters-in-law and eight grandchildren. *Submitted by Patricia Stufflebeam.*

**SULLIVAN** - After growing up in Iowa and as a single mom taking care of three girls, there came a time that Helen Sullivan knew there needed to be a change. By this time the first-born Tamra was married and had Helen's first grandchild.

A friend suggested Helen look at Missouri for a new life for the girls. So, after checking Kansas City and St. Louis she decided on a smaller town. Hindsight shows that God had the future planned for Helen and all she had to do was discover it.

Helen came to this area and applied for employment at the *News Leader* in Springfield and was hired to start the first of the year, 1979. She found a builder from the area and he owned property in Republic, MO. Arrangements were made to build a very inexpensive home on the property. Helen went back to Iowa, placed her home for sale and moved the children, Lisa and Denise, to the area.

The town of Republic is a wonderful place to live and raise children. It has been 25 years and many wonderful memories. Her daughter, Lisa L. Paswaters, still lives in Republic with her three children: Austin Paswaters, Eric Paswaters and Nikki Choate. She has never and says will never move from this area. The grandchildren have roots here and many, many wonderful friends.

They attend Calvary Baptist Church in Republic and feel that this is where God wants them to serve and learn and be closer to Jesus.

Helen and Lisa's family have so many wonderful friends in this area. Helen's husband Marty died in 2001 and her life has changed a lot. Helen does not know what her future brings but maybe it will be to stay in this area and enjoy the rest of her life. *Submitted by Helen M. Sullivan.*

**SWEARENGIN** – In the spring of 1951 the family moved to West Ave. in Republic from Sparta. Lester's wife had passed away, leaving him with six children to raise. He met a school teacher, Adah Rich, whom he married, and she insisted they move the family to a larger town, and closer to her home of Springfield. With three children left at home, Republic served as a strong community to work in and raise a family.

*Lester and Adah Swearengin.*

The whole family took a very active part in the community. Lester, was an elected city councilman and worked as a city employee for several years in the 60s in the waste water department. Before that he spent several years owning an auto repair shop on Main Street, the Republic Garage, in what used to be the Ford Garage. There he worked on several of the local residents' vehicles, including customizing many of the young people's vehicles. He maintained R-III School District's buses, of which he owned two, and was a driver.

Adah taught school for 29 years, and many of them were the one-room school houses in the area, so a lot of local folks were her students at one time. She worked at the garment factory for awhile, and later she and daughter Bonnie (now Volland), worked at the O'Dell Drug Store on Main Street. This was not only a thriving drug store, but also the popular soda fountain/young people after-school hang-out.

Son, Danny Joe, was very active in the school basketball and baseball teams. R-III had no football during this time so the whole town avidly turned out to support their boys during basketball season. He teamed up with dear friend, Bob Duvall, at Fred McCullah's service station after school and weekends. Having a short stint in the St. Louis Cardinals' baseball organization, he moved on to Army helicopters, later he was called back to start-up the Springfield army aviation repair facility. He became a city councilman, then member of the Republic R-III School Board and the first mayor of incorporated Battlefield. After 35 years of pastoring, Danny is an industrial chaplain and lives in Sedalia.

When Les and Adah retired, they bought 40 acres west of Republic and moved to the country. They still came to Republic to transact their business and visit with friends until they passed away, Lester in 1986, and Adah in 1996.

Janice married James Sparkman, of Battlefield, and they have significant businesses there with their children's families.

The family still have strong ties to the town, as Bonnie, husband Gary Volland, and their families have owned and operated Republic Printing for the past 20 years. Now their grandkids are calling Republic community their home. *Submitted by Bonnie Volland.*

**SWIFT/GHAN** - Robert "Bob" Eugene Swift of Billings married Republic native Kathryn Mae Ghan in 1941. The couple returned to Republic in 1945 after Bob lost his leg in the WWII Battle at Peleliu. Bob went to work for the Republic Post Office, but found it too hard with his leg. E.J. Short, a local friend of Harry Truman, offered to take Bob to Washington D.C. to see the president. Within two weeks, Bob was appointed a mail route in Billings which he kept until retirement.

After beginning his postal career, Bob and Kathryn also started their family with Larry (1947) and Rusty (1955).

Kathryn was always active. Besides being a homemaker, she hosted countless bridge clubs, sang in the Hood Methodist choir and belonged to many other organizations. She enjoyed oil painting. Most people remember her infectious smile and generous hospitality.

Bob served the Republic community on the city council for many years. His favorite accomplishments were getting the streets paved (at a time when there were many gravel streets in the city) and putting up the Hwy. 174 Water Tower.

Bob was an avid golfer and even managed to win a Republic doubles tennis league with Geri Gott in spite of his handicap. He was also known for his woodwork and stained glass creations. But his greatest interest was his kids and later his grandkids. He spent countless hours on the floor playing with the boys. When Larry became interested in model railroading, Bob and Larry constructed an amazing layout that took months to build. It was complete with hand-made buildings, houses, farms, towns, mountains and tunnels - the whole works, hand-painted with great detail. When Rusty became interested in model race cars, Bob was there to help and encourage; another several-month project was started and when completed would "WOW" anyone that saw it. He later hand-built a detailed doll house for granddaughter, Joetta, and spent many hours of his golden years playing with grandson, Cory.

Larry graduated from Rolla with an engineering degree. After serving in the Navy in the San Francisco area, Larry remained there where he met Mary Jo Pearce. They married in 1975 and have children: Robert (Peat) Hardison (1976), Kristen (1978) and Lauren (1981). The family moved to Salt Lake City in 1980, where Mary Jo was raised. Besides enjoying the mountains and outdoors, Larry plays mandolin in the group "Riding the Fault Line."

Rusty, a computer programmer married Glenda Loftin in 1984 and adopted her daughter Joetta (Josie) Mae (1979). The two had a son, Cory Randall (1988). Rusty is an avid sports fan and he also plays and sings for the group "Soul Witness." Glenda, a popular science teacher at Republic, was killed in an auto accident in 1999. Joetta, who loves the outdoors, attends Missouri State. Cory enjoys tennis and sings for the band "Straight Edge."

*Standing: Cory Swift, Michael Schmitt, Josie Swift. Seated: Rusty and Mary Ann Swift.*

Rusty married the former Mary Ann O'Neal in 2002. Mary Ann has a son Michael Schmitt from a previous marriage. The two enjoy supporting their church (where they first met in the crib) and their Tigers. *Submitted by Cory Swift.*

**THOMPSON/DISHEROON** - Dean Thompson was born April 6, 1913 in Checotah, OK, son of William Luster and Frances Elizabeth (Shipman) Thompson. He attended Alpena High School during the Depression years and dropped out to trap and work on the farm. Alpena Arkansas School District bought new buses and needed drivers. Dean wanted the job. The only way he could get the job was to attend high school. He drove one of Alpena's first school buses and graduated in 1934.

*Dean and Winnie Thompson.*

He fell in love with Winnie Disheroon, daughter of Burton M. and Ada (Leatherbury) Disheroon. She was born at Green Forest, Feb. 28, 1915, and graduated from Alpena High School in 1935.

Dean and Winnie married at Green Forest, AR, Jan. 6, 1936. Shortly after, they moved to Jerome, ID and worked on a sheep ranch. They moved back to Arkansas four and a half miles north of Alpena on Long Creek and began farming. On March 6, 1938, a tornado ripped through the community leveling the farm home and causing Dean to suffer from back and head injuries, a broken leg and fractures of ribs and collarbone. He spent months recovering from the injuries. As soon as his health improved, Dean and Winnie headed to California to pick grapes in the San Joaquin Valley near Exeter, CA. Later years they would call the job "Grapes of Wrath." Then it was on to Compton, CA, where Dean worked for U.S. Rubber and later at Long Beach, CA, during the war years as a welder making banana boats into warships.

Dean's dream was always to return to the farm in Arkansas. By working and saving, he was able to realize that dream in the 1940s. He and Winnie acquired 240 acres on Long Creek and built the first dairy barn in Boone County that would qualify for the Grade A market. Milk was first sold to Maple Leaf Dairy in Monett, MO, and later to CAMPA. The Thompsons were selected by Boone County as one of the "Farm Families of the Year" in the 1950s.

By 1962 the farm had 90 head of Jersey dairy cattle, "the little deers," and was milking 30 head of cattle averaging 9,000 pounds per cow. They sold 270,000 pounds of five percent butterfat milk during 1962. That year the Harrison Chamber of Commerce and Boone County Agricultural Workers Association recognized the farm with a pasture tour showcasing fescue, Bermuda, orchard grass, red clover, lespedeza, alfalfa, spring oats, and fescue ladino clover.

In 1971 Dean and Winnie retired, sold the farm, and moved to Green Forest, AR. Dean lived in Green Forest until his death in August 1992. He and Winnie were active in the Southern Baptist Church serving on several Boone-Carroll Association committees and Dean was an ordained deacon. Winnie moved to Republic to live with her daughter and son-in-law, Connie and Jack Buell, in 2002. She now lives at Sonshine Manor.

There are two grandchildren, Anthony Brian "Tony" Buell, and Teri Dawn Buell Watts of Republic. *Submitted by Winnie Thompson.*

**THOMPSON/MCNABB -** Harold Lee Thompson was born in Springfield, MO, the oldest child of Harry Lee and Pauline (Davis) Thompson on Aug. 20, 1950. He graduated from Rogersville High School and moved to Republic in 1972. He was active in the Republic Jaycees.

*Harold Thompson family in 1981. Standing: Michelle, Michael, and Gina. Harold and Janet, seated.*

Janet Sue McNabb was born in Springfield on April 19, 1947. She is the oldest of four children of John Isaac and Genevieve Josephine (Allen) McNabb. Her siblings are John Allen McNabb, Phyllis Jean Taylor and Linda Kay Pullen. Janet attended school at Republic until 1961 and moved to Tulsa with her family where she graduated from McLain High School in 1965. She moved back to Republic in 1970.

Janet married Harold Thompson on Sept. 8, 1981 at Warrenton, MO. They have a blended family of three children: Michelle Sue, Michael Lee and Gina Michelle. Michelle graduated in 1988 from Republic High School and is married to David Johnson who is a deputy chief with the Battlefield Fire Department. Michelle is a paramedic for Cox Ambulance Service. They have a blended family of seven children: Cory, Kristy, Scott, Blake, Kileigh, MaKenzie and Nicholas, they reside in Springfield. Michelle is a member of Republic Eastern Star and has served as Worthy Advisor of Republic Rainbow Assembly, IORG and as Mother Advisor. Cory and Kristy are also Past Worthy Advisors, Kileigh is now an officer, and MaKenzie is a member of the Republic Pledges. Scott is in the Marines in San Diego, California and Blake and Nick are active in soccer. Michael attended SMSU. He is a single parent with two daughters, Trinity and Eden. They reside in Omaha, NE. Gina resides in Springfield and is also an SMSU graduate.

Harold has worked in the printing business since 1970. This business closed in 1986, and he is now a government sales representative for Elkins Swyers Printing Company in Springfield.

Janet served as deputy city collector from 1972-78 under Dorothy Owen and Edna Mae Brashers, then was elected as city collector for three terms. Harold served on the Republic City Council in 1979-80 and was elected as mayor in 1980 and 1982. Janet was elected as mayor in 1984 for a two-year term and was the first woman to serve in this capacity. Janet is active in Eastern Star, having served as Worthy Matron in 1985 with Ernie Whitworth as Worthy Patron and was a Grand Chapter Officer in 2004-2005. She also continues to work with the Republic Rainbow Assembly. Janet is a retired office manager. *Submitted by Janet Thompson.*

**THURMAN/HAYMES -** Ellis Millard Thurman was born in Republic, MO, on Feb. 4, 1904 to Robert Ellis and Anna Godwin Thurman. As a youngster he was given the nickname "Bud" which remained with him throughout his life. Following high school graduation in Republic, he attended Southwest Missouri State Teachers' College (which has since become Missouri State University). He left college before graduating in order to pursue a career as a musical performer. He organized a band of musicians from the area known as "Buddy's Whizbangers" that performed throughout southwest Missouri and northwest Arkansas. Later he joined a vaudeville troupe which performed throughout the country.

*Ellis "Bud" Thurman, ca. 1950.*

While on tour, he was in an automobile accident in which he suffered a fractured skull. The injury was so severe that it was necessary for him to return to Republic for a lengthy convalescence. Since he had not yet completed his degree, he was hired by the Republic school system as a janitor, with the expectation that he would also teach choral and instrumental music. He later completed his music education degree and went on to teach music in the Republic school system for 20 years. While with the Republic school system, he also taught at various times: algebra, general math and science, as well as serving as the high school principal for a brief period. He married Elizabeth Haymes in 1934, and to that union four children were born: Robert (1939) married Dorothy Joslyn, Anne (1943) married Larry Cutberth, John (1945) married Patty Francis, and Thomas (1951) married Libby Musser.

Bud had exceptional success with the Republic instrumental music program. He challenged the students in his bands to play quality music literature, even though it was difficult and required intense rehearsals. He was loved and respected by his students, most of whom called him "Bud" instead of the more formal and acceptable "Mr. Thurman." The students' affection and respect led them to expend unusual effort to reach the musical goals he set for them. Their efforts were rewarded by consistently high ratings at state music festivals, both in ensemble and solo performances, and the acknowledgment that Republic had one of the outstanding music programs in Missouri. While he taught at Republic, several members of the community joined the high school band for Tuesday evening rehearsals in the high school gym. During the summer months, this expanded band performed on Saturday evenings in a band park across the street from Hood United Methodist Church. Citizens from Republic and the surrounding area would come to listen and enjoy these concerts as they sat and socialized on benches in front of the band shell or in cars parked around the periphery of the park.

Bud left the Republic school system in 1952 to teach instrumental music in the Springfield Public Schools, first at Study and then at Jarrett Junior High Schools and finally at Parkview Senior High School until his untimely death in 1963. *Submitted by John and Tom Thurman.*

**THURMAN/JENKINS -** Caleb Thurman (1834-1909) was born in Sevier County, TN to Barnabas Thurman (1794-1839) and Sarah Moon (1794-1837). Both parents died before Caleb was six and he lived with an older sister, Elizabeth Stafford, in Sevier County. In 1855, Caleb married Mary A.S. Jenkins (1835-1926), born in Sevier County to James and Hetty (Smith) Jenkins. Caleb and Mary Thurman's first child, William Harrison (1855-1927), was born in Tennessee. By 1857, the family had moved to Dunklin County, near Kennett, MO where they farmed near members of Mary Jenkins' family. There, sons Isaiah Jones (1857-1912) and Samuel G. (1860-1900) were born.

*Caleb and Mary A.S. Thurman with their youngest child, Mary Jane Wood on left – ca. 1900.*

By 1863, Caleb Thurman and family had moved near the towns of Prairie Grove and Fayetteville, Washington County, AR, where Caleb's older brother had lived since 1850. Caleb volunteered as a private in Company H of the 1st Arkansas Union Infantry Regiment, which was mustered in March 23, 1863 in Fayetteville. The regiment was formed from Arkansas residents in Washington and adjoining counties and participated in the Battle of Fayetteville on April 18, 1863, before uniforms had been issued to all of the troops. Thereafter, the division was marched in sequence to Springfield, MO; the Cherokee and Choctaw nations; Fort Smith, Moscow, Camden, Little Rock and Fort Smith in Arkansas; and back to Springfield, MO, with several skirmishes and battles over a two-year period.

Mary A.S. Thurman told one of her great-granddaughters that she, her three sons, and a woman friend walked from Prairie Grove, AR to Greene County, MO while Caleb was at war. They started this trek of over 120 miles with a mule, but it and some of their food was soon stolen. Mary and their sons reunited with Caleb when he was mustered out as a corporal on Aug. 19, 1865, and they decided to stay in Greene County, MO. Documented history tends to authenticate this story; many non-combatants from northern Arkansas were forced by guerrilla raids and bushwhacking to take refuge in the relative security of the Springfield, MO area during the later years of the Civil War.

Caleb Thurman told one of his sons that he started farming after the Civil War with 50 cents and a team of mules. On the 1870 census, he reported a value of $500 for real property. The Greene County Atlas of 1876 indicated that he had title to 80 acres 3/4 mile west of Republic, and an additional 40 acres two miles farther west. In 1909, his willed estate included 280 acres of farmland in the same area, with a substantial two-story house and outbuildings on the farmstead.

After Caleb and Mary Thurman settled near Republic, they had seven more children: twins-Robert Ellis (1866-1950) and Martha Caledonia Williams (1866-1965), James Grant (1868-1955), George W. (1870-1940), John (1872-1873), Nancy Sophronia A. O'Neal (1874-1965) and Mary Jane Wood (1878-1901). The Thurmans were involved in the building of the Hopewell Baptist Church in the 1870s. Most of their children became, or married, farmers in the Republic area. However, Robert E. first purchased a general mercantile store and then in 1908 started the R.E. Thurman Funeral Home in Republic, which he managed and owned until his death in 1950. George W. Thurman was part owner and active manager of the Republic Custom and Merchant Mill from after 1904, and later was involved in other Republic businesses.

Thirty-three of Caleb and Mary's grandchildren lived to be adults. Caleb and Mary, along with many descendants, were buried in the Wade Chapel Cemetery; other descendants were buried in Evergreen Cemetery. Several Thurman descendants still live in Republic and Greene County. *Submitted by Ivan L. Berry.*

**THURMAN/PICKERING** - Robert Ellis "Uncle Bob" Thurman was born in Republic on Aug. 27, 1866, along with his twin sister Martha. They were the ninth and tenth children of Caleb and Mary (Jenkins) Thurman. Caleb had moved to Republic with his family after being mustered out of the Confederate Army in Fayetteville, AR, at the close of the Civil War. Caleb and Mary purchased a farm just west of the town of Republic where he became a successful farmer, raising stock and grain. The farm eventually included 300 acres of land.

Robert married Ida Pickering in 1890 and they had three daughters: Stella (born 1890) married James Hood; Blanche (born 1894) married Walter Maxey; and Hazel (born 1896) married Herbert Chaffin. Ida died in 1899 while her children were still quite young. Three years later, Robert married Anna Godwin. Three children were born to this marriage: Ellis Millard (born 1904) married Elizabeth Haymes; an infant who died shortly after birth in 1908; and Daphne (born 1909) married H. Linzee Wells.

Robert and Anna owned a dry goods store on Main Street in Republic and also owned a mortuary. Eventually the dry goods store was sold and the mortuary was moved to 226 East Elm Street in Republic, where it was operat-

*From left: Hazel Thurman, Stella Thurman, Blanche Thurman, Anna Godwin Thurman, Daphne Thurman, Robert "Uncle Bob" Thurman, unknown, Ellis "Bud" Thurman. Picture taken during a Sunday afternoon hike to Billings along the railroad tracks sometime between 1910 and 1920.*

ed by Robert and his family until his death in 1950. It was truly a family operation, with his wife Anna keeping books for the business, his son Ellis, who became a licensed undertaker, assisting with the funeral business and with the ambulance service the business provided for the community, and his daughter Daphne playing the pump organ for funerals held in the funeral home on East Elm Street. He operated the funeral home for a period of 55 years. After his death the mortuary business was sold to Max Faucett of Mt. Vernon who moved it to the current location of Meadors Funeral Home on North Main Street in Republic.

Robert was a widely known and respected citizen of Republic and the surrounding area. He was a generous and friendly person, as exemplified by his practice during the "Great Depression" of carrying a number of customers on credit who had fallen on hard times and could not afford to pay their bills. Local residents affectionately called him "Uncle Bob" when they saw him on the street. He enjoyed the hobby of woodworking, and he spent many hours in his shop making desks, jewelry boxes, and other wooden objects for many of his family and friends. While his children were young, the family would enjoy Sunday afternoon hikes to Billings along the railroad right-of-way, returning to Republic via the passenger train on Sunday evening. *Submitted by Anne Thurman Cutberth and Robert Thurman II.*

**THURMAN/SMITH** - James Grant Thurman (1868-1955), born to Caleb and Mary A.S. Jenkins Thurman near Republic, MO, married Margaret Odessa Smith (1880-1947) around 1896. From family recollections, Jim made a living farming, owning an orchard, running the town power plant (owned by brother George W.), had a hardware store and even tried his hand at selling windmills. He had farms around Republic and near Powell, MO, a small town southeast of Republic that has since been deserted. The orchard was near Republic. He operated the power plant during the evening shift and on Tuesday mornings so the women of the town could do family ironing. The selling of windmills was a real learning experience for "Poppa" Thurman, as the first one he sold, he forgot to build a platform for the farmer to use later when repairing the windmill! Jim was gifted with music and played the violin and

*Trenton Smith Thurman, 1914, age 4 years.*

*Margaret Odessa Smith Thurman*

*James Grant Thurman*

a dulcimer which he made and taught himself to play. The violin remains in the family, but the dulcimer got away. Reports are he was quite good and played in area bands.

Jim and Odessa, along with other friends, were instrumental in establishing the First Baptist Church of Republic. When first organized, they met in a railroad car made possible by the "Frisco" railroad, soon however, they built the church on Main Street. The foundation of this building was discovered during excavation for "Thurman Hall" dedicated to the memories of Jim and Odessa Thurman.

*Orville Dewey Thurman, Student Army Training Corps, State Nomal College-Springfield, MO, Oct. 17, 1918.*

Five children were born to Jim and Odessa: Orville, Opal, Floriene, Iris and Trenton. Trenton celebrated his 95th birthday in 2005.

One story Trenton recalls is that a railroad car of bananas overturned in Republic, so the railroad sold the bananas for 25 cents a stalk. Turns out that Jim, Orville and Trenton each bought a stalk (without knowing the others had also bought a stalk) took them home, hung them in the basement and had bananas fixed every way possible for weeks later!

Orville Thurman, after returning home from World War I, purchased a new Model T truck pictured in front of the Republic Bottling Works with Orville and little brother Trenton, who would deliver soft drinks bottled at the Republic Bottling Works as far south as Arkansas and as far west as the Kansas line. The bottling plant closed down for four months in the winter for no one drank cold drinks then.

*Orville Thurman and little brother Trenton with their new Model T truck about 1918.*

The living descendents of the children of

*Four of the five Thurman children: Orville, Floriene, Opal and Iris.*

Jim and Odessa are Floriene - William James Watkinson and his son Brent; Iris - Nancy Green DeLapp and her children; Orville - Glen Gene Thurman, his two daughters, Dawn Kramer and Catherine Vinson, as well as six granddaughters.

The Thurman/Smith families have tried to live lives that would honor their forefathers and God. *Submitted by Gene Thurman. Editor's note: Trenton Thurman died 2006.*

**TIEDE -** John Tiede, born April 4, 1839, Hamburg, Germany was the son of Martin Friedrich Tiede and Dorothea Sophia Henriette Schildt. His mother died when he was 6 years old and his father died when he was 12 years old. Early in life he became a cabin boy on a ship, making trips to London. Later he became a sailor and made many ports to Great Britain and on the continent of Europe and to New York. On one of his trips to New York, he left ship and went to Iowa.

John Tiede married Emma (Engle) Huber, a young widow with twins, on March 16, 1864, at Fairfax, IA. They resided in Iowa from 1864 until about 1881. He then came to Missouri and secured several hundred acres of wild land in Christian and surrounding counties and resided in Billings for about two months. He moved with his family to Springfield to school his children and carry on a dairy business and remained there about six years. After moving back to Billings, he was first in the general merchandise business and afterward for about 16 years was widely known in the lumber business; this was disposed of about 1906. He also ran the ice house at one time. The old family home pictured in the Billings Centennial Book was built about 1890 on Elm Street, Hwy. 60 now.

John and Emma raised eight boys of their own and the two step children, Jacob and Mary Huber. Two young children died while they resided in Iowa. Charles married Freda Strohfield, John Jr. married Alice Fuhr, Martin married Carolina Lange, Adolph married Clara Kloss, Henry married Sarah Phillips, Edwin married Sarah DeWitt, William married Ida Wieck and Ralph married Alice Watkinson.

John died July 1, 1913 at his son's in Kansas and Emma died Jan. 10, 1914 at Billings, both are buried at Rose Hill Cemetery.

John Tiede Jr. was born Aug. 8, 1869, Norway, IA. He married Oct. 2, 1895, Christian County, MO to Alice Fuhr, who was born July 24, 1868. She was the daughter of John E. Fuhr (1824-1909) and Louise Phillips (1835-1916). All are buried at Kerr Cemetery in Greene County, MO. They had six children: Anna Louise who married Ellis Kerr; Hilda Otila married Robert W. Farmer; Ernest John married (l) Anna Norrine Norris and (2) Ruby J. Branstetter; Julia Huber married Milton C. Frazier; Walter William married Faye Smith; and Edna Grace married (l) Elmer Brown (2) William O. Clark and (3) Pat Baker. His farm was west of Republic, the house was built about 1905 and the youngest daughter Edna was born there. *Submitted by Vivian Lewis.*

*John Jr. and Alice (Fuhr) Tiede.*

**TOURVILLE -** During the early part of the 19th century, a young couple named d'Tourville came to the United States from Tourville, France. They first moved to Pittsburgh, PA. At this time the d' was dropped from the name. They did not stay in Pittsburgh very long, moving westward to Quincy, IL. In 1868, this was the birthplace of Peter Fredrick Tourville. A few years later, Susan Maude Ring was born in Belleville, IL. By some means, Peter met Susan and they married and settled in Bonne Terre, MO. To this union a son James Fredrick Tourville was born on May 6, 1895 and died in 1973. Jim had three sisters: Nellie, Edna and Minnie.

On May 28, 1895, a young lady by the name of Callie Katherine Hayes was born in Greene County, MO to George Washington Hayes and Malissa Ann Britain, who were married Oct. 6, 1878. Callie died in 1971. Other children were Nora, Elza and Ira. George, who had been born in Christian County, MO in 1857 and died in 1904, evidently gave in to Malissa and they moved to Greene County, where she had been born in 1859. Malissa outlived her husband by quite a few years and in her latter years became determined to build a large house like she always wanted. The house was located one mile west of Republic, MO and contained four bedrooms and a full basement.

Callie first married Clarence Logan who died at a very young age of pneumonia. One child named Lester was born to this union. Callie then moved to St. Louis, MO for work where she met her future husband, James. She then moved to Sullivan, MO and married James Tourville, who worked for the Frisco Railroad. A son named Jimmie was born in 1918 and died 1957. In 1934 upon the death of Malissa, Callie and James moved to Republic and occupied the home Malissa had built. Jimmie, a Republic graduate of 1937, married a lady named Alice Kelly from Ava, MO. A son Dan and a daughter Susan were born.

Another son named Timothy D. was born in 1940. Tim, a Republic graduate of 1958, married Sharon K. Hollis in 1961. A daughter Kim was born. Tim remarried in 1982 to Della R. Berger. *Submitted by Tim Tourville.*

**TROGDON/HALL –** In the year of 1927, Henry and Ica Ellen Trogdon bought a 220 acre farm, one and a half mile north of Brookline on MM Highway for the sum of $25,000. Mr. Trogdon sowed the land in orchard grass and clover seed. Henry and Ica lived on a farm near Ash Grove and never moved to the Brookline farm.

Two sons, Wayne and Jack, were born. When Wayne graduated from Ash Grove High School, he and Mabel Hall were dating. She graduated in 1931 and they were married Nov. 7, 1931 and moved to the Brookline farm. They farmed with his father at both farms for a number of years. More land was bought by Wayne and Mabel.

*Mabel and Wayne Trogdon – 50th Wedding Anniversary.*

In 1941, Robert Wayne was born. His schooling began at Brick School until the school was consolidated into the Republic Grade School. Robert graduated from Republic High and attended SMS College for two years. He and Donna Girth of Springfield were married and built a home just north of the family home on MM. Two sons were born, Kevin and Joel. They grew up attending Republic Grade and High School. Donna passed away when both boys were still in high school and college.

Kevin graduated from SMS and was married to Natalee Sneed after their graduation. Wayne passed away March 6, 1994. Joel and Hope Taylor were married June 28, 1997.

Bob lived in Quail Creek Nursing Home in Springfield until he passed away Oct. 4, 2006. Henry Trogdon was born in 1878 and passed away in 1950. Ica Ellen Trogdon was born in 1879 and passed away in 1946. Jack (1920-1994) and Dorothy Lee Gilmore (1921-1979) married in 1937. Kevin remarried and has two children, Bryson James (age 5 years) and Ashlyn (age 3 years). *Submitted by Mabel Trogdon.*

**TROGDON/MATTHEWS -** Daniel C. Trogdon was born in Oregon County, MO in 1889 to Bob and Amelia (Reiff) Trogdon. He had two brothers, Samuel (1885-1890) and John Randolph (1886-1979). They were orphaned at a very young age and were raised by their grandparents, Samuel and Mary (Craven) Trogdon, who lived south of Billings, and their Uncle George and Aunt Sophia Trogdon, who lived near a spring on Pickerel Creek. John and Dan attended school at St. Joe, west of Republic.

*Daniel and Ethel Trogdon.*

During the First World War, Daniel served in Battery E of the 129th FA, under the command of Harry Truman. He was in numerous battles including the Meuse-Argonne Offensive and Verdun. He was discharged in 1919 and returned to Missouri. In 1921, he married Ethel Matthews, a daughter of William and Martha Ann (Wrinkle) Matthews.

Their first child, Virginia, was born in Billings in 1922, but they moved to the farm on Pickerel Creek before Dan Matthew was born in 1924. Mary Sue and Jack were born there in 1927 and 1931. The old house was remodeled and a new chicken house and garage were built. In 1949, when electricity was finally made available to their neighborhood, they drilled a well, built a barn, and then they built a new house. All four children attended St. Elmo Grade School and graduated from Republic High School: Virginia in 1938, Dan in 1941, Sue in 1945 and Jack in 1949. All played in the band and all attended SMS.

In 1940, Virginia married Kenneth Lauderback, a teacher and school administrator. They had two children, Judy and Steven Kenneth. Virginia has three grandchildren and lives in Independence, MO.

Dan married Opal Wenkheimer in 1946 in Las Vegas. After his Navy enlistment was up, they came back to Missouri, where he finished his education at SMS. He worked for Martin Machinery for a time and lived at Carthage. After he bought an insurance agency in Mt. Vernon, they located there. They had four boys: Duane, Danny, Tim and Tom. There are five grandchildren. Dan lives in Mt. Vernon.

Mary Sue married Bob Steele, who was also in the Navy, and they lived near Forsyth. They built and operated a bait shop and vacation cabins for many years. After they retired, they moved into Forsyth. They had two boys, Mark and James. There are four grandchildren. Sue lives in Forsyth.

Jack enjoyed a successful basketball career at Republic, where he was All State for two years. He also played at SMS. He married Patsy Woodfill and they have four children: Debbie, who married Alan McMurtrey; Terry married Pat Mooneyham; Jerry married Shirley Wilkins; and Joe married Marilyn Evans. There are six grandchildren. Jack retired after 37 years as manager of the Credit Bureau of Springfield. They also raised Limousin cattle. *Submitted by Debbie (Trogdon) McMurtrey.*

**TURPIN/HOLIWAY** - Otto Lincoln Turpin was born at Versailes, MO in 1884. His family moved to the Brookline area where he attended Macedonia Baptist Church. There he met Myrtle Esther Holiway, and they were married in 1917. Myrtle was born in 1900. They moved to Elreno, OK where two daughters were born, LeVera in 1918 and Velma in 1920.

*Myrtle (Holiway) Otto Lincoln Turpin.*

The family returned to the Republic area in 1922. Irene was born in 1923, Charles Allen in 1926 and passed away at the age of two years. He is buried in the Brookline Cemetery. George W. was born in 1929. Calvin and Alvin were born in 1932, Alvin died shortly after birth and is buried in Brookline Cemetery. Juanita was born in 1935.

The children attended Lindsey and Republic Schools. LeVera and Velma graduated from Republic High School.

*Right to left, by age, LeVera Turpin Kerr, Velma Turpin Woolsey, Irene Turpin Henry, George W. Turpin, Calvin Turpin, Juanita Turpin Blankenship – 1983.*

Otto and Myrtle were charter members of Wilson Creek Baptist Church. Otto was a Baptist preacher.

The family moved to Seligman, MO in 1941. LeVera met and married Junior "June" Kerr in 1939. They lived in Republic and June worked at Thompson's Garage on Main Street. George worked for them in 1945 and 1946 and delivered ice to the homes in the area.

The children of June and LeVera Kerr are Deanna Warford and Jim Kerr. They attended and graduated school in Republic. June and LeVera are buried in Evergreen Cemetery.

Velma married Bob Woolsey and lives in Red Bluff, CA. Bob is buried in Red Bluff.

Irene married Onis Henry from Ponce De Leon and lived in Springfield. They are buried in Brookline Cemetery.

George married Helen Boggess from Exeter, MO and they live in the Nixa area. George is buried in Delaware Cemetery.

Calvin married Anna Wilbanks from Washburn then later married Barbara (Jones) Smith. They are buried in Rivermonte Memorial Gardens in Springfield, MO.

Juanita married Mike Blankenship and they live at Jenkins, MO. *Submitted by Helen Turpin.*

**TUTER/BOYD** - Solomon Forrester Tuter, born Sept. 28, 1883 in Greene County, Route 7, Springfield, MO (north of Brookline), son of Ballard Preston and Martha Catherine (Morris/Newsom) Tuter. At the age of 20 Solomon married Edna Earl Boyd, born Nov. 18, 1881 in Greene County, Republic, MO.

*Solomon and Edna Tuter.*

Edna was the daughter of George Washington Boyd and Tilitha Cuma Harrington. To this union nine children were born: Sherman Riley (Sept. 4, 1904-Nov. 6, 1984) married Pearl McGinnis; Sheridan (May l8, 1906, died same day); Ralph Boyd (June 4, 1907-Jan. 19, 1908); Georgia Mae Kathrine (Dec. 24, 1908-April 25, 2001) married Carl Logan; Edward Raymond (Feb. 4, 1911-March 19, 1994) married Hildred Batson; Litha Virginia "Jin" (Nov. 22, 1913-Oct. 5, 1984) married Clyde "Jim" Swearengin; Bessie Ruth (Dec. 8, 1915, Sept. 4, 1999) married Clarence Swearengin; Fern Nadine (March 18, 1919) married Elden Hood; and Kenneth Solomon (Jan. 2, 1922) married Rose Mary Cordia.

Sherman, Sheridan, Ralph and Georgia, were born east of Republic, while Edward, Litha "Jin" and Bessie were born northeast of Republic. Fern and Kenneth were both born at Bolivar, MO.

In 1916 Solomon, Edna and their five children moved into a log cabin in the country about four miles from Bolivar, MO. This log cabin had a living-dining area, with an attached kitchen on the ground floor and a very steep, narrow staircase to an upper floor. This log cabin was later donated to the city of Bolivar and is now part of the Bolivar Museum. The family lived there from 1916 to 1923. During this time, Solomon was what was called an "Old Time Medicine Man," and traveled around the countryside by horse and buggy selling McConan medicines and home remedies. He would spend one to two weeks away from home at a time, sometimes trading products for meals and lodging.

They returned to the Brookline-Springfield area in the early 1920s where he worked in the Frisco Railroad Shops. During the depression years, he worked as a carpenter and house painter in and around Springfield as well as working in the stone quarries. Being the gardener he was, he also sold produce to the business people in Springfield from his huge gardens. The early 1930s brought about the construction of many navigational dams and levees that significantly altered the Missouri River north of St. Louis. Solomon found an opportunity in this work and moved his family to areas along the river that included Parkville, Waldron and Nodaway, north of Kansas City, as he followed the river construction.

After spending a couple of years on the river construction, they returned to the Brookline area and spent the next few years there before building their home in Springfield. There, they spent the remainder of their lives together. Both Solomon and Edna, along with most of their children, are buried in the Harrington Cemetery east of Republic. *Submitted by Jami (Hood) and Clint Reilly.*

**UNDERWOOD/FULLER** - William Luther and Ebbie (Grisham) Underwood's relatives came from Tennessee to Everton, MO. W.L. and Ebbie had four children: Mildred Delma Spencer, Lois Alma Hayter, William Joseph Elbert "Bill" and Hubert Lee.

Bill attended his first eight years of school in Dade County at the Henry District #1 one-room school. He graduated the spring of 1946 from Everton High School. He had been allowed a war deferment until graduation. In September 1946 he was sent with the army occupation forces to Japan. After returning to the USA he worked for the Caterpillar Tractor Company in Peoria, IL. Later, he returned to Everton to help operate the Phillips 66 service station.

*Bill and Jean Underwood – 50th anniversary in 1999.*

In the summer of 1948, he began a plumbing apprenticeship under the GI Bill in Kansas City. Upon completion of the course he worked for a brother-in-law in Springfield. He began contract work that took him to Fort Leonard Wood, employment with Jess Wood, and 17 years with J.B. McCarty. Two large jobs he recalled were the building of Cox South Hospital and adding new equipment lines to 3-M. He retired from Connelly Plumbing in 1989. He holds a 50-year membership in the Plumbers and Fitters Local #178.

Bill was able to meet his future wife Iris Jean Fuller because Jean's dad was on the road board and Bill's dad did custom road work. Bill happened to be with his dad one day when he went to the Fuller home to discuss a job. Jean's parents are Garland and Stella (Hollingsworth) Fuller from Ash Grove. They had four other children: Genevieve Williams, Noel Duane, Nathan Hale and Jerry Max.

Jean attended the one-room school, Union Hall, in Lawrence County. She graduated from Ash Grove High School in 1948. Jean and Bill were married Dec. 22, 1949. They bought their first house in Springfield with the GI Bill. In 1966, with the help of realtor Vernon Davis, they found their home in Republic.

They have two children. Joe Don was born Sept. 24, 1953. He graduated from Republic in 1971 and is currently employed with Kraft. He married Judy Campbell and they had two daughters. Ashley Dawn does office work for St. John's Hospital and is married to Matt Tucker from Pleasant Hope. They live in Fair Grove. Their other daughter is Jamie Lynn. She worked for Harem and Company and graduated from Missouri State University in the spring of 2006. Her plans are to continue her education at the University of Arkansas.

Mark Alan born March 9, 1962 also graduated from RHS and lives in Republic with his wife Rhonda (Stump) Underwood. Rhonda is from Springfield. They were married in 1994. They have two sons, Cole Alan born in March 1996 and Camerin born in April 2001. Mark is employed by Legendary Auto Works as a painter.

Jean and Bill enjoy the activities of the

Heart of the Ozarks Model T Ford Club and the Early Days Gas Engine and Tractor Association. Bill enjoyed deer hunting in Colorado and Jean enjoys reading as well as crocheting. *Submitted by Bill and Jean Underwood.*

**UPDEGRAVE** - Dan and Tory have been a part of the Republic community for 10 years even though they have only been residents since May 2000. Both grew up in the outskirts of St. Louis. Dan grew up in Arnold, MO and attended Fox High School, graduating in 1994. Tory grew up in Chesterfield, MO and attended Parkway West High School, graduating in 1995. However, they did not meet until they came to Southwest Missouri State for college. They met while in the SMS Pride Marching Band.

*Tory and Dan Updegrave.*

Dan has a bachelor degree in music education, with an emphasis in vocal music, but he is also a very-proficient saxophone player, and Tory has a bachelor degree in accounting and a masters of business administration. They were married on June 5, 1999 in St. Louis. They began attending Calvary Baptist Church early in their college careers. In 1995 Dan became the interim song leader for Calvary.

After marrying and moving to Republic, Dan became the minister to students for Calvary in May 2000 and Tory became office manger for Calvary in September 2000. They have been active in many church and community events. They both were involved in the Republic Community Band for several years, Dan as conductor and Tory playing the E-flat Clarinet. They both sing in Calvary's choir, Dan also sings in the Praise Team, and Tory directs the hand bell choirs. They both enjoy working with Republic's youth, whether it is during church services, hanging out at the Hangar, Calvary's student center, on Friday nights, or attending one of the many activities in which the students of Calvary are involved. *Submitted by Dan Updegrave.*

**VERNICK/HUEBNER** - Milton Maxwell Vernick Jr. was born on July 6, 1946 at Lyons, KS. His father, Milton Maxwell Vernick, was born on July 20, 1920 in Brooklyn, NY and died Feb. 1, 1974 in Kansas. Milton's mother, Geraldine Mae Huebner, arrived on Jan. 28, 1925 in Bushton, KS. His grandparents, John and Martha Vernick, immigrated to the United States and started a family in New York. Families of Rex and Virginia Huebner were from England and Germany and they established homes in the Bushton, KS area.

The Vernick family was completed with the arrival of Timothy Glen, born April 12, 1949 in Texas and David Murray, Oct. 18, 1951 in Florida. The family moved many times because Milton Maxwell was a career military father. They lived in Okinawa for 18 months where they survived a

*Milton Vernick.*

hurricane. Traveling to Okinawa proved to be a horrible experience and one never to forget. The families were separated from the military personnel, had problems of being seasick, had cramped living space, and lacked fresh food and water. Milton was only six or seven at the time and the youngest son was a baby. Living around the country allowed the family to meet new people, different cultures, traditions and foods, all of which were enjoyable.

In 1962, the family moved to McPherson, KS. Milton graduated from high school in May 1964 and entered the local college. He graduated in 1968 with a bachelor of science degree.

In 1968, he started his Army career with basic training at Fort Dixon, NJ. In 1969 he trained at Fort Leonard Wood, MO where he completed his advanced individual training. Completion of this training made him eligible for Vietnam, but destiny had another job for him. He was sent to Fort Carson, CO until his discharge in 1970. After being discharged, he continued his schooling in Kansas and graduated in 1972 with a masters of science degree from Emporia College. In 1978, he received a direct commission with the Army as first lieutenant at Pine Bluff, AR in the Chemical Corps. He worked at the Pine Bluff Arsenal for four years while his Army career continued. Eventually he was sent to Dugway Proving Ground, UT until 1987. He was discharged from active duty and found himself in the Army Reserves. His military career ended in 1999 at Fort Leonard Wood with 31 years combined reserves and active duty. His final promotion was to lieutenant colonel.

In 1994 he was lucky to be introduced to his future wife, Ermal Hagewood Johnson, a native of Republic. After a long-distance romance, they married on Sept. 8, 1996. He finished his civilian employment with three years at Fort Leonard Wood before retirement. His wife retired from the Naval Reserves and the Veterans Administration at Mt. Vernon, MO. They enjoy volunteering with the Veterans Administration at Mt. Vernon and Missouri Conservation Dept. at Bois D'Arc, MO. They teach Hunters Education classes and help with special programs offered there. They are active at Macedonia Baptist Church, Springfield, MO and enjoy traveling, fishing, hunting and gardening. *Submitted by Geraldine Vernick.*

**VILES/ROGERS** - Oren Viles, born Nov. 30, 1911 in Spokane, MO and died June 7, 1993, was the third child of James C. "Cub" and Rebecca E. Richard Viles. As a child, Oren's family moved by wagon from Spokane, MO to Vinita, OK. As a teenager they moved, traveling by train, to Walville, WA, where Oren worked at a lumber mill at a very young age. The family returned to Greene County in 1929.

Oren met his wife to be at Gray School, which was a one-room country school located

*50th anniversary Nov. 15, 1988, l-r: Linda and Danny Viles, Orilla Keys, Joan and Oren Viles, Richard and Susan Viles.*

just west of Hood's Truck Stop on the outer road. On Nov. 15, 1938 Oren married Joan Rogers (born Nov. 20, 1919). She was the youngest child of James and Melvina (Stilwell) Rogers. They were blessed with three children: daughter Orilla Keys (born December 1939) and two sons, Richard (born December 1946) and Danny (born July 1952). In 1941 Oren and Joan moved to a farm north of Republic on Hwy. N just south of Route 66. They had a Grade A dairy farm, raising, grinding and mixing their own feed for their 50 milk cows. Oren insisted Joan take care of the house, and he took care of the farming chores.

They left the dairy farm after 12 years, purchasing 13 acres on PP Hwy. PP was a muddy dirt road at that time. Oren started working for Barnes General Store located on Hwy. 66 in the position of appliance serviceman. In 1963 he opened his own appliance and service store on Main Street in Republic. A few years later they built a shop at their home, where he worked the rest of his life servicing all home and commercial appliances. Their daughter Orilla lives in Virginia near D.C. where her husband is employed with the U.S. Government. They have a girl and a boy. Richard has three girls and now has two grandchildren. Danny and Linda have no children.

Joan worked at Woods Garment Factory when it first opened in Republic. She also operated Barnes Cafe at Barnes Store while Interstate 44 was being built, later working at Hood's Truck Stop, and 12 years at the Hillbilly Outpost located at Hood's. Oren and Joan enjoyed 55 wonderful years and 7 months together. They loved fishing and hunting. They hunted deer in Missouri and Colorado. Oren also enjoyed "coon" hunting. They loved spending time together and being with their children and their five grandchildren.

Joan has traveled a lot since Oren's death, making trips to the east coast, traveling from New York to Georgia and once to California. Flying for the first time in 1995, she flew to her granddaughter's in Italy.

Joan continues to live on the 13 acres they purchased in 1956. She loves traveling, attending music shows and attending church regularly at Yeakley Chapel where she and Oren joined in 1949. She says she has been blessed in so many ways. *Submitted by Joan Viles.*

**WADE** - Thomas Washington Wade was born Nov. 12, 1847, in Franklin County, GA. He came to Missouri as a young child with his parents, James and Nancy (Hearn) Wade, and other relatives in the early 1850s. A land record shows that James Wade bought land in 1851 in Greene County north of what was later to be the town of Republic. The other children of James and Nancy were Joshua Asbury, John Fletcher, Sarah A.C., Elizabeth, William P., James Benson, Martha and Wesley Osborne. Thomas was the youngest child of this marriage.

James had a later marriage, after Nancy's death, to Mrs. Mary (Hagewood) Robertson. The children of that marriage were Samuel and Sarepta. James died while living near Hindsville, AR, and was buried there. His remains were removed some years later to Wade Chapel Cemetery where he was buried beside the grave of his wife, Nancy, and near the log church where he, a Methodist minister, had preached.

Other relatives who came from Georgia during this period of time were James Wade's sister, Mary "Polly" Wade, sister Elizabeth and husband Tavner Rucker and their children Joshua, Frances, Anna; and Martha and husband Joel Skelton and family.

Thomas Wade married Sarepta Ellen Skelton Sept. 15, 1864. This was during the troubled times of the Civil War. Ellen's father, Joel Skelton, was shot and killed by bushwhackers at his home Nov. 8, 1862. Thomas's brother, William, a Confederate soldier, was wounded and taken prisoner in the Battle of Franklin, TN. He was taken to Camp Chase, OH, where he later died of pneumonia and was buried there.

Thomas and Ellen had 12 children. Thomas A., Mirtie, and Gussie, died in infancy. The others were Martha Elizabeth, Nancy Jane, Mary M., Eda Sarepta, Laura Etta, Lula Alice, Ira Clarence, Charles Wesley, and Maude Effie. All the children attended Prairie View School, a one-room school located northwest of Republic. Thomas and Ellen spent all their married life in Missouri except for a short time in Arkansas where daughter Eda was born. Speaking of this time to relatives, Thomas said he came back with a new baby on his arm and two dollars in his pocket. He later became a prosperous farmer and businessman. Assisted by his son Ira, he set up canning factories in Missouri, Arkansas and Louisiana. Other relatives joined him in this enterprise. He also served a term in the Missouri Legislature as a representative.

Most of the children of Thomas and Ellen spent at least part of their adult lives in the Republic area. Ira and his wife Alice Viola "Ola" Green lived out their lives on a farm north of Republic. Ira died Sept. 6, 1968 and Ola died March 13, 1977.

The farm where daughter Eda (Wade) Brown lived, also north of Republic, is still in the Brown family. Her grandson, Wade Brown, lived all of his life there, dying Sept. 5, 2001. His widow, Mae (Howard) Brown, remained on the farm until her death Dec. 14, 2005. *Submitted by Hilda E. Wade.*

**WADE/GARDNER** - Clyde "Cotton" Wade was born Jan. 29, 1912 west of Republic. His father was George Calvin Wade, grandfather Wesley O. Wade, grandmother Martha Susan Britain, great-grandfather James Wade, great-grandmother Nancy Hearn, who came to Greene County, MO from Franklin County, GA in 1852. His mother was Rosie Alice Laney Wade, grandfather William Marcellas Laney, grandmother Martha Susan Britain, great-grandfather George Marion Laney, great-grandmother Amy Bethia Garoutte.

*Clyde and Bonnie Wade wedding picture in 1934.*

Bonnie Bell Gardner was born Dec. 9, 1913 west of Republic. Her father was William Marion Gardner, grandfather George Gardner, grandmother Elizabeth Virginia Laney, great-grandfather Ephraim Laney, great-grandmother Margaret "Peggy" Miller. The Laneys came to Greene County, MO from Tennessee in the 1830s and settled west of Republic. Her mother was Rosa Elmeda Etheridge, grandfather Caleb E. Etheridge, grandmother Malinda A. Logan, great-grandfather John Etheridge, and great-grandmother Jane Bettis.

Clyde Wade and Bonnie Gardner were married Jan. 29, 1934 at the home of Rev. Efton Blades. As a young married couple, they took the train to California to find work during the Depression years. Bonnie had brothers and a sister living there, so Cotton was never out of work. Their first daughter, Juanita Marie, was born in Ontario, CA Oct. 25, 1934. They were soon homesick for Missouri so they returned for a short time, but there was no work to be had here, so they returned to California. Their second daughter Rosalene, was born in Ontario, CA Jan. 2, 1937. They were living in Pond Creek Township when Juanita started first grade at Grandview School. The California bug bit again in 1940 and back they went. Cotton worked at the General Electric Plant buffing irons and Bonnie worked in the fruit packing industry. Shortly after WWII started, the family returned to Republic for good. Their third daughter, Patricia Sue, was born Aug. 31, 1943.

Cotton had a milk route, worked delivering fertilizer and in the late 50s began to build houses. He also worked on several Republic School buildings. Bonnie worked at the Republic Garment Factory for many years. Cotton was a practical joker and always had time for fun. They were great fans of Republic basketball in 1963 when Republic won the state tournament and they followed the St. Louis Cardinal baseball team for many years. Bonnie and Cotton loved to fish and spent many happy hours on area lakes fishing for crappie. Bonnie suffered with rheumatoid arthritis but never complained and always had a smile, especially for her grandchildren. Bonnie died Feb. 10, 1986 and Cotton died May 8, 1988.

Juanita married Jack Bridges and their children are Teresa, Jack Jr. and Greg. Rosie married Max Bennett; their children are twins David and Neisha, Daniel, and Tracy. Patsy was married to Paul David McConnell, and they had a daughter Jody. Later Patsy married Gary Altman; their children are Gary Jr. and Jennifer. *Submitted by Patsy Altman.*

**WALKER** - Ken Walker moved his family from California to Republic in 1962. He purchased a lot on East Elm Street and built a house. The three Walker children: Karen, David and Linda, attended Republic Schools.

Ken went into the television business in 1964. The shop was located in a small building next to the old post office on Grant Street. In 1968 he purchased the pool hall on Main Street which was originally Doc O'Dells Drug Store.

A tornado struck Republic on Dec. 14, 1971 which was Ken's birthday. It came from the southwest. One of the first things it hit was the home of Laura Geren. Laura was a widow living alone on the west side of Republic on Highway 60. Laura's bed was in the southwest corner of her house. After the tornado went through, she got out of bed and walked across the room to the closet - which was not there. The only walls standing were the two by her bed. The rest of the house was across the highway. Laura was the mother of Marcella Garner, who along with others worked hard to found People Helping People for the community of Republic. People Helping People provides clothing and food for needy families.

After Laura's traumatic experience she naturally did not want to rebuild there, and put up a "For Sale" sign. Ken promptly bought the property. In 1973 he built his TV shop there. The building still stands.

Ken's TV is now owned and operated by David Denny, a long-time employee of Ken's.

Ken and Evelyn spent many winters of their retirement years as "R.V.ers". Their favorite destination was the Rio Grande Valley. The small town of Harlingen, TX was convenient for shopping trips and tours of Mexico. They enjoyed their vacations with Shearl and Helen Denny, Warren and Ruby Medlin, Pete and Ruby Kimmons and many others who returned to Texas year after year to enjoy the nice weather.

Fishing is now a big part of their lives, along with their dog Daisy, a German shorthair pointer dog.

Ken serves on the board of directors of the Republic Senior Friendship Center. He and Evelyn are active in the center's functions. *Submitted by Ken Walker.*

**WALKER/SKELTON** - Jim Walker was born Aug. 17, 1878. He came to Missouri in 1914 from Knoxville, TN. He bought the farm two miles south of Battlefield, MO on the James River. The price of the farm was $4,500. Jim stayed with his father and mother until his father passed away in 1921. At this time his mother went to Republic, MO to stay with her sister Grace Manley and brother Tom Nelson.

*Don and Von Walker.*

In 1923 Jim married Laura Skelton. To this marriage two sons were born. Twin sons, Von and Don were born July 1, 1925 in Battlefield, MO. They went to school at Green Ridge under the teaching of Mildred Howard. Her salary as a teacher was $50.00 a month.

The boys went to Republic High School. Their junior year in high school (1942) Von Walker fell dead on the basketball gym floor due to an earlier illness. His funeral service was held in the high school gym at Republic. Don went to military service for two years. At that time Jim Walker sold the farm and moved to Republic, MO. The farm sold for $25,000. Jim Walker died May 13, 1965. Laura Walker died in 1966. Both are buried in Wade Chapel Cemetery in Republic, MO.

Don Walker is married to June Dixon. *Submitted by Don Walker.*

**WALLACE** - Thomas Jefferson Wallace, born July 1823 in Tennessee, moved to Alabama, marrying Sarah M. Bayless in January 1847. She was born in September 1827. They moved to this area in 1860, with time spent in Arkansas. They are buried at Wade Chapel Cemetery. Thomas died in 1899 and Sarah in 1887. Eleven children were born: Sarah (O'Neal) 1847, Martha (Phelps) 1849, Nancy (O'Neal) 1851, Cynthia (Jackson) 1854, John 1856, Thomas 1860, Robert 1862, Mary 1864, Henry 1865, Alice (Williams) 1867, and Emma 1871. Thomas remarried after the death of Sarah in 1887 to Mary Black. To this union two children were born, Minnie (McConnell) 1890 and James 1891. Mary's death was in 1935.

The 7th child of Thomas and Sarah was Robert Grant Wallace, born in November 1862. He married Mary Catherine "Kate" Rector in January 1885. Mary, born July 1868, was the daughter of John Rector and Tina Davis. Robert and Mary had 10 children: infant son 1886, William Ernest 1887, Vesta 1889, Harry 1891, Charles 1893, John 1895, Neil 1897, Benjamin 1899, Richard 1903 and George 1906.

William Ernest, the 2nd child, was born October 1887 in Barry County, MO and married Mattie Myrtle Land in October 1909. Mattie was the daughter of Andrew Jackson Land and Viola (McKee) Land born in March 1891 in Kansas. They lived their early life in Cross Hollows, close to Jenkins, MO, moving to Elwood, MO in the early 1920s, and later to a house on Center Street in Springfield. Their children were Grace (Johnson) born in October 1910, who married Virgil Johnson in May 1939; Gladys (Robertson) born January 1914, married Finis Robertson in November 1936; Iris (Tinsley) born November 1917, married John Dee Tinsley in December 1940; Harold born July 1922, married Wilma Johnson in 1945 (Virgil's sister); Lois (Henry-Hacker) born December 1925, married Carroll Henry in May 1943. This marriage ended with a divorce and she married Jim Hacker in August 1968.

Back l-r: Grace, Iris, Lois, Gladys; front: Harold, Ernest and Myrtle Wallace.

In 1932, Ernest and family moved to a farm east of Republic which is now the Burl McConnell farm. Two of their children attended the Lindsey School, then high school in Republic. Ernest and Myrtle were active members of the Church of Christ in Republic. Ernest was the song leader for many years, as well as an elder and Bible scholar. Myrtle loved her church and enjoyed fulfilling the duties of an elder's wife. Ernest and Myrtle ran the farm very efficiently, milking, raising cattle, hogs, chickens and the likes. Myrtle canned all of their vegetables, cured their meat and also canned meats to keep over the winter months; she could prepare a meal fit for a king.

Myrtle could and did all the chores it took to make a home. Being a grandmother was one of her greatest gifts; the love she had for her family was to be envied by all. In the late 1950s they retired to a smaller home on North College Street in Republic, spending the remainder of their lives at this location. They died within two weeks of each other in 1961 and are buried at White Chapel Cemetery in Springfield. *Submitted by Lois Hacker.*

**WARD** - It was a warm Saturday morning in August 2000 when Steve and Linda Ward came to Republic to interview for the position of pastor at First Baptist Church. Their first impressions were of tree-shaded streets, new homes being built in many areas of the city, a crowded Highway 60 and a growing, thriving city. They realized immediately that Republic was a place with huge potential. It was far more than a bedroom community for Springfield. Even at this point they weren't aware of the effective and successful school system or major renovations to streets and to Highway 60. It was difficult for them to explain, but there was just a sense of expectancy and excitement in the air as they visited the area with eyes toward a move to Republic. While the Wards grew up in Springfield, they had been living in north central Florida for the last five years, and were looking for an opportunity to get back to the Ozarks. Little

*Steve and Linda Ward*

did they realize on that lovely summer day that they would have the privilege of living in such a great city in southwest Missouri.

In Republic, they discovered a city that puts an emphasis on family and family values, and they found a community that had strong faith-based ties—a community that valued God and godly values. The Wards found it to be a community that loves its children and promotes their welfare through wonderful parks, a new community center, the building of a beautiful new aquatics area that is state-of-the-art, and a great sports program for children and adults. The city has developed a system of walking trails for folks of all ages to encourage people's health and as a way to just get outdoors and enjoy the weather. Republic also offers a well-rounded program for senior adults at the newly renovated seniors' center—activities and benefits that will appeal to the Wards, even in retirement. The Wards are only minutes away from a national landmark at the Wilson's Creek National Battlefield. In addition, Steve and Linda found the people that make up this community as just "good people." Why wouldn't a person want to live in Republic?

The future of Republic is promising. It is certainly not a community in decline, but a community on the rise. New businesses keep coming to Republic, more expansion, and the economy is prosperous. For these reasons Republic will continue to grow and feel the pains that accompany such growth. More people will want to locate here and discover the treasure that is Republic, MO. Since Steve and Linda have located in Republic, both of their daughters and their families have as well. They include Wendy and Lance Renfrow and daughters, Ryley and Reese, and Allison and Bryan Smith and daughter Mavree. This extended family is discovering the fulfillment and satisfaction of others who have had the good fortune of growing up in Republic. They look forward to many more years, more grandchildren, and great-grandchildren who find Republic to be one the best kept secrets in the state. *Submitted by Steve Ward.*

**WARFORD** - Rev. and Mrs. C.C. Warford with five of their children, moved into west Republic in July 1946. Rev. Warford purchased 25 acres of vacant farm land on the south side of Elm Street for $100 an acre. This land was just outside the city in 1946 but is well within the city limits of Republic today. Rev. Warford and children set about building their small farm from scratch. The farm included a modest rock home, barn, chicken house and detached garage. Fencing and digging a well were also of top priority, and by the end of 1947, with the help of outside contractors, all the above improvements had been made.

C.C. Warford was a Southern Baptist minister and a farmer. He also had been a newspaper editor and printer for various small-town newspapers in Oklahoma and Texas. In the late 1940s, he printed the weekly newspaper of the old *Republic Record*. Rev. Warford was pastor of the Brookline Baptist Church from 1947 into 1949. He was pastor of the Bois D'Arc Baptist Church, 1949-1951, and pastor of Hopewell and New Hope Baptist churches west of Republic in the early to mid-1950s. He continued to preach as fill-in at several local churches until the late 1950s. In February 1959, Rev. and Mrs. Warford, along with their children, Fred, Richard and Duane, moved back to their home town of Stigler, OK.

*Rev. and Mrs. C.C. Warford, Republic, MO – 1950.*

Rev. Warford was born 1883 in Chismville, AR and died 1976 in Stigler, OK. Mrs. Warford was born in 1901 in Indian Territory and died in 1979 in Springfield, MO.

Aleta Jo married Ray Beach of Springfield in 1948. She was born 1933 in Lefors, TX and died 2002 in Springfield, MO. Duane C. was born 1936 in Lefors, TX and died 1989 in Muskogee, OK. He never married. Bill "David" was born 1939 in Lefors, TX and married Deanna K. Kerr of Republic in 1962. Their daughter Julie K. married Kirk Phillips. Julie has one daughter, Andrea K. Harris, all of Springfield, MO. Richard H. was born 1941 in Tahlequah, OK and died 1963 in Springfield, MO. He married Peggy Pettijohn of Stigler, OK. They had one son, Terry Van, born and died in 1962. Fred R. was born 1944 in Downey, CA and married Marcene Sadler of Muskogee, OK in 1968. They have one daughter Stacy R., and Stacy has one daughter, Kala Atkinson, all of Muskogee, OK. *Submitted by Julie Phillips.*

**WATTS/BUELL** - Michael Charles Watts was born Dec. 7, 1978, in Mission Viejo, CA, the son of Deborah Casey (Workman) and Ronald Dean Watts. He is the grandson of William Henry and Winifred Casey Workman of Springfield, IL, and Charles Howard and Dorothy Mae (Smith) Watts of Washington, IL.

Mike graduated from Republic High School in 1997. He was a pitcher for the high school and American Legion baseball teams. Mike attended Southwest Missouri State University and earned a bachelor of science

*Michael C. Watts, Teri (Buell) Watts and Lacey Watts.*

degree in finance and general business (2002) and master of business administration with a concentration in finance (2004). While pursuing his master's degree, he was a graduate assistant for the Citizenship and Service Learning office at SMSU.

Currently, Mike is employed as the sales manager of IPA Educational Supply in Springfield, MO. Teri Dawn (Buell) Watts was born April 1, 1979, in Springfield, MO, the daughter of Jack Carroll and Connie Jean (Thompson) Buell.

Teri attended Hurley Elementary and Republic Schools. She was active in music, singing with the Mid-America Singers Children's

Choirs for five years, and taking piano lessons from Carol Coggin for many years. At Republic, she was involved in a variety of activities, including FBLA, speech and debate, Student Council, YES and other academic organizations. During her senior year, Teri was crowned basketball homecoming queen and earned the honor of valedictorian.

Following high school graduation, Teri attended Southwest Missouri State University earning a bachelor of science degree in communications (2001) and a master of arts in communications (2003). While at Southwest Missouri State, Teri was involved in Student Government Association, Collegiate Chorale, Lamda Pi Êta Communication Honor Society and Gamma Sigma service sorority. During her junior year she was crowned university homecoming queen. During graduate school, Teri taught the "Introduction to University Life" course.

Teri is employed at CoxHealth in the Marketing and Planning Department as a public relations assistant. She is the editor of the Cox community magazine, *HealthSense*.

Teri and Mike were married May 7, 2005 and currently live in Republic. Lacey Watts, an 18-year-old Pomeranian, has been the family pet since 1988. *Submitted by Michael and Terri Watts.*

**WATTS/WORKMAN** - Deborah Casey (Workman) Watts was born in Springfield, IL, March 3, 1950. She is the daughter of Winifred Bernice Casey, born in Braidwood, IL, and William Henry Workman, born in Springfield, IL.

*Debbie and Ron Watts.*

Deborah graduated from South East High School in Springfield, IL, in 1968. She is the mother of three children and their spouses: Dena (Thorpe) Marques and her husband Alex of Dana Point, CA; Angela (Thorpe) Ford and her husband E. Gregg of Springfield, MO; and Michael Watts and his wife Teri of Republic, MO.

Ronald Dean Watts was born in New Orleans, LA, Aug. 7, 1945. He is the son of Charles Howard Watts of Chapin, IL, and Wilda Mareno of New Orleans, LA. Ron graduated from Springfield High School in Springfield, IL, in 1963. He served in the Navy from 1963-67. Ron has been employed by Chrysler since 1969. He is the father of three children and their spouses, Jeffrey Watts of Springfield, IL; Lori Estes and her husband David of Springfield, IL; and Michael Watts and his wife Teri of Republic, MO.

Ron and Deb had known each other many years and had been friends. Ron was at the hospital when Deb's husband passed away. The friendship deepened and they were married in 1977.

Deborah and Ron made a job transfer and are currently employed at Ozark Dodge in Ozark, MO. Even though they work in Ozark, as they were searching for a home and drove through Republic they liked the area and "it just really felt like home." They were able to find a house and have lived in Republic 18 years.

Deb enjoys reading and gardening, and Ron enjoys playing golf. *Submitted by Deb Watts.*

**WELCH** - Ronald E. Welch and Donna J. Woodfill were married April 18, 1958. They had two children, Kerry Lynette Welch born May 29, 1961 and Stanley Scott Welch born April 9, 1963. Ronald E. "Ron" is the son of Floyd E. Welch and Lois M. Welch and was born in Des Moines, IA. The family moved to Aurora, MO when Ron was young. Donna Jean is the daughter of Jack C. Woodfill and Mary Ann (Luttrell) Woodfill, longtime residents of Republic.

Ron attended Aurora Schools and moved to Republic when he and Donna were married. In school Ron was interested in art, photography and sports. He was active in scouts, reaching the level of Eagle Scout. Ron started working at Farmer's State Bank in Republic in 1962. He was vice president and treasurer of Safety Federal Savings and Loan in Springfield in 1966. Ron served as vice president and branch manager of the First Savings and Loan in Republic. In 1991 he retired banking and started working in real estate which he continues to do today. Ron and Donna worked at MWM Color Press while living in Aurora and attended college at SMS. Ron is a realtor for Murney Associates and serves on the board of directors for Billings Mutual and Missouri State Mutual Insurance companies.

Donna was born at 133 E. Mill Street. She attended Republic Schools. She was active in band, cheerleading and music. Donna was an outstanding clarinet player. One of Donna's first jobs during high school was working for Harley and Lil Sublett in the Trailways Cafe on Main Street. Donna attended Draughon's Business College. She worked for Montgomery GMC and Montgomery Buick in Springfield while attending SMS. There she met her husband. Donna worked for Madge Blades' Play and Learn Kindergarten. She also worked for the Republic Chamber of Commerce greeting newcomers into the community. She worked for approximately 10 years doing public relations and part-time teller work for Security State Bank. Donna started working in real estate in 1977. She worked at Continental Realty, Jacques Realtors, and later opened her own company, Welch and Associates. Wanting to get back into sales she closed her office in 1991 and went to work for Jones and Company Realtors. Ron and Donna both worked for Jones and Company Realtors, and then transferred their association to Murney Associates.

Kerry graduated from Republic in 1979. Kerry was active in band following her mother's footsteps of playing the clarinet. She participated in photography and track. Kerry worked at Pat's Pizza and Kentucky Fried Chicken. Kerry went to Southwest Baptist University in Bolivar. She transferred to SMS in Springfield. While attending SMS she worked at St. John's Child Development Center. Kerry graduated from SMSU in 1986 with her BS in elementary education and a master's degree in elementary education in 1993. In 1986 Kerry was hired by Republic Schools. She taught kindergarten, was a software coordinator, taught third and fourth grade eMINTS, and computer lab.

Stan graduated from Republic in 1981. His interests were art and playing drums. Stan had his first job at age 10 helping neighbor Shearl Denny haul hay. In high school he began working for Warren and Mable Davis at Cox-Davis Dairy Farms. Stan also had an interest in BMX biking. While in high school he began working for Mac and Reeda McKay and continued working at the Republic IGA for many years as produce manager.

He worked at Associated Grocers for several years, then Springfield Grocers and then went on into construction work which he continues to do today. Stan's favorite pastimes are fishing and hunting.

The family lived at 123 S. West Avenue and then in 1973 moved to a new home they built on Farm Road 174 west of Republic where Ron and Donna still reside. All of the family still live and work in the Republic and surrounding areas. *Submitted by Kerry Welch.*

**WELLS** - Daphne was born in Republic on Sept. 20, 1909 to Robert Ellis and Anna Godwin Thurman, and grew up on East Elm Street with her brother Ellis and three halfsisters: Stella, Blanche and Hazel. The family's neighbors were the Dr. Peebles family (a dentist) to the west, the Lees to the east, and the Burd O'Dell family to the north. Dr. O'Dell had the pharmacy just to the north of the post office on Main Street.

*Daphne (Thurman) Wells (1909-2003).*

As a child Daphne was both musical and athletic, playing the piano and various sports, including basketball. In addition to playing the pump organ for her father's funeral home, she played "action music" for the local movie theater. After graduation from high school Daphne attended Southwest Missouri State Teacher's College. Shortly before her graduation she was informed by her father that the Republic School needed a teacher for the next year, and "I told them you'd do it." Subsequently she got her teaching degree by attending summer school sessions, one in California.

Daphne taught at Republic School and at Bowerman in Springfield until around 1938 when she was offered a bite of postmaster Linzee Wells' hamburger in the cafe on Main Street. After a brief courtship they were married on Jan. 7, 1939 and she moved to his home, Wells Farm, northeast of Republic. Their three children were Mary Susanna, born in 1940; Linda Louise, 1942; and Donald Linzee, 1945. She spent the next few years raising the children. In 1948 Daphne returned to the classroom, teaching fifth and sixth grades for several years, then becoming the elementary music teacher. She was a very dedicated and conscientious teacher who instilled an appreciation for music in uncounted young students. During these years she also volunteered as an accompanist for innumerable soloists and ensembles during the spring music contests, in which Republic's showing was always outstanding.

After her retirement in 1972, Daphne continued to enjoy life and her many friends. She was active in the ABC (Arts, Books, Crafts) Club for many years and belonged to several bridge clubs. She was organist and pianist at the First Christian Church on Main Street for more than 70 years, until her eyesight no longer allowed her to play. Still, she continued to play music and entertain family and friends till the end of her life. She passed away in 2003 at the age of 94. *Submitted by Mary Anne Beck.*

**WELLS** - H. Linzee Wells was born on Oct. 4, 1890 in Paris, TX and raised in a family of six boys and two girls on a claim in Oklahoma, in Pierce City, MO and Aurora, MO where he graduated from high school. He served with the 35th Division, 110th Trench Artillery in France during World War I. In 1922 he used his war bonus to purchase a small run-down farm northeast of Republic and over the next few years he and his wife Edna built up a highly successful turkey business. With the help of neighborhood women, who plucked and processed the birds, Wells Farm turkeys were shipped all over the United States. In 1935, 700 turkeys were marketed. He also established a six-acre apple orchard, a vineyard, and raised chickens, guineas, hogs and dairy cattle.

*Herbert Linzee Wells (1890-1981).*

The Depression made it difficult to make a living on a small farm, so Linzee decided to apply for the position of Republic postmaster. His application was successful and his appointment was confirmed in September 1935. He continued in the position of postmaster for the next 25 years.

After the death of his first wife, Linzee married Daphne Thurman on Jan. 7, 1939 and they had three children: Mary Susanna, born 1940; Linda Louise, 1942; and Donald Linzee, 1945.

Linzee was a widely known and respected man in the community. He was a self-educated man and a voracious reader until his eyesight failed in his 80s. He was dedicated and committed to his work; for instance, on Christmas Day the Wells family's present-opening had to wait until he drove to the office and hand-delivered any packages which had come in the night before. At the same time he continued to keep dairy cows and had a large and highly productive vegetable garden until very late in his life. He was also active in the Masonic Lodge and a faithful tenor in the First Christian Church choir and their men's quartet. He was one of the three members of the building committee for the handsome stone church which sits at 443 N. Main Street and was dedicated in 1950.

He retired in 1960 and continued to enjoy his farm and his family, which came to include nine grandsons. He died in 1981 at the age of nearly 91. *Submitted by Linda Leonard.*

**WELLS FARM** - Wells Farm, at the intersection of Farm Roads 93 and 168 northeast of Republic, has been a family treasure and a local landmark for three generations. The 40-acre farm was part of a larger tract that was originally homesteaded in the 1850s. During the ensuing 70 years, the property changed hands no fewer than 20 times as various owners tried to make a living raising corn and cattle or used the property as a speculative investment.

In 1922, H. Linzee Wells of Aurora purchased the farm for $3,500. This was a very big step for a single man at age 32 with limited resources. Money saved during his service in France during World War I made the purchase possible.

Linzee faced major challenges at every turn. The farm was very run down and had been "corned to death." All the fences needed major repair or replacement. There was a charming, but poorly maintained house that lacked running water or electricity. The red barn (still in use today) was the best building on the place.

*Linzee Wells and guests on the west porch of his Wells farm home ca. 1930.*

In 1925, Linzee married Edna Belle Logan Lekinzie, a nurse originally from St. Louis. During the next 12 years, before Edna's death in 1937, Linzee and Edna made many improvements including remodeling and expanding the house and adding a vineyard, orchard and large garden. About 1930, Linzee, almost single-handedly, built a fieldstone garage and fences (still in use today) using a new masonry technique he developed.

Linzee and Edna also developed a very successful turkey operation. During the first year of production (1930), about 75 turkeys were sold to friends and acquaintances in the Republic/Springfield area. Largely as a result of word-of-mouth "advertising," annual production grew to more than 700 turkeys during the height of the operation (1932-35). The fieldstone garage was used as a processing and packing shed. Friends and neighbors were hired to help with the work. Shipments were made via overnight rail express to Oklahoma City, Kansas City, St. Louis, Chicago and many points in between and beyond.

In 1939, Linzee married Daphne Thurman of Republic, and they raised their three children: Mary Anne, Linda and Don, on the farm. Linzee and Daphne continued the turkey operation at a reduced level until about 1945. They operated the vineyard and orchard, milked a few cows, raised hay and maintained a large garden. Additional improvements were made to the house. In 1979, Linzee and Daphne moved to Republic. *(Please see articles on the Wells and Thurman families elsewhere in this volume.)*

Today, Mary Anne and her husband Dale Beck and Linda and her husband Roger Leonard live on the farm. The Leonards built a house in 1994, and the Becks extensively remodeled the original house in 2000. In 1990, a large pond was constructed.

A small Christmas tree operation was maintained during the 1990s.

While the farming heyday of Wells Farm is past, efforts continue to protect and improve the property for the benefit of generations to come. *Submitted by Don Wells.*

**WERNER** - There are currently three generations of Werners living in the city of Republic. Bill's grandparents (Bill and Betty) have lived in Republic since 1987 after moving from St. Louis where they lived most of their lives. They celebrated their 65th wedding anniversary in 2005. Their only daughter Deb also resides in Republic with her husband Jim. They raised two children, Jay and Melanie, who graduated from Republic HS. Their other son Bob lives in Defiance, MO with his wife Sherri. Their three daughters: Kim, Patty and Robyn still live in the St. Louis area with their husbands and children.

*Back: Barbara Werner, Bill, Mary, Bill Jr.; front: Betty Werner and Bill – September 2005.*

Bill's parents (Bill and Mary) moved to Republic from Nixa in October 2004. They have three children: Kathy who lives in Louisiana with her husband Bruce and their three children: Avalon, Shane and Chris. Bill "Jr." who lives in Republic with his wonderful loving wife Barbara. Kelly lives in Kentucky, where she spends her time working with horses.

Barbara came to Republic in the summer of 1997 from southern California to be closer to her mother Barbara and step-dad Larry, who has lived in Billings, MO since 1977.

She grew up in Calumet City, IL with her three sisters and two brothers. Currently, one sister lives in Liberty, MO with her husband where they raised one son. Her father John, his wife Tina, and her three sons and their families, along with one brother and his wife and her other two sisters with their husbands and children plus a grandchild, live in the suburbs of the Chicago/Joliet area. The youngest brother lives in Milwaukee with his wife and his youngest son. She met her loving husband, Bill Werner, in the fall of 1999, and they were married the following year in October. Barbara works in Springfield as an education coordinator for McKesson, but her biggest job is keeping the family in order making sure that everything runs smoothly. Her family would be lost without her organizational skills. She is an active member of the ladies auxiliary of the Republic VFW Post 4593. Barbara and Bill are the Mr. and Mrs. Chairpersons of the Buddy Poppies committee for the second year running.

Bill Werner Jr. grew up in Springfield and graduated from Marionville. He joined the Navy after graduation where he spent the next six years. During his tour he was privileged to have been part of the USS *Missouri* (BB-63) re-commissioning crew. He was in combat areas on both his ships, the USS *Missouri* (BB-63) and the USS *Tarawa* (LHA-1). His two girls, Kristina and Colleen, and grandson Mitchell live with their mother in Springfield. Currently he is an active life member of the local VFW Post 4593. He is also on the Republic Communication Committee and will be on the April 2006 election ticket running for a seat to help write the Home Rule Charter for Republic.

Currently Bill Jr. and his parents own BMW Realtors, Inc., a small real estate office here in Republic. Bill and Mary started the company and later asked Bill Jr. to join them in the family business. *Submitted by Bill and Barbara Werner.*

**WEST/COX -** Libby Cox West is the daughter of Beth "Puge" Snyder and Adrian Ervin "Heavy" Cox, living all of her life in Republic. She grew up in a house located at the southwest corner of Main and Highway 60, and at age 10, moved to the outer edge of the city to live on a farm on a dirt road. The current address is 613 E. Hines. This same area in which she continues to live is now considered a central part of the city. It is across the street from the city park. From her childhood she remembers the family telephone with the party lines and cranks used to ring them. She still remembers her phone number: 150M. Libby loved helping her dad on the farm, feeding the cows, gathering the eggs and bottle feeding the baby lambs. She always accused her older sister Phyllis of doing only one chore - putting water in the furnace humidifier.

Libby met Joe West when she was in the eighth grade and he was a junior in high school. He threw her in Terrell Creek for freshman initiation and told her to walk back to Republic. About halfway back to Republic, Libby got a ride, hidden in the trunk of a car. She enjoyed being active in numerous high school activities such as pep club, Future Homemakers of America, chorus, cheerleading, attending all sports activities and dancing with a youth square dance group. The Jig-A-Longs were regulars on a live television production "The Ozarks Jubilee," which was broadcast from the Springfield Jewell Theater, located on Jefferson Street downtown Springfield, MO. Libby served as a dancer and caller for the group. Joe and Libby dated in high school and were married on Dec. 15, 1962.

Joe was the son of Robert Fay and Tina Maxine (Marshal) West. The family moved to Republic from Greenfield, MO in 1957. Joe worked at Alton Box, Yale Forklift and Paul Mueller Company until his retirement. Libby did factory work and was later employed as a secretary for the Republic R-III School District where she continues to work.

Joe and Libby love camping, traveling, fishing, and nature. Fishing trips to Canada have been a real adventure for them. The Alaskan Cruise proved to be some of the most beautiful scenery they had visited.

Libby and Joe spend a lot of time with their four daughters: Jerri Reser, Barbie Luttrell, Mindy Kelley and Marti Clark, eight grandkids and seven great-grandkids.

In their youth, Libby and Joe loved fast cars and racing motorcycles. In their retirement years, they still love to ride their Harley. *Submitted by Jerri Reser. Editor's note: Joe passed away 2007.*

**WEST/DODD -** Kenneth West was born in 1903 in the rural Ash Grove area, and Deloris Louise Dodd was born in 1905 in rural Walnut Grove. Married when Deloris was 21, they lived in the same area until the early 30s when they moved to Springfield. Their only child, John William, was born in 1939. Deloris was a teacher and Kenneth became an electrician in the era when electricity was new and mysterious. In the 30s Kenneth was a contractor and built many of the tall AM radio towers surrounding Springfield in the early days of radio. He began a career with the Frisco Railroad in 1940.

Desiring to return to the farm, the couple bought 160 acres at the east end of current Farm Road 164, north of Republic in 1945. Electricity was not available so the family did not move until REA came through in 1948. A sawmill was located on the farm in 1946 and again in 1952 cutting and selling oak lumber.

This was an idyllic farm. Pond Creek wandered through the farm and was swelled by two large springs from which water was piped to the house. The Frisco Railroad held five acres for a lake from which water was pumped to a tower in Brookline for steam engines. By 1948 the dam had washed out but the remnants were still there, as was a rock washhouse.

*Loader made by Kenneth West. John, Lady (dog) and Kenneth.*

Orchard grass seed was profitable in those days. Binding, shocking and threshing this fragile crop was the most profitable method. Kenneth and John bought a Belle City thresher which was one of the last commercially operating machines. They built the loader shown in the picture. This machine was used with a 12 by 12 foot buck rake to bring shocks to the thresher. Later in the season it was used to build huge 20 foot tall ricks of hay when the orchard grass and lespedeza were cut.

In 1950 Kenneth and John became interested in the Soap Box Derby, a popular race in those days, and John built a streamlined racer. After entering in 1950 he won the race in Springfield the second year in 1951.

Kenneth worked for the Frisco Railroad until forced to retire for health reasons in 1967. He and Deloris bought a house in Republic on Fountain Street and moved from the farm. Kenneth remained active through a seven year struggle with cancer. He and Deloris loved their Lord and the First Baptist Church where both taught. Kenneth did the wiring in the current sanctuary. He remained active until his death in 1970.

The tornado of 1971 destroyed the two large barns built by Kenneth and John but spared the house and older barns on the farm. Deloris rented it out until she moved to Kansas in 1984 to be with her son and family. Deloris passed in 1993 in Paola, KS. Today the orchard grass fields have been developed into beautiful acreage, but the wooded part appears intact. *Submitted by John West.*

**WEST/ROBERTSON –** John W. and Mary K. (Robertson) West were raised in the Republic area during most of their young lives. John is the son of Francis Kenneth and Deloris Louise (Dodd) West and Mary the daughter of Wm. Finis Robertson and Gladys Lucille (Wallace) Robertson. John attended Mt. Aetna School and Mary attended Lindsey and Green Ridge Schools until the consolidation of schools when they entered the 7th

*John and Mary West – 1999.*

grade. They spent the remainder of their school years together. Both graduated from RHS in 1957 and from SMS in 1961. They were married following graduation on Aug. 6, 1961, in the old First Baptist Church building, Main Street, Republic.

They rented a house on West Anderson Street and Mary began teaching first grade at the Republic Elementary School, with 33 students. Quite a load for a new teacher but she dearly loved all of them. John was to enter the Army that winter so he taught shop, on a substitute basis in Springfield, then entered basic officer training. Mary finished the school year then joined John at Indianhead, MD. He was attending bomb disposal and demolition training. They relocated to Fort Riley, KS, where John was CO of the 98th Ordnance Detachment (ED), for the remainder of his three years of service. They lived in Manhattan, KS during this time and helped in the early days of the First Southern Baptist Church of Manhattan, now College Heights Baptist Church. Their first daughter, Kerry Sue, was born at the Fort Riley Army Hospital in April 1963.

After completing John's military obligation, the family moved back to Republic and bought an older house on Walnut Street. John worked for the Springday plant as an engineer and their second daughter, Karyl Kay, was born in October 1966. John had a chance to rejoin the Federal Service, this time as a civilian, at the U.S. Medical Center in Springfield. He had several positions and locations with the Bureau of Prisons ending with an assignment in Washington, D.C. Not liking the Washington scene he changed agencies and locations moving to a position with the Federal Aviation Administration in Kansas City, MO in 1970. This brought them back closer to their parents in Republic.

Their third daughter, Kendra Lee, was born in Olathe, KS, September 1974. John continued in several positions with FAA, in Kansas City and retired in 1994. During this period they purchased two small farms in the Spring Hill and Hillsdale areas and John farmed on the side. They were active in their church and helped start the Spring Hill Community Church, now Grace Community Church.

They now have eight grandchildren and live on a farm near Hillsdale, KS. Being semi-retired, John manages an apartment complex for the elderly and drives a school bus. They still visit family in Republic and really enjoy their high school class reunions with the class of '57. *Submitted by Karyl Morris.*

**WHITE –** Francis Jr. has lived in Republic all his life, since March 6, 1959. His dad Francis E. White Sr. was born on Oct. 14, 1904, in Gainesville, MO. His mom, Ellen G. White, was born on July 20, 1916, in Bruner, MO. They lived on West Street in Republic when Francis Jr. was born. Ellen had been married before and had six children: Robert, Johnny, Chuck, Velma, Jane and Ann. Francis Sr. had also been married before and had six children: Frank, James, Eugene, Betty, Bonnie, and Velma. Francis Jr. was the thirteenth child, but their first together.

As you can imagine Ellen was kept busy at home. In April of 1959 Francis Sr. got a job for Fugitt Farms, three miles south of Republic. He was always busy, trying to provide for all the children still at home.

This farm was a great place to grow up. Terrell Creek ran through the farm, and there were 1800 acres to play on. It was lonely at times. By the time Francis Jr. turned 6, all his brothers and sisters had married or moved

*White family in 1988. Left side is Whites, right side is Chathams and front center is Francis E. White Jr.*

away. The nearest neighbor was one-half mile away.

They raised most of their food. They raised cows for meat, milk and butter. They raised chickens for meat and eggs. They raised hogs for meat and extra money. They also raised goats, rabbits, guineas, turkeys and geese. They also had a large garden. Ellen was always picking, plucking, canning, butchering, or cleaning.

Francis Sr. worked from six in the morning until six at night, five days a week and from six until twelve on Saturday. After work he slopped and watered the hogs, milked the cows, and worked in the garden. On Saturday afternoon, they would go to town to get feed and groceries. About all they had to buy was salt, pepper, flour, sugar, and bread. Not much time for rest, but they made time for family and friends.

The old house they lived in has burnt down. There were a lot of good memories made there. They had an outhouse, and the only water was from an old pump on the porch. They heated with wood stoves. The house had a garage in the large basement, but it was built for buggies. Only small cars, like a Volkswagen, would fit. The house had six large rooms down stairs plus a bathroom Francis Sr. built around 1965. There were two rooms upstairs. The house didn't have any insulation, so it got pretty cold during the winter and took a lot of wood to heat. Francis Sr. retired and moved to town in 1970.

Francis Jr. bought the house in 1977, and has lived on College Street ever since. He married Debbie McGuire on March 8, 1981. Their first son, Francis E. "Frank" White III, was born Feb. 19, 1983, and second son, Bradley Lee "Brad" White was born Jan. 28, 1987. They like living in Republic! It's still a religious farming community. It's not as small and quiet as it used to be, but everything changes with time. *Submitted by Francis E. White Jr.*

**WHITE** – The family of Stanley and Georgia White includes six children: 1) Ruth Annella (born Dec. 8, 1951) married Gary Lee Sanders July 8, 1972. They live on a farm west of Miller and are active at Gray's Point Christian Church where her dad is minister. Two children, Carolyn Ann (born April 22, 1973) married Timothy O'Kelley on July 29, 1995. She works in the Hammond's Tower and he at Jack Henry. A daughter Alyssa was born Aug. 25, 2003. They live west of Halltown and attend Elm Branch Christian Church. Jonathan Lee (born Dec. 6, 1978) works on the farm and is superintendent at Gray's Point.

2) Paul Stanley (born Jan. 14, 1954) married Kelly Lee (Smith) on March 18, 1989. They live just southeast of his parents. He is self-employed doing vehicle seat and windshield repair, and mowing. He is an elder at Willard Community Christian Church. He adopted Kelly's three daughters: a.)Jacque (born Sept. 16, 1978) married Chris Burke on Dec. 20, 1997. He is minister at Rhinehart Christian Church. They have two daughters, Kayla Lee (born Jan. 22, 2002) and Bethany Grace (born Nov. 1, 2003). b.) Jessica Lynn (born Nov. 15, 1980) married Evan Valentine, Aug. 28, 1999, an irrigation specialist and part time youth minister at the church. Jessica and Evan have three children: Tia Star (born Aug. 13, 1997); Matthew Paul (born Dec. 16, 2001); and Hannah Lynn (born Feb. 8, 2003). c.) Jaime Laine (born Aug. 9, 1982) graduated OCC and works with premature births in Oklahoma City. Paul and Kelly also adopted the girls' half brother Nicholas Paul (born Sept. 4, 1984), who works at Wal-Mart, attends OTC, and runs the sound system at Willard.

3) Mary Ellen (born Nov. 28, 1955) married Patrick Timothy Otero on May 26, 1978 and works at General Mills and is a Hospice volunteer chaplain. Their five children are: Jason Timothy (born Dec. 19, 1982) teaches guitar, leads worship and installs security systems; Julia Maria (born April 28, 1985) is a nanny; Joanna Rachel (born Nov. 1, 1994), Jonathan David (born Dec. 3, 1996) and Joshua Daniel (born Jan. 6, 2000) are active at College Heights Christian Church.

4) David Lee (born Sept. 25, 1957) married Rebecca Ann (Byran) Aug. 27, 1988. He is an elementary guidance counselor. They have three daughters: Amy Rebecca (born June 24, 1990); Amber Ann (born April 4, 1993); and Amanda Jo (born Oct. 28, 1995). They built on the White farm and are active at Glendale Christian Church.

5) Lydia Ann (born Dec. 28, 1962) married Steve Copenhaver June 2, 1984. He took over his dad's electrical business. Steve's delight is serving as elder at Issaquah Christian Church where they are members. They have four children: Ashley Joanna (born Aug. 20, 1989); Heather Leanne (born Sept. 15, 1991); Stephanie Deanne (born Jan. 5, 1994); and Stephen Douglas II (born Aug. 24, 1998).

6) John Edwin (born Jan. 9, 1967) married Cynthia Kay (Grogg) May 14, 1988. He taught 10 years at Cookson Hills Christian School and now is a special education teacher at Republic. They have two sons, Adam John (born Dec. 15, 1993) and Caleb Benjamin (born Sept. 5, 1996). John also built on the farm where they were raised. They are active in the Glendale Christian Church. *Submitted by Paul Stanley White.*

**WHITE/JOHNSON** - During the hot summer evenings of the late 60s and early 70s, Bervin Junior White could be found doing what he loved most--working with children as a Little League umpire. Bervin believed there was no better preparation for life than participation in his beloved baseball. That is why during the summer he could be found nightly at the Kiwanis baseball field in Republic.

Although it could honestly be said that Bervin (born Sept. 9, 1935) loved all sports, he was especially fond of baseball and softball. He played softball and slow pitch softball until his death Aug. 23, 1978. He also umpired slow pitch softball, receiving the honor of being invited to umpire the National Tournament in 1975. Before his death, Bervin helped lay out the plans for the ball field complex on Miller Road. After his death, the city of Republic honored his devotion to the city of Republic and to the sports of baseball and softball by dedicating the new complex in his name. It is known as the Bervin White Memorial Ballfield.

*Bervin and Shirley White.*

Bervin was married to Shirley Johnson from Chesapeake, MO. They had three children: Larry, Brenda and Beverly. The family moved to Republic in 1965 where Bervin and Shirley became active members of the Republic community. Bervin was a member of the Republic Volunteer Fire Department and the Chief of the Republic Reserve Police Force. He worked for the Missouri Highway Department that was located in Republic.

Shirley worked in the community of Republic for many years. She was employed by Hagle Garment Factory, Republic R-III School District, Yocum Tire and Automotive, McDonalds as well as Wal-Mart. She also managed the concession stand at the Kiwanis baseball field for several years. Shirley's untimely death occurred May 1994.

Bervin and Shirley's children are very proud of their parents. They are proud of their positive roles in the growth of the Republic Parks Program's summer ball leagues. Because of their work and dedication in the early years of the program, Republic has a sound summer ball program for children and youth. *Submitted by Beverly White.*

**WHITE/SCOTT** - Georgia Ellan Scott (born Dec. 1, 1929) graduated from Lebanon High School and married Stanley L. White Aug. 30, 1950. Her ancestors can be traced on her mother's side to Sir Oliver Cromwell, Lord Protector of England, and three generations earlier to Thomas Cromwell, 1486.

Georgia's granddad George Parker Ingersoll (born March 11, 1878) was linotype operator for the *Ash Grove Commonwealth* and other newspapers. He married Milley Annella Fulks Dec. 27, 1899 who died in childbirth when Georgia's mother was only three. She and her older sister went to live with their uncle and aunt. In a few years her dad married Grace Meyer and they went to live with them.

Georgia's great-granddad John Scott was Irish but moved to England so he could teach his trade to others. He was a "puddler" (has to do with working with something like stucco). There, John C. Scott was born in West Hartleypool June 13, 1871. In 1883 they came to the U.S. when John C was 12. He married Ida Ella Tippy June 1, 1899. He became a medical doctor, who brought his family from Talma, IN to Lebanon in 1911. He came to Missouri for his health, intending to farm. When the flu epidemic hit in 1918, he was encouraged to return to his practice. He delivered his two grandchildren, Georgia Ellan (Dec, 1, 1929) and John Michael (Dec 29, 1937). He died in January 1938.

Stanley began preaching May 7, 1950 at McKinley Christian Church. His parents had a home built for them for $4,000.00 just south of

*Back: Mary, John, Paul, David; front: Ruth, Georgia, Stanley, Lydia White.*

the home place in 1952, where they continue to live. Stanley also preached for these Christian Churches: Marionville, High Prairie, Arcola, Halltown (his home church), Westside, Republic and is in his 24th year at Gray's Point. He has served the area in many ways, with his wife by his side. They were blessed with six children: Ruth Annella Sanders (Dec. 8, 1951); Paul Stanley (Jan. 14, 1954); Mary Ellen Otero (Nov. 28, 1955); David Lee (Sept. 25, 1957); Lydia Ann Copenhaver (Dec. 28, 1962) and John Edwin (Jan. 9, 1967).

The Whites are so thankful for those who have gone before them, and given direction, for the farm where they could raise their children. The hard work of dairying, row cropping, haying and beef cattle has been good for them. It paid the bills and gave time to work with the area churches. It gave their children and the generations to follow a reason to serve others. God has been so good in giving His Son, that ALL by accepting that gift can have hope for this life and the eternity God wants for everyone who obeys His Word.

Acts 4:12 is such a great truth. "Neither is there salvation in any other; for there is none other name under Heaven given among men, whereby we must be saved." They are grateful the way their children, grandchildren and great-grandchildren are serving others in Jesus name. *Submitted by Ruth Annella Sanders.*

**WILES** – It was the spring of 1942 when Jack and Maud Wiles, with their eight children, moved to Republic, MO. Jack's job as a glazier, putting in windows for airplane factories, had kept them on the move. This move from St. Joseph, MO to Republic was the last "move" for the family of 10.

*Back l-r: Jack Wiles (father) holding Jackie, Jack "Lin", Maud (mother). Front: Ramona, Joyce, Frank, Betty, Anna Mae, and June.*

They were barely settled into the little white house when they heard the radio broadcast announcing that the U.S. was "At War". Joyce remembered how worried her mother was because the oldest son, Jack "Lin", was a senior in high school, and her mom was so afraid that he would be called up. Her fears were realized, when following his graduation from Republic HS, he was in fact drafted into the Army to serve in Japan. Nevertheless, Republic HS had certainly not seen the end of the Wiles. Five more children walked its halls over the next several years. June, Anna Mae, Betty, Frank and Joyce, all graduated from Republic High. Lin's star hung in the window for two years and they were thrilled and thankful to be able to take it down when he returned home safe and sound. As with so many Americans, one did what could be done for the war effort; from entertaining soldiers for Sunday dinner to buying war bonds and stamps with extra money.

Upon graduation from Republic HS, several Wiles family members found employment at Woods Garment Factory. It was hard, grueling work as Joyce recalled, and she only lasted about six months before moving to Witchita, KS, where her older brother Lin and sister Betty were living. Joyce soon found a job and in the fall of 1951 was joined by her mother and two younger sisters, Ramona and Jackie.

One by one all left the sweet little town of Republic and started families of their own. Lin died at 79 leaving three children, June had three children, Anna Mae had five children, Betty died at 55 leaving one child, Frank had two children, Joyce had three children, Ramona had six children, and Jackie had three children.

They have never forgotten those days in Republic when they were so young. Although times were hard, the country was full of the same innocence and hope the Wiles family had. *Respectfully submitted by Joyce (Wiles) Smith.*

**WILHITE/ROBERTSON** - On Aug. 7, 1921, Charles Roscoe Wilhite (originally spelled Willhite) and Gertie S. Robertson were married in Springfield, MO. Charley was employed by the Frisco Railroad and Gertie attended Springfield State Normal College (presently known as Missouri State University) during the summer months, while teaching in rural Missouri schools during the school year.

*Gertie S. (Robertson) and Charles R. Wilhite.*

When the Frisco went out on strike, they moved to Detroit, MI where Charley found employment with the Ford Motor Company. During an extremely cold and severe winter, Charley came down with pneumonia and couldn't work. It was at that time they moved to Republic to be near friends and Gertie's family until he could regain his health and find employment.

Charles Roscoe Wilhite was the 10th child of Samuel Huston Wilhite (1843-1906) and Unity Jane (Turner) Wilhite (1852-1904). Charley was born on the family farm near Riverdale, in Christian County, MO on Sept. 27, 1888 and died April 20, 1957. He had four brothers and five sisters. Charley served in WWI in the U.S. Army, as a Corporal in the 11th Replacement Battalion, July 4, 1918 thru May 4, 1919, traveling via troopship to France. Many of the troops died of flu during their ocean-crossing.

Charley's father, Samuel Huston Wilhite, served in the U.S. Army during the Civil War, Company K Regiment, 21st Volunteers from Feb. 8, 1862 until he was honorably discharged on Feb. 11, 1865.

Gertie S. (Robertson) Wilhite was the 8th child of William Benjamin Robertson (1853-1923) and Sarah Alice (Johns) Robertson (1856-1937). Gertie was born on the family farm in Greene County, MO near the Wilson's Creek National Battlefield on Aug. 28, 1894 and died Aug. 29, 1984. She had two sisters and five brothers. Gertie's great-great-grandfather, known as Uncle Lindsey Robertson (1792-1861), organized the first Methodist church in Republic, the Methodist Episcopal Church, and was its pastor until his death.

Since there was no pastor available, a camp meeting was held each year at Robertson Spring to keep the interest alive and hold the group together until the present building (Hood United Methodist Church) was erected in 1891 (see *Republic, MO Home of 3,000 Good Neighbors*, page 98, published in 1971). Charley, Gertie, and their children were active members at Hood UMC until moving away from Republic.

During the Depression years and drought of the 1930s, Charley and Gertie suffered not only from several serious family illnesses, but also faced extreme economic hardship. As a result they lost their home in Republic. With the help of friends and family, and by their own industriousness and frugality, they were able to survive these trying times. They grew as much of their own food as possible, canned and preserved it; kept a cow for milk for the family; had chickens to eat and for eggs; raised a hog to butcher, and Gertie sewed her clothes and Betty Jane's from "hand-me-downs" and remnants given to her by friends and neighbors.

During the late 1930s, Charley found work with the State Highway Department where he was employed for several years. At that time they were able to purchase their own home on North Walnut Street.

In the early 1940s, during WWII, both Charley and Gertie were employed at the MFA Grocery & Feed Store on Main Street in Republic, retiring in the 1950s. The manager of the MFA Store was Lester "Bud" Logan and, later, Don Sneed.

Two children were born to Charley and Gertie, a son, Charles William Wilhite (born June 5, 1922 in Springfield, MO) and a daughter, Betty Jane Wilhite (born March 11, 1929), on a farm east of Republic near the Wilson's Creek National Battlefield. C.W. and Betty Jane graduated from Republic High School.

C.W. served in the U.S. Navy during WWII from 1942-46 in the South Pacific aboard the aircraft carrier USS *Yorktown*. On Sept. 13, 1952, he married Irene Willoughby (died Feb. 20, 2006) and they have two sons, Charles Daniel and William Burton Wilhite. Charles Daniel (born Oct. 2, 1954), has a BS degree from Missouri State University. He married Lana Norris on April 14, 1992. William Burton (born Jan. 20, 1957) has a BS degree from Missouri State University. He married Michele Ragland on Aug. 3, 1992. Bill and Michele have one son, Chad William Wilhite (born Jan. 24, 1994) who attends school in Republic, MO. *Submitted by Jane Wilhite.*

**WILLIAMS** - Enoch Williams was born about 1840 and at age 22 enlisted in Company D, 24th Regiment of the Iowa Volunteers and served from 1862 to 1865 in the Civil War fighting for the Union. He was discharged at Savannah, GA after surviving the war unwounded.

*Williams – l-r: Dorothy, Nannie, Lucille.*

Enoch was the father of Ralph, Jess and a daughter Mary, who married W.P. Lummis. Enoch, Ralph and his wife Nannie lived on South Main Street in the house built by them.

Enoch died in May 1939 at age 98 and is buried in the Evergreen Cemetery.

Ralph and Nannie married in 1902 and had two girls, Dorothy and Lucille. Ralph was a professional house painter and Nannie worked for the gas company, reading their charts, which was located close to their home which Ralph built on South Main Street. Ralph and Nannie are buried in Evergreen Cemetery in the Williams plot.

Lucille was a school teacher in Republic and St. Louis until Dr. Robert Mitchell came to Republic in 1931 to become the town physician. They married and lived on Elm Street and were lifelong residents. They had one son John who lives in Palmdale, CA. Robert died first with Lucille living several years afterward. Her hobby was playing bridge at which she was very proficient. Lucille and Robert are buried in the Mitchell plot in Evergreen Cemetery. *Submitted by Doug Hill.*

**WILLIAMS/COLLINS** - Hal L. Williams was born Nov. 27, 1933 to Hal K. Williams and Edna R. (Qualls) Williams near Mr. Vernon in Lawrence County, MO. His grandparents were Robert Williams and Melcina (Young) Williams and Jim Qualls and Cora (Moore) Qualls.

Naoma R. Collins was born June 12, 1938, to Troy O. Collins and Juanita (Box) Collins near the community of Lawrenceburg, also in Lawrence County, MO. Naoma's grandparents were Thomas H. Collins and Ella (Stines) Collins and William M. Box and Anna (Wynkoop) Box.

*Randy, Naoma, Hal, Karen Williams.*

Hal attended Edgewood grade school, Mt. Vernon High School and Southwest Missouri State College, graduating in 1955 with a BS in agriculture. He then served in the U.S. Army where he was stationed for 2-1/2 years at Toul Engineer Depot, Toul, France.

Naoma attended Lawrenceburg and Little Moore grade schools, Miller High School and Southwest Missouri State College where she majored in art.

Hal was discharged from the Army on Sept. 5, 1958, and he and Naoma were married on Oct. 25, 1958. They lived in Springfield for about a year before moving to the Republic area.

Hal and Naoma have two children, Karen and Randall "Randy." Karen (born Sept. 10, 1961) attended elementary and high school in Republic and is a graduate of Southwest Missouri State University. Karen now lives in Blue Springs, MO with her husband, Randy Fiene, and two daughters, Paige and Madison.

Randy Williams (born March 18, 1965) also attended Republic schools and is a graduate of Southwest Missouri State University. He now lives in Republic with his wife, Suni, and children, Jarred and Kaelei.

Hal and Naoma have enjoyed their married life which includes raising their children, their work and their social life. Hal worked in wholesale sales of agriculture and lawn and garden products, first with Lipscomb Agricultural Supply and later Springfield Seed Company, both in Springfield. Naoma worked for Southworth Printing Co, as a homemaker, a substitute teacher, and with Greenleaf Gardens in Republic. They are active members of Hood United Methodist Church. Hal has been a member of the Kiwanis Club of Republic for over 40 years. Naoma has also been a member of the American Home Club for over 40 years.

Both are now retired, and like most retired people, have trouble finding time to do everything that they want to do. Naoma enjoys painting, reading, and flower gardening. Hal enjoys gardening, watching sports and visiting with friends. *Submitted by Hal and Naoma Williams.*

**WILSON/JONES** – Florence Kathleen "Kay" Jones, daughter of Bert Isaac Jones and Ora Ellen (Coggin) Jones, was born Sept. 5, 1916. Florence married Paul A. Wilson (Sept. 27, 1914-June 1986) on Sept. 5, 1934. Initially they made their home on a farm north of Republic. In 1936, due to drought, they moved to Long Beach, CA to work in the Ford plant. A son, Gordon Lynn Wilson, was born Nov. 11, 1937. In 1938 the family moved back to Greene County on a dairy farm west of Springfield. Their daughter, Donna Kay Wilson was born Oct. 10, 1941.

*Kathleen "Kay," Donna K., Gordon L., Paul A. Wilson.*

Gordon Lynn Wilson and Donna May Walker (born Aug. 8, 1940) were married June 7, 1958. Gordon was in the U.S. Air Force at that time and was sent to England for 16 months. On returning, Gordon and Donna moved to Tulsa, OK, where Gordon worked for American Airlines. They had a son and daughter, Dan Jeffery Wilson (born Sept. 26, 1960) and Teresa Lynn Wilson (born July 17, 1962). In 1968 the family moved to a dairy farm northwest of Republic where they farmed for many years.

Dan Jeffery Wilson married Cathy Sue Hafley (born July 15, 1958) on March 21, 1982. They met at School of the Ozarks and were married after graduation. They made their home in Missouri initially, but later moved to Tulsa, OK. Their son, Bradley Michael Wilson was born July 26, 1990.

Teresa Lynn Wilson married Steven Mark Fletcher (born Nov. 1, 1961) on Feb. 19, 1983. They have made their home in Republic. Daughter Tiffany Lynn Wilson was born July 15, 1984 and son Cody Alan Fletcher was born May 13, 1987. Teresa is in banking and Steve is a Republic fireman.

Donna Kay Wilson married James Espy (born Aug. 1, 1938) on May 15, 1960. To this union were born three children: Scott M. Espy (Feb. 21, 1961), Dana A. Espy (Feb. 28, 1963) and Gina K. Espy (Feb. 20, 1967). Donna has taught school for many years and Jim is in the insurance business. Their home is in the Strafford area.

Scott Michael Espy and Lisa Gerst were married in 1982. Scott attended the University of Missouri Veterinarian School and began practicing in Marshfield. Lisa attended nursing school and has worked at various health institutions in the Springfield area. To this union was born Catherine Marie Espy (Feb. 28, 1990), Aaron Joseph Espy (Oct. 15, 1993) and Natalie Ann Espy (Oct. 20, 1994).

Dana Ann Espy and Jim Jones were married Nov. 26, 1988. To this union was born one son, Matthew Tyler Jones, on Sept. 15, 1993. Dana and family have resided in the St. Louis area since marriage. Dana is working in the medical field.

Gina Kay Espy and Jason Gannaway were married in 1991. To this union was born Lea Marie Gannaway (born May 17, 1993) and Justin Michael Gannaway (born June 21, 1995). Jason works with computers and Lisa in retail. They reside in the Strafford area. *Submitted by Gordon L. Wilson.*

**WOLFF** - Douglas Wolff was born and raised on a farm in southern Minnesota and his wife Mary was born and raised in Des Moines, IA. Douglas served with the Army Force in Europe during WWII. They were married in Des Moines in 1946 following Doug's discharge from the service. They then moved to Minnesota where they farmed the family century farm for seven years.

*Doug and Mary Wolff.*

In 1953 Doug obtained a position as a civilian employee of the U.S. Air Force at Luke AFB in Arizona where he served as a jet engine specialist. At the same time Mary was employed as a quality control inspector by Motorola Semi Conductors in Phoenix. Following Doug's retirement from Luke AFB, he was employed as an audio visual technician by the Phoenix Union High School District until again retiring.

In 1986 they moved to northern California where they lived until 2003 when they moved to Republic. They bought a house on a farm acreage adjacent to the Wilson's Creek National Battlefield. Their daughter Dr. Linda Vaught and her husband Dr. William Vaught built a new house on the farm acreage next to their place.

Linda is employed at Missouri State University. William manages their Vitro Fertilization Lab business in northern California with the use of computers and much air travel. Mary and Doug are members of the Hood United Methodist Church and Doug is a life member of a VFW post in Springfield.

They both grew up in the Midwest so coming to Republic is sort of a "homecoming" for them and they find the rural tempo of life in the country to be very pleasant. *Submitted by Doug Wolff.*

**WOODFILL/GREEN** - Jared Kingery Woodfill, a son of John Irons and Hannah Margaret (Kingery) Woodfill, was born in 1888 in Nichols, MO. He was married in 1907 to Georgia Elizabeth Green, daughter of George and Sarah (Twigger) Green, former neighbors in Nichols. Like their father and grandfather, Jared and his brothers learned telegraphy at a young age, and all worked for the railroads.

Jared, or "Jerry," worked from 1906 through 1914 for the Frisco Railroad as telegrapher and cashier at various points in the sys-

*Jared and Georgia Woodfill.*

tem, including Fort Scott, KS, Aurora, Logan, Lebanon and Republic, MO. In 1910, while at Logan, Katherine was born. Jack was born at Lebanon in 1912. That same year, they moved to Republic and lived on North Main Street for several years. In August 1914, he was hired by the Becker and Langenberg Milling Company as telegrapher and rate clerk. When the company sold out to Rae-Patterson Milling of Coffeyville, KS, in 1918, Jared was retained as the Republic Branch Manager. The family then moved across town to the McCleary house, also known as the miller's house, on E. Elm Street.

Jared and Georgia were active in the local lodge and Eastern Star, Civic Club, and the First Christian Church. He served on the school board. Although their children, Katherine and Jack, both worked at a young age, they also enjoyed music lessons and a busy social life. They picked strawberries on the family's small acreage north of town. Katherine packed daffodil bulbs and other plants for shipping while working for Mrs. Anna Howard at Howard's Gardens. Jack was the "soda jerk" at O'Dell's Drug Store and learned to press suits at the cleaning plant, located behind the barber shop.

In 1926, the Rae-Patterson Milling Company closed the Republic facility and combined operations with the Coffeyville branch. Although he was offered a transfer to Kansas, the family chose to stay in Republic. Jared then leased the mill storage area and went into the feed and flour business for himself.

Jared and Georgia began a second family when Mary Jean was born in 1926 and Jaredene in 1930. About the same time, Jack married Mary Luttrell, daughter of local grocer, John Luttrell, and they moved to Claremore, OK with her family. Katherine married Gus Verfurth, a native of Billings.

When the leased buildings were sold to Producers Ice and Manufacturing and converted to cold storage, Jared moved his family to Springfield. He attended classes at Drury College and was employed in general office work. Katherine worked at a beauty salon and eventually bought her own shop. Mary Jean and Jaredene attended schools in Springfield and graduated from Central High.

Jack and Mary returned to Republic with their daughter, Jacqueline. Patsy and Donna were born in Republic and all three graduated from the local high school. Jack worked in Springfield for Mary's brother Burley and his wife Mae. He later opened his own service station and grocery business.

Jared was working at Campbell 66 Freight Lines when he became ill and died in 1944. Georgia continued to live in Springfield where she died in 1982. She and Jared are buried at Clear Creek Cemetery. *Submitted by Patsy Woodfill Trogdon.*

**WOODFILL/LUTTRELL** - Jack Woodfill and Mary Luttrell were married in 1929. They were school sweethearts, passing notes during class from the time they attended the two-story grade school on West Elm to the new (1920) high school on Anderson Street. They purchased a house on Mill Street in 1933 from Bernice Noe, who had recently lost her husband, Marshall Mark Noe. She moved to the house next door

*Jack and Mary (Luttrell) Woodfill.*

and was a good friend and neighbor until her death in 1967. The house was on a large lot with a barn and room for chickens and two cows. It was behind the house on Elm Street where Jack had lived when his father was manager of the mill.

Jack and Mary's daughters, Jacqueline, Patsy and Donna, grew up there. The years were filled with working at their gas station, which later was L and W Market, a grocery on the corner of Sunshine and Scenic in Springfield. After they "retired", Jack was employed by O'Neal Lumber, Owen and Short Hardware, and Quessenberry Construction.

Mary worked at the grocery store and still managed to keep house, make a large garden, and sew for the girls. There often was a quilt set up to be finished and always a cake baked, ready for a visitor.

Jack's grandchildren thought he could fix anything and he was often called with a "how to fix" question. He might have to call later to retrieve a tool borrowed from his back porch.

Sunday afternoons were for long drives and going fishing. They would pack a picnic lunch, hook up the boat, and head to water. This love of fishing was passed along to their grandchildren.

Jackie married Ronald Brashear, nephew of Lynn and Irene Martin, who owned the local movie theater and Martin Insurance. They raised their family in Tulsa, OK.

Patsy married Jack Trogdon, a son of Dan and Ethel Trogdon. He grew up on the Trogdon farm, and attended St. Elmo School, and Republic High School. Living in "Wormeyville" and on the family farm, their children and grandchildren continued school, band, and sports activities that their parents had enjoyed.

Donna married Ronald Welch of Aurora and they have made their home in Republic. They and their children have always been involved in local business.

Jack and Mary lived in their home at 133 East Mill until Mary's death in 2001. They celebrated 72 years of marriage. Jack continued living in the house until his passing in 2004. They had always enjoyed their life in Republic. Their children, grandchildren, and great-grandchildren attended the same schools. They have been active members of the community, making positive contributions through organizations such as Kiwanis, school board, Historical Society, Chamber of Commerce, and BPW.

Many members of the family have earned their living in Republic, continuing the tradition begun by John Luttrell and Jared Woodfill, whose great-great-grandchildren are the fifth generation to attend First Christian Church on Main Street. "Papaw" and "Mamaw" often shared their stories of Republic. They always knew it would be the best place to live. *Submitted by Terry Trogdon Mooneyham.*

**YEAKLEY** - The Yeakley family came from Greene County, TN and settled in Greene County, MO on a farm just north of Republic in 1840. Thomas Yeakley set aside a parcel of land for church and cemetery purposes northwest of Republic, which is still in existence and is known as Yeakley Chapel.

*Front: George Yeakley, Lucy Yeakley Mansfield holding Robert Yeakley Mansfield, Minnie Yeakley Shook, Edwin Shook, Celestia Jane Redfern Yeakley; back: Hattie Yeakley Ricketts, Jacob Frame, Bessie Yeakley Frame, Robert E. Mansfield, Ed Shook, Pauline Yeakley Coggin.*

One son George Washington remained in the area. He married Celestia Jane Redfern and had five daughters, all of them married and settled in the same vicinity.

Pauline, the youngest daughter, married Frank Coggin, a farmer and livestock commission firm owner. They acquired the George Yeakley farm and raised a family on the farm. They had a daughter Helen Louise who died on her 14th birthday and a son Herbert Lee.

Herbert married Carol Elizabeth DeWitt, an accomplished pianist and piano teacher. Carol is the daughter of attorney Bruce T. DeWitt and Thirza May Garbee DeWitt. Herbert and Carol resided on the family farm (which they still own) until Herbert became postmaster of the Republic Post Office in 1961. Herbert and Carol have three sons, one daughter, seven grandsons, one granddaughter, three great-grandsons and one great-granddaughter. These great-grandchildren are the eighth generation descendants of the original Yeakley family that settled in this area. *Submitted by Brad Coggin.*

**ZELL** – The Zell family story in Republic, MO, actually started in Gustrow, Prussia, in 1866. It was a time of change in Germany, and many families left to look for a better life in America. The Zell family made a hard decision: Edward, the eldest son, who was single, would leave for America. He left his parents, one brother, and two sisters behind in Prussia. Later he did send for his brother. Because he had no money, he stowed away on a ship in Rostock, Germany, that was leaving for America. He said the trip was the hardest thing he had ever done. He was sick all the way. The stowaways had the hardest labor on the ship, but he made it to New York City.

*Edward and Willhemenia (VonLessing) Zell and daughters, Hattie and Millie.*

*Fred Carl Zell and Freda (Lehman) Zell.*

He worked on the docks for little pay until he found work in the coal mines in Bethlehem, PA. He became a United States citizen after five years. He moved to a German settlement in Blackhawk, WI. There he met Wilhemenia VonLessing, and they married in 1871. On Jan. 15, 1873, Fred Carl was born. Edward and Wilhemenia lost two babies the next year, so they moved to a warmer climate in Knierm, IA in 1876. During the next four years, Minnie, Hattie, Mary and Millie Zell were born.

In 1882, they heard of a settlement forming along a railroad line in Billings, MO. There was a new church called St. Peters being formed by families from the same region of their old country. Edward purchased a 145-acre farm which is now part of Eagle Crest Golf Course in Republic. Edward's wife Wilhemenia fell ill and died in 1892. Edward never re-married. Minnie, the eldest daughter, married Albert Bohm and had eight children. These descendants still live in the area. Fred Carl Zell married Freda Lehman. Fred and Freda had four children: Minnie (Arndt), Augusta (Stellwagen), Edward Emil and Anna (Byars). With Minnie and Fred Carl established and married, Edward took his other three daughters to California in 1902.

After Edward had his three daughters settled in California, he moved back to Republic to be with Fred Carl and Freda. In 1916, in order to be closer to a school, Fred Carl and Freda purchased a farm on the north edge of Billings. Today that farm is located on Zell Rd. and operated by Fred William and Diane Zell. Fred William is the grandson of Fred Carl and Freda Zell. The original farm in Eagle Crest was sold in 1920. Edward lived his last years with Fred Carl and Freda and died in 1923.

In 1940, Edward Emil, son of Fred Carl and Freda, married Deema Johnson from Everton, MO. That same year Ed and Deema bought the original farm at Eagle Crest and moved there. February 18, 1942 a daughter, Carolyn, was born and May 10, 1945 a son Fred William was born. By that time there had been three generations on the original Republic Eagle Crest farm. Once again, fate would play a role. In 1949, Ed and Deema sold the Eagle Crest farm in Republic so they could be closer to Fred Carl, who had suffered a stroke in Billings.

Ed and Deema's daughter Carolyn moved to Springfield, MO and worked at St. John's Hospital for 35 years. Fred William, son of Ed and Deema, married Diane Zoller in 1967. Fred W. and Diane had two daughters, Karen and Kathy. Karen married Zack Frazier. They have two daughters, Kristen and Marisa, and live in Nixa, MO. Kathy married Junior Murray of Republic. They have one son, Cole Murray, and they live in Republic. Now the family has come full circle, six generations have ties to Republic. Edward always said "Our hearts never left our old place in Republic." *Submitted by Fred Zell.*

**ZULAUF** - Alfred Zulauf's parents immigrated to America from Switzerland in the late 1800s. Alfred was born near New Glarus, WI Dec. 29, 1899. When he was seven years old, he and his family moved by train from New Glarus to Tipton, MO. When they arrived, they spent the first night in the Tipton Hotel, then hired a local Tipton resident to take their furniture, etc. by wagon to the farm they had purchased near Tipton.

*Alfred Zulauf.*

After Alfred graduated from Willow Fork Grade School he worked on the family farm for a few years. He took a short course at Missouri University in dairy and was employed by the Missouri Department of Agriculture to travel around the state of Missouri testing dairy farmer's cattle for diseases and the milk for butterfat. He would stay with local families for a night or two at a time while he worked in that area.

When he was working in the Republic, MO, area he stayed with the Albert Howard family. Albert's youngest daughter, Merle, and Alfred got acquainted and after 10 years of dating married Dec. 23, 1939.

Albert's wife, Sarah Permelia (Shelton) had just passed away, so Alfred and Merle lived with Albert on Albert's farm where Alfred managed the farm. Alfred and Merle had two daughters, Carolyn and Marian.

Alfred was a kind and gentle man, always ready to lend a hand to help a neighbor. It seemed he could "fix" anything from a broken toy to the farm machinery. It was Carolyn's job each day to help her daddy with the evening milking. She was glad to help as that gave her some one-on-one time with her daddy. They had many discussions while they waited for the milking machine to finish milking each cow. She felt privileged to be allowed to help with the threshing in the summer. She was given the task of putting on and removing the burlap sacks that caught the threshed grain. It was HOT, DUSTY work but she didn't mind as she was with her daddy! One job he would not let any of "his girls" do was drive the tractor.

Alfred was active in his community. He taught the adult Sunday school class at the Battlefield United Methodist Church. When the Green Ridge School was consolidated into the Republic R-III School District, he was elected to the school board. He also served on the Greene County Agricultural Board.

Alfred passed away March 8, 1968. *Submitted by Carolyn (Zulauf) Bunner.*

*Thurman Gathering* – The house stood on the north side of Highway 174 just west of where W. Elm joins Hwy. 174.

# Index


**A**

Abernathy, 10; V., 30
Abramson, Nick, 38
Ackerman, Nellie Geilert, 192
Adams, 31, 162, 191; Avis Steele, 209; B.B., 33; Bernice, 42; Bill, 35; Brandon, 242; Burl, 35; Cora Hart, 64; Grace Davis, 176; Harry, 209; Jenny, 88; Jessie Jo, 69; Joe, 53; Joetta, 176; Jo Ann Hays, 211; Karen, 131; Landon, 191; Marlene Blades, 238; Mary Ellen, 184; Maude Erminie, 211; Oran, 176; Paul, 242; Sallie Lou, 176; Shelly Walz, 242; Shilah, 75, 87; Taylor, 242
Adamson, Greg, 40
Adcock, John, 84
Addison, Beatrice L., 149
Aderhold, Clarence William, 182; Ellen Frances Richardson, 182; Johanna Christina Helling, 182; Laura Ann Courdin, 183; Ronald Willard, 183; William Frederick, 182
Admire, Mischa Myree, 245; William Timothy Creel, 245
Advance Tire and Wheel, Inc., 93
Albaugh, Susan, 237
Albough, Laura, 169
Albrecht, Gene, 241; Jana, 241; Linda Robertson, 241; Ryan, 241
Albright, Paula, 230
Alderman, Amy, 148; Bob, 75, 148; Bruce, 148; Carrie, 148; Cathy, 148; Colleen, 148; Curt, 148; Don, 75, 148; J.W., 148; Janice, 148; Jean, 148; Keith, 148; Laurie, 148; Linda, 148; Mrs. J.W., 148; Patricia, 148; Phyllis, 86, 148
Alexander, John B., 199; Karen Sue DeVore, 228; Karen Sue DeVore Kemppainen, 179; Reva, 252; Willis Gregory, 179
Alford, James, 82
Alien, Wendy, 170
Allen, Andrea Sanders, 245; Bernice, 228; Bertha Lanning, 213; Christopher, 245; Daylie, 245; Evelyn, 172; Genevieve Josephine, 222, 257; Glenn, 222; Golda, 173, 251; Heath Luttrull, 245; James Edward, 222; Jeff, 245; Kylie, 245; Lawrence, 222; Mabel Jenkins, 222; Natalie Beth Carlson, 167; Natalie Carlson, 251; Russ, 113; Sally, 229, 251
Alley, Jess, 148; Mary, 148; Opal, 148; Philip, 148; Troy Paul, 148; Veta, 148; Virgil Silas, 148
Allhands, Dixie, 169
Allison, 137; Bradley, 137
Allman, Bob, 148; Norma Blevins, 148
Alloway, Jean Alderman, 148; Malcolm, 148
Allred, Connie, 230; Cora Lee Batson, 159
Alms, Earlene, 251; Earline, 84, 235; Erlene, 87; Ernestine, 235
Alpheri, Jean, 165
Altis, Millard, 90
Altman, Gary, 262; Gary, Jr., 262; Jennifer, 262; Patricia, 154; Patricia Sue Wade, 162; Patricia Sue Wade McConnell, 262
Ambs, Dicie L. Maden, 148; Martha Jane, 148; Mary Elizabeth, 148; Michael P., 148; Susan, 148
Amsler, Bobby, 75, 87; Marjorie, 75
Anchor Baptist Church, 135
Anders, Erin, 85
Anderson, 9, 31, 154, 169, 254; Alexander, 29; Barbara Haladay, 210; Breta Jane, 149, 169; Carrie Jo, 210; Charles, 29, 36, 148; Coosie, 73, 148; David, 143; Della, 148; Don, 136; Donald, 90; Doug, 169, 254; Douglas, 69; E.T., 27, 144, 148; Earl Roscoe, 149, 169; Elijah, 29; Elijah Teague, 29, 148; Ella Nance, 148, 227; Elsie Lee Hinshaw, 149; Emma Nance, 148, 227; Eugene, 148; F.E., 105; Floss Isabelle Chumbley, 149, 169; George, 29, 66; George Edward, 149; Glen, 148; Henry, 29, 158; Henry Small, 149; Hettie E., 145; Hetty, 29; Hetty Looney, 29, 149; Isabelle Jane Kerr, 210; Jack, 148; Jackie, 69; Jacquelyn Lou, 149; James, 29, 148, 149; James W., 210; Jane, 29; Jenn Rawlings, 148; Jessie Mary, 149; Jessie Wiley, 158; Joan, 148, 227; John, 29; Joney, 29; Kate Costello, 148; Kendra Hubbard, 177; Lucretia M. Carson, 248; Luella, 73, 74; Lynn, 149; Marci Jane, 210; Marie, 77; Mark, 118, 149, 254; Martha Hollaway, 29; Martha Holloway, 149; Martha Jane, 29; Mary Clementine McCullah Robertson, 149; Mary Jo, 169; Mary Jo Stephenson, 149, 254; Mary Lorilla, 149; Maud, 73; Maude, 158; Melissa Garoutte, 148; Melissa Jane Garoutte, 29; Minnie, 29, 148; Mrs. P.L., 28; Myrtle, 29, 148; Nannie Payne, 149; Nellie, 211; P.L., 28, 29; Pascal Douglas, 149; Peter, 149; Peter L., 29, 148; Peter Looney, 149; Rebecca, 148; Reed, 210; Roberta, 74, 76, 77, 148, 227; Sarah Hazelton Luce, 149; Sarah Luce, 29; Sara Hazelton Luce, 149; Stella M., 149; Teague, 29, 39; Theresa Houtz, 148; Tresa, 229; W.P., 31, 36, 144, 227; Walter, 36; Wesley Reed, 210; William H., 29; William Peter, 29, 148; Zana, 29, 148
Andrew, Harriet V., 29
Andrews, Rolland, 53; W.P., 33
Andrus, Earl George, 149; Erlene, 149; George Edward, 149; Joan, 212; Kathy Mooneyham, 226; Mary Louise Conrad, 149; Ralph, 149, 226; Raymond, 149; Sarah Arminta Jones, 149
Angus, Myrtle, 157
Ankrom, Judy, 113
Appelquist, Gail, 88
Applegate, Bessie, 200
Applequist, Stephanie, 88
Ardeu, Jennifer, 160
Arehart, Benny, 73; Will, 74
Arms, Mahetable, 242
Armstrong, Agnes Brockhaus, 150; Florence, 116; Frankie, 75; Louise McCool, 150; Marjorie Moore, 150; Neil, 150; Orland Kay, 149, 150; Robert, 75; William Calvin, 150
Arndt, Albert, 150; Amber Anne, 150, 151; Bob, 207; Clarence, 150; Earl, 150; Edna Grace Gebhards, 150, 151; Ernest, 150; Frances, 150; Howard, 82, 150; Howard David, 150, 151; Hulda E. Bengsch, 150; Hulda Elizabeth Bengsch, 150; James O., 150; Jim, 165; Lloyd George, 150, 151; Mary Garrison, 174; Maxine, 207; Maxine Bull, 150, 165; Minnie Zell, 271; Otis, 150; Paula, 165, 207; Paula K., 150; Robert, 165; Robert F., 150; Robert Frederick, 150; Robert O., 150; Sylvia, 150; Wilford, 150, 165, 207
Arnold, James, 163; Jim, 207; John, 48; Margaret Ann, 163; Max, 163; Melinda, 48; Mike, 207; Pat, 207; Patrick, 76; Roberta, 196, 207, 227; Roberta Anderson, 77, 148; Rolland, 163; Ruby Mae Brown, 163; William, 31
Arrington, Eula, 116; John, 44, 45
Arthur, Chester, 127
Ashcroft, John, 155
Ashley, Thomas, 21
Atkinson, Jan, 239; Janice Lea O'Neal, 238; John A., 238; Kala, 263; Noel Wilber, 49
Aton, Benjamin Franklin, 151; Billy, 151; Bobby, 151; Clara, 151; Frances Wyles, 151; George, 151; Georgia Utley, 151; Ira Ervin, 151; Jerry, 131; Jerry Max, 151; Joe Bob, 151; John, 151; John, Jr., 151; John Perry, 151; Margaret Heaton, 151; Mary E., 151; Mrs. Jerry, 131; Rosa Belle Munhollon, 151; Ruth Irene, 151; Sidney Millard, 151; Thomas Nelson, 151; Tina Lois, 151; Walter W., 151
Austin, Genevieve, 175
Aven, W.F., 73, 74
Avery, Julie, 88

**B**

Baar, Sarah, 30
Babbington, Mary, 233
Babcock, Frank, 40, 45, 149, 233
Babington, Mary, 190
Backmann, Ruth Lutes, 119
Bachmann, John, 98
Bacon, 45, 172, 177, 212, 219, 241; Fay, Jr., 117; Garley, 214; Judy Kay, 214; Launa, 181; Lora Lee Day, 185; Reathel, 214; Terry, 191
Bailey, Allen Newton, 146; Betsy Ann, 162; Cora Elizabeth, 242
Bain, Maxine, 116; Pearl, 116
Baker, Edna Grace Tiede Brown Clark, 259; Juanita, 231; Lea, 178; Pat, 259; Rosina Sifferman, 248
Balcom, D.T., 28
Baldwin, 242; V.W., 117; Virgil, 129
Ball, Jamie, 166, 244
Ballard, Chris, 85
Banham, Mary Elizabeth Green, 194
Banister, H., 33
Barber, C., 33; Earlene, 86; Leon, 250; Leona Smith, 250
Bareford, Elenore, 68
Bareis, Robin, 88
Barker, Dorothea Jean Clutter, 170; Harold, 170; Teresa, 240
Barlett, 28
Barnes, 261; John, 24
Barnhart, Brandon, 88; Deidra, 225; Frank, 48
Barr, Darrell, 118
Barren, Mabel, 243; W.M., 31
Barrett, Allyson, 200; Brad, 200; Cathy Henderson, 200; Claudine, 121; Shealyn, 200
Barron, Alice, 116; Flora, 73, 74; Whitfield, 73; William, 36
Bartley, Jessie, 11
Barton, Brook, 248; Kathy, 248; Ryan, 248
Basham, Elizabeth, 161
Bashaw, Phyllis, 87
Basnett, Minnie Jackson, 206; Timotheus T., 206
Bass, Mildred Britain, 67
Bassore, Barbara Ellen, 176; Bernice Davis, 176; Bettie Rapp, 176; Bill Davis, 176; Brad Davis, 176; Brenda Kay, 176; Carolyn Sue, 176; Christopher Todd, 176; David Rapp, 176; Donald James, 176; Julie, 176; Kay Nations, 176; Kerry Grey, 176; Mary Ruth, 86, 176; Patricia Joan, 176; Russell, 176; Virginia Lee, 176
Bates, Jeanie, 183; Vanda Mae, 66
Batey, Andrea Lynn McNabb, 223
Batson, 76, 136, 157, 212; Alfred, 69; Benton W., 238; Bertha Blades, 151; Beryl, 27; Beryl Payne, 77; Bias, 64; Carl, 71; Cleo, 25; Cleo Blades, 25, 158, 180; Connie, 182; Cora Lee, 159; Daniel Paul, 152; Deffa, 74; Della, 163; Dennie, 182; Denzil, 182; Don, 47, 71; Donald Eugene, 151; Donnie, 25, 71, 189; Earl, 71, 159; Effie Jane Reynolds, 238; Erma, 84; Eugene, 69; Eva Etheridge, 182; Frank, 239; G. Lavon Gardner, 151, 152; George, 158; Herbert, 22, 189; Herbert Lawrence, 151, 152; Hildred, 260; Jessie Elizabeth Blanton, 158, 159; Jim, 64; Jimmy, 159; Joy Lee, 152; Lavonne, 25; Lavon Gardner, 189; Lawrence, 69, 151; Lawrence Wade, 152; Leo, 25, 151; Leo Arthur, 151; Leslie, 189; Lettie, 152; Louise, 71; Lydia Ricketts, 239; Mary Fadra, 221, 222; Mila, 74; Orville, 25, 47, 48, 151, 189; Orville Lesley, 151, 152; Pauline, 71; Ray, 25, 71, 76, 82, 189; Ray Leon, 151; Rebecca, 157; Rebecca L. Blades, 249; Renee, 88; Robert, 20, 90, 238; Ruby, 70; Ruby Lee, 197; Rutha Vileta, 189; Sonny, 25; Stephen, 20, 238; Steve, 48; Vesta, 238; Violet Ray Smith, 152; Virgil, 71; Wayne, 71; Willis Lesley, 151, 152
Battlefield United Methodist Church, 133
Baty, Mary, 184
Baucom, D.T., 141; Thomas, 141
Baum, Judy, 156, 225
Baumberger, Gary, 53, 76, 87; Reba, 66; Roland, 56
Baxter, 30; Cal, 35; John E., 145; Lucille, 91
Bayer, Cynthia Lipscomb, 121
Bayless, Sarah M., 262
Beach, Aleta Jo Warford, 263; Ray, 263
Beal, 9, 21, 45, 158, 164, 181, 201, 229; Anna Mae, 77; Carroll, 74; E.L., 24, 134, 178, 252; Edward D., 33; Edward L., 33, 34, 35, 36, 41, 43, 54; Luther, 33, 35; Mary, 116; Mary E. Landers, 33; W.A., 31
Bean, Hobart, 155; Iva Biglieni, 155; Marjorie Lee, 155
Beard, Alma Alice Dougherty, 152; Cathie Sue, 152, 171; Christina Fugitt, 152; Clara Hambelton, 152; Gerald Roger, 152; James, 152; Lisa, 152, 186; Lori, 152, 186; Melanie, 152; Nancy Evans, 152; Permelia Jane, 189; Rita Carol, 152; Tony Herbert, 152
Bears, Edwin C., 10
Beaver, Ralph, 117
Bebee, Lyle, 54
Beck, Anita, 152, 153; Anita Griffith, 152; Anna, 153; Bethany, 153; Christopher, 90, 152, 153; Clayton, 152, 153; Dale, 265; Dana Burrell, 152; Isaac, 153; Jericho, 153; Jessica, 153; Lauren, 153; Lincoln Christopher Ray, 152; Mary Anne Wells, 264, 265; Raymond, 152, 153; Rebekah, 153
Becker, 270; Latty, 235
Bedell, Troy, 123, 165
Befielb, Marcalene, 100
Beldon, Valerie, 88
Bell, Abbie, 153; Augusta White James, 207; Benjamon H., 153; David, 88; Elsie, 153; Fay DeBoard, 178; George, 153; Hazel, 243; Horace, 48, 153; Horrace, 207; J.R., 33; Jimmy, 75, 87; John, 153; Joseph, 153; Lawton, 153; Manford, 35; Mary, 153; Minty J. King, 153; Nora, 153; Robert, 31; Sarah, 153; W.R., 33; William, 153; William R., 33
Beltz, Jason, 166; Jason Wendell, 219; Jill McConnell, 166; Jill Renee McConnell, 219
Bender, Tim, 84
Benedict, Tomi, 112
Bengsch, Hulda E., 150; Hulda Elizabeth, 150
Bennett, 177, 245; Alvie, 127; Anna Mae Dennis, 38, 179; Anne T. Hood, 154; Bert, 154; Bruce, 53; Carl, 153, 190, 192; Carol, 48; Charlotte, 85; Charlotte Jean, 153, 154; Claude, 45, 52, 153, 154, 179, 233; Daniel, 262; Daniel M., 154; David, 262; David E., 154; David S., 154; David Samuel, 154; Edith, 153; Ernie, 66, 154; Ethel, 116; Ethel Click, 153, 154; Floyd, 154; Francis Alice Mooney, 154; Frank, 45, 119, 153, 214; Gene, 66, 87, 154; George Franklin, 153, 154; Gola, 154; Harold, 81, 86, 153; Hershel, 154; Ilene C. White, 154; Ilene White, 154; Imogene True, 214; James Martin, 153; Jean, 86; Jennifer Jameson Dyer, 154; John, 154; John Wesley, 153; Karen Schickram Duggan, 154; Kay, 153; Leah, 154; Leila, 154; Lon, 53; Louann, 154; Lynette, 154; Lynn, 47; Margie, 86; Martha Mooney, 154; Max, 154, 262; Mrs. Frank, 76; Nancy, 223; Neisha, 262; Neisha L., 154; Ray, 97; Rex, 87; Ronnie, 48; Rosalene (Rosie) Wade, 154; Rosalene Wade, 162, 262; Sarah Elizabeth Moore, 153; Shrimp, 35; Susan Adaline, 153; Susan Hays, 153; Tracy, 262; Tracy B., 154; W.P., 154; William E., 154; William P., 154
Benson, Dorothy Marie Green, 194; Sarah Erwin, 249
Bentley, Ceytru, 87; Della Marie, 176; Joe, 87
Berger, Della R., 259
Berkner, Nicole, 88
Berridge, Leslie, 75
Berry, 237; Dimitry, 154; Edmund, IV, 154; Edmund, V, 154; Irene, 77; Ivan L., 258; Kimberly, 154; Martha, 178; Naomi O'Neal, 67; Sondra, 190; Tracy B. Bennett, 154; Yana, 154
Bertino, Eula Lorene Maness, 216
Bertoldi, Helen, 75; Lucille, 75
Best, Ab, 155; Bertha, 155; Betty, 155; Bob, 119; Bonnie, 155; Dot, 155; Edythe Cutbirth Tyler, 154; Eva, 155; Gene, 155; James, 155; Leroy, 155; Leroy J., 155; Margaret, 74, 76, 77; Mary B., 155; Mildred White, 155; Orvie O., 154; Tony, 155; Troy, 155
Bethel, Ben, 211; Mary Eliza M.E. Kitchen, 211
Bettis, Jane, 262
Beyer, Fred, 166; John Raymond, 166; Judith Ann, 166; Rayetta Cantrell, 166
Bible Baptist Church, 135
Biellier, Anna, 248; Christian Alvin, 248; Elijah Dee, 248; Ernest,

248; Gertrude Mae, 248; Ivy Marshall, 248; Nancy Ellen Lile, 248; Nellie Frances, 248; Ralph Onas, 248; Rowena, 69; Wallace, 69; William Alexander Hamilton, 248
Biggers, Earl, 182; Gloria Ann, 182; Jeerl Dean Etheridge, 182
Biglieni, 129; Angie Compfortie, 155; Anthony, 155; Becky Salchow, 155; Belle, 155; Brenda, 47, 155; Brooke, 155; C.A., 155; Carl, 155; Carol, 69, 155; Charles, 72, 87, 155; Charles Anthony, 155; Charles Robert, 155; Charles William, 155; Clinton, 155; Danny Gene, 155; Ethel, 155; Eunice, 155; Eva Hunt, 155; Florella, 155, 157; Geralee, 155; Irene, 116; Irene Squibb, 155; Iva, 155; J.W., 75, 76, 82, 87; Jimmie, 69; Joseph, 155; Josephine, 155; Joseph Wesley, 155; Joshua, 155; Karen Robertson, 155; Laura McGuire, 155; Linda, 155; Lindy, 155; Madine, 155; Mae Phillips, 155; Margaret Sue, 155; Maxine, 155; Nancy Triggs, 155; Norma Jean Mosier, 155; Oblene, 155; Opal, 48; Opal McCroskey, 155; Sue, 47; Suzanne, 155; Tommy, 155; Travis, 155; W.R. Bill, 155; Wesley, 155; William, 155; William Lee, 155; William R., 155
Bilbo, Christy, 212
Bilbruck, Mary Frances, 234
Billings, Carrie, 194; M., 33
Billows, Brent, 152; Jason, 152; Matthew, 152; Rita Carol Beard, 152
Bills, Charles, 229; Dennis, 229; Wilma O'Dell, 229
Bingham, Edna, 207
Bird, Susan Caroline, 223
Bishop, Anna May Chastain, 169; Camille, 244; David F., 30; Dr., 21; Eunice Wilson, 30; J.W., 31, 32, 33; James Wilson, 30; Mary Meade, 30; Mike, 244; Savana, 244; Sierra, 244; Stehanie, 244; Stephanie Sanders, 177, 244
Black, George W., 28; Mary, 262
Blackman, May, 29; Wallace W., 29
Blackwell, Charles David, 156; Charles Robert, 156; Charlie, 160; Charlie Russell, 156; Clara Virginia Russell, 156; David, 160, 161; Dois Louise Trogdon, 156; Jim, 156; Joe Oliver, 156; Linda Conn, 156; Lori Lynn, 156; Louise Trogdon, 160; Sherry Ann Borovicka, 160; Sherry Borovicka, 156; Steven Lynn, 156; Tasha Ann, 156, 160
Blades, 9, 136, 141, 193, 194, 221; Adeline Dean, 177; Albert, 151; Alfred, 157; Alma, 224; Alonza, 43; Anna Marie, 68; Annie, 156; Annie Bethar Laney, 227; Ann Maria Lieser, 156; Becky, 167; Bertha, 151, 157; Bessie, 231; Betty, 67; Bonita, 84; Bonnie, 157, 216; Burl, 25; Burl L., 156; Burl Lester, 227; Butch, 82; Calvin, 127; Carl, 167; Carla, 167; Charles Lovett, 216; Chloe, 71; Chloe Susan, 227; Chole, 156; Clara, 151, 158, 180; Claude, 158; Claudia Sue, 158; Cleo, 25, 158, 180; Cleo Lavaughn, 151; Columbia A. Browning, 238; Columbia Ann Browning, 158; Cynthia Ann, 249; Cynthia Lee, 156; Danny Paul, 68; David, 68; Deborah Finn, 158; Dee, Jr., 67; Donald, 157, 216; Dorothy, 71, 151, 158, 180; Dorothy Vernell Rubison, 156; Drextle, 158; Dudley, 141; E.R., 66; Earl, 151, 157, 216; Edna, 25; Edward, 20, 141, 220, 224; Edward A., 157, 202, 216, 238; Edward Alvin Franklin, 248; Edward Alvin Franklin, Jr., 249; Edward, Jr., 157; Efton, 151, 262; Eleanor Penelope Maynard, 248; Eliza, 151; Elizabeth, 157, 249; Eliza Jane, 231; Ellen, 179; Ellen L. Maynard, 202; Ellen Maynor, 224; Ellen Penelope Maynard, 157; Elyjah, 231; Emma Browning, 157; Emmer, 48; Ethel, 116, 151, 157; Eugene, 32; Eva, 151, 157; Everett, 158; Florella Biglieni, 155, 157; Florence Erickson, 158; Floyd, 151, 152, 157; Frances Catherine, 248, 249; Frances Garoutte, 161, 242; Gary, 25, 71, 156; George W., 157; George Washington, 157, 249; Gid, 158; Gideon, 189, 231; Gladys, 75; Harold, 47, 158; Harold J., 238; Haven, 253; Helen, 4, 37, 38, 40, 67, 118, 155, 157; Hershel, 231; I.T., 66; Ike, 238; Ira, 156; Ira Harmon, 227; Isaac T., 157; Isaac Tillman, 158, 249; James, 157, 231; James G., 32; James M., 157, 238; James Melton, 158; James R., 157; James Reynolds, 156, 249; Jana, 158; Jeffrey Wayne, 156; Jess, 158; Jessie, 231; Jewel, 194; Jim, 35, 49, 52; Jimmie, 81, 87, 151, 157, 158, 180; Joe, 52, 117; John Henry, 156, 225; John Leroy, 151, 158; John M., 157, 238; Joseph, 157; Julie, 157, 158; JW Wayne, 156; Kelsey Elizabeth, 156; Ken, 52; Kenneth Dale, 156, 157; Kenny, 68, 82, 87; Larry, 158; Larry Michael, 158; Lawrence, 157; Lee, 67; Lena, 231; Lester, 67; Lettie, 230; Lillie, 157; Lilly, 151; Lissa Mooneyham, 179; Lorene, 75, 157, 216; Louisa Faye, 156, 225; Louisa Faye Rickman, 156; Louisa Gibson, 157; Louise, 231; Lucinda Sue, 158; Lucy, 253; Madge, 106, 157, 264; Madge McDaniel, 157, 158; Malissa, 157; Malissa Jane Mooneyham, 151, 158; Margaret Alice Howard, 156, 157; Margaret June Farmer, 158; Marion, 177; Marlene, 238; Martha, 161; Mary L., 141; Maude Anderson, 158; Micah, 158; Minnie McDaniel, 64, 179; Monroe, 157; Mrs. Dwight, 76; Mrs. Joe, 64; Myrtle Angus, 157; Myrtle M., 156; Nancy Ann Hood, 158; Nancy Ellen, 202; Nancy Emiline, 249; Nancy Hood, 157; Nathan Alexander, 156; Nellie Davis, 225; Nellie May Davis, 156; Nora Hayes, 158; Oliver, 231; Olive Hacking, 67; Opal, 67; Pamela Ann Cantrell Jones, 167; Patience, 141; Patricia Anne Rolufs, 158; Pauline, 157, 216; Penelope, 157, 220, 238; Penelope Ellen Maynard, 238; Polly French, 157; Rachael Ray, 158; Rachel Ray, 189, 231; Ralph, 155, 157; Ransom Dudley, 151, 157, 249; Ranson, 158; Ranson D., 238; Ranson Dudley, 161, 238, 242; Ray, 67; Reathel Wanda, 156, 225; Rebecca L., 249; Rex Wayne, 157; Roe, 231, 239; Rosa, 189; Rosalene, 84; Rosetta, 216; Rose Ann, 231; Roy, 157, 179; Samuel, 157; Sara, 220; Sarah Ann, 248; Sarah Jane, 161, 242; Shirley, 25; Stan, 157, 158; Susan, 157; Teresa Ann, 158; Terry Wayne, 158; Thelma, 151, 158, 179; Thomas, 157; Thomas Blackstone, 151, 157; Tressie Lovett, 157, 216; Triphany, 141; Velma, 157; Vesta Batson, 238; Wayne, 71, 151, 158, 180; William, 157; William Efton, 157; William W., 157; William Willis, 157, 249
Blades Chapel Church, 141
Blanchard, Phyllis, 131
Blanche, Keith, 83; Richard, 78, 87; Robert, 87
Bland, Martha Ann, 242
Blankenship, Donna, 185; Juanita Turpin, 260; Mike, 260
Blanton, Bert, 158, 159; Betty Crocker, 159; Bob, 159; Dorothy Mae, 158, 159; Elizabeth McAmis, 158; Frank, 158, 159; Frank, Jr., 158, 159; Glen, 159; Janie Wolfe, 159; Jeannie, 159; Jessie Elizabeth, 158, 159; Joe Hazel, 158, 159; John, 158; Lester, 159; Louella Gale, 159; Maude Anderson, 158, 159; Patrick, 159; Thelma, 182; Thelma Maude, 158, 159; Virginia Dameron, 159
Bledsoe, Jasper, 165
Blevins, Dale, 71; Norma, 148
Bloch, Henry, 104; Richard, 104
Block, G.W., 32
Blood, Alma Siplinger, 159; Jane, 159; Keith, 159; Penny, 159; Terry, 159
Bloom, Doc, 15
Blount, Charles, 124, 127
Bluebaum, Ashley, 223; Ashley Missy-Dawn, 222; Geoffrey Allen-Isaac, 222; Herbert Richard, III, 222; Herbie, III, 223; Jennifer Kay, 222; Phyllis Jean McNabb, 222
Blumenstock, Ryan, 84
Blunt, Matt, 97; Roy, 252
Boatright, 219, 242; Aaron Todd, 120, 159; Alexa Lynn, 159; Ashley Michele, 159; Austin, 69; Beverly, 120; Beverly Ann, 159; Dale, 54, 75, 120, 195, 241; Deborah Michele Evans, 159; Derek Todd, 159; Doug, 31, 57; Douglas Jay, 120, 159; Eathel Agnes Gaddy, 189; Eathel Gaddy, 159; Evan Owen, 159; Gene, 47, 48, 120, 159; Huba, 69; Jane, 50, 118; Jane Carolyn Owen, 120, 159, 233; Joe, 75; Kayla, 159; Leon, 70; Lorene Short, 159; Lorie Lynn Moreland, 159; Michael Gene, 159; Nancy, 159; Oscar Dale, 159; Roscoe, 159; Ross, 70; Shelia, 69; Sonny, 69; Stefanie Marie, 159; Susi, 100; Vicky, 159; Virginia, 215
Boatwright, Maxine, 77
Bock, Carol Carlson, 159, 160, 168; Jennifer Ardeu, 160; Jonathan, 160; Kurt, 160, 168; Rebecca, 160
Bodine, Eli, 166; Etta Mae, 166; Sarah Gray, 166
Boehm, C.H., 170; Sarilda, 170
Boggess, Helen, 260
Boggs, Elizabeth, 202
Bohannon, Shirley J., 177
Bohm, Albert, 271; Minnie Zell, 271
Bolier, 167
Bolin, Beatrice Louise, 149; Beverly, 85; Beverly Ann, 149; Mary Lorilla Anderson, 149; Nichole Gayle, 193, 250; Noel Eugene, 149
Boling, 90
Bolton, Lawrence, 70; Leroy, 70
Bond, Dale, 132
Bonham, Racheal, 203
Booher, George Robert, 242; JoAnne, 242, 243; Ruby Eulalia Ross, 242, 243; Virginia June, 242
Boone, Alexandra, 224; Daniel Morgan, 161; Janice Miller, 224; Jeffrey, 224; Jim, 224; Shannon, 224; Tanner, 224
Booth, Charles Noel, 160; Charlie, 25, 151; Clarence, 25; Gladys, 25, 151; Gladys Fay Cherry, 160; Irma, 160; Jane, 25; Jason, 177; Jewell, 25; Judy, 25; Kensington Elizabeth, 177; Madilynn Grace, 177; Mary, 160; Max, 25, 53, 160; Nancy, 160; Ron, 25, 160; Ronnie, 71; Steve, 160; Sue, 25, 71, 160; Tiffany Lynn Melton, 177
Boothe, Bessie, 160; Charles, 160; Charles Noel, 160; Clarence, 160; Ida, 48, 160; Ida Keltner, 160; Loyd, 160; Oral, 160; Spencer, 160; Winnie, 160
Borovicka, Brenda McKinney, 160, 161; Brian Lee, 160; Bruce Edward, 160; Bruce Edward, Jr., 160; Charley, 160; I.E. Ben, 156, 160; Joseph Lee, 161; Karen Hopkins, 160; Maggie Caylor, 160; Reba Hild, 156; Reba Maxine Hild, 160; Shannon Lynn, 160; Sherry, 156; Sherry Ann, 160
Borud, Nora Angeline, 243
Boston, Edna Mae, 208; Jim, 131; Mrs. Jim, 131; Vanlora, 116
Bottorf, Richard, 50
Bottorff, Frances, 74
Bough, Tom, 85
Bowen, George Sylvester, 162; Ida Augusta Bradford, 162; Ruby Margaret, 162
Bowers, Jasper Hoyt, 166, 219; Jennifer Jo McConnell, 219; Jennifer McConnell, 166; Jett Ellis, 166, 219; Michael, 166; Michael James, 219
Bowland, Emma V. Kerr, 210; R.A., 210
Bowling, Kenneth, 84; Pauline Hagewood, 221
Bowman, Lum, 15
Box, Anna Wynkoop, 269; Juanita, 269; William M., 269
Boyd, 42, 242; Anna Land, 212, 213; Barbara, 161; Betty Cassy, 161; Catherine Zumwalt, 161; Darrel, 161; David, 161; Dorothy Jean Chastain, 169; Edna Earl, 204, 260; Eleanor, 161; Elmer, 42; Freddie, 161; Gary, 161; George, 204; George Washington, 260; Grace, 161, 213; Homer, 70, 161, 213; Hugh, 161; Iva Mae Spurgeon, 161; James, 161, 213; John, 161, 212, 213; Johnnie, 161; John R., 161, 213; Julie, 161; Larry, 161; Lucile, 213; Lucille, 70, 161; Margaret Anna Land, 161; Margaret Harryman, 161; Martha Blades, 161; Mike, 161; Nancy, 161; Neal, 161; Pearl McGinnis, 260; Ruth, 215; Sarah, 212; Steve, 161; Terry, 161; Tilitha Cuma Harrington, 260
Boyer, La Verne, 47; Lorene, 47
Boyts, Janelle, 68
Bracken, Duncan, 54, 162
Brackens, Duncan, 35; Glen, 35
Bradfield, R.K., 33
Bradford, Ida Augusta, 162
Bradley, Leon, 47
Brake, Dee, 47
Brandenburg, Charlie, 202
Branson, C.C., 15; Christopher C., 15; Hannah, 169; Homer, 35; Jeff, 35; Joe, 35; Lawrence, 35; Lillian DeVoge, 35; Loge, 35; Lum, 15; Minnie, 24; Oliver, 35; Otis, 35; Roy, 24; Tom, 35
Branstetter, Ruby J., 259
Brashear, Jacqueline Woodfill, 270; Myrtle Anderson, 29, 148; Ronald, 270; Ronald Craig, 218; Will, 29, 148
Brashears, Bob, 75, 220; Donald, 220; Edith May McCullah, 220; J.J., 141; Joe, 188; Ota, 188, 243; Ota E., 187; Ota Ermine, 186; Robert, 220; Ronald, 24; Sarah, 157
Brashers, Amy, 212; Barbara, 87; Bessie, 223; Bettie, 161, 242; Bill, 161; Bruce, 76; Chelsea, 85; Dale Eugene, 227; Della, 161; Earline Sue Neil, 227; Edna Mae, 3, 6, 257; Elizabeth Basham, 161; Ella, 161; Hattie, 48; James Basham, 161, 162, 242; Jessie Rankin, 161; Juanita, 197; Larry, 75; Max, 117; Opal Blades, 67; Rayetta Elizabeth, 217; Sarah Jane Blades, 161, 162, 242; Walter, 161; William Walter, 161
Bray, Clejo, 189; Ronda, 224; Seltha, 129
Breakbill, 45; Edna Lee, 71; Harold, 71, 117; Johnny, 233; Junior, 71; LeRoy, 71
Breazeale, 254
Breshears, Edith, 116
Brewer, Ben, 24; Eva Ricketts, 239; Frank, 239; Franklin, 239; Katherine, 235; Richard, 55, 82
Bridges, 120, 235; Amber, 162; Amos, 162; Audrey, 162; Bryant, 162; Clementine, 162; Dixie, 162; Emilie, 162; Fanny, 162; Fay, 134; Fay Lawson, 162; Fide, 162; Frank, 32, 162; Gene, 162; Golden, 162; Greg, 162, 262; Jack, 134, 162, 262; Jack, Jr., 162, 262; Jackie, 75, 87; Johnny, 162; Juanita, 134, 154, 189; Juanita Marie Wade, 162, 262; Kelly, 162; Margaret, 162; Marvin, 162; Mary Clegg, 162; Mike, 162; Otho, 134, 162; Pam Wilcox, 162; Phillip, 162; Ruby, 162; Teresa, 47, 48, 162, 262
Bridwell, 15, 35, 37
Brienner, Bill, 230; Bonnie Long, 230; Grant, 230; Harris, 230; Henry, 230; Jillian, 230; Jordan, 230; Kimberly Perkins, 230; Lori Glenn, 230; Thomas, 230; Tim, 230
Brigman, Angela, 164; Carrie, 164; Dale, 164; Davin, 164; Effie Deloris Bruton, 164; Joy Dallas, 164; Joy Dallas, Jr., 164
Brim, 167, 186, 245; Bobby, 86; G.W., 31; John, 75, 167; R.C., 171, 224; Robert, 45, 78; Ruth, 116
Brimhall, Grace, 74
Brincks, Anne Elizabeth Comisky, 172; Benjamin Wyatt, 172; Caroline Elizabeth, 172; Michael, 172
Bristow, Martha, 229
Britain, 9, 20, 45, 121; Albert, 162; Aleck, 162; Amanda Belle, 162; Anna Johnson, 242; Bent, 119; Bertha, 227; Bessie, 242; Betsy Ann Bailey, 162; Bettie Jones, 242; Cassius, 242; Charles, 242; Charlie, 243; Clara, 74, 134; Delia Hagewood, 242; Diamma Sallee, 162; Donna, 67; E.H., 134; E.L., 81, 86; Edward, 173, 242; Edward L., 230; Edward L., III, 230; Edward L., Jr., 230; Eli, 119, 162; Elizabeth, 30, 162; Elizabeth Wade, 166; Eli H., 30; Ellen O'Neal, 229; Elsa, 242; Eugene, 234; Florence, 36, 232; Florence Pennoyer, 6, 234; Floyd, 48; Frank, 242; G.W., 33; George, 20, 30, 134, 221; George W., 30, 162, 179; George Washington, 121; Harry, 24; Helen, 116, 234; Helen M., 179; Henry I., 141; Ira, 162, 234; J.A., 32; J.T., 33; J.W., 33, 113; Jack, 162; James, 166; James Lafayette, 242; James M., 229; Janet, 75, 87; John, 121; John Thomas, 162; John W., 162; John Wesley, 30, 162; Kathleen Wilson, 230; Lawrence Ellis, 178; Louise, 234; Lucy A. Cox, 30; Lucy Cox, 162; Malissa, 162; Malissa Ann, 259; Marcellus L., 242; Margie, 67; Marie Hedrick, 230; Mark F., 162; Martha Jane, 166; Martha Susan, 262; Mary A. Paine, 242; Mary Jackson, 162; Mary Jane, 162; Mary Russell, 243; Melissa, 162; Mildred, 67, 77; Mrs. Havey, 64; Nick, 36;

Nora Sanford, 234; Rilla, 74, 230; Royal, 157; Ruby DeBoard, 178; Sarah, 162; Sarah Alice Rose, 242; Sarah Garrison, 162; Sarah Jane, 162; Stephen, 230; Velma Blades, 157; Vern, 119; Wanda Rose, 66
Britian, Audrey Allen, 251; Rebecca, 220
Britt, Lanna Daniel, 121
Brittain, 141; Edward, 64; Henry, 64
Brockerman, Day, 227; Margaret, 227; Pearl Nance, 227
Brockhaus, Agnes, 150
Brookline Cemetery Association, 143
Brookline First Baptist Church, 137
Brooks, 9; A.J., 15; Garth, 170; Hattie, 28; J.F., 90; James F., 33; Josiah F., 27, 29, 144; Lewis D., 32, 55; Mrs. J.F., 28
Brower, Louise Green, 195; Mary Joan, 194; Mary Louise Green, 194; Ramona Jean, 194; Vee, 194
Brown, 21, 223, 249; Alexander Elliott, 164; Allen, 53; Alvin, 131; Alvin E., 163; Alvin Earl, 162, 163; Andrew, 50; Andrew Tyler, 164; Angie Harris, 163; Angie L. Harris, 163; Ann, 202; Annie Jo, 210; Beatrice Ann, 163; Belle, 169, 178, 245; Beth Elaine, 245; Blake Austin, 245; Clara Alice Carter, 162; Clarke, 82, 163; Cora, 73; Cynthia Lynn Hough, 164; Danny, 212; Deloris, 71; Dicky, 71; Don, 71, 163, 172, 187, 219, 241; Don Truman, 245; Dorothy, 163; Earl, 155; Earl Sylvester, 162, 163; Eda Wade, 262; Edna, 181; Edna Grace Tiede, 259; Edna Maxine Green, 194; Elizabeth, 248; Elmer, 259; Elsie Butler, 163, 166; Erin, 212; Ethel, 182; Evelyn, 227; Evelyn Sue Tyler, 164; Gabe, 212; Garland, 71, 163, 187; Geneva, 71, 163; Geneva Mae, 187, 188; Gerald Allen, 245; Helen, 86, 187; I.D., 64; Janice Mooneyham, 179; Jefferson Davis, 162; Jerald, 194; JoAnn, 185; JoAnn Foust, 68, 163; Joel, 230; Josh, 212; Joyce, 194; Joyce Hayworth, 163; Kay, 72; Kenneth Ray, 163; Kim Lacey, 212; Lavinia, 245; Leland, 75, 82, 154, 155, 222; Leland Davis, 162, 163, 164; Leola, 223; Leslie, 194; Lestle Victor, 163; Lola, 116; Lucille, 163, 187; Mae Howard, 71, 262; Marcia, 245; Margaret Porter, 164; Margaret Roberts, 240; Marilyn, 163; Mark, 52; Mary, 170; Mary Alice, 177; Mary Patricia, 245; Max, 52, 71, 76, 163, 187; Michael, 163; Michael Davis, 164; Mildred, 163, 187; Mrs. Alvin, 131; Nancy, 163, 187; Nancy Ann, 178; Nancy Elizabeth, 163, 190; Nancy Emiline Blades Hood Batson, 249; Natalie Anne, 164; Norma, 87, 163, 187; Norma Francis, 192, 193; Norval, 68, 163; Nova, 163; Ola, 163; Omel, 71; Osha, 219; Osha Jackson, 163; Pat, 75; Pauline, 163; Peggy O'Neal, 230; Robert Allen, 245; Rose, 187; Rose Belle, 187; Rose Belle Newton, 163, 192; Rose Helen, 71, 163, 187; Rose Marie, 72; Ruby, 71, 155, 163, 187; Ruby Mae, 162, 163; Ruby Margaret Bowen, 162, 163; Ruth Ellen, 228; Sam, 166; Samuel, 163; Scott, 163; Sheridan, 163; Shirley Sanders, 245; Smith, 163, 178, 187, 192, 245; Smithy, 163, 178, 187; Stephen, 163; Stephen Max, 164; Sue, 154, 155; Sue Tyler, 163; Susan Marie, 163; Suzanne Myree, 245; Thomas Tolivar, 190; Thomas Toliver, 163; Tom, 71, 77, 152, 163, 187; Wade, 262; William Michael, 245; Wynona, 163; Wynonna, 187
Brownell, John, 33
Browning, Columbia A., 238; Emma, 157; George W., 66
Brownstone, Elizabeth, 48
Bruise, Nancy Jane Carson, 248
Brumley, Gladys, 155
Bruner, Angie Hiller, 188; Cynthia, 188; Mark, 188; Matthew, 188
Bruton, Clara Jane Peck, 164; Dana Machell, 164; Dean, 76, 118; Effie Deloris, 164; Helen, 164; James, 82; James C., 164; James Earl, 164; Jeff, 48, 164; Jim, Jr., 164; Judy Cox, 164; Kay Ratcliff, 164; Marthella Kline, 164; Marty, 118; Mary Beth, 164; Paula Dawn, 164; Rachel, 164; Thomas Delbert, 164; Thomas Delbert, Jr., 164; Timothy, 164; Tom, 93; Willard Dean, 164
Bryan, Alice, 164; Edna, 164; Florence, 164, 249; Frances Ann Kemper, 164; Jefferson Scott, 164; Lois, 164; Miles, 164; Neil, 164; Rebecca Ann, 267; Ruth, 164
Bryant, E.J., 145; Jim, 133; Marshall, 87; Shannon, 59
Buck, George, 74
Buckley, James, 72; Lavelle, 72; Louis, 72
Buckner, Brian Corbett, 193, 250; Diane Adele Smith, 193, 250; Ian Bradley, 193, 250
Budd, David, 134
Buechler, Mark, 88
Buell, Anthony Brian, 165, 257; Connie, 257; Connie Jean Thompson, 263; Connie Thompson, 165; J.B., 165; Jack, 257; Jack Carroll, 165, 263; Jill, 165; Loine Duncan, 165; Teri, 165; Teri Dawn, 165, 263
Buescher, Jerry, 83
Bull, 45; Betty, 165; Charles Bud, 165; Charles Olan, 165; Clora Hargas, 150; Clora Hargis, 165; Dorothy, 75, 165, 166; Evelyn, 86, 165; Jean Alpheri, 165; John, 165; Maxine, 86, 150, 165; Nina, 165; Olan, 150, 176; Steve, 165; Susie, 165
Bullard, Joretta, 166; Joretta A., 166
Bunch, 208
Bunner, Carolyn Zulauf, 271
Buoy, Carla, 219
Burbee, Steve, 90
Burdett, Rex, 207
Burford, D.W., 146
Burgess, B.C., 31; F.W., 31; J.W., 28; Janice, 100
Burk, Elmon, 179; Eva, 113; Jackson, 179; Jane McDaniel, 179; Ollie, 179; Ruby, 179
Burke, Bethany Grace, 267; Chris, 267; Cindy, 228; Jacque White, 267; Kayla Lee, 267
Burks, Andrea, 166; Barbara Joule, 166; Cindy, 50, 166; Edward, 166; Ethel Slagle, 166; James, 166; Jim, 117; Julia, 166; Katie, 166; Kimberly, 166; Melinda, 166; Nathan, 166; Patricia, 166; Robert, 166; Sonnie, 166; Thomas, 166
Burleson, Betty, 66, 213; Bobby, 75; Carolotte, 213; George, 66; Louise, 66
Burmingham, 12; Dorothy, 12, 133; Rocky, 12
Burnett, Jeannie, 226
Burney, F.J., 74; Mary Sifferman, 248
Burns, A., 33; Bruce Warren, 175; Calvin Ernest, 175; Carey Eugene, 175; Effie Sisk, 175; Nancy, 174; Ray Edwin, 175
Burr, Ruth, 196
Burrell, Dana, 152
Burris, Steve, 29
Burton, Clarence, 136; Clinton Earl, 235; Coy, 235; Danny, 235; David, 65; Eryn, 235; Jeff, 53; Joyce Anne Datema, 235; Keith William, 235
Bush, George, 50
Bushong, Mary Elizabeth, 232
Bussard, Iva Jane, 234; Linda, 156, 225
Bussey, 92; Colin Macway, 121; Lewis E., 121; Linda, 121; Lynn, 121, 173; Virginia Belle Cox, 121
Butcher, Frances, 85; Tony, 136
Butler, Andrea Hendricks, 166; Benjamin, 166; Clifford, 198; Danielle Anne, 154; E. Wayne, 166; Elsie, 163, 166; Emily Moreland, 166; Ernestine Tiede, 166; Frank, 166; Janet, 166, 244; Janet M., 244; Jewell, 70, 84, 166; Jimmie, 166; Jocelyn, 83, 166; Joel, 166; Joretta, 219; Joretta A. Bullard, 166; Joretta Bullard, 166; Joshua, 198; Judy, 47, 166, 219; Judy Elaine, 219; Leah Bennett, 154; Lela Vival, 245; Martha Britain, 225; Martha Jane Britain, 166; Maud, 156, 225; Maude, 166, 198; Maxine, 166; Merton, 198; Mirta Mooneyham, 166; Nadie, 166, 230; Nelson, 166, 225; Nelson Garrett, 166; Ray, 70, 81, 166; Ted, 198; Tommy, 154; Wayne, 70, 166, 191, 219
Butlin, J.T., 33
Butterfield, John, 13
Buxton, M.A., 122; Ranae, 100; Tressye, 116, 122
Byars, Anna Zell, 271
Byfield, 11; Wilma, 77
Byram, Lula Jackson, 206; Luther, 206
Byran, Rebecca Ann, 267

## C

Cafiero, Linda, 148
Cahill, John, 76
Cain, Dana, 118; Mary Gaddy, 189
Caldwell, Joan, 100; Scott, 48
Calhoun, Sandra Gaddy, 189
Calvary Baptist Church, 138
Cameron, Amy, 50
Camp, 21
Campbell, Angela Kay DeVore, 179; Betty, 87; Carson David, 179; Clinton Rex, 179; Dellie Mooneyham, 226; John Arnie, 226; Judy, 260; Linda, 131; Mike, 131; Morgan Rose, 179; Mrs. Russell, 131; Russell, 131; Samuel, 179; Terri, 88
Camron, Lena Elizabeth Langley, 212; Thomas Eugene, 212
Cannefax, Chesley, 174; Isabinda, 174; Radford, 166
Cantabary, Charles, 206; Christine, 206; Peter, 206
Cantrell, Addison, 167; Amanda, 167; Bill, 53, 86, 113, 117, 167, 205; Blake Edward, 167; Brent Raymond, 167; Brittnay, 167; Bryce William, 167; Cindy Wilson, 167; Darin, 84; Edward Raymond, 167; Etta Mae, 167; Etta Mae Bodine, 166; Gilda Sue, 167; Grace, 116; James Mathew, 167; James William, 167; Jaunita Lula, 166; Jean, 113, 167; Jeannie Whittaker, 167; Juanita, 86; Margie, 167; Michelle Gardner, 167; Morgan, 167; Nancy Buenta, 167; Pamela Ann, 167; Patty Crabb, 167; Rayetta, 166; Shirley Jean Tooley, 167; Thomas Darin, 167; Valerie Culley, 167; William, 117, 134; William Bodine, 166, 167; William Raymond, 166
Cardner, Layne, 84
Cardwell, Marvin, 48
Cargile, Susan Catherine, 242
Carlson, 239; Carol, 47, 159, 160, 167, 168; Carol Van Gelder, 167; Christine, 251; Christine Caroline, 167; Don, 82; Donald, 167, 174; Edith, 47, 48, 159; Edith Shelton, 167, 255; J.C., 87, 167; John, 47, 159, 167; John Charles, 167, 255; Natalie, 167, 251; Natalie Beth, 167; Phyllis Cox, 167, 174, 229, 251
Carnahan, 97; LaVada Ann Gardner Mooneyham, 189
Carpenter, Joe, 68, 88; John, 68; Marilyn, 68; Sue, 87
Carr, Ellen, 209; J.T., 32; Jack, 35; Richard, 71; Robert, 20; Tim, 131; Zelda Elaine, 220
Carrol, Isabell, 191
Carskaddon, Carolyn, 230
Carskaden, Lou, 32
Carson, Alta Beatrice, 248; Charles T., 248; Drucilla Ann, 248; Elijah C., 248; Ella Mae, 248; George Enoch, 248; James A., 248; John S., 248; Lilly Olive, 248; Lucretia M., 248; Mabel Madeline True, 214; Margie Britain, 67; Martha Ellen Raynor, 248; Melvina Porter, 248; Nancy Jane, 248; Rachel, 78; Richard H., 248; Sarah E., 248; Theresa Ann Evins, 248; W. Earl, 214; William Henry, 248; William Phillip, 248; William Raynor, 248
Carter, 81; Allison, 154; Alta Beatrice Carson, 248; Arabelle Rose, 242; Betty, 67; Beulah, 154; Caleb, 168; Cheryl Sue, 168; Clara Alice, 162; Cleo V. Kerr, 168; Connie, 48; Delphia, 177; Delphia Keltner, 168; Don, 69; Dwight Halbert, 168; Elizabeth Dorrell, 168; Ernest Wayne, 168; Frank, 168; Gerald Lafayette, 168; Gertrude M. Winter, 168; Gertrude Mae Biellier, 248; Glenda, 225; Gordon S., 56; Gordon Stephen, 168; Herman, 67; Jerry R., 100; Jessica, 154; John, 242; John Tolliver, 242; Junior, 87; Kay, 68; Kevin, 168; Larry, 52; Linda Kay, 168; Lynette Bennett, 154; Marie, 67; Mrs. Aaron, 64; Mrs. Frank, 64; Nancy Ferguson, 168; Naomi Snyder, 251; Phyllis W. O'Kelley, 168; Rhoda Dorrell O'Banion, 242; Robert J., 154; Rolla, 168; Ron, 69; Sarah Richard, 168; Stephen, 168; Steva Lynn, 168; William Rudolf, 168
Case, Gus, 177; Mary Zephi Dean, 177
Casey, Deborah, 263; Pat, 66; Winifred Bernice, 264
Cash, Della Brashers, 161
Cason, 39; Dee, 75; Pauline, 38; Viola, 211
Cassett, Helen, 209
Cassy, 245; Betty, 161, 168; Billy, 168; Bob, 168; Charley, 21, 168; Herschel, 168; Joann, 168; Margie, 21, 168; Roxie, 168; Virginia, 168; Wilma, 168
Castleberry, Christiana, 206
Castoe, J., 31
Castor, Tom, 117
Cave, Carolyn June, 197; Viola Pett, 209
Cavener, Martha, 221; Martha F., 197; Sarah, 190
Caylor, Maggie, 160
Chaffin, 39, 45, 243, 245; Harry, 35, 243; Hazel Thurman, 258; Herbert, 258; Lillian Russell, 243; P.A., 36; Peter, 31, 33
Chambers, Bud, 35; Jim, 84; Mary, 116
Champieux, Jim, 96; Norma, 96; Terri, 96
Chaney, Sarah, 202
Chapman, J.D., 33
Chastain, Anna May, 69, 168, 169; Betty Lou, 169; Claude, 175; Claude Oren, 168; Clay Thomas, 168; Clyde Ray, 168, 169; Dorothy Jean, 168, 169; Emma Smith, 250; Helen, 255; Helen Parker, 175; James Thomas, 168; Jane Lynette Dorrell, 180; Jimmie, 67; Joe, 250; Joseph Robert, 168; Lynette, 151; Mary Jane Offuitt, 168; Maude Mae Gildewell, 168; Pierre, 168; Reathel Maize Jones, 168, 169; Vernon, 180; William C., 33; Wilma Lee, 68, 175
Chatham, Ann, 266, 267; Chuck, 266, 267; Ellen, 266, 267; Jane, 266, 267; Johnny, 266, 267; Robert, 266, 267; Velma, 266, 267
Cheathan, Grace T., 154
Cheek, Marijo, 227
Cheeseman, J.M., 33
Cherry, Clem, 160; Gladys Fay, 160
Chestnut, Mary Francis, 237
Chevalier, Heather, 88
Chilcutt, Dale, 155; Donald Lee, 67; Eunice Biglieni, 155; Floyd, 67; J.W., 67; John, 155; Loyd, 67; Norma Pierce, 177; Patience Ann Lawson, 214; William Lee, 214
Childress, Linda, 156, 225
Chiles, Alton, 135
Chilton, Dan, 82; Laurie, 47
Choate, Nikki Paswaters, 256
Christian, Jeff, 233; Kelly, 233; Kristina, 233; Sean, 233
Christian Health Care, 111
Chronister, Cindy, 148; Gary, 148; Judy, 148; Mark, 148; Patricia Alderman, 148; Wayne, 148
Chumbley, Albert, 169; Ben, 169; Benjamin Thomas, 169; Bonnie Jean, 169; Charles, 169; Clinton, 169; Ed, 169; Ernest, 169; Floss Isabelle, 149, 169; Gladys, 169; Janie Wyn, 169; John, 169; Kathryn, 77; Lon, 169; Lucy, 169; Lucy Emily Wester, 169; Malinda Sharp, 169; Mary Eliza Goodman, 169; Samuel, 169; Victor, 169; Ward, 169; Wayne, 169
Cireco, Gina, 88
Clack, Mary E., 203; Racheal Bonham, 203; Robert, 203; Tennessee, 203
Claiborn, Lavega, 31, 45
Claiborne, Frank, 117; John, 33; John F.G., 32
Clanton, Leo, 83
Clark, Bill, 178; Cline, 151; Cole Joseph, 169; Collin Maus, 169; Cooper Douglas, 169; Diane, 169; Dixie Allhands, 169; Dixie L., 170; Donald, 169, 170; Dorothy, 87; Dorothy J., 116; Edna Grace Tiede Brown, 259; Elder E., 141; Gary, 169; Howard, 169; Jack, 169; Jeanette Merritt, 169; Jeffrey, 169; Jennifer, 169; Jim, 170; Joanna, 169; Jon, 44; Julie Dan, 203; Laura Albough, 169; Lizzie Alice, 156; Madison Dawn, 169; Mariah Sha'e, 169; Martha Goodwin, 169; Marti, 229, 266; Marti West, 266; Mary, 151; Mildred, 204; Natalie Maus, 169; Phyllis Ann Demanche, 169, 178; Richard, 178; Richard Joseph, 169; Rita, 170; Roger William, 169; Serilda, 169; Volney, 169; Volney, Jr., 169; Walter, 72; William, 169; William O., 259
Clarke, Rex, 74; Robert, 87
Clarkson, George, 24
Clawson, Mike, 133
Clay, Henry, 243
Clayborne, William, 183
Clayton, Jack, 71; James, 71; JoAn, 185; Linda Rae, 250
Clegg, Mary, 162
Clemenson, Cheryl Sue Carter, 168; James, 168

Clemons, Donald Edward, 194; Lisa Kay Gleghorn, 176, 194
Cliborne, 9; Charlotte Willis, 30; Drucilla Ann Gilbreth, 30; John F., 32; Jubal, 30; Mary Logan, 30; William, 30
Click, Ethel, 153
Clifton, Ira Milford, 68
Clinton, Bill, 50
Cloud, Bill, 72; Bob, 72
Clouse, Ferd, 67; Howard, 67
Clutter, Deborah Ann Day Melton, 177; Donald, 177; Dorothea, 87; Dorothea Jean, 170; Gladys, 170; Laura Haun, 170; Lewis, 170; Marjorie, 170; Paula, 177; Ramona, 177
Cobb, Oran, 135; Tom, 117
Cochran, Amber, 170; Debra, 170; Debra J. Gray, 170; Debra Jean Gray Wilson, 192, 193; Edna, 170; Elder W.B., 105; Evelyn, 170; Floyd, 170; James, 170; Jimmie, 170; Jimmie E., 170; Lucille, 170; Maurine, 170; Nathalee, 170; Richard, 170; Terry L., 170, 193; Wanda, 170
Cockran, 231
Cockrell, Rick, 90, 129
Coffer, 237
Coggin, Alvin, 35, 170; Barbara Search, 171; Beth, 152; Beth Allison, 171; Brad, 270; Brady, 152; Brady Kent, 171; Carol, 116, 264; Carol Elizabeth DeWitt, 171, 179, 270; Cathie Sue Beard, 152, 171; Clara Elizabeth, 171; Clarence B., 171; Daron Bradley, 171; Elizabeth Ellen Rose, 170, 171, 208; Frank, 170, 270; Garrett Alexander, 171; George V., 171; George W., 170, 208; George Washington, 170; Gladys, 171; Helen Louise, 171, 270; Herb, 47, 48, 53, 118; Herbert, 47, 52, 53, 69; Herbert L., 55, 171; Herbert Lee, 171, 179, 270; Ina Mae, 171; James A., 170, 171; James Bradley, 171, 179; John, 24, 170, 232; John Leon, 171; Joseph Frank, 171; Keturah Snyder, 251; Lafayette Alvin, 171; Laura Adrian, 171; Laura Coggin, 208; Laura Elizabeth, 171; Lawrence, 35, 39, 170; Lawrence Hershel, 171; Levi, 170; Lola, 39; Mada Maxine, 170; Martha Louise, 171, 179; Marti, 48; Martin L., 170; Mary A. Shropshire, 170; Mary Brown, 170, 171; Mattie B., 171; Melvina, 170; Mrs. Alvin, 170; Mrs. Lawrence, 64; Myrtle M., 171; Ora Ellen, 171, 202, 207, 208, 269; Pauline Yeakley, 171, 270; Quentin Nathaniel, 171; Randolph Joe, 171, 179; Randy, 82; Seth Alexander, 171; Stan, 134, 152; Stanley Kent, 171, 179; Stella, 170; Susan Diane Wimmer, 171; Tura, 48, 130; William E., 171; Zachary, 152; Zachery Kent, 171
Coggins, Gladys, 206; Laurence, 206; Nellie Jackson, 206
Cogley, E.J., 232
Coker, Brad, 88; Clay, 36; Dalton Wade, 171; Elizabeth Blades, 157; Holly Roberta Fuhr, 171, 187; James, 75; Jeremy Blaine, 171; Robert Joseph, 171; Sterling Wade, 171; Virginia Irene Vanderhoof, 171
Colbertson, Cordelia, 207
Cole, Anna Raper, 171; Dan, 171; Joe, 75, 171; Margaret, 171; Marilyn, 171; Novella, 171; Walter, 171
Coleman, Elizabeth Shaw, 247; J.I., 32; Lydia, 247; W.W., 33
Colemen, J.S., 32
Collier, Mrs. Don, 64
Collings, M.S., 74
Collins, Alexis Dianne, 194; Craig Steven, 194; Daniel, 171; Ella Stines, 269; James Burton, 194; Jim, 31, 90, 111, 117, 135, 171; Juanita Box, 269; Kathryn Jean, 194; Kristen, 85; Linda, 135, 171; Lisa, 171; Mary Fortner, 184; Nancy Jane, 248; Naoma R., 269; Sterling, 184; Thomas H., 269; Tom, 135; Troy O., 269; Willie Madine Green, 194
Collison, Bill, 32; E.F., 32; J.C., 33; William, 32
Colson, Bob, 182; Larry, 182; Patty, 182; Vetha Etheridge, 182
Combs, C., 33; Morris, 75; Zetta May, 255; Zetta May Stickney, 34, 35
Comisky, Alan, 4, 24, 40, 52, 53, 75, 76, 82, 118, 172, 173, 217; Alanna, 88; Alanna Rose, 172, 217; Anne Elizabeth, 172; Charles, 53, 75; Charles Edward, 171, 172; Charlotte Freeman, 172; David, 53; Evelyn Allen Koch, 172; Frank, 123, 176, 196; Frank Alan, 172; Frank J., 31, 172; Frank Joseph, 171, 172; Irene, 172; Irene Myrtle, 171; Irene Myrtle Wade, 172; Irene Wade, 176; James David, 172; Jeannette Elizabeth Gillham, 172; Lynda Sue, 172, 176; Michael Aaron, 172; Rosemary, 4, 30, 48, 58, 116, 118, 173, 217; Rosemary Maness, 172, 217
Commerce Bank, 99
Compton, Duane, 50, 55; Lou, 116; Susan Hays, 200
Comstock, Berniece Parker, 177; Frank, 177; Kenny, 177
Conklin, Torre McKay, 106
Conley, 10
Conn, Aileen, 156; Archie, 90; Linda, 156; Robert, 156
Conner, 20; Beverly Ann Boatright, 159; Douglas, 159; Elijah Vess, 159; Isabella Blue, 159
Conrad, Aubrey, 66; Mary Elizabeth Simpkins, 149; Mary Louise, 149; Samuel Labrenth, 149
Conroy, Betty Jean, 186; Marvin, 44, 86
Consalvo, Nick, 173
Cook, 237; Arbeleta, 70; Bonnie, 237; Charles, 82; Daisy Sifferman, 173, 248; Darren Keith, 175; Icia Marie, 175; Irvin, 175; Jack, 70; Kent, 48; Kevin Brent, 175; Lucille, 255; Michael Kent, 175; Oma Jean, 70; Robert Warren, 173; Shearl, 82; Sheral Max, 175; Viola Maxine Davis, 175
Coolidge, Calvin, 150
Coon, Faye, 29; Harriet V. Andrew, 29; Merle, 29; Mira A. Crudginton, 29; Teddy Benton, 29; Walter, 29; Walter A., 29, 55; William Benton, 29
Cooney, Alexandra Nicole, 241; Andrew Thomas, 241; Debbie, 242; Debra Sue Robertson, 241; Thomas Jeffery, 241
Cooper, Courtney, 88; Debbie, 47; Dustin, 133; Harry T., 49; Henry, 206; Jim, 23; Levina Elizabeth Jackson, 206; Norman, 211
Coover, Catherine Wilhelm, 29; Mary E. Gibson, 30; S.H., 29; Samuel Clyde, 30; W.W., 32, 33; Will, 134; William W., 29, 30, 32, 33, 55
Cope, Claudius, 31; Joy, 238
Copeland, Ada, 162; Beverly, 237
Copenhaver, Ashley Joanna, 267; Heather Leanne, 267; Lydia Ann White, 267, 268; Stephanie Deanne, 267; Stephen Douglas, II, 267; Steve, 267
Copes, Jeff, 140
Copley, Elizabeth Skelton, 249
Corbett, Sharon Henson Hook, 201
Corbin, Inez Patterson, 234
Cordia, Rose Mary, 260
Core, Amber Dawn, 193; Andy O., 193; Autumn Brooke, 193; Brandi Renee, 193; Vandeana Gray, 193
Costello, Kate, 148
Cotner, Marilyn Brown, 163
Cotter, J.M., 32; Lydia, 184; Travis, 236
Cotter-Grant, Margaret McSpadden, 223
Couch, James, 177; Johnna Lynn Day Murr, 177; Manerva, 212; Mitchell, 177; Stephanie, 177
Coulter, Elizabeth S., 29
Countryman, Amy Jo, 227
Countryside Bank, 100
Counts, Steve, 133
Courdin, Laura Ann, 183
Courtney, Terri, 47
Cowan, 78; Cavin, 84; Roger, 84
Coward, 242
Cowden, Amy Anne, 209; Amy Kerr, 209; Elizabeth, 209; John Albert, 209; Lena, 209; Liza, 209; Mary Frances Sullivan, 209; Matilda Frances, 209; Nancy, 209; Rachel Katie, 209; Walter, 209; William, 209
Cox, 92, 264; A.E., 207; Adrian, 167, 251; Adrian Ervin, 173, 174, 266; Amanda, 121; Amanda B., 121; Amanda Belle Britain, 121, 162; Amanda Britain, 116; Beatrice Ann Brown, 163; Beth, 55, 207; Beth Puge Snyder, 173, 174, 251, 266; Beth Snyder, 167; Beverly Copeland, 237; Bud, 173; Carrie, 88, 229, 232; Cathryn Lee, 121; Charlie, 173; Clara, 15; Claudine Barrett, 121; Clifford, 173; Dick, 173; Dorothy Vernell Wade, 172; Ethel, 121; Ethel M., 162; Ethel Mae, 121; George, 15; Hazel L. Ottendorf, 231; James, 162; James Mitchell, 121; Jane Owen, 232; Judy, 164; Larry, 31, 52; Lester, 144; Lester B., 121; Lester E., 36, 46, 121, 155, 162, 166, 173, 175, 205; Lester Lee, 121; Libby, 174, 207, 251, 266; Lucy, 162; Martha H., 242; Mary M., 234; Mary Margret Hill, 201, 234; Mildred Belle Lee, 121; Mona Marie Rose, 242; Mrs. Adrian, 76; Norma, 55; Phyllis, 76, 167, 173, 174, 207, 251, 266; Roy, 173; Sarah, 229, 232; Stanley William, 242; Vernell Wade, 67; Virginia Belle, 121
Coyle, 76
Crabb, Jessie, 12; Nettie Lou, 12; Patty, 167; Ray, 12
Crabtree, Cynthia, 80
Crader, Allan, 79; Allan B., 74
Craig, Charles E., Sr., 218; Colton Hamlin, 179; Irene Bonita, 218; Jeffrey Allen, 179; Lana Lundt, 218; Nancy Ruth DeVore, 179, 228; William, 25
Crain, Marlene Annette, 228
Craven, Mary, 259
Crawford, 92; Angie, 174; Chester, 174; Dorothy Hubbard, 174; Jack, 219; Linda, 243; Lisa, 100; Melvin Chester, 174; Mike, 174; Patty, 174; Robert, 174; Roland, 174; Susan, 174; Viola, 174
Crayne, W.S., 33
Creason, Floyd, 138
Creech, Charlotte Mae/May Oliver, 217, 246
Creed, Marci Jane Anderson, 210; Mark, 210; Wesley James, 210
Creighton, William, 33
Creson, Hazel, 250; Hazel Flood, 174; Ralph, 174
Creswell, T.F., 33
Crews, Glenda Carter, 225; Shari, 100
Crick, Darrell, 32
Crighton, 67; Clara, 72; John Tom, 72; Wilamenia, 72; Wilhemina, 72
Criswell, 9; Agnes Dennis, 179; Alfred, 179; Arminta, 28; Arrimba Greene, 30; Gregory, 30; H.G., 30, 134; Margaret, 76; Sarah Baar, 30; Theodore F., 30
Crocker, Betty Blanton, 159
Crockett, Scott, 84
Cromwell, Sir Oliver, 267; Thomas, 267
Crosswhite, Ollie, 41
Croston, Jenna, 88
Crow, Bryant, 174; Clifton, 174; Georgia, 174; Geraldine, 174; Henry, 174; Isabinda Cannefax, 174; Jessie, 174; Joseph Bryant, 174; Laura Taylor, 174; Lester, 174; Maggie, 174; Mary, 174; Melissa, 174; Monta, 174; Visa Jane, 174; Wilbur, 174; Winson, 174
Crowe, Gladys, 112
Crudginton, Mira A., 29; T.B., 29
Cruise, Roberta May, 188
Crum, Alvin, 74; Lilly, 212; Ruth, 216
Crume, Edna Mae, 76
Crumpley, Myrtle S. Sifferman, 248; Claudia, 76
Crumrine, Claudia, 76, 84
Cruse, Mary, 227; Mary Jo, 227
Culley, Valerie, 167; W.F., 203
Cummins, Al, 117; Hannah, 85; Harriet, 4
Cundiff, William, 117
Cunningham, Bernard Owen, 214; Carol Ann, 174, 175; Clark, 238; Donna, 71; Elda Gertrude Kerr, 210; Elizabeth Perry, 175; Emma May True, 214; Fred, 136; Genevieve Austin, 175; Ida, 169; Jeanne Lischer, 175; Katherine Rebecca, 175; Katherine Rebecca True, 214; LaZeta Redfearn Randolph, 238; Lucy Victoria Lile Potts, 248; Nancy, 159, 238; Nancy Burns, 174, 175; Nelson Perry, 174, 175; Peggy, 175; Richard William, 214; Robert William, 175; Ruby, 231; Terry, 90, 141; William Perry, 174, 175; Wilbur Perry, Jr., 175
Curtis, C.H. Skip, 24
Cutberth, Anne Thurman, 257, 258; Larry, 257
Cutbirth, Andrew Jackson, 155; Edythe, 154; Edythe Evelyna, 164; Herbert, 155; Myrtle Ryles, 155

## D

d'Tourville, 259
Dade, Kara, 188
Dahlstrom, Britt, 154; Chris, 154; Hugo, 154; Kelly, 154; Neisha L. Bennett, 154; Tara, 154
Dake, Ernie, 204; Julie, 212; Julie Hopper White, 204; Krista, 83
Dale, Cheri, 198; Dorothy, 99
Dalla Rosa, Genisse, 88
Dalton, Carrie Alderman, 148
Damene, Berry, 32
Damerel, B., 31
Dameron, Virginia, 159
Damitz, Irving, 86
Danhauer, Jean, 70
Daniel, Kayna, 85; Marilyn, 245
Daniels, Sarah Ellen, 214
Danielson, Dan, 231; Danny, 75, 87, 231; Hazel Ottendorf, 231
Darby, 134
Daren, Jerry, 52
Darling, Lucille Brown, 163
Datema, Alice, 234; Cornelius, 234; Elnora Joyce Phillips, 234, 235; Emma Grace, 235; Hank, 56; Hank C., 234; Homer Richard, 234; Hommo, 234; Joshua Hank, 235; Joyce Anne, 234; Mariah Elnora, 235; Mia Rae Weirich, 234; Michael Ross, 234, 235; Peter, 234; Ralph, 234; Sue, 234
Davidson, Allan, 157; Carey, 131; Holly, 83, 85; James, 157; Jennifer C., 177; Jerrold, 157; Lorene, 118; Lorene Blades, 157, 216; Sallie Lou Adams, 176; Steve, 216; Steven, 157; Thomas, 157; Tom, 118, 157, 176
Davis, 9, 39, 45, 92, 179, 264; Alma Lorene Jones, 175; Amy Anne Cowden, 209; B.W., 31; Barney, 127, 193; Barney Wilson, 176, 193; Bernard, 165, 176; Bernice, 176; Bettie Sarah, 176; Betty Jo Secrest, 175, 176; Blanche, 254; Bobby, 76; Bruce Allen, 175; Bryan, 185; Burl, 72; Candice, 175; Carl, 175; Charles, 201; Charles Richard, 172, 173, 176; Chris, 175; Clyde, 123, 127, 254; Clyde V., 254, 255; Connie Fortner, 185; Connie Mae Fortner, 219; Danny Wayne, 175; Della Marie Bentley, 176; Delores, 72; Deloris Mae McConnell, 219; Don, 86, 255; Donald Lee, 175; Doug, 53; Ed, 52; Edith Johnson, 219; Edward, 53, 75, 201; Emily Cordelia Pearce, 254; Eva Ann Harrington, 175; Everett, 75, 127; Everett L., 219; Francis Ellen, 245; George, 176; George Henry, 254; Ginger McElhaney, 222; Grace, 176; Guy, 36; Harold, 127, 254; Harold Wayne, 175; Harriett, 193; Harriet Hawkins O'Dell, 193; Helen, 72, 176; Henrietta, 72; Henry, 201; Henry Clay, 156; Hollie Jane, 176, 193; Howard, 38, 45, 165; Howard Leroy, 176; Ira, 201; Jack, 185, 219; James Robert, 175; Janet, 88; Janie, 175; Jared Blane, 172, 173, 176; Jayme Beth, 172, 173, 176; Jeanie, 47; Jean Elaine, 176; Jeffrey Robert, 176; Jerry Leslie, 175; Julie, 175; Karen, 180; Katy, 185; Kimberly Ann, 175; Laura Vesta, 176, 193; Lenore, 72; Leona, 201; Lester, 15, 66, 219; Lewis, 12; Linda Louise, 219; Lisa Ann, 175; Lizzie Alice Clark, 156; Louisa Little, 176; Lydia, 176; Lynda Sue Comisky, 172, 173, 176; Mabel Schad, 173, 175; Mable, 264; Marcella, 68, 255; Margaret Freeman O'Neal, 176; Martha Ella, 186; Marti Jenan Worley, 175; Mary Lou, 66; Mary Louella, 175; Mary Lou Tipton, 175; Mary Matilda Johnson, 175; Mattie, 201; Melody Ann, 219; Mildred, 254, 255; Mildred E., 220; Mina, 73, 74; Mrs. Bernard, 76; Mrs. Howard, 76; Mrs. W.R., 33; N.C., 32; N.D., 31; Nellie May, 156; Norman, 93; Pauline, 257; Penney Wilson, 173; Robert Leroy, 176; Sally, 87; Sandra Jean, 175; Sarah, 254; Sarah Elizabeth Hart, 176; Sarah Glenn, 201; Sherry Lynn, 175; Stanley Dale, 175; Stephen Lee, 175; Teresa Fay, 219; Thomas, 209; Thomas David, 175; Tina, 263; Tressie Alta, 176; Tressie R. Stewart, 254, 255; Tressie Stewart, 14, 254; Verdalea, 72; Vernon, 260; Vernon Lester, 175; Vernon M., 117; Vernon Monroe, 175; Virginia Marshall, 175; Viola Maxine, 175; W.H., 32; Walter, 175; Walter McKinley, 176; Warren, 173, 175, 264; Wayne, 66; William L., 176; Wilma Lee Chastain, 175
Day, Bearl, 177; Benton, 69, 177; Brittney, 85; Dana, 177; Debbie, 47, 177, 244; Deborah Ann, 177; Drenda, 48, 177; Edsel, 86; Emogene, 177; Imogene, 69; Jennifer C. Davidson, 177; John, 47; Johnna Lynn, 177; John Michael, 177; John Ryan, 177; John V., 177; Ken, 244; Kenneth, 48, 177; Leo, 177;

Marie, 244; Marie Parker, 177; Marion, 177, 216; Mark, 96; Mary Alice Brown, 177; Maude Looney, 177, 216; Mrs. Kenneth, 48; Pam, 229; Pamela, 243; Shirley J. Bohannon, 177; Terri Champieux, 96
Day-Bacon, Lora Lee, 163
Dean, Adeline, 177; Delphia Carter, 177; Edna Sneed, 251; Elisha, 177, 178, 189; Eli Pendleton, 177; Ella Lafollette, 177; Eula, 227; Friday, 250; Hardy, 177; Jess, 177; Lura, 177; Mae Martin, 177; Maggie, 177; Mary Catherine Hayes, 177; Mary Patterson, 177; Mary Zephi, 177; Melton Ratio, 177, 178, 189; Nancy Tinsley, 177; Naomi, 177; Nerva Garoutte, 177, 189, 190; Opal Smith, 250; Paul, 251; Pearly Garoutte, 177, 189, 190; Rufus, 177; Ted, 177; Thomas, Jr., 177; Tom, 177; Vanner, 177
DeBoard, Abner Copeland, 178; Elisha, 178; Fay, 178; Glynn, 178; Hulda Ellen Lane, 212; Lucy, 178; Mabel Irene, 212; Mary Elizabeth Harralson, 178; Ralph, 178; Roxie, 178; Ruby, 178; Susan Sewell, 178; Susie, 178; William, 178, 212; William Claude, 212
DeBorde, Ralph, 35; Roxie, 35
Deckard, Luther, 67
Decker, 31, 35, 139; Dorothy, 134; Ella, 28, 139; J.E., 29, 90, 144
DeLapp, Nancy Green, 259
Delarue, Percy, 52; William, 29
Demanche, Deborah L. Nakano Gold, 178; Dick, 169; Nancy, 169; Nancy Ann Brown, 178; Nancy Brown, 163; Phyllis Ann, 169, 178; Richard Eugene, 178; Richard S., 178; Thomas E., 178; Thomas Eugene, 178; Tom, 169
Demonbrum, Alta, 12; Louise, 12
Demore, Lula, 184
Dempsey, Evalee Gardner, 189; Lyman, 189; Rodney, 189
Dennis, Agnes, 76, 178, 179, 250; Anna, 178; Anna Mae, 38, 179; Darla Suzanne Highfill, 178; David, 178; George, 178, 179, 250; Gladys, 179; Hugh, 178; Jack, 178; Jeffery Mitchel, 178; Judith Ann Owen, 178, 233; Kaitlyn Suzanne, 178; Ollie Mae Smith, 178, 250; Robin Denise, 178; Sidney Claire, 178
Denny, 221; Artie Hart, 179; Calvin Leroy, 179; Clayborn, 179; Darthula, 179; David, 48, 109, 179, 234, 262; Diane, 48, 179; Earl, 179; Elbert, 179; Elbert S., 234; Eula, 179; Eva, 179; Helen, 262; Helen Britain, 234; Helen M. Britain, 179; Ina, 179; Karen, 131; Karen Walker, 179; Leo, 179; Linda, 109, 179; Lisa, 179; Maggie McDaniel, 179, 234; Mrs. David, 48; Mrs. Elbert, 64; Shearl, 179, 234, 262, 264; Sheral, 56; Velma, 179; Velma Irene, 157
Dent, Anna Katherine, 238; Katie, 194
Deragowski, Davis, 182; Lance, 182; Lauryn, 182; Sandy Etheridge, 159, 182
Derry, J.R., 105
DeVasure, Joyce Marie, 180
DeVoge, Lillian, 35
DeVore, Angela Kay, 179; Brenda Kay Vanderhoof, 179; Cherie Christine, 179; Derek Michael, 179; Edwina Ruth Nelson, 179, 228; Elizabeth Ann, 179; Karen Sue, 179, 228; Nancy Ruth, 179, 228; Walter Eugene, 179; Walter Eugene, Jr., 179, 228
Devries, Earl, 70
DeWett, 75, 242; Bertha, 70; DaMarous, 75, 87; Ed, 70; Flossie, 217, 243; Flossie Ann, 246; George Lewis, 246; Mildred Ruhamah Harrington, 246
Dewitt, Bryan, 211; Karen Kubat, 211; Porter, 211; Rob, 211; Mary Alice, 219
DeWitt, Alecia Kay, 179; Barbara Jean, 179; Brian David, 179; Bruce, 44; Bruce, Jr., 179; Bruce T., 171, 270; Bruce Tinsley, 179; Carol, 201; Carol Elizabeth, 86, 171, 179, 270; Cecil Virginia, 179; Don Porter, 179; Edward Harper, 179; Gary Bruce, 179; Gwendolyn Ann, 179; Henry Kent, 179; Janet Sue, 179; Karen, 85; Keith, 81, 86; Keith Garbee, 179; Kent, 23, 179, 201; Linda Erlene, 179; Michael Leon, 179; Nanny Kaye, 179; Nanny Kaye Eichenberger, 179; Patricia Lynn, 179; Porter, 75, 76, 82, 87; Robert Allen, 179; Sarah, 259; Steven Keith, 179; Thirza Garbee, 171; Thirza May Garbee, 179, 270; Virginia Sue, 179; William Drew, 179; William Drew, Jr., 179
Dial, Pearl, 75; Tonett, 45
Dickens, 77, Krista, 88
Dickerson, Charlotte, 227; Dorothy, 252; Margaret S.J. Lile Ruhl, 248
Dickover, Alice Roberts, 240
Dickson, Janelle Renee, 194
Diffie, Mary Ann, 216
Dillinger, Robert P., 141
Dillon, B.E., 134; Hazel, 116; Jim, 24
Dipper, Brady, 83; Brandy, 83
Dirks, Elsa, 108
Disheroon, Ada Leatherbury, 256; Burton M., 256; Winnie, 256
Dixon, June, 262; Mary Elizabeth, 227; Mary Sue, 85
Doak, Dell, 46
Dodd, Catherine, 214; Deloris Louise, 266; Elizabeth Jane, 226
Dodds, Thomas, 209
Dodson, Bill, 72; Don, 54, 117; Kathryn, 72; Terry, 75
Doerr, Mary, 110
Donnelly, Sybil Justine True, 214; Thomas John, 214
Donnelson, Emily, 110
Dorrah, James Alan, 176; Joetta Adams Engler, 176; Phillip Ray, 176; Ray Phillip, 176
Dorrell, Charles Leon, 179, 180; Charles Lyndle, 180; Delta Edna Swinney, 179; Elizabeth, 168; G.B., 21, 33; Green B., 33; Jane Lynette, 180; Jeremy James, 180; Karen Davis, 180; Kenneth, 179; Thelma Blades, 151, 158, 179, 180; Verbin, Jr., 179; Verbin Daniel, 179
Dorriss, Eula Denny, 179
Doty, Lucinda, 227
Dougherty, Alma Alice, 152; Dora Harris, 152; John, 152
Douglas, Mary Elizabeth, 226
Douglass, 218
Doverspike, Judy Harper, 199; Kim, 199
Dow, Gailya, 134
Downs, Paul, 123
Doyle, Terry, 84
Drain, Sherri Dunn, 181
Drake, Ray, 133
Drennon, John, 164
Droke, George, 148; Phyllis Alderman, 148; Thomas, 148
Dryden, C.F., 146
Duckman, E.C., 33
Duff, Charles, 70; Margaret, 70
Duggan, Alyssa, 154; Karen Schickram, 154; Kelly, 154
Duke, David L., 246; Iris Edwina Maness Jones, 217, 246
Dulin, Mary Norman, 221
Duncan, George, 216; Hayden, 216; Loine, 165; Mary Ann Shelton, 216; Nancy, 216; Sarah, 216; Scott, 88
Dunlavy, Albert, 165
Dunn, Caden Craig, 180, 181; Chester, 135; Connor Craig, 180, 181; Craig, 180, 181; Craig Elvin, 180; Elvin W., 180, 181; Kevin, 180, 181; Norma Blanche Hargis, 180; Sharon Gail Utke, 180, 181; Sherri, 84, 180, 181; Tricia Jo Jones, 180; William Lester, 180
Dunning, Darlene, 100
Dunshee, Nancy, 253
Durbin, Wanda Lee Fugitt, 186
Durham, Billie, 182; Gracie Estes, 182; Lora Mae, 182; Mary Sue, 182; Ray, 182; Ruth Simmons, 211
Duroni, Frank, 155
Dutton, Earl, 84
Duvall, Bill, 181; Billy, 70; Bob, 32, 52, 55, 181, 219, 256; David, 84; Ethel Keltner, 181, 219; Jess, 45, 245; Jesse, 219; Jessie Albert, 181; Jim, 52, 181; Joan, 70; Jo Ann, 181, 219; Peggy, 70, 181; Sue, 116
Dyer, Jamen, 154; Jennifer Jameson, 154
Dykens, Jim, 80

## E

Eagan, 216, 220, 254; Eddy, 35; Edgar, 181; Edna, 45, 122, 151; Edna Brown, 181; Elsie Merritt, 181; Gary, 122; Gary Lee, 181, 246; Harold, 181; Howard, 45, 86, 192, 204; Howard Lee, 122, 123, 181, 199, 246; Jo Ann, 45; Jo Ann Sellers, 77, 122, 181, 246; Launa Bacon, 181; Loleta, 86, 181; Mable, 181; Merle, 181; Michael, 181; Parolee, 181; Patrick, 181; S.V., 44, 45; Small, 35; Smallwood Van Buren, 181; Spike, 35
Eaglin, Opal Luna James, 207; Wayne, 207
Earl, Edna, 212
Earls, Janice, 191
Earnhardt, Emaline, 248
Earnhart, Clyde, 45
Earnheart, Carrie, 88
Easterday, Louise, 182
Eaton, A.T., 28
Eaves, Buck, 39; Etna Dallas, 215; James Patrick, 215; Sharon, 159; Sharon Rubison, 159; Violettie King Hamilton, 215
Eckley, Cindy Chronister, 148
Eddington, Aganeth, 184
Eddlemon, Marty, 82
Eddy, Mitchell, 66
Edgar, George, 73, 74; John F., 90; Leslie, 228; Sarah Jane, 193
Edmonds, Becky Viles, 174; Kala, 174; Kevin, 174; Loryn, 174; Paige, 174
Edmondson, E.M., 74; Elsie Belle, 222
Edwards, Elizabeth Jean, 176; Elsia, 230; Eugene, 68; Hubert, 176; James Wright, 219; Lydia Davis, 176; Matilda, 219; Ona, 207; Stacy, 83
Edward Jones, 98
Eichenberger, Nanny Kaye, 179
Eisenhower, 19, 150
Eitel, Roger, 39; Sandra, 212
Eliott, S.G., 31
Elkins, Donald, 70; Evelyn, 70; Jennifer, 223; Jennifer Kay Bluebaum, 222; Karlie Kay, 222; Leroy, 70; Russell, 222; Stephen Berry, 222
Elliott, Barbie, 181; Betty, 181, 182; Hollie, 182; Marilynn, 181; S.G., 28; W. Anson, 181, 182; Wallace, 69; Willie, 69; Wren Pullen, 236
Ellis, Joan Anderson, 148; Kerry, 83; Ransom, III, 148, 227; Ransom, Jr., 148; Sarah Ann, 209; Sarah Ann Elizabeth, 209; Sarah Elizabeth, 169
Elmore, Chester, 81
Elson, Venelia O., 158
Ely, Ethel, 46; Ethel Norman, 221
Emhoff, Eleanor, 68
Emory, Lyndon, 6
England, Kayla, 83
Engle, Emma, 259; Lisa, 47; Sally, 47
Engledow, Carolyn, 223; Eugene, 223; Grace Slagle, 223
Engler, Joan Paula, 176; Joetta Adams, 176; John Paul, 176
Enlow, Leslie Dale, 187; Linda Grace Hayley, 187; Manford Edward, 187; Michelle Diane, 187; Timothy Scott, 187
Ennis, Rosa, 189
Enyart, Aubrey, 179; Blake, 179; Diane Denny, 179; Wes, 179
Eppard, Billy, 72; Junior, 72; Kathryn, 72
Epps, Ethel, 212; Paul, 117
Erickson, Alvin, 151; Erica, 158; Florence, 158; Matt, 158
Erskin, Minnie, 202
Espy, Aaron Joseph, 269; Catherine Marie, 269; Dana Ann, 269; Donna Kay Wilson, 269; Gena Kay, 47; Gina Kay, 269; James, 269; Lisa Gerst, 269; Natalie Ann, 269; Scott Michael, 269
Essary, Judy Mitchell, 213
Estep, Waddell, 50
Esterling, Lucy DeBoard, 178
Estes, 237; Bill, 182; David, 264; Floried Pearce, 226; Gracie, 182; Hobert, 127; Lori Watts, 264; Sally Etheridge, 182
Etheridge, 136; Aaron, 182; Alfreda, 182; Betty Wells, 182; Brenda, 182; Caleb, 182, 189; Caleb E., 262; Cleta, 182; Debra Whittimore, 182; Dorothy, 182; Erik, 182; Ethel Brown, 182; Eva, 182; Everett, 182; Frances Iona Maness, 217; Frank, 182; Gary, 159, 182; George, 182; Gertrude, 182; Harold, 159, 182; Harold L., 182; Hazel, 182; Iona Maness, 182, 217; Jacob, 182; Janet, 182; Jeerly Salee, 182; Jeerl Dean, 182, 243; Jennie, 182; Jerlie Sallee, 243; Jewel, 182; Jill, 182; Joe, 182; John, 262; Lewis, 182, 243; Linda, 182; Lonnie, 182; Louise Easterday, 182; Malinda A. Logan, 262; Malinda Logan, 182, 189; Mary, 182; Mary Ellen, 190; Matthew, 182; Milinda Logan, 182; Myrtle Wade, 182; Nina Kay, 182; Ralph, 182; Ray, 182; Ray Wade, 217; Rilla Mayfield, 182; Rosa, 152; Rosa Elmeda, 189, 262; Rosie, 182; Sally, 182; Sandra, 182; Sandy, 159, 182; Sarah, 182; Steve, 182, 217; Steven, 182; Thelma Blanton, 182; Thelma Maude Blanton, 159; Vanessa, 182; Vetha, 87, 182; Vonda, 182; Warren, 182, 217
Etzler, Andrew, 132
Eubanks, Amy, 88; Carl, 55, 183, 226; Henry, 183; Jeanie, 182; Jeanie Bates, 183; John, 47; Martie Lee, 183; Ramona Harris, 183; Tony Scott, 183
Euler, Cindy, 88
Evans, Andy, 45, 183; Art, 133, 134; Beverly, 239; Carl, 45, 81, 183; Cindy, 47, 183; Crystal, 183; Dawna, 87; Deborah Michele, 159; Donna, 183; Ellen Roberts, 240; Fay Likens, 183; Gene, 183, 245; Hart, 183; J.S., 42; Jim, 45, 183; Jimmy, 183, 233; Lee, 45, 183; Marilyn, 260; Marjorie, 206; Marjorie Squibb, 183; Martha Stephenson, 183; Mrs. Jimmie, 77; Nancy, 152, 183; Stacy, 83; Steve, 183; Terri, 183; Terry, 183
Evatt, Juanita Lucille Gray, 176, 194; Lloyd Thomas, 194
Everett, Carole Guenther, 196; Colin, 196; Elise, 196; James Wilson, 196; L. Martin, Jr., 196; Lynn Caryl Yanyo, 196; Mark Tobin, 196
Evergreen Cemetery, 144
Everhart, James, 20
Everheart, William, 48
Evert, Chris, 192
Evins, Theresa Ann, 248

## F

Fabro, Barry, 179; Joshua, 179; Lisa Denny, 179; Ryan, 179
Fagg, Alta May McSpadden, 184; Cecil, 184
Fahl, Charles M., 164
Fair, Gene, 48
Fairbanks, Jonathan, 142
Family Pharmacy, 110
Fanning, Jamie, 88; Virginia, 116
Farley, A.C., 74; Mrs. A.C., 33
Farmer, Carl Celo, 158; Christopher, 158; Hilda Otila Tiede, 259; Isabelle, 247; James A., 158; Mary Elizabeth Willmington, 158; Olive Ann Porter, 158; Pauline Nicholson, 158; Robert W., 259
Farr, Bill, 55, 56, 226; Paula, 116
Farris, Lucy, 216
Farwell, 215; Derek, 183; Don, 162, 183; Greg, 86, 183; Jeff, 183; Wildon, 183; Wilena, 4, 86, 183
Faucett, Cleta Etheridge, 182; Leslie, 182; Max, 258
Faught, 254
Faulkner, Taylor, 85
Fault, Becky, 47
Feaster, Clemma Ethel, 220
Fees, Gary, 84
Feltus, Toby, 53
Ferguson, Amos, 64; Azie McNally, 183; David, 217; David Wallace, 184; E.B., 24, 123, 164, 226; Edna Bessie Wallace, 183, 184; Emmer, 64; Ernest, 52; Ernest Bly, 183, 184; James Wallace, 184; Jeanie Diane, 184; Jim, 82, 207; Jimmy, 207; John, 217; John Charles, 184; Julie Hedger, 184; Madison, 217; Madison Nicole, 184; Marilyn, 217; Marilyn Kay, 217; Marilyn Maness, 184; Maxine, 207; Maxine Riley, 77, 184; Mildred, 184; Nancy, 168; Nancy J. Wade Wallace, 184; Simon, 64; Thomas, 183; Thomas Wallace, 184; Wallace, 123, 207
Ferrell, 246; Vanessa, 88
Fiene, Karen Williams, 269; Madison, 269; Paige, 269; Randy, 269
Fikes, 42
Fillback, Heather, 88
Finn, Deborah, 158
First Baptist Church, 139
First Baptist Church of Battlefield, 136
First Christian Church, 130
Fishback, Mildred Ferguson, 184; Robert, 184; Wayne, 184; Woodson, 184
Fishburn, Loyd, 87
Fisher, Earmel Ada Evelene, 184; Gladys Mae, 184, 197; Ida, 184; John, 184; Johnny Robert, 184; Joseph Franklin, 184; Lamen Leslie, 184; Lula Irene, 184; Malena, 184; Mary Ellen Adams, 184; Merle Evelyn, 184; Mertie, 184; Minerva Jane Howard, 184; Nelson, 184; Payton, 184; Payton Townsend, 184; Sherman Earl, 184; Velva Lavanda, 184; William Deulen, 184
Fitzpatrick, J.D., 127; Ken, 100
Flanagan, 237; Mary, 237
Flanigan, Nancy, 47
Flatt, Kitty Fugitt, 186
Fleming, Mary Dawn, 228

Fletcher, Allen M., 178; Cody Alan, 269; Gary, 94; Jacqueline D., 178; Marcella C., 178; Steven Mark, 269; Sue, 200; Teresa Lynn Wilson, 269; Tiffany Lynn Wilson, 269
Flinn, Jane, 148
Flood, Hazel, 174; Janice, 219; Kris, 83; Lacey Kerr, 209
Floyd, Cletis, 69; Earnest, 69; Effie, 71; Elma, 69; Helen, 71; Jewell, 71; John, 71; Wanda Ottendorf, 217
Fly, T.B., 143
Followill, Goodwin H., 33
Forbis, Alta Carolyn King, 217; Ann, 246; Floyd, 231; Glen, 217; Jesse, 127; Jesse Greene, 217; Laura Ellen Maness, 216, 217; Ronnie, 217; Vernice Floyd, 217; Wanda Ottendorf, 217, 231
Ford, Angela Thorpe, 264; E. Gregg, 264; Sheila, 185
Forrester, S., 143
Forsythe, Sarah McCray, 242; Temperance Rose, 242; Thomas, 242; William, 242
Fortner, Aganeth Eddington, 184; Alma, 185; Alta May McSpadden Fagg, 184; Alta McSpadden, 223; Alva, 184; Bert, 184; Bertha Marsh, 184; Bob, 184; Connie, 185; Connie Mae, 219; Doris Fay McConnell, 219; Doris McConnell, 184, 185; Effie Jones, 184; Elick, 184; Elizabeth J., 184; Eula, 185; Eva, 184; Hannah, 184; Jacob, 184, 185; Jacob Lee, 184; James, 184; JoAn, 185; John, 184; Lewis, 184; Lidia, 184; Lula Demore, 184; Lydia Cotter, 184; Margaret Jones, 184; Martha, 184; Mary, 184; Mary Baty, 184; Mary Susan Steeley, 184; Monroe, 184; Norma, 185; Pleasant Witt, 184; Rachel, 184; Rachel Fortner, 184; Ramon, 185; Rebecca A., 184; Robert, 185; Robert D., 219; Robert Lee Bob, 184; Samuel, 184; Sarah, 185; Sarah Jane Haney/Haynie, 184; Tammy, 185; Tammy Fay, 219; Thomas, 185; William, 184
Fossett, Lelia, 113; Max L., 113
Foster, Anthony, 185; Arena, 157; Devon, 85; Evelyn Brown, 227; Geraldine, 116; Jason, 185, 188; Jennifer, 185, 188; Jessica, 185, 188; Karen, 185; Karen Fuhr, 185, 253; Karen Melinda Fuhr, 188; Maxine, 227; Robert, 188, 253; Robert, Jr., 185; Robert, Sr., 185; Roy, 227; Samantha, 185; Sheila Ford, 185
Foust, Charles B., 185; Dollie, 49, 183, 191; Dollie Garoutte, 163, 185, 241; Donna Blankenship, 185; JoAnn, 68, 163, 185; Lora Lee, 84, 163, 185; Lydia Harshbarger, 9; Mary Sue, 68, 163, 185, 241; Ollie Kimmons, 185; Sam, 163, 185, 241
Fraka, Jack, 52, 81, 87; Thelma, 38
Frame, Bessie Yeakley, 270; Edna, 192; Jacob, 270; Jessie Irene, 158; John Parker, 158; Venelia O. Elson, 158
Francis, Margie Cassy, 21, 168; Patty, 257; Ray A., 117
Frank, Eugene M., 134; M.E., 131; Mrs. M.E., 131
Franklin, Annalee, 198
Franks, Alice, 185, 196; Ivan, 185, 196; James Russell, 189; Laura Clarice, 189; Rosa Ennis, 189; Shirley, 185; Sondra, 185, 196
Frazier, Christopher Thomas, 167; David Solly, 48; Gilda Sue Cantrell, 167; Jessie, 48; Julia Huber Tiede, 259; Karen Zell, 271; Kristen, 271; Lori Ann, 167; Marisa, 271; Mike, 167; Milton C., 259; Vivian, 71; Zack, 271
Fredrick, Jennell, 116
Freeland, Carole Guenther, 196; Harold Eugene, 196
Freeman, Butch, 67; Charles, 12; Charles Jay, 237; Charlotte, 172; Donna, 116; Donna Jean Raper, 237; Elsie Ellen, 247; Joe, 69; Karen, 212; Margaret, 176; Maurice, 12; Randy, 211, 212; Rozella, 254; Samuel, 135; Sarah, 237; Shelley, 237
French, 12, 148; Aubyn, 52, 186; Betty, 207; Betty Jean Conroy, 186; Brian, 186; Clarissa Johnson, 186; Dakota, 186; David Clifton, 186; Deanna, 186; Diana Kay, 186; Doc, 45; Freda O. Miller, 186; Inez, 186; Jack, 117, 207; Jack Eugene, 186; Jennifer Louise, 186; Julia Ann, 186; Larry Omar, 186; Omar, 45, 186; Opal, 186; Pauline Louise Greismer, 186; Polly, 157; Richard Ulysses, 186; Ronald Dean, 186; Sallie, 116; Sallie Ann, 186; Sally Louise Johnson, 186; Sandra Faye, 186; Sandy, 207; Sarah Alcinda Turner, 185, 186; Steven Eugene, 186; Ulysses Simpson, 185, 186
Frieden, Jason, 230; Justin, 230; Tauna Kneale, 230; Tom, 230
Frisco Square, 92
Fritsch, Emilie Auguste, 191
Fronabarger, Jasen, 98
Fry, Ashley, 83; Edith Clara, 214; W.A., 11
Fugitt, 186, 237, 266; Barbara Lemons, 230; Beau, 230; Bedford, 186; Bette, 124; Bette Jane Sellers, 246; Bette Sellers, 186; Bill, 186, 230; Boyd, 43, 54, 123, 186; Cecil Garoutte, 190; Christina, 152, 186, 246; Connie Allred, 230; Frank, 186; J.W., 122, 123, 124, 126, 127, 186, 246; Jack, 186; James Waldo, 190; James William, 186; Jerry, 76; Jessica, 230; John, 126, 186; John H., 186; Jo Ann, 186, 230; Jo Ann Stewart, 77; Kathy, 186, 230; Kayla, 186, 230; Kim, 186, 230; Kitty 186; Leonard, 35, 52, 78, 117, 123, 124, 126, 127, 178, 186, 190, 255; Martha Ella Davis, 186; Mary Beth, 186; Sarah, 186; Terry, 48, 76, 122, 124, 125, 126, 127, 186, 246; Wanda, 230; Wanda Lee, 186; Wiley, 186
Fugitt Farms, 124
Fuhr, Abby Nicole, 187; Albert, 187; Alex Leo, 187; Alice, 187, 259; Anna, 187; Bill, 71, 187, 188; Bob, 23, 44, 187; Boyd, 186, 187, 188; Caroline, 187; Charles, 22, 37, 71, 187, 188; Charles E., 187; Charles Elbert, 188; Charles Thomas, 187; Cheryl Morin, 188; Clara, 187, 188; Ed, 37; Edd, 187; Eric Roger, 171, 187, 188; Geneva Brown, 163; Geneva Mae Brown, 187, 188; Geruisha, 187; Gloria, 75; Holly Roberta, 171, 187, 188; Jane Kerr, 188; Jerry, 187; Jerry C., 253; Jerry Charles, 188; Joe, 71, 187, 188; John E., 259; John Ernest, 187, 188; Judy, 187; Judy Mae, 188; Karen, 185, 187, 253; Karen Melinda, 188; Kyle, 187, 188; Leo, 187, 188; Louisa, 188; Louisa Phillippi, 187; Louise Phillips, 259; Mae Belle, 4, 23, 24, 27, 37, 118, 187, 188; Mae Belle Sparkman, 38, 78, 187, 188; Marcus, 187; Margaret Jane, 188; Margaret Jane Kerr, 187; Mary, 187; Michelle Diane Enlow, 187; Minnie, 187; Nina Roberta Warden, 171, 188; Nina Warden, 187; Ota Brashears, 188, 243; Ota E. Brashears, 187; Ota Ermine Brashears, 186; Ota Fuhr, 188; Otta Ermine Brashears, 187; Otto, 187, 188; Otto C., 22, 187; Ray, 187, 188; Robert, 187, 188, 243; Robert W., 186, 187, 188; Robert William, 187; Roger Leo, 171, 187, 188; Ted, 187, 188; Vesta, 187, 188, 243
Fulbright, 232
Fulks, Milley Annella, 267
Fuller, Garland, 260; Genevieve, 260; Iris Jean, 260; Jerry Max, 260; Nathan Hale, 260; Noel Duane, 260; Stella Hollingsworth, 260
Fullerton, Barbara, 75
Fuzzell, Bonnie, 155; Jack, 155

G

Gaddis, Jason, 140
Gaddy, Bletcher Holden, 189; Eathel, 159; Eathel Agnes, 189; Elisha Holden, 189; Ida May Runion, 189; Jerry, 189; Joe, 32; Joyce, 75; Mary, 189; Nola Careful, 189; Norma, 75, 189, 203; Ottie Bervin, 188, 189; Paul, 189; Sandra, 189; Sarah Marvilla Luna, 189; Willas May Norman, 188; Willie Marie Looney, 189; Willis Mae Norman, 77
Gaisford, Joel, 128
Galbraith, J.A., 74
Gale, Louella, 159
Gallagher, Arthur J., 180; Pat, 84
Gamble, 162, 166; R.A., 145; Richard, 134; Richard A., 33, 55; Sarah Britain, 162; W.L., 145; William R., 33
Gammel, Mike, 52
Gammon, Helen, 64; W. Ronald, 100
Gandy, Dorothy Mae Blanton, 158, 159; Raymond, 159; Sidney, 159
Gann, Lucille, 181
Gannaway, Gina Kay Espy, 269; Jason, 269; Justin Michael, 269; Lea Marie, 269
Garbee, 76; Connie, 75; Lucille, 116; Thirza, 171; Thirza May, 179
Garber, Barbara, 240; Barbara Zook, 240; John, 240
Gardner, Ailene, 151, 152, 189; Alex, 158; Alma, 152, 189; Alta Gertrude Pope, 189, 217; Amanda, 83; Archie, 189; Bonnie, 152; Bonnie Bell, 162, 189, 262; Brenda Kay, 189; Carrie, 206; Elizabeth Laney, 189; Elizabeth Virginia Laney, 262; Eric, 158; Evalee, 189; Evilana (Evalee), 152; Ferrell, 152, 189; Flossie Mary Pope, 217; G. Lavon, 151; George, 152, 189, 262; Gladys, 152, 189; Herbert, 152, 189; Herschel, 189; Hershal, 151; Hershel, 152; I.W. Jack, 15; Ishmael William, 189; Jim, 189; LaVada Ann, 189; Lavon, 152, 189; Lendsie, 189; Leo, 68, 189; Lettie Batson, 152; Lucille Annis Glidewell, 189; Marcella, 189; Marion, 22, 151, 152, 182, 189; Marion Richard, 189; Mark Allen, 189; Michelle, 167; Noel, 151, 152; Noel Juanita, 189; Oda Fay Tinsley, 189; Ola, 151, 152, 189; Ollie, 189; Ollie Robertson Phillips, 189; Otto, 151, 152, 189; Patience, 157; Rance William, 189; Richard Leo, 189; Robert, Jr., 158; Rosa, 151; Rosa Elmeda Etheridge, 189; Rosa Etheridge, 152; Rosie Etheridge, 182; Rutha Vileta Batson, 189; Susan Blades, 158; Vaunda Noreene Long, 189; William Marion, 189, 262; Zane Leroy, 189
Garner, 252; Charlie, 50; Chuck, 50; Janice, 148; Marcella, 50, 51, 240, 262
Garoutte, 9, 58, 117, 141, 157, 158, 194, 199, 221, 228, 238, 249; Allie, 90; Amanda Hazleton, 190; Amy Bethia, 262; Anna, 189, 190; Anthony, 20, 141, 191; Ava, 48, 185; Ava McDaniel, 179, 185, 190, 191; Carlos, 67; Cecil, 190; Cecil John, 190; Cecil Louise, 186; Charity Richards, 239; Charles Elmer, 190, 191; Charlie, 166, 185; Clejo Bray, 189; Columbus, 190; Darlene, 75; Delores Wright, 190; Dennie, 76; Dollie, 163, 179, 185, 191, 241; Elizabeth Smith, 190; Elva Emery, 190; Elve, 182; Eric, 190; Eric B., 190; Ethel May, 190; Frances, 157, 161, 242; Francis, 190; Gladys, 191; Glen, 190; Gose, 152; Harry, 189, 190; Harve, 11, 12; Henry, 239; Herschel, 190; Hershel, 190; Hettie, 190, 192; Hildred, 45; Homer, 190; James, 20; James E., 141; James E.D., 239; James Smith, 148, 190, 233; Jane Reynolds, 190; Jay D., 190; Jessie, 12; Jim, 191; Jimmy, 190; John, 189, 190; Joseph Mathias, 190; June Thigpein, 190; Katherine, 116; Katherine Hicks, 190; Laurence, 190; Leola Williams, 189; Leonard, 190; Leroy, 75; Lewis, 190; Lloyd, 23, 45, 191, 241; Louis, 190; Mark, 90, 189, 190; Marlynn Miller, 190; Mary, 157; Mary Babbington, 233; Mary Babington, 190; Mary Eliza, 194; Mary Ellen Etheridge, 190; Mary Eloise, 190; Mary Etheridge, 182; Mary Jane Richards, 239; Matt, 182; Mehetable Tannahill, 190; Melissa, 148; Melissa Jane, 29; Melvin, 182; Melvin Anderson, 190; Michael, 148, 189, 190; Michael Antoine, 233; Mildred McCoy, 190; Mrs. Charles, 64; Mrs. Sheral, 76; Nancy, 233; Nancy Caroline, 190; Nerva, 177, 189; Olive, 182; Olive Louelia, 190; Opal Jeanne, 190; Pauline Maness, 190; Pearly, 177, 189; Pearl Watson, 190; Rosa Blades, 189, 190; Sallie Robertson, 190; Samuel, 20, 190; Sarah Cavener, 190; Shearl, 54; Sheral, 31, 117, 122, 182; Sheral Joseph, 190; Sheral Kay, 190; Shirlene, 75; Sophia Smith, 190, 233; Thomas Waldo, 190; Warren, 189, 190; Warren W., 189; Willard Benton, 239; William, 20; William B., 238; William Babington, 148, 190; William D., 189
Garretson, Martha, 240
Garrett, Bonnie, 216; Bonnie Blades, 157; Donna, 157; Ed, 15; Richard, 157; Robert, 157; Robert, Jr., 157; Robin, 157; Ronald, 157
Garrison, Barbara, 67; Betty, 67; Bill, 174; Carol, 67; Gilbert, 174; Jerry, 67; Josephine, 67; Maggie Crow, 174; Mary, 174; Nancy, 67; Norma, 67; Robert, 67; Sarah, 162; Susan, 69
Garton, Alice, 221; Angie, 191; Awilda Owen, 191; Brad, 84, 191; Carl, 77; Dixie, 84; Dixie Joan, 191; Donna Rambo, 191; Elsie, 191; Glen, 191; Grace Pauline Inman, 191; Greg, 83, 191; J.B., 191; Jacob W., 221; Jacob Warren, Jr., 191; Jake, 191; Jamie, 191; Janice Earls, 191; John, 191; Johnnie, 76; Johnny, 49, 75, 82; Kathy, 191; Kayla, 48, 191; Kid, 35; Laurie, 191; Lorena, 191; Lura, 191; Marty, 191; Melissa, 191; Michelle, 191; Mike, 191; P.E. Rainey, 236; Penelope Elizabeth Rainey, 221; Ralph Sterling, 191; Richard Alan, 131; Rick, 191; Roberta, 191; Shirley Ann Walker, 191; Stacy, 191; Sterling Wayne, 191; Steve, 191; Thelma, 191; Tim, 191
Gates, Benjamin, 162; Kay, 162; Madeline, 162; Rick, 162
Gault, Bonnie, 72
Gaylor, Walter, 35
Gebhards, Anna Carolina Rother, 150; Bernhard Frederick, 150; Edna Grace, 150; Edwin, 150, 151; Etta, 150; Frederick, 150; Harry, 150; Tina, 150; Wilma, 150
Gee, Don, 131
Geilert, Elsa, 191, 192; Emil, 192; Helen, 192; Herbert, 192; Juanita, 192; Nellie, 192; Paul, 191, 192
Gentry, Charles E., 105; Maude, 74; Tony, 90
George, Amy, 208
Geren, Dennis, 90; Kinsey C., 209; Laura, 262; Richard, 48; Sarah A. Sullivan, 209
Gerst, Lisa, 269
Ghan, Charles, 73, 121; Charles Curtis, 192; Clarence, 149, 190; Clarence Talmadge, 192; Edith, 192; Hettie, 149; Hettie Garoutte, 190; Hettie Garroutte, 192; Jennie Guthrie, 192; Kathryn Mae, 190, 192, 256; Mae Kathryn, 77; Thomas Andrew, 192; Trish, 100; William Leslie, 192
Giacin, Cynthia Marie Gold, 192; Madison Paige, 192; Mark, 192
Gibson, Bertha DeWett, 70; Gene, 56; Louisa, 157; Mary E., 30; Rachel, 255; S.F., 30, 143
Giddens, Ben, 154; Ernie, 154; Louann Bennett, 154; Rhiannon, 154
Gideon, 237
Gilbert, Bill, 53; Raymond, 210; Sara Jo Johnson, 210
Gilbreth, Drucilla Ann, 30
Gildewell, Maude Mae, 168
Giles, Clara, 151; Clara Viles, 24; Vernie, 24, 151
Gill, Ed, 36
Gilland, Golda, 163
Gillham, Isabella, 229; Isaiah, 229; Jeannette Elizabeth, 172; Kara O'Bryant, 229
Gillian, Grace, 208
Gilliland, 249; Elnora, 71; Evelyn, 71; Lizzie, 238; Norma, 71; Wanda, 71
Gilmore, Billy, 72; Dorothy Lee, 259; Gene, 72
Gimlin, Amanda, 83
Gimmie, Hettie Ghan, 190
Ginn, Harold, 175; Viola Maxine Davis Cook, 175
Gipson, Jo Ann, 85
Girth, Donna, 259; Gina, 88; Jim, 138, 177; Mrs. Jim, 138; Scott, 88, 159; Vicky, 159
Gitson, Vicky Mitchell, 213
Gleghorn, Annabelle Gray, 159, 176, 194; Lisa Kay, 194; Randal, 232; Randall, 159; Randall Wiley, 194; Terry Lynn, 176, 194
Glenn, Ilene, 100; Lori, 230; Sarah, 201; Wayne, 15, 17, 18
Glessner, Krystal, 83, 85
Glidewell, 75; Albert, 192; Ann Lavina Perkins, 189; Archie, 192; Charles Thomas, 192; Davis Peter, 189; Emma, 192; Eula, 192; Ida Pratt, 192; Jack, 12, 13; James, 75; Joe, 15; LaVada Emaline Stiffler, 189; Lavada Stiffler Johnson, 192; Lucille, 192; Lucille Annis, 189; Myrtle Trogdon, 192; Perl, 70; Peter Wilson, 192; Rebecca Jennings, 189, 192; Sarah Perkins, 192; Tom, 15; Vernie, 192; William, 12; William B., 189; William David, 192; William Davis, 189; Wilson Peter, 189, 192
Gloyd, Ruthie, 88
Goddard, Don, 88
Godwin, 30, 162; Anna, 258, 264

Goff, Rose Helen Brown, 163
Goforth, Duane, 90; Shirley Franks, 185
Goheen, Ryan, 88
Gold, Anna Louise, 199; Charles, 192; Charley Efton, 192; Cynthia Marie, 192; Deborah L. Nakano, 178; Gregory Lee, 192; Jacqueline D. Fletcher, 178; Kathryn Sitzes, 192; Louise, 192; Morgan, 178; Nellie, 192; Nellie Heldstab, 192; Sarah Gray, 192; Shane, 88; Shane E., 178; Sydni, 178
Good, George Robert, 68
Goodin, 186; James H., 10; Urith, 242
Goodman, Mary Eliza, 169; Sampson, 169; Sarah Lyngar, 169
Goodnight, Jeff, 117
Goodwin, Ed, 159; James H., 253; Kathy, 47; Louisa, 169; Marion, 169; Martha, 169; Paul, 35, 169; Penny Blood, 159
Gordon, Karen, 76; Olivia, 222; Suzy, 99
Gott, Geri, 207, 256; Janice, 240; Jojohn, 207; Mrs. Jojohn, 76; Patricia Ruckman, 165; Terry, 207
Gower, John, 20
Grainge, Carolyn, 200; Emil, 200; Lois Wasson, 200
Grantham, Joe, 235; Katherine Brewer, 235; Kathy, 235; Larry, 235
Graves, 66; Allie Ann Lile, 248; Edgar, 66; Jerry, 131; Mrs. Jerry, 131; Roy, 32
Gray, 177; Ada, 193; Annabelle, 72, 176, 194; Annie, 30; Archie, 193; Arena Jane Russell, 193; Ava O. Skelton, 192; Avena, 193; Bill, 193, 194; Carolyn Jo, 176, 194; Dale, 69; Dallas, 193, 243; Dallas Barney, 176, 193, 228; Debra J., 170; Debra Jean, 192, 193; DeWayne B., 176, 194; Drucilla, 69; Earl V., 193; Elizabeth, 226; Elizabeth Grace Nelson, 176, 193, 228; Emma, 193; Emma E., 194; Emmett, 193, 194; Ernie, 192; George Washington, 193; Heather Nichole Hoskins, 194; Henry, 170; Henry Van, 192, 193; Hollie Davis, 194; Hollie Jane Davis, 176, 193; J.B., 72, 127, 176, 193, 194; Jake Bower, 194; James, 69; James Karr, 69; Jane Ruth, 176, 193, 228, 250; Jason Bryan, 194; Jerrod, 100; Jim, 53; Joe Emmett, 176, 193, 228, 250; John, 193, 194; John T., 193; Josiah, 193; Josiah Jefferson, 193; Juanita Lucille, 176, 194; Laura Vesta Davis, 176, 193; Lois June Swaney, 194; Maggie McNabb, 194; Margaretta, 207; Margaret L. McNabb, 193; Norma, 170; Norma Brown, 163; Norma Francis Brown, 192, 193; Robert, 30; Roy C., 192; Samuel, 193; Sarah, 166, 192; Sarah Ada, 194; Sarah Jane Edgar, 193; Theodore, 193; Travis, 194; Van, 69; Vandeana, 192, 193; Velma, 69, 87; Vesta Davis, 194; Vester, 69, 87; William Jefferson, 176, 193
Great Southern, 101
Green, 249; Agnes Jarmin, 194; Alice Viola, 194, 262; Alonzo, 194, 195; Alonzo, Jr., 194; Angie, 236; Berry Wesley, 194; Billy Joe, 194; Dora Lee, 194; Dorothy Marie, 194; Edgar, 123, 253; Edna Maxine, 194; Elijah, 194; Elizabeth, 194; Elizabeth Mahulda Mitchell, 194; Elma Jane Sparkman, 194; Elma Sparkman, 253; Ernest, 194; Everett Wan, 194; George, 269; Georgia Elizabeth, 269, 270; Halland Ernest, 194; Harold Eugene, 194; Helen Mae, 194; Helen Sager, 194; Ida Alice Wood, 194, 195; Imogene Whitehead, 194; Iris Thurman, 194; James Columbus, 194; Jane McMurtrey, 222; Jewel Blades, 194; John, 194; John Wesley, 194; John Willard, 194; Kay Ann, 194; Kenneth, 31; Kenneth Lee, 194; Lawrence Edgar, 194; Lawrence Loren, 194; Linda, 12; Lonnie, 35; Lucille Rivlet, 194; Martha Etta, 194; Marvin Lee, 194; Mary Elizabeth, 194; Mary Eliza Garoutte, 194; Mary Louise, 194; Max Douglas, 194; Mike, 90, 138; Myrtle Eva, 194; Nancy, 87, 194, 259; Nell, 116, 254; Norma, 253; Norma Jean, 66, 194; Ralph Arthur, 194; Rick, 56; Roberta, 238, 253; Roberta Elma, 194; Rosena, 66, 253; Rosena Lou, 194; Sarah Dean, 194; Sarah Twigger, 269; Susan Adella, 194; Thomas Jefferson, 194; Turk, 86; Victor Wayne, 194; Wanda Sue, 194; Willa LaFon, 194; Willie Madine, 194; Wuan, 81
Greene, Arrimba, 30; Nathaniel, 27; Patty, 47; Thomas, 30
Gregg, Betty Jean, 128; Floy, 128; George Wallace, 128
Gregory, Ollie, 74
Greismer, Pauline Louise, 186
Griesel, Cathy, 148
Griesmer, Louis, 27
Griffin, Aaron, 195; Adam, 195; Amy, 159, 195; Bobbie, 195; Eric, 195; Gary, 117, 159, 195; Sarah, 195; Terry, 195; Terry Blood, 159
Griffith, Anita, 152
Griffiths, Christina Fugitt, 186
Grills, Matilda, 142
Grimes, James, 210; Merle, 210; Peggy, 210; Rickey, 210
Grimmer, Nancy Elizabeth, 193
Grimmett, 69; Gladys Garoutte, 191; Hester, 69
Grisham, Dorothy, 72; Ebbie, 260
Grogg, Cynthia Kay, 267
Gromyko, Andre, 150
Groner, Wayne, 47
Grove, A.S., 32, 33; Abraham S., 33
Groves, Don, 56; Donald Louis, 195; Louis G., 195; Nellie Teaverbaugh, 195; Rebecca, 239; Robert E., 195; Roger Lee, 195; Ruby K. Klug, 195; Sharon Sue Hodge, 195; Sue, 134
Gruball, 45
Grubbs, Stacy, 237
Guenther, Arno, 196; Carole, 195; Carole Lina, 196; Debbie, 196; Diana, 196; Edris Laura Wilson, 195; Edward, 191; Emilie Auguste Fritsch, 191; Eric K.A., 196; Kenneth Arno, 195; Laura, 196; Loretta Rogers, 196; Marilyn, 196; Paul Arno, 195, 196; Paul Lee, 196
Gullett, J. June, 178
Gulley, Grace Ernestine, 227
Gunderson, Gary, 72; Kent, 72
Günther, Edris Laura Wilson, 195; Elsa, 195; Lina Becker Rost, 195; Otto, 195
Guthrie, Jennie, 192
Guy, Sandy, 226
Guyette, Iri, 64; Lycurgus, 64
Guyton, Elizabeth, 254

### H

H&R Block, 104
Hacker, Jim, 263; Lois Wallace Henry, 263
Hackett, Mary, 28
Hacking, Alice, 67; Olive, 67
Haddock, Angie, 88
Haden, Dorothy, 163; Myra, 194
Hadlin, Theresa Dorothy, 242
Hadlock, Bonnie, 75; Rosa May, 75
Haenig, James, 90; Jim, 131
Hafley, Cathy Sue, 269
Hagale, 49; Anthony, 38; John, 38
Hagerman, Bo, 196, 197; Heather, 196, 197; Jerry, 185, 196; Sondra Franks, 185, 196
Hagerty, John, 71
Hagewood, 9, 221; Anna Lucille, 197, 221; Ann Michelle, 197; Ben, Jr., 197; Benjamin, 197, 221; Berl, 67; Callie Marie, 197, 221; Carlos, 67; Carolyn June Cave, 197; Cordelia, 197; Delia, 242; Delta May, 197, 221; Donna Sue, 76; Dorothy, 75; Dorothy Mae, 197; Earl, 177; Edith Merle, 197, 221; Emma J., 197; Emmett Wesley, 197, 221; Ermal, 261; Ermal Lucille, 197; Gillian, 197; Gladys Fisher, 221; Gladys Mae Fisher, 184, 197; Hazel Pauline, 197, 221; Helen Irene, 197; James W., 197; Jimmie Gene, 197; Johnie Joseph, 197; John C., 197, 221; John Calvin, 197; John T., 197, 221; Joy Land, 70; Juanita Faye Brashers, 197; Leon, 135; Linda Kay, 197; Lucy, 197; Mae, 179; Maggie Ada McDaniel, 197, 221; Maggie McDaniel, 179, 221; Margaret, 197, 221; Marion, 197; Marion L., 197; Martha C., 221; Martha Cavener, 221; Martha F. Cavener, 197; Marvellus M., 197; Mary, 261; Mary A., 197; Mary Polly Robertson, 197, 241; Matilda F., 197; Michael Gene, 197; Mrs. John, 64; Nancy E., 197; Nancy Jane Reynolds, 197; Naomi Dean, 177; Oca, 184, 197, 221; Ocie, 179; Patsy Stephens, 197; Raymond, 197, 221; Ronald Lee, 197; Roy, 197; Roy Lee, 197; Ruby Lee Batson, 197; Sarah L., 197; Sarah R., 197; Sharon, 85; Sharon Kay, 197; Susie, 135; Thomas, 17, 197; William, 145, 197; William M., 197
Hagle, 191, 267
Hagler, Debbie, 47
Haguewood, 254
Hagwood, J.C., 66
Haile, Arthur Burton, 197, 198; Benson Columbus, 198; Columbus, 197; Della Newton, 197; Eric Kelly, 198; Hazel Wade, 197, 198; Jackson Overstreet, 197; Juanita Simpson, 198; Kelly, 85; Kelly Wade, 198; Kirby Dale, 198; Meade, II, 197
Hailey, Dickie, 48; Jonathan, 88
Hainer, Elizabeth, 28
Hainey, 237
Haladay, Barbara, 210
Hale, Betty, 153; Martha Jane, 228; Zella June, 209
Hall, Mabel, 259; Treva, 133
Hamilton, Aaron, 84; Cheri Dale, 198; Clayton, 198; Gretchen Marcia, 213; Juanita Geilert, 192; Katie, 198; Kendall, 198; Tim, 117, 198
Hammer, Dorothy Lanning, 213
Hammons, David, 200; Elsie Melton Pendergrass, 200; Roy, 200; Shirley B., 156
Hampton, Blanche, 255; Ray, 189
Hancock, Cathy, 53; Gene, 127
Haney/Haynie, Sarah Jane, 184
Hannan, Mary, 216
Hansen, Pete, 55
Hanson, Marjorie, 70; Minnie M., 41
Haptner, Jack, 241
Haralson, Darren, 171; Shannon, 171; Tricia, 171
Hardison, Glen, 67
Hargas, Clora, 150
Hargis, Clora, 165; Greg, 84; Laura Thompson, 165; Norma Blanche, 180; Rasberry, 165; Steve, 83
Hargrove, Carol, 85; Jeff, 84
Harlan, John, 88; Julie, 88
Harp, Eugene, 82
Harper, Annalee Franklin, 198; Betty, 198; Bill, 130, 198; Charles, 76, 87; Charles E., 198; Charles Earl, 198; Charles W., 198; Ella Mae, 198; Emma, 198; Frances, 198; Frances Riehn, 199; Grace, 198; Grace Elena, 202; Grace Knoebel, 199; James William, 199; John, 198; Judith Ann, 198, 199; Lula, 198; Lyndal, 199; Lyndal Vernell, 199; Mary, 198; Mattie, 198; Maude, 198; Minnie, 198; Minnie Erskin, 202; Nancy Wilson, 198; Patricia Nicholson, 198; Patty, 87; Patty Jean, 198; William Anthony, 199; William Charles, 198, 199; William Jule, 199; William L., 199; William Louis, 199; William Reilly, 198; William Riley, 202
Harralson, Amanda, 178; James, 178; Mary Elizabeth, 178; Myrtle Coggin, 170; Sterling, 178
Harrington, Ab Land, 212; Alfred, 90; Ellen, 90; Eva Ann, 175; Janet, 87; John, 214, 233; Kay, 85; Leila, 226; Martha Louella Link, 175; Mildred Ruhamah, 246; Nikki, 83; Roland, 233; Tilitha Cuma, 260; William, 212; William Sigel, 175
Harris, 212; Andrea K., 210, 263; Angie, 163; Angie L., 163; Anna Louise Gold, 199; Bill, 35; Bulger, 35; Bus, 35; Cheryl, 85, 192, 199; Dolly, 24; Donald, 199; Donnie, 192; Eula, 35; Floyd, 44, 117, 122, 192, 214; Floyd L., 199; Gladys, 35; Harold, 82, 192, 199; James, 77; Jenks, 35; Jim, 246; Joe, 24, 35; John W., 163; Linda, 246; Louise Gold, 192; Maggie, 35; Mattie Ethel, 243; Ora Payne, 163; Paula, 116; Peggy Louise Sellers, 246; Priscilla Jane, 191, 255; Ramona, 183; Robert, 246; Robert L., 246
Harrison, John, 202; M.F., 31; Mary Elizabeth, 202; Mrs. W.H., 139; Samual T., 32; Sarah Chaney, 202; T.J., 28; W.H., 28, 139; William Henry, 240
Harryman, Margaret, 161
Harshbarger, Lydia, 9
Hart, Artie, 179; Byron, 35; Cora, 64; Earl, 35, 250; Ernest, 64; Etter, 64; Hannah, 35; Hannah Branson, 169; John, 64, 208; Laurel, 35, 169; O.E. "Orie", 15; Sarah Elizabeth, 176; Will, 64; Zoa, 64
Harter, Bobby, 76
Hartley, Drucilla Ann Carson, 248
Hartline, Joyce, 245
Hartman, Don, 24; Mary, 24; Mary Jane, 131
Hartmayer, Gary, 239; Rebecca Reynolds, 239
Hartsell, Sam, 32
Hartz, J. Leslie, 56
Hartzog, Charles, 230; Jeanette O'Neal, 230; Jennifer, 230
Harvey, Jennifer, 204; Keith, 204
Harvill, Audie, 71; Audie Leonard, 66; Fred, 66, 71; Lena Mae, 71; Mildred, 250; Ruth, 71
Harwood, Alfred P., 143; Margaret, 143
Haseltine, 10, 161; Royal, 162; Thomas, 9
Hasket, E.E., 33; R.L., 134
Haskett, E.E., 33
Haslett, Bert, 12
Hastings, Jason, 88
Hathaway, Herrick, 74; Robert, 66
Haun, Laura, 170
Havener, Blanche Hughes, 205
Hawk, Ronda, 235
Hawkins, Emma, 213; Tricia, 88
Haworth, Thelma, 72
Hay, John, 33
Hayes, 9; Callie, 215; Callie Katherine, 259; Connor, 199; Connor Patrick, 173; Elza, 259; Emily, 199; Emily Nichole, 173; Eva McClure, 70; Frank, 64; Gary, 75; George, 158, 162; George Washington, 259; Henry, 31, 32, 33; Ira, 259; Jayme Beth Davis, 172, 173; Jeremiah, 177; Jimmie Ann, 75; Katie, 199; Kelly, 199; Lauren, 199; Lauren Elizabeth, 173; Lois, 199; Malissa Ann Britain, 259; Malissa Britain, 162; Mary Catherine, 177; Melissa Britain, 158, 162; Nancy Lowe, 177; Nora, 259; Patrick, 173, 199; R., 33; Suzanne, 199; Thomas, 199
Hayley, Linda Grace, 187
Haymes, Elizabeth, 257, 258
Haynie, Iva, 38, 238; Lora Belle, 238
Hays, 165; Agnes McCord, 200; Bessie Applegate, 200; Bonnie Ziegler, 200; Buddy, 75; E.M., 33; Ed, 200; Edward Lester, 200; Enoch M., 55; Enoch Monroe, 200; Ervin, 200; Ervin David, 200; George Purdy, 200; Hulda Dee Keller, 200; James, 226; James A., 66; James Arthur, 199, 200; James Purd, 200; James Tillman, 200; Jas. A., 66; Joann, 75; John Thomas, 200; Joseph, 66; Lillie King, 200; Lilly May King, 200; Lou Phelps, 200; Malinda Caroline Mooneyham, 199, 200; Malinda Mooneyham, 226; Martha Paulsell, 200; Pete, 64; Purd, 200; Rose, 200; Rose May, 200; Roxie Mae Pope, 200; Rutherford Berchard, 200; Rutherford Berchard, Jr., 200; Sue Fletcher, 200; Susan, 153; Violet, 86, 200; Violet Elizabeth, 200; William Henry, 200
Hayter, Lois Alma, 260
Hayward, Vickie, 50, 51
Hayworth, Joyce, 163
Hazelton, Adophus Hugh, 242; Alpheus, 66; Bert, 64; Lemie, 64; Lucy, 64; Mahetable Arms, 242; Marcellus, 64; Milbury Rose, 242; Otis, 64; Royal, 242
Hazen, Anna, 230; Bill, 230; Edith Payne, 230; Lori, 230; Matthew, 230; Michael, 230; Wanda Fugitt, 230; Wanda Lea, 14; William, 230
Hazleton, Amanda, 190
Head, Bill, 245; Jack, 75; Jill, 75
Headlee, Mary, 155; Sam, 155
Headley, Esther Mae, 161
Heagerty, Mildred, 77
Hearn, Nancy, 197, 261, 262
Hearnes, Warren E., 183
Heaven's Scent Flowers and Gifts, 108
Heavin, Bradley J., 194; Carolyn Jo Gray, 176, 194; Donald Gene, 194; Garrett Blayne, 194; Geni Jo, 194; Janelle Renee Dickson, 194; Kent Allen, 194; Megan Erin, 194
Hedger, Julie, 184
Hedgpeth, Pam, 74, 79, 182
Hedrick, Marie, 230
Heineman, Helene, 196; Kurt, 196
Heinemann, Georgia Mae Rader, 236; Richard, 236
Heinzler, Julie Bassore, 176
Heldstab, Anna Mabel Martin, 192; George Rayford, 192; Nellie, 192
Helling, Johanna Christina, 182
Helms, Mike, 131
Helton, 236; Eula, 87; Opha McSpadden, 223
Hemphill, Albert, 230; Brenda, 47; Etta O'Neal, 230; Harley, 47, 55, 219; Mark, 48
Henderson, 66; Annette, 200; Carolyn Grainge, 200; Cathy, 200; Donald R., 200; Fern Pendergrass, 200; Jim, 200; Kayla, 200; Richard, 200; Ryan, 200
Hendrick, Tom, 24

Hendricks, Andrea, 166; Beverly Carman, 167; Bryce, 71, 77, 166; Eugene, 71; Glen, 24; Jaunita Lula Cantrell, 166, 167; Jay Lynn, 167; Marcel, 42, 43; Mary Lou, 71, 84; Myrtle, 156; Rachel, 218
Hendrickson, Lisa, 230
Hendrix, Clara Ennis Wade, 172; L.V., 229; Lillard, 42, 43; Lucy, 203; Marcel, 35, 41; Marcell, 202, 229; N.J., 205; Otha, 137; Sarah, 205
Henry, 124; Carroll, 263; Gary, 56; Irene Turpin, 260; Lois Wallace, 263; Onis, 260
Hensley, Toni, 85
Henson, Barbara, 67; Brandon, 201; Cecil, 220; Charles Wayne, 200, 201; Edith May McCullah Brashears, 220; Geraldine, 67; Helen Tiede, 201; Jack, 200, 201; Josephine Medlin, 200; Kevin, 201; Laura Janes, 200, 201; Lee, 200; Lloyd Joseph, 200, 201; Sharon Sue, 200, 201; Terry, 67
Herbert, Flora Nance, 227; Robert, 227
Herndon, Holman, 12; Janet, 156, 225; Laura, 12
Herren, Nancy, 146
Herring, Jerry, 75
Hessee, Dick, 77; Maro, 48
Heying, Clarence, 35; Geneva Watson, 35; L, 35
Hicklin, Mary Elizabeth, 203; Mary Hood, 202; Mary Stogsdill, 203; William, 203
Hickman, D.C., 77; Dewey, 74
Hickok, Bill, 199
Hicks, 254; Artie, 175; John, 48; Katherine, 190; Peggy Mooneyham, 179; Susie, 212; W.H., 143
High, Bradley, 197; Brian Oca, 197; Dorothy Mae Hagewood, 197; Douglas Glen, 197; Glen Logan, 197; Kayla Sue, 197; Leslie Shawn, 197; Margie Anne, 197; Robbie Don, 197
Highfill, Darla Suzanne, 178
Hild, Joanne Maxine Testerman, 160; Kenneth Edgar, 160; Reba, 156; Reba Maxine, 160
Hill, Albion B., 201; Alexander, 234; Betty, 201; Bryce, 201; Doug, 269; Douglas, 201; Douglas Bohman, 234; Douglas E., 98; Douglas Patterson, 234; Eddie, 75; Erma, 201; Gary, 53; George, 201; J.M., 32; Jennifer, 201; Lorine, 201; Margret Hanna Patterson, 201; Margret Patterson, 234; Mary Margaret, 86; Mary Margret, 201, 234; Maurice, 201; Patsy, 75; Rodney, 201; Rodney Douglas, 234; Scott, 201, 234; Scott Patterson, 234; Shellie, 201
Hiller, Angie, 188
Hillhouse, Glenda, 86
Hilliard, Mildred May, 217
Hills, W.S., 33
Hilton, Carl, 161; Ellis, 161; Grace Boyd, 161; Janet, 204; Jimmie, 148; Joseph, 161; Loretta Faye, 205; Loy, 194; Pauline, 161; Ray, 24; Rosena Lou Green, 194; Susie, 148
Hindman, Adam, 88
Hines, Elizabeth, 231; John, 242; Kenneth, 209; Michelle, 88; Milbury Rose Hazelton, 242; Rosa Jones, 209; W.M., 223; William, 242
Hinshaw, Elsie Lee, 149; Jackson Ramsey, 149; Mary A. Mills, 149
Hock, Catherine Reeves, 201; Edward Joe, 201; Jess, 201; Lida, 201; Mary Ellen, 86, 201; Mattie, 116; Mattie Davis, 201; Myrtle, 201; Pearl, 201; Sam, 12, 201; Will, 201; William Francis, 201
Hodge, Ann Brown, 202; Carrie Lynn, 202; Chester Aaron Stewart, 202; Donald, 75, 87; Donald Ray, 195, 202; Ernest, 11; Etta Neill, 11; George Franklin, 202; Grace Harper, 198; Grace Elena Harper, 202; Harriett Taylor, 202; Jesse Ethel, 202; John Aubrey, 202; Kristin Marie, 202; Mary Elizabeth, 202; Mary Elizabeth Harrison, 202; Mary Elizabeth Severn, 202; Mary Etta Elizabeth Neill, 202; Maude, 198; Rachel, 208; Rachel Emilee, 202; Reason Ernest, 202; Rex, 87; Rex E., 195; Rex Eugene, 202; Robert Eugene, 202; Ruth, 134; Ruth M. Jones, 195; Ruth Mildred Jones, 202; Sara, 229; Sharon Sue, 195, 202; Susan Holster, 202; Wilbur, 202; William Orin, 195, 198, 202; William Orin, Jr., 202; William Stewart, 202
Hodges, Dana, 50; Della Fugitt, 186; Mary Jane, 209; Rita, 50
Hoerning, Louise Britain, 234; Robert, 234
Hoffman, Buck, 35; Little Buck, 35; Mrs. Waldon, 131; Pam, 212; Waldon, 131; Warren, 66
Hogenmiller, Alfred (Dutch), 24; Mildred, 24
Holbert, J.T., 141
Holbrook, Kirby, 133
Holiway, Myrtle Esther, 260
Holland, Danielle, 85
Hollaway, Martha, 29
Hollingsworth, Ada, 168; Stella, 260
Hollis, Debbie, 47; Gertrude Sarah, 208; Sharon K., 259
Holloway, Martha, 149
Hollyfield, Johnny, 75, 87
Holman, Sam, 24
Holmes, Breta, 169; Catherine M., 29; Cliff Cody, 239; Dawnnell Lea Hughes, 239; Kevin, 83
Holster, Susan, 202
Holt, Barbara, 71; Beverly, 71; Jake, 51; Josephine, 216; Kamrynn, 51; Kamrynn Riley, 214; Kyra, 51; Kyra Paige, 214; Linda, 210; Rodney Jake, 214; Shelly Kay Lehman, 51, 214; Wilda Jean, 212
Hood, 261; Anne, 75, 84, 87; Anne T., 154; Beverly, 203; Bill, 52; Brandee, 203, 204; Christina, 203, 204; Clyde, 202, 204; Clyde Henderson, 203; Cynthia, 157; Cynthia Ann Blades, 249; Duncan, 202, 203; Edward, 203; Elden, 203, 204, 260; Ellen E., 203; Eva M., 203; Fern Nadine Tuter, 260; Fern Tuter, 203, 204; Grace T. Cheathan, 154; Hildred Hadely Ted, 203, 204; Howard, Jr., 203, 204; Howard Wayne, 203, 204; Jack, 134; James, 20, 258; James D.A., Jr., 55; James Duncan, 202, 203, 204; Jami, 260; Jami Dawn, 204; Jennifer Rebecca, 204; Jim, 52, 134, 203; Jimmy, 203, 204; Jimmy Elden, 203, 204; John, 203; Johnny Elden, 204; Judith Mink, 204; Julie Robin, 204; Knox, 202; Knox H., 203; Lucille Turner, 154; Mae, 204; Mae Lenora Hughes, 203; Margaret, 202, 203; Mary, 203, 204; Mary E. Clack, 202, 203; Micagah E.A., 203; Mrs. Elden, 76; Nancy, 157; Nancy Ellen Blades, 202; Nora E., 203; Norma Gaddy, 203; Roscoe, 154; Ross, 52; Sarah A., 203; Sarah H., 141; Sharon Sargent, 203; Stella Thurman, 258; Victor, 203; W.E., 134; Wanda Mae, 203; William E., 154, 203
Hoodenpyle, Whitney Jones, 208
Hood United Methodist Church, 134
Hook, Cindy, 201; Dwayne, 201; Dwayne, II, 201; Karla, 201; Kelly, 201; Kim, 201; Sharon Sue Henson, 200, 201
Hooten, Frank, 49
Hopewell Baptist Church, 141
Hope Lutheran Church, 132
Hopkins, Karen, 160
Hopper, Brandie, 204; Brian, 204, 212; Donna, 212; Donna Lacey, 204; Jake, 204; Janet Hilton, 204; Julie, 204; Kelly, 204; Larry, 87; Lynne, 233; Rachel, 204; Roberta, 204; Wally, 204, 212
Horn, Elizabeth, 51; Penny, 50
Hornbuckle, Eliza, 164
Horne, Gerald D., 90
Horton, Bob, 15; Charlie, 15; Kelly, 88
Hosey, J.N., 143; Sybil Short, 70; T.N., 143
Hoskins, Heather Nichole, 194
Hosman, Alfred, 242; Elizabeth, 242; Martha H. Cox, 242; Nancy Elizabeth, 171
Hough, Cynthia Lynn, 164
House, 9; Arthur H., 178; Henry, 33; James, 74; John, 32, 33, 119; John H., 33; Josephine, 212; Mattie, 73; Susie DeBoard, 178
Houser, Charley, 41; Clara, 210; George Washington, 210; James Madison, 210; John Sherman, 210; Martha Elizabeth Kerr, 210; Sarah, 210
Housley, Esther Simmons, 211; Lenny, 84
Houston, Jim, 167; Millie, 167
Houtz, Finley, 74; Gail, 73, 74, 234; John W., 33; Theresa, 148
Hovey, Norma Gaddy, 189; Norma Della Gaddy, 189
Howard, 9, 96; A.M., 11; Agnes C., 209; Albert, 222, 271; Albert Marion, 221; Alice, 184; Anna, 270; Anna O'Neal, 38; Annie, 116, 148; Arch, 184; Arthur, 38; Birdie, 222; Birdie Pauline, 221; Clarence, 12; David, 184; Ed, 87, 205; Elizabeth, 141; Jasper, 184; John Ranson, 184; Katie, 184; Lee, 157; Lonnie, 184; Louis E., 204; M.L., 31; Mae, 71, 262; Margaret, 87; Margaret Alice, 156, 157; Martin, 38; Martin L., 55; Mary, 205; Mary Horton Montgomery, 18; Mary Lee, 66, 157; Merle, 271; Mildred, 70, 75, 262; Mildred Clark, 204; Minerva Jane, 184; Mollie Mae, 184; Nerva, 184; Oled, 184; Ollie Delena, 184; Paul, 38; Rachel Luzzi Noe, 184; Sarah Permelia Shelton, 221, 222, 271; Sue, 85; Thelma Faye, 157; Velma, 116; Velma Denny, 179; Velma Irene Denny, 157; Velma Mae, 157; William Monroe, 184; Woodson, 21
Howell, 9; Blanche, 15; Blanche Pierce, 15; C.A., 33; Clarence, 14, 15; Clarence August, 128; Curtis, 15; Edith, 15; Edward, 28; Elmer, 52; Florence, 15; Florence Lucille, 128; George, 15; James, 220; Jim, 35; Lou, 15; Marcella, 15; Minnie, 15; Minnie Annabell, 128; Orville, 15; Paul, 15; Paula, 57, 116, 118, 232
Hubbard, Cody, 177; Dana Day, 177; Doris, 76; Dorothy, 174; Katelin, 177; Kendra, 177; Mark, 177
Hubbert, Benjamin, 209; Margaret, 208, 209; Nancy, 209; Nancy Anne, 208; Rebecca Calvert, 209
Huber, Emma Engle, 259; Jacob, 259; Julia, 259; Mary, 259
Huckins, Nettie, 116
Hudson, Maggie, 6
Huebner, Geraldine Mae, 261; Rex, 261; Virginia, 261
Huff, Scott, 84
Huffman, Carl, 50; Marilyn, 97
Hughes, A.J., 32; Blanche Eulalia, 205; Breckin Allyn, 236; Chester Monroe, 205; Danny Ray, 239; Dawnnell Lea, 239; Donald Ray, 239; Elta Virginia Ross, 205; Ethel, 205; Frances, 75; Frances Zana, 205; Kristina Ann Smith, 239; Lucy, 205; Lucy Hendrix, 203; Lynn, 88; Mae, 205; Mae Lenora, 203; Michael Aaron, 239; Nell Elisabeth Richards, 236, 239; Rayben, 205; Sam, 129; Samual, 205; Samuel, 205; Samuel Meridieth, 203; Taylor Jo, 239; Wayne, 75; Wayne, III, 205; Wayne, Jr., 205; Wayne Woodard, 205; Webb, 45; Webster Wayne, 205; Zachary Loyd, 239
Hulston, John K., 121
Humes, Linda, 116
Humphery, Elizabeth Verch Rees, 208; Samuel, 208
Humphrey, Donald, 70; Sharon, 48
Hungerford, Jackie, 85
Hunt, Ashley, 128; Diana Morrison, 207; Eva, 155; Lou Agnes Pope, 217; LuDena Short, 15, 128; Mark, 128; Michael, 207; Rosa A. Lile Shipley Reynolds, 248; Warren, 36
Huntsinger, Doris, 205; James C., 205
Hussey, E.E., 134; Edward E., 33
Hutchenson, Mearl, 231
Hutchinson, Charles, 56
Hutchison, Anna Muriel, 231
Hutter, Elisabeth, 237
Hyde, Bobby, 66; Peggy Duvall, 181; Richard, 66

I

Ingersoll, Ann Josephine, 233; George Parker, 267; Grace Meyer, 267; Milley Annella Fulks, 267
Ingler, Adie, 74; H.B., 39; Hugh B., 55
Ingram, 21, 237; Eliza Jane, 234; M.V., 33
Inman, Elkanah, 219; Eugene, 12, 66; Finley Glover, 219; Grace Pauline, 191; Ida Mae, 219; Isabell Carrol, 191; John Henry, 191; John Watts, 191; John Wesley, 219; Lazarus, 219; Mae, 219; Mary Alice Dewitt, 219; Nancy Lavanda Wilson, 219; Ralsie, 219; Shirley, 12; Sophrena McCroskey, 191
Inmon, Beula M. Payne, 205; Charles H., 205; Charles Richard, 205, 206; John Michael, 206; Kay, 116; Loretta Faye Hilton, 205, 206; Peggy Ann, 205, 206; Raymond L., 205, 206; Ray Lee, 205, 206; Rolsie, 221
Ireland, Jim, 134, 195
Irvine, Cindy, 83
Iseminger, Amber, 88; Laura, 88
Isminger, Amber, 83
Ivins, Clara Coggin, 170

J

Jackson, 220, 249; Alf, 24; Andrew J., 206; Anna, 206; Bessie, 206, 212; Betty Jane, 190; Bill, 206; Billy Joe, 190; Bob, 206; Carlos, 206; Carrie Gardner, 206; Charlotte O'Neal, 206; Christiana Castleberry, 206; Christine Cantabary, 206; Clarence Newton, 206; Cynthia Wallace, 262; Deborah, 206; Della, 206; Della Batson, 163, 206; Diane, 212; Don, 56, 206; Earl, 190; Edith Idella, 206; Edward, 206; Edward R., 206; Edwina, 76; Emaline Williams, 206; Emmett, 163, 206; Ernie, 39; Ethel, 206; George, 20, 21, 160; George W., 146, 206; Glenn Edward, 206; Golda, 163, 206; Hattie Mae, 206; Hazel, 206; Helen, 116; Ida Belle, 206; Ila, 163, 206; Iri, 48; Jason, 163, 206; Jean, 206; Jill, 165; John, 25, 206; John H., 141; John Harry, 206; John M., 206; John M., Sr., 206; John Marion, Jr., 206; John Samuel Corum, 206; Joseph, 206; L. Fred, 31; Laura Edith, 206; Leroy, 206; Levina Elizabeth, 206; Lula, 206; Margaret Mae, 66; Mary, 162; Mattie, 206; Mildred, 206; Minnie, 64, 206; Mrs. Marshall, 64; Nancy Jane Liles, 206; Nellie, 64, 206; Nellie Looney, 206; Nettie Idella Newell, 206; Olive Garoutte, 182; Olive Louelia Garoutte, 190; Osha, 163, 206; Raymond, 66; Riley Deputy, 206; Sue Booth, 25, 160; Walter Andrew, 206; William, 91; William Andrew, 206
James, Augusta White, 207; Betty, 207; Betty Lou, 75; Charlie, 207; Frank Luther, 207; Freeman, 207; Judy, 207; Mary Ann, 207; Opal Luna, 207
Jameson, Eliza, 191; Liza, 221; Liza Jane, 241
Janes, Charles Boyd, 200; Laura, 200; Nancy Louraina Pendelton, 200
Jarmin, Agnes, 194
Jarrett, Jane Caroline, 240
Jeffery, Edith Anne, 237
Jeffries, Kellie, 51
Jenkins, Hetty Smith, 257; James, 257; Jamie, 84; Mabel, 222; Mary A.S., 257, 258
Jenkins-Rapp, Susan Marie Brown, 163
Jennings, Ardelia Ann Manley, 189; Rebecca, 189, 192; W.P., 192; William, 189
Jenson, Myron, 87
Jernigan, Ruby Stephenson, 254
Jett, Jeremy, 97
Jewell, Bonnie, 71; Clifton, 207; Edith, 71; Jerry, 207; Judy James, 207; Kandi, 207; Lola Fern, 71
Johns, Elizabeth, 242; Lum, 20; Milbury Redfearn, 242; Reese S., 242; Sarah Alice, 268
Johnson, 31, 115; Anna, 242; Anne E., 134; Anne E. Land, 232; Anne Elizabeth Land, 231; Anne Land, 209, 212; B., 142; Billie Rippee, 240; Clarissa, 186; Danny, 83; David, 257; Deema, 271; Don, 207; Donna, 69; Dora, 227; Eden, 257; Edith, 219; Edith Lanning Martin, 213; Eric, 88; Ermal Hagewood, 261; Gary, 52, 82; Gaylord, 192; Gladys, 66; Grace Wallace, 263; Gregg, 213, 231; Hallie, 207; Hubert, 66; Irene, 12; J.W., 33; Jimmy, 207; John, 192; John W., 31, 55; Joyce, 207; Karen, 67; Kathleen Marie Owen, 233; Kathryn, 231; Kenneth, 207; Laura, 212; Lawrence, 253; Lawrence Norva, 207; Lavada Stiffer, 192; Leon, 12; M.P., 30; Mark, 231; Mary Matilda, 175; Michelle, 223; Michelle Sue Thompson, 257; Mike, 240; Mrs. B., 142; Nancy Evans, 183; Ray, 38; Sally Louise, 186; Sara Jo, 210; Sharron A. Kerr, 210; Shirley, 267; Stella, 253; Stella Mae Sparkman, 207; Steven, 233; Terry, 183; Trevor, 233; Trinity, 257; Virgil, 263; Wilma, 263
Johnston, Donna Faye, 131; George, 87; James, 87
Jones, 242; Alice, 207; Alma Lorene, 175; Angela, 224, 243; Anna Carsten, 168; Anne, 227; Artie Hicks, 175; B.J., 110; Barbara, 260; Benjamin G.W., 207; Benjamin George Whitfield, 207;

Bert Isaac, 202, 207, 208, 269; Bettie, 242; Bunny Sawyer, 4, 243; Cameron, 224; Charles W., 207; Charley, 35, 45; Charlie, 32; Cheryl, 48; Dana Ann Espy, 269; Darrell, 208; Darrell Raymond, 208; Delilah, 221, 240, 241; Dwayne, 246; Dylan, 224; Edna Bingham, 207; Edna J., 207; Edward, 61; Edward D., Jr., 98; Edward D., Sr., 98; Effie, 184; Effie Keturah, 207; Eula Faye Wallace, 208; Florence Kathleen, 207, 208, 269; Forrest K., 209; Franklin R., 208; Fred Samuel, 207, 208; Gertrude Sarah Hollis, 208; Hannah Florence Pickering, 207, 208; Harold, 207; Helen, 116; Henry Bascomb, 207, 208; Howard Lee, 209; I.S., 105; Iris Edwina Maness, 246; Iris Maness, 243; Isaac Newton, 207; J.J., 105; J.N., 142; Jack, 207; James, 209; James Luther, 207; Jim, 269; Joan Mudd, 209; Joe, 69, 134; Joe Donald, 171, 207, 208; John, 18; Johnnie, 35; Jordan Kersee, 208; Joshua, 207; Joshua Lyman, 207; Joyce Marie DeVasure, 180; Katherine, 207; Kathleen, 171; Kathy, 224; Kelley, 224; Kelsey, 229; LaRae Dawn, 208; Larry, 134; Laura Coggin, 208; Linda, 134; Lois Faye, 208; Mabel Keith, 207, 208; Mandy, 110; Margaret, 184, 209; Martha, 142, 207; Martha McClure, 207; Mary Frances, 233; Matthew Tyler, 269; Michael, 243, 246; Mike, 243; Mose, 32, 35; Ora Coggin, 170; Ora Ellen Coggin, 171, 202, 207, 208, 269; Orvil E., 243; Orvil Eugene, 246; Otis, 246; Otto, 167; Pamela Ann Cantrell, 167; Paul, 60; Perry, 117; R.H., 11; Rachel Katie Cowden, 209; Ralph, 168; Ray, 208; Raymond R., 208; Reathel, 246; Reathel Maize, 168; Rhoda, 18; Rickie, 246; Rosa, 209; Rose Etta Rhodes, 209; Ruth, 171; Ruth M., 195; Ruth Mildred, 202, 207, 208; Sarah, 209, 229, 241; Sarah Arminta, 149; Sarah E., 207; Sarah Frances Kerr, 209; Shanni, 167; Shannon, 167; Sharon Elaine, 208; Sherman, 33; Summerfield, 209; Trevor, 224; Tricia Jo, 180; Whitney, 208; William, 209; Willis, 175; Willis Dean, 180; Yvonne, 246

Joplin, Alma, 230

Jordan, Francis, 186; Virginia, 255

Jorden, Fuzzy, 53

Jordon, Fuzzy, 87; Roger, 76; Susan, 76

Jorgenson, Kelly, 88; Mark, 88

Joslyn, Dorothy, 257

Joule, Aretha, 166; Barbara, 166; Ted, 166

Julian, 249; Benjamin Elliott, 216; Mary Ann Diffie, 216; Net, 64; Sarah, 242; Sylvania Jane, 216, 217, 243, 246

### K

Kackley, Jo Ann, 197

Kalas, 129

Kasper, Elsie Regina, 211

Kastendieck, Valentine, 70

Kates, 41

Kauffman, Alma, 66; Norman Kirby, 66; Reba, 66, 87

Kaykendall, Mattie, 73

Keatts, Belva Steele, 209; Charley, 35; Harold, 71; Lucille, 71; Nick, 209; Tom, 35

Keets, 165

Keith, Denzil, 70; Eugene, 75; Mabel, 207, 208; Orlis, 70

Keithley, Kody Lane, 222

Kellar, Price, 59

Keller, Alena, 83; Christine Carlson, 167; Christy, 251; Hulda Dee, 200

Kelley, James, 59; Jerry, 55; Joe, 50; Mark, 100; Mindy, 174; Mindy West, 266; Rod, 133

Kellogg, 24

Kellough, Ann, 67; Jesse J., 11; Kay, 67; Leah A., 11; Rocky, 67

Kelly, Alice, 259; James, 54; Kathy, 118; Opal, 71; Polly, 220; Rosalind, 191

Kelsey, Rachel, 110

Keltner, 254; Anna McCroskey, 234; Bent, 13; Carolyn, 69; Delphia, 168; Dixie, 11, 12, 19, 68, 208, 253, 254; Doris, 234; Dorothy, 208; E.W., 145; Ethel, 181; Ethyl Pierce, 208; Flo, 208; Fulton, 234; Grace Gillian Norman, 208; Harriet, 254; Ida, 160; Jerry Lee, 69; John, 208; Jo Ann, 208, 253; Kenneth, 208; Marcella, 68, 208; Margie Lee, 208; Mary, 208, 253; Patsy, 87; T.B., 133; Terry, 88; Victor, 208, 254

Kemper, Frances Ann, 164; Jonathon, 164; Rebecca Jane Sutor, 164

Kemppainen, Carl Ryan, 179; Karen Sue DeVore, 179; Lauren Nicole, 179; Patrick Lorne, 179

Ken's TV, 109

Kendrick, Amy, 158; Jana, 157, 158; Kolby, 158; Kurt, 158; Michael, 158; Mike, 158; Nancy, 247

Kendricks, Margaret Fruby, 246; Nancy, 246; Samuel James, 246

Kennedy, 24; Arthur, 237; Mary Flanagan, 237; Vera Louise, 237

Kenny, Elaine, 48

Kerr, 41, 229; Agnes C. Howard, 209; Agnes Leota, 210; Alexander, 209, 210, 212; Alexander Preston, 208, 210; Almeda, 210; Amanda, 210; Amy, 208, 209; Amy E., 209; Amy George, 208; Anderson, 208; Andrew J., 209; Andrew Jackson, 210; Anna Louise Tiede, 259; Benjamin Anderson, 209, 210; Bertha Frances, 210; Britta Mart, 210; Cecile, 209; Charles Walter, 210; Clarence, 209; Cleo V., 168; Clyde, 209; David, 209; Deanna, 260; Deanna K., 210, 263; Doyle John, 209; Earl, 209; Edith May, 210; Edna, 209; Edna A., 210; Edward Matthew, 209; Elda Gertrude, 210; Elizabeth, 90, 208; Ellis, 259; Elmer E., 210; Elmer Irvin, 210; Emma V., 210; Frances Short, 210; Harold Dale, 71; Isabelle Jane, 210; J.O., 32; Jacqueline Jane Little, 209; James A., 210; James Clifford, 210; James Jackson, 209; James Owen, 210; James Wiley, 209; Jane, 188; Jefferson Calvin, 209; Jim, 260; Jim L., 210; Johni Lynn, 209; John Ed, 209; John Ernest, 209; John George, 208; John T., 209; Joseph, 209; Judge, 41; Julianne Terigan, 210; Junior June, 210, 260; Kelli June, 209; Kelly L., 210; Lacey, 209; Lacey Jane, 209; LeVera Turpin, 210, 260; Lilly May Little, 209; Lisa Jo, 209; Liza Cowden, 209; Loyd M., 209; Lutrecia, 210; Margaret, 208; Margaret Hubbert, 208, 209, 210; Margaret Jane, 187; Marguerite Duerinda, 210; Marion C., 209; Marion Lee, 209; Martha, 208; Martha Elizabeth, 210; Mary E., 209, 210; Mary Jane Hodges, 209; Mary Lacey, 210; Mary Lavona O'Bryant, 209; Mary Lucille, 209; Mary Steele, 208; Mary Susan Pope, 209; Matthew, 209, 210; Matthew H., 209; Matthew Thomas, 210; Maxine, 71; Mrs. June, 76; Nancy, 209; Nancy Anne Hubbert, 208; Nancy Hubbert, 209; Nancy J., 210; Nellie Jewel Washam, 209; Olive M., 210; Orville, 209; R.C., 90; Rachael, 210; Rachel, 212; Rebecca, 208, 209; Rebecca Amanda, 210; Robert, 209; Robert, Jr., 208; Robert, Sr., 208; Robert, III, 208; Robert Clack, 209; Rosa Nina Laderach, 210; Rosa Phillips, 209; Ruth, 209; Sally Jane, 210; Sandra L. Muench, 210; Sarah, 210; Sarah Ann Elizabeth Ellis, 209; Sarah Ann Ellis, 209; Sarah Ann Reynolds, 209, 210; Sarah Frances, 209; Sarah J. Irvin, 210; Sarah J. Phelps, 210; Sarah Lou, 209; Sarah R., 209; Sharron A., 210; Spencer, 17; Spencer G., 90; Stacey, 209; Stacey Lee, 209; Stella Mae, 209; Stella Martha, 210; Thomas Jefferson, 208; Wesley Matthew, 209; Wilber Herbert, 210; William, 208, 209, 210, 212; William H., 209; William Preston, 210; William T., 209; Zella June Hale, 209

Key, Margaret Randolph, 238

Keyes, Grace, 136; Otis, 136

Keys, Orilla Viles, 261

Khomeini, Ayatollah, 80

Kiefner, Andy, 230; Beth, 230; John, 230; Pat Long, 230

Kile, Amber, 83

Killar, Marilyn, 48

Killingsworth, Margaret Rainey, 236; Scott, 136

Kimmons, Bessie McElhany, 221; Bess McElhaney, 34; Danavee, 88; John, 34; Ollie, 185; Pete, 262; Ruby, 231, 262

King, Alta Carolyn, 217; Andrew David, 200, 211; Anna, 73, 227; Beth, 84, 87; Chandler Colt, 210; Elizabeth Velma, 225; F., 32; Frederick, 31, 32, 33, 55; Fredrick, 66; Gary, 47, 48; Hattie Caroline, 211; Isaac, 10; J.E., 123; J.F., 133; James Lynn, 210; Jane, 66; Jaycee Lynn, 210; Jayde Lyndsay, 210; Jayma Lanae, 210; Jerry, 210; Jetta Irene, 211; Joe Lee, 210; Josie Lea, 210; Kevin, 83; Kim, 210; Lillie, 73, 200; Lilly May, 200, 211; Lula Jane, 211; Martha Elizabeth Lonon, 200, 211; Michelle, 88; Minty J., 153; Myrtle Rebecca Pope, 217; Orville F., 211; Peggy, 50, 61, 115, 117; Peggy Grimes, 210, 211; Roy, 225; Roy Edward, 211; Thomas, 66; Velma Short, 211, 225; Violettie, 215; Williams James, 210; William H., 211

Kingery, Hannah Margaret, 269

Kinkel, Betty Land, 213

Kinsey, Patty, 47

Kipper, Valetta, 47

Kirby, Jean Jackson, 206; Marion, 211; Peggy, 38, 87, 211; Viola Cason, 211

Kirk, Alexander, 248; Emaline Earnhardt, 248; Lunda Sophia, 248

Kirkes, Betty Bull, 165, 166; Bill, 166; Max, 165; Russell, 166

Kirkwood, Steve, 53

Kitchen, Anna Caroline Lullau, 211; Bernice, 211; Charles Ezekiel Burrow Fines, 211; Clara, 211; D.N., 134; Daniel Newton, 211; Isaac Young David Houston, 211; James Perry Daniel Lee, 211; Jessie, 211; Jim, 194; John Chapman Samuel Wra, 211; Mable Irene, 211; Margaret Harriet, 211; Margaret Irene, 211; Mary, 134; Mary Celeste, 211; Mary Eliza M.E., 211; Mary Thieme, 211; Maude Erminie Adams, 211; Nellie Anderson, 211; Nellie Louise, 211; Ruth B.C.S., 211; Sarah Myra Amanda Jane, 211; William Earl, 211; William Lilburn D.D., 211

Kitrell, Christy Scarlett, 198

Kiwanis Club, The, 117

Kizer, Sarah Fugitt, 186

Klatt, Gordy, 51

Klepees, Marlene, 108

Kline, Marthella, 164

Klingebiel, Jim, 162

Kloss, Clara, 259

Klug, Eva McNeely, 195; John, 195; Ruby K., 195

Knauer, Justin, 88

Kneal, Cheryl, 230

Kneale, Cheryl, 230; Leonard, 230; Misha, 230; Tauna, 230; Wilma, 230

Knetzer, Daryl, 85

Knoebel, Grace, 199

Knupp, Diana McGuire, 127

Koch, Evelyn Allen, 172; Larry, 172

Kokai, Jane Lovett, 216

Komrska, Barbara Malecek, 172; Francis, 172; Mildred Barbara, 172; Wencelaus, 172

Korage, Laura Taylor, 248

Kozemezak, Seth, 177

Kramer, Dawn Thurman, 259

Krause, Rose, 116

Kreider, Grace Marie, 72; James David, 72; Fritz, 82

Kromas, Lee, 116

Kruse, Aaron, 136

Krykendall, Jacob, 33

Kubat, Cliff, 167; Clifford, 134, 211; Elsie Regina Kasper, 211; Helen, 47, 167, 211; Jason, 212; Joseph Edward, 211; Karen, 211; Marcia, 212; Mike, 40, 211, 212; Rosemary, 211; Stan, 212; Suzanne, 212; Tim, 27, 39, 211, 212

Kubert, Karen, 85

Kubicek, Peggy, 50

Kuehn, Janie, 173; Michael, 175

Kuhn, Barbara, 113; Betty, 66; Bill, 66; Henrietta, 66

### L

Lacey, Adam, 212; Amy, 212; Carolyn Propps, 212; Diane Jackson, 212; Donna, 204, 212; Fred, 212; Freddy, 212; Greg, 212; Jason, 212; Kerri, 212; Kim, 212; Mary, 210; Susie Hicks, 212

Ladd, Mildred, 72; Susie Mooneyham, 179

Laderach, Rosa Nina, 210

LaFollett, Harold Dale, 68; Myrtle Evelyn, 71

Lafollette, 194; Ella, 177; Lundy Ann Sifferman, 248; Myrtle, 77; Nancy, 157; Oval, 41, 42, 43, 44, 229

LaFon, Jeannie, 48

Lake, Penny, 116

Lakey, Sharon, 59; Tim, 239

Lakins, Amy Brashers, 212; Bonie, 210; Bonnie Russell, 212; Carl, 212; Chandler, 212; Christy Bilbo, 212; David, 212; Douglas Wayne, 212; Ethan, 212; Frank, 212; Frank Monroe, 212; Frusa, 212; Hulda Lane, 212; Jennifer Ann, 212; Joe, 209, 210, 212; Joe Dean, 212; Joe L., 209; Joseph Frank, 212; Juanita, 212; Lousia, 212; Mary Ann Logan, 212; Micheal Wayne, 212; Norma, 212; Pam Hoffman, 212; Robert, 212; Sandra Eitel, 212; Wilda Jean, 212; Wiley, 212

Lamb, I.D., 141; Hattie, 250; Maude, 235

Land, 9, 161, 242; Ab, 212; Abigail, 213; Andrew Jackson, 263; Anna, 212, 213; Anne, 75, 87, 212, 213; Anne Elizabeth, 231; Bessie Jackson, 212; Betty, 76; Charles, 212; Edith, 212; Edna Earl, 212; Edna Sturman, 253; Grace, 116, 134; Grace B. Ottendorf, 213, 231; Grace Ottendorf, 212; Herbert, 212; J. Wilfred, 213, 231; James, 212; Jess, 213; Jesse, 212; John, 209, 212, 213; Josephine, 145; Josephine House, 212, 213; Joy, 70; Larry, 161, 213; Lilly Crum, 212; Luther, 70, 76, 145, 209, 212, 213; Manerva Couch, 212; Margaret Anna, 161; Mattie Myrtle, 263; Myrtle, 241; Ralph, 212; Ron, 213; Sarah, 212, 213; Sarah Boyd, 212; Sarah Kerr, 212; Sarah R. Kerr, 209; Sarah Robertson, 212; Stanley, 117; Viola McKee, 263; Wilford, 70, 134; Wilfred, 212; Will, 212; Willie, 213

Landers, Ellen J. Wilson, 33; John N., 33; Lynn, 156, 225; Mary E., 33

Landon, Ralph, 40

Lane, Hulda, 212; Hulda Ellen, 212; Lander, 212; Lela, 210; Rachel Kerr, 212; Robin Pullen, 236

Laney, 9, 141, 238, 249; Alice, 226; Amy Bethia Garoutte, 189, 262; Annie Bethar, 227; Charley, 71, 210; Elizabeth, 189, 197; Elizabeth Virginia, 262; Ephraim, 262; George Marion, 189, 262; Jeremiah H., 242; John, 20, 66, 197, 221; Lela Lane, 209, 210; Margaret, 141; Rosie Alice, 172; S.F., 66; Samiel F., 66; Sarah Elizabeth, 242; Sophia McAfee, 242; William Marcellas, 262

Lang, Vickie, 110

Lange, Carolina, 259

Langenberg, 270

Langiller-Hoppe, Josh, 133

Langley, Clarice, 212; Ethel Epps, 212; Lena Elizabeth, 212; Thomas, 212

Langston, Gordon, 66, 87

Langum, Connie, 19

Lankins, Bonnie, 210

Lanning, Aaron, 246; Bertha, 213; Betty Burleson, 213; Charles, 213; Charles J., 213; Charles Ted, 213; Delores, 213; Dorothy, 213; Edith, 213; Emma Hawkins, 213; Forrest, 213; Gretchen Marcia Hamilton, 213; Jim, 213; Linda O'Neal, 230, 246, 247; Paul, 230, 246; Ralph, 213; Ralph Doss, 213

Lappin, C., 31; J.M., 28

Larson, Arthur, 123; Dorothy, 87; Ruth, 87; Walter, 75

LaRue, Colter, 84

LaSalle, Tara, 88

Latimer, Eric, 88

Latshaw, Ira, 131; Judy, 47; Mrs. Ira, 131

Latta, Rebecca, 253

Lauderback, Judy, 259; Steven Kenneth, 259; Virginia Trogdon, 259

Lawrence, Bill, 75; Clarice, 118; Clarice Langley, 212; Clifford, 212; Kathy, 47; Nancy, 75

Lawson, 36; A.A., 143; Alex, 134; Alexander Ayers, 214; Arilla E., 214; Catherine Dodd, 214; Cora Powers, 162; Ernest Campbell, 211; Fay, 162; Guy, 162; Isham, 213; James Harvey, 214; Joanna Martin, 213; Lorenzo W., 162; Lumitta Elmina Long, 214; Martha Elizabeth, 214; Mary Martin, 213; Nelson, 213, 214; Patience Ann, 214; Ruth B.C.S. Kitchen, 211; W.W., 134; Walter, 211; Willie, 211; Winfield, 211

Lay, George, 77

Leabo, D.F., 210; Mary E. Kerr, 210

Leatherbury, Ada, 256

Leban, J.W., 33

Lebaw, J.W., 33

LeCompte, 12

Ledford, Kevin, 117

Lee, 237, 264; Anna Hagewood, 221; Edward Pete, 203; Jared, 223;

John, 130; Justin, 223; Mildred Belle, 121; Morean, 71; Pete, 71; Robert E., 121; Roger, 223; Vicki Carol Meadors, 223
Legan, Dwight, 122, 240
Lehman, Alicia Fisher, 214; Dorothy, 209; Fred, 209; Freda, 270, 271; Grace Steele, 209; Joe Rex, 214; Judy, 51; Judy Kay Bacon, 214; Kinley Kae, 214; Kolton Kent Fisher, 214; Lee, 237, 264; Leo, 214; Maxine, 214; Rex, 51, 233; Shelly Kay, 51, 214; Stacy Kent, 214
Leidenger, Carl, 45
Leidinger, Alan, 214; Elizabeth, 214; Karl, 53; Karl Josef, Jr., 214; Lee, 214; Lovetta Luce, 214
Leitz, Andrew, 194; Andy, 238; Kaleb, 238; Kaleb Nathaniel, 194; Kathryn Sue O'Neal, 194; Kathy O'Neal, 238; Kolby, 238; Kolby James, 194
Lekinzie, Edna Belle Logan, 265
Lemons, Barbara, 230
Lentz, Cletis Baker, 192; Mary, 15; Tom, 15
Leonard, Barbara, 75, 84, 87; C.K., 74, 123, 222, 226; Linda, 47; Linda Louise Wells, 265; Mrs. C.K., 226; Roger, 265
Letterman, Ab, 155; Betty, 155; Chad, 84
Lewallen, Wanda, 68
Lewis, D., 32; Ilonna, 214; Isabel, 174; James, 214; Janie, 47; Karen Faye, 214; Larry, 214; Lena Lorie, 214; Leonard Max, 214; Linda, 85; Linda Sue, 214; Michael, 214; Mike, 214; Paula, 214; Vivian, 259
Lieser, Ann Maria, 156
Likens, 45, 77; Fay, 183
Likins, Hannah E., 238
Lile, Allie Ann, 248; Frances, 157; Frances Catherine Blades, 248, 249; Green, 248; James Green, 248; John Alvin, 248; John Alvin, Jr., 248; Lucy Victoria, 248; Margaret S.J., 248; Nancy Ellen, 248; Nancy Jane Collins, 248; Rosa A., 248; Thomas Tillman, 248; William Elijah, 248
Liles, Green, 239; Jennie Ricketts, 239; Nancy Jane, 206
Lilie, Marvin, 132
Lillard, A.L., 72
Lincoln, 157, 239; Abraham, 20, 220, 238
Lindbergh, Charles, 150
Lindsey, Della Estella, 189; Edna, 176; Edwin, 66; Rick, 113
Lindsey Chapel Cemetery, 145
Link, Martha Louella, 175
Lipscomb, 92; Andrew, 121; Cathryn Lee Cox, 121; Cynthia, 121; Jack E., 121; Lawrence W., 121; Stephanie Amanda, 121; Stuart, 121
Lischer, Jeanne, 175
Lisenby, Bob, 244; JoAnna, 72; Naomi, 72; Stacye, 88; Wilma, 72
Little, Amy E. Kerr, 209; Arlie, 53; Charles, 72; Corleng, 88; Dale, 231; Elizabeth Jean Edwards, 176; Geneva, 72; Geneva Wilma Pope, 217; George C., 176; Jacqueline Jane, 209; Johnnie, 209; Lilly May, 209; Louisa, 176; Louise Ottendorf, 231; Sarah Lou Kerr, 209; Travis, 88; William Ellison, 209
Livingston, Harold, 74
Lloyd, Charley, 34; Delilah, 221; Fyan, 35; Harold, 33; Paul, 173; Virginia, 161
Lock, Kelsey, 83
Lockridge, Mary, 269
Loftin, Glenda, 256
Logan, 45, 161, 177, 212; Agnes, 214; Alice, 215; Andrea Sobotka, 251, 252; Anthony Mac, 215; Benjamin, 214, 215; Benjamin Levi, 215; Bud, 167, 235; Callie Hayes, 215; Callie Katherine Hayes, 259; Carl, 260; Clarence, 215, 259; Clarence Lee, 215; Daniel Lee, 215; David, 75, 76, 82, 87, 131; David Manuel, 214; David Roy, 215; Donna Sue Sifferman, 215; Don David, 215; Douglas Mark, 215; Elizabeth, 214; Elizabeth Jane, 225, 226; Ella Brashers, 161, 162; Emily May Paschall, 215; Ethel Smith, 250; Everette, 215; Frank, 215; Fronia, 215; George, 215; Georgia Mae Kathrine Tuter, 260; Glen, 250; Hattie, 215; Hugh, 215; James, 215; James M., 66; James Monroe, 214; Jane, 215; Jane Campbell, 214; Joan Andrus, 212; John, 212, 214, 215; Judy, 215; Kathy, 215; Kayla Pauline Word, 215; Lawrence, 215; Lem, 215; Lester, 207, 214, 215, 243, 259; Lester Bud, 190, 268; Liddie, 215; Malinda, 215; Malinda A., 262; Martha, 215; Mary, 30, 214, 215; Mary Ann, 212; Mike, 250; Milinda, 182; Mrs. David, 131; Nancy, 214, 229; Patricia Ann, 215; Patsy, 215; Robert, 215; Ruth Boyd, 215; Sadie Meyer, 215; Samiel, 66; Samuel J., 31; Samuel Jasper, 214; Sarah, 215; Tarlton, 66; Tarlton L., 214; Thomas, 33, 215; Tony, 76, 82, 207; Vanner Dean, 177; Victoria, 215; Virgie, 116, 167, 207; Virginia, 214; Virginia Boatright, 215; Viva Lee Smart, 215; W.R., 66; Walter, 177; Wesley Robert, 214; William Hood, 214
Lohkamp, Albert, 215; Austin, 215; Carol Saunders, 215; Dan, 85; Mike, 84; Steve, 99, 215; Wanda, 215
London, Robert P., 33
Long, Alyssa Myree, 245; B.L., 189; Bonnie, 230; Charles W., 189; Della Riley, 189; George, 141; Josey, 245; Jo Ann, 186; Jo Ann Fugitt, 186, 230; Kathy, 50, 100; Kevin, 83; Laura Clarice Franks, 189; Lee Russell, 189; Lumitta Elmina, 214; Mischa Myree Admire, 245; Pat, 230; Robert, 141; Sarah Ellen Daniels, 214; Stanley, 230; Tandy W., 214; Vaunda, 68; Vaunda Noreene, 189; Vonda, 87
Longfellow, 74
Lonon, 9; Lura, 169; Martha Elizabeth, 200, 211; Powell, 29, 148; Zana Anderson, 29, 148
Looney, Ben, 215, 216; Ben F., 215; Charlie, 71; Claud, 215, 216; Claude, 48; Clyde, 215; Dale, 71; Dewey, 215, 216; Dolen, 216; Edwin, 72; Elizabeth, 215; Etna Dallas Eaves, 215, 216; Frances Iona, 217; Glen, 215; Glenarven, 217; Hetty, 29, 149; James, 72; Jessie, 216; Keith, 76; Lelia, 215; Lloyd, 216; Maude, 177, 215; Merle, 215; Nellie, 206; Newell, 216; Odin, 216; Richard, 72; Robert, 215; Ruby, 216; Virginia, 75; Willie Marie, 189
Loonsfoot, Becky Ruckman, 165
Loose, John, 20
Loping, 28
Lorenze, Clara, 235
Loudermilk, Dr., 21
Love, Velma, 46
Lovejoy, Lilly Olive Carson, 248
Lovett, Acie, 216; AC Commadore, 216; Alberta, 216; Bethia, 216; Charles, 71, 216; Diana, 216; Eliza, 216; Floyd, 216; Jane, 216; Lela Sifferman, 216, 248; Loretta, 216; Lucy Farris, 216; Mary, 71, 216; Melissa Owens, 216; Michael G., 216; Olen, 216; Rosetta, 157; Rosetta Blades, 216; Ruth Crum, 216; Sophia, 216; Stanford, 216; Tressie, 157, 216; Valentine, 216
Loving, Tommy, 90
Lowe, Mark, 32; Nancy, 177
Lower, Ray, 61
Lowing, Fred H., 33
Loyd, Carol Joe, 161
Luce, John, 28; Lovetta, 214; Sarah, 29; Sarah Hazelton, 149; Sara Hazelton, 149; Sophrina, 28
Lugar, Chad, 88
Lullau, Anna Caroline, 211
Lummis, Mary Williams, 268; W.P., 268
Luna, Billy, 75; Charlie, 75; Howard, 75; Jessie Richard, 189; Jimmy, 75; Opal, 207; Permelia Jane Beard, 189; Sarah Marvilla, 189
Lundt, Lana, 218
Luttrell, Alonzo, 216; Barbie, 167; Barbie West, 266; Burley, 216, 270; Dora, 216; Faye Sharp, 216; John, 270; John J., 216; Josephine Holt, 216; Mae, 270; Mary, 270; Mary Ann, 216, 264; Mary Jo, 216; Nancy Duncan, 216
Lutz, O.D., 33
Lynch, Bill, 75, 87; Russell, 123; Russell J., 31
Lyngar, Sarah, 169
Lynn, Fred, 137
Lyon, 10, 161, 193, 197, 232; Nathaniel, 18, 19


### M

MacArthur, Douglas, 150, 192
MacDonald, Jenny, 88
Mace, 92
MacLean, Douglas, 39
Maden, Dicie L., 148
Magers, Billy, 161
Maggard, Clinton, 156, 225; Doris Jean, 156, 225; James, 135; Lily Jean, 222; Marietta, 156, 225; Patricia, 156, 225; Timmy, 156, 225; Wilda Louise Mooneyham, 156, 225
Mahan, Ray, 53; Robert, 53
Mahanay, A.T., 130
Mahaney, 76; A.T., 123
Maine, Reitha, 235
Malecek, Barbara, 172
Mallicoat, 69
Maness, 217, 242; Arthur L., 216; Donald, 70, 216; Donald S., 184, 217; Donald Sterling, 217; Eliza Ann Berry, 216; Elsie, 70; Elsie Gwendola, 217, 243, 246; Etta Jane, 217, 246; Etta Mae/May Short, 217, 243, 246; Eula, 217; Eula Lorene, 216; Flossie Ann DeWett, 246; Flossie DeWett, 217, 243; Francess Iona, 217; Glenarven Everett, 216; Harold Don, 217; Henry, 217; Henry Billingly, 216; Henry Elliott, 217, 243, 246; Henry Elliott, Jr., 217, 246; Homer, 73, 172, 182, 243; Homer E., 242; Homer Elliott, 216, 217, 246; Iona, 182, 217; Iona Vernell, 217; Iris, 243; Iris Edwina, 217, 246; John, 243; John Baldwin, 216, 217, 242, 246; Keith, 217; Laura, 217; Laura Ellen, 216; Lois Iona Pope, 217; Lois Pope, 172, 182; Luther Edwin, 217, 246; Marilyn, 76, 85, 184, 217; Marilyn Kay, 217; Mary, 217; Mary Alice Sparkman, 217; Mary Cordelia, 216; Mildred Mae, 217, 246; Paul, 217; Pauline, 190; Rayetta Elizabeth, 217, 246; Raymond, 243; Raymond Everett, 217, 243, 246; Raymond Everett, Jr., 217, 246; Regina, 116; Regina Sifferman, 25, 184, 248; Regina V., 249; Regina V. Sifferman, 217; Regina Vernell Sifferman, 217; Rosemary, 75, 87, 172, 217; Sandy, 116, 243; Scott, 217; Sterling, 217; Sterling Edward, 216; Sylvania Jane Julian, 216, 217, 243, 246; Velma Irene Martin, 246; Velma Martin, 217; Vernell, 85, 217; Virginia Lee, 217, 246
Manley, 189; Ardelia Ann, 189; C.B., 91; Caleb, 91, 192; Emma, 222; Grace, 262; Sarah J., 91; T.B., 91
Mann, Kelly, 212
Manners, Peggy, 75, 87
Manning, 221; Bob, 81; Irene, 116; John, 45; Nancy, 242; Wayne, 81
Mansfield, Lucy Yeakley, 270; Robert E., 270; Robert Yeakley, 270
Maple, Francis, 112
Maples, Annis, 47; Elias L., 227; Ethel Ruth, 179, 193, 227; Gracie Paralee Tabor, 227; Greta Jean, 75; Tim, 13; Timothy, 17
Maravilla, David, 90
Marcy, Edith Land, 212; James, 212
Mareno, Wilda, 264
Mark, Anita, 218; Emma, 218; Gene, 217; Imelda Joy, 218; Jacob, 218; Jeffrey, 218; Marcellene, 217; Paul, 217; Phyllis Peterson, 217, 218; Ron, 50, 54, 104; Ronald, 97; Ronald L., 217, 218; W.B., 217; Wyomia Marriott, 217
Markel, Don, 75, 87
Marques, Alex, 264; Dena Thorpe, 264
Marr, Aaron, 218; Amy, 218; Denny, 218; Dorothy Sanders, 218; Emily, 218
Marriott, Wyomia, 217
Marsh, Bernadine, 38; Bertha, 184; Burnadine, 87, 211; G.A., 33; Reba, 76
Marshal, Tina Maxine, 266
Marshall, Elizabeth Fortner, 184; Thomas, 184; Virginia, 175
Martien, Margaret Jones, 209; William, 209
Martin, 236, 245; Anna Mabel, 192; Anthony, 88; Charles Lyndell, 218; Danny, 182; Darlene, 182; Dorothy Etheridge, 182; Edith Lanning, 213; Eliza Jane, 246; Gilda, 167; Irene, 39, 45, 167, 270; Irene Bonita Craig, 218; J.R., 58, 189, 211; Jimmy, 182; Joanna, 213; Lester, 182; Lynn, 39, 45, 117, 119, 151, 167, 270; Mae, 177; Mary, 213; Milinda, 182; Nita, 99; Renae, 88; Thomas McNeese, 246; Velma, 217; Velma Irene, 246
Mashburn, Wiley, 41
Mason, 249; Betty, 4, 8, 10, 11, 18, 34, 91, 118, 222; Betty Jean McElhaney, 221, 222; Buell, 4, 118, 221, 222; Carolyn, 76; Gary, 194; Jeptha, 249; Jerry, 75, 76; Jimmie, 87; Kristen Ricketts, 240; Lucille Rivlet Green, 194; Martha J., 238; Mary Lockridge, 249; Rebecca, 221, 222; Sarah Erwin Benson, 249; Victor, 194
Massey, Ava, 73; Bonnie, 207; Carl, 207; Carla, 207; Dorothy, 86; Les, 45, 235; Tipton, 73
Mastin, 24
Matherly, Jackie, 67
Mathews, 219; Betty, 219; Josh, 90; Joshua, 140; Leon, 219; Lillian Willis Mecker, 219; Noel, 219; Ray, 32, 45, 49, 117, 180, 219; Sean, 219; Sharri Sittler, 219; Thelma, 180; Thelma Meeker, 219
Matney, Edith, 235; Latty Becker, 235; Thomas, 235
Matt, Becky, 75
Matteson, Judy Chronister, 148
Matthews, Ethel, 259; Martha Ann Wrinkle, 259; William, 259
Maus, Lindy, 51, 59; Natalie, 169; Stephen, 59
Mauss, Mark, 50
Maxey, 71; Blanche Thurman, 258; Walter, 258
Maxwell, Betty, 161; Hazel, 127, 213; J. Pres, 54; Kay, 161
Maybee, Mona Marie Rose Cox, 242; Orrin Smith, 242
Mayfield, Rilla, 182
Maynard, 254; Eleanor Penelope, 248; Ellen L., 202; Ellen Penelope, 157; Melissa, 158; Penelope Ellen, 238; Phillip, 158; Raymond, 158; Susan Blades Gardner, 158
Maynor, Ellen, 224
McAfee, Sophia, 242
McAmis, Elizabeth, 158
McAnally, Susie Bull, 165
McBride, Gene, 138
McCain, Amy Anne Cowden Davis, 209; Isaac, 209
McCall, John, 10, 253; T.C., 143
McCann, Lavina, 209
McCarty, J.B., 260; James, 20; Jerry, 71, 88; Virginia, 71
McCauley, George, 73
McCleary, 36, 270; Annie Gray, 30; Clara, 73; Eliza K. Smith, 30; Joseph C., 30; Margaret Smith, 30; Mrs. W.S., 28; W., 33; W.S., 28; William, 30
McCleasy, William S., 32
McClendon, America, 243; Permelia, 243; Robert, 243
McClure, 242; Charles, 137, 143, 207; Charles L., 242; Eglantine Smith, 242; Eva, 70; Kate, 70; Keturah Moon, 207; M.L., 143; Martha, 207
McConnell, Altha Pearce, 219, 220; Barbara Jean Miller, 219; Burl, 66, 161, 219, 263; Burl Russell, 219; C.H., 219; Carla Buoy, 219; Christie, 208, 254; Darrell, 131, 166; Darrell Dean, 219; Deloris, 66; Deloris Mae, 219; Dennis Russell, 219; Doris, 66, 184, 185; Doris Fay, 219; Edith, 219; Elene, 69; Fredona Tuter, 219; Gary, 131; Gary Lee, 219; Gene, 31, 72, 87, 127, 219, 220; Gertrude Roberts, 219; Harry, 219; Harry Lee, 131, 161, 219; Henry, 219; Henry Burl, 219; Ida Mae Inman, 219; Inas, 72, 84; Jane, 219; Jennifer, 166; Jennifer Jo, 219; Jessica, 166; Jessica Lyn, 219; Jill, 166; Jill Renee, 219; Jody, 262; John, 220; John Knox, 219; John Walter, 219; Jo Ann, 181, 219; Jo Ann Duvall, 219; Juanita, 23, 116; Judy Butler, 166, 219; Judy Elaine Butler, 219; Larry, 56, 57, 131; Larry Gene, 219; Linda Schroeder, 219; Mae Inman, 219; Mark, 118, 220; Mary Bell Ray, 219; Mary Lou, 66, 219; Matilda Edwards, 219; Mike, 220; Minnie Wallace, 262; Mrs. Gary, 131; Mrs. Harry Lee, 131; Nell, 220; Norma Sammons, 219; Patricia Sue Wade, 262; Paul, 23, 219; Paul David, 23, 87, 262; Phyllis, 220; Polly Parker, 219; Randy, 220; Randy Lee, 219; Richard, 23; Russell, 219, 220; Sharon Jean, 219; T.A., 143; Virgie Mae, 72; Walter, 219; William, 219; William Alexander, 219
McCool, A.M., 150; Louise, 150
McCord, Agnes, 200; Bryan Keith, 228; Greg, 53; Gregory Lane, 228; Kathleen Ruth, 228; Marlene Annette Crain, 228; Meagan Lane, 228; Norma, 156, 225; Raymond Gene, 228; Ruth Ellen Brown, 228
McCorkle, Crystal, 161; Judith, 66
McCoy, Gladys Coggin, 170; Mildred, 190
McCray, Sarah, 242
McCroskey, 67; Alden, 23; Allen, 209;

Angie Merle, 77; Bruce, 220, 255; C.W., 74; David, 220; Edna Thomas, 255; Eileen, 45; Elene, 158; Eual L., 220, 255; George, 117; Hobert, 72; James Madison, 255; June, 255; L.E., 11; M.C., 14; Matthew Carson, 191, 255; Mildred Davis, 255; Mildred E. Davis, 220; Mrs. Alden, 23; Nancy, 232; Nancy Caroline, 191; Opal, 155, 209; Pricilla, 14; Priscilla Jane Harris, 191, 255; Rachel Gibson, 255; Sammy, 88; Sophrena, 191; Steven, 220; Walter, 11
McCullah, Alexander, 247; Alexander, Jr., 241; Armour, 44; Armor Bascombe Bates, 220; Clemma Ethel Feaster, 220; Edith May, 220; Fred, 44, 152, 212, 244, 256; Fred Leroy, 220; Gary Leroy, 220; Lucy Robertson, 241, 246; Mary Clementine, 149; Mrs. Frank, 64; Rebecca, 246; W.F., 254; Zelda Elaine Carr, 220
McCulloch, 19; John, 113
McCullough, Harry, 165
McDaniel, 9, 141, 157, 237; Ava, 64, 185, 190, 191; Ava Ann, 221; Charles, 221, 255; Doris, 255; Elijah, 220; Eliza Jameson, 191; Ellen Blades, 179; Fred, 64; George, 151; Henderson, 220; Jackson, 220; James, 220; Jesse, 179, 220; John, 64, 220; Leon, 255; Liza Jameson, 221; Liza Jane Jameson, 241; Mabel, 64; Madge, 87, 157, 255; Maggie, 64, 179; Maggie Ada, 197, 221; Mary, 179; Minnie, 64; Nell, 87, 255; Olive Blades, 179; Pam, 255; Ralph, 12, 86, 255; Ransom, 221, 241; Ransom T., 179, 191, 220; Rebecca Britian, 220; Rebecca Eleanor, 220; Roy, 12, 157, 254, 255; Sarah, 141, 157; Sarah Ann Blades, 248; Sara Blades, 220, 221; Sara Jane Missouri, 220; Thomas, 220, 221; Verna, 12, 157; Vernalee, 255; Verna Lee, 12; Verna Stewart, 11, 254, 255; Virginia Jordan, 255; William, 20, 21, 185, 220, 221, 238
McDonald, 192
McDonald, E.L., 3
McDougal, Sarah, 209
McEagan, 181
McElhaney, 9; Bess, 34; Bessie, 255; Betty, 87, 222; Betty Jean, 66, 221; Birdie Howard, 222; Birdie Pauline Howard, 221; Bob, 222; Bryan, 6, 34, 221, 222; Dewey, 34; Dorothy Stewart, 18, 254, 255; E.L., 91; Florence Aven, 11; Frank, 11; George, 221; George L., 34; Ginger, 221, 222; Glen, 254; Guy, 70, 76; H.H., 210; Kay, 221, 222; Lou, 34; Lucy Pollard, 234; Maggie, 34; Mary Fadra Batson, 221, 222; Olive M. Kerr, 210; Robert, 221; Will, 11; William Bryan, 222
McElhany, 242; Alice, 221, 222; Alice Garton, 221; Bessie, 221; Bryan, 221; Charley, 221; Danny Leon, 219; Delilah, 221; Emma Manley, 222; George, 221, 222; George L., 221; Guy, 221; Henry, 221; Jane, 221; Janice Flood, 219; Kathy, 219; Leon, 77, 219, 221; Linna Mae, 219; Lucy Pollard, 221; Maggie, 221; Mary Appline, 221; Mary Cordelia Maness, 216; Mary Lou McConnell, 219; Myrtle, 221; Ralsie Inman, 219; Robert, 221; Rolsie Inmon, 221; Ronnie Lynn, 219; Stella Jane Robertson, 221, 241; Tammy Nolte, 219; Warham A., 221, 241; Warry, 219; Warry A., 221
McElroy, Florence Mae, 67; Opal, 67
McElwain, Beth Anne, 186
McGee, Joy, 67; Linda, 67; Margy, 249
McGeehee, Jerry, 71
McGehee, Culetta Schmidt, 153
McGill, Melissa, 83; Virginia Lee Maness, 217
McGilvery, Alice, 118
McGinnis, Edrie, 155; Helen Geilert, 192; Manilla, 234; May, 155; Pearl, 260
McGowan, Ceann Sifferman, 235
McGruder, Kenneth, 166; Maxine Butler, 166
McGuire, Catharine, 155; Cindy, 191; Corki, 191; Debbie, 267; Dwight, 191; John W, 155; Laura, 155; Penny, 191; Roberta Garton, 191
McHatton, Gladys, 116
McKay, Elbert, 106; Mac, 54, 264; Reeda, 106, 264; Torre, 106
McKee, 58; Viola, 263
McKeel, June, 87
McKimens, Patrica Ann, 223
McKinley, Lady Alice, 236
McKinney, Brenda, 160, 161
McKinsey, 45
McKinstry, Frank, 214; Ruth Lumitta True, 214
McLaughlin, Jaclyn, 235; Jordan, 235; Keith, 235, 236; Ronda Hawk, 235
McMullan, Burma, 252
McMurtrey, 76; Alan, 260; Alan Edward, 222; Amos, 74, 81, 82, 117, 162; Amos Eugene, 222; Andy, 222; Debbie Trogdon, 222, 260; Jane, 85; Jane Carol, 222; Olivia Gordon, 222; Patsy Ann, 222; Rosemary, 75, 87, 222
McNabb, 42; Andrea Lynn, 223; Bob, 81, 222; D.E., 41; David, 84; Elsie Belle Edmonson, 222; Evelyn, 222; Genevieve, 116, 222; Genevieve Josephine, 236; Genevieve Josephine Allen, 222, 223, 257; George, 81, 86; Janet Sue, 222, 257; John, 55, 236; John Allen, 222, 223, 236, 257; John Isaac, 222, 223, 236, 257; John Michael, 223; Keet, 222; Lilly, 236; Lilly McMillan, 223; Linda Kay, 222, 236, 257; Margaret L., 193; Phyllis Jean, 222, 257; Ray, 81; Virgil Lafayette, 222; W.T., 73
McNally, Azie, 183
McNeely, Eva, 195
McNeil, Clark, 130; J.W., 33; Jayme Beth Davis Hayes, 173; Sheldon, 173
McNiece, Bryant L., 174
McPhail, Ethel, 223; Kendall, 223; Kent, 223; Kevin, 223; Patrica Ann McKimens, 223; Ross, 117, 223; Ross K., 223
McPhayden, Jack, 3
McPherson, William, 141
McQuerter, Dave, 83
McSpadden, Alta, 223; Alta May, 184; Charlotte, 223; Dale, 223; Dee, 223; Doris, 223; Hattie, 223; Howard Vinton, 223; Jack, 223; James Bennett, 223; James Walker, 223; Jerry, 75; Jerry Vinton, 223; Jessie, 223; Juanita, 75, 223; Leola Brown, 223; Leonard, 223; Lillie, 223; Margaret, 223; Martha, 223; Mary, 223; Mary Matilda Young, 223; Mary Young, 185; Nancy Bennett, 223; Opha, 223; Rex, 223; Samuel, 223; Sarah, 223; Sharon, 223; Susan Caroline Bird, 223; Thomas Matthew, 223; Thomas Tom, 185; Tommy, 223
McTaggart, Ed, 24
McTaggert, E.D., 123
Meacheam, Lloyd, 134; Wanda, 134
Mead, Gail, 219
Meade, Mary, 30
Meadors, Bessie Brashers, 223; Carolyn, 4, 113, 118; Carolyn Engledow, 223, 224; Dale, 54, 102, 113, 117, 223; Elva Ray, 223; Jackie Dale, 223; Vicki Carol, 223
Meadors Funeral Home, 113
Meadows, Sid, 41
Meadowview Baptist Church, 140
Meads, Karen Jackson, 206
Mease, Narcissus W. Rainey, 236
Mecker, Lillian Willis, 219
Medley, Nellie, 73
Medlin, 92; Allie, 224; Angela Jones, 224; Clyde, 229; Emily, 229; Irene, 229; Jane, 224; Jarred, 224; Josephine, 200; Kent, 224; Kevin, 173, 224; Lacey, 224; Laura, 224; Leon, 50, 224; Mildred, 77; Ronda Bray, 224; Ruby, 262; Warren, 262
Meek, James T., 55
Meeker, Thelma, 219
Meese, Johnny, 253; Lucy, 254
Melton, B.T., 141; Deborah Ann Day, 177; Ron, 113, 117; Ronnie, 177; Taylor Paige, 236; Tiffany Lynn, 177
Meredith, James, 212
Merrell, T.N., 32, 33
Merrill, Irieta, 35
Merritt, Bertha, 239; David, 75; Elsie, 181; Jeanette, 169; Jimmy, 66; Marilyn, 66; Maxine, 69; Ola Mae, 70
Messenger, Eric, 85
Metcalf, Vicki, 225
Meyer, Grace, 267; Louisa, 224, 248; Sadie, 215
Meyers, Mary Jean, 67
Mid-Missouri Bank, 102
Miekley, June, 244; Melissa, 244; Melissa Rene, 244
Miller, 85, 136, 170, 199, 221; Abby, 224; Ada, 158; Alma, 158; Alma Blades, 224; Barbara Jean, 219; Bert, 137; Bertha, 64; Betty, 46; Billie, 179; Billy, 86, 107, 170, 224; Brenda, 224; Brenda Biglieni, 155; Charlie, 172; Cheryl Ruth, 247; Cody, 224; Daniel, 224; David, 50, 155, 224; Eddie, 84; Elmer, 135; Emmett, 224; Ethel, 64; Freda O., 186; James, 224; Janice, 224; Jesse, 10; Kay, 25, 107, 224; Keith, 31; Lester, 179; Lizzie, 224; Lucille, 107; Lucille Sifferman, 224; Malanie, 88; Margaret Peggy, 262; Marlynn, 190; Nancy, 179; Pearl, 158; Rebecca McDaniel, 221; Sarah, 209; Wyville, 86
Mills, Lillie McSpadden, 223; Lorene, 253; Louis, 69; M.A., 32; Mary A., 149; T.M., 10
Milton, Thomas, 141
Minier, Daniel George, 227; Danny, 227; Donna, 227; Earline Sue Neil Brashers, 227; Ellrey, 227; Florence, 227; George, 117; Harry, 227; Howard, 227; Irene, 227; Janet, 227; Jennie Cordelia Vogel, 227; Mary Ellen, 227; Oliver George, 227; Ora Mae, 227; Samuel, 227; Tammi Lynn, 227; Terri Sue, 227
Mink, Judith, 204
Minton, Thomas, 90; Thomas D., 130
Misemer, Bill, 22; Harr, 185; Mary, 185
Mitchell, 159; Anna Evelyn Teague, 213; C.A., 33, 74; Carole Guenther, 196; Charles, 213; Edward, 213; Elizabeth Mahulda, 194; Eugene, 156, 225; Greg, 140; Jennifer, 140, 225; John, 269; John Norris, 224, 225; Judy, 213; June, 213; Lucille Williams, 225, 269; Margaret, 148; Marilyn, 23, 225; Marilyn Ilene Mooneyham, 156, 225; Nancy, 225; Norris, 224; R.C., 44, 78, 107, 167, 178, 223, 241; Rhonda, 156, 225; Robert, 269; Robert Clarence, 224, 225; Roger Wayne, 196; Ronald, 156, 225; Vicky, 213
Mizell, Henry, 15
Monholland, Audrey, 225; Bill, 225; Cathy, 225; Clue, 225; Jean, 225; Lucas, 225; Vicki Metcalf, 225
Monroe, Marilyn, 78
Montague, A.W., 32; J.F., 74
Montgomery, Hiram, 224; Jack, 134; Mary Horton, 18; Opal, 224; Valle, 134
Moody, Margaret, 227; Randall, 90
Moon, Sarah, 257
Mooney, Francis Alice, 154; Martha, 154
Mooneyham, 9, 249; Aaron, 156, 225; Alan Lee, 225; Alysha Nikolet, 189; Ashley, 156, 225; Barbie, 225; Ben, 119; Bill, 179; Billy, 48; Brett, 156, 225; Brock, 225; Bud, 48; Burel, 39; Carl, 25, 68; Carrie, 156, 225; Casey, 156, 225; Chad, 156, 225; Charley, 158; Charlie, 226; Charlotte, 85; Charlotte Elaine, 156, 225; Chelsea, 85, 156, 225; Christina, 156, 225; Christopher, 225; Clara, 158; Clyde Leroy, 156, 225; Cody, 225; Curtis, 156, 225; Dale, 226; Daniel, 226; Darrel, 82; Darrell Lee, 156, 225; Deanna Toynton, 226; Deidra Barnhart, 225; Delia, 158; Dellie, 226; Dennis, 179; Donald Lee, 156, 225; Donna, 179; Dorothy, 25, 87; Dustin, 156, 225; Ed, 23, 158; Edward, 166; Edward Ellis, 225; Edward Leon, 156, 225; Elander Vaughn, 225, 226; Elizabeth Gray, 226; Elizabeth Jane Dodd, 226; Elizabeth Jane Logan, 158, 225, 226; Elizabeth Velma King, 225; Ellis, 70; Enoch, 12; Eric, 225; Fannie, 226; Gay, 48; George, 158; Gladys, 250; Gladys Dennis, 179; Glenna, 83, 156, 225; Glen Ray, 156, 225; Harold, 72, 160; Ina Gladys Wade, 172; Ina Wade, 67, 226; Janet Herndon, 156, 225; Janice, 179; Jean Neill, 226; Jean Studebaker, 156, 225; Jeff, 200; Jerry Leon, 156, 225; Jimmy, 87; Joan Reinert, 226; John, 158; John Edward, 156, 225; Judy, 226; Judy Baum, 156, 225; Kassie, 156, 225; Kathy, 226; Kay, 25, 68; Lake, 156, 225; LaVada Ann Gardner, 189; Leila Harrington, 226; Lewis, 226; Linda Bussard, 156, 225; Linda Childers, 156, 225; Lindsey, 156; Lisa, 156, 225; Lissa, 179; Louisa Faye Blades, 156, 225; Lucinda, 225, 226; Lyndsey, 225; Lynn Landers, 156, 225; Maggie Dean, 177; Malinda, 225, 226; Malinda Caroline, 199, 200; Malissa Jane, 151, 158; Marilyn Ilene, 156, 225; Martha Jane Mynatt, 166; Marty, 156, 225; Maud, 23; Maude Butler, 166; Maud Butler, 156, 225; Max Randall, 156, 225; Melinda, 156; Melissa, 156, 225; Merle, 25; Michaela, 225; Mindy, 225; Mirta, 166; Monroe, 35, 152, 158, 166, 177; Mrs. Burel, 39; Mrs. Terry, 48; Nick, 225; Nicole, 156, 225; Norma McCord, 156, 225; Pat, 260; Paul, 226; Pauline , 226; Peggy, 67, 179; Pernisa Reynolds, 226; Ralph, 25; Ray, 226; Ray Dean, 156, 225; Reathel Wanda Blades, 156, 225; Reva, 25, 68, 87; Robert, 179; Robert A., 179; Roger Ellis, 225; Ruby, 25, 68, 87; Ryan, 156, 225; Shane, 48, 156, 225; Sue Wade, 156, 225; Susie, 179; Taylor, 225; Terry, 48, 76, 82; Terry Lynn, 156, 225; Terry Trogdon, 270; Thelma, 160; Thomas Jefferson, 199, 225, 226; Thomas Jefferson, Jr., 226; Tim, 179; Tori, 83, 156, 225; Tracey, 156, 225; Ty, 156, 225; Velma Faye, 156, 225; Vera Lea, 161; Warren, 226; Warren M., 33; Wilda Louise, 156, 225; Willard Leon, 156, 225; William, 33, 158, 226; William J., 158, 225
Moore, 170; Artie, 74; Bob, 86; C.C., 223; Catherine E., 233; Cora, 269; Edna, 76; Edward, 33; Eual, 54, 117; Greg, 39; Lawrence, 85, 88; Loris, 66; Mary Catherine, 254; Mary Emily, 236; Paul, 211; Peggy Kirby, 211; Ruby Brown, 163; Sarah Elizabeth, 153; W.S., 74; Yolanda, 211
Moreland, Emily, 166; Lorie Lynn, 159
Moreno, Avelina, 228
Morgan, Dennis, 55; Hannah Kay, 226; Lawrence, 200; Lori Womack, 226; Mitchell, 66; Randy, 93; Rodney, 93; Sandy Guy, 226; Sidney Alfred, 226; Sidney Lynn, 226; Stan, 93; Tyler Allen, 226; Violet Elizabeth Hays, 200
Morin, Cheryl, 188
Morris, 10; Chad, 155; Charles C., 247; Dennis, 155; Dori, 247; Dorothy Ellen Shrum, 247; Dusty, 155; Gary, 247; Janet, 110; Karyl Kay West, 266; Lynn, 110; Margaret Sue Biglieni, 155; Mark D., 90; Ryleigh Ray, 155; Skyler, 247; Sue, 155
Morrison, Betty James, 207; Bron, 207; Diana, 207; Elwyn, 207
Morrow, Harold Lee, 191
Morton, Dennis, 226; Hugh, 42
Moses, 249
Mosier, Norma Jean, 155
Mosley, Floyd, 74
Mossbarger, Marcia, 47
Mount, Amos, 226; Amos Green, 226; Charaletta Woodsmall, 226; Floried, 76; Floried Pearce Estes, 226; Kate, 226; Letha Viola Smith, 226; Lloyd Russell, 226; Mary Elizabeth Douglas, 226; Mary Moses Asberry, 226; Rufus Walter, 226; Vencil, 88; Vencil Geoffrey, 226
Mudd, Joan, 209
Mueller, Paul, 266
Muench, Bryan, 226; Cyndy, 50; Cyndy Owsley, 226, 227; Effie, 226; Jack, 50, 100, 226, 227; Jackie, 226; Jack R., 100; Jeannie Burnett, 226; Leslie, 226; Ray, 226; Robert, 226; Sandra L., 210
Muir, Edward John, 172; Mildred Barbara Komrska, 172
Mummert, Patty Sue Reynolds, 239
Munhollon, Rosa Belle, 151
Murdaugh, Steve, 80
Murphy, Dale, 84; Doug, 45
Murr, Adam Scott, 177; Darcy, 177; Jacob Christopher, 177; Johnna Lynn Day, 177
Murray, 45; Cole, 271; Don, 55, 219; Johnston, 195; Junior, 271; Kathy Zell, 271; Sharon Jean McConnell, 219
Murren, Harold, 236
Musgrave, Pauline, 66
Musser, Libby, 257
Mustain, Miles, 66
Myers, 242; George, 123
Myhill, Laurie, 148
Mynatt, Martha Jane, 166

## N

Nakano, Deborah L., 178; J. June Gullett, 178; Stanley S., 178
Nance, Anna King, 227; Anne Jones, 227; Bertha, 48; Bertha Britain, 227; Charlotte, 227; Charlotte Parker, 227; Clement, 227; Cleve, 227; Dora Johnson, 227; Edgar, 227; Elizabeth Tilson, 227; Ella, 148, 227; Emma,

148, 227; Flora, 227; George, 227; Gerald, 227; Grace, 227; Helen, 227; John Calvin, 227; Josephine, 227; Kathleen, 227; Lillie, 227; Lon, 227; Lucinda Doty, 227; Pearl, 227; Roy, 227; Sidney Johnson, 227
Napier, Amy Jo Countryman, 227; Bryan Paul, 227; Clyde, 227; Dacey Abagale, 227; Emily Grace, 227; Grace Ernestine Gulley, 227; Marijo Cheek, 227; Mark, 227; Marvie Lee Robertson, 241; Maxine Foster, 227; Sara Michelle, 227; Shelley Jean, 227; William Ashford, 227
Napper, Lucille, 77, 225
Nations, Kay, 176
Nave, Darleen, 238
Naylor, Leslie, 209; Nelle Steele, 209
Neal, Chris, 247; Christopher James, 248; Marty, 248; Marty Robert, II, 248; Roxanna, 254; Tami Jeanette Shy, 247, 248; Zachary Allen, 248
Neece, W.W., 33
Neeley, Howard, 74
Neely, Brian Scott, 176; Bruce Keven, 176; Nancy, 176; Patricia Joan Bassore, 176; Richard Brent, 176; Richard Lee, 176
Neil, Chloe Blades, 76; Chloe Susan Blades, 227; Chole Blades, 156; David Baldwin, 227; Earline, 223; Earline Sue, 227; Earl David, 227; Lillie Mae White, 227; Marie, 71, 77; Mearl B., 227; N.B., 20; Opaline, 71
Neill, Barbara, 201; C.C. Allen, 11; Etta, 11; Jerry, 202; Jim, 201; Joe, 202; Karen, 201; Kate Phillips, 11; Mary, 11; Mary Ellen Hock, 201, 202; Mary Etta Elizabeth, 202; Mary Hock, 13; Tommy, 201, 202
Nelson, Andrew David, 228; Angela Lou Roy, 228; Avelina Moreno, 228; Beth Coggin, 152; Chloe Belle, 228; Cindy Burke, 228; Cloris, 231; David Joe, 228; Diane Kay, 228; Edgar Elijah, 179, 193, 227, 228; Edgar Jack, 228; Edwina Ruth, 179, 228; Elijah A., 227; Elizabeth Grace, 176, 193, 228; Erlene, 149; Ethel Ruth Maples, 179, 193, 227, 228; Frances Ann, 228; Frank R., 133; Greg, 228; Jacob, 152, 228; James M., 33; Jimmie, 228; Joe, 53, 127; Joe Ward, 228; John, 117; John A., 228; Kerry Jon, 228; Kevin Jack, 228; Kris, 228; Lamont, 228; Lennie M., 209; Leslie Edgar, 228; Marion C. Kerr, 209; Martha Jane Hale, 228; Mary Ann, 71; Mary Dawn Fleming, 228; Matthew Elijah, 228; Minerva Elizabeth Pearce, 227; Philip David, 228; Robert, 117; Rowdy, 228; Ruth, 72; Ruth Ellen Brown McCord, 228; Todd, 228; Tom, 262; Virginia Tiede, 228; Wanda, 71; Wilma, 71
Newberry, Anna, 28
Newcomb, Bettie Sarah Davis, 176; Carl Eugene, 176; Carol Lynn, 176; Donna Tierholm, 176; John Davis, 176; Katherine Ann, 176; Scott Timothy, 176; Victor A., 176
Newcomer, Jim, 84
Newell, Nettie Idella, 206
Newlin, Jeff, 17; Sherry, 17
Newton, Arthur, 15; Bud, 163; Della, 197; Rose Belle, 163, 192; Sarah Glowson, 163
Nichols, Jennifer, 83, 85; Mrs. C.E., 32
Nicholson, Jessie Irene Frame, 158; Johnathon Jefferson, 158; Mary Elizabeth Johns, 158; Patricia, 198; Pauline, 158; Walter David, 158
Nimmo, Jeff, 84
Nix, Eula Dean, 227
Noakes, David, 68; John A., 68
Noe, 9; A.S., 184; Archibald S., 184; Bernice, 270; Bernice Allen, 228, 229, 251; Catherine M. Holmes, 29; Clyde, 35; David, 184; Frank, 35, 74; H.A., 27, 33; Homer A., 29, 55; John, 184; L.F., 29; Larry, 69; Leona, 12; Lutecia, 184; M.S., 32; Margaret, 184; Margratt, 184; Mark, 35, 40, 41, 228, 270; Mark S., 41, 42, 43, 44, 229; Martha Wade, 184; Paul, 35; Rachel Luzzi, 184; Thomas, 184; Violet, 184; W.H., 27, 28, 29, 90, 144; William, 184; William H., 29
Noland, Terry, 52
Nolte, Tammy, 219
Norbury, Curtis, 186; Diana Kay French, 186; Hayes, 186; Ivy, 186; Max, 186; Preston, 186; Roni, 186; Tyler, 186
Norman, Ab, 149; Albert, 208; Alta, 208; Bertha, 208; Clara, 208; Della Estella Lindsey, 189; Eldon, 67, 221; Ethel, 221, George, 221; Glen, 46; Glen Lee, 25; Grace Gillian, 208; Hub, 35; Jane McElhany, 221; Katie Jane, 66; Katy, 87; Laura, 208; Lucille, 221; Mary, 221; Max, 66; Ruth, 68, 221; Virginia McCarty, 142; William Willis, 188, 189; Willas May, 188; Willis Mae, 77
Norris, Anna Norrine, 259; Lana, 268
North, Betty, 4

O

O'Banion, Alfred, 206, 248; Betsy, 248; Elmer, 206; Nancy Jane Collins Lile, 248; Nancy Liles, 206; Rhoda Dorrell, 242
O'Brien, Andrea Sell, 240
O'Bryant, 9, 37; A.J., 145; Andrew, 229; C.N., 73; Carolyn, 86, 229, 230; Carolyn Jane, 247; Carolyn Rainey, 229; Carrie, 116, 243; Carrie Maude Russell, 247; Carrie Russell, 229, 243; Clarence, 121; Edith Howell, 15; Eleanor, 229; Elias, 229, 241; Elias Jackson, 229; Ethel Cox, 116; Ethel M., 162; Floyd, 15; Frances, 116; Fred, 229, 243, 247; Fred Washington, 247; Gary, 75, 229; Henry, 203; Irene Medlin, 229; J.T., 145; Jack, 15; Joel, 229, 247; John E., 244; Kara, 88, 229; Kelly, 229; Louisa Phillips, 229; Lydia, 229, 232; Maggie, 203; Margaret Hood, 203; Mary Elizabeth, 76; Mary Lavona, 229; Nancy Short, 229; Opal, 15; Patrick, 229; Paul, 15; Russell, 229; Sarah Jones, 229, 241; Sarah Melcena Short, 247; Sarah Short, 229; Sharon, 229, 243; Victor, 15; William, 15, 16
O'Conner, Dick, 21
O'Connor, Dick, 189
O'Dell, 77, 167, 224, 245, 250, 256, 270; Burd, 48, 229, 264; Carson, 170; Dette, 229; Doc, 35, 44, 109, 211, 213; Gladys Clutter, 170; Harriet Hawkins, 176, 193; John, 229; Keith, 229; Lillian, 229; Loraine, 229; Margie, 229; Mary, 76; Mike, 229; Ralph, 44. 86, 229; Tresa, 116; Tresa Anderson, 229; Willard, 229; Wilma, 229
O'Kelley, Ada Hollingsworth, 168; Alyssa, 267; Carolyn Ann Sanders, 267; Charles, 168; Phyllis W., 168; Timothy, 267
O'Neal, 9, 212, 244, 270; Adith, 229; Adith Sallee, 230; Aideth Sallee, 243; Allison, 230; Alma Joplin, 230; Anna, 38; Anna Bess Townsend, 247; Anna Katherine Dent, 238; Annie Brown, 28; Betsy Townsend, 230; Bill, 4, 13, 14, 21, 22, 27, 36, 77, 81, 86, 118, 229, 230; Billie Saylers, 230; Billy Gene, 230, 247; Brady, 230; Brayden, 238; Brayden Isaac, 194; Carolyn, 4, 27, 116, 118; Carolyn Carskaddon, 230; Carolyn Jane O'Bryant, 247; Carolyn O'Bryant, 77, 229, 230, 247; Carol Ann, 76, 176; Carrie, 238; Carrie Billings, 194; Charlotte, 87, 206, 230, 231; Cheryl Kneal, 230; Cheryl Kneale, 230; Clarence, 229, 230, 243; D.R., 31, 74; Darrell, 238; Darrell Edward, 194; Dorris, 230; Duane, 230; Dustin R., 238; Dustin Ray, 194; Edith, 213; Elizabeth Hainer, 28; Ellen, 229; Ellis, 230, 231, 254; Elsia Edwards, 230; Elsie, 230, 231; Elsie M. Stewart, 254; Elsie Stewart, 14, 230; Elwin Norwood, 238; Ernest, 230; Etta, 230; Finis, 230; Frank, 230, 231; Fred, 230; Fronia Thurman, 230; G.W., 33, 166; George, 166, 230; George W., 33; Greg, 230; Gregory, 230; Guy, 230; Helen Lucille Reynolds, 238; Helen Reynolds, 238, 239; Hunter, 230; Irene Rapp, 230; James, 243; Janice, 76; Janice Lea, 238; Jarvis, 86; Jeanette, 230; Jesse, 28; Jim, 229, 230; Jimmie Lynn, 194, 238; Joan, 230; Joe, 81, 87, 230; Joe Bob, 229, 230, 247; John, 230; Joseph, 33; Joy, 230; Karen, 230; Kathryn Sue, 194; Kathy, 238; Katie Dent, 194; Laura Coggin, 170; Laura Jones, 208; Lester, 230; Lettie Blades, 230; Linda, 229, 230, 247; Lisa, 230; Lisa Hendrickson, 230; Maggie, 73; Margaret Freeman, 176; Martha Bristow, 229; Mary Ann, 47, 229, 230, 256; Max, 67; Maxie J., 176; Maxie James, 77; Minnie, 116; Moses, 229; Mrs. Norwood, 76; Myra Haden, 194; Myrtle, 74; Nadie Butler, 166, 230; Nancy Logan, 229; Nancy Sophronia A., 258; Nancy Wallace, 262; Naomi, 67; Nathan, 230; Nicholas, 238; Nickolas Alan, 194; Nora Stowe, 230; Norwood, 67; Oran, 208; Patty, 230; Paula, 230; Paula Albright, 230; Peggy, 230; Rilla Britain, 230; Robert, 230; Roberta Elma Green, 194; Roberta Green, 238; Ron, 230; Sarah, 157; Sarah Wallace, 262; Skylar, 238; Skylar Andrew, 194; Sophrina Luce, 28; Stan, 230; Steve, 230; Sylvia, 230, 247; Tony, 230, 231; Tony Ellis, 230; Vergie Robertson, 230; Victor, 230; Virginia, 68; Vivian, 68; W.J., 32; Wanda, 68; William B., 28; William Curtis, 230; William W., 229; Wilma, 68
O'Neill, Peggy Ann, 178
O'Reilly, 78, 109, 172
Odom, 237; Sarah Freeman, 237; Sophia, 237
Offuitt, Mary Jane, 168
Oglethorpe, 150
Olden, Mrs., 33
Oldham, Polly Ann, 236
Olinger, Mattie, 184
Oliver, A.J., 33; Charlotte Mae/May, 217, 246; Donald, 217, 246; Donald Wesley, Jr., 217, 246; Elsie Gwendola Maness, 217, 246; Elsie Maness, 70; John, 131; Malcolm, 117; Mary Deloris, 217, 246; Tony, 41
Orcutt, Charlene, 66; Delbert, 66
Order of the Eastern Star, 116
Orlando, Tony, 81
Orr, Sammy, 76
Orrell, Richard, 90
Osburn, Jim, 117
Oswalt, Kristina, 231; Leslie, 231; Linda Sneed, 231, 251; Ron, 231, 251; Ronda, 231; Sonya, 231
Otero, Jason Timothy, 267; Joanna Rachel, 267; Jonathan David, 267; Joshua Daniel, 267; Julia Maria, 267; Mary Ellen White, 267, 268; Patrick Timothy, 267
Otte, Rosemary McMurtrey, 222
Ottendorf, Anna Muriel Hutchison, 231, 232; Anne, 231; Bessie Blades, 231; Cloris Nelson, 231; Clyde, 231; Coral, 169; Don, 231; Doris, 67, 231; Elizabeth Hines, 231; Elmer, 231; Fred, 231; Fredrick, 231; Grace, 212; Grace B., 213, 231; Hazel L., 231; Joanna Clark, 169; Joan Clark, 231; Juanita Baker, 231; Loarn, 169, 231; Loren, 67; Louie, 231; Louie, Jr., 67; Louise, 231; Lue, 231; Maxine, 67; Mearl Hutchenson, 231; Merlin, 72; Muriel, 116; Roll, 35, 231; Rollie Eugene, 231, 232; Ruby Cunningham, 231; Stella, 231; Wanda, 231
Owen, 9, 12, 119, 154, 213, 245, 251, 252, 270; Alfred, 232; Allen, 144; Allen M., 232; Alwilda M.J., 232; Andrew, 20; Anna, 252; Awilda, 191; Carol, 68; Charles B., 11; Charles Baker, 191, 232; Charles J., 232; Charles Oscar, 178, 232, 233; Charles Russell, 233; Charles Sherman, 232, 233; Charles Thather, 233; Dorothy, 116, 134, 232, 257; Elizabeth, 233; Forrest, 232; Francis W., 232; George D., 232; Glen, 68, 175; Glenda, 72; Glenn, 35, 45, 179, 229, 232, 251; Harold, 35, 78, 229, 232, 243; Harry, 252; Inez, 12; Irma, 252; Jane, 229, 232; Jane Carolyn, 120, 159, 232; Jerry, 53, 236; JoAnn, 232; John S., 232; John Solomon, 232; Joseph L., 232; Judith Ann, 178, 232; Kathleen, 233; Kathleen Marie Russell, 233; Lela, 252; Leo, 32, 45, 117, 232, 252; Lottie, 232; Lydia, 116; Lydia O'Bryant, 229, 232; Lynne, 233; Lynne Hopper, 233; Margaret S., 232; Margie, 232; Martha Allene Stevenson, 178, 232, 233; Mary, 232; Mary Elizabeth Bushong, 232; Mickey, 52, 53, 191, 232; Myrtle, 252; Nancy Caroline McCroskey, 191; Nancy Ellen, 236; Nancy McCroskey, 232; Olivia, 233; P.W., 232; Pleasant Wade, 252; Rachel M., 232; Rita Belle, 70, 87; Rockford, 70; Sallie, 188, 252; Sarah Edith, 252; Sarah Yarborough, 232; Solomon H., 232; Steven A. Douglas, 232; Tommy, 52; W. Harold, 31; Wayne, 229, 232; William E., 232; Wilma Russell, 35, 39, 229, 232, 243
Owens, Adam, 254; Bob, 254; Catherine E. Moore, 233; James Henry, 233; Jeremiah M., 233, 236; Kristen Stephenson, 254; Lydia Ellen Porter, 233, 236; Melissa, 216; Mickey, 56; Nancy Caroline Garoutte, 190; Nancy Elizabeth, 190; Nancy Ellen, 233, 236; Nancy Garoutte, 233; Oral, 117; Oral R., 117; Richard, 190; Richard W., 233; Roberta, 254; Ruth, 236, 239; Terry, 233
Owsley, Carolyn Thompson, 227; Charles, 226, 227; Cyndy, 226, 227; Maurine, 226, 227

P

Paaree, Myrtle, 153
Packard, Curtis, 45, 119, 255
Padgett, Charles, 226; Judy Mooneyham, 226
Page, 71; Anna May, 71
Paine, Mary A., 242
Palen, Dan, 85
Palmer, Laura, 232; Laura Jane, 243
Parish, 24
Parker, Berniece, 177; Chad, 233; Charlotte, 227; Charlotte Bennett, 154; Clara, 158; Clara Blades, 151, 158, 180; Helen, 175; Henrietta, 177; Henry, 177; Jake, 233; Joe, 233; John, 40, 214, 233; John, Jr., 233; John C., 233; Katelyn, 233; Kayla, 233; Kelly, 233; Krisi, 233; Laighton, 233; Lolla, 244; Lolla Yingst, 177; Lori, 233; Margie, 233; Marie, 177; Mildred, 68; Polly, 219; Scott, 233; Valissa, 233; Vera, 177
Parkhurst, Parky, 174; Viola Crawford, 174
Parks, Christine, 50
Parnell, Gladys Denny, 179
Parson, Benjamin, 240; Martha Garretson, 240
Parsons, Rachael, 240
Parton, Ronnie, 76
Paschall, Emily May, 215
Paswaters, Austin, 256; Eric, 256; Nikki, 256; Lisa L. Sullivan, 256
Patrick, Patsy McMurtrey, 222
Patterson, Aldine, 29; Alfred, 234; Dr., 21; Elizabeth, 29; Elizabeth S. Coulter, 29; Eliza J., 201; Eliza Jane Ingram, 234; G.W., 32, 33; George W., 33; Inez, 234; J.A.N., 29; James, 234; Jimmy, 233, 234; John, 234; John A., 234; Margret, 234; Margret Hanna, 201; Mary, 177, 234; May, 29; May Blackman, 29; Nannie, 234; Pat, 12; Pearl, 73, 234; Robert, 201, 233, 234; Sally, 12, 69, 191; W.D., 234; William D., 201; William Douglas, 234; William P., 29
Patton, 71, 212; Beulah, 12; Gary, 69; LaDane, 68; LeRoy, 69; Lester, 71; Lorene, 71; Mary Jo, 12; Rassie, 12; Shirley Dean, 68; Vester, 71; Virginia, 77
Paulsell, Martha, 200; Milt, 35; Roxie DeBorde, 35
Paulson, Milton, 178; Roxie DeBoard, 178
Payne, 237; Beryl, 76; Beula M., 205; Edith, 230; J.M., 145; Jackie, 207; James, 17; Louise, 68; Nadine, 75; Nannie, 149; Norma Lee, 201; Ora, 163; Russell, 23, 86; Sophia Berry, 17; Wanda, 68
Payton, Ann, 85; Christy, 85; Lee, 212; Sarah Land, 212
Pearce, 162; Altha, 219; Andrew, 127; Ben, 219; Emily Cordelia, 254; Joseph, 32; Laura Fugitt, 186; Mary Davis, 219, 220; Mary Jo, 256; Merlin, 245; Minerva Elizabeth, 227; N. Bart, 19; Zalma Pauline, 77
Peck, Clara Jane, 164
Peebles, 264; Ada, 116
Peggy King Advertising, 115
Pendleton, Nancy Louraina, 200
Pendergast, 150
Pendergrass, 45; David, 200; Elsie Melton, 200; Fern, 69, 200
Penner, Dan, 84
Pennoyer, Augusta, 234; Eugene, 234; Florence, 6, 234; Gail, 116; Gail Houtz, 234; Gussie, 6; H.L., 36; Harmon, 6, 234; John B., 234; Mary Frances Bilbruck, 234
Perkins, Ann Lavina, 189; C.T., 11, 133; Conce, 243; Dora, 254, 255; Evelyn, 12, 116; Glen, 71; Hattie, 14, 230, 254; Hershel, 12; Jim, 32; John B., 91; Junior, 12; Kimberly, 230; Mae, 243; Marilyn, 12, 69; Mary E. Stewart, 243; Nancy, 66; Nancy Thomas, 128; Sarah, 91, 192; Virgie Mae,

244; W.G., 91, 143
Perryman, Diana Davis, 253
Peters, Delores Lanning, 213
Peterson, Albert, 243; John Russell, 243; Larry, 85; Mabel Russell, 243; Pete, 54; Phyllis, 217; W.A., 47
Pettey, George, 90
Pettijohn, John, 11
Pettijohn, Peggy, 263
Phelps, Lou, 200; Marsha, 227; Martha Wallace, 262; Sarah J., 210; Stephen, 10; W.S., 31
Phillippi, Louisa, 187
Phillips, 10; Amy, 116; Christopher, 235; Clellia Austin, 234; Columbus, 91, 234; Delmar, 235; Doris Isabell, 234; Doris Keltner, 234; Earnest Ray, 234; Elizabeth, 234; Elnora, 67; Elnora Joyce, 234; Emilla, 234; Finis Eugene, 234; Frankie, 235; Franklin, 235; Gary, 67; Gary Melvin, 234; Helen Pauline, 234; Hershel Owen, 234; Iva Jane Bussard, 234; J.T., 133; James, 235; Janet, 235; Janie Sue, 234; Jerry Lee, 235; Jimmy, 235; Joel, 91, 221, 234; Joel R., 234; John Dennis, 245; Joseph, 234; Julie K. Warford, 210, 263; Kate, 11; Kathy, 85; Kathy Grantham, 235; Katie, 234; Kirk, 210, 263; Lee Thelmar, 234; Lester, 165; Linda Kay, 69; Loren Lester, 234; Louisa, 229, 234; Louise, 259; Lucy, 91; Lucy Pollard McElhaney, 234; Mae, 155; Manilla McGinnis, 234; Martha, 235; Mary, 234; Mary Patricia Brown, 245; Mrs. Joe, 64; Nancy, 234; Nathan, 234; Nicholas, 235; Nick, 85; Odie Oren, 234; Ollie Robertson, 189; Patsy, 235; Raymond, 235; Reitha Maine, 235; Rosa, 209; Roscoe Emery, 234; Sarah, 259; Sarah Jane, 245; Sharon, 235; Teddy, 235; Terry Don, 245; Thetta Cynthia Manilla, 234; Thomas, 234; Tony, 235; Victor L., 60; Wanda, 87; Zina, 234
Philpott, Kayla, 159
Pickel, Denny, 250
Pickering, 9; C.R., 33; Claton R., 55; Guy Homer, 186; Hannah Florence, 207; Ida, 258; Jim, 186; Margaretta Gray, 207; Opal French, 186; Samuel Benton, 207
Pierce, Berniece Parker Comstock, 177; Blanche, 15; Chloe, 177; Ethyl, 208; F.B., 33; Frankie, 72, 87; Jeff, 143; Jennie, 116; Jerry, 68; Norma, 177
Piland, Edward, 75, 87
Pinegar, Ed, 94; Tad, 94
Pinegar Chevrolet, 94
Pinson, Chad, 117
Pipkin, W.D., 66
Pippin, Johnny, 88
Pitcher, Eldon, 50
Pitchford, Betty, 161; Bob, 161
Pittman, Lucille, 221; Lucille Norman, 76; Neil, 52; Norma, 67; Rex, 117; Shirley, 67
Plotner, Curtis L., 100
Plumlee, T.F., 32
Plummer, 38, 212, 245; Carl, 31, 45, 117, 129, 131, 235; Mrs. Carl, 131; Thelma, 45, 191, 235
Poe, Gilbert, 177; Lura Dean, 177; Pam, 110; Ralph, 86
Poerter, Orris, 235
Poindexter, Williedean, 213
Polk, R.M., 31
Pollard, Don, 44, 122, 199, 214; Lucy, 221; Vera, 48
Pool, Billy, 90, 235; Billy J., 135; Gerry, 31, 235
Poole, Harold, 162; Lucas, 162; Natalie, 162; Teresa Bridges, 162
Pope, Alta Gertrude, 189, 217; David Clarence, 217; Eula Pearl, 217; Flossie Mary, 217; Geneva Wilma, 217; Helen, 75; Jesse Stephen, 217; Lois, 182; Lois Iona, 217; Lou Agnes, 217; Mary Susan, 209; Myrtle Rebecca, 217; Ollie Elizabeth, 159; Roxie Mae, 200
Popejoy, 129
Porter, 162; Albert, 235, 236; Clara Lorenze, 235; Dorthy, 235; Edith, 236; Edith Matney, 235; Frank, 127; James Linden, 236; L. Max, 100; Lydia Ellen, 233, 236; Margaret, 164; Mary Emily Moore, 236; Melvina, 248; Nancy P. Richards, 236; Newt, 64; Olive Ann, 158; Orriss, 235; Polly Ann Oldham, 236; Presley, 158; Simeon Hall, 236; Stella, 64; Zeilda Morning Bently, 158
Potter, 10; Jessie McSpadden, 223; John, 10, 143
Potters, 24
Potts, 221; Ona, 158
Powell, Donald Max, 176; Dottie, 69; Kathy Nell, 176; Mary Ruth Bassore, 176
Powers, Cora, 162; Sue, 75
Pranger, Lester, 131; Mrs. Lester, 131; Norene, 131
Prater, F.G., 119; Sadie, 116
Pratt, Ernie, 47; Ida, 192; L.F., 61
Pressman, Holly, 110
Price, 190; B.J., 134; Francis, 68; John, 250; Mary, 68; Sterling, 19
Prickett, L.E., 35
Prine, Claudine, 67; Nora Belle, 67; Ray, 67
Propps, Carolyn, 212
Pruente, Barbara Ellen Bassore, 176; Beth Catherine, 176; Donald Mathias, 176; Dona Maria, 176; Jan Ellen, 176; Jill Ann, 176; Matt Donald, 176
Pullen, Amanda, 223; Amanda Jo, 236; Harl, 236; Heather, 223; Heather Nichole, 236; Joe Allen, 223, 236; Linda, 236; Linda Kay McNabb, 222, 223, 236, 257; Mary, 236; Michael Harl, 236; Robin, 236; Wren, 236
Pullen-Simpson, McKayla Jo, 236
Purselley, John, 140
Pyeatt, Bob, 25; Helen, 71; Jill, 131; Lesley, 48; Marla, 131; Orten, 25; Patsy Ann, 131

### Q

Qualls, Cora Moore, 269; Edna R., 269; Jim, 269
Queen, 24
Quessenberry, 270; Bonnie, 46, 47; Cindy, 47; Kerri, 47; Noel, 46, 48

### R

Rabe, Christie, 88
Rader, Alan, 48; Bill, 236; David, 236; Don, 236; Georgia Mae, 236; Judith, 236; Julia, 236; Linda, 85, 236; Oscar, 236; Sam, 236; Steve, 84
Rae-Patterson, 270
Ragland, Michele, 268
Ragsdale, 24; John, 169; Jordan, 169; Richard J., 91; Theodosia, 169; Victoria, 169
Rainey, 9; Betty, 70, 237; Betty Sue, 237; Carolyn, 229; Chesley O., 10, 253; Chesley Oren, 236, 242; Dee Owen, 237; Dorothy, 70; Dorothy Edith, 237; Edith Anne Jeffery, 237; Ellis Jeffery, 237; Estella, 237; George, 10; George Anderson, 237; Harold, 35, 236; Harold Ellis, 237; Harold Ellis, Jr., 237; James E.P., 236; Jane C., 253; Jane Catherine, 236, 246, 253; Jefferson W., 236; Jethro B., 236; John, 56; Josephine Ann, 242; Jospehine A., 236; Lawrence, 237; Linda Pullen, 236; Margaret, 236; Mary Francis Chestnut, 237; Mary Lou, 237; Minerva P., 236; Nancy C., 236; Narcissus W., 236; P.E., 236; Penelope Elizabeth, 221; Rosa, 237; Roscoe, 35, 237; Sarah B. White, 253; Sarah Barbara White, 236, 242; Sarah M., 236; Stella, 70; Stella Jean, 237
Rainwater, 24
Rambo, Bertha, 191; Donna, 191; Garry, 191; Robert, 191
Ramsey, Cletis, 253; Doug, 53; Hugh, 253; Leora, 253; Patsy, 47; Trent, 84
Rand, Alyssa, 230; Darrel, 230; Deidra, 230; Karen Sifferman, 230
Randles, Adam, 158; Harris, 53, 158; Jason, 158; Jerry, 53, 71; Julie Blades, 157, 158; Richard, 53, 71; Tara, 158
Randolph, Lazeta, 116; LaZeta Redfearn, 238; Margaret, 238; Wm., 238
Raney, Ellis, 77
Raper, 24; Angela Michelle, 237; Anna, 171; Anna May, 87; Ben, 76, 82; Beverly Copeland Cox, 237; Bill, 53; Bonnie Cook, 237; Charles Arthur, 237; Charles Arthur, II, 237; Donna Jean, 237; James, 237; James Arthur, Jr., 237; James Arthur, Sr., 237; James Bradley, 237; LeRoy, 67; Leroy, 66; Maryan, 237; Max, 81, 237; Roger, 237; Stacy Grubbs, 237; Susan Albaugh, 237; Vera Louise Kennedy, 237; William, 66
Rapp, Bettie, 176; Irene, 230
Ratcliff, Kay, 164; Lula Leota True, 214; Ora Sanford, 214
Ratliff, Rita, 100
Rauch, David, 237; Elisabeth Hutter, 237; George, 237; John, 237; Nikolaus, 237; Peter, 237; Philipp, 237
Rausch, Cathy Sifferman, 235
Rawlings, Jenn, 148
Ray, 169, 197; Alma, 250; Appolina, 254; Charles Edward, 254; Charley, 250; Earl, 76, 200, 250; Frances Elizabeth, 18, 254; Francis Elizabeth, 243, 254; George M., 219; Iva, 235, 250; John, 243; John A., 13, 18, 19, 210, 254; John Andrew, 240; John Wesley, 18, 254; Lester, 48; Livonia, 18, 254; Marcellus, 254; Marshall, 254; Martha H., 141; Mary Ann, 133; Mary Bell, 219; Olivia, 18, 254; Pat, 244; Rachel, 189, 231; Roxanna Neal Steele, 254; Roxanna Steele, 18, 240; Willie, 250
Raybourn, Eugene, 238; J.T., 237; Johnna, 238; John R., 238; John T., 238; Joseph, 237; Joy, 237; Joy Cope, 238; Leslie, 238; Loreese, 238
Rayl, Cora, 74; John, 33
Raymond, Bill, 131; John, 131
Raynor, Martha Ellen, 248
Reagan, 152; Ronald, 81
Reass, George, 117
Recknor, Leota Mae Ross Sawyer, 187
Rector, John, 263; Mary Catherine, 262, 263; Tina Davis, 263
Redfearn, 237; George H., 74, 238; Isaac, 242; Isaac Anthony, 242; LaZeta, 238; Lora Belle Haynie, 238; Margaret Ann, 242; Milbury, 242; Nancy Sarah Rose, 242; Penelope Taylor, 242; Ruth, 238
Redfern, Celestia Jane, 270; Iva, 45
Reed, Billy Mack, 71; Doris, 71, 87; Melvin, 55
Reek, Dirk, 132
Rees, Elizabeth Verch, 208
Reeves, Catherine, 201
Regions Bank, 103
Reiff, Amelia, 259
Reilly, Clint, 260; Jami Hood, 260
Reinert, Joan, 226
Renfrow, Lance, 263; Reese, 263; Ryley, 263; Wendy, 263
Republic Assembly of God, 129
Republic Free Will Baptist Church, 136
Republic Historical Society, 118
Republic License Office, 97
Republic Masonic Lodge, 119
Republic Monitor, The, 105
Reser, Jerri West, 266
Reynolds, 157, 249; Bert, 239; Chuck, 191; Dave, 249; David, 9, 20, 21, 91, 220, 238; David Alva, 238; David D., 238; Dixie Joan Garton, 191; Effie Jane, 238; Hannah, 238; Hannah E. Likins, 238; Harold William, 238; Hattie, 20; Helen, 238; Helen Lucille, 238; Henry, 20, 209, 210; James, 249; James H., 238; Jane, 190; Jennie Willie Mae Winter, 238; Jim, 20; John, 20, 220; John S., 238; Katy Ann, 239; Kenny, 191; Laura, 239; Lizzie Gilliland, 238; Margaret Hubbert Kerr, 210; Martha J. Mason, 238; Mrs. Alva, 64; Mrs. John, 64; Nancy Jane, 197; Nellie Jo Wiles, 239; Pam, 191; Patty Sue, 239; Paula, 191; Pernisa, 226; Polly, 238; Polly Kelly, 220; Rebecca, 239; Rebecca Eleanor, 220; Robert, 191; Sarah Ann, 209, 210; Sarah E., 238; Sarah Miller, 209; Susan J., 238; W.F., 238; Wilbert, 77, 239; Wilbert Levi, 239; William, 33
Rhodes, 237; Rose Etta, 209
Rice, Barbara, 85; F.R., 74; W.R., 74
Rich, Adah, 256
Richard, Rebecca E., 261; Sarah, 168
Richardon, 85
Richards, Andrew Alonzo, 239; Andrew Jackson, 239; Beverly Evans, 239; Charity, 239; David, 239; Ike, 239; Lisa Beth, 239; Loyd Alonzo, 236, 239; Loyd Alonzo, Jr., 236, 239; Mary Jane, 239; Mayflower Melissa Williams, 239; Nancy P., 236; Nell Elisabeth, 236, 239; Rebecca Groves, 239; Ruth Owens, 236, 239; S., 33; Virginia Ruth, 239
Richardson, 9; Cheryl Kay, 176; Ellen Frances, 182; Hal James, 176; J.C., 142; Jeffry Davis, 176; Lee Ann, 176; Terah, 234; Ural, 76; Virginia Lee Bassore, 176
Richey, Sallee, 6; Vesta, 6
Richter, Ronald, 67
Ricketts, Annie, 239; Artie, 239, 240; Asbury, 239; Bertha, 240; Bertha Merritt, 239; Christopher Columbus, 239; Claude Vernon, 239; Cliff, 100; Clifford, 88, 240; Doris, 71, 240; Eliza, 239; Eva, 239; Florie Smith, 239; Gilbert, 239; Hattie Yeakley, 239, 270; Herman, 239; Janice Gott, 240; Jennie, 239; Jim, 239; Josephus, 239; Josie, 239; Kristen, 240; Lawrence, 239; Lum, 239, 240; Lydia, 239; Ralph, 239; Raymond, 239; Rebecca, 239; Roe Blades, 239; Ryan, 240; Sara Bertha Smith, 239
Rickman, Ellen, 141; Louisa Faye, 156; Mary, 157; Rose, 141
Riddle, Charlie, 38, 49; Cora Elizabeth Bailey, 242; Eula Odessa Rose, 242; James Edmond, 242; Susan, 85; William Earnest, 242
Ridgeway, Matthew, 150
Ridley, Bea, 252
Riehn, Eugene Vernell, 199; Frances, 199
Riggin, Traci, 48
Riley, C. Earnest, 184; Charles E., 127; Della, 189; Mary Iona, 184; Maxine, 77, 184; Norma Jean, 87; S.W., 145
Ring, Susan Maude, 259
Rippee, Amy, 240; Bill, 240; Billie, 240; Cathy, 156, 225; Charlotte Elaine Mooneyham, 156, 225; Donna, 55, 240; Gary, 156, 225; Gina, 240; Jeff, 225; Jeffrey, 156; Sandra, 156; Sandy, 225
Ritter, 9; Aaron, 240; Adaline, 240; Barbara Garber, 240; Benjamin Franklin, 240; David, 240; Eliza, 240; Ellen, 240; Harriet, 240; Jacob, 240; John, 240; John, Jr., 240; John Newton, 240; John P., 240; Larrinda J., 240; Lorinda A., 240; Marcus, 240; Marcus D., 55; Marcus L., 240; Martha, 240; Martin, 240; Mary Ann, 240; Michael, 240; Phoebe Ann, 240; Rachael Parsons, 240; Samuel, 240; Sarah, 240; Susan, 240
Rivas, Antonio, 90
Robbins, James, 168; Joyce, 99; Kelly Lynn, 168; Linda Kay Carter, 168; Lori Ann, 168
Roberts, Alice, 240; Donna Mooneyham, 179; Ellen, 240; Georgia, 240; Gertrude, 219; Lee, 240; Lee Melvin, Jr., 240; Margaret, 240; Rebecca, 214; Ruth Norman, 221; Wilma Rubinson, 159
Robertson, 9, 242; A.M., 145; Abigail Ruth, 241; Alexander, 246; Allie, 74; Anthony, 134; Anthony M., 145; Benjamin Harrison, 214; Bill, 4, 14, 16, 20, 22, 25, 34, 37, 49, 118, 185, 229, 242, 250; Cecil, 70; Debra Sue, 241; Delilah, 145; Delilah Jones, 221, 240, 241; Delores, 241; Deloris, 70; Donald, 70; Effie, 73; Eleanor O'Bryant, 229; Finis, 12, 70, 241, 242, 263; Gertie S., 268; Gladys, 241; Gladys Lucille Wallace, 266; Gladys Wallace, 241, 242, 263; Glynn DeBoard, 178; H.E., 145; Hettie E. Anderson, 145; Ida, 74; Jack Samuel, 241; Jane Caroline Jarrett, 240; Jerry, 87; Jessie Pearl True, 214; Judy, 86, 241, 242; Karen, 155; Kerri Lee Ruth, 241; Linda, 85, 241, 242; Lindsey, 91, 134, 145, 216, 221, 240, 241, 268; Lucy, 241, 246; Marvie Lee, 241; Marvin, 241, 244; Mary, 241, 242, 266; Mary C., 145, 149, 240; Mary Clementine McCullah, 149; Mary Delores, 244; Mary Hagewood, 261; Mary K., 266; Mary Polly, 197, 241; Mary Sue, 4, 23, 118, 163, 185; Mary Sue Foust, 241; Mickey, 241; Nancy Conzadie Short, 244; R.E., 73; R.L., 145; Sallie, 190; Sam, 242; Samuel H., 241; Sarah, 212; Sarah Alice Johns, 268; Sherm, 35; Sherman, 31, 34, 43; Sloan, 197, 221; Sloan L., 241; Stella Jane, 221, 241; T.L., 70; Thomas, 33; Thomas Edward, 240, 241; Vera, 131; Vergie, 230; W.B., 68; William B., 241; William Benjamin, 268; William F., Jr., 241; William Finis, 241, 242, 266; William Finis, Jr., 241; William Foust, 241; Zade Short, 241
Robins, Emmett, 15
Robinson, Alpha, 15; Anne Ottendorf, 231; Brooke, 233; Fern, 15; Freda, 15; Huel, 15; Jeff, 233; Jessica, 233; Larry Bert, 15; Lori, 233; Marcus, 233; Raymond Buell, 15
Rodecker, William, 31
Rodgers, Donnie, 131; Mrs. Donnie, 131; Rex, 106; Rosemary, 106
Rodgers Co. Realty, 106
Roetto, Amanda, 170; Kenneth, 170;

Nathan, 170; Rita Clark, 170
Rogers, 91; Donald, 75, 76, 82; Ivoe, 49; James, 261; Jayne, 88; Jennifer Hill, 225; Joan, 261; Loretta, 87, 196; Melvina Stilwell, 261; Pruitt, 74
Rohlman, Brian, 88
Rolson, Arie, 15
Rolufs, Arthur, 117; Arthur Lloyd, 158; Beverly, 47; Beverly Jean, 158; Delighta Bell Vanderpool, 158; Henry, 158; Patricia Anne, 158; Phina Lang, 158; Sandra Sue, 158
Roop, 74; Alice, 192, 243; Charles, 148; Cora, 73, 74; Elmer, 29; Minnie Anderson, 29, 148
Roosevelt, 38, 77, 252; Eleanor, 5; Franklin, 223
Roper, Alice, 73; Janie, 73
Rose, 29, 249; Albert, 40, 242; Arabelle, 242; Arthur D., 242; Bettie Brashers, 161, 242; Beulah Helen, 242; Burl Efton, 242; Edward Y., 242; Eglantine Smith McClure, 242; Elizabeth Ellen, 171; Elizabeth Hosman, 242; Elizabeth Johns, 242; Eula Odessa, 242; Flora, 242; Franklin, 242; Gay Otto, 242; Ida Belle Jackson, 206; J.W., 33; John, 206; John W., 33, 55; John William, 242; Josephine Ann Rainey, 242; Jospehine A. Rainey, 236; Leroy, 242; Lula, 242; Margaret Ann Redfearn, 242; Mary Appline McElhany, 221; Meredith Marion, 242; Meredith Reddick, 242; Milbury, 242; Mona Marie, 242; Nancy Elizabeth Hosman, 171; Nancy Manning, 242; Nancy Sarah, 242; Richard, 171, 242; Sarah Alice, 242; Sarah Elizabeth Laney, 242; Savilla Belle Steele, 254; Temperance, 242; Thaddeus, 242; Theresa Dorothy Hadlin, 242; Townley, 242; Urith Goodin, 242; W.R., 33; Walter, 242; William R., 242
Ross, Betsy, 205, 243; Elta Virginia, 205; Eulalia Monroe Woodard, 242; John, 135; John Jacob, 242; Leota, 243; Marvin, 243; Ruby Eulalia, 242; Susan Catherine Cargile, 242; Thomas Francis, 242; Vesta Fuhr, 243
Rost, Lina Becker, 195
Rote, Brandy, 88; John, 84
Rother, Anna Carolina, 150
Roush, 35; Dollie Sallee, 243; John Allen, 253; Mary Troutwine, 253; Minnie, 188; Minnie Mae, 252, 253; Wesley, 243
Rowan, Greg, 88; Lisa, 48
Rowsey, 72; Richard, 72
Roy, Angela Lou, 228
Royster, Dustin, 100
Royston, F.E., 32
Ruark, Grant, 184; Hannah Fortner, 184; Martha Fortner, 184; Wayland, 184
Rubenstein, 37
Rubison, Barbara, 71, 159; Dorothy Vernell, 156; Everett E., 77; Henry, 68; Homer, 159; Ila, 163; Joe Hazel Blanton, 158, 159; Sharon, 159; Wilma, 159
Rucker, 249; Anna, 262; Elizabeth, 261; Elizabeth Wade, 249, 261, 262; Frances, 249, 262; John, 49; Joshua, 249, 262; Martha, 262; Martha E.A., 233, 249, 250; Mary, 49; Tavner, 249, 262
Ruckman, Becky, 47, 165; Dan, 165; Elmer, 36, 74; Evelyn, 166; Evelyn Bull, 165; Gene, 165; Jeffrey, 165; Kenneth, 165; Mark, 165; Patricia, 165
Ruhl, Clyde, 155; Edd, 155; Ethel Biglieni, 155; Marie, 155; Paul, 155
Rumsey, Hubert, 67; Sherman, 67; Ted, 67
Runion, Ida May, 189
Rusenstrom, Drenda Day, 177; Grace, 177; Ireland, 177; Kevin, 177; Rose, 177
Russell, Arena Jane, 193; Bill, 35; Bonnie, 212; Carrie, 73, 229, 243; Carrie Maude, 247; Clara Virginia, 156; Dave, 44, 105; David, 86, 131, 243; Ethel, 105; Isabinda Cannefax Crow, 174; J.N., 193; James, 212; Jefferson, 174; Joe, 68; John, 45, 243, 250; Johnnie, 35; Kent, 53; Laura Jane Palmer, 243; Laura Johnson, 212; Laura Palmer, 232; Lena Elizabeth Langley Camron, 212; Lillian, 243; Mabel, 243; Mabel Barren, 243; Mary, 243; Mrs. Dave, 44; Mrs. David, 131; Nancy Elizabeth Grimmer, 193; Paul, 243; Paul Densil, 212; Paul William, 212; William, 229, 232; William Riley, 243; William Ruel, 212; Wilma, 35, 39, 229, 232, 243; Zelma, 68
Rust, Caleb, 88
Ruth, Kerri Lee, 241
Rutherford, C.M., 66
Ruyle, Donna Britain, 67
Ryan, 41, 42; Charles, 69
Ryder, William, 33; William M., 33
Ryles, Myrtle, 155

## S

Sadler, Marcene, 263
Sagar, A.H., 42; Al, 42; Helen, 194
Salchow, Becky, 155; Burton Gene, 72; Hershal, 72; Lucille, 72; Raymond, 72
Salee, Jeerly, 182
Salkil, 242; Eldon, 66; Henry, 66; Howard, 68; Mamie Jo, 68
Salkill, Addison Mabel, 175; Dana, 175; Eldon, 70; Finis, 75; Henry, 70; Zoie, 175
Sallee, Adith, 230; Aideth, 243; America McClendon, 243; Berlie, 243; Diamma, 162; Dollie, 243; Emma, 74; Hazel Bell, 243; Jerlie, 243; John, 32, 119, 243; Levi, 162, 243; Mae, 73, 243; Permelia McClendon, 243
Sammons, Norma, 219; Norma Lee, 66, 87
Sample, Ryan, 88
Sampson, Ethel, 74
Sanders, 232, 242; Abby, 245; Alvin, 70; Alvin Lenard, 244; Amanda, 244; Amanda Brooke, 244; Andrea, 245; Angie, 116, 243, 244; Ava, 244; Billy, 12; Brad, 245; Carolyn Ann, 267; Cheryl, 245; Christina, 113; Dale, 166, 244; Debbie Day, 177, 244; Delores Robertson, 241; Deloris Robertson, 70; Dennis, 177, 244; Dorothy, 218; Duane, 244; Duane Alan, 244; Dylan, 110; Francis Elizabeth Ray, 243; Franklin M., 243; Gary Lee, 267; Holly, 245; Howard Don, 244, 245; Jacob Cole, 166, 244; Jamie Ball, 166, 244; Janet Butler, 166, 244; Janet M. Butler, 244; Jeffrey, 166, 244; Jeffrey Dale, 244; Joe, 15; Jonathan Lee, 267; Jordan, 244; Joshua, 177, 244; Joyce Hartline, 245; Julie, 83, 166, 244; Julie Dawn, 244; Justin, 110; Kevin, 83, 245; Kim, 245; Lenard, 87; Lenard Grant, 244, 245; Lige, 15; Lucas, 177, 244; Mae Perkins, 243; Marilyn, 116; Marilyn Daniel, 245; Marissa Tolliver, 244; Mary, 245; Mary Delores Robertson, 244; Mary Jane, 254; Melissa, 110; Melissa Miekley, 244; Melissa Rene Miekley, 244; Mildred, 218; Nora Angeline Borud, 243, 244; Norman, 218; Olivia, 110; Opal Sissel, 245; Oran Robert, 245; Ruby, 87; Ruth Annella White, 267, 268; Sam, 243; Samuel G., 243; Samuel Grant, 244; Sarah A. Wallace, 243; Shirley, 68, 245; Stephanie, 177, 244; Taylor, 110; Tera, 110; Tessa, 244; V. Dale, 244; Vernon, 37; Vernon A., 243, 244; Virgie Mae Perkins, 244; Wayne, 53, 68, 87
Saner, Marty, 136
Sanford, Nora, 234; T.M., 143
Santhuff, Chris, 88; Shelley, 100
Sargent, Sharon, 203
Saunders, Carol, 215; Gail, 215; R.V., 215
Sawyer, Bunny, 243; Charles, 243; Charles Ervin, 243; Judy, 85; Leota Ross, 243; Mattie Ethel Harris, 243
Sayers, R.A., 33; Robert A., 33
Saylers, Billie, 230
Scandrett, Frank, 48
Scarlet, Todd, 198
Scarlett, Christy, 198; Jerold, 198; Patty Jean Harper, 198
Schad, Carl, 173; Mabel, 173, 175
Schaefer, Barbara, 177; Max, 177; Vera Parker, 177
Schafffitzel, 36
Schatz, Bill, 52, 53, 80, 85, 162; Charles, 47, 219; Charley, 47, 48; Charlie, 55; Debbie, 88; Gail, 245; John, 245; Karen, 245; Lela Vival Butler, 245; Mike, 52, 245; Rosemary, 245; Sarah, 245; Vickie, 88; William, 74, 84, 245; William Louis, 245
Schaumann, Jean, 85
Scherer, Ann, 134
Schildt, Dorothea Sophia Henriette, 259
Schmidt, Alan, 133; Alma Gardner, 189; Billy J., 56; Frank, 189; George, 153; Jimmy, 189; Lee Roy, 189; Norene, 68; Sarah Bell, 153; Ted, 68; William, 153; Yvonne, 68
Schmitt, Michael, 229, 256
Schnell, Betty Mathews, 219; Kevin, 219; Kim, 219; Ray, 219
Schoenfeldon, Lorine Hill, 201; Walter, 201
Scholler, Don, 117; Donald L., 117; LaDonna, 85
Schon, Cynthia Lee Blades, 156; Madison Dale, 156; Paul Otto, 156
Schroeder, Linda, 219
Schudy, Jim, 136
Schulte, Jennifer Foster, 185; Michael, 185, 188
Schumaker, Mike, 50
Schumerth, Joe, 48
Scott, Ann Josephine Ingersoll, 233; Donald, 242; Georgia Ellan, 233, 267; Ida Ella Tippy, 267; J.E. Walter, 233; John, 267; John C., 267; John Michael, 267; Judy Robertson, 241, 242; Shelly, 242; William, 66; William T., 66
Scroggins, Bruce, 219; Jeff, 210; Jenna Layne, 210; Josie, 210; Justine Logan Buttercup, 210; Linda Louise Davis, 219
Scroggs, Cordelia, 189
Search, Barbara, 171
Searcy, A.E., 28; Hallie, 74; Mrs. W.B., 139; W.B., 28, 31, 33, 139, 160
Sears, David, 133
Seaton, Nancy Cunningham, 238
Secrest, Betty Jo, 175, 176; Edna Lindsey, 176; Louis Otto, 176
Sell, Andrea, 240; Doris Ricketts, 142, 240; Kevin, 240; Ron, 240
Sellers, 45, 77, 192, 243; Bette Jane, 245, 246; Betty, 77; Jo Ann, 77, 122, 181, 245, 246; Maude Silvers, 245; Melvin E., 245; Peggy, 86; Peggy Louise, 245, 246; Robert M., 245; Thomas E., 245
Selph, Mary Elizabeth, 40
Selvey, Jim, 23
Severn, Edwin, 202; Elizabeth Boggs, 202; Mary Elizabeth, 202
Severson, Lori, 88
Sewell, Annie, 215; Colten, 155; Harrison M., 215; Marshall F., 215; Michelle, 155; Shawn, 155; Stephanie, 88; Tristen, 155
Shackleford, Shelley, 88
Shadden, W.J., 33
Shakespeare, 77
Sharp, Bertha Frances Kerr, 210; Faye, 216; Joseph, 18; June Mitchell, 213; Malinda, 169; Mary Frances, 18; Richard, 64
Sharr, Bonnie, 76
Shatz, Carol Ann O'Neal, 176
Shaver, DyAnna Short, 15, 128; Ronald, 128; Sheldon, 128
Shaw, David, 222; Donna, 174; Elizabeth, 247; Jonathan, 222; Melissa Crow, 174; Rebecca Mason, 221, 222; Russell, 174
Sheldon, William, 133
Shelter Insurance Agency, 107
Shelton, 162; Abbie, 174; Arve, 12; Dale, 174; Edith, 167, 255; Ethel, 11; Fred, 15; Grace, 12; Josie, 255; Katie, 255; Kim Viles, 174; Levi, 174; Mary, 11; Mary Ann, 216; Myrtle McElhany, 221; Sarah Permelia, 221, 222, 271; Tressie, 255; Wallace, 255; William, 255
Sheridan, Vesta, 88
Sherman, Paula Arndt, 165
Sherron, John, 124, 127
Shevey, Allen, 152; Lisa Beard, 152, 186
Shields, Ada Marie, 75
Shilling, Dan, 83
Shinn, Ailene Gardner, 189; Charles, 189; Lloyd, 189; Marcia, 189; Vernon, 189; Wanda, 189
Shipley, Cindy, 116; John, 44
Shipman, Frances Elizabeth, 256; Joe, 127
Shoemaker, Adam, 199; Charles, 56; Gary, 56; Greg, 199; J.D., 56; Janet, 174; Jim, 56, 174; Kelly Hayes, 199; Olivia, 199; Rachel, 199
Shook, Ed, 270; Ellen, 116; Jacob, 142; Minnie Yeakley, 270; Tom, 53, 87
Short, 9, 119, 127, 147, 154, 213, 242, 245, 252, 270; Aaron, 246; Alice, 128; Alice Sparkman, 243; Ann Forbis, 246; Betty Jean Gregg, 128; Clara Britain, 134; Clell, 159; Delphia Jean, 66; Diana, 246; DyAnna, 15, 128; E.B., 145; E.J., 256; Eldon, 246; Elias Bates, 246; Emmit, 15; Eric, 128; Etta Mae/May, 217, 243, 246; Florence Howell, 15, 16; Florence Lucille Howell, 128; Frances, 210; Francis Alexander, 246; Francis Smiley, 246; Fred, 34, 44, 45, 232, 251; Fred R., 31; Gary, 15, 128; Gene, 16, 128; George, 246; Glenn Alice, 246; Greg, 15, 128; Helen, 16, 77, 128; Idelar, 128; Iona, 70; Isabelle Farmer, 247; Ivan, 16, 128; Jackson, 246; James, 145; James Monroe, 217, 243, 246; Jasper Newton, 246; John, 246, 247; John A., 246; John Asbury, 246; Julianne, 128; Julius, 246; Kelly, 15; Larriett, 246; Letha Margaret, 246; Lorene, 159; LuDena, 15, 128; Lutishe, 128; Lydia Coleman, 247; Lydia Elizabeth, 246, 247; Martha Jane, 128; Mary Alice Sparkman, 217, 246; Mary Frances, 128; Mary Malcena, 246; Megan, 128; Nancy, 229; Nancy Consadie, 128; Nancy Conzadie, 244; Nancy Kendrick, 247; Nancy Kendricks, 246; Nancy Thomas Perkins, 128; Natalie, 110, 128; Obie, 48; Ollie Elizabeth Pope, 159; Raymond James, 246; Rebecca McCullah, 246; Sam, 145; Samantha Caroline, 246; Samuel Emmit, 16, 128; Samuel James, 246; Sarah, 229; Sarah Elizabeth, 246; Sarah Melcena, 247; Standifer Rice, 246; Sybil, 70; Tom, 49; Velma, 211; W.C., 145; Wesley Bascombe, 246; William, 246; William Franklin, 128; Willis, 246, 247; Willis Bascombe, 246; Willis Calvin, 246; Zade, 241
Shropshire, Mary A., 170
Shrum, Dorothy Ellen, 247; Elsie Ellen Freeman, 247; Eugene Thurman, 247; Gene, 131; Mrs. Gene, 131
Shuler, Howard, 226; Pauline Mooneyham, 226
Shultz, Stacy, 51
Shy, Ann-Marie, 247, 248; Brandi Ruth, 247; Cheryl Ruth Miller, 247; Douglas Roy, 247; Elizabeth Ann, 247; Janet, 247, 248; Matthew Douglas, 247; Tami Jeanette, 247, 248
Siceluff, Harry, 77; Harry J., 74
Sifferman, Alex, 173; Alice, 173, 248; Birdie Smith, 173, 248; Bob, 230; Carl, 235; Caroline, 248; Catherine, 248; Cathy, 235; Cayla, 230; Ceann, 235; Charlotte O'Neal, 230; Craig, 235; Daisy, 173, 248; Dale, 248; Don, 190; Donald L., 235; Donna Sue, 71, 87, 215; Elizabeth Brown, 248; Ella Mae Carson, 248; Elmer, 25, 248; Elmer Nathaniel, 248; Ernestine Alms, 235; Ethel, 190; Ethel Mae Garoutte, 190; George, 248; Grace, 173, 248; Hazel, 248; Helen, 190; Henry, 117, 173, 248; Hildred, 248; Ina Denny, 179; Irene, 25, 45; Jayme, 230; John, 233, 248; John Adams, 248; John Alonzo, 248; Karen, 71, 87, 230; Lela, 216, 248; Lewis Dale, 248; Lewis Lafayette, 248; Lillie, 248; Louisa Meyer, 224, 248; Lucille, 71, 77, 197, 221, 224; Lunda Sophia Kirk, 248; Lundy, 248; Lundy Ann, 248; Mary, 248; Minnie, 173, 248; Myrtle S., 248; Nellie Frances Biellier, 248; Nichola, 224; Nicholas, 248; Norreva, 248; Norris, 248; Opal, 25; Opal Montgomery, 224; Ray, 173, 218, 248; Raymond, 69; Regina, 25, 184, 248; Regina V., 217; Regina Vernell, 217; Robert, 230, 248; Rosina, 248; Roy, 190; Ruby, 173, 248; Ruth, 173, 248; Ryan, 230; Stella, 248; T.A., 48; Thomas Alex, 248; Thomas Alexander, 248; Tricia Haralson, 171; True, 25, 224; Van, 230, 248; Wayne, 248
Sigel, 232; Franz, 18, 19
Silva, Betty Truman, 209, 210
Silvers, Maude, 245
Simmons, Andy, 249; Bea, 249; Blake, 249; Chad, 249; Claude, 249; Craig, 249; David, 211; Esther, 211; Evert, 48; Freddie, 211; James Leroy, 211; Nancy, 249; Norreva Sifferman Carter, 248; Paul Wesley, 211; Robert, 211; Ruth, 211; Sarah Myra Amanda Jane Kitchen, 211; Viva, 249
Simone, Vinnie, 56
Simpkins, Mary Elizabeth, 149
Simpson, Juanita, 198
Sims, Eddie, 75; Herbert, 72; John, 198; Leonard, 45; Margie, 72; Mrs. Leonard, 45; Nellie B., 197; Reva, 72; Stella Ottendorf, 231; Virgil, 72; Will, 231
Siplinger, Alma, 159
Sisco, Oren, 49
Sissel, Francis Ellen Davis, 245;

Opal, 245; Wilford Joel, 245
Sittler, Sharri, 219
Sitzes, Kathryn, 192
Sizemore, Bill, 140
Skelton, 157; Albert, 20, 21, 164, 249; Annie, 169, 249; Ava, 249; Ava O., 192; Bob, 86; Elizabeth, 197; Elmer, 21, 249; Fannie Mooneyham, 226; Florence Bryan, 164, 249; George, 20, 21, 249, 250; George V., 249; James, 249; Jeremiah, 249; Joel, 20, 262; Joel M., 233, 249; John, Jr., 249; John, Sr., 249; Laura, 64, 249, 262; Margy McGee, 249; Martha, 262; Martha E.A. Rucker, 233, 249, 250; Martha Hester Ann, 233; Mary, 69, 249; Mary Lockridge Mason, 249; Mollie, 20, 131; Noel, 249; Nora, 64, 249; Pearl, 64, 249; Robert, 131, 249; Roy, 76; Sarah, 249; Sarepta Ellen, 249, 262; Susan, 69; Vern, 249; Verne, 64; W.J., 226; William, 249
Skidmore, George, 41, 43, 44
Slagle, Ethel, 166; Grace, 223
Slavens, James H., 142
Slay, 254
Slentz, Bill, 39
Small, Henry, 178; Nancy, 178
Smart, Helen, 49; Ralph, 48, 49; Viva Lee, 215
Smith, Al, 245; Allan G., Jr., 196; Allison, 263; Anita, 250; Barbara Jones, 260; Birdie, 173, 248; Brenden, 229; Brook Barton, 248; Bryan, 263; Buddy, 250; Buster, 35; Carole Guenther, 196; Casey Carter, 168; Cheryl Rosa, 250; Clarence, 250; Clark, 130; Courtney Carter, 168; Craig, 166; David, 30; David Elliott, 193, 250; Dennis, 250; Diane Adele, 193, 250; Dorothy Bull, 166; Dorothy Mae, 263; Douglas Allen, 193, 250; Edward Myron, 250; Eglantine, 242; Elizabeth, 190; Eliza K., 30; Emma, 250; Ethel, 250; Faye, 259; Florie, 239; Gene, 250; Glenda, 75; H., 33; Harold, 177; Hattie Lamb, 250; Hazel Gladys Wilson, 250; Henrietta Parker, 177; Henry, 250; Hervey, 134; Hetty, 257; J.W., 141; James, 44; Jane, 193; Jane Ruth Gray, 176, 193, 228, 250; Jim, 47, 48, 105; Jimmy, 250; Johnny, 84; Joy, 116; Joyce Wiles, 268; Kelly Lee, 267; Kristina Ann Hughes, 239; Leona, 250; Letha Viola, 226; Linda Rae Clayton, 250; Margaret, 30; Margaret Odessa, 258; Martha, 250; Marvin, 35; Maryan Raper, 237; Mavree, 263; Michael, 177; Mick, 90; Mickey Robertson, 241; Mildred Harvill, 250; Minnie, 28; Misha Kneale, 230; Mollie Skelton, 165; Norman, 250; Ollie Mae, 178, 250; Oneida, 100; Opal, 250; Payton, 230; Ransom, 250; Ray, 90, 136; Regan, 230; S.P., 33; Samuel P., 33; Sarah Julian, 242; Sara Bertha, 239; Sophia, 190, 233; Stacy, 88; Stephen, 230; Steven, 230; Vicky, 83; Violet Ray, 152; Walter Luther, 193, 250; Walter Sherman, 250; Wayne, 177; William H., 55; William P., 242
Smythe, Rachel, 100
Sneed, Barbara, 251; Bob, 251; Carl, 250, 251; Don, 40, 250, 251, 268; Earlene Alms, 251; Earline Alms, 235; Edna, 75, 251; Evelyn, 251; Helen, 251; Helen Turner, 250; John, 251; Lillie, 250; Lillie Wheatley, 251; Linda, 231, 250, 251; Lloyd, 251; Natalee, 259; Peggy, 250, 251; Phillip, 235, 251; Raymond, 251; Sandy, 251; Ted, 251; Wanda, 251
Snider, Dale, 133
Snow, Ella, 6; Henager, 6; Mary, 6; Will, 6
Snowden, Lou Dean, 84
Snyder, Beth, 69, 167, 173; Beth Puge, 167, 173, 174, 251, 266; Golda Allen, 173, 251; Goldie, 35; Goldie Allen, 229; H.G., 41, 178; Harve, 35, 42, 45, 52, 173, 229, 251; Harve G., 43; Puge, 229; Ruth, 35, 45, 52, 167; Ruth Marie, 251
Sobotka, Andrea, 251; Bea Ridley, 251, 252; Randall, 45, 49; Randall J., 251, 252; Reva Alexander, 251, 252; Russell, 45; Russell B., 251, 252; Stephen Randall, 251; Susan Kay, 251
Sonshine Manor, 112
Sooter, Joe, 11
Sorrell, Malisa, 88
Souder, Jessie, 71; Paul, 71
Sowder, Calvin, 93
Spaethe, Cynthia, 253; Greg, 188
Spain, Jean Alice, 200; Rose May Hays, 200; Tommy, 200; Wesley Earl, 200
Spangler, Charles L., 100; Leon, 226; Virginia, 226
Sparkman, 9, 22, 23; Alaina, 83; Alberta Lovett, 216; Alice, 243; Allen, 253; Burma Jean McMullan, 252; Cassie, 253; Cletis Ramsey, 253; Don Lee, 252; Dorothy Dickerson, 252; Elizabeth, 253; Elizabeth Vestal, 253; Elma, 252, 253; Elma Jane, 194; George Earl, 191; Geraldine, 161; Guy, 27, 252, 253; James, 161, 253, 256; James M., 253; Jane C. Rainey, 253; Jane Catherine Rainey, 236, 246, 253; Janice Swearengin, 256; Jerry, 69; Jimmie, 191; John, 33, 207, 252, 253; John A., 188, 253; John Alexander, 252, 253; John Allen, 252, 253; John Arthur, 252, 253; Josie, 83; Junior, 191; Junior Ross, 70, 188, 252, 253; Kelly, 253; Leo, 161; Leora, 252, 253; Lorene Mills, 253; Lucy, 252, 253; Mae Belle, 38, 70, 187, 188, 252; Marjorie, 70, 188, 252; Mary, 70, 188, 252; Mary A., 253; Mary Alice, 217, 246; Minerva, 253; Minnie, 207; Minnie Mae Roush, 252, 253; Minnie Roush, 188; Mrs. Guy, 76; Norma Lee, 161; Oren, 253; Rebecca Latta, 253; Rosanna Williams, 253; Ross, 187, 188, 252, 253; S.A., 253; S. Elizabeth, 253; Sallie, 187; Sallie Owen, 188, 252; Sally Jean, 252; Sarah Edith Owen, 252, 253; Seth, 253; Stella, 252, 253; Stella Mae, 207; T.J., 33; Thomas Jefferson, 253; W.D., 90; William, III, 253; Williams, 253; William David, 246, 253; William Glen, 252; William Ross, 252, 253
Speaker, L.M., 74
Spellman, 10
Spellman, Mary, 75
Spencer, Anna, 6; Holley, 6; John W., 227; Mildred Delma, 260; Nancy, 50; Sherman, 66; Will, 33
Spickard, Ben, 100
Spillers, Sherri, 88
Spindler, Faye, 133
Spoon, Wendy, 88
Springston, Katherine, 83
Spurgeon, Iva Mae, 161
Spyres, Eberlee, 33
Squibb, 242; Benjamin, 206; Burchie, 206; Chester, 206; Dorothy, 206; George, 206; H., 52; Irene, 155; Johnnie Lucille, 206; June, 206; Marjorie, 183, 206; Minnie, 48; Minnie Jackson, 206; Mrs. Ben, 64; Ruel, 206
Squirrel, Bill, 55; Billy, 219
St. Clair, Angie Green, 236; Brandon, 236; Justin, 236; Nathan, 236; William, 235, 236
St. George, George, 239; Katy Ann Reynolds, 239
Stafford, Elizabeth, 257
Staires, Angela, 88
Staley, Jane, 71
Stam, 223
Stamps, Carrie, 15; Charles, 15; Doskie, 15; Herschell, 15; Jennings, 15; Lottie, 15; Richard, 15; Wesley, 15
Standlee, Jean, 67; JoAnn, 67
Stanley, Isaac, 141
Stapp, William B., 33
Stark, 150; Becky, 88; Jeanie Diane Ferguson, 184; John E., 184; Max, 138
Starkey, Audie, 50
Stater, Glen C., 251
Staton, Leona, 155
Steel, William, 210
Steele, Amy Kerr Cowden, 209; Andrew McCord, 254; Ann Elizabeth, 209, 254; Anna Elizabeth, 240, 241; Anne Elizabeth, 254; Avis, 209; Barbara, 12, 69, 253; Belva, 209; Bessie, 209; Bob, 259; Chris, 12; Christie, 253; Christie McConnell, 208, 254; Clyde, 208, 253, 254; Della Ione, 209; Emory Irl, 209; Evelyn Torrence, 254; Glen, 208, 253, 254; Grace, 209; Harry, 208, 253, 254; Helen Cassett, 209; J.W., 12, 253; James, 260; John, 209, 253, 254; John Almus, 208, 254; Lavina McCann, 209; Lena Leota, 254; Mark, 260; Mary, 208, 254; Mary Catherine Moore, 254; Mary Cornelia, 254; Mary Sue Trogdon, 259, 260; May, 209; Nancy Dunshee, 253, 254; Nelle, 209; Oscar Kenneth, 209; Robbie, 254; Robert, 253, 254; Robert Kerr, 209; Roxanna, 18, 240; Roxanna Neal, 254; Samuel Ferguson, 209; Sarah McDougal, 209; Savilla Belle, 254; Steve, 253; Viola Pett Cave, 209; Viva Dee, 209; William, 18, 254; William, Jr., 254; William F., 18, 240, 254; William Fletcher, 254; William Fletcher, Jr., 254
Steeley, Mary Susan, 184
Steere, Doug, 190; James, 190; Sheral Kay, 86, 116; Sheral Kay Garoutte, 190; Todd, 190
Steinbaugh, Arthur, 223; Juanita McSpadden, 223
Steinert, 254; Enid Stephenson, 254
Stellwagen, Augusta Zell, 271
Stephens, Patsy, 197
Stephenson, Anna, 254; Billy, 254; Clifford, 254; Dock, 254; Enid, 254; Harriet Keltner, 254; Inez, 70; Jack, 254; Jacob, 254; Jane, 149, 254; Janet Van Da Griff, 254; Joe, 149, 254; John, 254; Joseph Lonzo, 254; Kristen, 254; Martha, 183; Mary Jane Sanders, 254; Mary Jo, 149, 254; Matthew, 254; Rozella Freeman, 254; Ruby, 254; Sarah, 254; Tony, 41, 81, 118, 254
Sterling, Carline, 67; Edith, 67; Frank, 67; Margie, 67; Marilyn, 67
Stevens, David, 50; Jane, 200; Larry, 219; Melody Ann Davis, 219
Stevenson, Martha Allene, 178, 232
Steward, Ginger, 188; Jeremiah, 188; Judy, 253; Judy Mae Fuhr, 188; Paul, 188
Stewart, 78; Betty Young, 254, 255; Charlene, 12; Charles, 131; Claiborne, 254; Claiborne Jerome, 254; Clayborn, 18, 243; Dixie, 131; Dora, 12; Dora Perkins, 254, 255; Dorothy, 254; Ed, 11; Edmond, 254; Edwin J., 254; Edwin Jasper, 255; Elizabeth, 254; Elizabeth Guyton, 254; Elsie, 14, 230, 254; Elsie M., 254; Frances Elizabeth Ray, 18, 254; Gordon, 53; Grace, 254; Hattie Perkins, 14, 230, 254, 255; Henryettea, 254; Hobart, 81; Hobert, 87; Hubert, 254; Ivan, 117; J.B., 14; J.W., 133; James, 254; Jim, 68; Jo, 207; John, 6, 254; Jonathan, 254; Josie, 254; Josie Shelton, 255; Jo Ann, 77; Kate, 6; Keet, 68; L., 133; Linda, 207; Lisa, 254; Lucy, 14; Lucy Meese, 254; Martha, 254; Mary Beth Fugitt, 186; Mary E., 243; Mattie, 6; Mayme, 131; Paul, 67, 254; Ralph, 12, 254, 255; Roy, 14, 254; Ryan, 83; Sarah Davis, 254; Tommy, 254, 255; Tressie, 14; Tressie R., 254, 255; Verna, 11, 254, 255; Walter, 14, 127, 230, 254; Walter Lafayette, 254; Walter Layfette, 255; Will, 6; William, 254
Stewert, Linda, 207
Stickney, 45, 231; J.B., 35, 235; John B., 255; Zetta, 255; Zetta May, 34, 35, 255
Stiffler, Lavada, 192; LaVada Emaline, 189
Still, 10
Stilwell, Melvina, 261
Stines, Ella, 269
Stinger, Frances Hughes, 205
Stingle, Ann, 148
Stinnett, C.L.M., 74
Stockard, Alden, 47; Fenton T., 55
Stocker, Chris, 84; Dan, 84
Stockstill, John, 53
Stogdale, Johnathan, 141
Stogner, Dee, 90
Stogsdill, Mary, 203
Stokes, Charley, 47; Pat, 47
Stone, 245; E.T., 141; Loye, 135; Madison, 245; Marshall, 245; Meagan, 245; Murray C., 41, 42, 43, 44; R.C., 33, 35, 36, 63, 105
Stovall, 204
Stover, 229; V.W., 31
Stowe, Nora, 230
Strader, Alanna Rose Comisky, 172, 217; Alyssa Rose, 172; James Alan, 172; Steven James, 172
Strickland, Amanda Lynn, 158; Christopher Lee, 158; Jeffrey, 158; Teresa Ann Blades, 158
Strickrodt, Mary, 4, 13, 19, 21, 58; Mary Skelton, 78, 250
Stroesenreuther, Bonnie, 110
Strohfield, Freda, 259
Strong, 66; Delbert, 207; Edward, 207; Jack, 66, 207; Judson, 207; Mary Ann James, 207; Tom, 66
Strusz, Emily, 85
Studebaker, Jean, 156, 225
Stufflebeam, Charles E., 255; Jim, 255; Ken, 255; Mark, 255; Pat, 255; Patricia, 256
Stump, Rhonda, 260
Stumps, Cilia, 28
Sturgis, Samuel, 19
Sturman, Edna, 253
Sublet, Harley, 45; Lil, 45
Sublett, 175, 235, 246; Harley, 264; Lloyd, 44, 55; Lil, 264
Sullivan, Amy T., 209; Denise, 256; Eliza E., 209; Flora, 73; George D., 209; Helen M., 256; James W., 209; John G., 209; Lavina J., 209; Lisa L., 256; Marty, 256; Mary Frances, 209; Nancy Cowden, 209; Samuel J., 209; Sarah A., 209; Tamra, 256
Summer, John, 28
Sumner, Darrell, 105; Donald Joe, 67; Grace, 70; J.L., 31; John, 31; Nancy, 67
Sunderman, Nolan, 128
Sutherland, Karen Elaine, 47; Mrs. William, 47; William, 47
Sutor, Rebecca Jane, 164
Sutton, Jeff, 83; Keith, 84
Swadley, Lynn, 137
Swain, Effie, 64
Swaney, Lois June, 194
Swanson, Harold, 190; Harold, Jr., 190; Opal Garoutte, 190
Swearengin, Adah Rich, 256; Bessie, 213; Bessie Ruth Tuter, 260; Bonnie, 256; Clarence, 260; Clyde Jim, 260; Danny Joe, 256; Janice, 256; Lester, 256; Litha Virginia Tuter, 260; Terry, 83
Sweckard, Les, 47; Lester, 31; Lester T., 31
Sweeney, 19, 169; Cecil, 71
Swift, Bob, 192; Cory, 192, 256; Cory Randall, 256; Glenda Loftin, 256; Joetta Mae, 256; Josie, 256; Kathryn Mae Ghan, 192, 256; Kristen, 256; Larry, 192, 256; Lauren, 256; Mary Ann, 256; Mary Ann O'Neal, 230, 256; Mary Jo Pearce, 256; Robert Eugene, 256; Robert Hardison, 256; Rusty, 190, 230, 256
Swinehart, Shirley, 227
Swinney, 136; A.L., 48; Bessie, 131; Delta Edna, 179; Dorothy, 158; Dorothy Blades, 25, 151, 158, 180; Joe, 69; Maxine, 76; Sac, 35
Sykes, Bee, 6; Delia, 6; Eddie, 6; Sam, 6


## T


Tabor, 71; Gracie Paralee, 227
Talent, Charles, 127
Tannahill, Mehetable, 190
Tannehill, Magruder, 20
Tanner, 48; Colby, 88
Taylor, Andrew Jackson, 174; Chance, 156; Darrell, 223; Darrell Wayne, 222; George, 194; Grace Sifferman, 248; Harriett, 202; Hope, 259; Isabel Lewis, 174; Jack, 248; James, 50; Jeremy, 248; Kathy Barton, 248; Kent, 84; Krista, 88; Laura, 174, 248; Penelope, 242; Phyllis Jean McNabb, 223, 236, 257; Phyllis Jean McNabb Bluebaum, 222, 223; Sally Jane Kerr, 210; Sarah Ada Gray, 194; Zachary, 243
Teague, 161; Anna Evelyn, 213; Catherine, 161; Donna Shaw, 174; Earl, 161, 213; Evelyn, 161; Gladys, 161, 213; Isaac, 33; Jess, 213; Jesse, 161; Katherine, 213; Lucile Boyd, 213; Lucille Boyd, 161; Robert, 161, 213
Teaverbaugh, Nellie, 195
Tefft, J.E., 33
Tennis, Betty, 72
Tennison, Charles W., 31; Randy, 85
Terigan, Julianne, 210
Termin, Sally, 64
Tess, Arthur, 176; Helen Davis, 176; Kathy, 176; Michael, 176
Testerman, Joanne Maxine, 160
Tew, Lauren Daniel, 121
Thayer, Glen, 71; James, 71
Thieme, Mary, 211
Thigpein, June, 190
Thomas, Andy, 19; Dean, 47; Deann, 131; Edna, 255; Elsie, 255; Judy, 112; Pap, 30; Sherry, 48
Thompson, Almas, 44, 45; Almus, 127; Carolyn, 227; Connie, 165; Connie Jean, 263; Dean, 256, 257; Dean Patrick, 178; Deborah, 100; Dora Lee Green, 194; Eden, 257; Frances Elizabeth Shipman, 256; Frances Wade, 67; Gina, 223; Gina Michelle, 257; Harold, 31; Harold Lee, 223, 257; Harry Lee, 257; Janet, 31, 116, 222; Janet Sue McNabb, 223, 236, 257; Jena Layne, 244; Jenna Layne, 166; Jeremy, 166, 244; Josh, 85; Julie Dawn Sanders, 244; Julie Sanders, 166; M. Dean, 165; Malise Carrie, 178; Mary A., 210; Megan LeeAnn, 178; Michael, 223; Michael Lee, 257; Michelle Gwin, 236;

Michelle Sue, 257; Molly Ashton, 178; Pauline Davis, 257; Ray, 111, 117; Robin Denise Dennis, 178; Ryan Patrick, 178; Sarah M. Rainey, 236; Sherman, 162; Tommy, 47; Trinity, 257; William E., 210; William Luster, 256; Wilma, 194; Winnie, 165; Winnie Disheroon, 165, 256, 257
Thorne, Mike, 83
Thornton, Tony, 151
Thorpe, Angela, 264; Dena, 264
Thrasher, Brian, 88
Thummel, Claude, 209; Dorothy Lehman, 209
Thurman, 9, 39, 194, 252, 271; Ann, 85; Anna, 30, 113; Anna Godwin, 257, 258, 264; Anne, 85, 257; Barnabas, 257; Betty, 209; Blanche, 258, 264; Bob, 30, 35, 162; Bud, 47, 87, 192, 196; Caleb, 20, 238, 249, 257, 258; Catherine, 259; Cordie, 48; Daphne, 35, 39, 201, 258, 264, 265; Dawn, 259; Dorothy Joslyn, 257; E.A., 32; Elizabeth Haymes, 257, 258; Ellis, 35, 78, 86, 123, 264; Ellis Millard, 257, 258; Elvie, 41; Ewell, 227; Floriene, 258, 259; Fronia, 230; G.W., 32, 36, 37; Gene, 259; George, 52; George W., 258; Georgia, 238; Glen Gene, 259; Hazel, 258, 264; Howard, 52; Ida Pickering, 258; Iris, 194, 258, 259; Isaiah Jones, 257; James Grant, 258, 259; John, 82, 85, 257, 258; Libby Musser, 257; Lillie Nance, 227; Margaret Odessa Smith, 258, 259; Marie, 227; Martha Caledonia, 258; Martha Jane, 257; Mary, 238; Mary A.S. Jenkins, 257, 258; Mary Elizabeth Dixon, 227; Nancy Sophronia A., 258; Ollie, 36, 227; Opal, 258; Orville, 40; Orville Dewey, 258, 259; Patty Francis, 257; R.E. (Bob), 45, 113; Raymond, 227; Robert, 75, 87, 257; Robert, II, 258; Robert Ellis, 257, 258, 264; Samuel G., 257; Sarah Moon, 257; Stella, 258, 264; Thomas, 257; Tom, 257; Trenton Smith, 258, 259; William Harrison, 257
Thurston, Anna Jackson, 206; Hugh, 206
Tibbetts, Phoebe, 28
Tiede, Adolph, 259; Alice Fuhr, 259; Alice Watkinson, 259; Anna Louise, 259; Anna Norrine Norris, 259; Carolina Lange, 259; Charles, 259; Clara, 75, 87; Clara Kloss, 259; Dorothea Sophia Henriette Schildt, 259; Edna Grace, 259; Edwin, 259; Emma Engle Huber, 259; Ernestine, 71, 166; Ernest John, 259; Faye Smith, 259; Freda Strohfield, 259; Helen, 201; Henry, 259; Hilda Otila, 259; Ida Wieck, 259; JoAnn, 87; Joanne, 75; John, 259; John, Jr., 259; Julia Huber, 259; Leo, 71; Martin, 259; Martin Friedrich, 259; Ralph, 259; Richard, 71; Ruby J. Branstetter, 259; Sarah DeWitt, 259; Sarah Phillips, 259; Virginia, 228; Walter William, 259; William, 259
Tierholm, Donna, 176
Tillou, Nora, 169
Tilson, Elizabeth, 227
Tindell, Harold, 31
Tindle, Jr., Jerry, 93
Tinsley, Fred, 64; Iris Wallace, 263; John Dee, 263; Mae Hagewood, 221; Nancy, 177; Oda Fay, 189
Tinsour, G.A., 33
Tippy, Ida Ella, 267
Tipton, Blanche, 175; George, 175; Mary Lou, 175
Todd, Billy, 52; Elton, 52; Elton Ray, 117
Tolliver, Marissa, 244; Trudy, 85
Tooley, Shirley Jean, 167
Torrence, Evelyn, 254
Tourville, Alice Kelly, 259; Callie, 38; Callie Hayes Logan, 215; Callie Katherine Hayes Logan, 259; Dan, 259; Della R. Berger, 259; Edna, 259; James Fredrick, 259; Jim, 215; Jimmie, 259; Kim, 259; Michaelea, 88; Minnie, 259; Nellie, 259; Peter Fredrick, 259; Sharon K. Hollis, 259; Susan, 259; Susan Maude Ring, 259; Timmy, 75; Timothy D., 259
Towe, Blake Andrew, 171; Caleb Michael, 171; Judy, 50; Martha Louise Coggin, 171, 179; Randy Lee, 171; Trevor Paul, 171; Wesley, 53
Townsend, Anna Bess, 247; Betsy, 230
Toynton, Deanna, 226
Tractor Barn, 96
Trautwein, Amy, 116
Treesh, Edna A. Kerr, 210
Treesh, Ira J., 210
Tribble, Mae, 73; Roger, 233
Triggs, Nancy, 155
Trogdon, 24, 216; Amelia Reiff, 259; Ashlyn, 259; Bob, 56, 259; Bryson James, 259; Dan, 71, 270; Daniel C., 259; Danny, 259; Dan Matthew, 259; Debbie, 222, 260; Dois Louise, 156; Donna Girth, 259; Dorothy Lee Gilmore, 259; Duane, 259; Ethel, 270; Ethel Matthews, 259; George, 259; Henry, 259; Hope Taylor, 259; Ica Ellen, 259; Jack, 4, 52, 81, 87, 117, 118, 122, 199, 259, 260, 270; Jerry, 216, 260; Joe, 260; Joel, 88, 259; John Randolph, 259; Kevin, 259; Louise, 160; Mabel, 137; Mabel Hall, 259; Marilyn Evans, 260; Mary Craven, 259; Mary Sue, 259; Myrtle, 192; Myrtle Hendricks, 156; Natalee Sneed, 259; Opal Wenkheimer, 259; Orville, 156; Patsy, 4, 39, 65, 77, 118; Patsy Woodfill, 260, 270; Pat Mooneyham, 260; Robert Wayne, 259; Samuel, 259; Shirley Wilkins, 260; Sophia, 259; Terry, 47, 260, 270; Tim, 259; Tom, 53, 259; Virginia, 71, 77, 259; Wayne, 137, 259
Trout, Justin, 175
Troutwine, Mary, 253
Troxel, Daniel C., 199
True, Alice, 214; Bertha Ethel, 214; Edith, 67; Edith Clara Fry, 214; Emma May, 214; Gladys Marie Wright, 214; Hubert Paul, 214; Imogene, 84, 87, 214; Irene Amelia Wright, 214; James Nathan, 214; Jessie Pearl, 214; Katherine Rebecca, 214; Lillie Pearl Williams, 214; Lula Leota, 214; Mabel Madeline, 214; Martha Elizabeth Lawson, 214; Maudie, 214; Ralph Almus, 214; Rebecca Roberts, 214; Ruth Lumitta, 214; Sybil Justine, 214; William Albert, 214; William Henry, 214; Zachary Taylor, 214
Truman, Betty, 210; Harry, 256, 259
Tuck, Clyde Edwin, 142; Jane Blood, 159; Larry, 159
Tucker, Ashley Dawn Underwood, 260; Matt, 260
Turentine, James, 141
Turner, Helen, 250; Joseph W., 101; Lucille, 154; Rosa Isabell, 250; Sarah Alcinda, 185, 186; Unity Jane, 268; William V., 101
Turpin, Alvin, 260; Anna Wilbanks, 260; Barbara Jones Smith, 260; Calvin, 161, 260; Charles Allen, 260; G.W., 161; George W., 260; Helen Boggess, 260; Irene, 161, 260; Juanita, 260; LeVera, 77, 210, 260; Myrtle Esther Holiway, 260; Otto Lincoln, 260; Velma, 260
Tuter, Ballard, 204; Ballard Preston, 260; Bessie Ruth, 260; Edna Earl Boyd, 204, 260; Edward Raymond, 260; Fern, 203, 204; Fern Nadine, 260; Fredona, 219; Georgia Mae Kathrine, 260; Hildred Batson, 260; Kenneth Solomon, 260; Litha Virginia, 260; Lois, 77; Martha, 76; Martha Catherine Morris/Newsom, 260; Pearl McGinnis, 260; Ralph Boyd, 260; Rose Mary Cordia, 260; Sheridan, 260; Sherman Riley, 260; Solomon, 204; Solomon Forrester, 260
Tutor, Doug, 56
Twigger, Sarah, 269
Twist, Allison Carter, 154; Carter, 154; Erick, 154
Tyler, Alicia, 97; Edythe Cutbirth, 154; Edythe Evelyna Cutbirth, 164; Evelyn Sue, 155, 164; George, 155; Harwood H., 155; Herman Harwood, 164; Leona Staton, 155; Sue, 67, 87, 163
Tyndall, Betty Jane Jackson, 190

### U

Ulmer, Shania, 174
Ulrich, Al, 95; Dennis, 95; Fred, 95; Roy, 135
Ulrich Marine, 95
Underwood, Ashley Dawn, 260; Camerin, 260; Cole Alan, 260; Ebbie Grisham, 260; Hubert Lee, 260; Iris Jean Fuller, 260, 261; Jamie Lynn, 260; Joe Don, 260; Judy Campbell, 260; Lois Alma, 260; Mark Alan, 260; Mildred Delma, 260; Rhonda Stump, 260; William Joseph Elbert, 260, 261; William Luther, 260
Updegrave, Dan, 47, 261; Tory, 261
Updike, Chris, 88
Utchman, Janice, 156; Jim, 156; Lori Lynn Blackwell, 156; Riley Dean, 156; Shannon, 156
Utke, Lloyd S., 181; Sharon Gail, 180, 181; Winona Gail Willis, 181
Utley, Georgia, 151
Uzzell, 85

### V

Vaile, Hattie McSpadden, 223
Valentine, Evan, 267; Hannah Lynn, 267; Jessica Lynn White, 267; Matthew Paul, 267; Tia Star, 267
Vance, Cora, 74; Sarah, 162
Vandelicht, Ashley, 242; Kaycee, 242; Mike, 242; Shana, 242; Tracey Walz, 242
Vander, Fred, 131; Freddie, 131; Mrs. Fred, 131; Terry, 131
Vanderhoof, Brenda Kay, 179; Virginia Irene, 171
Vanderpool, Ed E., 158; Irene Bishop, 158
Van Da Griff, Janet, 254
Van Gelder, Carol, 167
Van Wyk, Mike, 85, 88
Varland, Joan O'Neal, 206, 230; Tom, 230
Varnes, Erling, 211; Rosemary Kubat, 211
Vaughn, Barbara, 85; Elander, 225; Jerry, 12; June, 12; Larry, 12; Lawrence, 12, 69; Mrs. Chester, 76
Vaught, Audrey, 226; Linda Wolff, 269; William, 269
Verfurth, Gus, 270; Katherine Woodfill, 270
Vernick, David Murray, 261; Ermal Hagewood Johnson, 261; Ermal L., 184; Geraldine Mae Huebner, 261; John, 261; Martha, 261; Milton Maxwell, 261; Milton Maxwell, Jr., 261; Timothy Glen, 261
Vernon, Bill, 131
Vestal, Dot, 155; Elizabeth, 253; Gene, 155
Viebrock, Jeff, 83; Jim, 111
Viles, Beatrice, 71; Becky, 71, 174; Billy, 152; Clara, 24; Danny, 261; Hollis, 24, 25; James C., 261; Joan, 25; Joan Rogers, 261; Kim, 174; Lori Beard, 152, 186; Matty, 25; Norene, 25; Norine, 71; Oren, 25, 261; Orilla, 71, 261; R.C., 33, 105; Rebecca E. Richard, 261; Richard, 174, 261; Robert C., 33; Shawn, 174; Susan Crawford, 174; Tina, 174
Vinson, Catherine Thurman, 259
Vogel, Jennie Cordelia Minier, 227
Volland, Bonnie Swearengin, 256; Gary, 256
VonLessing, Wilhemenia, 271; Willhemenia, 270
Von Lossow, Paul, 33
Voules, Jennifer, 88

### W

Waddle, Arilla E. Lawson, 214; Beulah Helen Rose, 242; Buck, 194; David C., 214; Helen Mae Green, 194; Henry Lee, 242; Idanna, 194; Kit, 194; Lonnie, 194; Phillip, 194
Wade, 37, 46, 136, 249; Ada, 64; Alice Laney, 226; Alice Viola Green, 262; Bonnie, 25; Bonnie Bell Gardner, 162, 189, 262; Bonnie Gardner, 154; Brick, 64; Calvin, 226; Charles Wesley, 262; Clara Ennis, 172; Clarence Emmet, 172; Cleve, 64; Clyde, 25, 262; Clyde Cotton, 189; Clyde D., 154, 162; Clyde Dee, 172; Darthula Denny, 179; Dorothy Vernell, 172; Eda Sarepta, 262; Elbert, 64; Elizabeth, 166, 249, 261; Elizabeth Skelton, 197; Ella, 197; Ervey, 197; Forest, 20; Forrest, 64; Frances, 67, 197; George Calvin, 172, 197, 262; Gertrude, 20; Gussie, 197, 262; Hazel, 197, 198; Helen, 189; Hilda E., 262; Ina, 67, 226; Ina Gladys, 172; Ira Clarence, 262; Irene Myrtle, 172; Iva, 64; James, 20, 91, 146, 197, 261, 262; James Benson, 179, 197, 261; James Ralph, 172; Jerry, 189, 206; Jim, 166; Joel Bence, 197; John Fletcher, 197, 261; Joshua, 197; Joshua Asbury, 261; Juanita, 25, 68, 154, 189; Juanita Marie, 162, 262; Laura Etta, 262; Lula Alice, 262; Luther, 206; Margaret, 68, 87; Marie Hagewood, 221; Martha, 184, 197, 261; Martha Elizabeth, 262; Marvin, 206; Mary Elizabeth, 197; Mary Hagewood Robertson, 261; Mary M., 262; Mary Polly, 261; Mattie Jackson, 206; Maude Effie, 262; Maxine Ottendorf, 67; Mertie, 206; Mirtie, 262; Mrs. Brick, 64; Mrs. Forrest, 64; Mrs. Ira, 48; Myrtle, 182; Nancy, 197; Nancy Hearn, 91, 197, 261; Nancy Herren, 146; Nancy J., 184; Nancy Jane, 262; Nellie B. Sims, 197; Noel Gardner, 189; Oscar, 64; Patricia, 154, 189; Patricia Sue, 162, 262; Patsy, 25; Rilla, 64; Rosalene, 162, 189, 262; Rosalene (Rosie), 154; Rosie, 25, 68, 87; Rosie Alice Laney, 172, 262; Roy, 81, 141, 189; Ruby Susan, 172; Ruth, 197; Samuel, 197, 261; Sarah A.C., 261; Sarah Ann, 197; Sarepta, 261; Sarepta Ellen Skelton, 262; Sue, 156, 225; Thomas A., 262; Thomas Washington, 197, 261; Vernell, 67; Wes, 20, 21; Wesley O., 262; Wesley Osborne, 197, 261; William, 262; William L., 197; William P., 197, 261
Wade Chapel Cemetery, 146
Wado, Grace, 64
Wagner, James, 83; John, 82, 117; John L., 117; Rosy, 100; Steve, 83
Wakeman, Howard, 123
Wal-Mart, 114
Waldron, Maureen, 100
Walker, Betty Sue, 87; David, 262; Delbert, 40; Don, 262; Donna, 87; Donna May, 269; Evelyn, 262; Giles D., 209; J.A., 11; Jim, 262; June Dixon, 262; Karen, 179, 262; Ken, 47, 109, 262; Laura Skelton, 262; Linda, 262; Mary Elizabeth Selph, 40; Mrs. Jim, 64; Norma Jean, 75; Shorty, 45, 252; Vardeman R., 40; Von, 262
Wallace, 24, 249; Alice, 262; Ann, 20; Benjamin, 263; Charles, 263; Cynthia, 262; Edna Bessie, 183, 184; Edna Mae Boston, 208; Emma, 262; Eula Faye, 208; Florabelle, 38; George, 263; George Washington, 208; Gertrude, 64; Gladys, 241, 263; Gladys Lucille, 266; Grace, 263; Harold, 263; Harry, 263; Henry, 262; Iris, 263; J.W., 141; James, 262; John, 20, 262, 263; Lois, 161, 263; Lucille, 35; Martha, 262; Mary, 262; Mary Black, 262; Mary Catherine Rector, 262; Mattie Myrtle Land, 263; Minnie, 262; Myrtle Land, 241; Nancy, 262; Nancy J. Wade, 184; Neil, 263; Richard, 263; Robert, 262; Robert Grant, 262; Sarah A., 243; Sarah M. Bayless, 262; Sarah O'Neal, 262; Thomas, 262; Thomas B., 184; Thomas J., 221; Thomas Jefferson, 262; Tommy, 35; Vesta, 263; William Ernest, 263; Wilma Johnson, 263; Wm. Ernest, 241
Wallis, Carl, 170; Marjorie Clutter, 170; Patsy, 72
Walter, Sue, 50, 98
Walters, Edward, 117
Walton, Bud, 114; James L., 114; Sam M., 114
Walz, Blake, 242; Buck, 242; Franklin Pete, 242; Judy Robertson Scott, 241, 242; Reid, 242; Shelly, 242; Tracey, 242
Wampler, Evelyn Sneed, 251; Harold, 251
Wankum, Allison Rose, 179; Cherie Christine DeVore, 179; Christopher John, 179; Patrick John, 179; Zachary Allan, 179
Ward, Allison, 263; Austin Daniel, 175; Blond, 127; Caroline Sifferman, 248; Carol Ann Cunningham, 174, 175; Catherine Sifferman, 248; Grandvall, 75; Helen, 76; Iona Vernell, 217; Jeremy, 217; John, 34; Lee Randell, 175; Linda, 263; Maggie McElhaney, 34; Maggie McElhany, 221; Max Perry, 175; Steve, 90, 263; Vernell Maness, 217; Windy, 263
Warden, Albert Reese, 188; Nina, 187; Nina Roberta, 171, 188; Roberta May Cruise, 188; Roger, 188; Tim, 188
Warford, Aleta Jo, 263; Bill, 78, 210; Bill David, 263; C.C., 263; David, 75; Deanna, 260; Deanna K. Kerr, 210, 263; Duane C., 263; Fred R., 263; Julie K., 210, 263; Marcene Sadler, 263; Mrs. C.C., 263; Peggy Pettijohn, 263; Richard H., 263; Stacy R., 263; Terry Van, 263
Warnock, William, 49, 50
Washam, Nellie Jewel, 209
Washon, George, 8
Wasson, 12; Lois, 200; Jim, 200
Waterman, Chris, 48

Watkinson, Alice, 259; Brent, 259; William James, 259
Watson, Darrell, 212; Debbie, 50; Ella, 169; Geneva, 35; Hildred Sifferman Wayman, 248; James, 31; Jennifer Ann Lakins, 212; Lane, 212; Logan, 212; Lula, 74; Mamie, 69; Pearl, 190
Watts, Charles Howard, 263, 264; Deborah Casey Workman, 263, 264; Dorothy Mae Smith, 263; Jeffrey, 264; Lori, 264; Michael, 264; Michael C., 165; Michael Charles, 263, 264; Ronald Dean, 263, 264; Teri Dawn Buell, 165, 257, 263, 264; Wilda Mareno, 264
Wears, Charles Jay, 237; Shelley, 116; Shelley Freeman, 237
Weatherford, Kenny, 176; Pam, 176; Rick, 176
Weatherwax, James, 76, 87
Weaver, Danny, 222; Kay McElhaney, 222; Sarah, 222
Webb, Anna, 4
Webster, H., 141
Weddle, James D., 98
Weinsaft, Tommy, 38, 241
Weirich, Mia Rae, 234
Weiss, Mrs. W.T., 33
Welch, Donna J. Woodfill, 264; Donna Woodfill, 270; Floyd E., 264; Kerry Lynette, 264; Lois M., 264; Ronald, 270; Ronald E., 264; Stanley Scott, 264
Wells, Betty, 182; Daphne, 24, 85; Daphne Thurman, 35, 39, 258, 264, 265; Daphnie Thurman, 192; Don, 265; Donald Linzee, 264, 265; Edna, 265; Edna Belle Logan Lekinzie, 265; Grover, 35; H. Linzee, 258, 265; Herbert Linzee, 55, 265; Linda, 85, 87; Linda Louise, 264, 265; Linzee, 24, 35, 45, 54, 123, 243, 252, 264; Mary Ann, 85; Mary Anne, 85, 87; Mary Susanna, 264, 265
Wenkheimer, Opal, 259
Werle, Roger, 39
Werner, Barbara, 265, 266; Betty, 265; Bill, 265, 266; Bill, Jr., 265, 266; Colleen, 265; Deb, 265; Kathy, 265; Kelly, 265; Kristina, 265; Mary, 265, 266
West, Barbie, 251, 266; Beth Anne McElwain, 186; Deloris Louise Dodd, 266; E.T., 32; Francis Kenneth, 266; Fred, 75; Jerri, 251, 266; Joe, 174, 266; John, 22, 186; John W., 266; John William, 266; Julia Ann French, 186; Karyl Kay, 266; Kendra Lee, 266; Kenneth, 266; Kerry Sue, 266; Libby, 80, 167; Libby Cox, 174, 229, 251, 266; Marti, 251, 266; Mary K. Robertson, 266; Mary Robertson, 241; Mindy, 251, 266; Ned, 75; Robert Fay, 266; Sabrina, 186; Robert Fay, 266; Sabrina, 186; Tina Maxine Marshal, 266
Wester, Henry Clay, 169; Jo Ann Keltner, 208; Krissi, 208; Lucy Emily, 169; Merle, 208; Sam, 208; Sarah Elizabeth Ellis, 169; Terri, 208; Terry, 208
Westfall, Dan, 50
Weston, Tammy, 116
Westside Christian Church, 131
Wetmore, Myetta, 6
Wharton, Robert, 196
Wheat, N.M., 28, 32
Wheatley, Lillie, 251
Wheeler, Ermal Lucille Hagewood, 197; Jack, 49; Robert Kelly, 197; Robert Luther, 197
Wheelis, Annette, 233
Whinrey, 249
White, 9, 21, 31; Adam John, 267; Amanda Jo, 267; Amber Ann, 267; Amy Rebecca, 267; Augusta, 207; Barbara, 154; Bervin, 52, 55, 57, 58, 219; Bervin Junior, 267; Betty, 154, 266; Beulah Carter, 154; Beverly, 48, 267; Bill, 219; Bonnie, 266; Bradley Lee, 267; Brenda, 267; Caleb Benjamin, 267; Cynthia Kay Grogg, 267; Daisy Sifferman, 248; David, 167; David Lee, 267, 268; Debbie McGuire, 267; Delano, 75; Dr., 21; Ed, 154; Edwin D., 233; Ellen G., 266, 267; Ernest D., 154; Eugene, 266; Francis E., III, 267; Francis E., Jr., 266, 267; Francis E., Sr., 266, 267; Frank, 266; Georgia, 267; Georgia Ellan Scott, 233; Gladene Looney, 216; Greg, 50; H.A., 27, 28, 31, 32; Harold, 154; Harvey A., 29; Ilene C., 154; Jacque, 267; Jaime Laine, 267; James, 266; Jane Anderson, 29; Jay, 167; Jennifer Jean, 167; Jerry E., 233; Jessica, 267; Joe, 47, 55, 219; John Edwin, 267, 268; John Wesley, 233; Josephine, 233; Julie Hopper, 204; Kathy McElhany, 219; Kelly Lee Smith, 267; Lacy, 204; Larry, 52, 204, 267; Lillie Mae, 227; Lydia Ann, 267, 268; Lynn, 191; Martha Hester Ann Skelton, 233; Mary Ellen, 267, 268; Mary Frances Jones, 233; Mildred, 155, 167; Nancy Buenta Cantrell, 167; Nancy Ellen Owens, 233; Nicholas Paul, 267; Nina, 73; Nola Careful Gaddy, 189; Norma Jean, 75; Ora Lee, 233; Paul Stanley, 267, 268; Pearl, 74; Rebecca Ann Byran, 267; Richard, 191; Ruth Annella, 267, 268; Sarah B., 253; Sarah Barbara, 236, 242; Shirley Johnson, 267; Stanley, 131, 267; Stanley L., 233, 267, 268; Ted, 75; Thelma, 154; Velma, 266; Vernon, 154; Walter, 233
Whitehead, Imogene, 194
Whitehurst, J.W., 33
Whitely, Barbara, 68; Kathryn, 68
Whitram, Alice, 201; Martha, 201
Whittaker, Bill, 25; Bruce, 25; Elmer, 25; Jeannie, 167; Linda, 25; Nettie, 25
Whittimore, Debra, 182; Greg, 83
Whittington, Greg, 83
Whittle, Brian, 90, 132
Whitworth, Ernie, 257; Lois, 116
Wiechert, Carole, 116
Wieck, Ida, 259
Wieland, Kenny, 76
Wiemer, Bill, 140
Wilbanks, Anna, 260
Wilbers, Chris, 50
Wilcox, Pam, 162
Wiles, Anna Mae, 268; Betty, 268; Frank, 268; Jack, 268; Jack Lin, 268; Jackie, 75, 268; Joyce, 268; June, 268; Maud, 268; Nellie Jo, 239; Ramona, 268
Wiley, George, 223; Jessie, 158; Lucy McElhany, 221
Wilhelm, Catherine, 29
Wilhite, Betty Jane, 268; C.W., 86; Chad William, 268; Charles, 23; Charles Daniel, 268; Charles Roscoe, 268; Charles William, 268; Gertie S. Robertson, 268; Irene Willoughby, 268; Lana Norris, 268; Michele Ragland, 268; Samuel Huston, 268; Unity Jane Turner, 268; William Burton, 268
Wilkerson, Bill, 215; Emma, 74; Wilma, 215
Wilkins, Helen Short, 16, 128; Robert Henry, 128; Shirley, 260
Wilkinson, Emma, 73; William, 32, 33
Willard, Cathryn Lynn, 121; Linda Bussey, 121
Williams, 6, 9, 208, 242; Alice Wallace, 262; Bill, 189; Billy, 81; Bob, 186; Bobby, 189; Bud, 68; Carl, 189; Celia Ann, 116; Colleen, 68; Daniel Lowell, 228; Debora, 189; Donnie, 189; Dorothy, 268, 269; Earl, 189; Edna R. Qualls, 269; Emaline, 206; Enoch, 233, 234, 268; Fay, 189; Ferrell Gardner, 189; Genevieve Fuller, 260; Gladys Gardner, 189; Hal, 48, 117; Hal K., 269; Hal L., 269; Jack, 189; Jarred, 269; Jennifer, 225; Jess, 268; Jim, 189; John, 66; Johnny, 189; John Wood, 12; Julia, 189; Kaelei, 269; Karen, 269; Kathleen Ruth McCord, 228; Kathy, 189; Leola, 189; Leon, 189; Lillie Pearl, 214; Linda, 189; Lucille, 225, 268, 269; Martha Caledonia, 258; Mary, 268; Mayflower Melissa, 239; Melcina Young, 269; Nancy, 48, 225; Nannie, 268, 269; Nannie Patterson, 234; Naoma, 134; Naoma R. Collins, 269; Pat, 45; Paul, 189; Ralph, 225, 268, 269; Randall, 269; Randy, 84; Richard, 117; Robert, 76, 269; Roberta, 68; Ronald, 189; Rosanna, 253; S.A., 33; Sam, 32; Sandra Faye French, 186; Sandy, 207; Sarah Catherine, 228; Sarah Jones, 209; Sharon, 189; Shelly, 186; Shirley, 189; Suni, 269; Thomas, 209; W.G., 33; Walter, 150; Wanda, 189
Willis, Charles A., 219; Charles Arthur, 181; Charlotte, 30; Gail Mead, 181, 219; Lillian, 219; Winona Gail, 181
Willmington, Mary Elizabeth, 158
Willoughby, Irene, 268
Wilmoth, Carole, 196; Carole Guenther, 195; Stephen Reece, 196
Wilson, Albert, 190; Andrea Annette, 197; Anna Garoutte, 190; Bradley Michael, 269; Cathy Sue Hafley, 269; Cecelia, 100; Cindy, 167; Dale, 170, 193; Dan Jeffery, 269; David William, 250; Debra Jean Gray, 193; Donna, 85, 87; Donna Kay, 269; Donna May Walker, 269; Donna Walker, 142; Doug, 170; Douglas, 170; Douglas Grant, 193; Dustin, 170; Dustin Anthony, 170, 193; Ed, 66; Eddie, 87; Edris Laura, 195; Ellen J., 33; Eunice, 30; Florence Kathleen Jones, 269; Garry Eugene, 197; Gary, 193; Gordon, 75, 87; Gordon Lynn, 269; Hazel Gladys, 250; Hazel Sifferman, 248; Iona Short, 70; J.E., 143; James, 8, 14, 195; Jason Ryan, 197; Kathleen, 230; Kathy, 183; Kathy Ann, 197; Kenneth Frank, 195; Laura Alice Wrinkle, 195; Makenna, 170; Makenna Lynn, 170; Mary, 6; Nancy, 198; Nancy Lavanda, 219; Paul, 134; Paul A., 269; Penney, 173; Rosa Isabell Turner, 250; Roy, 119; Sandi, 99; Sharon Kay Hagewood, 197; Stacie, 170; Stacie Wolden, 170; Teresa Lynn, 269; Warren, 183; Warren D., 117; Wendy Allen, 170
Wimmer, Jewell Butler, 166; Robert L., 166; Susan Diane, 171
Winkler, 195
Winn, Jim, 53
Winter, E.M., 31; Ernest, 64; Ernest M., 238; Frank, 64; Frank A., 238; Gertie, 64; Gertrude M., 168; Jennie Willie Mae, 238; Lafayette, 238; Lafe, 64; Lizzie Gilliland, 238; Margaret, 116; Mary F. Gertrude, 238; May, 64; Sarah E. Reynolds, 238; William, 238
Winters, Don, 86
Wise, Carolyn Sue Bassore, 176; Cindy, 83; John Wesley, 176; Kimberly Sue, 176; Mary Fugitt, 186; Sally Ann, 176
Witmer, E.A., 45, 46; Ed, 45

Witt, Dwayne, 131
Wittmer, Samuel, 170
Wojciechowski, Mike, 84
Wolden, Stacie, 170
Wolfe, Janie, 159
Wolff, Douglas, 269; Mary, 269
Wolfinbarger, Roy, 87
Wolken, Alan, 212; Kim Lacey Brown, 212
Womack, Linda, 50; Lori, 226
Wood, 155, 163, 170, 190, 235, 261, 268; Alma, 175; Austin Paul, 191; C. Virgil, 38; Etta Jane, 217; Henry, 175; Ida Alice, 194; Jack William, 175; Jess, 260; Kris, 47; Leroy, 53, 127; Lorena Garton, 191; Mary Jane Thurman, 257, 258; Mary Louella Davis, 175; Paul R., 191
Woodard, Eulalia Monroe, 242; Martha Ann Bland, 242; Monroe, 242
Woodfill, Donna, 75, 87, 216, 270; Donna J., 264; Georgia, 116; Georgia Elizabeth Green, 269, 270; Hannah Margaret Kingery, 269; J.K., 36; Jack, 216, 270; Jackie, 87, 211, 216; Jack C., 264; Jacqueline, 270; Jared, 270; Jaredene, 270; Jared Kingery, 269, 270; John Irons, 269; Katherine, 270; Mary Ann Luttrell, 216, 264; Mary Jean, 270; Mary Luttrell, 77, 270; Patsy, 75, 87, 216, 260, 270
Woods, Ola, 163; Pauline, 163
Woodsmall, Charaletta, 226
Woolsey, Bob, 260; Velma Turpin, 260
Word, Kayla Pauline, 215
Workman, Deborah Casey, 263, 264; Heather, 88; William Henry, 263, 264; Winifred Bernice Casey, 264; Winifred Casey, 263
Worley, Marti Jenan, 175
Worthington, Archie, 40; Dorothy Mae, 76; Little Joe, 35; Pete, 40; Popcorn Pete, 35
Worthy, Brad, 88
Wright, Delores, 190; Don, 48; Gladys Marie, 214; Harold Bell, 221; Irene Amelia, 214; Josh, 88; Mitchell, 90
Wrinkle, Alan, 195; Laura Alice, 195; Martha Ann, 259; Nancy S., 195; Thomas E., 195
Wyles, Frances, 151
Wynkoop, Anna, 269

**Y**

Yake, Mark Randall, 194; Shelby Lynn, 194; Taylor Anne, 194; Terry Lynn Gleghorn, 176, 194
Yanyo, Lynn Caryl, 196
Yarberry, Donnie Lee, 182; Hazel Etheridge, 182; John, 182
Yarborough, Sarah, 232
Yarbrough, Jerome, 254; Mary Cornelia Steele, 254
Yeakley, Carol Elizabeth DeWitt, 270; Celestia Jane Redfern, 270; George, 270; George Washington, 270; Hattie, 239; Helen Louise, 270; Henry, 142; Herbert Lee, 270; John, 91, 142; Matilda Grills, 142; Pauline, 171, 270; Susanna, 142; Thomas, 270
Yeakley Chapel, 142
Yingst, Lolla, 177
Yoachum, A., 32
Yocum, 267; Baker, 91; Carl, 69; Deana, 69; John, 31; Rodney, 84; Stanley, 69, 91
Yordon, Jon, 88
Young, 76, 170, 213, 254; Betty, 254, 255; C.H., 32; Eula Pearl Pope, 217; Frank, 119; Harry, 10, 35, 41, 42, 43, 44, 229; Jennings, 41, 229; Jessie, 243; Jim, 254; John, 191; Lena Leota Steele, 254; Lorena, 41; Mae Sallee, 243; Mary, 185; Mary Matilda, 223; Melcina, 269; Mollie, 12; Nancy C. Rainey, 236; P.M., 32; Paul, 41; T., 192; Theodore, 12, 13; Thomas J., 33; Vinita, 41
Youngblood, 9, 10; Anna, 74; Cleo, 35; Frank, 35; George G., 33; Grace, 35, 73; J.M., 33; J.P., 28, 139; John A., 33, 253; Leota, 35; Martha, 35, 116, 169; Mrs. J.P., 139; P.A., 28; Theodore, 10
Yount, Homer, 189; Howard, 189; Kenneth, 189; Mary Margaret, 68, 189; Ola Gardner, 189; Patricia Ann Logan Pyeatt, 215; Rose Marian, 84; Rose Marion, 189
Yunger, Alison, 183; Bob, 84; Carlie, 183; Casey, 152, 183; Melanie, 183; Melanie Beard, 152

**Z**

Zahn, Fredrick, 90
Zell, Anna, 271; Augusta, 271; Carolyn, 271; Deema Johnson, 271; Diane, 271; Diane Zoller, 271; Edward, 270, 271; Edward Emil, 271; Freda, 271; Freda Lehman, 270, 271; Fred Carl, 270, 271; Fred William, 271; Hattie, 271; Karen, 271; Kathy, 271; Mary, 271; Millie, 271; Minnie, 271; Wilhemenia VonLessing, 271; Willhemenia VonLessing, 270
Ziegler, Bonnie, 200; Nat, 6
Zieres, Beverly, 116
Zimmerman, Stella Sifferman Drum, 248
Zoller, Diane, 271
Zook, Barbara, 240
Zulauf, Alfred, 271; Carolyn, 12, 69, 191, 271; Marian, 12, 69, 271; Marion, 191; Merle, 13; Merle Howard, 12, 271
Zumwalt, Catherine, 161

*Looking south on Main Street, about 1907. R.C. Stone Milling Company on left, Little Red building on right.*

www.ingramcontent.com/pod-product-compliance
Lightning Source LLC
Chambersburg PA
CBHW080836230426
43665CB00021B/2856